Blackstone's Statutes
Commercial & Consumer Law

To Dominic and Sarah

Blackstone's Statutes

Commercial & Consumer Law

....

2006–2007

Fifteenth Edition

Edited by

F. D. Rose

MA, BCL, PhD, MA, of Gray's Inn, Barrister-at-Law

Professor of Commercial Law, University of Bristol

OXFORD
UNIVERSITY PRESS

OXFORD
UNIVERSITY PRESS

Great Clarendon Street, Oxford OX2 6DP

Oxford University Press is a department of the University of Oxford.
It furthers the University's objective of excellence in research, scholarship,
and education by publishing worldwide in

Oxford New York

Auckland Cape Town Dar es Salaam Hong Kong Karachi
Kuala Lumpur Madrid Melbourne Mexico City Nairobi
New Delhi Shanghai Taipei Toronto

With offices in

Argentina Austria Brazil Chile Czech Republic France Greece
Guatemala Hungary Italy Japan Poland Portugal Singapore
South Korea Switzerland Thailand Turkey Ukraine Vietnam

Oxford is a registered trade mark of Oxford University Press
in the UK and in certain other countries

Published in the United States
by Oxford University Press Inc., New York

First published by Blackstone Press

First edition 1989	Sixth edition 1997	Eleventh edition 2002
Second edition 1992	Seventh edition 1998	Twelfth edition 2003
Third edition 1994	Eighth edition 1999	Thirteenth edition 2004
Fourth edition 1995	Ninth edition 2000	Fourteenth edition 2005
Fifth edition 1996	Tenth edition 2001	Fifteenth edition 2006

British Library Cataloguing in Publication Data

Data available

Typeset by Newgen Imaging Systems (P) Ltd., Chennai, India
Printed in Great Britain
on acid-free paper by
CPI Bath

ISBN 0–19–928816–X   978–0–19–928816–8

1 3 5 7 9 10 8 6 4 2

CONTENTS

ALPHABETICAL CONTENTS

CHRONOLOGICAL CONTENTS

EDITOR'S PREFACE

As in previous editions, this book sets out to present the principle legislative materials in the conventionally central areas of commercial and consumer law (including particularly relevant topics of general common law) but (in order to keep the collection manageable and its price reasonable) generally omitting more specialist subjects.

This, of course, is more easily said than done. Commercial activity is infinitely varied and the pace of change continues to accelerate. For their part, our legislators are engaged in responding to, facilitating and promoting such changes. These elements, coupled with the volume of new material each year, make revision of this book both demanding and exciting. They also require increased selectivity in combining the core features of our commercial law with a flavour of its diversity.

Commercial and Consumer Law and statute have in common that they are all in a permanent state of flux, making it essential continually to update this collection of materials. The book therefore has the usual scattering of amendments to existing legislative provisions together with recent innovations.

This year's edition incorporates amendments to the Sale of Goods Act 1979, the Supply of Goods and Services Act 1982, the Consumer Protection Act 1987, the Arbitration Act 1996, the Contracts (Rights of Third Parties) Act 1999, the Financial Services and Markets Act 2000 and the Unfair Terms in Consumer Contracts Regulations 1999.

In addition, the General Product Safety Regulations 1994 have been replaced by the General Product Safety Regulations 2005 (implementing the European Parliament and Council Directive 2001/95/EC on general product safety). The UNCITRAL draft Instrument on Carriage of Goods wholly or partly by sea has appeared in a tidied up and updated form, overtly now as a draft Convention.

Most significantly, the Consumer Credit Act 2006 has been enacted, making major amendments to the Consumer Credit Act 1974 and with other knock-on effects.

As in previous editions, in most cases the material is reproduced in its complete, most recent form, amendments being enclosed in square brackets; occasional omissions are indicated by three dots. Supplementary notes and details of amending provisions, constantly changing and easily available in updated form elsewhere, are generally omitted for reasons of space.

As always, I am happy to acknowledge the holders' rights in copyright materials. Also, I continue to be grateful for suggestions as to possible revisions of this collection of materials.

Francis Rose
18 June 2006

PART I

Statutes

Life Assurance Act 1774
(14 Geo. III, c. 48)

An Act for regulating Insurances upon Lives, and for prohibiting all such Insurances except in cases where the Persons insuring shall have an Interest in the Life or Death of the Persons insured.

[1774]

Preamble

Whereas it hath been found by experience that the making insurances on lives or other events wherein the assured shall have no interest hath introduced a mischievous kind of gaming:

1 No insurance to be made on lives, etc., by persons having no interest, etc.

From and after the passing of this Act no insurance shall be made by any person or persons, bodies politick or corporate, on the life or lives of any person or persons, or on any other event or events whatsoever, wherein the person or persons for whose use, benefit, or on whose account such policy or policies shall be made, shall have no interest, or by way of gaming or wagering; and that every assurance made contrary to the true intent and meaning hereof shall be null and void to all intents and purposes whatsoever.

2 No policies on lives without inserting the names of persons interested, etc.

And [. . .] it shall not be lawful to make any policy or policies on the life or lives of any person or persons, or other event or events, without inserting in such policy or policies the person or persons name or names interested therein, or for whose use, benefit, or on whose account such policy is so made or underwrote.

3 How much may be recovered where the insured hath interest in lives

And [. . .] in all cases where the insured hath interest in such life or lives, event or events, no greater sum shall be recovered or received from the insurer or insurers than the amount of value of the interest of the insured in such life or lives, or other event or events.

4 Not to extend to insurances on ships, goods, etc.

Provided, always, that nothing herein contained shall extend or be construed to extend to insurances bona fide made by any person or persons on ships, goods, or merchandises, but every such insurance shall be as valid and effectual in the law as if this Act had not been made.

Bills of Lading Act 1855
(18 & 19 Vict., c. 111)

An Act to amend the Law relating to Bills of Lading. [14th August 1855]

Whereas by the Custom of Merchants a Bill of Lading of Goods being transferable by Endorsement the Property in the Goods may thereby pass to the Endorsee, but nevertheless all Rights in respect of the Contract contained in the Bill of Lading continue in the original Shipper or Owner, and it is expedient that such Rights should pass with the Property: And whereas it frequently happens that the Goods in respect of which Bills of Lading purport to be signed have not been laden on board, and it is proper that such Bills of Lading in the Hands of a bona fide Holder for Value should not be questioned by the Master or other Person signing the same on the Ground of the Goods not having been laden as aforesaid:

1   Rights under bills of lading to vest in consignee or endorsee
Every Consignee of Goods named in a Bill of Lading, and every Endorsee of a Bill of Lading to whom the Property in the Goods therein mentioned shall pass, upon or by reason of such Consignment or Endorsement, shall have transferred to and vested in him all Rights of Suit, and be subject to the same Liabilities in respect of such Goods as if the Contract contained in the Bill of Lading had been made with himself.

2   Not to affect right of stoppage in transitu or claims for freight
Nothing herein contained shall prejudice or affect any Right of Stoppage in transitu, or any Right to claim Freight against the original Shipper or Owner, or any Liability of the Consignee or Endorsee by reason or in consequence of his being such Consignee or Endorsee, or of his Receipt of the Goods by reason or in consequence of such Consignment or Endorsement.

3   Bill of lading in hands of consignee, &c. conclusive evidence of shipment as against master, &c.
Every Bill of Lading in the Hands of a Consignee or Endorsee for valuable Consideration representing Goods to have been shipped on board a Vessel shall be conclusive Evidence of such Shipment as against the Master or other Person signing the same, notwithstanding that such Goods or some Part thereof may not have been so shipped, unless such Holder of the Bill of Lading shall have had actual Notice at the Time of receiving the same that the Goods had not been in fact laden on board: Provided that the Master or other Person so signing may exonerate himself in respect of such Misrepresentation by showing that it was caused without any Default on his part, and wholly by the Fraud of the Shipper or of the Holder, or some person under whom the Holder claims.

[*This Act was repealed by the Carriage of Goods by Sea Act 1992.*]

Bills of Sale Act 1878
(41 & 42 Vict., c. 31)

An Act to consolidate and amend the Law for preventing Frauds upon Creditors by secret Bills of Sale of Personal Chattels.   [22nd July 1878]

3   Application
This Act shall apply to every bill of sale executed on or after the first day of January one thousand eight hundred and seventy-nine (whether the same be absolute, or subject or not subject to any trust) whereby the holder or grantee has power, either with or without notice, and either immediately or at any future time, to seize or take possession of any personal chattels comprised in or made subject to such bill of sale.

4   Interpretation of terms
In this Act the following words and expressions shall have the meanings in this section assigned to them respectively, unless there be something in the subject or context repugnant to such construction; (that is to say),

The expression 'bill of sale' shall include bills of sale, assignments, transfers, declarations of trust without transfer, inventories of goods with receipt thereto attached, or receipts for purchase moneys of goods, and other assurances of personal chattels, and also powers of attorney, authorities, or licenses to take possession of personal chattels as security for any debt, and also any agreement, whether intended or not to be followed by the execution of any other instrument, by which a right in equity to any personal chattels, or to any charge or security thereon, shall be conferred, but shall not include the following documents; that is to say, assignments for the benefit of the creditors of the person making or giving the same, marriage settlements, transfers or assignments of any ship or vessel or any share thereof, transfers of goods in the ordinary course of business of any trade or calling, bills of sale of goods in foreign parts or at sea, bills of lading, India warrants, warehouse-keepers' certificates, warrants or orders for the delivery of goods, or any other documents used in the ordinary course of business as proof of the possession or control of goods, or authorising or purporting to authorise, either by indorsement or by delivery, the possessor of such document to transfer or receive goods thereby represented:

The expression 'personal chattels' shall mean goods, furniture, and other articles capable of complete transfer by delivery, and (when separately assigned or charged) fixtures and growing crops, but shall not include chattel interests in real estate, nor fixtures (except trade machinery as herein-after defined), when assigned together with a freehold or leasehold interest in any land or building to which they are affixed, nor growing crops when assigned together with any interest in the land on which they grow, nor shares or interests in the stock, funds, or securities of any government, or in the capital or property of incorporated or joint stock companies, nor choses in action, nor any stock or produce upon any farm or lands which by virtue of any covenant or agreement or of the custom of the country ought not to be removed from any farm where the same are at the time of making or giving of such bill of sale:

Personal chattels shall be deemed to be in the 'apparent possession' of the person making or giving a bill of sale, so long as they remain or are in or upon any house, mill, warehouse, building, works, yard, land, or other premises occupied by him, or are used and enjoyed by him in any place whatsoever, notwithstanding that formal possession thereof may have been taken by or given to any other person:

'Prescribed' means prescribed by rules made under the provisions of this Act.

5   Application of Act to trade machinery

From and after the commencement of this Act trade machinery shall, for the purposes of this Act, be deemed to be personal chattels, and any mode of disposition of trade machinery by the owner thereof which would be a bill of sale as to any other personal chattels shall be deemed to be a bill of sale within the meaning of this Act.

For the purposes of this Act—

'Trade machinery' means the machinery used in or attached to any factory or workshop;

1st.   Exclusive of the fixed motive-powers, such as the water-wheels and steam-engines, and the steam-boilers, donkey-engines, and other fixed appurtenances of the said motive-powers; and

2nd. Exclusive of the fixed power machinery, such as the shafts, wheels, drums, and their fixed appurtenances, which transmit the action of the motive-powers to the other machinery, fixed and loose; and,

3rd.   Exclusive of the pipes for steam gas and water in the factory or workshop.

The machinery or effects excluded by this section from the definition of trade machinery shall not be deemed to be personal chattels within the meaning of this Act.

'Factory or workshop' means any premises on which any manual labour is exercised by way of trade, or for purposes of gain, in or incidental to the following purposes or any of them; that is to say,

(a) In or incidental to the making of any article or part of an article; or

(b) In or incidental to the altering repairing ornamenting finishing of any article; or

(c) In or incidental to the adapting for sale of any article.

6   Certain instruments giving powers of distress to be subject to this Act

Every attornment instrument or agreement, not being a mining lease, whereby a power of distress is given or agreed to be given by any person to any other person by way of security for any present future or contingent debt or advance, and whereby any rent is reserved or made payable as a mode of providing for the payment of interest on such debt or advance, or otherwise for the purpose of such security only, shall be deemed to be a bill of sale, within the meaning of this Act, of any personal chattels which may be seized or taken under such power of distress.

Provided, that nothing in this section shall extend to any mortgage of any estate or interest in any land tenement or hereditament which the mortgagee, being in possession, shall have demised to the mortgagor as his tenant at a fair and reasonable rent.

7   Fixtures or growing crops not to be deemed separately assigned when the land passes by the same instrument

No fixtures or growing crops shall be deemed, under this Act, to be separately assigned or charged by reason only that they are assigned by separate words, or that power is given to sever them from the land or building to which they are affixed, or from the land on which they grow, without otherwise taking possession of or dealing with such land or building, or land, if by the same instrument any freehold or leasehold interest in the land or building to which such fixtures are affixed, or in the land on which such crops grow, is also conveyed or assigned to the same persons or person.

The same rule of construction shall be applied to all deeds or instruments, including fixtures or growing crops, executed before the commencement of this Act, and then subsisting and in force, in all questions arising under any bankruptcy liquidation assignment for the benefit of creditors, or execution of any process of any court, which shall take place or be issued after the commencement of this Act.

8   Avoidance of unregistered bills of sale in certain cases

Every bill of sale to which this Act applies shall be duly attested and shall be registered under this Act, within seven days after the making or giving thereof, and shall set forth the consideration for which such bill of sale was given, otherwise such bill of sale, as against all trustees or assignees of the estate of the person whose chattels, or any of them, are comprised in such bill of sale under the law relating to bankruptcy or liquidation, or under any assignment for the benefit of the creditors of such person, and also as against all sheriffs officers and other persons seizing any chattels comprised in such bill of sale, in the execution of any process of any court authorising the seizure of the chattels of the person by whom or of whose chattels such bill has been made, and also as against every person on whose behalf such process shall have been issued, shall be deemed fraudulent and void so far as regards the property in or right to the possession of any chattels comprised in such bill of sale which, at or after the time of filing the petition for bankruptcy or liquidation, or of the execution of such assignment, or of executing such process (as the case may be), and after the expiration of such seven days are in the possession or apparent possession of the person making such bill of sale (or of any person against whom the process has issued under or in the execution of which such bill has been made or given, as the case may be).

9   Avoidance of certain duplicate bills of sale

Where a subsequent bill of sale is executed within or on the expiration of seven days after the execution of a prior unregistered bill of sale, and comprises all or any part of the personal chattels comprised in such prior bill of sale, then, if such subsequent bill of sale is given as a security for the same debt as is secured by the prior bill of sale, or for any part of such debt, it shall, to the extent to which it is a security for the same debt or part thereof, and so far as respects the personal chattels or part thereof comprised in the prior bill, be absolutely void, unless it is proved to the satisfaction of the court having cognizance of the case that the subsequent bill of sale was bona fide given for the purpose of correcting some material error in the prior bill of sale, and not for the purpose of evading this Act.

10   Mode of registering bills of sale

A bill of sale shall be attested and registered under this Act in the following manner:

(1) The execution of every bill of sale shall be attested by a solicitor of the [Senior Courts], and the attestation shall state that before the execution of the bill of sale the effect thereof has been explained to the grantor by the attesting solicitor.

(2) Such bill, with every schedule or inventory thereto annexed or therein referred to, and also a true copy of such bill and of every such schedule or inventory, and of every attestation of the execution of such bill of sale, together with an affidavit of the time of such bill of sale being made or given, and of its due execution and attestation, and a description of the residence and occupation of the person making or giving the same (or in case the same is made or given by any person under or in the execution of any process, then a description of the residence and occupation of the person against whom such process issued), and of every attesting witness to such bill of sale, shall be presented to and the said copy and affidavit shall be filed with the registrar within seven clear days after the making or giving of such bill of sale, in like manner as a warrant of attorney in any personal action given by a trader is now by law required to be filed:

(3) If the bill of sale is made or given subject to any defeasance or condition, or declaration of trust not contained in the body thereof, such defeasance, condition, or declaration shall be deemed to be part of the bill, and shall be written on the same paper or parchment therewith before the registration, and shall be truly set forth in the copy filed under this Act therewith and as part thereof, otherwise the registration shall be void.

In case two or more bills of sale are given, comprising in whole or in part any of the same chattels, they shall have priority in the order of the date of their registration respectively as regards such chattels.

A transfer or assignment of a registered bill of sale need not be registered.

11   Renewal of registration

The registration of a bill of sale, whether executed before or after the commencement of this Act, must be renewed once at least every five years, and if a period of five years elapses from the registration or renewed registration of a bill of sale without a renewal or further renewal (as the case may be), the registration shall become void.

The renewal of a registration shall be effected by filing with the registrar an affidavit stating the date of the bill of sale and of the last registration thereof, and the names, residences, and occupations of the parties thereto as stated therein, and that the bill of sale is still a subsisting security.

Every such affidavit may be in the form set forth in the Schedule (A) to this Act annexed.

A renewal of registration shall not become necessary by reason only of a transfer or assignment of a bill of sale.

12   Form of register

The registrar shall keep a book (in this Act called 'the register') for the purposes of this Act, and shall, upon the filing of any bill of sale or copy under this Act, enter therein in the form set forth in the second schedule (B) to this Act annexed, or in any other prescribed form, the name residence and occupation of the person by whom the bill was made or given (or in case the same was made or given by any person under or in the execution of process, then the name residence and occupation of the person against whom such process was issued, and also the name of the person or persons to whom or in whose favour the bill was given), and the other particulars shown in the said schedule or to be prescribed under this Act, and shall number all such bills registered in each year consecutively, according to the respective dates of their registration.

Upon the registration of any affidavit of renewal the like entry shall be made, with the addition of the date and number of the last previous entry relating to the same bill, and the bill of sale or copy originally filed shall be thereupon marked with the number affixed to such affidavit of renewal.

The registrar shall also keep an index of the names of the grantors of registered bills of sale with reference to entries in the register of the bills of sale given by each such grantor.

Such index shall be arranged in divisions corresponding with the letters of the alphabet, so that all grantors whose surnames begin with the same letter (and no others) shall be comprised in one division, but the arrangement within each such division need not be strictly alphabetical.

13 The registrar

The masters of the [Senior Courts] attached to the Queen's Bench Division of the High Court of Justice, or such other officers as may for the time being be assigned for this purpose under the provisions of the Supreme Court of Judicature Acts 1873 and 1875, shall be the registrar for the purposes of this Act, and any one of the said masters may perform all or any of the duties of the registrar.

14 Rectification of register

Any judge of the High Court of Justice on being satisfied that the omission to register a bill of sale or an affidavit or renewal thereof within the time prescribed by this Act, or the omission or mis-statement of the name residence or occupation of any person, was accidental or due to inadvertence, may in his discretion order such omission or mis-statement to be rectified by the insertion in the register of the true name residence or occupation, or by extending the time for such registration on such terms and conditions (if any) as to security, notice by advertisement or otherwise, or as to any other matter, as he thinks fit to direct.

15 Entry of satisfaction

Subject to and in accordance with any rules to be made under and for the purposes of this Act, the registrar may order a memorandum of satisfaction to be written upon any registered copy of a bill of sale, upon the prescribed evidence being given that the debt (if any) for which such bill of sale was made or given has been satisfied or discharged.

16 Copies may be taken, etc.

Any person shall be entitled to have an office copy or extract of any registered bill of sale, and affidavit of execution filed therewith, or copy thereof, and of any affidavit filed therewith, if any, or registered affidavit of renewal, upon paying for the same at the like rate as for office copies of judgments of the High Court of Justice, and any copy of a registered bill of sale, and affidavit purporting to be an office copy thereof, shall in all courts and before all arbitrators or other persons, be admitted as prima facie evidence thereof, and of the fact and date of registration as shown thereon [. . .].

20 Order and disposition

Chattels comprised in a bill of sale which has been and continues to be duly registered under this Act shall not be deemed to be in the possession, order, or disposition of the grantor of the bill of sale within the meaning of the Bankruptcy Act 1869.

21 Rules

Rules for the purposes of this Act may be made and altered from time to time by the like persons and in the like manner in which rules and regulations may be made under and for the purposes of the Supreme Court of Judicature Acts 1873 and 1875.

22 Time for registration

When the time for registering a bill of sale expires on a Sunday, or other day on which the registrar's office is closed, the registration shall be valid if made on the next following day on which the office is open.

24 Extent of Act

This Act shall not extend to Scotland or to Ireland.

SCHEDULES

Section 11   SCHEDULE (A)

I [*A.B.*]   of   do swear that a bill of sale, bearing date the   day of   18 [*insert the date of the bill*], and made between [*insert the names and descriptions of the parties in the original bill of sale*] and which said bill of sale [*or,* and a copy of which said bill of sale, *as the case may be*] was registered on the   day of   18 [*insert date of registration*], is still a subsisting security.
     Sworn, &c.

SCHEDULE (B)

Satis-faction entered	No	By whom given (or against whom process issued)			To whom given	Nature of Instrument	Date	Date of Registration	Date of Registration of affidavit of renewal
		Name	Residence	Occupation					

Bills of Exchange Act 1882
(45 & 46 Vict., c. 61)

An Act to codify the law relating to Bills of Exchange, Cheques, and Promissory Notes.
                                        [18th August 1882]

PART I   PRELIMINARY

1   Short title
This Act may be cited as the Bills of Exchange Act, 1882.

2   Interpretation of terms
In this Act, unless the context otherwise requires,—
     'Acceptance' means an acceptance completed by delivery or notification.
     'Action' includes counter claim and set off.
     'Banker' includes a body of persons whether incorporated or not who carry on the business of banking.
     'Bankrupt' includes any person whose estate is vested in a trustee or assignee under the law for the time being in force relating to bankruptcy.
     'Bearer' means the person in possession of a bill or note which is payable to bearer.
     'Bill' means bill of exchange, and 'note' means promissory note.

'Delivery' means transfer of possession, actual or constructive, from one person to another.

'Holder' means the payee or indorsee of a bill or note who is in possession of it, or the bearer thereof.

'Indorsement' means an indorsement completed by delivery.

'Issue' means the first delivery of a bill or note, complete in form to a person who takes it as a holder.

'Person' includes a body of persons whether incorporated or not.

['postal operator' has the meaning given by section 125(1) of the Postal Services Act 2000.]

'Value' means valuable consideration.

'Written' includes printed, and 'writing' includes print.

PART II   BILLS OF EXCHANGE

Form and interpretation

3   Bill of exchange defined

(1) A bill of exchange is an unconditional order in writing, addressed by one person to another, signed by the person giving it, requiring the person to whom it is addressed to pay on demand or at a fixed or determinable future time a sum certain in money to or to the order of a specified person, or to bearer.

(2) An instrument which does not comply with these conditions, or which orders any act to be done in addition to the payment of money, is not a bill of exchange.

(3) An order to pay out of a particular fund is not unconditional within the meaning of this section; but an unqualified order to pay, coupled with (a) an indication of a particular fund out of which the drawee is to re-imburse himself or a particular account to be debited with the amount, or (b) a statement of the transaction which gives rise to the bill, is unconditional.

(4) A bill is not invalid by reason—

(a) That it is not dated;

(b) That it does not specify the value given, or that any value has been given therefor;

(c) That it does not specify the place where it is drawn or the place where it is payable.

4   Inland and foreign bills

(1) An inland bill is a bill which is or on the face of it purports to be (a) both drawn and payable within the British Islands, or (b) drawn within the British Islands upon some person resident therein. Any other bill is a foreign bill.

For the purposes of this Act 'British Islands' means any part of the United Kingdom of Great Britain and Ireland, the islands of Man, Guernsey, Jersey, Alderney, and Sark, and the islands adjacent to any of them being part of the dominions of Her Majesty.

(2) Unless the contrary appear on the face of the bill the holder may treat it as an inland bill.

5   Effect where different parties to bill are the same person

(1) A bill may be drawn payable to, or to the order of, the drawer; or it may be drawn payable to, or to the order of, the drawee.

(2) Where in a bill drawer and drawee are the same person, or where the drawee is a fictitious person or a person not having capacity to contract, the holder may treat the instrument, at his option, either as a bill of exchange or as a promissory note.

6   Address to drawee

(1) The drawee must be named or otherwise indicated in a bill with reasonable certainty.

(2) A bill may be addressed to two or more drawees whether they are partners or not, but an order addressed to two drawees in the alternative or to two or more drawees in succession is not a bill of exchange.

7 Certainty required as to payee

(1) Where a bill is not payable to bearer, the payee must be named or otherwise indicated therein with reasonable certainty.

(2) A bill may be made payable to two or more payees jointly, or it may be made payable in the alternative to one of two, or one or some of several payees. A bill may also be made payable to the holder of an office for the time being.

(3) Where the payee is a fictitious or non-existing person the bill may be treated as payable to bearer.

8 What bills are negotiable

(1) When a bill contains words prohibiting transfer, or indicating an intention that it should not be transferable, it is valid as between the parties thereto, but is not negotiable.

(2) A negotiable bill may be payable either to order or to bearer.

(3) A bill is payable to bearer which is expressed to be so payable, or on which the only or last indorsement is an indorsement in blank.

(4) A bill is payable to order which is expressed to be so payable, or which is expressed to be payable to a particular person, and does not contain words prohibiting transfer or indicating an intention that it should not be transferable.

(5) Where a bill, either originally or by indorsement, is expressed to be payable to the order of a specified person, and not to him or his order, it is nevertheless payable to him or his order at his option.

9 Sum payable

(1) The sum payable by a bill is a sum certain within the meaning of this Act, although it is required to be paid—

    (a) With interest.

    (b) By stated instalments.

    (c) By stated instalments, with a provision that upon default in payment of any instalment the whole shall become due.

    (d) According to an indicated rate of exchange or according to a rate of exchange to be ascertained as directed by the bill.

(2) Where the sum payable is expressed in words and also in figures, and there is a discrepancy between the two, the sum denoted by the words is the amount payable.

(3) Where a bill is expressed to be payable with interest, unless the instrument otherwise provides, interest runs from the date of the bill, and if the bill is undated from the issue thereof.

10 Bill payable on demand

(1) A bill is payable on demand—

    (a) Which is expressed to be payable on demand, or at sight, or on presentation; or

    (b) In which no time for payment is expressed.

(2) Where a bill is accepted or indorsed when it is overdue, it shall, as regards the acceptor who so accepts, or any indorser who so indorses it, be deemed a bill payable on demand.

11 Bill payable at a future time

A bill is payable at a determinable future time within the meaning of this Act which is expressed to be payable—

(1) At a fixed period after date or sight.

(2) On or at a fixed period after the occurrence of a specified event which is certain to happen, though the time of happening may be uncertain.

An instrument expressed to be payable on a contingency is not a bill, and the happening of the event does not cure the defect.

12 Omission of date in bill payable after date

Where a bill expressed to be payable at a fixed period after date is issued undated, or where the acceptance of a bill payable at a fixed period after sight is undated, any holder may insert therein the true date of issue or acceptance, and the bill shall be payable accordingly.

Provided that (1) where the holder in good faith and by mistake inserts a wrong date, and (2) in every case where a wrong date is inserted, if the bill subsequently comes into the hands of a holder in due course the bill shall not be avoided thereby, but shall operate and be payable as if the date so inserted had been the true date.

13   Ante-dating and post-dating

(1) Where a bill or an acceptance or any indorsement on a bill is dated, the date shall, unless the contrary be proved, be deemed to be the true date of the drawing, acceptance, or indorsement, as the case may be.

(2) A bill is not invalid by reason only that it is ante-dated or post-dated, or that it bears date on a Sunday.

14   Computation of time of payment

Where a bill is not payable on demand the day on which it falls due is determined as follows:

[(1) The bill is due and payable in all cases on the last day of the time of payment as fixed by the bill or, if that is a non-business day, on the succeeding business day.]

(2) Where a bill is payable at a fixed period after date, after sight, or after the happening of a specified event, the time of payment is determined by excluding the day from which the time is to begin to run and by including the day of payment.

(3) Where a bill is payable at a fixed period after sight, the time begins to run from the date of the acceptance if the bill be accepted, and from the date of noting or protest if the bill be noted or protested for non-acceptance, or for non-delivery.

15   Case of need

The drawer of a bill and any indorser may insert therein the name of a person to whom the holder may resort in case of need, that is to say, in case the bill is dishonoured by non—acceptance or non-payment. Such person is called the referee in case of need. It is in the option of the holder to resort to the referee in case of need or not as he may think fit.

16   Optional stipulations by drawer or indorser

The drawer of a bill, and any indorser may insert therein an express stipulation—

(1) Negativing or limiting his own liability to the holder:

(2) Waiving as regards himself some or all of the holder's duties.

17   Definition and requisites of acceptance

(1) The acceptance of a bill is the signification by the drawee of his assent to the order of the drawer.

(2) An acceptance is invalid unless it complies with the following conditions, namely:

    (a) It must be written on the bill and be signed by the drawee. The mere signature of the drawee without additional words is sufficient.

    (b) It must not express that the drawee will perform his promise by any other means than the payment of money.

18   Time for acceptance

A bill may be accepted—

(1) before it has been signed by the drawer, or while otherwise incomplete:

(2) When it is overdue, or after it has been dishonoured by a previous refusal to accept, or by non-payment:

(3) When a bill payable after sight is dishonoured by non-acceptance, and the drawee subsequently accepts it, the holder, in the absence of any different agreement, is entitled to have the bill accepted as of the date of first presentment to the drawee for acceptance.

19   General and qualified acceptance

(1) An acceptance is either (a) general or (b) qualified.

(2) A general acceptance assents without qualification to the order of the drawer. A qualified acceptance in express terms varies the effect of the bill as drawn.

In particular an acceptance is qualified which is—

    (a) conditional, that is to say, which makes payment by the acceptor dependent on the fulfilment of a condition therein stated:

    (b) partial, that is to say, an acceptance to pay part only of the amount for which the bill is drawn:

    (c) local, that is to say, an acceptance to pay only at a particular specified place: An acceptance to pay at a particular place is a general acceptance, unless it expressly states that the bill is to be paid there only and not elsewhere:

    (d) qualified as to time:

    (e) the acceptance of some one or more of the drawees, but not of all.

20   Inchoate instruments

(1) Where a simple signature on a blank paper is delivered by the signer in order that it may be converted into a bill, it operates as a prima facie authority to fill it up as a complete bill for any amount [. . .] using the signature for that of the drawer, or the acceptor, or an indorser; and, in like manner, when a bill is wanting in any material particular, the person in possession of it has a prima facie authority to fill up the omission in any way he thinks fit.

(2) In order that any such instrument when completed may be enforceable against any person who became a party thereto prior to its completion, it must be filled up within a reasonable time, and strictly in accordance with the authority given. Reasonable time for this purpose is a question of fact.

Provided that if any such instrument after completion is negotiated to a holder in due course it shall be valid and effectual for all purposes in his hands and he may enforce it as if it had been filled up within a reasonable time and strictly in accordance with the authority given.

21   Delivery

(1) Every contract on a bill, whether it be the drawer's, the acceptor's, or an indorser's is incomplete and revocable, until delivery of the instrument in order to give effect thereto.

Provided that where an acceptance is written on a bill, and the drawee gives notice to or according to the directions of the person entitled to the bill that he has accepted it, the acceptance then becomes complete and irrevocable.

(2) As between immediate parties, and as regards a remote party other than a holder in due course, the delivery—

    (a) in order to be effectual must be made either by or under the authority of the party drawing, accepting, or indorsing, as the case may be:

    (b) may be shown to have been conditional or for a special purpose only, and not for the purpose of transferring the property in the bill.

But if the bill be in the hands of a holder in due course a valid delivery of the bill by all parties prior to him so as to make them liable to him is conclusively presumed.

(3) Where a bill is no longer in the possession of a party who has signed it as drawer, acceptor, or indorser, a valid and unconditional delivery by him is presumed until the contrary is proved.

Capacity and authority of parties

22   Capacity of parties

(1) Capacity to incur liability as a party to a bill is coextensive with capacity to contract. Provided that nothing in this section shall enable a corporation to make itself liable as drawer, acceptor, or indorser of a bill unless it is competent to it so to do under the law for the time being in force relating to corporations.

(2) Where a bill is drawn or indorsed by an infant, minor, or corporation having no capacity or power to incur liability on a bill, the drawing or indorsement entitles the holder to receive payment of the bill, and to enforce it against any other party thereto.

23 Signature essential to liability

No person is liable as drawer, indorser, or acceptor of a bill who has not signed it as such: Provided that

(1) Where a person signs a bill in a trade or assumed name, he is liable thereon as if he had signed it in his own name:

(2) The signature of the name of a firm is equivalent to the signature by the person so signing of the names of all persons liable as partners in that firm.

24 Forged or unauthorised signature

Subject to the provisions of this Act, where a signature on a bill is forged or placed thereon without the authority of the person whose signature it purports to be, the forged or unauthorised signature is wholly inoperative, and no right to retain the bill or to give a discharge therefor or to enforce payment thereof against any party thereto can be acquired through or under that signature, unless the party against whom it is sought to retain or enforce payment of the bill is precluded from setting up the forgery or want of authority.

Provided that nothing in this section shall affect the ratification of an unauthorised signature not amounting to a forgery.

25 Procuration signatures

A signature by procuration operates as notice that the agent has but a limited authority to sign, and the principal is only bound by such signature if the agent in so signing was acting within the actual limits of his authority.

26 Person signing as agent or in representative capacity

(1) Where a person signs a bill as drawer, indorser, or acceptor, and adds words to his signature, indicating that he signs for or on behalf of a principal, or in a representative character, he is not personally liable thereon; but the mere addition to his signature of words describing him as an agent, or as filling a representative character, does not exempt him from personal liability.

(2) In determining whether a signature on a bill is that of the principal or that of the agent by whose hand it is written, the construction most favourable to the validity of the instrument shall be adopted.

The consideration for a bill

27 Value and holder for value

(1) Valuable consideration for a bill may be constituted by,—

    (a) Any consideration sufficient to support a simple contract;

    (b) An antecedent debt or liability. Such a debt or liability is deemed valuable consideration whether the bill is payable on demand or at a future time.

(2) Where value has at any time been given for a bill the holder is deemed to be a holder for value as regards the acceptor and all parties to the bill who became parties prior to such time.

(3) Where the holder of a bill has a lien on it, arising either from contract or by implication of law, he is deemed to be a holder for value to the extent of the sum for which he has a lien.

28 Accommodation bill or party

(1) An accommodation party to a bill is a person who has signed a bill as drawer, acceptor, or indorser, without receiving value therefor, and for the purpose of lending his name to some other person.

(2) An accommodation party is liable on the bill to a holder for value; and it is immaterial whether, when such holder took the bill, he knew such party to be an accommodation party or not.

29 Holder in due course

(1) A holder in due course is a holder who has taken a bill, complete and regular on the face of it, under the following conditions, namely,

(a) That he became the holder of it before it was overdue, and without notice that it had been previously dishonoured, if such was the fact:

(b) That he took the bill in good faith and for value, and that at the time the bill was negotiated to him he had no notice of any defect in the title of the person who negotiated it.

(2) In particular the title of a person who negotiates a bill is defective within the meaning of this Act when he obtained the bill, or the acceptance thereof, by fraud, duress or force and fear, or other unlawful means, or for an illegal consideration, or when he negotiates it in breach of faith, or under such circumstances as amount to a fraud.

(3) A holder (whether for value or not), who derives his title to a bill through a holder in due course, and who is not himself a party to any fraud or illegality affecting it, has all the rights of that holder in due course as regards the acceptor and all parties to the bill prior to that holder.

30 Presumption of value and good faith

(1) Every party whose signature appears on a bill is prima facie deemed to have become a party thereto for value.

(2) Every holder of a bill is prima facie deemed to be a holder in due course; but if in an action on a bill it is admitted or proved that the acceptance, issue, or subsequent negotiation of the bill is affected with fraud, duress, or force and fear, or illegality, the burden of proof is shifted, unless and until the holder proves that, subsequent to the alleged fraud or illegality, value has in good faith been given for the bill.

Negotiation of bills

31 Negotiation of bill

(1) A bill is negotiated when it is transferred from one person to another in such a manner as to constitute the transferee the holder of the bill.

(2) A bill payable to bearer is negotiated by delivery.

(3) A bill payable to order is negotiated by the indorsement of the holder completed by delivery.

(4) Where, the holder of a bill payable to his order transfers it for value without indorsing it, the transfer gives the transferee such title as the transferor had in the bill, and the transferee in addition acquires the right to have the indorsement of the transferor.

(5) Where any person is under obligation to indorse a bill in a representative capacity, he may indorse a bill in such terms as to negative personal liability.

32 Requisites of a valid indorsement

An indorsement in order to operate as a negotiation must comply with the following conditions, namely:—

(1) It must be written on the bill itself and signed by the indorser. The simple signature of the indorser on the bill, without additional words, is sufficient.

An indorsement written on an allonge or a 'copy' of a bill issued or negotiated in a country where 'copies' are recognised, is deemed to have been written on the bill itself.

(2) It must be an indorsement of the entire bill. A partial indorsement, that is to say, an indorsement which purports to transfer to the indorsee a part only of the amount payable, or which purports to transfer the bill to two or more indorsees severally, does not operate as a negotiation of the bill.

(3) Where a bill is payable to the order of two or more payees or indorsees who are not partners all must indorse, unless the one indorsing has authority to indorse for the others.

(4) Where, in a bill payable to order, the payee or indorsee is wrongly designated, or his name is mis-spelt, he may indorse the bill as therein described, adding, if he think fit, his proper signature.

(5) Where there are two or more indorsements on a bill, each indorsement is deemed to have been made in the order in which it appears on the bill, until the contrary is proved.

(6) An indorsement may be made in blank or special. It may also contain terms making it restrictive.

33 Conditional indorsement

Where a bill purports to be indorsed conditionally the condition may be disregarded by the payer, and payment to the indorsee is valid whether the condition has been fulfilled or not.

34 Indorsement in blank and special indorsement

(1) An indorsement in blank specifies no indorsee, and a bill so indorsed becomes payable to bearer.

(2) A special indorsement specifies the person to whom, or to whose order, the bill is to be payable.

(3) The provisions of this Act relating to a payee apply with the necessary modifications to an indorsee under a special indorsement.

(4) When a bill has been indorsed in blank, any holder may convert the blank indorsement into a special indorsement by writing above the indorser's signature a direction to pay the bill to or to the order of himself or some other person.

35 Restrictive indorsement

(1) An indorsement is restrictive which prohibits the further negotiation of the bill or which expresses that it is a mere authority to deal with the bill as thereby directed and not a transfer of ownership thereof, as, for example, if a bill be indorsed 'Pay D. only', or 'Pay D. for the account of X.,' or 'Pay D. or order for collection.'

(2) A restrictive indorsement gives the indorsee the right to receive payment of the bill and to sue any party thereto that his indorser could have sued, but gives him no power to transfer his rights as indorsee unless it expressly authorise him to do so.

(3) Where a restrictive indorsement authorises further transfer, all subsequent indorsees take the bill with the same rights and subject to the same liabilities as the first indorsee under the restrictive indorsement.

36 Negotiation of overdue or dishonoured bills

(1) Where a bill is negotiable in its origin it continues to be negotiable until it has been (a) restrictively indorsed or (b) discharged by payment or otherwise.

(2) Where an overdue bill is negotiated, it can only be negotiated subject to any defect of title affecting it at its maturity, and thenceforward no person who takes it can acquire or give a better title than that which the person from whom he took it had.

(3) A bill payable on demand is deemed to be overdue within the meaning and for the purposes of this section, when it appears on the face of it to have been in circulation for an unreasonable length of time. What is an unreasonable length of time for this purpose is a question of fact.

(4) Except where an indorsement bears date after the maturity of the bill, every negotiation is prima facie deemed to have been effected before the bill was overdue.

(5) Where a bill which is not overdue has been dishonoured any person who takes it with notice of the dishonour takes it subject to any defect of title attaching thereto at the time of dishonour, but nothing in this sub-section shall affect the rights of a holder in due course.

37 Negotiation of bill to party already liable thereon

Where a bill is negotiated back to the drawer, or to a prior indorser or to the acceptor, such party may, subject to the provisions of this Act, reissue and further negotiate the bill, but he is not entitled to enforce payment of the bill against any intervening party to whom he was previously liable.

38 Rights of the holder

The rights and powers of the holder of a bill are as follows:

(1) He may sue on the bill in his own name:

(2) Where he is a holder in due course, he holds the bill free from any defect of title of prior parties, as well as from mere personal defences available to prior parties among themselves, and may enforce payment against all parties liable on the bill:

(3) Where his title is defective (a) if he negotiates the bill to a holder in due course, that holder obtains a good and complete title to the bill, and (b) if he obtains payment of the bill the person who pays him in due course gets a valid discharge for the bill.

General duties of the holder

39 When presentment for acceptance is necessary

(1) Where a bill is payable after sight, presentment for acceptance is necessary in order to fix the maturity of the instrument.

(2) Where a bill expressly stipulates that it shall be presented for acceptance, or where a bill is drawn payable elsewhere than at the residence or place of business of the drawee, it must be presented for acceptance before it can be presented for payment.

(3) In no other case is presentment for acceptance necessary in order to render liable any party to the bill.

(4) Where the holder of a bill, drawn payable elsewhere than at the place of business or residence of the drawee, has not time, with the exercise of reasonable diligence, to present the bill for acceptance before presenting it for payment on the day that it falls due, the delay caused by presenting the bill for acceptance before presenting it for payment is excused, and does not discharge the drawer and the indorsers.

40 Time for presenting bill payable after sight

(1) Subject to the provisions of this Act, when a bill payable after sight is negotiated, the holder must either present it for acceptance or negotiate it within a reasonable time.

(2) If he do not do so, the drawer and all indorsers prior to that holder are discharged.

(3) In determining what is a reasonable time within the meaning of this section, regard shall be had to the nature of the bill, the usage of trade with respect to similar bills, and the facts of the particular case.

41 Rules as to presentment for acceptance and excuses for non-presentment

(1) A bill is duly presented for acceptance which is presented in accordance with the following rules:

    (a) The presentment must be made by or on behalf of the holder to the drawee or to some person authorised to accept or refuse acceptance on his behalf at a reasonable hour on a business day and before the bill is overdue:

    (b) Where a bill is addressed to two or more drawees, who are not partners, presentment must be made to them all, unless one has authority to accept for them all, then presentment must be made to him only:

    (c) Where the drawee is dead presentment may be made to his personal representative:

    (d) Where the drawee is bankrupt, presentment may be made to him or to his trustee:

    (e) Where authorised by agreement or usage, a presentment through [a postal operator] is sufficient.

(2) Presentment in accordance with these rules is excused, and a bill may be treated as dishonoured by non-acceptance—

    (a) Where the drawee is dead or bankrupt, or is a fictitious person or a person not having capacity to contract by bill:

    (b) Where, after the exercise of reasonable diligence, such presentment cannot be effected:

    (c) Where although the presentment has been irregular, acceptance has been refused on some other ground.

(3) The fact that the holder has reason to believe that the bill, on presentment, will be dishonoured does not excuse presentment.

42 Non-acceptance

(1) When a bill is duly presented for acceptance and is not accepted within the customary time, the person presenting it must treat it as dishonoured by non-acceptance. If he do not, the holder shall lose his right of recourse against the drawer and indorsers.

43 Dishonour by non-acceptance and its consequences

(1) A bill is dishonoured by non-acceptance—

(a) when it is duly presented for acceptance, and such an acceptance as is prescribed by this Act is refused or cannot be obtained; or

(b) when presentment for acceptance is excused and the bill is not accepted.

(2) Subject to the provisions of this Act when a bill is dishonoured by non-acceptance an immediate right of recourse against the drawer and indorsers accrues to the holder, and no presentment for payment is necessary.

44 Duties as to qualified acceptances

(1) The holder of a bill may refuse to take a qualified acceptance, and if he does not obtain an unqualified acceptance may treat the bill as dishonoured by non-acceptance.

(2) Where a qualified acceptance is taken, and the drawer or an indorser has not expressly or impliedly authorised the holder to take a qualified acceptance, or does not subsequently assent thereto, such drawer or indorser is discharged from his liability on the bill.

The provisions of this sub-section do not apply to a partial acceptance, whereof due notice has been given. Where a foreign bill has been accepted as to part, it must be protested as to the balance.

(3) When the drawer or indorser of a bill receives notice of a qualified acceptance, and does not within a reasonable time express his dissent to the holder he shall be deemed to have assented thereto.

45 Rules as to presentment for payment

Subject to the provisions of this Act a bill must be duly presented for payment. If it be not so presented the drawer and indorsers shall be discharged.

A bill is duly presented for payment which is presented in accordance with the following rules:—

(1) Where the bill is not payable on demand, presentment must be made on the day it falls due.

(2) Where the bill is payable on demand then, subject to the provisions of this Act, presentment must be made within a reasonable time after its issue in order to render the drawer liable, and within a reasonable time after the indorsement, in order to render the indorser liable.

In determining what is a reasonable time, regard shall be had to the nature of the bill, the usage of trade with regard to similar bills, and the facts of the particular case.

(3) Presentment must be made by the holder or by some person authorised to receive payment on his behalf at a reasonable hour on a business day, at the proper place as hereinafter defined, either to the person designated by the bill as payer, or to some person authorised to pay or refuse payment on his behalf if with the exercise of reasonable diligence such person can there be found.

(4) A bill is presented at the proper place:—

(a) Where a place of payment is specified in the bill and the bill is there presented.

(b) Where no place of payment is specified, but the address of the drawee or acceptor is given in the bill, and the bill is there presented.

(c) Where no place of payment is specified and no address given, and the bill is presented at the drawees or acceptor's place of business if known, and if not, at his ordinary residence if known.

(d) In any other case if presented to the drawer or acceptor wherever he can be found, or if presented at his last known place of business or residence.

(5) Where a bill is presented at the proper place, and after the exercise of reasonable diligence no person authorised to pay or refuse payment can be found there, no further presentment to the drawee or acceptor is required.

(6) Where a bill is drawn upon, or accepted by two or more persons who are not partners, and no place of payment is specified, presentment must be made to them all.

(7) Where the drawee or acceptor of a bill is dead, and no place of payment is specified, presentment must be made to a personal representative, if such there be, and with the exercise of reasonable diligence he can be found.

(8) Where authorised by agreement or usage a presentment through [a postal operator] is sufficient.

46 Excuses for delay or non-presentment for payment

(1) Delay in making presentment for payment is excused when the delay is caused by circumstances beyond the control of the holder, and not imputable to his default, misconduct, or negligence. When the cause of delay ceases to operate presentment must be made with reasonable diligence.

(2) Presentment for payment is dispensed with,—

(a) Where, after the exercise of reasonable diligence presentment, as required by this Act, cannot be effected.
The fact that the holder has reason to believe that the bill will, on presentment, be dishonoured, does not dispense with the necessity for presentment.

(b) Where the drawee is a fictitious person.

(c) As regards the drawer where the drawee or acceptor is not bound, as between himself and the drawee, to accept or pay the bill, and the drawer has no reason to believe that the bill would be paid if presented.

(d) As regards an indorser, where the bill was accepted or made for the accommodation of the indorser, and he has no reason to expect that the bill would be paid if presented.

(e) By waiver of presentment, expressed or implied.

47 Dishonour by non-payment

(1) A bill is dishonoured by non-payment (a) when it is duly presented for payment and payment is refused or cannot be obtained, or (b) when presentment is excused and the bill is overdue and unpaid.

(2) Subject to the provisions of this Act, when a bill is dishonoured by non-payment, an immediate right of recourse against the drawer and indorsers accrues to the holder.

48 Notice of dishonour and effect of non-notice

Subject to the provisions of this Act, when a bill has been dishonoured by non-acceptance or by non-payment, notice of dishonour must be given to the drawer and each indorser, and any drawer or indorser to whom such notice is not given is discharged; Provided that—

(1) Where a bill is dishonoured by non-acceptance, and notice of dishonour is not given, the rights of the holder in due course subsequent to the omission, shall not be prejudiced by the omission.

(2) Where a bill is dishonoured by non-acceptance and due notice of dishonour is given, it shall not be necessary to give notice of a subsequent dishonour by nonpayment unless the bill shall in the meantime have been accepted.

49   Rules as of notice of dishonour

Notice of dishonour in order to be valid and effectual must be given in accordance with the following rules:—

(1) The notice must be given by or on behalf of the holder, or by or on behalf of an indorser who, at the time of giving it, is himself liable on the bill.

(2) Notice of dishonour may be given by an agent either in his own name, or in the name of any party entitled to give notice whether that party be his principal or not.

(3) Where the notice is given by on on behalf of the holder, it enures for the benefit of all subsequent holders and all prior indorsers who have a right of recourse against the party to whom it is given.

(4) Where notice is given by or on behalf of an indorser entitled to give notice as hereinbefore provided, it enures for the benefit of the holder and all indorsers subsequent to the party to whom notice is given.

(5) The notice may be given in writing or by personal communication, and may be given in any terms which sufficiently identify the bill, and intimate that the bill has been dishonoured by non-acceptance or non-payment.

(6) The return of a dishonoured bill to the drawer or an indorser is, in point of form, deemed a sufficient notice of dishonour.

(7) A written notice need not be signed, and an insufficient written notice may be supplemented and validated by verbal communication. A misdescription of the bill shall not vitiate the notice unless the party to whom the notice is given is in fact misled thereby.

(8) Where notice of dishonour is required to be given to any person, it may be given either to the party himself, or to his agent in that behalf.

(9) Where the drawer or indorser is dead, and the party giving notice knows it, the notice must be given to a personal representative if such there be, and with the exercise of reasonable diligence he can be found.

(10) Where the drawer or indorser is bankrupt, notice may be given either to the party himself or to the trustee.

(11) Where there are two or more drawers or indorsers who are not partners, notice must be given to each of them, unless one of them has authority to receive such notice for the others.

(12) The notice may be given as soon as the bill is dishonoured and must be given within a reasonable time thereafter.

In the absence of special circumstances notice is not deemed to have been given within a reasonable time, unless—

    (a) where the person giving and the person to receive notice reside in the same place, the notice is given or sent off in time to reach the latter on the day after the dishonour of the bill.

    (b) where the person giving and the person to receive notice reside in different places, the notice is sent off on the day after the dishonour of the bill, if there be a post at a convenient hour on that day, and if there be no such post on that day then by the next post thereafter.

(13) Where a bill when dishonoured is in the hands of an agent, he may either himself give notice to the parties liable on the bill, or he may give notice to his principal. If he gives notice to his principal, he must do so within the same time as if he were the holder, and the principal upon receipt of such notice has himself the same time for giving notice as if the agent had been an independent holder.

(14) Where a party to a bill receives due notice of dishonour, he has after the receipt of such notice the same period of time for giving notice to antecedent parties that the holder has after the dishonour.

(15) Where a notice of dishonour is duly addressed and posted, the sender is deemed to have given due notice of dishonour, notwithstanding any miscarriage by the [postal operator concerned].

50   Excuses for non-notice and delay

(1) Delay in giving notice of dishonour is excused where the delay is caused by circumstances beyond the control of the party giving notice, and not imputable to his default, misconduct, or negligence. When the cause of delay ceases to operate the notice must be given with reasonable diligence.

(2) Notice of dishonour is dispensed with—

(a) When, after the exercise of reasonable diligence, notice as required by this Act cannot be given to or does not reach the drawer or indorser sought to be charged:

(b) By waiver express or implied. Notice of dishonour may be waived before the time of giving notice has arrived, or after the omission to give due notice:

(c) As regards the drawer in the following cases, namely, (1) where drawer and drawee are the same person, (2) where the drawee is a fictitious person or a person not having capacity to contract, (3) where the drawer is the person to whom the bill is presented for payment, (4) where the drawee or acceptor is as between himself and the drawer under no obligation to accept or pay the bill, (5) where the drawer has countermanded payment:

(d) As regards the indorser in the following cases, namely (1) where the drawee is a fictitious person or a person not having the capacity to contract and the indorser was aware of the fact at the time he indorsed the bill, (2) where the indorser is the person to whom the bill is presented for payment, (3) where the bill was accepted or made for his accommodation.

51   Noting or protest of bill

(1) Where an inland bill has been dishonoured it may, if the holder think fit, be noted for non-acceptance or non-payment, as the case may be; but it shall not be necessary to note or protest any such bill in order to preserve the recourse against the drawer or indorser.

(2) Where a foreign bill, appearing on the face of it to be such, has been dishonoured by non-acceptance it must be duly protested for non-acceptance and where such a bill, which has not been previously dishonoured by non-acceptance, is dishonoured by non-payment it must be duly protested for non-payment. If it be not so protested the drawer and indorsers are discharged. Where a bill does not appear on the face of it to be a foreign bill, protest thereof in the case of dishonour is unnecessary.

(3) A bill which has been protested for non-acceptance may be subsequently protested for non-payment.

(4) Subject to the provisions of this Act, when a bill is noted or protested, [it may be noted on the day of its dishonour and must be noted not later than the next succeeding business day]. When a bill has been duly noted, the protest may be subsequently extended as of the date of the noting.

(5) Where the acceptor of the bill becomes bankrupt or insolvent or suspends payment before it matures, the holder may cause the bill to be protested for better security against the drawer and indorsers.

(6) A bill must be protested at the place where it is dishonoured: Provided that—

(a) When a bill is presented through [a postal operator], and returned by post dishonoured, it may be protested at the place to which it is returned and on the day of its return if received during business hours, and if not received during business hours, then not later than the next business day;

(b) When a bill drawn payable at the place of business or residence of some person other than the drawee, has been dishonoured by non-acceptance, it must be protested for non-payment at the place where it is expressed to be payable, and no further presentment for payment to, or demand on, the drawee is necessary.

(7) A protest must contain a copy of the bill, and must be signed by the notary making it, and must specify—

   (a) The person at whose request the bill is protested:

   (b) The place and date of protest, the cause or reason for protesting the bill, the demand made, and the answer given, if any, or the fact that the drawee or acceptor could not be found.

   (8) Where a bill is lost or destroyed, or is wrongly detained from the person entitled to hold it, protest may be made on a copy or written particulars thereof.

   (9) Protest is dispensed with by any circumstance which would dispense with notice of dishonour. Delay in noting or protesting is excused when the delay is caused by circumstances beyond the control of the holder, and not imputable to his default, misconduct, or negligence. When the cause of delay ceases to operate the bill must be noted or protested with reasonable diligence.

52 Duties of holder as regards drawee or acceptor

   (1) When a bill is accepted generally presentment for payment is not necessary in order to render the acceptor liable.

   (2) When by the terms of a qualified acceptance presentment for payment is required, the acceptor, in the absence of an express stipulation to that effect, is not discharged by the omission to present the bill for payment on the day that it matures.

   (3) In order to render the acceptor of a bill liable it is not necessary to protest it, or that notice of dishonour should be given to him.

   (4) Where the holder of a bill presents it for payment, he shall exhibit the bill to the person from whom he demands payment, and when a bill is paid the holder shall forthwith deliver it up to the party paying it.

Liabilities of parties

53 Funds in hands of drawee

   (1) A bill, of itself, does not operate as an assignment of funds in the hands of the drawee available for the payment thereof, and the drawee of a bill who does not accept as required by this Act is not liable on the instrument. This sub-section shall not extend to Scotland.

   (2) In Scotland, where the drawee of a bill has in his hands funds available for the payment thereof, the bill operates as an assignment of the sum, for which it is drawn in favour of the holder, from the time when the bill is presented to the drawee.

54 Liability of acceptor

The acceptor of a bill, by accepting it—

   (1) Engages that he will pay it according to the tenor of his acceptance:

   (2) Is precluded from denying to a holder in due course:

      (a) The existence of the drawer, the genuineness of his signature, and his capacity and authority to draw the bill;

      (b) In the case of a bill payable to drawer's order, the then capacity of the drawer to indorse, but not the genuineness or validity of his indorsement;

      (c) In the case of a bill payable to the order of a third person, the existence of the payee and his then capacity to indorse, but not the genuineness or validity of his indorsement.

55 Liability of drawer or indorser

   (1) The drawer of a bill by drawing it—

      (a) Engages that on due presentment it shall be accepted and paid according to its tenor, and that if it be dishonoured he will compensate the holder or any indorser who is compelled to pay it, provided that the requisite proceedings on dishonour be duly taken;

      (b) Is precluded from denying to a holder in due course the existence of the payee and his then capacity to indorse.

(2) The indorser of a bill by indorsing it—

    (a) Engages that on due presentment it shall be accepted and paid according to its tenor, and that if it be dishonoured he will compensate the holder or a subsequent indorser who is compelled to pay it, provided that the requisite proceedings on dishonour be duly taken;

    (b) Is precluded from denying to a holder in due course the genuineness and regularity in all respects of the drawer's signature and all previous indorsements;

    (c) Is precluded from denying to his immediate or a subsequent indorsee that the bill was at the time of his indorsement a valid and subsisting bill, and that he had then a good title thereto.

56   Stranger signing bill liable as indorser

Where a person signs a bill otherwise than as drawer or acceptor, he thereby incurs the liabilities of an indorser to a holder in due course.

57   Measure of damages against parties to dishonoured bill

Where a bill is dishonoured, the measure of damages, which shall be deemed to be liquidated damages, shall be as follows:

(1) The holder may recover from any party liable on the bill, and the drawer who has been compelled to pay the bill may recover from the acceptor, and an indorser who has been compelled to pay the bill may recover from the acceptor or from the drawer, or from a prior indorser—

    (a) The amount of the bill:

    (b) Interest thereon from the time of presentment for payment if the bill is payable on demand, and from the maturity of the bill in any other case:

    (c) The expenses of noting, or, when protest is necessary, and the protest has been extended, the expenses of protest.

[...]

(3) Where by this Act interest may be recovered as damages, such interest may, if justice require it, be withheld wholly or in part, and where a bill is expressed to be payable with interest at a given rate, interest as damages may or may not be given at the same rate as interest proper.

58   Transferor by delivery and transferee

(1) Where the holder of a bill payable to bearer negotiates it by delivery without indorsing it, he is called a 'transferor by delivery.'

(2) A transferor by delivery is not liable on the instrument.

(3) A transferor by delivery who negotiates a bill thereby warrants to his immediate transferee being a holder for value that the bill is what it purports to be, that he has a right to transfer it, and that at the time of the transfer he is not aware of any fact which renders it valueless.

Discharge of bill

59   Payment in due course

(1) A bill is discharged by payment in due course by or on behalf of the drawee or acceptor. 'Payment in due course' means payment made at or after the maturity of the bill to the holder thereof in good faith and without notice that his title to the bill is defective.

(2) Subject to the provisions herein-after contained, when a bill is paid by the drawer or an indorser it is not discharged; but

    (a) Where a bill payable to, or to the order of, a third party is paid by the drawer, the drawer may enforce payment thereof against the acceptor, but may not reissue the bill.

    (b) Where a bill is paid by an indorser, or where a bill payable to drawer's order is paid by the drawer, the party paying it is remitted to his former rights as regards the acceptor or antecedent parties, and he may, if he thinks fit, strike out his own and subsequent indorsements, and again negotiate the bill.

(3) Where an accommodation bill is paid in due course by the party accommodated the bill is discharged.

60   Banker paying demand draft whereon indorsement is forged

When a bill payable to order on demand is drawn on a banker, and the banker on whom it is drawn, pays the bill in good faith and in the ordinary course of business, it is not incumbent on the banker to show that the indorsement of the payee or any subsequent indorsement was made by or under the authority of the person whose indorsement it purports to be, and the banker is deemed to have paid the bill in due course, although such indorsement has been forged or made without authority.

61   Acceptor the holder at maturity

When the acceptor of a bill is or becomes the holder of it at or after its maturity, in his own right, the bill is discharged.

62   Express waiver

(1) When the holder of a bill at or after its maturity absolutely and unconditionally renounces his rights against the acceptor the bill is discharged.

The renunciation must be in writing, unless the bill is delivered up to the acceptor.

(2) The liabilities of any party to a bill may in like manner be renounced by the holder before, at, or after its maturity; but nothing in this section shall affect the rights of a holder in due course without notice of the renunciation.

63   Cancellation

(1) Where a bill is intentionally cancelled by the holder or his agent, and the cancellation is apparent thereon, the bill is discharged.

(2) In like manner any party liable on a bill may be discharged by the intentional cancellation of his signature by the holder or his agent. In such case any indorser who would have had a right of recourse against the party whose signature is cancelled, is also discharged.

(3) A cancellation made unintentionally, or under a mistake, or without the authority of the holder is inoperative; but where a bill or any signature thereon appears to have been cancelled the burden of proof lies on the party who alleges that the cancellation was made unintentionally, or under a mistake, or without authority.

64   Alteration of bill

(1) Where a bill or acceptance is materially altered without the assent of all parties liable on the bill, the bill is avoided except as against a party who has himself made, authorised, or assented to the alteration, and subsequent indorsers.

Provided that,

Where a bill has been materially altered, but the alteration is not apparent, and the bill is in the hands of a holder in due course, such holder may avail himself of the bill as if it had not been altered, and may enforce payment of it according to its original tenour.

(2) In particular the following alterations are material, namely, any alteration of the date, the sum payable, the time of payment, the place of payment, and where a bill has been accepted generally, the addition of a place of payment without the acceptor's assent.

Acceptance and payment for honour

65   Acceptance for honour supra protest

(1) Where a bill of exchange has been protested for dishonour by non-acceptance, or protested for better security, and is not overdue, any person, not being a party already liable thereon, may, with the consent of the holder, intervene and accept the bill *supra protest,* for the honour of any party liable thereon, or for the honour of the person for whose account the bill is drawn.

(2) A bill may be accepted for honour for part only of the sum for which it is drawn.

(3) An acceptance for honour supra protest in order to be valid must—

(a) be written on the bill, and indicate that it is an acceptance for honour;

(b) be signed by the acceptor for honour:

(4) Where an acceptance for honour does not expressly state for whose honour it is made, it is deemed to be an acceptance for the honour of the drawer.

(5) Where a bill payable after sight is accepted for honour, its maturity is calculated from the date of the noting for non-acceptance, and not from the date of the acceptance for honour.

66 Liability of acceptor for honour

(1) The acceptor for honour of a bill by accepting it engages that he will, on due presentment, pay the bill according to the tenor of his acceptance, if it is not paid by the drawee, provided it has been duly presented for payment, and protested for non-payment, and that he receives notice of these facts.

(2) The acceptor for honour is liable to the holder and to all parties to the bill subsequent to the party for whose honour he has accepted.

67 Presentment to acceptor for honour

(1) Where a dishonoured bill has been accepted for honour supra protest, or contains a reference in case of need, it must be protested for non-payment before it is presented for payment to the acceptor for honour, or referee in case of need.

(2) Where the address of the acceptor for honour is in the same place where the bill is protested for non-payment, the bill must be presented to him not later than the day following its maturity; and where the address of the acceptor for honour is in some place other than the place where it was protested for non-payment, the bill must be forwarded not later than the day following its maturity for presentment to him.

(3) Delay in presentment or non-presentment is excused by any circumstances which would excuse delay in presentment for payment or non-presentment for payment.

(4) When a bill of exchange is dishonoured by the acceptor for honour it must be protested for non-payment by him.

68 Payment for honour supra protest

(1) Where a bill has been protested for non-payment any person may intervene and pay it *supra protest* for the honour of any party liable thereon, or for the honour of the person for whose account the bill is drawn.

(2) Where two or more persons offer to pay a bill for the honour of different parties, the person whose payment will discharge most parties to the bill shall have the preference.

(3) Payment for honour *supra protest,* in order to operate as such and not as a mere voluntary payment, must be attested by a notarial act of honour which may be appended to the protest or form an extension of it.

(4) The notarial act of honour must be founded on a declaration made by the payer for honour, or his agent in that behalf, declaring his intention to pay the bill for honour, and for whose honour he pays.

(5) Where a bill has been paid for honour, all parties subsequent to the party for whose honour it is paid are discharged, but the payer for honour is subrogated for, and succeeds to both the rights and duties of, the holder as regards the party for whose honour he pays, and all parties liable to that party.

(6) The payer for honour on paying to the holder the amount of the bill and the notarial expenses incidental to its dishonour is entitled to receive both the bill itself and the protest. If the holder do not on demand deliver them up he shall be liable to the payer for honour in damages.

(7) Where the holder of a bill refuses to receive payment *supra protest* he shall lose his right of recourse against any party who would have been discharged by such payment.

Lost instruments

69   Holder's right to duplicate of lost bill

Where a bill has been lost before it is overdue, the person who was the holder of it may apply to the drawer to give him another bill of the same tenor, giving security to the drawer if required to indemnify him against all persons whatever in case the bill alleged to have been lost shall be found again.

If the drawer on request as aforesaid refuses to give such duplicate bill, he may be compelled to do so.

70   Action on lost bill

In any action or proceeding upon a bill, the court or a judge may order that the loss of the instrument shall not be set up, provided an indemnity be given to the satisfaction of the court or judge against the claims of any other person upon the instrument in question.

Bill in a set

71   Rules as to sets

(1) Where a bill is drawn in a set, each part of the set being numbered and containing a reference to the other parts, the whole of the parts constitute one bill.

(2) Where the holder of a set indorses two or more parts to different persons, he is liable to every such part, and every indorser subsequent to him is liable on the part he has himself indorsed as if the said parts were separate bills.

(3) Where two or more parts of a set are negotiated to different holders in due course, the holder whose title first accrues is as between such holders deemed the true owner of the bill; but nothing in this sub-section shall affect the rights of a person who in the course accepts or pays the part first presented to him.

(4) The acceptance may be written on any part, and it must be written on one part only. If the drawee accepts more than one part, and such accepted parts get into the hands of different holders in due course, he is liable on every such part as if it were a separate bill.

(5) When the acceptor of a bill drawn in a set pays it without requiring the part bearing the acceptance to be delivered up to him, and that part at maturity is outstanding in the hands of a holder in due course, he is liable to the holder thereof.

(6) Subject to the preceding rules, where any one part of a bill drawn in a set is discharged by payment or otherwise, the whole bill is discharged.

Conflict of laws

72   Rules where laws conflict

Where a bill drawn in one country is negotiated, accepted, or payable in another, the rights, duties, and liabilities of the parties thereto are determined as follows:

(1) The validity of a bill as regards requisites in form is determined by the law of the place of issue, and the validity as regards requisites in form of the supervening contracts, such as acceptance, or indorsement, or acceptance supra protest, is determined by the law of the place where such contract was made.

Provided that—

(a) Where a bill is issued out of the United Kingdom it is not invalid by reason only that it is not stamped in accordance with the law of the place of issue:

(b) Where a bill, issued out of the United Kingdom, conforms, as regards requisites in form, to the law of the United Kingdom, it may, for the purpose of enforcing payment thereof, be treated as valid as between all persons who negotiate, hold, or become parties to it in the United Kingdom.

(2) Subject to the provisions of this Act, the interpretation of the drawing, indorsement, acceptance, or acceptance supra protest of a bill, is determined by the law of the place where such contract is made.

Provided that where an inland bill is indorsed in a foreign country the indorsement shall as regards the payer be interpreted according to the law of the United Kingdom.

(3) The duties of the holder with respect to presentment for acceptance or payment and the necessity for or sufficiency of a protest or notice of dishonour, or otherwise, are determined by the law of the place where the act is done or the bill is dishonoured.

[...]

(5) Where a bill is drawn in one country and is payable in another, the due date thereof is determined according to the law of the place where it is payable.

PART III   CHEQUES ON A BANKER

73   Cheque defined

A cheque is a bill of exchange drawn on a banker payable on demand. Except as otherwise provided in this Part, the provisions of this Act applicable to a bill of exchange payable on demand apply to a cheque.

74   Presentment of cheque for payment

Subject to the provisions of this Act—

(1) Where a cheque is not presented for payment within a reasonable time of its issue, and the drawer or the person on whose account it is drawn had the right at the time of such presentment as between him and the banker to have the cheque paid and suffers actual damage through the delay, he is discharged to the extent of such damage, that is to say, to the extent to which such drawer or person is a creditor of such banker to a larger amount than he would have been had such cheque been paid.

(2) In determining what is a reasonable time regard shall be had to the nature of the instrument, the usage of trade and of bankers, and the facts of the particular case.

(3) The holder of such cheque as to which such drawer or person is discharged shall be a creditor, in lieu of such drawer or person, of such banker to the extent of such discharge, and entitled to recover the amount from him.

[74A   Presentment of cheque for payment: alternative place of presentment

Where the banker on whom a cheque is drawn—

(a) has by notice published in the London, Edinburgh and Belfast Gazettes specified an address at which cheques drawn on him may be presented, and

(b) has not by notice so published cancelled the specification of that address, the cheque is also presented at the proper place if it is presented there.]

[74B   Presentment of cheque for payment: alternative means of presentment by banker

(1) A banker may present a cheque for payment to the banker on whom it is drawn by notifying him of its essential features by electronic means or otherwise, instead of by presenting the cheque itself.

(2) If a cheque is presented for payment under this section, presentment need not be made at the proper place or at a reasonable hour on a business day.

(3) If, before the close of business on the next business day following presentment of a cheque under this section, the banker on whom the cheque is drawn requests the banker by whom the cheque was presented to present the cheque itself—

(a) the presentment under this section shall be disregarded, and

(b) this section shall not apply in relation to the subsequent presentment of the cheque.

(4) A request under subsection (3) above for the presentment of a cheque shall not constitute dishonour of the cheque by non-payment.

(5) Where presentment of a cheque is made under this section, the banker who presented the cheque and the banker on whom it is drawn shall be subject to the same duties in relation

to the collection and payment of the cheque as if the cheque itself had been presented for payment.

    (6) For the purposes of this section, the essential features of a cheque are—

        (a) the serial number of the cheque,

        (b) the code which identifies the banker on whom the cheque is drawn,

        (c) the account number of the drawer of the cheque, and

        (d) the amount of the cheque is entered by the drawer of the cheque.]

[74C   Cheques presented for payment under section 74B: disapplication of section 52(4)

Section 52(4) above—

        (a) so far as relating to presenting a bill for payment, shall not apply to presenting a cheque for payment under section 74B above, and

        (b) so far as relating to a bill which is paid, shall not apply to a cheque which is paid following presentment under that section.]

75   Revocation of banker's authority

The duty and authority of a banker to pay a cheque drawn on him by his customer are determined by—

    (1) Countermand of payment:

    (2) Notice of the customer's death.

[75A

    (1) On the countermand of payment of a cheque, the banker shall be treated as having no funds available for the payment of the cheque.

    (2) This section applies to Scotland only.]

Crossed cheques

76   General and special crossings defined

    (1) Where a cheque bears across its face an addition of—

        (a) The words 'and company' or any abbreviation thereof between two parallel transverse lines either with or without the words 'not negotiable'; or

        (b) Two parallel transverse lines simply, either with or without the words 'not negotiable';

that addition constitutes a crossing, and the cheque is crossed generally.

    (2) Where a cheque bears across its face an addition of the name of a banker, either with or without the words 'not negotiable', that addition constitutes a crossing, and the cheque is crossed specially and to that banker.

77   Crossing by drawer or after issue

    (1) A cheque may be crossed generally or specially by the drawer.

    (2) Where a cheque is uncrossed, the holder may cross it generally or specially.

    (3) Where a cheque is crossed generally the holder may cross it specially.

    (4) Where a cheque is crossed generally or specially, the holder may add the words 'not negotiable.'

    (5) Where a cheque is crossed specially, the banker to whom it is crossed may again cross it specially to another banker for collection.

    (6) Where an uncrossed cheque, or a cheque crossed generally is sent to a banker for collection, he may cross it specially to himself.

78   Crossing a material part of cheque

A crossing authorised by this Act is a material part of the cheque; it shall not be lawful for any person to obliterate or except as authorised by this Act, to add to or alter the crossing.

79   Duties of banker as to crossed cheques

    (1) Where a cheque is crossed specially to more than one banker except when crossed to an agent for collection being a banker, the banker on whom it is drawn shall refuse payment thereof.

(2) Where the banker on whom a cheque is drawn which is so crossed nevertheless pays the same, or pays a cheque crossed generally otherwise than to a banker, or if crossed specially otherwise than to the banker to whom it is crossed, or his agent for collection being a banker, he is liable to the true owner of the cheque for any loss he may sustain owing to the cheque having been so paid.

Provided that where a cheque is presented for payment which does not at the time of presentment appear to be crossed, or to have had a crossing which had been obliterated, or to have been added to or altered otherwise than as authorised by this Act, the banker paying the cheque in good faith and without negligence shall not be responsible or incur any liability, nor shall the payment be questioned by reason of the cheque having been crossed, or of the crossing having been obliterated on having been added to or altered otherwise than as authorised by this Act, and of payment having been made otherwise than to a banker or to the banker to whom the cheque is or was crossed, or to his agent for collection being a banker as the case may be.

80   Protection to banker and drawer where cheque is crossed

Where the banker, on whom a crossed cheque [(including a cheque which under section 81A below or otherwise is not transferable)] is drawn in good faith and without negligence pays it, if crossed generally to a banker, and if crossed specially, to the banker to whom it is crossed, or his agent for collection being a banker the banker paying the cheque, and, if the cheque has come into the hands of the payee, the drawer, shall respectively be entitled to the same rights and be placed in the same position as if payment of the cheque had been made to the true owner thereof.

81   Effect of crossing on holder

Where a person takes a crossed cheque which bears on it the words 'not negotiable,' he shall not have and shall not be capable of giving a better title to the cheque than that which the person from whom he took it had.

[81A   Non-transferable cheques

(1) Where a cheque is crossed and bears across its face the words 'account payee' or 'a/c payee', either with or without the words 'only', the cheque shall not be transferable, but shall only be valid as between the parties thereto.

(2) A banker is not to be treated for the purposes of section 80 above as having been negligent by reason only of his failure to concern himself with any purported indorsement of a cheque which under subsection (1) above or otherwise is not transferable.]

[...]

PART IV   PROMISSORY NOTES

83   Promissory note defined

(1) A promissory note is an unconditional promise in writing made by one person to another signed by the maker, engaging to pay, on demand or at a fixed or determinable future time, a sum certain in money, to, or to the order of, a specified person or to bearer.

(2) An instrument in the form of a note payable to maker's order is not a note within the meaning of this section unless and until it is indorsed by the maker.

(3) A note is not invalid by reason only that it contains also a pledge of collateral security with authority to sell or dispose thereof.

(4) A note which is, or on the face of it purports to be, both made and payable within the British Islands is an inland note. Any other note is a foreign note.

84   Delivery necessary

A promissory note is inchoate and incomplete until delivery thereof to the payee or bearer.

85   Joint and several notes

(1) A promissory note may be made by two or more makers, and they may be liable thereon jointly, or jointly and severally according to its tenour.

(2) Where a note runs 'I promise to pay' and is signed by two or more persons it is deemed to be their joint and several note.

86   Note payable on demand

(1) Where a note payable on demand has been indorsed, it must be presented for payment within a reasonable time of the indorsement. If it be not so presented the indorser is discharged.

(2) In determining what is a reasonable time, regard shall be had to the nature of the instrument, the usage of trade, and the facts of the particular case.

(3) Where a note payable on demand is negotiated, it is not deemed to be overdue for the purpose of affecting the holder with defects of title of which he had no notice, by reason that it appears that a reasonable time for presenting it for payment has elapsed since its issue.

87   Presentment of note for payment

(1) Where a promissory note is in the body of it made payable at a particular place, it must be presented for payment at that place in order to render the maker liable. In any other case, presentment for payment is not necessary to render the maker liable.

(2) Presentment for payment is necessary in order to render the indorser of a note liable.

(3) Where a note is in the body of it made payable at a particular place, presentment at that place is necessary in order to render an indorser liable; but when a place of payment is indicated by way of memorandum only, presentment at that place is sufficient to render the indorser liable, but a presentment to the maker elsewhere, if sufficient in other respects, shall also suffice.

88   Liability of maker

The maker of a promissory note by making it—

(1) Engages that he will pay it according to its tenour;

(2) Is precluded from denying to a holder in due course the existence of the payee and his then capacity to indorse.

89   Application of Part II to notes

(1) Subject to the provisions in this part and, except as by this section provided, the provisions of this Act relating to bills of exchange apply, with the necessary modifications, to promissory notes.

(2) In applying those provisions the maker of a note shall be deemed to correspond with the acceptor of a bill, and the first indorser of a note shall be deemed to correspond with the drawer of an accepted bill payable to drawer's order.

(3) The following provisions as to bills do not apply to notes; namely, provisions relating to—

(a) Presentment for acceptance;

(b) Acceptance;

(c) Acceptance supra protest;

(d) Bills in a set.

(4) Where a foreign note is dishonoured, protest thereof is unnecessary.

PART V   SUPPLEMENTARY

90   Good faith

A thing is deemed to be done in good faith, within the meaning of this Act, where it is in fact done honestly, whether it is done negligently or not.

91 Signature

(1) Where, by this Act, any instrument or writing is required to be signed by any person, it is not necessary that he should sign it with his own hand, but it is sufficient if his signature is written thereon by some other person by or under his authority.

(2) In the case of a corporation, where, by this Act, any instrument or writing is required to be signed, it is sufficient if the instrument or writing be sealed with the corporate seal.

But nothing in this section shall be construed as requiring the bill or note of a corporation to be under seal.

92 Computation of time

Where by this Act, the time limited for doing any act or thing is less than three days, in reckoning time, non-business days are excluded.

'Non-business days' for the purposes of this Act mean—

(a) [Saturday,] Sunday, Good Friday, Christmas Day:

(b) A bank holiday under [the Banking and Financial Dealings Act 1971.]

(c) A day appointed by Royal proclamation as a public fast or thanksgiving day.

[(d) a day declared by an order under section 2 of the Banking and Financial Dealings Act 1971 to be a non-business day.]

Any other day is a business day.

93 When noting equivalent to protest

For the purposes of this Act, where a bill or note is required to be protested within a specified time or before some further proceeding is taken, it is sufficient that the bill has been noted for protest before the expiration of the specified time or the taking of the proceeding; and the formal protest may be extended at any time thereafter as of the date of the noting.

94 Protest when notary not accessible

Where a dishonoured bill or note is authorised or required to be protested, and the services of a notary cannot be obtained at the place where the bill is dishonoured, any householder, or substantial resident of the place may, in the presence of two witnesses, give a certificate, signed by them, attesting to the dishonour of the bill, and the certificate shall in all respects operate as if it were a formal protest of the bill.

The form given in Schedule I to this Act may be used with necessary modifications, and if used shall be sufficient.

95 Dividend warrants may be crossed

The provisions of this Act as to crossed cheques shall apply to a warrant for payment of dividend.

[...]

97 Savings

(1) The rules in bankruptcy relating to bills of exchange, promissory notes, and cheques, shall continue to apply thereto notwithstanding anything in this Act contained.

(2) The rules of common law including the law merchant, save in so far as they are inconsistent with the express provisions of this Act, shall continue to apply to bills of exchange, promissory notes, and cheques—

(3) Nothing in this Act or in any repeal effected thereby shall affect—

(a) [...] any law or enactment for the time being in force relating to the revenue;

(b) The provisions of the Companies Act, 1862, or Acts amending it, or any Act relating to joint stock banks or companies:

(c) The provisions of any Act relating to or confirming the privileges of the Bank of England or the Bank of Ireland respectively:

(d) The validity of any usage relating to dividend warrants, or the indorsements thereof.

98   Saving of summary diligence in Scotland
Nothing in this Act or in any repeal effected thereby shall extend or restrict, or in any way alter the law and practice in Scotland in regard to summary diligence.

99   Construction with other Acts, etc.
Where any Act or document refers to any enactment repealed by this Act, the Act or document shall be construed, and shall operate as if it referred to the corresponding provisions of this Act.

100   Parole evidence allowed in certain judicial proceedings in Scotland
In any judicial proceeding in Scotland, any fact relating to a bill of exchange, bank cheque, or promissory note, which is relevant to any question of liability thereon, may be proved by parole evidence: Provided that this enactment shall not in any way affect the existing law and practice whereby the party who is, according to the tenour of any bill of exchange, bank cheque, or promissory note, debtor to the holder in the amount thereof, may be required, as a condition of obtaining a sist of diligence, or suspension of a charge, or threatened charge, to make such consignation, or to find such caution as the court or judge before whom the cause is depending may require. [...]

SCHEDULES

Section 94   FIRST SCHEDULE

Form of protest which may be used when the services of a notary cannot
be obtained.
Know all men that I, *A. B.* [householder], of   in the county of
in the United Kingdom, at the request of *C. D.*, there being no notary
public available, did on the   day of   188   at————
demand payment [*or* acceptance] of the bill of exchange hereunder written, from *E. F*, to which demand he made answer [state answer, if any] wherefore I now, in the presence of *G. H.* and *J. K.* do protest the said bill of exchange.

(Signed)   A. B.⎫
           G. H.⎬ *Witnesses*
           J. K. ⎭

N.B.—The bill itself should be annexed, or a copy of the bill and all that is written thereon should be underwritten.

Bills of Sale Act (1878) Amendment Act 1882
(45 & 46 Vict., c. 43)

An Act to amend the Bills of Sale Act 1878.   [18th August 1882]

1   Short title
This Act may be cited for all purposes as the Bills of Sale Act (1878) Amendment Act 1882; and this Act and the Bills of Sale Act 1878 may be cited together as the Bills of Sale Acts 1878 and 1882.
. . .

3   Construction of Act
The Bills of Sale Act 1878 is herein-after referred to as 'the principal Act', and this Act shall, so far as is consistent with the tenor thereof, be construed as one with the principal Act; but unless the context otherwise requires shall not apply to any bill of sale duly registered before the commencement of this Act so long as the registration thereof is not avoided by non-renewal or otherwise.

The expression 'bill of sale', and other expressions in this Act, have the same meaning as in the principal Act, except as to bills of sale or other documents mentioned in section four of the principal Act, which may be given otherwise than by way of security for the payment of money, to which last-mentioned bills of sale and other documents this Act shall not apply.

4 Bill of sale to have schedule of property attached thereto
Every bill of sale shall have annexed thereto or written thereon a schedule containing an inventory of the personal chattels comprised in the bill of sale; and such bill of sale, save as herein-after mentioned, shall have effect only in respect of the personal chattels specifically described in the said schedule; and shall be void, except as against the grantor, in respect of any personal chattels not so specifically described.

5 Bill of sale not to affect after acquired property
Save as herein-after mentioned, a bill of sale shall be void, except as against the grantor, in respect of any personal chattels specifically described in the schedule thereto of which the grantor was not the true owner at the time of the execution of the bill of sale.

6 Exception as to certain things
Nothing contained in the foregoing sections of this Act shall render a bill of sale void in respect of any of the following things; (that is to say,)

(1) Any growing crops separately assigned or charged where such crops were actually growing at the time when the bill of sale was executed.

(2) Any fixtures separately assigned or charged, and any plant, or trade machinery where such fixtures, plant, or trade machinery are used in, attached to, or brought upon any land, farm, factory, workshop, shop, house, warehouse, or other place in substitution for any of the like fixtures, plant, or trade machinery specifically described in the schedule to such bill of sale.

7 Bill of sale with power to seize except in certain events to be void
Personal chattels assigned under a bill of sale shall not be liable to be seized or taken possession of by the grantee for any other than the following causes:—

(1) If the grantor shall make default in payment of the sum or sums of money thereby secured at the time therein provided for payment, or in the performance of any covenant or agreement contained in the bill of sale and necessary for maintaining the security;

(2) If the grantor shall become a bankrupt, or suffer the said goods or any of them to be distrained for rent, rates, or taxes;

(3) If the grantor shall fraudulently either remove or suffer the said goods, or any of them, to be removed from the premises;

(4) If the grantor shall not, without reasonable excuse, upon demand in writing by the grantee, produce to him his last receipts for rent, rates, and taxes;

(5) If execution shall have been levied against the goods of the grantor under any judgment at law:

Provided that the grantor may within five days from the seizure or taking possession of any chattels on account of any of the above-mentioned causes, apply to the High Court, or to a judge thereof in chambers, and such court or judge, if satisfied that by payment of money or otherwise the said cause of seizure no longer exists, may restrain the grantee from removing or selling the said chattels, or may make such other order as may seem just.

[7A Defaults under consumer credit agreements
(1) Paragraph (1) of section 7 of this Act does not apply to a default relating to a bill of sale given by way of security for the payment of money under a regulated agreement to which section 87(1) of the Consumer Credit Act 1974 applies—

(a) unless the restriction imposed by section 88(2) of that Act has ceased to apply to the bill of sale; or

(b) if, by virtue of section 89 of that Act, the default is to be treated as not having occurred.

(2) Where paragraph (1) of section 7 of this Act does apply in relation to a bill of sale such as is mentioned in subsection (1) of this section, the proviso to that section shall have effect with the substitution of 'county court' for 'High Court'.]

8   Bill of sale to be void unless attested and registered

Every bill of sale shall be duly attested, and shall be registered under the principal Act within seven clear days after the execution thereof, or if it is executed in any place out of England then within seven clear days after the time at which it would in the ordinary course of post arrive in England if posted immediately after the execution thereof; and shall truly set forth the consideration for which it was given; otherwise such bill of sale shall be void in respect of the personal chattels comprised therein.

9   Form of bill of sale

A bill of sale made or given by way of security for the payment of money by the grantor thereof shall be void unless made in accordance with the form in the schedule to this Act annexed.

10   Attestation

The execution of every bill of sale by the grantor shall be attested by one or more credible witness or witnesses, not being a party or parties thereto. . . .

11   Local registration of contents of bills of sale

Where the affidavit (which under section ten of the principal Act is required to accompany a bill of sale when presented for registration) describes the residence of the person making or giving the same or of the person against whom the process is issued to be in some place outside [the London insolvency district] or where the bill of sale describes the chattels enumerated therein as being in some place outside [the London insolvency district], the registrar under the principal Act shall forthwith and within three clear days after registration in the principal registry, and in accordance with the prescribed directions, transmit an abstract in the prescribed form of the contents of such bill of sale to the county court registrar in whose district such places are situate, and if such places are in the districts of different registrars to each such registrar.

Every abstract so transmitted shall be filed, kept, and indexed by the registrar of the county court in the prescribed manner, and any person may search, inspect, make extracts from, and obtain copies of the abstract so registered in the like manner and upon the like terms as to payment or otherwise as near as may be as in the case of bills of sale registered by the registrar under the principal Act.

12   Bill of sale under £30 to be void

Every bill of sale made or given in consideration of any sum under thirty pounds shall be void.

13   Chattels not to be removed or sold

All personal chattels seized or of which possession is taken . . . under or by virtue of any bill of sale (whether registered before or after the commencement of this Act), shall remain on the premises where they were so seized or so taken possession of, and shall not be removed or sold until after the expiration of five clear days from the day they were so seized or so taken possession of.

14   Bill of sale not to protect chattels against poor and parochial rates

A bill of sale to which this Act applies shall be no protection in respect of personal chattels included in such bill of sale which but for such bill of sale would have been liable to distress under a warrant for the recovery of taxes and poor and other parochial rates.

15   Repeal of part of Bills of Sale Act 1878

. . . All . . . enactments contained in the principal Act which are inconsistent with this Act are repealed . . .

16 Inspection of registered bills of sale

... Any person shall be entitled at all reasonable times to search the register, on payment of a fee of one shilling, or such other fee as may be prescribed, and subject to such regulations as may be prescribed, and shall be entitled at all reasonable times to inspect, examine, and make extracts from any and every registered bill of sale without being required to make a written application, or to specify any particulars in reference thereto, upon payment of one shilling for each bill of sale inspected, and such payment shall be made by a judicature stamp. Provided that the said extracts shall be limited to the dates of execution, registration, renewal of registration, and satisfaction, to the names, addresses, and occupations of the parties, to the amount of the consideration, and to any further prescribed particulars.

17 Debentures to which Act not to apply

Nothing in this Act shall apply to any debentures issued by any mortgage, loan, or other incorporated company [or by any limited liability partnership], and secured upon the capital stock or goods, chattels, and effects of such company [or a limited liability partnership].

18 Extent of Act

This Act shall not extend to Scotland or Ireland.

Section 9   SCHEDULE

                          FORM OF BILL OF SALE

This Indenture made the   day of   between *A.B.* of   of the one part, and *C.D.* of   of the other part, witnesseth that in consideration of the sum of £   now paid to *A.B.* by *C.D.*, the receipt of which the said *A.B.* hereby acknowledges [*or whatever else the consideration may be*], he the said *A.B.* doth hereby assign unto *C.D.*, his executors, administrators, and assigns, all and singular the several chattels and things specifically described in the schedule hereto annexed by way of security for the payment of the sum of £   and interest thereon at the rate of   per cent per annum [*or whatever else may be the rate*]. And the said *A.B.* doth further agree and declare that he will duly pay to the said *C.D.* the principal sum aforesaid, together with the interest then due, by equal   payments of £   on the
        day of [*or whatever else may be the stipulated times or time of payment*]. And the said *A.B.* doth also agree with the said *C.D.* that he will [*here insert terms as to insurance, payment of rent, or otherwise, which the parties may agree to for the maintenance or defeasance of the security*].
        Provided always, that the chattels hereby assigned shall not be liable to seizure or to be taken possession of by the said *C.D.* for any cause other than those specified in section seven of the Bills of Sale Act (1878) Amendment Act 1882.
                          In witness, &c.
        Signed and sealed by the said *A.B.* in the presence of me *E.F.* [*add witness' name, address, and description*].

Factors Act 1889
(52 & 53 Vict., c. 45)

An Act to amend and consolidate the Factors Acts.   [26th August 1889]

Preliminary

1 Definitions

For the purposes of this Act—

(1) The expression 'mercantile agent' shall mean a mercantile agent having in the customary course of his business as such agent authority either to sell goods or to consign goods for the purpose of sale, or to buy goods, or to raise money on the security of goods:

(2) A person shall be deemed to be in possession of goods or of the documents of title to goods, where the goods or documents are in the actual custody or are held by any other person subject to his control or for him or on his behalf:

(3) The expression 'goods' shall include wares and merchandise:

(4) The expression 'document of title' shall include any bill of lading, dock warrant, warehouse-keeper's certificate, and warrant or order for the delivery of goods, and any other document used in the ordinary course of business as proof of the possession or control of goods, or authorising or purporting to authorise, either by endorsement or by delivery, the possessor of the document to transfer or receive goods thereby represented:

(5) The expression 'pledge' shall include any contract pledging, or giving a lien or security on, goods, whether in consideration of an original advance or of any further or continuing advance or of any pecuniary liability:

(6) The expression 'person' shall include any body of persons corporate or unincorporate.

Dispositions by mercantile agents

2   Powers of mercantile agent with respect to disposition of goods

(1) Where a mercantile agent is, with the consent of the owner, in possession of goods or of the documents of title to goods, any sale, pledge, or other disposition of the goods, made by him when acting in the ordinary course of business of a mercantile agent, shall, subject to the provisions of this Act, be as valid as if he were expressly authorised by the owner of the goods to make the same; provided that the person taking under the disposition acts in good faith, and has not at the time of the disposition notice that the person making the disposition has not authority to make the same.

(2) Where a mercantile agent has, with the consent of the owner, been in possession of goods or of the documents of title to goods, any sale, pledge, or other disposition, which would have been valid if the consent had continued, shall be valid notwithstanding the determination of the consent; provided that the person taking under the disposition has not at the time thereof notice that the consent has been determined.

(3) Where a mercantile agent has obtained possession of any documents of title to goods by reason of his being or having been, with the consent of the owner, in possession of the goods represented thereby, or of any other documents of title to the goods, his possession of the first-mentioned documents shall, for the purposes of this Act, be deemed to be with the consent of the owner.

(4) For the purposes of this Act the consent of the owner shall be presumed in the absence of evidence to the contrary.

3   Effect of pledges of documents of title
A pledge of the documents of title to goods shall be deemed to be a pledge of the goods.

4   Pledge for antecedent debt
Where a mercantile agent pledges goods as security for a debt or liability due from the pledgor to the pledgee before the time of the pledge, the pledgee shall acquire no further right to the goods than could have been enforced by the pledgor at the time of the pledge.

5   Rights acquired by exchange of goods or documents
The consideration necessary for the validity of a sale, pledge, or other disposition of goods, in pursuance of this Act, may be either a payment in cash, or the delivery or transfer of other goods, or of a document of title to goods, or of a negotiable security, or any other valuable consideration; but where goods are pledged by a mercantile agent in consideration of the delivery or transfer of other goods, or of a document of title to goods, or of a negotiable security, the pledgee shall acquire no right or interest in the goods so pledged in excess of the value of the goods, documents, or security when so delivered or transferred in exchange.

6 Agreements through clerks, &c.

For the purposes of this Act an agreement made with a mercantile agent through a clerk or other person authorised in the ordinary course of business to make contracts of sale or pledge on his behalf shall be deemed to be an agreement with the agent.

7 Provisions as to consignors and consignees

(1) Where the owner of goods has given possession of the goods to another person for the purpose of consignment or sale, or has shipped the goods in the name of another person, and the consignee of the goods has not had notice that such person is not the owner of the goods, the consignee shall, in respect of advances made to or for the use of such person, have the same lien on the goods as if such person were the owner of the goods, and may transfer any such lien to another person.

(2) Nothing in this section shall limit or affect the validity of any sale, pledge, or disposition, by a mercantile agent.

Dispositions by sellers and buyers of goods

8 Disposition by seller remaining in possession

Where a person, having sold goods, continues, or is, in possession of the goods or of the documents of title to the goods, the delivery or transfer by that person, or by a mercantile agent acting for him, of the goods or documents of title under any sale, pledge, or other disposition thereof, or under any agreement for sale, pledge, or other disposition thereof, to any person receiving the same in good faith and without notice of the previous sale, shall have the same effect as if the person making the delivery or transfer were expressly authorised by the owner of the goods to make the same.

9 Disposition by buyer obtaining possession

Where a person, having bought or agreed to buy goods, obtains with the consent of the seller possession of the goods or the documents of title to the goods, the delivery or transfer, by that person or by a mercantile agent acting for him, of the goods or documents of title under any sale, pledge, or other disposition thereof, or under any agreement for sale, pledge, or other disposition thereof, to any person receiving the same in good faith and without notice of any lien or other right of the original seller in respect of the goods, shall have the same effect as if the person making the delivery or transfer were a mercantile agent in possession of the goods or documents of title with the consent of the owner.

[For the purposes of this section—

    (i)   the buyer under a conditional sale agreement shall be deemed not to be a person who has bought or agreed to buy goods, and

   (ii) 'conditional sale agreement' means an agreement for the sale of goods which is a consumer credit agreement within the meaning of the Consumer Credit Act 1974 under which the purchase price or part of it is payable in instalments, and the property in the goods is to remain in the seller (notwithstanding that the buyer is to be in possession of the goods) until such conditions as to the payment of instalments or otherwise as may be specified in the agreement are fulfilled.]

10 Effect of transfer of documents on vendor's lien or right of stoppage in transitu

Where a document of title to goods has been lawfully transferred to a person as a buyer or owner of the goods, and that person transfers the document to a person who takes the document in good faith and for valuable consideration, the last-mentioned transfer shall have the same effect for defeating any vendor's lien or right of stoppage in transitu as the transfer of a bill of lading has for defeating the right of stoppage in transitu.

Supplemental

11 Mode of transferring documents
For the purposes of this Act, the transfer of a document may be by endorsement, or, where the document is by custom or by its express terms transferable by delivery or makes the goods deliverable to the bearer, then by delivery.

12 Saving for rights of true owner
(1) Nothing in this Act shall authorise an agent to exceed or depart from his authority as between himself and his principal, or exempt him from any liability, civil or criminal, for so doing.

(2) Nothing in this Act shall prevent the owner of goods from recovering the goods from any agent or his trustee in bankruptcy at any time before the sale or pledge thereof, or shall prevent the owner of goods pledged by an agent from having the right to redeem the goods at any time before the sale thereof, on satisfying the claim for which the goods were pledged, and paying to the agent, if by him required, any money in respect of which the agent would by law be entitled to retain the goods or the documents of title thereto, or any of them, by way of lien as against the owner, or from recovering from any person with whom the goods have been pledged any balance of money remaining in his hands as the produce of the sale of the goods after deducting the amount of his lien.

(3) Nothing in this Act shall prevent the owner of goods sold by an agent from recovering from the buyer the price agreed to be paid for the same, or any part of that price, subject to any right of set off on the part of the buyer against the agent.

13 Saving for common law powers of agent
The provisions of this Act shall be construed in amplification and not in derogation of the powers exercisable by an agent independently of this Act.

[…]

16 Extent of Act
This Act shall not extend to Scotland.

17 Short title
This Act may be cited as the Factors Act, 1889.

Bills of Sale Act 1890
(53 & 54 Vict., c. 53)

An Act to exempt certain letters of hypothecation from the operation of the Bills of Sale Act 1882.
[10th August 1890]

1 Exemption of letters of hypothecation of imported goods from 41 & 42 Vict., c. 31, and 45 & 46 Vict., c. 43, s. 9
[An instrument charging or creating any security on or declaring trusts of imported goods given or executed at any time prior to their deposit in a warehouse, factory, or store, or to their being reshipped for export, or delivered to a purchaser not being the person giving or executing such instrument, shall not be deemed a bill of sale within the meaning of the Bills of Sale Acts 1878 and 1882.]

2 Saving of 46 & 47 Vict., c. 52, s. 44
Nothing in this Act shall affect the operation of section forty-four of the Bankruptcy Act 1883 in respect of any goods comprised in any such instrument as is hereinbefore described, if such goods would but for this Act be goods within the meaning of subsection three of that section.

Partnership Act 1890

(53 & 54 Vict., c. 39)

An Act to declare and amend the Law of Partnership.   [14th August 1890]

Nature of partnership

1   Definition of partnership

(1) Partnership is the relation which subsists between persons carrying on a business in common with a view of profit.

(2) But the relation between members of any company or association which is—

(a) Registered as a company under the Companies Act, 1862, or any other Act of Parliament for the time being in force and relating to the registration of joint stock companies; or

(b) Formed or incorporated by or in pursuance of any other Act of Parliament or letters patent, or Royal Charter [. . .]

is not a partnership within the meaning of this Act.

2   Rules for determining existence of partnership

In determining whether a partnership does or does not exist, regard shall be had to the following rules:

(1) joint tenancy, tenancy in common, joint property, common property, or part ownership does not of itself create a partnership as to anything so held or owned, whether the tenants or owners do or do not share any profits made by the use thereof.

(2) The sharing of gross returns does not of itself create a partnership, whether the persons sharing such returns have or have not a joint or common right or interest in any property from which or from the use of which the returns are derived.

(3) The receipt by a person of a share of the profits of a business is prima facie evidence that he is a partner in the business, but the receipt of such a share, or of a payment contingent on or varying with the profits of a business, does not of itself make him a partner in the business; and in particular—

(a) The receipt by a person of a debt or other liquidated amount by instalments, or otherwise out of the accruing profits of a business does not of itself make him a partner in the business or liable as such:

(b) A contract for the remuneration of a servant or agent of a person engaged in a business by a share of the profits of the business does not of itself make the servant or agent a partner in the business or liable as such:

(c) A person being the widow[, widower, surviving civil partner,] or child of a deceased partner, and receiving by way of annuity a portion of the profits made in the business in which the deceased person was a partner, is not by reason only of such receipt a partner in the business or liable as such:

(d) The advance of money by way of loan to a person engaged or about to engage in any business on a contract with that person that the lender shall receive a rate of interest varying with the profits, or shall receive a share of the profits arising from carrying on the business, does not of itself make the lender a partner with the person or persons carrying on the business or liable as such. Provided that the contract is in writing, and signed by or on behalf of all the parties thereto:

(e) A person receiving by way of annuity or otherwise a portion of the profits of a business in consideration of the sale by him of the goodwill of the business is not by reason only of such receipt a partner in the business or liable as such.

3   Postponement of rights of person lending or selling in consideration of share of profits in case of insolvency

In the event of any person to whom money has been advanced by way of loan upon such a contract as is mentioned in the last foregoing section, or of any buyer of a goodwill in consideration of a share of the profits of the business, being adjudged a bankrupt, entering into an arrangement to pay his creditors less than twenty shillings in the pound, or dying in insolvent circumstances, the lender of the loan shall not be entitled to recover anything in respect of the loan, and the seller of the goodwill shall not be entitled to recover anything in respect of the share of profits contracted for, until the claims of the other creditors of the borrower or buyer for valuable consideration in money or money's worth have been satisfied.

4   Meaning of firm

(1) Persons who have entered into partnership with one another are for the purposes of this Act called collectively a firm, and the name under which their business is carried on is called the firm-name.

(2) In Scotland a firm is a legal person distinct from the partners of whom it is composed, but an individual partner may be charged on a decree or diligence directed against the firm, and on payment of the debts is entitled to relief pro rata from the firm and its other members.

Relations of Partners to persons dealing with them

5   Power of partner to bind the firm

Every partner is an agent of the firm and his other partners for the purpose of the business of the partnership; and the acts of every partner who does any act for carrying on in the usual way business of the kind carried on by the firm of which he is a member bind the firm and his partners, unless the partner so acting has in fact no authority to act for the firm in the particular matter, and the person with whom he is dealing either knows that he has no authority, or does not know or believe him to be a partner.

6   Partners bound by acts on behalf of firm

An act or instrument relating to the business of the firm and done or executed in the firm-name, or in any other manner showing an intention to bind the firm, by any person thereto authorised, whether a partner or not, is binding on the firm and all the partners.

Provided that this section shall not affect any general rule of law relating to the execution of deeds or negotiable instruments.

7   Partner using credit of firm for private purposes

Where one partner pledges the credit of the firm for a purpose apparently not connected with the firm's ordinary course of business, the firm is not bound, unless he is in fact specially authorised by the other partners; but this section does not affect any personal liability incurred by an individual partner.

8   Effect of notice that firm will not be bound by acts of partner

If it has been agreed between the partners that any restriction shall be placed on the power of any one or more of them to bind the firm, no act done in contravention of the agreement is binding on the firm with respect to persons having notice of the agreement.

9   Liability of partners

Every partner in a firm is liable jointly with the other partners, and in Scotland severally also, for all debts and obligations of the firm incurred while he is a partner; and after his death his estate is also severally liable in a due course of administration for such debts and obligations, so far as they remain unsatisfied, but subject in England or Ireland to the prior payment of his separate debts.

10   Liability of the firm for wrongs

Where, by any wrongful act or omission of any partner acting in the ordinary course of the business of the firm, or with the authority of his co-partners, loss or injury is caused to any person not being a partner in the firm, or any penalty is incurred, the firm is liable therefor to the same extent as the partner so acting or omitting to act.

11   Misapplication of money or property received for or in custody of the firm
In the following cases; namely—

   (a) Where one partner acting within the scope of his apparent authority receives the money or property of a third person and misapplies it; and

   (b) Where a firm in the course of its business receives money or property of a third person, and the money or property so received is misapplied by one or more of the partners while it is in the custody of the firm;

the firm is liable to make good the loss.!

12   Liability for wrongs joint and several
Every partner is liable jointly with his co-partners and also severally for everything for which the firm while he is a partner therein becomes hable under either of the two last preceding sections.

13   Improper employment of trust-property for partnership purposes
If a partner, being a trustee, improperly employs trust property in the business or on the account of the partnership, no other partner is liable for the trust-property to the persons beneficially interested therein.

   Provided as follows:—

   (1) This section shall not affect any liability incurred by any partner by reason of his having notice of a breach of trust; and

   (2) Nothing in this section shall prevent trust money from being followed and recovered from the firm if still in its possession or under its control.

14   Persons liable by 'holding out'
   (1) Every one who by words spoken or written or by conduct represents himself, or who knowingly suffers himself to be represented, as a partner in a particular firm, is liable as a partner to one who has on the faith of any such representation given credit to the firm, whether the representation has or has not been made or communicated to the person so giving credit by or with the knowledge of the apparent partner making the representation or suffering it to be made.

   (2) Provided that where after a partner's death the partnership business is continued in the old firm-name, the continued use of that name or of the deceased partner's name as part thereof shall not of itself make his executors or administrators estate or effects liable for any partnership debts contracted after his death.

15   Admissions and representations of partners
An admission or representation made by any partner concerning the partnership affairs, and in the ordinary course of its business, is evidence against the firm.

16   Notice to acting partner to be notice to the firm
Notice to any partner who habitually acts in the partnership business of any matter relating to partnership affairs operates as a notice to the firm, except in the case of a fraud on the firm committed by or with the consent of that partner.

17   Liabilities of incoming and outgoing partners
   (1) A person who is admitted as a partner into an existing firm does not thereby become liable to the creditors of the firm for anything done before he became a partner.

   (2) A partner who retires from a firm does not thereby cease to be liable for partnership debts or obligations incurred before his retirement.

   (3) A retiring partner may be discharged from any existing liabilities, by an agreement to that effect between himself and the members of the firm as newly constituted and the creditors, and this agreement may be either express or inferred, as a fact from the course of dealing between the creditors and the firm as newly constituted.

18   Revocation of continuing guaranty by change in firm
A continuing guaranty or cautionary obligation given either to a firm or to a third person in respect of the transactions of a firm is, in the absence of agreement to the contrary, revoked as

to future transactions by any change in the constitution of the firm to which, or of the firm in respect of the transactions of which, the guaranty or obligation was given.

Relations of partners to one another

19   Variation by consent of terms of partnership

The mutual rights and duties of partners, whether ascertained by agreement or defined by this Act, may be varied by the consent of all the partners, and such consent may be either express or inferred from a course of dealing.

20   Partnership property

(1) All property and rights and interests in property originally brought into the partnership stock or acquired, whether by purchase or otherwise, on account of the firm or for the purposes and in the course of the partnership business, are called in this Act partnership property, and must be held and applied by the partners exclusively for the purposes of the partnership and in accordance with the partnership agreement.

(2) Provided that the legal estate or interest in any land, or in Scotland the title to and interest in any heritable estate, which belongs to the partnership shall devolve according to the nature and tenure thereof, and the general rules of law thereto applicable, but in trust, so far as necessary, for the persons beneficially interested in the land under this section.

(3) Where co-owners of an estate or interest in any land, or in Scotland of any heritable estate, not being itself partnership property, are partners as to profits made by the use of that land or estate, and purchase other land or estate out of the profits to be used in like manner, the land or estate so purchased belongs to them, in the absence of an agreement to the contrary, not as partners but as co-owners for the same respective estates and interests as are held by them in the land or estate first mentioned at the date of the purchase.

21   Property bought with partnership money

Unless the contrary intention appears, property bought with money belonging to the firm is deemed to have been bought on account of the firm.

23   Procedure against partnership property for a partner's separate judgment debt

(1) [...] a writ of execution shall not issue against any partnership property except on a judgment against the firm.

(2) The High Court, or a judge thereof, [...] or a county court, may, on the application by summons of any judgment creditor of a partner, make an order charging that partner's interest in the partnership property and profits with payment of the amount of the judgment debt and interest thereon, and may by the same or a subsequent order appoint a receiver of that partner's share of profits (whether already declared or accruing), and of any other money which may be coming to him in respect of the partnership, and direct all accounts and inquiries, and give all other orders and directions which might have been directed or given if the charge had been made in favour of the judgment creditor by the partner, or which the circumstances of the case may require.

(3) The other partner or partners shall be at liberty at any time to redeem the interest charged, or in case of a sale being directed, to purchase the same.

[...]

(5) This section shall not apply in Scotland.

24   Rules as to interests and duties of partners subject to special agreement

The interests of partners in the partnership property and their rights and duties in relation to the partnership shall be determined, subject to any agreement express or implied between the partners, by the following rules:

(1) All the partners are entitled to share equally in the capital and profits of the business, and must contribute equally towards the losses whether of capital or otherwise sustained by the firm.

(2) The firm must indemnify every partner in respect of payments made and personal liabilities incurred by him—

    (a) In the ordinary and proper conduct of the business of the firm—, or,

    (b) In or about anything necessarily done for the preservation of the business or property of the firm.

(3) A partner making, for the purpose of the partnership, any actual payment or advance beyond the amount of capital which he has agreed to subscribe, is entitled to interest at the rate of five per cent. per annum from the date of the payment or advance.

(4) A partner is not entitled, before the ascertainment of profits, to interest on the capital subscribed by him.

(5) Every partner may take part in the management of the partnership business.

(6) No partner shall be entitled to remuneration for acting in the partnership business.

(7) No person may be introduced as a partner without the consent of all existing partners.

(8) Any difference arising as to ordinary matters connected with the partnership business may be decided by a majority of the partners, but no change may be made in the nature of the partnership business without the consent of all existing partners.

(9) The partnership books are to be kept at the place of business of the partnership (or the principal place, if there is more than one), and every partner may, when he thinks fit, have access to and inspect and copy any of them.

25 Expulsion of partner

No majority of the partners can expel any partner unless a power to do so has been conferred by express agreement between the partners.

26 Retirement from partnership at will

(1) Where no fixed term has been agreed upon for the duration of the partnership, any partner may determine the partnership at any time on giving notice of his intention so to do to all the other partners.

(2) Where the partnership has originally been constituted by deed, a notice in writing, signed by the partner giving it, shall be sufficient for this purpose.

27 Where partnership for term is continued over, continuance on old terms presumed

(1) Where a partnership entered into for a fixed term is continued after the term has expired, and without any express new agreement, the rights and duties of the partners remain the same as they were at the expiration of the term, so far as is consistent with the incidents of a partnership at will.

(2) A continuance of the business by the partners or such of them as habitually acted therein during the term, without any settlement or liquidation of the partnership affairs, is presumed to be a continuance of the partnership.

28 Duty of partners to render accounts, &c.

Partners are bound to render true accounts and full information of all things affecting the partnership to any partner or his legal representatives.

29 Accountability of partners for private profits

(1) Every partner must account to the firm for any benefit derived by him without the consent of the other partners from any transaction concerning the partnership, or from any use by him of the partnership property name or business connexion.

(2) This section applies also to transactions undertaken after a partnership has been dissolved by the death of a partner, and before the affairs thereof have been completely wound up, either by any surviving partner or by the representatives of the deceased partner.

30 Duty of partner not to compete with firm
If a partner, without the consent of the other partners, carries on any business of the same nature as and competing with that of the firm, he must account for and pay over to the firm all profits made by him in that business.

31 Rights of assignee of share in partnership
(1) An assignment by any partner of his share in the partnership, either absolute or by way of mortgage or redeemable charge, does not, as against the other partners, entitle the assignee, during the continuance of the partnership, to interfere in the management or administration of the partnership business or affairs, or to require any accounts of the partnership transactions, or to inspect the partnership books, but entitles the assignee only to receive the share of profits to which the assigning partner would otherwise be entitled, and the assignee must accept the account of profits agreed to by the partners.

(2) In the case of a dissolution of the partnership, whether as respects all the partners or as respects the assigning partner, the assignee is entitled to receive the share of the partnership assets to which the assigning partner is entitled as between himself and the other partners, and, for the purpose of ascertaining that share, to an account as from the date of the dissolution.

Dissolution of partnership, and its consequences

32 Dissolution by expiration or notice
Subject to any agreement between the partners a partnership is dissolved—
  (a) If entered into for a fixed term, by the expiration of that term:
  (b) If entered into for a single adventure or undertaking, by the termination of that adventure or undertaking:
  (c) If entered into for an undefined time, by any partner giving notice to the other or others of his intention to dissolve the partnership.

In the last-mentioned case the partnership is dissolved as from the date mentioned in the notice as the date of dissolution, or, if no date is so mentioned, as from the date of the communication of the notice.

33 Dissolution by bankruptcy, death, or charge
(1) Subject to any agreement between the partners, every partnership is dissolved as regards all partners by the death or bankruptcy of any partner.

(2) A partnership may, at the option of the other partners, be dissolved if any partner suffers his share of the partnership property to be charged under this Act for his separate debt.

34 Dissolution by illegality of partnership
A partnership is in every case dissolved by the happening of any event which makes it unlawful for the business of the firm to be carried on or for the members of the firm to carry it on in partnership.

35 Dissolution by the Court
On application by a partner the Court may decree a dissolution of the partnership in any of the following cases:
  [...]
  (b) When a partner, other than the partner suing, becomes in any other way permanently incapable of performing his part of the partnership contract:
  (c) When a partner, other than the partner suing, has been guilty of such conduct as, in the opinion of the Court, regard being had to the nature of the business, is calculated to prejudicially affect the carrying on of the business:
  (d) When a partner, other than the partner suing, wilfully or persistently commits a breach of the partnership agreement, or otherwise so conducts himself in matters relating to the partnership business that it is not reasonably practicable for the other partner or partners to carry on the business in partnership with him:
  (e) When the business of the partnership can only be carried on at a loss:

(f) Whenever in any case circumstances have arisen which, in the opinion of the Court, render it just and equitable that the partnership be dissolved.

36 Rights of persons dealing with firm against apparent members of firm

(1) Where a person deals with a firm after a change in its constitution he is entitled to treat all apparent members of the old firm as still being members of the firm until he has notice of the change.

(2) An advertisement in the London Gazette as to a firm whose principal place of business is in England or Wales, in the Edinburgh Gazette as to a firm whose principal place of business is in Scotland, and in the Dublin Gazette as to a firm whose principal place of business is in Ireland, shall be notice as to persons who had not dealings with the firm before the date of the dissolution or change so advertised.

(3) The estate of a partner who dies, or who becomes bankrupt, or of a partner who, not having been known to the person dealing with the firm to be a partner, retires from the firm, is not liable for partnership debts contracted after the date of the death, bankruptcy, or retirement respectively.

37 Right of partners to notify dissolution

On dissolution of a partnership or retirement of a partner any partner may publicly notify the same, and may require the other partner or partners to concur for that purpose in all necessary or proper acts, if any, which cannot be done without his or their concurrence.

38 Continuing authority of partners for purposes of winding up

After the dissolution of a partnership the authority of each partner to bind the firm, and the other rights and obligations of the partners, continue notwithstanding the dissolution so far as may be necessary to wind up the affairs of the partnership, and to complete transactions begun but unfinished at the time of the dissolution, but not otherwise.

Provided that the firm is in no case bound by the acts of a partner who has become bankrupt; but this proviso does not affect the liability of any person who has after the bankruptcy represented himself or knowingly suffered himself to be represented as a partner of the bankrupt.

39 Rights of partners as to application of partnership property

On the dissolution of a partnership every partner is entitled, as against the other partners in the firm, and all persons claiming through them in respect of their interests as partners, to have the property of the partnership applied in payment of the debts and liabilities of the firm, and to have the surplus assets after such payment applied in payment of what may be due to the partners respectively after deducting what may be due from them as partners to the firm; and for that purpose any partner or his representatives may on the termination of the partnership apply to the Court to wind up the business and affairs of the firm.

40 Apportionment of premium where partnership prematurely dissolved

Where one partner has paid a premium to another on entering into a partnership for a fixed term, and the partnership is dissolved before the expiration of that term otherwise than by the death of a partner, the Court may order the repayment of the premium, or of such part thereof as it thinks just, having regard to the terms of the partnership contract and to the length of time during which the partnership has continued; unless

(a) the dissolution is, in the judgment of the Court, wholly or chiefly due to the misconduct of the partner who paid the premium, or

(b) the partnership has been dissolved by an agreement containing no provision for a return of any part of the premium.

41 Rights where partnership dissolved for fraud or misrepresentation

Where a partnership contract is rescinded on the ground of fraud or misrepresentation of one of the parties thereto, the party entitled to rescind is, without prejudice to any other right, entitled—

(a) to a lien on, or right of retention of, the surplus of the partnership assets, after satisfying the partnership liabilities, for any sum of money paid by him for the purchase of a share in the partnership and for any capital contributed by him, and is

(b) to stand in the place of the creditors of the firm for any payments made by him in respect of the partnership liabilities, and

(c) to be indemnified by the person guilty of the fraud or making the representation against all the debts and liabilities of the firm.

42   Right of outgoing partner in certain cases to share in profits made after dissolution

(1) Where any member of a firm has died or otherwise ceased to be a partner, and the surviving or continuing partners carry on the business of the firm with its capital or assets without any final settlement of accounts as between the firm and the outgoing partner or his estate, then, in the absence of any agreement to the contrary, the outgoing partner or his estate is entitled at the option of himself or his representatives to such share of the profits made since the dissolution as the Court may find to be attributable to the use of his share of the partnership assets, or to interest at the rate of five per cent. per annum on the amount of his share of the partnership assets.

(2) Provided that where by the partnership contract an option is given to surviving or continuing partners to purchase the interest of a deceased or outgoing partner, and that option is duly exercised, the estate of the deceased partner, or the outgoing partner or his estate, as the case may be, is not entitled to any further or other share of profits; but if any partner assuming to act in exercise of the option does not in all material respects comply with the terms thereof, he is liable to account under the foregoing provisions of this section.

43   Retiring or deceased partner's share to be a debt

Subject to any agreement between the partners, the amount due from surviving or continuing partners to an outgoing partner or the representatives of a deceased partner in respect of the outgoing or deceased partner's share is a debt accruing at the date of the dissolution or death.

44   Rule for distribution of assets on final settlement of accounts

In settling accounts between the partners after a dissolution of partnership, the following rules shall, subject to any agreement, be observed:

(a) Losses, including losses and deficiencies of capital, shall be paid first out of profits, next out of capital, and lastly, if necessary, by the partners individually in the proportion in which they were entitled to share profits:

(b) The assets of the firm including the sums, if any, contributed by the partners to make up losses or deficiencies of capital, shall be applied in the following manner and order:

1. In paying the debts and liabilities of the firm to persons who are not partners therein:

2. In paying to each partner rateably what is due from the firm to him for advances as distinguished from capital:

3. In paying to each partner rateably what is due from the firm to him in respect of capital:

4. The ultimate residue, if any, shall be divided among the partners in the proportion in which the profits are divisible.

Supplemental

45   Definitions of 'court' and 'business'

In this Act, unless the contrary intention appears—

The expression 'court' includes every court and judge having jurisdiction in the case:

The expression 'business' includes every trade, occupation or profession.

46   Saving for rules of equity and common law

The rules of equity and of common law applicable to partnership shall continue in force except so far as they are inconsistent with the express provisions of this Act.

47   Provision as to bankruptcy in Scotland

. . .

50   Short title

This Act may be cited as the Partnership Act, 1890.

Marine Insurance Act 1906
(6 Edw. 7, c. 41)

An Act to codify the Law relating to Marine Insurance.   [21st December 1906]

Marine insurance

1   Marine insurance defined

A contract of marine insurance is a contract whereby the insurer undertakes to indemnify the assured, in manner and to the extent thereby agreed, against marine losses, that is to say, the losses incident to marine adventure.

2   Mixed sea and land risks

(1) A contract of marine insurance may, by its express terms, or by usage of trade, be extended so as to protect the assured against losses on inland waters or on any land risk which may be incidental to any sea voyage.

(2) Where a ship in course of building, or the launch of a ship, or any adventure analogous to marine adventure, is covered by a policy in the form of a marine policy, the provisions of this Act, in so far as applicable, shall apply thereto; but, except as by this section provided, nothing in this Act shall alter or affect any rule of law applicable to any contract of insurance other than a contract of marine insurance as by this Act defined.

3   Marine adventure and maritime perils defined

(1) Subject to the provisions of this Act, every lawful marine adventure may be the subject of marine insurance.

(2) In particular there is a marine adventure where—

    (a) Any ship goods or other moveables are exposed to maritime perils. Such property is in this Act referred to as 'insurable property';

    (b) The earning or acquisition of any freight, passage money, commission, profit, or other pecuniary benefit, or the security for any advances, loan or disbursements, is endangered by the exposure of insurable property to maritime perils;

    (c) Any liability to a third party may be incurred by the owner of, or other person interested in or responsible for, insurable property, by reason of maritime perils.

'Maritime perils' means the perils consequent on, or incidental to, the navigation of the sea, that is to say, perils of the seas, fire, war perils, pirates, rovers, thieves, captures, seisures, restraints, and detainments of princes and peoples, jettisons, barratry, and any other perils, either of the like kind or which may be designated by the policy.

Insurable interest

4   Avoidance of wagering or gaming contracts

(1) Every contract of marine insurance by way of gaming or wagering is void.

(2) A contract of marine insurance is deemed to be a gaming or wagering contract—

    (a) Where the assured has not an insurable interest as defined by this Act, and the contract is entered into with no expectation of acquiring such an interest; or

    (b) Where the policy is made 'interest or no interest,' or 'without further proof of interest than the policy itself,' or 'without benefit of salvage to the insurer,' or subject to any other like term:

Provided that, where there is no possibility of salvage, a policy may be effected without benefit of salvage to the insurer.

5 Insurable interest defined

(1) Subject to the provisions of this Act, every person has an insurable interest who is interested in a marine adventure.

(2) In particular a person is interested in a marine adventure where he stands in any legal or equitable relation to the adventure or to any insurable property at risk therein, in consequence of which he may benefit by the safety or due arrival of insurable property, or may be prejudiced by its loss, or damage thereto, or by the detention thereof, or may incur liability in respect thereof.

6 When interest must attach

(1) The assured must be interested in the subject-matter insured at the time of the loss though he need not be interested when the insurance is effected:

Provided that where the subject-matter is insured 'lost or not lost,' the assured may recover although he may not have acquired his interest until after the loss, unless at the time of effecting the contract of insurance the assured was aware of the loss, and the insurer was not.

(2) Where the assured has no interest at the time of the loss, he cannot acquire interest by any act or election after he is aware of the loss.

7 Defeasible or contingent interest

(1) A defeasible interest is insurable, as also is a contingent interest.

(2) In particular, where the buyer of goods has insured them, he has an insurable interest, notwithstanding that he might, at his election, have rejected the goods, or have treated them as at the seller's risk, by reason of the latter's delay in making delivery or otherwise.

8 Partial interest

A partial interest of any nature is insurable.

9 Re-insurance

(1) The insurer under a contract of marine insurance has an insurable interest in his risk, and may re-insure in respect of it.

(2) Unless the policy otherwise provides, the original assured has no right or interest in respect of such re-insurance.

10 Bottomry

The lender of money on bottomry or respondentia has an insurable interest in respect of the loan.

11 Master's and seamen's wages

The master or any member of the crew of a ship has an insurable interest in respect of his wages.

12 Advance freight

In the case of advance freight, the person advancing the freight has an insurable interest, in so far as such freight is not repayable in case of loss.

13 Charges of insurance

The assured has an insurable interest in the charges of any insurance which he may effect.

14 Quantum of interest

(1) Where the subject-matter insured is mortgaged, the mortgagor has an insurable interest in the full value thereof, and the mortgagee has an insurable interest in respect of any sum due or to become due under the mortgage.

(2) A mortgagee, consignee, or other person having an interest in the subject-matter insured may insure on his own behalf and for the benefit of other persons interested as well as for his own benefit.

(3) The owner of insurable property has an insurable interest in respect of the full value thereof, notwithstanding that some third person may have agreed, or be liable, to indemnify him in case of loss.

15   Assignment of interest

Where the assured assigns or otherwise parts with his interest in the subject-matter insured, he does not thereby transfer to the assignee his rights under the contract of insurance, unless there be an express or implied agreement with the assignee to that effect.

But the provisions of this section do not affect a transmission of interest by operation of law.

Insurable value

16   Measure of insurable value

Subject to any express provision or valuation in the policy, the insurable value of the subject-matter insured must be ascertained as follows:—

(1) In insurance on ship, the insurable value is the value, at the commencement of the risk, of the ship, including her outfit, provisions and stores for the officers and crew, money advanced for seamen's wages, and other disbursements (if any) incurred to make the ship fit for the voyage or adventure contemplated by the policy, plus the charges of insurance upon the whole:

The insurable value, in the case of a steamship, includes also the machinery, boilers, and coals and engine stores if owned by the assured, and, in the case of a ship engaged in a special trade, the ordinary fittings requisite for that trade:

(2) In insurance on freight, whether paid in advance or otherwise, the insurable value is the gross amount of freight at the risk of the assured, plus the charges of insurance:

(3) In insurance on goods or merchandise, the insurable value is the prime cost of the property insured, plus the expenses of and incidental to shipping and the charges of insurance upon the whole:

(4) In insurance on any other subject-matter, the insurable value is the amount at the risk of the assured when the policy attaches, plus the charges of insurance.

Disclosure and representations

17   Insurance is uberrimae fidei

A contract of marine insurance is a contract based upon the utmost good faith, and, if the utmost good faith is not observed by either party, the contract may be avoided by the other party.

18   Disclosure by assured

(1) Subject to the provisions of this section, the assured must disclose to the insurer, before the contract is concluded, every material circumstance which is known to the assured, and the assured is deemed to know every circumstance which, in the ordinary course of business, ought to be known by him. If the assured fails to make such disclosure, the insurer may avoid the contract.

(2) Every circumstance is material which would influence the judgment of a prudent insurer in fixing the premium, or determining whether he will take the risk.

(3) In the absence of inquiry the following circumstances need not be disclosed, namely:—

(a) Any circumstance which diminishes the risk;

(b) Any circumstance which is known or presumed to be known to the insurer. The insurer is presumed to know matters of common notoriety or knowledge, and matters which an insurer in the ordinary course of his business, as such, ought to know;

(c) Any circumstance as to which information is waived by the insurer.

(d) Any circumstance which it is superfluous to disclose by reason of any express or implied warranty.

(4) Whether any particular circumstance, which is not disclosed, be material or not is, in each case, a question of fact.

(5) The term 'circumstance' includes any communication made to, or information received by, the assured.

19 Disclosure by agent effecting insurance

Subject to the provisions of the preceding section as to circumstances which need not be disclosed, where an insurance is effected for the assured by an agent, the agent must disclose to the insurer—

    (a) Every material circumstance which is known to himself, and an agent to insure is deemed to know every circumstance which, in the ordinary course of business, ought to be known by, or to have been communicated to, him; and

    (b) Every material circumstance which the assured is bound to disclose, unless it come to his knowledge too late to communicate it to the agent.

20 Representations pending negotiation of contract

(1) Every material representation made by the assured or his agent to the insurer during the negotiations for contract, and before the contract is concluded, must be true. If it be untrue the insurer may avoid the contract.

(2) A representation is material which would influence the judgment of a prudent insurer in fixing the premium, or determining whether he will take the risk.

(3) A representation may be either a representation as to a matter of fact, or as to a matter of expectation or belief.

(4) A representation as to matter of fact is true, if it be substantially correct, that is to say, if the difference between what is represented and what is actually correct would not be considered material by a prudent insurer.

(5) A representation as to a matter of expectation or belief is true if it be made in good faith.

(6) A representation may be withdrawn or corrected before the contract is concluded.

(7) Whether a particular representation be material or not is, in each case, a question of fact.

21 When contract is deemed to be concluded

A contract of marine insurance is deemed to be concluded when the proposal of the assured is accepted by the insurer, whether the policy be then issued or not; and, for the purpose of showing when the proposal was accepted, reference may be made to the slip or covering note or other customary memorandum of the contract, [. . .]

The policy

22 Contract must be embedded in policy

Subject to the provisions of any statute, a contract of marine insurance is inadmissible in evidence unless it is embodied in a marine policy in accordance with this Act. The policy may be executed and issued either at the time when the contract is concluded or afterwards.

23 What policy must specify

A marine policy must specify—

(1) The name of the assured, or of some person who effects the insurance on his behalf: [. . .]

24 Signature of insurer

(1) A marine policy must be signed by or on behalf of the insurer, provided that in the case of a corporation the corporate seal may be sufficient, but nothing in this section shall be construed as requiring the subscription of a corporation to be under seal.

(2) Where a policy is subscribed by or on behalf of two or more insurers, each subscription, unless the contrary be expressed, constitutes a distinct contract with the assured.

25 Voyage and time policies

(1) Where the contract is to insure the subject-matter 'at and from', or from one place to another or others, the policy is called a 'voyage policy', and where the contract is to insure

the subject-matter for a definite period of time the policy is called a 'time policy'. A contract for both voyage and time may be included in the same policy.

[...]

26 Designation of subject-matter

(1) The subject-matter insured must be designated in a marine policy with reasonable certainty.

(2) The nature and extent of the interest of the assured in the subject-matter insured need not be specified in the policy.

(3) Where the policy designates the subject-matter insured in general terms, it shall be construed to apply to the interest intended by the assured to be covered.

(4) In the application of this section regard shall be had to any usage regulating the designation of the subject-matter insured.

27 Valued policy

(1) A policy may be either valued or unvalued.

(2) A valued policy is a policy which specifies the agreed value of the subject-matter insured.

(3) Subject to the provisions of this Act, and in the absence of fraud, the value fixed by the policy is, as between the insurer and the assured, conclusive of the insurable value of the subject intended to be insured, whether the loss be total or partial.

(4) Unless the policy otherwise provides, the value fixed by the policy is not conclusive for the purpose of determining whether there has been a constructive total loss.

28 Unvalued policy

An unvalued policy is a policy which does not specify the value of the subject-matter insured, but, subject to the limit of the sum insured, leaves the insurable value to be subsequently ascertained, in the manner herein-before specified.

29 Floating policy by ship or ships

(1) A floating policy is a policy which describes the insurance in general terms, and leaves the name of the ship or ships and other particulars to be defined by subsequent declaration.

(2) The subsequent declaration or declarations may be made by indorsement on the policy, or in other customary manner.

(3) Unless the policy otherwise provides, the declarations must be made in the order of dispatch or shipment. They must, in the case of goods, comprise all consignments within the terms of the policy, and the value of the goods or other property must be honestly stated, but an omission or erroneous declaration may be rectified even after loss or arrival, provided the omission or declaration was made in good faith.

(4) Unless the policy otherwise provides, where a declaration of value is not made until after notice of loss or arrival, the policy must be treated as an unvalued policy as regards the subject-matter of that declaration.

30 Construction of terms in policy

(1) A policy may be in the form in the First Schedule to this Act.

(2) Subject to the provisions of this Act, and unless the context of the policy otherwise requires, the terms and expressions mentioned in the First Schedule to this Act shall be construed as having the scope and meaning in that schedule assigned to them.

31 Premium to be arranged

(1) Where an insurance is effected at a premium to be arranged, and no arrangement is made, a reasonable premium is payable.

(2) Where an insurance is effected on the terms that an additional premium is to be arranged in a given event, and that event happens but no arrangement is made, then a reasonable additional premium is payable.

Double insurance

32   Double insurance

(1) Where two or more policies are effected by or on behalf of the assured on the same adventure and interest or any part thereof, and the sums insured exceed the indemnity allowed by this Act, the assured is said to be over-insured by double insurance.

(2) Where the assured is over-insured by double insurance—

    (a) The assured, unless the policy otherwise provides, may claim payment from the insurers in such order as he may think fit, provided that he is not entitled to receive any sum in excess of the indemnity allowed by this Act;

    (b) Where the policy under which the assured claims is a valued policy, the assured must give credit as against the valuation for any sum received by him under any other policy without regard to the actual value of the subject-matter insured;

    (c) Where the policy under which the assured claims is an unvalued policy he must give credit, as against the full insurable value, for any sum received by him under any other policy.

    (d) Where the assured receives any sum in excess of the indemnity allowed by this Act, he is deemed to hold such sum in trust for the insurers, according to their right of contribution among themselves.

Warranties, etc.

33   Nature of warranty

(1) A warranty, in the following sections relating to warranties, means a promissory warranty, that is to say, a warranty by which the assured undertakes that some particular thing shall or shall not be done, or that some condition shall be fulfilled, or whereby he affirms or negatives the existence of a particular state of facts.

(2) A warranty may be express or implied.

(3) A warranty, as above defined, is a condition which must be exactly complied with, whether it be material to the risk or not. If it be not so complied with, then, subject to any express provision in the policy, the insurer is discharged from liability as from the date of the breach of warranty, but without prejudice to any liability incurred by him before that date.

34   When breach of warranty excused

(1) Non-compliance with a warranty is excused when, by reason of a change of circumstances, the warranty ceases to be applicable to the circumstances of the contract, or when compliance with the warranty is rendered unlawful by any subsequent law.

(2) Where a warranty is broken, the assured cannot avail himself of the defence that the breach has been remedied, and the warranty complied with, before loss.

(3) A breach of warranty may be waived by the insurer.

35   Express warranties

(1) An express warranty may be in any form of words from which the intention to warrant is to be inferred.

(2) An express warranty must be included in, or written upon, the policy, or must be contained in some document incorporated by reference into the policy.

(3) An express warranty does not exclude an implied warranty, unless it be inconsistent therewith.

36   Warranty of neutrality

(1) Where insurable property, whether ship or goods, is expressly warranted neutral, there is an implied condition that the property shall have a neutral character at the commencement of the risk, and that, so far as the assured can control the matter, its neutral character shall be preserved during the risk.

(2) Where a ship is expressly warranted 'neutral' there is also an implied condition that, so far as the assured can control the matter, she shall be properly documented, that is to say, that she shall carry the necessary papers to establish her neutrality, and that she shall not falsify or suppress her papers, or use simulated papers. If any loss occurs through breach of this condition, the insurer may avoid the contract.

37   No implied warranty of nationality
There is no implied warranty as to the nationality of a ship, or that her nationality shall not be changed during the risk.

38   Warranty of good safety
Where the subject-matter insured is warranted 'well' or 'in good safety' on a particularday, it is sufficient if it be safe at any time during that day.

39   Warranty of seaworthiness of ship
(1) In a voyage policy there is an implied warranty that at the commencement of the voyage the ship shall be seaworthy for the purpose of the particular adventure insured.

(2) Where the policy attaches while the ship is in port, there is also an implied warranty that she shall, at the commencement of the risk, be reasonably fit to encounter the ordinary perils of the port.

(3) Where the policy relates to a voyage which is performed in different stages, during which the ship requires different kinds of or further preparation or equipment, there is an implied warranty that at the commencement of each stage the ship is seaworthy in respect of such preparation or equipment for the purposes of that stage.

(4) A ship is deemed to be seaworthy when she is reasonably fit in all respects to encounter the ordinary perils of the seas of the adventure insured.

(5) In a time policy there is no implied warranty that the ship shall be seaworthy at any stage of the adventure, but where, with the privity of the assured, the ship is sent to sea in an unseaworthy state, the insurer is not liable for any loss attributable to unseaworthiness.

40   No implied warranty that goods are seaworthy
(1) In a policy on goods or other moveables there is no implied warranty that the goods or moveables are seaworthy.

(2) In a voyage policy on goods or other moveables there is an implied warranty that at the commencement of the voyage the ship is not only seaworthy as a ship, but also that she is reasonably fit to carry the goods or other moveables to the destination contemplated by the policy.

41   Warranty of legality
There is an implied warranty that the adventure insured is a lawful one, and that, so far as the assured can control the matter, the adventure shall be carried out in a lawful manner.

The voyage

42   Implied condition as to commencement of risk
(1) Where the subject-matter is insured by a voyage policy 'at and from' or 'from' a particular place, it is not necessary that the ship should be at that place when the contract is concluded, but there is an implied condition that the adventure shall be commenced within a reasonable time, and that if the adventure be not so commenced the insurer may avoid the contract.

(2) The implied condition may be negatived by showing that the delay was caused by circumstances known to the insurer before the contract was concluded, or by showing that he waived the condition.

43   Alteration of port of departure
Where the place of departure is specified by the policy, and the ship instead of sailing from that place sails from any other place, the risk does not attach.

44 Sailing for different destination
Where the destination is specified in the policy, and the ship, instead of sailing for that destination, sails for any other destination, the risk does not attach.

45 Change of voyage
(1) Where, after the commencement of the risk, the destination of the ship is voluntarily changed from the destination contemplated by the policy, there is said to be a change of voyage.

(2) Unless the policy otherwise provides, where there is a change of voyage, the insurer is discharged from liability as from the time of the change, that it to say, as from the time when the determination to change it is manifested; and it is immaterial that the ship may not have left the course of voyage contemplated by the policy when the loss occurs.

46 Deviation
(1) Where a ship, without lawful excuse, deviates from the voyage contemplated by the policy, the insurer is discharged from liability as from the time of deviation, and it is immaterial that the ship may have regained her route before any loss occurs.

(2) There is a deviation from the voyage contemplated by the policy—
　　(a) Where the course of the voyage is specifically designated by the policy, and that course is departed from; or
　　(b) Where the course of the voyage is not specifically designated by the policy, but the usual and customary course is departed from.

(3) The intention to deviate is immaterial; there must be a deviation in fact to discharge the insurer from his liability under the contract.

47 Several ports of discharge
(1) Where several ports of discharge are specified by the policy, the ship may proceed to all or any of them, but, in the absence of any usage or sufficient cause to the contrary, she must proceed to them, or such of them as she goes to, in the order designated by the policy. If she does not there is a deviation.

(2) Where the policy is to 'ports of discharge', within a given area, which are not named, the ship must, in the absence of any usage or sufficient cause to the contrary, proceed to them, or such of them as she goes to, in their geographical order. If she does not there is a deviation.

48 Delay in voyage
In the case of a voyage policy, the adventure insured must be prosecuted throughout its course with reasonable dispatch, and, if without lawful excuse it is not so prosecuted, the insurer is discharged from liability as from the time when the delay becomes unreasonable.

49 Excuses for deviation or delay
(1) Deviation or delay in prosecuting the voyage contemplated by the policy is excused—
　　(a) Where authorised by any special term in the policy; or
　　(b) Where caused by circumstances beyond the control of the master and his employer; or
　　(c) Where reasonably necessary in order to comply with an express or implied warranty; or
　　(d) Where reasonably necessary for the safety of the ship or subject-matter insured; or
　　(e) For the purpose of saving human life, or aiding a ship in distress where human life may be in danger; or
　　(f) Where reasonably necessary for the purpose of obtaining medical or surgical aid for any person on board the ship; or
　　(g) Where caused by the barratrous conduct of the master or crew, if barratry be one of the perils insured against.

(2) When the cause excusing the deviation or delay ceases to operate, the ship must resume her course, and prosecute her voyage, with reasonable dispatch.

Assignment of policy

50 When and how policy is assignable

(1) A marine policy is assignable unless it contains terms expressly prohibiting assignment. It may be assigned either before or after loss.

(2) Where a marine policy has been assigned so as to pass the beneficial interest in such policy, the assignee of the policy is entitled to sue thereon in his own name; and the defendant is entitled to make any defence arising out of the contract which he would have been entitled to make if the action had been brought in the name of the person by or on behalf of whom the policy was effected.

(3) A marine policy may be assigned by indorsement thereon or in other customary manner.

51 Assured who has no interest cannot assign

Where the assured has parted with or lost his interest in the subject-matter insured, and has not, before or at the time of so doing, expressly or impliedly agreed to assign the policy, any subsequent assignment of the policy is inoperative:

Provided that nothing in this section affects the assignment of a policy after loss.

The premium

52 When premium payable

Unless otherwise agreed, the duty of the assured or his agent to pay the premium, and the duty of the insurer to issue the policy to the assured or his agent, are concurrent conditions, and the insurer is not bound to issue the policy until payment or tender of the premium.

53 Policy effected through broker

(1) Unless otherwise agreed, where a marine policy is effected on behalf of the assured by a broker, the broker is directly responsible to the insurer for the premium, and the insurer is directly responsible to the assured for the amount which may be payable in respect of losses, or in respect of returnable premium.

(2) Unless otherwise agreed, the broker has, as against the assured, a lien upon the policy for the amount of the premium and his charges in respect of effecting the policy; and, where he has dealt with the person who employs him as a principal, he has also a lien on the policy in respect of any balance on any insurance account which may be due to him from such person, unless when the debt was incurred he had reason to believe that such person was only an agent.

54 Effect of receipt on policy

Where a marine policy effected on behalf of the assured by a broker acknowledges the receipt of the premium, such acknowledgement is, in the absence of fraud, conclusive as between the insurer and the assured, but not as between the insurer and broker.

Loss and abandonment

55 Included and excluded losses

(1) Subject to the provisions of this Act, and unless the policy otherwise provides, the insurer is liable for any loss proximately caused by a peril insured against, but, subject as aforesaid, he is not liable for any loss which is not proximately caused by a peril insured against.

(2) In particular,—

    (a) The insurer is not liable for any loss attributable to the wilful misconduct of the assured, but, unless the policy otherwise provides, he is liable for any loss proximately caused by a peril insured against, even though the loss would not have happened but for the misconduct or negligence of the master or crew;

(b) Unless the policy otherwise provides, the insurer on ship or goods is not liable for any loss proximately caused by delay, although the delay be caused by a peril insured against.

(c) Unless the policy otherwise provides, the insurer is not liable for ordinary wear and tear, ordinary leakage and breakage, inherent vice or nature of the subject-matter insured, or for any loss proximately caused by rats or vermin, or for any injury to machinery not proximately caused by maritime perils.

56 Partial and total loss

(1) A loss may be either total or partial. Any loss other than a total loss, as herein-after defined, is a partial loss.

(2) A total loss may be either an actual total loss, or a constructive total loss.

(3) Unless a different intention appears from the terms of the policy, an insurance against total loss includes a constructive, as well as an actual, total loss.

(4) Where the assured brings an action for a total loss and the evidence proves only a partial loss, he may, unless the policy otherwise provides, recover for a partial loss.

(5) Where goods reach their destination in specie, but by reason of obliteration of marks, or otherwise, they are incapable of identification, the loss, if any, is partial, and not total.

57 Actual total loss

(1) Where the subject-matter insured is destroyed, or so damaged as to cease to be a thing of the kind insured, or where the assured is irretrievably deprived thereof, there is an actual total loss.

(2) In the case of an actual total loss no notice of abandonment need be given.

58 Missing ship

Where the ship concerned in the adventure is missing, and after the lapse of a reasonable time no news of her has been received, an actual total loss may be presumed.

59 Effect of transhipment, etc.

Where, by a peril insured against, the voyage is interrupted at any intermediate port or place, under such circumstances as apart from any special stipulation in the contract of affreightment, to justify the master in landing and re-shipping the goods or other moveables, or in transhipping them, and sending them on to their destination, the liability of the insurer continues, notwithstanding the landing or transhipment.

60 Constructive total loss defined

(1) Subject to any express provision in the policy, there is a constructive total loss where the subject-matter insured is reasonably abandoned on account of its total loss appearing to be unavoidable, or because it could not be preserved from actual total loss without an expenditure which would exceed its value when the expenditure had been incurred.

(2) In particular, there is a constructive total loss—

(i) Where the assured is deprived of the possession of his ship or goods by a peril insured against, and (a) it is unlikely that he can recover the ship or goods, as the case may be, or (b) the cost of recovering the ship or goods, as the case may be, would exceed their value when recovered; or

(ii) In the case of damage to a ship, where she is so damaged by a peril insured against that the cost of repairing the damage would exceed the value of the ship when repaired.

In estimating the cost of repairs, no deduction is to be made in respect of general average contributions to those repairs payable by other interests, but account is to be taken of the expense of future salvage operations and of any future general average contributions to which the ship would be liable if repaired; or

(iii) In the case of damage to goods, where the cost of repairing the damage and forwarding the goods to their destination would exceed their value on arrival.

61 Effect of constructive total loss

Where there is a constructive total loss the assured may either treat the loss as a partial loss, or abandon the subject-matter insured to the insurer and treat the loss as if it were an actual total loss.

62 Notice of abandonment

(1) Subject to the provisions of this section, where the assured elects to abandon the subject-matter insured to the insurer, he must give notice of the abandonment. If he fails to do so the loss can only be treated as a partial loss.

(2) Notice of abandonment may be given in writing, or by word of mouth, or partly in writing and partly by word of mouth, and may be given in terms which indicate the intention of the assured to abandon his insured interest in the subject-matter insured unconditionally to the insurer.

(3) Notice of abandonment must be given with reasonable diligence after the receipt of reliable information of the loss, but where the information is of a doubtful character the assured is entitled to a reasonable time to make inquiry.

(4) Where notice of abandonment is properly given, the rights of the assured are not prejudiced by the fact that the insurer refuses to accept the abandonment.

(5) The acceptance of an abandonment may be either express or implied from the conduct of the insurer. The mere silence of the insurer after notice is not an acceptance.

(6) Where a notice of abandonment is accepted the abandonment is irrevocable. The acceptance of the notice conclusively admits liability for the loss and the sufficiency of the notice.

(7) Notice of abandonment is unnecessary where, at the time when the assured receives information of the loss, there would be no possibility of benefit to the insurer if notice were given to him.

(8) Notice of abandonment may be waived by the insurer.

(9) Where an insurer has re-insured his risk, no notice of abandonment need be given by him.

63 Effect of abandonment

(1) Where there is a valid abandonment the insurer is entitled to take over the interest of the assured in whatever may remain of the subject-matter insured, and all proprietary rights incidental thereto.

(2) Upon the abandonment of a ship, the insurer thereof is entitled to any freight in course of being earned, and which is earned by her subsequent to the casualty causing the loss, less the expenses of earning it incurred after the casualty; and, where a ship is carrying the owner's goods, the insurer is entitled to a reasonable remuneration for the carriage of them subsequent to the casualty causing the loss.

Partial losses (including salvage and general average and particular charges)

64 Particular average loss

(1) A particular average loss is a partial loss of the subject-matter insured, caused by a peril insured against, and which is not a general average loss.

(2) Expenses incurred by or on behalf of the assured for the safety or preservation of the subject-matter insured, other than general average and salvage charges, are called particular charges. Particular charges are not included in particular average.

65 Salvage charges

(1) Subject to any express provision in the policy, salvage charges incurred in preventing a loss by perils insured against may be recovered as a loss by those perils.

(2) 'Salvage charges' means the charges recoverable under maritime law by a salvor independently of contract. They do not include the expenses of services in the nature of salvage rendered by the assured or his agents, or any person employed for hire by them, for the purpose of averting a peril insured against. Such expenses, where properly incurred, may

be recovered as particular charges or as a general average loss, according to the circumstances under which they were incurred.

66   General average loss

(1) A general average loss is a loss caused by or directly consequential on a general average act. It includes a general average expenditure as well as a general average sacrifice.

(2) There is a general average act where any extraordinary sacrifice or expenditure is voluntarily and reasonably made or incurred in the time of peril for the purpose of preserving the property imperilled in the common adventure.

(3) Where there is a general average loss, the party on whom it falls is entitled, subject to the conditions imposed by maritime law, to a rateable contribution from the other parties interested, and such contribution is called a general average contribution.

(4) Subject to any express provision in the policy, where the assured has incurred a general average expenditure, he may recover from the insurer in respect of the proportion of the loss which falls upon him; and, in the case of a general average sacrifice, he may recover from the insurer in respect of the whole loss without having enforced his right of contribution from the other parties liable to contribute.

(5) Subject to any express provision in the policy, where the assured has paid, or is liable to pay, a general average contribution in respect of the subject insured, he may recover therefor from the insurer.

(6) In the absence of express stipulation, the insurer is not liable for any general average loss or contribution where the loss was not incurred for the purpose of avoiding, or in connexion with the avoidance of, a peril insured against.

(7) Where ship, freight, and cargo, or any two of those interests, are owned by the same assured, the liability of the insurer in respect of general average losses or contributions is to be determined as if those subjects were owned by different persons.

Measure of indemnity

67   Extent of liability of insurer for loss

(1) The sum which the assured can recover in respect of a loss on a policy by which he is insured, in the case of an unvalued policy to the full extent of the insurable value, or in the case of a valued policy to the full extent of the value fixed by the policy, is called the measure of indemnity.

(2) Where there is a loss recoverable under the policy, the insurer, or each insurer if there be more than one, is liable for such proportion of the measure of indemnity as the amount of his subscription bears to the value fixed by the policy in the case of a valued policy, or to the insurable value in the case of an unvalued policy.

68   Total loss

Subject to the provisions of this Act and to any express provision in the policy, where there is a total loss of the subject-matter insured,—

(1) If the policy be a valued policy, the measure of indemnity is the sum fixed by the policy:

(2) If the policy be an unvalued policy, the measure of indemnity is the insurable value of the subject-matter insured.

69   Partial loss of ship

Where a ship is damaged, but not totally lost, the measure of indemnity, subject to any express provision in the policy, is as follows:—

(1) Where the ship has been repaired, the assured is entitled to the reasonable cost of the repairs, less the customary deductions, but not exceeding the sum insured in respect of any one casualty:

(2) Where the ship has been only partially repaired, the assured is entitled to the reasonable cost of such repairs, computed as above, and also to be indemnified for the

reasonable depreciation, if any, arising from the unrepaired damage, provided that the aggregate amount shall not exceed the cost of repairing the whole damage, computed as above:

(3) Where the ship has not been repaired, and has not been sold in her damaged state during the risk, the assured is entitled to be indemnified for the reasonable depreciation arising from the unrepaired damage, but not exceeding the reasonable cost of repairing such damage, computed as above.

70   Partial loss of freight

Subject to any express provision in the policy, where there is a partial loss of freight, the measure of indemnity is such proportion of the sum fixed by the policy in the case of a valued policy, or of the insurable value in the case of an unvalued policy, as the proportion of freight lost by the assured bears to the whole freight at the risk of the assured under the policy.

71   Partial loss of goods, merchandise, etc.

Where there is a partial loss of goods, merchandise, or other moveables, the measure of indemnity, subject to any express provision in the policy, is as follows:—

(1) Where part of the goods, merchandise, or other moveables insured by a valued policy is totally lost, the measure of indemnity is such proportion of the sum fixed by the policy as the insurable value of the part lost bears to the insurable value of the whole, ascertained as in the case of an unvalued policy:

(2) Where part of the goods, merchandise, or other moveables insured by an unvalued policy is totally lost, the measure of indemnity is the insurable value of the part lost, ascertained as in the case of total loss:

(3) Where the whole or any part of the goods or merchandise insured has been delivered damaged at its destination, the measure of indemnity is such proportion of the sum fixed by the policy in the case of a valued policy, or of the insurable value in the case of an unvalued policy, as the difference between the gross sound and damaged values at the place of arrival bears to the gross sound value:

(4) 'Gross value' means the wholesale price or, if there be no such price, the estimated value, with, in either case, freight, landing charges, and duty paid before-hand; provided that, in the case of goods or merchandise customarily sold in bond, the bonded price is deemed to be the gross value. 'Gross proceeds' means the actual price obtained at a sale where all charges on sale are paid by the sellers.

72   Apportionment of valuation

(1) Where different species of property are insured under a single valuation, the valuation must be apportioned over the different species in proportion to their respective insurable values, as in the case of an unvalued policy. The insured value of any part of a species is such proportion of the total insured value of the same as the insurable value of the part bears to the insurable value of the whole, ascertained in both cases as provided by this Act.

(2) Where a valuation has to be apportioned, and particulars of the prime cost of each separate species, quality, or description of goods cannot be ascertained, the division of the valuation may be made over the net arrived sound values of the different species, qualities, or descriptions of goods.

73   General average contributions and salvage charges

(1) Subject to any express provision in the policy, where the assured has paid, or is liable for, any general average contribution, the measure of indemnity is the full amount of such contribution, if the subject-matter liable to contribution is insured for its full contributory value; but, if such subject-matter be not insured for its full contributory value, or if only part of it be insured, the indemnity payable by the insurer must be reduced in proportion to the under insurance, and where there has been a particular average loss which constitutes a deduction from the contributory value, and for which the insurer is liable, that amount must be deducted from the insured value in order to ascertain what the insurer is liable to contribute.

(2) Where the insurer is liable for salvage charges the extent of his liability must be determined on the like principle.

74 Liabilities to third parties

Where the assured has effected an insurance in express terms against any liability to a third party, the measure of indemnity, subject to any express provision in the policy, is the amount paid or payable by him to such third party in respect of such liability.

75 General provisions as to measure of indemnity

(1) Where there has been a loss in respect of any subject-matter not expressly provided for in the foregoing provisions of this Act, the measure of indemnity shall be ascertained, as nearly as may be, in accordance with those provisions, in so far as applicable to the particular case.

(2) Nothing in the provisions of this Act relating to the measure of indemnity shall affect the rules relating to double insurance, or prohibit the insurer from disproving interest wholly or in part, or from showing that at the time of the loss the whole or any part of the subject-matter insured was not at risk under the policy.

76 Particular average warranties

(1) Where the subject-matter insured is warranted free from particular average, the assured cannot recover for a loss of part, other than a loss incurred by a general average sacrificel unless the contract contained in the policy be apportionable; but, if the contract be apportionable, the assured may recover for a total loss of any apportionable part.

(2) Where the subject-matter insured is warranted free from particular average, either wholly or under a certain percentage, the insurer is nevertheless liable for salvage charges, and for particular charges and other expenses properly incurred pursuant to the provisions of the suing and labouring clause in order to avert a loss insured against.

(3) Unless the policy otherwise provides, where the subject-matter is warranted free from particular average under a specified percentage, a general average loss cannot be added to a particular average loss to make up the specified percentage.

(4) For the purpose of ascertaining whether the specified percentage has been reached, regard shall be had only to the actual loss suffered by the subject-matter insured. Particular charges and the expenses of and incidental to ascertaining and proving the loss must be excluded.

77 Successive losses

(1) Unless the policy otherwise provides, and subject to the provisions of this Act, the insurer is liable for successive losses, even though the total amount of such losses may exceed the sum insured.

(2) Where, under the same policy, a partial loss, which has not been repaired or otherwise made good, is followed by a total loss, the assured can only recover in respect of the total loss:

Provided that nothing in this section shall affect the liability of the insurer under the suing and labouring clause.

78 Suing and labouring clause

(1) Where the policy contains a suing and labouring clause, the engagement thereby entered into is deemed to be supplementary to the contract of insurance, and the assured may recover from the insurer any expenses properly incurred pursuant to the clause, notwithstanding that the insurer may have paid for a total loss, or that the subject-matter may have been warranted free from particular average, either wholly or under a certain percentage.

(2) General average losses and contributions and salvage charges, as defined by this Act, are not recoverable under the suing and labouring clause.

(3) Expenses incurred for the purpose of averting or diminishing any loss not covered by the policy are not recoverable under the suing and labouring clause.

(4) It is the duty of the assured and his agents, in all cases, to take such measures as may be reasonable for the purpose of averting or minimising a loss.

Rights of insurer on payment

79   Right of subrogation

(1) Where the insurer pays for a total loss, either of the whole, or in the case of goods of any apportionable part, of the subject-matter insured, he thereupon becomes entitled to take over the interest of the assured in whatever may remain of the subject-matter so paid for, and he is thereby subrogated to all the rights and remedies of the assured in and in respect of that subject-matter as from the time of the casualty causing the loss.

(2) Subject to the foregoing provisions, where the insurer pays for a partial loss, he acquires no title to the subject-matter insured, or such part of it as may remain, but he is thereupon subrogated to all rights and remedies of the assured in and in respect of the subject-matter insured as from the time of the casualty causing the loss, in so far as the assured has been indemnified, according to this Act, by such payment for the loss.

80   Right of contribution

(1) Where the assured is over-insured by double insurance, each insurer is bound, as between himself and the other insurers, to contribute rateably to the loss in proportion to the amount for which he is liable under his contract.

(2) If any insurer pays more than his proportion of the loss, he is entitled to maintain an action for contribution against the other insurers, and is entitled to the like remedies as a surety who has paid more than his proportion of the debt.

81   Effect of under insurance

Where the assured is insured for an amount less than the insurable value or, in the case of a valued policy, for an amount less than the policy valuation, he is deemed to be his own insurer in respect of the uninsured balance.

Return of premium

82   Enforcement of return

Where the premium or a proportionate part thereof is, by this Act, declared to be returnable,—

(a) If already paid, it may be recovered by the assured from the insurer; and

(b) If unpaid, it may be retained by the assured or his agent.

83   Return by agreement

Where the policy contains a stipulation for the return of the premium, or a proportionate part thereof, on the happening of a certain event, and that event happens, the premium, or, as the case may be, the proportionate part thereof, is thereupon returnable to the assured.

84   Return for failure of consideration

(1) Where the consideration for the payment of the premium totally fails, and there has been no fraud or illegality on the part of the assured or his agents, the premium is thereupon returnable to the assured.

(2) Where the consideration for the payment of the premium is apportionable and there is a total failure of any apportionable part of the consideration, a proportionate part of the premium is, under the like conditions, thereupon returnable to the assured.

(3) In particular—

(a) Where the policy is void, or is avoided by the insurer as from the commencement of the risk, the premium is returnable, provided that there has been no fraud or illegality on the part of the assured; but if the risk is not apportionable, and has once attached, the premium is not returnable;

(b) Where the subject-matter insured, or part thereof, has never been imperilled, the premium, or, as the case may be, a proportionate part thereof, is returnable: Provided that where the subject-matter has been insured 'lost or not lost' and has arrived in safety at the time when the contract is concluded, the premium is not returnable unless, at such time, the insurer knew of the safe arrival.

(c) Where the assured has no insurable interest throughout the currency of the risk, the premium is returnable, provided that this rule does not apply to a policy effected by way of gaming or wagering;

(d) Where the assured has a defeasible interest which is terminated during the currency of the risk, the premium is not returnable;

(e) Where the assured has over-insured under an unvalued policy, a proportionate part of the premium is returnable;

(f) Subject to the foregoing provisions, where the assured has over-insured by double insurance, a proportionate part of the several premiums is returnable:

Provided that, if the policies are effected at different times, and any earlier policy has at any time borne the entire risk, or if a claim has been paid on the policy in respect of the full sum insured thereby, no premium is returnable in respect of that policy, and when the double insurance is effected knowingly by the assured no premium is returnable.

Mutual insurance

85   Modification of Act in case of mutual insurance

(1) Where two or more persons mutually agree to insure each other against marine losses there is said to be a mutual insurance.

(2) The provisions of this Act relating to the premium do not apply to mutual insurance, but a guarantee, or such other arrangement as may be agreed upon, may be substituted for the premium.

(3) The provisions of this Act, in so far as they may be modified by the agreement of the parties, may in the case of mutual insurance be modified by the terms of the policies issued by the association, or by the rules and regulations of the association.

(4) Subject to the expectations mentioned in this section, the provisions of this Act apply to a mutual insurance.

Supplemental

86   Ratification by assured

Where a contract of marine insurance is in good faith effected by one person on behalf of another, the person on whose behalf it is effected may ratify the contract even after he is aware of a loss.

87   Implied obligations varied by agreement or usage

(1) Where any right, duty, or liability would arise under a contract of marine insurance by implication of law, it may be negatived or varied by express agreement or by usage, if the usage be such as to bind both parties to the contract.

(2) The provisions of this section extend to any right, duty, or liability declared by this Act which may be lawfully modified by agreement.

88   Reasonable time, etc, a question of fact

Where by this Act any reference is made to reasonable time, reasonable premium, or reasonable diligence, the question what is reasonable is a question of fact.

89   Slip as evidence

Where there is a duly stamped policy, reference may be made, as heretofore, to the slip or covering note, in any legal proceeding.

90   Interpretation of terms

In this Act, unless the context or subject-matter otherwise requires,—

'Action' includes counter-claim and set off:

'Freight' includes the profit derivable by a shipowner from the employment of his ship to carry his own goods or moveables, as well as freight payable by a third party, but does not include passage money:

'Moveables' means any moveable tangible property, other than the ship, and includes money, valuable securities, and other documents.

'Policy' means a marine policy.

91 Savings

(1) Nothing in this Act, or in any repeal effected thereby, shall affect—

    (a) The provisions of the Stamp Act 1891, or any enactment for the time being in force relating to the revenue;

    (b) The provisions of the Companies Act 1862, or any enactment amending or substituted for the same;

    (c) The provisions of any statute not expressly repealed by this Act.

(2) The rules of the common law including the law merchant, save in so far as they are inconsistent with the express provisions of this Act, shall continue to apply to contracts of marine insurance.

94 Short title

This Act may be cited as the Marine Insurance Act 1906.

SCHEDULES

Section 30   SCHEDULE 1

FORM OF POLICY

BE IT KNOWN THAT ...... as well in ...... own name as for and in the name and names of all and every other person or persons to whom the same doth, may, or shall appertain, in part or in all doth make assurance and cause and them, and every of them, to be insured lost or not lost, at and from ......

Upon any kind of goods and merchandise, and also upon the body, tackle, apparel, ordnance, munition, artillery, boat, and other furniture, of and in the good ship or vessel called the .... whereof is master under God, for this present voyage, ... or whosoever else shall go for master in the said ship, or by whatsoever other name or names the said ship, or the master thereof, is or shall be named or called; beginning the adventure upon the said goods and merchandises from the loading thereof aboard the said ship. upon the said ship, etc.

and so shall continue and endure, during her abode there, upon the said ship, etc. And further, until the said ship, with all her ordnance, tackle, apparel, etc., and goods and merchandises whatsoever shall be arrived at .... upon the said ship, etc., until she hath moored at anchor for twenty-four hours in good safety; and upon the goods and merchandises, until the same be there discharged and safely landed. And it shall be lawful for the said ship, etc., in this voyage to proceed and sail to and touch and stay at any ports or places whatsoever without prejudice to this insurance. The said ship, etc., goods and merchandises, etc., for so much as concerns the assured by agreement between the assured and assurers in this policy, are and shall be valued at ......

Touching the adventures and perils which we the assurers are contented to bear and do take upon us in this voyage: they are of the seas, men of war, fire, enemies, pirates, rovers, thieves, jettisons, letters of mart and countermart, surprisals, takings at sea, arrests, restraints, and detainments of all kings, princes, and people, of what nation, condition, or quality soever, barratry of the master and mariners, and of all other perils, losses, and misfortunes, that have or shall come to the hurt, detriment, or damage of the said goods and merchandises, and ship, etc., or any part thereof. And in case of any loss or misfortune it shall be lawful to the assured, their factors, servants and assigns, to sue, labour, and travel for, in and about the defence, safeguards, and recovery of the said goods and merchandises, and ship, etc., or any part thereof, without prejudice to this insurance; to the charges whereof we, the assurers, will contribute each one according to the rate and quantity of his sum herein assured. And it is especially declared and agreed that no acts of the insurer or insured in recovering, saving, or preserving the property insured shall be considered as a waiver, or acceptance of abandonment. And it is agreed by us, the insurers, that this writing or policy of assurance shall be of as much force and effect as the surest writing or policy of assurance heretofore made in Lombard Street, or in the Royal Exchange, or elsewhere in London. And so we, the assurers, are contented, and do hereby promise and bind ourselves, each one for his own part, our heirs, executors, and goods to the assured, their executors, administrators, and assigns, for the true performance of the premises, confessing ourselves paid the consideration due unto us for this assurance by the assured, at and after the rate of ......

IN WITNESS whereof we, the assurers, have subscribed our names and sums assured in London. N.B.—Corn, fish, salt, fruit, flour, and seed are warranted free from average, unless general, or the ship be stranded-sugar, tobacco, hemp, flax, hides and skins are warranted free from average, under five pounds per cent., and all other goods, also the ship and freight, are warranted free from average, under three pounds per cent. unless general, or the ship be stranded.

Rules for construction of policy

The following are the rules referred to by this Act for the construction of a policy in the above or other like form, where the context does not otherwise require:—

1. Where the subject-matter is insured 'lost or not lost,' and the loss has occurred before the contract is concluded, the risk attaches, unless at such time the assured was aware of the loss, and the insurer was not.

2. Where the subject-matter is insured 'from' a particular place, the risk does not attach until the ship starts on the voyage insured.

3. (a) Where a ship is insured 'at and from' a particular place, and she is at that place in good safety when the contract is concluded, the risk attaches immediately.

    (b) If she be not at that place when the contract is concluded, the risk attaches as soon as she arrives there in good safety, and, unless the policy otherwise provides, it is immaterial that she is covered by another policy for a specified time after arrival.

    (c) Where chartered freight is insured 'at and from' a particular place, and the ship is at that place in good safety when the contract is concluded the risk attaches immediately. If she be not there when the contract is concluded, the risk attaches as soon as she arrives there in good safety.

    (d) Where freight, other than chartered freight, is payable without special conditions and is insured 'at and from' a particular place, the risk attaches pro rata as the goods or merchandise are shipped; provided that if there be cargo in readiness which belongs to the shipowner, or which some other person has contracted with him to ship, the risk attaches as soon as the ship is ready to receive such cargo.

4. Where goods or other moveables are insured 'from the loading thereof,' the risk does not attach until such goods or moveables are actually on board, and the insurer is not liable for them while in transit from shore to ship.

5. Where the risk on goods or other moveables continues until they are 'safely landed,' they must be landed in the customary manner and within a reasonable time after arrival at the port of discharge, and if they are not so landed the risk ceases.

6. In the absence of any further licence or usage, the liberty to touch and stay 'at any port or place whatsoever' does not authorise the ship to depart from the course of her voyage from the port of departure to the port of destination.

7. The term 'perils of the seas' refers only to fortuitous accidents or casualties of the seas. It does not include the ordinary action of the winds and waves.

8. The term 'pirates' includes passengers who mutiny and rioters who attack the ship from the shore.

9. The term 'thieves' does not cover clandestine theft or a theft committed by anyone of the ship's company, whether crew or passengers.

10. The term 'arrests, etc., of kings, princes, and people' refers to political or executive acts, and does not include a loss caused by riot or by ordinary judicial process.

11. The term 'barratry' includes every wrongful act wilfully committed by the master or crew to the prejudice of the owner, or, as the case may be, the charterer.

12. The term 'all other perils' includes only perils similar in kind to the perils specifically mentioned in the policy.

13. The term 'average unless general' means a partial loss of the subject-matter insured other than a general average loss, and does not include 'particular charges.'

14. Where the ship has stranded, the insurer is liable for the excepted losses, although the loss is not attributable to the stranding, provided that when the stranding takes place the risk has attached and, if the policy be on goods, that the damaged goods are on board.

15. The term 'ship' includes the hull, materials and outfit, stores and provisions for the officers and crew, and, in the case of vessels engaged in a special trade, the ordinary fittings requisite for the trade, and also, in the case of a steamship, the machinery, boilers, and coals and engine stores, if owned by the assured.

16. The term 'freight' includes the profit derivable by a shipowner from the employment of his ship to carry his own goods or moveables, as well as freight payable by a third party, but does not include passage money.

17. The term 'goods' means goods in the nature of merchandise, and does not include personal effects or provisions and stores for use on board.

In the absence of any usage to the contrary, deck cargo and living animals must be insured specifically, and not under the general denomination of goods.

Marine Insurance (Gambling Policies) Act 1909
(9 Edw. 7, c. 12)

An Act to prohibit Gambling on loss by Maritime Perils.   [20th October 1909]

1   Prohibition of gambling on loss by maritime perils

(1) If—
   (a) any person effects a contract of marine insurance without having any bonâ fide interest, direct or indirect, either in the safe arrival of the ship in relation to which the contract is made or in the safety or preservation of the subject-matter insured, or a bonâ fide expectation of acquiring such an interest; or
   (b) any person in the employment of the owner of a ship, not being a part owner of the ship, effects a contract of marine insurance in relation to the ship, and the contract is made 'interest or no interest,' or 'without further proof of interest than the policy itself,' or 'without benefit of salvage to the insurer,' or subject to any other like term, the contract shall be deemed to be a contract by way of gambling on loss by maritime perils, and the person effecting it shall be guilty of an offence, and shall be liable, on summary conviction, to imprisonment [...] for a term not exceeding six months or to a fine not exceeding one hundred pounds, and in either case to forfeit to the Crown any money he may receive under the contract.

(2) Any broker or other person through whom, and any insurer with whom, any such contract is effected shall be guilty of an offence and liable on summary conviction to the like penalties if he acted knowing that the contract was by way of gambling on loss by maritime perils within the meaning of this Act.

(3) Proceedings under this Act shall not be instituted without the consent in England of the Attorney-General, in Scotland of the Lord Advocate, and in Ireland of the Attorney-General for Ireland.

(4) Proceedings shall not be instituted under this Act against a person (other than a person in the employment of the owner of the ship in relation to which the contract was made) alleged to have effected a contract by way of gambling on loss by maritime perils until an opportunity has been afforded him of showing that the contract was not such a contract as aforesaid, and any information given by that person for that purpose shall not be admissible in evidence against him in any prosecution under this Act.

(5) If proceedings under this Act are taken against any person (other than a person in the employment of the owner of the ship in relation to which the contract was made) for effecting such a contract, and the contract was made 'interest or no interest,' or 'without further proof of interest than the policy itself,' or 'without benefit of salvage to the insurer,' or subject to any other like term, the contract shall be deemed to be a contract by way of gambling on loss by maritime perils unless the contrary is proved.

(6) For the purpose of giving jurisdiction under this Act, every offence shall be deemed to have been committed either in the place in which the same actually was committed or in any place in which the offender may be.

(7) Any person aggrieved by an order or decision of a court of summary jurisdiction under this Act, may appeal to [the Crown Court].

(8) For the purposes of this Act the expression 'owner' includes charterer.

(9) Subsection (7) of this section shall not apply to Scotland.

2   Short title
This Act may be cited as the Marine Insurance (Gambling Policies) Act 1909, and the Marine Insurance Act 1906, and this Act may be cited together as the Marine Insurance Acts 1906 and 1909.

Law of Property Act 1925
(15 Geo. 5, c. 20)

An Act to consolidate the enactments relating to conveyancing and the law of property in England and Wales.   [9th April 1925]

136   Legal assignments of things in action
(1) Any absolute assignment by writing under the hand of the assignor (not purporting to be by way of charge only) of any debt or other legal thing in action, of which express notice in writing has been given to the debtor, trustee or other person from whom the assignor would have been entitled to claim such debt or thing in action, is effectual in law (subject to equities having priority over the right of the assignee) to pass and transfer from the date of such notice—
   (a) the legal right to such debt or thing in action;
   (b) all legal and other remedies for the same; and
   (c) the power to give a good discharge for the same without the concurrence of the assignor:
Provided that, if the debtor, trustee or other person liable in respect of such debt or thing in action has notice—
   (a) that the assignment is disputed by the assignor or any person claiming under him; or
   (b) of any other opposing or conflicting claims to such debt or thing in action; he may, if he thinks fit, either call upon the persons making claim thereto to interplead concerning the same, or pay the debt or other thing in action into court under the provisions of the Trustee Act, 1925.

(2) This section does not affect the provisions of the Policies of Assurance Act, 1867.

137   Dealings with life interests, reversions and other equitable interests
(1) The law applicable to dealings with equitable things in action which regulates the priority of competing interests therein, shall, as respects dealings with equitable interests in

land, capital money, and securities representing capital money effected after the commencement of this Act, apply to and regulate the priority of competing interests therein.

This subsection applies whether or not the money or securities are in court.

(3) A notice, otherwise than in writing, given to, or received by, a trustee after the commencement of this Act as respects any dealing with an equitable interest in real or personal property, shall not affect the priority of competing claims of purchasers in that equitable interest.

Third Parties (Rights Against Insurers) Act 1930
(20 & 21 Geo. V, c. 25)

An Act to confer on third parties rights against insurers of third-party risks in the event of the insured becoming insolvent, and in certain other events.   [10th July 1930]

1   Rights of third parties against insurers on bankruptcy, etc., of the insured

(1) Where under any contract of insurance a person (hereinafter referred to as the insured) is insured against liabilities to third parties which he may incur, then

  (a) in the event of the insured becoming bankrupt or making a composition or arrangement with his creditors; or

  (b) in the case of the insured being a company, in the event of a winding-up order [...] being made, or a resolution for a voluntary winding-up being passed, with respect to the company, [or of the company entering administration] or of a receiver or manager of the company's business or undertaking being duly appointed, or of possession being taken, by or on behalf of the holders of any debentures secured by a floating charge, of any property comprised in or subject to that charge [or of a voluntary arrangement proposed for the purposes of Part I of the Insolvency Act 1986 being approved under that Part];

if, either before or after that event, any such liability as aforesaid is incurred by the insured, his rights against the insurer under the contract in respect of the liability shall, notwithstanding anything in any Act or rule of law to the contrary, be transferred to and vest in the third party to whom the liability was so incurred.

(2) Where [the estate of any person falls to be administered in accordance with an order under section 421 of the Insolvency Act 1986] then, if any debt provable in bankruptcy [(in Scotland, any claim accepted in the sequestration)] is owing by the deceased in respect of a liability against which he was insured under a contract of insurance as being a liability to a third party, the deceased debtor's rights against the insurer under the contract in respect of that liability shall, notwithstanding anything in [any such order], be transferred to and vest in the person to whom the debt is owing.

(3) In so far as any contract of insurance made after the commencement of this Act in respect of any liability of the insured to third parties purports, whether directly or indirectly, to avoid the contract or to alter the rights of the parties thereunder upon the happening to the insured of the events specified in paragraph (a) or paragraph (b) of subsection (1) of this section or upon the [estate of any person falling to be administered in accordance with an order under section 421 of the Insolvency Act 1986], the contract shall be of no effect.

(4) Upon a transfer under subsection (1) or subsection (2) of this section, the insurer shall, subject to the provisions of section three of this Act, be under the same liability to the third party as he would have been under to the insured, but—

  (a) if the liability of the insurer to the insured exceeds the liability of the insured to the third party, nothing in this Act shall affect the rights of the third party against the insured in respect of the excess; and

(b) if the liability of the insurer to the insured is less than the liability of the insured to the third party, nothing in this Act shall affect the rights of the third party against the insured in respect of the balance.

(5) For the purposes of this Act, the expression 'liabilities to third parties', in relation to a person insured under any contract of insurance, shall not include any liability of that person in the capacity of insurer under some other contract of insurance.

(6) This Act shall not apply—

(a) where a company is wound up voluntarily merely for the purposes of reconstruction or of amalgamation with another company; or

(b) to any case to which subsections (1) and (2) of section seven of the Workmen's Compensation Act 1925 applies.

2   Duty to give necessary information to third parties

(1) In the event of any person becoming bankrupt or making a composition or arrangement with his creditors, or in the event of [the estate of any person falling to be administered in accordance with an order under section 421 of the Insolvency Act 1986], or in the event of a winding-up order [. . .] being made, or a resolution for a voluntary winding-up being passed, with respect to any company [or of the company entering administration] or of a receiver or manager of the company's business or undertaking being duly appointed, or of possession being taken, by or on behalf of the holders of any debentures secured by a floating charge, of any property comprised in or subject to the charge it shall be the duty of the bankrupt, debtor, personal representative of the deceased debtor or company, and, as the case may be, of the trustee in bankruptcy, trustee, liquidator, [administrator], receiver, or manager, or person in possession of the property to give at the request of any person claiming that the bankrupt, debtor, deceased debtor, or company is under a liability to him such information as may be reasonably required by him for the purpose of ascertaining whether any rights have been transferred to and vested in him by this Act and for the purpose of enforcing such rights, if any, and any contract of insurance, in so far as it purports, whether directly or indirectly, to avoid the contract or to alter the rights of the parties thereunder upon the giving of any such information in the events aforesaid or otherwise to prohibit or prevent the giving thereof in the said events shall be of no effect.

[(1A) The reference in subsection (1) of this section to a trustee includes a reference to the supervisor of a voluntary arrangement proposed for the purposes of, and approved under, Part I or Part VIII of the Insolvency Act 1986.]

(2) If the information given to any person in pursuance of subsection (1) of this section discloses reasonable ground for supposing that there have or may have been transferred to him under this Act rights against any particular insurer, that insurer shall be subject to the same duty as is imposed by the said subsection on the persons therein mentioned.

(3) The duty to give information imposed by this section shall include a duty to allow all contracts of insurance, receipts for premiums, and other relevant documents in the possession or power of the person on whom the duty is so imposed to be inspected and copies thereof to be taken.

3   Settlement between insurers and insured persons

Where the insured has become bankrupt or where in the case of the insured being a company, a winding-up order [or an administration order] has been made or a resolution for a voluntary winding-up has been passed, with respect to the company, no agreement made between the insurer and the insured after liability has been incurred to a third party and after the commencement of the bankruptcy or winding-up [or the day of the administration order], as the case may be, nor any waiver, assignment, or other disposition made by, or payment made to the insured after the commencement [or day] aforesaid shall be effective to defeat or affect the rights transferred to the third party under this Act, but those rights shall be the same as if no such agreement, waiver, assignment, disposition or payment had been made.

[**3A Application to limited liability partnerships**

(1) This Act applies to limited liability partnerships as it applies to companies.

(2) In its application to limited liability partnerships, references to a resolution for a voluntary winding-up being passed are references to a determination for a voluntary winding-up being made.]

4 Application to Scotland

[…]

5 Short title

This Act may be cited as the Third Parties (Rights Against Insurers) Act 1930.

Law Reform (Frustrated Contracts) Act 1943
(6 & 7 Geo. VI, c. 40)

An Act to amend the law relating to the frustration of contracts.   [5th August 1943]

1 Adjustment of rights and liabilities of parties to frustrated contracts

(1) Where a contract governed by English law has become impossible of performance or been otherwise frustrated, and the parties thereto have for that reason been discharged from the further performance of the contract, the following provisions of this section shall, subject to the provisions of section two of this Act, have effect in relation thereto.

(2) All sums paid or payable to any party in pursuance of the contract before the time when the parties were so discharged (in this Act referred to as 'the time of discharge') shall, in the case of sums so paid, be recoverable from him as money received by him for the use of the party by whom the sums were paid, and, in the case of sums so payable, cease to be so payable:Provided that, if the party to whom the sums were so paid or payable incurred expenses before the time of discharge in, or for the purpose of, the performance of the contract, the court may, if it considers it just to do so having regard to all the circumstances of the case, allow him to retain or, as the case may be, recover the whole or any part of the sums so paid or payable, not being an amount in excess of the expenses so incurred.

(3) Where any party to the contract has, by reason of anything done by any other party thereto in, or for the purpose of, the performance of the contract, obtained a valuable benefit (other than a payment of money to which the last foregoing subsection applies) before the time of discharge there shall be recoverable from him by the said other party such sum (if any), not exceeding the value of the said benefit to the party obtaining it, as the court considers just, having regard to all the circumstances of the case and, in particular,—

    (a) the amount of any expenses incurred before the time of discharge by the benefited party in, or for the purpose of, the performance of the contract, including any sums paid or payable by him to any other party in pursuance of the contract and retained or recoverable by that party under the last foregoing sub-section, and

    (b) the effect, in relation to the said benefit, of the circumstances giving rise to the frustration of the contract.

(4) In estimating, for the purposes of the foregoing provisions of this section, the amount of any expenses incurred by any party to the contract, the court may, without prejudice to the generality of the said provisions, include any sum as appears to be reasonable in respect of overhead expenses and in respect of any work or services performed personally by the said party.

(5) In considering whether any sum ought to be recovered or retained under the foregoing provisions of this section by any party to the contract, the court shall not take into account any sums which have, by reason of the circumstances giving rise to the frustration of

the contract, become payable to that party under any contract of insurance unless there was an obligation to insure imposed by an express term of the frustrated contract or by or under any enactment.

(6) Where any person has assumed obligations under the contract in consideration of the conferring of a benefit by any other party to the contract upon any other person, whether a party to the contract or not, the court may, if in all the circumstances of the case it considers it just to do so, treat for the purposes of subsection (3) of this section any benefit so conferred as a benefit obtained by the person who has assumed the obligations as aforesaid.

2   Provision as to application of this Act

(1) This Act shall apply to contracts, whether made before or after the commencement of this Act, as respects which the time of discharge is on or after the first day of July, nineteen hundred and forty-three, but not to contracts as respects which the time of discharge is before the said date.

(2) This Act shall apply to contracts to which the Crown is a party in like manner as to contracts between subjects.

(3) Where any contract to which this Act applies contains any provision which, upon the true construction of the contract, is intended to have effect in the event of circumstances arising which operate, or would but for the said provision operate, to frustrate the contract, or is intended to have effect whether such circumstances arise or not, the court shall give effect to the said provision and shall only give effect to the foregoing section of this Act to such extent, if any, as appears to the court to be consistent with the said provision.

(4) Where it appears to the court that a part of any contract to which this Act applies can be properly severed from the remainder of the contract, being a part wholly performed before the time of discharge, or so performed except for the payment in respect of that part of the contract of sums which are or can be ascertained under the contract, the court shall treat that part of the contract as if it were a separate contract and had not been frustrated and shall treat the foregoing section of this Act as only applicable to the remainder of that contract.

(5) This Act shall not apply—

  (a) to any charterparty, except a time charterparty or a charterparty by way of demise, or to any contract (other than a charterparty) for the carriage of goods by sea; or

  (b) to any contract of insurance, save as is provided by subsection (5) of the foregoing section; or

  (c) to any contract to which [section 7 of the Sale of Goods Act 1979] (which avoids contracts for the sale of specific goods which perish before the risk has passed to the buyer) applies, or to any other contract for the sale, or for the sale and delivery, of specific goods, where the contract is frustrated by reason of the fact that the goods have perished.

3   Short title and interpretation

(1) This Act may be cited as the Law Reform (Frustrated Contracts) Act, 1943.

(2) In this Act the expression 'court' means, in relation to any matter, the court or arbitrator by or before whom the matter falls to be determined.

Cheques Act 1957
(5 & 6 Eliz. 2, c. 36)

An Act to amend the law relating to cheques and certain other instruments.   [17th July 1957]

1   Protection of bankers paying unindorsed or irregularly indorsed cheques, etc.

(1) Where a banker in good faith and in the ordinary course of business pays a cheque drawn on him which is not indorsed or is irregularly indorsed, he does not in doing so, incur

any liability by reason only of the absence of, or irregularity in indorsement, and he is deemed to have paid it in due course.

(2) Where a banker in good faith and in the ordinary course of business pays any such instrument as the following namely—

(a) a document issued by a customer of his which, though not a bill of exchange, is intended to enable a person to obtain payment from him of the sum mentioned in the document;

(b) a draft payable on demand drawn by him upon himself, whether payable at the head office or some other office of his bank; he does not, in so doing, incur any liability by reason only of the absence of, or irregularity in, indorsement, and the payment discharges the instrument.

2 Rights of bankers collecting cheques not indorsed by holders

A banker who gives value for, or has a lien on, a cheque payable to order which the holder delivers to him for collection without indorsing it, has such (if any) rights as he would have had if, upon delivery, the holder had indorsed it in blank.

3 Unindorsed cheques as evidence of payment

[(1)] An unindorsed cheque which appears to have been paid by the banker on whom it is drawn is evidence of the receipt by the payee of the sum payable by the cheque.

[(2) For the purposes of subsection (1) above, a copy of a cheque to which that subsection applies is evidence of the cheque if—

(a) the copy is made by the banker in whose possession the cheque is after present-ment and,

(b) it is certified by him to be a true copy of the original.]

4 Protection of bankers collecting payment of cheques, &c.

(1) Where a banker, in good faith and without negligence—

(a) receives payment for a customer of an instrument to which this section applies; or

(b) having credited a customer's account with the amount of such an instrument, receives payment thereof for himself;

and the customer has no title, or a defective title, to the instrument, the banker does not incur any liability to the true owner of the instrument by reason only of having received payment thereof.

(2) This section applies to the following instruments, namely:—

(a) cheques [(including cheques which under section 81A(1) of the Bills of Exchange Act 1882 or otherwise are not transferable)];

(b) any document issued by a customer of a banker which, though not a bill of exchange, is intended to enable a person to obtain payment from that banker of the sum mentioned in the document;

(c) any document issued by a public officer is intended to enable a person to obtain payment from the Paymaster General or the Queen's and Lord Treasurer's Remembrancer of the sum mentioned in the document but is not a bill of exchange;

(d) any draft payable on demand drawn by a banker upon himself whether payable at the head office or some other office of his bank.

(3) A banker is not to be treated for the purposes of this section as having been negligent by reason only of his failure to concern himself with absence of, or irregularity in, indorse-ment of an instrument.

5 Application of certain provisions of Bills of Exchange Act, 1882, to instruments not being bills of exchange

The provisions of the Bills of Exchange Act, 1882, relating to crossed cheques shall, so far as applicable, have effect in relation to instruments (other than cheques) to which the last foregoing section applies as they have effect in relation to cheques.

6   Construction, saving and repeal

(1) This Act shall be construed as one with the Bills of Exchange Act, 1882.

(2) The foregoing provisions of this Act do not make negotiable any instrument which, apart from them, is not negotiable.

[...]

7   Provisions as to Northern Ireland

This Act extends to Northern Ireland, [...]

8   Short title and commencement

(1) This Act may be cited as the Cheques Act, 1957.

(2) This Act shall come into operation at the expiration of a period of three months beginning with the day on which it is passed.

Hire-Purchase Act 1964
(1964, c. 53)

An Act to amend the law relating to hire-purchase and credit-sale, and, in relation thereto, to amend the enactments relating to the sale of goods; to make provision with respect to dispositions of motor vehicles which have been let or agreed to be sold by way of hire-purchase or conditional sale; to amend the Advertisements (Hire-Purchase) Act, 1957; and for purposes connected with the matters aforesaid.
[16th July 1964]

PART III   TITLE TO MOTOR VEHICLES ON HIRE-PURCHASE OR CONDITIONAL SALE

27   Protection of purchasers of motor vehicles

(1) This section applies where a motor vehicle has been bailed or (in Scotland) hired under a hire-purchase agreement, or has been agreed to be sold under a conditional sale agreement, and, before the property in the vehicle has become vested in the debtor, he disposes of the vehicle to another person.

(2) Where the disposition referred to in subsection (1) above is to a private purchaser, and he is a purchaser of the motor vehicle in good faith without notice of the hire-purchase or conditional sale agreement (the 'relevant agreement') that disposition shall have effect as if the creditor's title to the vehicle has been vested in the debtor immediately before that disposition.

(3) Where the person to whom the disposition referred to in subsection (1) above is made (the 'original purchaser') is a trade or finance purchaser, then if the person who is the first private purchaser of the motor vehicle after that disposition (the 'first private purchaser') is a purchaser of the vehicle in good faith without notice of the relevant agreement, the disposition of the vehicle to the first private purchaser shall have effect as if the title of the creditor to the vehicle had been vested in the debtor immediately before he disposed of it to the original purchaser.

(4) Where, in a case within subsection (3) above—

(a) the disposition by which the first private purchaser becomes a purchaser of the motor vehicle in good faith without notice of the relevant agreement is itself a bailment or hiring under a hire-purchase agreement, and

(b) the person who is the creditor in relation to that agreement disposes of the vehicle to the first private purchaser, or a person claiming under him, by transferring to him the property in the vehicle in pursuance of a provision in the agreement in that behalf, the disposition referred to in paragraph (b) above (whether or not the person to whom it is made is a purchaser in good faith without notice of the relevant agreement) shall as well as the disposition referred to in paragraph (a) above, have effect as mentioned in subsection (3) above.

(5) The preceding provisions of this section apply—

(a) notwithstanding anything in [section 21 of the Sale of Goods Act 19791 (sale of goods by a person not the owner), but

(b) without prejudice to the provisions of the Factors Acts (as defined by [section 61(1) of the said Act of 1979]) or any other enactment enabling the apparent owner of goods to dispose of them as if he were the true owner.

(6) Nothing in this section shall exonerate the debtor from any liability (whether criminal or civil) to which he would be subject apart from this section; and, in a case where the debtor disposes of the motor vehicle to a trade or finance purchaser, nothing in this section shall exonerate—

(a) that trade or finance purchaser, or

(b) any other trade or finance purchaser who becomes a purchaser of the vehicle and is not a person claiming under the first private purchaser,

from any liability (whether criminal or civil) to which he would be subject apart from this section.

28 Presumptions relating to dealings with motor vehicles

(1) Where in any proceedings (whether criminal or civil) relating to a motor vehicle it is proved—

(a) that the vehicle was bailed or (in Scotland) hired under a hire-purchase agreement, or was agreed to be sold under a conditional sale agreement and

(b) that a person (whether a party to the proceedings or not) became a private purchaser of the vehicle in good faith without notice of the hire-purchase or conditional sale agreement (the 'relevant agreement'), this section shall have effect for the purposes of the operation of section 27 of this Act in relation to those proceedings.

(2) It shall be presumed for those purposes unless the contrary is proved, that the disposition of the vehicle to the person referred to in subsection (1)(b) above (the 'relevant purchaser') was made by the debtor.

(3) If it is proved that that disposition was not made by the debtor, then it shall be presumed for those purposes, unless the contrary is proved—

(a) that the debtor disposed of the vehicle to a private purchaser purchasing in good faith without notice of the relevant agreement, and

(b) that the relevant purchaser is or was a person claiming under the person to whom the debtor so disposed of the vehicle.

(4) If it is proved that the disposition of the vehicle to the relevant purchaser was not made by the debtor, and that the person to whom the debtor disposed of the vehicle (the 'original purchaser') was a trade or finance purchaser, then it shall be presumed for those purposes, unless the contrary is proved,

(a) that the person who, after the disposition of the vehicle to the original purchaser, first became a private purchaser of the vehicle was a purchaser in good faith without notice of the relevant agreement, and

(b) that the relevant purchaser is or was a person claiming under the original purchaser.

(5) Without prejudice to any other method of proof, where in any proceedings a party thereto admits a fact, that fact shall, for the purposes of this section, be taken as against him to be proved in relation to those proceedings.

29 Interpretation of Part III

(1) In this Part of this Act—

'conditional sale agreement' means an agreement for the sale of goods under which the purchase price or part of it is payable by instalments, and the property in the goods is to remain in the seller (notwithstanding that the buyer is to be in possession of the goods) until such conditions as to the payment of instalments or otherwise as may be specified in the agreement are fulfilled;

'creditor' means the person by whom goods are bailed or (in Scotland) hired under a hire-purchase agreement or as the case may be, the seller under a conditional sale agreement, or the person to whom his rights and duties have passed by assignment or operation of law;

'disposition' means any sale or contract of sale (including a conditional sale agreement), any bailment or (in Scotland) hiring under a hire-purchase agreement and any transfer of the property of goods in pursuance of a provision in that behalf contained in a hire-purchase agreement, and includes any transaction purporting to be a disposition (as so defined), and 'dispose of' shall be construed accordingly:

'hire-purchase agreement' means an agreement, other than a conditional sale agreement, under which—

> (a) goods are bailed or (in Scotland) hired in return for periodical payments by the person to whom they are bailed or hired, and
> (b) the property in the goods will pass to that person if the terms of the agreement are complied with and one or more of the following occurs—
>> (i) the exercise of an option to purchase by that person,
>> (ii) the doing of any other specified act by any party to the agreement,
>> (iii) the happening of any other specified events; and

'motor vehicle' means a mechanically propelled vehicle intended or adapted for use on roads to which the public has access.

(2) In this Part of this Act 'trade or finance purchaser' means a purchaser who, at the time of the disposition made to him, carries on a business which consists, wholly or partly—

> (a) of purchasing motor vehicles for the purpose of offering or exposing them for sale, or
> (b) of providing finance by purchasing motor vehicles for the purpose of bailing or (in Scotland) hiring them under hire-purchase agreements or agreeing to sell them under conditional sale agreements,

and 'private purchaser' means a purchaser who, at the time of the disposition made to him, does not carry on any such business.

(3) For the purposes of this Part of this Act a person becomes a purchaser of a motor vehicle if, and at the time when, a disposition of the vehicle is made to him; and a person shall be taken to be a purchaser of a motor vehicle without notice of a hire-purchase agreement or conditional sale agreement if, at the time of the disposition made to him, he has no actual notice that the vehicle is or was the subject of any such agreement.

(4) In this Part of this Act the 'debtor' in relation to a motor vehicle which has been bailed or hired under a hire-purchase agreement, or, as the case may be, agreed to be sold under a conditional sale agreement, means the person who at the material time (whether the agreement has before that time been terminated or not) either—

> (a) is the person to whom the vehicle is bailed or hired under that agreement, or
> (b) is, in relation to the agreement, the buyer, including a person who at that time is, by virtue of section 130(4) of the Consumer Credit Act 1974 treated as a bailee or (in Scotland) a custodier of the vehicle.

(5) In this Part of this Act any reference to the title of the creditor to a motor vehicle which has been bailed or (in Scotland) hired under a hire-purchase agreement or agreed to be sold under a conditional sale agreement, and is disposed of by the debtor, is a reference to such title (if any) to the vehicle as, immediately before that disposition, was vested in the person who then was the creditor in relation to the agreement.]

Carriage of Goods by Road Act 1965
(1965, c. 37)

An Act to give effect to the Convention on the Contract for the International Carriage of Goods by Road signed at Geneva on 19th May 1956; and for purposes connected therewith.   [5th August 1965]

1 Convention to have force of law
Subject to the following provisions of this Act, the provisions of the Convention on the Contract for the International Carriage of Goods by Road (in this Act referred to as 'the Convention'), as set out in the Schedule to this Act, shall have the force of law in the United Kingdom so far as they relate to the rights and liabilities of persons concerned in the carriage of goods by road under a contract to which the Convention applies.

2 Designation of High Contracting Parties
(1) Her Majesty may by Order in Council from time to time certify who are the High Contracting Parties to the Convention and in respect of what territories they are respectively parties.

(2) An Order in Council under this section shall, except so far as it has been superseded by a subsequent Order, be conclusive evidence of the matters so certified.

3 Power of court to take account of other proceedings
(1) A court before which proceedings are brought to enforce a liability which is limited by article 23 in the Schedule to this Act may at any stage of the proceedings make any such order as appears to the court to be just and equitable in view of the provisions of the said article 23 and of any other proceedings which have been, or are likely to be, commenced in the United Kingdom or elsewhere to enforce the liability in whole or in part.

(2) Without prejudice to the preceding subsection, a court before which proceedings are brought to enforce a liability which is limited by the said article 23 shall, where the liability is, or may be, partly enforceable in other proceedings in the United Kingdom or elsewhere, have jurisdiction to award an amount less than the court would have awarded if the limitation applied solely to the proceedings before the court, or to make any part of its award conditional on the result of any other proceedings.

4 Registration of foreign judgments
(1) Subject to the next following subsection, Part I of the Foreign judgments (Reciprocal Enforcement) Act 1933 (in this section referred to as 'the Act of 1933') shall apply whether or not it would otherwise have so applied, to any judgment which—

    (a) has been given in any such action as is referred to in paragraph 1 of article 31 in the Schedule to this Act and

    (b) has been so given by any court or tribunal of a territory in respect of which one of the High Contracting Parties other than the United Kingdom, is a party to the Convention, and

    (c) has become enforceable in that territory.

(2) In the application of Part I of the Act of 1933 in relation to any such judgment as is referred to in the preceding subsection, section 4 of that Act shall have effect with the omission of subsections (2) and (3).

(3) The registration, in accordance with Part I of the Act of 1933, of any such judgment as is referred to in subsection (1) of this section shall constitute, in relation to that judgment compliance with the formalities for the purposes of paragraph 3 of article 31 in the Schedule to this Act.

5 Contribution between carriers
(1) Where a carrier under a contract to which the Convention applies is liable in respect of any loss or damage for which compensation is payable under the Convention, nothing in [section 1 of the Civil Liability (Contribution) Act 1978] or section 3 (2) of the Law Reform (Miscellaneous Provisions) (Scotland) Act 1940 shall confer on him any right to recover

contribution in respect of that loss or damage from any other carrier who, in accordance with article 34 in the Schedule to this Act, is a party to the contract of carriage.

(2) The preceding subsection shall be without prejudice to the operation of article 37 in the Schedule to this Act.

6   Actions against High Contracting Parties

Every High Contracting Party to the Convention shall, for the purposes of any proceedings brought in a court in the United Kingdom in accordance with the provisions of article 31 in the Schedule to this Act to enforce a claim in respect of carriage undertaken by that Party, be deemed to have submitted to the jurisdiction of that court, and accordingly rules of court may provide for the manner in which any such action is to be commenced and carried on; but nothing in this section shall authorise the issue of execution, or in Scotland the execution of diligence, against the property of any High Contracting Party.

7   Arbitrations

(1) Any reference in the preceding provisions of this Act to a court includes a reference to an arbitration tribunal acting by virtue of article 33 in the Schedule to this Act.

(2) For the purposes of article 32 in the Schedule to this Act, as it has effect (by virtue of the said article 33) in relation to arbitrations,—

[(a) as respects England and Wales and Northern Ireland, the provisions of section 14(3) to (5) of the Arbitration Act 1996 (which determine the time at which an arbitration is commenced) apply;]

(c) as respects Scotland, an arbitration shall be deemed to be commenced when one party to the arbitration serves on the other party or parties a notice requiring him or them to appoint an arbiter or to agree to the appointment of an arbiter or, where the arbitration agreement provides that the reference shall be to a person named or designated in the agreement, requiring him or them to submit the dispute to the person so named or designated.

8   Resolution of conflicts between Conventions on carriage of goods

(1) If it appears to Her Majesty in Council that there is any conflict between the provisions of this Act (including the provisions of the Convention as set out in the Schedule to this Act) and any provisions relating to the carriage of goods for reward by land, sea or air contained in—

(a) any other Convention which has been signed or ratified by or on behalf of Her Majesty's Government in the United Kingdom before the passing of this Act, or

(b) any enactment of the Parliament of the United Kingdom giving effect to such a Convention, Her Majesty may by Order in Council make such provision as may seem to her to be appropriate for resolving that conflict by amending or modifying this Act or any such enactment.

(2) Any statutory instrument made by virtue of this section shall be subject to annulment in pursuance of a resolution of either House of Parliament.

[8A   Amendments consequential on revision of Convention

(1) If at any time it appears to Her Majesty in Council that Her Majesty's Government in the United Kingdom have agreed to any revision of the Convention, Her Majesty may by Order in Council make such amendment of—

[(a) this Act; and]

(c) section 5(1) of the Carriage by Air and Road Act 1979, as appear to Her to be appropriate in consequence of the revision.

(2) In the preceding subsection 'revision' means an omission from, addition to or alteration of the Convention and includes replacement of the Convention or part of it by another Convention.

(3) An Order in Council under this section shall not be made unless a draft of the Order has been laid before Parliament and approved by a resolution of each House of Parliament.

[...]

9   Application to British possessions, etc.

Her Majesty may by Order in Council direct that this Act shall extend, subject to such exceptions, adaptations and modifications as may be specified in the Order, to—

    (a) the Isle of Man;

    (b) any of the Channel Islands;

    (c) any colony

10   Application to Scotland

. . .

11   Application to Northern Ireland

. . .

12   Orders in Council

An Order in Council made under any of the preceding provisions of this Act may contain such transitional and supplementary provisions as appear to Her Majesty to be expedient and may be varied or revoked by a subsequent Order in Council made under that provision.

13   Application to Crown

This Act shall bind the Crown.

14   Short title, interpretation and commencement

    (1) This Act may be cited as the Carriage of Goods by Road Act 1965.

    (2) The persons who, for the purposes of this Act, are persons concerned in the carriage of goods by road under a contract to which the Convention applies are—

    (a) the sender,

    (b) the consignee,

    (c) any carrier who, in accordance with article 34 in the Schedule to this Act or otherwise, is a party to the contract of carriage,

    (d) any person for whom such a carrier is responsible by virtue of article 3 in the Schedule to this Act,

    (e) any person to whom the rights and liabilities of any of the persons referred to in paragraphs (a) to (d) of this subsection have passed (whether by assignment or assignation or by operation of law).

    (3) Except in so far as the context otherwise requires, any reference in this Act to an enactment shall be construed as a reference to that enactment as amended or extended by or under any other enactment.

    (4) This Act shall come into operation on such day as Her Majesty may by Order in Council appoint; but nothing in this Act shall apply in relation to any contract for the carriage of goods by road made before the day so appointed.

Section 1   SCHEDULE

CONVENTION ON THE CONTRACT FOR THE INTERNATIONAL CARRIAGE OF GOODS BY ROAD (CMR)

CHAPTER I

Scope of application

Article 1

    1. This Convention shall apply to every contract for the carriage of goods by road in vehicles for reward, when the place of taking over of the goods and the place designated for delivery, as specified in the contract, are situated in two different countries, of which at least one is a contracting country, irrespective of the place of residence and the nationality of the parties.

2. For the purposes of this Convention, 'vehicles' means motor vehicles, articulated vehicles, trailers and semi-trailers as defined in article 4 of the Convention on Road Traffic dated 19th September 1949.

3. This Convention shall apply also where carriage coming within its scope is carried out by States or by governmental institutions or organisations.

4. This Convention shall not apply:

(a) To carriage performed under the terms of any international postal convention;

(b) To funeral consignments;

(c) To furniture removal.

5. The Contracting Parties agree not to vary any of the provisions of this Convention by special agreements between two or more of them, except to make it inapplicable to their frontier traffic or to authorize the use in transport operations entirely confined to their territory of consignment notes representing a title to the goods.

Article 2

1. Where the vehicle containing the goods is carried over part of the journey by sea, rail, inland waterways or air, and except where the provisions of article 14 are applicable, the goods are not unloaded from the vehicle, this Convention shall nevertheless apply to the whole of the carriage. Provided that to the extent that it is proved that any loss, damage or delay in delivery of the goods which occurs during the carriage by the other means of transport was not caused by an act or omission of the carrier by road, but by some event which could only have occurred in the course of and by reason of the carriage by that other means of transport, the liability of the carrier by road shall be determined not by this Convention but in the manner in which the liability of the carrier by the other means of transport would have been determined if a contract for the carriage of the goods alone had been made by the sender with the carrier by the other means of transport in accordance with the conditions prescribed by law for the carriage of goods by that means of transport. If, however, there be no such prescribed conditions, the liability of the carrier by road shall be determined by this Convention.

2. If the carrier by road is also himself the carrier by the other means of transport, his liability shall also be determined in accordance with the provisions of paragraph 1 of this article, but as if, in his capacities as carrier by road and as carrier by the other means of transport, he were two separate persons.

CHAPTER II

Persons for whom the carrier is responsible

Article 3

For the purposes of this Convention the carrier shall be responsible for the acts and omissions of his agents and servants and of any other persons of whose services he makes use for the performance of the carriage, when such agents, servants or other persons are acting within the scope of their employment, as if such acts or omissions were his own.

CHAPTER III

Conclusion and performance of the contract of carriage

Article 4

The contract of carriage shall be confirmed by the making out of a consignment note. The absence, irregularity or loss of the consignment note shall not affect the existence or the validity of the contract of carriage which shall remain subject to the provisions of this Convention.

Article 5

1. The consignment note shall be made out in three original copies signed by the sender and by the carrier. These signatures may be printed or replaced by the stamps of the sender and the carrier if the law of the country in which the consignment note has been made out so

permits. The first copy shall be handed to the sender, the second shall accompany the goods and the third shall be retained by the carrier.

2. When the goods which are to be carried have to be loaded in different vehicles, or are of different kinds or are divided into different lots, the sender or the carrier shall have the right to require a separate consignment note to be made out for each vehicle used, or for each kind or lot of goods.

Article 6

1. The consignment note shall contain the following particulars:
    (a) The date of the consignment note and the place at which it is made out;
    (b) The name and address of the sender;
    (c) The name and address of the carrier;
    (d) The place and the date of taking over of the goods and the place designated for delivery;
    (e) The name and address of the consignee;
    (f) The description in common use of the nature of the goods and the method of packing, and, in the case of dangerous goods, their generally recognised description;
    (g) The number of packages and their special marks and numbers;
    (h) The gross weight of the goods or their quantity otherwise expressed;
    (i) Charges relating to the carriage (carriage charges, supplementary charges, customs duties and other charges incurred from the making of the contract to the time of delivery);
    (j) The requisite instructions for Customs and other formalities;
    (k) A statement that the carriage is subject, notwithstanding any clause to the contrary, to the provisions of this Convention.
2. Where applicable, the consignment note shall also contain the following particulars:
    (a) A statement that transshipment is not allowed;
    (b) The charges which the sender undertakes to pay;
    (c) The amount of 'cash on delivery' charges;
    (d) A declaration of the value of the goods and the amount representing special interest on delivery;
    (e) The sender's instructions to the carrier regarding insurance of the goods;
    (f) The agreed time-limit within which the carriage is to be carried out;
    (g) A list of documents handed to the carrier.
3. The parties may enter in the consignment note any other particulars which they deem useful.

Article 7

1. The sender shall be responsible for all expenses, loss and damage sustained by the carrier by reason of the inaccuracy or inadequacy of
    (a) The particulars specified in article 6, paragraph 1, (b), (d), (e), (f), (g), (h) and (j);
    (b) The particulars specified in article 6, paragraph 2;
    (c) Any other particulars or instructions given by him to enable the consignment note to be made out or for the purpose of their being entered therein.
2. If, at the request of the sender, the carrier enters in the consignment note the particulars referred to in paragraph 1 of this article, he shall be deemed, unless the contrary is proved to have done so on behalf of the sender.
3. If the consignment note does not contain the statement specified in article 6, paragraph 1(k), the carrier shall be liable for all expenses, loss and damage sustained through such omission by the person entitled to dispose of the goods.

Article 8

1. On taking over the goods, the carrier shall check:
    (a) The accuracy of the statements in the consignment note as to the number of packages and their marks and numbers, and

(b) The apparent condition of the goods and their packaging.

2. Where the carrier has no reasonable means of checking the accuracy of the statements referred to in paragraph 1 (a) of this article, he shall enter his reservations in the consignment note together with the grounds on which they are based. He shall likewise specify the grounds for any reservations which he makes with regard to the apparent condition of the goods and their packaging. Such reservations shall not bind the sender unless he has expressly agreed to be bound by them in the consignment note.

3. The sender shall be entitled to require the carrier to check the gross weight of the goods or their quantity otherwise expressed. He may also require the contents of the packages to be checked. The carrier shall be entitled to claim the cost of such checking. The result of the checks shall be entered in the consignment note.

Article 9

1. The consignment note shall be prima facie evidence of the making of the contract of carriage, the conditions of the contract and the receipt of the goods by the carrier.

2. If the consignment note contains no specific reservations by the carrier, it shall be presumed, unless the contrary is proved, that the goods and their packaging appeared to be in good condition when the carrier took them over and that the number of packages, their marks and numbers corresponded with the statements in the consignment note.

Article 10

The sender shall be liable to the carrier for damage to persons, equipment or other goods, and for any expenses due to defective packing of the goods, unless the defect was apparent or known to the carrier at the time when he took over the goods and he made no reservations concerning it.

Article 11

1. For the purposes of the Customs or other formalities which have to be completed before delivery of the goods, the sender shall attach the necessary documents to the consignment note or place them at the disposal of the carrier and shall furnish him with all the information which he requires.

2. The carrier shall not be under any duty to enquire into either the accuracy or the adequacy of such documents and information. The sender shall be liable to the carrier for any damage caused by the absence, inadequacy or irregularity of such documents and information, except in the case of some wrongful act or neglect on the part of the carrier.

3. The tiability of the carrier for the consequences arising from the loss or incorrect use of the documents specified in and accompanying the consignment note or deposited with the carrier shall be that of an agent, provided that the compensation payable by the carrier shall not exceed that payable in the event of loss of the goods.

Article 12

1. The sender has a right to dispose of the goods in particular by asking the carrier to stop the goods in transit, to change the place at which delivery is to take place or to deliver the goods to a consignee other than the consignee indicated in the consignment note.

2. This right shall cease to exist when the second copy of the consignment note is handed to the consignee or when the consignee exercises his right under article 13, paragraph 1; from that time onwards the carrier shall obey the orders of the consignee.

3. The consignee shall, however, have the right of disposal from the time when the consignment note is drawn up, if the sender makes an entry to that effect in the consignment note.

4. If in exercising his right of disposal the consignee has ordered the delivery of the goods to another person, that other person shall not be entitled to name other consignees.

5. The exercise of the right of disposal shall be subject to the following conditions:

(a) That the sender or, in the case referred to in paragraph 3 of this article, the consignee who wishes to exercise the right produces the first copy of the consignment note on which the new instructions to the carrier have been entered and indemnifies the carrier against all expenses, loss and damage involved in carrying out such instructions;

(b) That the carrying out of such instructions is possible at the time when the instructions reach the person who is to carry them out and does not either interfere with the normal working of the carrier's undertaking or prejudice the senders or consignees of other consignments;

(c) That the instructions do not result in a division of the consignment.

6. When, by reason of the provisions of paragraph 5(b) of this article, the carrier cannot carry out the instructions which he receives he shall immediately notify the person who gave him such instructions.

7. A carrier who has not carried out the instructions given under the conditions provided for in this article, or who has carried them out without requiring the first copy of the consignment note to be produced, shall be liable to the person entitled to make a claim for any loss or damage caused thereby.

Article 13

1. After arrival of the goods at the place designated for delivery, the consignee shall be entitled to require the carrier to deliver to him, against a receipt, the second copy of the consignment note and the goods. If the loss of the goods is established or if the goods have not arrived after the expiry of the period provided for in article 19, the consignee shall be entitled to enforce in his own name against the carrier any rights arising from the contract of carriage.

2. The consignee who avails himself of the rights granted to him under paragraph 1 of this article shall pay the charges shown to be due on the consignment note, but in the event of dispute on this matter the carrier shall not be required to deliver the goods unless security has been furnished by the consignee.

Article 14

1. If for any reason it is or becomes impossible to carry out the contract in accordance with the terms laid down in the consignment note before the goods reach the place designated for delivery, the carrier shall ask for instructions from the person entitled to dispose of the goods in accordance with the provisions of article 12.

2. Nevertheless, if circumstances are such as to allow the carriage to be carried out under conditions differing from those laid down in the consignment note and if the carrier has been unable to obtain instructions in reasonable time from the person entitled to dispose of the goods in accordance with the provisions of article 12, he shall take such steps as seem to him to be in the best interests of the person entitled to dispose of the goods.

Article 15

1. Where circumstances prevent delivery of the goods after their arrival at the place designated for delivery, the carrier shall ask the sender for his instructions. If the consignee refuses the goods the sender shall be entitled to dispose of them without being obliged to produce the first copy of the consignment note.

2. Even if he has refused the goods, the consignee may nevertheless require delivery so long as the carrier has not received instructions to the contrary from the sender.

3. When circumstances preventing delivery of the goods arise from the consignee, in exercise of his rights under article 12, paragraph 3, has given an order for the goods to be delivered to another person, paragraphs 1 and 2 of this article shall apply as if the consignee were the sender and that other person were the consignee.

Article 16

1. The carrier shall be entitled to recover the cost of his request for instructions and any expenses entailed in carrying out such instructions, unless such expenses were caused by the wrongful act or neglect of the carrier.

2. In the cases referred to in article 14, paragraph 1, and in article 15, the carrier may immediately unload the goods for account of the person entitled to dispose of them and thereupon the carriage shall be deemed to be at an end. The carrier shall then hold the goods on behalf of the person so entitled. He may however entrust them to a third party, and in that case he shall not be under any liability except for the exercise of reasonable care in the choice of such third party. The charges due under the consignment note and all other expenses shall remain chargeable against the goods.

3. The carrier may sell the goods, without awaiting instructions from the person entitled to dispose of them, if the goods are perishable or their condition warrants such a course, or when the storage expenses would be out of proportion to the value of the goods. He may also proceed to the sale of the goods in other cases if after the expiry of a reasonable period he has not received from the person entitled to dispose of the goods instructions to the contrary which he may reasonably be required to carry out.

4. If the goods have been sold pursuant to this article, the proceeds of sale, after deduction of the expenses chargeable against the goods, shall be placed at the disposal of the person entitled to dispose of the goods. If these charges exceed the proceeds of sale, the carrier shall be entitled to the difference.

5. The procedure in the case of sale shall be determined by the law or custom of the place where the goods are situated.

CHAPTER IV

Liability of the carrier

Article 17

1. The carrier shall be liable for the total or partial loss of the goods and for damage thereto occurring between the time when he takes over the goods and the time of delivery, as well as for any delay in delivery.

2. The carrier shall however be relieved of liability if the loss, damage or delay was caused by the wrongful act or neglect of the claimant, by the instructions of the claimant given otherwise than as the result of a wrongful act or neglect on the part of the carrier, by inherent vice of the goods or through circumstances which the carrier could not avoid and the consequences of which he was unable to prevent.

3. The carrier shall not be relieved of liability by reason of the defective condition of the vehicle used by him in order to perform the carriage, or by reason of the wrongful act or neglect of the person from whom he may have hired the vehicle or of the agents or servants of the latter.

4. Subject to article 18, paragraphs 2 to 5 the carrier shall be relieved of liability when the loss or damage arises from the special risks inherent in one or more of the following circumstances:

    (a) Use of open unsheeted vehicles, when their use has been expressly agreed and specified in the consignment note;

    (b) The lack of, or defective condition of packing in the case of goods which, by their nature, are liable to wastage or to be damaged when not packed or when not properly packed;

    (c) Handling, loading, stowage or unloading of the goods by the sender, the consignee or person acting on behalf of the sender or consignee;

    (d) The nature of certain kinds of goods which particularly exposes them to total or partial loss or to damage, especially through breakage, rust, decay, desiccation, leakage, normal wastage, or the action of moth or vermin;

(e) Insufficiency or inadequacy of marks or numbers on the packages;

(f) The carriage of livestock.

5. Where under this article the carrier is not under any liability in respect of some of the factors causing the loss, damage or delay, he shall only be hable to the extent that those factors for which he is hable under this article have contributed to the loss, damage or delay.

Article 18

1. The burden of proving that loss, damage or delay was due to one of the causes specified in article 17, paragraph 2, shall rest upon the carrier.

2. When the carrier establishes that in the circumstances of the case, the loss or damage could be attributed to one or more of the special risks referred to in article 17, paragraph 4, it shall be presumed that it was so caused. The claimant shall however be entitled to prove that the loss or damage was not, in fact, attributable either wholly or partly to one of these risks.

3. This presumption shall not apply in the circumstances set out in article 17, paragraph 4 (a), if there has been an abnormal shortage, or a loss of any package.

4. If the carriage is performed in vehicles specially equipped to protect the goods from the effects of heat, cold, variations in temperature or the humidity of the air, the carrier shall not be entitled to claim the benefit of article 17, paragraph 4 (d) unless he proves that all steps incumbent on him in the circumstances with respect to the choice, maintenance and use of such equipment were taken and that he complied with any special instructions issued to him.

5. The carrier shall not be entitled to claim the benefit of article 17, paragraph 4 (f), unless he proves that all steps normally incumbent on him in the circumstances were taken and that he complied with any special instructions issued to him.

Article 19

Delay in delivery shall be said to occur when the goods have not been delivered within the agreed time-limit or when, failing an agreed time-limit, the actual duration of the carriage having regard to the circumstances of the case, and in particular, in the case of partial loads, the time required for making up a complete load in the normal way, exceeds the time it would be reasonable to allow a diligent carrier.

Article 20

1. The fact that the goods have not been delivered within thirty days following the expiry of the agreed time-limit, or if there is no agreed time-limit, within sixty days from the time when the carrier took over the goods, shall be conclusive evidence of the loss of the goods, and the person entitled to make a claim may thereupon treat them as lost.

2. The person so entitled may, on receipt of compensation for the missing goods, request in writing that he shall be notified immediately should the goods be recovered in the course of the year following the payment of compensation. He shall be given a written acknowledgement of such request.

3. Within the thirty days following receipt of such notification, the person entitled as aforesaid may require the goods to be delivered to him against payment of the charges shown to be due on the consignment note and also against refund of the compensation he received less any charges included therein but without prejudice to any claims to compensation for delay in delivery under article 23 and, where applicable, article 26.

4. In the absence of the request mentioned in paragraph 2 or of any instructions given within the period of thirty days specified in paragraph 3, or if the goods are not recovered until more than one year after the payment of compensation, the carrier shall be entitled to deal with them in accordance with the law of the place where the goods are situated.

Article 21

Should the goods have been delivered to the consignee without collection of the 'cash on delivery' charge which should have been collected by the carrier under the terms of the contract of carriage, the carrier shall be liable to the sender for compensation not exceeding the amount of such charge without prejudice to his right of action against the consignee.

Article 22

1. When the sender hands goods of a dangerous nature to the carrier, he shall inform the carrier of the exact nature of the danger and indicate, if necessary, the precautions to be taken. If this information has not been entered in the consignment note, the burden of proving, by some other means, that the carrier knew the exact nature of the danger constituted by the carriage of the said goods shall rest upon the sender or the consignee.

2. Goods of a dangerous nature which, in the circumstances referred to in paragraph 1 of this article, the carrier did not know were dangerous, may, at any time or place, be unloaded, destroyed or rendered harmless by the carrier without compensation; further, the sender shall be liable for all expenses, loss or damage arising out of their handing over for carriage or of their carriage.

Article 23

1. When, under the provisions of this Convention, a carrier is liable for compensation in respect of total or partial loss of goods, such compensation shall be calculated by reference to the value of the goods at the place and time at which they were accepted for carriage.

2. The value of the goods shall be fixed according to the commodity exchange price or, if there is no such price, according to the current market price, or, if there is no commodity exchange price or current market price, by reference to the normal value of goods of the same kind and quality.

[3. Compensation shall not, however, exceed 8.33 units of account per kilogram of gross weight short.]

4. In addition, the carriage charges, Customs duties and other charges incurred in respect of the carriage of the goods shall be refunded in full in case of total loss and in proportion to the loss sustained in case of partial loss, but no further damages shall be payable.

5. In the case of delay, if the claimant proves that damage has resulted therefrom the carrier shall pay compensation for such damage not exceeding the carriage charges.

6. Higher compensation may only be claimed where the value of the goods or a special interest in delivery has been declared in accordance with articles 24 and 26.

[7. The unit of account mentioned in this Convention is the Special Drawing Right as defined by the International Monetary Fund. The amount mentioned in paragraph 3 of this article shall be converted into the national currency of the State of the Court seised of the case on the basis of the value of that currency on the date of judgment or the date agreed upon by the Parties.]

Article 24

The sender may, against payment of a surcharge to be agreed upon, declare in the consignment note a value for the goods exceeding the limit laid down in article 23, paragraph 3, and in that case the amount of the declared value shall be substituted for that limit.

Article 25

1. In case of damage, the carrier shall be liable for the amount by which the goods have diminished in value, calculated by reference to the value of the goods fixed in accordance with article 23, paragraphs 1, 2 and 4.

2. The compensation may not, however, exceed:
   (a) If the whole consignment has been damaged, the amount payable in the case of total loss;
   (b) If part only of the consignment has been damaged, the amount payable in the case of loss of the part affected.

Article 26

1. The sender may, against payment of a surcharge to be agreed upon, fix the amount of a special interest in delivery in the case of loss or damage or of the agreed time-limit being

exceeded, by entering such amount in the consignment note.

2. If a declaration of a special interest in delivery has been made, compensation for the additional loss or damage proved may be claimed, up to the total amount of the interest declared, independently of the compensation provided for in articles 23, 24 and 25.

Article 27

1. The claimant shall be entitled to claim interest on compensation payable. Such interest, calculated at five per centum per annum, shall accrue from the date on which the claim was sent in writing to the carrier or, if no such claim has been made, from the date on which legal proceedings were instituted.

2. When the amounts on which the calculation of the compensation is based are not expressed in the currency of the country in which payment is claimed, conversion shall be at the rate of exchange applicable on the day and at the place of payment of compensation.

Article 28

1. In cases where, under the law applicable, loss, damage or delay arising out of carriage under this Convention gives rise to an extra-contractual claim, the carrier may avail himself of the provisions of this Convention which exclude his liability or which fix or limit the compensation due.

2. In cases where the extra-contractual liability for loss, damage or delay of one of the persons for whom the carrier is responsible under the terms of article 3 is in issue, such person may also avail himself of the provisions of this Convention which exclude the liability of the carrier or which fix or limit the compensation due.

Article 29

1. The carrier shall not be entitled to avail himself of the provisions of this chapter which exclude or limit his liability or which shift the burden of proof if the damage was caused by his wilful misconduct or by such default on his part as, in accordance with the law of the court or tribunal seised of the case, is considered as equivalent to misconduct.

2. The same provision shall apply if the wilful misconduct or default is committed by the agents or servants of the carrier or by any other persons of whose services he makes use for the performance of the carriage, when such agents, servants or other persons are acting within the scope of their employment. Furthermore, in such a case such agents, servants or other persons shall not be entitled to avail themselves, with regard to their personal liability, of the provisions of this chapter referred to in paragraph 1.

CHAPTER V

Claims and actions

Article 30

1. If the consignee takes delivery of the goods without duly checking their condition with the carrier or without sending him reservations giving a general indication of the loss or damage, not later than the time of delivery in the case of apparent loss or damage and within seven days of delivery, Sundays and public holidays excepted, in the case of loss or damage which is not apparent, the fact of his taking delivery shall be prima facie evidence that he has received the goods in the condition described in the consignment note. In the case of loss or damage which is not apparent the reservations referred to shall be made in writing.

2. When the condition of the goods has been duly checked by the consignee and the carrier, evidence contradicting the result of this checking shall only be admissible in the case of loss or damage which is not apparent and provided that the consignee has duly sent reservations in writing to the carrier within seven days, Sundays and public holidays excepted, from the date of checking.

3. No compensation shall be payable for delay in delivery unless a reservation has been sent in writing to the carrier, within twenty-one days from the time that the goods were placed at the disposal of the consignee.

4. In calculating the time-limits provided for in this article the date of delivery, or the date of checking, or the date when the goods were placed at the disposal of the consignee, as the case may be, shall not be included.

5. The carrier and the consignee shall give each other every reasonable facility for making the requisite investigations and checks.

Article 31

1. In legal proceedings arising out of carriage under this Convention, the plaintiff may bring an action in any court or tribunal of a contracting country designated by agreement between the parties and, in addition, in the courts or tribunals of a country within whose territory:

    (a) The defendant is ordinarily resident, or has his principal place of business, or the branch or agency through which the contract of carriage was made, or

    (b) The place where the goods were taken over by the carrier or the place designated for delivery is situated, and in no other courts or tribunals.

2. Where in respect of a claim referred to in paragraph 1 of this article an action is pending before a court or tribunal competent under that paragraph, or where in respect of such a claim a judgment has been entered by such a court or tribunal no new action shall be started between the same parties on the same grounds unless the judgment of the court or tribunal before which the first action was brought is not enforceable in the country in which the fresh proceedings are brought.

3. When a judgment entered by a court or tribunal of a contracting country in any such action as is referred to in paragraph 1 of this article has become enforceable in that country, it shall also become enforceable in each of the other contracting States, as soon as the formalities required in the country concerned have been complied with. These formalities shall not permit the merits of the case to be re-opened.

4. The provisions of paragraph 3 of this article shall apply to judgments after trial, judgments by default and settlements confirmed by an order of the court, but shall not apply to interim judgments or to awards of damages, in addition to costs against a plaintiff who wholly or partly fails in his action.

5. Security for costs shall not be required in proceedings arising out of carriage under this Convention from nationals of contracting countries resident or having their place of business in one of those countries.

Article 32

1. The period of limitation for an action arising out of carriage under this Convention shall be one year. Nevertheless, in the case of wilful misconduct, or such default as in accordance with the law of the court or tribunal seised of the case, is considered as equivalent to wilful misconduct, the period of limitation shall be three years. The period of limitation shall begin to run:

    (a) In the case of partial loss, damage or delay in delivery, from the date of delivery;

    (b) In the case of total loss, from the thirtieth day after the expiry of the agreed time-limit or where there is no agreed time-limit from the sixtieth day from the date on which the goods were taken over by the carrier;

    (c) In all other cases, on the expiry of a period of three months after the making of the contract of carriage.

The day on which the period of limitation begins to run shall not be included in the period.

2. A written claim shall suspend the period of limitation until such date as the carrier rejects the claim by notification in writing and returns the documents attached thereto. If a part of the claim is admitted the period of limitation shall start to run again only in respect of that part of the claim still in dispute. The burden of proof of the receipt of the claim, or of the reply and of

the return of the documents, shall rest with the party relying upon these facts. The running of the period of limitation shall not be suspended by further claims having the same object.

3. Subject to the provisions of paragraph 2 above, the extension of the period of limitation shall be governed by the law of the court or tribunal seised of the case. That law shall also govern the fresh accrual rights of action.

4. A right of action which has become barred by lapse of time may not be exercised by way of counter-claim or set-off.

Article 33

The contract of carriage may contain a clause conferring competence on an arbitration tribunal if the clause conferring competence on the tribunal provides that the tribunal shall apply this Convention.

CHAPTER VI

Provisions relating to carriage performed by successive carriers

Article 34

If carriage governed by a single contract is performed by successive road carriers, each of them shall be responsible for the performance of the whole operation, the second carrier and each succeeding carrier becoming a party to the contract of carriage, under the terms of the consignment note, by reason of his acceptance of the goods and the consignment note.

Article 35

1. A carrier accepting the goods from a previous carrier shall give the latter a dated and signed receipt. He shall enter his name and address on the second copy of the consignment note. Where applicable, he shall enter on the second copy of the consignment note and on the receipt reservations of the kind provided for in article 8, paragraph 2.

2. The provisions of article 9 shall apply to the relations between successive carriers.

Article 36

Except in the case of a counter-claim or a set-off raised in an action concerning a claim based on the same contract of carriage, legal proceedings in respect of liability for loss, damage or delay may only be brought against the first carrier, the last carrier or the carrier who was performing that portion of the carriage during which the event causing the loss, damage or delay occurred; an action may be brought at the same time against several of these carriers.

Article 37

A carrier who has paid compensation in compliance with the provisions of this Convention, shall be entitled to recover such compensation, together with interest thereon and all costs and expenses incurred by reason of the claim, from the other carriers who have taken part in the carriage, subject to the following provisions:

(a) The carrier responsible for the loss or damage shall be solely liable for the compensation whether paid by himself or by another carrier;

(b) When the loss or damage has been caused by the action of two or more carriers, each of them shall pay an amount proportionate to his share of liability; should it be impossible to apportion the liability, each carrier shall be liable in proportion to the share of the payment for the carriage which is due to him;

(c) If it cannot be ascertained to which carriers liability is attributable for the loss or damage, the amount of the compensation shall be apportioned between all the carriers as laid down in (b) above.

Article 38

If one of the carriers is insolvent, the share of the compensation due from him and unpaid by him shall be divided among the other carriers in proportion to the share of the payment for the carriage due to them.

Article 39

1. No carrier against whom a claim is made under articles 37 and 38 shall be entitled to dispute the validity of the payment made by the carrier making the claim if the amount of the compensation was determined by judicial authority after the first mentioned carrier had been given due notice of the proceedings and afforded an opportunity of entering an appearance.

2. A carrier wishing to take proceedings to enforce his right of recovery may make his claim before the competent court or tribunal of the country in which one of the carriers concerned is ordinarily resident, or has his principal place of business or the branch or agency through which the contract of carriage was made. All the carriers concerned may be made defendants in the same action.

3. The provisions of article 31, paragraphs 3 and 4 shall apply to judgments entered in the proceedings referred to in articles 37 and 38.

4. The provisions of article 32 shall apply to claims between carriers. The period of limitation shall, however, begin to run either on the date of the final judicial decision fixing the amount of compensation payable under the provisions of this Convention, or, if there is no such judicial decision, from the actual date of payment.

Article 40

Carriers shall be free to agree among themselves on provisions other than those laid down in articles 37 and 38.

CHAPTER VII

Nullity of stipulations contrary to the Convention

Article 41

1. Subject to the provisions of article 40, any stipulation which would directly or indirectly derogate from the provisions of this Convention shall be null and void. The nullity of such a stipulation shall not involve the nullity of the other provisions of the contract.

2. In particular, a benefit of insurance in favour of the carrier or any other similar clause, or any clause shifting the burden of proof shall be null and void.

CHAPTER VIII

Final provisions

Article 42

1. This Convention is open for signature or accession by countries members of the Economic Commission for Europe and countries admitted to the Commission in a consultative capacity under paragraph 8 of the Commission's terms of reference.

2. Such countries as may participate in certain activities of the Economic Commission for Europe in accordance with paragraph 11 of the Commission's terms of reference may become Contracting Parties to this Convention by acceding thereto after its entry into force.

3. The Convention shall be open for signature until 31 August 1956 inclusive. Thereafter, it shall be open for accession.

4. This Convention shall be ratified.

5. Ratification or accession shall be effected by the deposit of an instrument with the Secretary-General of the United Nations.

Article 43

1. This Convention shall come into force on the ninetieth day after five of the countries referred to in article 42, paragraph 1, have deposited their instruments of ratification or accession.

2. For any country ratifying or acceding to it after five countries have deposited their instruments of ratification or accession, this Convention shall enter into force on the ninetieth day after the said country has deposited its instrument of ratification or accession.

Article 44

1. Any Contracting Party may denounce this Convention by so notifying the Secretary-General of the United Nations.

2. Denunciation shall take effect twelve months after the date of receipt by the Secretary-General of the notification of denunciation.

Article 45

If, after the entry into force of this Convention, the number of Contracting Parties is reduced, as a result of denunciations, to less than five, the Convention shall cease to be in force from the date on which the last day of such denunciations takes effect.

Article 46

1. Any country may, at the time of depositing its instrument of ratification or accession or at any time thereafter, declare by notification addressed to the Secretary-General of the United Nations that this Convention shall extend to all or any of the territories for the international relations of which it is responsible. The Convention shall extend to the territory or territories named in the notification as from the ninetieth day after its receipt by the Secretary- General or, if on that day the Convention has not yet entered into force, at the time of its entry into force.

2. Any country which has made a declaration under the preceding paragraph extending this Convention to any territory for whose international relations it is responsible may denounce the Convention separately in respect of that territory in accordance with the provisions of article 44.

Article 47

Any dispute between two or more Contracting Parties relating to the interpretation or application of this Convention, which the parties are unable to settle by negotiation or other means may, at the request of any one of the Contracting Parties concerned, be referred for settlement to the International Court of Justice.

Article 48

1. Each Contracting Party may, at the time of signing, ratifying, or acceding to, this Convention, declare that it does not consider itself as bound by article 47 of the Convention. Other Contracting Parties shall not be bound by article 47 in respect of any Contracting Party which has entered such a reservation.

2. Any Contracting Party having entered a reservation as provided for in paragraph 1 may at any time withdraw such reservation by notifying the Secretary-General of the United Nations.

3. No other reservation to this Convention shall be permitted.

Article 49

1. After this Convention has been in force for three years, any Contracting Party may, by notification to the Secretary-General of the United Nations, request that a conference be convened for the purpose of reviewing the Convention. The Secretary-General shall notify all Contracting Parties of the request and a review conference shall be convened by the Secretary- General if, within a period of four months following the date of notification by the Secretary- General, not less than one-fourth of the Contracting Parties notify him of their concurrence with the request.

2. If a conference is convened in accordance with the preceding paragraph, the Secretary-General shall notify all the Contracting Parties and invite them to submit within a period of three months such proposals as they may wish the Conference to consider. The Secretary-General shall circulate to all Contracting Parties the provisional agenda for the conference

together with the texts of such proposals at least three months before the date on which the conference is to meet.

3. The Secretary-General shall invite to any conference convened in accordance with this article all countries referred to in article 42, paragraph 1, and countries which have become Contracting Parties under article 42, paragraph 2.

Article 50

In addition to the notifications provided for in article 49, the Secretary-General of the United Nations shall notify the countries referred to in article 42, paragraph 1, and the countries which have become Contracting Parties under article 42, paragraph 2, of:

      (a) Ratifications and accessions under article 42;

      (b) The dates of entry into force of this Convention in accordance with article 43;

      (c) Denunciations under article 44;

      (d) The termination of this Convention in accordance with article 45;

      (e) Notifications received in accordance with article 46;

      (f) Declarations and notifications received in accordance with article 48, paragraphs 1 and 2.

Article 51

After 31 August 1956, the original of this Convention shall be deposited with the Secretary-General of the United Nations, who shall transmit certified true copies to each of the countries mentioned in article 42, paragraphs 1 and 2.

Misrepresentation Act 1967
(1967, c. 7)

An Act to amend the law relating to innocent misrepresentations and to amend sections 11 and 35 of the Sale of Goods Act 1893.   [22nd March 1967]

1   Removal of certain bars to rescission for innocent misrepresentation

Where a person has entered into a contract after a misrepresentation has been made to him, and—

      (a) the misrepresentation has become a term of the contract, or

      (b) the contract has been performed;

or both, then, if otherwise he would be entitled to rescind the contract without alleging fraud, he shall be so entitled, subject to the provisions of this Act, notwithstanding the matters mentioned in paragraphs (a) and (b) of this section.

2   Damages for misrepresentation

(1) Where a person has entered into a contract after a misrepresentation has been made to him by another party thereto and as a result thereof he has suffered loss, then, if the person making the misrepresentation would be liable to damages in respect thereof had the misrepresentation been made fraudulently, that person shall be so liable notwithstanding that the misrepresentation was not made fraudulently, unless he proves that he had reasonable ground to believe and did believe up to the time the contract was made that the facts represented were true.

(2) Where a person has entered into a contract after a misrepresentation has been made to him otherwise than fraudulently, and he would be entitled, by reason of the misrepresentation, to rescind the contract, then, if it is claimed, in any proceedings arising out of the contract, that the contract ought to be or has been rescinded, the court or arbitrator may declare the contract subsisting and award damages in lieu of rescission, if of opinion that it would be equitable to do so having regard to the nature of the

misrepresentation and the loss that would be caused by it if the contract were upheld, as well as to the loss that rescission would cause to the other party.

(3) Damages may be awarded against a person under subsection (2) of this section whether or not he is liable to damages under subsection (1) thereof, but where he is so liable any award under the said subsection (2) shall be taken into account in assessing his liability under the said subsection (1).

3   Avoidance of provision excluding liability for misrepresentation
[If a contract contains a term which would exclude or restrict—
> (a) any liability to which a party to a contract may be subject by reason of any misrepresentation made by him before the contract was made; or
> (b) any remedy available to another party to the contract by reason of such a misrepresentation,

that term shall be of no effect except in so far as it satisfies the requirement of reasonableness as stated in section 11(1) of the Unfair Contract Terms Act 1977; and it is for those claiming that the term satisfies that requirement to show that it does.]

4   Amendments of Sale of Goods Act 1893
. . .

5   Saving for past transactions
Nothing in this Act shall apply in relation to any misrepresentation or contract of sale which is made before the commencement of this Act.

Trade Descriptions Act 1968
(1968, c. 29)

An Act to replace the Merchandise Marks Acts 1887 to 1953 by fresh provisions prohibiting misdescriptions of goods, services, accommodation and facilities provided in the course of trade; to prohibit false or misleading indications as to the price of goods; to confer power to require information or instructions relating to goods to be marked on or to accompany the goods or to be included in advertisements; to prohibit the unauthorised use of devices or emblems signifying royal awards; to enable the Parliament of Northern Ireland to make laws relating to merchandise marks; and for purposes connected with those matters.   [30th May 1968]

Prohibition of false trade descriptions

1   Prohibition of false trade descriptions
(1) Any person who, in the course of a trade or business,—
> (a) applies a false trade description to any goods; or
> (b) supplies or offers to supply any goods to which a false trade description is applied;
> shall, subject to the provisions of this Act, be guilty of an offence.

(2) Sections 2 to 6 of this Act shall have effect for the purposes of this section and for the interpretation of expressions used in this section, wherever they occur in this Act.

2   Trade description
(1) A trade description is an indication, direct or indirect, and by whatever means given, of any of the following matters with respect to any goods or parts of goods, that is to say—
> (a) quantity, size or gauge;
> (b) method of manufacture, production, processing or re-conditioning;
> (c) composition;
> (d) fitness for purpose, strength, performance, behaviour or accuracy;
> (e) any physical characteristics not included in the preceding paragraphs;
> (f) testing by any person and results thereof;

    (g) approval by any person or conformity with a type approved by any person;

    (h) place or date of manufacture, production, processing or reconditioning;

    (i) person by whom manufactured, produced, processed or reconditioned;

    (j) other history, including previous ownership or use.

  (2) The matters specified in subsection (1) of this section shall be taken—

    (a) in relation to any animal, to include sex, breed or cross, fertility and soundness;

    (b) in relation to any semen, to include the identity and characteristics of the animal from which it as taken and measure of dilution.

  (3) In this section 'quantity' includes length, width, height, area, volume, capacity, weight and number.

  (4) Notwithstanding anything in the preceding provisions of this section, the following shall be deemed not to be trade descriptions, that is to say, any description or mark applied in pursuance of—

    (a) [...]

    (b) section 2 of the Agricultural Produce (Grading and Marking) Act 1928 (as amended by the Agricultural Produce (Grading and Marking) Amendment Act 1931) or any corresponding enactment of the Parliament of Northern Ireland;

    (c) the Plant Varieties and Seeds Act 1964;

    (d) the Agriculture and Horticulture Act 1964 [or any Community grading rules within the meaning of Part III of that Act];

    (e) the Seeds Act (Northern Ireland) 1965;

    (f) the Horticulture Act (Northern Ireland) 1966;

    [(g) the Consumer Protection Act 1987];

    [(h) the Plant Varieties Act 1997];

[any statement made in respect of, or mark applied to, any material in pursuance of Part IV of the Agriculture Act 1970, any name or expression to which a meaning has been assigned under section 70 of that Act when applied to any material in the circumstances specified in that section] [...] anymark prescribed by a system of classification compiled under section 5 of the Agriculture Act 1967 [and any designation, mark or description applied in pursuance of a scheme brought into force under Section 6(1) or an order made under section 25(1) of the Agriculture Act 1970.]

  (5) Notwithstanding anything in the preceding provisions of this section,

    (a) where provision is made under [the Food Safety Act 1990] or the Food and Drugs Act (Northern Ireland) 1958 [or the Consumer Protection Act 1987] prohibiting the application of a description except to goods in the case of which the requirements specified in that provision are complied with, that description, when applied to such goods, shall be deemed not to be a trade description.

    [(b) where by virtue of any provision made under Part V of the Medicines Act 1968 (or made under any provisions of the said Part V as applied by an order made under section 104 or section 105 of that Act) anything which in accordance with this Act, constitutes the application of a trade description to goods is subject to any requirements or restrictions imposed by that provision, any particular description specified in that provision, when applied to goods in circumstances to which those requirements or restrictions are applicable, shall be deemed not to be a trade description.]

3 False trade description

  (1) A false trade description is a trade description which is false to a material degree.

  (2) A trade description which, though not false, is misleading, that is to say, likely to be taken for such an indication of any of the matters specified in section 2 of this Act as would be false to a material degree, shall be deemed to be a false trade description.

(3) Anything which, though not a trade description, is likely to be taken for an indication of any of those matters and, as such an indication, would be false to a material degree, shall be deemed to be a false trade description.

(4) A false indication, or anything likely to be taken as an indication which would be false, that any goods comply with a standard specified or recognised by any person or implied by the approval of any person shall be deemed to be a false trade description, if there is no such person or no standard so specified, recognised or implied.

4   Applying a trade description to goods

(1) A person applies a trade description to goods if he—
- (a) affixes or annexes it to or in any manner marks it on or incorporates it with—
  - (i)   the goods themselves, or
  - (ii) anything in, on or with which the goods are supplied; or
- (b) places the goods in, on or with anything which the trade description has been affixed or annexed to, marked on or incorporated with, or places any such thing with the goods; or
- (c) uses the trade description in any manner likely to be taken as referring to the goods.

(2) An oral statement may amount to the use of a trade description.

(3) Where goods are supplied in pursuance of a request in which a trade description is used and the circumstances are such as to make it reasonable to infer that the goods are supplied as goods corresponding to that trade description, the person supplying the goods shall be deemed to have applied the trade description to the goods.

5   Trade descriptions used in advertisements

(1) The following provisions of this section shall have effect where in an advertisement a trade description is used in relation to any class of goods.

(2) The trade description shall be taken as referring to all goods of the class, whether or not in existence at the time the advertisement is published—
- (a) for the purpose of determining whether an offence has been committed under paragraph (a) of section 1 (1) of this Act; and
- (b) where goods of the class are supplied or offered to be supplied by a person publishing or displaying the advertisement, also for the purpose of determining whether an offence has been committed under paragraph (b) of the said section 1(1).

(3) In determining for the purposes of this section whether any goods are of a class to which a trade description used in an advertisement relates regard shall be had not only to the form and content of the advertisement but also to the time, place, manner and frequency of its publication and all other matters making it likely or unlikely that a person to whom the goods are supplied would think of the goods as belonging to the class in relation to which the trade description is used in the advertisement.

6   Offer to supply

A person exposing goods for supply or having goods in his possession for supply shall be deemed to offer to supply them.

Power to define terms and to require display, etc. of information

7   Definition orders

Where it appears to the Board of Trade—
- (a) that it would be in the interest of persons to whom any goods are supplied; or
- (b) that it would be in the interest of persons by whom any goods are exported and would not be contrary to the interest of persons to whom such goods are supplied in the United Kingdom;

that any expressions used in relation to the goods should be understood as having definite meanings, the Board may by order assign such meanings either—

      (i) to those expressions when used in the course of a trade or business as, or as part of, a trade description applied to the goods; or

     (ii) to those expressions when so used in such circumstances as may be specified in the order;

and where such a meaning is so assigned to an expression it shall be deemed for the purposes of this Act to have that meaning when used as mentioned in paragraph (i), or as the case may be, paragraph (ii) of this section.

8 Marking orders

(1) Where it appears to the Board of Trade necessary or expedient in the interests of persons to whom any goods are supplied that the goods should be marked with or accompanied by any information (whether or not amounting to or including a trade description) or instruction relating to the goods, the Board may subject to the provisions of this Act, by order impose requirements for securing that the goods are so marked or accompanied, and regulate or prohibit the supply of goods with respect to which the requirements are not complied with; and the requirements may extend to the form and manner in which the information or instruction is to be given.

(2) Where an order under this section is in force with respect to goods of any description, any person who, in the course of any trade or business, supplies or offers to supply goods of that description in contravention of the order shall, subject to the provisions of this Act, be guilty of an offence.

(3) An order under this section may make different provision for different circumstances and may, in the case of goods supplied in circumstances where the information or instruction required by the order would not be conveyed until after delivery, require the whole or part thereof to be also displayed near the goods.

9 Information etc. to be given in advertisements

(1) Where it appears to the Board of Trade necessary or expedient in the interest of persons to whom any goods are to be supplied that any description of advertisements of the goods should contain or refer to any information (whether or not amounting to or including a trade description) relating to the goods the Board may, subject to the provisions of this Act, by order impose requirements as to the inclusion of that information, or of an indication of the means by which it may be obtained, in such description of advertisements of the goods as may be specified in the order.

(2) An order under this section may specify the form and manner in which any such information or indication is to be included in advertisements of any description and may take different provision for different circumstances.

(3) Where an advertisement of any goods to be supplied in the course of any trade or business fails to comply with any requirement imposed under this section, any person who publishes the advertisement shall, subject to the provisions of this Act, be guilty of an offence.

10 Provisions supplementary to sections 8 and 9

(1) A requirement imposed by an order under section 8 or section 9 of this Act in relation to any goods shall not be confined to goods manufactured or produced in any one country or any one of a number of countries or to goods manufactured or produced outside any one or more countries, unless—

    (a) it is imposed with respect to a description of goods in the case of which the Board of Trade are satisfied that the interest of persons in the United Kingdom to whom goods of that description are supplied will be sufficiently protected if the requirement is so confined; and

    (b) the Board of Trade are satisfied that the order is compatible with the international obligations of the United Kingdom.

(2) Where any requirements with respect to any goods are for the time being imposed by such an order and the Board of Trade are satisfied, on the representation of persons appearing to the Board to have a substantial interest in the matter, that greater hardship would be caused to such persons if the requirements continued to apply than is justified by the interest of persons to whom the goods are supplied, the power of the Board to relax or discontinue the requirements by a further order may be exercised without the consultation and notice required by section 38(3) of this Act.

Misstatements other than false trade descriptions

11 […]

12 False representations as to royal approval or award, etc.

(1) If any person in the course of any trade or business, gives, by whatever means, any false indication, direct or indirect, that any goods or services supplied by him or any methods adopted by him are or are of a kind supplied to or approved by Her Majesty or any member of the Royal Family, he shall, subject to the provisions of this Act be guilty of an offence.

(2) If any person, in the course of any trade or business, uses, without the authority of Her Majesty, any device or emblem signifying the Queen's Award to Industry or anything so nearly resembling such a device or emblem as to be likely to deceive, he shall, subject to the provisions of this Act, be guilty of an offence.

13 False representations as to supply of goods or services

If any person, in the course of any trade or business, gives, by whatever means, any false indication, direct or indirect, that any goods or services supplied by him are of a kind supplied to any person he shall, subject to the provisions of this Act, be guilty of an offence.

14 False or misleading statements as to services, etc.

(1) It shall be an offence for any person in the course of any trade or business—
    (a) to make a statement which he knows to be false; or
    (b) recklessly to make a statement which is false; as to any of the following matters, that is to say,—
        (i) the provision in the course of any trade or business of any services, accommodation or facilities;
        (ii) the nature of any services, accommodation or facilities provided in the course of any trade or business;
        (iii) the time at which, manner in which or persons by whom any services, accommodation or facilities are so provided;
        (iv) the examination, approval or evaluation by any person of any services, accommodation or facilities so provided; or
        (v) the location or amenities of any accommodation so provided.
(2) For the purposes of this section—
    (a) anything (whether or not a statement as to any of the matters specified in the preceding subsection) likely to be taken for such a statement as to any of those matters as would be false shall be deemed to be a false statement as to that matter; and
    (b) a statement made regardless of whether it is true or false shall be deemed to be made recklessly, whether or not the person making it had reasons for believing that it might be false.
(3) In relation to any services consisting of or including the application of any treatment or process or the carrying out of any repair, the matters specified in subsection (1) of this section shall be taken to include the effect of the treatment, process or repair.
(4) In this section 'false' means false to a material degree and 'services' does not include anything done under a contract of service.

15 Orders defining terms for purposes of section 14

Where it appears to the Board of Trade that it would be in the interest of persons for whom any services, accommodation or facilities are provided in the course of any trade or business that any expressions used with respect thereto should be understood as having definite meanings, the Board may by order assign such meanings to those expressions when used as, or as part of, such statements as are mentioned in section 14 of this Act with respect to those services, accommodation or facilities; and where such a meaning is so assigned to an expression it shall be deemed for the purposes of this Act to have that meaning when so used.

Prohibition of importation of certain goods

16 Prohibition of importation of goods bearing false indication of origin

Where a false trade description is applied to any goods outside the United Kingdom and the false indication, or one of the false indications, given, or likely to be taken as given, thereby is an indication of the place of manufacture, production, processing or reconditioning of the goods or any part thereof, the goods shall not be imported into the United Kingdom.

17 Restriction on importation of goods bearing infringing trade marks

. . .

Provisions as to offences

18 Penalty for offences

A person guilty of an offence under this Act for which no other penalty is specified shall be liable—

    (a) on summary conviction, to a fine not exceeding [the prescribed sum]; and

    (b) on conviction on indictment, to a fine or imprisonment for a term not exceeding two years or both.

19 Time limit for prosecutions

(1) No prosecution for an offence under this Act shall be commenced after the expiration of three years from the commission of the offence or one year from its discovery by the prosecutor, whichever is the earlier.

(2) Not withstanding anything in [section 127(1) of the Magistrates' Courts Act 1980], a magistrates' court may try an information for an offence under this Act if the information was laid at any time within twelve months from the commission of the offence.

(3) Notwithstanding anything in section 23 of the Summary Jurisdiction (Scotland) Act 1954 (limitation of time for proceedings in statutory offences) summary proceedings in Scotland for an offence under this section may be commenced at any time within twelve months from the time when the offence was committed, and subsection (2) of the said section 23 shall apply for the purposes of this subsection as it applies for the purposes of that section.

(4) Subsections (2) and (3) of this section do not apply where—

    (a) the offence was committed by the making of an oral statement; or

    (b) the offence was one of supplying goods to which a false trade description is applied, and the trade description was applied by an oral statement; or

    (c) the offence was one where a false trade description is deemed to have been applied to goods by virtue of section 4(3) of this Act and the goods were supplied in pursuance of an oral request.

20 Offences by corporations

(1) Where an offence under this Act which has been committed by a body corporate is proved to have been committed with the consent and connivance of, or to be attributable to any neglect on the part of, any director, manager, secretary or other similar officer of the body corporate, or any person who was purporting to act in any such capacity, he as well as

the body corporate shall be liable to be proceeded against and punished accordingly.

(2) In this section 'director', in relation to any body corporate established by or under any enactment for the purpose of carrying on under national ownership any industry or part of an industry or undertaking, being a body corporate whose affairs are managed by the members thereof, means a member of that body corporate.

21 Accessories to offences committed abroad

(1) Any person who, in the United Kingdom, assists in or induces the commission in any other country of an act in respect of goods which, if the act were committed in the United Kingdom, would be an offence under section 1 of this Act shall be guilty of an offence, except as provided by subsection (2) of this section, but only if either—

  (a) the false trade description concerned is an indication (or anything likely to be taken as an indication) that the goods or any part thereof were manufactured, produced, processed or reconditioned in the United Kingdom; or
  (b) the false trade description concerned—
    (i) consists of or comprises an expression (or anything likely to be taken as an expression) to which a meaning is assigned by an order made by virtue of section 7(b) of this Act, and
    (ii) where that meaning is so assigned only in circumstances specified in the order, the trade description is used in those circumstances.

(2) A person shall not be guilty of an offence under subsection (1) of this section, if by virtue of section 32 of this Act, the act, though committed in the United Kingdom would not be an offence under section 1 of this Act had the goods been intended for despatch to the other country.

(3) Any person who, in the United Kingdom, assists in or induces the commission outside the United Kingdom of an act which if committed in the United Kingdom, would be an offence under section 12 of this Act shall be guilty of an offence.

22 Restrictions on institution of proceedings and admission of evidence

(1) Where any act or omission constitutes both an offence under this Act and an offence under any provision contained in or having effect by virtue of Part IV of the [Weights and Measures Act 1985] or Part IV of the Weights and Measures Act (Northern Ireland) 1967—

  (a) proceedings for the offence shall not be instituted under this Act, except by virtue of section 23 thereof, without the service of such a notice as is required by [subsection (3) of section 83 of the said Act of 19851 or, as the case may be, subsection (2) of section 33 of the said Act of 1967, nor after the expiration of the period mentioned in paragraph (c) of that subsection; and
  (b) [sections 35, 36 and 37(1) of the said Act of 1985] or, as the case may be, of section 20 of the said Act of 1967, shall, with the necessary modifications, apply as if the offence under this Act were an offence under Part IV of that Act or any instrument made thereunder.

(2) Where any act or omission constitutes both an offence under this Act and an offence under the food and drugs laws, evidence on behalf of the prosecution concerning any sample procured for analysis shall not be admissible in proceedings for the offence under this Act unless the relevant provisions of those laws have been complied with.

[(2A) In subsection (2) of this section—

'the food and drugs laws' means the Food Safety Act 1990, the Medicines Act 1968 and the Food (Northern Ireland) Order 1989 and any instrument made thereunder;

'the relevant provisions' means—

  (i) in relation to the said Act of 1990, section 31 and regulations made thereunder;
  (ii) in relation to the said Act of 1968, so much of Schedule 3 to that Act as is applicable to the circumstances in which the sample was procured; and

(iii) in relation to the said Order, Articles 40 and 44, or any provisions replacing any of those provisions by virtue of section 17 of the said Act of 1990, paragraph 27 of Schedule 3 to the said Act of 1968 or Article 72 or 73 of the said Order.]

(3) The Board of Trade may by order provide that in proceedings for an offence under this Act in relation to such goods as may be specified in the order (other than proceedings for an offence failing within the preceding provisions of this section) evidence on behalf of the prosecution concerning any sample procured for analysis shall not be admissible unless the sample has been dealt with in such manner as may be specified in the order.

23   Offences due to fault of other person

Where the commission by any person of an offence under this Act is due to the act or default of some other person that other person shall be guilty of the offence, and a person may be charged with and convicted of the offence by virtue of this section whether or not proceedings are taken against the first-mentioned person.

Defences

24   Defence of mistake, accident, etc.

(1) In any proceedings for an offence under this Act it shall, subject to subsection (2) of this section, be a defence for the person charged to prove—

(a) that the commission of the offence was due to a mistake or to reliance on information supplied to him or to the act or default of another person, an accident or some other cause beyond his control; and

(b) that he took all reasonable precautions and exercised all due diligence to avoid the commission of such an offence by himself or any person under his control.

(2) If in any case the defence provided by the last foregoing subsection involves the allegation that the commission of the offence was due to the act or default of another person or to reliance on information supplied by another person, the person charged shall not, without leave of the court, be entitled to rely on that defence unless, within a period ending seven clear days before the hearing, he has served on the prosecutor a notice in writing giving such information identifying or assisting in the identification of that other person as was then in his possession.

(3) In any proceedings for an offence under this Act of supplying or offering to supply goods to which a false trade description is applied it shall be a defence for the person charged to prove that he did not know, and could not with reasonable diligence have ascertained, that the goods did not conform to the description or that the description had been applied to the goods.

25   Innocent publication of advertisement

In proceedings for an offence under this Act committed by the publication of an advertisement it shall be a defence for the person charged to prove that he is a person whose business it is to publish or arrange for the publication of advertisements and that he received the advertisement for publication in the ordinary course of business and did not know and had no reason to suspect that its publication would amount to an offence under this Act.

Enforcement

26   Enforcing authorities

(1) It shall be the duty of every local weights and measures authority [as defined in section 69(3) of the Weights and Measures Act 1985] to enforce within their area the provisions of this Act and of any order made under this Act [. . .]

(2) Every local weights and measures authority shall, whenever the Board of Trade so direct, make to the Board a report on the exercise of their functions under this Act in such form and containing such particulars as the Board may direct.

[...]

(5) Nothing in this section shall be taken as authorising a local weights and measures authority in Scotland to institute proceedings for an offence.

27   Power to make test purchases

A local weights and measures authority shall have power to make, or to authorise any of their officers to make on their behalf, such purchases of goods, and to authorise any of their officers to secure the provision of such services, accommodation or facilities, as may appear expedient for the purpose of determining whether or not the provisions of this Act and any order made thereunder are being complied with.

28   Power to enter premises and inspect and seize goods and documents

(1) A duly authorised officer of a local weights and measures authority or of a Government department may, at all reasonable hours and on production, if required, of his credentials, exercise the following powers, that is to say,—

(a) he may, for the purpose of ascertaining whether any offence under this Act has been committed, inspect any goods and enter any premises other than premises used only as a dwelling;

(b) if he has reasonable cause to suspect that an offence under this Act has been committed, he may, for the purpose of ascertaining whether it has been committed, require any person carrying on a trade or business or employed in connection with a trade or business to produce any books or documents relating to the trade or business and may take copies of, or of any entry in, any such book or document;

(c) if he has reasonable cause to believe that an offence under this Act has been committed, he may seize and detain any goods for the purpose of ascertaining, by testing or otherwise, whether the offence has been committed;

(d) he may seize and detain any goods or documents which he has reason to believe may be required as evidence in proceedings for an offence under this Act;

(e) he may, for the purpose of exercising his powers under this subsection to seize goods, but only if and to the extent that it is reasonably necessary in order to secure that the provisions of this Act and of any order made thereunder are duly observed, require any person having authority to do so to break open any container or open any vending machine and, if that person does not comply with the requirement, he may do so himself.

(2) An officer seizing any goods or documents in the exercise of his powers under this section shall inform the person from whom they are seized and, in the case of goods seized from a vending machine, the person whose name and address are stated on the machine as being the proprietor's or, if no name and address are so stated, the occupier of the premises on which the machine stands or to which it is affixed.

(3) If a justice of the peace, on sworn information in writing—

(a) is satisfied that there is reasonable ground to believe either—

(i) that any goods, books or documents which a duly authorised officer has power under this section to inspect are on any premises and that their inspection is likely to disclose evidence of the commission of an offence under this Act; or

(ii) that any offence under this Act has been, is being or is about to be committed on any premises; and

(b) is also satisfied either—

(i) that admission to the premises has been or is likely to be refused and that notice of intention to apply for a warrant under this subsection has been given to the occupier; or

(ii) that an application for admission, or the giving of such a notice would defeat the object of the entry or that the premises are unoccupied or that the occupier is temporarily absent and it might defeat the object of the entry to await his return, the justice may by warrant under his hand, which shall continue in force for a period of one month, authorise an officer of a local weights and measures authority or of a Government department to enter the premises, if need be by force.

In the application of this subsection to Scotland, 'justice of the peace' shall be construed as including a sheriff and a magistrate.

(4) An officer entering any premises by virtue of this section may take with him such other persons and such equipment as may appear to him necessary; and on leaving any premises which he has entered by virtue of a warrant under the preceding subsection he shall, if the premises are unoccupied or the occupier is temporarily absent, leave them as effectively secured against trespassers as he found them.

[...]

(6) If any person who is not a duly authorised officer of a local weights and measures authority or of a Government department purports to act as such under this section he shall be guilty of an offence.

(7) Nothing in this section shall be taken to compel the production by a solicitor of a document containing a privileged communication made by or to him in that capacity or to authorise the taking of possession of any such document which is in his possession.

29   Obstruction of authorised officers

(1) Any person who—

(a) wilfully obstructs an officer of a local weights and measures authority or of a Government department acting in pursuance of this Act; or

(b) wilfully fails to comply with any requirement properly made to him by such an officer under section 28 of this Act; or

(c) without reasonable cause fails to give such an officer so acting any other assistance or information which he may reasonably require of him for the purpose of the performance of his functions under this Act,

shall be guilty of an offence and liable, on summary conviction to a fine not exceeding [level 3 on the standard scale].

(2) If any person in giving any such information as is mentioned in the preceding subsection, makes any statement which he knows to be false, he shall be guilty of an offence.

(3) Nothing in this section shall be construed as requiring a person to answer any question or give any information if to do so might incriminate him.

30   Notice of test and intended prosecution

(1) Where any goods seized or purchased by an officer in pursuance of this Act are submitted to a test, then—

(a) if the goods were seized the officer shall inform the person mentioned in section 28(2) of this Act of the result of the test;

(b) if the goods were purchased and the test leads to the institution of proceedings for an offence under this Act, the officer shall inform the person from whom the goods were purchased, or, in the case of goods sold through a vending machine, the person mentioned in section 28(2) of this Act, of the result of the test; and shall, where as a result of the test proceedings for an offence under this Act are instituted against any person, allow him to have the goods tested on his behalf if it is reasonably practicable to do so.

[...]

31   Evidence by certificate

(1) The Board of Trade may by regulations provide that certificates issued by such persons as may be specified by the regulations in relation to such matters as may be so specified shall,

subject to the provisions of this section be received in evidence of those matters in any proceedings under this Act.

(2) Such a certificate shall not be received in evidence—

(a) unless the party against whom it is to be given in evidence has been served with a copy thereof not less than seven days before the hearing; or

(b) if that party has, not less than three days before the hearing, served on the other party a notice requiring the attendance of the person issuing the certificate.

(3) In any proceedings under this Act in Scotland, a certificate received in evidence by virtue of this section or, where the attendance of a person issuing a certificate is required under subsection (2)(b) of this section, the evidence of that person, shall be sufficient evidence of the matters stated in the certificate.

(4) For the purposes of this section any document purporting to be such a certificate as is mentioned in this section shall be deemed to be such a certificate unless the contrary is shown.

(5) Regulations under this section shall be made by statutory instrument which shall be subject to annulment in pursuance of a resolution of either House of Parliament.

Miscellaneous and supplemental

32 Power to exempt goods sold for export, etc.
In relation to goods which are intended—

(a) for despatch to a destination outside the United Kingdom and any designated country within the meaning of [section 24(2)(b) of the Weights and Measures Act 1985] or section 15(5)(b) of the Weights and Measures Act (Northern Ireland) 1967; or

(b) for use as stores within the meaning of the Customs and Excise Act 1952 in a ship or aircraft on a voyage or flight to an eventual destination outside the United Kingdom; or

(c) for use by Her Majesty's forces or by a visiting force within the meaning of any of the provisions of Part I of the Visiting Forces Act 1952; or

[(d) for industrial use within the meaning of the Weights and Measures Act 1985 or for constructional use;]

section 1 of this Act shall apply as if there were omitted from the matters included in section 2(1) of this Act those specified in paragraph (a) thereof; and, if the Board of Trade by order specify any other of those matters for the purposes of this section with respect to any description of goods, the said section 1 shall apply, in relation to goods of that description which are intended for despatch to a destination outside the United Kingdom and such country (if any) as may be specified in the order, as if the matters so specified were also omitted from those included in the said section 2(1).

[(2) In this section 'constructional use', in relation to any goods, means the use of those goods in constructional work (or, if the goods are explosives within the meaning of the Manufacture and Storage of Explosives Regulations 2005, in mining, quarrying or demolition work) in the course of the carrying on of a business;]

33 Compensation for loss, etc. of goods seized under s. 28
(1) Where, in the exercise of his powers under section 28 of this Act, an officer of a local weights and measures authority or of a Government department seizes and detains any goods and their owner suffers loss by reason thereof or by reason that the goods, during the detention, are lost or damaged or deteriorate, then, unless the owner is convicted of an offence under this Act committed in relation to the goods, the authority or department shall be liable to compensate him for the loss so suffered.

(2) Any disputed question as to the right to or the amount of any compensation payable under this section shall be determined by arbitration and, in Scotland, by a single arbiter appointed, failing agreement between the parties, by the sheriff.

34 Trade marks containing trade descriptions

The fact that a trade description is a trade mark, or part of a trade mark, within the meaning of the Trade Marks Act 1938 does not prevent it from being a false trade description when applied to any goods, except where the following conditions are satisfied, that is to say—

(a) that it could have been lawfully applied to the goods if this Act had not been passed; and

(b) that on the day this Act is passed the trade mark either is registered under the Trade Marks Act 1938 or is in use to indicate a connection in the course of trade between such goods and the proprietor of the trade mark; and

(c) that the trade mark as applied is used to indicate such a connection between the goods and the proprietor of the trade mark or a person registered under section 28 of the Trade Marks Act 1938 as a registered user of the trade mark; and

(d) that the person who is the proprietor of the trade mark is the same person as, or a successor in title of, the proprietor on the day this Act is passed.

35 Saving for civil rights

A contract for the supply of any goods shall not be void or unenforceable by reason only of a contravention of any provision of this Act.

36 Country of origin

For the purposes of this Act goods shall be deemed to have been manufactured or produced in the country in which they last underwent a treatment or process resulting in a substantial change.

(2) The Board of Trade may by order specify—

(a) in relation to any description of goods, what treatment or process is to be regarded for the purposes of this section as resulting or not resulting in a substantial change;

(b) in relation to any description of goods different parts of which were manufactured or produced in different countries, or of goods assembled in a country different from that in which their parts were manufactured or produced, in which of those countries the goods are to be regarded for the purposes of this Act as having been manufactured or produced.

37 Market research experiments

(1) In this section 'market research experiment' means any activities conducted for the purpose of ascertaining the opinion of persons (in this section referred to as 'participants' of—

(a) any goods; or

(b) anything in, on or with which the goods are supplied; or

(c) the appearance or any other characteristic of the goods or of any such thing; or

(d) the name or description under which the goods are supplied.

(2) This section applies to any market research experiment with respect to which the following conditions are satisfied, that is to say,—

(a) that any participant to whom the goods are supplied in the course of the experiment is informed, at or before the time at which they are supplied to him, that they are supplied for such a purpose as is mentioned in subsection (1) of this section, and

(b) that no consideration in money or money's worth is given by a participant for the goods or any goods supplied to him for comparison.

(3) Neither section 1 nor section 8 of this Act shall apply in relation to goods supplied or offered to be supplied, whether to a participant or any other person, in the course of a market research experiment to which this section applies.

38 Orders

(1) Any power to make an order under the preceding provisions of this Act shall be exercisable by statutory instrument, which shall be subject to annulment in pursuance of a

resolution of either House of Parliament, and includes power to vary or revoke such an order by a subsequent order.

(2) Any order under the preceding provisions of this Act which relates to any agricultural, horticultural or fishery produce, whether processed or not, food, feeding stuffs or ingredients of food or feeding stuffs, fertilisers or any goods used as pesticides or for similar purposes shall be made by the Board of Trade acting jointly with the following Ministers, that is to say, if the order extends to England and Wales, the Minister of Agriculture, Fisheries and Food, and if it extends to Scotland or Northern Ireland, the Secretary of State concerned.

(3) The following provisions shall apply to the making of an order under section 7, 8, 9, 15 or 36 of this Act, except in the case mentioned in section 10(2) thereof, that is to say—

> (a) before making the order the Board of Trade shall consult with such organisations as appear to them to be representative of interests substantially affected by it and shall publish, in such manner as the Board think appropriate, notice of their intention to make the order and of the place where copies of the proposed order may be obtained; and
>
> (b) the order shall not be made until the expiration of a period of twenty-eight days from the publication of the notice and may then be made with such modifications (if any) as the Board of Trade think appropriate having regard to any representations received by them.

39   Interpretation

(1) The following provisions shall have effect in addition to sections 2 to 6 of this Act, for the interpretation in this Act of expressions used therein, that is to say,—

'advertisement' includes a catalogue, a circular and a price list;

'goods' includes ships and aircraft, things attached to land and growing crops;

'premises' includes any place and any stall, vehicle, ship or aircraft; and

'ship' includes any boat and any other description of vessel used in navigation.

(2) For the purposes of this Act, a trade description or statement published in any newspaper, book or periodical or in any film or sound or television broadcast [or in any programme included in any programme service (within the meaning of the Broadcasting Act 1990) other than a sound or television broadcasting service] shall not be deemed to be a trade description applied or statement made in the course of a trade or business unless it is or forms part of an advertisement.

40   Provisions as to Northern Ireland

. . .

41   Consequential amendments and repeals

. . .

[…]

43   Short title and commencement

(1) This Act may be cited as the Trade Descriptions Act 1968.

(2) This Act shall come into force on the expiration of the period of six months beginning with the day on which it is passed.

Conveyancing and Feudal Reform (Scotland) Act 1970
(1970, c. 35)

9   The standard security

(1) The provisions of this Part of this Act shall have effect for the purpose of enabling a new form of heritable security to be created to be known as a standard security.

(2) It shall be competent to grant and record in the Register of Sasines a standard security over any [land or real right in land] to be expressed in conformity with one of the forms prescribed in Schedule 2 to this Act.

[(2A) It shall not be competent to grant a standard security over a conservation burden (within the meaning of Part 4 of the Abolition of Feudal Tenure etc. (Scotland) Act 2000 (asp 5)).]

[(2B) It shall not be competent to grant a standard security over a personal pre-emption burden or personal redemption burden (both within the meaning of Part 4 of the Abolition of Feudal Tenure etc. (Scotland) Act 2000 (asp 5)).]

(3) A grant of any right over [land or a real right] in land for the purpose of securing any debt by way of a heritable security shall only be capable of being effected at law if it is embodied in a standard security.

(4) Where for the purpose last-mentioned any deed which is not in the form of a standard security contains a disposition or assignation [of land or of a real right] in land, it shall to that extent be void and unenforceable, and where that deed has been duly recorded the creditor in the purported security may be required, by any person having an interest, to grant any deed which may be appropriate to clear the Register of Sasines of that security.

(5) A standard security may be used for any other purpose for which a heritable security may be used if any of the said forms is appropriate to that purpose, and for the purpose of any enactment affecting heritable securities a standard security, if so used, or if used as is required by this Act instead of a heritable security as defined therein, shall be a heritable security for the purposes of that enactment.

(6) The Bankruptcy Act 1696, in so far as it renders a heritable security of no effect in relation to a debt contracted after the recording of that security, and any rule of law which requires that a real burden for money may only be created in respect of a sum specified in the deed of creation, shall not apply in relation to a standard security.

(8) For the purposes of this Part of this Act—

    (a) 'heritable security' (except in subsection (5) of this section if the context otherwise requires) means any security capable of being constituted over any [land or real right] in land by disposition or assignation of that [land or real right] in security of any debt and of being recorded in the Register of Sasines;

    (b) ['real right in land' means any such right, other than ownership or a real burden, which is capable of being held separately and to which a title may be recorded in the Register of Sasines;]

    (c) 'debt' means any obligation due, or which will or may become due, to repay or pay money, including any such obligation arising from a transaction or part of a transaction in the course of any trade, business or profession, and any obligation to pay an annuity or *ad factum praestandum,* but does not include an obligation to pay any [. . .] rent or other periodical sum payable in respect of land, and 'creditor' and 'debtor', in relation to a standard security, shall be construed accordingly.

10   Import of forms of, and certain clauses in, standard security

(1) The import of the clause relating to the personal obligation contained in Form A of Schedule 2 to this Act expressed in any standard security shall, unless specially qualified, be as follows—

    (a) where the security is for a fixed amount advanced or payable at, or prior to, the delivery of the deed, the clause undertaking to make payment to the creditor shall import an acknowledgment of receipt by the debtor of the principal sum advanced or an acknowledgment by the debtor of liability to pay that sum and a personal obligation undertaken by the debtor to repay or pay to the creditor on demand in writing at any time after the date of delivery of the standard security the said sum, with interest at the rate stated payable on the dates specified, together with all expenses for which the debtor is liable by virtue of the deed or of this Part of this Act;

(b) where the security is for a fluctuating amount, whether subject to a maximum amount or not and whether advanced or due partly before and partly after delivery of the deed or whether to be advanced or to become due wholly after such delivery, the clause undertaking to make payment to the creditor shall import a personal obligation by the debtor to repay or pay to the creditor on demand in writing the amount, not being greater than the maximum amount, if any, specified in the deed, advanced or due and outstanding at the time of demand, with interest on each advance from the date when it was made until repayment thereof, or on each sum payable from the date on which it became due until payment thereof, and at the rate stated payable on the dates specified, together with all expenses for which the debtor is liable by virtue of the deed or of this Part of this Act.

(2) The clause of warrandice in the forms of standard security contained in Schedule 2 to this Act expressed in any standard security shall, unless specially qualified, import absolute warrandice as regards the [land or real right] in land over which the security is granted and the title deeds thereof, and warrandice from fact and deed as regards the rents thereof.

(3) The clause relating to consent to registration for execution contained in Form A of Schedule 2 to this Act expressed in any standard security shall, unless specially qualified, import a consent to registration in the Books of Council and Session, or, as the case may be, in the books of the appropriate sheriff court, for execution.

(4) The forms of standard security contained in Schedule 2 to this Act shall, unless specially qualified, import an assignation to the creditor of the title deeds, including searches, and all conveyances not duly recorded, affecting the security subjects or any part thereof, with power to the creditor in the event of a sale under the powers conferred by the security, but subject to the rights of any person holding prior rights to possession of those title deeds, to deliver them, so far as in the creditor's possession, to the purchaser, and to assign to the purchaser any right he may possess to have the title deeds made forthcoming.

11   Effect of recorded standard security, and incorporation of standard conditions

(1) Where a standard security is duly recorded, it shall operate to vest [in the grantee a real right in security] for the performance of the contract to which the security relates.

(2) Subject to the provisions of this Part of this Act, the conditions set out in Schedule 3 to this Act, either as so set out or with such variations as have been agreed by the parties in the exercise of the powers conferred by the said Part (which conditions are hereinafter in this Act referred to as 'the standard conditions'), shall regulate every standard security.

(3) Subject to the provisions of this Part of this Act, the creditor and debtor in a standard security may vary any of the standard conditions, other than [standard condition 11 (procedure on redemption) and] the provisions of Schedule 3 to this Act relating to the powers of sale, [ ] and foreclosure and to the exercise of those powers, but no condition capable of being varied shall be varied in a manner inconsistent with any condition which may not be varied by virtue of this subsection.

(4) In this Part of this Act—

(a) any reference to a variation of the standard conditions shall include a reference to the inclusion of an additional condition and to the exclusion of a standard condition;

(b) any purported variation of a standard condition which contravenes the provisions of subsection (3) of this section shall be void and unenforceable.

12   Standard security may be granted by person uninfeft

(1) Notwithstanding any rule of law, a standard security may be granted over [land or real right] in land by a person [. . .] whose title thereto has not been completed by being duly recorded, if in the deed expressing that security the grantor deduces his title to that [land or

real right] from the person who appears in the Register of Sasines as having the last recorded title thereto.

(2) A deduction of title in a deed for the purposes of the foregoing subsection shall be expressed in the form prescribed by Note 2 or 3 of Schedule 2 to this Act, and on such a deed being recorded as aforesaid the title of the grantee shall, for the purposes of the rights and obligations between the grantor and the grantee thereof and those deriving right from them, but for no other purpose, in all respects be of the same effect as if the title of the grantor of the deed to the [land or real right in land] to which he has deduced title therein had been duly completed; and any references to a proprietor or to a person [having the last recorded title] shall in this Part of this Act be construed accordingly.

(3) There may be specified for the purposes of any deduction of title in pursuance of any provision of this Part of this Act any writing which it is competent to specify as a title, midcouple, or link in title for the purposes of section 5 of the Conveyancing (Scotland) Act 1924 (deduction of title).

13 Ranking of standard securities

(1) Where the creditor in a standard security duly recorded has received notice of the creation of a subsequent security over the same [land or real right in land or over any part thereof, or of the subsequent assignation or conveyance of that land or real right] in whole or in part, being a security, assignation or conveyance so recorded, the preference in ranking of the security of that creditor shall be restricted to security for
>   (a) the present debt incurred (whenever payable); and
>   (b) any future debt which, under the contract to which the security relates, he is required to allow the debtor in the security to incur,]

and interest present or future due thereon (including any such interest which has accrued or may accrue) and for any expenses or outlays (including interest thereon) which may be, or may have been, reasonably incurred in the exercise of any power conferred on any creditor by the deed expressing the existing security.

(2) For the purposes of the foregoing subsection—
>   (a) a creditor in an existing standard security duly recorded shall not be held to have had any notice referred to in that subsection, by reason only of the subsequent recording of the relevant deed in the Register of Sasines;
>   (b) any assignation, conveyance or vesting in favour of or in any other person of the interest of the debtor in the security subjects or in any part thereof resulting from any judicial decree, or otherwise by operation of law, shall constitute sufficient notice thereof to the creditor.

(3) Nothing in the foregoing provisions of this section shall affect—
>   (a) any preference in ranking enjoyed by the Crown; and
>   (b) any powers of the creditor and debtor in any heritable security to regulate the preference to be enjoyed by creditors in such manner as they may think fit.

14 Assignation of standard security

(1) Any standard security duly recorded may be transferred, in whole or in part, by the creditor by an assignation in conformity with Form A or B of Schedule 4 to this Act, and upon such an assignation being duly recorded, the security, or, as the case may be, part thereof, shall be vested in the assignee as effectually as if the security or the part had been granted in his favour.

(2) An assignation of a standard security shall, except so far as otherwise therein stated, be deemed to convey to the grantee all rights competent to the grantor to the writs, and shall have the effect *inter alia* of vesting in the assignee—
>   (a) the full benefit of all corroborative or substitutional obligations for the debt, or any part thereof, whether those obligations are contained in any deed or arise by operation of law or otherwise,
>   (b) the right to recover payment from the debtor of all expenses properly incurred by the creditor in connection with the security, and

(c) the entitlement to the benefit of any notices served and of all procedure instituted by the creditor in respect of the security to the effect that the grantee may proceed as if he had originally served or instituted such notices or procedure.

15 Restriction of standard security

(1) The security constituted by any standard security duly recorded may be restricted, as regards any part of the [land or real right] in land burdened by the security, by a deed of restriction in conformity with Form C of Schedule 4 to this Act, and, upon that deed being duly recorded, the security shall be restricted [to the land or real right contained in the standard security other than the part of that land or real right disburdened by the deed; and the land or real right] thereby disburdened shall be released from the security wholly or to the extent specified in the deed.

(2) A partial discharge and deed of restriction of a standard security, which has been duly recorded, may be combined in one deed, which shall be in conformity with Form D of the said Schedule 4.

16 Variation of standard security

(1) Any alteration in the provisions (including any standard condition) of a standard security duly recorded, other than an alteration which may appropriately be effected by an assignation, discharge or restriction of that standard security, or an alteration which involves an addition to, or an extension of, the [land or real right] in land mentioned therein, may be effected by a variation endorsed on the standard security in conformity with Form E of Schedule 4 to this Act, or by a variation contained in a separate deed in a form appropriate for that purpose, duly recorded in either case.

(2) Where a standard security has been duly recorded, but the personal obligation or any other provision (including any standard condition) relating to the security has been created or specified in a deed which has not been so recorded, nothing contained in this section shall prevent any alteration in that personal obligation or provision, other than an alteration which may be appropriately effected by an assignation, discharge or restriction of the standard security, or an alteration which involves an addition to, or an extension of, the [land or real right] in land mentioned therein, by a variation contained in any form of deed appropriate for that purpose, and such a variation shall not require to be recorded in the Register of Sasines.

(4) Any variation effected in accordance with this section shall not prejudice any other security or right over the same [land or real right in land, or over], or any part thereof, effectively constituted before the variation is recorded, or, where the variation is effected by an unrecorded deed, before that deed is executed, as the case may be.

17 Discharge of standard security

A standard security duly recorded may be discharged, and the [land or real right] in land burdened by that security may be disburdened thereof, in whole or in part, by a discharge in conformity with Form F of Schedule 4 to this Act, duly recorded.

18 Redemption of standard security

(1) [Subject to the provisions of subsection (1A) of this section,] The debtor in a standard security or, where the debtor is not the proprietor, the proprietor of the security subjects shall be entitled to redeem the security [on giving two months' notice of his intention to do so, and] in conformity with the terms of standard condition 11 and the appropriate Forms of Schedule 5 to this Act.

[(1A) The provisions of the foregoing subsection shall be subject to any agreement to the contrary, but any right to redeem the security shall be exercisable in conformity with the terms and Forms referred to in that subsection.]

(2) Where owing to the death or absence of the creditor, or to any other cause, the debtor in a standard security or, as the case may be, the proprietor of the security subjects [(being in

either case a person entitled to redeem the security)] is unable to obtain a discharge under the [foregoing provisions], he may—

    (a) where the security was granted in respect of any obligation to repay or pay money, consign in any bank in Scotland, incorporated by or under Act of Parliament or by Royal Charter, the whole amount due to the creditor on redemption, other than any unascertained expenses of the creditor, for the person appearing to have the best right thereto, and

    (b) in any other case, apply to the court for declarator that the whole obligations under the contract to which the security relates have been performed.

(3) On consignation, or on the court granting declarator as aforesaid, a certificate to that effect may be expede by a solicitor in the appropriate form prescribed by Form D of Schedule 5 to this Act, which on being duly recorded shall disburden the [land or real right] in land, to which the standard security relates, of that security.

(4) For the purposes of this section, 'whole amount due' means the debt to which the security relates, so far as outstanding, and any other sums due thereunder by way of interest or otherwise.

19   Calling-up of standard security

(1) Where a creditor in a standard security intends to require discharge of the debt thereby secured and, failing that discharge, to exercise any power conferred by the security to sell any subjects of the security or any other power which he may appropriately exercise on the default of the debtor within the meaning of standard condition 9(1)(a), he shall serve a notice calling-up the security in conformity with Form A of Schedule 6 to this Act (herein after in this Act referred to as a 'calling-up notice'), in accordance with the following provisions of this section.

(2) Subject to the following provisions of this section, a calling-up notice shall be served on the person [having the last recorded title to] the security subjects and appearing on the record as the proprietor, and should the proprietor of those subjects, or any part thereof, be dead then on his representative or the person entitled to the subjects in terms of the last recorded title thereto, notwithstanding any alteration of the succession not appearing in the Register of Sasines.

(3) Where the person [having the last recorded title to] the security subjects was an incorporated company which has been removed from the Register of Companies, or a person deceased who has left no representatives, a calling-up notice shall be served on the Lord Advocate and, where the estates of the person [having the last recorded title have] been sequestrated under the Bankruptcy (Scotland) Act 1913, the notice shall be served on the trustee in the sequestration (unless such trustee has been discharged) as well as on the bankrupt.

(4) If the proprietor be a body of trustees, it shall be sufficient if the notice is served on a majority of the trustees [having title to] the security subjects.

(5) It shall be an obligation on the creditor to serve a copy of the calling-up notice on any other person against whom he wishes to preserve any right of recourse in respect of the debt.

(6) For the purposes of the foregoing provisions of this section, the service of a calling-up notice may be made by delivery to the person on whom it is desired to be served or the notice may be sent by registered post or by the recorded delivery service to him at his last known address, or, in the case of the Lord Advocate, at the Crown Office, Edinburgh, and an acknowledgment, signed by the person on whom service has been made, in conformity with Form C of Schedule 6 to this Act, or, as the case may be, a certificate in conformity with Form D of that Schedule, accompanied by the postal receipt shall be sufficient evidence of the service of that notice; and if the address of the person on whom the notice is desired to be served is not known, or if it is not known whether that person is still alive, or if the packet containing a calling-up notice is returned to the creditor with an intimation that it could not be delivered, that notice shall be sent to the Extractor of the Court of Session, and

shall be equivalent to the service of a calling-up notice on the person on whom it is desired to be served.

(7) For the purposes of the last foregoing subsection, an acknowledgment of receipt by the said Extractor on a copy of a calling-up notice shall be sufficient evidence of the receipt by him of that notice.

(8) A calling-up notice served by post shall be held to have been served on the next day after the day of posting.

(9) Where a creditor in a standard security has indicated in a calling-up notice that any sum and any interest thereon due under the contract may be subject to adjustment in amount, he shall, if the person on whom notice has been served so requests, furnish the debtor with a statement of the amount as finally determined within a period of one month from the date of service of the calling-up notice, and a failure by the creditor to comply with the provisions of this subsection shall cause the calling-up notice to be of no effect.

(10) The period of notice mentioned in the calling-up notice may be effectively dispensed with or shortened by the person on whom it is served, with the consent of the creditors, if any, holding securities *pari passu* with, or postponed to, the security held by the creditor serving the calling-up notice, by a minute written or endorsed upon the said notice, or a copy thereof, in conformity with Form C of Schedule 6 to this Act.

[Provided that, without prejudice to the foregoing generality, if the standard security is over a matrimonial home as defined in section 22 of the Matrimonial Homes (Family Protection) (Scotland) Act 1981, the spouse on whom the calling-up notice has been served may not dispense with or shorten the said period without the consent in writing of the other spouse.]

(11) A calling-up notice shall cease to have effect for the purpose of a sale in the exercise of any power conferred by the security on the expiration of a period of five years, which period shall run—

    (a) in the case where the subjects of the security, or any part thereof, have not been offered for or exposed to sale, from the date of the notice,

    (b) in the case where there has been such an offer or exposure, from the date of the last offer or exposure.

[19A Notice to occupier of calling-up

(1) Where a creditor in a standard security over [land or a real right] in land used to any extent for residential purposes serves a calling-up notice, he shall serve a notice in conformity with Form BB (notice to occupier) of Schedule 6 to this Act together with a copy of the calling-up notice.

(2) Notices under subsection (1) above shall be sent by recorded delivery letter addressed to 'The Occupier' at the security subjects.

(3) If a creditor fails to comply with subsections (1) and (2) above, the calling-up notice shall be of no effect.]

[19B Notice to local authority of calling-up

(1) Where a creditor in a standard security over an interest in land used to any extent for residential purposes serves a calling-up notice, the creditor shall give notice of that fact to the local authority in whose area the security subjects are situated, unless the creditor is that local authority.

(2) Notice under subsection (1) shall be given in the form and manner prescribed under section 11(3) of the Homelessness etc. (Scotland) Act 2003 (asp 10).]

20 Exercise of rights of creditor on default of debtor in complying with a calling-up notice

(1) Where the debtor in a standard security is in default within the meaning of standard condition 9(1)(a), the creditor may exercise such of his rights under the security as he may consider appropriate, and any such right shall be in addition to and not in derogation from

any other remedy arising from the contract to which the security relates or from any right conferred by any enactment or by any rule of law on the creditor in a heritable security.

(2) Where the debtor is in default as aforesaid, the creditor shall have the right to sell the security subjects, or any part thereof, in accordance with the provisions of this Part of this Act.

(3) A creditor in a standard security who is in lawful possession of the security subjects may let the security subjects, or any part thereof, for any period not exceeding seven years, or may make application to the court for warrant to let those subjects, or any part thereof, for a period exceeding seven years, and the application shall state the proposed tenant, and the duration and conditions of the proposed lease, and shall be served on the proprietor of the subjects and on any other heritable creditor having interest as such a creditor in the subjects.

(4) The court, on such an application as aforesaid and after such inquiry and such further intimation of the application as it may think fit, may grant the application as submitted, or subject to such variation as it may consider reasonable in all the circumstances of the case, or may refuse the application.

(5) There shall be deemed to be assigned to a creditor who is in lawful possession of the security subjects all rights and obligations of the proprietor relating to—

(a) leases, or any permission or right of occupancy, granted in respect of those subjects or any part thereof, and
(b) the management and maintenance of the subjects and the effecting of any reconstruction, alteration or improvement reasonably required for the purpose of maintaining the market value of the subjects.

21 Notice of default

(1) Where the debtor in a standard security is in default within the meaning of standard condition 9(1)(b), and the default is remediable, the creditor may, without prejudice to any other powers he may have by virtue of this Act or otherwise, proceed in accordance with the provisions of this section to call on the debtor and on the proprietor, where he is not the debtor, to purge the default.

(2) For the aforesaid purpose the creditor may serve on the debtor and, as the case may be, on the proprietor a notice in conformity with Form B of Schedule 6 to this Act (herein after in this Act referred to as a 'notice of default') which shall be served in the like manner and with the like requirements as to proof of service as a calling-up notice.

[(2A) Section 19A and19B of this Act apply where the creditor serves a notice of default as it applies where he serves a calling-up notice.]

(3) For the purpose of dispensing with, or shortening, the period of notice mentioned in a notice of default, section 19(10) of this Act shall apply as it applies in relation to a calling-up notice.

(4) Notwithstanding the failure to comply with any requirement contained in the notice, a notice of default shall cease to be authority for the exercise of the rights mentioned in section 23(2) of this Act on the expiration of a period of five years from the date of the notice.

22 Objections to notice of default

(1) Where a person on whom a notice of default has been served considers himself aggrieved by any requirement of that notice he may, within a period of fourteen days of the service of the notice, object to the notice by way of application to the court; and the applicant shall, not later than the lodging of that application, serve a copy of his application on the creditor, and on any other party on whom the notice has been served by the creditor.

(2) On any such application the court, after hearing the parties and making such inquiry as it may think fit, may order the notice appealed against to be set aside, in whole or in part, or otherwise to be varied, or to be upheld.

(3) The respondent in any such application may make a counter-application craving for any of the remedies conferred on him by this Act or by any other enactment relating to heritable securities, and the court may grant any such remedy as aforesaid as it may think proper.

(4) For the purposes of such a counter-application as aforesaid, a certificate which conforms with the requirements of Schedule 7 to this Act may be lodged in court by the creditor, and that certificate shall be *prima facie* evidence of the facts directed by the said Schedule to be contained therein.

23 Rights and duties of parties after service of notice of default to which objection is not taken, or where the notice is not set aside

(1) Where a person does not object to a notice of default in accordance with the provisions of the last foregoing section, or where he has so objected and the notice has been upheld or varied under that section, it shall be his duty to comply with any requirement, due to be performed or fulfilled by him, contained in the notice or, as the case may be, in the notice as so varied.

(2) Subject to the provisions of section 21(4) of this Act, where a person fails to comply as aforesaid, the creditor, subject to the next following subsection, may proceed to exercise such of his rights on default under standard condition 10(2), (6) and (7) as he may consider appropriate.

(3) At any time after the expiry of the period stated in a notice of default, or in a notice varied as aforesaid, but before the conclusion of any enforceable contract to sell the security subjects, or any part thereof, by virtue of the last foregoing subsection, the debtor or proprietor [(being in either case a person entitled to redeem the security)] may, subject to any agreement to the contrary, redeem the security without the necessity of observance of any requirement as to notice.

24 Application by creditor to court for remedies on default

(1) Without prejudice to his proceeding by way of notice of default in respect of a default within the meaning of standard condition 9(1)(b), a creditor in a standard security, where the debtor is in default within the meaning of that standard condition or standard condition 9(1)(c), may apply to the court for warrant to exercise any of the remedies which he is entitled to exercise on a default within the meaning of standard condition 9(1)(a).

(2) For the purposes of such an application as aforesaid in respect of a default within the meaning of standard condition 9(1)(b), a certificate which conforms with the requirements of Schedule 7 to this Act may be lodged in court by the creditor, and that certificate shall be *prima facie* evidence of the facts directed by the said Schedule to be contained therein.

[(3) Where the creditor applies to the court under subsection (1) above, he shall, if the standard security is over [land or a real right] in land used to any extent for residential purposes—

   (a) serve on the debtor and (where the proprietor is not the debtor) on the proprietor a notice in conformity with Form E of Schedule 6 to this Act, [...]
   (b) serve on the occupier of the security subjects a notice in conformity with Form F of that Schedule. [, and
   (c) give notice of the application to the local authority in whose area the security subjects are situated, unless the creditor is that local authority.]

(4) Notices under subsection (3) above shall be sent by recorded delivery letter addressed—

   (a) in the case of a notice under subsection (3)(a), to the debtor or, as the case may be, the proprietor at his last known address,
   (b) in the case of a notice under subsection (3)(b), to 'The Occupier' at the security subjects.]

25 Exercise of power of sale

A creditor in a standard security having right to sell the security subjects may [subject to sections 37(5)(e) or 40(1) of the Land Reform (Scotland) Act 2003 (asp 2) (prohibition of transfer of land registered under that Act except in accordance with its provisions),] exercise that right either by private bargain or by exposure to sale, and in either event it shall be the duty of the creditor to advertise the sale and to take all reasonable steps to ensure that the price at which all or any of the subjects are sold is the best that can be reasonably obtained.

26 Disposition by creditor on sale

(1) Where a creditor in a standard security has effected a sale of the security subjects, or any part thereof, and grants to the purchaser or his nominee a disposition of the subjects sold thereby, which bears to be in implement of the sale, then, on that disposition being duly recorded, those subjects shall be disburdened of the standard security and of all other heritable securities and diligences ranking *pari passu* with, or postponed to, that security.

(2) Where on a sale as aforesaid the security subjects remain subject to a prior security, the recording of a disposition under the foregoing subsection shall not affect the rights of the creditor in that security, but to the creditor who has effected the sale shall have the like right as the debtor to redeem the security.

27 Application of proceeds of sale

(1) The money which is received by the creditor in a standard security, arising from any sale by him of the security subjects, shall be held by him in trust to be applied by him in accordance with the following order of priority—

(a) first, in payment of all expenses properly incurred by him in connection with the sale, or any attempted sale;

(b) secondly, in payment of the whole amount due under any prior security to which the sale is not made subject;

(c) thirdly, in payment of the whole amount due under the standard security, and in payment, in due proportion, of the whole amount due under a security, if any, ranking *pari passu* with his own security, which has been duly recorded;

(d) fourthly, in payment of any amounts due under any securities with a ranking postponed to that of his own security, according to their ranking, and any residue of the money so received shall be paid to the person entitled to the security subjects at the time of sale, or to any person authorised to give receipts for the proceeds of the sale thereof.

(2) Where owing to the death or absence of any other creditor, or to any other cause, a creditor is unable to obtain a receipt or discharge for any payment he is required to make under the provisions of the foregoing subsection, he may, without prejudice to his liability to account therefor, consign the amount due (so far as ascertainable) in the sheriff court for the person appearing to have the best right thereto; and where consignation is so made, the creditor shall lodge in court a statement of the amount consigned.

(3) A consignation made in pursuance of the last foregoing subsection shall operate as a discharge of the payment of the amount due, and a certificate under the hand of the sheriff clerk shall be sufficient evidence thereof.

28 Foreclosure

(1) Where the creditor in a standard security has exposed the security subjects to sale at a price not exceeding the amount due under the security and under any security ranking prior to, or *pari passu* with, the security, and has failed to find a purchaser, or where, having so failed, he has succeeded in selling only a part of the subjects at a price which is less than the amount due as aforesaid, he may, on the expiration of a period of two months from the date of the first exposure to sale, apply to the court for a decree of foreclosure.

(2) In any application under the last foregoing subsection the creditor shall lodge a statement setting out the whole amount due under the security but, without prejudice to the right of the debtor or of the proprietor to challenge that statement, it shall be sufficient for the purposes of the application for the creditor to establish to the satisfaction of the court that the amount so stated is not less than the price at which the security subjects have been exposed to sale or sold, where part of the subjects has been sold as aforesaid.

(3) Any application under subsection (1) of this section shall be served on the debtor in the standard security, the proprietor of the security subjects (if he is a person other than the debtor) and the creditor in any other heritable security affecting the security subjects as disclosed by a search of the Register of Sasines for a period of twenty years immediately preceding the last date to which the appropriate Minute Book of the said Register has been completed at the time when the application is made [or by an examination of the title sheet of the security subjects in the Land Register of Scotland].

(4) The court may order such intimation and inquiry as it thinks fit and may in its discretion allow the debtor or the proprietor of the security subjects a period not exceeding three months in which to pay the whole amount due under the security and, subject to any such allowance, may—

(a) appoint the security subjects or the unsold part thereof to be re-exposed to sale at a price to be fixed by the court, in which event the creditor in the security may bid and purchase at the sale, or

(b) grant a decree of foreclosure in conformity with the provisions of the next following subsection.

(5) A decree of foreclosure shall contain a declaration that, on the extract of the decree being duly recorded, [any right to redeem the security] has been extinguished and that the creditor has right to the security subjects or the unsold part thereof, described by means of a particular description or by reference to a description thereof as in Schedule D to the Conveyancing (Scotland) Act 1924 or in Schedule G to the Titles to Land Consolidation (Scotland) Act 1868, including a reference to any conditions or clauses affecting the subjects or the unsold part thereof [or in accordance with section 15 of the Land Registration (Scotland) Act 1979]; at the price at which the said subjects were last exposed to sale under deduction of the price received for any part thereof sold, and shall also contain a warrant for recording the extract of the decree in the Register of Sasines.

(6) Upon an extract of the decree of foreclosure being duly recorded, the following provisions of this subsection shall have effect in relation to the security subjects to which the decree relates—

(a) [any right to redeem the security] shall be extinguished, and the creditor shall have right to, and be vested in, the subjects as if he had received an irredeemable disposition thereof duly recorded from the proprietor of the subjects at the date of the recording of the extract of the decree;

(b) the subjects shall be disburdened of the standard security and all securities and diligences postponed thereto;

(c) the creditor who has obtained the decree shall have the like right as the debtor to redeem any security prior to, or *pari passu* with, his own security.

(7) Notwithstanding the due recording of an extract of a decree of foreclosure, any personal obligation of the debtor under the standard security shall remain in full force and effect so far as not extinguished by the price at which the security subjects have been acquired and the price for which any part thereof has been sold.

(8) Where the security subjects or any part thereof have been acquired by a creditor in the security by virtue of a decree of foreclosure under the provisions of this section, the title thereto of the creditor shall not be challengeable on the ground of any irregularity in the proceedings for foreclosure or on calling-up or default which preceded it; but nothing in the provisions of this subsection shall affect the competency of any claim for damages in respect of such proceedings against the creditor.

29 Procedure

(1) The court for the purposes of this Part of this Act, and for the operation of section 11 of the Heritable Securities (Scotland) Act 1894 (application by *pari passu* creditor to sell), in relation to a standard security, shall be the sheriff having jurisdiction over any part of the security subjects, and the sheriff shall be deemed to have such jurisdiction whatever the value of the subjects.

30 Interpretation of Part II

(1) In this Part of this Act, unless the context otherwise requires, the following expressions have the meanings hereby respectively assigned to them, that is to say—

'creditor' and 'debtor' shall include any successor in title, assignee or representative of a creditor or debtor;

'debt' and 'creditor' and 'debtor', in relation to a standard security, have the meanings assigned to them by section 9(8) of this Act;

'duly recorded' means recorded in the appropriate division of the General Register of Sasines;

'exposure to sale' means exposure to sale by public roup, and exposed or re-exposed to sale shall be construed accordingly;

'heritable security' has the meaning assigned to it by the said section 9(8);

['real right in land' has the meaning assigned to it by the said section 9(8)];

'Register of Sasines' means the appropriate division of the General Register of Sasines;

'the standard conditions' are the conditions (whether varied or not) referred to in section 11(2) of this Act;

'whole amount due' has the meaning assigned to it by section 18(4) of this Act.

(2) For the purpose of construing this Part of this Act in relation to the creation of a security over a registered lease and to any subsequent transactions connected with that security, the following expressions shall have the meanings hereby respectively assigned to them, that is to say—

'conveyance' or 'disposition' means assignation;

'convey' or 'dispone' means assign;

[...]

'proprietor' means lessee;

'security subjects' means a registered lease subject to a security.

31 Saving

Nothing in the provisions of this Part of this Act shall affect the validity of any heritable security within the meaning of this Part which has been duly recorded before the commencement of this Act, and any such security may be dealt with, and shall be as capable of being enforced, as if this Part had not been passed.

32 Application of enactments

The provisions of any enactment relating to a bond and disposition or assignation in security shall apply to a standard security, except in so far as such provisions are inconsistent with the provisions of this Part of this Act, but, without prejudice to the generality of that exception, the enactments specified in Schedule 8 to this Act shall not so apply.

Sections 9 and 10   SCHEDULE 2

FORMS OF STANDARD SECURITY

FORM A

[To be used where the personal obligation is included in the deed]

I, A.B. (*designation*), hereby undertake to pay to C.D. (*designation*), the sum of £   (*or* a maximum sum of £   ) *or* all sums due and that may become due by me to the said C.D. in respect of .... (*here specify the matter for which the undertaking is granted*)) with-interest from .... (*or* from the respective times of advance) at .... percentum per annum (*or otherwise as the case may be*) (annually, half-yearly, *or otherwise as the case may be*) on .... in each year commencing on ....; For which I grant a standard security in favour of the said C.D. over ALL and WHOLE (*here describe the security subjects as indicated in* Note 1 hereto): The standard conditions specified in Schedule 3 to the Conveyancing and Feudal Reform (Scotland) Act 1970, and any lawful variation thereof operative for the time being, shall apply: And I grant warrandice: And I consent to registration for execution.

[To be attested]

FORM B

[To be used where the personal obligation is constituted in a separate instrument or instruments]

I, A.B. (*designation*) hereby in security of (*here specify the nature of the debt or obligation in respect of which the security is given and the instrument(s) by which it is constituted in such manner as will identify these instruments*) grant a standard security in favour of C.D. (*designation*) over ALL and WHOLE (*here describe the security subjects as indicated in Note 1 hereto*): The standard conditions specified in Schedule 3 to the Conveyancing and Feudal Reform (Scotland) Act 1970, and any lawful variation thereof operative for the time being, shall apply: And I grant warrandice.

[To be attested]

NOTES TO SCHEDULE 2

[*Note 1.*—The security subjects shall be described sufficiently to identify them; but this note is without prejudice to any additional requirement imposed as respects any register.]

Note 2.—Where the grantor has not a recorded title to the security subjects, insert after the description thereof a clause of deduction of title as follows:—*Which subjects* (or [. . .] *lease* (or *tack*) or, as the case may be) *were last vested* (or *are part of the subjects last vested*) *in E.F. whose title thereto was recorded in the Register for* .... (or the said Register of Sasines) on .... (or, if the last [recorded title] has already been mentioned, say *in the said E.F. as aforesaid), and from whom I acquired right by* (here specify shortly the writ or writs by which that right was so acquired).

Note 3.—Where the grantor of a standard security has granted a conveyance *ex facie* absolute of the security subjects, or any part thereof, that conveyance shall be referred to in accordance with Note 5 to this Schedule. In any such case:—(a) where the grantor [has a recorded title to] the security subjects, no clause of deduction of title is required in the standard security, (b) where the grantor [does not have a recorded title to] the security subjects but has right thereto by virtue of an unrecorded title insert in the standard security after the description of the security subjects a clause of deduction of title as follows.—*Which subjects* (or [...] *lease* (or *tack*) or, as the case may be) *were formerly vested in* (or *are part of the subjects formerly vested in*) (give name of person [who last had a recorded title to] the subjects before the grantor acquired right thereto) *whose title thereto was recorded in the Register for* .... (or *the said Register of Sasines*) on .... (or if such [recorded title] has already been mentioned say *in the said* .... *as aforesaid) and from whom I acquired right by* (here specify shortly the writ or writs by which that right was so acquired).

Note 4.—Where it is desired to vary any of the standard conditions contained in Schedule 3 to this Act, such variations shall be effected either by an instrument or instruments other than the standard security, and any such instrument shall not require to be recorded in the Register of Sasines or by inserting in the standard security after the description of the security subjects (and after the clause of deduction of title, if any) *And I agree that the standard conditions shall be varied to the effect that* (here insert particulars of the variations desired).

(As regards future variations, see section 16 of, and Form E and Notes 5 and 6 in Schedule 4 to, this Act.)

Note 5.—Where the security subjects are burdened by any other standard security or heritable security, or by any security by way of *ex facie* absolute conveyance which ranks prior to the standard security which is being granted, insert immediately before the clause of warrandice the following:—*But the security hereby granted is subject to* (here specify any deed by which such preferable rights were created and any deed modifying or altering such rights), and amend the clause of warrandice to read *And, subject as aforesaid, I grant warrandice.* Where the standard security is to rank prior or postponed to, or *pari passu* with, any other existing heritable security or any other standard security, a ranking clause may be inserted in appropriate terms immediately prior to the warrandice clause, and the warrandice clause shall, where necessary, be qualified accordingly.

Note 6.—Where a standard security is granted in Form A for a fluctuating or uncertain amount, provisions for ascertaining the amount due at any time may be inserted immediately prior to the clause of granting of the security, and the registration clause shall, where necessary, be amended accordingly.

Note 7.—In the case of a standard security for a non-monetary obligation, the forms in this Schedule shall be adapted as appropriate.

Section 11   SCHEDULE 3

THE STANDARD CONDITIONS

Maintenance and repair
  1. It shall be an obligation on the debtor—
      (a) to maintain the security subjects in good and sufficient repair to the reasonable satisfaction of the creditor;
      (b) to permit, after seven clear days notice in writing, the creditor or his agent to enter upon the security subjects at all reasonable times to examine the condition thereof;
      (c) to make all necessary repairs and make good all defects in pursuance of his obligation under head (a) of this condition within such reasonable period as the creditor may require by notice in writing.

Completion of buildings etc. and prohibition of alterations etc.

  2. It shall be an obligation on the debtor—
      (a) to complete, as soon as may be practicable, any unfinished buildings or works forming part of the security subjects to the reasonable satisfaction of the creditor;
      (b) not to demolish, alter or add to any buildings or works forming part of the security subjects, except in accordance with the terms of a prior written consent of the creditor and in compliance with any consent, licence or approval required by law;
      (c) to exhibit to the creditor at his request evidence of that consent, licence or approval.

Observance of conditions in title, payment of duties, charges, etc., and general compliance with requirements of law relating to security subjects
  3. It shall be an obligation on the debtor—
      (a) to observe any condition or perform any obligation in respect of the security subjects lawfully binding on him in relation to the security subjects;
      (b) to make due and punctual payment of any ground burden, teind, stipend, or standard charge, and any rates, taxes and other public burdens, and any other payments exigible in respect of the security subjects;
      (c) to comply with any requirement imposed upon him in relation to the security subjects by virtue of any enactment.

Planning notices, etc.

4. It shall be an obligation on the debtor—

    (a) where he has received any notice or order, issued or made by virtue of the Town and Country Planning (Scotland) Acts 1947 to 1969 or any amendment thereof, or any proposal so made for the making or issuing of any such notice or order, or any other notice or document affecting or likely to affect the security subjects, to give to the creditor, within fourteen days of the receipt of that notice, order or proposal, full particulars thereof;

    (b) to take, as soon as practicable, all reasonable or necessary steps to comply with such a notice or order or, as the case may be, duly to object thereto;

    (c) in the event of the creditor so requiring, to object or to join with the creditor in objecting to any such notice or order or in making representations against any proposal therefor.

Insurance

5. It shall be an obligation on the debtor—

    (a) to insure the security subjects or, at the option of the creditor, to permit the creditor to insure the security subjects in the names of the creditor and the debtor to the extent of the market value thereof against the risk of fire and such other risks as the creditor may reasonably require;

    (b) to deposit any policy of insurance effected by the debtor for the aforesaid purpose with the creditor;

    (c) to pay any premium due in respect of any such policy, and, where the creditor so requests, to exhibit a receipt therefor not later than the fourteenth day after the renewal date of the policy;

    (d) to intimate to the creditor, within fourteen days of the occurrence, any occurrence which may give rise to a claim under the policy, and to authorise the creditor to negotiate the settlement of the claim;

    (e) without prejudice to any obligation to the contrary enforceable against him, to comply with any reasonable requirement of the creditor as to the application of any sum received in respect of such a claim;

    (f) to refrain from any act or omission which would invalidate the policy.

Restriction on letting

6. It shall be an obligation on the debtor not to let, or agree to let, the security subjects, or any part thereof, without the prior consent in writing of the creditor, and 'to let' in this condition includes to sub-let.

General power of creditor to perform obligations etc. on failure of debtor and power to charge debtor

7. (1) The creditor shall be entitled to perform any obligation imposed by the standard conditions on the debtor, which the debtor has failed to perform.

(2) Where it is necessary for the performance of any obligation as aforesaid, the creditor may, after giving seven clear days notice in writing to the debtor, enter upon the security subjects at all reasonable times.

(3) All expenses and charges (including any interest thereon), reasonably incurred by the creditor in the exercise of a right conferred by this condition, shall be recoverable from the debtor and shall be deemed to be secured by the security subjects under the standard security, and the rate of any such interest shall be the rate in force at the relevant time in respect of advances secured by the security, or, where no such rate is prescribed, shall be the bank rate in force at the relevant time.

Calling-up

8. The creditor shall be entitled, subject to the terms of the security and to any requirement of law, to call-up a standard security in the manner prescribed by section 19 of this Act.

Default

9. (1) The debtor shall he held to be in default in any of the following circumstances, that is to say—

    (a) where a calling-up notice in respect of the security has been served and has not been complied with;

    (b) where there has been a failure to comply with any other requirement arising out of the security;

    (c) where the proprietor of the security subjects has become insolvent.

(2) For the purposes of this condition, the proprietor shall be taken to be insolvent if—

    (a) he has become notour bankrupt, or he has executed a trust deed for behoof of, or has made a composition contract or arrangement with, his creditors;

    (b) he has died and a judicial factor has been appointed under section [11A of the Judicial Factors (Scotland) Act 1889] to divide his insolvent estate among his creditors, [or his estate falls to be administered in accordance with an order under section 421 of the Insolvency Act 1986];

    (c) where the proprietor is a company, a winding-up order has been made with respect to it, or a resolution for voluntary winding-up (other than a Members' voluntary winding-up) has been passed with respect to it, or a receiver or manager of its undertaking has been duly appointed, or possession has been taken, by or on behalf of the holders of any debentures secured by a floating charge, of any property of the company comprised in or subject to the charge.

Rights of creditor on default

10. (1) Where the debtor is in default, the creditor may, without prejudice to his exercising any other remedy arising from the contract to which the standard security relates, exercise, in accordance with the provisions of Part II of this Act and of any other enactment applying to standard securities, such of the remedies specified in the following sub-paragraphs of this standard condition as he may consider appropriate.

(2) He may proceed to sell the security subjects or any part thereof.

(3) He may enter into possession of the security subjects and may receive or recover [...], as the case may be, the rents of those subjects or any part thereof.

(4) Where he has entered into possession as aforesaid, he may let the security subjects or any part thereof.

(5) Where he has entered into possession as aforesaid there shall be transferred to him all the rights of the debtor in relation to the granting of leases or rights of occupancy over the security subjects and to the management and maintenance of those subjects.

(6) He may effect all such repairs and may make good such defects as are necessary to maintain the security subjects in good and sufficient repair, and may effect such reconstruction, alteration and improvement on the subjects as would be expected of a prudent proprietor to maintain the market value of the subjects, and for the aforesaid purposes may enter on the subjects at all reasonable times.

(7) He may apply to the court for a decree of foreclosure.

Exercise of right of redemption

11. (1) The debtor shall be entitled to exercise his [right (if any) to redeem the security on giving notice] of his intention so to do, being a notice in writing (hereinafter referred to as a 'notice of redemption').

(2) Nothing in the provisions of [this Act] shall preclude a creditor from waiving the necessity for a notice of redemption, or from agreeing to a period of notice of less than [that to which he is entitled].

(3) (a) A notice of redemption may be delivered to the creditor or sent by registered post or recorded delivery to him at his last known address, and an acknowledgment signed by the creditor or his agent or a certificate of postage by the person giving the notice accompanied by the postal receipt shall be sufficient evidence of such notice having been given.

(b) If the address of the creditor is not known, or if the packet containing the notice of redemption is returned to the sender with intimation that it could not be delivered, a notice of redemption may be sent to the Extractor of the Court of Session and an acknowledgment of receipt by him shall be sufficient evidence of such notice having been given.

(c) A notice of redemption sent by post shall be held to have been given on the day next after the day of posting.

(4) When a notice of redemption states that a specified amount will be repaid, and it is subsequently ascertained that the whole amount due to be repaid is more or less than the amount specified in the notice, the notice shall nevertheless be effective as a notice of repayment of the amount due as subsequently ascertained.

(5) [Where the debtor has exercised a right to redeem] the whole amount due, or [has performed] the whole obligations of the debtor under the contract to which the security relates, the creditor shall grant a discharge in the terms prescribed in section 17 of this Act.

12. The debtor shall be personally liable to the creditor for the whole expenses of the preparation and execution of the standard security and any variation, restriction and discharge thereof and, where any of those deeds are recorded, the recording thereof, and all expenses reasonably incurred by the creditor in calling-up the security and realising or attempting to realise the security subjects, or any part thereof, and exercising any other powers conferred upon him by the security.

Interpretation

In this Schedule, where the debtor is not the proprietor of the security subjects, 'debtor' means 'proprietor', except

(a) in standard conditions 9(1), 10(1) and 12, and

(b) in standard condition 11, where 'debtor' includes the proprietor.

Carriage of Goods by Sea Act 1971
(1971, c. 19)

An Act to amend the law with respect to the carriage of goods by sea.   [8th April 1971]

1   Application of Hague Rules as amended

(1) In this Act, 'the Rules' means the International Convention for the unification of certain rules of law relating to bills of lading signed at Brussels on 25th August 1924, as amended by the Protocol signed at Brussels on 23rd February 1968 [and by the protocol signed at Brussels on 21 December 1979].

(2) The provisions of the Rules, as set out in the Schedule to this Act, shall have the force of law.

(3) Without prejudice to subsection (2) above, the said provisions shall have effect (and have the force of law) in relation to and in connection with the carriage of goods by sea in ships where the port of shipment is a port in the United Kingdom, whether or not the carriage is between ports in two different States within the meaning of Article X of the Rules.

(4) Subject to subsection (6) below, nothing in this section shall be taken as applying anything in the Rules to any contract for the carriage of goods by sea, unless the contract expressly or by implication provides for the issue of a bill of lading or any similar document of title.

(5) […]

(6) Without prejudice to Article X (c) of the Rules, the Rules shall have the force of law in relation to—

    (a) any bill of lading if the contract contained in or evidenced by it expressly provides that the Rules shall govern the contract, and

    (b) any receipt which is a non-negotiable document marked as such if the contract contained in or evidenced by it is a contract for the carriage of goods by sea which expressly provides that the Rules are to govern the contract as if the receipt were a bill of lading, but subject, where paragraph (b) applies, to any necessary modifications and in particular with the omission in Article III of the Rules of the second sentence of paragraph 4 and of paragraph 7.

(7) If and so far as the contract contained in or evidenced by a bill of lading or receipt within paragraph (a) or (b) of subsection (6) above applies to deck cargo or live animals, the Rules as given the force of law by that subsection shall have effect as if Article I(c) did not exclude deck cargo and live animals.

In this subsection 'deck cargo' means cargo which by the contract of carriage is stated as being carried on deck and is so carried.

2   Contracting States, etc.

(1) If Her Majesty by Order in Council certifies to the following effect, that is to say, that for the purposes of the Rules—

    (a) a State specified in the Order is a contracting State, or is a contracting State in respect of any place or territory so specified; or

    (b) any place or territory specified in the Order forms part of a State so specified (whether a contracting State or not),

the Order shall, except so far as it has been superseded by a subsequent Order, be conclusive evidence of the matters so certified.

(2) An Order in Council under this section may be varied or revoked by a subsequent Order in Council.

3   Absolute warranty of seaworthiness not to be implied in contracts to which Rules apply

There shall not be implied in any contract for the carriage of goods by sea to which the Rules apply by virtue of this Act any absolute undertaking by the carrier of the goods to provide a seaworthy ship.

4   Application of Act to British possessions, etc.

(1) Her Majesty may by Order in Council direct that this Act shall extend, subject to such exceptions, adaptations and modifications as may be specified in the Order, to all or any of the following territories, that is—

    (a) any colony (not being a colony for whose external relations a country other than the United Kingdom is responsible),

    (b) any country outside Her Majesty's dominions in which Her Majesty has jurisdiction in right of Her Majesty's Government of the United Kingdom.

(2) An Order in Council under this section may contain such transitional and other consequential and incidental provisions as appear to Her Majesty to be expedient, including provisions amending or repealing any legislation about the carriage of goods by sea forming part of the law of any of the territories mentioned in paragraphs (a) and (b) above.

(3) An Order in Council under this section may be varied or revoked by a subsequent Order in Council.

5   Extension of application of Rules to carriage from ports in British possessions, etc.

(1) Her Majesty may by Order in Council provide that section 1(3) of this Act shall have effect as if the reference therein to the United Kingdom included a reference to all or any of the following territories, that is—

(a) the Isle of Man;

(b) any of the Channel Islands specified in the Order;

(c) any colony specified in the Order (not being a colony for whose external relations a country other than the United Kingdom is responsible);

(d) any associated state (as defined by section 1(3) of the West Indies Act 1967) specified in the Order;

(e) any country specified in the Order, being a country outside Her Majesty's dominions in which Her Majesty has jurisdiction in right of Her Majesty's Government of the United Kingdom.

(2) An Order in Council under this section may be varied or revoked by a subsequent Order in Council.

6 Supplemental

(1) This Act may be cited as the Carriage of Goods by Sea Act 1971.

(2) It is hereby declared that this Act extends to Northern Ireland.

(3) The following enactments shall be repealed, that is—

(a) the Carriage of Goods by Sea Act 1924,

(b) section 12(4)(a) of the Nuclear Installations Act 1965, and without prejudice to section 38(1) of the Interpretation Act 1889, the reference to the said Act of 1924 in section 1(1)(i)(ii) of the Hovercraft Act 1968 shall include a reference to this Act.

(4) It is hereby declared that for the purposes of Article VIII of the Rules [section 18 of the Merchant Shipping Act 1979 (which] entirely exempts shipowners and others in certain circumstances from liability for loss of, or damage to, goods) is a provision relating to limitation of liability.

(5) This Act shall come into force on such day as Her Majesty may by Order in Council appoint, and, for the purposes of the transition from the law in force immediately before the day appointed under this subsection to the provisions of this Act, the Order appointing the day may provide that those provisions shall have effect subject to such transitional provisions as may be contained in the Order.

SCHEDULE

THE HAGUE RULES AS AMENDED BY THE
BRUSSELS PROTOCOL 1968

Article I

In these Rules the following words are employed, with the meanings set out below:—

(a) 'Carrier' includes the owner or the charterer who enters into a contract of carriage with a shipper.

(b) 'Contract of carriage' applies only to contracts of carriage covered by a bill of lading or any similar document of title, in so far as such document relates to the carriage of goods by sea, including any bill of lading or any similar document as aforesaid issued under or pursuant to a charter party from the moment at which such bill of lading or similar document of title regulates the relations between a carrier and a holder of the same.

(c) 'Goods' includes goods, wares, merchandise, and articles of every kind whatsoever except live animals and cargo which by the contract of carriage is stated as being carried on deck and is so carried.

(d) 'Ship' means any vessel used for the carriage of goods by sea.

(e) (e) 'Carriage of goods' covers the period from the time when the goods are loaded on to the time they are discharged from the ship.

Article II

Subject to the provisions of Article VI, under every contract of carriage of goods by sea the carrier, in relation to the loading, handling, stowage, carriage, custody, care and discharge of such goods, shall be subject to the responsibilities and liabilities, and entitled to the rights and immunities hereinafter set forth.

Article III

(1) The carrier shall be bound before and at the beginning of the voyage to exercise due diligence to—

(a) Make the ship seaworthy.

(b) Properly man, equip and supply the ship.

(c) Make the holds, refrigerating and cool chambers, and all other parts of the ship in which goods are carried, fit and safe for their reception, carriage and preservation.

(2) Subject to the provisions of Article IV, the carrier shall properly and carefully load, handle, stow, carry, keep, care for, and discharge the goods carried.

(3) After receiving the goods into his charge the carrier or the master or agent of the carrier shall, on demand of the shipper, issue to the shipper a bill of lading showing among other things—

(a) The leading marks necessary for identification of the goods as the same are furnished in writing by the shipper before the loading of such goods starts, provided such marks are stamped or otherwise shown clearly upon the goods if uncovered, or on the cases or coverings in which such goods are contained, in such a manner as should ordinarily remain legible until the end of the voyage.

(b) Either the number of packages or pieces, or the quantity, or weight, as the case may be, as furnished in writing by the shipper.

(c) The apparent order and condition of the goods. Provided that no carrier, master or agent of the carrier shall be bound to state or show in the bill of lading any marks, number, quantity, or weight which he has reasonable ground for suspecting not accurately to represent the goods actually received, or which he has had no reasonable means of checking.

(4) Such a bill of lading shall be prima facie evidence of the receipt by the carrier of the goods as therein described in accordance with paragraph 3(a), (b) and (c). However, proof to the contrary shall not be admissible when the bill of lading has been transferred to a third party acting in good faith.

(5) The shipper shall be deemed to have guaranteed to the carrier the accuracy at the time of shipment of the marks, number, quantity and weight, as furnished by him, and the shipper shall indemnify the carrier against all loss, damages and expenses arising or resulting from inaccuracies in such particulars. The right of the carrier to such indemnity shall in no way limit his responsibility and liability under the contract of carriage to any person other than the shipper.

(6) Unless notice of loss or damage and the general nature of such loss or damage be given in writing to the carrier or his agent at the port of discharge before or at the time of the removal of the goods into the custody of the person entitled to delivery thereof under the contract of carriage, or, if the loss or damage be not apparent, within three days, such removal shall be prima facie evidence of the delivery by the carrier of the goods as described in the bill of lading.

The notice in writing need not be given if the state of the goods has, at the time of their receipt, been the subject of joint survey or inspection.

Subject to paragraph 6bis the carrier and the ship shall in any event be discharged from all liability whatsoever in respect of the goods, unless suit is brought within one year of their delivery or of the date when they should have been delivered. This period may, however, be extended if the parties so agree after the cause of action has arisen.

In the case of any actual or apprehended loss or damage the carrier and the receiver shall give all reasonable facilities to each other for inspecting and tallying the goods.

(6bis) An action for indemnity against a third person may be brought even after the expiration of the year provided for in the preceding paragraph if brought within the time allowed by the law of the Court seized of the case. However, the time allowed shall be not less than three months, commencing from the day when the person bringing such action for indemnity has settled the claim or has been served with process in the action against himself.

(7) After the goods are loaded the bill of lading to be issued by the carrier, master, or agent of the carrier, to the shipper shall, if the shipper so demands, be a 'shipped' bill of lading, provided that if the shipper shall have previously taken up any document of title to such goods, he shall surrender the same as against the issue of the 'shipped' bill of lading, but at the option of the carrier such document of title may be noted at the port of shipment by the carrier, master, or agent with the name or names of the ship or ships upon which the goods have been shipped and the date or dates of shipment, and when so noted if it shows the particulars mentioned in paragraph 3 of Article III, shall for the purpose of this article be deemed to constitute a 'shipped' bill of lading.

(8) Any clause, covenant, or agreement in a contract of carriage relieving the carrier or the ship from liability for loss or damage to, or in connection with, goods arising from negligence, fault, or failure in the duties and obligations provided in this article or lessening such liability otherwise than as provided in these Rules, shall be null and void and of no effect. A benefit of insurance in favour of the carrier or similar clause shall be deemed to be a clause relieving the carrier from liability.

Article IV

(1) Neither the carrier nor the ship shall be liable for loss or damage arising or resulting from unseaworthiness unless caused by want of due diligence on the part of the carrier to make the ship seaworthy, and to secure that the ship is properly manned, equipped and supplied, and to make the holds, refrigerating and cool chambers and all other parts of the ship in which goods are carried fit and safe for their reception, carriage and preservation in accordance with the provisions of paragraph 1 of Article III. Whenever loss or damage has resulted from unseaworthiness the burden of proving the exercise of due diligence shall be on the carrier or other person claiming exemption under this article.

(2) Neither the carrier nor the ship shall be responsible for loss or damage arising or resulting from—

(a) Act, neglect, or default of the master, mariner, pilot, or the servants of the carrier in the navigation or in the management of the ship.
(b) Fire, unless caused by the actual fault or privity of the carrier.
(c) Perils, dangers and accidents of the sea or other navigable waters.
(d) Act of God.
(e) Act of war.
(f) Act of public enemies.
(g) Arrest or restraint of princes, rulers or people, or seizure under legal process.
(h) Quarantine restrictions.
(i) Act or omission of the shipper or owner of the goods, his agent or representative.
(j) Strikes or lockouts or stoppage or restraint of labour from whatever cause, whether partial or general.
(k) Riots and civil commotions.
(l) Saving or attempting to save life or property at sea.
(m)Wastage in bulk or weight or any other loss or damage arising from inherent defect, quality or vice of the goods.
(n) Insufficiency of packing.
(o) Insufficiency or inadequacy of marks.
(p) Latent defects not discoverable by due diligence.
(q) Any other cause arising without the actual fault or privity of the carrier, or without the fault or neglect of the agents or servants of the carrier, but the burden of proof shall be on the person claiming the benefit of this exception to show that

neither the actual fault or privity of the carrier nor the fault or neglect of the agents or servants of the carrier contributed to the loss or damage.

(3) The shipper shall not be responsible for the loss or damage sustained by the carrier or the ship arising or resulting from any cause without the act, fault or neglect of the shipper, his agents or his servants.

(4) Any deviation in saving or attempting to save life or property at sea or any reasonable deviation shall not be deemed to be an infringement or breach of these Rules or of the contract of carriage, and the carrier shall not be liable for any loss or damage resulting therefrom.

(5) (a) Unless the nature and value of such goods have been declared by the shipper before shipment and inserted in the bill of lading, neither the carrier nor the ship shall in any event be or become liable for any loss or damage to or in connection with the goods in an amount exceeding [666.67 units of account] per package or unit or [2 units of account per kilogramme] of gross weight of the goods lost or damaged, whichever is the higher.

(b) The total amount recoverable shall be calculated by reference to the value of such goods at the place and time at which the goods are discharged from the ship in accordance with the contract or should have been so discharged.

The value of the goods shall be fixed according to the commodity exchange price, or, if there be no such price, according to the current market price, or, if there be no commodity exchange price or current market price, by reference to the normal value of goods of the same kind and quality.

(c) Where a container, pallet or similar article of transport is used to consolidate goods, the number of packages or units enumerated in the bill of lading as packed in such article of transport shall be deemed the number of packages or units for the purpose of this paragraph as far as these packages or units are concerned. Except as aforesaid such article of transport shall be considered the package or unit.

[(d) The unit of account mentioned in this Article is the special drawing right as defined by the International Monetary Fund. The amounts mentioned in sub-paragraph (a) of this paragraph shall be converted into national currency on the basis of the value of that currency on a date to be determined by the law of the court seised of the case.]

(e) Neither the carrier nor the ship shall be entitled to the benefit of the limitation of liability provided for in this paragraph if it is proved that the damage resulted from an act or omission of the carrier done with intent to cause damage, or recklessly and with knowledge that damage would probably result.

(f) The declaration mentioned in sub-paragraph (a) of this paragraph, if embodied in the bill of lading, shall be prima facie evidence, but shall not be binding or conclusive on the carrier.

(g) By agreement between the carrier, master or agent of the carrier and the shipper other maximum amounts than those mentioned in sub-paragraph (a) of this paragraph may be fixed, provided that no maximum amount so fixed shall be less than the appropriate maximum mentioned in that sub-paragraph.

(h) Neither the carrier nor the ship shall be responsible in any event for loss or damage to, or in connection with, goods if the nature or value thereof has been knowingly mis-stated by the shipper in the bill of lading.

(6) Goods of an inflammable, explosive or dangerous nature to the shipment whereof the carrier, master or agent of the carrier has not consented with knowledge of their nature and character, may at any time before discharge be landed at any place, or destroyed or rendered innocuous by the carrier without compensation and the shipper of such goods shall be liable for all damages and expenses directly or indirectly arising out of or resulting from such shipment. If any such goods shipped with such knowledge and consent shall become a danger to the ship or cargo, they may in like manner be landed at any place, or destroyed or

rendered innocuous by the carrier without liability on the part of the carrier except to general average, if any.

Article IV bis

(1) The defences and limits of liability provided for in these Rules shall apply in any action against the carrier in respect of loss or damage to goods covered by a contract of carriage whether the action be founded in contract or in tort.

(2) If such an action is brought against a servant or agent of the carrier (such servant or agent not being an independent contractor), such servant or agent shall be entitled to avail himself of the defences and limits of liability which the carrier is entitled to invoke under these Rules.

(3) The aggregate of the amounts recoverable from the carrier, and such servants and agents, shall in no case exceed the limit provided for in these Rules.

(4) Nevertheless, a servant or agent of the carrier shall not be entitled to avail himself of the provisions of this article, if it is proved that the damage resulted from an act or omission of the servant or agent done with intent to cause damage or recklessly and with knowledge that damage would probably result.

Article V

A carrier shall be at liberty to surrender in whole or in part all or any of his rights and immunities or to increase any of his responsibilities and obligations under these Rules, provided such surrender or increase shall be embodied in the bill of lading issued to the shipper. The provisions of the Rules shall not be applicable to charter parties, but if bills of lading are issued in the case of a ship under a charter party they shall comply with the terms of these Rules. Nothing in these Rules shall be held to prevent the insertion in a bill of lading of any lawful provisions regarding general average.

Article VI

Notwithstanding the provisions of the preceding articles, a carrier, master or agent of the carrier and a shipper shall in regard to any particular goods be at liberty to enter into any agreement in any terms as to the responsibility and liability of the carrier for such goods, and as to the rights and immunities of the carrier in respect of such goods, or his obligation as to seaworthiness, so far as this stipulation is not contrary to public policy, or the care or diligence of his servants or agents in regard to the loading, handling, stowage, carriage, custody, care and discharge of the goods carried by sea, provided that in this case no bill of lading has been or shall be issued and that the terms agreed shall be embodied in a receipt which shall be a non-negotiable document and shall be marked as such.

Any agreement so entered into shall have full legal effect.

Provided that this article shall not apply to ordinary commercial shipment made in the ordinary course of trade, but only to other shipments where the character or condition of the property to be carried or the circumstances, terms and conditions under which the carriage is to be performed are such as reasonably to justify a special agreement.

Article VII

Nothing herein contained shall prevent a carrier or a shipper from entering into any agreement, stipulation, condition, reservation or exemption as to the responsibility and liability of the carrier or the ship for the loss or damage to, or in connection with, the custody and care and handling of goods prior to the loading on, and subsequent to the discharge from, the ship on which the goods are carried by sea.

Article VIII

The provisions of these Rules shall not affect the rights and obligations of the carrier under any statute for the time being in force relating to the limitation of the liability of owners of sea-going vessels.

Article IX

These rules shall not affect the provisions of any international Convention or national law governing liability for nuclear damage.

Article X

The provisions of these Rules shall apply to every bill of lading relating to the carriage of goods between ports in two different States if:

    (a) the bill of lading is issued in a contracting State, or

    (b) the carriage is from a port in a contracting State, or

    (c) the contract contained in or evidenced by the bill of lading provides that these Rules or legislation of any State giving effect to them are to govern the contract, whatever may be the nationality of the ship, the carrier, the shipper, the consignee, or any other interested person.

[*The last two paragraphs of this article are not reproduced. They require contracting States to apply the Rules to bills of lading mentioned in the article and authorise them to apply the Rules to other bills of lading.*]

[*Articles 11 to 16 of the international Convention for the unification of certain rules of law relating to bills of lading signed at Brussels on August 25 1974 are not reproduced. They deal with the coming into force of the Convention, procedure for ratification, accession and denunciation and the right to call for a fresh conference to consider amendments to the Rules contained in the Convention.*]

Unsolicited Goods and Services Act 1971
(1971, c. 30)

An Act to make provision for the greater protection of persons receiving unsolicited goods, and to amend the law with respect to charges for entries in directories.   [12th May 1971]

2 Demands and threats regarding payment

(1) A person who, not having reasonable cause to believe there is a right to payment, in the course of any trade or business makes a demand for payment, or asserts a present or prospective right to payment, for what he knows are unsolicited goods sent (after the commencement of this Act) to another person with a view to his acquiring them [for the purposes of his trade or business], shall be guilty of an offence and on summary conviction shall be liable to a fine not exceeding £200.

(2) A person who, not having reasonable cause to believe there is a right to payment in the course of any trade or business and with a view to obtaining any payment for what he knows are unsolicited goods sent as aforesaid—

    (a) threatens to bring any legal proceedings; or

    (b) places or causes to be placed the name of any person on a list of defaulters or debtors or threatens to do so; or

    (c) invokes or causes to be invoked any other collection procedure or threatens to do so,

shall be guilty of an offence and shall be liable on summary conviction to a fine not exceeding £400.

3 Directory entries

[(1) A person ('the purchaser') shall not be liable to make any payment, and shall be entitled to recover any payment made by him, by way of charge for including or arranging for the inclusion in a directory of an entry relating to that person or his trade or business, unless—

    (a) there has been signed by the purchaser or on his behalf an order complying with this section,

    (b) there has been signed by the purchaser or on his behalf a note complying with this section of his agreement to the charge and before the note was signed, a copy of it was supplied, for retention by him, to him or a person acting on his behalf, [. . .]

(c) there has been transmitted by the purchaser or a person acting on his behalf an electronic communication which includes a statement that the purchaser agrees to the charge and the relevant condition is satisfied in relation to that communication[, or

(d) the charge arises under a contract in relation to which the conditions in section 3B(1) (renewed and extended contracts) are met].

(2) A person shall be guilty of an offence punishable on summary conviction with a fine not exceeding £400 if, in a case where a payment in respect of a charge would [. . .] be recoverable from him in accordance with the terms of subsection (1) above, he demands payment, or asserts a present or prospective right to payment, of the charge or any part of it, without knowing or having reasonable cause to believe [that—

(a) the entry to which the charge relates was ordered in accordance with this section,

(b) a proper note of the agreement has been duly signed, or

(c) the requirements set out in subsection (1)(c) or (d) above have been met.]

(3) For the purposes of [this section—

(a) an order for an entry in a directory must be made by means of an order form or other stationery belonging to the purchaser, which may be sent electronically but which must bear his name and address (or one or more of his addresses); and

(b) the note of a person's agreement to a charge must—

    (i) specify the particulars set out in Part 1 of the Schedule to the Regulatory Reform (Unsolicited Goods and Services Act 1971) (Directory Entries and Demands for Payment) Order 2005, and

    (ii) give reasonable particulars of the entry in respect of which the charge would be payable.]

[(3A) In relation to an electronic communication which includes a statement that the purchaser agrees to a charge for including or arranging the inclusion in a directory of any entry, the relevant condition is that—

(a) before the electronic communication was transmitted the information referred to in subsection (3B) below was communicated to the purchaser, and

(b) the electronic communication can readily be produced and retained in a visible and legible form.

(3B) that information is—

(a) the following particulars—

    (i) the amount of the charge;

    (ii) the name of the directory or proposed directory;

    (iii) the name of the person producing the directory;

    (iv) the geographic address at which that person is established;

    (v) if the directory is or is to be available in printed form, the proposed date of publication of the directory or of the issue in which the entry is to be included;

    (vi) if the directory or the issue in which the entry is to be included is to be put on sale, the price at which it is to be offered for sale and the minimum number of copies which are to be available for sale;

    (vii) if the directory or the issue in which the entry is to be included is to be distributed free of charge (whether or not it is also to be put on sale), the minimum number of copies which are to be so distributed;

    (viii) if the directory is or is to be available in a form other than in printed form, adequate details of how it may be accessed; and

(b) reasonable particulars of the entry in respect of which the charge would be payable.

(3C) In this section 'electronic communication' has the same meaning as in the Electronic Communications Act 2000.]

(4) Nothing in this section shall apply to a payment due under a contract entered into before the commencement of this Act, or entered into by the acceptance of an offer made before that commencement.

[3B   Renewed and extended contracts

(1) The conditions referred to in section 3(1)(d) above are met in relation to a contract ('the new contract') if—

    (a) a person ('the purchaser') has entered into an earlier contract ('the earlier contract') for including or arranging for the inclusion in a particular issue or version of a directory ('the earlier directory') of an entry ('the earlier entry') relating to him or his trade or business;

    (b) the purchaser was liable to make a payment by way of a charge arising under the earlier contract for including or arranging for the inclusion of the earlier entry in the earlier directory;

    (c) the new contract is a contract for including or arranging for the inclusion in a later issue or version of a directory ('the later directory') of an entry ('the later entry') relating to the purchaser or his trade or business;

    (d) the form, content and distribution of the later directory is materially the same as the form, content and distribution of the earlier directory;

    (e) the form and content of the later entry is materially the same as the form and content of the earlier entry;

    (f) if the later directory is published other than in electronic form—

        (i)   the earlier directory was the last, or the last but one, issue or version of the directory to be published before the later directory, and

        (ii) the date of publication of the later directory is not more than 13 months after the date of publication of the earlier directory;

    (g) if the later directory is published in electronic form, the first date on which the new contract requires the later entry to be published is not more than the relevant period after the last date on which the earlier contract required the earlier entry to be published;

    (h) if it was a term of the earlier contract that the purchaser renew or extend the contract—

        (i)   before the start of the new contract the relevant publisher has given notice in writing to the purchaser containing the information set out in Part 3 of the Schedule to the Regulatory Reform (Unsolicited Goods and Services Act 1971) (Directory Entries and Demands for Payment) Order 2005; and

        (ii) the purchaser has not written to the relevant publisher withdrawing his agreement to the renewal or extension of the earlier contract within the period of 21 days starting when he receives the notice referred to in sub-paragraph (i); and

    (i) if the parties to the earlier contract and the new contract are different—

        (i)   the parties to both contracts have entered into a novation agreement in respect of the earlier contract; or

        (ii) the relevant publisher has given the purchaser the information set out in Part 4 of the Schedule to the Regulatory Reform (Unsolicited Goods and Services Act 1971) (Directory Entries and Demands for Payment) Order 2005.

(2) For the purposes of subsection (1)(d) and (e), the form, content or distribution of the later directory, or the form or content of the later entry, shall be taken to be materially the same as that of the earlier directory or the earlier entry (as the case may be), if a reasonable person in the position of the purchaser would—

    (a) view the two as being materially the same; or

    (b) view that of the later directory or the later entry as being an improvement on that of the earlier directory or the earlier entry.

(3) For the purposes of subsection (1)(g) 'the relevant period' means the period of 13 months or (if shorter) the period of time between the first and last dates on which the earlier contract required the earlier entry to be published.

(4) For the purposes of subsection (1)(h) and (i) 'the relevant publisher' is the person with whom the purchaser has entered into the new contract.

(5) The information referred to in subsection (1)(i)(ii) must be given to the purchaser prior to the conclusion of the new contract.]

4   Unsolicited publications

(1) A person shall be guilty of an offence if he sends or causes to be sent to another person any book, magazine or leaflet (or advertising material for any such publication which he knows or ought reasonably to know is unsolicited and which describes or illustrates human sexual techniques.

(2) A person found guilty of an offence under this section shall be liable on summary conviction to a fine not exceeding £100 for a first offence and to a fine not exceeding £400 for any subsequent offence.

(3) A prosecution for an offence under this section shall not in England and Wales be instituted except by, or with the consent of, the Director of Public Prosecutions.

5   Offences by corporations

(1) Where an offence under this Act which has been committed by a body corporate is proved to have been committed with the consent or connivance of, or to be attributable to any neglect on the part of, any director, manager, secretary, or other similar officer of the body corporate, or of any person who was purporting to act in any such capacity, he as well as the body corporate shall be guilty of that offence and shall be liable to be proceeded against and punished accordingly.

(2) Where the affairs of a body corporate are managed by its members, this section shall apply in relation to the acts or defaults of a member in connection with his functions of management as if he were a director of the body corporate.

6   Interpretation

(1) In this Act, unless the context or subject matter otherwise requires,—

'acquire' includes hire;

'send' includes deliver, and 'sender' shall be construed accordingly;

'unsolicited' means, in relation to goods sent to any person, that they are sent without any prior request made by him or on his behalf.

[(2) For the purposes of the Act, any invoice or similar document stating the amount of any payment shall be regarded as asserting a right to the payment unless it complies with the conditions set out in Part 2 of the Schedule to the Regulatory Reform (Unsolicited Goods and Services Act 1971) (Directory Entries and Demands for Payment) Order 2005.]

[(3) Nothing in sections 3 or 3B shall affect the rights of any consumer under the Consumer Protection (Distance Selling) Regulations 2000.]

Fair Trading Act 1973
(1973, c. 41)

An Act to provide for the appointment of a Director General of Fair Trading and of a Consumer Protection Advisory Committee, and to confer on the Director General and the Committee so appointed, on the Secretary of State, on the Restrictive Practices Court and on certain other courts new functions for the protection of consumers; to make provision, in substitution for the Monopolies and Restrictive Practices (Inquiry and Control) Act 1948 and the Monopolies and Mergers Act 1965, for the matters dealt with in those Acts and related matters, including restrictive labour practices; to amend the Restrictive Trade Practices Act 1956 and the Restrictive Trade Practices Act 1968, to make provision for extending the said Act of 1956 to agreements relating to services, and to transfer to the Director General of Fair Trading the functions of the Registrar of Restrictive Trading Agreements; to make provision with respect to pyramid selling and similar trading schemes; to make new provision in place of section 30(2) to (4) of the Trade Descriptions Act 1968; and for Purposes connected with those matters.

[25th July 1973]

Order in pursuance of report of Advisory Committee

[22   Order of Secretary of State in pursuance of report on reference to which s. 17 applies
Repealed]

23   Penalties for contravention of order under s. 22
Subject to the following provisions of this Part of this Act, any person who contravenes a prohibition imposed by an order under section 22 of this Act, or who does not comply with a requirement imposed by such an order which applies to him, shall be guilty of an offence and shall be liable—

> (a) on summary conviction, to a fine not exceeding £400;
> (b) on conviction on indictment, to a fine or to imprisonment for a term not exceeding two years or both.

24   Offences due to default of other person
Where the commission by any person of an offence under section 23 of this Act is due to the act or default of some other person, that other person shall be guilty of the offence, and a person may be charged with and convicted of the offence by virtue of this section whether or not proceedings are taken against the first-mentioned person.

25   Defences in proceedings under s. 23
(1) In any proceedings for an offence under section 23 of this Act it shall, subject to subsection (2) of this section, be a defence for the person charged to prove—

> (a) that the commission of the offence was due to a mistake, or to reliance on information supplied to him, or to the act or default of another person, an accident or some other cause beyond his control, and
> (b) that he took all reasonable precautions and exercised an due diligence to avoid the commission of such an offence by himself or any person under his control.

(2) If in any case the defence provided by the preceding subsection involves the allegation that the commission of the offence was due to the act or default of another person or to reliance on information supplied by another person, the person charged shall not, without leave of the court, be entitled to rely on that defence unless, within a period ending seven clear days before the hearing, he has served on the prosecutor a notice in writing giving such information identifying or assisting in the identification of that other person as was then in his possession.

(3) In proceedings for an offence under section 23 of this Act committed by the publication of an advertisement, it shall be a defence for the person charged to prove that he is a person whose business it is to publish or arrange for the publication of advertisements, and that he received the advertisement for publication in the ordinary course of business and did not know and had no reason to suspect that its publication would amount to an offence under section 23 of this Act.

26   Limitation of effect of orders under s. 22
A contract for the supply of goods or services shall not be void or unenforceable by reason only of a contravention of an order made under section 22 of this Act; and, subject to the provisions of section 33 of the Interpretation Act 1889 (which relates to offences under two or more laws), the provisions of this Part of this Act shall not be construed as—

> (a) conferring a right of action in any civil proceedings (other than proceedings for the recovery of a fine) in respect of any contravention of such an order, or

(b) affecting any restriction imposed by or under any other enactment, whether public or private, or

(c) derogating from any right of action or other remedy (whether civil or criminal) in proceedings instituted otherwise than under this Part of this Act.

Enforcement of orders

27   Enforcing authorities

(1) It shall be the duty of every local weights and measures authority to enforce within their area the provisions of any order made under section 22 of this Act; and section 37 of the Weights and Measures Act 1963 (power of local authorities to combine) shall apply with respect to the functions of such authorities under this Part of this Act as it applies with respect to their functions under that Act.

(2) Nothing in subsection (1) shall be taken as authorising a local weights and measures authority in Scotland to institute proceedings for an offence.

28   Power to make test purchases

A local weights and measures authority may make, or may authorise any of their officers to make on their behalf, such purchases of goods, and may authorise any of their officers to obtain such services, as may be expedient for the purpose of determining whether or not the provisions of any order made under section 22 of this Act are being complied with.

29   Power to enter premises and inspect and seize goods and documents

(1) A duly authorised officer of a local weights and measures authority, or a person duly authorised in writing by the Secretary of State, may at all reasonable hours, and on production, if required, of his credentials, exercise the following powers, that is to say—

(a) he may, for the purpose of ascertaining whether any offence under section 23 of this Act has been committed, inspect any goods and enter any premises other than premises used only as a dwelling.

(b) if he has reasonable cause to suspect that an offence under that section has been committed, he may, for the purpose of ascertaining whether it has been committed, require any person carrying on a business or employed in connection with a business to produce any books or documents relating to the business and may take copies of, or of any entry in, any such book or document;

(c) if he has reasonable cause to believe that such an offence has been committed he may seize and detain any goods for the purpose of ascertaining, by testing or otherwise, whether the offence has been committed;

(d) he may seize and detain any goods or documents which he has reason to believe may be required as evidence in proceedings for such an offence;

(e) he may, for the purpose of exercising his powers under this subsection to seize goods, but only if and to the extent that it is reasonably necessary in order to secure that the provisions of an order made under section 22 of this Act are duly observed, require any person having authority to do so to break open any container or open any vending machine and, if that person does not comply with the requirement, he may do so himself.

(2) A person seizing any goods or documents in the exercise of his powers under this section shall inform the person from whom they are seized and, in the case of goods seized from a vending machine, the person whose name and address are stated on the machine as being the proprietor's or, if no name and address are so stated, the occupier of the premises on which the machine stands or to which it is affixed.

(3) If a justice of the peace, on sworn information in writing,—

(a) is satisfied that there is reasonable ground to believe either—

(i)   that any goods, books or documents which a person has power under this section to inspect are on any premises and that their inspection is likely to disclose evidence of the commission of an offence under section 23 of this Act, or

(ii) that any offence under section 23 has been, is being or is about to be committed on any premises, and

(b) is also satisfied either—

(i) that admission to the premises has been or is likely to be refused and that notice of intention to apply for a warrant under this subsection has been given to the occupier, or

(ii) that an application for admission, or the giving of such a notice, would defeat the object of the entry or that the premises are unoccupied or that the occupier is temporarily absent, and it might defeat the object of the entry to await his return, the justice may by warrant under his hand, which shall continue in force for a period of one month, authorise any such officer or other person as is mentioned in subsection of this section to enter the premises, if need be by force. In the application of this subsection to Scotland 'justice of the peace' shall be construed as including a sheriff and a magistrate.

(4) A person entering any premises by virtue of this section may take with him such other persons and such equipment as may appear to him necessary and on leaving any premises which he has entered by virtue of a warrant under subsection (3) of this section he shall, if the premises are unoccupied or the occupier is temporarily absent, leave them as effectively secured against trespassers as he found them.

(5) Nothing in this section shall be taken to compel the production by a barrister, advocate or solicitor of a document containing a privileged communication made by or to him in that capacity or to authorise the taking of possession of any such document which is in his possession.

30 Offences in connection with exercise of powers under s. 29

(1) Subject to subsection (6) of this section, any person who—

(a) wilfully obstructs any such officer or person as is mentioned in subsection (1) of section 29 of this Act acting in the exercise of any powers conferred on him by or under that section, or

(b) wilfully fails to comply with any requirement properly made to him by such an officer or person under that section, or

(c) without reasonable cause fails to give to such an officer or person so acting any other assistance or information which he may reasonably require of him for the purpose of the performance of his functions under this Part of this Act,

shall be guilty of an offence.

(2) If any person, in giving any such information as is mentioned in subsection (1) (c) of this section, makes any statement which he knows to be false, he shall be guilty of an offence.

[...]

(4) If any person who is neither a duly authorised officer of a weights and measures authority nor a person duly authorised in that behalf by the Secretary of State purports to act as such under section 29 of this Act or under this section, he shall be guilty of an offence.

(5) Any person guilty of an offence under subsection (1) of this section shall be liable on summary conviction to a fine not exceeding £50; and any person guilty of an offence under subsection (2), [...] or subsection (4) of this section shall be liable—

(a) on summary conviction, to a fine not exceeding £400;

(b) on conviction on indictment, to a fine or to imprisonnent for a term not exceeding two years or to both.

(6) Nothing in this section shall be construed as requiring a person to answer any question or give any information if to do so might incriminate that person or (where that person is [married or a civil partner) the spouse or civil partner].

31 Notice of test

Where any goods seized or purchased by a person in pursuance of this Part of this Act are submitted to a test, then—

    (a) if the goods were seized, he shall inform any such person as is mentioned in section 29(2) of this Act of the result of the test—,

    (b) if the goods were purchased and the test leads to the institution of proceedings for an offence under section 23 of this Act, he shall inform the person from whom the goods were purchased, or, in the case of goods sold through a vending machine, the person mentioned in relation to such goods in section 29(2) of this Act, of the result of the test; and where, as a result of the test, proceedings for an offence under section 23 of this Act are instituted against any person, he shall allow that person to have the goods tested on his behalf if it is reasonably practicable to do so.

32 Compensation for loss in respect of goods seized under s. 29

(1) Where in the exercise of his powers under section 29 of this Act a person seizes and detains any goods, and their owner suffers loss by reason of their being damaged or deteriorate, unless the owner is convicted of an offence under section 23 of this Act committed in relation to the goods, the appropriate authority shall be liable to compensate him for the loss so suffered.

(2) Any disputed question as to the right to or the amount of any compensation payable under this section shall be determined by arbitration and, in Scotland, by a single arbiter appointed, failing agreement between the parties, by the sheriff.

(3) In this section 'the appropriate authority'—

    (a) in relation to goods seized by an officer of a local weights and measures authority, means that authority, and

    (b) in any other case, means the Secretary of State.

33 Application of Part II to Northern Ireland

. . .

Supply of Goods (Implied Terms) Act 1973
(1973, c. 13)

An Act to amend the law with respect to the terms to be implied in contracts of sale of goods and hire-purchase agreements and on the exchange of goods for trading stamps, and with respect to the terms of conditional sale agreements; and for connected purposes.   [18th April 1973]

8 Implied terms as title

[(1) In every hire-purchase agreement, other than one to which subsection (2) below applies, there is—

    (a) an implied term on the part of the creditor that he will have a right to sell the goods at the time when the property is to pass; and

    (b) an implied term that—

        (i) the goods are free, and will remain free until the time when the property is to pass, from any charge or encumbrance not disclosed or known to the person to whom the goods are bailed or (in Scotland) hired before the agreement is made, and

        (ii) that person will enjoy quiet possession of the goods except so far as it may be disturbed by any person entitled to the benefit of any charge or encumbrance so disclosed or known.

(2) In a hire-purchase agreement, in the case of which there appears from the agreement or is to be inferred from the circumstances of the agreement an intention that the creditor should transfer only such title as he or a third person may have, there is—

    (a) an implied term that all charges or encumbrances known to the creditor and not known to the person to whom the goods are bailed or hired have been disclosed to that person before the agreement is made; and

    (b) an implied term that neither—

        (i) the creditor; nor

        (ii) in a case where the parties to the agreement intend that any title which may be transferred shall be only such title as a third person may have, that person; nor

        (iii) anyone claiming through or under the creditor or that third person not otherwise than under a charge or encumbrance disclosed or known to the person to whom the goods are bailed or hired, before the agreement is made; will disturb the quiet possession of the person to whom the goods are bailed or hired.

    (3) As regards England and Wales and Northern Ireland, the term implied by subsection (1)(a) above is a condition and the terms implied by subsections (1)(b), (2)(a) and (2)(b) above are warranties.]

9 Bailing or hiring by description

    [(1) Where under a hire-purchase agreement goods are bailed or (in Scotland) hired by description, there is an implied term that the goods will correspond with the description, and if under the agreement the goods are bailed or hired by reference to a sample as well as a description, it is not sufficient that the bulk of the goods corresponds with the sample if the goods do not also correspond with the description.

    (1A) As regards England and Wales and Northern Ireland, the term implied by sub-section (1) above is a condition.

    (2) Goods shall not be prevented from being bailed or hired by description by reason only that, being exposed for sale, bailment or hire, they are selected by the person to whom they are bailed or hired.]

10 Implied undertakings as to quality or fitness

    [(1) Except as provided by this section and section 11 below and subject to the provisions of any other enactment, including any enactment of the Parliament of Northern Ireland or the Northern Ireland Assembly, there is no implied term as to the quality or fitness for any particular purpose of goods bailed or (in Scotland) hired under a hire-purchase agreement.

    (2) Where the creditor bails or hires goods under a hire purchase agreement in the course of a business, there is an implied term that the goods supplied under the agreement are of satisfactory quality.

    (2A) For the purposes of this Act, goods are of satisfactory quality if they meet the standard that a reasonable person would regard as satisfactory, taking account of any description of the goods, the price (if relevant) and all the other relevant circumstances.

    (2B) For the purposes of this Act, the quality of goods includes their state and condition and the following (among others) are in appropriate cases aspects of the quality of goods—

    (a) fitness for all the purposes for which goods of the kind in question are commonly supplied,

    (b) appearance and finish.

    (c) freedom from minor defects,

    (d) safety, and

    (e) durability.

    (2C) The term implied by subsection (2) above does not extend to any matter making the quality of goods unsatisfactory—

    (a) which is specifically drawn to the attention of the person to whom the goods are bailed or hired before the agreement is made,

    (b) where that person examines the goods before the agreement is made, which that examination ought to reveal, or

(c) where the goods are bailed or hired by reference to a sample, which would have been apparent on a reasonable examination of the sample.

[(2D) If the person to whom the goods are bailed or hired deals as consumer or, in Scotland, if the goods are hired to a person under a consumer contract, the relevant circumstances mentioned in subsection (2A) above include any public statements on the specific characteristics of the goods made about them by the creditor, the producer or his representative, particularly in advertising or on labelling.

(2E) A public statement is not by virtue of subsection (2D) above a relevant circumstance for the purposes of subsection (2A) above in the case of a contract of hire-purchase, if the creditor shows that—

(a) at the time the contract was made, he was not, and could not reasonably have been, aware of the statement,

(b) before the contract was made, the statement had been withdrawn in public or, to the extent that it contained anything which was incorrect or misleading, it had been corrected in public, or

(c) the decision to acquire the goods could not have been influenced by the statement.

(2F) Subsections (2D) and (2E) above do not prevent any public statement from being a relevant circumstance for the purposes of subsection (2A) above (whether or not the person to whom the goods are bailed or hired deals as consumer or, in Scotland, whether or not the goods are hired to a person under a consumer contract) if the statement would have been such a circumstance apart from those subsections.]

(3) Where the creditor bails or hires goods under a hire-purchase agreement in the course of a business and the person to whom the goods are bailed or hired, expressly or by implication, makes known—

(a) to the creditor in the course of negotiations conducted by the creditor in relation to the making of the hire-purchase agreement, or

(b) to a credit-broker in the course of negotiations conducted by that broker in relation to goods sold by him to the creditor before forming the subject matter of the hire-purchase agreement,

any particular purpose for which the goods are being bailed or hired, there is an implied term that the goods supplied under the agreement are reasonably fit for that purpose, whether or not that is a purpose for which such goods are commonly supplied, except where the circumstances show that the person to whom the goods are bailed or hired does not rely, or that it is unreasonable for him to rely, on the skill or judgment of the creditor or credit-broker.

(4) An implied term as to quality or fitness for a particular purpose may be annexed to a hire-purchase agreement by usage.

(5) The preceding provisions of this section apply to a hire-purchase agreement made by a person who in the course of a business is acting as agent for the creditor as they apply to an agreement made by the creditor in the course of a business, except where the creditor is not bailing or hiring in the course of a business and either the person to whom the goods are bailed or hired knows that fact or reasonable steps are taken to bring it to the notice of that person before the agreement is made.

(6) In subsection (3) above and this subsection—

(a) 'credit-broker' means a person acting in the course of a business of credit brokerage;

(b) 'credit brokerage' means the effecting of introductions of individuals desiring to obtain credit—

(i) to persons carrying on any business so far as it relates to the provision of credit, or

(ii) to other persons engaged in credit brokerage.

(7) As regards England and Wales and Northern Ireland, the terms implied by subsections (2) and (3) above are conditions.]

[(8) In Scotland, 'consumer contract' in this section has the same meaning as in section 12A(3) below.]

11   Samples

[(1) Where under a hire-purchase agreement goods are bailed or (in Scotland) hired by reference to a sample, there is an implied term—

(a) that the bulk will correspond with the sample in quality; and

(b) that the person to whom the goods are bailed or hired will have a reasonable opportunity of comparing the bulk with the sample; and

(c) that the goods will be free from any defect, making their quality unsatisfactory, which would not be apparent on reasonable examination of the sample.

(2) As regards England and Wales and Northern Ireland, the term implied by subsection (1) above is a condition.]

[11A   Modification of remedies for breach of statutory condition in non-consumer cases

(1) Where in the case of a hire purchase agreement—

(a) the person to whom goods are bailed would, apart from this subsection, have the right to reject them by reason of a breach on the part of the creditor of a term implied by section 9, 10 or 11(1)(a) or (c) above, but

(b) the breach is so slight that it would be unreasonable for him to reject them, then, if the person to whom the goods are bailed does not deal as consumer, the breach is not to be treated as a breach of condition but may be treated as a breach of warranty.

(2) This section applies unless a contrary intention appears in, or is to be implied from, the agreement.

(3) It is for the creditor to show—

(a) that a breach fell within subsection (1)(b) above, and

(b) that the person to whom the goods were bailed did not deal as consumer.

(4) The references in this section to dealing as consumer are to be construed in accordance with Part I of the Unfair Contract Terms Act 1977.

(5) This section does not apply to Scotland.]

[12   Exclusion of implied terms

An express term does not negative a term implied by this Act unless inconsistent with it.]

[12A   Remedies for breach of hire-purchase agreements as respects Scotland ...]

14   Special provisions as to conditional sale agreements

[(1) Section 11(4) of the Sale of Goods Act 1979 (whereby in certain circumstances a breach of a condition in a contract of sale is treated only as a breach of warranty) shall not apply to [a conditional sale agreement where the buyer deals as consumer within Part I of the Unfair Contract Terms Act 1977 ...

(2) In England and Wales and Northern Ireland a breach of a condition (whether express or implied) to be fulfilled by the seller under any such agreement shall be treated as a breach of warranty, and not as grounds for rejecting the goods and treating the agreement as repudiated, if (but only if) it would have fallen to be so treated had the condition been contained or implied in a corresponding hire-purchase agreement as a condition to be fulfilled by the creditor.]

15   Supplementary

[(1) In sections 8 to 14 above and this section—

'business' includes a profession and the activities of any government department (including a Northern Ireland department), [or local or public authority];

'buyer' and 'seller' includes a person to whom rights and duties under a conditional sale agreement have passed by assignment or operation of law;

'conditional sale agreement' means an agreement for the sale of goods under which the purchase price or part of it is payable by instalments, and the property in the goods is to remain in the seller (notwithstanding that the buyer is to be in possession of the goods) until such conditions as to the payment of instalments or otherwise as may be specified in the agreement are fulfilled;

['consumer sale' has the same meaning as in section 5 5 of the Sale of Goods Act 1979 (as set out in paragraph 11 of Schedule 1 to that Act)];

'creditor' means the person by whom the goods are bailed or (in Scotland) hired under a hire-purchase agreement or the person to whom his rights and duties under the agreement have passed by assignment or operation of law; and

'hire-purchase agreement' means an agreement, other than conditional sale agreement, under which—

> (a) goods are bailed or (in Scotland) hired in return for periodical payments by the person to whom they are bailed or hired, and
> (b) the property in the goods will pass to that person if the terms of the agreement are complied with and one or more of the following occurs—
>   (i)   the exercise of an option to purchase by that person,
>   (ii) the doing of any other specified act by any party to the agreement,
>   (iii) the happening of any other specified event.

['producer' means the manufacturer of goods, the importer of goods into the European Economic Area or any person purporting to be a producer by placing his name, trade mark or other distinctive sign on the goods;]

(3) In section 14(2) above 'corresponding hire-purchase agreement' means, in relation to a conditional sale agreement, a hire-purchase agreement relating to the same goods as the conditional sale agreement and made between the same parties and at the same time and in the same circumstances and, as nearly as may be, in the same terms as the conditional sale agreement.

(4) Nothing in sections 8 to 13 above shall prejudice the operation of any other enactment including any enactment of the Parliament of Northern Ireland or the Northern Ireland Assembly or any rule of law whereby any term, other than one relating to quality or fitness, is to be implied in any hire-purchase agreement.]

Consumer Credit Act 1974
(1974, c. 39)

An Act to establish for the protection of consumers a new system, administered by the Director General of Fair Trading, of licensing and other control of traders concerned with the provision of credit, or the supply of goods on hire or hire-purchase, and their transactions, in place of the present enactments regulating moneylenders, pawnbrokers and hire-purchase traders and their transactions; and for related matters.   [31st July 1974]

PART I   [OFFICE OF FAIR TRADING]

1   General functions of [OFT]

> (1) It is the duty of [the Office of Fair Trading ('the OFT'])—
>   (a) to administer the licensing system set up by this Act,
>   (b) to exercise the adjudicating functions conferred on [it] by this Act in relation to the issue, renewal, variation, suspension and revocation of licences, and other matters,
>   [(ba) to monitor, as it sees fit, businesses being carried on under licences;]
>   (c) generally to superintend the working and enforcement of this Act, and regulations made under it, and
>   (d) where necessary or expedient, [itself] to take steps to enforce this Act, and regulations so made.

(2) It is the duty of the [OFT], so far as appears to [it] to be practicable and having regard both to the national interest and the interests of persons carrying on businesses to which this Act applies and their customers, to keep under review and from time to time advise the Secretary of State about—

(a) social and commercial developments in the United Kingdom and elsewhere relating to the provision of credit or bailment or (in Scotland) hiring of goods to individuals, and related activities; and

(b) the working and enforcement of this Act and orders and regulations made under it.

2   Powers of Secretary of State

(1) The Secretary of State may by order—

(a) confer on the [OFT] additional functions concerning the provision of credit or bailment or (in Scotland) hiring of goods to individuals, and related activities, and

(b) regulate the carrying out by the [OFT] of [its] functions under this Act.

(2) The Secretary of State may give general directions indicating considerations to which the [OFT] should have particular regard in carrying out [its] functions under this Act, and may give specific directions on any matter connected with the carrying out by the [OFT] of those functions.

(3) The Secretary of State, on giving any directions under subsection (2), shall arrange for them to be published in such manner as he thinks most suitable for drawing them to the attention of interested persons.

(4) With the approval of the Secretary of State and the Treasury, the [OFT] may charge, for any service or facility provided by [it] under this Act, a fee of an amount specified by general notice (the 'specified fee').

(5) Provision may be made under subsection (4) for reduced fees, or no fees at all, to be paid for certain services or facilities by persons of a specified description, and references in this Act to the specified fee shall, in such cases, be construed accordingly.

(6) An order under subsection (1)(a) shall be made by statutory instrument and shall be of no effect unless a draft of the order has been laid before and approved by each House of Parliament.

(7) References in subsection (2) to the functions of the [OFT] under this Act do not include the making of a determination to which section 41 [...] (appeals from [OFT] to [the Tribunal]) applies.

4   Dissemination of information and advice

The [OFT] shall arrange for the dissemination, in such form and manner as [it] considers appropriate, of such information and advice as it may appear to [it] expedient to give to the public in the United Kingdom about the operation of this Act, [the consumer credit jurisdiction under Part 16 of the Financial Services and Markets Act 2000,] the credit facilities available to them, and other matters within the scope of [its] functions under this Act.

5   Annual and other reports

6   Form etc. of applications

(1) An application to the [OFT] under this Act is of no effect unless the requirements of this section are satisfied.

(2) The application must be in writing, and in such form, and accompanied by such [information and documents], as the [OFT] may specify [or describe in a] general notice, [...].

[(2A) The application must also be accompanied—

(a) in the case of an application for a licence or for the renewal of a licence, by the charge payable by virtue of section 6A;

(b) in any other case, by the specified fee.]

[(3) Where the OFT receives an application, it may by notice to the applicant at any time before the determination of the application require him to provide such information or documents relevant to the application as may be specified or described in the notice.]

(4) The [OFT] may by notice require the applicant to publish details of his applicant at a time or times and in a manner specified in the notice

[(5) Subsection (6) applies where a general notice under subsection (2) comes into effect—

    (a) after an application has been made; but

    (b) before its determination.

(6) The applicant shall, within such period as may be specified in the general notice, provide the OFT with any information or document—

    (a) which he has not previously provided in relation to the application by virtue of this section;

    (b) which he would have been required to provide with his application had it been made after the general notice came into effect; and

    (c) which the general notice requires to be provided for the purposes of this subsection.

(7) An applicant shall notify the OFT, giving details, if before his application is determined—

    (a) any information or document provided by him in relation to the application by virtue of this section is, to any extent, superseded or otherwise affected by a change in circumstances; or

    (b) he becomes aware of an error in or omission from any such information or document.

(8) A notification for the purposes of subsection (7) shall be given within the period of 28 days beginning with the day on which (as the case may be)—

    (a) the information or document is superseded;

    (b) the change in circumstances occurs; or

    (c) the applicant becomes aware of the error or omission.

(9) Subsection (7) does not require an applicant to notify the OFT about—

    (a) anything of which he is required to notify it under section 36; or

    (b) an error in or omission from any information or document which is a clerical error or omission not affecting the substance of the information or document.]

[6A   Charge on applicants for licences etc.

(1) An applicant for a licence, or for the renewal of a licence, shall pay the OFT a charge towards the costs of carrying out its functions under this Act.

(2) The amount of the charge payable by an applicant shall be determined in accordance with provision made by the OFT by general notice.

(3) The provision that may be made by the OFT under subsection (2) includes—

    (a) different provision in relation to persons of different descriptions;

    (b) provision for no charge at all to be payable by persons of specified descriptions.

(4) The approval of the Secretary of State and the Treasury is required for a general notice under subsection (2).]

[7   Penalty for false information

A person commits an offence if, for the purposes of, or in connection with, any requirement imposed or other provision made by or under this Act, he knowingly or recklessly gives information to the OFT, or to an officer of the OFT, which, in a material particular, is false or misleading.]

PART II   CREDIT AGREEMENTS, HIRE AGREEMENTS
AND LINKED TRANSACTIONS

8   Consumer credit agreements

(1) A [consumer] credit agreement is an agreement between an individual ('the debtor') and any other person ('the creditor') by which the creditor provides the debtor with credit of any amount.

[...]

(3) A consumer credit agreement is a regulated agreement within the meaning of this Act if it is not an agreement (an 'exempt agreement') specified in or under section 16 [, 16A or 16B.].

9   Meaning of credit

(1) In this Act 'credit' includes a cash loan, and any other form of financial accommodation.

(2) Where credit is provided otherwise than in sterling it shall be treated for the purposes of this Act as provided in sterling of an equivalent amount.

(3) Without prejudice to the generality of subsection (1), the person by whom goods are bailed or (in Scotland) hired to an individual under a hire-purchase agreement shall be taken to provide him with fixed-sum credit to finance the transaction of an amount equal to the total price of the goods less the aggregate of the deposit (if any) and the total charge for credit.

(4) For the purposes of this Act, an item entering into the total charge for credit shall not be treated as credit even though time is allowed for its payment.

10   Running-account credit and fixed-sum credit

(1) For the purposes of this Act—

    (a) running-account credit is a facility under a [consumer] credit agreement whereby the debtor is enabled to receive from time to time (whether in his own person, or by another person) from the creditor or a third party cash, goods and services (or any of them) to an amount or value such that, taking into account payments made by or to the credit of the debtor, the credit limit (if any) is not at any time exceeded; and

    (b) fixed-sum credit is any other facility under a [consumer] credit agreement whereby the debtor is enabled to receive credit (whether in one amount or by instalments).

(2) In relation to running-account credit, 'credit limit' means, as respects any period, the maximum debit balance which, under the credit agreement, is allowed to stand on the account during that period, disregarding any term of the agreement allowing that maximum to be exceeded merely temporarily.

(3) For the purposes of [paragraph (a) of section 16B(1)] , running-account credit shall be taken not to exceed the amount specified in that [paragraph] ('the specified amount') if—

    (a) the credit limit does not exceed the specified amount; or

    (b) whether or not there is a credit limit, and if there is, notwithstanding that it exceeds the specified amount,—

        (i)   the debtor is not enabled to draw at any one time an amount which, so far as (having regard to section 9(4)) it represents credit, exceeds the specified amount, or

        (ii) the agreement provides that, if the debit balance rises above a given amount (not exceeding the specified amount), the rate of the total charge for credit increases or any other condition favouring the creditor or his associate comes into operation, or

        (iii) at the time the agreement is made it is probable, having regard to the terms of the agreement and any other relevant considerations, that the debit balance will not at any time rise above the specified amount.

11   Restricted-use credit and unrestricted-use credit

(1) A restricted-use credit agreement is a regulated consumer credit agreement—

    (a) to finance a transaction between the debtor and the creditor, whether forming part of that agreement or not, or

(b) to finance a transaction between the debtor and a person (the 'supplier') other than the creditor, or

(c) to refinance any existing indebtedness of the debtor's, whether to the creditor or another person, and 'restricted-use credit' shall be construed accordingly.

(2) An unrestricted-use credit agreement is a regulated consumer credit agreement not falling within subsection (1), and 'unrestricted-use credit' shall be construed accordingly.

(3) An agreement does not fall within subsection (1) if the credit is in fact provided in such a way as to leave the debtor free to use it as he chooses, even though certain uses would contravene that or any other agreement.

(4) An agreement may fall within subsection (1)(b) although the identity of the supplier is unknown at the time the agreement is made.

12   Debtor-creditor supplier agreements

A debtor-creditor-supplier agreement is a regulated consumer credit agreement being—

(a) a restricted-use credit agreement which falls within section 11(1)(a), or

(b) a restricted-use credit agreement which falls within section 11(1)(b) and is made by the creditor under pre-existing arrangements, or in contemplation of future arrangements, between himself and the supplier, or

(c) an unrestricted-use credit agreement which is made by the creditor under pre-existing arrangements between himself and a person (the 'supplier') other than the debtor in the knowledge that the credit is to be used to finance a transaction between the debtor and the supplier.

13   Debtor-creditor agreements

A debtor-creditor agreement is a regulated consumer credit agreement being—

(a) a restricted-use credit agreement which falls within section 11(1)(b) but is not made by the creditor under pre-existing arrangements, or in contemplation of future arrangements, between himself and the supplier, or

(b) a restricted-use credit agreement which falls within section 11(1)(c), or

(c) an unrestricted-use credit agreement which is not made by the creditor under preexisting arrangements between himself and a person (the 'supplier') other than the debtor in the knowledge that the credit is to be used to finance a transaction between the debtor and the supplier.

14   Credit-token agreements

(1) A credit-token is a card, check, voucher, coupon, stamp, form, booklet or other document or thing given to an individual by a person carrying on a consumer credit business, who undertakes—

(a) that on the production of it (whether or not some other action is also required) he will supply cash, goods and services (or any of them) on credit, or

(b) that where, on the production of it to a third party (whether or not any other action is also required), the third party supplies cash, goods and services (or any of them), he will pay the third party for them (whether or not deducting any discount or commission), in return for payment to him by the individual.

(2) A credit-token agreement is a regulated agreement for the provision of credit in connection with the use of a credit-token.

(3) Without prejudice to the generality of section 9(1), the person who gives to an individual an undertaking falling within subsection (1)(b) shall be taken to provide him with credit drawn on whenever a third party supplies him with cash, goods or services.

(4) For the purposes of subsection (1), use of an object to operate a machine provided by the person giving the object or a third party shall be treated as the production of the object to him.

15   Consumer hire agreements

(1) A consumer hire agreement is an agreement made by a person with an individual (the 'hirer') for the bailment or (in Scotland) the hiring of goods to the hirer, being an agreement which—

  (a) is not a hire-purchase agreement, and

  (b) is capable of subsisting for more than three months, [...].

(2) A consumer hire agreement is a regulated agreement if it is not an exempt agreement.

16 Exempt agreements

(1) This Act does not regulate a consumer credit agreement where the creditor is a local authority [...], or a body specified, or of a description specified, in an order made by the Secretary of State, being—

  [(a) an insurer;]

  (b) a friendly society,

  (c) an organisation of employers or organisation of workers,

  (d) a charity,

  (e) a land improvement company, or

  (f) a body corporate named or specifically referred to in any public general Act.

  [(ff) a body corporate named or specifically referred to in an order made under—

    section 156(4) or 447(2)(a) of the Housing Act 1985,

    section 156(4) of that Act as it has effect by virtue of section 17 of the Housing Act 1996 (the right to acquire),

    section 223 or 229 of the Housing (Scotland) Act 1987, or

    Article 154(1)(a) or 156AA of the Housing (Northern Ireland) Order 1981 or Article 10(6A) of the Housing (Northern Ireland) Order 1983; or]

  (g) a building society, or

  [(h) a deposit taker.]

(2) Subsection (1) applies only where the agreement is—

  (a) a debtor-creditor-supplier agreement financing—

    (i) the purchase of land, or

    (ii) the provision of dwellings on any land, and secured by a land mortgage on that land; or

  (b) a debtor-creditor agreement secured by any land mortgage; or

  (c) a debtor-creditor-supplier agreement financing a transaction which is a linked transaction in relation to—

    (i) an agreement falling within paragraph (a), or

    (ii) an agreement failing within paragraph (b) financing—

      (aa) the purchase of any land, or

      (bb) the provision of dwellings on any land, and secured by a land mortgage on the land referred to in paragraph (a) or, as the case may be, the land referred to in sub-paragraph (ii).

  [(3) Before he makes, varies or revokes an order under subsection (1), the Secretary of State must undertake the necessary consultation.

  (3A) The necessary consultation means consultation with the bodies mentioned in the following table in relation to the provision under which the order is to be made, varied or revoked:

TABLE

Provision of subsection (1)	Consultee
Paragraph (a) or (b)	The Financial Services Authority
Paragraph (d)	The Charity Commissioners
Paragraph (e), (f) or (ff)	Any Minister of the Crown with responsibilities in relation to the body in question
Paragraph (g) or (h)	The Treasury and the Financial Services Authority]

(4) An order under subsection (1) relating to a body may be limited so as to apply only to agreements by that body of a description specified in the order.

(5) The Secretary of State may by order provide that this Act shall not regulate other consumer credit agreements where—

> (a) the number of payments to be made by the debtor does not exceed the number specified for that purpose in the order, or
> (b) the rate of the total charge for credit does not exceed the rate so specified, or
> (c) an agreement has a connection with a country outside the United Kingdom.

(6) The Secretary of State may by order provide that this Act shall not regulate consumer hire agreements of a description specified in the order where—

> (a) the owner is a body corporate authorised by or under any enactment to supply electricity, gas or water, and
> (b) the subject of the agreement is a meter or metering equipment [or where the owner is a provider of a public electronic communications service who is specified in the order].

[(6A) This Act does not regulate a consumer credit agreement where the creditor is a housing authority and the agreement is secured by a land mortgage of a dwelling.

(6B) In subsection (6A) 'housing authority' means—

> (a) as regards England and Wales, the Housing Corporation, . . . and an authority or body within section 80(1) of the Housing Act 1985 (the landlord condition for secure tenancies), other than a housing association or a housing trust which is a charity;
> (b) as regards Scotland, a development corporation established under an order made, or having effect as if made under the New Towns (Scotland) Act 1968, the Scottish Special Housing Association or the Housing Corporation;
> (c) as regards Northern Ireland, the Northern Ireland Housing Executive.]

[(6C) This Act does not regulate a consumer credit agreement if—

> (a) it is secured by a land mortgage; and
> (b) entering into that agreement as lender is a regulated activity for the purposes of the Financial Services and Markets Act 2000.

(6D) But section 126, and any other provision so far as it relates to section 126, applies to an agreement which would (but for subsection (6C)) be a regulated agreement.

(6E) Subsection (6C) must be read with—

> (a) section 22 of the Financial Services and Markets Act 2000 (regulated activities: power to specify classes of activity and categories of investment);
> (b) any order for the time being in force under that section; and
> (c) Schedule 2 to that Act.]

[. . .]

[(7A) Nothing in this section affects the application of sections 140A to 140C.]

[(8) In the application of this section to Scotland, subsection (3A) shall have effect as if the reference to the Charity Commissioners were a reference to the Lord Advocate.]

(9) In the application of this section to Northern Ireland [subsection (3A)] shall have effect as if any reference to a Minister of the Crown were a reference to a Northern Ireland department, [. . .] and any reference to the Charity Commissioners were a reference to the Department of Finance for Northern Ireland.

[(10) In this section—

> (a) 'deposit-taker' means—
>> (i) a person who has permission under Part 4 of the Financial Services and Markets Act 2000 to accept deposits,
>> (ii) an EEA firm of the kind mentioned in paragraph 5(b) of Schedule 3 to that Act which has permission under paragraph 15 of that Schedule (as a result of qualifying for authorisation under paragraph 12 of that Schedule) to accept deposits,

(iii) any wholly owned subsidiary (within the meaning of the Companies Act 1985) of a person mentioned in sub-paragraph (i), or

(iv) any undertaking which, in relation to a person mentioned in sub-paragraph (ii), is a subsidiary undertaking within the meaning of any rule of law in force in the EEA State in question for purposes connected with the implementation of the European Council Seventh Company Law Directive of 13 June 1983 on consolidated accounts (No. 83/349/EEC), and which has no members other than that person;

(b) 'insurer' means—

(i) a person who has permission under Part 4 of the Financial Services and Markets Act 2000 to effect or carry out contracts of insurance, or

(ii) an EEA firm of the kind mentioned in paragraph 5(d) of Schedule 3 to that Act, which has permission under paragraph 15 of that Schedule (as a result of qualifying for authorisation under paragraph 12 of that Schedule) to effect or carry out contracts of insurance,

but does not include a friendly society or an organisation of workers or of employers.

(11) Subsection (10) must be read with—

(a) section 22 of the Financial Services and Markets Act 2000;

(b) any relevant order under that section; and

(c) Schedule 2 to that Act.]

[16A   Exemption relating to high net worth debtors and hirers

(1) The Secretary of State may by order provide that this Act shall not regulate a consumer credit agreement or a consumer hire agreement where—

(a) the debtor or hirer is a natural person;

(b) the agreement includes a declaration made by him to the effect that he agrees to forgo the protection and remedies that would be available to him under this Act if the agreement were a regulated agreement;

(c) a statement of high net worth has been made in relation to him; and

(d) that statement is current in relation to the agreement and a copy of it was provided to the creditor or owner before the agreement was made.

(2) For the purposes of this section a statement of high net worth is a statement to the effect that, in the opinion of the person making it, the natural person in relation to whom it is made—

(a) received during the previous financial year income of a specified description totalling an amount of not less than the specified amount; or

(b) had throughout that year net assets of a specified description with a total value of not less than the specified value.

(3) Such a statement—

(a) may not be made by the person in relation to whom it is made;

(b) must be made by a person of a specified description; and

(c) is current in relation to an agreement if it was made during the period of one year ending with the day on which the agreement is made.

(4) An order under this section may make provision about—

(a) how amounts of income and values of net assets are to be determined for the purposes of subsection (2)(a) and (b);

(b) the form, content and signing of—

(i) statements of high net worth;

(ii) declarations for the purposes of subsection (1)(b).

(5) Where an agreement has two or more debtors or hirers, for the purposes of paragraph (c) of subsection (1) a separate statement of high net worth must have been made in relation to each of them; and paragraph (d) of that subsection shall have effect accordingly.

(6) In this section—

'previous financial year' means, in relation to a statement of high net worth, the financial year immediately preceding the financial year during which the statement is made;

'specified' means specified in an order under this section.

(7) In subsection (6) 'financial year' means a period of one year ending with 31st March.

(8) Nothing in this section affects the application of sections 140A to 140C.]

[16B Exemption relating to businesses

(1) This Act does not regulate—

(a) a consumer credit agreement by which the creditor provides the debtor with credit exceeding £25,000, or

(b) a consumer hire agreement that requires the hirer to make payments exceeding £25,000,

if the agreement is entered into by the debtor or hirer wholly or predominantly for the purposes of a business carried on, or intended to be carried on, by him.

(2) If an agreement includes a declaration made by the debtor or hirer to the effect that the agreement is entered into by him wholly or predominantly for the purposes of a business carried on, or intended to be carried on, by him, the agreement shall be presumed to have been entered into by him wholly or predominantly for such purposes.

(3) But that presumption does not apply if, when the agreement is entered into—

(a) the creditor or owner, or

(b) any person who has acted on his behalf in connection with the entering into of the agreement,

knows, or has reasonable cause to suspect, that the agreement is not entered into by the debtor or hirer wholly or predominantly for the purposes of a business carried on, or intended to be carried on, by him.

(4) The Secretary of State may by order make provision about the form, content and signing of declarations for the purposes of subsection (2).

(5) Where an agreement has two or more creditors or owners, in subsection (3) references to the creditor or owner are references to any one or more of them.

(6) Nothing in this section affects the application of sections 140A to 140C.]

17 Small agreements

(1) A small agreement is—

(a) a regulated consumer credit agreement for credit not exceeding [£50], other than a hire-purchase or conditional sale agreement; or

(b) a regulated consumer hire agreement which does not require the hirer to make payments exceeding [£50],

being an agreement which is either unsecured or secured by a guarantee or indemnity only (whether or not the guarantee or indemnity is itself secured).

(2) Section 10(3)(a) applies for the purposes of subsection (1) as it applies for the purposes of section [16B(1)(a)].

(3) Where—

(a) two or more small agreements are made at or about the same time between the same parties, and

(b) it appears probable that they would instead have been made as a single agreement but for the desire to avoid the operation of provisions of this Act which would have applied to that single agreement but, apart from this subsection, are not applicable to the small agreements,

this Act applies to the small agreements as if they were regulated agreements other than small agreements.

(4) If, apart from this subsection, subsection (3) does not apply to any agreements but would apply if, for any party or parties to any of the agreements, there were substituted an

associate of that party, or associates of each of those parties, as the case may be, then subsection (3) shall apply to the agreements.

18 Multiple agreements

(1) This section applies to an agreement (a 'multiple agreement') if its terms are such as—

    (a) to place a part of it within one category of agreement mentioned in this Act, and another part of it within a different category of agreement so mentioned, or within a category of agreement not so mentioned, or

    (b) to place it, or a part of it, within two or more categories of agreement so mentioned.

(2) Where a part of an agreement falls within subsection (1), that part shall be treated for the purposes of this Act as a separate agreement.

(3) Where an agreement falls within subsection (1)(b), it shall be treated as an agreement in each of the categories in question, and this Act shall apply to it accordingly.

(4) Where under subsection (2) a part of a multiple agreement is to be treated as a separate agreement, the multiple agreement shall (with any necessary modifications) be construed accordingly; and any sum payable under the multiple agreement, if not apportioned by the parties, shall for the purposes of proceedings in any court relating to the multiple agreement be apportioned by the court as may be requisite.

(5) In the case of an agreement for running-account credit, a term of the agreement allowing the credit limit to be exceeded merely temporarily shall not be treated as a separate agreement or as providing fixed-sum credit in respect of the excess.

(6) This Act does not apply to a multiple agreement so far as the agreement relates to goods if under the agreement payments are to be made in respect of the goods in the form of rent (other than a rentcharge) issuing out of land.

19 Linked transactions

(1) A transaction entered into by the debtor or hirer, or a relative of his, with any other person ('the other party'), except one for the provision of security, is a linked transaction in relation to an actual or prospective regulated agreement (the 'principal agreement') of which it does not form part if—

    (a) the transaction is entered into in compliance with a term of the principal agreement; or

    (b) the principal agreement is a debtor-creditor-supplier agreement and the transaction is financed, or to be financed, by the principal agreement; or

    (c) the other party is a person mentioned in subsection (2), and a person so mentioned initiated the transaction by suggesting it to the debtor or hirer, or his relative, who enters into it—

        (i) to induce the creditor or owner to enter into the principal agreement, or

        (ii) for another purpose related to the principal agreement, or

        (iii) where the principal agreement is a restricted-use credit agreement, for a purpose related to a transaction financed, or to be financed, by the principal agreement.

(2) The persons referred to in subsection (1)(c) are—

    (a) the creditor or owner, or his associate;

    (b) a person who, in the negotiation of the transaction, is represented by a credit-broker who is also a negotiator in antecedent negotiations for the principal agreement;

    (c) a person who, at the time the transaction is initiated, knows that the principal agreement has been made or contemplates that it might be made.

(3) A linked transaction entered into before the making of the principal agreement has no effect until such time (if any) as that agreement is made.

(4) Regulations may exclude linked transactions of the prescribed description from the operation of subsection (3).

20   Total charge for credit

(1) The Secretary of State shall make regulations containing such provisions as appear to him appropriate for determining the true cost to the debtor of the credit provided or to be provided under an actual or prospective consumer credit agreement (the 'total charge for credit'), and regulations so made shall prescribe—

> (a) what items are to be treated as entering into the total charge for credit, and how their amount is to be ascertained;
>
> (b) the method of calculating the rate of the total charge for credit.

(2) Regulations under subsection (1) may provide for the whole or part of the amount payable by the debtor or his relative under any linked transaction to be included in the total charge for credit, whether or not the creditor is a party to the transaction or derives benefit from it.

PART III   LICENSING OF CREDIT AND HIRE BUSINESSES

Licensing principles

21   Businesses needing a licence

(1) Subject to this section, a licence is required to carry on a consumer credit business or [a consumer hire business or an ancillary credit business].

(2) A local authority does not need a licence to carry on a business.

(3) A body corporate empowered by a public general Act naming it to carry on a business does not need a licence to do so.

22   Standard and group licences

(1) A licence may be—

> (a) a standard licence, that is a licence, issued by the [OFT] to a person named in the licence on an application made by him, which, [whilst the licence is in effect], covers such activities as are described in the licence, or
>
> (b) a group licence, that is a licence, issued by the [OFT] (whether on the application of any person or of [its] own motion), which, [whilst the licence is in effect], covers such persons and activities as are described in the licence.

[(1A) The terms of a licence shall specify—

> (a) whether it has effect indefinitely or only for a limited period; and
>
> (b) if it has effect for a limited period, that period.

(1B) For the purposes of subsection (1A)(b) the period specified shall be such period not exceeding the prescribed period as the OFT thinks fit (subject to subsection (1E)).

(1C) A standard licence shall have effect indefinitely unless—

> (a) the application for its issue requests that it have effect for a limited period only; or
>
> (b) the OFT otherwise thinks there is good reason why it should have effect for such a period only.

(1D) A group licence shall have effect for a limited period only unless the OFT thinks there is good reason why it should have effect indefinitely.

(1E) Where a licence which has effect indefinitely is to be varied under section 30 or 31 for the purpose of limiting the licence's duration, the variation shall provide for the licence to expire—

> (a) in the case of a variation under section 30, at the end of such period from the time of the variation as is set out in the application for the variation; or
>
> (b) in the case of a variation under section 31, at the end of such period from the time of the variation as the OFT thinks fit;

but a period mentioned in paragraph (a) or (b) shall not exceed the prescribed period.]

(2) A licence is not assignable or, subject to section 37, transmissible on death or in any other way.

(3) Except in the case of a partnership or an unincorporated body of persons, a standard licence shall not be issued to more than one person.

(4) A standard licence issued to a partnership or an unincorporated body of persons shall be issued in the name of the partnership or body.

(5) The [OFT] may issue a group licence only if it appears to [it] that the public interest is better served by doing so than by obliging the persons concerned to apply separately for standard licences.

[(5A) A group licence to carry on a business may limit the activities it covers in any way the OFT thinks fit.]

(6) The persons covered by a group licence may be described by general words, whether or not coupled with the exclusion of named persons, or in any other way the [OFT] thinks fit.

(7) The fact that a person is covered by a group licence in respect of certain activities does not prevent a standard licence being issued to him in respect of those activities or any of them.

(8) A group licence issued on the application of any person shall be issued to that person, and general notice shall be given of the issue of any group licence (whether on application or not).

[...]

23   Authorisation of specific activities

(1) Subject to [the terms of the licence], a licence to carry on a business covers all lawful activities done in the course of that business, whether by the licensee or other persons on his behalf.

[...]

(3) A licence covers the canvassing off trade premises of debtor-creditor-supplier agreements or regulated consumer hire agreements only if, and to the extent that, the licence specifically so provides; and such provision shall not be included in a group licence.

(4) [The OFT may by general notice specify] other activities which, if engaged in by or on behalf of the person carrying on a business, require to be covered by an express term in his licence.

24   Control of name of business

A standard licence authorises the licensee to carry on a business under the name or names specified in the licence, but not under any other name.

[24A   Applications for standard licences

(1) An application for a standard licence shall, in relation to each type of business which is covered by the application, state whether the applicant is applying—

  (a) for the licence to cover the carrying on of that type of business with no limitation; or

  (b) for the licence to cover the carrying on of that type of business only so far as it falls within one or more descriptions of business.

(2) An application within subsection (1)(b) in relation to a type of business shall set out the description or descriptions of business in question.

(3) References in this Part to a type of business are references to a type of business within subsection (4).

(4) The types of business within this subsection are—

  (a) a consumer credit business;

  (b) a consumer hire business;

  (c) a business so far as it comprises or relates to credit brokerage;

  (d) a business so far as it comprises or relates to debt-adjusting;

  (e) a business so far as it comprises or relates to debt-counselling;

  (f) a business so far as it comprises or relates to debt-collecting;

  (g) a business so far as it comprises or relates to debt administration;

(h) a business so far as it comprises or relates to the provision of credit information services;

(i) a business so far as it comprises or relates to the operation of a credit reference agency.

(5) The OFT—

    (a) shall by general notice specify the descriptions of business which can be set out in an application for the purposes of subsection (2) in relation to a type of business;

    (b) may by general notice provide that applications within subsection (1)(b) cannot be made in relation to one or more of the types of business within subsection (4)(c) to (i).

(6) The power of the OFT under subsection (5) includes power to make different provision for different cases or classes of case.]

25   Licensee to be a fit person

[(1) If an applicant for a standard licence—

    (a) makes an application within section 24A(1)(a) in relation to a type of business, and

    (b) satisfies the OFT that he is a fit person to carry on that type of business with no limitation,

he shall be entitled to be issued with a standard licence covering the carrying on of that type of business with no limitation.

(1AA) If such an applicant—

    (a) makes an application within subsection (1)(b) of section 24A in relation to a type of business, and

    (b) satisfies the OFT that he is a fit person to carry on that type of business so far as it falls within the description or descriptions of business set out in his application in accordance with subsection (2) of that section,

he shall be entitled to be issued with a standard licence covering the carrying on of that type of business so far as it falls within the description or descriptions in question.

(1AB) If such an applicant makes an application within section 24A(1)(a) or (b) in relation to a type of business but fails to satisfy the OFT as mentioned in subsection (1) or (1AA) (as the case may be), he shall nevertheless be entitled to be issued with a standard licence covering the carrying on of that type of business so far as it falls within one or more descriptions of business if—

    (a) he satisfies the OFT that he is a fit person to carry on that type of business so far as it falls within the description or descriptions in question;

    (b) he could have applied for the licence to be limited in that way; and

    (c) the licence would not cover any activity which was not covered by his application.

(1AC) In this section 'description of business' means, in relation to a type of business, a description of business specified in a general notice under section 24A(5)(a).

(1AD) An applicant shall not, by virtue of this section, be issued with a licence unless he satisfies the OFT that the name or names under which he would be licensed is or are not misleading or otherwise undesirable.]

(1B) If an application for the grant of a standard licence—

    (a) is made by a person with permission under Part 4 of the Financial Services and Markets Act 2000 to accept deposits, and

    (b) relates to a listed activity,

the Financial Services Authority may, if it considers that the [OFT] ought to refuse the application, notify him of that fact.

(1C) In subsection (1B) 'listed activity' means an activity listed in Annex 1 to the banking consolidation directive (2000/12/EC) or in the Annex to the investment services directive (93/22/EEC) and references to deposits and to their acceptance must be read with—

    (a) section 22 of the Financial Services and Markets Act 2000;

    (b) any relevant order under that section; and

    (c) Schedule 2 to that Act.]

[(2) In determining whether an applicant for a licence is a fit person for the purposes of this section the OFT shall have regard to any matters appearing to it to be relevant including (amongst other things)—

    (a) the applicant's skills, knowledge and experience in relation to consumer credit businesses, consumer hire businesses or ancillary credit businesses;

    (b) such skills, knowledge and experience of other persons who the applicant proposes will participate in any business that would be carried on by him under the licence;

    (c) practices and procedures that the applicant proposes to implement in connection with any such business;

    (d) evidence of the kind mentioned in subsection (2A).

(2A) That evidence is evidence tending to show that the applicant, or any of the applicant's employees, agents or associates (whether past or present) or, where the applicant is a body corporate, any person appearing to the OFT to be a controller of the body corporate or an associate of any such person, has—

    (a) committed any offence involving fraud or other dishonesty or violence;

    (b) contravened any provision made by or under—

        (i) this Act;

        (ii) Part 16 of the Financial Services and Markets Act 2000 so far as it relates to the consumer credit jurisdiction under that Part;

        (iii) any other enactment regulating the provision of credit to individuals or other transactions with individuals;

    (c) contravened any provision in force in an EEA State which corresponds to a provision of the kind mentioned in paragraph (b);

    (d) practised discrimination on grounds of sex, colour, race or ethnic or national origins in, or in connection with, the carrying on of any business; or

    (e) engaged in business practices appearing to the OFT to be deceitful or oppressive or otherwise unfair or improper (whether unlawful or not).

(2B) For the purposes of subsection (2A)(e), the business practices which the OFT may consider to be deceitful or oppressive or otherwise unfair or improper include practices in the carrying on of a consumer credit business that appear to the OFT to involve irresponsible lending.]

(3) In subsection [(2A)], 'associate', in addition to the persons specified in section 184, includes a business associate.

[25A Guidance on fitness test

(1) The OFT shall prepare and publish guidance in relation to how it determines, or how it proposes to determine, whether persons are fit persons as mentioned in section 25.

(2) If the OFT revises the guidance at any time after it has been published, the OFT shall publish it as revised.

(3) The guidance shall be published in such manner as the OFT thinks fit for the purpose of bringing it to the attention of those likely to be affected by it.

(4) In preparing or revising the guidance the OFT shall consult such persons as it thinks fit.

(5) In carrying out its functions under this Part the OFT shall have regard to the guidance as most recently published.]

[26   Conduct of business

(1) Regulations may be made as to—
- (a) the conduct by a licensee of his business; and
- (b) the conduct by a consumer credit EEA firm of its business in the United Kingdom.

(2) The regulations may in particular specify—
- (a) the books or other records to be kept by any person to whom the regulations apply;
- (b) the information to be furnished by such a person to those persons with whom—
  - (i)   that person does business, or
  - (ii) that person seeks to do business, and the way in which that information is to be furnished.]

Issue of licences

27   Determination of applications

(1) Unless the [OFT] determines to issue a licence in accordance with an application [it] shall, before determining the application, by notice—
- (a) inform the applicant, giving [its] reasons, that, as the case may be, [it] is minded to refuse the application, or to grant it in terms different from those applied for, describing them, and
- (b) invite the applicant to submit to the [OFT] representations in support of his application in accordance with section 34.

(2) If the [OFT] grants the application in terms different from those applied for then, whether or not the applicant appeals, the [OFT] shall issue the licence in the terms approved by [it] unless the applicant by notice informs [it] that he does not desire a licence in those terms.

[27A   Consumer credit EEA firms

(1) Where—
- (a) a consumer credit EEA firm makes an application for a standard licence, and
- (b) the activities covered by the application are all permitted activities,

the OFT shall refuse the application.

(2) Subsection (3) applies where—
- (a) a consumer credit EEA firm makes an application for a standard licence; and
- (b) some (but not all) of the activities covered by the application are permitted activities.

(3) In order to be entitled to be issued with a standard licence in accordance with section 25(1) to (1AB) in relation to a type of business, the firm need not satisfy the OFT that it is a fit person to carry on that type of business so far as it would involve any of the permitted activities covered by the application.

(4) A standard licence held by a consumer credit EEA firm does not at any time authorise the carrying on of an activity which is a permitted activity at that time.

(5) In this section 'permitted activity' means, in relation to a consumer credit EEA firm, an activity for which the firm has, or could obtain, permission under paragraph 15 of Schedule 3 to the Financial Services and Markets Act 2000.]

28   Exclusion from group licence

Where the [OFT] is minded to issue a group licence (whether on the application of any person or not), and in doing so to exclude any person from the group by name, [it] shall, before determining the matter,—
- (a) give notice of that fact to the person proposed to be excluded, giving [its] reasons, and
- (b) invite that person to submit to the [OFT] representations against his exclusion in accordance with section 34.

Charges for indefinite licences

[28A   Charges to be paid by licensees etc. before end of payment periods

(1) The licensee under a standard licence which has effect indefinitely shall, before the end of each payment period of his, pay the OFT a charge towards the costs of carrying out its functions under this Act.

(2) The original applicant for a group licence which has effect indefinitely shall, before the end of each payment period of his, pay the OFT such a charge.

(3) The amount of the charge payable by a person under subsection (1) or (2) before the end of a payment period shall be determined in accordance with provision which—

    (a) is made by the OFT by general notice; and

    (b) is current on such day as may be determined in accordance with provision made by regulations.

(4) The provision that may be made by the OFT under subsection (3)(a) includes—

    (a) different provision in relation to persons of different descriptions (including persons whose payment periods end at different times);

    (b) provision for no charge at all to be payable by persons of specified descriptions.

(5) The approval of the Secretary of State and the Treasury is required for a general notice under subsection (3)(a).

(6) For the purposes of this section a person's payment periods are to be determined in accordance with provision made by regulations.]

[28B   Extension of period to pay charge under s. 28A

(1) A person who is required under section 28A to pay a charge before the end of a period may apply once to the OFT for that period to be extended.

(2) The application shall be made before such day as may be determined in accordance with provision made by the OFT by general notice.

(3) If the OFT is satisfied that there is a good reason—

    (a) why the applicant has not paid that charge prior to his making of the application, and

    (b) why he cannot pay that charge before the end of that period,

it may, if it thinks fit, by notice to him extend that period by such time as it thinks fit having regard to that reason.

(4) The power of the OFT under this section to extend a period in relation to a charge—

    (a) includes the power to extend the period in relation to a part of the charge only;

    (b) may be exercised even though the period has ended.]

[28C   Failure to pay charge under s. 28A

(1) This section applies if a person (the 'defaulter') fails to pay a charge—

    (a) before the end of a period (the 'payment period') as required under section 28A; or

    (b) where the payment period is extended under section 28B, before the end of the payment period as extended (subject to subsection (2)).

(2) Where the payment period is extended under section 28B in relation to a part of the charge only, this section applies if the defaulter fails—

    (a) to pay so much of the charge as is not covered by the extension before the end of the payment period disregarding the extension; or

    (b) to pay so much of the charge as is covered by the extension before the end of the payment period as extended.

(3) Subject to subsection (4), if the charge is a charge under section 28A(1), the defaulter's licence terminates.

(4) If the defaulter has applied to the OFT under section 28B for the payment period to be extended and that application has not been determined—

    (a) his licence shall not terminate before the application has been determined and the OFT has notified him of the determination; and

(b) if the OFT extends the payment period on that application, this section shall have effect accordingly.

(5) If the charge is a charge under section 28A(2), the charge shall be recoverable by the OFT.]

Renewal, variation, suspension and revocation of licences

29 Renewal

(1) If the licensee under a standard licence [of limited duration], or the original applicant for, or any licensee under, a group licence of limited duration, wishes the [OFT] to renew the licence, whether on the same terms (except as to expiry) or on varied terms, he must, during the period specified by the [OFT] by general notice or such longer period as the [OFT] may allow, make an application to the Director for its renewal.

(2) The [OFT] may of [its] own motion renew any group licence.

(3) The preceding provisions of this Part apply to the renewal of a licence as they apply to the issue of a licence, except that section 28 does not apply to a person who was already excluded in the licence up for renewal.

[(3A) In its application to the renewal of standard licences by virtue of subsection (3) of this section, section 27(1) shall have effect as if for paragraph (b) there were substituted—

'(b) invite the applicant to submit to the OFT in accordance with section 34 representations—
   (i)   in support of his application; and
   (ii) about the provision (if any) that should be included under section 34A as part of the determination were the OFT to refuse the application or grant it in terms different from those applied for.']

(4) Until the determination of an application under subsection (1) and, where an appeal lies from the determination, until the end of the appeal period, the licence shall continue [to have effect], notwithstanding that apart from this subsection it would expire earlier.

[...]

(6) General notice shall be given of the renewal of a group licence.

30 Variation by request

[(1) If it thinks fit, the OFT may by notice to the licensee under a standard licence—
   (a) in the case of a licence which covers the carrying on of a type of business only so far as it falls within one or more descriptions of business, vary the licence by—
      (i)   removing that limitation;
      (ii) adding a description of business to that limitation; or
      (iii) removing a description of business from that limitation;
   (b) in the case of a licence which covers the carrying on of a type of business with no limitation, vary the licence so that it covers the carrying on of that type of business only so far as it falls within one or more descriptions of business;
   (c) vary the licence so that it no longer covers the carrying on of a type of business at all;
   (d) vary the licence so that a type of business the carrying on of which is not covered at all by the licence is covered either—
      (i)   with no limitation; or
      (ii) only so far as it falls within one or more descriptions of business; or
   (e) vary the licence in any other way except for the purpose of varying the descriptions of activities covered by the licence.

(1A) The OFT may vary a licence under subsection (1) only in accordance with an application made by the licensee.

(1B) References in this section to a description of business in relation to a type of business—
   (a) are references to a description of business specified in a general notice under section 24A(5)(a); and

(b) in subsection (1)(a) (apart from sub-paragraph (ii)) include references to a description of business that was, but is no longer, so specified.]

(2) In the case of a group licence issued on the application of any person, the [OFT], on an application made by that person, may if [it] thinks fit by notice to that person vary the terms of the licence in accordance with the application; but the [OFT] shall not vary a group licence under this subsection by excluding a named person, other than the person making the request, unless that named person consents in writing to his exclusion.

(3) In the case of a group licence from which (whether by name or description) a person is excluded, the [OFT], on an application made by that person, may if [it] thinks fit, by notice to that person, vary the terms of the licence so as to remove the exclusion.

(4) Unless the [OFT] determines to vary a licence in accordance with an application [it] shall, before determining the application, by notice—

(a) inform the applicant, giving [its] reasons, that [it] is minded to refuse the application, and

(b) invite the applicant to submit to the [OFT] representations in suppprt of his application in accordance with section 34.

(5) General notice shall be given that a variation of a group licence has been made under this section.

31 Compulsory variation

(1) Where at a time during the currency of a licence the [OFT] is of the opinion that, if the licence had expired at that time [(assuming, in the case of a licence which has effect indefinitely, that it were a licence of limited duration)], [it] would on an application for its renewal or futher renewal on the same terms (except as to expiry), have been minded to grant the application but on different terms, and that therefore [it should take steps mentioned in subsection (1A)], [it] shall proceed as follows.

[(1A) Those steps are—

(a) in the case of a standard licence, steps mentioned in section 30(1)(a)(ii) and (iii), (b), (c) and (e);

(b) in the case of a group licence, the varying of terms of the licence.]

[(1B) The OFT shall also proceed as follows if, having regard to section 22 (1B) to (1E), it is of the opinion—

(a) that a licence which has effect indefinitely should have its duration limited; or

(b) in the case of a licence of limited duration, that the period during which it has effect should be shortened.]

(2) In the case of a standard licence the [OFT] shall, by notice—

(a) inform the licensee of the variations the [OFT] is minded to make in the terms of the licence, stating [its] reasons, and

[(b) invite him to submit to the OFT in accordance with section 34 representations—

(i) as to the proposed variations; and

(ii) about the provision (if any) that should be included under section 34A as part of the determination were the OFT to vary the licence.]

(3) In the case of a group licence the [OFT] shall—

(a) give general notice of the variations [it] is minded to make in the terms of the licence, stating [its] reasons, and

(b) in the notice invite any licensee to submit to [it] representations as to the proposed variations in accordance with section 34.

(4) In the case of a group licence issued on application the [OFT] shall also—

(a) inform the original applicant of the variations the [OFT] is minded to make in the terms of the licence, stating [its] reasons, and

(b) invite him to submit to the [OFT] representations as to the proposed variations in accordance with section 34.

(5) If the [OFT] is minded to vary a group licence by excluding any person (other than the original applicant) from the group by name the [OFT] shall, in addition, take the like steps under section 28 as are required in the case mentioned in that section.

(6) General notice shall be given that a variation of any group licence has been made under this section.

(7) A variation under this section shall not take effect before the end of the appeal period.

[(8) Subsection (1) shall have effect in relation to a standard licence as if an application could be made for the renewal or further renewal of the licence on the same terms (except as to expiry) even if such an application could not be made because of provision made in a general notice under section 24A(5).

(9) Accordingly, in applying subsection (1AA) of section 25 in relation to the licence for the purposes of this section, the OFT shall treat references in that subsection to the description or descriptions of business in relation to a type of business as references to the description or descriptions of business included in the licence in relation to that type of business, notwithstanding that provision under section 24A(5).]

32   Suspension and revocation

(1) Where at a time during the currency of a licence the [OFT] is of the opinion that if the licence had expired at that time [(assuming, in the case of a licence which has effect indefinitely, that it were a licence of limited duration)] [it] would have been minded not to renew it, and that therefore it should be revoked or suspended, [it] shall proceed as follows.

(2) In the case of a standard licence the [OFT] shall, by notice—
    (a) inform the licensee that, as the case may be, the [OFT] is minded to revoke the licence, or suspend it until a specified date or indefinitely, stating [its] reasons, and
    [(b) invite him to submit to the OFT in accordance with section 34 representations—
        (i) as to the proposed revocation or suspension; and
        (ii) about the provision (if any) that should be included under section 34A as part of the determination were the OFT to revoke or suspend the licence.]

(3) In the case of a group licence the [OFT] shall—
    (a) give general notice that, as the case may be, [it] is minded to revoke the licence, or suspend it until a specified date or indefinitely, stating [its] reasons, and
    (b) in the notice invite any licensee to submit to [it] representations as to the proposed revocation or suspension in accordance with section 34.

(4) In the case of a group licence issued on application the [OFT] shall also—
    (a) inform the original applicant that, as the case may be, the [OFT] is minded to revoke the licence, or suspend it until a specified date or indefinitely, stating [its] reasons, and
    (b) invite him to submit representations as to the proposed revocation or suspension in accordance with section 34.

[...]

(6) General notice shall be given of the revocation or suspension of a group licence.

(7) A revocation or suspension under this section shall not take effect before the end of the appeal period.

(8) Except for the purposes of section 29, a licensee under a suspended licence shall be treated, in respect of the period of suspension, as if the licence had not been issued; and where the suspension is not expressed to end on a specified date it may, if the [OFT] thinks fit, be ended by notice given by [it] to the licensee or, in the case of a group licence, by general notice.

[(9) The OFT has no power to revoke or to suspend a standard licence simply because, by virtue of provision made in a general notice under sections 24A(5), a person cannot apply for the renewal of such a licence on terms which are the same as the terms of the licence in question.]

33   Application to end suspension

(1) On an application made by a licensee the [OFT] may, if [it] thinks fit, by notice to the licensee end the suspension of a licence, whether the suspension was for a fixed or indefinite period.

(2) Unless the [OFT] determines to end the suspension in accordance with the application [it] shall, before determining the application, by notice—

    (a) inform the applicant, giving [its] reasons, that [it] is minded to refuse the application, and

    (b) invite the applicant to submit to the [OFT] representations in support of his application in accordance with section 34.

(3) General notice shall be given that a suspension of a group licence has been ended under this section.

(4) In the case of a group licence issued on application—

    (a) the references in subsection (1) to a licensee include the original applicant;

    (b) the [OFT] shall inform the original applicant that a suspension of a group licence has been ended under this section.

[Further powers of OFT to regulate conduct of licensees etc.]

[33A   Power of OFT to impose requirements on licensees

(1) This section applies where the OFT is dissatisfied with any matter in connection with—

    (a) a business being carried on, or which has been carried on, by a licensee or by an associate or a former associate of a licensee;

    (b) a proposal to carry on a business which has been made by a licensee or by an associate or a former associate of a licensee; or

    (c) any conduct not covered by paragraph (a) or (b) of a licensee or of an associate or a former associate of a licensee.

(2) The OFT may by notice to the licensee require him to do or not to do (or to cease doing) anything specified in the notice for purposes connected with—

    (a) addressing the matter with which the OFT is dissatisfied; or

    (b) securing that matters of the same or a similar kind do not arise.

(3) A requirement imposed under this section on a licensee shall only relate to a business which the licensee is carrying on, or is proposing to carry on, under the licence under which he is a licensee.

(4) Such a requirement may be framed by reference to a named person other than the licensee.

(5) For the purposes of subsection (1) it is immaterial whether the matter with which the OFT is dissatisfied arose before or after the licensee became a licensee.

(6) If—

    (a) a person makes an application for a standard licence, and

    (b) while dealing with that application the OFT forms the opinion that, if such a licence were to be issued to that person, it would be minded to impose on him a requirement under this section,

the OFT may, before issuing such a licence to that person, do (in whole or in part) anything that it must do under section 33D or 34(1) or (2) in relation to the imposing of the requirement.

(7) In this section 'associate', in addition to the persons specified in section 184, includes a business associate.]

[33B   Power of OFT to impose requirements on supervisory bodies

(1) This section applies where the OFT is dissatisfied with the way in which a responsible person in relation to a group licence—

    (a) is regulating or otherwise supervising, or has regulated or otherwise supervised, persons who are licensees under that licence; or

    (b) is proposing to regulate or otherwise to supervise such persons.

(2) The OFT may by notice to the responsible person require him to do or not to do (or to cease doing) anything specified in the notice for purposes connected with—

    (a) addressing the matters giving rise to the OFT's dissatisfaction; or

(b) securing that matters of the same or a similar kind do not arise.

(3) A requirement imposed under this section on a responsible person in relation to a group licence shall only relate to practices and procedures for regulating or otherwise supervising licensees under the licence in connection with their carrying on of businesses under the licence.

(4) For the purposes of subsection (1) it is immaterial whether the matters giving rise to the OFT's dissatisfaction arose before or after the issue of the group licence in question.

(5) If—

(a) a person makes an application for a group licence, and

(b) while dealing with that application the OFT forms the opinion that, if such a licence were to be issued to that person, it would be minded to impose on him a requirement under this section,

the OFT may, before issuing such a licence to that person, do (in whole or in part) anything that it must do under section 33D or 34(1) or (2) in relation to the imposing of the requirement.

(6) For the purposes of this Part a person is a responsible person in relation to a group licence if—

(a) he is the original applicant for it; and

(b) he has a responsibility (whether by virtue of an enactment, an agreement or otherwise) for regulating or otherwise supervising persons who are licensees under the licence.]

[33C   Supplementary provision relating to requirements

(1) A notice imposing a requirement under section 33A or 33B may include provision about the time at or by which, or the period during which, the requirement is to be complied with.

(2) A requirement imposed under section 33A or 33B shall not have effect after the licence by reference to which it is imposed has itself ceased to have effect.

(3) A person shall not be required under section 33A or 33B to compensate, or otherwise to make amends to, another person.

(4) The OFT may by notice to the person on whom a requirement has been imposed under section 33A or 33B vary or revoke the requirement (including any provision made under subsection (1) of this section in relation to it) with effect from such date as may be specified in the notice.

(5) The OFT may exercise its power under subsection (4) in relation to a requirement either on its own motion or on the application of a person falling within subsection (6) or (7) in relation to the requirement.

(6) A person falls within this subsection in relation to a requirement if he is the person on whom the requirement is imposed.

(7) A person falls within this subsection in relation to a requirement if—

(a) the requirement is imposed under section 33A;

(b) he is not the person on whom the requirement is imposed;

(c) the requirement is framed by reference to him by name; and

(d) the effect of the requirement is—

(i) to prevent him being an employee of the person on whom the requirement is imposed;

(ii) to restrict the activities that he may engage in as an employee of that person; or

(iii) otherwise to prevent him from doing something, or to restrict his doing something, in connection with a business being carried on by that person.]

[33D   Procedure in relation to requirements

(1) Before making a determination—

(a) to impose a requirement on a person under section 33A or 33B,

(b) to refuse an application under section 33C(5) in relation to a requirement imposed under either of those sections, or

(c) to vary or to revoke a requirement so imposed,

the OFT shall proceed as follows.

(2) The OFT shall give a notice to every person to whom subsection (3) applies in relation to the determination—

(a) informing him, with reasons, that it is minded to make the determination; and

(b) inviting him to submit to it representations as to the determination under section 34.

(3) This subsection applies to a person in relation to the determination if he falls within, or as a consequence of the determination would fall within, section 33C(6) or (7) in relation to the requirement in question.

(4) This section does not require the OFT to give a notice to a person if the determination in question is in the same terms as a proposal made to the OFT by that person (whether as part of an application under this Part or otherwise).]

[33E   Guidance on requirements

(1) The OFT shall prepare and publish guidance in relation to how it exercises, or how it proposes to exercise, its powers under sections 33A to 33C.

(2) If the OFT revises the guidance at any time after it has been published, the OFT shall publish it as revised.

(3) The guidance shall be published in such manner as the OFT thinks fit for the purpose of bringing it to the attention of those likely to be affected by it.

(4) In preparing or revising the guidance the OFT shall consult such persons as it thinks fit.

(5) In exercising its powers under sections 33A to 33C the OFT shall have regard to the guidance as most recently published.]

Miscellaneous

34   Representations to [OFT]

(1) Where this section applies to an invitation by the [OFT] to any person to submit representations, the [OFT] shall invite that person, within 21 days after the notice containing the invitation is given to him or published, or such longer period as the [OFT] may allow—

(a) to submit his representations in writing to the [OFT], and

(b) to give notice to the [OFT], if he thinks fit, that he wishes to make representations orally,

and where notice is given under paragraph (b) the [OFT] shall arrange for the oral representations to be heard.

(2) In reaching [its] determination the [OFT] shall take into account any representations submitted or made under this section.

(3) The [OFT] shall give notice of [its] determination to the persons who were required to be invited to submit representations about it or, where the invitation to submit representations was required to be given by general notice, shall give general notice of the determination.

[34A   Winding-up of standard licensee's business

(1) If it thinks fit, the OFT may, for the purpose of enabling the licensee's business, or any part of his business, to be transferred or wound up, include as part of a determination to which subsection (2) applies provision authorising the licensee to carry on for a specified period—

(a) specified activities, or

(b) activities of specified descriptions,

which, because of that determination, the licensee will no longer be licensed to carry on.

(2) This subsection applies to the following determinations—

    (a) a determination to refuse to renew a standard licence in accordance with the terms of the application for its renewal;

    (b) a determination to vary such a licence under section 31;

    (c) a determination to suspend or revoke such a licence.

(3) Such provision—

    (a) may specify different periods for different activities or activities of different description;

    (b) may provide for persons other than the licensee to carry on activities under the authorisation;

    (c) may specify requirements which must be complied with by a person carrying on activities under the authorisation in relation to those activities;

and, if a requirement specified under paragraph (c) is not complied with, the OFT may by notice to a person carrying on activities under the authorisation terminate the authorisation (in whole or in part) from a specified date.

(4) Without prejudice to the generality of paragraph (c) of subsection (3), a requirement specified under that paragraph may have the effect of—

    (a) preventing a named person from being an employee of a person carrying on activities under the authorisation, or restricting the activities he may engage in as an employee of such a person;

    (b) preventing a named person from doing something, or restricting his doing something, in connection with activities being carried on by a person under the authorisation;

    (c) securing that access to premises is given to officers of the OFT for the purpose of enabling them to inspect documents or to observe the carrying on of activities.

(5) Activities carried on under an authorisation shall be treated for the purposes of sections 39(1), 40, 148 and 149 as if carried on under a standard licence.]

35 The register

(1) The [OFT] shall establish and maintain a register, in which [it] shall cause to be kept particulars of—

    (a) applications not yet determined for the issue, variation or renewal of licences, or for ending the suspension of a licence;

    (b) licences which are in [effect], or have at any time been suspended or revoked [or terminated by section 28C], with details of any variation of the terms of a licence;

    [(ba) requirements imposed under section 33A or 33B which are in effect or which have been in effect, with details of any variation of such a requirement;]

    (c) decisions given by [it] under this Act, and any appeal from those decisions; and

    (d) such other matters (if any) as he thinks fit.

[(1A) The [OFT] shall also cause to be kept in the register any copy of any notice or other document relating to a consumer credit EEA firm which is given to the [OFT] by the Financial Services Authority for inclusion in the register.]

(2) The [OFT] shall give general notice of the various matters required to be entered in the register, and of any change in them made under subsection (1)(d).

(3) Any person shall be entitled on payment of the specified fee—

    (a) to inspect the register during ordinary office hours and take copies of any entry, or

    (b) to obtain from the [OFT] a copy, certified by the [OFT] to be correct, of any entry in the register.

(4) The [OFT] may, if [it] thinks fit, determine that the right conferred by subsection (3)(a) shall be exercisable in relation to a copy of the register instead of, or in addition to, the original.

(5) The [OFT] shall give general notice of the place or places where, and times when, the register or a copy of it may be inspected.

36 Duty to notify changes

(1) Within 21 working days after change takes place in any particulars entered in the register in respect of a standard licence or the licensee under section 35(1)(d) (not being a change resulting from action taken by the [OFT]), the licensee shall give the [OFT] notice of the change; and the [OFT] shall cause any necessary amendment to be made in the register.

(2) Within 21 working days after—

    (a) any change takes place in the officers of—

        (i)   a body corporate, or an unincorporated body of persons, which is the icensee under a standard licence, or

        (ii)   a body corporate which is a controller of a body corporate which is such a Licensee, or

    (b) a body corporate which is such a licensee becomes aware that a person has become or ceased to be a controller of the body corporate, or

    (c) any change takes place in the members of a partnership which is such a licensee (including a change on the amalgamation of the partnership with another firm, or a change whereby the number of partners is reduced to one), the licensee shall give the [OFT] notice of the change.

(3) Within 14 working days after any change takes place in the officers of a body corporate which is a controller of another body corporate which is a licensee under a standard licence, the controller shall give the licensee notice of the change.

(4) Within 14 working days after a person becomes or ceases to be a controller of a body corporate which is a licensee under a standard licence, that person shall give the licensee notice of the fact.

(5) Where a change in a partnership has the result that the business ceases to be carried on under the name, or any of the names, specified in a standard licence the licence shall cease to have effect.

    […]

[36A Further duties to notify changes etc.

(1) Subsections (2) to (4) apply where a general notice under section 6(2) comes into effect.

(2) A person who is the licensee under a standard licence or who is the original applicant for a group licence shall, in relation to each relevant application which he has made and which was determined before the general notice came into effect, provide the OFT with any information or document—

    (a) which he would have been required to provide with the application had the application been made after the general notice came into effect; and

    (b) which the general notice requires to be provided for the purposes of this subsection.

(3) Any such information or document shall be provided within such period as may be specified in the general notice.

(4) Subsection (2) does not require a person to provide any information or document—

    (a) which he provided in relation to the application by virtue of section 6;

    (b) which he has previously provided in relation to the application by virtue of this section; or

    (c) which he would have been required to provide in relation to the application by virtue of subsection (5) but for subsection (6).

(5) A person who is the licensee under a standard licence or who is the original applicant for a group licence shall, in relation to each relevant application which he has made, notify the OFT giving details if, after the application is determined, any information or document which he—

    (a) provided in relation to the application by virtue of section 6, or

    (b) has so provided by virtue of this section,

is, to any extent, superseded or otherwise affected by a change in circumstances.

(6) Subsection (5) does not require a person to notify the OFT about a matter unless it falls within a description of matters specified by the OFT in a general notice.

(7) A description may be specified for the purposes of subsection (6) only if the OFT is satisfied that the matters which would fall within that description are matters which would be relevant to the question of—

    (a) whether, having regard to section 25(2), a person is a fit person to carry on a business under a standard licence; or

    (b) whether the public interest is better served by a group licence remaining in effect than by obliging the licensees under it to apply separately for standard licences.

(8) A person who is the licensee under a standard licence or who is the original applicant for a group licence shall, in relation to each relevant application which he has made, notify the OFT about every error or omission—

    (a) in or from any information or document which he provided by virtue of section 6, or which he has provided by virtue of this section, in relation to the application; and

    (b) of which he becomes aware after the determination of the application.

(9) A notification for the purposes of subsection (5) or (8) shall be given within the period of 28 days beginning with the day on which (as the case may be)—

    (a) the information or document is superseded;

    (b) the change in circumstances occurs; or

    (c) the licensee or the original applicant becomes aware of the error or omission.

(10) This section does not require a person to notify the OFT about—

    (a) anything of which he is required to notify it under section 36; or

    (b) an error in or omission from any information or document which is a clerical error or omission not affecting the substance of the information or document.

(11) In this section 'relevant application' means, in relation to a person who is the licensee under a standard licence or who is the original applicant for a group licence—

    (a) the original application for the licence; or

    (b) an application for its renewal or for its variation.]

[36B Power of OFT to require information generally

(1) The OFT may by notice to a person require him—

    (a) to provide such information as may be specified or described in the notice; or

    (b) to produce such documents as may be so specified or described.

(2) The notice shall set out the reasons why the OFT requires the information or documents to be provided or produced.

(3) The information or documents shall be provided or produced—

    (a) before the end of such reasonable period as may be specified in the notice; and

    (b) at such place as may be so specified.

(4) A requirement may be imposed under subsection (1) on a person who is—

    (a) the licensee under a standard licence, or

    (b) the original applicant for a group licence,

only if the provision or production of the information or documents in question is reasonably required for purposes connected with the OFT's functions under this Act.

(5) A requirement may be imposed under subsection (1) on any other person only if—

    (a) an act or omission mentioned in subsection (6) has occurred or the OFT has reason to suspect that such an act or omission has occurred; and

    (b) the provision or production of the information or documents in question is reasonably required for purposes connected with—

        (i) the taking by the OFT of steps under this Part as a consequence; or

        (ii) its consideration of whether to take such steps as a consequence.

(6) Those acts or omissions are acts or omissions which—

(a) cast doubt on whether, having regard to section 25(2), a person is a fit person to carry on a business under a standard licence;

(b) cast doubt on whether the public interest is better served by a group licence remaining in effect, or being issued, than by obliging the persons who are licensees under it, or who would be licensees under it, to apply separately for standard licences;

(c) give rise, or are likely to give rise, to dissatisfaction for the purposes of section 33A(1) or 33B(1); or

(d) constitute or give rise to a failure of the kind mentioned in section 39A(1).]

[36C   Power of OFT to require access to premises

(1) The OFT may by notice to a licensee under a licence require him to secure that access to the premises specified or described in the notice is given to an officer of an enforcement authority in order for the officer—

(a) to observe the carrying on of a business under the licence by the licensee; or

(b) to inspect such documents of the licensee relating to such a business as are—

(i)   specified or described in the notice; and

(ii) situated on the premises.

(2) The notice shall set out the reasons why the access is required.

(3) The premises which may be specified or described in the notice—

(a) include premises which are not premises of the licensee if they are premises from which he carries on activities in connection with the business in question; but

(b) do not include premises which are used only as a dwelling.

(4) The licensee shall secure that the required access is given at such times as the OFT reasonably requires.

(5) The OFT shall give reasonable notice of those times.

(6) Where an officer is given access to any premises by virtue of this section, the licensee shall also secure that persons on the premises give the officer such assistance or information as he may reasonably require in connection with his observation or inspection of documents (as the case may be).

(7) The assistance that may be required under subsection (6) includes (amongst other things) the giving to the officer of an explanation of a document which he is inspecting.

(8) A requirement may be imposed under subsection (1) on a person who is—

(a) the licensee under a standard licence, or

(b) the original applicant for a group licence,

only if the observation or inspection in question is reasonably required for purposes connected with the OFT's functions under this Act.

(9) A requirement may be imposed under subsection (1) on any other person only if—

(a) an act or omission mentioned in section 36B(6) has occurred or the OFT has reason to suspect that such an act or omission has occurred; and

(b) the observation or inspection in question is reasonably required for purposes connected with—

(i)   the taking by the OFT of steps under this Part as a consequence; or

(ii) its consideration of whether to take such steps as a consequence.

(10) In this section—

(a) references to a licensee under a licence include, in relation to a group licence issued on application, references to the original applicant; and

(b) references to a business being carried on under a licence by a licensee include, in relation to the original applicant for a group licence, activities being carried on by him for the purpose of regulating or otherwise supervising (whether by virtue of an enactment, an agreement or otherwise) licensees under that licence in connection with their carrying on of businesses under that licence.]

[36D   Entry to premises under warrant

(1) A justice of the peace may issue a warrant under this section if satisfied on information on oath given on behalf of the OFT that there are reasonable grounds for believing that the following conditions are satisfied.

(2) Those conditions are—

(a) that there is on the premises specified in the warrant information or documents in relation to which a requirement could be imposed under section 36B; and

(b) that if such a requirement were to be imposed in relation to the information or documents—

(i)   it would not be complied with; or

(ii) the information or documents would be tampered with.

(3) A warrant under this section shall authorise an officer of an enforcement authority—

(a) to enter the premises specified in the warrant;

(b) to search the premises and to seize and detain any information or documents appearing to be information or documents specified in the warrant or information or documents of a description so specified;

(c) to take any other steps which may appear to be reasonably necessary for preserving such information or documents or preventing interference with them; and

(d) to use such force as may be reasonably necessary.

(4) An officer entering premises by virtue of this section may take such persons and equipment with him as he thinks necessary.

(5) In the application of this section to Scotland—

(a) the reference to a justice of the peace includes a reference to a sheriff;

(b) for 'information on oath' there is substituted 'evidence on oath'.

(6) In the application of this section to Northern Ireland the reference to a justice of the peace shall be construed as a reference to a lay magistrate.]

[36E   Failure to comply with information requirement

(1) If on an application made by the OFT it appears to the court that a person (the 'information defaulter') has failed to do something that he was required to do by virtue of section 36B or 36C, the court may make an order under this section.

(2) An order under this section may require the information defaulter—

(a) to do the thing that it appears he failed to do within such period as may be specified in the order;

(b) otherwise to take such steps to remedy the consequences of the failure as may be so specified.

(3) If the information defaulter is a body corporate, a partnership or an unincorporated body of persons which is not a partnership, the order may require any officer who is (wholly or partly) responsible for the failure to meet such costs of the application as are specified in the order.

(4) In this section—

'court' means—

(a) in England and Wales and Northern Ireland, the High Court or the county court;

(b) in Scotland, the Court of Session or the sheriff;

'officer' means—

(a) in relation to a body corporate, a person holding a position of director, manager or secretary of the body or any similar position;

(b) in relation to a partnership or to an unincorporated body of persons, a member of the partnership or body.

(5) In subsection (4) 'director' means, in relation to a body corporate whose affairs are managed by its members, a member of the body.]

[36F   Officers of enforcement authorities other than OFT

(1) A relevant officer may only exercise powers by virtue of section 36C or 36D in pursuance of arrangements made with the OFT by or on behalf of the enforcement authority of which he is an officer.

(2) Anything done or omitted to be done by, or in relation to, a relevant officer in the exercise or purported exercise of a power by virtue of section 36C or 36D shall be treated for all purposes as having been done or omitted to be done by, or in relation to, an officer of the OFT.

(3) Subsection (2) does not apply for the purposes of any criminal proceedings brought against the officer, the enforcement authority of which he is an officer or the OFT in respect of anything done or omitted to be done by the officer.

(4) A relevant officer shall not disclose to a person other than the OFT information obtained by his exercise of a power by virtue of section 36C or 36D unless—

(a) he has the approval of the OFT to do so; or

(b) he is under a duty to make the disclosure.

(5) In this section 'relevant officer' means an officer of an enforcement authority other than the OFT.]

37   Death, bankruptcy etc. of licensee

(1) A licence held by one individual terminates if he—

(a) dies, or

(b) is adjudged bankrupt, or

[(c) becomes a person who lacks capacity (within the meaning of the Mental Capacity Act 2005) to carry on the activities covered by the licence.]

[(1A) A licence terminates if the licensee gives the OFT a notice under subsection (1B).

(1B) A notice under this subsection shall—

(a) be in such form as the OFT may by general notice specify;

(b) contain such information as may be so specified;

(c) be accompanied by the licence or give reasons as to why it is not accompanied by the licence; and

(d) be signed by or on behalf of the licensee.]

(2) In relation to a licence held by one individual, or a partnership or other unincorporated body of persons, or a body corporate, regulations may specify other events relating to the licensee on the occurrence of which the licence is to terminate.

(3) Regulations may—

(a) provide for the termination of a licence by subsection (1) [or (1A)], or under subsection (2), to be deferred for a period not exceeding 12 months, and

(b) authorise the business of the licensee to be carried on under the licence by some other person during the period of deferment, subject to such conditions as may be prescribed.

(4) This section does not apply to group licences.

38   Application of s. 37 to Scotland and Northern Ireland

. . .

39   Offences against Part III

(1) A person who engages in any activities for which a licence is required when he is not a licensee under a licence covering those activities commits an offence.

(2) A licensee under a standard licence who carries on business under a name not specified in the licence commits an offence.

(3) A person who fails to give the [OFT] or a licensee notice under section 36 within the period required commits an offence.

[39A   Power of OFT to impose civil penalties

(1) Where the OFT is satisfied that a person (the 'defaulter') has failed or is failing to comply with a requirement imposed on him by virtue of section 33A, 33B or 36A, it may by notice to him (a 'penalty notice') impose on him a penalty of such amount as it thinks fit.

The penalty notice shall—
- (a) specify the amount of the penalty that is being imposed;
- (b) set out the OFT's reasons for imposing a penalty and for specifying that amount;
- (c) specify how the payment of the penalty may be made to the OFT; and
- (d) specify the period within which the penalty is required to be paid.

(3) The amount of the penalty shall not exceed £50,000.

(4) The period specified in the penalty notice for the purposes of subsection (2)(d) shall not end earlier than the end of the period during which an appeal may be brought against the imposition of the penalty under section 41.

(5) If the defaulter does not pay the penalty to the OFT within the period so specified—
- (a) the unpaid balance from time to time shall carry interest at the rate for the time being specified in section 17 of the Judgments Act 1838; and
- (b) the penalty and any interest payable on it shall be recoverable by the OFT.]

[39B Further provision relating to civil penalties

(1) Before determining to impose a penalty on a person under section 39A the OFT shall give a notice to that person—
- (a) informing him that it is minded to impose a penalty on him;
- (b) stating the proposed amount of the penalty;
- (c) setting out its reasons for being minded to impose a penalty on him and for proposing that amount;
- (d) setting out the proposed period for the payment of the penalty; and
- (e) inviting him to submit representations to it about the matters mentioned in the preceding paragraphs in accordance with section 34.

(2) In determining whether and how to exercise its powers under section 39A in relation to a person's failure, the OFT shall have regard to (amongst other things)—
- (a) any penalty or fine that has been imposed on that person by another body in relation to the conduct giving rise to the failure;
- (b) other steps that the OFT has taken or might take under this Part in relation to that conduct.

(3) General notice shall be given of the imposition of a penalty under section 39A on a person who is a responsible person in relation to a group licence.

(4) That notice shall include the matters set out in the notice imposing the penalty in accordance with section 39A(2)(a) and (b).]

[39C Statement of policy in relation to civil penalties

(1) The OFT shall prepare and publish a statement of policy in relation to how it exercises, or how it proposes to exercise, its powers under section 39A.

(2) If the OFT revises the statement of policy at any time after it has been published, the OFT shall publish it as revised.

(3) No statement of policy shall be published without the approval of the Secretary of State.

(4) The statement of policy shall be published in such manner as the OFT thinks fit for the purpose of bringing it to the attention of those likely to be affected by it.

(5) In preparing or revising the statement of policy the OFT shall consult such persons as it thinks fit.

(6) In determining whether and how to exercise its powers under section 39A in relation to a person's failure, the OFT shall have regard to the statement of policy as most recently published at the time the failure occurred.

(7) The OFT shall not impose a penalty on a person under section 39A in relation to a failure occurring before it has published a statement of policy.]

40 Enforcement of agreements made by unlicensed trader

[(1) A regulated agreement is not enforceable against the debtor or hirer by a person acting in the course of a consumer credit business or a consumer hire business (as the case may be) if that person is not licensed to carry on a consumer credit business or a consumer hire business (as the case may be) of a description which covers the enforcement of the agreement.

(1A) Unless the OFT has made an order under subsection (2) which applies to the agreement, a regulated agreement is not enforceable against the debtor or hirer if—

    (a) it was made by the creditor or owner in the course of a consumer credit business or a consumer hire business (as the case may be); and

    (b) at the time the agreement was made he was not licensed to carry on a consumer credit business or a consumer hire business (as the case may be) of a description which covered the making of the agreement.

  (2) Where—

    (a) during any period a person (the 'trader' has) made regulated agreements in the course of a consumer credit business or a consumer hire business (as the case may be), and

    (b) during that period he was not licensed to carry on a consumer credit business or a consumer hire business (as the case may be) of a description which covered the making of those agreements,

he or his successor in title may apply to the OFT for an order that the agreements are to be treated for the purposes of subsection (1A) as if he had been licensed as required.]

(3) Unless the [OFT] determines to make an order under subsection (2) in accordance with the application, [it] shall, before determining the application, by notice—

    (a) inform the applicant, giving [its] reasons, that, as the case may be, [it] is minded to refuse the application, or to grant it in terms different from those applied for, describing them, and

    (b) invite the applicant to submit to the [OFT] representations in support of his application in accordance with section 34.

(4) In determining whether or not to make an order under subsection (2) in respect of any period the [OFT] shall consider, in addition to any other relevant factors—

    (a) how far, if at all, debtors or hirers under [the regulated agreements in question] were prejudiced by the trader's conduct,

    (b) whether or not the [OFT] would have been likely to grant a licence covering [the making of those agreements during] that period on an application by the trader, and

    (c) the degree of culpability for the failure to [be licensed as required].

(5) If the [OFT] thinks fit, [it] may in an order under subsection (2)—

    (a) limit the order to specified agreements, or agreements of a specified description or made at a specified time;

    (b) make the order conditional on the doing of specified acts by the applicant.

[(6) This section (apart from subsection (1)) does not apply to a regulated agreement [...] made by a consumer credit EEA firm unless at the time it was made that firm was precluded from entering into it as a result of—

    (a) a consumer credit prohibition imposed under section 203 of the Financial Services and Markets Act 2000; or

    (b) a restriction imposed on the firm under section 204 of that Act.]

[(7) Subsection (1) does not apply to the enforcement of a regulated agreement by a consumer credit EEA firm unless that firm is precluded from enforcing it as a result of a prohibition or restriction mentioned in subsection (6)(a) or (b).

(8) This section (apart from subsection (1)) does not apply to a regulated agreement made by a person if by virtue of section 21(2) or (3) he was not required to be licensed to make the agreement.

(9) Subsection (1) does not apply to the enforcement of a regulated agreement by a person if by virtue of section 21(2) or (3) he is not required to be licensed to enforce the agreement.]

[*Appeals*]

[40A   The Consumer Credit Appeals Tribunal

(1) There shall be a tribunal known as the Consumer Credit Appeals Tribunal ('the Tribunal').

(2) The Tribunal shall have the functions conferred on it by or under this Part.

(3) The Lord Chancellor may by rules make such provision as he thinks fit for regulating the conduct and disposal of appeals before the Tribunal.

(4) Schedule A1 (which makes provision about the Tribunal and proceedings before it) shall have effect.

(5) But that Schedule does not limit the Lord Chancellor's powers under subsection (3).]

41   Appeals to Secretary of State under Part III

(1) If, in the case of a determination by the [OFT] such as is mentioned in column 1 of the table set out at the end of this section, a person mentioned in relation to that determination in column 2 of the table is aggrieved by the determination he may, within the [specified period, appeal to the Tribunal].

[(1A) The means for making an appeal is by sending the Tribunal a notice of appeal.

(1B) The notice of appeal shall—

(a) be in the specified form;

(b) set out the grounds of appeal in the specified manner; and

(c) include the specified information and documents.

(1C) An appeal to the Tribunal is to be by way of a rehearing of the determination appealed against.

(1D) In this section 'specified' means specified by rules under section 40A(3).]

TABLE

Determination	Appellant
Refusal to issue, renew or vary licence in accordance with terms of application.	The applicant.
Exclusion of person from group licence.	The person excluded.
[...]	

Determination	Appellant
Compulsory variation, or suspension or revocation, of standard licence.	The licensee.
Compulsory variation, or suspension or revocation, of group licence.	The original applicant or any licensee.
Refusal to end suspension of licence in accordance with terms of application.	The applicant.
[Determination— (a) to impose a requirement under section 33A or 33B; (b) to refuse an application under section 33C(5) in relation to a requirement imposed under either of those sections; or (c) to vary or revoke a requirement so imposed.	A person who falls within section 33C(6) or (7) in relation to the requirement unless the OFT was not required to give a notice to him in relation to the determination by virtue of section 33D(4).]

[Imposition of penalty under section 39A	The person on whom the penalty is imposed.]
Refusal to make order under section 40(2)[,148(2) or 149(2)] in accordance with terms of application.	The applicant.
[Imposition of, or refusal to withdraw, consumer credit prohibition under section 203 of the Financial Services and Markets Act 2000.	The consumer credit EEA firm concerned.
Imposition of, or refusal to withdraw, a restriction under section 204 of the Financial Services and Markets Act 2000.	The consumer credit EEA firm concerned.]

[41A   Appeals from the Consumer Credit Appeals Tribunal

(1) A party to an appeal to the Tribunal may with leave appeal—

    (a) in England and Wales and Northern Ireland, to the Court of Appeal, or

    (b) in Scotland, to the Court of Session,

on a point of law arising from a decision of the Tribunal.

(2) For the purposes of subsection (1) leave to appeal may be given by—

    (a) the Tribunal; or

    (b) the Court of Appeal or the Court of Session.

(3) An application for leave to appeal may be made to the Court of Appeal or the Court of Session only if the Tribunal has refused such leave.

(4) If on an appeal under this section the court considers that the decision of the Tribunal was wrong in law, it may do one or more of the following—

    (a) quash or vary that decision;

    (b) substitute for that decision a decision of its own;

    (c) remit the matter to the Tribunal for rehearing and determination in accordance with the directions (if any) given to it by the court.

(5) An appeal may be brought from a decision of the Court of Appeal under this section only if leave to do so is given by the Court of Appeal or the House of Lords.

(6) Rules under section 40A(3) may make provision for regulating or prescribing any matters incidental to or consequential on an appeal under this section.

(7) In this section 'party' means, in relation to an appeal to the Tribunal, the appellant or the OFT.]

PART IV   SEEKING BUSINESS

Advertising

43   Advertisements to which Part IV applies

(1) This Part applies to any advertisement, published for the purposes of a business carried on by the advertiser, indicating that he is willing—

    (a) to provide credit, or

    (b) to enter into an agreement for the bailment or (in Scotland) the hiring of goods by him.

(2) An advertisement does not fall within subsection (1) if the advertiser does not carry on—

    (a) a consumer credit business or consumer hire business, or

    (b) a business in the course of which he provides credit to individuals secured on land, or

    (c) a business which comprises or relates to unregulated agreements where—

(i)   the [law applicable to] the agreement is the law of a country outside the United Kingdom, and

(ii)   if the [law applicable to] the agreement were the law of a part of the United Kingdom it would be a regulated agreement.

(3) An advertisement does not fall within subsection (1)(a) if it indicates—

[...]

(b) that the credit is available only to a body corporate.

[(3A) An advertisement does not fall within subsection (1)(a) in so far as it is a communication of an invitation or inducement to engage in investment activity within the meaning of section 21 of the Financial Services and Markets Act 2000, other than an exempt generic communication.

(3B) An 'exempt generic communication' is a communication to which subsection (1) of section 21 of the Financial Services and Markets Act 2000 does not apply, as a result of an order under subsection (5) of that section, because it does not identify a person as providing an investment or as carrying on an activity to which the communication relates.]

(4) An advertisement does not fall within subsection (1)(b) if it indicates that the advertiser is not willing to enter into a consumer hire agreement.

(5) The Secretary of State may by order provide that this Part shall not apply to other advertisements of a description specified in the order.

44   Form and content of advertisements

(1) The Secretary of State shall make regulations as to the form and content of advertisements to which this Part applies, and the regulations shall contain such provisions as appear to him appropriate with a view to ensuring that, having regard to its subject-matter and the amount of detail included in it, an advertisement conveys a fair and reasonably comprehensive indication of the nature of the credit or hire facilities offered by the advertiser and of their true cost to persons using them.

(2) Regulations under subsection (1) may in particular—

(a) require specified information to be included in the prescribed manner in advertisements, and other specified material to be excluded;

(b) contain requirements to ensure that specified information is clearly brought to the attention of persons to whom advertisements are directed, and that one part of an advertisement is not given insufficient or excessive prominence compared with another.

45   Prohibition of advertisement where goods etc. not sold for cash

If an advertisement to which this Part applies indicates that the advertiser is willing to provide credit under a restricted-use credit agreement relating to goods or services to be supplied by any person, but at the time when the advertisement is published that person is not holding himself out as prepared to sell the goods or provide the services (as the case may be) for cash, the advertiser commits an offence.

46   False or misleading advertisements

(1) If an advertisement to which this Part applies conveys information which in a material respect is false or misleading the advertiser commits an offence.

(2) Information stating or implying an intention on the advertiser's part which he has not got is false.

47   Advertising infringements

(1) Where an advertiser commits an offence against regulations made under section 44 or against section 45 or 46 or would be taken to commit such an offence but for the defence provided by section 168, a like offence is committed by—

(a) the publisher of the advertisement, and

(b) any person who, in the course of a business carried on by him, devised the advertisement, or a part of it relevant to the first-mentioned offence, and

(c) where the advertiser did not procure the publication of the advertisement, the person who did procure it.

(2) In proceedings for an offence under subsection (1)(a) it is a defence for the person charged to prove that—

(a) the advertisement was published in the course of a business carried on by him, and

(b) he received the advertisement in the course of that business, and did not know and had no reason to suspect that its publication would be an offence under this Part.

Canvassing, etc.

48 **Definition of canvassing off trade premises (regulated agreements)**

(1) An individual (the 'canvasser') canvasses a regulated agreement off trade premises if he solicits the entry (as debtor or hirer) of another individual (the 'consumer') into the agreement by making oral representations to the consumer, or any other individual, during a visit by the canvasser to any place (not excluded by subsection (2)) where the consumer, or that other individual, as the case may be, is, being a visit—

(a) carried out for the purpose of making such oral representations to individuals who are at that place, but

(b) not carried out in response to a request made on a previous occasion.

(2) A place is excluded from subsection (1) if it is a place where a business is carried on (whether on a permanent or temporary basis) by—

(a) the creditor or owner, or

(b) a supplier, or

(c) the canvasser, or the person whose employee or agent the canvasser is, or

(d) the consumer.

49 **Prohibition of canvassing debtor-creditor agreements off trade premises**

(1) It is an offence to canvass debtor-creditor agreements off trade premises.

(2) It is also an offence to solicit the entry of an individual (as debtor) into a debtor-creditor agreement during a visit carried out in response to a request made on a previous occasion, where—

(a) the request was not in writing signed by or on behalf of the person making it, and

(b) if no request for the visit had been made, the soliciting would have constituted the canvassing of a debtor-creditor agreement off trade premises.

(3) Subsections (1) and (2) do not apply to any soliciting for an agreement enabling the debtor to overdraw on a current account of any description kept with the creditor, where—

(a) the [OFT] has determined that current accounts of that description kept with the creditor are excluded from subsections (1) and (2), and

(b) the debtor already keeps an account with the creditor (whether a current account or not).

(4) A determination under subsection (3)(a)—

(a) may be made subject to such conditions as the [OFT] thinks fit, and

(b) shall be made only where the [OFT] is of opinion that it is not against the interests of debtors.

(5) If soliciting is done in breach of a condition imposed under subsection (4)(a), the determination under subsection (3)(a) does not apply to it.

50 Circulars to minors

(1) A person commits an offence who, with a view to financial gain, sends to a minor any document inviting him to—

   (a) borrow money, or

   (b) obtain goods on credit or hire, or

   (c) obtain services on credit, or

   (d) apply for information or advice on borrowing money or otherwise obtaining credit, or hiring goods.

(2) In proceedings under subsection (1) in respect of the sending of a document to a minor, it is a defence for the person charged to prove that he did not know, and had no reasonable cause to suspect, that he was a minor.

(3) Where a document is received by a minor at any school or other educational establishment for minors, a person sending it to him at that establishment knowing or suspecting it to be such an establishment shall be taken to have reasonable cause to suspect that he is a minor.

51 Prohibition of unsolicited credit-tokens

(1) It is an offence to give a person a credit-token if he has not asked for it.

(2) To comply with subsection (1) a request must be contained in a document signed by the person making the request, unless the credit-token agreement is a small debtor-creditor-supplier agreement.

(3) Subsection (1) does not apply to the giving of a credit-token to a person—

   (a) for use under a credit-token agreement already made, or

   (b) in renewal or replacement of a credit-token previously accepted by him under a credit-token agreement which continues in force, whether or not varied.

Miscellaneous

52 Quotations

(1) Regulations may be made—

   (a) as to the form and content of any document (a 'quotation') by which a person who carries on a consumer credit business or consumer hire business, or a business in the course of which he provides credit to individuals secured on land, gives prospective customers information about the terms on which he is prepared to do business;

   (b) requiring a person carrying on such a business to provide quotations to such persons and in such circumstances as are prescribed.

(2) Regulations under subsection (1)(a) may in particular contain provisions relating to quotations such as are set out in relation to advertisements in section 44.

[(3) In this section, 'quotation' does not include—

   (a) any document which is a communication of an invitation or inducement to engage in investment activity within the meaning of section 21 of the Financial Services and Markets Act 2000; or

   (b) any document (other than one falling within paragraph (a)) provided by an authorised person (within the meaning of that Act) in connection with an agreement which would or might be an exempt agreement as a result of section 16(6C).]

53 Duty to display information

Regulations may require a person who carries on a consumer credit business or consumer hire business, or a business in the course of which he provides credit to individuals secured on land [(other than credit provided under an agreement which is an exempt agreement as a result of section 16(6C)], to display in the prescribed manner, at any premises where the business is carried on to which the public have access, prescribed information about the business.

54 Conduct of business regulations

Without prejudice to the generality of section 26, regulations under that section may include provisions further regulating the seeking of business by [a person to whom the regulations apply] who carries on a consumer credit business or a consumer hire business.

PART V   ENTRY INTO CREDIT OR HIRE AGREEMENTS

Preliminary matters

55 Disclosure of information

(1) Regulations may require specified information to be disclosed in the prescribed manner to the debtor or hirer before a regulated agreement is made.

(2) A regulated agreement is not properly executed unless regulations under subsection (1) were complied with before the making of the agreement.

56 Antecedent negotiations

(1) In this Act 'antecedent negotiations' means any negotiations with the debtor or hirer—

   (a) conducted by the creditor or owner in relation to the making of any regulated agreement, or

   (b) conducted by a credit-broker in relation to goods sold or proposed to be sold by the credit-broker to the creditor before forming the subject-matter of a debtor-creditor-supplier agreement within section 12(a), or

   (c) conducted by the supplier in relation to a transaction financed or proposed to be financed by a debtor-creditor-supplier agreement within section 12(b) or (c), and 'negotiator' means the person by whom negotiations are so conducted with the debtor or hirer.

(2) Negotiations with the debtor in a case falling within subsection (1)(b) or (c) shall be deemed to be conducted by the negotiator in the capacity of agent of the creditor as well as in his actual capacity.

(3) An agreement is void if, and to the extent that, it purports in relation to an actual or prospective regulated agreement—

   (a) to provide that a person acting as, or on behalf of, a negotiator is to be treated as the agent of the debtor or hirer, or

   (b) to relieve a person from liability for acts or omissions of any person acting as, or on behalf of, a negotiator.

(4) For the purposes of this Act, antecedent negotiations shall be taken to begin when the negotiator and the debtor or hirer first enter into communication (including communication by advertisement), and to include any representations made by the negotiator to the debtor or hirer and any other dealings between them.

57 Withdrawal from prospective agreement

(1) The withdrawal of a party from a prospective regulated agreement shall operate to apply this Part to the agreement, any linked transaction and any other thing done in anticipation of the making of the agreement as it would apply if the agreement were made and then cancelled under section 69.

(2) The giving to a party of a written or oral notice which, however expressed, indicates the intention of the other party to withdraw from a prospective regulated agreement operates as a withdrawal from it.

(3) Each of the following shall be deemed to be the agent of the creditor or owner for the purpose of receiving a notice under subsection (2)—

   (a) a credit-broker or supplier who is the negotiator in antecedent negotiations,

   (b) any person who, in the course of a business carried on by him, acts on behalf of the debtor or hirer in any negotiations for the agreement.

(4) Where the agreement, if made, would not be a cancellable agreement, subsection (1) shall nevertheless apply as if the contrary were the case.

58 Opportunity for withdrawal from prospective land mortgage

(1) Before sending to the debtor or hirer, for his signature, an unexecuted agreement in a case where the prospective regulated agreement is to be secured on land (the 'mortgaged land'), the creditor or owner shall give the debtor or hirer a copy of the unexecuted agreement which contains a notice in the prescribed form indicating the right of the debtor or hirer to withdraw from the prospective agreement, and how and when the right is exercisable, together with a copy of any other document referred to in the unexecuted agreement.

(2) Subsection (1) does not apply to—

   (a) a restricted-use credit agreement to finance the purchase of the mortgaged land, or

   (b) an agreement for a bridging loan in connection with the purchase of the mortgaged land or other land.

59 Agreement to enter future agreement void

(1) An agreement is void if, and to the extent that, it purports to bind a person to enter as debtor or hirer into a prospective regulated agreement.

(2) Regulations may exclude from the operation of subsection (1) agreements such as are described in the regulations.

Making the agreement

60 Form and content of agreements

(1) The Secretary of State shall make regulations as to the form and content of documents embodying regulated agreements, and the regulations shall contain such provisions as appear to him appropriate with a view to ensuring that the debtor or hirer is made aware of—

   (a) the rights and duties conferred or imposed on him by the agreement,

   (b) the amount and rate of the total charge for credit (in the case of a consumer credit agreement),

   (c) the protection and remedies available to him under this Act, and

   (d) any other matters which, in the opinion of the Secretary of State, it is desirable for him to know about in connection with the agreement.

(2) Regulations under subsection (1) may in particular—

   (a) require specified information to be included in the prescribed manner in documents, and other specified material to be excluded;

   (b) contain requirements to ensure that specified information is clearly brought to the attention of the debtor or hirer, and that one part of a document is not given insufficient or excessive prominence compared with another.

(3) If, on an application made to the [OFT] by a person carrying on a consumer credit business or a consumer hire business, it appears to the [OFT] impracticable for the applicant to comply with any requirement of regulations under subsection (1) in a particular case, [it] may, by notice to the applicant direct that the requirement be waived or varied in relation to such agreements, and subject to such conditions (if any), as [it] may specify, and this Act and the regulations shall have effect accordingly.

(4) The [OFT] shall give a notice under subsection (3) only if [it] is satisfied that to do so would not prejudice the interests of debtors or hirers'.

61 Signing of agreement

(1) A regulated agreement is not properly executed unless—

   (a) a document in the prescribed form itself containing all the prescribed terms and conforming to regulations under section 60(1) is signed in the prescribed manner both by the debtor or hirer and by or on behalf of the creditor or owner, and

(b) the document embodies all the terms of the agreement, other than implied terms, and

(c) the document is, when presented or sent to the debtor or hirer for signature, in such a state that all its terms are readily legible.

(2) In addition, where the agreement is one to which section 58(1) applies, it is not properly executed unless—

(a) the requirements of section 58(1) were complied with, and

(b) the unexecuted agreement was sent, for his signature, to the debtor or hirer [by an appropriate method] not less than seven days after a copy of it was given to him under section 58(1), and

(c) during the consideration period, the creditor or owner refrained from approaching the debtor or hirer (whether in person, by telephone or letter, or in any other way) except in response to a specific request made by the debtor or hirer after the beginning of the consideration period, and

(d) no notice of withdrawal by the debtor or hirer was received by the creditor or owner before the sending of the unexecuted agreement.

(3) In subsection (2)(c), 'the consideration period' means the period beginning with the giving of the copy under section 58(1) and ending—

(a) at the expiry of seven days after the day on which the unexecuted agreement is sent, for his signature, to the debtor or hirer, or

(b) on its return by the debtor or hirer after signature by him, whichever first occurs.

(4) Where the debtor or hirer is a partnership or an unincorporated body of persons, subsection (1)(a) shall apply with the substitution for 'by the debtor or hirer' of 'by or on behalf of the debtor or hirer's'.

62   Duty to supply copy of unexecuted agreement

(1) If the unexecuted agreement is presented personally to the debtor or hirer for his signature, but on the occasion when he signs it the document does not become an executed agreement, a copy of it, and of any other document referred to in it, must be there and then delivered to him.

(2) If the unexecuted agreement is sent to the debtor or hirer for his signature, a copy of it, and of any other document referred to in it, must be sent to him at the same time.

(3) A regulated agreement is not properly executed if the requirements of this section are not observed.

63   Duty to supply copy of executed agreement

(1) If the unexecuted agreement is presented personally to the debtor or hirer for his signature, and on the occasion when he signs it the document becomes an executed agreement, a copy of the executed agreement, and of any other document referred to in it, must be there and then delivered to him.

(2) A copy of the executed agreement, and of any other document referred to in it, must be given to the debtor or hirer within the seven days following the making of the agreement unless—

(a) subsection (1) applies, or

(b) the unexecuted agreement was sent to the debtor or hirer for his signature and, on the occasion of his signing it, the document became an executed agreement.

(3) In the case of a cancellable agreement, a copy under subsection (2) must be sent [by an appropriate method].

(4) In the case of a credit-token agreement, a copy under subsection (2) need not be given within the seven days following the making of the agreement if it is given before or at the time when the credit-token is given to the debtor.

(5) A regulated agreement is not properly executed if the requirements of this section are not observed.

64 Duty to give notice of cancellation rights

(1) In the case of a cancellable agreement, a notice in the prescribed form indicating the right of the debtor or hirer to cancel the agreement, how and when that right is exercisable, and the name and address of a person to whom notice of cancellation may be given,—

(a) must be included in every copy given to the debtor or hirer under section 62 or 63, and

(b) except where section 63(2) applied, must also be sent [by an appropriate method] to the debtor or hirer within the seven days following the making of the agreement.

(2) In the case of a credit-token agreement, a notice under subsection (1)(b) need not be sent [by an appropriate method] within the seven days following the making of the agreement if either—

(a) it is sent [by an appropriate method] to the debtor or hirer before the credit-token is given to him, or

(b) it is sent [by an appropriate method] to him together with the credit-token.

(3) Regulations may provide that except where section 63(2) applied a notice sent under subsection (1)(b) shall be accompanied by a further copy of the executed agreement, and of any other document referred to in it.

(4) Regulations may provide that subsection (1)(b) is not to apply in the case of agreements such as are described in the regulations, being agreements made by a particular person, if—

(a) on an application by that person to the [OFT], the [OFT] has determined that, having regard to—

(i) the manner in which antecedent negotiations for agreements with the applicant of that description are conducted, and

(ii) the information provided to debtors or hirers before such agreements are made, the requirement imposed by subsection (1)(b) can be dispensed with without prejudicing the interests of debtors or hirers, and

(b) any conditions imposed by the [OFT] in making the determination are complied with.

(5) A cancellable agreement is not properly executed if the requirements of this section are not observed.

65 Consequences of improper execution

(1) An improperly-executed regulated agreement is enforceable against the debtor or hirer on an order of the court only.

(2) A retaking of goods or land to which a regulated agreement relates is an enforcement of the agreement.

66 Acceptance of credit-tokens

(1) The debtor shall not be liable under a credit-token agreement for use made of the credit-token by any person unless the debtor had previously accepted the credit-token, or the use constituted an acceptance of it by him.

(2) The debtor accepts a credit-token when—

(a) it is signed, or

(b) a receipt for it is signed, or

(c) it is first used, either by the debtor himself or by a person who, pursuant to the agreement, is authorised by him to use it.

Cancellation of certain agreements within cooling-off period

67 Cancellable agreements

A regulated agreement may be cancelled by the debtor or hirer in accordance with this Part if the antecedent negotiations included oral representations made when in the presence of the debtor or hirer by an individual acting as, or on behalf of, the negotiator, unless—

> (a) the agreement is secured on land, or is a restricted-use credit agreement to finance the purchase of land or is an agreement for a bridging loan in connection with the purchase of land, or
> (b) the unexecuted agreement is signed by the debtor or hirer at premises at which any of the following is carrying on any business (whether on a permanent or temporary basis)—
> > (i)   the creditor or owner;
> > (ii) any party to a linked transaction (other than the debtor or hirer or a relative of his);
> > (iii) the negotiator in any antecedent negotiations.

68 Cooling-off period

The debtor or hirer may serve notice of cancellation of a cancellable agreement between his signing of the unexecuted agreement and—

> (a) the end of the fifth day following the day on which he received a copy under section 63(2) or a notice under section 64(1)(b), or
> (b) if (by virtue of regulations made under section 64(4) section 64(1)(b) does not apply, the end of the fourteenth day following the day on which he signed the unexecuted agreement.

69 Notice of cancellation

(1) If within the period specified in section 68 the debtor or hirer under a cancellable agreement serves on—

> (a) the creditor or owner, or
> (b) the person specified in the notice under section 64(1), or
> (c) a person who (whether by virtue of subsection (6) or otherwise) is the agent of the creditor or owner, a notice (a 'notice of cancellation') which, however expressed and whether or not conforming to the notice given under section 64(1), indicates the intention of the debtor or hirer to withdraw from the agreement, the notice shall operate—
> > (i) to cancel the agreement, and any linked transaction, and
> > (ii) to withdraw any offer by the debtor or hirer, or his relative, to enter into a linked transaction.

(2) In the case of a debtor-creditor-supplier agreement for restricted-use credit financing—

> (a) the doing of work or supply of goods to meet an emergency, or
> (b) the supply of goods which, before service of the notice of cancellation, had by the act of the debtor or his relative become incorporated in any land or thing not comprised in the agreement or any linked transaction,

subsection (1) shall apply with the substitution of the following for paragraph (i)—

> '(i) to cancel only such provisions of the agreement and any linked transaction as—
> > (aa) relate to the provision of credit, or
> > (bb) require the debtor to pay an item in the total charge for credit, or
> > (cc) subject the debtor to any obligation other than to pay for the doing of the said work, or the supply of the said goods'.

(3) Except so far as is otherwise provided, references in this Act to the cancellation of an agreement or transaction do not include a case within subsection (2).

(4) Except as otherwise provided by or under this Act, an agreement or transaction cancelled under subsection (1) shall be treated as if it had never been entered into.

(5) Regulations may exclude linked transactions of the prescribed description from subsection (1)(i) or (ii).

(6) Each of the following shall be deemed to be the agent of the creditor or owner for the purpose of receiving a notice of cancellation—

(a) a credit-broker or supplier who is the negotiator in antecedent negotiations,

(b) any person who, in the course of a business carried on by him, acts on behalf of the debtor or hirer in any negotiations for the agreement.

[(7) Whether or not it is actually received by him, a notice of cancellation sent to a person shall be deemed to be served on him—

(a) in the case of a notice sent by post, at the time of posting, and

(b) in the case of a notice transmitted in the form of an electronic communication in accordance with section 176A(1), at the time of the transmission.]

70   Cancellation: recovery of money paid by debtor or hirer

(1) On the cancellation of a regulated agreement, and of any linked transaction,—

(a) any sum paid by the debtor or hirer, or his relative, under or in contemplation of the agreement or transaction, including any item in the total charge for credit, shall become repayable, and

(b) any sum, including any item in the total charge for credit, which but for the cancellation is, or would or might become, payable by the debtor or hirer, or his relative, under the agreement or transaction shall cease to be, or shall not become, so payable, and

(c) in the case of a debtor-creditor-supplier agreement falling within section 12(b), any sum paid on the debtor's behalf by the creditor to the supplier shall become repayable to the creditor.

(2) If, under the terms of a cancelled agreement or transaction, the debtor or hirer, or his relative, is in possession of any goods, he shall have a lien on them for any sum repayable to him under subsection (1) in respect of that agreement or transaction, or any other linked transaction.

(3) A sum repayable under subsection (1) is repayable by the person to whom it was originally paid, but in the case of a debtor-creditor-supplier agreement falling within section 12(b) the creditor and the supplier shall be under a joint and several liability to repay sums paid by the debtor, or his relative, under the agreement or under a linked transaction falling within section 19(1)(b) and accordingly, in such a case, the creditor shall be entitled, in accordance with rules of court, to have the supplier made a party to any proceedings brought against the creditor to recover any such sums.

(4) Subject to any agreement between them, the creditor shall be entitled to be indemnified by the supplier for loss suffered by the creditor in satisfying his liability under subsection (3), including costs reasonably incurred by him in defending proceedings instituted by the debtor.

(5) Subsection (1) does not apply to any sum which, if not paid by a debtor, would be payable by virtue of section 71, and applies to a sum paid or payable by a debtor for the issue of a credit-token only where the credit-token has been returned to the creditor or surrendered to a supplier.

(6) If the total charge for credit includes an item in respect of a fee or commission charged by a credit-broker, the amount repayable under subsection (1) in respect of that item shall be the excess over [£5] of the fee or commission.

(7) If the total charge for credit includes any sum payable or paid by the debtor to a credit-broker otherwise than in respect of a fee or commission charged by him, that sum shall for the purposes of subsection (6) be treated as if it were such a fee or commission.

(8) So far only as is necessary to give effect to section 69(2), this section applies to an agreeement or transaction within that subsection as it applies to a cancelled agreement or transaction.

71 Cancellation: repayment of credit

(1) Notwithstanding the cancellation of a regulated consumer credit agreement, other than a debtor-creditor-supplier agreement for restricted-use credit, the agreement shall continue in force so far as it relates to repayment of credit and payment of interest.

(2) If, following the cancellation of a regulated consumer credit agreement, the debtor repays the whole or a portion of the credit—

    (a) before the expiry of one month following service of the notice of cancellation, or

    (b) in the case of a credit repayable by instalments, before the date on which the first instalment is due,

no interest shall be payable on the amount repaid.

(3) If the whole of a credit repayable by instalments is not repaid on or before the date specified in subsection (2)(b), the debtor shall not be liable to repay any of the credit except on receipt of a request in writing in the prescribed form, signed by or on behalf of the creditor, stating the amounts of the remaining instalments (recalculated by the creditor as nearly as may be in accordance with the agreement and without extending the repayment period), but excluding any sum other than principal and interest.

(4) Repayment of a credit, or payment of interest, under a cancelled agreement shall be treated as duly made if it is made to any person on whom, under section 69, a notice of cancellation could have been served, other than a person referred to in section 69(6)(b).

72 Cancellation: return of goods

(1) This section applies where any agreement or transaction relating to goods, being—

    (a) a restricted-use debtor-creditor-supplier agreement, a consumer hire agreement, or a linked transaction to which the debtor or hirer under any regulated agreement is a party, or

    (b) a linked transaction to which a relative of the debtor or hirer under any regulated agreement is a party,

is cancelled after the debtor or hirer (in a case within paragraph (a)) or the relative (in a case within paragraph (b)) has acquired possession of the goods by virtue of the agreement or transaction.

(2) In this section—

    (a) 'the possessor' means the person who has acquired possession of the goods as mentioned in subsection (1),

    (b) 'the other party' means the person from whom the possessor acquired possession, and

    (c) 'the pre-cancellation period' means the period beginning when the possessor acquired possession and ending with the cancellation.

(3) The possessor shall be treated as having been under a duty throughout the pre-cancellation period—

    (a) to retain possession of the goods, and

    (b) to take reasonable care of them.

(4) On the cancellation, the possessor shall be under a duty, subject to any restore the goods to the other party in accordance with this section, and meanwhile to retain possession of the goods and take reasonable care of them.

(5) The possessor shall not be under any duty to deliver the goods except at his own premises and in pursuance of a request in writing signed by or on behalf of the other party and served on the possessor either before, or at the time when, the goods are collected from those premises.

(6) If the possessor—

    (a) delivers the goods (whether at his own premises or elsewhere) to any person on whom, under section 69, a notice of cancellation could have been served (other than a person referred to in section 69(6)(b), or

(b) sends the goods at his own expense to such a person, he shall be discharged from any duty to retain the goods or deliver them to any person.

(7) Where the possessor delivers the goods as mentioned in subsection (6)(a), his obligation to take care of the goods shall cease: and if he sends the goods as mentioned in subsection (6)(b), he shall be under a duty to take reasonable care to see that they are received by the other party and not damaged in transit, but in other respects his duty to take care of the goods shall cease.

(8) Where, at any time during the period of 21 days following the cancellation, the possessor receives such a request as is mentioned in subsection (5), and unreasonably refuses or unreasonably fails to comply with it, his duty to take reasonable care of the goods shall continue until he delivers or sends the goods as mentioned in subsection (6), but if within that period he does not receive such a request his duty to take reasonable care of the goods shall cease at the end of that period.

(9) The preceding provisions of this section do not apply to—
    (a) perishable goods, or
    (b) goods which by their nature are consumed by use and which, before the cancellation, were so consumed, or
    (c) goods supplied to meet an emergency, or
    (d) goods which, before the cancellation, had become incorporated in any land or thing not comprised in the cancelled agreement or a linked transaction.

(10) Where the address of the possessor is specified in the executed agreement, references in this section to his own premises are to that address and no other.

(11) Breach of a duty imposed by this section is actionable as a breach of statutory duty.

73 Cancellation: goods given in part-exchange

(1) This section applies on the cancellation of a regulated agreement where, in antecedent negotiations, the negotiator agreed to take goods in part-exchange (the 'part-exchange goods') and those goods have been delivered to him.

(2) Unless, before the end of the period of ten days beginning with the date of cancellation, the part-exchange goods are returned to the debtor or hirer in a condition substantially as good as when they were delivered to the negotiator, the debtor or hirer shall be entitled to recover from the negotiator a sum equal to the part-exchange allowance (as defined in subsection (7)(b)).

(3) In the case of a debtor-creditor-supplier agreement within section 12(b), the negotiator and the creditor shall be under a joint and several liability to pay to the debtor a sum recoverable under subsection (2).

(4) Subject to any agreement between them, the creditor shall be entitled to be indemnified by the negotiator for loss suffered by the creditor in satisfying his liability under subsection (3), including costs reasonably incurred by him in defending proceedings instituted by the debtor.

(5) During the period of ten days beginning with the date of cancellation, the debtor or hirer, if he is in possession of goods to which the cancelled agreement relates, shall have a lien on them for—
    (a) delivery of the part-exchange goods, in a condition substantially as good as when they were delivered to the negotiator, or
    (b) a sum equal to the part-exchange allowance; and if the lien continues to the end of that period it shall thereafter subsist only as a lien for a sum equal to the part-exchange allowance.

(6) Where the debtor or hirer recovers from the negotiator or creditor, or both of them jointly, a sum equal to the part-exchange allowance, then, if the title of the debtor or hirer to the part-exchange goods has not vested in the negotiator, it shall so vest on the recovery of that sum.

(7) For the purposes of this section—

    (a) the negotiator shall be treated as having agreed to take goods in part-exchange if, in pursuance of the antecedent negotiations, he either purchased or agreed to purchase those goods or accepted or agreed to accept them as part of the consideration for the cancelled agreement, and

    (b) the part-exchange allowance shall be the sum agreed as such in the antecedent negotiations or, if no such agreement was arrived at, such sum as it would have been reasonable to allow in respect of the part-exchange goods if no notice of cancellation had been served.

(8) In an action brought against the creditor for a sum recoverable under subsection (2), he shall be entitled, in accordance with rules of court, to have the negotiator made a party to the proceedings.

Exclusion of certain agreements from Part V

74   Exclusion of certain agreements from Part V

(1) This Part (except section 56) does not apply to—

    (a) a non-commercial agreement, or

    (b) a debtor-creditor agreement enabling the debtor to overdraw on a current account, or

    (c) a debtor-creditor agreement to finance the making of such payments arising on, or connected with, the death of a person as may be prescribed.

(2) This Part (except sections 55 and 56) does not apply to a small debtor-creditor-supplier agreement for restricted-use credit.

[(2A) In the case of an agreement to which the Consumer Protection (Cancellation of Contracts Concluded Away from Business Premises) Regulations 1987 apply the reference in subsection (2) to a small agreement shall be construed as if in section 17(1)(a) and (b) '£35' were substituted for '£50'.]

(3) Subsection (1)(b) or (c) applies only where the [OFT] so determines, and such a determination—

    (a) may be made subject to such conditions as the [OFT] thinks fit, and

    (b) shall be made only if the [OFT] is of opinion that it is not against the interests of debtors.

[(3A) Notwithstanding anything in subsection (3)(b) above, in relation to a debtor-creditor agreement under which the creditor is the Bank of England or a bank within the meaning of the Bankers' Books Evidence Act 1879, the [OFT] shall make a determination that subsection (1)(b) above applies unless [it] considers that it would be against the public interest to do so.]

(4) If any term of an agreement falling within subsection [(1)(c)] or (2) is expressed in writing, regulations under section 60(1) shall apply to that term (subject to section 60(3)) as if the agreement were a regulated agreement not falling within subsection [(1)(c)] or (2).

PART VI   MATTERS ARISING DURING CURRENCY OF CREDIT OR HIRE AGREEMENTS

75   Liability of creditor for breaches by supplier

(1) If the debtor under a debtor-creditor-supplier agreement falling within section 12(b) or (c) has, in relation to a transaction financed by the agreement, any claim against the supplier in respect of a misrepresentation or breach of contract, he shall have a like claim against the creditor, who, with the supplier, shall accordingly be jointly and severally liable to the debtor.

(2) Subject to any agreement between them, the creditor shall be entitled to be indemnified by the supplier for loss suffered by the creditor in satisfying his liability under subsection (1), including costs reasonably incurred by him in defending proceedings instituted by the debtor. (3) Subsection (1) does not apply to a claim—

    (a) under a non-commercial agreement, or

    (b) so far as the claim relates to any single item to which the supplier has attached a cash price not exceeding [£100] or more than [£30,000].

(4) This section applies notwithstanding that the debtor, in entering into the transaction, exceeded the credit limit or otherwise contravened any term of the agreement.

(5) In an action brought against the creditor under subsection (1) he shall be entitled, in accordance with rules of court, to have the supplier made a party to the proceedings.

76   Duty to give notice before taking certain action

(1) The creditor or owner is not entitled to enforce a term of a regulated agreement by—

    (a) demanding earlier payment of any sum, or

    (b) recovering possession of any goods or land, or

    (c) treating any right conferred on the debtor or hirer by the agreement as terminated, restricted or deferred,

except by or after giving the debtor or hirer not less than seven days' notice of his intention to do so.

(2) Subsection (1) applies only where—

    (a) a period for the duration of the agreement is specified in the agreement, and

    (b) that period has not ended when the creditor or owner does an act mentioned in subsection (1),

but so applies notwithstanding that, under the agreement, any party is entitled to terminate it before the end of the period so specified.

(3) A notice under subsection (1) is ineffective if not in the prescribed form.

(4) Subsection (1) does not prevent a creditor from treating the right to draw on any credit as restricted or deferred and taking such steps as may be necessary to make the restriction or deferment effective.

(5) Regulations may provide that subsection (1) is not to apply to agreements described by the regulations.

(6) Subsection (1) does not apply to a right of enforcement arising by reason of any breach by the debtor or hirer of the regulated agreement.

77   Duty to give information to debtor under fixed-sum credit agreement

(1) The creditor under a regulated agreement for fixed-sum credit, within the prescribed period after receiving a request in writing to that effect from the debtor and payment of a fee of [£1], shall give the debtor a copy of the executed agreement (if any) and of any other document referred to in it, together with a statement signed by or on behalf of the creditor showing, according to the information to which it is practicable for him to refer,—

    (a) the total sum paid under the agreement by the debtor;

    (b) the total sum which has become payable under the agreement by the debtor but remains unpaid, and the various amounts comprised in that total sum, with the date when each became due; and

    (c) the total sum which is to become payable under the agreement by the debtor, and the various amounts comprised in that total sum, with the date, or mode of determining the date, when each becomes due.

(2) If the creditor possesses insufficient information to enable him to ascertain the amounts and dates mentioned in subsection (1)(c), he shall be taken to comply with that paragraph if his statement under subsection (1) gives the basis on which, under the regulated agreement, they would fall to be ascertained.

(3) Subsection (1) does not apply to—
  (a) an agreement under which no sum is, or will or may become, payable by the debtor, or
  (b) a request made less than one month after a previous request under that subsection relating to the same agreement was complied with.
(4) If the creditor under an agreement fails to comply with subsection (1)—
  (a) he is not entitied, while the default continues, to enforce the agreement; and
  (b) if the default continues for one month he commits an offence.
(5) This section does not apply to a non-commercial agreement.

[77A Statements to be provided in relation to fixed-sum credit agreements
  (1) The creditor under a regulated agreement for fixed-sum credit—
  (a) shall, within the period of one year beginning with the day after the day on which the agreement is made, give the debtor a statement under this section; and
  (b) after the giving of that statement, shall give the debtor further statements under this section at intervals of not more than one year.
  (2) Regulations may make provision about the form and content of statements under this section.
  (3) The debtor shall have no liability to pay any sum in connection with the preparation or the giving to him of a statement under this section.
  (4) The creditor is not required to give the debtor any statement under this section once the following conditions are satisfied—
  (a) that there is no sum payable under the agreement by the debtor; and
  (b) that there is no sum which will or may become so payable.
  (5) Subsection (6) applies if at a time before the conditions mentioned in subsection (4) are satisfied the creditor fails to give the debtor—
  (a) a statement under this section within the period mentioned in subsection (1)(a); or
  (b) such a statement within the period of one year beginning with the day after the day on which such a statement was last given to him.
  (6) Where this subsection applies in relation to a failure to give a statement under this section to the debtor—
  (a) the creditor shall not be entitled to enforce the agreement during the period of non-compliance;
  (b) the debtor shall have no liability to pay any sum of interest to the extent calculated by reference to the period of non-compliance or to any part of it; and
  (c) the debtor shall have no liability to pay any default sum which (apart from this paragraph)—
    (i) would have become payable during the period of non-compliance; or
    (ii) would have become payable after the end of that period in connection with a breach of the agreement which occurs during that period (whether or not the breach continues after the end of that period).
  (7) In this section 'the period of non-compliance' means, in relation to a failure to give a statement under this section to the debtor, the period which—
  (a) begins immediately after the end of the period mentioned in paragraph (a) or (as the case may be) paragraph (b) of subsection (5); and
  (b) ends at the end of the day on which the statement is given to the debtor or on which the conditions mentioned in subsection (4) are satisfied, whichever is earlier.
  (8) This section does not apply in relation to a non-commercial agreement or to a small agreement.]

78 Duty to give information to debtor under running-account credit agreement
  (1) The creditor under a regulated agreement for running-account credit, within the prescribed period after receiving a request in writing to that effect from the debtor and

payment of a fee of [£1], shall give the debtor a copy of the executed agreement (if any) and of any other document referred to in it, together with a statement signed by or on behalf of the creditor showing, according to the information to which it is practicable for him to refer,—

    (a) the state of the account, and

    (b) the amount, if any, currently payable under the agreement by the debtor to the creditor, and

    (c) the amounts and due dates of any payments which, if the debtor does not draw further on the account, will later become payable under the agreement by the debtor to the creditor.

    (2) If the creditor possesses insufficient information to enable him to ascertain the amounts and dates mentioned in subsection (1)(c), he shall be taken to comply with that paragraph if his statement under subsection (1) gives the basis on which, under the regulated agreement, they would fall to be ascertained.

    (3) Subsection (1) does not apply to—

    (a) an agreement under which no sum is, or will or may become, payable by the debtor, or

    (b) a request made less than one month after a previous request under that subsection relating to the same agreement was complied with.

    (4) Where running-account credit is provided under a regulated agreement, the creditor shall give the debtor statements in the prescribed form, and with the prescribed contents—

    (a) showing according to the information to which it is practicable for him to refer, the state of the account at regular intervals of not more than twelve months, and

    (b) where the agreement provides, in relation to specified periods, for the making of payments by the debtor, or the charging against him of interest or any other sum, showing according to the information to which it is practicable for him to refer the state of the account at the end of each of those periods during which there is any movement in the account.

    [(4A) Regulations may require a statement under subsection (4) to contain also information in the prescribed terms about the consequences of the debtor—

    (a) failing to make payments as required by the agreement; or

    (b) only making payments of a prescribed description in prescribed circumstances.]

    (5) A statement under subsection (4) shall be given within the prescribed period after the end of the period to which the statement relates.

    (6) If the creditor under an agreement fails to comply with subsection (1)—

    (a) he is not entitled, while the default continues, to enforce the agreement; and

    (b) if the default continues for one month he commits an offence.

    (7) This section does not apply to a non-commercial agreement, and subsections [(4) to (5)] do not apply to a small agreement.

79 Duty to give hirer information

    (1) The owner under a regulated consumer hire agreement, within the prescribed period after receiving a request in writing to that effect from the hirer and payment of a fee of [£1], shall give to the hirer a copy of the executed agreement and of any other document referred to in it, together with a statement signed by or on behalf of the owner showing, according to the information to which it is practicable for him to refer, the total sum which has become payable under the agreement by the hirer but remains unpaid and the various amounts comprised in that total sum, with the date when each became due.

    (2) Subsection (1) does not apply to—

    (a) an agreement under which no sum is, or will or may become, payable by the hirer, or

    (b) a request made less than one month after a previous request under that subsection relating to the same agreement was complied with.

    (3) If the owner under an agreement fails to comply with subsection (1)—

    (a) he is not entitled, while the default continues, to enforce the agreement; and

(b) if the default continues for one month he commits an offence.
(4) This section does not apply to a non-commercial agreement.

80   Debtor or hirer to give information about goods

(1) Where a regulated agreement, other than a non-commercial agreement, requires the debtor or hirer to keep goods to which the agreement relates in his possession or control, he shall, within seven working days after he has received a request in writing to that effect from the creditor or owner, tell the creditor or owner where the goods are.

(2) If the debtor or hirer fails to comply with subsection (1), and the default continues for 14 days, he commits an offence.

81   Appropriation of payments

(1) Where a debtor or hirer is liable to make to the same person payments in respect of two or more regulated agreements, he shall be entitled, on making any payment in respect of the agreements which is not sufficient to discharge the total amount then due under all the agreements, to appropriate the sum so paid by him—

(a) in or towards the satisfaction of the sum due under any one of the agreements, or
(b) in or towards the satisfaction of the sums due under any two or more of the agreements in such proportions as he thinks fit.

(2) If the debtor or hirer fails to make any such appropriation where one or more of the agreements is—

(a) a hire-purchase agreement or conditional sale agreement, or
(b) a consumer hire agreement, or
(c) an agreement in relation to which any security is provided, the payment shall be appropriated towards the satisfaction of the sums due under the several agreements respectively in the proportions which those sums bear to one another.

82   Variation of agreements

(1) Where, under a power contained in a regulated agreement, the creditor or owner varies the agreement, the variation shall not take effect before notice of it is given to the debtor or hirer in the prescribed manner.

(2) Where an agreement (a 'modifying agreement') varies or supplements an earlier agreement, the modifying agreement shall for the purposes of this Act be treated as—

(a) revoking the earlier agreement, and
(b) containing provisions reproducing the combined effect of the two agreements, and obligations outstanding in relation to the earlier agreement shall accordingly be treated as outstanding instead in relation to the modifying agreement.

(3) If the earlier agreement is a regulated agreement but (apart from this subsection) the modifying agreement is not then, unless the modifying agreement is for running-account credit, it shall be treated as a regulated agreement.

(4) If the earlier agreement is a regulated agreement for running-account credit, and by the modifying agreement the creditor allows the credit limit to be exceeded but intends the excess to be merely temporary, Part V (except section 56) shall not apply to the modifying agreement.

(5) If—

(a) the earlier agreement is a cancellable agreement, and
(b) the modifying agreement is made within the period applicable under section 68 to the earlier agreement,

then, whether or not the modifying agreement would, apart from this subsection, be a cancellable agreement, it shall be treated as a cancellable agreement in respect of which a notice may be served under section 68 not later than the end of the period applicable under that section to the earlier agreement.

(6) Except under subsection (5), a modifying agreement shall not be treated as a cancellable agreement.

(7) This section does not apply to a non-commercial agreement.

83 Liability for misuse of credit facilities

(1) The debtor under a regulated consumer credit agreement shall not be liable to the creditor for any loss arising from use of the credit facility by another person not acting, or to be treated as acting, as the debtor's agent.

(2) This section does not apply to a non-commercial agreement, or to any loss in so far as it arises from misuse of an instrument to which section 4 of the Cheques Act 1957 applies.

84 Misuse of credit-tokens

(1) Section 83 does not prevent the debtor under a credit-token agreement from being made liable to the extent of [£50] (or the credit limit if lower) for loss to the creditor arising from use of the credit-token by other persons during a period beginning when the credit-token ceases to be in the possession of any authorized person and ending when the credit-token is once more in the possession of an authorised person.

(2) Section 83 does not prevent the debtor under a credit-token agreement from being made liable to any extent for loss to the creditor from use of the credit-token by a person who acquired possession of it with the debtor's consent.

(3) Subsection (1) and (2) shall not apply to any use of the credit-token after the creditor has been given oral or written notice that it is lost or stolen, or is for any other reason liable to misuse.

[(3A) Subsections (1) and (2) shall not apply to any use, in connection with a distance contract (other than an excepted contract), of a card which is a credit-token.

(3B) In subsection (3A), 'distance contract' and 'excepted contract' have the meanings given in the Consumer Protection (Distance Selling) Regulations 2000.]

[(3C) Subsections (1) and (2) shall not apply to any use, in connection with a distance contract within the meaning of the Financial Services (Distance Marketing) Regulations 2004, of a card which is a credit-token.]

(4) Subsections (1) and (2) shall not apply unless there are contained in the credit-token agreement in the prescribed manner particulars of the name, address and telephone number of a person stated to be the person to whom notice is to be given under subsection (3).

(5) Notice under subsection (3) takes effect when received, but where it is given orally, and the agreement so requires, it shall be treated as not taking effect if not confirmed in writing within seven days.

(6) Any sum paid by the debtor for the issue of the credit-token to the extent (if any) that it has not been previously offset by use made of the credit-token, shall be treated as paid towards satisfaction of any liability under subsection (1) or (2).

(7) The debtor, the creditor, and any person authorised by the debtor to use the credit-token, shall be authorised persons for the purposes of subsection (1).

(8) Where two or more credit-tokens are given under one credit-token agreement, the preceding provisions of this section apply to each credit-token separately.

85 Duty on issue of new credit-tokens

(1) Whenever, in connection with a credit-token agreement, a credit-token (other than the first) is given by the creditor to the debtor, the creditor shall give the debtor a copy of the executed agreement (if any) and of any other document referred to in it.

(2) If the creditor fails to comply with this section—

(a) he is not entitled, while the default continues, to enforce the agreement, and

(b) if the default continues for one month he commits an offence.

(3) This section does not apply to a small agreement.

86   Death of debtor or hirer

(1) The creditor or owner under a regulated agreement is not entitied, by reason of the death of the debtor or hirer, to do an act specified in paragraphs (a) to (e) of section 87(1) if at the death the agreement is fully secured.

(2) If at the death of the debtor or hirer a regulated agreement is only partly secured or is unsecured, the creditor or owner is entitled, by reason of the death of the debtor or hirer, to do an act specified in paragraphs (a) to (e) of section 87(1) on an order of the court only.

(3) This section applies in relation to the termination of an agreement only where—

(a) a period for its duration is specified in the agreement, and

(b) that period has not ended when the creditor or owner purports to terminate the agreement,

but so applies notwithstanding that, under the agreement, any party is entitled to terminate it before the end of the period so specified.

(4) This section does not prevent the creditor from treating the right to draw on any credit as restricted or deferred, and taking such steps as may be necessary to make the restriction or deferment effective.

(5) This section does not affect the operation of any agreement providing for payment of sums—

(a) due under the regulated agreement, or

(b) becoming due under it on the death of the debtor or hirer, out of the proceeds of a policy of assurance on his life.

(6) For the purposes of this section an act is done by reason of the death of the debtor or hirer if it is done under a power conferred by the agreement which is—

(a) exercisable on his death, or

(b) exercisable at will and exercised at any time after his death.

PART VII   DEFAULT AND TERMINATION

[Information sheets]

[86A   OFT to prepare information sheets on arrears and default

(1) The OFT shall prepare, and give general notice of, an arrears information sheet and a default information sheet.

(2) The arrears information sheet shall include information to help debtors and hirers who receive notices under section 86B or 86C.

(3) The default information sheet shall include information to help debtors and hirers who receive default notices.

(4) Regulations may make provision about the information to be included in an information sheet.

(5) An information sheet takes effect for the purposes of this Part at the end of the period of three months beginning with the day on which general notice of it is given.

(6) If the OFT revises an information sheet after general notice of it has been given, it shall give general notice of the information sheet as revised.

(7) A revised information sheet takes effect for the purposes of this Part at the end of the period of three months beginning with the day on which general notice of it is given.]

[Sums in arrears and default sums]

[86B   Notice of sums in arrears under fixed-sum credit agreements etc.

(1) This section applies where at any time the following conditions are satisfied—

(a) that the debtor or hirer under an applicable agreement is required to have made at least two payments under the agreement before that time;

    (b) that the total sum paid under the agreement by him is less than the total sum which he is required to have paid before that time;

    (c) that the amount of the shortfall is no less than the sum of the last two payments which he is required to have made before that time;

    (d) that the creditor or owner is not already under a duty to give him notices under this section in relation to the agreement; and

    (e) if a judgment has been given in relation to the agreement before that time, that there is no sum still to be paid under the judgment by the debtor or hirer.

  (2) The creditor or owner—

    (a) shall, within the period of 14 days beginning with the day on which the conditions mentioned in subsection (1) are satisfied, give the debtor or hirer a notice under this section; and

    (b) after the giving of that notice, shall give him further notices under this section at intervals of not more than six months.

  (3) The duty of the creditor or owner to give the debtor or hirer notices under this section shall cease when either of the conditions mentioned in subsection (4) is satisfied; but if either of those conditions is satisfied before the notice required by subsection (2)(a) is given, the duty shall not cease until that notice is given.

  (4) The conditions referred to in subsection (3) are—

    (a) that the debtor or hirer ceases to be in arrears;

    (b) that a judgment is given in relation to the agreement under which a sum is required to be paid by the debtor or hirer.

  (5) For the purposes of subsection (4)(a) the debtor or hirer ceases to be in arrears when—

    (a) no sum, which he has ever failed to pay under the agreement when required, is still owing;

    (b) no default sum, which has ever become payable under the agreement in connection with his failure to pay any sum under the agreement when required, is still owing;

    (c) no sum of interest, which has ever become payable under the agreement in connection with such a default sum, is still owing; and

    (d) no other sum of interest, which has ever become payable under the agreement in connection with his failure to pay any sum under the agreement when required, is still owing.

  (6) A notice under this section shall include a copy of the current arrears information sheet under section 86A.

  (7) The debtor or hirer shall have no liability to pay any sum in connection with the preparation or the giving to him of a notice under this section.

  (8) Regulations may make provision about the form and content of notices under this section.

  (9) In the case of an applicable agreement under which the debtor or hirer must make all payments he is required to make at intervals of one week or less, this section shall have effect as if in subsection (1)(a) and (c) for 'two' there were substituted 'four'.

  (10) If an agreement mentioned in subsection (9) was made before the beginning of the relevant period, only amounts resulting from failures by the debtor or hirer to make payments he is required to have made during that period shall be taken into account in determining any shortfall for the purposes of subsection (1)(c).

  (11) In subsection (10) 'relevant period' means the period of 20 weeks ending with the day on which the debtor or hirer is required to have made the most recent payment under the agreement.

  (12) In this section 'applicable agreement' means an agreement which—

    (a) is a regulated agreement for fixed-sum credit or a regulated consumer hire agreement; and

    (b) is neither a non-commercial agreement nor a small agreement.]

[86C   Notice of sums in arrears under running-account credit agreements

(1) This section applies where at any time the following conditions are satisfied—

(a) that the debtor under an applicable agreement is required to have made at least two payments under the agreement before that time;

(b) that the last two payments which he is required to have made before that time have not been made;

(c) that the creditor has not already been required to give a notice under this section in relation to either of those payments; and

(d) if a judgment has been given in relation to the agreement before that time, that there is no sum still to be paid under the judgment by the debtor.

(2) The creditor shall, no later than the end of the period within which he is next required to give a statement under section 78(4) in relation to the agreement, give the debtor a notice under this section.

(3) The notice shall include a copy of the current arrears information sheet under section 86A.

(4) The notice may be incorporated in a statement or other notice which the creditor gives the debtor in relation to the agreement by virtue of another provision of this Act.

(5) The debtor shall have no liability to pay any sum in connection with the preparation or the giving to him of the notice.

(6) Regulations may make provision about the form and content of notices under this section.

(7) In this section 'applicable agreement' means an agreement which—

(a) is a regulated agreement for running-account credit; and

(b) is neither a non-commercial agreement nor a small agreement.]

[86D   Failure to give notice of sums in arrears

(1) This section applies where the creditor or owner under an agreement is under a duty to give the debtor or hirer notices under section 86B but fails to give him such a notice—

(a) within the period mentioned in subsection (2)(a) of that section; or

(b) within the period of six months beginning with the day after the day on which such a notice was last given to him.

(2) This section also applies where the creditor under an agreement is under a duty to give the debtor a notice under section 86C but fails to do so before the end of the period mentioned in subsection (2) of that section.

(3) The creditor or owner shall not be entitled to enforce the agreement during the period of non-compliance.

(4) The debtor or hirer shall have no liability to pay—

(a) any sum of interest to the extent calculated by reference to the period of non-compliance or to any part of it; or

(b) any default sum which (apart from this paragraph)—

(i)   would have become payable during the period of non-compliance; or

(ii)   would have become payable after the end of that period in connection with a breach of the agreement which occurs during that period (whether or not the breach continues after the end of that period).

(5) In this section 'the period of non-compliance' means, in relation to a failure to give a notice under section 86B or 86C to the debtor or hirer, the period which—

(a) begins immediately after the end of the period mentioned in (as the case may be) subsection (1)(a) or (b) or (2); and

(b) ends at the end of the day mentioned in subsection (6).

(6) That day is—

(a) in the case of a failure to give a notice under section 86B as mentioned in sub-section (1)(a) of this section, the day on which the notice is given to the debtor or hirer;

(b) in the case of a failure to give a notice under that section as mentioned in sub-section (1)(b) of this section, the earlier of the following—

    (i) the day on which the notice is given to the debtor or hirer;

    (ii) the day on which the condition mentioned in subsection (4)(a) of that section is satisfied;

(c) in the case of a failure to give a notice under section 86C, the day on which the notice is given to the debtor.]

[86E Notice of default sums

(1) This section applies where a default sum becomes payable under a regulated agreement by the debtor or hirer.

(2) The creditor or owner shall, within the prescribed period after the default sum becomes payable, give the debtor or hirer a notice under this section.

(3) The notice under this section may be incorporated in a statement or other notice which the creditor or owner gives the debtor or hirer in relation to the agreement by virtue of another provision of this Act.

(4) The debtor or hirer shall have no liability to pay interest in connection with the default sum to the extent that the interest is calculated by reference to a period occurring before the 29th day after the day on which the debtor or hirer is given the notice under this section.

(5) If the creditor or owner fails to give the debtor or hirer the notice under this section within the period mentioned in subsection (2), he shall not be entitled to enforce the agreement until the notice is given to the debtor or hirer.

(6) The debtor or hirer shall have no liability to pay any sum in connection with the preparation or the giving to him of the notice under this section.

(7) Regulations may—

    (a) provide that this section does not apply in relation to a default sum which is less than a prescribed amount;

    (b) make provision about the form and content of notices under this section.

(8) This section does not apply in relation to a non-commercial agreement or to a small agreement.]

[86F Interest on default sums

(1) This section applies where a default sum becomes payable under a regulated agreement by the debtor or hirer.

(2) The debtor or hirer shall only be liable to pay interest in connection with the default sum if the interest is simple interest.]

Default notices

87 Need for default notice

(1) Service of a notice on the debtor or hirer in accordance with section 88 (a 'default notice') is necessary before the creditor or owner can become entitled, by reason of any breach by the debtor or hirer of a regulated agreement,—

    (a) to terminate the agreement, or

    (b) to demand earlier payment of any sum, or

    (c) to recover possession of any goods or land, or

    (d) to treat any right conferred on the debtor or hirer by the agreement as terminated, restricted or deferred, or

    (e) to enforce any security.

(2) Subsection (1) does not prevent the creditor from treating the right to draw upon any credit as restricted or deferred, and taking such steps as may be necessary to make the restriction or deferment effective.

(3) The doing of an act by which a floating charge becomes fixed is not enforcement of a security.

(4) Regulations may provide that section (1) is not to apply to agreements described by the regulations.

88   Contents and effect of default notice

(1) The default notice must be in the prescribed form and specify—
   (a) the nature of the alleged breach;
   (b) if the breach is capable of remedy, what action is required to remedy it and the date before which that action is to be taken;
   (c) if the breach is not capable of remedy, the sum (if any) required to be paid as compensation for the breach, and the date before which it is to be paid.

(2) A date specified under subsection (1) must not be less than [14] days after the date of service of the default notice, and the creditor or owner shall not take action such as is mentioned in section 87(1) before the date so specified or (if no requirement is made under subsection (1)) before those [14] days have elapsed.

(3) The default notice must not treat as a breach failure to comply with a provision of the agreement which becomes operative only on breach of some other provision, but if the breach of that other provision is not duly remedied or compensation demanded under subsection (1) is not duly paid, or (where no requirement is made under subsection (1)) if the seven days mentioned in subsection (2) have elapsed, the creditor or owner may treat the failure as a breach and section 87(1) shall not apply to it.

(4) The default notice must contain information in the prescribed terms about the consequences of failure to comply with it [and any other prescribed matters relating to the agreement].

[(4A) The default notice must also include a copy of the current default information sheet under section 86A.]

(5) A default notice making a requirement under subsection (1) may include a provision for the taking of action such as is mentioned in section 87(1) at any time after the restriction imposed by subsection (2) will cease, together with a statement that the provision will be ineffective if the breach is duly remedied or the compensation duly paid.

89   Compliance with default notice

If before the date specified for that purpose in the default notice the debtor or hirer takes the action specified under section 88(1)(b) or (c) the breach shall be treated as not having occurred.

Further restriction of remedies for default

90   Retaking of protected hire-purchase etc. goods

(1) At any time when—
   (a) the debtor is in breach of a regulated hire-purchase or a regulated conditional sale agreement relating to goods, and
   (b) the debtor has paid to the creditor one-third or more of the total price of the goods and
   (c) the property in the goods remains in the creditor, the creditor is not entitled to recover possession of the goods from the debtor except on an order of the court.

(2) Where under a hire-purchase or conditional sale agreement the creditor is required to carry out any installation and the agreement specifies, as part of the total price, the amount to be paid in respect of the installation (the 'installation charge') the reference in subsection (1)(b) to one-third of the total price shall be construed as a reference to the aggregate of the installation charge and one-third of the remainder of the total price.

(3) In a case where—
  (a) subsection (1)(a) is satisfied, but not subsection (1)(b), and
  (b) subsection (1)(b) was satisfied on a previous occasion in relation to an earlier agreement, being a regulated hire-purchase or regulated conditional sale agreement, between the same parties, and relating to any of the goods comprised in the later agreement (whether or not other goods were also included),
subsection (1) shall apply to the later agreement with the omission of paragraph (b).

(4) If the later agreement is a modifying agreement, subsection (3) shall apply with the substitution, for the second reference to the later agreement, of a reference to the modifying agreement.

(5) Subsection (1) shall not apply, or shall cease to apply, to an agreement if the debtor has terminated, or terminates, the agreement.

(6) Where subsection (1) applies to an agreement at the death of the debtor, it shall continue to apply (in relation to the possessor of the goods) until the grant of probate or administration, or (in Scotland) confirmation (on which the personal representative would fall to be treated as the debtor).

(7) Goods falling within this section are in this Act referred to as 'protected goods'.

91 Consequences of breach of s. 90
If goods are recovered by the creditor in contravention of section 90—
  (a) the regulated agreement, if not previously terminated, shall terminate, and
  (b) the debtor shall be released from all liability under the agreement, and shall be entitled to recover from the creditor all sums paid by the debtor under the agreement.

92 Recovery of possession of goods or land
(1) Except under an order of the court, the creditor or owner shall not be entitled to enter any premises to take possession of goods subject to a regulated hire-purchase agreement, regulated conditional sale agreement or regulated consumer hire agreement.

(2) At any time when the debtor is in breach of a regulated conditional sale agreement relating to land, the creditor is entitled to recover possession of the land from the debtor, or any person claiming under him, on an order of the court only.

(3) An entry in contravention of section (1) or (2) is actionable as a breach of statutory duty.

93 Interest not to be increased on default
The debtor under a regulated consumer credit agreement shall not be obliged to pay interest on sums which, in breach of the agreement, are unpaid by him at a rate—
  (a) where the total charge for credit includes an item in respect of interest, exceeding the rate of that interest, or
  (b) in any other case, exceeding what would be the rate of the total charge for credit if any items included in the total charge for credit by virtue of section 20(2) were disregarded.

[93A Summary diligence not competent in Scotland
...]

Early payment by debtor

94 Right to complete payments ahead of time
(1) The debtor under a regulated consumer credit agreement is entitled at any time, by notice to the creditor and the payment to the creditor of all amounts payable by the debtor to him under the agreement (less any rebate allowable under section 95), to discharge the debtor's indebtedness under the agreement.

(2) A notice under subsection (1) may embody the exercise by the debtor of any option to purchase goods conferred on him by the agreement, and deal with any other matter arising on, or in relation to, the termination of the agreement.

95 Rebate on early settlement

(1) Regulations may provide for the allowance of a rebate of charges for credit to the debtor under a regulated consumer credit agreement where, under section 94, on refinancing, on breach of the agreement, or for any other reason, his indebtedness is discharged or becomes payable before the time fixed by the agreement, or any sum becomes payable by him before the time so fixed.

(2) Regulations under subsection (1) may provide for calculation of the rebate by reference to any sums paid or payable by the debtor or his relative under or in connection with the agreement (whether to the creditor or some other person), including sums under linked transactions and other items in the total charge for credit.

96 Effect on linked transactions

(1) Where for any reason the indebtedness of the debtor under a regulated consumer credit agreement is discharged before the time fixed by the agreement, he, and any relative of his, shall at the same time be discharged from any liability under a linked transaction, other than a debt which has already become payable.

(2) Subsection (1) does not apply to a linked transaction which is itself an agreement providing the debtor or his relative with credit.

(3) Regulations may exclude linked transactions of the prescribed description from the operation of subsection (1).

97 Duty to give information

(1) The creditor under a regulated consumer credit agreement, within the prescribed period after he has received a request in writing to that effect from the debtor, shall give the debtor a statement in the prescribed form indicating, according to the information to which it is practicable for him to refer, the amount of the payment required to discharge the debtor's indebtedness under the agreement, together with the prescribed particulars showing how the amount is arrived at.

(2) Subsection (1) does not apply to a request made less than one month after a previous request under that subsection relating to the same agreement was complied with.

(3) If the creditor fails to comply with subsection (1)—

 (a) he is not entitled, while the default continues, to enforce the agreement; and

 (b) if the default continues for one month he commits an offence.

Termination of agreements

98 Duty to give notice of termination (non-default cases)

(1) The creditor or owner is not entitled to terminate a regulated agreement except by or after giving the debtor or hirer not less than seven days' notice of the termination.

(2) Subsection (1) applies only where—

 (a) a period for the duration of the agreement is specified in the agreement, and

 (b) that period has not ended when the creditor or owner does an act mentioned in subsection (1),

but so applies notwithstanding that, under the agreement, any party is entitled to terminate it before the end of the period so specified.

(3) A notice under subsection (1) is ineffective if not in the prescribed form.

(4) Subsection (1) does not prevent a creditor from treating the right to draw on any credit as restricted or deferred and taking such steps as may be necessary to make the restriction or deferment effective.

(5) Regulations may provide that subsection (1) is not to apply to agreements described by the regulations.

(6) Subsection (1) does not apply to the termination of a regulated agreement by reason of any breach by the debtor or hirer of the agreement.

99   Right to terminate hire-purchase etc. agreements

(1) At any time before the final payment by the debtor under a regulated hire-purchase or regulated conditional sale agreement falls due, the debtor shall be entitled to terminate the agreement by giving notice to any person entitled or authorised to receive the sums payable under the agreement.

(2) Termination of an agreement under subsection (1) does not affect any liability under the agreement which has accrued before the termination.

(3) Subsection (1) does not apply to a conditional sale agreement relating to land after the title to the land has passed to the debtor.

(4) In the case of a conditional sale agreement relating to goods, where the property in the goods, having become vested in the debtor, is transferred to a person who does not become the debtor under the agreement, the debtor shall not thereafter be entitled to terminate the agreement under subsection (1).

(5) Subject to subsection (4), where a debtor under a conditional sale agreement relating to goods terminates the agreement under this section after the property in the goods has become vested in him, the property in the goods shall thereupon vest in the person (the 'previous owner') in whom it was vested immediately before it became vested in the debtor:

Provided that if the previous owner has died, or any other event has occurred whereby that property, if vested in him immediately before that event, would thereupon have vested in some other person, the property shall be treated as having devolved as if it had been vested in the previous owner immediately before his death or immediately before that event, as the case may be.

100   Liability of debtor on termination of hire-purchase etc. agreement

(1) Where a regulated hire-purchase or regulated conditional sale agreement is terminated under section 99 the debtor shall be liable, unless the agreement provides for a smaller payment, or does not provide for any payment, to pay to the creditor the amount (if any) by which one-half of the total price exceeds the aggregate of the sums paid and the sums due in respect of the total price immediately before the termination.

(2) Where under a hire-purchase or conditional sale agreement the creditor is required to carry out any installation and the agreement specifies, as part of the total price, the amount to be paid in respect of the installation (the 'installation charge') the reference in subsection (1) to one-half of the total price shall be construed as a reference to the aggregate of the installation charge and one-half of the remainder of the total price.

(3) If in any action the court is satisfied that a sum less than the amount specified in subsection (1) would be equal to the loss sustained by the creditor in consequence of the termination of the agreement by the debtor, the court may make an order for the payment of that sum in lieu of the amount specified in subsection (1).

(4) If the debtor has contravened an obligation to take reasonable care of the goods or land, the amount arrived at under subsection (1) shall be increased by the sum required to recompense the creditor for that contravention, and subsection (2) shall have effect accordingly.

(5) Where the debtor, on the termination of the agreement, wrongfully retains possession of goods to which the agreement relates, then, in any action brought by the creditor to recover possession of the goods from the debtor, the court, unless it is satisfied that having regard to the circumstances it would not be just to do so, shall order the goods to be delivered to the creditor without giving the debtor an option to pay the value of the goods.

101 Right to termininate hire agreement

(1) The hirer under a regulated consumer hire agreement is entitled to terminate the agreement by giving notice to any person entitled or authorised to receive the sums payable under the agreement.

(2) Termination of an agreement under subsection (1) does not affect any liability under the agreement which has accrued before the termination.

(3) A notice under subsection (1) shall not expire earlier than eighteen months after the making of the agreement, but apart from that the minimum period of notice to be given under subsection (1), unless the agreement provides for a shorter period, is as follows.

(4) If the agreement provides for the making of payments by the hirer to the owner at equal intervals, the minimum period of notice is the length of one interval or three months, whichever is less.

(5) If the agreement provides for the making of such payments at differing intervals, the minimum period of notice is the length of the shortest interval or three months, whichever is less.

(6) In any other case, the minimum period of notice is three months.

(7) This section does not apply to—

(a) any agreement which provides for the making by the hirer of payments which in total (and without breach of the agreement) exceed [£1,500] in any year, or

(b) any agreement where—

(i) goods are bailed or (in Scotland) hired to the hirer for the purposes of a business carried on by him, or the hirer holds himself out as requiring the goods for those purposes, and

(ii) the goods are selected by the hirer, and acquired by the owner for the purposes of the agreement at the request of the hirer from any person other than the owner's associate, or

(c) any agreement where the hirer requires, or holds himself out as requiring, the goods for the purpose of bailing or hiring them to other persons in the course of a business carried on by him.

(8) If, on an application made to the [OFT] by a person carrying on a consumer hire business, it appears to the [OFT] that it would be in the interest of hirers to do so, [it] may by notice to the applicant direct that [, subject to such conditions (if any) as it may specify, this section shall not apply to consumer hire agreements made by the applicant; and this Act shall have effect accordingly].

[(8A) If it appears to the OFT that it would be in the interests of hirers to do so, it may by general notice direct that, subject to such conditions (if any) as it may specify, this section shall not apply to a consumer hire agreement if the agreement falls within a specified description; and this Act shall have effect accordingly.]

(9) In the case of a modifying agreement, subsection (3) shall apply with the substitution for 'the making of the agreement' of 'the making of the original agreement'.

102 Agency for receiving notice of rescission

(1) Where the debtor or hirer under a regulated agreement claims to have a right to rescind the agreement, each of the following shall be deemed to be the agent of the creditor or owner for the purpose of receiving any notice rescinding the agreement which is served by the debtor or hirer—

(a) a credit-broker or supplier who was the negotiator in antecedent negotiations, and

(b) any person who, in the course of a business carried on by him, acted on behalf of the debtor or hirer in any negotiations for the agreement.

(2) In subsection (1) 'rescind' does not include—

(a) service of a notice of cancellation, or

(b) termination of an agreement under section 99 or 101 or by the exercise of a right or power in that behalf expressly conferred by the agreement.

103   Termination statements

(1) If an individual (the 'customer') serves on any person (the 'trader') a notice—

    (a) stating that—

        (i)   the customer was the debtor or hirer under a regulated agreement described in the notice, and the trader was the creditor or owner under the agreement, and

        (ii) the customer has discharged his indebtedness to the trader under the agreement, and

        (iii) the agreement has ceased to have any operation; and

    (b) requiring the trader to give the customer a notice, signed by or on behalf of the trader, confirming that those statements are correct,

the trader shall, within the prescribed period after receiving the notice, either comply with it or serve on the customer a counter-notice stating that, as the case may be, he disputes the correctness of the notice or asserts that the customer is not indebted to him under the agreement.

(2) Where the trader disputes the correctness of the notice he shall give particulars of the way in which he alleges it to be wrong.

(3) Subsection (1) does not apply in relation to any agreement if the trader has previously complied with that subsection on the service of a notice under it with respect to that agreement.

(4) Subsection (1) does not apply to a non-commercial agreement.

(5) If the trader fails to comply with subsection (1), and the default continues for one month, he commits an offence.

104   Goods not to be treated as subject to landlord's hypothec in Scotland

Goods comprised in a hire-purchase agreement or goods comprised in a conditional sale agreement which have not become vested in the debtor shall not be treated in Scotland as subject to the landlord's hypothec—

    (a) during the period between the service of a default notice in respect of the goods and the date on which the notice expires or is earlier complied with; or

    (b) if the agreement is enforceable on an order of the court only, during the period between the commencement and termination of an action by the creditor to enforce the agreement.

PART VIII   SECURITY

General

105   Form and content of securities

(1) Any security provided in relation to a regulated agreement shall be expressed in writing.

(2) Regulations may prescribe the form and content of documents ('security instruments') to be made in compliance with subsection (1).

(3) Regulations under subsection (2) may in particular—

    (a) require specified information to be included in the prescribed manner in documents, and other specified material to be excluded;

    (b) contain requirements to ensure that specified information is clearly brought to the attention of the surety, and that one part of a document is not given insufficient or excessive prominence compared with another.

(4) A security instrument is not properly executed unless—

    (a) a document in the prescribed form, itself containing all the prescribed terms and conforming to regulations under subsection (2), is signed in the prescribed manner by or on behalf of the surety, and

  (b) the document embodies all the terms of the security, other than implied terms, and
  (c) the document, when presented or sent for the purpose of being signed by or on behalf of the surety, is in such state that its terms are readily legible, and
  (d) when the document is presented or sent for the purpose of being signed by or on behalf of the surety there is also presented or sent a copy of the document.
 (5) A security instrument is not properly executed unless—
  (a) where the security is provided after, or at the time when, the regulated agreement is made, a copy of the executed agreement, together with a copy of any other document referred to in it, is given to the surety at the time the security is provided, or
  (b) where the security is provided before the regulated agreement is made, a copy of the executed agreement, together with a copy of any other document referred to in it, is given to the surety within seven days after the regulated agreement is made.
 (6) Subsection (1) does not apply to a security provided by the debtor or hirer.
 (7) If—
  (a) in contravention of subsection (1) a security is not expressed in writing, or
  (b) a security instrument is improperly executed, the security, so far as provided in relation to a regulated agreement, is enforceable against the surety on an order of the court only.
 (8) If an application for an order under subsection (7) is dismissed (except on technical grounds only) section 106 (ineffective securities) shall apply to the security.
 (9) Regulations under section 60(1) shall include provision requiring documents embodying regulated agreements also to embody any security provided in relation to a regulated agreement by the debtor or hirer.

106   Ineffective securities

Where, under any provision of this Act, this section is applied to any security provided in relation to a regulated agreement, then, subject to section 177 (saving for registered charges)—
  (a) the security, so far as it is so provided, shall be treated as never having effect;
  (b) any property lodged with the creditor or owner solely for the purposes of the security as so provided shall be returned by him forthwith;
  (c) the creditor or owner shall take any necessary action to remove or cancel an entry in any register, so far as the entry relates to the security as so provided; and
  (d) any amount received by the creditor or owner on realisation of the security shall, so far as it is referable to the agreement, be repaid to the surety.

107   Duty to give information to surety under fixed-sum credit agreement

 (1) The creditor under a regulated agreement for fixed-sum credit in relation to which security is provided, within the prescribed period after receiving a request in writing to that effect from the surety and payment of a fee of [£1], shall give to the surety (if a different person from the debtor)—
  (a) a copy of the executed agreement (if any) and of any other document referred to in it;
  (b) a copy of the security instrument (if any); and
  (c) a statement signed by or on behalf of the creditor showing, according to the information to which it is practicable for him to refer,—
   (i)   the total sum paid under the agreement by the debtor,
   (ii) the total sum which has become payable under the agreement by the debtor but remains unpaid, and the various amounts comprised in that total sum, with the date when each became due, and
   (iii) the total sum which is to become payable under the agreement by the debtor, and the various amounts comprised in that total sum, with the date, or mode of determining the date, when each becomes due.

(2) If the creditor possesses insufficient information to enable him to ascertain the amounts and dates mentioned in subsection (1)(c)(iii), he shall be taken to comply with that sub-paragraph if his statement under subsection (1)(c) gives the basis on which, under the regulated agreement, they would fall to be ascertained.

(3) Subsection (1) does not apply to—

(a) an agreement under which no sum is, or will or may become, payable by the debtor, or

(b) a request made less than one month after a previous request under that subsection relating to the same agreement was complied with.

(4) If the creditor under an agreement fails to comply with subsection (1)—

(a) he is not entitled, while the default continues, to enforce the security, so far as provided in relation to the agreement; and

(b) if the default continues for one month he commits an offence.

(5) This section does not apply to a non-commercial agreement.

108   Duty to give information to surety under running-account credit agreement

(1) The creditor under a regulated agreement for running-account credit in relation to which security is provided, within the prescribed period after receiving a request in writing to that effect from the surety and payment of a fee of [£1], shall give to the surety (if a different person from the debtor)—

(a) a copy of the executed agreement (if any) and of any other document referred to in it;

(b) a copy of the security instrument (if any); and

(c) a statement signed by or on behalf of the creditor showing, according to the information to which it is practicable for him to refer,—

(i)   the state of the account, and

(ii) the amount, if any, currently payable under the agreement by the debtor to the creditor, and

(iii) the amounts and due dates of any payments which, if the debtor does not draw further on the account, will later become payable under the agreement by the debtor to the creditor.

(2) If the creditor possesses insufficient information to enable him to ascertain the amounts and dates mentioned in subsection (1)(c)(iii), he shall be taken to comply with that sub-paragraph if his statement under subsection (1)(c) gives the basis on which, under the regulated agreement, they would fall to be ascertained.

(3) Subsection (1) does not apply to—

(a) an agreement under which no sum is, or will or may become, payable by the debtor, or

(b) a request made less than one month after a previous request under that subsection relating to the same agreement was complied with.

(4) If the creditor under an agreement fails to comply with subsection (1)—

(a) he is not entitled, while the default continues, to enforce the security, so far as provided in relation to the agreement; and

(b) if the default continues for one month he commits an offence.

(5) This section does not apply to a non-commercial agreement.

109   Duty to give information to surety under consumer hire agreement

(1) The owner under a regulated consumer hire agreement in relation to which security is provided, within the prescribed period after receiving a request in writing to that effect from the surety and payment of a fee of [£1], shall give to the surety (if a different person from the hirer)—

(a) a copy of the executed agreement and of any other document referred to in it;

(b) a copy of the security instrument (if any); and

(c) a statement signed by or on behalf of the owner showing, according to the information to which it is practicable for him to refer, the total sum which has become payable under the agreement by the hirer but remains unpaid and the various amounts comprised in that total sum, with the date when each became due.

(2) Subsection (1) does not apply to—

(a) an agreement under which no sum is, or will or may become, payable by the hirer, or

(b) a request made less than one month after a previous request under that subsection relating to the same agreement was complied with.

(3) If the owner under an agreement fails to comply with subsection (1)—

(a) he is not entitled, while the default continues, to enforce the security, so far as provided in relation to the agreement; and

(b) if the default continues for one month he commits an offence.

(4) This section does not apply to a non-commercial agreement.

110   Duty to give information to debtor or hirer

(1) The creditor or owner under a regulated agreement, within the prescribed period after receiving a request in writing to that effect from the debtor or hirer and payment of a fee of [£1], shall give the debtor or hirer a copy of any security instrument executed in relation to the agreement after the making of the agreement.

(2) Subsection (1) does not apply to—

(a) a non-commercial agreement, or

(b) an agreement under which no sum is, or will or may become, payable by the debtor or hirer, or

(c) a request made less than one month after a previous request under subsection (1) relating to the same agreement was complied with.

(3) If the creditor or owner under an agreement fails to comply with subsection (1)—

(a) he is not entitled, while the default continues, to enforce the security (so far as provided in relation to the agreement); and

(b) if the default continues for one month he commits an offence.

111   Duty to give surety copy of default etc. notice

(1) When a default notice or a notice under section 76(1) or 98(1) is served on a debtor or hirer, a copy of the notice shall be served by the creditor or owner on any surety (if a different person from the debtor or hirer).

(2) If the creditor or owner fails to comply with subsection (1) in the case of any surety, the security is enforceable against the surety (in respect of the breach or other matter to which the notice relates) on an order of the court only.

112   Realisation of securities

Subject to section 121, regulations may provide for any matters relating to the sale or other realisation, by the creditor or owner, of property over which any right has been provided by way of security in relation to an actual or prospective regulated agreement, other than a non-commercial agreement.

113   Act not to be evaded by use of security

(1) Where a security is provided in relation to an actual or prospective regulated agreement, the security shall not be enforced so as to benefit the creditor or owner, directly or indirectly, to an extent greater (whether as respects the amount of any payment or the time or manner of its being made) than would be the case if the security were not provided and any obligations of the debtor or hirer, or his relative, under or in relation to the agreement were carried out to the extent (if any) to which they would be enforced under this Act.

(2) In accordance with subsection (1), where a regulated agreement is enforceable on an order of the court or the [OFT] only, any security provided in relation to the agreement is

enforceable (so far as provided in relation to the agreement) where such an order has been made in relation to the agreement, but not otherwise.

(3) Where—

(a) a regulated agreement is cancelled under section 69(1) or becomes subject to section 69(2), or

(b) a regulated agreement is terminated under section 91, or

(c) in relation to any agreement an application for an order under section 40(2), 65(1), 124(1) or 149(2) is dismissed (except on technical grounds only), or

(d) a declaration is made by the court under section 142(1) (refusal of enforcement order) as respects any regulated agreement,

section 106 shall apply to any security provided in relation to the agreement.

(4) Where subsection (3)(d) applies and the declaration relates to a part only of the regulated agreement, section 106 shall apply to the security only so far as it concerns that part.

(5) In the case of a cancelled agreement, the duty imposed on the debtor or hirer by section 71 or 72 shall not be enforceable before the creditor or owner has discharged any duty imposed on him by section 106 (as applied by subsection (3)(a)).

(6) If the security is provided in relation to a prospective agreement or transaction, the security shall be enforceable in relation to the agreement or transaction only after the time (if any) when the agreement is made; and until that time the person providing the security shall be entitled, by notice to the creditor or owner, to require that section 106 shall thereupon apply to the security.

(7) Where an indemnity [or guarantee] is given in a case where the debtor or hirer is a minor, or [an indemnity is given in a case where he] is otherwise not of full capacity, the reference in subsection (1) to the extent to which his obligations would be enforced shall be read in relation to the indemnity [or guarantee] as a reference to the extent to which [those obligations] would be enforced if he were of full capacity.

(8) Subsections (1) and (3) also apply where a security is provided in relation to an actual or prospective linked transaction, and in that case—

(a) references to the agreement shall be read as references to the linked transaction, and

(b) references to the creditor or owner shall be read as references to any person (other than the debtor or hirer, or his relative) who is a party, or prospective party, to the linked transaction.

Pledges

114 Pawn-receipts

(1) At the time he receives the article, a person who takes any article in pawn under a regulated agreement shall give to the person from whom he receives it a receipt in the prescribed form (a 'pawn-receipt').

(2) A person who takes any article in pawn from an individual whom he knows to be, or who appears to be and is, a minor commits an offence.

(3) This section and sections 115 to 122 do not apply to—

(a) a pledge of documents of title [or of bearer bonds], or

(b) a non-commercial agreement.

115 Penalty for failure to supply copies of pledge agreement, etc.

If the creditor under a regulated agreement to take any article in pawn fails to observe the requirements of section 62 to 64 or 114(1) in relation to the agreement he commits an offence.

116 Redemption period

(1) A pawn is redeemable at any time within six months after it was taken.

(2) Subject to subsection (1), the period within which a pawn is redeemable shall be the same as the period fixed by the parties for the duration of the credit secured by the pledge, or such longer period as they may agree.

(3) If the pawn is not redeemed by the end of the period laid down by subsections (1) and (2) (the 'redemption period'), it nevertheless remains redeemable until it is realised by the pawnee under section 121 except where under section 120(1)(a) the property in it passes to the pawnee.

(4) No special charge shall be made for redemption of a pawn after the end of the redemption period, and charges in respect of the safe keeping of the pawn shall not be at a higher rate after the end of the redemption period than before.

117 Redemption procedure

(1) On surrender of the pawn-receipt, and payment of the amount owing, at any time when the pawn is redeemable, the pawnee shall deliver the pawn to the bearer of the pawn-receipt.

(2) Subsection (1) does not apply if the pawnee knows or has reasonable cause to suspect that the bearer of the pawn-receipt is neither the owner of the pawn nor authorised by the owner to redeem it.

(3) The pawnee is not liable to any person in tort or delict for delivering the pawn where subsection (1) applies, or refusing to deliver it where the person demanding delivery does not comply with subsection (1) or, by reason of subsection (2), subsection (1) does not apply.

118 Loss etc. of pawn-receipt

(1) A person (the 'claimant') who is not in possession of the pawn-receipt but claims to be the owner of the pawn, or to be otherwise entitled or authorised to redeem it, may do so at any time when it is redeemable by tendering to the pawnee in place of the pawn-receipt—

(a) a statutory declaration made by the claimant in the prescribed form, and with the prescribed contents, or

(b) where the pawn is security for fixed-sum credit not exceeding [£75] or running-account credit on which the credit limit does not exceed [£75], and the pawnee agrees, a statement in writing in the prescribed form, and with the prescribed contents, signed by the claimant.

(2) On compliance by the claimant with subsection (1), section 117 shall apply as if the declaration or statement were the pawn-receipt, and the pawn-receipt itself shall become inoperative for the purposes of section 117.

119 Unreasonable refusal to deliver pawn

(1) If a person who has taken a pawn under a regulated agreement refuses without reasonable cause to allow the pawn to be redeemed, he commits an offence.

(2) On the conviction in England and Wales of a pawnee under subsection (1) where the offence does not amount to theft, [section 148 of the Powers of Criminal Courts (Sentencing) Act 2000 (restitution orders)] shall apply as if the pawnee had been convicted of stealing the pawn.

(3) On the conviction in Northern Ireland of a pawnee under subsection (1) where the offence does not amount to theft, section 27 (orders for restitution) of the Theft Act (Northern Ireland) 1969, and any provision of the Theft Act (Northern Ireland) 1969 relating to that section, shall apply as if the pawnee had been convicted of stealing the pawn.

120 Consequence of failure to redeem

(1) If at the end of the redemption period the pawn has not been redeemed—

(a) notwithstanding anything in section 113, the property in the pawn passes to the pawnee where the redemption period is six months and the pawn is security for fixed-sum credit not exceeding [£75] or running-account credit on which the credit limit does not exceed [£75]; or

(b) in any other case the pawn becomes realisable by the pawnee.

(2) Where the debtor or hirer is entitled to apply to the court for a time order under section 129, subsection (1) shall apply with the substitution, for 'at the end of the redemption period' of 'after the expiry of five days following the end of the redemption period'.

121   Realisation of pawn

(1) When a pawn has become realisable by him, the pawnee may sell it, after giving to the pawnor (except in such cases as may be prescribed) not less than the prescribed period of notice of the intention to sell, indicating in the notice the asking price and such other particulars as may be prescribed.

(2) Within the prescribed period after the sale takes place, the pawnee shall give the pawnor the prescribed information in writing as to the sale, its proceeds and expenses.

(3) Where the net proceeds of sale are not less than the sum which, if the pawn had been redeemed on the date of the sale, would have been payable for its redemption, the debt secured by the pawn is discharged and any surplus shall be paid by the pawnee to the pawnor.

(4) Where subsection (3) does not apply, the debt shall be treated as from the date of sale as equal to the amount by which the net proceeds of sale fall short of the sum which would have been payable for the redemption of the pawn on that date.

(5) In this section the 'net proceeds of sale' is the amount realised (the 'gross amount') less the expenses (if any) of the sale.

(6) If the pawnor alleges that the gross amount is less than the true market value of the pawn on the date of sale, it is for the pawnee to prove that he and any agents employed by him in the sale used reasonable care to ensure that the true market value was obtained, and if he fails to do so subsections (3) and (4) shall have effect as if the reference in subsection (5) to the gross amount were a reference to the true market value.

(7) If the pawnor alleges that the expenses of the sale were unreasonably high, it is for the pawnee to prove that they were reasonable, and if he fails to do so subsections (3) and (4) shall have effect as if the reference in subsection (5) to expenses were a reference to reasonable expenses.

122   Order in Scotland to deliver pawn

. . .

Negotiable instruments

123   Restrictions on taking and negotiating instruments

(1) A creditor or owner shall not take a negotiable instrument, other than a bank note or cheque, in discharge of any sum payable—

(a) by the debtor or hirer under a regulated agreement, or

(b) by any person as surety in relation to the agreement.

(2) The creditor or owner shall not negotiate a cheque taken by him in discharge of a sum payable as mentioned in subsection (1) except to a banker (within the meaning of the Bills of Exchange Act 1882).

(3) The creditor or owner shall not take a negotiable instrument as security for the discharge of any sum payable as mentioned in subsection (1).

(4) A person takes a negotiable instrument as security for the discharge of a sum if the sum is intended to be paid in some other way, and the negotiable instrument is to be presented for payment only if the sum is not paid in that way.

(5) This section does not apply where the regulated agreement is a non-commercial agreement.

(6) The Secretary of State may by order provide that this section shall not apply where the regulated agreement has a connection with a country outside the United Kingdom.

124   Consequences of breach of s. 123

(1) After any contravention of section 123 has occurred in relation to a sum payable as mentioned in section 123(1)(a), the agreement under which the sum is payable is enforceable against the debtor or hirer on an order of the court only.

(2) After any contravention of section 123 has occurred in relation to a sum payable by any surety, the security is enforceable on an order of the court only.

(3) Where an application for an order under subsection (2) is dismissed (except on technical grounds only) section 106 shall apply to the security.

125   Holders in due course

(1) A person who takes a negotiable instrument in contravention of section 123(1) or (3) is not a holder in due course, and is not entitled to enforce the instrument.

(2) Where a person negotiates a cheque in contravention of section 123(2), his doing so constitutes a defect in his title within the meaning of the Bills of Exchange Act 1882.

(3) If a person mentioned in section 123(1)(a) and (b) ('the protected person') becomes liable to a holder in due course of an instrument taken from the protected person in contravention of section 123(1) or (3), or taken from the protected person and negotiated in contravention of section 123(2), the creditor or owner shall indemnify the protected person in respect of that liability.

(4) Nothing in this Act affects the rights of the holder in due course of any negotiable instrument.

Land mortgages

126   Enforcement of land mortgages

A land mortgage securing a regulated agreement is enforceable (so far as provided in relation to the agreement) on an order of the court only.

PART IX   JUDICIAL CONTROL

Enforcement of certain regulated agreements and securities

127   Enforcement orders in cases of infringement

(1) In the case of an application for an enforcement order under—

    (a) section 65(1) (improperly executed agreements), or

    (b) section 105(7)(a) or (b) (improperly executed security instruments), or

    (c) section 111(2) (failure to serve copy of notice on surety), or

    (d) section 124(1) or (2) (taking of negotiable instrument in contravention of section 123),

the court shall dismiss the application if, but [. . .] only if, it considers it just to do so having regard to—

        (i)   prejudice caused to any person by the contravention in question, and the degree of culpability for it; and

        (ii)   the powers conferred on the court by subsection (2) and sections 135 and 136.

(2) If it appears to the court just to do so, it may in an enforcement order reduce or discharge any sum payable by the debtor or hirer, or any surety, so as to compensate him for prejudice suffered as a result of the contravention in question.

[. . .]

128   Enforcement orders on death of debtor or hirer

The court shall make an order under section 86(2) if, but only if, the creditor or owner proves that he has been unable to satisfy himself that the present and future obligations of the debtor or hirer under the agreement are likely to be discharged.

Extension of time

129 Time orders

(1) If it appears to the court just to do so—

(a) on an application for an enforcement order; or

(b) on an application made by a debtor or hirer under this paragraph after service on him of—

(i) a default notice, or

(ii) a notice under section 76(1) or 98(1);

[(ba) on an application made by a debtor or hirer under this paragraph after he has been given a notice under section 86B or 86c; or]

(c) in an action brought by a creditor or owner to enforce a regulated agreement or any security, or recover possession of any goods or land to which a regulated agreement relates,

the court may make an order under this section (a 'time order').

(2) A time order shall provide for one or both of the following, as the court considers just—

(a) the payment by the debtor or hirer or any surety of any sum owed under a regulated agreement or a security by such instalments, payable at such times, as the court having regard to the means of the debtor or hirer and any surety, considers reasonable;

(b) the remedying by the debtor or hirer of any breach of a regulated agreement (other than non-payment of money) within such period as the court may specify.

[(3) Where in Scotland a time to pay direction or a time order has been made in relation to a debt, it shall not thereafter be competent to make a time order in relation to the same debt.]

[129A Debtor or hirer to give notice of intent etc. to creditor or owner

(1) A debtor or hirer may make an application under section 129(1)(ba) in relation to a regulated agreement only if—

(a) following his being given the notice under section 86B or 86C, he gave a notice within subsection (2) to the creditor or owner; and

(b) a period of at least 14 days has elapsed after the day on which he gave that notice to the creditor or owner.

(2) A notice is within this subsection if it—

(a) indicates that the debtor or hirer intends to make the application;

(b) indicates that he wants to make a proposal to the creditor or owner in relation to his making of payments under the agreement; and

(c) gives details of that proposal.]

130 Supplemental provisions about time orders

(1) Where in accordance with rules of court an offer to pay any sum by instalments is made by the debtor or hirer and accepted by the creditor or owner, the court may in accordance with rules of court make a time order under section 129(2)(a) giving effect to the offer without hearing evidence of means.

(2) In the case of a hire-purchase or conditional sale agreement only, a time order under section 129(2)(a) may deal with sums which, although not payable by the debtor at the time the order is made, would if the agreement continued in force become payable under it subsequently.

(3) A time order under section 129(2)(a) shall not be made where the regulated agreement is secured by a pledge if, by virtue of regulations made under section 76(5), 87(4) or 98(5), service of a notice is not necessary for enforcement of the pledge.

(4) Where, following the making of a time order in relation to a regulated hire-purchase or conditional sale agreement or a regulated consumer hire agreement, the debtor or hirer is

in possession of the goods, he shall be treated (except in the case of a debtor to whom the creditor's title has passed) as a bailee or (in Scotland) a custodier of the goods under the terms of the agreement, notwithstanding that the agreement has been terminated.

(5) Without prejudice to anything done by the creditor or owner before the commencement of the period specified in a time order made under section 129(2)(b) ('the relevant period'),—

(a) he shall not while the relevant period subsists take in relation to the agreement any action such as is mentioned in section 87(1);

(b) where—

(i) a provision of the agreement ('the secondary provision') becomes operative only on breach of another provision of the agreement ('the primary provision'), and

(ii) the time order provides for the remedying of such a breach of the primary provision within the relevant period,

he shall not treat the secondary provision as operative before the end of that period;

(c) if while the relevant period subsists the breach to which the order relates is remedied it shall be treated as not having occurred.

(6) On the application of any person affected by a time order, the court may vary or revoke the order.

[Interest]

[130A   Interest payable on judgment debts etc.

(1) If the creditor or owner under a regulated agreement wants to be able to recover from the debtor or hirer post-judgment interest in connection with a sum that is required to be paid under a judgment given in relation to the agreement (the 'judgment sum'), he—

(a) after the giving of that judgment, shall give the debtor or hirer a notice under this section (the 'first required notice'); and

(b) after the giving of the first required notice, shall give the debtor or hirer further notices under this section at intervals of not more than six months.

(2) The debtor or hirer shall have no liability to pay post-judgment interest in connection with the judgment sum to the extent that the interest is calculated by reference to a period occurring before the day on which he is given the first required notice.

(3) If the creditor or owner fails to give the debtor or hirer a notice under this section within the period of six months beginning with the day after the day on which such a notice was last given to the debtor or hirer, the debtor or hirer shall have no liability to pay post-judgment interest in connection with the judgment sum to the extent that the interest is calculated by reference to the whole or to a part of the period which—

(a) begins immediately after the end of that period of six months; and

(b) ends at the end of the day on which the notice is given to the debtor or hirer.

(4) The debtor or hirer shall have no liability to pay any sum in connection with the preparation or the giving to him of a notice under this section.

(5) A notice under this section may be incorporated in a statement or other notice which the creditor or owner gives the debtor or hirer in relation to the agreement by virtue of another provision of this Act.

(6) Regulations may make provision about the form and content of notices under this section.

(7) This section does not apply in relation to post-judgment interest which is required to be paid by virtue of any of the following—

(a) section 4 of the Administration of Justice (Scotland) Act 1972;

(b) Article 127 of the Judgments Enforcement (Northern Ireland) Order 1981;

(c) section 74 of the County Courts Act 1984.

(8) This section does not apply in relation to a non-commercial agreement or to a small agreement.

(9) In this section 'post-judgment interest' means interest to the extent calculated by reference to a period occurring after the giving of the judgment under which the judgment sum is required to be paid.]

Protection of property pending proceedings

131   Protection orders

The court, on application of the creditor or owner under a regulated agreement, may make such orders as it thinks just for protecting any property of the creditor or owner, or property subject to any security, from damage or depreciation pending the determination of any proceedings under this Act, including orders restricting or prohibiting use of the property or giving directions as to its custody.

Hire and hire-purchase etc. agreements

132   Financial relief for hirer

(1) Where the owner under a regulated consumer hire agreement recovers possession of goods to which the agreement relates otherwise than by action, the hirer may apply to the court for an order that—

    (a) the whole or part of any sum paid by the hirer to the owner in respect of the goods shall be repaid, and

    (b) the obligation to pay the whole or part of any sum owed by the hirer to the owner in respect of the goods shall cease,

and if it appears to the court just to do so, having regard to the extent of the enjoyment of the goods by the hirer, the court shall grant the application in full or in part.

(2) Where in proceedings relating to a regulated consumer hire agreement the court makes an order for the delivery to the owner of goods to which the agreement relates the court may include in the order the like provision as may be made in an order under subsection (1).

133   Hire-purchase etc. agreements: special powers of court

(1) If, in relation to a regulated hire-purchase or conditional sale agreement, it appears to the court just to do so—

    (a) on an application for an enforcement order or time order; or

    (b) in an action brought by the creditor to recover possession of goods to which the agreement relates,

the court may—

    (i)   make an order (a 'return order') for the return to the creditor of goods to which the agreement relates;

    (ii) make an order (a 'transfer order') for the transfer to the debtor of the creditor's title to certain goods to which the agreement relates ('the transferred goods'), and the return to the creditor of the remainder of the goods.

(2) In determining for the purposes of this section how much of the total price has been paid ('the paid-up sum'), the court may—

    (a) treat any sum paid by the debtor, or owed by the creditor, in relation to the goods as part of the paid-up sum;

    (b) deduct any sum owed by the debtor in relation to the goods (otherwise than as part of the total price) from the paid-up sum,

and make corresponding reductions in amounts so owed.

(3) Where a transfer order is made, the transferred goods shall be such of the goods to which the agreement relates as the court thinks just; but a transfer order shall be made only where the paid-up sum exceeds the part of the total price referable to the transferred goods by an amount equal to at least one-third of the unpaid balance of the total price.

(4) Notwithstanding the making of a return order or transfer order, the debtor may at any time before the goods enter the possession of the creditor, on payment of the balance of the total price and the fulfilment of any other necessary conditions, claim the goods ordered to be returned to the creditor.

(5) When, in pursuance of a time order or under this section, the total price of goods under a regulated hire-purchase agreement or regulated conditional sale agreement is paid and any other necessary conditions are fulfilled, the creditor's title to the goods vests in the debtor.

(6) If, in contravention of a return order or transfer order, any goods to which the order relates are not returned to the creditor, the court, on the application of the creditor, may—

    (a) revoke so much of the order as relates to those goods, and

    (b) order the debtor to pay the creditor the unpaid portion of so much of the total price as is referable to those goods.

(7) For the purposes of this section, the part of the total price referable to any goods is the part assigned to those goods by the agreement or (if no such assignment is made) the part determined by the court to be reasonable.

134 Evidence of adverse detention in hire-purchase etc. cases

(1) Where goods are comprised in a regulated hire-purchase agreement, regulated conditional sale agreement or regulated consumer hire agreement, and the creditor or owner—

    (a) brings an action or makes an application to enforce a right to recover possession of the goods from the debtor or hirer and

    (b) proves that a demand for the delivery of the goods was included in the default notice under section 88(5), or that, after the right to recover possession of the goods accrued but before the action was begun or the application was made, he made a request in writing to the debtor or hirer to surrender the goods,

then, for the purposes of the claim of the creditor or owner to recover possession of the goods, the possession of them by the debtor or hirer shall be deemed to be adverse to the creditor or owner.

(2) In subsection (1) 'the debtor or hirer' includes a person in possession of the goods at any time between the debtor's or hirer's death and the grant of probate or administration, or (in Scotland) confirmation.

(3) Nothing in this section affects a claim for damages for conversion or (in Scotland) for delict.

Supplemental provisions as to orders

135 Power to impose conditions, or suspend operation of order

(1) If it considers it just to do so, the court may in an order made by it in relation to a regulated agreement include provisions—

    (a) making the operation of any term of the order conditional on the doing of specified acts by any party to the proceedings;

    (b) suspending the operation of any term of the order either—

        (i) until such time as the court subsequently directs, or

        (ii) until the occurrence of a specified act or omission.

(2) The court shall not suspend the operation of a term requiring the delivery up of goods by any person unless satisfied that the goods are in his possession or control.

(3) In the case of a consumer hire agreement, the court shall not so use its powers under subsection (1)(b) as to extend the period for which, under the terms of the agreement, the hirer is entitled to possession of the goods to which the agreement relates.

(4) On the application of any person affected by a provision included under subsection (1), the court may vary the provision.

136 Power to vary agreements and securities

(1) The court may in an order made by it under this Act include such provision as it considers just for amending any agreement or security in consequence of a term of the order.

[. . .]

[Unfair relationships]

[140A Unfair relationships between creditors and debtors

(1) The court may make an order under section 140B in connection with a credit agreement if it determines that the relationship between the creditor and the debtor arising out of the agreement (or the agreement taken with any related agreement) is unfair to the debtor because of one or more of the following—

(a) any of the terms of the agreement or of any related agreement;

(b) the way in which the creditor has exercised or enforced any of his rights under the agreement or any related agreement;

(c) any other thing done (or not done) by, or on behalf of, the creditor (either before or after the making of the agreement or any related agreement).

(2) In deciding whether to make a determination under this section the court shall have regard to all matters it thinks relevant (including matters relating to the creditor and matters relating to the debtor).

(3) For the purposes of this section the court shall (except to the extent that it is not appropriate to do so) treat anything done (or not done) by, or on behalf of, or in relation to, an associate or a former associate of the creditor as if done (or not done) by, or on behalf of, or in relation to, the creditor.

(4) A determination may be made under this section in relation to a relationship notwithstanding that the relationship may have ended.

(5) An order under section 140B shall not be made in connection with a credit agreement which is an exempt agreement by virtue of section 16(6C).]

[140B Powers of court in relation to unfair relationships

(1) An order under this section in connection with a credit agreement may do one or more of the following—

(a) require the creditor, or any associate or former associate of his, to repay (in whole or in part) any sum paid by the debtor or by a surety by virtue of the agreement or any related agreement (whether paid to the creditor, the associate or the former associate or to any other person);

(b) require the creditor, or any associate or former associate of his, to do or not to do (or to cease doing) anything specified in the order in connection with the agreement or any related agreement;

(c) reduce or discharge any sum payable by the debtor or by a surety by virtue of the agreement or any related agreement;

(d) direct the return to a surety of any property provided by him for the purposes of a security;

(e) otherwise set aside (in whole or in part) any duty imposed on the debtor or on a surety by virtue of the agreement or any related agreement;

(f) alter the terms of the agreement or of any related agreement;

(g) direct accounts to be taken, or (in Scotland) an accounting to be made, between any persons.

(2) An order under this section may be made in connection with a credit agreement only—

(a) on an application made by the debtor or by a surety;

(b) at the instance of the debtor or a surety in any proceedings in any court to which the debtor and the creditor are parties, being proceedings to enforce the agreement or any related agreement; or

(c) at the instance of the debtor or a surety in any other proceedings in any court where the amount paid or payable under the agreement or any related agreement is relevant.

(3) An order under this section may be made notwithstanding that its effect is to place on the creditor, or any associate or former associate of his, a burden in respect of an advantage enjoyed by another person.

(4) An application under subsection (2)(a) may only be made—

(a) in England and Wales, to the county court;

(b) in Scotland, to the sheriff court;

(c) in Northern Ireland, to the High Court (subject to subsection (6)).

(5) In Scotland such an application may be made in the sheriff court for the district in which the debtor or surety resides or carries on business.

(6) In Northern Ireland such an application may be made to the county court if the credit agreement is an agreement under which the creditor provides the debtor with—

(a) fixed-sum credit not exceeding £15,000; or

(b) running-account credit on which the credit limit does not exceed £15,000.

(7) Without prejudice to any provision which may be made by rules of court made in relation to county courts in Northern Ireland, such rules may provide that an application made by virtue of subsection (6) may be made in the county court for the division in which the debtor or surety resides or carries on business.

(8) A party to any proceedings mentioned in subsection (2) shall be entitled, in accordance with rules of court, to have any person who might be the subject of an order under this section made a party to the proceedings.

(9) If, in any such proceedings, the debtor or a surety alleges that the relationship between the creditor and the debtor is unfair to the debtor, it is for the creditor to prove to the contrary.]

[140C   Interpretation of ss. 140A and 140B

(1) In this section and in sections 140A and 140B 'credit agreement' means any agreement between an individual (the 'debtor') and any other person (the 'creditor') by which the creditor provides the debtor with credit of any amount.

(2) References in this section and in sections 140A and 140B to the creditor or to the debtor under a credit agreement include—

(a) references to the person to whom his rights and duties under the agreement have passed by assignment or operation of law;

(b) where two or more persons are the creditor or the debtor, references to any one or more of those persons.

(3) The definition of 'court' in section 189(1) does not apply for the purposes of sections 140A and 140B.

(4) References in sections 140A and 140B to an agreement related to a credit agreement (the 'main agreement') are references to—

(a) a credit agreement consolidated by the main agreement;

(b) a linked transaction in relation to the main agreement or to a credit agreement within paragraph (a);

(c) a security provided in relation to the main agreement, to a credit agreement within paragraph (a) or to a linked transaction within paragraph (b).

(5) In the case of a credit agreement which is not a regulated consumer credit agreement, for the purposes of subsection (4) a transaction shall be treated as being a linked transaction in relation to that agreement if it would have been such a transaction had that agreement been a regulated consumer credit agreement.

(6) For the purposes of this section and section 140B the definitions of 'security' and 'surety' in section 189(1) apply (with any appropriate changes) in relation to—

(a) a credit agreement which is not a consumer credit agreement as if it were a consumer credit agreement; and

(b) a transaction which is a linked transaction by virtue of subsection (5).

(7) For the purposes of this section a credit agreement (the 'earlier agreement') is consolidated by another credit agreement (the 'later agreement') if—

    (a) the later agreement is entered into by the debtor (in whole or in part) for purposes connected with debts owed by virtue of the earlier agreement; and

    (b) at any time prior to the later agreement being entered into the parties to the earlier agreement included—

        (i) the debtor under the later agreement; and

        (ii) the creditor under the later agreement or an associate or a former associate of his.

(8) Further, if the later agreement is itself consolidated by another credit agreement (whether by virtue of this subsection or subsection (7)), then the earlier agreement is consolidated by that other agreement as well.]

[140D   Advice and information

The advice and information published by the OFT under section 229 of the Enterprise Act 2002 shall indicate how the OFT expects sections 140A to 140C of this Act to interact with Part 8 of that Act.]

Miscellaneous

141   Jurisdiction and parties

(1) In England and Wales the county court shall have jurisdiction to hear and determine—

    (a) any action by the creditor or owner to enforce a regulated agreement or any security relating to it;

    (b) any action to enforce any linked transaction against the debtor or hirer or his relative,

and such an action shall not be brought in any other court.

(2) Where an action or application is brought in the High Court which, by virtue of this Act, ought to have been brought in the county court it shall not be treated as improperly brought, but shall be transferred to the county court.

[(3) In Scotland the sheriff court shall have jurisdiction to hear and determine any action falling within subsection (1) and such an action shall not be brought in any other court.]

[(3A) Subject to subsection (3B) an action which is brought in the sheriff court by virtue of subsection (3) shall be brought only in one of the following courts, namely—

    (a) the court for the place where the debtor or hirer is domiciled (within the meaning of section 41 or 42 of the Civil Jurisdiction and Judgments Act 1982);

    (b) the court for the place where the debtor or hirer carries on business; and

    (c) where the purpose of the action is to assert, declare or determine proprietary or possessory rights, or rights of security, in or over movable property, or to obtain authority to dispose of movable property, the court for the place where the property is situated.

(3B) Subsection (3A) shall not apply—

    (a) where Rule 3 of Schedule 8 to the said Act of 1982 applies; or

    (b) where the jurisdiction of another court has been prorogated by an agreement entered into after the dispute has arisen.]

(4) In Northern Ireland the county court shall have jurisdiction to hear and determine any action or application falling within subsection (1).

(5) Except as may be provided by rules of court, all the parties to a regulated agreement, and any surety, shall be made parties to any proceedings relating to the agreement.

142 Power to declare rights of parties

(1) Where under any provision of this Act a thing can be done by a creditor or owner on an enforcement order only, and either—

    (a) the court dismisses (except on technical grounds only) an application for an enforcement order, or

    (b) where no such application has been made or such an application has been dismissed on technical grounds only an interested party applies to the court for a declaration under this subsection,

the court may if it thinks just make a declaration that the creditor or owner is not entitled to do that thing, and thereafter no application for an enforcement order in respect of it shall be entertained.

(2) Where—

    (a) a regulated agreement or linked transaction is cancelled under section 69(1), or becomes subject to section 69(2), or

    (b) a regulated agreement is terminated under section 91, and an interested party applies to the court for a declaration under this subsection, the court may make a declaration to that effect.

Northern Ireland

143 Jurisdiction of county court in Northern Ireland

. . .

144 Appeal from county court in Northern Ireland

. . .

PART X   ANCILLARY CREDIT BUSINESSES

Definitions

145 Types of ancillary credit business

(1) An ancillary credit business is any business so far as it comprises or relates to—

    (a) credit brokerage,

    (b) debt-adjusting,

    (c) debt-counselling,

    (d) debt-collecting,

  [(da) debt administration,]

  [(db) the provision of credit information services, or]

    (e) the operation of a credit reference agency.

(2) Subject to section 146(5) [and (5A)], credit brokerage is the effecting of introductions—

    (a) of individuals desiring to obtain credit—

        (i) to persons carrying on businesses to which this sub-paragraph applies, or

        (ii) in the case of an individual desiring to obtain credit to finance the acquisition or provision of a dwelling occupied by himself or his relative, to any person carrying on a business in the course of which he provides credit secured on land, or

    (b) of individuals desiring to obtain goods on hire to persons carrying on businesses to which this paragraph applies, or

    (c) of individuals desiring to obtain credit, or to obtain goods on hire, to other credit-brokers.

(3) Subsection (2)(a)(i) applies to—

    (a) a consumer credit business;

(b) a business which comprises or relates to consumer credit agreements being, otherwise than by virtue of section 16(5)(a), exempt agreements;

(c) a business which comprises or relates to unregulated agreements where—

(i) the [law applicable to] the agreement is the law of a country outside the United Kingdom, and

(ii) if the [law applicable to] the agreement were the law of a part of the United Kingdom it would be a regulated consumer credit agreement.

(4) Subsection (2)(b) applies to—

(a) a consumer hire business;

[(aa) a business which comprises or relates to consumer hire agreements being, otherwise than by virtue of section 16(6), exempt agreements;]

(b) a business which comprises or relates to unregulated agreements where—

(i) the [law applicable to] the agreement is the law of a country outside the United Kingdom, and

(ii) if the [law applicable to] the agreement were the law of a part of the United Kingdom it would be a regulated consumer hire agreement.

(5) Subject to [section 146(5B) and (6)], debt-adjusting is, in relation to debts due under consumer credit agreements or consumer hire agreements,—

(a) negotiating with the creditor or owner, on behalf of the debtor or hirer, terms for the discharge of a debt, or

(b) taking over, in return for payments by the debtor or hirer, his obligation to discharge a debt, or

(c) any similar activity concerned with the liquidation of a debt.

(6) Subject to [section 146 (5C) and (6)], debt-counselling is the giving of advice to debtors or hirers about the liquidation of debts due under consumer credit agreements or consumer hire agreements.

(7) Subject to section 146(6), debt-collecting is the taking of steps to procure payment of debts due under consumer credit agreements or consumer hire agreements.

[(7A) Subject to section 146(7), debt administration is the taking of steps—

(a) to perform duties under a consumer credit agreement or a consumer hire agreement on behalf of the creditor or owner, or

(b) to exercise or to enforce rights under such an agreement on behalf of the creditor or owner,

so far as the taking of such steps is not debt-collecting.]

[(7B) A person provides credit information services if—

(a) he takes any steps mentioned in subsection (7C) on behalf of an individual; or

(b) he gives advice to an individual in relation to the taking of any such steps.

(7C) Those steps are steps taken with a view—

(a) to ascertaining whether a credit information agency (other than that person himself if he is one) holds information relevant to the financial standing of an individual;

(b) to ascertaining the contents of such information held by such an agency;

(c) to securing the correction of, the omission of anything from, or the making of any other kind of modification of, such information so held; or

(d) to securing that such an agency which holds such information—

(i) stops holding it; or

(ii) does not provide it to another person.

(7D) In subsection (7C) 'credit information agency' means—

(a) a person carrying on a consumer credit business or a consumer hire business;

(b) a person carrying on a business so far as it comprises or relates to credit brokerage, debt-adjusting, debt-counselling, debt-collecting, debt administration or the operation of a credit reference agency;

    (c) a person carrying on a business which would be a consumer credit business except that it comprises or relates to consumer credit agreements being, otherwise than by virtue of section 16(5)(a), exempt agreements; or

    (d) a person carrying on a business which would be a consumer hire business except that it comprises or relates to consumer hire agreements being, otherwise than by virtue of section 16(6), exempt agreements.]

(8) A credit reference agency is a person carrying on a business comprising the furnishing of persons with information relevant to the financial standing of individuals, being information collected by the agency for that purpose.

146 Exceptions from section 145

(1) A barrister or advocate acting in that capacity is not to be treated as doing so in the course of any ancillary credit business.

(2) A solicitor engaging in contentious business (as defined in [section 87(1) of the Solicitors Act 1974]) is not to be treated as doing so in the course of any ancillary credit business.

(3) A solicitor within the meaning of the Solicitors (Scotland) Act 1933 engaging in business done in or for the purposes of proceedings before a court or before an arbiter is not to be treated as doing so in the course of any ancillary credit business.

(4) A solicitor in Northern Ireland engaging in [contentious business (as defined in Article 3(2) of the Solicitors (Northern Ireland) Order 1976], is not to be treated as doing so in the course of any ancillary credit business.

(5) For the purposes of section 145(2), introductions effected by an individual by canvassing off trade premises either debtor-creditor-supplier agreements falling within section 12(a) or regulated consumer hire agreements shall be disregarded if—

    (a) the introductions are not effected by him in the capacity of an employee, and

    (b) he does not by any other method effect introductions falling within section 145(2).

[(5A) It is not credit brokerage for a person to effect the introduction of an individual desiring to obtain credit if the introduction is made—

    (a) to an authorised person, within the meaning of the 2000 Act, who has permission under that Act to enter as lender into relevant agreements; or

    (b) to a qualifying broker,

with a view to that individual obtaining credit under a relevant agreement.

(5B) It is not debt-adjusting for a person to carry on an activity mentioned in paragraph (a), (b) or (c) of section 145(5) if—

    (a) the debt in question is due under a relevant agreement; and

    (b) that activity is a regulated activity for the purposes of the 2000 Act.

(5C) It is not debt-counselling for a person to give advice to debtors about the liquidation of debts if—

    (a) the debt in question is due under a relevant agreement; and

    (b) giving that advice is a regulated activity for the purposes of the 2000 Act.

(5D) In this section—

'the 2000 Act' means the Financial Services and Markets Act 2000;

'relevant agreement' means a consumer credit agreement which is secured by a land mortgage, where entering into that agreement as lender is a regulated activity for the purposes of the 2000 Act;

'qualifying broker' means a person who may effect introductions of the kind mentioned in subsection (5A) without contravening the general prohibition, within the meaning of section 19 of the 2000 Act, and references to 'regulated activities' and the definition of 'qualifying broker' must be read with—

    (a) section 22 of the 2000 Act (regulated activities: power to specify classes of activity and categories of investment);

(b) any order for the time being in force under that section; and

(c) Schedule 2 to that Act.]

(6) It is not debt-adjusting, debt-counselling or debt-collecting for a person to do anything in relation to a debt arising under an agreement if [any of the following conditions is satisfied]—

[...]

[(aa) that he is the creditor or owner under the agreement, or]

(c)   [that] he is the supplier in relation to the agreement, or

(d)   [that] he is a credit-broker who has acquired the business of the person who was the supplier in relation to the agreement, or

(e)   [that] he is a person prevented by subsection (5) from being treated as a credit-broker, and the agreement was made in consequence of an introduction (whether made by him or another person) which, under subsection (5), is to be disregarded.

[(7) It is not debt administration for a person to take steps to perform duties, or to exercise or enforce rights, under an agreement on behalf of the creditor or owner if any of the conditions mentioned in subsection (6)(aa) to (e) is satisfied in relation to that person.]

Licensing

147   Application of Part III

[...]

(2) Without prejudice to the generality of section 26, regulations under that section [...] may include provisions regulating the collection and dissemination of information by credit reference agencies.

148   Agreement for services of unlicensed trader

(1) An agreement for the services of a person carrying on ancillary credit business (the 'trader'), if made when the trader was unlicensed, is enforceable against the other party (the 'customer') only where the [OFT] has made an order under subsection (2) which applies to the agreement.

(2) The trader or his successor in title may apply to the [OFT] for an order that agreements within subsection (1) are to be treated as if made when the trader was licensed.

(3) Unless the [OFT] determines to make an order under subsection (2) in accordance with the application, [it] shall, before determining the application, by notice—

(a) inform the trader, giving [its] reasons, that, as the case may be, [it] is minded to refuse the application, or to grant it in terms different from those applied for, describing them, and

(b) invite the trader to submit to the [OFT] representations in support of his application in accordance with section 34.

(4) In determining whether or not to make an order under subsection (2) in respect of any period the [OFT] shall consider, in addition to any other relevant factors,—

(a) how far, if at all, customers under agreements made by the trader during that period were prejudiced by the trader's conduct,

(b) whether or not the [OFT] would have been likely to grant a licence covering that period on an application by the trader, and

(c) the degree of culpability for the failure to obtain a licence.

(5) If the [OFT] thinks fit, [it] may in an order under subsection (2)—

(a) limit the order to specified agreements, or agreements of a specified description or made at a specified time;

(b) make the order conditional on the doing of specified acts by the trader.

[(6) This section does not apply to an agreement made by a consumer credit EEA firm unless at the time it was made that firm was precluded from entering into it as a result of—

(a) a consumer credit prohibition imposed under section 203 of the Financial Services and Markets Act 2000; or

(b) a restriction imposed on the firm under section 204 of that Act.]

149   Regulated agreements made on introductions by unlicensed credit-broker

(1) A regulated agreement made by a debtor or hirer who, for the purpose of making that agreement, was introduced to the creditor or owner by an unlicensed credit-broker is enforceable against the debtor or hirer only where—

(a) on the application of the credit-broker, the [OFT] has made an order under section 148(2) in respect of a period including the time when the introduction was made, and the order does not (whether in general terms or specifically) exclude the application of this paragraph to the regulated agreement, or

(b) the [OFT] has made an order under subsection (2) which applies to the agreement.

(2) Where during any period individuals were introduced to a person carrying on a consumer credit business or consumer hire business by an unlicensed credit-broker for the purpose of making regulated agreements with the person carrying on that business, that person or his successor in title may apply to the Director for an order that regulated agreements so made are to be treated as if the credit-broker had been licensed at the time of the introduction.

(3) Unless the [OFT] determines to make an order under subsection (2) in accordance with the application, [it] shall, before determining the application, by notice—

(a) inform the applicant, giving [its] reasons, that, as the case may be, [it] is minded to refuse the application, or to grant it in terms different from those applied for, describing them, and

(b) invite the applicant to submit to the [OFT] representations in support of his application in accordance with section 34.

(4) In determining whether or not to make an order under subsection (2) the [OFT] shall consider, in addition to any other relevant factors—

(a) how far, if at all, debtors or hirers under regulated agreements to which the application relates were prejudiced by the credit-broker's conduct, and

(b) the degree of culpability of the applicant in facilitating the carrying on by the credit-broker of his business when unlicensed.

(5) If the [OFT] thinks fit, [it] may in an order under subsection (2)—

(a) limit the order to specified agreements, or agreements of a specified description or made at a specified time;

(b) make the order conditional on the doing of specified acts by the applicant.

[(6) For the purposes of this section, 'unlicensed credit-broker' does not include a consumer credit EEA firm unless at the time the introduction was made that firm was precluded from making it as a result of—

(a) a consumer credit prohibition imposed under section 203 of the Financial Services and Markets Act 2000; or

(b) a restriction imposed on the firm under section 204 of that Act.]

[...]

Seeking business

151   Advertisements

(1) Sections 44 to 47 apply to an advertisement published for the purposes of a business of credit brokerage carried on by any person, whether it advertises the services of that person or the services of persons to whom he effects introductions, as they apply to an advertisement to which Part IV applies.

(2) Sections 44, 46 and 47 apply to an advertisement, published for the purposes of a business carried on by the advertiser, indicating that he is willing to advise on debts, [to] engage in transactions concerned with the liquidation of debts [or to provide credit information, services], as they apply to an advertisement to which Part IV applies.

[(2A) An advertisement does not fall within subsection (1) or (2) in so far as it is a communication of an invitation or inducement to engage in investment activity within the meaning of section 21 of the Financial Services and Markets Act 2000, other than an exempt generic communication (as defined in section 43(3B)).]

(3) The Secretary of State may by order provide that an advertisement published for the purposes of a business of credit brokerage, debt adjusting[, debt-counselling or the provision of credit information services] shall not fall within subsection (1) or (2) if it is of a description specified in the order.

(4) An advertisement [(other than one for credit information services)] does not fall within subsection (2) if it indicates that the advertiser is not willing to act in relation to consumer credit agreements and consumer hire agreements.

(5) In subsections (1) and (3) 'credit brokerage' includes the effecting of introduc-tions of individuals desiring to obtain credit to any person carrying on a business in the course of which he provides credit secured on land.

152 Application of sections 52 to 54 to credit brokerage etc.

(1) Sections 52 to 54 apply to a business of credit brokerage, debt-adjusting[, debt-counselling or the provision of credit information services] as they apply to a consumer credit business.

(2) In their application to a business of credit brokerage, sections 52 and 53 shall apply to the giving of quotations and information about the business of any person to whom the credit-broker effects introductions as well as to the giving of quotations and information about his own business.

153 Definition of canvassing off trade premises (agreements for ancillary credit services)

(1) An individual (the 'canvasser') canvasses off trade premises the services of a person carrying on an ancillary credit business if he solicits the entry of another individual (the 'consumer') into an agreement for the provision to the consumer of those services by making oral representations to the consumer, or any other individual, during a visit by the canvasser to any place (not excluded by subsection (2)) where the consumer, or that other individual as the case may be, is, being a visit—

    (a) carried out for the purpose of making such oral representations to individuals who are at that place, but

    (b) not carried out in response to a request made on a previous occasion.

(2) A place is excluded from subsection (1) if it is a place where (whether on a permanent or temporary basis)—

    (a) the ancillary credit business is carried on, or

    (b) any business is carried on by the canvasser or the person whose employee or agent the canvasser is, or by the consumer.

154 Prohibition of canvassing certain ancillary credit services off trade premises

It is an offence to canvass off trade premises the services of a person carrying on a business of credit-brokerage, debt-adjusting[, debt-counselling or the provision of credit information services].

155 Right to recover brokerage fees

(1) [Subject to subsection (2A),] The excess over [£5] of a fee or commission for his ser-vices charged by a credit-broker to an individual to whom this subsection applies shall cease to be payable or, as the case may be, shall be recoverable by the individual if the introduction does not result in his entering into a relevant agreement within the six months following the introduction (disregarding any agreement which is cancelled under section 69(1) or becomes subject to section 69(2)).

(2) Subsection (1) applies to an individual who sought an introduction for a purpose which would have been fulfilled by his entry into—

(a) a regulated agreement, or

(b) in the case of an individual such as is referred to in section 145(2)(a)(ii), an agreement for credit secured on land, or

(c) an agreement such as is referred to in section 145(3)(b) or (c) or (4)(b).

[(2A) But subsection (1) does not apply where—

(a) the fee or commission relates to the effecting of an introduction of a kind mentioned in section 146(5A); and

(b) the person charging that fee or commission is an authorised person or an appointed representative, within the meaning of the Financial Services and Markets Act 2000.]

(3) An agreement is a relevant agreement for the purposes of subsection (1) in relation to an individual if it is an agreement such as is referred to in subsection (2) in relation to that individual.

(4) In the case of an individual desiring to obtain credit under a consumer credit agreement, any sum payable or paid by him to a credit-broker otherwise than as a fee or commission for the credit-broker's services shall for the purposes of subsection (1) be treated as such a fee or commission if it enters, or would enter, into the total charge for credit.

Entry into agreements

156   Entry into agreements

Regulations may make provision, in relation to agreements entered into in the course of a business of credit brokerage, debt-adjusting[, debt-counselling or the provision of credit information services], corresponding, with such modifications as the Secretary of State thinks fit, to the provision which is or may be made by or under sections 55, 60, 61, 62, 63, 65, 127, 179 or 180 in relation to agreements to which those sections apply.

Credit reference agencies

157   Duty to disclose name etc. of agency

(1) A creditor, owner or negotiator, within the prescribed period after receiving a request in writing to that effect from the debtor or hirer, shall give him notice of the name and address of any credit reference agency from which the creditor, owner or negotiator has, during the antecedent negotiations, applied for information about his financial standing.

(2) Subsection (1) does not apply to a request received more than 28 days after the termination of the antecedent negotiations, whether on the making of the regulated agreement or otherwise.

(3) If the creditor, owner or negotiator fails to comply with subsection (1) he commits an offence.

158   Duty of agency to disclose filed information

(1) A credit reference agency, within the prescribed period after receiving,—

[(a) a request in writing to that effect from a consumer,] and

(b) such particulars as the agency may reasonably require to enable them to identify the file, and

(c) a fee of [£2],

shall give the consumer a copy of the file relating to it kept by the agency.

(2) When giving a copy of the file under subsection (1), the agency shall also give the consumer a statement in the prescribed form of [the consumer's] rights under section 159.

(3) If the agency does not keep a file relating to the consumer it shall give [the consumer] notice of that fact, but need not return any money paid.

(4) If the agency contravenes any provision of this section it commits an offence.

[(4A) In this section 'consumer' means—

(a) a partnership consisting of two or three persons not all of whom are bodies corporate; or

(b) an unincorporated body of persons which does not consist entirely of bodies corporate and is not a partnership.]

(5) In this Act 'file', in relation to an individual, means all the information about him kept by a credit reference agency, regardless of how the information is stored, and 'copy of the file', as respects information not in plain English, means a transcript reduced into plain English.

159 Correction of wrong information

[(1) Any individual (the 'objector') given—
  (a) information under section 7 of the Data Protection Act 1998 by a credit reference agency, or
  (b) information under section 158, who considers that an entry in his file is incorrect, and that if it is not corrected he is likely to be prejudiced, may give notice to the agency requiring it either to remove the entry from the file or amend it.]

(2) Within 28 days after receiving a notice under subsection (1), the agency shall by notice inform the [objector] that it has—
  (a) removed the entry from the file, or
  (b) amended the entry, or
  (c) taken no action, and if the notice states that the agency has amended the entry it shall include a copy of the file so far as it comprises the amended entry.

(3) Within 28 days after receiving a notice under subsection (2), or where no such notice was given, within 28 days after the expiry of the period mentioned in subsection (2), the [objector] may, unless he has been informed by the agency that it has removed the entry from his file, serve a further notice on the agency requiring it to add to the file an accompanying notice of correction (not exceeding 200 words) drawn up by the [objector], and include a copy of it when furnishing information included in or based on that entry.

(4) Within 28 days after receiving a notice under subsection (3), the agency, unless it intends to apply to the [the relevant authority] under subsection (5), shall by notice inform the [objector] that it has received the notice under subsection (3) and intends to comply with it.

(5) If—
  (a) the [objector] has not received a notice under subsection (4) within the time required, or
  (b) it appears to the agency that it would be improper for it to publish a notice of correction because it is incorrect, or unjustly defames any person, or is frivolous or scandalous, or is for any other reason unsuitable, the [objector] or, as the case may be, the agency may, in the prescribed manner and on payment of the specified fee, apply to the [the relevant authority], who may make such order on the application as he thinks fit.

(6) If a person to whom an order under this section is directed fails to comply with it within the period specified in the order he commits an offence.

[(7) The Data Protection Commissioner may vary or revoke any order made by him under this section.

(8) In this section 'the relevant authority' means
  (a) where the objector is a partnership or other unincorporated body of persons, the [OFT], and
  (b) in any other case, the Data Protection Commissioner.]

160 Alternative procedure for business consumers

(1) The [OFT], on an application made by a credit reference agency, may direct that this section shall apply to the agency if [it] is satisfied—
  (a) that compliance with section 158 in the case of consumers who carry on a business would adversely affect the service provided to its customers by the agency, and
  (b) that, having regard to the methods employed by the agency and to any other relevant facts, it is probable that consumers carrying on a business would not be prejudiced by the making of the direction.

(2) Where an agency to which this section applies receives a request, particulars and a fee under section 158(1) from a consumer who carries on a business and section 158(3) does not apply, the agency, instead of complying with section 158, may elect to deal with the matter under the following subsections.

(3) Instead of giving the consumer a copy of the file, the agency shall within the prescribed period give notice to the consumer that it is proceeding under this section, and by notice give the consumer such information included in or based on entries in the file as the [OFT] may direct, together with a statement in the prescribed form of the consumer's rights under subsections (4) and (5).

(4) If within 28 days after receiving the information given [to the consumer] under subsection (3), or such longer period as the [OFT] may allow, the consumer—

    (a) gives notice to the [OFT] that [the consumer] is dissatisfied with the information, and

    (b) satisfies the [OFT] that [the consumer] has taken such steps in relation to the agency as may be reasonable with a view to removing the cause of [the consumer's] dissatisfaction, and

    (c) pays the [OFT] the specified fee, the [OFT] may direct the agency to give the [OFT] a copy of the file, and the [OFT] may disclose to the consumer such of the information on the file as the [OFT] thinks fit.

(5) Section 159 applies with any necessary modifications to information given to the consumer under this section as it applies to information given under section 158.

(6) If an agency making an election under subsection (2) fails to comply with subsection (3) or (4) it commits an offence.

[(7) In this section 'consumer' has the same meaning as in section 158.]

PART XI   ENFORCEMENT OF ACT

161   Enforcement authorities

(1) The following authorities ('enforcement authorities') have a duty to enforce this Act and regulations made under it—

    (a) the [OFT],

    (b) in Great Britain, the local weights and measures authority,

    (c) In Northern Ireland, the Department of Commerce for Northern Ireland.

    [...]

(3) Every local weights and measures authority shall, whenever the [OFT] requires, report to [it] in such form and with such particulars as [it] requires on the exercise of their functions under this Act.

    [...]

162   Powers of entry and inspection

(1) A duly authorised officer of an enforcement authority, at all reasonable hours and on production, if required, of his credentials, may—

    (a) in order to ascertain whether a breach of any provision of or under this Act has been committed, inspect any goods and enter any premises (other than premises used only as a dwelling);

    (b) if he has reasonable cause to suspect that a breach of any provision of or under this Act has been committed, in order to ascertain whether it has been committed, require any person—

        (i) carrying on, or employed in connection with, a business to produce any [...] documents relating to it; or

        (ii) having control of any information relating to a business [to provide him with that information],

        [...]

(c) if he has reasonable cause to believe that a breach of any provision of or under this Act has been committed, seize and detain any goods in order to ascertain (by testing or otherwise) whether such a breach has been committed;

(d) seize and detain any goods, [...] or documents which he has reason to believe may be required as evidence in proceedings for an offence under this Act;

(e) for the purpose of exercising his powers under this subsection to seize goods, [...] or documents, but only if and to the extent that it is reasonably necessary for securing that the provision of this Act and of any regulations made under it are duly observed, require any person having authority to do so to break open any container and, if that person does not comply, break it open himself.

(2) An officer seizing goods, [...] or documents in exercise of his powers under this section shall not do so without informing the person he seizes them from.

(3) If a justice of the peace, on sworn information in writing, or, in Scotland, a sheriff or a magistrate or justice of the peace, on evidence on oath,—

(a) is satisfied that there is reasonable ground to believe either—

(i) that any goods, [...] or documents which a duly authorised officer has power to inspect under this section are on any premises and their inspection is likely to disclose evidence of a breach of any provision of or under this Act; or

(ii) that a breach of any provision of or under this Act has been, is being or is about to be committed on any premises; and

(b) is also satisfied either—

(i) that admission to the premises has been or is likely to be refused and that notice of intention to apply for a warrant under this subsection has been given to the occupier; or

(ii) that an application for admission, or the giving of such a notice, would defeat the object of the entry or that the premises are unoccupied or that the occupier is temporarily absent and it might defeat the object of the entry to wait for his return, the justice or, as the case may be, the sheriff or magistrate may by warrant under his hand, which shall continue in force for a period of one month, authorise an officer of an enforcement authority to enter the premises (by force if need be).

(4) An officer entering premises by virtue of this section may take such other persons and equipment with him as he thinks necessary; and on leaving premises entered by virtue of a warrant under subsection (3) shall, if they are unoccupied or the occupier is temporarily absent, leave them as effectively secured against trespassers as he found them.

(5) Regulations may provide that, in cases described by the regulations, an officer of a local weights and measures authority is not to be taken to be duly authorised for the purposes of this section unless he is authorised by the [OFT].

(6) A person who is not a duly authorised officer of an enforcement authority, but purports to act as such under this section, commits an offence.

[...]

[(8) References in this section to a breach of any provision of or under this Act do not include references to—

(a) a failure to comply with a requirement imposed under section 33A or 33B;

(b) a failure to comply with section 36A; or

(c) a failure in relation to which the OFT can apply for an order under section 36E.]

163 Compensation for loss

(1) Where, in exercising his powers under section 162, an officer of an enforcement authority seizes and detains goods and their owner suffers loss by reason of—

(a) that seizure, or

  (b) the loss, damage or deterioration of the goods during detention, then, unless the owner is convicted of an offence under this Act committed in relation to the goods, the authority shall compensate him for the loss so suffered.

 (2) Any dispute as to the right to or amount of any compensation under subsection (1) shall be determined by arbitration.

164 Power to make test purchases etc.

 (1) An enforcement authority may—

  (a) make, or authorise any of their officers to make on their behalf, such purchases of goods; and

  (b) authorise any of their officers to procure the provision of such services or facilities or to enter into such agreements or other transactions, as may appear to them expedient for determining whether any provisions made by or under this Act are being complied with.

 (2) Any act done by an officer authorised to do it under subsection (1) shall be treated for the purposes of this Act as done by him as an individual on his own behalf.

 (3) Any goods seized by an officer under this Act may be tested, and in the event of such a test he shall inform the person mentioned in section 162(2) of the test results.

 (4) Where any test leads to proceedings under this Act, the enforcement authority shall—

  (a) if the goods were purchased, inform the person they were purchased from of the test results, and

  (b) allow any person against whom the proceedings are taken to have the goods tested on his behalf if it is reasonably practicable to do so.

165 Obstruction of authorised officers

 (1) Any person who—

  (a) wilfully obstructs an officer of an enforcement authority acting in pursuance of this Act; or

  (b) wilfully fails to comply with any requirement properly made to him by such an officer under section 162; or

  (c) without reasonable cause fails to give such an officer (so acting) other assistance or information he may reasonably require in performing his functions under this Act, commits an offence.

 [(1A) A failure to give assistance or information shall not constitute an offence under subsection (1)(c) if it is also—

  (a) a failure to comply with a requirement imposed under section 33A or 33B;

  (b) a failure to comply with section 36A; or

  (c) a failure in relation to which the OFT can apply for an order under section 36E.]

 (2) If any person, in giving such information as is mentioned in subsection (1)(c), makes any statement which he knows to be false, he commits an offence.

 (3) Nothing in this section requires a person to answer any question or give any information if to do so might incriminate that person or (where that person is [married or a civil partner) the spouse or civil partner].

166 Notification of convictions and judgments to Director

Where a person is convicted of an offence or has a judgment given against him by or before any court in the United Kingdom and it appears to the court—

  (a) having regard to the functions of the [OFT] under this Act, that the conviction or judgment should be brought to the [OFT's] attention, and

  (b) that it may not be brought to [its] attention unless arrangements for that purpose are made by the court,

the court may make such arrangements notwithstanding that the proceedings have been finally disposed of.

167 Penalties

(1) An offence under a provision of this Act specified in column 1 of Schedule 1 is triable in the mode or modes indicated in column 3, and on conviction is punishable as indicated in column 4 (where a period of time indicates the maximum term of imprisonment, and a monetary amount indicates the maximum fine, for the offence in question).

(2) A person who contravenes any regulations made under section 44, 52, 53, or 112, or made under section 26 by virtue of section 54, commits an offence.

168 Defences

(1) In any proceedings for an offence under this Act it is a defence for the person charged to prove—

   (a) that his act or omission was due to a mistake, or to reliance on information supplied to him, or to an act or omission by another person, or to an accident or some other cause beyond his control, and

   (b) that he took all reasonable precautions and exercised all due diligence to avoid such an act or omission by himself or any person under his control.

(2) If in any case the defence provided by subsection (1) involves the allegation that the act or omission was due to an act or omission by another person or to reliance on information supplied by another person, the person charged shall not, without leave of the court, be entitled to rely on that defence unless, within a period ending seven clear days before the hearing, he has served on the prosecutor a notice giving such information identifying or assisting in the identification of that other person as was then in his possession.

169 Offences by bodies corporate

Where at any time a body corporate commits an offence under this Act with the consent or connivance of, or because of neglect by, any individual, the individual commits the like offence if at that time—

   (a) he is a director, manager, secretary or similar officer of the body corporate, or

   (b) he is purporting to act as such an officer, or

   (c) the body corporate is managed by its members of whom he is one.

170 No further sanctions for breach of Act

(1) A breach of any requirement made (otherwise than by any court) by or under this Act shall incur no civil or criminal sanction as being such a breach, except to the extent (if any) expressly provided by or under this Act.

(2) In exercising [its] functions under this Act the [OFT] may take account of any matter appearing to [it] to constitute a breach of a requirement made by or under this Act, whether or not any sanction for that breach is provided by or under this Act and, if it is so provided, whether or not proceedings have been brought in respect of the breach.

(3) Subsection (1) does not prevent the grant of an injunction, or the making of an order of certiorari, mandamus or prohibition or as respects Scotland the grant of an interdict or of an order under section 91 of the Court of Session Act 1868 (order for specific performance of statutory duty).

171 Onus of proof in various proceedings

(1) If an agreement contains a term signifying that in the opinion of the parties section 10(3)(b)(iii) does not apply to the agreement, it shall be taken not to apply unless the contrary is proved.

(2) It shall be assumed in any proceedings, unless the contrary is proved, that when a person initiated a transaction as mentioned in section 19(1)(c) he knew the principal agreement had been made, or contemplated that it might be made.

(3) Regulations under section 44 or 52 may make provision as to the onus of proof in any proceedings to enforce the regulations.

(4) In proceedings brought by the creditor under a credit-token agreement—

    (a) it is for the creditor to prove that the credit-token was lawfully supplied to the debtor, and was accepted by him, and

    (b) if the debtor alleges that any use made of the credit-token was not authorised by him, it is for the creditor to prove either—

        (i) that the use was so authorised, or

        (ii) that the use occurred before the creditor had been given notice under section 84(3).

(5) In proceedings under section 50(1) in respect of a document received by a minor at any school or other educational establishment for minors, it is for the person sending it to him at that establishment to prove that he did not know or suspect it to be such an establishment.

(6) In proceedings under section 119(1) it is for the pawnee to prove that he had reasonable cause to refuse to allow the pawn to be redeemed.

    [...]

172   Statements by creditor or owner to be binding

(1) A statement by a creditor or owner is binding on him if given under—

section 77(1),

section 78(1),

section 79(1),

section 97(1),

section 107(1)(c),

section 108(1)(c), or

section 109(1)(c).

(2) Where a trader—

    (a) gives a customer a notice in compliance with section 103(1)(b), or

    (b) gives a customer a notice under section 103(1) asserting that the customer is not indebted to him under an agreement,

the notice is binding on the trader.

(3) Where in proceedings before any court—

    (a) it is sought to reply on a statement or notice given as mentioned in subsection (1) or (2), and

    (b) the statement or notice is shown to be incorrect, the court may direct such relief (if any) to be given to the creditor or owner from the operation of subsection (1) or (2) as appears to the court to be just.

173   Contracting-out forbidden

(1) A term contained in a regulated agreement or linked transaction, or in any other agreement relating to an actual or prospective regulated agreement or linked transaction, is void if, and to the extent that, it is inconsistent with a provision for the protection of the debtor or hirer or his relative or any surety contained in this Act or in any regulation made under this Act.

(2) Where a provision specifies the duty or liability of the debtor or hirer or his relative or any surety in certain circumstances, a term is inconsistent with that provision if it purports to impose, directly or indirectly, an additional duty or liability on him in those circumstances.

(3) Notwithstanding subsection (1), a provision of this Act under which a thing may be done in relation to any person on an order of the court or the [OFT] only shall not be taken to prevent its being done at any time with that person's consent given at that time, but the refusal of such consent shall not give rise to any liability.

PART XII   SUPPLEMENTAL

[174   Restrictions on disclosure of information]
[*1. Repealed by the Enterprise Act 2002, s. 278, Sch. 26.*]

[174A   Powers to require provision of information or documents etc.

(1) Every power conferred on a relevant authority by or under this Act (however expressed) to require the provision or production of information or documents includes the power—

(a) to require information to be provided or produced in such form as the authority may specify, including, in relation to information recorded otherwise than in a legible form, in a legible form;

(b) to take copies of, or extracts from, any documents provided or produced by virtue of the exercise of the power;

(c) to require the person who is required to provide or produce any information or document by virtue of the exercise of the power—

(i)   to state, to the best of his knowledge and belief, where the information or document is;

(ii) to give an explanation of the information or document;

(iii) to secure that any information provided or produced, whether in a document or otherwise, is verified in such manner as may be specified by the authority;

(iv) to secure that any document provided or produced is authenticated in such manner as may be so specified;

(d) to specify a time at or by which a requirement imposed by virtue of paragraph (c) must be complied with.

(2) Every power conferred on a relevant authority by or under this Act (however expressed) to inspect or to seize documents at any premises includes the power to take copies of, or extracts from, any documents inspected or seized by virtue of the exercise of the power.

(3) But a relevant authority has no power under this Act—

(a) to require another person to provide or to produce,

(b) to seize from another person, or

(c) to require another person to give access to premises for the purposes of the inspection of,

any information or document which the other person would be entitled to refuse to provide or produce in proceedings in the High Court on the grounds of legal professional privilege or (in Scotland) in proceedings in the Court of Session on the grounds of confidentiality of communications.

(4) In subsection (3) 'communications' means—

(a) communications between a professional legal adviser and his client;

(b) communications made in connection with or in contemplation of legal proceedings and for the purposes of those proceedings.

(5) In this section 'relevant authority' means—

(a) the OFT or an enforcement authority (other than the OFT);

(b) an officer of the OFT or of an enforcement authority (other than the OFT).]

175   Duty of persons deemed to be agents

Where under this Act a person is deemed to receive a notice or payment as agent of the creditor or owner under regulated agreement, he shall be deemed to be under a contractual duty to the creditor or owner to transmit the notice, or remit the payment, to him forthwith.

176   Service of documents

(1) A document to be served under this Act by one person ('the server') on another person ('the subject') is to be treated as properly served on the subject if dealt with as mentioned in the following subsections.

2) The document may be delivered or sent by post to the subject, or addressed to him by name and left at his proper address.

(3) For the purposes of this Act, a document sent by post to, or left at, the address last known to the server as the address of a person shall be treated as sent by post to, or left at, his proper address.

(4) Where the document is to be served on the subject as being the person having any interest in land, and it is not practicable after reasonable inquiry to ascertain the subject's name or address, the document may be served by—

    (a) addressing it to the subject by the description of the person having that interest in the land (naming it), and

    (b) delivering the document to some responsible person on the land or affixing it, or a copy of it, in a conspicuous position on the land.

(5) Where a document to be served on the subject as being a debtor, hirer or surety, or as having any other capacity relevant for the purposes of this Act, is served at any time on another person who—

    (a) is the person last known to the server as having that capacity, but

    (b) before that time had ceased to have it, the document shall be treated as having been served at that time on the subject.

(6) Anything done to a document in relation to a person who (whether to the knowledge of the server or not) has died shall be treated for the purposes of subsection (5) as service of the document on that person if it would have been so treated had he not died.

[(7) The following enactments shall not be construed as authorising service on the Public Trustee (in England and Wales) or the Probate Judge (in Northern Ireland) of any document which is to be served under this Act—

section 9 of the Administration of Estates Act 1925;

section 3 of the Administration of Estates Act (Northern Ireland) 1955.]

(8) References in the preceding subsections to the serving of a document on a person include the giving of the document to that person.

[176A   Electronic transmission of documents

(1) A document is transmitted in accordance with this subsection if—

    (a) the person to whom it is transmitted agrees that it may be delivered to him by being transmitted to a particular electronic address in a particular electronic form,

    (b) it is transmitted to that address in that form, and

    (c) the form in which the document is transmitted is such that any information in the document which is addressed to the person to whom the document is transmitted is capable of being stored for future reference for an appropriate period in a way which allows the information to be reproduced without change.

(2) A document transmitted in accordance with subsection (1) shall, unless the contrary is proved, be treated for the purposes of this Act, except section 69, as having been delivered on the working day immediately following the day on which it is transmitted.

(3) In this section, 'electronic address' includes any number or address used for the purposes of receiving electronic communications.]

177   Saving for registered charges

(1) Nothing in this Act affects the rights of a proprietor of a registered charge (within the meaning of the [Land Registration Act 2002]), who—

    (a) became the proprietor under a transfer for valuable consideration without notice of any defect in the title arising (apart from this section) by virtue of this Act, or

    (b) derives title from such a proprietor.

(2) Nothing in this Act affects the operation of section 104 of the Law of Property Act 1925 (protection of purchaser where mortgagee exercises power of sale).

(3) Subsection (1) does not apply to a proprietor carrying on a business of debt-collecting.

(4) Where, by virtue of subsection (1), a land mortgage is enforced which apart from this section would be treated as never having effect, the original creditor or owner shall be liable to indemnify the debtor or hirer against any loss thereby suffered by him.

(5) In the application of this section to Scotland for subsections (1) to (3) there shall be substituted the following subsections—

'(1) Nothing in this Act affects the rights of a creditor in a heritable security who—

    (a) became the creditor under a transfer for value without notice of any defect in the title arising (apart from this section) by virtue of this Act; or

    (b) derives title from such a creditor.

(2) Nothing in this Act affects the operation of section 41 of the Conveyancing (Scotland) Act 1924 (protection of purchasers), or of that section as applied to standard securities by section 32 of the Conveyancing and Feudal Reform (Scotland) Act 1970.

(3) Subsection (1) does not apply to a creditor carrying on [a consumer credit business, a consumer hire business or a business of debt-collecting or debt administration].'

(6) In the application of this section to Northern Ireland—

    (a) any reference to the proprietor of a registered charge (within the meaning of the [Land Registration Act 2002]) shall be construed as a reference to the registered owner of a charge under the Local Registration of Title (Ireland) Act 1891 or Part IV of the Land Registration Act (Northern Ireland) 1970, and

    (b) for the reference to section 104 of the Law Property Act 1925 there shall be substituted a reference to section 21 of the Conveyancing and Law Property Act 1881 and section 5 of the Conveyancing Act 1911.

178   Local Acts

The Secretary of State or the Department of Commerce for Northern Ireland may by order make such amendments or repeals of any provision of any local Act as appears to the Secretary of State or, as the case may be, the Department, necessary or expedient in consequence of the replacement by this Act of the enactments relating to pawnbrokers and moneylenders.

Regulations, orders, etc.

179   Power to prescribe form etc. of secondary documents

(1) Regulations may be made as to the form and content of credit-cards, trading-checks, receipts, vouchers and other documents or things issued by creditors, owners or suppliers under or in connection with regulated agreements or by other persons in connection with linked transactions, and may in particular—

    (a) require specified information to be included in the prescribed manner in documents, and other specified material to be excluded;

    (b) contain requirements to ensure that specified information is clearly brought to the attention of the debtor or hirer, or his relative, and that one part of a document is not given insufficient or excessive prominence compared with another.

(2) If a person issues any document or thing in contravention of regulations under subsection (1) then, as from the time of the contravention but without prejudice to anything done before it, this Act shall apply as if the regulated agreement had been improperly executed by reason of a contravention of regulations under section 60(1).

180   Power to prescribe form etc. of copies

(1) Regulations may be made as to the form and content of documents to be issued as copies of any executed agreement, security instrument or other document referred to in this Act, and may in particular—

    (a) require specified information to be included in the prescribed manner in any copy, and contain requirements to ensure that such information is clearly brought to the attention of a reader of the copy;

    (b) authorise the omission from a copy of certain material contained in the original, or the inclusion of such material in condensed form.

(2) A duty imposed by any provision of this Act (except section 35) to supply a copy of any document—

    (a) is not safisfied unless the copy supplied is in the prescribed form and conforms to the prescribed requirements;

    (b) is not infringed by the omission of any material, or its inclusion in condensed form, if that is authorised by regulations;

and references in this Act to copies shall be construed accordingly.

(3) Regulations may provide that a duty imposed by this Act to supply a copy of a document referred to in an unexecuted agreement or an executed agreement shall not apply to documents of a kind specified in the regulations.

181   Power to alter monetary limits etc.

(1) The Secretary of State may by order made by statutory instrument amend, or further amend, any of the following provisions of this Act so as to reduce or increase a sum mentioned in that provision, namely, sections [16B(1)], 17(1), [39A(3)], 70(6), 75(3)(b), 77(1), 78(1), 79(1), 84(1), 101(7)(a), 107(1), 108(1), 109(1), 110(1), 118(1)(b), 120(1)(a), [140B(6),] 155(1) and 158(1).

(2) An order under subsection (1) amending section [16B(1),] 17(1), [39A(3),] 75(3)(b) [or 140B(6)] shall be of no effect unless a draft of the order has been laid before and approved by each House of Parliament.

182   Regulations and orders

(1) Any power of the Secretary of State to make regulations or orders under this Act, except the power conferred by sections 2(1)(a), 181 and 192 shall be exercisable by statutory instrument subject to annulment in pursuance of a resolution of either House of Parliament.

[(1A) The power of the Lord Chancellor to make rules under section 40A(3) shall be exercisable by statutory instrument subject to annulment in pursuance of a resolution of either House of Parliament.]

(2) Where a power to make regulations or orders [or rules] is exercisable by the Secretary of State [or by the Lord Chancellor] by virtue of this Act, regulations or orders [or rules] made in the exercise of that power may—

    (a) make different provision in relation to different cases or classes of case, and

    (b) exclude certain cases or classes of case, and

    (c) contain such transitional provision as the [person making them] thinks fit.

(3) Regulations may provide that specified expressions, when used as described by the regulations, are to be given the prescribed meaning, notwithstanding that another meaning is intended by the person using them.

(4) Any power conferred on the Secretary of State by this Act to make orders includes power to vary or revoke an order so made.

[183   Determinations etc. by OFT

(1) The OFT may vary or revoke any determination made, or direction given, by it under this Act.

(2) Subsection (1) does not apply to—

    (a) a determination to issue, renew or vary a licence;

    (b) a determination to extend a period under section 28B or to refuse to extend a period under that section;

    (c) a determination to end a suspension under section 33;

    (d) a determination to make an order under section 40(2), 148(2) or 149(2);

    (e) a determination mentioned in column 1 of the Table in section 41.]

Interpretation

184   Associates

(1) A person is an associate of an individual if that person is the individual's husband or wife, or is a relative, or the husband or wife of a relative, of the individual or of the individual's husband or wife.

(2) A person is an associate of any person with whom he is in partnership, and of the husband or wife [or civil partner] or a relative of any individual with whom he is in partnership.

(3) A body corporate is an associate of another body corporate—

(a) if the same person is a controller of both, or a person is a controller of one and persons who are his associates, or he and persons who are his associates, are controllers of the other; or

(b) if a group of two or more persons is controller of each company, and the groups either consist of the same persons or could be regarded as consisting of the same persons by treating (in one or more cases) a member of either group as replaced by a person of whom he is an associate.

(4) A body corporate is an associate of another person if that person is a controller of it or if that person and persons who are his associates together are controllers of it.

(5) In this section 'relative' means brother, sister, uncle, aunt, nephew, niece, lineal ancestor or lineal descendant, [...] references to a husband or wife include a former husband or wife and a reputed husband [or wife, and references to a civil partner include a former civil partner;] and for the purposes of this subsection a relationship shall be established as if any illegitimate child, step-child or adopted child of a person [were the legitimate child of the relationship in question].

185 Agreement with more than one debtor or hirer

(1) Where an actual or prospective regulated agreement has two or more debtors or hirers (not being a partnership or an unincorporated body of persons)—

(a) anything required by or under this Act to be done to or in relation to the debtor or hirer shall be done to or in relation to each of them; and

(b) anything done under this Act by or on behalf of one of them shall have effect as if done by or on behalf of all of them.

[(2) Notwithstanding subsection (1)(a), where credit is provided under an agreement to two or more debtors jointly, in performing his duties—

(a) in the case of fixed-sum credit, under section 77A, or

(b) in the case of running-account credit, under section 78(4),

the creditor need not give statements to any debtor who has signed and given to him a notice (a 'dispensing notice') authorising him not to comply in the debtor's case with section 77A or (as the case may be) 78(4).

(2A) A dispensing notice given by a debtor is operative from when it is given to the creditor until it is revoked by a further notice given to the creditor by the debtor.

(2B) But subsection (2) does not apply if (apart from this subsection) dispensing notices would be operative in relation to all of the debtors to whom the credit is provided.

(2C) Any dispensing notices operative in relation to an agreement shall cease to have effect if any of the debtors dies.

(2D) A dispensing notice which is operative in relation to an agreement shall be operative also in relation to any subsequent agreement which, in relation to the earlier agreement, is a modifying agreement.]

(3) Subsection (1)(b) does not apply for the purposes of section 61(1)(a) [...].

(4) Where a regulated agreement has two or more debtors or hirers (not being a partnership or an unincorporated body of persons), section 86 applies to the death of any of them.

(5) An agreement for the provision of credit, or the bailment or (in Scotland) the hiring of goods, to two or more persons jointly where—

(a) one or more of those persons is an individual, and

(b) one or more of them is [not an individual], is a consumer credit agreement or consumer hire agreement if it would have been one had they all been individuals; and [each person within paragraph (b)] shall accordingly be included among the debtors or hirers under the agreement.

(6) Where subsection (5) applies, references in this Act to the signing of any document by the debtor or hirer shall be construed in relation to a body corporate [within paragraph (b) of that subsection] as referring to a signing on behalf of the body corporate.

186   Agreement with more than one creditor or owner

Where an actual or prospective regulated agreement has two or more creditors or owners, anything required by or under this Act to be done to, or in relation to, or by, the creditor or owner shall be effective if done to, or in relation to, or by, any one of them.

187   Arrangements between creditor and supplier

(1) A consumer credit agreement shall be treated as entered into under pre-existing arrangements between a creditor and a supplier if it is entered into in accordance with, or in furtherance of, arrangements previously made between persons mentioned in subsection (4)(a), (b) or (c).

(2) A consumer credit agreement shall be treated as entered into in contemplation of future arrangements between a creditor and a supplier if it is entered into in the expectation that arrangements will subsequently be made between persons mentioned in subsection (4)(a), (b) or (c) for the supply of cash, goods and services (or any of them) to be financed by the consumer credit agreement.

(3) Arrangements shall be disregarded for the purposes of subsection (1) or (2) if—
  (a) they are arrangements for the making, in specified circumstances, of pay-ments to the supplier by the creditor, and
  (b) the creditor holds himself out as willing to make, in such circumstances, pay-ments of the kind to suppliers generally.

[(3A) Arrangements shall also be disregarded for the purposes of subsections (1) and (2) if they are arrangements for the electronic transfer of funds from a current account at a bank within the meaning of the Bankers' Book Evidence Act 1879.]

(4) The persons referred to in subsections (1) and (2) are—
  (a) the creditor and the supplier;
  (b) one of them and an associate of the other's;
  (c) an associate of one and an associate of the other's.

(5) Where the creditor is an associate of the supplier's. the consumer credit agreement shall be treated, unless the contrary is proved, as entered into under pre-existing arrange-ments between the creditor and the supplier.

[187A   Definition of 'default sum'

(1) In this Act 'default sum' means, in relation to the debtor or hirer under a regulated agreement, a sum (other than a sum of interest) which is payable by him under the agree-ment in connection with a breach of the agreement by him.

(2) But a sum is not a default sum in relation to the debtor or hirer simply because, as a consequence of his breach of the agreement, he is required to pay it earlier than he would otherwise have had to.]

188   Examples of use of new terminology

(1) Schedule 2 shall have effect for illustrating the use of terminology employed in this Act.

(2) The examples given in Schedule 2 are not exhaustive.

(3) In the case of conflict between Schedule 2 and any other provision of this Act, that other provision shall prevail.

(4) The Secretary of State may by order amend Schedule 2 by adding further examples or in any other way.

189   Definitions

(1) In this Act, unless the context otherwise requires—
'advertisement' includes every form of advertising, whether in a publication, by televi-sion or radio, by display of notices, signs, labels, showcards or goods, by distribution of

samples, circulars, catalogues, price lists or other material, by exhibition of pictures, models or films, or in any other way, and references to the publishing of advertisements shall be construed accordingly;

'advertiser' in relation to an advertisement, means any person indicated by the advertisement as willing to enter into transactions to which the advertisement relates;

'ancillary credit business' has the meaning given by section 145(1), 'antecedent negotiations' has the meaning given by section 56;

'appeal period' means the period beginning on the first day on which an appeal to the [Tribunal] may be brought and ending on the last day on which it may be brought or, if it is brought, ending on its final determination, or abandonment;

['appropriate method' means—
    (a) post, or
    (b) transmission in the form of an electronic communication in accordance with section 176A(1);]

'assignment', in relation to Scotland, means assignation;

'associate' shall be construed in accordance with section 184; ['authorised institution' means an institution authorised under the Banking Act 1987;]

[...]

'bill of sale' has the meaning given by section 4 of the Bills of Sale Act 1878 or, for Northern Ireland, by section 4 of the Bills of Sale (Ireland) Act 1879; ['building society' means a building society within the meaning of the Building Societies Act 1986;]

'business' includes profession or trade, and references to a business apply subject to subsection (2);

'cancellable agreement' means a regulated agreement which, by virtue of section 67, may be cancelled by the debtor or hirer;

'canvass' shall be construed in accordance with sections 48 and 153;

'cash' includes money in any form;

'charity' means as respects England and Wales a charity registered under [the Charities Act 1993] or an exempt charity (within the meaning of that Act), and as respects Scotland and Northern Ireland an institution or other organization established for charitable purposes only ('organisation' including any persons administering a trust and 'charitable' being construed in the same way as if it were contained in the Income Tax Acts);

'conditional sale agreement' means an agreement for the sale of goods or land under which the purchase price or part of it is payable by instalments, and the property in the goods or land is to remain in the seller (notwithstanding that the buyer is to be in possession of the goods or land) until such conditions as to the payment of instalments or otherwise as may be specified in the agreement are fulfilled;

'consumer credit agreement' has the meaning given by section 8, and includes a consumer credit agreement which is cancelled under section 69(1), or becomes subject to section 69(2), so far as the agreement remains in force;

['consumer credit business' means any business being carried on by a person so far as it comprises or relates to—
    (a) the provision of credit by him, or
    (b) otherwise his being a creditor,
under regulated consumer credit agreements;]

'consumer hire agreement' has the meaning given by section 15;

['consumer hire business' means any business being carried on by a person so far as it comprises or relates to—
    (a) the bailment or (in Scotland) the hiring of goods by him, or
    (b) otherwise his being an owner,
under regulated consumer hire agreements;]

'controller', in relation to a body corporate, means a person—

(a) in accordance with whose directions or instructions the directors of the body corporate or of another body corporate which is its controller (or any of them) are accustomed to act, or

(b) who, either alone or with any associate or associates, is entitled to exercise, or control the exercise of, one third or more of the voting power at any general meeting of the body corporate or of another body corporate which is its controller;

'copy' shall be construed in accordance with section 180;

[…]

'court' means in relation to England and Wales the county court, in relation to Scotland the sheriff court and in relation to Northern Ireland the High Court or the county court;

'credit' shall be construed in accordance with section 9;

'credit-broker' means a person carrying on a business of credit-brokerage;

'credit-brokerage' has the meaning given by section 145(2);

['credit information services' has the meaning given by section 145(7B);]

'credit limit' has the meaning given by section 10(2);

'creditor' means the person providing credit under a consumer credit agreement or the person to whom his rights and duties under the agreement have passed by assignment or operation of law, and in relation to a prospective consumer agreement, includes the prospective creditor;

'credit reference agency' has the meaning given by section 145(8);

'credit-sale agreement' means an agreement for the sale of goods, under which the purchase price or part of it is payable by instalments, but which is not a conditional sale agreement;

'credit-token' has the meaning given by section 14(1);

'credit-token agreement' means a regulated agreement for the provision of credit in connection with the use of a credit-token;

'debt-adjusting' has the meaning given by section 145(5);

['debt administration' has the meaning given by section 145(7A);]

'debt-collecting' has the meaning given by section 145(7);

'debt-counselling' has the meaning given by section 145(6);

'debtor' means the individual receiving credit under a consumer credit agreement or the person to whom his rights and duties under the agreement have passed by assignment or operation of law, and in relation to a prospective consumer credit agreement includes the prospective debtor;

'debtor-creditor agreement' has the meaning given by section 13;

'debtor-creditor-supplier agreement' has the meaning given by section 12;

'default notice' has the meaning given by section 87(1);

['default sum' has the meaning given by section 187A;]

'deposit' means [(except in section 16(10) and 25(1B)] any sum payable by a debtor or hirer by way of deposit or downpayment, or credited or to be credited to him on account of any deposit or downpayment, whether the sum is to be or has been paid to the creditor or owner or any other person, or is to be or has been discharged by a payment of money or a transfer or delivery of goods or by any other means;

['documents' includes information recorded in any form;]

[…]

'electric line' has the meaning given by [the Electricity Act 1989] or, for Northern Ireland the Electricity Supply (Northern Ireland) Order 1972;

['electronic communication' means an electronic communication within the meaning of the Electronic Communications Act 2000 (c.7);]

'embodies' and related words shall be construed in accordance with subsection (4);

'enforcement authority' has the meaning given by section 161(1);

'enforcement order' means an order under section 65(1), 105(7)(a) or (b), 111(2) or 124(1) or (2);

'executed agreement' means a document, signed by or on behalf of the parties, embodying the terms of a regulated agreement, or such of them as have been reduced to writing;

'exempt agreement' means an agreement specified in or under section 16[, 16A or 16B];

'finance' means to finance wholly or partly, and 'financed' and 'refinanced' shall be construed accordingly;

'file' and 'copy of the file' have the meanings given by section 158(5);

'fixed-sum credit' has the meaning given by section 10(1)(b);

'friendly society' means a society registered [or treated as registered under the Friendly Societies Act 1974 or the Friendly Societies Act 1992] [...];

'future arrangements' shall be construed in accordance with section 187;

'general notice' means a notice published by the [OFT] at a time and in a manner appearing to [it] suitable for securing that the notice is seen within a reasonable time by persons likely to be affected by it;

'give' means deliver or send [by an appropriate method] to;

'goods' has the meaning given by [section 61(1) of the Sale of Goods Act 1979];

'group licence' has the meaning given by section 22(1)(b);

'High Court' means Her Majesty's High Court of Justice, or the Court of Session in Scotland or the High Court of Justice in Northern Ireland;

'hire-purchase agreement' means an agreement, other than a conditional sale agreement, under which—

   (a) goods are bailed or (in Scotland) hired in return for periodical payments by the person to whom they are bailed or hired, and

   (b) the property in the goods will pass to that person if the terms of the agreement are complied with and one or more of the following occurs—

      (i) the exercise of an option to purchase by that person,

      (ii) the doing of any other specified act by any party to the agreement,

      (iii) the happening of any other specified event;

'hirer' means the individual to whom goods are bailed or (in Scotland) hired under a consumer hire agreement, or the person to whom his rights and duties under the agreement have passed by assignment or operation of law, and in relation to a prospective consumer hire agreement includes the prospective hirer;

'individual' includes—

   (a) a partnership consisting of two or three persons not all of whom are bodies corporate; and

   (a) an unincorporated body of persons which does not consist entirely of bodies corporate and is not a partnership;]

'installation' means—

   (a) the installing of any electric line or any gas or water pipe,

   (b) the fixing of goods to the premises where they are to be used, and the alteration of premises to enable goods to be used on them,

   (c) where it is reasonably necessary that goods should be constructed or erected on the premises where they are to be used, any work carried out for the purpose of constructing or erecting them on those premises;

   [...]

'judgment' includes an order or decree made by any court;

'land' includes an interest in land, and in relation to Scotland includes heritable subjects of whatever description;

'land improvement company' means an improvement company as defined by section 7 of the improvement of Land Act 1899;

'land mortgage' includes any security charged on land;

'licence' means a licence under Part III [...];

'licensed', in relation to any act, means authorised by a licence to do the act or cause or permit another person to do it;

'licensee', in the case of a group licence, includes any person covered by the licence;

'linked transaction' has the meaning given by section 19(1);

'local authority', in relation to England and Wales, means the Greater London Council, a county council, a London borough council, a district council, the Common Council of the City of London, or the Council of the Isles of Scilly, and in relation to Scotland, means a [council constituted under section 2 of the Local Government etc. (Scotland) Act 1994], and, in relation to Northern Ireland, means a district council;

'modifying agreement' has the meaning given by section 82(2);

'mortgage', in relation to Scotland, includes any heritable security;

'multiple agreement' has the meaning given by section 18(1);

'negotiator' has the meaning given by section 56(1);

'non-commercial agreement' means a consumer credit agreement or a consumer hire agreement not made by the creditor or owner in the course of a business carried on by him;

'notice' means notice in writing;

'notice of cancellation' has the meaning given by section 69(1);

['OFT' means the Office of Fair Trading;]

'owner' means a person who bails or (in Scotland) hires out goods under a consumer hire agreement or the person to whom his rights and duties under the agreement have passed by assignment or operation of law, and in relation to a prospective consumer hire agreement, includes the prospective bailor or person from whom the goods are to be hired;

'pawn' means any article subject to a pledge;

'pawn-receipt' has the meaning given by section 114;

'pawnee' and 'pawnor' include any person to whom the rights and duties of the original pawnee or the original pawnor, as the case may be, have passed by assignment or operation of law;

'payment' includes tender;

[...]

'pledge' means the pawnee's rights over an article taken in pawn;

'prescribed' means prescribed by regulations made by the Secretary of State;

'pre-existing arrangements' shall be construed in accordance with section 187;

'principal agreement' has the meaning given by section 19(1);

'protected goods' has the meaning given by section 90(7);

'quotation' has the meaning given by section 52(1)(a);

'redemption period' has the meaning given by section 116(3);

'register' means the register kept by the [OFT] under section 35;

'regulated agreement' means a consumer credit agreement, or consumer hire agreement, other than an exempt agreement, and 'regulated' and 'unregulated' shall be construed accordingly;

'regulations' means regulations made by the Secretary of State;

'relative', except in section 184, means a person who is an associate by virtue of section 184(1);

'representation' includes any condition or warranty, and any other statement or undertaking, whether oral or in writing;

'restricted-use credit agreement' and 'restricted-use credit' have the meanings given by section 11(1);

'rules of court', in relation to Northern Ireland means, in relation to the High Court, rules made under section 7 of the Northern Ireland Act 1962, and, in relation to any other court, rules made by the authority having for the time being power to make rules regulating the practice and procedure in that court;

'running-account credit' shall be construed in accordance with section 10;

'security', in relation to an actual or prospective consumer credit agreement or consumer hire agreement, or any linked transaction, means a mortgage, charge, pledge, bond, debenture, indemnity, guarantee, bill, note or other right provided by the debtor or hirer, or at his request (express or implied), to secure the carrying out of the obligations of the debtor or hirer under the agreement;

'security instrument' has the meaning given by section 105(2);

'serve on' means deliver or send [by an appropriate method] to;

'signed' shall be construed in accordance with subsection (3);

'small agreement' has the meaning given by section 17(1), and 'small' in relation to an agreement within any category shall be construed accordingly;

'specified fee' shall be construed in accordance with section 2(4) and (5);

'standard licence' has the meaning given by section 22(1)(a);

'supplier' has the meaning given by section 11(1)(b) or 12(c) or 13(c) or, in relation to an agreement failing within section 11(1)(a), means the creditor, and includes a person to whom the rights and duties of a supplier (as so defined) have passed by assignment or operation of law, or (in relation to a prospective agreement) the prospective supplier;

'surety' means the person by whom any security is provided, or the person to whom his rights and duties in relation to the security have passed by assignment or operation of law;

'technical grounds' shall be construed in accordance with subsection (5);

'time order' has the meaning given by section 129(1);

'total charge for credit' means a sum calculated in accordance with regulations under section 20(1);

'total price' means the total sum payable by the debtor under a hire-purchase agreement or a conditional sale agreement, including any sum payable on the exercise of an option to purchase, but excluding any sum payable as a penalty or as compensation or damages for a breach of the agreement;

['the Tribunal' means the Consumer Credit Appeals Tribunal;]

'unexecuted agreement' means a document embodying the terms of a prospective regulated agreement, or such of them as it is intended to reduce to writing;

'unlicensed' means without a licence, but applies only in relation to acts for which a licence is required;

'unrestricted-use credit agreement' and 'unrestricted-use credit' have the meanings given by section 11(2);

'working day' means any day other than—

    (a) Saturday or Sunday,

    (b) Christmas Day or Good Friday,

    (c) a bank holiday within the meaning given by section 1 of the Banking and Financial Dealings Act 1971.

[(1A) In sections 36E(3), 70(4), 73(4) and 75(2) and paragraphs 14 and 15 of Schedule A1 'costs', in relation to proceedings in Scotland, means expenses.]

(2) A person is not to be treated as carrying on a particular type of business merely because occasionally he enters into transactions belonging to a business of that type.

(3) Any provision of this Act requiring a document to be signed is complied with by a body corporate if the document is sealed by that body.

This subsection does not apply to Scotland.

(4) A document embodies a provision if the provision is set out either in the document itself or in another document referred to in it.

(5) An application dismissed by the court or the Director shall, if the court or the Director (as the case may be) so certifies, be taken to be dismissed on technical grounds only.

(6) Except in so far as the context otherwise requires, any reference in this Act to an enactment shall be construed as a reference to that enactment as amended by or under any other enactment, including this Act.

(7) In this Act, except where otherwise indicated—

    (a) a reference to a numbered Part, section or Schedule is a reference to the Part or section of, or the Schedule to, this Act so numbered, and

    (b) a reference in a section to a numbered subsection is a reference to the subsection of that section so numbered, and

    (c) a reference in a section, subsection or Schedule to a numbered paragraph is a reference to the paragraph of that section, subsection or Schedule so numbered.

[189A Meaning of 'consumer credit EEA firm'

In this Act 'consumer credit EEA firm' means an EEA firm falling within sub-paragraph (a), (b) or (c) of paragraph 5 of Schedule 3 to the Financial Services and Markets Act 2000 carrying on, or seeking to carry on, consumer credit business, consumer hire business or ancillary credit business for which a licence would be required under this Act but for paragraph 15(3) of Schedule 3 to the Financial Services and Markets Act 2000.]

190 Financial provisions

    (1) There shall be defrayed out of money provided by Parliament—

        (a) all expenses incurred by the Secretary of State in consequence of the provisions of this Act;

        (b) any expenses incurred in consequence of those provisions by any other Minister of the Crown or Government department;

        (c) any increase attributable to this Act in the sums payable out of money so provided under the Superannuation Act 1972 or the Fair Trading Act 1973.

    (2) Any fees[, charges, penalties or others sums] received by the [OFT] under this Act shall be paid into the Consolidated Fund.

191 Special provisions as to Northern Ireland

. . .

192 Transitional and commencement provisions, amendments and repeals

    (1) The provisions of Schedule 3 shall have effect for the purposes of this Act.

    (2) The appointment of a day for the purposes of any provision of Schedule 3 shall be effected by an order of the Secretary of State made by statutory instrument; and any such order shall include a provision amending Schedule 3 so as to insert an express reference to the day appointed.

    (3) Subject to subsection (4)—

        (a) the enactments specified in Schedule 4 shall have effect subject to the amendments specified in that Schedule (being minor amendments or amendments consequential on the preceding provisions of thsi Act), and

        (b) the enactments specified in Schedule 5 are hereby repealed to the extent shown in column 3 of that Schedule.

    (4) The Secretary of State shall by order made by statutory instrument provide for the coming into operation of the amendments contained in Schedule 4 and the repeals contained in Schedule 5, and those amendments and repeals shall have effect only as provided by an order so made.

193 Short title and extent

    (1) This Act may be cited as the Consumer Credit Act 1974.

    (2) This Act extend to Northern Ireland.

[SCHEDULE A1

THE CONSUMER CREDIT APPEALS TRIBUNAL

PART 1

INTERPRETATION

1 In this Schedule—

"the Deputy President" means the Deputy President of the Consumer Credit Appeals Tribunal;

"lay panel" means the panel established under paragraph 3(3);

"panel of chairmen" means the panel established under paragraph 3(1);

"party" means, in relation to an appeal, the appellant or the OFT;

"the President" means the President of the Consumer Credit Appeals Tribunal;

"rules" means rules under section 40A(3) of this Act;

"specified" means specified by rules.

PART 2

THE TRIBUNAL

2 The President and the Deputy President

(1) The Lord Chancellor shall appoint one of the members of the panel of chairmen to preside over the discharge of the Tribunal's functions.

(2) The person so appointed shall be known as the President of the Consumer Credit Appeals Tribunal.

(3) The Lord Chancellor may appoint one of the members of the panel of chairmen to be the Deputy President of the Consumer Credit Appeals Tribunal.

(4) The Deputy President shall have such functions in relation to the Tribunal as the President may assign to him.

(5) If the President or the Deputy President ceases to be a member of the panel of chairmen, he shall also cease to be the President or (as the case may be) the Deputy President.

(6) The functions of the President may, if he is absent or is otherwise unable to act, be discharged—

(a) by the Deputy President; or

(b) if there is no Deputy President or he too is absent or otherwise unable to act, by a person appointed for that purpose from the panel of chairmen by the Lord Chancellor.

3 Panels

(1) The Lord Chancellor shall appoint a panel of persons for the purpose of serving as chairmen of the Tribunal.

(2) A person shall not be appointed to the panel of chairmen unless he—

(a) has a seven year general qualification within the meaning of section 71 of the Courts and Legal Services Act 1990;

(b) is an advocate or solicitor in Scotland of at least seven years' standing; or

(c) is a member of the Bar of Northern Ireland, or a solicitor of the Supreme Court of Northern Ireland, of at least seven years' standing.

(3) The Lord Chancellor shall also appoint a panel of persons who appear to him to be qualified by experience or otherwise to deal with appeals of the kind that may be made to the Tribunal.

4 Terms of office etc.

(1) Each member of the panel of chairmen or the lay panel shall hold and vacate office in accordance with the terms of his appointment.

(2) The Lord Chancellor may remove a member of either panel from office on the ground of incapacity or misbehaviour.

(3) A member of either panel—

(a) may at any time resign office by notice in writing to the Lord Chancellor;

(b) is eligible for re-appointment if he ceases to hold office.

5 Remuneration and allowances

The Lord Chancellor may pay to a person in respect of his service—

(a) as the President or the Deputy President,

(b) as a member of the Tribunal, or

(c) as a person appointed under paragraph 7(4),
such remuneration and allowances as the Lord Chancellor may determine.

6 Staff and costs
(1) The Lord Chancellor may appoint such staff for the Tribunal as he may determine.
(2) The Lord Chancellor shall defray—
    (a) the remuneration of the Tribunal's staff; and
    (b) such other costs of the Tribunal as he may determine.

PART 3

CONSTITUTION OF THE TRIBUNAL

7 (1) On an appeal to the Tribunal, the persons to act as members of the Tribunal for the purposes of the appeal shall be selected from the panel of chairmen or the lay panel.

(2) The selection shall be in accordance with arrangements made by the President for the purposes of this paragraph.

(3) Those arrangements shall provide for at least one member to be a person selected from the panel of chairmen.

(4) If it appears to the Tribunal that a matter before it involves a question of fact of special difficulty, it may appoint one or more experts to provide assistance.

PART 4

TRIBUNAL POWERS AND PROCEDURE

8 Sittings
The Tribunal shall sit at such times and in such places as the Lord Chancellor may direct.

9 Evidence
(1) Subject to sub-paragraph (2), the Tribunal may, on an appeal, consider any evidence that it thinks relevant, whether or not it was available to the OFT at the time it made the determination appealed against.

(2) Rules may make provision restricting the evidence that the Tribunal may consider on an appeal in specified circumstances.

10 Rules on procedure
Rules may include, amongst other things, provision—
    (a) about the withdrawal of appeals;
    (b) about persons who may appear on behalf of a party to an appeal;
    (c) about how an appeal is to be dealt with if a person acting as member of the Tribunal in respect of the appeal becomes unable to act;
    (d) setting time limits in relation to anything that is to be done for the purposes of an appeal or for such limits to be set by the Tribunal or a member of the panel of chairmen;
    (e) for time limits (including the period specified for the purposes of section 41(1) of this Act) to be extended by the Tribunal or a member of the panel of chairmen;
    (f) conferring powers on the Tribunal or a member of the panel of chairmen to give such directions to the parties to an appeal as it or he thinks fit for purposes connected with the conduct and disposal of the appeal;
    (g) about the holding of hearings by the Tribunal or a member of the panel of chairmen (including for such hearings to be held in private);
    (h) placing restrictions on the disclosure of information and documents or for such restrictions to be imposed by the Tribunal or a member of the panel of chairmen;

(i) about the consequences of a failure to comply with a requirement imposed by or under any rule (including for the immediate dismissal or allowing of an appeal if the Tribunal or a member of the panel of chairmen thinks fit);

(j) for proceedings on different appeals (including appeals with different appellants) to take place concurrently;

(k) for the suspension of determinations of the OFT;

(l) for the suspension of decisions of the Tribunal;

(m) for the Tribunal to reconsider its decision disposing of an appeal where it has reason to believe that the decision was wrongly made because of an administrative error made by a member of its staff.

11 Council on Tribunals

A member of the Council on Tribunals or of its Scottish Committee shall be entitled—

(a) to attend any hearing held by the Tribunal or a member of the panel of chairmen whether or not it is held in public; and

(b) to attend any deliberations of the Tribunal in relation to an appeal.

12 Disposal of appeals

(1) The Tribunal shall decide an appeal by reference to the grounds of appeal set out in the notice of appeal.

(2) In disposing of an appeal the Tribunal may do one or more of the following—

(a) confirm the determination appealed against;

(b) quash that determination;

(c) vary that determination;

(d) remit the matter to the OFT for reconsideration and determination in accordance with the directions (if any) given to it by the Tribunal;

(e) give the OFT directions for the purpose of giving effect to its decision.

(3) In the case of an appeal against a determination to impose a penalty, the Tribunal—

(a) has no power by virtue of sub-paragraph (2)(c) to increase the penalty;

(b) may extend the period within which the penalty is to be paid (including in cases where that period has already ended).

(4) Sub-paragraph (3) does not affect—

(a) the Tribunal's power to give directions to the OFT under sub-paragraph (2)(d); or

(b) what the OFT can do where a matter is remitted to it under sub-paragraph (2)(d).

(5) Where the Tribunal remits a matter to the OFT, it may direct that the requirements of section 34 of this Act are not to apply, or are only to apply to a specified extent, in relation to the OFT's reconsideration of the matter.

(6) Subject to sub-paragraphs (7) and (8), where the Tribunal remits an application to the OFT, section 6(1) and (3) to (9) of this Act shall apply as if the application had not been previously determined by the OFT.

(7) In the case of a general notice which came into effect after the determination appealed against was made but before the application was remitted, the applicant shall provide any information or document which he is required to provide under section 6(6) within—

(a) the period of 28 days beginning with the day on which the application was remitted; or

(b) such longer period as the OFT may allow.

(8) In the case of—

(a) any information or document which was superseded,

(b) any change in circumstances which occurred, or

(c) any error or omission of which the applicant became aware,

after the determination appealed against was made but before the application was remitted, any notification that is required to be given by the applicant under section 6(7) shall be given within the period of 28 days beginning with the day on which the application was remitted.

13 Decisions of the Tribunal

(1) A decision of the Tribunal may be taken by majority.

(2) A decision of the Tribunal disposing of an appeal shall—

(a) state whether it was unanimous or taken by majority; and

(b) be recorded in a document which—

　　(i) contains a statement of the reasons for the decision and any other specified information; and

　　(ii) is signed and dated by a member of the panel of chairmen.

(3) Where the Tribunal disposes of an appeal it shall—

(a) send to each party to the appeal a copy of the document mentioned in sub-paragraph (2)(b); and

(b) publish that document in such manner as it thinks fit.

(4) The Tribunal may exclude from what it publishes under sub-paragraph (3)(b) information of a specified description.

Costs

14 (1) Where the Tribunal disposes of an appeal and—

(a) it decides that the OFT was wrong to make the determination appealed against, or

(b) during the course of the appeal the OFT accepted that it was wrong to make that determination,

it may order the OFT to pay to the appellant the whole or a part of the costs incurred by the appellant in relation to the appeal.

(2) In determining whether to make such an order, and the terms of such an order, the Tribunal shall have regard to whether it was unreasonable for the OFT to make the determination appealed against.

15 Where—

(a) the Tribunal disposes of an appeal or an appeal is withdrawn before the Tribunal disposes of it, and

(b) the Tribunal thinks that a party to the appeal acted vexatiously, frivolously or unreasonably in bringing the appeal or otherwise in relation to the appeal,

it may order that party to pay to the other party the whole or a part of the costs incurred by the other party in relation to the appeal.

16 An order of the Tribunal under paragraph 14 or 15 may be enforced—

(a) as if it were an order of the county court; or

(b) in Scotland, as if it were an interlocutor of the Court of Session.

Continued

Section 167

SCHEDULE 1

PROSECUTION AND PUNISHMENT OF OFFENCES

1 Section	2 Offence	3 Mode of prosecution	4 Imprisonment or fine
7 ...	Knowingly or recklessly giving false information to [OFT].	(a) Summarily. (b) On indictment.	[The prescribed sum.] 2 years or a fine or both.
39(1) ...	Engaging in activities requiring a licence when not a licensee.	(a) Summarily. (b) On indictment.	[The prescribed sum.] 2 years or a fine or both.
39(2) ...	Carrying on a business under a name not specified in licence.	(a) Summarily. (b) On indictment.	[The prescribed sum.] 2 years or a fine or both.
39(3) ...	Failure to notify changes in registered particulars.	(a) Summarily. (b) On indictment.	[The prescribed sum.] 2 years or a fine or both.
45 ...	Advertising credit where goods etc. not available for cash.	(a) Summarily. (b) On indictment.	[The prescribed sum.] 2 years or a fine or both.
46(1) ...	False or misleading advertisements.	(a) Summarily. (b) On indictment.	[The prescribed sum.] 2 years or a fine or both.
47(1) ...	Advertising infringements.	(a) Summarily. (b) On indictment.	[The prescribed sum.] 2 years or a fine or both.
49(1) ...	Canvassing debtor-creditor agreements off trade premises.	(a) Summarily. (b) On indictment.	[The prescribed sum.] 2 years or a fine or both.
49(2) ...	Soliciting debtor-creditor agreements during visits made inresponse to previous oral requests.	(a) Summarily. (b) On indictment.	[The prescribed sum.] 2 years or a fine or both.
50(1) ...	Sending circulars to minors.	(a) Summarily. (b) On indictment.	[The prescribed sum.] 2 years or a fine or both.
51(1) ...	Supplying unsolicited credit-tokens.	(a) Summarily. (b) On indictment.	[The prescribed sum.] 2 years or a fine or both.
77(4) ...	Failure of creditor under fixed-sum credit agreement to supply copies of documents etc.	(a) Summarily.	[Level 4 on the standard scale.]

Schedule 1 Continued

1 Section	2 Offence	3 Mode of prosecution	4 Imprisonment or fine
78(6)	Failure of creditor under running-account credit agreement to supply copies of documents etc.	(a) Summarily.	[Level 4 on the standard scale.]
79(3) ...	Failure of owner under consumer hire agreement to supply copies of documents etc.	(a) Summarily.	[Level 4 on the standard scale.]
80(2) ...	Failure to tell creditor or owner whereabouts of goods.	(a) Summarily.	[Level 3 on the standard scale.]
85(2) ...	Failure of creditor to supply copy of credit-token agreement.	(a) Summarily.	[Level 4 on the standard scale.]
97(3) ...	Failure to supply debtor with statement of amount required to discharge agreement.	(a) Summarily.	[Level 3 on the standard scale.]
103(5) ...	Failure to deliver notice relating to discharge of agreements.	(a) Summarily.	[Level 3 on the standard scale.]
107(4) ...	Failure of creditor to give information to surety under fixed-sum credit agreement.	(a) Summarily.	[Level 4 on the standard scale.]
108(4) ...	Failure of creditor to give information to surety under running-account credit agreement.	(a) Summarily.	[Level 4 on the standard scale.]
109(3) ...	Failure of owner to give information to surety under consumer hire agreements.	(a) Summarily.	[Level 4 on the standard scale.]
110(3) ...	Failure of creditor or owner to supply a copy of any security instrument to debtor or hirer.	(a) Summarily.	[Level 4 on the standard scale.]
114(2) ...	Taking pledges from minors.	(a) Summarily. (b) On indictment.	[The prescribed sum.] 1 year or a fine or both.
115 ...	Failure to supply copies of a pledge agreement or pawn-receipt.	(a) Summarily.	[Level 4 on the standard scale.]

Section	Offence	Mode of prosecution	Penalty
119(1)	Unreasonable refusal to allow pawn to be redeemed.	(a) Summarily.	[Level 4 on the standard scale.]
154 ...	Canvassing ancillary credit services off trade premises.	(a) Summarily.	[The prescribed sum.]
		(b) On indictment.	1 year or a fine or both.
157(3) ...	Refusal to give name etc. of credit reference agency.	(a) Summarily.	[Level 4 on the standard scale.]
158(4) ...	Failure of credit reference agency to disclose filed information.	(a) Summarily.	[Level 4 on the standard scale.]
159(6) ...	Failure of credit reference agency to correct information.	(a) Summarily.	[Level 4 on the standard scale.]
160(6) ...	Failure of credit reference agency to comply with section 160(3) or (4).	(a) Summarily.	[Level 4 on the standard scale.]
		(b) On indictment.	[1 year or a fine or both.]
162(6) ...	Impersonation of enforcement authority officers.	(a) Summarily.	[The prescribed sum.]
		(b) On indictment.	[1 year or a fine or both.]
165(1) ...	Impersonation of enforcement authority officers.	(a) Summarily.	[The prescribed sum.]
		(b) On indictment.	[1 year or a fine or both.]
165(1) ...	Objection of enforcement authority officers.	(a) Summarily.	[Level 4 on the standard scale.]
165(2) ...	Giving false information to enforcement authority officers.	(a) Summarily.	[The prescribed sum].
		(b) On indictment.	[2 years or a fine or both.]
167(2) ...	Contravention of regulations under section 44, 52, 53, 54, or 112.	(a) Summarily.	[Level 4 on the standard scale.]
		(b) On indictment.	[2 years or a fine or both.]
174(5) ...	Wrongful disclosure of information.	(a) Summarily.	[Level 4 on the standard scale.]
		(b) On indictment.	[2 years or a fine or both.]

Section 188(1)   SCHEDULE 2

EXAMPLES OF USE OF NEW TERMINOLOGY

PART I   LIST OF TERMS

Term	Defined in section	Illustrated by examples (s)
Advertisement	189(1)	2
Advertiser	189(1)	2
Antecedent negotiations	56	1, 2, 3, 4
Cancellable agreement	67	4
Consumer credit agreement ...	8	5, 6, 7, 15, 19, 21
Consumer hire agreement ...	15	20, 24
Credit	9	16, 19, 21
Credit-broker	189(1)	2
Credit limit	10(2)	6, 7, 19, 22, 23
Creditor	189(1)	1, 2, 3, 4
Credit-sale agreement	189(1)	5
Credit-token	14	3, 14, 16
Credit-token agreement ...	14	3, 14, 16, 21
Debtor-creditor agreement ...	13	8, 16, 17, 18
Debtor-creditor-supplier agreement ..	12	8, 16
Fixed-sum credit	10	9, 10, 17, 23
Hire-purchase agreement ...	189(1)	10
Individual	189(1)	19, 24
Linked transaction	19	11
Modifying agreement	82(2)	24
Multiple agreement	18	16, 18
Negotiator	56(1)	1, 2, 3, 4
[...]		
Pre-existing arrangements	187	8, 21
Restricted-use credit	11	10, 12, 13, 14, 16
Running-account credit ...	10	15, 16, 18, 23
Small agreement	17	16, 17, 22
Supplier	189(1)	3, 14
Total charge for credit	20	5, 10
Total price	189(1)	10
Unrestricted-use credit	11	8, 12, 16, 17, 18

PART II   EXAMPLES

Example 1

Facts Correspondence passes between an employee of a money-lending company (writing on behalf of the company) and an individual about the terms on which the company would grant him a loan under a regulated agreement.

Analysis The correspondence constitutes antecedent negotiations falling within section 56(1)(a), the moneylending company being both creditor and negotiator.

Example 2

Facts Representations are made about goods in a poster displayed by a shopkeeper near the goods, the goods being selected by a customer who has read the poster and then sold by the shopkeeper to a finance company introduced by him (with whom he has a business relationship). The goods are disposed of by the finance company to the customer under a regulated hire-purchase agreement.

Analysis The representations in the poster constitute antecedent negotiations falling within section 56(1)(b), the shopkeeper being the credit-broker and negotiator and the finance company being the creditor. The poster is an advertisement and the shopkeeper is the advertiser.

Example 3

Facts Discussions take place between a shopkeeper and a customer about goods the customer wishes to buy using a credit-card issued by the D Bank under a regulated agreement.

Analysis The discussions constitute antecedent negotiations falling within section 56(1)(c), the shopkeeper being the supplier and negotiator and the D Bank the creditor. The credit-card is a credit-token as defined in section 14(1), and the regulated agreement under which it was issued is a credit-token agreement as defined in section 14(2).

Example 4

Facts Discussions take place and correspondence passes between a secondhand car dealer and a customer about a car, which is then sold by the dealer to the customer under a regulated conditional sale agreement. Subsequently, on a revocation of that agreement by consent, the car is resold by the dealer to a finance company introduced by him (with whom he has a business relationship), who in turn dispose of it to the same customer under a regulated hire-purchase agreement.

Analysis The discussions and correspondence constitute antecedent negotiations in relation both to the conditional sale agreement and the hire-purchase agreement. They fall under section 56(1)(a) in relation to the conditional sale agreement, the dealer being the creditor and the negotiator. In relation to the hire-purchase agreement they fall within section 56(1)(b), the dealer continuing to be treated as the negotiator but the finance company now being the creditor. Both agreements are cancellable if the discussions took place when the individual conducting the negotiations (whether the 'negotiator' or his employee or agent) was in the presence of the debtor, unless the unexecuted agreement was signed by the debtor at trade premises (as defined in section 67(b)). If the discussions all took place by telephone however, or the unexecuted agreement was signed by the debtor on trade premises (as so defined) the agreements are not cancellable.

Example 5

Facts E agrees to sell to F (an individual) an item of furniture in return for 24 monthly instalments of £10 payable in arrear. The property in the goods passes to F immediately.

Analysis This is a credit-sale agreement (see definition of 'credit-sale agreement' in section 189(1)). The credit provided amounts to £240 less the amount which, according to regulations made under section 20(1), constitutes the total charge for credit. (This amount is required to be deducted by section 9(4).) Accordingly the agreement falls within section 8(2) and is a consumer credit agreement.

Example 6

Facts The G Bank grants H (an individual) an unlimited over-draft, with an increased rate of interest on so much of any debit balance as exceeds £2,000.

Analysis Although the overdraft purports to be unlimited, the stipulation for increased interest above £2,000 brings the agreement within section 10(3)(b)(ii) and it is a consumer credit agreement.

Example 7

Facts J is an individual who owns a small shop which usually carries a stock worth about £1,000. K makes a stocking agreement under which he undertakes to provide on short-term credit the stock needed from time to time by J without any specified limit.

Analysis Although the agreement appears to provide unlimited credit, it is probable, having regard to the stock usually carried by J, that his indebtedness to K will not at any time rise above £5,000. Accordingly the agreement falls within section 10(3)(b)(iii) and is a consumer credit agreement.

Example 8

Facts U, a moneylender, lends £500 to V (an individual) knowing he intends to use it to buy office equipment from W. W introduced V to U, it being his practice to introduce customers needing finance to him. Sometimes U gives W a commission for this and sometimes not. U pays the £500 direct to V.

Analysis Although this appears to fall under section 11(1)(b), it is excluded by section 11(3) and is therefore (by section 11(2)) an unrestricted-use credit agreement. Whether it is a debtor-creditor agreement (by section 13(c)) or a debtor-creditor-supplier agreement (by section 12(c)) depends on whether the previous dealings between U and W amount to 'preexisting arrangements', that is whether the agreement can be taken to have been entered into 'in accordance with, or in furtherance of' arrangements previously made between U and W, as laid down in section 187(1).

Example 9

Facts A agrees to lend B (an individual) £4,500 in nine monthly instalments of £500.

Analysis This is a cash loan and is a form of credit (see section 9 and definition of 'cash' in section 189(1)). Accordingly it falls within section 10(1)(b) and is fixed-sum credit amounting to £4,500.

Example 10

Facts C (in England) agrees to bail goods to D (an individual) in return for periodical payments. The agreement provides for the property in the goods to pass to D on payment of a total of £7,500 and the exercise by D of an option to purchase. The sum of £7,500 includes a down-payment of £1,000. It also includes an amount which, according to regulations made under section 20(1), constitutes a total charge for credit of £1,500.

Analysis This is a hire-purchase agreement with a deposit of £1,000 and a total price of £7,500 (see definitions of 'hire-purchase agreement', 'deposit' and 'total price' in section 189(1)). By section 9(3), it is taken to provide credit amounting to £7,500 − (£1,500 + £1,000), which equals £5,000. Under section 8(2), the agreement is therefore a consumer credit agreement, and under sections 9(3) and 11(l) it is a restricted-use credit agreement for fixed-sum credit. A similar result would follow if the agreement by C had been a hiring agreement in Scotland.

Example 11

Facts X (an individual) borrows £500 from Y (Finance). As a condition of the granting of the loan X is required—

(a) to execute a second mortgage on his house in favour of Y (Finance), and

(b) to take out a policy of insurance on his life with Y (Insurances).

In accordance with the loan agreement, the policy is charged to Y (Finance) as collateral security for the loan. The two companies are associates within the meaning of section 184(3).

Analysis The second mortgage is a transaction for the provision of security and accordingly does not fall within section 19(1), but the taking out of the insurance policy is a linked transaction falling within section 19(1)(a). The charging of the policy is a separate transaction (made between different parties) for the provision of security and again is excluded from section 19(1). The only linked transaction is therefore the taking out of the insurance policy. If X had not been required by the loan agreement to take out the policy, but it had been done at the suggestion of Y (Finance) to induce them to enter into the loan agreement, it would have been a linked transaction under section 19(1)(c)(i) by virtue of section 19(2)(a).

Example 12

Facts The N Bank agrees to lend 0 (an individual) £2,000 to buy a car from P. To make sure the loan is used as intended, the N Bank stipulates that the money must be paid by it direct to P.

Analysis The agreement is a consumer credit agreement by virtue of section 8(2). Since it falls within section 11(1)(b), it is a restricted-use credit agreement, P being the supplier. If the N Bank had not stipulated for direct payment to the supplier, section 11(3) would have operated and made the agreement into one for unrestricted-use credit.

Example 13

Facts Q, a debt-adjuster, agrees to pay off debts owed by R (an individual) to various money-lenders. For this purpose the agreement provides for the making of a loan by Q to R in return for R's agreeing to repay the loan by instalments with interest. The loan money is not paid over to R but retained by Q and used to pay off the money lenders.

Analysis This is an agreement to refinance existing indebtedness of the debtor's, and if the loan by Q does not exceed £5,000 is a restricted-use credit agreement falling within section 11(1)(c).

Example 14

Facts On payment of £1, S issues to T (an individual) a trading check under which T can spend up to £20 at any shop which has agreed, or in future agrees, to accept S's trading checks.

Analysis The trading check is a credit-token falling within section 14(1)(b). The credit-token agreement is a restricted-use credit agreement within section 11(1)(b), any shop in which the credit-token is used being the 'supplier'. The fact that further shops may be added after the issue of the credit-token is irrelevant in view of section 11(4).

Example 15

Facts A retailer L agrees with M (an individual) to open an account in M's name and, in return for M's promise to pay a specified minimum sum into the account each month and to pay a monthly charge for credit, agrees to allow to be debited to the account, in respect of purchases made by M from L, such sums as will not increase the debit balance at any time beyond the credit limit, defined in the agreement as a given multiple of the specified minimum sum.

Analysis This agreement provides credit falling within the definition of running-account credit in section 10(1)(a). Provided the credit limit is not over £5,000, the agreement falls within section 8(2) and is a consumer credit agreement for running-account credit.

Example 16

Facts Under an unsecured agreement, A (Credit), an associate of the A Bank, issues to B (an individual) a credit-card for use in obtaining cash on credit from A (Credit), to be paid by branches of the A Bank (acting as agent of A (Credit)), or goods or cash from suppliers or banks who have agreed to honour credit-cards issued by A (Credit). The credit limit is £30.

Analysis This is a credit-token agreement falling within section 14(1)(a) and (b). It is a regulated consumer credit agreement for running-account credit. Since the credit limit does not exceed £30, the agreement is a small agreement. So far as the agreement relates to goods it is a debtor-creditor-supplier agreement within section 12(b), since it provides restricted-use credit under section 11(1)(b). So far as it relates to cash it is a debtor-creditor agreement within section 13(c) and the credit it provides is unrestricted-use credit. This is therefore a multiple agreement. In that the whole agreement falls within several of the categories of agreement mentioned in this Act, it is, by section 18(3), to be treated as an agreement in each of those categories. So far as it is a debtor-creditor-supplier agreement providing restricted-use credit it is, by section 18(2), to be treated as a separate agreement; and similarly so far as it is a debtor-creditor agreement providing unrestricted-use credit. (See also Example 22.)

Example 17

Facts The manager of the C Bank agrees orally with D (an individual) to open a current account in D's name. Nothing is said about overdraft facilities. After maintaining the account in credit for some weeks, D draws a cheque in favour of E for an amount exceeding D's credit balance by £20. E presents the cheque and the Bank pay it.

Analysis In drawing the cheque D, by implication, requests the Bank to grant him an overdraft of £20 on its usual terms as to interest and other charges. In deciding to honour the cheque, the Bank by implication accept the offer. This constitutes a regulated small consumer credit agreement for unrestricted-use, fixed sum credit. It is a debtor-creditor agreement, and falls within section 74(1)(b) if covered by a determination under section 74(3). (Compare Example 18.)

Example 18

Facts F (an individual) has had a current account with the G Bank for many years. Although usually in credit, the account has been allowed by the Bank to become overdrawn from time to time. The maximum such overdraft has been is about £1,000. No explicit agreement has ever been made about overdraft facilities. Now, with a credit balance of £500, F draws a cheque for £1,300.

Analysis It might well be held that the agreement with F (express or implied) under which the Bank operate his account includes an implied term giving him the right to overdraft facilities up to say £1,000. If so, the agreement is a regulated consumer credit agreement for unrestricted-use, running-account credit. It is a debtor-creditor agreement, and falls within section 74(1)(b) if covered by a direction under section 74(3). It is also a multiple agreement, part of which (i.e. the part not dealing with the overdraft), as referred to in section 18(1)(a), falls within a category of agreement not mentioned in this Act. (Compare Example 17.)

Example 19

Facts H (a finance house) agrees with J (a partnership of individuals) to open an un- secured loan account in J's name on which the debit balance is not to exceed £7,500 (having regard to payments into the account made from time to time by J). Interest is to be payable in advance on this sum, with provision for yearly adjustments. H is entitled to debit the account with interest, a 'setting-up' charge, and other charges. Before J has an opportunity to draw on the account it is initially debited with £2,250 for advance interest and other charges.

Analysis This is a personal running-account credit agreement (see sections 8(1) and 10(1)(a), and definition of 'individual' in section 189(1)). By section 10(2) the credit limit is £7,000. By section 9(4) however the initial debit of £2,250, and any other charges later debited to the account by H, are not to be treated as credit even though time is allowed for their payment. Effect is given to this by section 10(3). Although the credit limit of £7,000 exceeds the amount (£5,000) specified in section 8(2) as the maximum for a consumer credit agreement, so that the agreement is not within section 10(3)(a), it is caught by section 10(3)(b)(i). At the beginning J can effectively draw (as credit) no more than £4,750, so the agreement is a consumer credit agreement.

Example 20

Facts K (in England) agrees with L (an individual) to bail goods to L for a period of three years certain at £2,200 a year, payable quarterly. The agreement contains no provision for the passing of the property in the goods to L.

Analysis This is not a hire-purchase agreement (see paragraph (b) of the definition of that term in section 189(1)), and is capable of subsisting for more than three months. Paragraphs(a) and (b) of section 15(1) are therefore satisfied, but paragraph (c) is not. The payments by L must exceed £5,000 if he conforms to the agreement. It is true that under section 101 L has a right to terminate the agreement on giving K three month's notice expiring not earlier than eighteen months after the making of the agreement, but that section applies only where the agreement is a regulated consumer hire agreement apart from the section (see subsection (1)). So the agreement is not a consumer hire agreement, though it would be if the hire charge were say £1,500 a year, or there were a 'break' clause in it operable by either party before the hire charges exceeded £5,000. A similar result would follow if the agreement by K had been a hiring agreement in Scotland.

Example 21

Facts The P Bank decides to issue cheque cards to its customers under a scheme whereby the bank undertakes to honour cheques of up to £30 in every case where the payee has taken the cheque in reliance on the cheque card, whether the customer has funds in his account or not. The P Bank writes to the major retailers advising them of this scheme and also publicises it by advertising. The Bank issues a cheque card to Q (an individual), who uses it to pay by cheque for goods costing £20 bought by Q from R, a major retailer. At the time, Q has £500 in his account at the P Bank.

Analysis The agreement under which the cheque card is issued to Q is a consumer credit agreement even though at all relevant times Q has more than £30 in his account. This is because Q is free to draw out his whole balance and then use the cheque card, in which case the Bank has bound itself to honour the cheque. In other words the cheque card agreement provides Q with credit, whether he avails himself of it or not. Since the amount of the credit is not subject to any express limit, the cheque card can be used any number of times. It may be presumed however that section 10(3)(b)(iii) will apply. The agreement is an unrestricted-use debtor-creditor agreement (by section 13(c)). Although the P Bank wrote to R informing R of the P Bank's willingness to honour any cheque taken by R in reliance on a cheque card, this does not constitute pre-existing arrangements as mentioned in section 13(c) because section 187(3) operates to prevent it. The agreement is not a credit-token agreement within section 14(1)(b) because payment by the P Bank to R, would be a payment of the cheque and not a payment for the goods.

Example 22

Facts The facts are as in Example 16. On one occasion B uses the credit-card in a way which increases his debit balance with A (Credit) to £40. A (Credit) writes to B agreeing to allow the excess on that occasion only, but stating that it must be paid off within one month.

Analysis In exceeding his credit limit B, by implication, requests A (Credit) to allow him a temporary excess (compare Example 17). A (Credit) is thus faced by B's action with the choice of treating it as a breach of contract or granting his implied request. He does the latter. If he had done the former, B would be treated as taking credit to which he was not entitled (see section 14(3)) and, subject to the terms of his contract with A (Credit), would be liable to damages for breach of contract. As it is, the agreement to allow the excess varies the original credit-token agreement by adding a new term. Under section 10(2), the new term is to be disregarded in arriving at the credit limit, so that the credit-token agreement at no time ceases to be a small agreement. By section 82(2) the later agreement is deemed to revoke the original agreement and contain provisions reproducing the combined effect of the two agreements. By section 82(4), this later agreement is exempted from Part V (except section 56).

Example 23

Facts Under an oral agreement made on 10th January, X (an individual) has an overdraft on his current account at the Y bank with a credit limit of £100. On 15th February, when his overdraft stands at £90, X draws a cheque for £25. It is the first time that X has exceeded his credit limit, and on 16th February the bank honours the cheque.

Analysis The agreement of 10th January is a consumer credit agreement for running-account credit. The agreement of 15th-16th February varies the earlier agreement by adding a term allowing the credit limit to be exceeded merely temporarily. By section 82(2) the later agreement is deemed to revoke the earlier agreement and reproduce the combined effect of the two agreements. By section 82(4), Part V of this Act (except section 56) does not apply to the later agreement. By section 18(5), a term allowing a merely temporary excess over the credit limit is not to be treated as a separate agreement, or as providing fixed-sum credit. The whole of the £115 owed to the bank by X on 16th February is therefore running-account credit.

Example 24

Facts On 1st March 1975 Z (in England) enters into an agreement with A (an unincorporated body of persons) to bail to A equipment consisting of two components (component P and component Q). The agreement is not a hire-purchase agreement and is for a fixed term of 3 years, so paragraphs (a) and (b) of section 15(1) are both satisfied. The rental is payable monthly at a rate of £2,400 a year, but the agreement provides that this is to be reduced to £1,200 a year for the remainder of the agreement if at any time during its currency A returns component Q to the owner Z. On 5th May 1976 A is incorporated as A Ltd., taking over A's assets and liabilities. On 1st March 1977, A Ltd. returns component Q. On 1st January 1978, Z and A Ltd. agree to extend the earlier agreement by one year, increasing the rental for the final year by £250 to £1,450.

Analysis When entered into on 1st March 1975, the agreement is a consumer hire agreement. A falls within the definition of 'individual' in section 189(1) and if A returns component Q before 1st May 1976 the total rental will not exceed £5,000 (see section 15(1)(c)). When this date is passed without component Q having been returned it is obvious that the total rental must now exceed £5,000. Does this mean that the agreement then ceases to be a consumer hire agreement? The answer is no, because there has been no change in the terms of the agreement, and without such a change the agreement cannot move from one category to the other. Similarly, the fact that A's rights and duties under the agreement pass to a body corporate on 5th May 1976 does not cause the agreement to cease to be a consumer hire agreement (see definition of 'hirer' in section 189(1)).

The effect of the modifying agreement of 1st January 1978 is governed by section 82(2), which requires it to be treated as containing provisions reproducing the combined effect of the two actual agreements, that is to say as providing that—

(a) obligations outstanding on 1st January 1978 are to be treated as outstanding under the modifying agreement;

(b) the modifying agreement applies at the old rate of hire for the months of January and February 1978, and

(c) for the year beginning 1st March 1978 A Ltd. will be the bailee of component P at a rental of £1,450.

The total rental under the modifying agreement is £1,850. Accordingly the modifying agreement is a regulated agreement. Even if the total rental under the modifying agreement exceeded £5,000 it would still be regulated because of the provisions of section 82(3).

[*Scheds. 3 (transitional and commencement provisions), 4 (minor and consequential amendments) and 5 (repeals) are omitted.*]

Torts (Interference with Goods) Act 1977
(1977, c. 32)

An Act to amend the law concerning conversion and other torts affecting goods.   [22nd July 1977]

1 Definition of 'wrongful interference with goods'
In this Act 'wrongful interference', or 'wrongful interference with goods', means—

(a) conversion of goods (also called trover),

(b) trespass to goods,

(c) negligence so far as it results in damage to goods or to an interest in goods,

(d) subject to section 2, any other tort so far as it results in damage to goods or to an interest in goods

[and references in this Act (however worded) to proceedings for wrongful interference or to a claim or right to claim for wrongful interference shall include references to proceedings by virtue of Part I of the Consumer Protection Act 1987 (product liability) in respect of any damage to goods and to the interest in goods or, as the case may be, to a claim or right to claim by virtue of that Part in respect of any such damage].

2 Abolition of detinue
(1) Detinue is abolished.

(2) An action lies in conversion for loss or destruction of goods which a bailee has allowed to happen in breach of his duty to his bailor (that is to say it lies in a case which is not otherwise conversion, but would have been detinue before detinue was abolished).

3 Forms of judgment where goods are detained
(1) In proceedings for wrongful interference against a person who is in possession or in control of the goods relief may be given in accordance with this section, so far as appropriate.

(2) The relief is—

(a) an order for delivery of goods, and for payment of any consequential damages, or

(b) an order for delivery of the goods, but giving the defendant the alternative of paying damages by reference to the value of the goods, together in either alternative with payment of any consequential damages, or

(c) damages.

(3) Subject to rules of court—

(a) relief shall be given under only one of paragraphs (a), (b) and (c) of subsection (2),

(b) relief under paragraph (a) of subsection (2) is at the discretion of the court, and the claimant may choose between the others.

(4) If it is shown to the satisfaction of the court that an order under subsection (2)(a) had not been complied with, the court may—

(a) revoke the order, or the relevant part of it, and

(b) make an order for payment of damages by reference to the value of the goods.

(5) Where an order is made under subsection (2)(b) the defendant may satisfy the order by returning the goods at any time before execution of judgment, but without prejudice to liability to pay any consequential damages.

(6) An order for delivery of the goods under subsection (2)(a) or (b) may impose such conditions as may be determined by the court, or pursuant to rules of court, and in particular, where damages by reference to the value of the goods would not be the whole of the value of the goods, may require an allowance to be made by the claimant to reflect the difference.

For example, a bailor's action against the bailee may be one in which the measure of damages is not the full value of the goods, and then the court may order delivery of the goods, but require the bailor to pay the bailee a sum reflecting the difference.

(7) Where under subsection (1) or subsection (2) of section 6 an allowance is to be made in respect of an improvement of the goods, and an order is made under subsection (2)(a) or (b), the court may assess the allowance to be made in respect of the improvement, and by the order require, as a condition for delivery of the goods, that allowance to be made by the claimant.

(8) This section is without prejudice—

(a) to the remedies afforded by section 133 of the Consumer Credit Act, or

. . .

(c) to any jurisdiction to afford ancillary or incidental relief.

4   Interlocutory relief where goods are detained

(1) In this section 'proceedings' means proceedings for wrongful interference.

(2) On the application of any person in accordance with rules of court, the High Court shall, in such circumstances as may be specified in the rules, have power to make an order providing for the delivery up of any goods which are or may become subject matter of subsequent proceedings in the court, or as to which any question may arise in proceedings.

(3) Delivery shall be, as the order may provide, to the claimant or to a person appointed by the court for the purpose, and shall be on such terms and conditions as may be specified in the order.

5   Extinction of title on satisfaction of claim for damages

(1) Where damages for wrongful interference are, or would fall to be, assessed on the footing that the claimant is being compensated—

(a) for the whole of his interest in the goods, or

(b) for the whole of his interest in the goods subject to a reduction for contributory negligence,

payment of the assessed damages (under all heads), or as the case may be settlement of a claim for damages for the wrong (under all heads), extinguishes the claimant's title to that interest.

(2) In subsection (1) the reference to the settlement of the claim includes—

(a) where the claim is made in court proceedings, and the defendant has paid a sum into court to meet the whole claim, the taking of that sum by the claimant, and

(b) where the claim is made in court proceedings, and the proceedings are settled or compromised, the payment of what is due in accordance with the settlement or compromise, and

(c) where the claim is made out of court and is settled or compromised, the payment of what is due in accordance with the settlement or compromise.

(3) It is hereby declared that subsection (1) does not apply where damages are assessed on the footing that the claimant is being compensated for the whole of his interest in the goods, but the damages paid are limited to some lesser amount by virtue of any enactment or rule of law.

(4) Where under section 7(3) the claimant accounts over to another person (the 'third party') so as to compensate (under all heads) the third party for the whole of his interest in the goods, the third party's title to that interest is extinguished.

(5) This section has effect subject to any agreement varying the respective rights of the parties to the agreement, and where the claim is made in court proceedings has effect subject to any court.

6   Allowance for improvement of the goods

(1) If in proceedings for wrongful interference against a person (the 'improver') who has improved the goods, it is shown that the improver acted in the mistaken but honest belief that he had a good title to them, an allowance shall be made for the extent to which, at the time as at which the goods fall to be valued in assessing damages, the value of the goods is attributable to the improvement.

(2) If, in proceedings for wrongful interference against a person ('the purchaser') who has purported to purchase the goods—

   (a) from the improver, or

   (b) where after such a purported sale the goods passed by a further purported sale on one or more occasions, on any such occasion,

it is shown that the purchaser acted in good faith, an allowance shall be made on the principle set out in subsection (1).

For example, where a person in good faith buys a stolen car from the improver and is sued in conversion by the true owner the damages may be reduced to reflect the improvement, but if the person who bought the stolen car from the improver sues the improver for failure of consideration, and the improver acted in good faith, subsection (3) below will ordinarily make a comparable reduction in the damages he recovers from the improver.

(3) If in a case within subsection (2) the person purporting to sell the goods acted in good faith, then in proceedings by the purchaser for recovery of the purchase price because of failure of consideration, or in any other proceedings founded on that failure of consideration, an allowance shall, where appropriate, be made on the principle set out in subsection (1).

(4) This section applies, with the necessary modifications, to a purported bailment or other disposition of goods as it applies to a purported sale of goods.

7   Double liability

(1) In this section 'double liability' means the double liability of the wrongdoer which can arise—

   (a) where one of two or more rights of action for wrongful interference is founded on a possessory title, or

   (b) where the measure of damages in an action for wrongful interference founded on a proprietary title is or includes the entire value of the goods, although the interest is one of two or more interests in the goods.

(2) In proceedings to which any two or more claimants are parties, the relief shall be such as to avoid double liability of the wrongdoer as between those claimants.

(3) On satisfaction, in whole or in part, of any claim for an amount exceeding that recoverable if subsection (2) applied, the claimant is liable to account over to the other person having a right to claim to such extent as will avoid double liability.

(4) Where, as the result of enforcement of a double liability, any claimant is unjustly enriched to an extent, he shall be liable to reimburse the wrongdoer to that extent.

For example, if a converter of goods pays damages first to a finder of the goods, and then to the true owner, the finder is unjustly enriched unless he accounts over to the true owner under subsection (3); and then the true owner is unjustly enriched and becomes liable to reimburse the converter of the goods.

8   Competing rights to the goods

(1) The defendant in an action for wrongful interference shall be entitled to show, in accordance with rules of court, that a third party has a better right than the plaintiff as respects all or any part of the interest claimed by the plaintiff, or in right of which he sues, and any rule of law (sometimes called jus tertii) to the contrary is abolished.

(2) Rules of court relating to proceedings for wrongful interference may—

    (a) require the plaintiff to give particulars of his title,

    (b) require the plaintiff to identify any person who, to his knowledge, has or claims any interest in the goods,

    (c) authorise the defendant to apply for directions as to whether any person should be joined with a view to establishing whether he has a better right than the plaintiff, or has a claim of a result of which the defendant might be doubly liable,

    (d) where a party fails to appear on an application within paragraph (c), or to comply with any direction given by the court on such an application, authorise the court to deprive him of any right of action against the defendant for the wrong either unconditionally, or subject to such terms or conditions as may be specified.

(3) Subsection (2) is without prejudice to any power of making rules of court.

9 Concurrent actions

. . .

10 Co-owners

(1) Co-ownership is no defence to an action founded on conversion or trespass to goods where the defendant without the authority of the other co-owner—

    (a) destroys the goods, or disposes of the goods in a way giving a good title to the entire property in the goods, or otherwise does anything equivalent to the destruction of the other's interest in the goods, or

    (b) purports to dispose of the goods in a way which would give a good title to the entire property in the goods if he was acting with the authority of all co-owners of the goods.

(2) Subsection (1) shall not affect the law concerning execution or enforcement of judgments, or concerning any form of distress.

(3) Subsection (1)(a) is by the way of restatement of existing law so far as it relates to conversion.

11 Minor amendments

(1) Contributory negligence is no defence in proceedings founded on conversion, or on intentional trespass to goods.

(2) Receipt of goods by way of pledge is conversion if the delivery of the goods is conversion.

(3) Denial of title is not of itself conversion.

12 Bailee's power of sale

(1) This section applies to goods in the possession or under the control of a bailee where—

    (a) the bailor is in breach of an obligation to take delivery of the goods or, if the terms of the bailment so provide, to give directions as to their delivery, or

    (b) the bailee could impose such an obligation by giving notice to the bailor, but is unable to trace or communicate with the bailor, or

    (c) the bailee can reasonably expect to be relieved of any duty to safeguard the goods on giving notice to the bailor, but is unable to trace or communicate with the bailor.

(2) In the cases of Part I of Schedule 1 to this Act a bailee may, for the purposes of subsection (1), impose an obligation on the bailor to take delivery of the goods, or as the case may be to give directions as to their delivery, and in those cases the said Part I sets out the method of notification.

(3) If the bailee—

    (a) has in accordance with Part II of Schedule 1 to this Act given notice to the bailor of his intention to sell the goods under this subsection, or

(b) has failed to trace or communicate with the bailor with a view to giving him such a notice, after having taken reasonable steps for the purpose, and is reasonably satisfied that the bailor owns the goods, he shall be entitled, as against the bailor, to sell the goods.

(4) Where subsection (3) applies but the bailor did not in fact own the goods, a sale under this section, or under section 13, shall not give a good title as against the owner, or as against a person claiming under the owner.

(5) A bailee exercising his powers under subsection (3) shall be liable to account to the bailor for the proceeds of sale, less any cost of sale, and—

(a) the account shall be taken on the footing that the bailee should have adopted the best method of sale reasonably available in the circumstances, and

(b) where subsection (3)(a) applies, any sum payable in respect of the goods by the bailor to the bailee which accrued due before the bailee gave notice of intention to sell the goods shall be deductible from the proceeds of sale.

(6) A sale duly made under this section gives a good title to the purchaser as against the bailor.

(7) In this section, section 13, and Schedule 1 to the Act,

(a) 'bailor' and 'bailee' include their respective successors in title, and

(b) references to what is payable, paid or due to the bailee in respect of the goods include references to what would be payable by the bailor to the bailee as a condition of delivery of the goods at the relevant time.

(8) This section, and Schedule 1 to this Act, have effect subject to the terms of the bailment.

(9) this section shall not apply where the goods were bailed before the commencement of this Act.

13   Sale authorised by the court

(1) If a bailee of the goods to which section 12 applies satisfies the court that he is entitled to see the goods under section 12, or that he would be so entitled if he had given any notice required in accordance with Schedule 1 to this Act, the court—

(a) may authorise the sale of the goods subject to such terms and conditions, if any, as may be specified in the order and,

(b) may authorise the bailee to deduct from the proceeds of sale any costs of sale and any amount due from the bailor to the bailee in respect of the goods, and

(c) may direct the payment into court of the net proceeds of sale, less any amount deducted under paragraph (b), to be held to the credit of the bailor.

(2) A decision of the court authorising a sale under this section shall, subject to any right of appeal, be conclusive, as against the bailor, of the bailee's entitlement to sell the goods, and gives a good title to the purchaser as against the bailor.

(3) In this section 'the court' means the High Court or a county court, and a county court shall have jurisdiction in the proceedings if the value of the goods does not exceed the county court limit.

14   Interpretation

(1) In this Act, unless the context otherwise requires—

. . .

'goods' includes all chattels personal other than things in action and money.

. . .

15   . . .

16   Extent and application to the Crown

(3) This Act shall bind the Crown, but as regards the Crown's liability in tort shall not bind the Crown further than the Crown is made liable in tort by the Crown Proceedings Act 1947.

SCHEDULES

SCHEDULE 1

UNCOLLECTED GOODS

PART I   POWER TO IMPOSE OBLIGATION TO COLLECT GOODS

1. (1) For the purposes of section 12(1) a bailee may, in the circumstances specified in this Part of this Schedule, by notice given to the bailor impose on him an obligation to take delivery of the goods.

(2) The notice shall be in writing, and may be given either—

    (a) by delivering it to the bailor, or

    (b) by leaving it at his proper address, or

    (c) by post.

(3) The notice shall—

    (a) specify the name and address of the bailee, and give sufficient particulars of the goods and the address or place where they are held, and

    (b) state that the goods are ready for delivery to the bailor, or where combined with a notice terminating the contract of bailment, will be ready for delivery when the contract is terminated, and

    (c) specify the amount, if any, which is payable by the bailor to the bailee in respect of the goods and which became due before the giving of the notice.

(4) Where the notice is sent by post it may be combined with a notice under Part II of this Schedule if the notice is sent by post in a way complying with paragraph 6(4).

(5) References in this Part of this Schedule to taking delivery of the goods include, where the terms of the bailment admit, references to giving directions as to their delivery.

(6) This Part of this Schedule is without prejudice to the provisions of any contract requiring the bailor to take delivery of the goods.

Goods accepted for repair or other treatment

2. If a bailee has accepted goods for repair or other treatment on the terms (expressed or implied) that they will be re-delivered to the bailor when the repair or other treatment has been carried out, the notice may be given at any time after the repair or other treatment has been carried out.

Goods accepted for valuation or appraisal

3. If a bailee has accepted goods in order to value or appraise them, the notice may be given at any time after the bailee has carried out the valuation or appraisal.

Storage, warehousing, etc.

4. (1) If a bailee is in possession of goods which he has held as custodian, and his obligation as custodian has come to an end, the notice may be given at any time after the ending of the obligation, or may be combined with any notice terminating his obligation as custodian.

(2) This paragraph shall not apply to goods held by a person as mercantile agent, that is to say by a person having in the customary course of his business as a mercantile agent authority either to sell goods or to consign goods for the purpose of sale, or to buy goods, or to raise money on the security of goods.

Supplemental

5. Paragraphs 2, 3 and 4 apply whether or not the bailor has paid any amount due to the bailee in respect of the goods, and whether or not the bailment is for reward, or in the course of business, or gratuitous.

PART II   NOTICE OF INTENTION TO SELL GOODS

6. (1) A notice under section 12(3) shall—
   (a) specify the name and address of the bailee, and give sufficient particulars of the goods and the address or place where they are held, and
   (b) specify the date on or after which the bailee proposes to sell the goods, and
   (c) specify the amount, if any, which is payable by the bailor to the bailee in respect of the goods, and which became due before giving of the notice.

(2) The period between giving of the notice and the date specified in the notice as that on or after which the bailee proposes to exercise the power of sale shall be such as will afford the bailor a reasonable opportunity of taking delivery of the goods.

(3) If any amount is payable in respect of the goods by the bailor to the bailee, and become due before giving of the notice, the said period shall be not less than three months.

(4) The notice shall be in writing and shall be sent by post in a registered letter, or by the recorded delivery service.

7. (1) The bailee shall not give a notice under section 12(3), or exercise his right to send the goods pursuant to such a notice, at a time when he has notice that, because of a dispute concerning the goods, the bailor is questioning or refusing to pay all or any part of what the bailee claims to be due to him in respect of the goods.

(2) This paragraph shall be left out of account in determining under section 13(1) whether a bailee of goods is entitled to see the goods under section 12, or would be so entitled if he had given any notice required in accordance with this Schedule.

Unfair Contract Terms Act 1977
(1977, c. 50)

An act to impose further limits on the extent to which under the law of England and Wales and Northern Ireland civil liability for breach of contract, or for negligence or other breach of duty, can be avoided by means of contract terms and otherwise, and under the law of Scotland civil liability can be avoided by means of contract terms.   [26th October 1977]

PART I

1 Scope of Part I
   (1) For the purposes of this Part of this Act, 'negligence' means the breach—
   (a) of any obligation, arising from the express or implied terms of a contract, to take reasonable care or exercise reasonable skill in the performance of the contract;
   (b) of any common law duty to take reasonable care or exercise reasonable skill (but not any stricter duty);
   (c) of the common duty of care imposed by the Occupiers' Liability Act 1957 or the Occupier's Liability Act (Northern Ireland) 1957.

(2) This Part of the Act is subject to Part III; and in relation to contracts, the operation of sections 2 to 4 and 7 is subject to the exceptions made by Schedule I.

(3) In the case of both contract and tort, sections 2 to 7 apply (except where the contrary is stated in section 6(4)) only to business liability, that is liability to breach of obligations or duties arising—
   (a) from things done or to be done by a person in the course of a business (whether his own business or another's); or
   (b) from the occupation of premises used for business purposes of the occupier; and references to liability are to be read accordingly [but liability of an occupier of

premises for breach of an obligation or duty towards a person obtaining access to the premises for recreational or educational purposes, being liability for loss or damage suffered by reason of the dangerous state of the premises, is not a business liability of the occupier unless granting that person such access for the purposes concerned falls within the business purposes of the occupier].

(4) In relation to any breach of duty or obligation, it is immaterial for any purpose of this Part of this Act whether the breach was inadvertent or intentional, or whether liability for it arises directly or vicariously.

2   Negligence liability

(1) A person cannot by reference to any contract term or to a notice given to persons generally or to particular persons exclude or restrict his liability for death or personal injury resulting from negligence.

(2) In the case of other loss or damage, a person cannot so exclude or restrict his liability for negligence except in so far as the term or notice satisfies the requirement of reasonableness.

(3) Where a contract term or notice purports to exclude or restrict liability for negligence a person's agreement to or awareness of it is not of itself to be taken as indicating his voluntary acceptance of any risk.

3   Liability arising in contract

(1) This section applies as between contracting parties where one of them deals as consumer or on the other's written standard terms of business.

(2) As against that party, the other cannot by reference to any contract term—

    (a) when himself in breach of contract, exclude or restrict any liability of his in respect of the breach; or

    (b) claim to be entitled—

        (i)   to render a contractual performance substantially different from that which was reasonably expected of him, or

        (ii) in respect of the whole of any part of his contractual obligation, to render no performance at all,

except in so far as (in any of the cases mentioned above in this subsection) the contract term satisfies the requirement of reasonableness.

4   Unreasonable indemnity clauses

(1) A person dealing as consumer cannot by reference to any contract term be made to indemnify another person (whether a party to the contract or not) in respect of liability that may be incurred by the other for negligence or breach of contract, except in so far as the contract term satisfies the requirement of reasonableness.

(2) This section applies whether the liability in question—

    (a) is directly that of the person to be indemnified or is incurred by him vicariously;

    (b) is to the person dealing as consumer or to someone else.

5   'Guarantee' of consumer goods

(1) In the case of goods of a type ordinarily supplied for private use of consumption, where loss or damage—

    (a) arises from the goods proving defective while in consumer use; and

    (b) results from the negligence of a person concerned in the manufacture or distribution of the goods,

liability for the loss or damage cannot be excluded or restricted by reference to any contract term or notice contained in or operating by reference to a guarantee of the goods.

(2) For these purposes—

    (a) goods are to be regarded as 'in consumer use' when a person is using them, or has them in his possession for use, otherwise than exclusively for the purposes of a business; and

(b) anything in writing is a guarantee if it contains or purports to contain some promise or assurance (however worded or presented) that defects will be made good by complete or partial replacement, or by repair, monetary compensation or otherwise.

(3) This section does not apply as between the parties to a contract under or in pursuance of which possession or ownership of the goods passed.

6 Sale and hire-purchase

(1) Liability for breach of the obligations arising from—

(a) [section 12 of the Sale of Goods Act 1979] (seller's implied undertakings as to title, etc.);

(b) section 8 of the Supply of Goods (Implied Terms) Act 1973 (the corresponding thing in relation to hire-purchase),

cannot be excluded or restricted by reference to any contract term.

(2) As against a person dealing as consumer, liability for breach of the obligations arising from—

(a) [section 13, 14 or 15 of the [1979] Act] (seller's implied undertakings as to conformity of goods with description or sample, or as to their quality of fitness for a particular purpose);

(b) section 9, 10 or 11 of the 1973 Act (the corresponding things in relation to hire-purchase),

cannot be excluded or restricted by reference to any contract term.

(3) As against a person dealing otherwise than as consumer, the liability specified in subsection (2) above can be excluded or restricted by reference to a contract term, but only in so far as the term satisfies the requirement of reasonableness.

(4) The liabilities referred to in this section are not only the business liabilities defined by section 1(3), but include those arising under any contract of sale of goods or hire-purchase agreement.

7 Miscellaneous contracts under which goods pass

(1) Where the possession or ownership of goods passes under or in pursuance of a contract not governed by the law of sale of goods or hire-purchase, subsections (2) to (4) below apply as regards the effect (if any) to be given to contract terms excluding or restricting liability for breach of obligation arising by implication of law from the nature of the contract.

(2) As against a person dealing as consumer, liability in respect of the goods' correspondence with description or sample, or their quality or fitness for any particular purpose, cannot be excluded or restricted by reference to any such term.

(3) As against a person dealing otherwise than as consumer, that liability can be excluded or restricted by reference to such a term, but only in so far as the term satisfies the requirement of reasonableness.

[(3A) Liability for breach of the obligations arising under section 2 of the Supply of Goods and Services Act 1982 (implied terms about title etc. in certain contracts for the transfer of the property in goods) cannot be excluded or restricted by reference to any such term.]

(4) Liability in respect of—

(a) the right to transfer ownership of the goods, or give possession; or

(b) the assurance of quiet possession to a person taking goods in pursuance of the contract,

cannot [(in a case to which subsection (3A) above does not apply)] be excluded or restricted by reference to any such term except in so far as the term satisfies the requirement of reasonableness.

(c) This section does not apply in the case of goods passing on a redemption of trading stamps within the Trading Stamps Act 1964 or the Tradings Stamps Act (Northern Ireland) 1965.

9   Effect of breach

(1) Where for reliance upon it a contract term has to satisfy the requirement of reasonableness, it may be found to do so-and be given effect accordingly notwithstanding that the contract has been terminated either by breach or by a party electing to treat it as repudiated.

(2) Where on a breach the contract is nevertheless affirmed by a party entitled to treat it as repudiated, this does not of itself exclude the requirement of reasonableness in relation to any contract term.

10   Evasion by means of secondary contract

A person is not bound by any contract term prejudicing or taking away rights of his which arise under, or in connection with the performance of, another contract, so far as those rights extend to the enforcement of another's liability which this Part of this Act prevents that other from excluding or restricting.

11   The 'reasonableness' test

(1) In relation to a contract term, the requirement of reasonableness for the purposes of this Part of this Act, section 3 of the Misrepresentation Act 1967 and section 3 of the Misrepresentation Act (Northern Ireland) 1967 is that the term shall have been a fair and reasonable one to be included having regard to the circumstances which were, or ought reasonably to have been, known to or in the contemplation of the parties when the contract was made.

(2) In determining for the purposes of section 6 or 7 above whether a contract term satisfies the requirement of reasonableness, regard shall be had in particular to the matters specified in Schedule 2 to this Act; but this subsection does not prevent the court or arbitrator from holding, in accordance with any rule of law, that a term which purports to exclude or restrict any relevant liability is not a term of the contract.

(3) In relation to a notice (not being a notice having contractual effect), the requirement of reasonableness under this Act is that it should be fair and reasonable to allow reliance on it, having regard to all the circumstances obtaining when the liability arose or (but for the notice) would have arisen.

(4) Where by reference to a contract term or notice a person seeks to restrict liability to a specified sum of money, and the question arises (under this or any other Act) whether the term or notice satisfies the requirement of reasonableness, regard shall be had in particular (but without prejudice to subsection (2) above in the case of contract terms) to—

      (a) the resources which he could expect to be available to him for the purpose of meeting the liability should it arise; and

      (b) how far it was open to him to cover himself by insurance.

(5) It is for those claiming that a contract term or notice satisfies the requirement of reasonableness to show that it does.

12   'Dealing as consumer'

(1) A party to contract 'deals as consumer' in relation to another party if—

      (a) he neither makes the contract in the course of a business nor holds himself out as doing so; and

      (b) the other party does make the contract in the course of a business; and

      (c) in the case of a contract governed by the law of sale of goods or hire-purchase, or by section 7 of this Act, the goods passing under or in pursuance of the contract are of a type ordinarily supplied for private use or consumption.

[But if the first party mentioned in subsection (1) is an individual paragraph (c) of that subsection must be ignored.]

    [(2) But the buyer is not in any circumstances to be regarded as dealing as consumer—

      (a) if he is an individual and the goods are second hand goods sold at public auction at which individuals have the opportunity of attending the sale in person;

      (b) if he is not an individual and the goods are sold by auction or by competitive tender.]

(3) Subject to this, it is for those claiming that a party does not deal as consumer to show that he does not.

13 Varieties of exemption clause

(1) To the extent that this Part of this Act prevents the exclusion or restriction of any liability it also prevents—

(a) making the liability or its enforcement subject to restrictive or onerous conditions;

(b) excluding or restricting any right or remedy in respect of the liability, or subjecting a person to any prejudice in consequence of his pursuing any such right or remedy;

(c) excluding or restricting rules of evidence or procedure; and (to that extent) sections 2 and 5 to 7 also prevent excluding or restricting liability by reference to terms and notices which exclude or restrict the relevant obligation or duty.

(2) But an agreement in writing to submit present or future differences to arbitration is not to be treated under this Part of this Act as excluding or restricting any liability.

14 Interpretation of Part I

In this Part of the Act—

'business' includes a profession and the activities of any government department or local or public authority;

'goods' has the same meaning as in [the Sales of Goods Act 1979]; 'hire-purchase agreement' has the same meaning as in the Consumer Credit Act 1974;

'negligence' has the meaning given by section 1(1); 'notice' includes an announcement, whether or not in writing, and any other communication or pretended communication; and

'personal injury' includes any disease and any impairment of physical or mental condition.

PART II

15 Scope of Part II

(1) This Part of this Act [. . .] issubject to Part III of this Act and does not affect the validity of any discharge or indemnity given by a person in consideration of the receipt by him of compensation in settlement of any claim which he has.

(2) Subject to subsection (3) below, sections 16 to 18 of this Act apply to any contract only to the extent that the contract—

(a) relates to the transfer of the ownership or possession of goods from one person to another (with or without work having been done on them);

(b) constitutes a contract of service or apprenticeship;

(c) relates to services of whatever kind, including (without prejudice to the foregoing generality) carriage, deposit and pledge, care and custody, mandate, agency, loan and services relating to the use of land;

(d) relates to the liability of an occupier of land to persons entering upon or using that land;

(e) relates to a grant of any right or permission to enter upon or use land not amounting to an estate or interest in the land.

(3) Notwithstanding anything in subsection (2) above, sections 16 to 18—

(a) do not apply to any contract to the extent that the contract—

(i) is a contract of insurance (including a contract to pay an annuity on human life);

(ii) relates to the formation, constitution or dissolution of any body corporate or unincorporated association or partnership;

(a) apply to—

a contract of marine salvage or towage;

a charter party of a ship or hovercraft;

a contract for the carriage of goods by ship or hovercraft;

or a contract to which subsection (4) below relates,

only to the extent that—

> (i)   both parties deal or hold themselves out as dealing in the course of a business (and then only in so far as the contract purports to exclude or restrict liability for breach of duty in respect of death or personal injury); or
>
> (ii) the contract is a consumer contract (and then only in favour of the consumer).

(4) This subsection relates to a contract in pursuance of which goods are carried by ship or hovercraft and which either—

> (a) specifies ship or hovercraft as the means of carriage over part of the journey to be covered; or
>
> (b) makes no provision as to the means of carriage and does not exclude ship or hovercraft as that means,

in so far as the contract operates for and in relation to the carriage of the goods by that means.

16 Liability for breach of duty

(1) [Subject to subsection (1A) below,] Where a term of a contract [, or a provision of a notice given to persons generally or to particular persons,] purports to exclude or restrict liability for breach of duty arising in the course of any business or from the occupation of any premises used for business purposes of the occupier, that term [or provision]—

> (a) shall be void in any case where such exclusion or restriction is in respect of death or personal injury;
>
> (b) shall, in any other case, have no effect if it was not fair and reasonable to incorporate the term in the contract [or, as the case may be, if it is not fair and reasonable to allow reliance on the provision].

[(1A) Nothing in paragraph (b) of subsection (1) above shall be taken as implying that a provision of a notice has effect in circumstances where, apart from that paragraph, it would not have effect.]

(2) Subsection (1)(a) above does not affect the validity of any discharge and indemnity given by a person, on or in connection with an award to him of compensation for pneumoconiosis attributable to employment in the coal industry, in respect of any further claim arising from his contracting that disease.

(3) Where under subsection (1) above a term of a contract [or a provision of a notice] is void or has no effect, the fact that a person agreed to, or was aware of, the term [or provision] shall not of itself be sufficient evidence that he knowingly and voluntarily assumed any risk.

17 Control of unreasonable exemptions in consumer or standard form contracts

(1) Any term of a contract which is a consumer contract or a standard form contract shall have no effect for the purpose of enabling a party to the contract—

> (a) who is in breach of a contractual obligation, to exclude or restrict any liability of his to the consumer or customer in respect of the breach;
>
> (b) in respect of a contractual obligation, to render no performance, or to render a performance substantially different from that which the consumer or customer reasonably expected from the contract;

if it was not fair and reasonable to incorporate the term in the contract.

(2) In this section 'customer' means a party to a standard form contract who deals on the basis of written standard terms of business of the other party to the contract who himself deals in the course of a business.

18 Unreasonable indemnity clauses in consumer contracts

(1) Any term of a contract which is a consumer contract shall have no effect for the purpose of making the consumer indemnify another person (whether a party to the contract or not) in respect of liability which that other person may incur as a result of breach of duty or breach of contract, if it was not fair and reasonable to incorporate the term in the contract.

(2) In this section 'liability' means liability arising in the course of any business or from the occupation of any premises used for business purposes of the occupier.

19 'Guarantee' of consumer goods

(1) This section applies to a guarantee—

    (a) in relation to goods which are of a type ordinarily supplied for private use or consumption; and

    (b) which is not a guarantee given by one party to the other party to a contract under or in pursuance of which the ownership or possession of the goods to which the guarantee relates is transferred.

(2) A term of a guarantee to which this section applies shall be void in so far as it purports to exclude or restrict liability for loss or damage (including death or personal injury)—

    (a) arising from the goods proving defective while—

        (i) in use otherwise than exclusively for the purposes of a business; or

        (ii) in the possession of a person for such use; and

    (b) resulting from the breach of duty of a person concerned in the manufacture or distribution of the goods.

(3) For the purposes of this section, any document is a guarantee if it contains or purports to contain some promise or assurance (however worded or presented) that defects will be made good by complete or partial replacement, or by repair, monetary compensation or otherwise.

20 Obligations implied by law in sale and hire-purchase contracts

(1) Any term of a contract which purports to exclude or restrict liability for breach of the obligations arising from—

    (a) section 12 of the Sale of Goods Act [1979] (seller's implied undertakings as to title etc.);

    (b) section 8 of the Supply of Goods (Implied Terms) Act 1973 (implied terms as to title in hire-purchase agreements),

shall be void.

(2) Any term of a contract which purports to exclude or restrict liability for breach of the obligations arising from—

    (a) section 13, 14 or 15 of the said Act of [1979] (seller's implied undertakings as to conformity of goods with description or sample, or as to their quality or fitness for a particular purpose);

    (b) section 9, 10 or 11 of the said Act of 1973 (the corresponding provisions in relation to hire-purchase),

shall—

    (i) in the case of a consumer contract, be void against the consumer;

    (ii) in any other case, have no effect if it was not fair and reasonable to incorporate the term in the contract.

21 Obligations implied by law in other contracts for the supply of goods

(1) Any term of a contract to which this section applies purporting to exclude or restrict liability for breach of an obligation—

    (a) such as is referred to in subsection (3)(a) below—

        (i) in the case of a consumer contract, shall be void against the consumer, and

        (ii) in any other case, shall have no effect if it was not fair and reasonable to incorporate the term in the contract;

    (b) such as is referred to in subsection (3)(b) below, shall have no effect if it was not fair and reasonable to incorporate the term in the contract.

(2) This section applies to any contract to the extent that it relates to any such matter as is referred to in section 15(2)(a) of this Act, but does not apply to—

    (a) a contract of sale of goods or a hire-purchase agreement; or

    (b) a charterparty of a ship or hovercraft unless it is a consumer contract (and then only in favour of the consumer).

(3) An obligation referred to in this subsection is an obligation incurred under a contract in the course of a business and arising by implication of law from the nature of the contract which relates—

> (a) to the correspondence of goods with description or sample, or to the quality or fitness of goods for any particular purpose; or
>
> (b) to any right to transfer ownership or possession of goods, or to the enjoyment of quiet possession of goods.

[(3A) Notwithstanding anything in the foregoing provisions of this section, any term of a contract which purports to exclude or restrict liability for breach of the obligations arising under section 11B of the Supply of Goods and Services Act 1982 (implied terms about title, freedom from encumbrances and quiet possession in certain contracts for the transfer of property in goods) shall be void.]

(4) Nothing in this section applies to the supply of goods on a redemption of trading stamps within the Trading Stamps Act 1964.

22 Consequence of breach

For the avoidance of doubt, where any provision of this Part of this Act requires that the incorporation of a term in a contract must be fair and reasonable for that term to have effect—

> (a) if that requirement is satisfied, the term may be given effect to notwithstanding that the contract has been terminated in consequence of breach of that contract;
>
> (b) for the term to be given effect to, that requirement must be satisfied even where a party who is entitled to rescind the contract elects not to rescind it.

23 Evasion by means of secondary contract

Any term of any contract shall be void which purports to exclude or restrict, or has the effect of excluding or restricting—

> (a) the exercise, by a party to any other contract, of any right or remedy which arises in respect of that other contract in consequence of breach of duty, or of obligation, liability for which could not by virtue of the provisions of this Part of this Act be excluded or restricted by a term of that other contract;
>
> (b) the application of the provisions of this Part of this Act in respect of that or any other contract.

24 The 'reasonableness' test

(1) In determining for the purposes of this Part of this Act whether it was fair and reasonable to incorporate a term in a contract, regard shall be had only to the circumstances which were, or ought reasonably to have been, known to or in the contemplation of the parties to the contract at the time the contract was made.

(2) In determining for the purposes of section 20 or 21 of this Act whether it was fair and reasonable to incorporate a term in a contract, regard shall be had in particular to the matters specified in Schedule 2 to this Act; but this sub-section shall not prevent a court or arbiter from holding in accordance with any rule of law, that a term which purports to exclude or restrict any relevant liability is not a term of the contract.

[(2A) In determining for the purposes of this Part of this Act whether it is fair and reasonable to allow reliance on a provision of a notice (not being a notice having contractual effect), regard shall be had to all the circumstances obtaining when the liability arose or (but for the provision) would have arisen.]

(3) Where a term in a contract [or a provision of a notice] purports to restrict liability to a specified sum of money, and the question arises for the purposes of this Part of this Act whether it was fair and reasonable to incorporate the term in the contract [or whether it is fair and reasonable to allow reliance on the provision], then, without prejudice to subsection (2) above [in the case of a term in a contract], regard shall be had in particular to—

> (a) the resources which the party seeking to rely on that term [or provision] could expect to be available to him for the purpose of meeting the liability should it arise;

(b) how far it was open to that party to cover himself by insurance.

(4) The onus of proving that it was fair and reasonable to incorporate a term in a contract [or that it is fair and reasonable to allow reliance on a provision of a notice] shall lie on the party so contending.

25 Interpretation of Part II

(1) In this Part of this Act—

'breach of duty' means the breach—

(a) of any obligation, arising from the express or implied terms of a contract, to take reasonable care or exercise reasonable skill in the performance of the contract;

(b) of any common law duty to take reasonable care or exercise reasonable skill;

(c) of the duty of reasonable care imposed by section 2(1) of the Occupiers' Liability (Scotland) Act 1960;

'business' includes a profession and the activities of any government department or local or public authority;

'consumer' has the meaning assigned to that expression in the definition in this section of 'consumer contract';

'consumer contract' means [subject to subsections (1A) and (1B) below] a contract [. . .] in which—

(a) one party to the contract deals, and the other party to the contract ('the consumer') does not deal or hold himself out as dealing, in the course of a business, and

(b) in the case of a contract such as is mentioned in section 15(2)(a) of this Act, the goods are of a type ordinarily supplied for private use or consumption; and for the purposes of this Part of this Act the onus of proving that a contract is not to be regarded as a consumer contract shall lie on the party so contending; 'goods' has the same meaning as in the Sale of Goods Act [1979];

'hire-purchase agreement' has the same meaning as in section 189(1) of the Consumer Credit Act 1974;

['notice' includes an announcement, whether or not in writing, and any other communication or pretended communication;]

'personal injury' includes any disease and any impairment of physical or mental condition.

[(1A) Where the consumer is an individual, paragraph (b) in the definition of 'consumer contract' in subsection (1) must be disregarded.

(1B) The expression of 'consumer contract' does not include a contract in which—

(a) the buyer is an individual and the goods are second hand goods sold by public auction at which individuals have the opportunity of attending in person; or

(b) the buyer is not an individual and the goods are sold by auction or competitive tender.][1]

(2) In relation to any breach of duty or obligation, it is immaterial for any purpose of this Part of this Act whether the act or omission giving rise to that breach was inadvertent or intentional or whether liability for it arises directly or vicariously.

(3) In this Part of this Act, any reference to excluding or restricting any liability includes—

(a) making the liability or its enforcement subject to any restrictive or onerous conditions;

(b) excluding or restricting any right or remedy in respect of the liability, or subjecting a person to any prejudice in consequence of his pursuing any such right or remedy;

(c) excluding or restricting any rule of evidence or procedure;

[. . .]

(5) In section 15 and 16 and 19 to 21 of this Act, any reference to excluding or restricting liability for breach of any obligation or duty shall include a reference to excluding or restricting the obligation or duty itself.

PART III

26 International supply contracts

(1) The limits imposed by this Act on the extent to which a person may exclude or restrict liability by reference to a contract term do not apply to liability arising under such a contract as is described in subsection (3) below.

(2) The terms of such a contract are not subject to any requirement of reason-ableness under section 3 or 4: and nothing in Part II of this Act should require the incorporation of the terms of such a contract to be fair and reasonable for them to have effect.

(3) Subject to subsection (4), that description of contract is one whose characteristics are the following—

  (a) either it is a contract of sale of goods or it is one under or in pursuance of which the possession of ownership of goods passes, and

  (b) it is made by parties whose places of business (or, if they have none, habitual residences) are in the territories of different States (the Channel Islands and the Isle of Man being treated for this purpose as different States from the United Kingdom).

(4) A contract falls within subsection (3) above only if either—

  (a) the goods in question are, at the time of the conclusion of the contract, in the course of carriage, or will be carried, from the territory of one State to the territory of another; or

  (b) the acts constituting the offer and acceptance have been done in the territories of different States; or

  (c) the contract provides for the goods to be delivered to the territory of a state other than that within whose territory those acts were done.

27 Choice of law clauses

(1) Where the [law applicable to] a contract is the law of any part of the United Kingdom only by choice of the parties (and apart from that choice would be the law of some country outside the United Kingdom) sections 2 to 7 and 16 to 21 of this Act do not operate as part [of the law applicable to the contract].

(2) This Act has effect notwithstanding any contract term which applies or purports to apply the law of some country outside the United Kingdom, where (either or both)—

  (a) the term appears to the court, or arbitrator or arbiter to have been imposed wholly or mainly for the purpose of enabling the party imposing it to evade the operation of this Act; or

  (b) in the making of the contract one of the parties dealt as consumer, and he was then habitually resident in the United Kingdom, and the essential steps necessary for the making of the contract were taken there, whether by him or by others on his behalf.

28 ...

29 Saving for other relevant legislation

(1) Nothing in this Act removes or restricts the effect of, or prevents reliance upon, any contractual provision which—

  (a) is authorised or required by the express terms or necessary implication of an enactment; or

  (b) being made with a view to compliance with an international agreement to which the United Kingdom is a party, does not operate more restrictively than is contemplated by the agreement.

(2) A contract terms is to be taken—

  (a) for the purposes of Part I of this Act, as satisfying the requirement of reason-ableness . . .

if it is incorporated or approved by, or incorporated pursuant to a decision or ruling of, a competent authority acting in the exercise of any statutory jurisdiction or function and is not a term in a contract to which the competent authority is itself a party.

(3) In this section—

'competent authority' means any court, arbitrator or arbiter, government department or public authority;

'enactment' means any legislation (including subordinate legislation) of the United Kingdom or Northern Ireland and any instrument having effect by virtue of such legislation; and

'statutory' means conferred by an enactment.

SCHEDULES

Section 1(2)   SCHEDULE 1

SCOPE OF SECTIONS 2 TO 4 AND 7

1. Sections 2 to 4 of this Act do not extend to—
    (a) any contract of insurance (including a contract to pay an annuity on human life);
    (b) any contract so far as it relates to the creation or transfer of an interest in land, or to the termination of such an interest, whether by extinction, merger, surrender, forfeiture or otherwise;
    (c) any contract so far as it relates to the creation or transfer of a right or interest in any patent, trade mark, copyright, registered design, technical or commercial information or other intellectual property, or relates to the termination of any such right or interest;
    (d) any contract so far as it relates—
        (i) to the formation or dissolution of a company (which means any body corporate or unincorporated association and includes a partnership), or
        (ii) to its constitution or the rights or obligations of its corporators or members;
    (e) any contract so far as it relates to the creation or transfer of securities or of any right or interest in securities.
2. Section 2(1) extends to—
    (a) any contract of marine salvage or towage;
    (b) any charterparty of a ship or hovercraft; and
    (c) any contract for the carriage of goods by ship or hovercraft;
but subject to this sections 2 to 4 and 7 do not extend to any such contract except in favour of a person dealing as a consumer.
3. Where goods are carried by ship or hovercraft in pursuance of a contract which either—
    (a) specifies that as the means of carriage over part of the journey to be covered, or
    (b) makes no provision as to the means of carriage and does not exclude that means, then sections 2(2), 3 and 4 do not, except in favour of a person dealing as consumer, extend to the contract as it operates for and in relation to the carriage of the goods by that means.
4. Section 2(1) and (2) do not extend to a contract of employment, except in favour of the employee.
5. Section 2(1) does not affect the validity of any discharge and indemnity given by a person, on or in connection with an award to him of compensation for pneumoconiosis attributable to employment in the coal industry, in respect of any further claim arising from his contracting the disease.

Sections 11(2) and 24(2)   SCHEDULE 2

'GUIDELINES' FOR APPLICATION OF REASONABLENESS TEST

The matters to which regard is to be had in particular for the purposes of sections 6(3), 7(3) and (4), 20 and 21 are any of the following which appear to be relevant—

(a) the strength of the bargaining positions of the parties relative to each other, taking into account (among other things) alternative means by which the customer's requirements could have been met;

(b) whether the customer received an inducement to agree to the term, or in accepting it had an opportunity of entering into a similar contract with other persons, but without having to accept a similar term;

(c) whether the customer knew or ought reasonably to have known of the existence and extent of the term (having regard, among other things, to any custom of the trade and any previous course of dealing between the parties);

(d) where the term excludes or restricts any relevant liability if some condition is not complied with, whether it was reasonable at the time of the contract to expect that compliance with that condition would be practicable;

(e) whether the goods were manufactured, processed or adapted to the special order of the customer.

Civil Liability (Contribution) Act 1978
(1978, c. 47)

An Act to make new provision for contribution between persons who are jointly or severally, or both jointly and severally, liable for the same damage and in certain other similar cases where two or more persons have paid or may be required to pay compensation for the same damage; and to amend the law relating to proceedings against persons jointly liable for the same debt or jointly or severally, or both jointly or severally, liable for the same damage.   [31st July 1978]

1 Entitlement to contribution

(1) Subject to the following provisions of this section, any person liable in respect of any damage suffered by another person may recover contribution from any other person liable in respect of the same damage (whether jointly with him or otherwise).

(2) A person shall be entitled to recover contribution by virtue of subsection (1) above notwithstanding that he has ceased to be liable in respect of the damage in question since the time when the damage occurred, provided that he was so liable immediately before he made or was ordered or agreed to make the payment in respect of which the contribution is sought.

(3) A person shall be liable to make contribution by virtue of subsection (1) above notwithstanding that he has ceased to be liable in respect of the damage in question since the time when the damage occurred, unless he ceased to be liable by virtue of the expiry of a period of limitation or prescription which extinguished the right on which the claim against him in respect of the damage was based.

(4) A person who has made or agreed to make any payment in bona fide settlement or compromise of any claim made against him in respect of any damage (including a payment into court which as been accepted) shall be entitled to recover contribution in accordance with this section without regard to whether or not he himself is or ever was liable in respect of the damage, provided, however, that he would have been liable assuming that the factual basis of the claim against him could be established.

(5) A judgment given in any action brought in any part of the United Kingdom by or on behalf of the person who suffered the damage in question against any person from whom

contribution is sought under this section shall be conclusive in the proceedings for contribution as to any issue determined by that judgment in favour of the person from whom the contribution is sought.

(6) References in this section to a person's liability in respect of any damage are references to any such liability which has been or could be established in an action brought against him in England and Wales by or on behalf of the person who suffered the damage; but it is immaterial whether any issue arising in any such action was or would be determined (in accordance with the rules of private international law) by reference to the law of a country outside England and Wales.

2   Assessment of contribution

(1) Subject to subsection (3) below, in any proceedings for contribution under section 1 above the amount of the contribution recoverable from any person shall be such as may be found by the court to be just and equitable having regard to the extent of that person's responsibility for the damage in question.

(2) Subject to subsection (3) below, the court shall have power in any such proceedings to exempt any person from liability to make contribution or to direct that the contribution to be recovered from any person shall amount to a complete indemnity.

(3) Where the amount of the damages which have or might have been awarded in respect of the damage in question in any action brought in England and Wales by or on behalf of the person who suffered it against the person from whom the contribution is sought was or would have been subject to—

(a) any limit imposed by or under any enactment or by any agreement made before the damage occurred;

(b) any reduction by virtue of section 1 of the Law Reform (Contributory Negligence) Act 1945 or section 5 of the Fatal Accidents Act 1976; or

(c) any corresponding limit or reduction under the law of a country outside England and Wales;

the person from whom the contribution is sought shall not by virtue of any contribution awarded under section 1 above be required to pay in respect of the damage a greater amount than the amount of those damages as so limited or reduced.

3   Proceedings against persons jointly liable for the same debt or damage

Judgment recovered against any person liable in respect of any debt or damage shall not be a bar to an action, or to the continuance of an action, against any person who is (apart from any such bar) jointly liable with him in respect of the same debt or damage.

4   Successive actions against persons liable (jointly or otherwise) for the same damage

If more than one action is bought in respect of any damage by or on behalf of the person by whom it was suffered against persons liable in respect of the damage (whether jointly or otherwise) the plaintiff shall not be entitled to costs in any of those actions, other than that in which judgment is first given, unless the court is of the opinion that there was reasonable ground for bringing the action.

5   Application to the Crown

Without prejudice to section 4(1) of the Crown Proceedings Act 1947 (indemnity and contribution), this Act shall bind the Crown, but nothing in this Act shall be construed as in any way affecting Her Majesty in Her private capacity (including in right of Her Duchy of Lancaster) or the Duchy of Cornwall.

6   Interpretation

(1) A person is liable in respect of any damage for the purposes of this Act if the person who suffered it (or anyone representing his estate or dependants) is entitled to recover

compensation from him in respect of that damage (whatever the legal basis of his liability, whether tort, breach of contract, breach of trust or otherwise).

(2) References in this Act to an action brought by or on behalf of the person who suffered any damage include references to an action brought for the benefit of his estate or dependents.

(3) In this Act 'dependants' has the same meaning as in the Fatal Accidents Act 1976.

(4) In this Act, except in section 1(5) above, 'action' means an action brought in England and Wales.

7 Savings

. . .

(3) The right to recover contribution in accordance with section 1 above supersedes any right, other than an express contractual right, to recover contribution (as distinct from indemnity) otherwise than under this Act in corresponding circumstances; but nothing in this Act shall affect—

(a) any express or implied contractual or other right to indemnity; or

(b) any express contractual provision regulating or excluding contribution; which would be enforceable apart from this Act (or render enforceable any agreement for indemnity or contribution which would not be enforceable apart from this Act).

Sale of Goods Act 1979
(1979, c. 54)

An Act to consolidate the law relating to the sale of goods.   [6th December 1979]

PART I   CONTRACTS TO WHICH ACT APPLIES

1 Contracts to which Act applies

(1) This Act applies to contracts of sale of goods made on or after (but not to those made before) 1 January 1894.

(2) In relation to contracts made on certain dates, this Act applies subject to the modification of certain of its sections as mentioned in Schedule 1 below.

(3) Any such modification is indicated in the section concerned by a reference to Schedule 1 below.

(4) Accordingly, where a section does not contain such a reference, this Act applies in relation to the contract concerned without such modification of the section.

PART II   FORMATION OF THE CONTRACT

Contract of sale

2 Contract of sale

(1) A contract of sale of goods is a contract by which the seller transfers or agrees to transfer the property in goods to the buyer for a money consideration, called the price.

(2) There may a contract of sale between one part owner and another.

(3) A contract of sale may be absolute or conditional.

(4) Where under a contract of sale the property in the goods is transferred from the seller to the buyer the contact is called a sale.

(5) Where under a contract of sale the transfer of the property in the goods is to take place at a future time or subject to some condition later to be fulfilled the contract is called an agreement to sell.

(6) An agreement to sell becomes a sale when the time elapses or the conditions are fulfilled subject to which the property in the goods is to be transferred.

3 Capacity to buy and sell

(1) Capacity to buy and sell is regulated by the general law concerning capacity to contract and to transfer and acquire property.

(2) Where necessaries are sold and delivered [to a minor][1] or to a person who by reason of [mental incapacity or][2] drunkenness is incompetent to contract, he must pay a reasonable price for them.

(3) In subsection (2) above 'necessaries' means goods suitable to the condition in life of the [minor or other][1] person concerned and to his actual requirements at the time of the sale and delivery.

[*1. The words 'to a minor or' in s. 3(2) and 'minor or other' in s. 3(3) were repealed, for Scotland only, by the Age of Legal Capacity (Scotland) Act 1991, s. 10, Sched. 2.*]

[*2. The words 'mental capacity or' no long have effect in England and Wales: Mental Capacity Act 2005, s 67(1), Sched 6, para 24.*]

Formalities of contract

4 How contract of sale is made

(1) Subject to this and any other Act, a contract of sale may be made in writing (either with or without seal), or by word of mouth, or partly in writing and partly by word of mouth, or may be implied from the conduct of the parties.

(2) Nothing in this section affects the law relating to corporations.

Subject matter of contract

5 Existing or future goods

(1) The goods which form the subject of a contract of sale may be either existing goods, owned or possessed by the seller, or goods to be manufactured or acquired by him after the making of the contract of sale, in this Act called future goods.

(2) There may be a contract for the sale of goods the acquisition of which by the seller depends on a contingency which may or may not happen.

(3) Where by a contract of sale the seller purports to effect a present sale of future goods, the contract operates as an agreement to sell the goods.

6 Goods which have perished

Where there is a contract for the sale of specific goods, and the goods without the knowledge of the seller have perished at the time when a contract is made, the contract is void.

7 Goods perishing before sale but after agreement to sell

Where there is an agreement to sell specific goods and subsequently the goods, without any fault on the part of the seller or buyer, perish before the risk passes to the buyer, the agreement is avoided.

The price

8 Ascertainment of price

(1) The price in a contract of sale may be fixed by the contract, or may be left to be fixed in a manner agreed by the contract, or may be determined by the course of dealing between the parties.

(2) Where the price is not determined as mentioned in subsection (1) above the buyer must pay a reasonable price.

(3) What is a reasonable price is a question of fact dependent on the circumstances of each particular case.

9   Agreement to sell at valuation

(1) Where there is an agreement to sell goods on the terms that the price is to be fixed by the valuation of a third party, and he cannot or does not make the valuation, the agreement is avoided; but if the goods or any part of them have been delivered to and appropriated by the buyer he must pay a reasonable price for them.

(2) Where the third party is prevented from making the valuation by the fault of the seller or buyer, the party not at fault may maintain an action for damages against the party at fault.

[Implied terms etc.]

10   Stipulations about time

(1) Unless a different intention appears from the terms of the contract, stipulations as to time of payment are not of the essence of a contract of sale.

(2) Whether any other stipulation as to time is or is not of the essence of the contract depends on the terms of the contract.

(3) In a contract of sale 'month' prima facie means calendar month.

11   When condition to be treated as warranty

[(1) This section does not apply to Scotland.]

(2) Where a contract of sale is subject to a condition to be fulfilled by the seller, the buyer may waive the condition, or may elect to treat the breach of the condition as a breach of warranty and not as a ground for treating the contract as repudiated.

(3) Whether a stipulation in a contract of sale is a condition, the breach of which may give rise to a right to treat the contract as repudiated, or a warranty, the breach of which may give rise to a claim for damages but not to a right to reject the goods and treat the contract as repudiated, depends in each case on the construction of the contract; and a stipulation may be a condition, though called a warranty in the contract.

(4) [Subject to section 35A below] Where a contract of sale is not severable and the buyer has accepted the goods or part of them, the breach of a condition to be fulfilled by the seller can only be treated as a breach of warranty, and not as a ground for rejecting the goods and treating the contract as repudiated, unless there is an express or implied term of the contract to that effect.

(6) Nothing in this section affects a condition or warranty whose fulfilment is excused by law by reason of impossibility or otherwise.

(7) Paragraph 2 of Schedule 1 below applies in relation to a contract made before 22 April 1967 or (in the application of this Act to Northern Ireland) 28 July 1967.

12   Implied terms about title, etc.

(1) In a contract of sale, other than one to which subsection (3) below applies, there is an implied [term] on the part of the seller that in the case of a sale he has a right to sell the goods, and in the case of an agreement to sell he will have such a right at the time when the property is to pass.

(2) In a contract of sale, other than one to which subsection (3) below applies, there is also an implied [term] that—

    (a) the goods are free, and will remain free until the time when the property is to pass, from any charge or encumbrance not disclosed or known to the buyer before the contract is made, and

    (b) the buyer will enjoy quiet possession of the goods except so far as it may be disturbed by the owner or other person entitled to the benefit of any charge or encumbrance so disclosed or known.

(3) This subsection applies to a contract of sale in the case of which there appears from the contract or is to be inferred from its circumstances an intention that the seller should transfer only such title as he or a third person may have.

(4) In a contract to which subsection (3) above applies there is an implied [term] that all charges or encumbrances known to the seller and not known to the buyer have been disclosed to the buyer before the contract is made.

(5) In a contract to which subsection (3) above applies there is also an implied [term] that none of the following will disturb the buyer's quiet possession of the goods, namely—

   (a) the seller;

   (b) in a case where the parties to the contract intend that the seller should transfer only such title as a third person may have, that person;

   (c) anyone claiming through or under the seller or that third person otherwise than under a charge or encumbrance disclosed or known to the buyer before the contract is made.

[(5A) As regards England and Wales and Northern Ireland, the term implied by subsection (1) above is a condition and the terms implied by subsections (2), (4) and (5) above are warranties.]

(6) Paragraph 3 of Schedule 1 below applies in relation to a contract made before 18 May 1973.

13 Sale by description

(1) Where there is a contract for the sale of goods by description, there is an implied [term] that the goods will correspond with the description.

[(1A) As regards England and Wales and Northern Ireland, the term implied by subsection (1) above is a condition.]

(2) If the sale is by sample as well as by description it is not sufficient that the bulk of the goods corresponds with the sample if the goods do not also correspond with the description.

(3) A sale of goods is not prevented from being a sale by description by reason only that, being exposed for sale or hire, they are selected by the buyer.

(4) Paragraph 4 of Schedule 1 below applies in relation to a contract made before 18 May 1973.

14 Implied terms about quality or fitness

(1) Except as provided by this section and section 15 below and subject to any other enactment, there is no implied [term] about the quality or fitness for any particular purpose of goods supplied under a contract of sale.

[(2) Where the seller sells goods in the course of a business, there is an implied term that the goods supplied under the contract are of satisfactory quality.

(2A) For the purposes of this Act, goods are of satisfactory quality if they meet the standard that a reasonable person would regard as satisfactory, taking account of any description of the goods, the price (if relevant) and all the other relevant circumstances.

(2B) For the purposes of this Act, the quality of goods includes their state and condition and the following (among others) are in appropriate cases aspects of the quality of goods—

   (a) fitness for all the purposes for which goods of the kind in question are commonly supplied,

   (b) appearance and finish,

   (c) freedom from minor defects,

   (d) safety, and

   (e) durability.

(2C) The term implied by subsection (2) above does not extend to any matter making the quality of goods unsatisfactory—

   (a) which is specifically drawn to the buyer's attention before the contract is made,

   (b) where the buyer examines the goods before the contract is made, which that examination ought to reveal, or

   (c) in the case of a contract for sale by sample, which would have been apparent on a reasonable examination of the sample.]

[(2D) If the buyer deals as consumer or, in Scotland, if a contract of sale is a consumer contract, the relevant circumstances mentioned in subsection (2A) above include any public statements on the specific characteristics of the goods made about them by the seller, the producer or his representative, particularly in advertising or on labelling.

(2E) A public statement is not by virtue of subsection (2D) above a relevant circumstance for the purposes of subsection (2A) above in the case of a contract of sale, if the seller shows that—

(a) at the time the contract was made, he was not, and could not reasonably have been aware of the statement,

(b) before the contract was made, the statement had been withdrawn in public or, to the extent that it contained anything which was incorrect or misleading, it had been corrected in public, or

(c) the decision to buy the goods could not have been influenced by the statement.

(2F) Subsections (2D) and (2E) above do not prevent any public statement from being a relevant circumstance for the purposes of subsection (2A) above (whether or not the buyer deals as consumer or, in Scotland, whether or not the contract of sale is a consumer contract) if the statement would have been such a circumstance apart from those subsections.]

(3) Where the seller sells goods in the course of a business and the buyer, expressly or by implication, makes known—

(a) to the seller, or

(b) where the purchase price of part of it is payable by instalments and the goods were previously sold by a credit-broker to the seller, to that credit-broker,

any particular purpose for which the goods are being bought, there is an implied [term] that the goods supplied under the contract are reasonably fit for that purpose, whether or not that is a purpose for which such goods are commonly supplied, except where the circumstances show that the buyer does not rely, or that it is unreasonable for him to rely, on the skill or judgment of the seller or credit-broker.

(4) An implied [term] about quality or fitness for a particular purpose may be annexed to a contract of sale by usage.

(5) The preceding provisions of this section apply to a sale by a person who in the course of a business is acting as agent for another as they apply to a sale by a principal in the course of a business, except where that other is not selling in the course of a business and either the buyer knows that fact or reasonable steps are taken to bring it to the notice of the buyer before the contract is made.

[(6) As regards England and Wales and Northern Ireland, the terms implied by subsections (2) and (3) above are conditions.]

(7) Paragraph 5 of Schedule 1 below applies in relation to a contract made on or after 18 May 1973 and before the appointed day, and paragraph 6 in relation to one made before 18 May 1973.

(8) In subsection (7) above and paragraph 5 of Schedule 1 below references to the appointed day are to the day appointed for the purposes of those provisions by an order of the Secretary of State made by statutory instrument.

Sale by sample

15 Sale by sample

(1) A contract of sale is a contract for sale by sample where there is an express or implied term to that effect in the contract.

(2) In the case of a contract for sale by sample there is an implied [term]—

(a) that the bulk will correspond with the sample in quality;

[...]

(c) that the goods will be free from any defect, making their quality unsatisfactory, which would not be apparent on reasonable examination of the sample.

[(3) As regards England and Wales and Northern Ireland, the term implied by subsection (2) above is a condition.]

(4) Paragraph 7 of Schedule 1 below applies in relation to a contract made before 18 May 1973.

Miscellaneous

[15A   Modification of remedies for breach of condition in non-consumer cases

(1) Where in the case of a contract of sale—

   (a) the buyer would, apart from this subsection, have the right to reject goods by reason of a breach on the part of the seller of a term implied by section 13, 14 or 15 above, but

   (b) the breach is so slight that it would be unreasonable for him to reject them, then, if the buyer does not deal as consumer, the breach is not to be treated as a breach of condition but may be treated as a breach of warranty.

(2) This section applies unless a contrary intention appears in, or is to be implied from, the contract.

(3) It is for the seller to show that a breach fell within subsection (1)(b) above.

(4) This section does not apply to Scotland.]

[15B   Remedies for breach of contract as respects Scotland

(1) Where in a contract of sale the seller is in breach of any term of the contract (express or implied), the buyer shall be entitled—

   (a) to claim damages, and

   (b) if the breach is material, to reject any goods delivered under the contract and treat it as repudiated.

(2) Where a contract of sale is a consumer contract, then, for the purposes of subsection (1)(b) above, breach by the seller of any term (express or implied)—

   (a) as to the quality of the goods or their fitness for a purpose,

   (b) if the goods are, or are to be, sold by description, that the goods will correspond with the description,

   (c) if the goods are, or are to be, sold by reference to a sample, that the bulk will correspond with the sample in quality,

shall be deemed to be a material breach.

(3) This section applies to Scotland only.]

PART III   EFFECTS OF THE CONTRACT

Transfer of property as between seller and buyer

16   Goods must be ascertained

[Subject to section 20A below] Where there is a contract for the sale of unascertained goods no property in the goods is transferred to the buyer unless and until the goods are ascertained.

17   Property passes when intended to pass

(1) Where there is a contract for the sale of specific or ascertained goods the property in them is transferred to the buyer at such time as the parties to the contract intend it to be transferred.

(2) For the purpose of ascertaining the intention of the parties regard shall be had to the terms of the contract, the conduct of the parties and the circumstances of the case.

18   Rules for ascertaining intention

Unless a different intention appears, the following are rules for ascertaining the intention of the parties as to the time at which the property in the goods is to pass to the buyer.

Rule 1.—Where there is an unconditional contract for the sale of specific goods in a deliverable state the property in the goods passes to the buyer when the contract is made, and it is immaterial whether the time of payment or the time of delivery, or both, be postponed.

Rule 2.—Where there is a contract for the sale of specific goods and the seller is bound to do something to the goods for the purpose of putting them into a deliverable state, the property does not pass until the thing is done and the buyer has notice that it has been done.

Rule 3.—Where there is a contract for the sale of specific goods in a deliverable state but the seller is bound to weigh, measure, test, or do some other act or thing with reference to the goods for the purpose of ascertaining the price, the property does not pass until the act or thing is done and the buyer has notice that it has been done.

Rule 4.—When goods are delivered to the buyer on approval or on sale or return or other similar terms the property in the goods passes to the buyer:—

(a) when he signifies his approval or acceptance to the seller or does any other act adopting the transaction;

(b) if he does not signify his approval or acceptance to the seller but retains the goods without giving notice of rejection, then, if a time has been fixed for the return of the goods, on the expiration of that time, and, if no time has been fixed, on the expiration of a reasonable time.

Rule 5.—(1) Where there is a contract for the sale of unascertained or future goods by description, and goods of that description and in a deliverable state are unconditionally appropriated to the contract, either by the seller with the assent of the buyer or by the buyer with the assent of the seller, the property in the goods then passes to the buyer; and the assent may be express or implied, and may be given either before of after the appropriation is made.

(2) Where, in pursuance of the contract, the seller delivers the goods to the buyer or to a carrier or other bailee or custodier (whether named by the buyer or not) for the purpose of transmission to the buyer, and does not reserve the right of disposal, he is to be taken to have unconditionally appropriated the goods to the contract.

[(3) Where there is a contract for the sale of a specified quantity of unascertained goods in a deliverable state forming part of a bulk which is identified either in the contract or by subsequent agreement between the parties and the bulk is reduced to (or to less than) that quantity, then, if the buyer under that contract is the only buyer to whom goods are then due out of the bulk—

(a) the remaining goods are to be taken as appropriated to that contract at the time when the bulk is so reduced; and

(b) the property in those goods then passes to that buyer.

(4) Paragraph (3) above applies also (with the necessary modifications) where a bulk is reduced to (or to less than) the aggregate of the quantities due to a single buyer under separate contracts relating to that bulk and he is the only buyer to whom goods are then due out of that bulk.]

19 Reservation of right of disposal

(1) Where there is a contract for the sale of specific goods or where goods are subsequently appropriated to the contract, the seller may, by the terms of the contract or appropriation, reserve the right of disposal of the goods until certain conditions are fulfilled; and in such a case, notwithstanding the delivery of the goods to the buyer, or to a carrier or other bailee or custodier for the purpose of transmission to the buyer, the property in the goods does not pass to the buyer until the conditions imposed by the seller are fulfilled.

(2) Where goods are shipped, and by the bill of lading the goods are deliverable to the order of the seller or his agent, the seller is prima facie to be taken to reserve the right of disposal.

(3) Where the seller of goods draws on the buyer for the price, and transmits the bill of exchange and bill of lading to the buyer together to secure acceptance or payment of the bill of exchange, the buyer is bound to return the bill of lading if he does not honour the bill of

exchange, and if he wrongfully retains the bill of lading the property in the goods does not pass to him.

20   [Passing of risk]

(1) Unless otherwise agreed, the goods remain at the seller's risk until the property in them is transferred to the buyer, but when the property in them is transferred to the buyer the goods are at the buyer's risk whether delivery has been made or not.

(2) But where delivery has been delayed through the fault of either buyer or seller the goods are at the risk of the party at fault as regards any loss which might not have occurred but for such fault.

(3) Nothing in this section affects the duties or liabilities of either seller or buyer as a bailee or custodier of the goods of the other party.

[(4) In a case where the buyer deals as consumer or, in Scotland, where there is a consumer contract in which the buyer is a consumer, subsections (1) to (3) above must be ignored and the goods remain at the seller's risk until they are delivered to the consumer.]

[20A   Undivided shares in goods forming part of a bulk

(1) This section applies to a contract for the sale of a specified quantity of unascertained goods if the following conditions are met—

(a) the goods or some of them form part of a bulk which is identified either in the contract or by subsequent agreement between the parties; and

(b) the buyer has paid the price for some or all of the goods which are the subject of the contract and which form part of the bulk.

(2) Where this section applies, then (unless the parties agree otherwise), as soon as the conditions specified in paragraphs (a) and (b) of subsection (1) above are met or at such later time as the parties may agree—

(a) property in an undivided share in the bulk is transferred to the buyer; and

(b) the buyer becomes an owner in common of the bulk.

(3) Subject to subsection (4) below, for the purposes of this section, the undivided share of a buyer in a bulk at any time shall be such share as the quantity of goods paid for and due to the buyer out of the bulk bears to the quantity of goods in the bulk at that time.

(4) Where the aggregate of the undivided shares of buyers in a bulk determined under subsection (3) above would at any time exceed the whole of the bulk at that time, the undivided share in the bulk of each buyer shall be reduced proportionately so that the aggregate of the undivided shares is equal to the whole bulk.

(5) Where a buyer has paid the price for only some of the goods due to him out of a bulk, any delivery to the buyer out of the bulk shall, for the purposes of this section, be ascribed in the first place to the goods in respect of which payment has been made.

(6) For the purpose of this section payment of part of the price for any goods shall be treated as payment for a corresponding part of the goods.]

[20B   Deemed consent by co-owner to dealings in bulk goods

(1) A person who has become an owner in common of a bulk by virtue of section 20A above shall be deemed to have consented to—

(a) any delivery of goods out of the bulk to any other owner in common of the bulk, being goods which are due to him under his contract;

(b) any removal, dealing with, delivery or disposal of goods in the bulk by any other person who is an owner in common of the bulk in so far as the goods fall within that co-owner's undivided share in the bulk at the time of the removal, dealing, delivery or disposal.

(2) No cause of action shall accrue to anyone against a person by reason of that person having acted in accordance with paragraph (a) or (b) of subsection (1) above in reliance on any consent deemed to have been given under that subsection.

(3) Nothing in this section or section 20A above shall—

    (a) impose an obligation on a buyer of goods out of a bulk to compensate any other buyer of goods out of that bulk for any shortfall in the goods received by that other buyer;

    (b) affects any contractual arrangement between buyers of goods out of a bulk for adjustments between themselves; or

    (c) affect the rights of any buyer under his contract.]

Transfer of title

21 Sale by person not the owner

(1) Subject to this Act, where goods are sold by a person who is not their owner, and who does not sell them under the authority or with the consent of the owner, the buyer acquires no better title to the goods than the seller had, unless the owner of the goods is by his conduct precluded from denying the seller's authority to sell.

(2) Nothing in this Act affects—

    (a) the provisions of the Factors Acts or any enactment enabling the apparent owner of goods to dispose of them as if he were their true owner;

    (b) the validity of any contract of sale under any special common law or statutory power of sale or under the order of a court of competent jurisdiction.

22 Market overt

[…]

(2) This section does not apply to Scotland.

(3) Paragraph 8 of Schedule 1 below applies in relation to a contract under which goods were sold before 1 January 1968 or (in the application of this Act to Northern Ireland) 29 August 1967.

23 Sale under voidable title

When the seller of goods has a voidable title to them, but his title has not been avoided at the time of the sale, the buyer acquires a good title to the goods, provided he buys them in good faith and without notice of the seller's defect of title.

24 Seller in possession after sale

Where a person having sold goods continues or is in possession of the goods, or of the documents of title to the goods, the delivery or transfer by that person, or by a mercantile agent acting for him, of the goods or documents of title under any sale, pledge, or other disposition thereof, to any person receiving the same in good faith and without notice of the previous sale, has the same effect as if the person making the delivery or transfer were expressly authorised by the owner of the goods to make the same.

25 Buyer in possession after sale

(1) Where a person having bought or agreed to buy goods obtains, with the consent of the seller, possession of the goods or the documents of title to the goods, the delivery or transfer by that person, or by a mercantile agent acting for him, of the goods or documents of title, under any sale, pledge, or other disposition thereof, to any person receiving the same in good faith and without notice of any lien or other right of the original seller in respect of the goods, has the same effect as if the person making the delivery or transfer were a mercantile agent in possession of the goods or documents of title with the consent of the owner.

(2) For the purposes of subsection (1) above—

    (a) the buyer under a conditional sale agreement is to be taken not to be a person who has bought or agreed to buy goods, and

    (b) 'conditional sale agreement' means an agreement for the sale of goods which is a consumer credit agreement within the meaning of the Consumer Credit Act 1974 under which the purchase price or part of it is payable by instalments, and the property in the goods is to remain in the seller (notwithstanding that the buyer is to be in possession of the goods) until such conditions as to the payment of instalments or otherwise as may be specified in the agreement are fulfilled.

(3) Paragraph 9 of Schedule 1 below applies in relation to a contract under which a person buys or agrees to buy goods and which is made before the appointed day.

(4) In subsection (3) above and paragraph 9 of Schedule 1 below references to the appointed day are to the day appointed for the purposes of those provisions by an order of the Secretary of State made by statutory instrument.

26 Supplementary to sections 24 and 25
In sections 24 and 25 above 'mercantile agent' means a mercantile agent having in the customary course of his business as such agent authority either—

  (a) to sell goods, or
  (b) to consign goods for the purpose of sale, or
  (c) (c) to buy goods, or
  (d) to raise money on the security of goods.

PART IV   PERFORMANCE OF THE CONTRACT

27 Duties of seller and buyer
It is the duty of the seller to deliver the goods, and of the buyer to accept and pay for them, in accordance with the terms of the contract of sale.

28 Payment and delivery are concurrent conditions
Unless otherwise agreed, delivery of the goods and payment of the price are concurrent conditions, that is to say, the seller must be ready and willing to give possession of the goods to the buyer in exchange for the price and the buyer must be ready and willing to pay the price in exchange for possession of the goods.

29 Rules about delivery
(1) Whether it is for the buyer to take possession of the goods or for the seller to send them to the buyer is a question depending in each case on the contract, express or implied, between the parties.

(2) Apart from any such contract, express or implied, the place of delivery is the seller's place of business if he has one, and if not, his residence; except that, if the contract is for the sale of specific goods, which to the knowledge of the parties when the contract is made are in some other place, then that place is the place of delivery.

(3) Where under the contract of sale the seller is bound to send the goods to the buyer, but no time for sending them is fixed, the seller is bound to send them within a reasonable time.

(4) Where the goods at the time of sale are in the possession of a third person, there is no delivery by seller to buyer unless and until the third person acknowledges to the buyer that he holds the goods on his behalf; but nothing in this section affects the operation of the issue or transfer of any document of title to goods.

(5) Demand or tender of delivery may be treated as ineffectual unless made at a reasonable hour; and what is a reasonable hour is a question of fact.

(6) Unless otherwise agreed, the expenses of and incidental to putting the goods into a deliverable state must be borne by the seller.

30 Delivery of wrong quantity
(1) Where the seller delivers to the buyer a quantity of goods less than he contracted to sell, the buyer may reject them, but if the buyer accepts the goods so delivered he must pay for them at the contract rate.

(2) Where the seller delivers to the buyer a quantity of goods larger than he contracted to sell, the buyer may accept the goods included in the contract and reject the rest, or he may reject the whole.

[(2A) A buyer who does not deal as consumer may not—

(a) where the seller delivers a quantity of goods less than he contracted to sell, reject the goods under subsection (1) above, or

(b) where the seller delivers a quantity of goods larger than he contracted to sell, reject the whole under subsection (2) above,

if the shortfall or, as the case may be, excess is so slight that it would be unreasonable for him to do so.

(2B) It is for the seller to show that a shortfall or excess fell within subsection (2A) above.

(2C) Subsections (2A) and (2B) above do not apply to Scotland. (2D) Where the seller delivers a quantity of goods—

(a) less than he contracted to sell, the buyer shall not be entitled to reject the goods under subsection (1) above,

(b) larger than he contracted to sell, the buyer shall not be entitled to reject the whole under subsection (2) above,

unless the shortfall or excess is material.

(2E) Subsection (2D) above applies to Scotland only.]

(3) Where the seller delivers to the buyer a quantity of goods larger than he contracted to sell and the buyer accepts the whole of the goods so delivered he must pay for them at the contract rate.

(5) This section is subject to any usage of trade, special agreement, or course of dealing between the parties.

31   Instalment deliveries

(1) Unless otherwise agreed, the buyer of goods is not bound to accept delivery of them by instalments.

(2) Where there is a contract for the sale of goods to be delivered by stated instalments, which are to be separately paid for, and the seller makes defective deliveries in respect of one or more instalments, or the buyer neglects or refuses to take delivery of or pay for one or more instalments, it is a question in each case depending on the terms of the contract and the circumstances of the case whether the breach of contract is a repudiation of the whole contract or whether it is a severable breach giving rise to a claim for compensation but not to a right to treat the whole contract as repudiated.

32   Delivery to carrier

(1) Where, in pursuance of a contract of sale, the seller is authorised or required to send the goods to the buyer, delivery of the goods to a carrier (whether named by the buyer or not) for the purpose of transmission to the buyer is prima facie deemed to be delivery of the goods to the buyer.

(2) Unless otherwise authorised by the buyer, the seller must make such contact with the carrier on behalf of the buyer as may be reasonable having regard to the nature of the goods and the other circumstances of the case; and if the seller omits to do so, and the goods are lost or damaged in course of transit, the buyer may decline to treat the delivery to the carrier as a delivery to himself or may hold the seller responsible in damages.

(3) Unless otherwise agreed, where goods are sent by the seller to the buyer by a route involving sea transit, under circumstances in which it is usual to insure, the seller must give such notice to the buyer as may enable him to insure them during their sea transit, and if the seller fails to do so, the goods are at his risk during such sea transit.

[(4) In a case where the buyer deals as consumer or, in Scotland where there is a consumer contract in which the buyer is a consumer, subsections (1) to (3) above must be ignored, but if in pursuance of a contract of sale the seller is authorised or required to send the goods to the buyer, delivery of the goods to the carrier is not delivery of the goods to the buyer.]

33 Risk where goods are delivered at distant place

Where the seller of goods agrees to deliver them at his own risk at a place other than that where they are when sold, the buyer must nevertheless (unless otherwise agreed) take any risk of deterioration in the goods necessarily incident to the course of transit.

34 Buyer's right of examining the goods

[Unless otherwise agreed, when the seller tenders delivery of goods to the buyer, he is bound on request to afford the buyer a reasonable opportunity of examining the goods for the purpose of ascertaining whether they are in conformity with the contract [and, in the case of a contract for sale by sample, of comparing the bulk with the sample.]

35 Acceptance

(1) The buyer is deemed to have accepted the goods [subject to subsection (2) below—
   (a) when he intimates to the seller that he has accepted them, or
   (b) when the goods have been delivered to him and he does any act in relation to them which is inconsistent with the ownership of the seller.

(2) Where goods are delivered to the buyer, and he has not previously examined them, he is not deemed to have accepted them under subsection (1) above until he has had a reasonable opportunity of examining them for the purpose—
   (a) of ascertaining whether they are in conformity with the contract, and
   (b) in the case of a contract for sale by sample, of comparing the bulk with the sample.

(3) Where the buyer deals as consumer or (in Scotland) the contract of sale is a consumer contract, the buyer cannot lose his right to rely on subsection (2) above by agreement, waiver or otherwise.

(4) The buyer is also deemed to have accepted the goods when after the lapse of a reasonable time he retains the goods without intimating to the seller that he has rejected them.

(5) The questions that are material in determining for the purposes of subsection (4) above whether a reasonable time has elapsed include whether the buyer has had a reasonable opportunity of examining the goods for the purpose mentioned in subsection (2) above.

(6) The buyer is not by virtue of this section deemed to have accepted the goods merely because—
   (a) he asks for, or agrees to, their repair by or under an arrangement with the seller, or
   (b) the goods are delivered to another under a sub-sale or other disposition.

(7) Where the contract is for the sale of goods making one or more commercial units, a buyer accepting any goods included in a unit is deemed to have accepted all the goods making the unit; and in this subsection 'commercial unit' means a unit division of which would materially impair the value of the goods or the character of the unit.

(8)] Paragraph 10 of Schedule 1 below applies in relation to a contract made before 22 April 1967 or (in the application of this Act to Northern Ireland) 28 July 1967.

[35A Right of partial rejection

(1) If the buyer—
   (a) has the right to reject the goods by reason of a breach on the part of the seller that affects some or all of them, but
   (b) accepts some of the goods, including, where there are any goods unaffected by the breach, all such goods,
he does not by accepting them lose his right to reject the rest.

(2) In the case of a buyer having the right to reject an instalment of goods, subsection (1) above applies as if references to the goods were references to the goods comprised in the instalment.

(3) For the purposes of subsection (1) above, goods are affected by a breach if by reason of the breach they are not in conformity with the contract.

(4) This section applies unless a contrary intention appears in, or is to be implied from, the contract.]

36 Buyer not bound to return rejected goods
Unless otherwise agreed, where goods are delivered to the buyer, and he refuses to accept them, having the right to do so, he is not bound to return them to the seller, but it is sufficient if he intimates to the seller that he refuses to accept them.

37 Buyer's liability for not taking delivery of goods
(1) When the seller is ready and willing to deliver the goods, and requests the buyer to take delivery, and the buyer does not within a reasonable time after such request take delivery of the goods, he is liable to the seller for any loss occasioned by his neglect or refusal to take delivery, and also for a reasonable charge for the care and custody of the goods.

(2) Nothing in this section affects the rights of the seller where the neglect or refusal of the buyer to take delivery amounts to a repudiation of the contract.

PART V   RIGHTS OF UNPAID SELLER AGAINST THE GOODS

Preliminary

38 Unpaid seller defined
(1) The seller of goods is an unpaid seller within the meaning of this Act—
  (a) when the whole of the price has not been paid or tendered;
  (b) when a bill of exchange or other negotiable instrument has been received as conditional payment, and the condition on which it was received has not been fulfilled by reason of the dishonour of the instrument or otherwise.

(2) In this Part of this Act 'seller' includes any person who is in the position of a seller, as, for instance, an agent of the seller to whom the bill of lading has been indorsed, or a consignor or agent who has himself paid (or is directly responsible for) the price.

39 Unpaid seller's rights
(1) Subject to this and any other Act, notwithstanding that the property in the goods may have passed to the buyer, the unpaid seller of goods, as such, has by implication of law—
  (a) a lien on the goods or right to retain them for the price while he is in possession of them;
  (b) in the case of the insolvency of the buyer, a right of stopping the goods in transit after he has parted with the possession of them;
  (c) a right of re-sale as limited by this Act.

(2) Where the property in goods has not passed to the buyer, the unpaid seller has (in addition to his other remedies) a right of withholding delivery similar to and coextensive with his rights of lien or retention and stoppage in transit where the property has passed to the buyer.

Unpaid seller's lien

41 Seller's lien
(1) Subject to this Act, the unpaid seller of goods who is in possession of them is entitled to retain possession of them until payment or tender of the price in the following cases:—
  (a) where the goods have been sold without any stipulation as to credit;
  (b) where the goods have been sold on credit but the term of credit has expired;
  (c) where the buyer becomes insolvent.

(2) The seller may exercise his lien or right of retention notwithstanding that he is in possession of the goods as agent or bailee or custodier for the buyer.

42 Part delivery
Where an unpaid seller has made part delivery of the goods, he may exercise his lien or right of retention on the remainder, unless such part delivery has been made under such circumstances as to show an agreement to waive the lien or right of retention.

43 Termination of lien

(1) The unpaid seller of goods loses his lien or right of retention in respect of them—

(a) when he delivers the goods to a carrier or other bailee or custodier for the purpose of transmission to the buyer without reserving the right of disposal of the goods;

(b) when the buyer or his agent lawfully obtains possession of the goods;

(c) by waiver of the lien or right of retention.

(2) An unpaid seller of goods who has a lien or right of retention in respect of them does not lose his lien or right of retention by reason only that he has obtained judgment or decree for the price of the goods.

Stoppage in transit

44 Right of stoppage in transit

Subject to this Act, when the buyer of goods becomes insolvent the unpaid seller who has parted with the possession of the goods has the right of stopping them in transit, that is to say, he may resume possession of the goods as long as they are in course of transit, and may retain them until payment or tender of the price.

45 Duration of transit

(1) Goods are deemed to be in course of transit from the time when they are delivered to a carrier or other bailee or custodier for the purpose of transmission to the buyer, until the buyer or his agent in that behalf takes delivery of them from the carrier or other bailee or custodier.

(2) If the buyer or his agent in that behalf obtains delivery of the goods before their arrival at the appointed destination, the transit is at an end.

(3) If, after the arrival of the goods at the appointed destination, the carrier or other bailee or custodier acknowledges to the buyer or his agent that he holds the goods on his behalf and continues in possession of them as bailee or custodier for the buyer or his agent, the transit is at an end, and it is immaterial that a further destination for the goods may have been indicated by the buyer.

(4) If the goods are rejected by the buyer, and the carrier or other bailee or custodier continues in possession of them, the transit is not deemed to be at an end, even if the seller has refused to receive them back.

(5) When goods are delivered to a ship chartered by the buyer it is a question depending on the circumstances of the particular case whether they are in the possession of the master as a carrier or as agent to the buyer.

(6) Where the carrier or other bailee or custodier wrongfully refuses to deliver the goods to the buyer or his agent in that behalf, the transit is deemed to be at an end.

(7) Where part delivery of the goods has been made to the buyer or his agent in that behalf, the remainder of the goods may be stopped in transit, unless such part delivery has been made under such circumstances as to show an agreement to give up possession of the whole of the goods.

46 How stoppage in transit is effected

(1) The unpaid seller may exercise his right of stoppage in transit either by taking actual possession of the goods or by giving notice of his claim to the carrier or other bailee or custodier in whose possession the goods are.

(2) The notice may be given either to the person in actual possession of the goods or to his principal.

(3) If given to the principal, the notice is ineffective unless given at such time and under such circumstances that the principal, by the exercise of reasonable diligence, may communicate it to his servant or agent in time to prevent a delivery to the buyer.

(4) When notice of stoppage in transit is given by the seller to the carrier or other bailee or custodier in possession of the goods, he must re-deliver the goods to, or according to the directions of, the seller; and the expenses of the re-delivery must be borne by the seller.

Re-sale etc. by buyer

47   Effect of sub-sale etc. by buyer

(1) Subject to this Act, the unpaid seller's right of lien or retention or stoppage in transit is not affected by any sale or other disposition of the goods which the buyer may have made, unless the seller has assented to it.

(2) Where a document of title to goods has been lawfully transferred to any person as buyer or owner of the goods, and that person transfers the document to a person who takes it in good faith and for valuable consideration, then—

    (a) if the last-mentioned transfer was by way of sale the unpaid seller's right of lien or retention or stoppage in transit is defeated; and

    (b) if the last-mentioned transfer was made by way of pledge or other disposition for value, the unpaid seller's right of lien or retention of stoppage in transit can only be exercised subject to the rights of the transferee.

Rescission: and re-sale by seller

48   Rescission: and re-sale by seller

(1) Subject to this section, a contract of sale is not rescinded by the mere exercise by an unpaid seller of his right of lien or retention or stoppage in transit.

(2) Where an unpaid seller who has exercised his right of lien or retention or stoppage in transit re-sells the goods, the buyer acquires a good title to them as against the original buyer.

(3) Where the goods are of a perishable nature, or where the unpaid seller gives notice to the buyer of his intention to re-sell, and the buyer does not within a reasonable time pay or tender the price, the unpaid seller may re-sell the goods and recover from the original buyer damages for any loss occasioned by his breach of contract.

(4) Where the seller expressly reserves the right of re-sale in case the buyer should make default, and on the buyer making default re-sells the goods, the original contract of sale is rescinded but without prejudice to any claim the seller may have for damages.

[PART 5A

ADDITIONAL RIGHTS OF BUYER IN CONSUMER CASES

48A   Introductory

(1) This section applies if—

    (a) the buyer deals as consumer or, in Scotland, there is a consumer contract in which the buyer is a consumer, and

    (b) the goods do not conform to the contract of sale at the time of delivery.

(2) If this section applies, the buyer has the right—

    (a) under and in accordance with section 48B below, to require the seller to repair or replace the goods, or

    (b) under and in accordance with section 48C below—

        (i) to require the seller to reduce the purchase price of the goods to the buyer by an appropriate amount, or

        (ii) to rescind the contract with regard to the goods in question.

(3) For the purposes of subsection (1)(b) above goods which do not conform to the contract of sale at any time within the period of six months starting with the date on which the goods were delivered to the buyer must be taken not to have so conformed at that date.

(4) Subsection (3) above does not apply if—

    (a) it is established that the goods did so conform at that date;

    (b) its application is incompatible with the nature of the goods or the nature of the lack of conformity.

48B   Repair or replacement of the goods
   (1) If section 48A above applies, the buyer may require the seller—
     (a) to repair the goods, or
     (b) to replace the goods.
   (2) If the buyer requires the seller to repair or replace the goods, the seller must—
     (a) repair or, as the case may be, replace the goods within a reasonable time but without causing significant inconvenience to the buyer;
     (b) bear any necessary costs incurred in doing so (including in particular the cost of any labour, materials or postage).
   (3) The buyer must not require the seller to repair or, as the case may be, replace the goods if that remedy is—
     (a) impossible, or
     (b) disproportionate in comparison to the other of those remedies, or
     (c) disproportionate in comparison to an appropriate reduction in the purchase price under paragraph (a), or rescission under paragraph (b), of section 48C(1) below.
   (4) One remedy is disproportionate in comparison to the other if the one imposes costs on the seller which, in comparison to those imposed on him by the other, are unreasonable, taking into account—
     (a) the value which the goods would have if they conformed to the contract of sale,
     (b) the significance of the lack of conformity, and
     (c) whether the other remedy could be effected without significant inconvenience to the buyer.
   (5) Any question as to what is a reasonable time or significant inconvenience is to be determined by reference to—
     (a) the nature of the goods, and
     (b) the purpose for which the goods were acquired.

48C   Reduction of purchase price or rescission of contract
   (1) If section 48A above applies, the buyer may—
     (a) require the seller to reduce the purchase price of the goods in question to the buyer by an appropriate amount, or
     (b) rescind the contract with regard to those goods,
if the condition in subsection (2) below is satisfied.
   (2) The condition is that—
     (a) by virtue of section 48B(3) above the buyer may require neither repair nor replacement of the goods; or
     (b) the buyer has required the seller to repair or replace the goods, but the seller is in breach of the requirement of section 48B(2)(a) above to do so within a reasonable time and without significant inconvenience to the buyer.
   (3) For the purposes of this Part, if the buyer rescinds the contract, any reimbursement to the buyer may be reduced to take account of the use he has had of the goods since they were delivered to him.

48D   Relation to other remedies etc.
   (1) If the buyer requires the seller to repair or replace the goods the buyer must not act under subsection (2) until he has given the seller a reasonable time in which to repair or replace (as the case may be) the goods.
   (2) The buyer acts under this subsection if—
     (a) in England and Wales or Northern Ireland he rejects the goods and terminates the contract for breach of condition;
     (b) in Scotland he rejects any goods delivered under the contract and treats it as repudiated;
     (c) he requires the goods to be replaced or repaired (as the case may be).

48E   Powers of the court

(1) In any proceedings in which a remedy is sought by virtue of this Part the court, in addition to any other power it has, may act under this section.

(2) On the application of the buyer the court may make an order requiring specific performance or, in Scotland, specific implement by the seller of any obligation imposed on him by virtue of section 48B above.

(3) Subsection (4) applies if—

(a) the buyer requires the seller to give effect to a remedy under section 48B or 48C above or has claims to rescind under section 48C, but

(b) the court decides that another remedy under section 48B or 48C is appropriate.

(4) The court may proceed—

(a) as if the buyer had required the seller to give effect to the other remedy, or if the other remedy is rescission under section 48C

(b) as if the buyer had claimed to rescind the contract under that section.

(5) If the buyer has claimed to rescind the contract the court may order that any reimbursement to the buyer is reduced to take account of the use he has had of the goods since they were delivered to him.

(6) The court may make an order under this section unconditionally or on such terms and conditions as to damages, payment of the price and otherwise as it thinks just.

48F   Conformity with the contract

For the purposes of this Part, goods do not conform to a contract of sale if there is, in relation to the goods, a breach of an express term of the contract or a term implied by section 13, 14 or 15 above.]

PART VI   ACTIONS FOR BREACH OF THE CONTRACT

Seller's remedies

49   Action for price

(1) Where, under a contract of sale, the property in the goods has passed to the buyer and he wrongfully neglects or refuses to pay for the goods according to the terms of the contract, the seller may maintain an action against him for the price of the goods.

(2) Where, under a contract of sale, the price is payable on a day certain irrespective of delivery and the buyer wrongfully neglects or refuses to pay such price, the seller may maintain an action for the price, although the property in goods has not passed and the goods have not been appropriated to the contract.

(3) Nothing in this section prejudices the right of the seller in Scotland to recover interest on the price from the date of tender of the goods, or from the date on which the price was payable, as the case may be.

50   Damages for non-acceptance

(1) Where the buyer wrongfully neglects or refuses to accept and pay for the goods, the seller may maintain an action against him for damages for non-acceptance.

(2) The measure of damages is the estimated loss directly and naturally resulting in the ordinary course of events, from the buyer's breach of contract.

(3) Where there is an available market for the goods in question the measure of damages is prima facie to be ascertained by the difference between the contract price and the market or current price at the time or times when the goods ought to have been accepted or (if no time was fixed for acceptance) at the time of the refusal to accept.

Buyer's remedies

51 Damages for non-delivery

(1) Where the seller wrongfully neglects or refuses to deliver the goods to the buyer, the buyer may maintain an action against the seller for damages for non-delivery.

(2) The measure of damages is the estimated loss directly and naturally resulting, in the ordinary course of events, from the seller's breach of contract.

(3) Where there is an available market for the goods in question the measure of damages is prima facie to be ascertained by the difference between the contract price and the market or current price of the goods at the time or times when they ought to have been delivered or (if no time was fixed) at the time of the refusal to deliver.

52 Specific performance

(1) If any action for breach of contract to deliver specific or ascertained goods the court may, if it thinks fit, on the plaintiff s application, by its judgment or decree direct that the contract shall be performed specifically, without giving the defendant the option of retaining the goods on payment of damages.

(2) The plaintiff s application may be made at any time before judgment or decree.

(3) The judgment or decree may be unconditional, or on such terms and conditions as to damages, payment of the price and otherwise as seem just to the court.

(4) The provisions of this section shall be deemed to be supplementary to, and not in derogation of, the right of specific implement in Scotland.

53 Remedy for breach of warranty

(1) Where there is a breach of warranty by the seller, or where the buyer elects (or is compelled) to treat any breach of a condition on the part of the seller as a breach of warranty, the buyer is not by reason only of such breach of warranty entitled to reject the goods; but he may—

   (a) set up against the seller the breach of warranty in diminution of extinction of the price, or

   (b) maintain an action against the seller for damages for the breach of warranty.

(2) The measure of damages for breach of warranty is the estimated loss directly and naturally resulting, in the ordinary course of events, from the breach of warranty.

(3) In the case of breach of warranty of quality such loss is prima facie the difference between the value of the goods at the time of delivery to the buyer and the value they would have had if they had fulfilled the warranty.

(4) The fact that the buyer has set up the breach of warranty in diminution or extinction of the price does not prevent him from maintaining an action for the same breach of warranty if he has suffered further damage.

[(5) This section does not apply to Scotland.]

[53A Measure of damages as respects Scotland

(1) The measure of damages for the seller's breach of contract is the estimated loss directly and naturally resulting, in the ordinary course of events, from the breach.

(2) Where the seller's breach consists of the delivery of goods which are not of the quality required by the contract and the buyer retains the goods, such loss as aforesaid is prima facie the difference between the value of the goods at the time of delivery to the buyer and the value they would have had if they had fulfilled the contract.

(3) This section applies to Scotland only.]

Interest, etc.

54   Interest, etc.
Nothing in this Act affects the right of the buyer or the seller to recover interest or special damages in any case where by law interest or special damages may be recoverable, or to recover money paid where the consideration for the payment of it has failed.

PART VII   SUPPLEMENTARY

55   Exclusion of implied terms
(1) Where a right duty or liability would arise under a contract of sale of goods by implication of law, it may (subject to the Unfair Contract Terms Act 1977) be negatived or varied by express agreement, or by the course of dealing between the parties, or by such usage as binds both parties to the contract.

(2) An express [term] does not negative a [term] implied by this Act unless inconsistent with it.

(3) Paragraph 11 of Schedule 1 below applies in relation to a contract made on or after 18 May 1973 and before 1 February 1978, and paragraph 12 in relation to one made before 18 May 1973.

56   Conflict of laws
Paragraph 13 of Schedule 1 below applies in relation to a contract made on or after 18 May 1973 and before 1 February 1978, so as to make provision about conflict of laws in relation to such a contract.

57   Auction sales
(1) Where goods are put up for sale by auction in lots, each lot is prima facie deemed to be the subject of a separate contract of sale.

(2) A sale by auction is complete when the auctioneer announces its completion by the fall of the hammer, or in other customary manner; and until the announcement is made any bidder may retract his bid.

(3) A sale by auction may be notified to be subject to a reserve or upset price, and a right to bid may also be reserved expressly by or on behalf of the seller.

(4) Where a sale by auction is not notified to be subject to a right to bid by or on behalf of the seller, it is not lawful for the seller to bid himself or to employ any person to bid at the sale, or for the auctioneer knowingly to take any bid from the seller or any such person.

(5) A sale contravening subsection (4) above may be treated as fraudulent by the buyer.

(6) Where, in respect of a sale by auction, a right to bid is expressly reserved (but not otherwise) the seller or any one person on his behalf may bid at the auction.

58   Payment into court in Scotland
In Scotland where a buyer has elected to accept goods which he might have rejected, and to treat a breach of contract as only giving rise to a claim for damages, he may, in an action by the seller for the price, be required, in the discretion of the court before which the action depends, to consign or pay into court the price of the goods, or part of the price, or to give other reasonable security for its due payment.

59   Reasonable time a question of fact
Where a reference is made in this Act to a reasonable time the question what is a reasonable time is a question of fact.

60   Rights, etc. enforceable by action
Where a right, duty or liability is declared by this Act, it may (unless otherwise provided by this Act) be enforced by action.

61 Interpretation

(1) In this Act, unless the context or subject matter otherwise requires,— 'action' includes counterclaim and set-off, and in Scotland condescendence and claim and compensation;

['bulk' means a mass or collection of goods of the same kind which—

(a) is contained in a defined space or area; and

(b) is such that any goods in the bulk are interchangeable with any other goods therein of the same number or quantity;]

'business' includes a profession and the activities of any government department (including a Northern Ireland department) or local or public authority;

'buyer' means a person who buys or agrees to buy goods;

['consumer contract' has the same meaning as in section 25(1) of the Unfair Contract Terms Act 1977; and for the purposes of this Act the onus of proving that a contract is not to be regarded as a consumer contract shall lie on the seller] 'contract of sale' includes an agreement to sell as well as a sale,

'credit-broker' means a person acting in the course of a business of credit brokerage carried on by him, that is a business of effecting introductions of individuals desiring to obtain credit—

(a) to persons carrying on any business so far as it relates to the provision of credit, or

(b) to other persons engaged in credit brokerage;

'defendant' includes in Scotland defender, respondent, and claimant in a multiplepoinding;

'delivery' means voluntary transfer of possession from one person to another; [except that in relation to sections 20A and 20B above it includes such appropriation of goods to the contract as results in property in the goods being transferred to the buyer;]

'document of title to goods' has the same meaning as it has in the Factors Acts;

'Factors Acts' means the Factors Act 1889, the Factors (Scotland) Act 1890, and any enactment amending or substituted for the same;

'fault' means wrongful act or default;

'future goods' means goods to be manufactured or acquired by the seller after the making of the contract of sale;

'goods' includes all personal chattels other than things in action and money, and in Scotland all corporeal moveables except money; and in particular 'goods' includes emblements, industrial growing crops, and things attached to or forming part of the land which are agreed to be severed before sale or under the contract of sale; [and includes an undivided share in goods;]

'plaintiff' includes pursuer, complainer, claimant in a multiplepoinding and defendant or defender counter-claiming;

['producer' means the manufacturer of goods, the importer of goods into the European Economic Area or any person purporting to be a producer by placing his name, trade mark or other distinctive sign on the goods;]

'property' means the general property in goods, and not merely a special property;

['repair' means, in cases where there is a lack of conformity in goods for purposes of section 48F of this Act, to bring the goods into conformity with the contract;]

'sale' includes a bargain and sale as well as a sale and delivery;

'seller' means a person who sells or agrees to sell goods;

'specific goods' means goods identified and agreed on at the time a contract of sale is made; [and includes an undivided share, specified as a fraction or percentage, of goods identified and agreed on as aforesaid;]

'warranty' (as regards England and Wales and Northern Ireland) means an agreement with reference to goods which are the subject of a contract of sale, but collateral to the main purpose of such contract, the breach of which gives rise to a claim for damages, but not to a right to reject the goods and treat the contract as repudiated.

(3) A thing is deemed to be done in good faith within the meaning of this Act when it is in fact done honestly, whether it is done negligently or not.

(4) A person is deemed to be insolvent within the meaning of this Act if he has either ceased to pay his debts in the ordinary course of business or he cannot pay his debts as they become due, [. . .]

(5) Goods are in a deliverable state within the meaning of this Act when they are in such a state that the buyer would under the contract be bound to take delivery of them.

[(5A) References in this Act to dealing as consumer are to be construed in accordance with Part I of the Unfair Contract Terms Act 1977; and, for the purposes of this Act, it is for a seller claiming that the buyer does not deal as consumer to show that he does not.]

(6) As regards the definition of 'business' in subsection (1) above, paragraph 14 of Schedule 1 below applies in relation to a contract made on or after 18 May 1973 and before 1 February 1978, and paragraph 15 in relation to one made before 18 May 1973.

62   Savings: rules of law, etc.

(1) The rules in bankruptcy relating to contracts of sale apply to those contracts, notwithstanding anything in this Act.

(2) The rules of the common law, including the law merchant, except in so far as they are inconsistent with the provisions of this Act, and in particular the rules relating to the law of principal and agent and the effect of fraud, misrepresentation, duress or coercion, mistake, or other invalidating cause, apply to contracts for the sale of goods.

(3) Nothing in this Act or the Sale of Goods Act 1893 affects the enactments relating to bills of sale, or any enactment relating to the sale of goods which is not expressly repealed or amended by this Act or that.

(4) The provisions of this Act about contracts of sale do not apply to a transaction in the form of a contract of sale which is intended to operate by way of mortgage, pledge, charge, or other security.

(5) Nothing in this Act prejudices or affects the landlord's right of hypothec or sequestration for rent in Scotland.

63   Consequential amendments, repeals and savings

. . .

64   Short title and commencement

(1) This Act may be cited as the Sale of Goods Act 1979.

(2) This act comes into force on 1 January 1980.

Supply of Goods and Services Act 1982
(1982, c. 29)

An Act to amend the law with respect to the terms to be implied in certain contracts for the transfer of property in goods, in certain contracts for the hire of goods and in certain contracts for the supply of a service; and for connected purposes.   [13th July 1982]

PART I   SUPPLY OF GOODS

Contracts for the transfer of property in goods

1   The contracts concerned

(1) In this Act [in its application to England and Wales and Northern Ireland] a 'contract for the transfer of goods' means a contract under which one person transfers or agrees to transfer to another the property in goods, other than an excepted contract.

(2) For the purposes of this section an excepted contract means any of the following:—

    (a) a contract of sale of goods;

    (b) a hire-purchase agreement;

    [...]

    (d) a transfer or agreement to transfer which is made by deed and for which there is no consideration other than the presumed consideration imported by the deed;

    (e) a contract intended to operate by way of mortgage, pledge, charge or other security.

(3) For the purposes of this Act [in its application to England and Wales and Northern Ireland] a contract is a contract for the transfer of goods whether or not services are also provided or to be provided under the contract, and (subject to subsection (2) above) whatever is the nature of the consideration for the transfer or agreement to transfer.

2   Implied terms about title, etc.

(1) In a contract for the transfer of goods, other than one to which subsection (3) below applies, there is an implied condition on the part of the transferor that in the case of a transfer of the property in the goods he has a right to transfer the property and in the case of an agreement to transfer the property in the goods he will have such a right at the time when the property is to be transferred.

(2) In a contract for the transfer of goods, other than one to which subsection (3) below applies, there is also an implied warranty that—

    (a) the goods are free, and will remain free until the time when the property is to be transferred, from any charge or encumbrance not disclosed or known to the transferee before the contract is made, and

    (b) the transferee will enjoy quiet possession of the goods except so far as it may be disturbed by the owner or other person entitled to the benefit of any charge or encumbrance so disclosed or known.

(3) This subsection applies to a contract for the transfer of goods in the case of which there appears from the contract or is to be inferred from its circumstances an intention that the transferor should transfer only such title as he or a third person may have.

(4) In a contract to which subsection (3) above applies there is an implied warranty that all charges or encumbrances known to the transferor and not known to the transferee have been disclosed to the transferee before the contract is made.

(5) In a contract to which subsection (3) above applies, there is also an implied warranty that none of the following will disturb the transferee's quiet possession of the goods, namely—

    (a) the transferor;

    (b) in a case where the parties to the contract intend that the transferor should transfer only such title as a third person may have, that person;

    (c) anyone claiming through or under the transferor or that third person otherwise than under a charge or encumbrance disclosed or known to the transferee before the contract is made.

3   Implied terms where transfer is by description

(1) This section applies where, under a contract for the transfer of goods, the transferor transfers or agrees to transfer the property in the goods by description.

(2) In such case there is an implied condition that the goods will correspond with the description.

(3) If the transferor transfers or agrees to transfer the property in the goods by sample as well as by description it is not sufficient that the bulk of the goods corresponds with the sample if the goods do not also correspond with the description.

(4) A contract is not prevented from falling within subsection (1) above by reason only that, being exposed for supply, the goods are selected by the transferee.

4 Implied terms about quality or fitness

(1) Except as provided by this section and section 5 below and subject to the provision of any other enactment, there is no implied condition or warranty about the quality or fitness for any particular purpose of goods supplied under a contract for the transfer of goods.

[(2) Where, under such a contract, the transferor transfers the property in goods in the course of a business, there is an implied condition that the goods supplied under the contract are of satisfactory quality.

(2A) For the purposes of this section and section 5 below, goods are of satisfactory quality if they meet the standard that a reasonable person would regard as satisfactory, taking account of any description of the goods, the price (if relevant) and all the other relevant circumstances.]

[(2B) If the transferee deals as consumer, the relevant circumstances mentioned in sub-section (2A) above include any public statements on the specific characteristics of the goods made about them by the transferor, the producer or his representative, particularly in advertising or on labelling.

(2C) A public statement is not by virtue of subsection (2B) above a relevant circumstance for the purposes of subsection (2A) above in the case of a contract for the transfer of goods, if the transferor shows that—

(a) at the time the contract was made, he was not, and could not reasonably have been, aware of the statement,

(b) before the contract was made, the statement had been withdrawn in public or, to the extent that it contained anything which was incorrect or misleading, it had been corrected in public, or

(c) the decision to acquire the goods could not have been influenced by the statement.

(2D) Subsections (2B) and (2C) above do not prevent any public statement from being a relevant circumstance for the purposes of subsection (2A) above (whether or not the transferee deals as consumer) if the statement would have been such a circumstance apart from those subsections.]

[(3) The condition implied by subsection (2) above does not extend to any matter making the quality of goods unsatisfactory—

(a) which is specifically drawn to the transferee's attention before the contract is made,

(b) where the transferee examines the goods before the contract is made, which that examination ought to reveal, or

(c) where the property in the goods is transferred by reference to a sample, which would have been apparent on a reasonable examination of the sample.]

(4) Subsection (5) below applies where, under a contract for the transfer of goods, the transferor transfers the property in goods in the course of a business and the transferee, expressly or by implication, makes known—

(a) to the transferor, or

(b) where the consideration or part of the consideration for the transfer is a sum payable by instalments and the goods were previously sold by a credit-broker to the transferor, to that credit-broker,

any particular purpose for which the goods are being acquired.

(5) In that case there is (subject to subsection (6) below) an implied condition that the goods supplied under the contract are reasonably fit for that purpose, whether or not that is a purpose for which such goods are commonly supplied.

(6) Subsection (5) above does not apply where the circumstances show that the transferee does not rely, or that it is unreasonable for him to rely, on the skill or judgment of the transferor or credit-broker.

(7) An implied condition or warranty about quality or fitness for a particular purpose may be annexed by usage to a contract for the transfer of goods.

(8) The preceding provisions of this section apply to a transfer by a person who in the course of a business is acting as agent for another as they apply to a transfer by a principal in the course of a business, except where that other is not transferring in the course of a business and either the transferee knows that fact or reasonable steps are taken to bring it to the transferee's notice before the contract concerned is made.

5 Implied terms where transfer is by sample

(1) This section applies where, under a contract for the transfer of goods, the transferor transfers or agrees to transfer the property in the goods by reference to a sample.

(2) In such a case there is an implied condition—

    (a) that the bulk will correspond with the sample in quality; and

    (b) that the transferee will have a reasonable opportunity of comparing the bulk with the sample; and

    (c) that the goods will be free from any defect, [making their quality unsatisfactory], which would not be apparent on reasonable examination of the sample.

(4) For the purposes of this section a transferor transfers or agrees to transfer the property in goods by reference to a sample where there is an express or implied term to that effect in the contract concerned.

[5A Modification of remedies for breach of statutory condition in non- consumer cases

(1) Where in the case of a contract for the transfer of goods—

    (a) the transferee would, apart from this subsection, have the right to treat the contract as repudiated by reason of a breach on the part of the transferor of a term implied by section 3, 4 or 5(2)(a) or (c) above, but

    (b) the breach is so slight that it would be unreasonable for him to do so,

then, if the transferee does not deal as consumer, the breach is not to be treated as a breach of condition but may be treated as a breach of warranty.

(2) This section applies unless a contrary intention appears in, or is to be implied from, the contract.

(3) It is for the transferor to show that a breach fell within subsection (1)(b) above.]

Contracts for the hire of goods

6 The contracts concerned

(1) In this Act [in its application to England and Wales and Northern Ireland] a 'contract for the hire of goods' means a contract under which one person bails or agrees to bail goods to another by way of hire, other than [a hire-purchase agreement].

    [...]

(3) For the purposes of this Act [in its application to England and Wales and Northern Ireland] a contract is a contract for the hire of goods whether or not services are also provided or to be provided under the contract, and [...] whatever is the nature of the consideration for the bailment or agreement to bail by way of hire.

7 Implied terms about right to transfer possession, etc.

(1) In a contract for the hire of goods there is an implied condition on the part of the bailor that in the case of a bailment he has a right to transfer possession of the goods by way of hire for the period of the bailment and in the case of an agreement to bail he will have such a right at the time of the bailment.

(2) In a contract for the hire of goods there is also an implied warranty that the bailee will enjoy quiet possession of the goods for the period of the bailment except so far as the possession may be disturbed by the owner or other person entitled to the benefit of any charge or encumbrance disclosed or known to the bailee before the contract is made.

(3) The preceding provisions of this section do not affect the right of the bailor to repossess the goods under an express or implied term of contract.

8   Implied terms where hire is by description

(1) This section applies where, under a contract for the hire of goods, the bailor bails or agrees to bail the goods by description.

(2) In such a case there is an implied condition that the goods will correspond with the description.

(3) If under the contract the bailor bails or agrees to bail the goods by reference to a sample as well as a description it is not sufficient that the bulk of the goods corresponds with the sample if the goods do not also correspond with the description.

(4) A contract is not prevented from falling within subsection (1) above by reason only that, being exposed for supply, the goods are selected by the bailee.

9   Implied terms about quality or fitness

(1) Except as provided by this section and section 10 below and subject to the provisions of any other enactment, there is no implied condition or warranty about the quality or fitness for any particular purpose of goods bailed under a contract for the hire of goods.

[(2) Where, under such a contract, the bailor bails goods in the course of a business, there is an implied condition that the goods supplied under the contract are of satisfactory quality.

(2A) For the purposes of this section and section 10 below, goods are of satisfactory quality if they meet the standard that a reasonable person would regard as satisfactory, taking account of any description of the goods, the consideration for the bailment (if relevant) and all the other relevant circumstances.]

[(2B) If the bailee deals as consumer, the relevant circumstances mentioned in subsection (2A) above include any public statements on the specific characteristics of the goods made about them by the bailor, the producer or his representative, particularly in advertising or on labelling.

(2C) A public statement is not by virtue of subsection (2B) above a relevant circumstance for the purposes of subsection (2A) above in the case of a contract for the hire of goods, if the bailor shows that—

   (a) at the time the contract was made, he was not, and could not reasonably have been, aware of the statement,
   (b) before the contract was made, the statement had been withdrawn in public or, to the extent that it contained anything which was incorrect or misleading, it had been corrected in public, or
   (c) the decision to acquire the goods could not have been influenced by the statement.

(2D) Subsections (2B) and (2C) above do not prevent any public statement from being a relevant circumstance for the purposes of subsection (2A) above (whether or not the bailee deals as consumer) if the statement would have been such a circumstance apart from those subsections.]

[(3) The condition implied by subsection (2) above does not extend to any matter making the quality of goods unsatisfactory—

   (a) which is specifically drawn to the bailee's attention before the contract is made,
   (b) where the bailee examines the goods before the contract is made, which that examination ought to reveal, or
   (c) where the goods are bailed by reference to a sample, which would have been apparent on a reasonable examination of the sample.]

(4) Subsection (5) below applies where, under a contract for the hire of goods, the bailor bails goods in the course of a business and the bailee, expressly or by implication, makes known—

   (a) to the bailor in the course of negotiations conducted by him in relation to the making of the contract, or
   (b) to a credit-broker in the course of negotiations conducted by that broker in relation to goods sold by him to the bailor before forming the subject matter of the contract,

any particular purpose for which the goods are being bailed.

(5) In that case there is (subject to subsection (6) below) an implied condition that the goods supplied under the contract are reasonably fit for that purpose, whether or not that is a purpose for which such goods are commonly supplied.

(6) Subsection (5) above does not apply where the circumstances show that the bailee does not rely, or that it is unreasonable for him to rely, on the skill or judgment of the bailor or credit-broker.

(7) An implied condition or warranty about quality or fitness for a particular purpose may be annexed by usage to a contract for the hire of goods.

(8) The preceding provisions of this section apply to a bailment by a person who in the course of a business is acting as agent for another as they apply to a bailment by a principal in the course of a business, except where that other is not bailing in the course of a business and either the bailee knows that fact or reasonable steps are taken to bring it to the bailee's notice before the contract concerned is made.

10   Implied terms where hire is by sample

(1) This section applies where, under a contract for the hire of goods, the bailor bails or agrees to bail the goods by reference to a sample.

(2) In such a case there is an implied condition—

(a) that the bulk will correspond with the sample in quality; and

(b) that the bailee will have a reasonable opportunity of comparing the bulk with the sample; and

(c) that the goods will be free from any defect, [making their quality unsatisfactory], which would not be apparent on reasonable examination of the sample.

(4) For the purposes of this section a bailor bails or agrees to bail goods by reference to a sample where there is an express or implied term to that effect in the contract concerned.

[10A   Modification of remedies for breach of statutory condition in non-consumer cases

(1) Where in the case of a contract for the hire of goods—

(a) the bailee would, apart from this subsection, have the right to treat the contract as repudiated by reason of a breach on the part of the bailor of a term implied by section 8, 9 or 10(2)(a) or (c) above, but

(b) the breach is so slight that it would be unreasonable for him to do so, then, if the bailee does not deal as consumer, the breach is not to be treated as a breach of condition but may be treated as a breach of warranty.

(2) This section applies unless a contrary intention appears in, or is to be implied from, the contract.

(3) It is for the bailor to show that a breach fell within subsection (1)(b) above.]

Exclusion of implied terms, etc.

11   Exclusion of implied terms, etc.

(1) Where a right, duty or liability would arise under a contract for the transfer of goods or a contract for the hire of goods by implication of law, it may (subject to subsection (2) below and the 1977 Act) be negatived or varied by express agreement, or by the course of dealing between the parties, or by such usage as binds both parties to the contract.

(2) An express condition or warranty does not negative a condition or warranty implied by the preceding provisions of this Act unless inconsistent with it.

(3) Nothing in the preceding provisions of this Act prejudices the operation of any other enactment or any rule of law whereby any condition or warranty (other than one relating to quality or fitness) is to be implied in a contract for the transfer of goods or a contract for hire of goods.

[PART IA   SUPPLY OF GOODS AS RESPECTS SCOTLAND

Contracts for the transfer of property in goods

11A   The contracts concerned

(1) In this Act in its application to Scotland a 'contract for the transfer of goods' means a contract under which one person transfers or agrees to transfer to another the property in goods, other than an excepted contract.

(2) For the purposes of this section an excepted contract means any of the following—

(a) a contract of sale of goods;

(b) a hire-purchase agreement;

[...]

(d) a transfer or agreement to transfer for which there is no consideration;

(e) a contract intended to operate by way of mortgage, pledge, charge or other security.

(3) For the purposes of this Act in its application to Scotland a contract is a contract for the transfer of goods whether or not services are also provided or to be provided under the contract, and (subject to subsection (2) above) whatever is the nature of the consideration for the transfer or agreement to transfer.

11B   Implied terms about title, etc.

(1) In a contract for the transfer of goods, other than one to which subsection (3) below applies, there is an implied term on the part of the transferor that in the case of a transfer of the property in the goods he has a right to transfer the property and in the case of an agreement to transfer the property in the goods he will have such a right at the time when the property is to be transferred.

(2) In a contract for the transfer of goods, other than one to which subsection (3) below applies, there is also an implied term that—

(a) the goods are free, and will remain free until the time when the property is to be transferred, from any charge or encumbrance not disclosed or known to the transferee before the contract is made, and

(b) the transferee will enjoy quiet possession of the goods except so far as it may be disturbed by the owner or other person entitled to the benefit of any charge or encumbrance so disclosed or known.

(3) This subsection applies to a contract for the transfer of goods in the case of which there appears from the contract or is to be inferred from its circumstances an intention that the transferor should transfer only such title as he or a third person may have.

(4) In a contract to which subsection (3) above applies there is an implied term that all charges or encumbrances known to the transferor and not known to the transferee have been disclosed to the transferee before the contract is made.

(5) In a contract to which subsection (3) above applies there is also an implied term that none of the following will disturb the transferee's quiet possession of the goods, namely—

(a) the transferor;

(b) in a case where the parties to the contract intend that the transferor should transfer only such title as a third person may have, that person;

(c) anyone claiming through or under the transferor or that third person otherwise than under a charge or encumbrance disclosed or known to the transferee before the contract is made.

11C   Implied terms where transfer is by description

(1) This section applies where, under a contract for the transfer of goods, the transferor transfers or agrees to transfer the property in the goods by description.

(2) In such a case there is an implied term that the goods will correspond with the description.

(3) If the transferor transfers or agrees to transfer the property in the goods by reference to a sample as well as by description it is not sufficient that the bulk of the goods corresponds with the sample if the goods do not also correspond with the description.

(4) A contract is not prevented from falling within subsection (1) above by reason only that, being exposed for supply, the goods are selected by the transferee.

11D   Implied terms about quality or fitness

(1) Except as provided by this section and section 11E below and subject to the provisions of any other enactment, there is no implied term about the quality or fitness for any particular purpose of goods supplied under a contract for the transfer of goods.

(2) Where, under such a contract, the transferor transfers the property in goods in the course of a business, there is an implied term that the goods supplied under the contract are of satisfactory quality.

(3) For the purposes of this section and section 11E below, goods are of satisfactory quality if they meet the standard that a reasonable person would regard as satisfactory, taking account of any description of the goods, the price (if relevant) and all the other relevant circumstances.

[(3A) If the contract for the transfer of goods is a consumer contract, the relevant circumstances mentioned in subsection (3) above include any public statements on the specific characteristics of the goods made about them by the transferor, the producer or his representative, particularly in advertising or on labelling.

(3B) A public statement is not by virtue of subsection (3A) above a relevant circumstance for the purposes of subsection (3) above in the case of a contract for the transfer of goods, if the transferor shows that—

    (a) at the time the contract was made, he was not, and could not reasonably have been, aware of the statement,

    (b) before the contract was made, the statement had been withdrawn in public or, to the extent that it contained anything which was incorrect or misleading, it had been corrected in public, or

    (c) the decision to acquire the goods could not have been influenced by the statement.

(3C) Subsections (3A) and (3B) above do not prevent any public statement from being a relevant circumstance for the purposes of subsection (3) above (whether or not the contract for the transfer of goods is a consumer contract) if the statement would have been such a circumstance apart from those subsections.]

(4) The term implied by subsection (2) above does not extend to any matter making the quality of goods unsatisfactory—

    (a) which is specifically drawn to the transferee's attention before the contract is made,

    (b) where the transferee examines the goods before the contract is made, which that examination ought to reveal, or

    (c) where the property in the goods is, or is to be, transferred by reference to a sample, which would have been apparent on a reasonable examination of the sample.

(5) Subsection (6) below applies where, under a contract for the transfer of goods, the transferor transfers the property in goods in the course of a business and the transferee, expressly or by implication, makes known—

    (a) to the transferor, or

    (b) where the consideration or part of the consideration for the transfer is a sum payable by instalments and the goods were previously sold by a credit-broker to the transferor, to that credit-broker,

any particular purpose for which the goods are being acquired.

(6) In that case there is (subject to subsection (7) below) an implied term that the goods supplied under the contract are reasonably fit for the purpose, whether or not that is a purpose for which such goods are commonly supplied.

(7) Subsection (6) above does not apply where the circumstances show that the transferee does not rely or that it is unreasonable for him to rely, on the skill or judgment of the transferor or credit-broker.

(8) An implied term about quality or fitness for a particular purpose may be annexed by usage to a contract for the transfer of goods.

(9) The preceding provisions of this section apply to a transfer by a person who in the course of a business is acting as agent for another as they apply to a transfer by a principal in the course of a business, except where that other is not transferring in the course of a business and either the transferee knows that fact or reasonable steps are taken to bring it to the transferee's notice before the contract concerned is made.

[(10) For the purposes of this section, 'consumer contract' has the same meaning as in section 11F(3) below.]

11E   Implied terms where transfer is by sample

(1) This section applies where, under a contract for the transfer of goods, the transferor transfers or agrees to transfer the property in the goods by reference to a sample.

(2) In such a case there is an implied term—
- (a) that the bulk will correspond with the sample in quality;
- (b) that the transferee will have a reasonable opportunity of comparing the bulk with the sample; and
- (c) that the goods will be free from any defect, making their quality unsatisfactory, which would not be apparent on reasonable examination of the sample.

(3) For the purposes of this section a transferor transfers or agrees to transfer the property in goods by reference to a sample where there is an express or implied term to that effect in the contract concerned.

11F   Remedies for breach of contract

(1) Where in a contract for the transfer of goods a transferor is in breach of any term of the contract (express or implied), the other party to the contract (in this section referred to as 'the transferee') shall be entitled—
- (a) to claim damages; and
- (b) if the breach is material, to reject any goods delivered under the contract and treat it as repudiated.

(2) Where a contract for the transfer of goods is a consumer contract and the transferee is the consumer, then, for the purposes of subsection (1)(b) above, breach by the transferor of any term (express or implied)—
- (a) as to the quality of the goods or their fitness for a purpose;
- (b) if the goods are, or are to be, transferred by description, that the goods will correspond with the description;
- (c) if the goods are, or are to be, transferred by reference to a sample, that the bulk will correspond with the sample in quality,

shall be deemed to be a material breach.

(3) In subsection (2) above, 'consumer contract' has the same meaning as in section 25(1) of the 1977 Act; and for the purposes of that subsection the onus of proving that a contract is not to be regarded as a consumer contract shall lie on the transferor.

Contracts for the hire of goods

11G   The contracts concerned

(1) In this Act in its application to Scotland a 'contract for the hire of goods' means a contract under which one person ('the supplier') hires or agrees to hire goods to another, other than [a hire-purchase agreement].

[...]

(3) For the purposes of this Act in its application to Scotland a contract is a contract for the hire of goods whether or not services are also provided or to be provided under the contract, and [...] whatever is the nature of the consideration for the hire or agreement to hire.

11H   Implied terms about right to transfer possession etc.

(1) In a contract for the hire of goods there is an implied term on the part of the supplier that—

    (a) in the case of a hire, he has a right to transfer possession of the goods by way of hire for the period of the hire; and

    (b) in the case of an agreement to hire, he will have such a right at the time of commencement of the period of the hire.

(2) In a contract for the hire of goods there is also an implied term that the person to whom the goods are hired will enjoy quiet possession of the goods for the period of the hire except so far as the possession may be disturbed by the owner or other person entitled to the benefit of any charge or encumbrance disclosed or known to the person to whom the goods are hired before the contract is made.

(3) The preceding provisions of this section do not affect the right of the supplier to repossess the goods under an express or implied term of the contract.

11I   Implied terms where hire is by description

(1) This section applies where, under a contract for the hire of goods, the supplier hires or agrees to hire the goods by description.

(2) In such a case there is an implied term that the goods will correspond with the description.

(3) If under the contract the supplier hires or agrees to hire the goods by reference to a sample as well as by description it is not sufficient that the bulk of the goods corresponds with the sample if the goods do not also correspond with the description.

(4) A contract is not prevented from falling within subsection (1) above by reason only that, being exposed for supply, the goods are selected by the person to whom the goods are hired.

11J   Implied terms about quality or fitness

(1) Except as provided by this section and section 11K below and subject to the provisions of any other enactment, there is no implied term about the quality or fitness for any particular purpose of goods hired under a contract for the hire of goods.

(2) Where, under such a contract, the supplier hires goods in the course of a business, there is an implied term that the goods supplied under the contract are of satisfactory quality.

(3) For the purposes of this section and section 11K below, goods are of satisfactory quality if they meet the standard that a reasonable person would regard as satisfactory, taking account of any description of the goods, the consideration for the hire (if relevant) and all the other relevant circumstances.

[(3A) If the contract for the hire of goods is a consumer contract, the relevant circumstances mentioned in subsection (3) above include any public statements on the specific characteristics of the goods made about them by the hirer, the producer or his representative, particularly in advertising or on labelling.

(3B) A public statement is not by virtue of subsection (3A) above a relevant circumstance for the purposes of subsection (3) above in the case of a contract for the hire of goods, if the hirer shows that—

    (a) at the time the contract was made, he was not, and could not reasonably have been, aware of the statement,

    (b) by the time the contract was made, the statement had been withdrawn in public or, to the extent that it contained anything which was incorrect or misleading, it had been corrected in public, or

    (c) the decision to acquire the goods could not have been influenced by the statement.

(3C) Subsections (3A) and (3B) above do not prevent any public statement from being a relevant circumstance for the purposes of subsection (3) above (whether or not the contract for the hire of goods is a consumer contract) if the statement would have been such a circumstance apart from those subsections.]

(4) The term implied by subsection (2) above does not extend to any matter making the quality of goods unsatisfactory—

 (a) which is specifically drawn to the attention of the person to whom the goods are hired before the contract is made, or

 (b) where that person examines the goods before the contract is made, which that examination ought to reveal; or

 (c) where the goods are hired by reference to a sample, which would have been apparent on reasonable examination of the sample.

(5) Subsection (6) below applies where, under a contract for the hire of goods, the supplier hires goods in the course of a business and the person to whom the goods are hired, expressly or by implication, makes known—

 (a) to the supplier in the course of negotiations conducted by him in relation to the making of the contract; or

 (b) to a credit-broker in the course of negotiations conducted by that broker in relation to goods sold by him to the supplier before forming the subject matter of the contract, any particular purpose for which the goods are being hired.

(6) In that case there is (subject to subsection (7) below) an implied term that the goods supplied under the contract are reasonably fit for that purpose, whether or not that is a purpose for which such goods are commonly supplied.

(7) Subsection (6) above does not apply where the circumstances show that the person to whom the goods are hired does not rely, or that it is unreasonable for him to rely, on the skill or judgment of the hirer or credit-broker.

(8) An implied term about quality or fitness for a particular purpose may be annexed by usage to a contract for the hire of goods.

(9) The preceding provisions of this section apply to a hire by a person who in the course of a business is acting as agent for another as they apply to a hire by a principal in the course of a business, except where that other is not hiring in the course of a business and either the person to whom the goods are hired knows that fact or reasonable steps are taken to bring it to that person's notice before the contract concerned is made.

[(10) For the purposes of this section, 'consumer contract' has the same meaning as in section 11F(3) above.]

11K Implied terms where hire is by sample

(1) This section applies where, under a contract of the hire of goods, the supplier hires or agrees to hire the goods by reference to a sample.

(2) In such a case there is an implied term—

 (a) that the bulk will correspond with the sample in quality; and

 (b) that the person to whom the goods are hired will have a reasonable opportunity of comparing the bulk with the sample; and

 (c) that the goods will be free from any defect, making their quality unsatisfactory, which would not be apparent on reasonable examination of the sample.

(3) For the purposes of this section a supplier hires or agrees to hire goods by reference to a sample where there is an express or implied term to that effect in the contract concerned.

Exclusion of implied terms, etc.

11L Exclusion of implied terms etc.

(1) Where a right, duty or liability would arise under a contract for the transfer of goods or a contract for the hire of goods by implication of law, it may (subject to subsection (2)

below and the 1977 Act) be negatived or varied by express agreement, or by the course of dealing between the parties, or by such usage as binds both parties to the contract.

(2) An express term does not negative a term implied by the preceding provisions of this Part of this Act unless inconsistent with it.

(3) Nothing in the preceding provisions of this Part of this Act prejudices the operation of any other enactment or any rule of law whereby any term (other than one relating to quality or fitness) is to be implied in a contract for the transfer of goods or a contract for the hire of goods.]

[PART 1B

ADDITIONAL RIGHTS OF TRANSFEREE IN CONSUMER CASES]

[11M Introductory
(1) This section applies if—
  (a) the transferee deals as consumer or, in Scotland, there is a consumer contract in which the transferee is a consumer, and
  (b) the goods do not conform to the contract for the transfer of goods at the time of delivery.
(2) If this section applies, the transferee has the right—
  (a) under and in accordance with section 11N below, to require the transferor to repair or replace the goods, or
  (b) under and in accordance with section 11P below—
    (i) to require the transferor to reduce the amount to be paid for the transfer by the transferee by an appropriate amount, or
    (ii) to rescind the contract with regard to the goods in question.
(3) For the purposes of subsection (1)(b) above, goods which do not conform to the contract for the transfer of goods at any time within the period of six months starting with the date on which the goods were delivered to the transferee must be taken not to have so conformed at that date.
(4) Subsection (3) above does not apply if—
  (a) it is established that the goods did so conform at that date;
  (b) its application is incompatible with the nature of the goods or the nature of the lack of conformity.
(5) For the purposes of this section, 'consumer contract' has the same meaning as in section 11F(3) above.

11N Repair or replacement of the goods
(1) If section 11M above applies, the transferee may require the transferor—
  (a) to repair the goods, or
  (b) to replace the goods.
(2) If the transferee requires the transferor to repair or replace the goods, the transferor must—
  (a) repair or, as the case may be, replace the goods within a reasonable time but without causing significant inconvenience to the transferee;
  (b) bear any necessary costs incurred in doing so (including in particular the cost of any labour, materials or postage).
(3) The transferee must not require the transferor to repair or, as the case may be, replace the goods if that remedy is—
  (a) impossible,
  (b) disproportionate in comparison to the other of those remedies, or
  (c) disproportionate in comparison to an appropriate reduction in the purchase price under paragraph (a), or rescission under paragraph (b), of section 11P(1) below.

(4) One remedy is disproportionate in comparison to the other if the one imposes costs on the transferor which, in comparison to those imposed on him by the other, are unreasonable, taking into account—

    (a) the value which the goods would have if they conformed to the contract for the transfer of goods,

    (b) the significance of the lack of conformity to the contract for the transfer of goods, and

    (c) whether the other remedy could be effected without significant inconvenience to the transferee.

(5) Any question as to what is a reasonable time or significant inconvenience is to be determined by reference to—

    (a) the nature of the goods, and

    (b) the purpose for which the goods were acquired.

11P   Reduction of purchase price or rescission of contract

(1) If section 11M above applies, the transferee may—

    (a) require the transferor to reduce the purchase price of the goods in question to the transferee by an appropriate amount, or

    (b) rescind the contract with regard to those goods,

if the condition in subsection (2) below is satisfied.

(2) The condition is that—

    (a) by virtue of section 11N(3) above the transferee may require neither repair nor replacement of the goods, or

    (b) the transferee has required the transferor to repair or replace the goods, but the transferor is in breach of the requirement of section 11N(2)(a) above to do so within a reasonable time and without significant inconvenience to the transferee.

(3) If the transferee rescinds the contract, any reimbursement to the transferee may be reduced to take account of the use he has had of the goods since they were delivered to him.

11Q   Relation to other remedies, etc.

(1) If the transferee requires the transferor to repair or replace the goods the transferee must not act under subsection (2) until he has given the transferor a reasonable time in which to repair or replace (as the case may be) the goods.

(2) The transferee acts under this subsection if—

    (a) in England and Wales or Northern Ireland he rejects the goods and terminates the contract for breach of condition;

    (b) in Scotland he rejects any goods delivered under the contract and treats it as repudiated; or

    (c) he requires the goods to be replaced or repaired (as the case may be).

11R   Powers of the court

(1) In any proceedings in which a remedy is sought by virtue of this Part the court, in addition to any other power it has, may act under this section.

(2) On the application of the transferee the court may make an order requiring specific performance or, in Scotland, specific implement by the transferor of any obligation imposed on him by virtue of section 11N above.

(3) Subsection (4) applies if—

    (a) the transferee requires the transferor to give effect to a remedy under section 11N or 11P above or has claims to rescind under section 11P, but

    (b) the court decides that another remedy under section 11N or 11P is appropriate.

(4) The court may proceed—

    (a) as if the transferee had required the transferor to give effect to the other remedy, or if the other remedy is rescission under section 11P,

    (b) as if the transferee had claimed to rescind the contract under that section.

(5) If the transferee has claimed to rescind the contract the court may order that any reimbursement to the transferee is reduced to take account of the use he has had of the goods since they were delivered to him.

(6) The court may make an order under this section unconditionally or on such terms and conditions as to damages, payment of the price and otherwise as it thinks just.

11S   Conformity with the contract
(1) Goods do not conform to a contract for the supply or transfer of goods if—
(a) there is, in relation to the goods, a breach of an express term of the contract or a term implied by section 3, 4 or 5 above or, in Scotland, by section 11C, 11D or 11E above, or
(b) installation of the goods forms part of the contract for the transfer of goods, and the goods were installed by the transferor, or under his responsibility, in breach of the term implied by section 13 below or (in Scotland) in breach of any term implied by any rule of law as to the manner in which the installation is carried out.]

PART II   SUPPLY OF SERVICES

12   The contracts concerned
(1) In this Act a 'contract for the supply of a service' means, subject to subsection (2) below a contract under which a person ('the supplier') agrees to carry out a service.

(2) For the purposes of this Act, a contract of service or apprenticeship is not a contract for the supply of a service.

(3) Subject to subsection (2) above, a contract is a contract for the supply of a service for the purposes of this Act whether or not goods are also—
(a) transferred or to be transferred, or
(b) bailed or to be bailed by way of hire, under the contract, and whatever is the nature of the consideration for which the service is to be carried out.

(4) The Secretary of State may by order provide that one or more of sections 13 to 15 below shall not apply to services of a description specified in the order, and such an order may make different provision for different circumstances.

(5) The power to make an order under subsection (4) above shall be exercisable by statutory instrument subject to annulment in pursuance of a resolution of either House of Parliament.

13   Implied term about care and skill
In a contract for the supply of a service where the supplier is acting in the course of a business, there is an implied term that the supplier will carry out the service with reasonable care and skill.

14   Implied term about time of performance
(1) Where, under a contract for the supply of a service by a supplier acting in the course of a business, the time for the service to be carried out is not fixed by the contract, left to be fixed in a manner agreed by the contract or determined by the course of dealing between the parties, there is an implied term that the supplier will carry out the service within a reasonable time.

(2) What is a reasonable time is a question of fact.

15   Implied term about consideration
(1) Where, under a contract for the supply of a service, the consideration for the service is not determined by the contract, left to be determined in a manner agreed by the contract or determined by the course of dealing between the parties, there is an implied term that the party contracting with the supplier will pay a reasonable charge.

(2) What is a reasonable charge is a question of fact.

16   Exclusion of implied terms, etc.

(1) Where a right, duty or liability would arise under contract for the supply of a service by virtue of this Part of this Act, it may (subject to subsection (2) below and the 1977 Act) be negatived or varied by express agreement, or by the course of dealing between the parties, or by such usage as binds both parties to the contract.

(2) An express term does not negative a term implied by this Part of this Act unless inconsistent with it.

(3) Nothing in this Part of this Act prejudices—

   (a) any rule of law which imposes on the supplier a duty stricter than that imposed by section 13 or 14 above; or

   (b) subject to paragraph (a) above, any rule of law whereby any term not inconsistent with this Part of this Act is to be implied in a contract for the supply of a service.

(4) This Part of this Act has effect to any other enactment which defines or restricts the rights, duties or liabilities arising in connection with a service of any description.

PART III   SUPPLEMENTARY

18   Interpretation: general

(1) In the preceding provisions of this Act and this section—

'bailee', in relation to a contract for the hire of goods means (depending on the context) a person to whom the goods are bailed under a contract, or a person to whom they are to be so bailed, or a person to whom the rights under the contract of either of those persons have passed;

'bailor', in relation to a contract for the hire of goods, means (depending on the context) a person who bails the goods under the contract, or a person who agrees to do so, or a person to whom the duties under the contract of either of those persons have passed;

'business' includes a profession and the activities of any government department or local or public authority;

'credit-broker' means a person acting in the course of a business of credit brokerage carried on by him;

'credit brokerage' means the effecting of introductions—

   (a) of individuals desiring to obtain credit to persons carrying on any business so far as it relates to the provision of credit; or

   (b) of individuals desiring to obtain goods on hire to persons carrying on a business which comprises or relates to the bailment [or as regards Scotland the hire] of goods under a contract for the hire of goods; or

   (c) of individuals desiring to obtain credit, or to obtain goods on hire, to other credit-brokers;

'enactment' means any legislation (including subordinate legislation) of the United Kingdom or Northern Ireland;

'goods' [includes all personal chattels, other than things in action and money, and as regards Scotland all corporeal moveables; and in particular 'goods' includes] emblements, industrial growing crops, and things attached to or forming part of the land which are agreed to be severed before the transfer [bailment or hire] concerned or under the contract concerned [. . .];

'hire-purchase agreement' has the same meaning as in the 1974 Act;

['producer' means the manufacturer of goods, the importer of goods into the European Economic Area or any person purporting to be a producer by placing his name, trade mark or other distinctive sign on the goods;]

'property', in relation to goods, means the general property in them and not merely a special property;

[...]

['repair' means, in cases where there is a lack of conformity in goods for the purposes of this Act, to bring the goods into conformity with the contract.]

[...]

'transferee', in relation to a contract for the transfer of goods, means (depending on the context) a person to whom the property in the goods is transferred under the contract, or a person to whom the property is to be so transferred, or a person to whom the rights under the contract of either of those persons have passed;

'transferor', in relation to a contract for the transfer of goods, means (depending on the context) a person who transfers the property in the goods under the contract, or a person who agrees to do so, or a person to whom the duties under the contract of either of those persons have passed.

(2) In subsection (1) above, in the definitions of bailee, bailor, transferee and transferor, a reference to rights or duties passing is to their passing by assignment, [assignation] operation of law or otherwise.

[(3) For the purposes of this Act, the quality of goods includes their state and condition and the following (among others) are in appropriate cases aspects of the quality of goods—

(a) fitness for all the purposes for which goods of the kind in question are commonly supplied,

(b) appearance and finish,

(c) freedom from minor defects,

(d) safety, and

(e) durability.

(4) References in this Act to dealing as consumer are to be construed in accordance with Part I of the Unfair Contract Terms Act 1977; and, for the purposes of this Act, it is for the transferor or bailor claiming that the transferee or bailee does not deal as consumer to show that he does not.]

19   Interpretation: references to Acts

In this Act—

'the 1973 Act' means the Supply of Goods (Implied Terms) Act 1973;

'the 1974 Act' means the Consumer Credit Act 1974;

'the 1977 Act' means the Unfair Contract Terms Act 1977;

and 'the 1979 Act' means the Sale of Goods Act 1979.

20   Citation, transitional provisions, commencement and extent

(1) This Act may be cited as the Supply of Goods and Services Act 1982.

. . .

Companies Act 1985

(1985, c. 6)

An Act to consolidate the greater part of the Companies Acts.   [11th March 1985]

[35A   Power of directors to bind the company

(1) In favour of a person dealing with a company in good faith, the power of the board of directors to bind the company, or authorise others to do so, shall be deemed to be free of any limitation under the company's constitution.

(2) For this purpose—

(a) a person 'deals with' a company if he is a party to any transaction or other act to which the company is a party;

(b) a person shall not be regarded as acting in bad faith by reason only of his knowing that an act is beyond the powers of the directors under the company's constitution; and

(c) a person shall be presumed to have acted in good faith unless the contrary is proved.

(3) The references above to limitations on the directors' powers under the company's constitution include limitations deriving—

      (a) from a resolution of the company in general meeting or a meeting of any class of shareholders, or

      (b) from any agreement between the members of the company or of any class of shareholders.

(4) Subsection (1) does not affect any right of a member of the company to bring proceedings to restrain the doing of an act which is beyond the powers of the directors; but no such proceedings shall lie in respect of an act to be done in fulfilment of a legal obligation arising from a previous act of the company.

(5) Nor does that subsection affect any liability incurred by the directors, or any other person, by reason of the directors' exceeding their powers . . .]

[35B   No duty to enquire as to capacity of company or authority of directors

A party to a transaction with a company is not bound to enquire as to whether it is permitted by the company's memorandum or as to any limitation on the powers of the board of directors to bind the company or authorise others to do so.]

[36C   Pre-incorporation contracts, deeds and obligations

(1) A contract which purports to be made by or on behalf of a company at a time when the company has not been formed has effect, subject to any agreement to the contrary, as one made with the person purporting to act for the company or as agent for it, and he is personally liable on the contract accordingly.

(2) Subsection (1) applies—

      (a) to the making of a deed under the law of England and Wales, and

      (b) . . .

as it applies to the making of a contract.]

[196   {*Payment of debts out of assets subject to floating charge (England and Wales)*}

(1) The following applies in the case of a company registered in England and Wales, where debentures of the company are secured by a charge which, as created, was a floating charge.

(2) If possession is taken, by or on behalf of the holders of any of the debentures, of any property comprised in or subject to the charge, and the company is not at that time in course of being wound up, the company's preferential debts shall be paid out of assets coming to the hands of the person taking possession in priority to any claims for principal or interest in respect of the debentures.

(3) 'Preferential debts' means the categories of debts listed in Schedule 6 to the Insolvency Act; and for the purposes of that Schedule 'the relevant date' is the date of possession being taken as above mentioned.

(4) Payments made under this section shall be recouped, as far as may be, out of the assets of the company available for payment of general creditors.]

349   Company's name to appear in its correspondence, etc.

(4) If an officer of a company or a person on its behalf signs or authorises to be signed on behalf of the company any bill of exchange, promissory note, endorsement, cheque or order for money or goods in which the company's name is not mentioned as required by subsection (1), he is liable to a fine; and he is further personally liable to the holder of the bill of exchange, promissory note, cheque or order for money or goods for the amount of it (unless it is duly paid by the company).

395   Certain charges void if not registered

(1) Subject to the provisions of this Chapter, a charge created by a company registered in England and Wales and being a charge to which this section applies is, so far as any security on the company's property or undertaking is conferred by the charge, void against the liquidator [or administrator] and any creditor of the company, unless the prescribed particulars of the charge together with the instrument (if any) by which the charge is created or

evidenced, are delivered to or received by the registrar of companies for registration in the manner required by this Chapter within 21 days after the date of the charge's creation.

(2) Subsection (1) is without prejudice to any contract or obligation for repayment of the money secured by the charge; and when a charge becomes void under this section, the money secured by it immediately becomes payable.

396 Charges which have to be registered

(1) Section 395 applies to the following charges—

(a) a charge for the purpose of securing any issue of debentures,

(b) a charge on uncalled share capital of the company,

(c) a charge created or evidenced by an instrument which, if executed by an individual, would require registration as a bill of sale,

(d) a charge on land (wherever situated) or any interest in it, but not including a charge for any rent or other periodical sum issuing out of the land,

(e) a charge on book debts of the company,

(f) (f) a floating charge on the company's undertaking or property,

(g) a charge on calls made but not paid,

(h) a charge on a ship or aircraft, or any share in a ship,

(j) a charge on goodwill, [or on any intellectual property].

(2) Where a negotiable instrument has been given to secure the payment of any book debts of a company, the deposit of the instrument for the purpose of securing an advance to the company is not, for purposes of section 395, to be treated as a charge on those book debts.

(3) The holding of debentures entitling the holder to a charge on land is not for purposes of this section deemed to be an interest in land.

[(3A) The following are 'intellectual property' for the purposes of this section—

(a) any patent, trade mark, . . . registered design, copyright or design right;

(b) any licence under or in respect of any such right.]

(4) In this Chapter, 'charge' includes mortgage.

PART XII   REGISTRATION OF CHARGES

CHAPTER II   REGISTRATION OF CHARGES (SCOTLAND)

410 Charges void unless registered

(1) The following provisions of this Chapter have effect for the purpose of securing the registration in Scotland of charges created by companies.

(2) Every charge created by a company, being a charge to which this section applies, is, so far as any security on the company's property or any part of it is conferred by the charge, void against the liquidator and any creditor of the company unless the prescribed particulars of the charge, together with a copy (certified in the prescribed manner to be a correct copy) of the instrument (if any) by which the charge is created or evidenced, are delivered to or received by the registrar of companies for registration in the manner required by this Chapter within 21 days after the date of the creation of the charge.

(3) Subsection (2) is without prejudice to any contract or obligation for repayment of the money secured by the charge; and when a charge becomes void under this section the money secured by it immediately becomes payable.

(4) This section applies to the following charges—

(a) a charge on land wherever situated, or any interest in such land (not including a charge for any rent, ground annual or other periodical sum payable in respect of the land, but including a charge created by a heritable security within the meaning of section 9(8) of the Conveyancing and Feudal Reform (Scotland) Act 1970),

(b) a security over the uncalled share capital of the company,

  (c) a security over incorporeal moveable property of any of the following categories—
    (i) the book debts of the company,
    (ii) calls made but not paid,
    (iii) goodwill,
    (iv) a patent or a licence under a patent,
    (v) a trademark,
    (vi) a copyright or a licence under a copyright,
  (d) a security over a ship or aircraft or any share in a ship, and
  (e) a floating charge.

(5) In this Chapter 'company' (except in section 424) means an incorporated company registered in Scotland; 'registrar of companies' means the registrar or other officer performing under this Act the duty of registration of companies in Scotland; and references to the date of creation of a charge are—
  (a) in the case of a floating charge, the date on which the instrument creating the floating charge was executed by the company creating the charge, and
  (b) in any other case, the date on which the right of the person entitled to the benefit of the charge was constituted as a real right.

PART XVIII   FLOATING CHARGES AND RECEIVERS (SCOTLAND)

CHAPTER 1   FLOATING CHARGES

462   Power of incorporated company to create floating charge

(1) It is competent under the law of Scotland for an incorporated company (whether a company within the meaning of this Act or not), for the purpose of securing any debt or other obligation (including a cautionary obligation) incurred or to be incurred by, or binding upon, the company or any other person, to create in favour of the creditor in the debt or obligation a charge, in this Part referred to as a floating charge, over all or any part of the property (including uncalled capital) which may from time to time be comprised in its property and undertaking.

(2) A floating charge may be created, in the case of a company which the Court of Session has jurisdiction to wind up, only by the execution, under the seal of the company, of an instrument or bond or other written acknowledgment of debt or obligation which purports to create such a charge.

(3) Execution in accordance with this section incudes execution by an attorney authorised for such purpose by the company by writing under its common seal; and any such execution on behalf of the company binds the company.

(4) References in this Part to the instrument by which a floating charge was created are, in the case of a floating charge created by words in a bond or other written acknowledgment, references to the bond or, as the case may be, the other written acknowledgment.

(5) Subject to this Act, a floating charge has effect in accordance with this Part in relation to any heritable property in Scotland to which it relates, notwithstanding that the instrument creating it is not recorded in the Register of Sasines or, as appropriate, registered in accordance with the Land Registration (Scotland) Act 1979.

463   Effect of floating charge on winding up

(1) On the commencement of the winding up of a company, a floating charge created by the company attaches to the property then comprised in the company's property and undertaking or, as the case may be, in part of that property and undertaking, but does so subject to the rights of any person who—
  (a) has effectually executed diligence on the property or any part of it; or
  (b) holds a fixed security over the property or any part of it ranking in priority to the floating charge; or

(c) holds over the property or any part of it another floating charge so ranking.

(2) The provisions on Part XX (except section 623(4)) have effect in relation to a floating charge, subject to subsection (1), as if the charge were a fixed security over the property to which it has attached in respect of the principal of the debt or obligation to which it relates and any interest due or to become due thereon.

(3) Nothing in this section—

(a) prejudices the operation of section 614(2);

(b) derogates from the provisions of sections 469(7) and 470(6) in this Part.

(4) Subject to section 617, interest accrues, in respect of a floating charge which after 16th November 1972 attaches to the property of the company, until payment of the sum due under the charge is made.

464 Ranking of floating charges

(1) Subject to subsection (2), the instrument creating a floating charge over all or any part of the company's property under section 462 may contain—

(a) provisions prohibiting or restricting the creation of any fixed security or any other floating charge having priority over, or ranking pari passu with, the floating charge; or

(b) provisions regulating the order in which the floating charge shall rank with any other subsisting or future floating charges or fixed securities over that property or any part of it.

(2) Where all or any part of the property of a company is subject both to a floating charge and to a fixed security arising by operation of law, the fixed security has priority over the floating charge.

(3) Where the order of ranking of the floating charge with any other subsisting or future floating charges or fixed securities over all or any part of the company's property is not regulated by provisions contained in the instrument creating the floating charge, the order of ranking is determined in accordance with the following provisions of this section.

(4) Subject to the provisions of this section—

(a) a fixed security, the right to which has been constituted as a real right before a floating charge has attached to all or any part of the property of the company, has priority of ranking over the floating charge;

(b) floating charges rank with one another according to the time of registration in accordance with Chapter II of Part XII;

(c) floating charges which have been received by the registrar for registration by the same postal delivery rank with one another equally.

(5) Where the holder of a floating charge over all or any part of the company's property which has been registered in accordance with Chapter II of Part XII has received intimation in writing of the subsequent registration in accordance with that Chapter of another floating charge over the same property or any part thereof, the preference in ranking of the first-mentioned floating charge is restricted to security for—

(a) the holder's present advances;

(b) future advances which he may be required to make under the instrument creating the floating charge or under any ancillary document;

(c) interest due or to become due on all such advances; and

(d) any expenses or outlays which may reasonably be incurred by the holder.

(6) This section is subject to section 614(2) (preferential debts in winding up).

465 Continued effect of certain charges validated by Act of 1972

(1) Any floating charge which—

(a) purported to subsist as a floating charge on 17th November 1972, and

(b) if it had been created on or after that date, would have been validly created by virtue of the Companies (Floating Charges and Receivers) (Scotland) Act 1972,

is deemed to have subsisted as a valid floating charge as from the date of its creation.

(2) Any provision which—

    (a) is contained in an instrument creating a floating charge or in any ancillary document executed prior to, and still subsisting at, the commencement of that Act,

    (b) relates to the ranking of charges, and

    (c) if it had been made after the commencement of that Act, would have been a valid provision,

is deemed to have been a valid provision as from the date of its making.

Insolvency Act 1986
(1986, c. 45)

An Act to consolidate the enactments relating to company insolvency and winding up (including the winding up of companies that are not insolvent, and of unregistered companies); enactments relating to the insolvency and bankruptcy of individuals; and other enactments bearing on those two subject matters, including the functions and qualification of insolvency practitioners, the public administration of insolvency, the penalisation and redress of malpractice and wrongdoing, and the avoidance of certain transactions at an undervalue.   **[25th July 1986]**

8   Power of court to make order

(1) Subject to this section, if the court—

    (a) is satisfied that a company is or is likely to become unable to pay its debts (within the meaning given to that expression by section 123 of this Act), and

    (b) considers that the making of an order under this section would be likely to achieve one or more of the purposes mentioned below,

the court may make an administration order in relation to the company.

(2) An administration order is an order directing that, during the period for which the order is in force, the affairs, business and property of the company shall be managed by a person ('the administrator') appointed for the purpose by the court.

(3) The purposes for whose achievement an administration order may be made are—

    (a) the survival of the company, and the whole or any part of its undertaking, as a going concern;

    (b) the approval of a voluntary arrangement under Part I;

    ...

    (d) a more advantageous realisation of the company's assets than would be effected on a winding up;

and the order shall specify the purpose or purposes for which it is made.

[(4) An administration order shall not be made in relation to a company after it has gone into liquidation.]

10   Effect of application

(1) During the period beginning with the presentation of a petition for an administration order and ending with the making of such an order or the dismissal of the petition—

    (a) no resolution may be passed or order made for the winding up of the company;

    [(aa) no landlord or other person to whom rent is payable may exercise any right of forfeiture by peaceable re-entry in relation to premises let to the company in respect of a failure by the company to comply with any term or condition of its tenancy of such premises, except with the leave of the court and subject to such terms as the court may impose]

(4) References in this section and the next to hire-purchase agreements include conditional sale agreements, chattel leasing agreements and retention of title agreements.

11   Effect of order

(3) During the period for which an administration order is in force—

(a) no resolution may be passed or order made for the winding up of the company;

(b) no administrative receiver of the company may be appointed;

[(ba) no landlord or other person to whom rent is payable may exercise any right of forfeiture by peaceable re-entry in relation to premises let to the company in respect of a failure by the company to comply with any term or condition of its tenancy of such premises, except with the consent of the administrator or the leave of the court and subject (where the court gives leave) to such terms as the court may impose]

(c) no other steps may be taken to enforce any security over the company's property, or to repossess goods in the company's possession under any hire-purchase agreement, except with the consent of the administrator or the leave of the court and subject (where the court gives leave) to such terms as the court may impose; and

(d) no other proceedings and no execution or other legal process may be commenced or continued, and no distress may be levied, against the company or its property except with the consent of the administrator or the leave of the court and subject (where the court gives leave) to such terms as aforesaid.

15   Power to deal with charged property, etc.

(2) Where, on an application by the administrator, the court is satisfied that the disposal (with or without other assets) of—

(a) any property of the company subject to a security to which this subsection applies, or

(b) any goods in the possession of the company under a hire-purchase agreement, would be likely to promote the purpose or one or more of the purposes specified in the administration order, the court may by order authorise the administrator to dispose of the property as if it were not subject to the security or to dispose of the goods as if all rights of the owner under the hire-purchase agreement were vested in the company.

[(3) Subsection (2) applies to any security other than one which, as created, was a floating charge.]

(4) Where property is disposed of under subsection (1), the holder of the security has the same priority in respect of any property of the company directly or indirectly representing the property disposed of as he would have had in respect of the property subject to the security.

(5) It shall be a condition of an order under subsection (2) that—

(a) the net proceeds of the disposal, and

(b) where those proceeds are less than such amount as may be determined by the court to be the net amount which would be realised on a sale of the property or goods in the open market by a willing vendor, such sums as may be required to make good the deficiency,

shall be applied towards discharging the sums secured by the security or payable under the hire-purchase agreement.

(6) Where a condition imposed in pursuance of subsection (5) relates to two or more securities, that condition requires the net proceeds of the disposal and, where paragraph (b) of that subsection applies, the sums mentioned in that paragraph to be applied towards discharging the sums secured by those securities in the order of their priorities.

(7) An office copy of an order under subsection (2) shall, within 14 days after the making of the order, be sent by the administrator to the registrar of companies.

(8) If the administrator without reasonable excuse fails to comply with subsection (7), he is liable to a fine and, for continued contravention, to a daily default fine.

(9) References in this section to hire-purchase agreements include conditional sale agreements, chattel leasing agreements and retention of title agreements.

40   Payment of debts out of assets subject to floating charge

(1) The following applies, in the case of a company, where a receiver is appointed on behalf of the holders of any debentures of the company secured by a charge which, as created, was a floating charge.

(2) If the company is not at the time in course of being wound up, its preferential debts (within the meaning given to that expression by section 386 in Part XII) shall be paid out of the assets coming to the hands of the receiver in priority to any claims for principal or interest in respect of the debentures.

(3) Payments made under this section shall be recouped, as far as may be, out of the assets of the company available for payment of general creditors.

127   Avoidance of property dispositions, etc.

[(1)] In a winding up by the court, any disposition of the company's property, and any transfer of shares, or alteration in the status of the company's members, made after the commencement of the winding up is, unless the court otherwise orders, void.

[(2) This section has no effect in respect of anything done by an administrator of a company while a winding-up petition is suspended under paragraph 40 of Schedule B1.]

175   Preferential debts (general provision)

(1) In a winding up the company's preferential debts (within the meaning given by section 386 in Part XII) shall be paid in priority to all other debts.

(2) Preferential debts—

(a) rank equally among themselves after the expenses of the winding up and shall be paid in full, unless the assets are insufficient to meet them, in which case they abate in equal proportions; and

(b) so far as the assets of the company available for payment of general creditors are insufficient to meet them, have priority over the claims of holders of debentures secured by, or holders of, any floating charge created by the company, and shall be paid accordingly out of any property comprised in or subject to that charge.

[176A   Share of assets for unsecured creditors

(1) This section applies where a floating charge relates to property of a company—

(a) which has gone into liquidation,

(b) which is in administration,

(c) of which there is a provisional liquidator, or

(d) of which there is a receiver.

(2) The liquidator, administrator or receiver—

(a) shall make a prescribed part of the company's net property available for the satisfaction of unsecured debts, and

(b) shall not distribute that part to the proprietor of a floating charge except in so far as it exceeds the amount required for the satisfaction of unsecured debts.

(3) Subsection (2) shall not apply to a company if—

(a) the company's net property is less than the prescribed minimum, and

(b) the liquidator, administrator or receiver thinks that the cost of making a distribution to unsecured creditors would be disproportionate to the benefits.

(4) Subsection (2) shall also not apply to a company if or in so far as it is disapplied by—

(a) a voluntary arrangement in respect of the company, or

(b) a compromise or arrangement agreed under section 425 of the Companies Act (compromise with creditors and members).

(5) Subsection (2) shall also not apply to a company if—

(a) the liquidator, administrator or receiver applies to the court for an order under this subsection on the ground that the cost of making a distribution to unsecured creditors would be disproportionate to the benefits, and

(b) the court orders that subsection (2) shall not apply.

(6) In subsections (2) and (3) a company's net property is the amount of its property which would, but for this section, be available for satisfaction of claims of holders of debentures secured by, or holders of, any floating charge created by the company.

(7) An order under subsection (2) prescribing part of a company's net property may, in particular, provide for its calculation—

(a) as a percentage of the company's net property, or

(b) as an aggregate of different percentages of different parts of the company's net property.

(8) An order under this section—

(a) must be made by statutory instrument, and

(b) shall be subject to annulment pursuant to a resolution of either House of Parliament.

(9) In this section—

'floating charge' means a charge which is a floating charge on its creation and which is created after the first order under subsection (2)(a) comes into force, and

'prescribed' means prescribed by order by the Secretary of State.

(10) An order under this section may include transitional or incidental provision.]

213   Fraudulent trading

(1) If in the course of the winding up of a company it appears that any business of the company has been carried on with intent to defraud creditors of the company or creditors of any other person, or for any fraudulent purpose, the following has effect.

(2) The court, on the application of the liquidator may declare that any persons who were knowingly parties to the carrying on of the business in the manner above-mentioned are to be liable to make such contributions (if any) to the company's assets as the court thinks proper.

238   Transactions at an undervalue (England and Wales)

(1) This section applies in the case of a company where—

[(a) the company enters administration,]

(b) the company goes into liquidation;

and 'the office-holder' means the administrator or the liquidator, as the case may be.

(2) Where the company has at a relevant time (defined in section 240) entered into a transaction with any person at an undervalue, the office-holder may apply to the court for an order under this section.

(3) Subject as follows, the court shall, on such an application, make such order as it thinks fit for restoring the position to what it would have been if the company had not entered into that transaction.

(4) For the purposes of this section and section 241, a company enters into a transaction with a person at an undervalue if—

(a) the company makes a gift to that person or otherwise enters into a transaction with that person on terms that provide for the company to receive no consideration, or

(b) the company enters into a transaction with that person for a consideration the value of which, in money or money's worth, is significantly less than the value, in money or money's worth, of the consideration provided by the company.

(5) The court shall not make an order under this section in respect of a transaction at an undervalue if it is satisfied—

(a) that the company which entered into the transaction did so in good faith and for the purpose of carrying on its business, and

(b) that at the time it did so there were reasonable grounds for believing that the transaction would benefit the company.

239   Preferences (England and Wales)

(1) This section applies as does section 238.

(2) Where the company has at a relevant time (defined in the next section) given a preference to any person, the office-holder may apply to the court for an order under this section.

(3) Subject as follows, the court shall, on such an application, make such order as it thinks fit for restoring the position to what it would have been if the company had not given that preference.

(4) For the purposes of this section and section 241, a company gives a preference to a person if—

(a) that person is one of the company's creditors or a surety or guarantor for any of the company's debts or other liabilities, and

(b) the company does anything or suffers anything to be done which (in either case) has the effect of putting that person into a position which, in the event of the company going into insolvent liquidation, will be better than the position he would have been in if that thing had not been done.

(5) The court shall not make an order under this section in respect of a preference given to any person unless the company which gave the preference was influenced in deciding to give it by a desire to produce in relation to that person the effect mentioned in subsection (4)(b).

(6) A company which has given a preference to a person connected with the company (otherwise than by reason only of being its employee) at the time the preference was given is presumed, unless the contrary is shown, to have been influenced in deciding to give it by such a desire as is mentioned in subsection (5).

(7) The fact that something has been done in pursuance of the order of a court does not, without more, prevent the doing or suffering of that thing from constituting the giving of a preference.

240   'Relevant time' under ss. 238, 239

. . .

241   Orders under ss. 238, 239

(1) Without prejudice to the generality of sections 238(3) and 239(3), an order under either of those sections with respect to a transaction or preference entered into or given by a company may (subject to the next subsection)—

(a) require any property transferred as part of the transaction, or in connection with the giving of the preference, to be vested in the company,

(b) require any property to be so vested if it represents in any person's hands the application either of the proceeds of sale of property so transferred or of money so transferred,

(c) release or discharge (in whole or in part) any security given by the company,

(d) require any person to pay, in respect of benefits received by him from the company, such sums to the office-holder as the court may direct,

(e) provide for any surety or guarantor whose obligations to any person were released or discharged (in whole or in part) under the transaction, or by the giving of the preference, to be under such new or revived obligations to that person as the court thinks appropriate,

(f) provide for security to be provided for the discharge of any obligation imposed by or arising under the order, for such an obligation to be charged on any property and for the security or charge to have the same priority as a security or charge released or discharged (in whole or in part) under the transaction or by the giving of the preference, and

(g) provide for the extent to which any person whose property is vested by the order in the company, or on whom obligations are imposed by the order, is to be able to prove in the winding up of the company for debts or other liabilities which arose from, or were released or discharged (in whole or in part) under or by, the transaction or the giving of the preference.

(2) An order under section 238 or 239 may affect the property of, or impose any obligation on, any person whether or not he is the person with whom the company in question entered into the transaction or (as the case may be) the person to whom the preference was given; but such an order—

(a) shall not prejudice any interest in property which was acquired from a person other than the company and was acquired [in good faith and for value], or prejudice any interest deriving from such an interest, and

(b) shall not require a person who received a benefit from the transaction or preference [in good faith and for value] to pay a sum to the office-holder, except where that person was a party to the transaction or the payment is to be in respect of a preference given to that person at a time when he was a creditor of the company.

[(2A) Where a person has acquired an interest in property from a person other than the company in question, or has received a benefit from the transaction or preference, and at the time of that acquisition or receipt—

(a) he had notice of the relevant surrounding circumstances and of the relevant proceedings, or

(b) he was connected with, or was an associate of, either the company in question or the person with whom that company entered into the transaction or to whom that company gave the preference,

then, unless the contrary is shown, it shall be presumed for the purposes of paragraph (a) or (as the case may be) paragraph (b) of subsection (2) that the interest was acquired or the benefit was received otherwise than in good faith.]

[(3) For the purposes of subsection (2A)(a), the relevant surrounding circumstances are (as the case may require)—

(a) the fact that the company in question entered into the transaction at an undervalue; or

(b) the circumstances which amounted to the giving of the preference by the company in question;

and subsections (3A) to (3C) have effect to determine whether, for those purposes, a person has notice of the relevant proceedings.]

[(3A) Where section 238 or 239 applies by reason of a company's entering administration, a person has notice of the relevant proceedings if he has notice that—

(a) an administration application has been made,

(b) an administration order has been made,

(c) a copy of a notice of intention to appoint an administrator under paragraph 14 or 22 of Schedule B1 has been filed, or

(d) notice of the appointment of an administrator has been filed under paragraph 18 or 29 of that Schedule.

(3B) Where section 238 or 239 applies by reason of a company's going into liquidation at the time when the appointment of an administrator of the company ceases to have effect, a person has notice of the relevant proceedings if he has notice that—

(a) an administration application has been made,

(b) an administration order has been made,

(c) a copy of a notice of intention to appoint an administrator under paragraph 14 or 22 of Schedule B1 has been filed,

(d) notice of the appointment of an administrator has been filed under paragraph 18 or 29 of that Schedule, or

(e) the company has gone into liquidation.]

(3C) In a case where section 238 or 239 applies by reason of the company in question going into liquidation at any other time, a person has notice of the relevant proceedings if he has notice—

    (a) where the company goes into liquidation on the making of a winding-up order, of the fact that the petition on which the winding-up order is made has been presented or of the fact that the company has gone into liquidation;

    (b) in any other case, of the fact that the company has gone into liquidation.]

(4) The provisions of sections 238 to 241 apply without prejudice to the availability of any other remedy, even in relation to a transaction or preference which the company had no power to enter into or give.

244 Extortionate credit transactions

(1) This section applies as does section 238, and where the company is, or has been, a party to a transaction for, or involving, the provision of credit to the company.

(2) The court may, on the application of the office-holder, make an order with respect to the transaction if the transaction is or was extortionate and was entered into in the period of 3 years ending with [the day on which the company entered administration or went into liquidation.]

(3) For the purposes of this section a transaction is extortionate if, having regard to the risk accepted by the person providing the credit—

    (a) the terms of it are or were such as to require grossly exorbitant payments to be made (whether unconditionally or in certain contingencies) in respect of the provision of the credit, or

    (b) it otherwise grossly contravened ordinary principles of fair dealing;

and it shall be presumed, unless the contrary is proved, that a transaction with respect to which an application is made under this section is or, as the case may be, was extortionate.

(4) An order under this section with respect to any transaction may contain such one or more of the following as the court thinks fit, that is to say—

    (a) provision setting aside the whole or part of any obligation created by the transaction,

    (b) provision otherwise varying the terms of the transaction or varying the terms on which any security for the purposes of the transaction is held,

    (c) provision requiring any person who is or was a party to the transaction to pay to the office-holder any sums paid to that person, by virtue of the transaction, by the company,

    (d) provision requiring any person to surrender to the office-holder any property held by him as security for the purposes of the transaction,

    (e) provision directing accounts to be taken between any persons.

(5) The powers conferred by this section are exercisable in relation to any transaction concurrently with any powers exercisable in relation to that transaction as a transaction at an undervalue or under section 242 (gratuitous alienations in Scotland).

245 Avoidance of certain floating charges

(1) This section applies as does section 238, but applies to Scotland as well as to England and Wales.

(2) Subject as follows, a floating charge on the company's undertaking or property created at a relevant time is invalid except to the extent of the aggregate of—

    (a) the value of so much of the consideration for the creation of the charge as consists of money paid, or goods or services supplied, to the company at the same time as, or after, the creation of the charge,

    (b) the value of so much of that consideration as consists of the discharge or reduction, at the same time as, or after, the creation of the charge, of any debt of the company, and

(c) the amount of such interest (if any) as is payable on the amount falling within paragraph (a) or (b) in pursuance of any agreement under which the money was so paid, the goods or services were so supplied or the debt was so discharged or reduced.

(3) Subject to the next subsection, the time at which a floating charge is created by a company is a relevant time for the purposes of this section if the charge is created—

(a) in the case of a charge which is created in favour of a person who is connected with the company, at a time in the period of 2 years ending with the onset of insolvency,

(b) in the case of a charge which is created in favour of any other person, at a time in the period of 12 months ending with the onset of insolvency,

(c) in either case, at a time between the making of an administration application in respect of the company and the making of an administration order on that application, or

(d) in either case, at a time between the filing with the court of a copy of notice of intention to appoint an administrator under paragraph 14 or 22 of Schedule B1 and the making of an appointment under that paragraph.

(4) Where a company creates a floating charge at a time mentioned in subsection (3)(b) and the person in favour of whom the charge is created is not connected with the company, that time is not a relevant time for the purposes of this section unless the company—

(a) is at that time unable to pay its debts within the meaning of section 123 in Chapter VI of Part IV, or

(b) becomes unable to pay its debts within the meaning of that section in consequence of the transaction under which the charge is created.

(5) For the purposes of subsection (3), the onset of insolvency is—

[(a) in a case where this section applies by reason of an administrator of a company being appointed by administration order, the date on which the administration application is made,

(b) in a case where this section applies by reason of an administrator of a company being appointed under paragraph 14 or 22 of Schedule B1 following filing with the court of a copy of notice of intention to appoint under that paragraph, the date on which the copy of the notice is filed,

(c) in a case where this section applies by reason of an administrator of a company being appointed otherwise than as mentioned in paragraph (a) or (b), the date on which the appointment takes effect, and

(d) in a case where this section applies by reason of a company going into liquidation, the date of the commencement of the winding up.]

(6) For the purposes of subsection (2)(a) the value of any goods or services supplied by way of consideration for a floating charge is the amount in money which at the time they were supplied could reasonably have been expected to be obtained for supplying the goods or services in the ordinary course of business and on the same terms (apart from the consideration) as those on which they were supplied to the company.

251 Expressions used generally

In this Group of Parts, except in so far as the context otherwise requires— ...

'administrative receiver' means—

(a) an administrative receiver as defined by section 29(2) in Chapter I of Part III, or

(b) a receiver appointed under section 51 in Chapter II of that Part in a case where the whole (or substantially the whole) of the company's property is attached by the floating charge;

'business day' means any day other than a Saturday, a Sunday, Christmas Day, Good Friday or a day which is a bank holiday in any part of Great Britain;

'chattel leasing agreement' means an agreement for the bailment or, in Scotland, the hiring of goods which is capable of subsisting for more than 3 months;

'contributory' has the meaning given by section 79;

'director' includes any person occupying the position of director, by whatever named called;

'floating charge' means a charge which, as created, was a floating charge and includes a floating charge within section 462 of the Companies Act (Scottish floating charges);

'office copy', in relation to Scotland, means a copy certified by the clerk of court;

'the official rate', in relation to interest, means the rate payable under section 189(4);

'prescribed' means prescribed by the rules;

'receiver', in the expression 'receiver or manager', does not include a receiver appointed under section 51 in Chapter II of Part III;

'retention of title agreement' means an agreement for the sale of goods to a company, being an agreement—

(a) which does not constitute a charge on the goods, but

(b) under which, if the seller is not paid and the company is wound up, the seller will have priority over all other creditors of the company as respects the goods or any property representing the goods;

'the rules' means rules under section 411 in Part XV; and

'shadow director', in relation to a company, means a person in accordance with whose directions or instructions the directors of the company are accustomed to act (but so that a person is not deemed a shadow director by reason only that the directors act on advice given by him in a professional capacity);

and any expression for whose interpretation provision is made by Part XXVI of the Companies Act, other than an expression defined above in this section, is to be constructed in accordance with that provision.

344   Avoidance of general assignment of book debts

(1) The following applies where a person engaged in any business makes a general assignment to another person of his existing or future book debts, or any class of them, and is subsequently adjudged bankrupt.

(2) The assignment is void against the trustee of the bankrupt's estate as regards book debts which were not paid before the presentation of the bankruptcy petition, unless the assignment has been registered under the Bills of Sale Act 1878.

(3) For the purpose of subsections (1) and (2)—

(a) 'assignment' includes an assignment by way of security or charge on book debts, and

(b) 'general assignment' does not include—

(i) an assignment of book debts due at the date of the assignment from specified debtors or of debts becoming due under specified contracts, or

(ii) an assignment of book debts included either in a transfer of a business made in good faith and for value or in an assignment of assets for the benefit of creditors generally.

(4) For the purposes of registration under the Act of 1878 an assignment of book debts is to be treated as if it were a bill of sale given otherwise than by way of security for the payment of a sum of money; and the provisions of that Act with respect to the registration of bills of sale apply accordingly with such necessary modifications as may be made by rules under that Act.

423   Transactions defrauding creditors

(1) This section relates to transactions entered into at an undervalue; and a person enters into such a transaction with another person if—

(a) he makes a gift to the other person or he otherwise enters into a transaction with the other on terms that provide for him to receive no consideration;

(b) he enters into a transaction with the other in consideration of marriage [or the formation of a civil partnership]; or

(c) he enters into a transaction with the other for a consideration the value of which, in money or money's worth, is significantly less than the value, in money or money's worth, of the consideration provided by himself.

(2) Where a person has entered into such a transaction, the court may, if satisfied under the next subsection, make such order as it thinks fit for—

(a) restoring the position to what it would have been if the transaction had not been entered into, and

(b) protecting the interests of persons who are victims of the transaction.

(3) In the case of a person entering into such a transaction, an order shall only be made if the court is satisfied that it was entered into by him for the purpose—

(a) of putting assets beyond the reach of a person who is making, or may at some time make, a claim against him, or

(b) of otherwise prejudicing the interests of such a person in relation to the claim which he is making or may make.

(5) In relation to a transaction at an undervalue, references here and below to a victim of the transaction are to a person who is, or is capable of being, prejudiced by it; and in the following two sections the person entering into the transaction is referred to as 'the debtor'.

425 Provision which may be made by order under s. 423

(1) Without prejudice to the generality of section 423, an order made under that section with respect to a transaction may (subject as follows)—

(a) require any property transferred as part of the transaction to be vested in any person, either absolutely or for the benefit of all the persons on whose behalf the application for the order is treated as made;

(b) require any property to be so vested if it represents, in any person's hands, the application either of the proceeds of sale of property so transferred or of money so transferred;

(c) release or discharge (in whole or in part) any security given by the debtor;

(d) require any person to pay to any other person in respect of benefits received from the debtor such sums as the court may direct;

(e) provide for any surety or guarantor whose obligations to any person were released or discharged (in whole or in part) under the transaction to be under such new or revived obligations as the court thinks appropriate;

(f) provide for security to be provided for the discharge of any obligation imposed by or arising under the order, for such an obligation to be charged on any property and for such security or charge to have the same priority as a security or charge released or discharged (in whole or in part) under the transaction.

(2) An order under section 423 may affect the property of, or impose any obligation on, any person whether or not he is the person with whom the debtor entered into the transaction; but such an order—

(a) shall not prejudice any interest in property which was acquired from a person other than the debtor and was acquired in good faith, for value and without notice of the relevant circumstances, or prejudice any interest deriving from such an interest, and

(b) shall not require a person who received a benefit from the transaction in good faith, for value and without notice of the relevant circumstances to pay any sum unless he was a party to the transaction.

(3) For the purposes of this section the relevant circumstances in relation to a transaction are the circumstances by virtue of which an order under section 423 may be made in respect of the transaction.

(4) In this section 'security' means any mortgage, charge, lien or other security.

Consumer Protection Act 1987
(1987, c. 43)

An Act to make provision with respect to the liability of persons for damage caused by defective products; to consolidate with amendments the Consumer Safety Act 1978 and the Consumer Safety (Amendment) Act 1986; to make provision with respect to the giving of price indications; to amend Part I of the Health and Safety at Work etc. Act 1974 and sections 31 and 80 of the Explosives Act 1875; to repeal the Trade Descriptions Act 1972 and the Fabrics (Misdescription) Act 1913; and for connected purposes.   [15th May 1987]

PART I   PRODUCT LIABILITY

1   Purpose and construction of Part I

(1) This Part shall have effect for the purpose of making such provision as is necessary in order to comply with the product liability Directive and shall be construed accordingly.

(2) In this Part, except in so far as the context otherwise requires—

[…]

'dependant' and 'relative' have the same meaning as they have in, respectively, the Fatal Accidents Act 1976 and the Damages (Scotland) Act 1976;

'producer', in relation to a product, means—

(a) the person who manufactured it;

(b) in the case of a substance which has not been manufactured but has been won or abstracted, the person who won or abstracted it;

(c) in the case of a product which has not been manufactured, won or abstracted but essential characteristics of which are attributable to an industrial or other process having been carried out (for example, in relation to agricultural produce), the person who carried out that process;

'product, means any goods or electricity and (subject to subsection (3) below) includes a product which is comprised in another product, whether by virtue of being a component part or raw material or otherwise; and

'the product liability Directive' means the Directive of the Council of the European Communities, dated 25th July 1985, (No. 85/374/EEC) on the approximation of the laws, regulations and administrative provisions of the member States concerning liability for defective products.

(3) For the purposes of this Part a person who supplies any product in which products are comprised, whether by virtue of being component parts or raw materials or otherwise, shall not be treated by reason only of his supply of that product as supplying any of the products so comprised.

2   Liability for defective products

(1) Subject to the following provisions of this Part, where any damage is caused wholly or partly by a defect in a product, every person to whom subsection (2) below applies shall be liable for the damage.

(2) This subsection applies to—

(a) the producer of the product;

(b) any person who, by putting his name on the product or using a trade mark or other distinguishing mark in relation to the product, has held himself out to be the producer of the product;

(c) any person who has imported the product into a member State from a place outside the member States in order, in the course of any business of his, to supply it to another.

(3) Subject as aforesaid, where any damage is caused wholly or partly by a defect in a product, any person who supplied the product (whether to the person who suffered the

damage, to the producer of any product in which the product in question is comprised or to any other person) shall be liable for the damage if—

(a) the person who suffered the damage requests the supplier to identify one or more of the persons (whether still in existence or not) to whom subsection (2) above applies in relation to the product;

(b) that request is made within a reasonable period after the damage occurs and at a time when it is not reasonably practicable for the person making the request to identify all those persons; and

(c) the supplier fails, within a reasonable period after receiving the request, either to comply with the request or to identify the person who supplied the product to him.

(5) Where two or more persons are liable by virtue of this Part for the same damage, their liability shall be joint and several.

(6) This section shall be without prejudice to any liability arising otherwise than by virtue of this Part.

3 Meaning of 'defect'

(1) Subject to the following provisions of the section, there is a defect in a product for the purposes of this Part if the safety of the product is not such as persons generally are entitled to expect; and for those purposes 'safety', in relation to a product, shall include safety with respect to products comprised in that product and safety in the context of risks of damage to property, as well as in the context of risks of death or personal injury.

(2) In determining for the purposes of subsection (1) above what persons generally are entitled to expect in relation to a product all the circumstances shall be taken into account, including—

(a) the manner in which, and purposes for which, the product has been marketed, its get-up, the use of any mark in relation to the product and any instructions for, or warnings with respect to, doing or refraining from doing anything with or in relation to the product;

(b) what might reasonably be expected to be done with or in relation to the product; and

(c) the time when the product was supplied by its producer to another;

and nothing in this section shall require a defect to be inferred from the fact alone that the safety of a product which is supplied after that time is greater than the safety of the product in question.

4 Defences

(1) In any civil proceedings by virtue of this Part against any person ('the person proceeded against') in respect of a defect in a product it shall be a defence for him to show—

(a) that the defect is attributable to compliance with any requirement imposed by or under any enactment or with any Community obligation; or

(b) that the person proceeded against did not at any time supply the product to another; or

(c) that the following conditions are satisfied, that is to say—

(i) that the only supply of the product to another by the person proceeded against was otherwise than in the course of a business of that person's; and

(ii) that section 2(2) above does not apply to that person or applies to him by virtue only of things done otherwise than with a view to profit; or

(d) that the defect did not exist in the product at the relevant time; or

(e) that the state of scientific and technical knowledge at the relevant time was not such that a producer of products of the same description as the product in question might be expected to have discovered the defect if it had existed in his products while they were under his control; or

(f) that the defect—
  (i) constituted a defect in a product ('the subsequent product') in which the product in question had been comprised; and
  (ii) was wholly attributable to the design of the subsequent product or to compliance by the producer of the product in question with instructions given by the producer of the subsequent product.

(2) In this section 'the relevant time', in relation to electricity, means the time at which it was generated, being a time before it was transmitted or distributed, and in relation to any other product, means—
  (a) if the person proceeded against is a person to whom subsection (2) of section 2 above applies in relation to the product, the time when he supplied the product to another;
  (b) if that subsection does not apply to that person in relation to the product, the time when the product was last supplied by a person to whom that subsection does apply in relation to the product.

5 Damage giving rise to liability

(1) Subject to the following provisions of this section, in this Part 'damages' means death or personal injury or any loss of or damage to any property (including land).

(2) A person shall not be liable under section 2 above in respect of any defect in a product for the loss of or any damage to the product itself or for the loss of or any damage to the whole or any part of any product which has been supplied with the product in question comprised in it.

(3) A person shall not be liable under section 2 above for any loss of or damage to any property which, at the time it is lost or damaged, is not—
  (a) of a description of property ordinarily intended for private use, occupation or consumption; and
  (b) intended by the person suffering the loss or damage mainly for his own private use, occupation or consumption.

(4) No damages shall be awarded to any person by virtue of this Part in respect of any loss of or damage to any property if the amount which would fall to be so awarded to that person, apart from this subsection and any liability for interest, does not exceed £275.

(5) In determining for the purposes of this Part who has suffered any loss of or damage to property and when any such loss or damage occurred, the loss or damage shall be regarded as having occurred at the earliest time at which a person with an interest in the property had knowledge of the material facts about the loss or damage.

(6) For the purposes of subsection (5) above the material facts about any loss of or damage to any property are such facts about the loss or damage as would lead a reasonable person with an interest in the property to consider the loss or damage sufficiently serious to justify his instituting proceedings for damages against a defendant who did not dispute liability and was able to satisfy a judgment.

(7) For the purposes of subsection (5) above a person's knowledge includes knowledge which he might reasonably have been expected to acquire—
  (a) from facts observable or ascertainable by him; or
  (b) from facts ascertainable by him with help of appropriate expert advice which it is reasonable for him to seek;
but a person shall not be taken by virtue of this subsection to have knowledge of a fact ascertainable by him only with the help of expert advice unless he has failed to take all reasonable steps to obtain (and, where appropriate, to act on) that advice.

(8) Subsections (5) to (7) above shall not extend to Scotland.

6 Application of certain enactments etc.

(1) Any damage for which a person is liable under section 2 above shall be deemed to have been caused—

(a) for the purposes of the Fatal Accidents Act 1976, by that person's wrongful act, neglect or default;

(b) for the purposes of section 3 of the Law Reform (Miscellaneous Provisions) (Scotland) Act 1940 (contribution among joint wrongdoers), by that person's wrongful act or negligent act or omission;

(c) for the purposes of section 1 of the Damages (Scotland) Act 1976 (rights of relatives of a deceased), by that person's act or omission, and

(d) for the purposes of Part II of the Administration of Justice Act 1982 (damages for personal injuries, etc.—Scotland), by an act or omission giving rise to liability in that person to pay damages.

(2) Where—

(a) a person's death is caused wholly or partly by a defect in a product, or a person dies after suffering damage which has been so caused;

(b) a request such as mentioned in paragraph (a) of subsection (3) of section 2 above is made to a supplier of the product by that person's personal representatives or, in the case of a person whose death is caused wholly or partly by the defect, by any dependant or relative of that person; and

(c) the conditions specified in paragraphs (b) and (c) of that subsection are satisfied in relation to that request,

this Part shall have effect for the purposes of the Law Reform (Miscellaneous Provisions) Act 1934, the Fatal Accidents Acts 1976 and the Damages (Scotland) Act 1976 as if liability of the supplier to that person under that subsection did not depend on that person having requested the supplier to identify certain persons or on the said conditions having been satisfied in relation to a request made by that person.

(3) Section 1 of the Congenital Disabilities (Civil Liability) Act 1976 shall have effect for the purposes of this Part as if—

(a) a person were answerable to a child in respect of an occurrence caused wholly or partly by a defect in a product if he is or has been liable under section 2 above in respect of any effect of the occurrence on a parent of the child, or would be so liable if the occurrence caused a parent of the child to suffer damage;

(b) the provisions of this Part relating to liability under section 2 above applied in relation to liability by virtue of paragraph (a) above under the said section 1; and

(c) subsection (6) of the said section 1 (exclusion of liability) were omitted.

(4) Where any damage is caused partly by a defect in a product and partly by the fault of the person suffering the damage, the Law Reform (Contributory Negligence) Act 1945 and section 5 of the Fatal Accidents Act 1976 (contributory negligence) shall have effect as if the defect were the fault of every person liable by virtue of this Part for the damage caused by the defect.

(5) In subsection (4) above 'fault' has the same meaning as in the said Act of 1945.

(6) Schedule 1 to this Act shall have effect for the purpose of amending the Limitation Act 1980 and the Prescription and Limitation (Scotland) Act 1973 in their application in relation to the bringing of actions by virtue of this Part.

(7) It is hereby declared that liability by virtue of this Part is to be treated as liability in tort for the purposes of any enactment conferring jurisdiction on any court with respect to any matter.

(8) Nothing in this Part shall prejudice the operation of section 12 of the Nuclear Installations Act 1965 (rights to compensation for certain breaches of duties confined to rights under that Act).

7 Prohibition on exclusions from liability

The liability of a person by virtue of this Part to person who has suffered damage caused wholly or partly by a defect in a product, or to a dependant or relative of such a person, shall not be limited or excluded by any contract term, by any notice or by any other provision.

8   Power to modify Part I

(1) Her Majesty may by Order in Council make such modifications of this Part and of any other enactment (including an enactment contained in the following Parts of this Act, or in an Act passed after this Act) as appear to Her Majesty in Council to be necessary or expedient in consequence of any modification of the product liability Directive which is made at any time after the passing of this Act.

(2) An Order in Council under subsection (1) above shall not be submitted to Her Majesty in Council unless a draft of the Order has been laid before, and approved by a resolution of, each House of Parliament.

9   Application of Part I to Crown

(1) Subject to subsection (2) below, this Part shall bind the Crown.

(2) The Crown shall not, as regards the Crown's liability by virtue of this Part, be bound by this Part further than the Crown is made liable in tort or in reparation under the Crown Proceedings Act 1947, as that Act has effect from time to time.

PART II   CONSUMER SAFETY

[...]

11   Safety regulations

(1) The Secretary of State may by regulations under this section ('safety regulations') make such provision as he considers appropriate [...] for the purpose of securing—

(a) that goods to which this section applies are safe;

(b) that goods to which this section applies which are unsafe, or would be unsafe in the hands of persons of a particular description, are not made available to persons generally or, as the case may be, to persons of that description, and

(c) that appropriate information is, and inappropriate information is not, provided in relation to goods to which this section applies.

(2) Without prejudice to the generality of subsection (1) above, safety regulations may contain provision—

(a) with respect to the composition or contents, design, construction, finish or packing of goods to which this section applies, with respect to standards for such goods and with respect to other matters relating to such goods;

(b) with respect to the giving, refusal, alteration or cancellation of approvals of such goods, of descriptions of such goods or of standards for such goods;

(c) with respect to the conditions that may be attached to any approval given under the regulations;

(d) for requiring such fees as may be determined by or under the regulations to be paid on the giving or alteration of any approval under the regulations and on the making of an application for such an approval or alteration;

(e) with respect to appeals against refusals, alterations and cancellations of approvals given under the regulations and against the conditions contained in such approvals;

(f) for requiring goods to which this section applies to be approved under the regulations or to conform to the requirements of the regulations or to descriptions or standards specified in or approved by or under the regulations;

(g) with respect to the testing or inspection of goods to which this section applies (including provision for determining the standards to be applied in carrying out any test or inspection);

(h) with respect to the way of dealing with goods of which some or all do not satisfy a test required by or under the regulations or a standard connected with a procedure so required;

    (i) for requiring a mark, warning or instruction or any other information relating to goods to be put on or to accompany the goods or to be used or provided in some other manner in relation to the goods, and for securing that inappropriate information is not given in relation to goods either by means of misleading marks or otherwise;

    (j) for prohibiting persons from supplying, or from offering to supply, agreeing to supply, exposing for supply or possessing for supply, goods to which this section applies and component parts and raw materials for such goods;

    (k) for requiring information to be given to any such person as may be determined by or under the regulations for the purpose of enabling that person to exercise any function conferred on him by the regulations.

  (3) Without prejudice as aforesaid, safety regulations may contain provision—

    (a) for requiring persons on whom functions are conferred by or under section 27 below to have regard, in exercising their functions so far as relating to any provision of safety regulations, to matters specified in a direction issued by the Secretary of State with respect to that provision;

    (b) for securing that a person shall not be guilty of an offence under section 12 below unless it is shown that the goods in question do not conform to a particular standard;

    (c) for securing that proceedings for such an offence are not brought in England and Wales except by or with the consent of the Secretary of State or the Director of Public Prosecutions;

    (d) for securing that proceedings for such an offence are not brought in Northern Ireland except by or with consent of the Secretary of State or the Director of Public Prosecutions for Northern Ireland;

    (e) for enabling a magistrate's court in England and Wales or Northern Ireland to try an information or, in Northern Ireland, a complaint in respect of such an offence if the information was laid or the complaint made within twelve months from the time when the offence was committed;

    (f) for enabling summary proceedings for such an offence to be brought in Scotland at any time within twelve months from the time when the offence was committed; and

    (g) for determining the persons by whom, and the manner in which, anything required to be done by or under the regulations is to be done.

  (4) Safety regulations shall not provide for any contravention of the regulations to be an offence.

  (5) Where the Secretary of State proposes to make safety regulations it shall be his duty before he makes them—

    (a) to consult such organisations as appear to him to be representative of interests substantially affected by the proposal;

    (b) to consult such other persons as he considers appropriate; and

    (c) in the case of proposed regulations relating to goods suitable for use at work to consult the Health and Safety Commission in relation to the application of the proposed regulations to Great Britain;

but the preceding provisions of this subsection shall not apply in the case of regulations which provide for the regulations to cease to have effect at the end of a period of not more than twelve months beginning with the day on which they come into force and which contain a statement that it appears to the Secretary of State that the need to protect the public requires that the regulations should be made without delay.

  (6) The power to make safety regulations shall be exercisable by statutory instrument subject to annulment in pursuance of a resolution of either House of Parliament and shall include power—

    (a) to make different provision for different cases; and

(b) to make such supplemental, consequential and transitional provision as the Secretary of State considers appropriate.

(7) This section applies to any goods other than—

(a) growing crops and things comprised in land by virtue of being attached to it;

(b) water, food, feeding stuff and fertiliser;

(c) gas which is, is to be or has been supplied by a person authorised to supply it by or under [section 7A of the Gas Act 1986 (licensing of gas suppliers and gas shippers) …];

(d) controlled drugs and licensed medicinal products.

12   Offences against the safety regulations

(1) Where safety regulations prohibit a person from supplying or offering or agreeing to supply any goods or from exposing or possessing any goods for supply that person shall be guilty of an offence if he contravenes the prohibition.

(2) Where safety regulations require a person who makes or processes any goods in the course of carrying on a business—

(a) to carry out a particular test or use a particular procedure in connection with the making or processing of the goods with a view to ascertaining whether the goods satisfy any requirements of such regulations; or

(b) to deal or not to deal in a particular way with a quantity of the goods of which the whole or part does not satisfy such a test or does not satisfy standards connected with such a procedure,

that person shall be guilty of an offence if he does not comply with the requirement.

(3) If a person contravenes a provision of safety regulations which prohibits or requires the provision, by means of a mark or otherwise, of information of a particular kind in relation to goods, he shall be guilty of an offence.

(4) Where safety regulations require any person to give information to another for the purpose of enabling that other to exercise any function, that person shall be guilty of an offence if—

(a) he fails without reasonable cause to comply with the requirement; or

(b) in giving the information which is required of him—

(i)   he makes any statement which he knows is false in a material particular; or

(ii) he recklessly makes any statement which is false in a material particular.

(5) A person guilty of an offence under this section shall be liable on summary conviction to imprisonment for a term not exceeding six months or to a fine not exceeding level 5 on the standard scale or to both.

13   Prohibition notices and notices to warn

(1) The Secretary of State may—

(a) serve on any person a notice ('a prohibition notice') prohibiting that person, except with the consent of the Secretary of State, from supplying, or from offering to supply, agreeing to supply or possessing for supply, any relevant goods which the Secretary of State considers are unsafe and which are described in the notice;

(b) serve on any person a notice ('a notice to warn') requiring that person at his own expense to publish, in a form and manner and on occasions specified in the notice, a warning about any relevant goods which the Secretary of State considers are unsafe, which that person supplies or has supplied and which are described in the notice.

(2) Schedule 2 to this Act shall have effect with respect to prohibition notices and notices to warn, and the Secretary of State may by regulations make provision specifying the manner in which information is to be given to any person under that Schedule.

(3) A consent given by the Secretary of State for the purposes of a prohibition notice may impose such conditions on the doing of anything for which the consent is required as the Secretary of State considers appropriate.

(4) A person who contravenes a prohibition notice or a notice to warn shall be guilty of an offence and liable on summary conviction to imprisonment for a term not exceeding six months or to a fine not exceeding level 5 on the standard scale or to both.

(5) The power to make regulations under subsection (2) above shall be exercisable by statutory instrument subject to annulment in pursuance of a resolution of either House of Parliament and shall include power—

(a) to make different provision for different cases; and

(b) to make such supplemental, consequential and transitional provision as the Secretary of State considers appropriate.

(6) In this section 'relevant goods' means—

(a) in relation to a prohibition notice, any goods to which section 11 above applies; and

(b) in relation to a notice to warn, any goods to which that section applies or any growing crops or things comprised in land by virtue of being attached to it.

[(7) A notice may not be given under this section in respect of any aspect of the safety of goods, or any risk or category of risk associated with goods, concerning which provision is contained in the General Product Safety Regulations 2005.]

14 Suspension notices

(1) Where an enforcement authority has reasonable grounds for suspecting that any safety provision has been contravened in relation to any goods, the authority may serve a notice ('suspension notice') prohibiting the person on whom it is served, for such period ending not more than six months after the date of the notice as is specified therein, from doing any of the following things without the consent of the authority, that is to say, supplying the goods, offering to supply them, agreeing to supply them or exposing them for supply.

(2) A suspension notice served by an enforcement authority in respect of any goods shall—

(a) describe the goods in a manner sufficient to identify them;

(b) set out the grounds on which the authority suspects that a safety provision has been contravened in relation to the goods, and

(c) state that, and the manner in which, the person on whom the notice is served may appeal against the notice under section 15 below.

(3) A suspension notice served by an enforcement authority for the purpose of prohibiting a person for any period from doing the things mentioned in subsection (1) above in relation to any goods may also require that person to keep the authority informed of the whereabouts throughout that period of any of those goods in which he has an interest.

(4) Where a suspension notice has been served on any person in respect of any goods, no further such notice shall be served on that person in respect of the same goods unless—

(a) proceedings against that person for an offence in respect of a contravention in relation to the goods of a safety provision (not being an offence under this section); or

(b) proceedings for the forfeiture of the goods under section 16 or 17 below, are pending at the end of the period specified in the first-mentioned notice.

(5) A consent given by an enforcement authority for the purposes of subsection (1) above may impose such conditions on the doing of anything for which the consent is required as the authority considers appropriate.

(6) Any person who contravenes a suspension notice shall be guilty of an offence and liable on summary conviction to imprisonment for a term not exceeding six months or to a fine not exceeding level 5 on the standard scale or to both.

(7) Where an enforcement authority serves a suspension notice in respect of any goods, the authority shall be liable to pay compensation to any person having an interest in the goods in respect of any loss or damage caused by reason of the service of the notice if—

(a) there has been no contravention in relation to the goods of any safety provision; and

(b) the exercise of the power is not attributable to any neglect or default by that person.

(8) Any disputed question as to the right to or the amount of any compensation payable under this section shall be determined by arbitration or, in Scotland, by a single arbiter appointed, failing agreement between the parties, by the sheriff.

15 Appeals against suspension notices

(1) Any person having an interest in any goods in respect of which a suspension notice is for the time being in force may apply for an order setting aside the notice.

(2) An application under this section may be made—

    (a) to any magistrates' court in which proceedings have been brought in England and Wales or Northern Ireland—

        (i) for an offence in respect of a contravention in relation to the goods of any safety provision; or

        (ii) for the forfeiture of the goods under section 16 below;

    (b) where no such proceedings have been so brought, by way of complaint to a magistrates' court; or

    (c) in Scotland, by summary application to the sheriff.

(3) On an application under this section to a magistrates' court in England and Wales or Northern Ireland the court shall make an order setting aside the suspension notice only if the court is satisfied that there has been no contravention in relation to the goods of any safety provision.

(4) On an application under this section to the sheriff he shall make an order setting aside the suspension notice only if he is sasified that at the date of making the order—

    (a) proceedings for an offence in respect of a contravention in relation to the goods of any safety provision; or

    (b) proceedings for the forfeiture of the goods under section 17 below, have not been brought or, having been brought, have been concluded.

(5) Any person aggrieved by an order made under this section by a magistrates' court in England and Wales or Northern Ireland, or by a decision of such a court not to make such an order, may appeal against that order or decision—

    (a) in England and Wales, to the Crown Court;

    (b) in Northern Ireland, to the county court;

and an order so made may contain such provision as appears to the court to be appropriate for delaying the coming into force of the order pending the making and determination of any appeal (including any application under section Ill of the Magistrates' Courts Act 1980 or Article 146 of the Magistrates' Courts (Northern Ireland) Order 1981 (statement of case)).

16 Forfeiture: England and Wales and Northern Ireland

(1) An enforcement authority in England and Wales or Northern Ireland may apply under this section for an order for the forfeiture of any goods on the grounds that there has been a contravention in relation to the goods of a safety provision.

(2) An application under this section may be made—

    (a) where proceedings have been brought in a magistrates' court for an offence in respect of a contravention in relation to some or all of the goods of any safety provision, to that court;

    (b) where an application with respect to some or all of the goods has been made to a magistrates' court under section 15 above or section 33 below, to that court; and

    (c) where no application for the forfeiture of the goods has been made under paragraph (a) or (b) above, by way of complaint to a magistrates' court.

(3) On an application under this section the court shall make an order for the forfeiture of any goods only if it is satisfied that there has been a contravention in relation to the goods of a safety provision.

(4) For the avoidance of doubt it is declared that a court may infer for the purposes of this section that there has been a contravention in relation to any goods of a safety provision if it is satisfied that any such provision has been contravened in relation to goods which are representative of those goods (whether by reason of being of the same design or part of the same consignment or batch or otherwise).

(5) Any person aggrieved by an order made under this section by a magistrates' court, or by a decision of such a court not to make such an order, may appeal against that order or decision—

(a) in England and Wales, to the Crown Court;

(b) in Northern Ireland, to the county court;

and an order so made may contain such provision as appears to the court to be appropriate for delaying the coming into force of the order pending the making and determination of any appeal (including any application under section III of the Magistrates' Courts Act 1980 or Article 146 of the Magistrates' Courts (Northern Ireland) Order 1981 (statement of case)).

(6) Subject to subsection (7) below, where any goods are forfeited under this section they shall be destroyed in accordance with such directions as the court may give.

(7) On making an order under this section a magistrates' court may, if it considers it appropriate to do so, direct that the goods to which the order relates shall (instead of being destroyed) be released, to such person as the court may specify, on condition that that person—

(a) does not supply those goods to any person otherwise than as mentioned in section 46(7)(a) or (b) below, and

(b) complies with any order to pay costs or expenses (including any order under section 35 below) which has been made against that person in the proceedings for the order for forfeiture.

17　Forfeiture: Scotland

(1) In Scotland a sheriff may make an order for forfeiture of any goods in relation to which there has been a contravention of a safety provision—

(a) on an application by the procurator-fiscal made in the manner specified in section 310 of the Criminal Procedure (Scotland) Act 1975; or

(b) where a person is convicted of any offence in respect of any such contravention, in addition to any other penalty which the sheriff may impose.

(2) The procurator-fiscal making an application under subsection (1)(a) above shall serve on any person appearing to him to be the owner of, or otherwise to have an interest in, the goods to which the application relates a copy of the application, together with a notice giving him the opportunity to appear at the hearing of the application to show cause why the goods should not be forfeited.

(3) Service under subsection (2) above shall be carried out, and such service may be proved, in the manner specified for citation of an accused in summary proceedings under the Criminal Procedure (Scotland) Act 1975.

(4) Any person upon whom notice is served under subsection (2) above and any other person claiming to be the owner of, or otherwise to have an interest in, goods to which an application under this section relates shall be entitled to appear at the hearing of the application to show cause why the goods should not be forfeited.

(5) The sheriff shall not make an order following an application under subsection (1)(a) above—

(a) if any person on whom notice is served under subsection (2) above does not appear, unless service of the notice on that person is proved; or

(b) if no notice under subsection (2) above has been served, unless the court is satisfied that in the circumstances it was reasonable not to serve notice on any person.

(6) The sheriff shall make an order under this section only if he is satisfied that there has been a contravention in relation to those goods of a safety provision.

(7) For the avoidance of doubt it is declared that the sheriff may infer for the purposes of this section that there has been a contravention in relation to any goods of a safety provision if he is satisfied that any such provision has been contravened in relation to any goods which are representative of those goods (whether by reason of being of the same design or part of the same consignment or batch or otherwise).

(8) Where an order for the forfeiture of any goods is made following an application by the procurator-fiscal under subsection (1)(a) above, any person who appeared, or was entitled to appear, to show cause why goods should not be forfeited may, within twenty-one days of the making of the order, appeal to the High Court by Bill of Suspension on the ground of an alleged miscarriage of justice; [and section 182(5)(a) to (e) of the Criminal Procedure (Scotland) Act 1995 shall apply to an appeal under this subsection as it applies to a stated case under Part X of that Act].

(9) An order following an application under subsection (1)(a) above shall not take effect—

(a) until the end of the period of twenty-one days beginning with the day after the day on which the order is made; or

(b) if an appeal is made under subsection (8) above within that period, until the appeal is determined or abandoned.

(10) An order under subsection (1)(b) above shall not take effect—

(a) until the end of the period within which an appeal against the order could be brought under the Criminal Procedure (Scotland) Act 1975; or

(b) if an appeal is made within that period, until the appeal is determined or abandoned.

(11) Subject to subsection (12) below, goods forfeited under this section shall be destroyed in accordance with such directions as the sheriff may give.

(12) If he thinks fit the sheriff may direct that the goods be released, to such person as he may specify, on condition that that person does not supply those goods to any other person otherwise than as mentioned in section 46(7)(a) or (b) below.

18   Power to obtain information

(1) If the Secretary of State considers that, for the purpose of deciding whether—

(a) to make, vary or revoke any safety regulations; or

(b) to serve, vary or revoke a prohibition notice; or

(c) to serve or revoke a notice to warn,

he requires information which another person is likely to be able to furnish, the Secretary of State may serve on the other person a notice under this section.

(2) A notice served on any person under this section may require that person—

(a) to furnish to the Secretary of State, within a period specified in the notice, such information as is so specified;

(b) to produce such records as are specified in the notice at a time and place so specified and to permit a person appointed by the Secretary of State for the purpose to take copies of the records at that time and place.

(3) A person shall be guilty of an offence if he—

(a) fails, without reasonable cause, to comply with a notice served on him under this section; or

(b) in purporting to comply with a requirement which by virtue of paragraph (a) of subsection (2) above is contained in such a notice—

(i) furnishes information which he knows is false in a material particular;

(ii) recklessly furnishes information which is false in a material particular.

(4) A person guilty of an offence under subsection (3) above shall—

(a) in the case of an offence under paragraph (a) of that subsection, be liable on summary conviction to a fine not exceeding level 5 on the standard scale; and

(b) in the case of an offence under paragraph (b) of that subsection be liable—

(i) on conviction on indictment, to a fine,

(ii) on summary conviction, to a fine not exceeding the statutory maximum.

19 Interpretation of Part II

(1) In this Part— '

'controlled drug' means a controlled drug within the meaning of the Misuse of Drugs Act 1971;

'feeding stuff' and 'fertiliser' have the same meaning as in Part IV of the Agriculture Act 1970;

'food' does not include anything containing tobacco but, subject to that, has the same meaning as in the [Food Safety Act 1990] or, in relation to Northern Ireland, the same meaning as in the Food and Drugs Act (Northern Ireland) 1958;

'licensed medicinal product' means—

(a) any medicinal product within the meaning of the Medicines Act 1968 in respect of which a product licence within the meaning of that Act is for the time being in force; or

(b) any other article or substance in respect of which any such licence is for the time being in force in pursuance of an order under section 104 or 105 of that Act (application of Act to other articles and substances);

'safe', in relation to any goods, means such that there is no risk, or no risk apart from one reduced to a minimum, that any of the following will (whether immediately or after a definite or indefinite period) cause the death of, or any personal injury to, any person whatsoever, that is to say—

(a) the goods;

(b) the keeping, use or consumption of the goods;

(c) the assembly of any of the goods which are, or are to be supplied unassembled;

(d) any emission or leakage from the goods or, as a result of the keeping, use or consumption of the goods, from anything else; or

(e) reliance on the accuracy of any measurement, calculation or other reading made by or by means of the goods,

and [...] 'unsafe' shall be construed accordingly;

'tobacco' includes any tobacco product within the meaning of the Tobacco Products Duty Act 1979 and any article or substance containing tobacco and intended for oral or nasal use.

(2) In the definition of 'safe' in subsection (1) above, references to the keeping, use or consumption of any goods are references to—

(a) the keeping, use or consumption of the goods by the persons by whom, and in all or any of the ways or circumstances in which, they might reasonably be expected to be kept, used or consumed; and

(b) the keeping, use or consumption of the goods either alone or in conjunction with other goods in conjunction with which they might reasonably be expected to be kept, used or consumed.

PART III   MISLEADING PRICE INDICATIONS

20 Offence of giving misleading indication

(1) Subject to the following provisions of this Part, a person shall be guilty of an offence if, in the course of any business of his, he gives (by any means whatever) to any consumers an indication which is misleading as to the price at which any goods, services, accommodation or facilities are available (whether generally or from particular persons).

(2) Subject as aforesaid, a person shall be guilty of an offence if—

    (a) in the course of any business of his, he has given an indication to any consumers which, after it was given, has become misleading as mentioned in subsection (1) above; and

    (b) some or all of those consumers might reasonably be expected to rely on the indication at a time after it has become misleading; and

    (c) he fails to take all such steps as are reasonable to prevent those consumers from relying on the indication.

(3) For the purposes of this section it shall be immaterial—

    (a) whether the person who gives or gave the indication is or was acting on his own behalf or on behalf of another;

    (b) whether or not that person is the person, or included among the persons, from whom the goods, services, accommodation or facilities are available; and

    (c) whether the indication is or has become misleading in relation to all the consumers to whom it is or was given or only in relation to some of them.

(4) A person guilty of an offence under subsection (1) or (2) above shall be liable—

    (a) on conviction on indictment, to a fine;

    (b) on summary conviction, to a fine not exceeding the statutory maximum.

(5) No prosecution for an offence under subsection (1) or (2) above shall be brought after whichever is the earlier of the following, that is to say—

    (a) the end of the period of three years beginning with the day on which the offence was committed; and

    (b) the end of the period of one year beginning with the day on which the person bringing the prosecution discovered that the offence had been committed.

[(5A) A person is not guilty of an offence under subsection (1) or (2) above if, in giving the misleading indication which would otherwise constitute an offence under either of those subsections, he is guilty of an offence under section 397 of the Financial Services and Markets Act 2000 (misleading statements and practices).]

(6) In this Part—

'consumer'—

    (a) in relation to any goods, means any person who might wish to be supplied with the goods for his own private use or consumption;

    (b) in relation to any services or facilities, means any person who might wish to be provided with the services or facilities otherwise than for the purposes of any business of his; and

    (c) in relation to any accommodation, means any person who might wish to occupy the accommodation otherwise than for the purposes of any business of his;

'price', in relation to any goods, services, accommodation or facilities, means—

    (a) the aggregate of the sums required to be paid by a consumer for or otherwise in respect of the supply of the goods or the provision of the services, accommodation or facilities; or

    (b) except in section 21 below, any method which will be or has been applied for the purpose of determining that aggregate.

21   Meaning of 'misleading'

(1) For the purposes of section 20 above an indication given to any consumers is misleading as to a price if what is conveyed by the indication, or what those consumers might reasonably be expected to infer from the indication or any omission from it, includes any of the following, that is to say—

    (a) that the price is less than in fact it is;

    (b) that the applicability of the price does not depend on facts or circumstances on which its applicability does in fact depend;

    (c) that the price covers matters in respect of which an additional charge is in fact made;

(d) that a person who in fact has no such expectation—
  (i) expects the price to be increased or reduced (whether or not at a particular time or by a particular amount); or
  (ii) expects the price, or the price as increased or reduced, to be maintained (whether or not for a particular period); or
(e) that the facts or circumstances by reference to which the consumers might reasonably be expected to judge the validity of any relevant comparison made or implied by the indication are not what in fact they are.

(2) For the purpose of section 20 above, an indication given to any consumers is misleading as to a method of determining a price if what is conveyed by the indication, or what those consumers might reasonably be expected to infer from the indication or any omission from it, includes any of the following, that is to say—
(a) that the method is not what in fact it is;
(b) that the applicability of the method does not depend on facts or circumstances on which its applicability does in fact depend;
(c) that the method takes into account matters in respect of which an additional charge will in fact be made;
(d) that a person who in fact has no such expectation—
  (i) expects the method to be altered (whether or not at a particular time or in a particular respect); or
  (ii) expects the method, or that method as altered, to remain unaltered (whether or not for a particular period); or
(e) that the facts or circumstances by reference to which the consumers might reasonably be expected to judge the validity of any relevant comparison made or implied by the indication are not what in fact they are.

(3) For the purposes of subsection (1)(e) and (2)(e) above a comparison is a relevant comparison in relation to a price or method of determining a price if it is made between that price or that method, or any price which has been or may be determined by that method, and
(a) any price or value which is stated or implied to be, to have been or to be likely to be attributed to the goods, services, accommodation or facilities in question or to any other goods, services, accommodation or facilities; or
(b) any method, or other method, which is stated or implied to be, to have been or to be likely to be applied or applicable for the determination of the price or value of the goods, services, accommodation or facilities in question or of the price or value of any other goods, services, accommodation or facilities.

22 Application to provision of services and facilities
(1) Subject to the following provisions of this section, references in this Part to services or facilities are references to any services or facilities whatever including, in particular—
(a) the provision of credit or of banking or insurance services and the provision of facilities incidental to the provision of such services;
(b) the purchase or sale of foreign currency;
(c) the supply of electricity;
(d) the provision of a place, other than on a highway, for the parking of a motor vehicle;
(e) the making of arrangements for a person to put or keep a caravan on any land other than arrangements by virtue of which that person may occupy the caravan as his only or main residence.

(2) References in this Part to services shall not include references to services provided to an employer under a contract of employment.
  [...]
(4) In relation to a service consisting in the purchase or sale of foreign currency, references in this Part to the method by which the price of the service is determined shall include references to the rate of exchange.

(5) In this section—

[. . .]

'caravan' has the meaning as in the Caravan Sites and Control of Development Act 1960;

'contract of employment' and 'employer' have the same meanings as in [the Employment Rights Act 1996];

'credit' has the same meaning as in the Consumer Credit Act 1974.

23   Application to provision of accommodation etc.

(1) Subject to subsection (2) below, references in this Part to accommodation or facilities being available shall not include references to accommodation or facilities being available to be provided by means of the creation or disposal of an interest in land except where—

(a) the person who is to create or dispose of the interest will do so in the course of any business of his; and

(b) the interest to be created or disposed of is a relevant interest in a new dwelling and is to be created or disposed of for the purpose of enabling that dwelling to be occupied as a residence, or one of the residences, of the person acquiring the interest.

(2) Subsection (1) above shall not prevent the application of any provision of this Part in relation to—

(a) the supply of any goods as part of the same transaction as any creation or disposal of an interest in land; or

(b) the provision of any services or facilities for the purpose of, or in connection with, any transaction for the creation or disposal of such an interest.

(3) In this section—

'new dwelling' means any building or part of a building in Great Britain which—

(a) has been constructed or adapted to be occupied as a residence; and

(b) has not previously been so occupied or has been so occupied only with other premises or as more than one residence,

and includes any yard, garden, out-houses or appurtenances which belong to that building or part or are to be enjoyed with it;

'relevant interest'—

(a) in relation to a new dwelling in England and Wales, means the freehold estate in the dwelling or a leasehold interest in the dwelling for a term of years absolute of more than twenty-one years, not being a term of which twenty-one years or less remains unexpired;

(b) in relation to a new dwelling in Scotland, means the [ownership] of the land comprising the dwelling, or a leasehold interest in the dwelling where twenty-one years or more remains unexpired.

24   Defences

(1) In any proceedings against a person for an offence under subsection (1) or (2) of section 20 above in respect of any indication it shall be a defence for that person to show that his acts or omissions were authorised for the purposes of this subsection by regulations made under section 26 below.

(2) In proceedings against a person for an offence under subsection (1) or (2) of section 20 above in respect of an indication published in a book, newspaper, magazine [or film or in a programme included in a programme service (within the meaning of the Broadcasting Act 1990),] it shall be a defence for that person to show that the indication was not contained in an advertisement.

(3) In proceedings against a person for an offence under subsection (1) or (2) of section 20 above in respect of an indication published in an advertisement it shall be a defence for that person to show that—

(a) he is a person who carries on a business of publishing or arranging for the publication of advertisements;

(b) he received the advertisement for publication in the ordinary course of that business; and

(c) at the time of publication he did not know and had no grounds for suspecting that the publication would involve the commission of the offence.

(4) In any proceedings against a person for an offence under subsection (1) of section 20 above in respect of any indication, it shall be a defence for that person to show that—

(a) the indication did not relate to the availability from him of any goods, services, accommodation or facilities;

(b) a price had been recommended to every person from whom the goods, services, accommodation or facilities were indicated as being available;

(c) the indication related to that price and was misleading as to that price only by reason of a failure by any person to follow the recommendation; and

(d) it was reasonable for the person who gave the indication to assume that the recommendation was for the most part being followed.

(5) The provisions of this section are without prejudice to the provisions of section 39 below.

(6) In this section—

'advertisement' includes a catalogue, a circular and a price list.

25 Code of practice

(1) The Secretary of State may, after consulting [the Office of Fair Trading] and such other persons as the Secretary of State considers it appropriate to consult, by order approve any code of practice issued (whether by the Secretary of State or another person) for the purpose of—

(a) giving practical guidance with respect to any of the requirements of section 20 above; and

(b) promoting what appear to the Secretary of State to be desirable practices as to the circumstances and manner in which any person gives an indication as to the price at which any goods, services, accommodation or facilities are available or indicates any other matter in respect of which any such indication may be misleading.

(2) A contravention of a code of practice approved under this section shall not of itself give rise to any criminal or civil liability, but in any proceedings against any person for an offence under section 20(1) or (2) above—

(a) any contravention by that person of such a code may be relied on in relation to any matter for the purpose of establishing that that person committed the offence or of negativing any defence; and

(b) compliance by that person with such a code may be relied on in relation to any matter for the purpose of showing that the commission of the offence by that person has not been established or that that person has a defence.

(3) Where the Secretary of State approves a code of practice under this section he may, after such consultation as is mentioned in subsection (1) above, at any time by order—

(a) approve any modification of the code; or

(b) withdraw his approval;

and references in subsection (2) above to a code of practice approved under this section shall be construed accordingly.

(4) The power to make an order under this section shall be exercisable by statutory instrument subject to annulment in pursuance of a resolution of either House of Parliament.

26 Power to make regulations

(1) The Secretary of State may, after consulting [the Office of Fair Trading] and such other persons as the Secretary of State considers it appropriate to consult, by regulations make provision—

(a) for the purpose of regulating the circumstances and manner in which any person—

(i) gives any indication as to the price at which any goods, services, accommodation or facilities will be or are available or have been supplied or provided; or

       (ii) indicates any other matter in respect of which any such indication may be misleading;

  (b) for the purpose of facilitating the enforcement of the provisions of section 20 above or of any regulations made under this section.

(2) The Secretary of State shall not make regulations by virtue of subsection (1)(a) above except in relation to—

  (a) indications given by persons in the course of business; and

  (b) such indications given otherwise than in the course of business as—

       (i) are given by or on behalf of persons by whom accommodation is provided to others by means of leases or licences; and

       (ii) relate goods, services or facilities supplied or provided to those others in connection with the provision of the accommodation.

(3) Without prejudice to the generality of subsection (1) above, regulations under this section may—

  (a) prohibit an indication as to a price from referring to such matters as may be prescribed by the regulations;

  (b) require an indication as to a price or other matter to be accompanied or supplemented by such explanation or such additional information as may be prescribed by the regulations;

  (c) require information or explanations with respect to a price or other matter to be given to an officer of an enforcement authority and to authorise such an officer to require such information or explanations to be given;

  (d) require any information or explanation provided for the purposes of any regulations made by virtue of paragraph (b) or (c) above to be accurate;

  (e) prohibit the inclusion in indications as to a price or other matter of statements that the indications are not to be relied upon;

  (f) provide that expressions used in any indication as to a price or other matter shall be construed in a particular way for the purposes of this Part;

  (g) provide that a contravention of any provision of the regulations shall constitute a criminal offence punishable—

       (i) on conviction on indictment, by a fine;

       (ii) on summary conviction, by a fine not exceeding the statutory maximum;

  (h) apply any provision of this Act which relates to a criminal offence created by virtue of paragraph (g) above.

(4) The power to make regulations under this section shall be exercisable by statutory instrument subject to annulment in pursuance of a resolution of either House of Parliament and shall include power—

  (a) to make different provision for different cases; and

  (b) to make such supplemental, consequential and transitional provision as the Secretary of State considers appropriate.

(5) In this section 'lease' includes a sub-lease and an agreement for a lease and a statutory tenancy (within the meaning of the Landlord and Tenant Act 1985 or the Rent (Scotland) Act 1984).

PART IV   ENFORCEMENT OF PARTS II AND III

27   Enforcement

(1) Subject to the following provisions of this section—

  (a) it shall be the duty of every weights and measures authority in Great Britain to enforce within their area the safety provisions and the provisions made by or under Part III of this Act; and

(b) it shall be the duty of every district council in Northern Ireland to enforce within their area the safety provisions.

(2) The Secretary of State may by regulations—

(a) wholly or partly transfer any duty imposed by subsection (1) above on a weights and measures authority or a district council in Northern Ireland to such other person who has agreed to the transfer as is specified in the regulations;

(b) relieve such an authority or council of any such duty so far as it is exercisable in relation to such goods as may be described in the regulations.

(3) The power to make regulations under subsection (2) above shall be exercisable by statutory instrument subject to annulment in pursuance of a resolution of either House of Parliament and shall include power—

(a) to make different provision for different cases; and

(b) to make such supplemental, consequential and transitional provision as the Secretary of State considers appropriate.

(4) Nothing in this section shall authorise any weights and measures authority, or any person whom functions are conferred by regulations under subsection (2) above, to bring proceedings in Scotland for an offence.

28   Test purchases

(1) An enforcement authority shall have power, for the purpose of ascertaining whether any safety provision or any provision made by or under Part III of this Act has been contravened in relation to any goods, services, accommodation or facilities—

(a) to make, or to authorise an officer of the authority to make, any purchase of any goods; or

(b) to secure, or to authorise an officer of the authority to secure, the provision of any services, accommodation or facilities.

(2) Where—

(a) any goods purchased under this section by or on behalf of an enforcement authority are submitted to a test; and

(b) the test leads to—

(i)   the bringing of proceedings for an offence in respect of a contravention in relation to the goods of any safety provision or of any provision made by or under Part III of this Act or for the forfeiture of the goods under section 16 or 17 above; or

(ii) the serving of a suspension notice in respect of any goods; and

(c) the authority is requested to do so and it is practicable for the authority to comply with the request,

the authority shall allow the person from whom the goods were purchased or any person who is a party to the proceedings or has an interest in any goods to which the notice relates to have the goods tested.

(3) The Secretary of State may by regulations provide that any test of goods under this section by or on behalf of an enforcement authority shall—

(a) be carried out at the expense of the authority in a manner and by a person prescribed by or determined under the regulations; or

(b) be carried out either as mentioned in paragraph (a) above or by the authority in a manner prescribed by the regulations.

(4) The power to make regulations under subsection (3) above shall be exercisable by statutory instrument subject to annulment in pursuance of a resolution of either House of Parliament and shall include power—

(a) to make different provision for different cases; and

(b) to make such supplemental, consequential and transitional provision as the Secretary of State considers appropriate.

(5) Nothing in this section shall authorise the acquisition by or on behalf of an enforcement authority of any interest in land.

29   Powers of search etc.

(1) Subject to the following provisions of this Part, a duly authorised officer of an enforcement authority may at any reasonable hour and on production, if required, of his credentials exercise any of the powers conferred by the following provisions of this section.

(2) The officer may, for the purpose of ascertaining whether there has been any contravention of any safety provision or of any provision made by or under Part III of this Act, inspect any goods and enter any premises other than premises occupied only as a person's residence.

(3) The officer may, for the purpose of ascertaining whether there has been any contravention of any safety provision, examine any procedure (including any arrangements for carrying out a test) connected with the production of any goods.

(4) If the officer has reasonable grounds for suspecting that any goods are manufactured or imported goods which have not been supplied in the United Kingdom since they were manufactured or imported he may—

    (a) for the purpose of ascertaining whether there has been any contravention of any safety provision in relation to the goods, require any person carrying on a business, or employed in connection with a business, to produce any records relating to the business;

    (b) for the purpose of ascertaining (by testing or otherwise) whether there has been any such contravention, seize and detain the goods;

    (c) take copies of, or of any entry in, any records produced by virtue of paragraph (a) above.

(5) If the officer has reasonable grounds for suspecting that there has been a contravention in relation to any goods of any safety provision or of any provision made by or under Part III of this Act, he may—

    (a) for the purpose of ascertaining whether there has been any such contravention, require any person carrying on a business, or employed in connection with a business, to produce any records relating to the business;

    (b) for the purpose of ascertaining (by testing or otherwise) whether there has been any such contravention, seize and detain the goods;

    (c) take copies of, or of any entry in, any records produced by virtue of paragraph (a) above.

(6) The fficer may seize and detain—

    (a) any goods or records which he has reasonable grounds for believing may be required as evidence in proceedings for an offence in respect of a contravention of any safety provision or of any provision made by or under Part III of this Act;

    (b) any goods which he has reasonable grounds for suspecting may be hable to be forfeited under section 16 or 17 above.

(7) If and to the extent that it is reasonably necessary to do so to prevent a contravention of any safety provision or of any provision made by or under Part III of this Act, the officer may, for the purpose of exercising his power under subsection (4), (5) or (6) above to seize any goods or records—

    (a) require any person having authority to do so to open any container or to open any vending machine; and

    (b) himself open or break open any such container or machine where a requirement made under paragraph (a) above in relation to the container or machine has not been complied with.

30   Provisions supplemental to s. 29

(1) An officer seizing any goods or records under section 29 above shall inform the following persons that the goods or records have been so seized, that is to say—

    (a) the person from whom they are seized; and

    (b) in the case of imported goods seized on any premises under the control of the Commissioners of Customs and Excise, the importer of those goods (within the meaning of the Customs and Excise Management Act 1979).

  (2) If a justice of the peace—

    (a) is satisfied by any written information on oath that there are reasonable grounds for believing either—

      (i) that any goods or records which any officer has power to inspect under section 29 above are on any premises and that their inspection is likely to disclose evidence that there has been a contravention of any safety provision or of any provision made by or under Part III of this Act; or

      (ii) that such a contravention has taken place, is taking place or is about to take place on any premises; and

    (b) is also satisfied by any such information either—

      (i) that admission to the premises has been or is likely to be refused and that notice of intention to apply for a warrant under this section has been given to the occupier; or

      (ii) that an application for admission, or the giving of such a notice, would defeat the object of entry or that the premises are unoccupied or that the occupier is temporarily absent and it might defeat the object of the entry to await his return, the justice may by warrant under his hand, which shall continue in force for a period of one month, authorise any officer of an enforcement authority to enter the premises, if need be by force.

  (3) An officer entering any premises by virtue of section 29 above or a warrant under subsection (2) above may take with him such other persons and such equipment as may appear to him necessary.

  (4) On leaving any premises which a person is authorised to enter by a warrant under subsection (2) above, that person shall, if the premises are unoccupied or the occupier is temporarily absent, leave the premises as effectively secured against trespassers as he found them.

  (5) If any person who is not an officer of an enforcement authority purports to act as such under section 29 above of this section he shall be guilty of an offence and liable on summary conviction to a fine not exceeding level 5 on the standard scale.

  (6) Where any goods seized by an officer under section 29 above are submitted to a test, the officer shall inform the persons mentioned in subsection (1) above of the result of the test and, if—

    (a) proceedings are brought for an offence in respect of a contravention in relation to the goods of any safety provision or of any provision made by or under Part III of this Act or for the forfeiture of the goods under section 16 or 17 above, or a suspension notice is served in respect of any goods; and

    (b) the officer is requested to do so and it is practicable to comply with the request, the officer shall allow any person who is a party to the proceedings or, as the case may be, has an interest in the goods to which the notice relates to have the goods tested.

  (7) The Secretary of State may by regulations provide that any test of goods seized under section 29 above by an officer of an enforcement authority shall—

    (a) be carried out at the expense of the authority in a manner and by a person prescribed by or determined under the regulations; or

    (b) be carried out either as mentioned in paragraph (a) above or by the authority in a manner prescribed by the regulations.

  (8) The power to make regulations under subsection (7) above shall be exercisable by statutory instrument subject to annulment in pursuance of a resolution of either House of Parliament and shall include power—

    (a) to make different provision for different cases; and

(b) to make such supplemental, consequential and transitional provisions as the Secretary of State considers appropriate.

(9) In the application of this section to Scotland, the reference in subsection (2) above to a justice of the peace shall include a reference to a sheriff and the references to written information on oath shall be construed as references to evidence on oath.

(10) In the application of this section to Northern Ireland, the references in subsection (2) above to any information on oath shall be construed as references to any complaint on oath.

31   Power of customs officer to detain goods

(1) A customs officer may, for the purpose of facilitating the exercise by an enforcement authority or officer of such an authority of any functions conferred on the authority or officer by or under Part II of this Act, or by or under this Part in its application for the purposes of the safety provisions, seize any imported goods and detain them for not more than two working days.

(2) Anything seized and detained under this section shall be dealt with during the period of its detention in such manner as the Commissioners of Customs and Excise may direct.

(3) In subsection (1) above the reference to two working days is a reference to a period of forty-eight hours calculated from the time when the goods in question are seized but disregarding so much of any period as falls on a Saturday or Sunday or on Christmas Day, Good Friday or a day which is a bank holiday under the Banking and Financial Dealings Act 1971 in the part of the United Kingdom where the goods are seized.

(4) In this section and section 32 below 'customs officer' means any officer within the meaning of the Customs and Excise Management Act 1979.

32   Obstruction of authorised officer

(1) Any person who—
(a) intentionally obstructs any officer of an enforcement authority who is acting in pursuance of any provision of this Part or any customs officer who is so acting; or
(b) intentionally fails to comply with any requirements made of him by any officer of an enforcement authority under any provision of this Part, or
(c) without reasonable cause fails to give any officer of an enforcement authority who is so acting any other assistance or information which the officer may reasonably require of him for the purposes of the exercise of the officer's functions under any provision of this Part,

shall be guilty of an offence and liable on summary conviction to a fine not exceeding level 5 on the standard scale.

(2) A person shall be guilty of an offence if, in giving any information which is required of him by virtue of subsection (1)(c) above—
(a) he makes any statement which he knows is false in a material particular, or
(b) he recklessly makes a statement which is false in a material particular.

(3) A person guilty of an offence under subsection (2) above shall be liable—
(a) on conviction on indictment to a fine;
(b) on summary conviction, to a fine not exceeding the statutory maximum.

33   Appeals against detention of goods

(1) Any person having an interest in any goods which are for the time being detained under any provision of this Part by an enforcement authority or by an officer of such an authority may apply for an order requiring the goods to be released to him or to another person.

(2) An application under this section may be made—
(a) to any magistrates' court in which proceedings have been brought in England and Wales or Northern Ireland—
(i) for an offence in respect of a contravention in relation to the goods of any safety provision or of any provision made by or under Part III of this Act; or
(ii) for the forfeiture of the goods under section 16 above;

(b) where no such proceedings have been so brought, by way of complaint to a magistrates' court; or

(c) makes an order under section 16 or 17 above for the forfeiture of any goods.

35 Recovery of expenses of enforcement

(2) The court may (in addition to any other order it may make as to costs or expenses) order the person convicted or, as the case may be, any person having an interest in the goods to reimburse an enforcement authority for any expenditure which has been or may be incurred by that authority—

(a) in connection with any seizure or detention of the goods by or on behalf of the authority; or

(b) in connection with any compliance by the authority with directions given by the court for the purposes of any order for the forfeiture of the goods.

PART V   MISCELLANEOUS AND SUPPLEMENTAL

36 Amendments of Part I of the Health and Safety at Work etc. Act 1974

. . .

37 [Power of Commissioners for Revenue and Customs to disclose information]

(1) If they think it appropriate to do so for the purpose of facilitating the exercise by any person to whom subsection (2) below applies of any function conferred on that person by or under Part II of this Act, or by or under Part IV of this Act in its application for the purposes of the safety provisions, [the Commissioners for Her Majesty's Revenue and Customs] may authorise the disclosure to that person of any information obtained [or held] for the purposes of the exercise [by Her Majesty's Revenue and Customs] of their functions in relation to imported goods.

(2) This subsection applies to an enforcement authority and to any officer of an enforcement authority.

(3) A disclosure of information made to any person under subsection (1) above shall be made in such manner as may be directed by [the Commissioners for Her Majesty's Revenue and Customs] and may be through such persons acting on behalf of that person as may be so directed.

(4) Information may be disclosed to a person under subsection (1) above whether or not the disclosure of the information has been requested by or on behalf of that person.

39 Defence of due diligence

(1) Subject to the following provisions of this section, in proceedings against any person for an offence to which this section applies it shall be a defence for that person to show that he took all reasonable steps and exercised all due diligence to avoid committing the offence.

(2) Where in any proceedings against any person for such an offence the defence provided by subsection (1) above involves an allegation that the commission of the offence was due—

(a) to the act or default of another; or

(b) to reliance on information given by another,

that person shall not, without the leave of the court, be entitled to rely on the defence unless, not less than seven clear days before the hearing of the proceedings, he has served a notice under subsection (3) below on the person bringing the proceedings.

(3) A notice under this subsection shall give such information identifying or assisting in the identification of the person who committed the act or default or gave the information as is in the possession of the person serving the notice at the time he serves it.

(4) It is hereby declared that a person shall not be entitled to rely on the defence provided by subsection (1) above by reason of his reliance on information supplied by another, unless he shows that it was reasonable in all the circumstances for him to have relied on the information, having regard in particular—

>   (a) to the steps which he took, and those which might reasonably have been taken, for the purpose of verifying the information, and

>   (b) to whether he had any reason to disbelieve the information.

(5) This section shall apply to an offence under section [...] 12(1), (2) or (3), 13(4), 14(6) or 20(1) above.

40   Liability of persons other than principal offender

(1) Where the commission by any person of an offence to which section 39 above applies is due to an act or default committed by some other person in the course of any business of his, the other person shall be guilty of the offence and may be proceeded against and punished by virtue of this subsection whether or not proceedings are taken against the first-mentioned person.

(2) Where a body corporate is guilty of an offence under this Act (including where it is so guilty by virtue of subsection (1) above) in respect of any act or default which is shown to have been committed with the consent or connivance of, or to be attributable to any neglect on the part of, any director, manager, secretary or other similar officer of the body corporate or any person who was purporting to act in any such capacity he, as well as the body corporate, shall be guilty of that offence and shall be liable to be proceeded against and punished accordingly.

(3) Where the affairs of a body corporate are managed by its members, subsection (2) above shall apply in relation to the acts and defaults of a member in connection with his functions of management as if he were a director of the body corporate.

41   Civil proceedings

(1) An obligation imposed by safety regulations shall be a duty owed to any person who may be affected by a contravention of the obligation and, subject to any provisions to the contrary in the regulations and to the defences and other incidents applying to actions for breach of statutory duty, a contravention of any such obligation shall be actionable accordingly.

(2) This Act shall not be construed as conferring any other right of action in civil proceedings, apart from the right conferred by virtue of Part I of this Act, in respect of any loss or damage suffered in consequence of a contravention of a safety provision or of a provision made by or under Part III of this Act.

(3) Subject to any provision to the contrary in the agreement itself, an agreement shall not be void or unenforceable by reason only of a contravention of a safety provision or of a provision made by or under Part III of this Act.

(4) Liability by virtue of subsection (1) above shall not be limited or excluded by any contract term, by any notice or (subject to the power contained in subsection (1) above to limit or exclude it in safety regulations) by any other provision.

(5) Nothing in subsection (1) above shall prejudice the operation of section 12 of the Nuclear Installations Act 1965 (rights to compensation for certain breaches of duties confined to rights under that Act).

(6) In this section 'damage' includes personal injury and death.

42   Reports etc.

(1) It shall be the duty of the Secretary of State at least once in every five years to lay before each House of Parliament a report on the exercise during the period to which the report relates of the functions which under Part II of this Act, or under Part IV of this Act in its application for the purposes of the safety provisions, are exercisable by the Secretary of State,

weights and measures authorities, district councils in Northern Ireland and persons on whom functions are conferred by regulations made under section 27(2) above.

(2) The Secretary of State may from time to time prepare and lay before each House of Parliament such other reports on the exercise of those functions as he considers appropriate.

(3) Every weights and measures authority, every district council in Northern Ireland and every person on whom functions are conferred by regulations under subsection (2) of section 27 above shall, whenever the Secretary of State so directs, make a report to the Secretary of State on the exercise of the functions exercisable by that authority or council under that section or by that person by virtue of any such regulations.

(4) A report under subsection (3) above shall be in such form and shall contain such particulars as are specified in the direction of the Secretary of State.

(5) The first report under subsection (1) above shall be laid before each House of Parliament not more than five years after the laying of the last report under section 8(2) of the Consumer Safety Act 1978.

43 Financial provisions

(1) There shall be paid out of money provided by Parliament—
   (a) any expenses incurred or compensation payable by a Minister of the Crown or Government department in consequence of any provision of this Act; and
   (b) any increase attributable to this Act in the sums payable out of money so provided under any other Act.

(2) Any sums received by a Minister of the Crown or Government department by virtue of this Act shall be paid into the Consolidated Fund.

44 Service of documents etc.

(1) Any documents required or authorised by virtue of this Act to be served on a person may be so served—
   (a) by delivering it to him or by leaving it at his proper address or by sending it by post to him at that address; or
   (b) if the person is a body corporate, by serving it in accordance with paragraph (a) above on the secretary or clerk of that body; or
   (c) if the person is a partnership, by serving it in accordance with that paragraph on a partner or on a person having control or management of the partnership business.

(2) For the purposes of subsection (1) above, and for the purposes of section 7 of the Interpretation Act 1978 (which relates to the service of documents by post) in its application to that subsection, the proper address of any person on whom a document is to be served by virtue of this Act shall be his last known address except that—
   (a) in the case of service on a body corporate or its secretary or clerk, it shall be the address of the registered or principal office of the body corporate;
   (b) in the case of service on a partnership or a partner or a person having the control or management of a partnership business, it shall be the principal office of the partnership; and for the purposes of this subsection the principal office of a company registered outside the United Kingdom or of a partnership carrying on business outside the United Kingdom is its principal office within the United Kingdom.

(3) The Secretary of State may by regulations make provision for the manner in which any information is to be given to any person under any provision of Part IV of this Act.

(4) Without prejudice to the generality of subsection (3) above regulations made by the Secretary of State may prescribe the person, or manner of determining the person, who is to be treated for the purposes of section 28(2) or 30 above as the person from whom goods were purchased or seized where the goods were purchased or seized from a vending machine.

(5) The power to make regulations under subsection (3) or (4) above shall be exercisable by statutory instrument subject to annulment in pursuance of a resolution of either House of Parliament and shall include power—

    (a) to make different provision for different cases; and

    (b) to make such supplemental, consequential and transitional provision as the Secretary of State considers appropriate.

45 Interpretation

(1) In this Act, expect in so far as the context otherwise requires—

'aircraft' includes gliders, balloons and hovercraft;

'business' includes a trade or profession and the activities of a professional or trade association or of a local authority or other public authority;

'conditional sale agreement', 'credit-sale agreement' and 'hire-purchase agreement' have the same meanings as in the Consumer Credit Act 1974 but as if in the definitions in that Act 'goods' had the same meaning as in this Act;

'contravention' includes a failure to comply and cognate expressions shall be construed accordingly;

'enforcement authority' means the Secretary of State, any other Minister of the Crown in charge of a Government department, any such department and any authority, council or other person on whom functions under this Act are conferred by or under section 27 above;

'gas' has the same meaning as in Part I of the Gas Act 1986;

'goods' includes substances, growing crops and things comprised in land by virtue of being attached to it and any ship, aircraft or vehicle;

'information' includes accounts, estimates and returns;

'magistrates' court', in relation to Northern Ireland, means a court of summary jurisdiction;

'modifications' includes additions, alterations and omissions, and cognate expressions shall be construed accordingly;

'motor vehicle' has the same meaning as in the Road Traffic Act 1972;

'notice' means a notice in writing;

'notice to warn' means a notice under section 13(1)(b) above;

'officer', in relation to an enforcement authority, means a person authorised in writing to assist the authority in carrying out its functions under or for the purposes of the enforcement of any of the safety provisions or of any of the provisions made by or under Part III of this Act;

'personal injury' includes any disease and any other impairment of a person's physical or mental condition;

'premises' includes any place and any ship, aircraft or vehicle;

'prohibition notice' means a notice under section 13(1)(a) above;

'records' includes any books or documents and any records in non-documentary form;

'safety provision' means [. . .] any provision of safety regulations, a prohibition notice or a suspension notice;

'safety regulations' means regulations under section 11 above;

'ship' includes any boat and any other description of vessel used in navigation;

'subordinate legislation' has the same meaning as in the Interpretation Act 1978;

'substance' means any natural or artificial substance, whether in solid, liquid or gaseous form or in the form of a vapour, and includes substances that are comprised in or mixed with other goods;

'supply' and cognate expressions shall be construed in accordance with section 46 below;

'suspension notice' means a notice under section 14 above.

(2) Except in so far as the context otherwise requires, references in this Act to a contravention of a safety provision shall, in relation to any goods, include references to anything which would constitute such a contravention if the goods were supplied to any person.

(3) References in this Act to any goods in relation to which any safety provision has been or may have been contravened shall include references to any goods which it is not reasonably practicable to separate from any such goods.

(4) Section 68(2) of the Trade Marks Act 1938 (construction of references to use of a mark) shall apply for the purposes of this Act as it applies for the purposes of that Act.

(5) In Scotland, any reference in this Act to things comprised in land by virtue of being attached to it is a reference to moveables which have become heritable by accession to heritable property.

46 Meaning of 'supply'

(1) Subject to the following provisions of this section, references in this Act to supplying goods shall be construed as references to doing any of the following, whether as principal or agent, that is to say—

   (a) selling, hiring out or lending the goods;

   (b) entering into a hire-purchase agreement to furnish the goods;

   (c) the performance of any contract for work and materials to furnish the goods;

   (d) providing the goods in exchange for any consideration [...] other than money;

   (e) providing the goods in or in connection with the performance of any statutory function; or

   (f) giving the goods as a prize or otherwise making a gift of the goods;

and, in relation to gas or water, those references shall be construed as including references to providing the service by which the gas or water is made available for use.

(2) For the purposes of any reference in this Act to supplying goods, where a person ('the ostensible supplier') supplies goods to another person ('the customer') under a hire-purchase agreement, conditional sale agreement or credit-sale agreement or under an agreement for the hiring of goods (other than a hire-purchase agreement) and the ostensible supplier—

   (a) carries on the business of financing the provision of goods for others by means of such agreements; and

   (b) in the course of that business acquired his interest in the goods supplied to the customer as a means of financing the provision of them for the customer by a further person ('the effective supplier'),

the effective supplier and not the ostensible supplier shall be treated as supplying the goods to the customer.

(3) Subject to subsection (4) below, the performance of any contract by the erection of any building or structure on any land or by the carrying out of any other building works shall be treated for the purposes of this Act as a supply of goods in so far as, but only in so far as, it involves the provision of any goods to any person by means of their incorporation into the building, structure or works.

(4) Except for the purposes of, and in relation to, notices to warn or any provision made by or under Part III of this Act, references in this Act to supplying goods shall not include references to supplying goods comprised in land where the supply is effected by the creation or disposal of an interest in the land.

(5) Except in Part I of this Act references in this Act to a person's supplying goods shall be confined to references to that person's supplying goods in the course of a business of his, but for the purposes of this subsection it shall be immaterial whether the business is a business of dealing in the goods.

(6) For the purposes of subsection (5) above goods shall not be treated as supplied in the course of a business if they are supplied, in pursuance of an obligation arising under or in connection with the insurance of the goods, to the person with whom they were insured.

(7) Except for the purposes of, and in relation to, prohibition notices or suspension notices, references in Parts II to IV of this Act to supplying goods shall not include—

   (a) references to supplying goods where the person supplied carries on a business of buying goods of the same description as those goods and repairing or reconditioning them,

(b) references to supplying goods by a sale of articles as scrap (that is to say, for the value of materials included in the articles rather that for the value of the articles themselves).

(8) Where any goods have at any time been supplied by being hired out or lent to any person, neither a continuation or renewal of the hire or loan (whether on the same or different terms) nor any transaction for the transfer after that time of any interest in the goods to the person to whom they were hired or lent shall be treated for the purposes of this Act as a further supply of the goods to that person.

(9) A ship, aircraft or motor vehicle shall not be treated for the purposes of this Act as supplied to any person by reason only that services consisting in the carriage of goods or passengers in that ship, aircraft or vehicle, or in its use for any other purpose, are provided to that person in pursuance of an agreement relating to the use of the ship, aircraft or vehicle for a particular period or for particular voyages, flights or journeys.

47   Savings for certain privileges

(1) Nothing in this Act shall be taken as requiring any person to produce any records if he would be entitled to refuse to produce those records in any proceedings in any court on the ground that they are the subject of legal professional privilege or, in Scotland, that they contain a confidential communication made by or to an advocate or solicitor in that capacity, or as authorising any person to take possession of any records which are in the possession of a person who would be so entitled.

(2) Nothing in this Act shall be construed as requiring a person to answer any question or give any information if to do so would incriminate that person or that person's spouse [or civil partner].

48   Minor and consequential amendments and repeals

. . .

49   Northern Ireland

(1) This Act shall extend to Northern Ireland with the exception of—
(a) the provisions of Parts I and III;
(b) any provision amending or repealing an enactment which does not so extend; and
(c) any other provision so far as it has effect for the purposes of, or in relation to, a provision falling within paragraph (a) or (b) above.

. . .

50   Short title, commencement and transitional provision

(1) This Act may be cited as the Consumer Protection Act 1987.

(2) This Act shall come into force on such day as the Secretary of State may by order made by statutory instrument appoint, and different days may be so appointed for different provisions or for different purposes.

(3) The Secretary of State shall not make an order under subsection (2) above bringing into force the repeal of the Trade Descriptions Act 1972, a repeal of any provision of that Act or a repeal of that Act or of any provision of it for any purposes, unless a draft of the order has been laid before, and approved by a resolution of, each House of Parliament.

(4) An order under subsection (2) above bringing a provision into force may contain such transitional provision in connection with the coming into force of that provision as the Secretary of State considers appropriate.

(5) Without prejudice to the generality of the power conferred by subsection (4) above, the Secretary of State may by order provide for any regulations made under the Consumer Protection Act 1961 or the Consumer Protection Act (Northern Ireland) 1965 to have effect as if made under section 11 above and for any regulations to have effect with such modifications as he considers appropriate for that purpose.

(6) The power of the Secretary of State by order to make such provision as is mentioned in subsection (5) above, shall, in so far as it is not exercised by an order under subsection (2) above, be exercisable by statutory instrument subject to annul-ment in pursuance of a resolution of either House of Parliament.

(7) Nothing in this Act or in any order under subsection (2) above shall make any person liable by virtue of Part I of this Act for any damage caused wholly or partly by a defect in a product which was supplied to any person by its producer before the coming into force of Part I of this Act.

(8) Expressions used in subsection (7) above and in Part I of this Act have the same meaning in that subsection as in that Part.

SCHEDULES

Section 13   **SCHEDULE 2**

PROHIBITION NOTICES AND NOTICES TO WARN

PART I   PROHIBITION NOTICES

1. A prohibition notice in respect of any goods shall—
    (a) state that the Secretary of State considers that the goods are unsafe;
    (b) set out the reasons why the Secretary of State considers that the goods are unsafe;
    (c) specify the day on which the notice is to come into force; and
    (d) state that the trader may at any time make representations in writing to the Secretary of State for the purpose of establishing that the goods are safe.

2.—(1) If representations in writing about a prohibition notice are made by the trader to the Secretary of State, it shall be the duty of the Secretary of State to consider whether to revoke the notice and—
    (a) if he decides to revoke it, to do so;
    (b) in any other case, to appoint a person to consider those representations, any further representations made (whether in writing or orally) by the trader about the notice and the statements of any witnesses examined under this Part of this Schedule.

(2) Where the Secretary of State has appointed a person to consider representations about a prohibition notice, he shall serve a notification on the trader which—
    (a) states that the trader may make oral representations to the appointed person for the purpose of establishing that the goods to which the notice relates are safe; and
    (b) specifies the place and time at which the oral representations may be made.

(3) The time specified in a notification served under sub-paragraph (2) above shall not be before the end of the period of twenty-one days beginning with the day on which the notification is served, unless the trader otherwise agrees.

(4) A person on whom a notification has been served under sub-paragraph (2) above or his representative may, at the place and time specified in the notification—
    (a) make oral representations to the appointed person for the purpose of establishing that the goods in question are safe; and
    (b) call and examine witnesses in connection with representations.

3.—(1) Where representations in writing about a prohibition notice are made by the trader to the Secretary of State at any time after a person has been appointed to consider representations about that notice, then, whether or not the appointed person has made a report to the Secretary of State, the following provisions of this paragraph shall apply instead of paragraph 2 above.

(2) The Secretary of State shall, before the end of the period of one month beginning with the day on which he receives the representations, serve a notification on the trader which states—

    (a) that the Secretary of State has decided to revoke the notice, has decided to vary it or, as the case may be, has decided neither to revoke nor to vary it; or

    (b) that, a person having been appointed to consider representations about the notice, the trader may, at a place and time specified in the notification, make oral representations to the appointed person for the purpose of establishing that the goods to which the notice relates are safe.

(3) The time specified in a notification served for the purposes of sub-paragraph (2)(b) above shall not be before the end of the period of twenty-one days beginning with the day on which the notification is served, unless the trader otherwise agrees or the time is the time already specified for the purposes of paragraph 2(2)(b) above.

(4) A person on whom a notification has been served for the purposes of sub-paragraph (2)(b) above or his representative may, at the place and time specified in the notification—

    (a) make oral representations to the appointed person for the purpose of establishing that the goods in question are safe; and

    (b) call and examine witnesses in connection with the representations.

4.—(1) Where a person is appointed to consider representations about a prohibition notice, it shall be his duty to consider—

    (a) any written representations made by the trader about the notice, other than those in respect of which a notification is served under paragraph 3(2)(a) above;

    (b) any oral representations made under paragraph 2(4) or 3(4) above; and

    (c) any statements made by witnesses in connection with the oral representations, and after considering any matters under this paragraph, to make a report (including recommendations) to the Secretary of State about the matters considered by him and the notice.

(2) It shall be the duty of the Secretary of State to consider any report made to him under sub-paragraph (1) above and, after considering the report, to inform the trader of his decision with respect to the prohibition notice to which the report relates.

5.—(1) The Secretary of State may revoke or vary a prohibition notice by serving on the trader a notification stating that the notice is revoked or, as the case may be, is varied as specified in the notification.

(2) The Secretary of State shall not vary a prohibition notice so as to make the effect of the notice more restrictive for the trader.

(3) Without prejudice to the power conferred by section 13(2) of this Act, the service of a notification under sub-paragraph (1) above shall be sufficient to satisfy the requirement of paragraph 4(2) above that the trader shall be informed of the Secretary of State's decision.

PART II   NOTICES TO WARN

6.—(1) If the Secretary of State proposes to serve a notice to warn on any person in respect of any goods, the Secretary of State, before he serves the notice shall serve on that person a notification which—

    (a) contains a draft of the proposed notice;

    (b) states that the Secretary of State proposes to serve a notice in the form of the draft on that person;

    (c) states that the Secretary of State considers that the goods described in the draft are unsafe;

    (d) sets out the reasons why the Secretary of State considers that those goods are unsafe; and

    (e) states that that person may make representations to the Secretary of State for the purpose of establishing that the goods are safe if, before the end of the period of

fourteen days beginning with the day on which the notification is served, he informs the Secretary of State—
  (i) of his intention to make representations; and
  (ii) whether the representations will be made only in writing or both in writing and orally.
(2) Where the Secretary of State has served a notification containing a draft of a proposed notice to warn on any person, he shall not serve a notice to warn on that person in respect of the goods to which the proposed notice relates unless—
  (a) the period of fourteen days beginning with the day on which the notification was served expires without the Secretary of State being informed as mentioned in subparagraph (1)(e) above;
  (b) the period of twenty-eight days beginning with that day expires without any written representations being made by that person to the Secretary of State about the proposed notice; or
  (c) the Secretary of State has considered a report about the proposed notice by a person appointed under paragraph 7(1) below.
7.—(1) Where a person on whom a notification containing a draft of a proposed notice to warn has been served—
  (a) informs the Secretary of State as mentioned in paragraph 6(1)(e) above before the end of the period of fourteen days beginning with the day on which the notification was served; and
  (b) makes written representations to the Secretary of State about the proposed notice before the end of the period of twenty-eight days beginning with that day, the Secretary of State shall appoint a person to consider those representations, any further representations made by that person about the draft notice and the statements of any witnesses examined under this Part of this Schedule.
(2) Where—
  (a) the Secretary of State has appointed a person to consider representations about a proposed notice to warn; and
  (b) the person whose representations are to be considered has informed the Secretary of State for the purposes of paragraph 6(1)(e) above that the representations he intends to make will include oral representations,
the Secretary of State shall inform the person intending to make the representations of the place and time at which oral representations may be made to the appointed person.
(3) Where a person on whom a notification containing a draft of a proposed notice to warn has been served is informed of a time for the purposes of sub-paragraph (2) above, that time shall not be—
  (a) before the end of the period of twenty-eight days beginning with the day on which the notification was served; or
  (b) before the end of the period of seven days beginning with the day on which that person is informed of the time.
(4) A person who has been informed of a place and time for the purposes of subparagraph (2) above or his representative may, at that place and time—
  (a) make oral representations to the appointed person for the purpose of establishing that the goods to which the proposed notice relates are safe; and
  (b) call and examine witnesses in connection with the representations.
8.—(1) Where a person is appointed to consider representations about a proposed notice to warn, it shall be his duty to consider—
  (a) any written representations made by the person on whom it is proposed to serve the notice; and
  (b) in a case where a place and time has been appointed under paragraph 7(2) above for oral representations to be made by that person or his representative, any representations so made and any statements made by witnesses in connection with those representations,

and, after considering those matters to make a report (including recommendations) to the Secretary of State about the matters considered by him and the proposal to serve the notice.

(2) It shall be the duty of the Secretary of State to consider any report made to him under sub-paragraph (1) above, and after considering the report, to inform the person on whom it was proposed that a notice to warn should be served of his decision with respect to the proposal.

(3) If at any time after serving a notification on a person under paragraph 6 above the Secretary of State decides not to serve on that person either the proposed notice to warn or that notice with modifications, the Secretary of State shall inform that person of the decision, and nothing done for the purposes of any of the preceding provisions of this Part
of this Schedule before that person was so informed shall—

> (a) entitle the Secretary of State subsequently to serve the proposed notice or the notice with modifications; or
> (b) require the Secretary of State, or any person appointed to consider representations about the proposed notice, subsequently to do anything in respect of, or in consequence of, any such representations.

(4) Where a notification containing a draft of a proposed notice to warn is served on a person in respect of any goods, a notice to warn served on him in consequence of a decision made under sub-paragraph (2) above shall either be in the form of the draft or shall be less onerous than the draft.

9. The Secretary of State may revoke a notice to warn by serving on the person on whom the notice was served a notification stating that the notice is revoked.

PART III   GENERAL

10.—(1) Where in a notification served on any person under this Schedule the Secretary of State has appointed a time for the making of oral representations or the examination of witnesses, he may, by giving that person such notification as the Secretary of State considers appropriate, change that time to a later time or appoint further times at which further representations may be made or the examination of witnesses may be continued; and paragraphs 2(4), 3(4) and 7(4) above shall have effect accordingly.

(2) For the purposes of this Schedule the Secretary of State may appoint a person (instead of the appointed person) to consider any representations or statements, if the person originally appointed, or last appointed under this sub-paragraph, to consider those representations or statements has died or appears to the Secretary of State to be otherwise unable to act.

11. In this Schedule— '

'the appointed person' in relation to a prohibition notice or a proposal to serve a notice to warn, means the person for the time being appointed under this Schedule to consider representations about the notice or, as the case may be, about the proposed notice;

'notification' means a notification in writing;

'trader', in relation to a prohibition notice, means the person on whom the notice is or was served.

Food Safety Act 1990
(1990, c. 16)

[29th June 1990]

PART I   PRELIMINARY

2   Extended meaning of 'sale' etc.

(1) For the purposes of this Act—

> (a) the supply of food, otherwise than on sale, in the course of a business; and

(b) any other thing which is done with respect to food and is specified in an order made by [the Secretary of State],

shall be deemed to be a sale of the food, and references to purchasers and purchasing shall be construed accordingly.

(2) This Act shall apply—

(a) in relation to any food which is offered as a prize or reward or given away in connection with any entertainment to which the public are admitted, whether on payment of money or not, as if the food were, or had been, exposed for sale by each person concerned in the organisation of the entertainment;

(b) in relation to any food which, for the purpose of advertisement or in furtherance of any trade or business, is offered as a prize or reward or given away, as if the food were, or had been, exposed for sale by the person offering or giving away the food; and

(c) in relation to any food which is exposed or deposited in any premises for the purpose of being so offered or given away as mentioned in paragraph (a) or (b) above, as if the food were, or had been, exposed for sale by the occupier of the premises; and in this subsection 'entertainment' includes any social gathering, amusement, exhibition, performance, game, sport or trial of skill.

PART II   MAIN PROVISIONS

8   Selling food not complying with food safety requirements

(1) Any person who—

(a) sells for human consumption, or offers, exposes or advertises for sale for such consumption, or has in his possession for the purpose of such sale or of preparation for such sale; or

(b) deposits with, or consigns to, any other person for the purpose of such sale or of preparation for such sale,

any food which fails to comply with food safety requirements shall be guilty of an offence.

(2) For the purposes of this Part food fails to comply with food safety requirements if—

(a) it has been rendered injurious to health by means of any of the operations mentioned in section 7(1) above;

(b) it is unfit for human consumption; or

(c) it is so contaminated (whether by extraneous matter or otherwise) that it would not be reasonable to expect it to be used for human consumption in that state; and references to such requirements or to food complying with such requirements shall be construed accordingly.

Consumer protection

14   Selling food not of the nature or substance or quality demanded

(1) Any person who sells to the purchaser's prejudice any food which is not of the nature or substance or quality demanded by the purchaser shall be guilty of an offence.

(2) In subsection (1) above the reference to sale shall be construed as a reference to sale for human consumption; and in proceedings under that subsection it shall not be a defence that the purchaser was not prejudiced because he bought for analysis or examination.

15   Falsely describing or presenting food

(1) Any person who gives with any food sold by him, or displays with any food offered or exposed by him for sale or in his possession for the purpose of sale, a label, whether or not attached to or printed on the wrapper or container, which—

(a) falsely describes the food; or

(b) is likely to mislead as to the nature or substance or quality of the food, shall be guilty of an offence.

(2) Any person who publishes, or is a party to the publication of, an advertisement (not being such a label given or displayed by him as mentioned in subsection (1) above) which—

(a) falsely describes any food; or

(b) is likely to mislead as to the nature or substance or quality of any food, shall be guilty of an offence.

(3) Any person who sells, or offers or exposes for sale, or has in his possession for the purpose of sale, any food the presentation of which is likely to mislead as to the nature or substance or quality of the food shall be guilty of an offence.

(4) In proceedings for an offence under subsection (1) or (2) above, the fact that a label or advertisement in respect of which the offence is alleged to have been committed contained an accurate statement of the composition of the food shall not preclude the court from finding that the offence was committed.

(5) In this section references to sale shall be construed as references to sale for human consumption.

Property Misdescriptions Act 1991
(1991, c. 29)

An Act to prohibit the making of false or misleading statements about property matters in the course of estate agency business and property development business.   [27th June 1991]

1   Offence of property misdescription

(1) Where a false or misleading statement about a prescribed matter is made in the course of an estate agency business or a property development business, otherwise than in providing conveyancing services, the person by whom the business is carried on shall be guilty of an offence under this section.

(2) Where the making of the statement is due to the act or default of an employee the employee shall be guilty of an offence under this section; and the employee may be proceeded against and punished whether or not proceedings are also taken against his employer.

(4) No contract shall be void or unenforceable, and no right of action in civil proceedings in respect of any loss shall arise, by reason only of the commission of an offence under this section.

(5) For the purposes of this section—

(a) 'false' means false to a material degree,

(b) a statement is misleading if (though not false) what a reasonable person may be expected to infer from it, or from any omission from it, is false,

(c) a statement may be made by pictures or any other method of signifying meaning as well as by words and, if made by words, may be made orally or in writing,

(d) a prescribed matter is any matter relating to land which is specified in an order made by the Secretary of State,

(e) a statement is made in the course of an estate agency business if (but only if) the making of the statement is a thing done as mentioned in subsection (1) of section 1 of the Estate Agents Act 1979 and that Act either applies to it or would apply to it but for subsection (2)(a) of that section (exception for things done in course of profession by practising solicitor or employee),

(f) a statement is made in the course of a property development business if (but only if) it is made—

(i)   in the course of a business (including a business in which the person making the statement is employed) concerned wholly or substantially with the development of land, and

      (ii)   for the purpose of, or with a view to disposing of an interest in land con-
sisting of or including a building, or a part of a building, constructed or
renovated in the course of the business, and

   (g) 'conveyancing services' means the preparation of any transfer, conveyance, writ,
contract or other document in connection with the disposal or acquisition of an
interest in land, and services ancillary to that, but does not include anything done
as mentioned in section 1(1)(a) of the Estate Agents Act 1979.

(6) For the purposes of this section any reference in this section or section 1 of the Estate
Agents Act 1979 to disposing of or acquiring an interest in land—

   (a) in England and Wales and Northern Ireland shall be construed in accordance with
section 2 of that Act....

2 Due diligence defence

(1) In proceedings against a person for an offence under section 1 above it shall be a
defence for him to show that he took all reasonable steps and exercised all due diligence to
avoid committing the offence.

(2) A person shall not be entitled to rely on the defence provided by subsection (1) above
by reason of his reliance on information given by another unless he shows that it was reasonable in all the circumstances for him to have relied on the information, having regard in
particular—

   (a) to the steps which he took, and those which might reasonably have been taken,
for the purpose of verifying the information, and

   (b) to whether he had any reason to disbelieve the information.

(3) Where in any proceedings against a person for an offence under section 1 above the
defence provided by subsection (1) above involves an allegation that the commission of the
offence was due—

   (a) to the act or default of another, or

   (b) to reliance on information given by another,

the person shall not, without the leave of the court, be entitled to rely on the defence unless he
has served a notice under subsection (4) below on the person bringing the proceedings not less
than seven clear days before the hearing of the proceedings or, in Scotland, the diet of trial.

(4) A notice under this subsection shall give such information identifying or assisting in
the identification of the person who committed the act or default, or gave the information, as
is in the possession of the person serving the notice at the time he serves it.

Carriage of Goods by Sea Act 1992
(1992, c. 50)

*An Act to replace the Bills of Lading Act 1855 with new provision with respect to bills of lading and
certain other shipping documents.*   *[16th July 1992]*

1 Shipping documents etc. to which Act applies

(1) This Act applies to the following documents, that is to say—

   (a) any bill of lading;

   (b) any sea waybill; and

   (c) any ship's delivery order.

(2) References in this Act to a bill of lading—

   (a) do not include references to a document which is incapable of transfer either by
indorsement or, as a bearer bill, by delivery without indorsement; but

   (b) subject to that, do include references to a received for shipment bill of lading.

(3) References in this Act to a sea waybill are references to any document which is not a bill of lading but—

  (a) is such a receipt for goods as contains or evidences a contract for the carriage of goods by sea; and

  (b) identifies the person to whom delivery of the goods is to be made by the carrier in accordance with that contract.

(4) References in this Act to a ship's delivery order are references to any document which is neither a bill of lading nor a sea waybill but contains an undertaking which—

  (a) is given under or for the purposes of a contract for the carriage by sea of the goods to which the document relates, or of goods which include those goods; and

  (b) is an undertaking by the carrier to a person identified in the document to deliver the goods to which the document relates to that person.

(5) The Secretary of State may by regulations make provision for the application of this Act to cases where [an electronic communications network] or any other information technology is used for effecting transactions corresponding to—

  (a) the issue of a document to which this Act applies;

  (b) the indorsement, delivery or other transfer of such a document; or

  (c) the doing of anything else in relation to such a document.

(6) Regulations under subsection (5) above may—

  (a) make such modifications of the following provisions of this Act as the Secretary of State considers appropriate in connection with the application of this Act to any case mentioned in that subsection; and

  (b) contain supplemental, incidental, consequential and transitional provision; and the power to make regulations under that subsection shall be exercisable by statutory instrument subject to annulment in pursuance of a resolution of either House of Parliament.

2   Rights under shipping documents

(1) Subject to the following provisions of this section, a person who becomes—

  (a) the lawful holder of a bill of lading;

  (b) the person who (without being an original party to the contract of carriage) is the person to whom delivery of the goods to which a sea waybill relates is to be made by the carrier in accordance with that contract; or

  (c) the person to whom delivery of the goods to which a ship's delivery order relates is to be made in accordance with the undertaking contained in the order,

shall (by virtue of becoming the holder of the bill or, as the case may be, the person to whom delivery is to be made) have transferred to and vested in him all rights of suit under the contract of carriage as if he had been a party to that contract.

(2) Where, when a person becomes the lawful holder of a bill of lading, possession of the bill no longer gives a right (as against the carrier) to possession of the goods to which the bill relates, that person shall not have any rights transferred to him by virtue of subsection (1) above unless he becomes the holder of the bill—

  (a) by virtue of a transaction effected in pursuance of any contractual or other arrangements made before the time when such a right to possession ceased to attach to possession of the bill; or

  (b) as a result of the rejection to that person by another person of goods or documents delivered to the other person in pursuance of any such arrangements.

(3) The rights vested in any person by virtue of the operation of subsection (1) above in relation to a ship's delivery order—

  (a) shall be so vested subject to the terms of the order; and

  (b) where the goods to which the order relates form a part only of the goods to which the contract of carriage relates, shall be confined to rights in respect of the goods to which the order relates.

(4) Where, in the case of any document to which this Act applies—

    (a) a person with any interest or right in or in relation to goods to which the document relates sustains loss or damage in consequence of a breach of the contract of carriage; but

    (b) subsection (1) above operates in relation to that document so that rights of suit in respect of that breach are vested in another person,

the other person shall be entitled to exercise those rights for the benefit of the person who sustained the loss or damage to the same extent as they could have been exercised if they had been vested in the person for whose benefit they are exercised.

(5) Where rights are transferred by virtue of the operation of subsection (1) above in relation to any document, the transfer for which that subsection provides shall extinguish any entitlement to those rights which derives—

    (a) where that document is a bill of lading, from a person's having been an original party to the contract of carriage; or

    (b) in the case of any document to which this Act applies, from the previous operation of that subsection in relation to that document;

but the operation of that subsection shall be without prejudice to any rights which derive from a person's having been an original party to the contract contained in, or evidenced by, a sea waybill and, in relation to a ship's delivery order, shall be without prejudice to any rights deriving otherwise than from the previous operation of that subsection in relation to that order.

3   Liabilities under shipping documents

(1) Where subsection (1) of section 2 of this Act operates in relation to any document to which this Act applies and the person in whom rights are vested by virtue of that subsection—

    (a) takes or demands delivery from the carrier of any of the goods to which the document relates;

    (b) makes a claim under the contract of carriage against the carrier in respect of any of those goods; or

    (c) is a person who, at a time before those rights were vested in him, took or demanded delivery from the carrier of any of those goods,

that person shall (by virtue of taking or demanding delivery or making the claim or, in a case falling within paragraph (c) above, of having the rights vested in him) become subject to the same liabilities under that contract as if he had been a party to that contract.

(2) Where the goods to which a ship's delivery order relates form a part only of the goods to which the contract of carriage relates, the liabilities to which any person is subject by virtue of the operation of this section in relation to that order shall exclude liabilities in respect of any goods to which the order does not relate.

(3) This section, so far as it imposes liabilities under any contract on any person, shall be without prejudice to the liabilities under the contract of any person as an original party to the contract.

4   Representations in bills of lading

A bill of lading which—

    (a) represents goods to have been shipped on board a vessel or to have been received for shipment on board a vessel; and

    (b) has been signed by the master of the vessel or by a person who was not the master but had the express, implied or apparent authority of the carrier to sign bills of lading,

shall, in favour of a person who has become the lawful holder of the bill, be conclusive evidence against the carrier of the shipment of the goods or, as the case may be, of their receipt for shipment.

5   Interpretation etc.

(1) In this Act—

'bill of lading', 'sea waybill' and 'ship's delivery order' shall be construed in accordance with section 1 above;

'the contract of carriage'—

    (a) in relation to a bill of lading or sea waybill, means the contract contained in or evidenced by that bill or waybill; and

    (b) in relation to a ship's delivery order, means the contract under or for the purposes of which the undertaking contained in the order is given;

'holder', in relation to a bill of lading, shall be construed in accordance with subsection (2) below;

'information technology' includes any computer or other technology by means of which information or other matter may be recorded or communicated without being reduced to documentary form; [...].

(2) References in this Act to the holder of a bill of lading are references to any of the following persons, that is to say—

    (a) a person with possession of the bill who, by virtue of being the person identified in the bill, is the consignee of the goods to which the bill relates;

    (b) a person with possession of the bill as a result of the completion, by delivery of the bill, of any indorsement of the bill or, in the case of a bearer bill, of any other transfer of the bill;

    (c) a person with possession of the bill as a result of any transaction by virtue of which he would have become a holder falling within paragraph (a) or (b) above had not the transaction been effected at a time when possession of the bill no longer gave a right (as against the carrier) to possession of the goods to which the bill relates;

and a person shall be regarded for the purposes of this Act as having become the lawful holder of a bill of lading wherever he has become the holder of the bill in good faith.

(3) References in this Act to a person's being identified in a document include references to his being identified by a description which allows for the identity of the person in question to be varied, in accordance with the terms of the document, after its issue; and the reference in section 1(3)(b) of this Act to a document's identifying a person shall be construed accordingly.

(4) Without prejudice to sections 2(2) and 4 above, nothing in this Act shall preclude its operation in relation to a case where the goods to which a document relates—

    (a) cease to exist after the issue of the document; or

    (b) cannot be identified (whether because they are mixed with other goods or for any other reason);

and references in this Act to the goods to which a document relates shall be construed accordingly.

(5) The preceding provisions of this Act shall have effect without prejudice to the application, in relation to any case, of the rules (the Hague-Visby Rules) which for the time being have the force of law by virtue of section 1 of the Carriage of Goods by Sea Act 1971.

6   Short title, repeal, commencement and extent

(1) This Act may be cited as the Carriage of Goods by Sea Act 1992.

(2) The Bills of Lading Act 1855 is hereby repealed.

(3) This Act shall come into force at the end of the period of two months beginning with the day on which it is passed; but nothing in this Act shall have effect in relation to any document issued before the coming into force of this Act.

(4) This Act extends to Northern Ireland.

Timeshare Act 1992
(1992, c. 35)

An Act to provide for rights to cancel certain agreements about timeshare accommodation.
[16th March 1992]

1 Application of Act

(1) In this Act—

    (a) 'timeshare accommodation' means any living accommodation, in the United Kingdom or elsewhere, used or intended to be used, wholly or partly, for leisure purposes by a class of persons (referred to below in this section as 'timeshare users') all of whom have rights to use, or participate in arrangements under which they may use, that accommodation, or accommodation within a pool of accommodation to which that accommodation belongs, for [a specified or ascertainable period of the year] ...

(4) In this Act 'timeshare agreement' means [...] an agreement under which timeshare rights are conferred or purport to be conferred on any person and in this Act, in relation to a timeshare agreement—

    (a) references to the offeree are to the person on whom timeshare rights are conferred, or purport to be conferred, and

    (b) references to the offeror are to the other party to the agreement,

and, in relation to any time before the agreement is entered into, references in this Act to the offeree or the offeror are to the persons who become the offeree and offeror when it is entered into.

[(5) In this Act 'timeshare credit agreement' means an agreement, not being a timeshare agreement, under which credit which fully or partly covers the price under a timeshare agreement is granted—

    (a) by the offeror, or

    (b) by another person, under an arrangement between that person and the offeror; and a person who grants credit under a timeshare credit agreement is in this Act referred to as 'the creditor'.]

[(6A) No timeshare agreement or timeshare credit agreement to which this Act applies may be cancelled under section 67 of the Consumer Credit Act 1974.]

(7) This Act applies to any timeshare agreement or timeshare credit agreement if—

    (a) the agreement is to any extent governed by the law of the United Kingdom or of a part of the United Kingdom, or

    (b) when the agreement is entered into, one or both of the parties are in the United Kingdom.

[(7A) This Act also applies to any timeshare agreement if—

    (a) the relevant accommodation is situated in the United Kingdom,

    (ab) the relevant accommodation is situated in another EEA State and the parties to the agreement are to any extent subject to the jurisdiction of any court in the United Kingdom in relation to the agreement, or

    (b) when the agreement is entered into, the offeree is ordinarily resident in the United Kingdom and the relevant accommodation is situated in another EEA State.

(7B) For the purposes of subsection (7A) above, 'the relevant accommodation' means—

    (a) the accommodation which is the subject of the agreement, or

    (b) some or all of the accommodation in the pool of accommodation which is the subject of the agreement,

as the case may be.]

[1A   Obligations to provide information

(1) A person who proposes in the course of a business to enter into a timeshare agreement to which this Act applies as offeror (an 'operator') must provide any person who requests information on the proposed accommodation with a document complying with subsection (2) below.

(2) The document shall provide—

(a) a general description of the proposed accommodation,

(b) information (which may be brief) on the matters referred to in paragraphs (a) to (g) [and (i) of Schedule 1 to this Act,]

[(ba) information (which may be brief) on the rights under this Act to cancel a timeshare agreement and the effect of cancellation on any related timeshare credit agreement to which this Act applies, and]

(c) information on how further information may be obtained.

[(2A) In subsection (2)(ba) above 'related timeshare credit agreement' means a timeshare credit agreement under which credit which fully or partly covers the price under the timeshare agreement is granted.]

(3) Where an operator—

(a) provides a person with a document containing information on the proposed accommodation, and

(b) subsequently enters as offeror into a timeshare agreement to which this Act applies the subject of which is the proposed accommodation,

subsection (4) below applies.

(4) If the offeree under the agreement is an individual who—

(a) is not acting in the course of a business, and

(b) has received the document mentioned in subsection (3) above, any information contained in that document which was, or would on request have been, required to be provided under section (2)(b) above shall be deemed to be a term of the agreement.

(5) If, in a case where subsection (4) above applies, a change in the information contained in the document is communicated to the offeree in writing before the timeshare agreement is entered into, the change shall be deemed for the purposes of this Act always to have been incorporated in the information contained in the document if—

(a) the change arises from circumstances beyond the offeror's control, or

(b) the offeror and the offeree expressly agree to the change before entering into the timeshare agreement,

and the change is expressly mentioned in the timeshare agreement.

(6) A person who contravenes subsection (1) above is guilty of an offence and liable—

(a) on summary conviction, to a fine not exceeding the statutory maximum, and

(b) on conviction on indictment, to a fine.

(7) In this section 'the proposed accommodation' means—

(a) the accommodation which is the subject of the proposed agreement, or

(b) the accommodation in the pool of accommodation which is the subject of the proposed agreement,

as the case may be.

(8) This section only applies if—

(a) the accommodation which is the subject of the proposed agreement or agreement is accommodation in a building, or

(b) some or all of the accommodation in the pool of accommodation which is the subject of the proposed agreement or agreement is accommodation in a building,

as the case may be.]

[1B   Advertising of timeshare rights

(1) No person shall advertise timeshare rights in the course of a business unless the advertisement indicates the possibility of obtaining the document referred to in section 1A(1) of this Act and where it may be obtained.

(2) A person who contravenes this section is guilty of an offence and liable—

(a) on summary conviction, to a fine not exceeding the statutory maximum, and

(b) on conviction on indictment, to a fine.

(3) In proceedings against a person for an offence under this section it shall be a defence for that person to show that at the time when he advertised the timeshare rights—

(a) he did not know and had no reasonable cause to suspect that he was advertising timeshare rights, or

(b) he had reasonable cause to believe that the advertisement complied with the requirements of subsection (1) above.

(4) This section only applies if—

(a) the timeshare accommodation concerned is, or appears from the advertisement to be, accommodation in a building, or

(b) some or all of the accommodation in the pool of accommodation concerned is, or appears from the advertisement to be, accommodation in a building,

as the case may be.]

[1C   Obligatory terms of timeshare agreement

(1) A person must not in the course of a business enter into a timeshare agreement to which this Act applies as offeror unless the agreement includes, as terms set out in it, the information referred to in Schedule 1 to this Act.

(2) If and to the extent that any information set out in an agreement in accordance with subsection (1) above is inconsistent with any term (the 'deemed term') which is deemed to be included in the agreement under section 1A(4) of this Act, the agreement shall be treated for all purposes of this Act as if the deemed term, and not that information, were set out and included in the agreement.

(3) A person who contravenes subsection (1) above is guilty of an offence and liable—

(a) on summary conviction, to a fine not exceeding the statutory maximum, and

(b) on conviction on indictment, to a fine.

(4) This section only applies if the offeree—

(a) is an individual, and

(b) is not acting in the course of a business.

(5) This section only applies if—

(a) the accommodation which is the subject of the agreement is accommodation in a building, or

(b) some or all of the accommodation in the pool of accommodation which is the subject of the agreement is accommodation in a building,

as the case may be.]

[1D   Form of agreement and language of brochure and agreement

(1) A person must not in the course of a business enter into a timeshare agreement to which this Act applies as offeror unless the agreement is in writing and complies with sub-sections (3) to (5) below, so far as applicable.

(2) A person who is required to provide a document under subsection (1) of section 1A of this Act contravenes that subsection if he does not provide a document which complies with subsections (3) and (4) below, so far as applicable.

(3) If the customer is resident in, or a national of, an EEA State, the agreement or document (as the case may be) must be drawn up in a language which is—

(a) the language, or one of the languages, of the EEA State in which he is resident, or

(b) the language, or one of the languages, of the EEA State of which he is a national,

and is an official language of an EEA State.

(4) If, in a case falling within subsection (3) above, there are two or more languages in which the agreement or document may be drawn up in compliance with that subsection and the customer nominates one of those languages, the agreement or document must be drawn up in the language he nominates.

(5) If the offeree is resident in the United Kingdom and the agreement would not, apart from this subsection, be required to be drawn up in English, it must be drawn up in English (in addition to any other language in which it is drawn up).

(6) A person who contravenes subsection (1) above is guilty of an offence and liable—

(a) on summary conviction, to a fine not exceeding the statutory maximum, and

(b) on conviction on indictment, to a fine.

(7) In this section 'the customer' means—

(a) for the purposes of subsection (1) above, the offeree, and

(b) for the purposes of subsection (2) above, the person to whom the document is required to be provided.

(8) Subsection (1) above only applies if the offeree—

(a) is an individual, and

(b) is not acting in the course of a business.

(9) Subsection (1) above only applies if—

(a) the accommodation which is the subject of the agreement is accommodation in a building, or

(b) some or all of the accommodation in the pool of accommodation which is the subject of the agreement is accommodation in a building,

as the case may be.]

[1E   Translation of agreement

(1) A person must not in the course of a business enter into a timeshare agreement to which this Act applies as offeror unless he complies with subsection (2) below.

(2) If the timeshare accommodation which is the subject of the agreement, or any of the accommodation in the pool of accommodation which is the subject of the agreement, is situated in an EEA State, the offeror must provide the offeree with a certified translation of the agreement in the language, or one of the languages, of that State.

(3) The language of the translation must be an official language of an EEA State.

(4) Subsection (1) above does not apply if the agreement is drawn up in a language in which the translation is required or permitted to be made.

(5) A person who contravenes subsection (1) above is guilty of an offence and liable—

(a) on summary conviction, to a fine not exceeding the statutory maximum, and

(b) on conviction on indictment, to a fine.

(6) In this section 'certified translation' means a translation which is certified to be accurate by a person authorised to make or verify translations for the purposes of court proceedings.

(7) This section only applies if the offeree—

(a) is an individual, and

(b) is not acting in the course of a business.

(8) This section only applies if—

(a) the accommodation which is the subject of the agreement is accommodation in a building, or

(b) some or all of the accommodation in the pool of accommodation which is the subject of the agreement is accommodation in a building.

as the case may be.]

2 [Obligation for timeshare agreement to contain information on cancellation rights]

(1) A person must not in the course of a business enter into a timeshare agreement to which this Act applies as offeror unless [the offeree has received the agreement and it complies with the following requirements.]

(2) [The agreement] must state—

(a) that the offeree is entitled to give notice of cancellation of the agreement to the offeror at any time on or before the date specified [in the agreement], being a day falling not less than fourteen days after the day on which the agreement is entered into, and

(b) that if the offeree gives such a notice to the offeror on or before that date he will [(subject to section 5(9) of this Act)] have no further rights or obligations under the agreement, but will have the right to recover any sums paid under or in contemplation of the agreement.

[(2A) If the agreement includes provision for providing credit for or in respect of the offeree, it must state that, notwithstanding the giving of notice of cancellation under section 5 or 5A of this Act, so far as the agreement relates to repayment of the credit and payment of interest, it will continue to be enforceable, subject to section 7 of this Act.

(2B) Subsection (2C) below applies if—

(a) the price under the timeshare agreement is covered fully or partly by credit granted under a timeshare credit agreement to which this Act applies,

(b) the offeree is an individual, and

(c) the accommodation which is the subject of the timeshare agreement is accommodation in a building, or some or all of the accommodation in the pool of accommodation which is the subject of the agreement is accommodation in a building.

(2C) The timeshare agreement must state that, if the offeree gives to the offeror a notice as mentioned in subsection (2)(b) above or a notice of cancellation of the agreement under section 5A of this Act which has the effect of cancelling the agreement—

(a) the notice will also have the effect of cancelling the timeshare credit agreement,

(b) so far as the timeshare credit agreement relates to repayment of credit and payment of interest, it shall have effect subject to section 7 of this Act, and

(c) subject to paragraph (b) above, the offeree will have no further rights or obligations under the timeshare credit agreement.

(2D) Subsection (2E) below applies if—

(a) the offeree is an individual, and

(b) the accommodation which is the subject of the timeshare agreement is accommodation in a building, or some or all of the accommodation in the pool of accommodation which is the subject of the agreement is accommodation in a building.

(2E) The agreement must state that the offeree may have, in addition to the rights mentioned in subsection (2) above, further rights under section 5A of this Act to cancel the timeshare agreement.

(2F) The agreement must contain a blank notice of cancellation.]

(3) A person who contravenes this section is guilty of an offence ...

3 [Obligation for timeshare credit agreement to contain information on cancellation rights]

(1) A person must not in the course of a business enter into a timeshare credit agreement to which this Act applies as creditor unless [the offeree has received the agreement and it complies with the following requirements.]

(2) [The agreement] must state—

(a) that the offeree is entitled to give notice of cancellation of the agreement to the creditor at any time on or before the date specified [in the agreement], being a day falling not less than fourteen days after the day on which the agreement is entered into, and

    (b) that, if the offeree gives such a notice to the creditor on or before that date, then—

        (i) so far as the agreement relates to repayment of credit and payment of interest, it shall have effect subject to section 7 of this Act, and

        (ii) subject to sub-paragraph (i) above, the offeree will have no further rights or obligations under the agreement.

[(3) [The agreement must state that it] is a timeshare credit agreement for the purposes of this Act.]

[(4) Subsection (5) below applies if—

    (a) the offeree is an individual, and

    (b) the accommodation which is the subject of the timeshare agreement to which the timeshare credit agreement relates is accommodation in a building, or some or all of the accommodation in the pool of accommodation which is the subject of that timeshare agreement is accommodation in a building.

(5) The timeshare credit agreement must state that, if the offeree gives a notice under section 5 or 5A of this Act of cancellation of the timeshare agreement which has the effect of cancelling it, the notice will also have the effect of cancelling the timeshare credit agreement (with the same consequences as mentioned in subsection (2)(b)(i) and (ii) above).

(6) The agreement must contain a blank notice of cancellation.]

4 Provisions supplementary to sections 2 and 3

(1) Sections 2 and 3 of this Act do not apply where, in entering into the agreement, the offeree is acting in the course of a business.

(2) [A timeshare agreement to which this Act applies and a timeshare credit agreement to which this Act applies must each—]

    (a) be in such form as may be prescribed, and

    (b) comply with such requirements (whether as to type, size, colour or disposition or lettering, quality or colour of paper, or otherwise) as may be prescribed for securing that [the matters required to be stated or contained in the agreement by virtue of section 2 or 3 are] prominent and easily legible.

(3) An agreement is not invalidated by reason of a contravention of section 2 or 3.

5 Right to cancel timeshare agreement

(1) Where a person—

    (a) has entered, or proposes to enter, into a timeshare agreement to which this Act applies as offeree, and

    [(b) the agreement complies with the requirements of sections 2 and 4 of this Act,] the agreement may not be enforced against him on or before the date specified [in the agreement in pursuance of section 2(2)(a) above]. and he may give notice of cancellation of the agreement to the offeror at any time on or before that date.

(2) Subject to subsection (3) below, where

    [(a) a person enters into a timeshare agreement to which this Act applies as offeree, but

    (b) the agreement does not comply with the requirements of sections 2 and 4 of this Act,]

the agreement may not be enforced against him and he may give notice of cancellation of the agreement to the offeror at any time.

(3) If in a case falling within subsection (2) above the offeree affirms the agreement at any time after the expiry of the period of fourteen days beginning with the day on which the agreement is entered into—

    (a) subsection (2) above does not prevent the agreement being enforced against him, and

    (b) he may not at any subsequent time give notice of cancellation of the agreement to the offeror [under subsection (2) above].

[(3A) Where—
- (a) the offeree is an individual, and
- (b) the accommodation which is the subject of the agreement is accommodation in a building, or some or all of the accommodation in the pool of accommodation which is the subject of the agreement is accommodation in a building,

subsection (3) above applies as if for 'fourteen days' there were substituted 'three months and ten days'.

(3B) If in a case falling within subsection (3A) above the last day of the period of three months and ten days is a public holiday, the period shall not end until the end of the first working day after the public holiday.]

(4) The offeree's giving, within the time allowed under this section [or subsection 5A of this Act], notice of cancellation of the agreement to the offeror at a time when the agreement has been entered into shall have the effect of cancelling the agreement.

(5) The offeree's giving notice of cancellation of the agreement [under this section] to the offeror before the agreement has been entered into shall have the effect of withdrawing any offer to enter into the agreement.

(6) Where a timeshare agreement is cancelled under this section [or section 5A of this Act], then, subject to subsection (9) below—
- (a) the agreement shall cease to be enforceable, and
- (b) subsection (8) below shall apply.

(7) Subsection (8) below shall also apply where giving a notice of cancellation has the effect of withdrawing an offer to enter into a timeshare agreement.

(8) Where this subsection applies—
- (a) any sum which the offeree has paid under or in contemplation of the agreement to the offeror, or to any person who is the offeror's agent for the purpose of receiving that sum, shall be recoverable from the offeror by the offeree and shall be due and payable at the time the notice of cancellation is given, but
- (b) no sum may be recovered by or on behalf of the offeror from the offeree in respect of the agreement.

(9) Where a timeshare agreement includes provision for providing credit for or in respect of the offeree, then, notwithstanding the giving of notice of cancellation under this section [or section 5A of this Act], so far as the agreement relates to repayment of the credit and payment of interest—
- (a) it shall continue to be enforceable, subject to section 7 of this Act, [...]

[5A Additional right to cancel timeshare agreement

(1) If a timeshare agreement to which this Act applies does not include, as terms set out in it, the information referred to in paragraph (a), (b), (c), (d)(i), (d)(ii), (h), (i), (k) [and (m)] of Schedule 1 to this Act, the agreement may not be enforced against the offeree before the end of the period of three months and ten days beginning with the day on which the agreement was entered into, and the offeree may give notice of cancellation of the agreement to the offeror at any time during that period.

(2) If the information referred to in subsection (1) above is provided to the offeree before the end of the period of three months beginning with the day on which the agreement was entered into—
- (a) the offeree may give notice of cancellation of the agreement to the offeror at any time within the period of ten days beginning with the day on which the information is received by the offeree, but
- (b) the offeree may not at any subsequent time give notice of cancellation of the agreement to the offeror under subsection (1) above.

(3) If the last day of the period referred to in subsection (1) above or the last day of the period of ten days referred to in subsection (2) above is a public holiday, the period concerned shall not end until the end of the first working day after the public holiday.

(4) The reference in subsection (1) above to a timeshare agreement to which this Act applies includes a reference to a binding preliminary agreement.

(5) This section only applies if [*sic*] the offeree—

    (a) is an individual, and

    (b) is not acting in the course of a business.

(6) This section only applies if—

    (a) the accommodation which is the subject of the agreement is accommodation in a building, or

    (b) some or all of the accommodation in the pool of accommodation which is the subject of the agreement is accommodation in a building,

as the case may be.]

[5B   Advance payments

(1) A person who enters, or proposes to enter, in the course of a business into a timeshare agreement to which this Act applies as offeror must not (either in person or through another person) request or accept from the offeree or proposed offeree any advance payment before the end of the period during which notice of cancellation of the agreement may be given under section 5 or 5A of this Act.

(2) A person who contravenes this section is guilty of an offence and liable—

    (a) on summary conviction, to a fine not exceeding the statutory maximum, and

    (b) on conviction on indictment, to a fine.

(3) Subsection (1) above only applies if the offeree or proposed offeree—

    (a) is an individual, and

    (b) is not acting in the course of a business.

(4) Subsection (1) above only applies if—

    (a) the accommodation which is the subject of the agreement or proposed agreement is accommodation in a building, or

    (b) some or all of the accommodation in the pool of accommodation which is the subject of the agreement or proposed agreement is accommodation in a building, as the case may be.]

[6   Right to cancel timeshare credit agreement by giving notice/b]

(1) Where a person—

    (a) has entered into a timeshare credit agreement to which this Act applies as offeree, and

    [(b) the agreement complies with the requirements of section 3 and 4 of this Act,]

he may give notice of cancellation of the agreement to the creditor at any time on or before the date specified [in the agreement in pursuance of section 3(2)(a) above].

(2) Subject to subsection (3) below, where

    [(a) a person enters into a timeshare credit agreement to which this Act applies as offeree, but

    (b) the agreement does not comply with the requirements of sections 3 and 4 of this Act,]

he may give notice of cancellation of the agreement to the creditor at any time.

(3) If in a case falling within subsection (2) above the offeree affirms the agreement at any time after the expiry of the period of fourteen days beginning with the day on which the agreement is entered into, he may not at any subsequent time give notice of cancellation of the agreement to the creditor.

(4) The offeree's giving, within the time allowed under this section, notice of cancellation of the agreement to the creditor at a time when the agreement has been entered into shall have the effect of cancelling the agreement.

(5) Where a timeshare credit agreement is cancelled under this section [or section 6A of this Act]—

(a) the agreement shall continue in force, subject to section 7 of this Act, so far as it relates to repayment of the credit and payment of interest, and

(b) subject to paragraph (a) above, the agreement shall cease to be enforceable.

[6A   Automatic cancellation of timeshare credit agreement

(1) Where—

(a) a notice of cancellation of a timeshare agreement is given under section 5 or 5A of this Act, and

(b) the giving of the notice has the effect of cancelling the agreement,

the notice shall also have the effect of cancelling any related timeshare credit agreement to which this Act applies.

(2) Where a timeshare credit agreement is cancelled as mentioned in subsection (1) above, the offeror shall, if he is not the same person as the creditor under the related timeshare credit agreement, forthwith on receipt of the notice inform the creditor that the notice has been given.

(3) A timeshare credit agreement is related to a timeshare agreement for the purposes of this section if credit under the timeshare credit agreement fully or partly covers the price under the timeshare agreement.

(4) Subsection (1) above only applies if the offeree under the timeshare agreement concerned is an individual.

(5) Subsection (1) above only applies if—

(a) the accommodation which is the subject of the timeshare agreement is accommodation in a building, or

(b) some or all of the accommodation in the pool of accommodation which is the subject of the timeshare agreement is accommodation in a building,

as the case may be.]

7   Repayment of credit and interest

(1) This section applies following—

(a) the giving of notice of cancellation of a timeshare agreement in accordance with section 5 of this Act in a case where subsection (9) of that section applies, [. . .]

(b) the giving of notice of cancellation of a timeshare credit agreement in accordance with section 6 of this Act [or

(c) the cancellation of a timeshare credit agreement by virtue of section 6A of this Act.]

(2) If the offeree repays the whole or a portion of the credit—

(a) before the expiry of one month following the giving of the notice [or the cancellation of the timeshare credit agreement by virtue of section 6A of this Act], or

(b) in the case of a credit repayable by instalments, before the date on which the first instalment is due,

no interest shall be payable on the amount repaid.

(3) If the whole of a credit repayable by instalments is not repaid on or before the date specified in subsection (2)(b) above, the offeree shall not be liable to repay any of the credit except on receipt of a request in writing in such form as may be prescribed, signed by or on behalf of the offeror or (as the case may be) creditor, stating the amounts of the remaining instalments (recalculated by the offeror or creditor as nearly as may be in accordance with the agreement and without extending the repayment period), but excluding any sum other than principal and interest.

8   Defence of due diligence

(1) In proceedings against a person for an offence under section [1A(6), 1B(2), 1C(3), 1D(6), 1E(5), 2(3) or 5B(2)] of this Act it shall be a defence for that person to show that he took all reasonable steps and exercised all due diligence to avoid committing the offence.

[10A   Civil proceedings

(1) The obligation to comply with subsection (1) of section 1A of this Act shall be a duty owed by the person who proposes to enter into a timeshare agreement to any person whom he is required to provide with a document under that subsection and a contravention of the obligation shall be actionable accordingly.

(2) The obligation to comply with section 1C(1), 1D(1), [1E(1), and 2(1)] of this Act shall in each case be a duty owed by the person who enters into a timeshare agreement as offeror to the offeree and a contravention of the obligation shall be actionable accordingly.

(3) The obligation to comply with section 6A(2) of this Act shall be a duty owed by the offeror under the timeshare agreement to the creditor under the related timeshare credit agreement and a contravention of the obligation shall be actionable accordingly.]

12   General provisions

(1) For the purposes of this Act, a notice of cancellation of an agreement is a notice (however expressed) showing that the offeree wishes unconditionally to cancel the agreement, whether or not it is in a prescribed form.

(2) The rights conferred and duties imposed by sections [1A] to 7 of this Act are in addition to any rights conferred or duties imposed by or under any other Act.

(3) For the purposes of this Act, if the offeree sends a notice by post in a properly addressed and pre-paid letter the notice is to be treated as given at the time of posting.

(4) This Act shall have effect in relation to any timeshare agreement or timeshare credit agreement notwithstanding any agreement or notice.

[SCHEDULE 1   MINIMUM LIST OF ITEMS TO BE INCLUDED IN A TIMESHARE AGREEMENT TO WHICH SECTION 1C APPLIES

(a) The identities and domiciles of the parties, including specific information on the offeror's legal status at the time of the conclusion of the agreement and the identity and domicile of the owner.

(b) the exact nature of the right which is the subject of the agreement and, if the accommodation concerned, or any of the accommodation in the pool of accommodation concerned, is situated in the territory of an EEA State, a clause setting out the conditions governing the exercise of that right within the territory of that State and if those conditions have been fulfilled or, if they have not, what conditions remain to be fulfilled.

(c) When the timeshare accommodation has been determined, an accurate description of that accommodation and its location.

(d) Where the timeshare accommodation is under construction—
   (i)   the state of completion,
   (ii) a reasonable estimate of the deadline for completion of the timeshare accommodation,
   (iii) where it concerns specific timeshare accommodation, the number of the building permit and the name and full address of the competent authority or authorities,
   (iv) the state of completion of the services rendering the timeshare accommodation fully operational (gas, electricity, water and telephone connections),
   (v)   a guarantee regarding completion of the timeshare accommodation or a guarantee regarding reimbursement of any payment made if the accommodation is not completed and, where appropriate, the conditions governing the operation of those guarantees.

(e) The services (lighting, water, maintenance, refuse collection) to which the offeree has or will have access and on what conditions.

(f) The common facilities, such as swimming pool, sauna, etc., to which the offeree has or may have access, and where appropriate, on what conditions.

(g) The principles on the basis of which the maintenance of and repairs to the timeshare accommodation and its administration and management will be arranged.

(h) The exact period within which the right which is the subject of the agreement may be exercised and, if necessary, its duration; the date on which the offeree may start to exercise that right.

(i) The price to be paid by the offeree to exercise the right under the agreement; an estimate of the amount to be paid by the offeree for the use of common facilities and services; the basis for the calculation of the amount of charges relating to occupation of the timeshare accommodation, the mandatory statutory charges (for example, taxes and fees) and the administrative overheads (for example, management, maintenance and repairs).

(j) A clause stating that acquisitions will not result in costs, charges or obligations other than those specified in the agreement.

(k) Whether or not it is possible to join a scheme for the exchange or resale of the rights under the agreement, and any costs involved should an exchange or resale scheme be organised by the offeror or by a third party designated by him in the agreement.

[...]

(m)The date and place of each party's signing of the agreement.]

Arbitration Act 1996
(1996, c. 23)

An Act to restate and improve the law relating to arbitration pursuant to an arbitration agreement; to make other provision relating to arbitration and arbitration awards; and for connected purposes.

[17th June 1996]

PART I   ARBITRATION PURSUANT TO AN ARBITRATION AGREEMENT

Introductory

1   General principles
The provisions of this Part are founded on the following principles, and shall be construed accordingly—

(a) the object of arbitration is to obtain the fair resolution of disputes by an impartial tribunal without unnecessary delay or expense;

(b) the parties should be free to agree how their disputes are resolved, subject only to such safeguards as are necessary in the public interest;

(c) in matters governed by this Part the court should not intervene except as provided by this Part.

2   Scope of application of provisions
(1) The provisions of this Part apply where the seat of the arbitration is in England and Wales or Northern Ireland.

(2) The following sections apply even if the seat of the arbitration is outside England and Wales or Northern Ireland or no seat has been designated or determined–

(a) sections 9 to 11 (stay of legal proceedings, &c.), and

(b) section 66 (enforcement of arbitral awards).

(3) The powers conferred by the following sections apply even if the seat of the arbitration is outside England and Wales or Northern Ireland or no seat has been designated or determined—

(a) section 43 (securing the attendance of witnesses), and

(b) section 44 (court powers exercisable in support of arbitral proceedings);

but the court may refuse to exercise any such power if, in the opinion of the court, the fact that the seat of the arbitration is outside England and Wales or Northern Ireland, or that when designated or determined the seat is likely to be outside England and Wales or Northern Ireland, makes it inappropriate to do so.

(4) The court may exercise a power conferred by any provision of this Part not mentioned in subsection (2) or (3) for the purpose of supporting the arbitral process where–

(a) no seat of the arbitration has been designated or determined, and

(b) by reason of a connection with England and Wales or Northern Ireland the court is satisfied that it is appropriate to do so.

(5) Section 7 (separability of arbitration agreement) and section 8 (death of a party) apply where the law applicable to the arbitration agreement is the law of England and Wales or Northern Ireland even if the seat of the arbitration is outside England and Wales or Northern Ireland or has not been designated or determined.

3 The seat of the arbitration

In this Part 'the seat of the arbitration' means the juridical seat of the arbitration designated—

(a) by the parties to the arbitration agreement, or

(b) by any arbitral or other institution or person vested by the parties with powers in that regard, or

(c) by the arbitral tribunal if so authorised by the parties,

or determined, in the absence of any such designation, having regard to the parties' agreement and all the relevant circumstances.

4 Mandatory and non-mandatory provisions

(1) The mandatory provisions of this Part are listed in Schedule 1 and have effect notwithstanding any agreement to the contrary.

(2) The other provisions of this Part (the 'non-mandatory provisions') allow the parties to make their own arrangements by agreement but provide rules which apply in the absence of such agreement.

(3) The parties may make such arrangements by agreeing to the application of institutional rules or providing any other means by which a matter may be decided.

(4) It is immaterial whether or not the law applicable to the parties' agreement is the law of England and Wales or, as the case may be, Northern Ireland.

(5) The choice of a law other than the law of England and Wales or Northern Ireland as the applicable law in respect of a matter provided for by a non-mandatory provision of this Part is equivalent to an agreement making provision about that matter.

For this purpose an applicable law determined in accordance with the parties' agreement, or which is objectively determined in the absence of any express or implied choice, shall be treated as chosen by the parties.

5 Agreements to be in writing

(1) The provisions of this Part apply only where the arbitration agreement is in writing, and any other agreement between the parties as to any matter is effective for the purposes of this Part only if in writing.

The expressions 'agreement', 'agree' and 'agreed' shall be construed accordingly.

(2) There is an agreement in writing—

(a) if the agreement is made in writing (whether or not it is signed by the parties),

(b) if the agreement is made by exchange of communications in writing, or

(c) if the agreement is evidenced in writing.

(3) Where parties agree otherwise than in writing by reference to terms which are in writing, they make an agreement in writing.

(4) An agreement is evidenced in writing if an agreement made otherwise than in writing is recorded by one of the parties, or by a third party, with the authority of the parties to the agreement.

(5) An exchange of written submissions in arbitral or legal proceedings in which the existence of an agreement otherwise than in writing is alleged by one party against another party and not denied by the other party in his response constitutes as between those parties an agreement in writing to the effect alleged.

(6) References in this Part to anything being written or in writing include its being recorded by any means.

6   Definition of arbitration agreement

(1) In this Part an 'arbitration agreement' means an agreement to submit to arbitration present or future disputes (whether they are contractual or not).

(2) The reference in an agreement to a written form of arbitration clause or to a document containing an arbitration clause constitutes an arbitration agreement if the reference is such as to make that clause part of the agreement.

7   Separability of arbitration agreement

Unless otherwise agreed by the parties, an arbitration agreement which forms or was intended to form part of another agreement (whether or not in writing) shall not be regarded as invalid, non-existent or ineffective because that other agreement is invalid, or did not come into existence or has become ineffective, and it shall for that purpose be treated as a distinct agreement.

8   Whether agreement discharged by death of a party

(1) Unless otherwise agreed by the parties, an arbitration agreement is not discharged by the death of a party and may be enforced by or against the personal representatives of that party.

(2) Subsection (1) does not affect the operation of any enactment or rule of law by virtue of which a substantive right or obligation is extinguished by death.

Stay of legal proceedings

9   Stay of legal proceedings

(1) A party to an arbitration agreement against whom legal proceedings are brought (whether by way of claim or counterclaim) in respect of a matter which under the agreement is to be referred to arbitration may (upon notice to the other parties to the proceedings) apply to the court in which the proceedings have been brought to stay the proceedings so far as they concern that matter.

(2) An application may be made notwithstanding that the matter is to be referred to arbitration only after the exhaustion of other dispute resolution procedures.

(3) An application may not be made by a person before taking the appropriate procedural step (if any) to acknowledge the legal proceedings against him or after he has taken any step in those proceedings to answer the substantive claim.

(4) On an application under this section the court shall grant a stay unless satisfied that the arbitration agreement is null and void, inoperative, or incapable of being performed.

(5) If the court refuses to stay the legal proceedings, any provision that an award is a condition precedent to the bringing of legal proceedings in respect of any matter is of no effect in relation to those proceedings.

10   Reference of interpleader issue to arbitration

(1) Where in legal proceedings relief by way of interpleader is granted and any issue between the claimants is one in respect of which there is an arbitration agreement between them, the court granting the relief shall direct that the issue be determined in accordance with the agreement unless the circumstances are such that proceedings brought by a claimant in respect of the matter would not be stayed.

(2) Where subsection (1) applies but the court does not direct that the issue be determined in accordance with the arbitration agreement, any provision that an award is a condition precedent to the bringing of legal proceedings in respect of any matter shall not affect the determination of that issue by the court.

11   Retention of security where Admiralty proceedings stayed

(1) Where Admiralty proceedings are stayed on the ground that the dispute in question should be submitted to arbitration, the court granting the stay may, if in those proceedings property has been arrested or bail or other security has been given to prevent or obtain release from arrest—

(a) order that the property arrested be retained as security for the satisfaction of any award given in the arbitration in respect of that dispute, or

(b) order that the stay of those proceedings be conditional on the provision of equivalent security for the satisfaction of any such award.

(2) Subject to any provision made by rules of court and to any necessary modifications, the same law and practice shall apply in relation to property retained in pursuance of an order as would apply if it were held for the purposes of proceedings in the court making the order.

Commencement of arbitral proceedings

12   Power of court to extend time for beginning arbitral proceedings, &c.

(1) Where an arbitration agreement to refer future disputes to arbitration provides that a claim shall be barred, or the claimant's right extinguished, unless the claimant takes within a time fixed by the agreement some step–

(a) to begin arbitral proceedings, or

(b) to begin other dispute resolution procedures which must be exhausted before arbitral proceedings can be begun,

the court may by order extend the time for taking that step.

(2) Any party to the arbitration agreement may apply for such an order (upon notice to the other parties), but only after a claim has arisen and after exhausting any available arbitral process for obtaining an extension of time.

(3) The court shall make an order only if satisfied—

(a) that the circumstances are such as were outside the reasonable contmplation of the parties when they agreed the provision in question, and that it would be just to extend the time, or

(b) that the conduct of one party makes it unjust to hold the other party to the strict terms of the provision in question.

(4) The court may extend the time for such period and on such terms as it thinks fit, and may do so whether or not the time previously fixed (by agreement or by a previous order) has expired.

(5) An order under this section does not affect the operation of the Limitation Acts (see section 13).

(6) The leave of the court is required for any appeal from a decision of the court under this section.

13   Application of limitation acts

(1) The Limitation Acts apply to arbitral proceedings as they apply to legal proceedings.

(2) The court may order that in computing the time prescribed by the Limitation Acts for the commencement of proceedings (including arbitral proceedings) in respect of a dispute which was the subject matter—

(a) of an award which the court orders to be set aside or declares to be of no effect, or

(b) of the affected part of an award which the court orders to be set aside in part, or declares to be in part of no effect,

the period between the commencement of the arbitration and the date of the order referred to in paragraph (a) or (b) shall be excluded.

(3) In determining for the purposes of the Limitation Acts when a cause of action accrued, any provision that an award is a condition precedent to the bringing of legal proceedings in respect of a matter to which an arbitration agreement applies shall be disregarded.

(4) In this Part 'the Limitation Acts' means—

(a) in England and Wales, the Limitation Act 1980, the Foreign Limitation Periods Act 1984 and any other enactment (whenever passed) relating to the limitation of actions;

(b) in Northern Ireland, the Limitation (Northern Ireland) Order 1989, the Foreign Limitation Periods (Northern Ireland) Order 1985 and any other enactment (whenever passed) relating to the limitation of actions.

14   Commencement of arbitral proceedings

(1) The parties are free to agree when arbitral proceedings are to be regarded as commenced for the purposes of this Part and for the purposes of the Limitation Acts.

(2) If there is no such agreement the following provisions apply.

(3) Where the arbitrator is named or designated in the arbitration agreement, arbitral proceedings are commenced in respect of a matter when one party serves on the other party or parties a notice in writing requiring him or them to submit that matter to the person so named or designated.

(4) Where the arbitrator or arbitrators are to be appointed by the parties, arbitral proceedings are commenced in respect of a matter when one party serves on the other party or parties notice in writing requiring him or them to appoint an arbitrator or to agree to the appointment of an arbitrator in respect of that matter.

(5) Where the arbitrator or arbitrators are to be appointed by a person other than a party to the proceedings, arbitral proceedings are commenced in respect of a matter when one party gives notice in writing to that person requesting him to make the appointment in respect of that matter.

The arbitral tribunal

15   The arbitral tribunal

(1) The parties are free to agree on the number of arbitrators to form the tribunal and whether there is to be a chairman or umpire.

(2) Unless otherwise agreed by the parties, an agreement that the number of arbitrators shall be two or any other even number shall be understood as requiring the appointment of an additional arbitrator as chairman of the tribunal.

(3) If there is no agreement as to the number of arbitrators, the tribunal shall consist of a sole arbitrator.

16   Procedure for appointment of arbitrators

(1) The parties are free to agree on the procedure for appointing the arbitrator or arbitrators, including the procedure for appointing any chairman or umpire.

(2) If or to the extent that there is no such agreement, the following provisions apply.

(3) If the tribunal is to consist of a sole arbitrator, the parties shall jointly appoint the arbitrator not later than 28 days after service of a request in writing by either party to do so.

(4) If the tribunal is to consist of two arbitrators, each party shall appoint one arbitrator not later than 14 days after service of a request in writing by either party to do so.

(5) If the tribunal is to consist of three arbitrators—

(a) each party shall appoint one arbitrator not later than 14 days after service of a request in writing by either party to do so, and

(b) the two so appointed shall forthwith appoint a third arbitrator as the chairman of the tribunal.

(6) If the tribunal is to consist of two arbitrators and an umpire—

(a) each party shall appoint one arbitrator not later than 14 days after service of a request in writing by either party to do so, and

(b) the two so appointed may appoint an umpire at any time after they themselves are appointed and shall do so before any substantive hearing or forthwith if they cannot agree on a matter relating to the arbitration.

(7) In any other case (in particular, if there are more than two parties) section 18 applies as in the case of a failure of the agreed appointment procedure.

17 Power in case of default to appoint sole arbitrator

(1) Unless the parties otherwise agree, where each of two parties to an arbitration agreement is to appoint an arbitrator and one party ('the party in default') refuses to do so, or fails to do so within the time specified, the other party, having duly appointed his arbitrator, may give notice in writing to the party in default that he proposes to appoint his arbitrator to act as sole arbitrator.

(2) If the party in default does not within 7 clear days of that notice being given—

(a) make the required appointment, and

(b) notify the other party that he has done so,

the other party may appoint his arbitrator as sole arbitrator whose award shall be binding on both parties as if he had been so appointed by agreement.

(3) Where a sole arbitrator has been appointed under subsection (2), the party in default may (upon notice to the appointing party) apply to the court which may set aside the appointment.

(4) The leave of the court is required for any appeal from a decision of the court under this section.

18 Failure of appointment procedure

(1) The parties are free to agree what is to happen in the event of a failure of the procedure for the appointment of the arbitral tribunal.

There is no failure if an appointment is duly made under section 17 (power in case of default to appoint sole arbitrator), unless that appointment is set aside.

(2) If or to the extent that there is no such agreement any party to the arbitration agreement may (upon notice to the other parties) apply to the court to exercise its powers under this section.

(3) Those powers are—

(a) to give directions as to the making of any necessary appointments;

(b) to direct that the tribunal shall be constituted by such appointments (or any one or more of them) as have been made;

(c) to revoke any appointments already made;

(d) to make any necessary appointments itself.

(4) An appointment made by the court under this section has effect as if made with the agreement of the parties.

(5) The leave of the court is required for any appeal from a decision of the court under this section.

19   Court to have regard to agreed qualifications

In deciding whether to exercise, and in considering how to exercise, any of its powers under section 16 (procedure for appointment of arbitrators) or section 18 (failure of appointment procedure), the court shall have due regard to any agreement of the parties as to the qualifications required of the arbitrators.

20   Chairman

(1) Where the parties have agreed that there is to be a chairman, they are free to agree what the functions of the chairman are to be in relation to the making of decisions, orders and awards.

(2) If or to the extent that there is no such agreement, the following provisions apply.

(3) Decisions, orders and awards shall be made by all or a majority of the arbitrators (including the chairman).

(4) The view of the chairman shall prevail in relation to a decision, order or award in respect of which there is neither unanimity nor a majority under subsection (3).

21   Umpire

(1) Where the parties have agreed that there is to be an umpire, they are free to agree what the functions of the umpire are to be, and in particular—

    (a) whether he is to attend the proceedings, and

    (b) when he is to replace the other arbitrators as the tribunal with power to make decisions, orders and awards.

(2) If or to the extent that there is no such agreement, the following provisions apply.

(3) The umpire shall attend the proceedings and be supplied with the same documents and other materials as are supplied to the other arbitrators.

(4) Decisions, orders and awards shall be made by the other arbitrators unless and until they cannot agree on a matter relating to the arbitration.

In that event they shall forthwith give notice in writing to the parties and the umpire, whereupon the umpire shall replace them as the tribunal with power to make decisions, orders and awards as if he were sole arbitrator.

(5) If the arbitrators cannot agree but fail to give notice of that fact, or if any of them fails to join in the giving of notice, any party to the arbitral proceedings may (upon notice to the other parties and to the tribunal) apply to the court which may order that the umpire shall replace the other arbitrators as the tribunal with power to make decisions, orders and awards as if he were sole arbitrator.

(6) The leave of the court is required for any appeal from a decision of the court under this section.

22   Decision-making where no chairman or umpire

(1) Where the parties agree that there shall be two or more arbitrators with no chairman or umpire, the parties are free to agree how the tribunal is to make decisions, orders and awards.

(2) If there is no such agreement, decisions, orders and awards shall be made by all or a majority of the arbitrators.

23   Revocation of arbitrator's authority

(1) The parties are free to agree in what circumstances the authority of an arbitrator may be revoked.

(2) If or to the extent that there is no such agreement the following provisions apply.

(3) The authority of an arbitrator may not be revoked except—

    (a) by the parties acting jointly, or

    (b) by an arbitral or other institution or person vested by the parties with powers in that regard.

(4) Revocation of the authority of an arbitrator by the parties acting jointly must be agreed in writing unless the parties also agree (whether or not in writing) to terminate the arbitration agreement.

(5) Nothing in this section affects the power of the court—

    (a) to revoke an appointment under section 18 (powers exercisable in case of failure of appointment procedure), or

    (b) to remove an arbitrator on the grounds specified in section 24.

24 Power of court to remove arbitrator

(1) A party to arbitral proceedings may (upon notice to the other parties, to the arbitrator concerned and to any other arbitrator) apply to the court to remove an arbitrator on any of the following grounds—

    (a) that circumstances exist that give rise to justifiable doubts as to his impartiality;

    (b) that he does not possess the qualifications required by the arbitration agreement;

    (c) that he is physically or mentally incapable of conducting the proceedings or there are justifiable doubts as to his capacity to do so;

    (d) that he has refused or failed—

        (i) properly to conduct the proceedings, or

        (ii) to use all reasonable despatch in conducting the proceedings or making an award,

and that substantial injustice has been or will be caused to the applicant.

(2) If there is an arbitral or other institution or person vested by the parties with power to remove an arbitrator, the court shall not exercise its power of removal unless satisfied that the applicant has first exhausted any available recourse to that institution or person.

(3) The arbitral tribunal may continue the arbitral proceedings and make an award while an application to the court under this section is pending.

(4) Where the court removes an arbitrator, it may make such order as it thinks fit with respect to his entitlement (if any) to fees or expenses, or the repayment of any fees or expenses already paid.

(5) The arbitrator concerned is entitled to appear and be heard by the court before it makes any order under this section.

(6) The leave of the court is required for any appeal from a decision of the court under this section.

25 Resignation of arbitrator

(1) The parties are free to agree with an arbitrator as to the consequences of his resignation as regards—

    (a) his entitlement (if any) to fees or expenses, and

    (b) any liability thereby incurred by him.

(2) If or to the extent that there is no such agreement the following provisions apply.

(3) An arbitrator who resigns his appointment may (upon notice to the parties) apply to the court—

    (a) to grant him relief from any liability thereby incurred by him, and

    (b) to make such order as it thinks fit with respect to his entitlement (if any) to fees or expenses or the repayment of any fees or expenses already paid.

(4) If the court is satisfied that in all the circumstances it was reasonable for the arbitrator to resign, it may grant such relief as is mentioned in subsection (3)(a) on such terms as it thinks fit.

(5) The leave of the court is required for any appeal from a decision of the court under this section.

26 Death of arbitrator or person appointing him

(1) The authority of an arbitrator is personal and ceases on his death.

(2) Unless otherwise agreed by the parties, the death of the person by whom an arbitrator was appointed does not revoke the arbitrator's authority.

27 Filling of vacancy, &c.

(1) Where an arbitrator ceases to hold office, the parties are free to agree—

   (a) whether and if so how the vacancy is to be filled,

   (b) whether and if so to what extent the previous proceedings should stand, and

   (c) what effect (if any) his ceasing to hold office has on any appointment made by him (alone or jointly).

(2) If or to the extent that there is no such agreement, the following provisions apply.

(3) The provisions of sections 16 (procedure for appointment of arbitrators) and 18 (failure of appointment procedure) apply in relation to the filling of the vacancy as in relation to an original appointment.

(4) The tribunal (when reconstituted) shall determine whether and if so to what extent the previous proceedings should stand.

This does not affect any right of a party to challenge those proceedings on any ground which had arisen before the arbitrator ceased to hold office.

(5) His ceasing to hold office does not affect any appointment by him (alone or jointly) of another arbitrator, in particular any appointment of a chairman or umpire.

28 Joint and several liability of parties to arbitrators for fees and expenses

(1) The parties are jointly and severally liable to pay to the arbitrators such reasonable fees and expenses (if any) as are appropriate in the circumstances.

(2) Any party may apply to the court (upon notice to the other parties and to the arbitrators) which may order that the amount of the arbitrators' fees and expenses shall be considered and adjusted by such means and upon such terms as it may direct.

(3) If the application is made after any amount has been paid to the arbitrators by way of fees or expenses, the court may order the repayment of such amount (if any) as is shown to be excessive, but shall not do so unless it is shown that it is reasonable in the circumstances to order repayment.

(4) The above provisions have effect subject to any order of the court under section 24(4) or 25(3)(b) (order as to entitlement to fees or expenses in case of removal or resignation of arbitrator).

(5) Nothing in this section affects any liability of a party to any other party to pay all or any of the costs of the arbitration (see sections 59 to 65) or any contractual right of an arbitrator to payment of his fees and expenses.

(6) In this section references to arbitrators include an arbitrator who has ceased to act and an umpire who has not replaced the other arbitrators.

29 Immunity of arbitrator

(1) An arbitrator is not liable for anything done or omitted in the discharge or purported discharge of his functions as arbitrator unless the act or omission is shown to have been in bad faith.

(2) Subsection (1) applies to an employee or agent of an arbitrator as it applies to the arbitrator himself.

(3) This section does not affect any liability incurred by an arbitrator by reason of his resigning (but see section 25).

Jurisdiction of the arbitral tribunal

30 Competence of tribunal to rule on its own jurisdiction

(1) Unless otherwise agreed by the parties, the arbitral tribunal may rule on its own substantive jurisdiction, that is, as to—

   (a) whether there is a valid arbitration agreement,

   (b) whether the tribunal is properly constituted, and

   (c) what matters have been submitted to arbitration in accordance with the arbitration agreement.

(2) Any such ruling may be challenged by any available arbitral process of appeal or review or in accordance with the provisions of this Part.

31   Objection to substantive jurisdiction of tribunal

(1) An objection that the arbitral tribunal lacks substantive jurisdiction at the outset of the proceedings must be raised by a party not later than the time he takes the first step in the proceedings to contest the merits of any matter in relation to which he challenges the tribunal's jurisdiction.

A party is not precluded from raising such an objection by the fact that he has appointed or participated in the appointment of an arbitrator.

(2) Any objection during the course of the arbitral proceedings that the arbitral tribunal is exceeding its substantive jurisdiction must be made as soon as possible after the matter alleged to be beyond its jurisdiction is raised.

(3) The arbitral tribunal may admit an objection later than the time specified in subsection (1) or (2) if it considers the delay justified.

(4) Where an objection is duly taken to the tribunal's substantive jurisdiction and the tribunal has power to rule on its own jurisdiction, it may—

(a) rule on the matter in an award as to jurisdiction, or

(b) deal with the objection in its award on the merits.

If the parties agree which of these courses the tribunal should take, the tribunal shall proceed accordingly.

(5) The tribunal may in any case, and shall if the parties so agree, stay proceedings whilst an application is made to the court under section 32 (determination of preliminary point of jurisdiction).

32   Determination of preliminary point of jurisdiction

(1) The court may, on the application of a party to arbitral proceedings (upon notice to the other parties), determine any question as to the substantive jurisdiction of the tribunal.

A party may lose the right to object (see section 73).

(2) An application under this section shall not be considered unless—

(a) it is made with the agreement in writing of all the other parties to the proceedings, or

(b) it is made with the permission of the tribunal and the court is satisfied—

(i) that the determination of the question is likely to produce substantial savings in costs,

(ii) that the application was made without delay, and

(iii) that there is good reason why the matter should be decided by the court.

(3) An application under this section, unless made with the agreement of all the other parties to the proceedings, shall state the grounds on which it is said that the matter should be decided by the court.

(4) Unless otherwise agreed by the parties, the arbitral tribunal may continue the arbitral proceedings and make an award while an application to the court under this section is pending.

(5) Unless the court gives leave, no appeal lies from a decision of the court whether the conditions specified in subsection (2) are met.

(6) The decision of the court on the question of jurisdiction shall be treated as a judgment of the court for the purposes of an appeal.

But no appeal lies without the leave of the court which shall not be given unless the court considers that the question involves a point of law which is one of general importance or is one which for some other special reason should be considered by the Court of Appeal.

The arbitral proceedings

33   General duty of the tribunal

(1) The tribunal shall—

(a) act fairly and impartially as between the parties, giving each party a reasonable opportunity of putting his case and dealing with that of his opponent, and

(b) adopt procedures suitable to the circumstances of the particular case, avoiding unnecessary delay or expense, so as to provide a fair means for the resolution of the matters falling to be determined.

(2) The tribunal shall comply with that general duty in conducting the arbitral proceedings, in its decisions on matters of procedure and evidence and in the exercise of all other powers conferred on it.

34 Procedural and evidential matters

(1) It shall be for the tribunal to decide all procedural and evidential matters, subject to the right of the parties to agree any matter.

(2) Procedural and evidential matters include—

(a) when and where any part of the proceedings is to be held;

(b) the language or languages to be used in the proceedings and whether translations of any relevant documents are to be supplied;

(c) whether any and if so what form of written statements of claim and defence are to be used, when these should be supplied and the extent to which such statements can be later amended;

(d) whether any and if so which documents or classes of documents should be disclosed between and produced by the parties and at what stage;

(e) whether any and if so what questions should be put to and answered by the respective parties and when and in what form this should be done;

(f) whether to apply strict rules of evidence (or any other rules) as to the admissibility, relevance or weight of any material (oral, written or other) sought to be tendered on any matters of fact or opinion, and the time, manner and form in which such material should be exchanged and presented;

(g) whether and to what extent the tribunal should itself take the initiative in ascertaining the facts and the law;

(h) whether and to what extent there should be oral or written evidence or submissions.

(3) The tribunal may fix the time within which any directions given by it are to be complied with, and may if it thinks fit extend the time so fixed (whether or not it has expired).

35 Consolidation of proceedings and concurrent hearings

(1) The parties are free to agree—

(a) that the arbitral proceedings shall be consolidated with other arbitral proceedings, or

(b) that concurrent hearings shall be held,

on such terms as may be agreed.

(2) Unless the parties agree to confer such power on the tribunal, the tribunal has no power to order consolidation of proceedings or concurrent hearings.

36 Legal or other representation

Unless otherwise agreed by the parties, a party to arbitral proceedings may be represented in the proceedings by a lawyer or other person chosen by him.

37 Power to appoint experts, legal advisers or assessors

(1) Unless otherwise agreed by the parties—

(a) the tribunal may—

(i) appoint experts or legal advisers to report to it and the parties, or

(ii) appoint assessors to assist it on technical matters,

and may allow any such expert, legal adviser or assessor to attend the proceedings; and

(b) the parties shall be given a reasonable opportunity to comment on any information, opinion or advice offered by any such person.

(2) The fees and expenses of an expert, legal adviser or assessor appointed by the tribunal for which the arbitrators are liable are expenses of the arbitrators for the purposes of this Part.

38   General powers exercisable by the tribunal

(1) The parties are free to agree on the powers exercisable by the arbitral tribunal for the purposes of and in relation to the proceedings.

(2) Unless otherwise agreed by the parties the tribunal has the following powers.

(3) The tribunal may order a claimant to provide security for the costs of the arbitration. This power shall not be exercised on the ground that the claimant is—

(a) an individual ordinarily resident outside the United Kingdom, or

(b) a corporation or association incorporated or formed under the law of a country outside the United Kingdom, or whose central management and control is exercised outside the United Kingdom.

(4) The tribunal may give directions in relation to any property which is the subject of the proceedings or as to which any question arises in the proceedings, and which is owned by or is in the possession of a party to the proceedings—

(a) for the inspection, photographing, preservation, custody or detention of the property by the tribunal, an expert or a party, or

(b) ordering that samples be taken from, or any observation be made of or experiment conducted upon, the property.

(5) The tribunal may direct that a party or witness shall be examined on oath or affirmation, and may for that purpose administer any necessary oath or take any necessary affirmation.

(6) The tribunal may give directions to a party for the preservation for the purposes of the proceedings of any evidence in his custody or control.

39   Power to make provisional awards

(1) The parties are free to agree that the tribunal shall have power to order on a provisional basis any relief which it would have power to grant in a final award.

(2) This includes, for instance, making—

(a) a provisional order for the payment of money or the disposition of property as between the parties, or

(b) an order to make an interim payment on account of the costs of the arbitration.

(3) Any such order shall be subject to the tribunal's final adjudication; and the tribunal's final award, on the merits or as to costs, shall take account of any such order.

(4) Unless the parties agree to confer such power on the tribunal, the tribunal has no such power.

This does not affect its powers under section 47 (awards on different issues, &c.).

40   General duty of parties

(1) The parties shall do all things necessary for the proper and expeditious conduct of the arbitral proceedings.

(2) This includes—

(a) complying without delay with any determination of the tribunal as to procedural or evidential matters, or with any order or directions of the tribunal, and

(b) where appropriate, taking without delay any necessary steps to obtain a decision of the court on a preliminary question of jurisdiction or law (see sections 32 and 45).

41   Powers of tribunal in case of party's default

(1) The parties are free to agree on the powers of the tribunal in case of a party's failure to do something necessary for the proper and expeditious conduct of the arbitration.

(2) Unless otherwise agreed by the parties, the following provisions apply.

(3) If the tribunal is satisfied that there has been inordinate and inexcusable delay on the part of the claimant in pursuing his claim and that the delay—

(a) gives rise, or is likely to give rise, to a substantial risk that it is not possible to have a fair resolution of the issues in that claim, or

(b) has caused, or is likely to cause, serious prejudice to the respondent, the tribunal may make an award dismissing the claim.

(4) If without showing sufficient cause a party—

(a) fails to attend or be represented at an oral hearing of which due notice was given, or

(b) where matters are to be dealt with in writing, fails after due notice to submit written evidence or make written submissions,

the tribunal may continue the proceedings in the absence of that party or, as the case may be, without any written evidence or submissions on his behalf, and may make an award on the basis of the evidence before it.

(5) If without showing sufficient cause a party fails to comply with any order or directions of the tribunal, the tribunal may make a peremptory order to the same effect, prescribing such time for compliance with it as the tribunal considers appropriate.

(6) If a claimant fails to comply with a peremptory order of the tribunal to provide security for costs, the tribunal may make an award dismissing his claim.

(7) If a party fails to comply with any other kind of peremptory order, then, without prejudice to section 42 (enforcement by court of tribunal's peremptory orders), the tribunal may do any of the following—

(a) direct that the party in default shall not be entitled to rely upon any allegation or material which was the subject matter of the order;

(b) draw such adverse inferences from the act of non-compliance as the circumstances justify;

(c) proceed to an award on the basis of such materials as have been properly provided to it;

(d) make such order as it thinks fit as to the payment of costs of the arbitration incurred in consequence of the non-compliance.

Powers of court in relation to arbitral proceedings

42 Enforcement of peremptory orders of tribunal

(1) Unless otherwise agreed by the parties, the court may make an order requiring a party to comply with a peremptory order made by the tribunal.

(2) An application for an order under this section may be made—

(a) by the tribunal (upon notice to the parties),

(b) by a party to the arbitral proceedings with the permission of the tribunal (and upon notice to the other parties), or

(c) where the parties have agreed that the powers of the court under this section shall be available.

(3) The court shall not act unless it is satisfied that the applicant has exhausted any available arbitral process in respect of failure to comply with the tribunal's order.

(4) No order shall be made under this section unless the court is satisfied that the person to whom the tribunal's order was directed has failed to comply with it within the time prescribed in the order or, if no time was prescribed, within a reasonable time.

(5) The leave of the court is required for any appeal from a decision of the court under this section.

43 Securing the attendance of witnesses

(1) A party to arbitral proceedings may use the same court procedures as are available in relation to legal proceedings to secure the attendance before the tribunal of a witness in order to give oral testimony or to produce documents or other material evidence.

(2) This may only be done with the permission of the tribunal or the agreement of the other parties.

(3) The court procedures may only be used if—
  (a) the witness is in the United Kingdom, and
  (b) the arbitral proceedings are being conducted in England and Wales or, as the case may be, Northern Ireland.

(4) A person shall not be compelled by virtue of this section to produce any document or other material evidence which he could not be compelled to produce in legal proceedings.

44 Court powers exercisable in support of arbitral proceedings

(1) Unless otherwise agreed by the parties, the court has for the purposes of and in relation to arbitral proceedings the same power of making orders about the matters listed below as it has for the purposes of and in relation to legal proceedings.

(2) Those matters are—
  (a) the taking of the evidence of witnesses;
  (b) the preservation of evidence;
  (c) making orders relating to property which is the subject of the proceedings or as to which any question arises in the proceedings—
    (i) for the inspection, photographing, preservation, custody or detention of the property, or
    (ii) ordering that samples be taken from, or any observation be made of or experiment conducted upon, the property; and for that purpose authorising any person to enter any premises in the possession or control of a party to the arbitration;
  (d) the sale of any goods the subject of the proceedings;
  (e) the granting of an interim injunction or the appointment of a receiver.

(3) If the case is one of urgency, the court may, on the application of a party or proposed party to the arbitral proceedings, make such orders as it thinks necessary for the purpose of preserving evidence or assets.

(4) If the case is not one of urgency, the court shall act only on the application of a party to the arbitral proceedings (upon notice to the other parties and to the tribunal) made with the permission of the tribunal or the agreement in writing of the other parties.

(5) In any case the court shall act only if or to the extent that the arbitral tribunal, and any arbitral or other institution or person vested by the parties with power in that regard, has no power or is unable for the time being to act effectively.

(6) If the court so orders, an order made by it under this section shall cease to have effect in whole or in part on the order of the tribunal or of any such arbitral or other institution or person having power to act in relation to the subject-matter of the order.

(7) The leave of the court is required for any appeal from a decision of the court under this section.

45 Determination of preliminary point of law

(1) Unless otherwise agreed by the parties, the court may on the application of a party to arbitral proceedings (upon notice to the other parties) determine any question of law arising in the course of the proceedings which the court is satisfied substantially affects the rights of one or more of the parties.

An agreement to dispense with reasons for the tribunal's award shall be considered an agreement to exclude the court's jurisdiction under this section.

(2) An application under this section shall not be considered unless—
  (a) it is made with the agreement of all the other parties to the proceedings, or
  (b) it is made with the permission of the tribunal and the court is satisfied—
    (i) that the determination of the question is likely to produce substantial savings in costs, and
    (ii) that the application was made without delay.

(3) The application shall identify the question of law to be determined and, unless made with the agreement of all the other parties to the proceedings, shall state the grounds on which it is said that the question should be decided by the court.

(4) Unless otherwise agreed by the parties, the arbitral tribunal may continue the arbitral proceedings and make an award while an application to the court under this section is pending.

(5) Unless the court gives leave, no appeal lies from a decision of the court whether the conditions specified in subsection (2) are met.

(6) The decision of the court on the question of law shall be treated as a judgment of the court for the purposes of an appeal.

But no appeal lies without the leave of the court which shall not be given unless the court considers that the question is one of general importance, or is one which for some other special reason should be considered by the Court of Appeal.

The award

46 Rules applicable to substance of dispute
(1) The arbitral tribunal shall decide the dispute—
  (a) in accordance with the law chosen by the parties as applicable to the substance of the dispute, or
  (b) if the parties so agree, in accordance with such other considerations as are agreed by them or determined by the tribunal.

(2) For this purpose the choice of the laws of a country shall be understood to refer to the substantive laws of that country and not its conflict of laws rules.

(3) If or to the extent that there is no such choice or agreement, the tribunal shall apply the law determined by the conflict of laws rules which it considers applicable.

47 Awards on different issues, &c.
(1) Unless otherwise agreed by the parties, the tribunal may make more than one award at different times on different aspects of the matters to be determined.

(2) The tribunal may, in particular, make an award relating—
  (a) to an issue affecting the whole claim, or
  (b) to a part only of the claims or cross-claims submitted to it for decision.

(3) If the tribunal does so, it shall specify in its award the issue, or the claim or part of a claim, which is the subject matter of the award.

48 Remedies
(1) The parties are free to agree on the powers exercisable by the arbitral tribunal as regards remedies.

(2) Unless otherwise agreed by the parties, the tribunal has the following powers.

(3) The tribunal may make a declaration as to any matter to be determined in the proceedings.

(4) The tribunal may order the payment of a sum of money, in any currency.

(5) The tribunal has the same powers as the court—
  (a) to order a party to do or refrain from doing anything;
  (b) to order specific performance of a contract (other than a contract relating to land);
  (c) to order the rectification, setting aside or cancellation of a deed or other document.

49 Interest
(1) The parties are free to agree on the powers of the tribunal as regards the award of interest.

(2) Unless otherwise agreed by the parties the following provisions apply.

(3) The tribunal may award simple or compound interest from such dates, at such rates and with such rests as it considers meets the justice of the case—
  (a) on the whole or part of any amount awarded by the tribunal, in respect of any period up to the date of the award;

(b) on the whole or part of any amount claimed in the arbitration and outstanding at the commencement of the arbitral proceedings but paid before the award was made, in respect of any period up to the date of payment.

(4) The tribunal may award simple or compound interest from the date of the award (or any later date) until payment, at such rates and with such rests as it considers meets the justice of the case, on the outstanding amount of any award (including any award of interest under subsection (3) and any award as to costs).

(5) References in this section to an amount awarded by the tribunal include an amount payable in consequence of a declaratory award by the tribunal.

(6) The above provisions do not affect any other power of the tribunal to award interest.

50   Extension of time for making award

(1) Where the time for making an award is limited by or in pursuance of the arbitration agreement, then, unless otherwise agreed by the parties, the court may in accordance with the following provisions by order extend that time.

(2) An application for an order under this section may be made—
(a) by the tribunal (upon notice to the parties), or
(b) by any party to the proceedings (upon notice to the tribunal and the other parties),
but only after exhausting any available arbitral process for obtaining an extension of time.

(3) The court shall only make an order if satisfied that a substantial injustice would otherwise be done.

(4) The court may extend the time for such period and on such terms as it thinks fit, and may do so whether or not the time previously fixed (by or under the agreement or by a previous order) has expired.

(5) The leave of the court is required for any appeal from a decision of the court under this section.

51   Settlement

(1) If during arbitral proceedings the parties settle the dispute, the following provisions apply unless otherwise agreed by the parties.

(2) The tribunal shall terminate the substantive proceedings and, if so requested by the parties and not objected to by the tribunal, shall record the settlement in the form of an agreed award.

(3) An agreed award shall state that it is an award of the tribunal and shall have the same status and effect as any other award on the merits of the case.

(4) The following provisions of this Part relating to awards (sections 52 to 58) apply to an agreed award.

(5) Unless the parties have also settled the matter of the payment of the costs of the arbitration, the provisions of this Part relating to costs (sections 59 to 65) continue to apply.

52   Form of award

(1) The parties are free to agree on the form of an award.

(2) If or to the extent that there is no such agreement, the following provisions apply.

(3) The award shall be in writing signed by all the arbitrators or all those assenting to the award.

(4) The award shall contain the reasons for the award unless it is an agreed award or the parties have agreed to dispense with reasons.

(5) The award shall state the seat of the arbitration and the date when the award is made.

53   Place where award treated as made

Unless otherwise agreed by the parties, where the seat of the arbitration is in England and Wales or Northern Ireland, any award in the proceedings shall be treated as made there, regardless of where it was signed, despatched or delivered to any of the parties.

54 Date of award

(1) Unless otherwise agreed by the parties, the tribunal may decide what is to be taken to be the date on which the award was made.

(2) In the absence of any such decision, the date of the award shall be taken to be the date on which it is signed by the arbitrator or, where more than one arbitrator signs the award, by the last of them.

55 Notification of award

(1) The parties are free to agree on the requirements as to notification of the award to the parties.

(2) If there is no such agreement, the award shall be notified to the parties by service on them of copies of the award, which shall be done without delay after the award is made.

(3) Nothing in this section affects section 56 (power to withhold award in case of non-payment).

56 Power to withhold award in case of non-payment

(1) The tribunal may refuse to deliver an award to the parties except upon full payment of the fees and expenses of the arbitrators.

(2) If the tribunal refuses on that ground to deliver an award, a party to the arbitral proceedings may (upon notice to the other parties and the tribunal) apply to the court, which may order that—

(a) the tribunal shall deliver the award on the payment into court by the applicant of the fees and expenses demanded, or such lesser amount as the court may specify,

(b) the amount of the fees and expenses properly payable shall be determined by such means and upon such terms as the court may direct, and

(c) that out of the money paid into court there shall be paid out such fees and expenses as may be found to be properly payable and the balance of the money (if any) shall be paid out to the applicant.

(3) For this purpose the amount of fees and expenses properly payable is the amount the applicant is liable to pay under section 28 or any agreement relating to the payment of the arbitrators.

(4) No application to the court may be made where there is any available arbitral process for appeal or review of the amount of the fees or expenses demanded.

(5) References in this section to arbitrators include an arbitrator who has ceased to act and an umpire who has not replaced the other arbitrators.

(6) The above provisions of this section also apply in relation to any arbitral or other institution or person vested by the parties with powers in relation to the delivery of the tribunal's award.

As they so apply, the references to the fees and expenses of the arbitrators shall be construed as including the fees and expenses of that institution or person.

(7) The leave of the court is required for any appeal from a decision of the court under this section.

(8) Nothing in this section shall be construed as excluding an application under section 28 where payment has been made to the arbitrators in order to obtain the award.

57 Correction of award or additional award

(1) The parties are free to agree on the powers of the tribunal to correct an award or make an additional award.

(2) If or to the extent there is no such agreement, the following provisions apply.

(3) The tribunal may on its own initiative or on the application of a party—

(a) correct an award so as to remove any clerical mistake or error arising from an accidental slip or omission or clarify or remove any ambiguity in the award, or

(b) make an additional award in respect of any claim (including a claim for interest or costs) which was presented to the tribunal but was not dealt with in the award.

These powers shall not be exercised without first affording the other parties a reasonable opportunity to make representations to the tribunal.

(4) Any application for the exercise of those powers must be made within 28 days of the date of the award or such longer period as the parties may agree.

(5) Any correction of an award shall be made within 28 days of the date the application was received by the tribunal or, where the correction is made by the tribunal on its own initiative, within 28 days of the date of the award or, in either case, such longer period as the parties may agree.

(6) Any additional award shall be made within 56 days of the date of the original award or such longer period as the parties may agree.

(7) Any correction of an award shall form part of the award.

58 Effect of award

(1) Unless otherwise agreed by the parties, an award made by the tribunal pursuant to an arbitration agreement is final and binding both on the parties and on any persons claiming through or under them.

(2) This does not affect the right of a person to challenge the award by any available arbitral process of appeal or review or in accordance with the provisions of this Part.

Costs of the arbitration

59 Costs of the arbitration

(1) References in this Part to the costs of the arbitration are to—
  (a) the arbitrators' fees and expenses,
  (b) the fees and expenses of any arbitral institution concerned, and
  (c) the legal or other costs of the parties.

(2) Any such reference includes the costs of or incidental to any proceedings to determine the amount of the recoverable costs of the arbitration (see section 63).

60 Agreement to pay costs in any event

An agreement which has the effect that a party is to pay the whole or part of the costs of the arbitration in any event is only valid if made after the dispute in question has arisen.

61 Award of costs

(1) The tribunal may make an award allocating the costs of the arbitration as between the parties, subject to any agreement of the parties.

(2) Unless the parties otherwise agree, the tribunal shall award costs on the general principle that costs should follow the event except where it appears to the tribunal that in the circumstances this is not appropriate in relation to the whole or part of the costs.

62 Effect of agreement or award about costs

Unless the parties otherwise agree, any obligation under an agreement between them as to how the costs of the arbitration are to be borne, or under an award allocating the costs of the arbitration, extends only to such costs as are recoverable.

63 The recoverable costs of the arbitration

(1) The parties are free to agree what costs of the arbitration are recoverable.

(2) If or to the extent there is no such agreement, the following provisions apply.

(3) The tribunal may determine by award the recoverable costs of the arbitration on such basis as it thinks fit.

If it does so, it shall specify—
  (a) the basis on which it has acted, and

(b) the items of recoverable costs and the amount referable to each.

(4) If the tribunal does not determine the recoverable costs of the arbitration, any party to the arbitral proceedings may apply to the court (upon notice to the other parties) which may—

(a) determine the recoverable costs of the arbitration on such basis as it thinks fit, or

(b) order that they shall be determined by such means and upon such terms as it may specify.

(5) Unless the tribunal or the court determines otherwise—

(a) the recoverable costs of the arbitration shall be determined on the basis that there shall be allowed a reasonable amount in respect of all costs reasonably incurred, and

(b) any doubt as to whether costs were reasonably incurred or were reasonable in amount shall be resolved in favour of the paying party.

(6) The above provisions have effect subject to section 64 (recoverable fees and expenses of arbitrators).

(7) Nothing in this section affects any right of the arbitrators, any expert, legal adviser or assessor appointed by the tribunal, or any arbitral institution, to payment of their fees and expenses.

64   Recoverable fees and expenses of arbitrators

(1) Unless otherwise agreed by the parties, the recoverable costs of the arbitration shall include in respect of the fees and expenses of the arbitrators only such reasonable fees and expenses as are appropriate in the circumstances.

(2) If there is any question as to what reasonable fees and expenses are appropriate in the circumstances, and the matter is not already before the court on an application under section 63(4), the court may on the application of any party (upon notice to the other parties)—

(a) determine the matter, or

(b) order that it be determined by such means and upon such terms as the court may specify.

(3) Subsection (1) has effect subject to any order of the court under section 24(4) or 25(3)(b) (order as to entitlement to fees or expenses in case of removal or resignation of arbitrator).

(4) Nothing in this section affects any right of the arbitrator to payment of his fees and expenses.

65   Power to limit recoverable costs

(1) Unless otherwise agreed by the parties, the tribunal may direct that the recoverable costs of the arbitration, or of any part of the arbitral proceedings, shall be limited to a specified amount.

(2) Any direction may be made or varied at any stage, but this must be done sufficiently in advance of the incurring of costs to which it relates, or the taking of any steps in the proceedings which may be affected by it, for the limit to be taken into account.

Powers of the court in relation to award

66   Enforcement of the award

(1) An award made by the tribunal pursuant to an arbitration agreement may, by leave of the court, be enforced in the same manner as a judgment or order of the court to the same effect.

(2) Where leave is so given, judgment may be entered in terms of the award.

(3) Leave to enforce an award shall not be given where, or to the extent that, the person against whom it is sought to be enforced shows that the tribunal lacked substantive jurisdiction to make the award.

The right to raise such an objection may have been lost (see section 73).

(4) Nothing in this section affects the recognition or enforcement of an award under any other enactment or rule of law, in particular under Part II of the Arbitration Act 1950 (enforcement of awards under Geneva Convention) or the provisions of Part III of this Act relating to the recognition and enforcement of awards under the New York Convention or by an action on the award.

67 Challenging the award: substantive jurisdiction

(1) A party to arbitral proceedings may (upon notice to the other parties and to the tribunal) apply to the court—

(a) challenging any award of the arbitral tribunal as to its substantive jurisdiction; or

(b) for an order declaring an award made by the tribunal on the merits to be of no effect, in whole or in part, because the tribunal did not have substantive jurisdiction.

A party may lose the right to object (see section 73) and the right to apply is subject to the restrictions in section 70(2) and (3).

(2) The arbitral tribunal may continue the arbitral proceedings and make a further award while an application to the court under this section is pending in relation to an award as to jurisdiction.

(3) On an application under this section challenging an award of the arbitral tribunal as to its substantive jurisdiction, the court may by order—

(a) confirm the award,

(b) vary the award, or

(c) set aside the award in whole or in part.

(4) The leave of the court is required for any appeal from a decision of the court under this section.

68 Challenging the award: serious irregularity

(1) A party to arbitral proceedings may (upon notice to the other parties and to the tribunal) apply to the court challenging an award in the proceedings on the ground of serious irregularity affecting the tribunal, the proceedings or the award.

A party may lose the right to object (see section 73) and the right to apply is subject to the restrictions in section 70(2) and (3).

(2) Serious irregularity means an irregularity of one or more of the following kinds which the court considers has caused or will cause substantial injustice to the applicant—

(a) failure by the tribunal to comply with section 33 (general duty of tribunal);

(b) the tribunal exceeding its powers (otherwise than by exceeding its substantive jurisdiction: see section 67);

(c) failure by the tribunal to conduct the proceedings in accordance with the procedure agreed by the parties;

(d) failure by the tribunal to deal with all the issues that were put to it;

(e) any arbitral or other institution or person vested by the parties with powers in relation to the proceedings or the award exceeding its powers;

(f) uncertainty or ambiguity as to the effect of the award;

(g) the award being obtained by fraud or the award or the way in which it was procured being contrary to public policy;

(h) failure to comply with the requirements as to the form of the award; or

(i) any irregularity in the conduct of the proceedings or in the award which is admitted by the tribunal or by any arbitral or other institution or person vested by the parties with powers in relation to the proceedings or the award.

(3) If there is shown to be serious irregularity affecting the tribunal, the proceed-ings or the award, the court may—

(a) remit the award to the tribunal, in whole or in part, for reconsideration,

(b) set the award aside in whole or in part, or

(c) declare the award to be of no effect, in whole or in part.

The court shall not exercise its power to set aside or to declare an award to be of no effect, in whole or in part, unless it is satisfied that it would be inappropriate to remit the matters in question to the tribunal for reconsideration.

(4) The leave of the court is required for any appeal from a decision of the court under this section.

69 Appeal on point of law

(1) Unless otherwise agreed by the parties, a party to arbitral proceedings may (upon notice to the other parties and to the tribunal) appeal to the court on a question of law arising out of an award made in the proceedings.

An agreement to dispense with reasons for the tribunal's award shall be considered an agreement to exclude the court's jurisdiction under this section.

(2) An appeal shall not be brought under this section except—

    (a) with the agreement of all the other parties to the proceedings, or

    (b) with the leave of the court.

The right to appeal is also subject to the restrictions in section 70(2) and (3).

(3) Leave to appeal shall be given only if the court is satisfied—

    (a) that the determination of the question will substantially affect the rights of one or more of the parties,

    (b) that the question is one which the tribunal was asked to determine,

    (c) that, on the basis of the findings of fact in the award—

        (i) the decision of the tribunal on the question is obviously wrong, or

        (ii) the question is one of general public importance and the decision of the tribunal is at least open to serious doubt, and

    (d) that, despite the agreement of the parties to resolve the matter by arbitration, it is just and proper in all the circumstances for the court to determine the question.

(4) An application for leave to appeal under this section shall identify the question of law to be determined and state the grounds on which it is alleged that leave to appeal should be granted.

(5) The court shall determine an application for leave to appeal under this section without a hearing unless it appears to the court that a hearing is required.

(6) The leave of the court is required for any appeal from a decision of the court under this section to grant or refuse leave to appeal.

(7) On an appeal under this section the court may by order—

    (a) confirm the award,

    (b) vary the award,

    (c) remit the award to the tribunal, in whole or in part, for reconsideration in the light of the court's determination, or

    (d) set aside the award in whole or in part.

The court shall not exercise its power to set aside an award, in whole or in part, unless it is satisfied that it would be inappropriate to remit the matters in question to the tribunal for reconsideration.

(8) The decision of the court on an appeal under this section shall be treated as a judgment of the court for the purposes of a further appeal.

But no such appeal lies without the leave of the court which shall not be given unless the court considers that the question is one of general importance or is one which for some other special reason should be considered by the Court of Appeal.

70 Challenge or appeal: supplementary provisions

(1) The following provisions apply to an application or appeal under section 67, 68 or 69.

(2) An application or appeal may not be brought if the applicant or appellant has not first exhausted—

(a) any available arbitral process of appeal or review, and

(b) any available recourse under section 57 (correction of award or additional award).

(3) Any application or appeal must be brought within 28 days of the date of the award or, if there has been any arbitral process of appeal or review, of the date when the applicant or appellant was notified of the result of that process.

(4) If on an application or appeal it appears to the court that the award—

(a) does not contain the tribunal's reasons, or

(b) does not set out the tribunal's reasons in sufficient detail to enable the court properly to consider the application or appeal,

the court may order the tribunal to state the reasons for its award in sufficient detail for that purpose.

(5) Where the court makes an order under subsection (4), it may make such further order as it thinks fit with respect to any additional costs of the arbitration resulting from its order.

(6) The court may order the applicant or appellant to provide security for the costs of the application or appeal, and may direct that the application or appeal be dismissed if the order is not complied with.

The power to order security for costs shall not be exercised on the ground that the applicant or appellant is—

(a) an individual ordinarily resident outside the United Kingdom, or

(b) a corporation or association incorporated or formed under the law of a country outside the United Kingdom, or whose central management and control is exercised outside the United Kingdom.

(7) The court may order that any money payable under the award shall be brought into court or otherwise secured pending the determination of the application or appeal, and may direct that the application or appeal be dismissed if the order is not complied with.

(8) The court may grant leave to appeal subject to conditions to the same or similar effect as an order under subsection (6) or (7).

This does not affect the general discretion of the court to grant leave subject to conditions.

71   Challenge or appeal: effect of order of court

(1) The following provisions have effect where the court makes an order under section 67, 68 or 69 with respect to an award.

(2) Where the award is varied, the variation has effect as part of the tribunal's award.

(3) Where the award is remitted to the tribunal, in whole or in part, for reconsideration, the tribunal shall make a fresh award in respect of the matters remitted within three months of the date of the order for remission or such longer or shorter period as the court may direct.

(4) Where the award is set aside or declared to be of no effect, in whole or in part, the court may also order that any provision that an award is a condition precedent to the bringing of legal proceedings in respect of a matter to which the arbitration agreement applies, is of no effect as regards the subject matter of the award or, as the case may be, the relevant part of the award.

Miscellaneous

72   Saving for rights of person who takes no part in proceedings

(1) A person alleged to be a party to arbitral proceedings but who takes no part in the proceedings may question—

(a) whether there is a valid arbitration agreement,

(b) whether the tribunal is properly constituted, or

(c) what matters have been submitted to arbitration in accordance with the arbitration agreement,

by proceedings in the court for a declaration or injunction or other appropriate relief.

(2) He also has the same right as a party to the arbitral proceedings to challenge an award—

      (a) by an application under section 67 on the ground of lack of substantive jurisdiction in relation to him, or

      (b) by an application under section 68 on the ground of serious irregularity (within the meaning of that section) affecting him;

and section 70(2) (duty to exhaust arbitral procedures) does not apply in his case.

73   Loss of right to object

(1) If a party to arbitral proceedings takes part, or continues to take part, in the proceedings without making, either forthwith or within such time as is allowed by the arbitration agreement or the tribunal or by any provision of this Part, any objection—

      (a) that the tribunal lacks substantive jurisdiction,

      (b) that the proceedings have been improperly conducted,

      (c) that there has been a failure to comply with the arbitration agreement or with any provision of this Part, or

      (d) that there has been any other irregularity affecting the tribunal or the proceedings,

he may not raise that objection later, before the tribunal or the court, unless he shows that, at the time he took part or continued to take part in the proceedings, he did not know and could not with reasonable diligence have discovered the grounds for the objection.

(2) Where the arbitral tribunal rules that it has substantive jurisdiction and a party to arbitral proceedings who could have questioned that ruling—

      (a) by any available arbitral process of appeal or review, or

      (b) by challenging the award,

does not do so, or does not do so within the time allowed by the arbitration agreement or any provision of this Part, he may not object later to the tribunal's substantive jurisdiction on any ground which was the subject of that ruling.

74   Immunity of arbitral institutions, &c.

(1) An arbitral or other institution or person designated or requested by the parties to appoint or nominate an arbitrator is not liable for anything done or omitted in the discharge or purported discharge of that function unless the act or omission is shown to have been in bad faith.

(2) An arbitral or other institution or person by whom an arbitrator is appointed or nominated is not liable, by reason of having appointed or nominated him, for anything done or omitted by the arbitrator (or his employees or agents) in the discharge or purported discharge of his functions as arbitrator.

(3) The above provisions apply to an employee or agent of an arbitral or other institution or person as they apply to the institution or the person himself.

75   Charge to secure payment of solicitors' costs

The powers of the court to make declarations and orders under section 73 of the Solicitors Act 1974 or Article 71H of the Solicitors (Northern Ireland) Order 1976 (power to charge property recovered in the proceedings with the payment of solicitors' costs) may be exercised in relation to arbitral proceedings as if those proceedings were proceedings in the court.

Supplementary

76   Service of notices, &c.

(1) The parties are free to agree on the manner of service of any notice or other document required or authorised to be given or served in pursuance of the arbitration agreement or for the purposes of the arbitral proceedings.

(2) If or to the extent that there is no such agreement the following provisions apply.

(3) A notice or other document may be served on a person by any effective means.

(4) If a notice or other document is addressed, pre-paid and delivered by post—

    (a) to the addressee's last known principal residence or, if he is or has been carrying on a trade, profession or business, his last known principal business address, or

    (b) where the addressee is a body corporate, to the body's registered or principal office,

it shall be treated as effectively served.

(5) This section does not apply to the service of documents for the purposes of legal proceedings, for which provision is made by rules of court.

(6) References in this Part to a notice or other document include any form of communication in writing and references to giving or serving a notice or other document shall be construed accordingly.

77 Powers of court in relation to service of documents

(1) This section applies where service of a document on a person in the manner agreed by the parties, or in accordance with provisions of section 76 having effect in default of agreement, is not reasonably practicable.

(2) Unless otherwise agreed by the parties, the court may make such order as it thinks fit—

    (a) for service in such manner as the court may direct, or

    (b) dispensing with service of the document.

(3) Any party to the arbitration agreement may apply for an order, but only after exhausting any available arbitral process for resolving the matter.

(4) The leave of the court is required for any appeal from a decision of the court under this section.

78 Reckoning periods of time

(1) The parties are free to agree on the method of reckoning periods of time for the purposes of any provision agreed by them or any provision of this Part having effect in default of such agreement.

(2) If or to the extent there is no such agreement, periods of time shall be reckoned in accordance with the following provisions.

(3) Where the act is required to be done within a specified period after or from a specified date, the period begins immediately after that date.

(4) Where the act is required to be done a specified number of clear days after a specified date, at least that number of days must intervene between the day on which the act is done and that date.

(5) Where the period is a period of seven days or less which would include a Saturday, Sunday or a public holiday in the place where anything which has to be done within the period falls to be done, that day shall be excluded.

In relation to England and Wales or Northern Ireland, a 'public holiday' means Christmas Day, Good Friday or a day which under the Banking and Financial Dealings Act 1971 is a bank holiday.

79 Power of court to extend time limits relating to arbitral proceedings

(1) Unless the parties otherwise agree, the court may by order extend any time limit agreed by them in relation to any matter relating to the arbitral proceedings or specified in any provision of this Part having effect in default of such agreement.

This section does not apply to a time limit to which section 12 applies (power of court to extend time for beginning arbitral proceedings, &c.).

(2) An application for an order may be made—

    (a) by any party to the arbitral proceedings (upon notice to the other parties and to the tribunal), or

    (b) by the arbitral tribunal (upon notice to the parties).

(3) The court shall not exercise its power to extend a time limit unless it is satisfied—

(a) that any available recourse to the tribunal, or to any arbitral or other institution or person vested by the parties with power in that regard, has first been exhausted, and

(b) that a substantial injustice would otherwise be done.

(4) The court's power under this section may be exercised whether or not the time has already expired.

(5) An order under this section may be made on such terms as the court thinks fit.

(6) The leave of the court is required for any appeal from a decision of the court under this section.

80   Notice and other requirements in connection with legal proceedings

(1) References in this Part to an application, appeal or other step in relation to legal proceedings being taken 'upon notice' to the other parties to the arbitral proceedings, or to the tribunal, are to such notice of the originating process as is required by rules of court and do not impose any separate requirement.

(2) Rules of court shall be made—

(a) requiring such notice to be given as indicated by any provision of this Part, and

(b) as to the manner, form and content of any such notice.

(3) Subject to any provision made by rules of court, a requirement to give notice to the tribunal of legal proceedings shall be construed—

(a) if there is more than one arbitrator, as a requirement to give notice to each of them; and

(b) if the tribunal is not fully constituted, as a requirement to give notice to any arbitrator who has been appointed.

(4) References in this Part to making an application or appeal to the court within a specified period are to the issue within that period of the appropriate originating process in accordance with rules of court.

(5) Where any provision of this Part requires an application or appeal to be made to the court within a specified time, the rules of court relating to the reckoning of periods, the extending or abridging of periods, and the consequences of not taking a step within the period prescribed by the rules, apply in relation to that requirement.

(6) Provision may be made by rules of court amending the provisions of this Part—

(a) with respect to the time within which any application or appeal to the court must be made,

(b) so as to keep any provision made by this Part in relation to arbitral proceedings in step with the corresponding provision of rules of court applying in relation to proceedings in the court, or

(c) so as to keep any provision made by this Part in relation to legal proceedings in step with the corresponding provision of rules of court applying generally in relation to proceedings in the court.

(7) Nothing in this section affects the generality of the power to make rules of court.

81   Saving for certain matters governed by common law

(1) Nothing in this Part shall be construed as excluding the operation of any rule of law consistent with the provisions of this Part, in particular, any rule of law as to—

(a) matters which are not capable of settlement by arbitration;

(b) the effect of an oral arbitration agreement; or

(c) the refusal of recognition or enforcement of an arbitral award on grounds of public policy.

(2) Nothing in this Act shall be construed as reviving any jurisdiction of the court to set aside or remit an award on the ground of errors of fact or law on the face of the award.

82 Minor definitions

(1) In this Part—

'arbitrator', unless the context otherwise requires, includes an umpire;

'available arbitral process', in relation to any matter, includes any process of appeal to or review by an arbitral or other institution or person vested by the parties with powers in relation to that matter;

'claimant', unless the context otherwise requires, includes a counterclaimant, and related expressions shall be construed accordingly;

'dispute' includes any difference;

'enactment' includes an enactment contained in Northern Ireland legislation;

'legal proceedings' means civil proceedings in the High Court or a county court;

'peremptory order' means an order made under section 41(5) or made in exercise of any corresponding power conferred by the parties;

'premises' includes land, buildings, moveable structures, vehicles, vessels, aircraft and hovercraft;

'question of law' means—

      (a) for a court in England and Wales, a question of the law of England and Wales, and

      (b) for a court in Northern Ireland, a question of the law of Northern Ireland;

'substantive jurisdiction', in relation to an arbitral tribunal, refers to the matters specified in section 30(1)(a) to (c), and references to the tribunal exceeding its substantive jurisdiction shall be construed accordingly.

(2) References in this Part to a party to an arbitration agreement include any person claiming under or through a party to the agreement.

83 Index of defined expressions: Part I

In this Part the expressions listed below are defined or otherwise explained by the provisions indicated—

agreement, agree and agreed	section 5(1)
agreement in writing	section 5(2) to (5)
arbitration agreement	sections 6 and 5(1)
arbitrator	section 82(1)
available arbitral process	section 82(1)
claimant	section 82(1)
commencement (in relation to arbitral proceedings)	section 14
costs of the arbitration	section 59
the court	section 105
dispute	section 82(1)
enactment	section 82(1)
legal proceedings	section 82(1)
Limitation Acts	section 13(4)
notice (or other document)	section 76(6)
party—	
—in relation to an arbitration agreement	section 82(2)
—where section 106(4) or (3) applies	section 106(4)
Question of law	section 82(1)
peremptory order	section 82(1) (and see section 41(5))
premises	section 82(1)
question of law	section 82(1)
recoverable costs	sections 63 and 64
seat of the arbitration	section 3

serve and service (of notice or other document)	section 76(6)
substantive jurisdiction (in relation to an arbitral tribunal)	section 82(1) (and see section 30(1)(a) to (c))
upon notice (to the parties or the tribunal)	section 80
written and in writing	section 5(6)

84 Transitional provisions

(1) The provisions of this Part do not apply to arbitral proceedings commenced before the date on which this Part comes into force.

(2) They apply to arbitral proceedings commenced on or after that date under an arbitration agreement whenever made.

(3) The above provisions have effect subject to any transitional provision made by an order under section 109(2) (power to include transitional provisions in commencement order).

PART II OTHER PROVISIONS RELATING TO ARBITRATION

Domestic arbitration agreements

85 Modification of Part I in relation to domestic arbitration agreement

(1) In the case of a domestic arbitration agreement the provisions of Part I are modified in accordance with the following sections.

(2) For this purpose a 'domestic arbitration agreement' means an arbitration agreement to which none of the parties is—

(a) an individual who is a national of, or habitually resident in, a state other than the United Kingdom, or

(b) a body corporate which is incorporated in, or whose central control and management is exercised in, a state other than the United Kingdom,

and under which the seat of the arbitration (if the seat has been designated or determined) is in the United Kingdom.

(3) In subsection (2) 'arbitration agreement' and 'seat of the arbitration' have the same meaning as in Part I (see sections 3, 5(1) and 6).

86 Staying of legal proceedings

(1) In section 9 (stay of legal proceedings), subsection (4) (stay unless the arbitration agreement is null and void, inoperative, or incapable of being performed) does not apply to a domestic arbitration agreement.

(2) On an application under that section in relation to a domestic arbitration agreement the court shall grant a stay unless satisfied—

(a) that the arbitration agreement is null and void, inoperative, or incapable of being performed, or

(b) that there are other sufficient grounds for not requiring the parties to abide by the arbitration agreement.

(3) The court may treat as a sufficient ground under subsection (2)(b) the fact that the applicant is or was at any material time not ready and willing to do all things necessary for the proper conduct of the arbitration or of any other dispute resolution procedures required to be exhausted before resorting to arbitration.

(4) For the purposes of this section the question whether an arbitration agreement is a domestic arbitration agreement shall be determined by reference to the facts at the time the legal proceedings are commenced.

87   Effectiveness of agreement to exclude court's jurisdiction

(1) In the case of a domestic arbitration agreement any agreement to exclude the jurisdiction of the court under—

(a) section 45 (determination of preliminary point of law), or

(b) section 69 (challenging the award: appeal on point of law),

is not effective unless entered into after the commencement of the arbitral proceedings in which the question arises or the award is made.

(2) For this purpose the commencement of the arbitral proceedings has the same meaning as in Part I (see section 14).

(3) For the purposes of this section the question whether an arbitration agreement is a domestic arbitration agreement shall be determined by reference to the facts at the time the agreement is entered into.

88   Power to repeal or amend sections 85 to 87

(1) The Secretary of State may by order repeal or amend the provisions of sections 85 to 87.

(2) An order under this section may contain such supplementary, incidental and transitional provisions as appear to the Secretary of State to be appropriate.

(3) An order under this section shall be made by statutory instrument and no such order shall be made unless a draft of it has been laid before and approved by a resolution of each House of Parliament.

Consumer arbitration agreements

89   Application of unfair terms regulations to consumer arbitration agreements

(1) The following sections extend the application of the Unfair Terms in Consumer Contracts Regulations 1994 in relation to a term which constitutes an arbitration agreement.

For this purpose 'arbitration agreement' means an agreement to submit to arbitration present or future disputes or differences (whether or not contractual).

(2) In those sections 'the Regulations' means those regulations and includes any regulations amending or replacing those regulations.

(3) Those sections apply whatever the law applicable to the arbitration agreement.

90   Regulations apply where consumer is a legal person

The Regulations apply where the consumer is a legal person as they apply where the consumer is a natural person.

91   Arbitration agreement unfair where modest amount sought

(1) A term which constitutes an arbitration agreement is unfair for the purposes of the Regulations so far as it relates to a claim for a pecuniary remedy which does not exceed the amount specified by order for the purposes of this section.

(2) Orders under this section may make different provision for different cases and for different purposes.

(3) The power to make orders under this section is exercisable—

(a) for England and Wales, by the Secretary of State with the concurrence of the Lord Chancellor,

(b) for Scotland, by the Secretary of State [. . .], and

(c) for Northern Ireland, by the Department of Economic Development for Northern Ireland with the concurrence of the Lord Chancellor.

(4) Any such order for England and Wales or Scotland shall be made by statutory instrument which shall be subject to annulment in pursuance of a resolution of either House of Parliament.

(5) Any such order for Northern Ireland shall be a statutory rule for the purposes of the Statutory Rules (Northern Ireland) Order 1979 and shall be subject to negative resolution, within the meaning of section 41(6) of the Interpretation Act (Northern Ireland) 1954.

Small claims arbitration in the county court

92   Exclusion of Part I in relation to small claims arbitration in the county court

Nothing in Part I of this Act applies to arbitration under section 64 of the County Courts Act 1984.

Appointment of judges as arbitrators

93   Appointment of judges as arbitrators

(1) A judge of the Commercial Court or an official referee may, if in all the circumstances he thinks fit, accept appointment as a sole arbitrator or as umpire by or by virtue of an arbitration agreement.

(2) A judge of the Commercial Court shall not do so unless the Lord Chief Justice has informed him that, having regard to the state of business in the High Court and the Crown Court, he can be made available.

(3) An official referee shall not do so unless the Lord Chief Justice has informed him that, having regard to the state of official referees' business, he can be made available.

(4) The fees payable for the services of a judge of the Commercial Court or official referee as arbitrator or umpire shall be taken in the High Court.

(5) In this section—

'arbitration agreement' has the same meaning as in Part I; and

'official referee' means a person nominated under section 68(1)(a) of [the Senior Courts Act 1981] to deal with official referees' business.

(6) The provisions of Part I of this Act apply to arbitration before a person appointed under this section with the modifications specified in Schedule 2.

Statutory arbitrations

94   Application of Part I to statutory arbitrations

(1) The provisions of Part I apply to every arbitration under an enactment (a 'statutory arbitration'), whether the enactment was passed or made before or after the commencement of this Act, subject to the adaptations and exclusions specified in sections 95 to 98.

(2) The provisions of Part I do not apply to a statutory arbitration if or to the extent that their application—

    (a) is inconsistent with the provisions of the enactment concerned, with any rules or procedure authorised or recognised by it, or

    (b) is excluded by any other enactment.

(3) In this section and the following provisions of this Part 'enactment'—

    (a) in England and Wales, includes an enactment contained in subordinate legislation within the meaning of the Interpretation Act 1978;

    (b) in Northern Ireland, means a statutory provision within the meaning of section 1(f) of the Interpretation Act (Northern Ireland) 1954.

95   General adaptation of provisions in relation to statutory arbitrations

(1) The provisions of Part I apply to a statutory arbitration—

    (a) as if the arbitration were pursuant to an arbitration agreement and as if the enactment were that agreement, and

    (b) as if the persons by and against whom a claim subject to arbitration in pursuance of the enactment may be or has been made were parties to that agreement.

(2) Every statutory arbitration shall be taken to have its seat in England and Wales, or, as the case may be, in Northern Ireland.

96   Specific adaptations of provisions in relation to statutory arbitrations

(1) The following provisions of Part I apply to a statutory arbitration with the following adaptations.

(2) In section 30(1) (competence of tribunal to rule on its own jurisdiction), the reference in paragraph (a) to whether there is a valid arbitration agreement shall be construed as a reference to whether the enactment applies to the dispute or difference in question.

(3) Section 35 (consolidation of proceedings and concurrent hearings) applies only so as to authorise the consolidation of proceedings, or concurrent hearings in proceedings, under the same enactment.

(4) Section 46 (rules applicable to substance of dispute) applies with the omission of subsection (1)(b) (determination in accordance with considerations agreed by parties).

97 Provisions excluded from applying to statutory arbitrations
The following provisions of Part I do not apply in relation to a statutory arbitration—
- (a) section 8 (whether agreement discharged by death of a party);
- (b) section 12 (power of court to extend agreed time limits);
- (c) sections 9(5), 10(2) and 71(4) (restrictions on effect of provision that award condition precedent to right to bring legal proceedings).

98 Power to make further provision by regulations
(1) The Secretary of State may make provision by regulations for adapting or excluding any provision of Part I in relation to statutory arbitrations in general or statutory arbitrations of any particular description.

(2) The power is exercisable whether the enactment concerned is passed or made before or after the commencement of this Act.

(3) Regulations under this section shall be made by statutory instrument which shall be subject to annulment in pursuance of a resolution of either House of Parliament.

PART III   RECOGNITION AND ENFORCEMENT OF CERTAIN FOREIGN AWARDS

Enforcement of Geneva Convention awards

99 Continuation of Part II of the Arbitration Act 1950
Part II of the Arbitration Act 1950 (enforcement of certain foreign awards) continues to apply in relation to foreign awards within the meaning of that Part which are not also New York Convention awards.

Recognition and enforcement of New York Convention awards

100 New York Convention awards
(1) In this Part a 'New York Convention award' means an award made, in pursuance of an arbitration agreement, in the territory of a state (other than the United Kingdom) which is a party to the New York Convention.

(2) For the purposes of subsection (1) and of the provisions of this Part relating to such awards—
- (a) 'arbitration agreement' means an arbitration agreement in writing, and
- (b) an award shall be treated as made at the seat of the arbitration, regardless of where it was signed, despatched or delivered to any of the parties.

In this subsection 'agreement in writing' and 'seat of the arbitration' have the same meaning as in Part I.

(3) If Her Majesty by Order in Council declares that a state specified in the Order is a party to the New York Convention, or is a party in respect of any territory so specified, the Order shall, while in force, be conclusive evidence of that fact.

(4) In this section 'the New York Convention' means the Convention on the Recognition and Enforcement of Foreign Arbitral Awards adopted by the United Nations Conference on International Commercial Arbitration on 10th June 1958.

101 Recognition and enforcement of awards

(1) A New York Convention award shall be recognised as binding on the persons as between whom it was made, and may accordingly be relied on by those persons by way of defence, set-off or otherwise in any legal proceedings in England and Wales or Northern Ireland.

(2) A New York Convention award may, by leave of the court, be enforced in the same manner as a judgment or order of the court to the same effect.

As to the meaning of 'the court' see section 105.

(3) Where leave is so given, judgment may be entered in terms of the award.

102 Evidence to be produced by party seeking recognition or enforcement

(1) A party seeking the recognition or enforcement of a New York Convention award must produce—

(a) the duly authenticated original award or a duly certified copy of it, and

(b) the original arbitration agreement or a duly certified copy of it.

(2) If the award or agreement is in a foreign language, the party must also produce a translation of it certified by an official or sworn translator or by a diplomatic or consular agent.

103 Refusal of recognition or enforcement

(1) Recognition or enforcement of a New York Convention award shall not be refused except in the following cases.

(2) Recognition or enforcement of the award may be refused if the person against whom it is revoked proves—

(a) that a party to the arbitration agreement was (under the law applicable to him) under some incapacity;

(b) that the arbitration agreement was not valid under the law to which the parties subjected it or, failing any indication thereon, under the law of the country where the award was made;

(c) that he was not given proper notice of the appointment of the arbitrator or of the arbitration proceedings or was otherwise unable to present his case;

(d) that the award deals with a difference not contemplated by or not falling within the terms of the submission to arbitration or contains decisions on matters beyond the scope of the submission to arbitration (but see subsection (4))

(e) that the composition of the arbitral tribunal or the arbitral procedure was not in accordance with the agreement of the parties or, failing such arrangement, withe the law of the country in which the arbitration took place;

(f) that the award has not yet become binding on the parties, or has been set aside or suspended by a competent authority of the country in which, or under the law of which, it was made.

(3) Recognition or enforcement of the award may also be refused if the award is in respect of a matter which is not capable of settlement by arbitration, or if it would be contrary to public policy to recognise or enforce the award.

(4) An award which contains decisions on matters not submitted to arbitration may be recognised or enforced to the extent that it contains decisions on matters submitted to arbitration which can be separated from those on matters not so submitted.

(5) Where an application for the setting aside or suspension of the award has been made to such a competent authority as is mentioned in subsection (2)(f), the court before which the award is sought to be relied upon may, if it considers it proper, adjourn the decision on the recognition or enforcement of the award.

It may also on the application of the party claiming recognition or enforcement of the award order the other party to give suitable security.

104 Saving for other bases of recognition or enforcement

Nothing in the preceding provisions of this Part affects any right to rely upon or enforce a New York Convention award at common law or under section 66.

PART IV   GENERAL PROVISIONS

105   Meaning of 'the court': jurisdiction of High Court and county court

(1) In this Act 'the court' means the High Court or a county court, subject to the following provisions.

(2) The Lord Chancellor may by order make provision—

(a) allocating proceedings under this Act to the High Court or to county courts; or

(b) specifying proceedings under this Act which may be commenced or taken only in the High Court or in a county court.

(3) The Lord Chancellor may by order make provision requiring proceedings of any specified description under this Act in relation to which a county court has jurisdiction to be commenced or taken in one or more specified county courts.

Any jurisdiction so exercisable by a specified county court is exercisable throughout England and Wales or, as the case may be, Northern Ireland.

['(3A) The Lord Chancellor must consult the Lord Chief Justice of England and Wales or the Lord Chief Justice of Northern Ireland (as the case may be) before making an order under this section.

(3B) The Lord Chief Justice of England and Wales may nominate a judicial office holder (as defined in section 109(4) of the Constitutional Reform Act 2005) to exercise his functions under this section.

(3C) The Lord Chief Justice of Northern Ireland may nominate any of the following to exercise his functions under this section—

(a) the holder of one of the offices listed in Schedule 1 to the Justice (Northern Ireland) Act 2002;

(b) a Lord Justice of Appeal (as defined in section 88 of that Act).]

(4) An order under this section—

(a) may differentiate between categories of proceedings by reference to such criteria as the Lord Chancellor sees fit to specify, and

(b) may make such incidental or transitional provision as the Lord Chancellor considers necessary or expedient.

(5) An order under this section for England and Wales shall be made by statutory instrument which shall be subject to annulment in pursuance of a resolution of either House of Parliament.

(6) An order under this section for Northern Ireland shall be a statutory rule for the purposes of the Statutory Rules (Northern Ireland) Order 1979 which shall be subject to annulment in pursuance of a resolution of either House of Parliament in like manner as a statutory instrument and section 5 of the Statutory Instruments Act 1946 shall apply accordingly.

106   Crown application

(1) Part I of this Act applies to any arbitration agreement to which Her Majesty, either in right of the Crown or of the Duchy of Lancaster or otherwise, or the Duke of Cornwall, is a party.

(2) Where Her Majesty is party to an arbitration agreement otherwise than in right of the Crown, Her Majesty shall be represented for the purposes of any arbitral proceedings—

(a) where the agreement was entered into by Her Majesty in right of the Duchy of Lancaster, by the Chancellor of the Duchy or such person as he may appoint, and

(b) in any other case, by such person as Her Majesty may appoint in writing under the Royal Sign Manual.

(3) Where the Duke of Cornwall is party to an arbitration agreement, he shall be represented for the purposes of any arbitral proceedings by such person as he may appoint.

(4) References in Part I to a party or the parties to the arbitration agreement or to arbitral proceedings shall be construed, where subsection (2) or (3) applies, as references to the person representing Her Majesty or the Duke of Cornwall.

108   Extent

(1) The provisions of this Act extend to England and Wales and, except as mentioned below, to Northern Ireland.

(2) The following provisions of Part II do not extend to Northern Ireland—section 92 (exclusion of Part I in relation to small claims arbitration in the county court), and

section 93 and Schedule 2 (appointment of judges as arbitrators).

(3) Sections 89, 90 and 91 (consumer arbitration agreements) extend to Scotland and the provisions of Schedules 3 and 4 (consequential amendments and repeals) extend to Scotland so far as they relate to enactments which so extend, subject as follows.

(4) The repeal of the Arbitration Act 1975 extends only to England and Wales and Northern Ireland.

109   Commencement

(1) The provisions of this Act come into force on such day as the Secretary of State may appoint by order made by statutory instrument, and different days may be appointed for different purposes.

(2) An order under subsection (1) may contain such transitional provisions as appear to the Secretary of State to be appropriate.

110   Short title

This Act may be cited as the Arbitration Act 1996.

SCHEDULES

Section 4(1)   SCHEDULE 1

MANDATORY PROVISIONS OF PART I

sections 9 to 11 (stay of legal proceedings);
section 12 (power of court to extend agreed time limits);
section 13 (application of Limitation Acts);
section 24 (power of court to remove arbitrator);
section 26(1) (effect of death of arbitrator);
section 28 (liability of parties for fees and expenses of arbitrators);
section 29 (immunity of arbitrator);
section 31 (objection to substantive jurisdiction of tribunal);
section 32 (determination of preliminary point of jurisdiction);
section 33 (general duty of tribunal);
section 37(2) (items to be treated as expenses of arbitrators);
section 40 (general duty of parties);
section 43 (securing the attendance of witnesses);
section 56 (power to withhold award in case of non-payment);
section 60 (effectiveness of agreement for payment of costs in any event);
section 66 (enforcement of award);
sections 67 and 68 (challenging the award: substantive jurisdiction and serious irregularity),
    and sections 70 and 71 (supplementary provisions; effect of order of court) so far as relating
    to those sections;
section 72 (saving for rights of person who takes no part in proceedings);
section 73 (loss of right to object);
section 74 (immunity of arbitral institutions, &c.);
section 75 (charge to secure payment of solicitors' costs).

Section 93(6)   SCHEDULE 2

MODIFICATIONS OF PART I IN RELATION TO JUDGE-ARBITRATORS

Introductory

1. In this Schedule 'judge-arbitrator' means a judge of the Commercial Court or official referee appointed as arbitrator or umpire under section 93.

General

2.—(1) Subject to the following provisions of this Schedule, references in Part I to the court shall be construed in relation to a judge-arbitrator, or in relation to the appointment of a judge-arbitrator, as references to the Court of Appeal.

(2) The references in sections 32(6), 45(6) and 69(8) to the Court of Appeal shall in such a case be construed as references to the House of Lords.

[*1. "Supreme Court" will be substituted for "House of Lords" when the Constitutional Reform Act 2005, s 26, Sched 9, para 60 is in force.*]

Arbitrator's fees

3.—(1) The power of the court in section 28(2) to order consideration and adjustment of the liability of a party for the fees of an arbitrator may be exercised by a judge-arbitrator.

(2) Any such exercise of the power is subject to the powers of the Court of Appeal under sections 24(4) and 25(3)(b) (directions as to entitlement to fees or expenses in case of removal or resignation).

Exercise of court powers in support of arbitration

4.—(1) Where the arbitral tribunal consists of or includes a judge-arbitrator the powers of the court under sections 42 to 44 (enforcement of peremptory orders, summoning witnesses, and other court powers) are exercisable by the High Court and also by the judge-arbitrator himself.

(2) Anything done by a judge-arbitrator in the exercise of those powers shall be regarded as done by him in his capacity as judge of the High Court and have effect as if done by that court.

Nothing in this sub-paragraph prejudices any power vested in him as arbitrator or umpire.

Extension of time for making award

5.—(1) The power conferred by section 50 (extension of time for making award) is exercisable by the judge-arbitrator himself.

(2) Any appeal from a decision of a judge-arbitrator under that section lies to the Court of Appeal with the leave of that court.

Withholding award in case of non-payment

6.—(1) The provisions of paragraph 7 apply in place of the provisions of section 56 (power to withhold award in the case of non-payment) in relation to the withholding of an award for non-payment of the fees and expenses of a judge-arbitrator.

(2) This does not affect the application of section 56 in relation to the delivery of such an award by an arbitral or other institution or person vested by the parties with powers in relation to the delivery of the award

7.—(1) A judge-arbitrator may refuse to deliver an award except upon payment of the fees and expenses mentioned in section 56(1).

(2) The judge-arbitrator may, on an application by a party to the arbitral proceedings, order that if he pays into the High Court the fees and expenses demanded, or such lesser amount as the judge-arbitrator may specify—

    (a) the award shall be delivered,

    (b) the amount of the fees and expenses properly payable shall be determined by such means and upon such terms as he may direct, and

    (c) out of the money paid into court there shall be paid out such fees and expenses as may be found to be properly payable and the balance of the money (if any) shall be paid out to the applicant.

(3) For this purpose the amount of fees and expenses properly payable is the amount the applicant is liable to pay under section 28 or any agreement relating to the payment of the` arbitrator.

(4) No application to the judge-arbitrator under this paragraph may be made where there is any available arbitral process for appeal or review of the amount of the fees or expenses demanded.

(5) Any appeal from a decision of a judge-arbitrator under this paragraph lies to the Court of Appeal with the leave of that court.

(6) Where a party to arbitral proceedings appeals under sub-paragraph (5), an arbitrator is entitled to appear and be heard.

Correction of award or additional award

8. Subsections (4) to (6) of section 57 (correction of award or additional award: time limit for application or exercise of power) do not apply to a judge-arbitrator.

Costs

9. Where the arbitral tribunal consists of or includes a judge-arbitrator the powers of the court under section 63(4) (determination of recoverable costs) shall be exercised by the High Court.

10.—(1) The power of the court under section 64 to determine an arbitrator's reasonable fees and expenses may be exercised by a judge-arbitrator.

(2) Any such exercise of the power is subject to the powers of the Court of Appeal under sections 24(4) and 25(3)(b) (directions as to entitlement to fees or expenses in case of removal or resignation).

Enforcement of award

11. The leave of the court required by section 66 (enforcement of award) may in the case of an award of a judge-arbitrator be given by the judge-arbitrator himself.

Solicitors' costs

12. The powers of the court to make declarations and orders under the provisions applied by section 75 (power to charge property recovered in arbitral proceedings with the payment of solicitors' costs) may be exercised by the judge-arbitrator.

Powers of court in relation to service of documents

13.—(1) The power of the court under section 77(2) (powers of court in relation to service of documents) is exercisable by the judge-arbitrator.

(2) Any appeal from a decision of a judge-arbitrator under that section lies to the Court of Appeal with the leave of that court.

Powers of court to extend time limits relating to arbitral proceedings

14.—(1) The power conferred by section 79 (power of court to extend time limits relating to arbitral proceedings) is exercisable by the judge-arbitrator himself.

(2) Any appeal from a decision of a judge-arbitrator under that section lies to the Court of Appeal with the leave of that court.

Contract (Scotland) Act 1997
(1997, c. 34)

An Act to reform the law of Scotland relating to the admissibility of extrinsic evidence to prove an additional term of a contract or unilateral voluntary obligation, to the supersession of a contract by a deed executed in implement of it and to the obtaining of damages for breach of contract of sale; and for connected purposes.   [22nd March 1997]

3 Damages for breach of contract of sale

Any rule of law which precludes the buyer in a contract of sale of property from obtaining damages for breach of that contract by the seller unless the buyer rejects the property and rescinds the contract shall cease to have effect.

4 Short title, extent etc.

(4) This Act extends to Scotland only.

Late Payment of Commercial Debts (Interest) Act 1998
(1998, c. 20)

An Act to make provision with respect to interest on the late payment of certain debts arising under commercial contracts for the supply of goods or services; and for connected purposes.

[11th June 1998]

[Application: The Act is amended for Scotland by SSI 2002/335.]

PART I   STATUTORY INTEREST ON QUALIFYING DEBTS

1 Statutory interest

(1) It is an implied term in a contract to which this Act applies that any qualifying debt created by the contract carries simple interest subject to and in accordance with this Part.

(2) Interest carried under that implied term (in this Act referred to as 'statutory interest') shall be treated, for the purposes of any rule of law or enactment (other than this Act) relating to interest on debts, in the same way as interest carried under an express contract term.

(3) This Part has effect subject to Part II (which in certain circumstances permits contract terms to oust or vary the right to statutory interest that would otherwise be conferred by virtue of the term implied by subsection (1)).

2 Contracts to which Act applies

(1) This Act applies to a contract for the supply of goods or services where the purchaser and the supplier are each acting in the course of a business, other than an excepted contract.

(2) In this Act 'contract for the supply of goods or services' means—

    (a) a contract of sale of goods; or

    (b) a contract (other than a contract of sale of goods) by which a person does any, or any combination, of the things mentioned in subsection (3) for a consideration that is (or includes) a money consideration.

(3) Those things are—

    (a) transferring or agreeing to transfer to another the property in goods;

    (b) bailing or agreeing to bail goods to another by way of hire or, in Scotland, hiring or agreeing to hire goods to another; and

    (c) agreeing to carry out a service

(4) For the avoidance of doubt a contract of service or apprenticeship is nor a contract for the supply of goods or services.

(5) The following are expected contracts—

    (a) a consumer credit agreement;

    (b) a contract intended to operate by way of mortgage, pledge, charge or other security; and

[. . .]

(7) In this section—

'business' includes a profession and the activities of any government department or local or public authority;

'consumer credit agreement' has the same meaning as in the Consumer Credit Act 1974;

'contract of sale of goods' and 'goods' have the same meaning as in the Sale of Goods Act 1979;

['government department' includes any part of the Scottish Administration;]

'property in goods' means the general property in them and not merely a special property.

3   Qualifying debts

(1) A debt created by virtue of an obligation under a contract to which this Act applies to pay the whole or any part of the contract price is a 'qualifying debt' for the purposes of this Act, unless (when created) the whole of the debt is prevented from carrying statutory interest by this section.

(2) A debt does not carry statutory interest if or to the extent that it consists of a sum to which a right to interest or to charge interest applies by virtue of any enactment (other than section 1 of this Act).

This subsection does not prevent a sum from carrying statutory interest by reason of the fact that a court, arbitrator or arbiter would, apart from this Act, have power to award interest on it.

(3) A debt does not carry (and shall be treated as never having carried) statutory interest if or to the extent that a right to demand interest on it, which exists by virtue of any rule of law, is exercised.

[…]

4   Period for which statutory interest runs

(1) Statutory interest runs in relation to a qualifying debt in accordance with this section (unless section 5 applies).

(2) Statutory interest starts to run on the day after the relevant day for the debt, at the rate prevailing under section 6 at the end of the relevant day.

(3) Where the supplier and the purchaser agree a date for payment of the debt (that is, the day on which the debt is to be created by the contract), that is the relevant day unless the debt relates to an obligation to make an advance payment.

A date so agreed may be a fixed one or may depend on the happening of an event or the failure of an event to happen.

(4) Where the debt relates to an obligation to make an advance payment, the relevant day is the day on which the debt is treated by section 11 as having been created.

(5) In any other case, the relevant day is the last day of the period of 30 days beginning with—

  (a) the day on which the obligation of the supplier to which the debt relates is performed; or

  (b) the day on which the purchaser has notice of the amount of the debt or (where that amount is unascertained) the sum which the supplier claims is the amount of the debt,

whichever is the later.

(6) Where the debt is created by virtue of an obligation to pay a sum due in respect of a period of hire of goods, subsection (5)(a) has effect as if it referred to the last day of that period.

(7) Statutory interest ceases to run when the interest would cease to run if it were carried under an express contract term.

(8) In this section 'advance payment' has the same meaning as in section 11.

5   Remission of statutory interest

(1) This section applies where, by reason of any conduct of the supplier, the interests of justice require that statutory interest should be remitted in whole or part in respect of a period for which it would otherwise run in relation to a qualifying debt.

(2) If the interests of justice require that the supplier should receive no statutory interest for a period, statutory interest shall not run for that period.

(3) If the interests of justice require that the supplier should receive statutory interest at a reduced rate for a period, statutory interest shall run at such rate as meets the justice of the case for that period.

(4) Remission of statutory interest under this section may be required—

(a) by reason of conduct at any time (whether before or after the time at which the debt is created); and

(b) for the whole period for which statutory interest would otherwise run or for one or more parts of that period.

(5) In this section 'conduct' includes any act or omission.

[5A Compensation arising out of late payment

(1) Once statutory interest begins to run in relation to a qualifying debt, the supplier shall be entitled to a fixed sum (in addition to the statutory interest on the debt).

(2) That sum shall be—

(a) for a debt less than £1,000, the sum of £40;

(b) for a debt of £1,000 or more, but less than £10,000, the sum of £70;

(c) for a debt of £10,000 or more, the sum of £100.

(3) The obligation to pay an additional fixed sum under this section in respect of a qualifying debt shall be treated as part of the term implied by section 1(1) in the contract creating the debt.]

6 Rate of statutory interest

(1) The Secretary of State shall by order made with the consent of the Treasury set the rate of statutory interest by prescribing—

(a) a formula for calculating the rate of statutory interest; or

(b) the rate of statutory interest.

(2) Before making such an order the Secretary of State shall, among other things, consider the extent to which it may be desirable to set the rate so as to—

(a) protect suppliers whose financial position makes them particularly vulnerable if their qualifying debts are paid late; and

(b) deter generally the late payment of qualifying debts.

PART II   CONTRACT TERMS RELATING TO LATE PAYMENT OF QUALIFYING DEBTS

7 Purpose of Part II

(1) This Part deals with the extent to which the parties to a contract to which this Act applies may by reference to contract terms oust or vary the right to statutory interest that would otherwise apply when a qualifying debt created by the contract (in this Part referred to as 'the debt') is not paid.

(2) This Part applies to contract terms agreed before the debt is created; after that time the parties are free to agree terms dealing with the debt.

(3) This Part has effect without prejudice to any other ground which may affect the validity of a contract term.

8 Circumstances where statutory interest may be ousted or varied

(1) Any contract terms are void to the extent that they purport to exclude the right to statutory interest in relation to the debt, unless there is a substantial contractual remedy for late payment of the debt.

(2) Where the parties agree a contractual remedy for late payment of the debt that is a substantial remedy, statutory interest is not carried by the debt (unless they agree otherwise).

(3) The parties may not agree to vary the right to statutory interest in relation to the debt unless either the right to statutory interest as varied or the overall remedy for late payment of the debt is a substantial remedy.

(4) Any contract terms are void to the extent that they purport to—

    (a) confer a contractual right to interest that is not a substantial remedy for late payment of the debt, or

    (b) vary the right to statutory interest so as to provide for a right to statutory interest that is not a substantial remedy for late payment of the debt,

unless the overall remedy for late payment of the debt is a substantial remedy.

(5) Subject to this section, the parties are free to agree contract terms which deal with the consequences of late payment of the debt.

9 Meaning of 'substantial remedy'

(1) A remedy for the late payment of the debt shall be regarded as a substantial remedy unless—

    (a) the remedy is insufficient either for the purpose of compensating the supplier for late payment or for deterring late payment; and

    (b) it would not be fair or reasonable to allow the remedy to be relied on to oust or (as the case may be) to vary the right to statutory interest that would otherwise apply in relation to the debt.

(2) In determining whether a remedy is not a substantial remedy, regard shall be had to all the relevant circumstances at the time the terms in question are agreed.

(3) In determining whether subsection (1)(b) applies, regard shall be had (without prejudice to the generality of subsection (2)) to the following matters—

    (a) the benefits of commercial certainty;

    (b) the strength of the bargaining positions of the parties relative to each other;

    (c) whether the term was imposed by one party to the detriment of the other (whether by the use of standard terms or otherwise); and

    (d) whether the supplier received an inducement to agree to the term.

10 Interpretation of Part II

(1) In this Part—

'contract term' means a term of the contract creating the debt or any other contract term binding the parties (or either of them);

'contractual remedy' means a contractual right to interest or any contractual remedy other than interest;

'contractual right to interest' includes a reference to a contractual right to charge interest;

'overall remedy', in relation to the late payment of the debt, means any combination of a contractual right to interest, a varied right to statutory interest or a contractual remedy other than interest;

'substantial remedy' shall be construed in accordance with section 9.

(2) In this Part a reference (however worded) to contract terms which vary the right to statutory interest is a reference to terms altering in any way the effect of Part I in relation to the debt (for example by postponing the time at which interest starts to run or by imposing conditions on the right to interest).

(3) In this Part a reference to late payment of the debt is a reference to late payment of the sum due when the debt is created (excluding any part of that sum which is prevented from carrying statutory interest by section 3).

PART III GENERAL AND SUPPLEMENTARY

11 Treatment of advance payments of the contract price

(1) A qualifying debt created by virtue of an obligation to make an advance payment shall be treated for the purposes of this Act as if it was created on the day mentioned in subsection (3), (4) or (5) (as the case may be).

(2) In this section 'advance payment' means a payment falling due before the obligation of the supplier to which the whole contract price relates ('the supplier's obligation') is performed, other than a payment of a part of the contract price that is due in respect of any

part performance of that obligation and payable on or after the day on which that part performance is completed.

(3) Where the advance payment is the whole contract price, the debt shall be treated as created on the day on which the supplier's obligation is performed.

(4) Where the advance payment is a part of the contract price, but the sum is not due in respect of any part performance of the supplier's obligation, the debt shall be treated as created on the day on which the supplier's obligation is performed.

(5) Where the advance payment is a part of the contract price due in respect of any part performance of the supplier's obligation, but is payable before that part performance is completed, the debt shall be treated as created on the day on which the relevant part performance is completed.

(6) Where the debt is created by virtue of an obligation to pay a sum due in respect of a period of hire of goods, this section has effect as if—

> (a) references to the day on which the supplier's obligation is performed were references to the last day of that period; and
>
> (b) references to part performance of that obligation were references to part of that period.

(7) For the purposes of this section an obligation to pay the whole outstanding balance of the contract price shall be regarded as an obligation to pay the whole contract price and not as an obligation to pay a part of the contract price.

12   Conflict of laws

(1) This Act does not have effect in relation to a contract governed by the law of a part of the United Kingdom by choice of the parties if—

> (a) there is no significant connection between the contract and that part of the United Kingdom; and
>
> (b) but for that choice, the applicable law would be a foreign law.

(2) This Act has effect in relation to a contract governed by a foreign law by choice of the parties if—

> (a) but for that choice, the applicable law would be the law of a part of the United Kingdom; and
>
> (b) there is no significant connection between the contract and any country other than that part of the United Kingdom.

(3) In this section—

'contract' means a contract falling within section 2(1);and

'foreign law' means the law of a country outside the United Kingdom.

13   Assignments, etc.

(1) The operation of this Act in relation to a qualifying debt is not affected by—

> (a) any change in the identity of the parties to the contract creating the debt; or
>
> (b) the passing of the right to be paid the debt, or the duty to pay it (in whole or in part) to a person other than the person who is the original creditor or the original debtor when the debt is created.

(2) Any reference in this Act to the supplier or the purchaser is a reference to the person who is for the time being the supplier or the purchaser or, in relation to a time after the debt in question has been created, the person who is for the time being the creditor or the debtor, as the case may be.

(3) Where the right to be paid part of a debt passes to a person other than the person who is the original creditor when the debt is created, any reference in this Act to a debt shall be construed as (or, if the context so requires, as including) a reference to part of a debt.

(4) A reference in this section to the identity of the parties to a contract changing, or to a right or duty passing, is a reference to it changing or passing by assignment or assignation, by operation of law or otherwise.

14   Contract terms relating to the date for payment of the contract price

(1) This section applies to any contract term which purports to have the effect of postponing the time at which a qualifying debt would otherwise be created by a contract to which this Act applies.

(2) Sections 3(2)(b) and 17(1)(b) of the Unfair Contract Terms Act 1977 (no reliance to be placed on certain contract terms) shall apply in cases where such a contract term is not contained in written standard terms of the purchaser as well as in cases where the term is contained in such standard terms.

(3) In this section 'contract term' has the same meaning as in section 10(1).

15   Orders and regulations

(1) Any power to make an order or regulations under this Act is exercisable by statutory instrument.

(2) Any statutory instrument containing an order or regulations under this Act, other than an order under section 17(2), shall be subject to annulment in pursuance of a resolution of either House of Parliament.

16   Interpretation

(1) In this Act—

'contract for the supply of goods or services' has the meaning given in section 2(2);

'contract price' means the price in a contract of sale of goods or the money consideration referred to in section 2(2)(b) in any other contract for the supply of goods or services;

'purchaser' means (subject to section 13(2)) the seller in a contract of sale or the person who contracts with the supplier in any other contract for the supply of goods or services;

'qualifiying debt' means a debt falling within section 3(1);

'statutory interest' means interest carried by virtue of the term implied by section 1(1); and

'supplier' means (subject to section 13(2)) the seller in a contract of sale of goods or the person who does one or more of the things mentioned in section 2(3) in any other contract for the supply of goods or services

(2) In this Act any reference (however worded) to an agreement or to contract terms includes a reference to both express and implied terms (including terms established by a course of dealing or by such usage as binds the parties).

17   Short title, commencement and extent

(2) This Act (apart from this section) shall come into force on such day as the Secretary of State may by order appoint; and different days may be appointed for different descriptions of contract or for other different purposes.

An order under this subsection may specify a description of contract by reference to any feature of the contract (including the parties).

(3) The Secretary of State may by regulations make such transitional, supplemental or incidental provision (including provision modifying any provision of this Act) as the Secretary of State may consider necessary or expedient in connection with the operation of this Act while it is not fully in force.

(4) This Act does not affect contracts of any description made before this Act comes into force for contracts of that description.

(5) This Act extends to Northern Ireland.

Contracts (Rights of Third Parties) Act 1999
(1999, c. 31)

An Act to make provision for the enforcement of contractual terms by third parties.
[11th November 1999]

1   Right of third party to enforce contractual term

(1) Subject to the provisions of this Act, a person who is not a party to a contract (a 'third party') may in his own right enforce a term of the contract if—

(a) the contract expressly provides that he may, or

(b) subject to subsection (2), the term purports to confer a benefit on him.

(2) Subsection (1)(b) does not apply if on a proper construction of the contract it appears that the parties did not intend the term to be enforceable by the third party.

(3) The third party must be expressly identified in the contract by name, as a member of a class or as answering a particular description but need not be in existence when the contract is entered into.

(4) This section does not confer a right on a third party to enforce a term of a contract otherwise than subject to and in accordance with any other relevant terms of the contract.

(5) For the purpose of exercising his right to enforce a term of the contract, there shall be available to the third party any remedy that would have been available to him in an action for breach of contract if he had been a party to the contract (and the rules relating to damages, injunctions, specific performance and other relief shall apply accordingly).

(6) Where a term of a contract excludes or limits liability in relation to any matter references in this Act to the third party enforcing the term shall be construed as references to his availing himself of the exclusion or limitation.

(7) In this Act, in relation to a term of a contract which is enforceable by a third party—

'the promisor' means the party to the contract against whom the term is enforceable by the third party, and

'the promisee' means the party to the contract by whom the term is enforceable against the promisor.

2 Variation and rescission of contract

(1) Subject to the provisions of this section, where a third party has a right under section 1 to enforce a term of the contract, the parties to the contract may not, by agreement, rescind the contract, or vary it in such a way as to extinguish or alter his entitlement under that right, without his consent if—

(a) the third party has communicated his assent to the term to the promisor,

(b) the promisor is aware that the third party has relied on the term, or

(c) the promisor can reasonably be expected to have foreseen that the third party would rely on the term and the third party has in fact relied on it.

(2) The assent referred to in subsection (1)(a)—

(a) may be by words or conduct, and

(b) if sent to the promisor by post or other means, shall not be regarded as communicated to the promisor until received by him.

(3) Subsection (1) is subject to any express term of the contract under which—

(a) the parties to the contract may by agreement rescind or vary the contract without the consent of the third party, or

(b) the consent of the third party is required in circumstances specified in the contract instead of those set out in subsection (1)(a) to (c).

(4) Where the consent of a third party is required under subsection (1) or (3), the court or arbitral tribunal may, on the application of the parties to the contract, dispense with his consent if satisfied—

(a) that his consent cannot be obtained because his whereabouts cannot reasonably be ascertained, or

(b) that he is mentally incapable of giving his consent.

(5) The court or arbital tribunal may, on the application of the parties to a contract, dispense with any consent that may be required under subsection (1)(c) if satisfied that it cannot reasonably be ascertained whether or not the third party has in fact relied on the term.

(6) If the court or arbitral tribunal dispenses with a third party's consent, it may impose such conditions as it thinks fit, including a condition requiring the payment of compensation to the third party.

(7) The jurisdiction conferred on the court by subsections (4) to (6) is exercisable by both the High Court and a county court.

3 Defences etc. available to promisor

(1) Subsections (2) to (5) apply where, in reliance on section 1, proceedings for the enforcement of a term of a contract are brought by a third party.

(2) The promisor shall have available to him by way of defence or set-off any matter that—

(a) arises from or in connection with the contract and is relevant to the term, and

(b) would have been available to him by way of defence or set-off if the proceedings had been brought by the promisee.

(3) The promisor shall also have available to him by way of defence or set-off any matter if—

(a) an express term of the contract provides for it to be available to him in proceedings brought by the third party, and

(b) it would have been available to him by way of defence or set-off if the proceedings had been brought by the promisee.

(4) The promisor shall also have available to him—

(a) by way of defence or set-off any matter, and

(b) by way of counterclaim any matter not arising from the contract,

that would have been available to him by way of defence or set-off or, as the case may be, by way of counterclaim against the third party if the third party had been a party to the contract.

(5) Subsections (2) and (4) are subject to any express term of the contract as to the matters that are not available to the promisor by way of defence, set-off or counterclaim.

(6) Where in any proceedings brought against him a third party seeks in reliance on section 1 to enforce a term of a contract (including, in particular, a term purporting to exclude or limit liability), he may not do so if he could not have done so (whether by reason of any particular circumstances relating to him or otherwise) had he been a party to the contract.

4 Enforcement of contract by promisee

Section 1 does not affect any right of the promisee to enforce any term of contract.

5 Protection of promisor from double liability

Where under section 1 a term of a contract is enforceable by a third party, and the promisee has recovered from the promisor a sum in respect of—

(a) the third party's loss in respect of the term, or

(b) the expense to the promisee of making good to the third party the default of the promisor,

then, in any proceedings brought in reliance on that section by the third party, the court or arbital tribunal shall reduce any award to the third party to such extent as it thinks appropriate to take account of the sum recovered by the promisee.

6 Exceptions

(1) Section 1 confers no rights on a third party in the case of a contract on a bill of exchange, promissory note or other negotiable instrument.

(2) Section 1 confers no rights on a third party in the case of any contract binding on a company and its members under section 14 of the Companies Act 1985.

[(2A) Section 1 confers no rights on a third party in the case of any incorporation document of a limited liability partnership or any limited liability partnership agreement as defined in the Limited Liability Partnerships Regulations 2001 (S.I. No. 2001/1090).]

(3) Section 1 confers no right on a third party to enforce—

(a) any term of a contract of employment against an employee,

(b) any term of a worker's contract against a worker (including a home worker), or

(c) any term of a relevant contract against an agency worker.

(4) In subsection (3)—

(a) 'contract of employment', 'employee', 'worker's contract', and 'worker' have the meaning given by section 54 of the National Minimum Wage Act 1998,

(b) 'home worker' has the meaning given by section 35(2) of that Act

(c) 'agency worker' has the same meaning as in section 34(1) of that Act, and

(d) 'relevant contract' means a contract entered into, in a case where section 34 of that Act applies, by the agency worker as respects work falling within subsection (1)(a) of that section.

(5) Section 1 confers no rights on a third party in the case of—

(a) a contract for the carriage of goods by sea, or

(b) a contract for the carriage of goods by rail or road, or for the carriage of cargo by air, which is subject to the rules of the appropriate international transport convention,

except that a third party may in reliance on that section avail himself of an exclusion or limitation of liability in such a contract.

(6) In subsection (5) 'contract for the carriage of goods by sea' means a contract of carriage—

(a) contained in or evidenced by a bill of lading, sea waybill or a corresponding electronic transaction, or

(b) under or for the purposes of which there is given an undertaking which is contained in a ship's delivery order or a corresponding electronic transaction.

(7) For the purposes of subsection (6)—

(a) 'bill of lading', 'sea waybill' and 'ship's delivery order' have the same meaning as in the Carriage of Goods by Sea Act 1992, and

(b) a corresponding electronic transaction is a transaction within section 1(5) of that Act which corresponds to the issue, indorsement, delivery or transfer of a bill of lading, sea waybill or ship's delivery order.

(8) In subsection (5) 'the appropriate international transport convention' means—

(a) in relation to a contract for the carriage of goods by rail, the Convention which has the force of law in the United Kindgom under [regulation 3 of the Railways (Convention on International Carriage by Rail) Regulations 2005],

(b) in relation to a contract for the carriage of goods by road, the Convention which has the force of law in the United Kingdom under section 1 of the Carriage of Goods by road Act 1965, and

(c) in relation to a contract for the carriage of cargo by air—

(i) the Convention which has the force of law in the United Kingdom under section 1 of the Carriage by Air act 1961, or

(ii) the Convention which has the force of law under section 1 of the Carriage by Air (Supplementary Provisions) Act 1962, or

(iii) either of the amended Conventions set out in Part B of Schedule 2 or 3 to the Carriage by Air Acts (Application of Provisions) Order 1967.

7 Supplementary provisions relating to third party

(1) Section 1 does not affect any right or remedy of a third party that exists or is available from this Act.

(2) Section 2(2) of the Unfair Contract Terms Act 1977 (restriction on exclusion etc. of liability for negligence) shall not apply where the negligence consists of the breach of an obligation arising from a term of a contract and the person seeking to enforce it is a third party acting in reliance on section 1.

(3) In sections 5 and 8 of the Limitation Act 1980 the references to an action founded on a simple contract and an action upon a specialty shall respectively include references to an

action brought in reliance on section 1 relating to a simple contract and an action brought in reliance on that section relating to a specialty.

(4) A third party shall not, by virtue of section 1(5) or 3(4) or (6), be treated as a party to the contract for the purposes of any other Act (or any instrument made under any other Act).

8 Arbitration provisions

(1) Where—

    (a) a right under section 1 to enforce a term ('the substantive term') is subject to a term providing for the submission of disputes to arbitration ('the arbitration agreement'), and

    (b) the arbitration agreement is an agreement in writing for the purposes of Part I of the Arbitration Act 1996,

the third party shall be treated for the purposes of that Act as a party to the arbitration agreement as regards disputes between himself and the promisor relating to the enforcement of the substantive term by the third party.

(2) Where—

    (a) a third party has a right under section 1 to enforce a term providing for one or more descriptions of dispute between the third party and the promisor to be submitted to arbitration ('the arbitration agreement'),

    (b) the arbitration agreement is an agreement in writing for the purposes of Part I of the Arbitration Act 1996, and

    (c) the third party does not fall to be treated under subsection (1) as a party to the arbitration agreement,

the third party shall, if he exercises the right, be treated for the purposes of that Act as a party to the arbitration agreement in relation to the matter with respect to which the right is exercised, and be treated as having been so immediately before the exercise of the right.

9 Northern Ireland

(1) In its application to Northern Ireland, this Act has effect with the modifications specified in subsections (2) and (3).

(2) In section 6(2), for 'section 14 of the Companies Act 1985' there is substituted 'Article 25 of the Companies (Northern Ireland) Order 1986'.

(3) In section 7, for subsection (3) there is substituted—

'(3) In articles 4(a) and 15 of the Limitation (Northern Ireland) Order 1981, the references to an action founded on a simple contract and an action upon an instrument under seal shall respectively include references to an action brought in reliance of section 1 relating to a simple contract and an action brought in reliance on that section relating to a contract under seal.'.

   ...

10 Short title, commencement and extent

   ...

(2) This Act comes into force on the day on which it is passed but, subject to subsection (3), does nor apply in relation to a contract entered into before the end of the period of six months beginning with that day.

(3) The restriction in subsection (2) does not apply in relation to a contract which—

    (a) is entered into on or after the day on which this Act is passed, and

    (b) expressly provides for the application of this Act.

(4) This Act extends as follows—

    (a) section 9 extends to Northern Ireland only;

    (b) the remaining provisions extend to England and Wales and Northern Ireland only.

EXPLANATORY NOTES

1. These explanatory notes ... have been prepared by the Lord Chancellor's Department in order to assist the reader in understanding the Act. They do not form part of the Act and have not been endorsed by Parliament.

Section 3: Defences etc. available to promisor

15. *Section 3* enables the promisor, in a claim by the third party, to rely on any defence or set-off arising out of the contract and relevant to the term being enforced, which would have been available to him had the claim been by the promisee. He may also rely on any defence or set-off, or make any counterclaim, where this would have been possible had the third party been a party to the contract.

16. *Subsection (2)* can be illustrated as follows—

   (I) a third party can no more enforce a void, discharged or unenforceable contract than a promisee could;

   (II) P1 (the promisor) and P2 (the promisee) contract that P2 will sell goods to P1, who will pay the contract price to P3 (the third party). In breach of contract, P2 delivers goods that are not of the standard contracted for. In an action for the price by P3 (just as in an action for the price by P2) P1 is entitled to reduce or extinguish the price by reason of the damages for breach of contract.

17. *Subsection (3)* can be illustrated as follows—

P1 and P2 contract that P1 will pay P3 if P2 transfers his car to P1. P2 owes P1 money under a wholly unrelated contract. P1 and P2 agree to an express term in the contract which provides that P1 can raise against a claim by P3 any matter which would have given P1 a defence or setoff to a claim by P2.

18. *Subsection (4)* makes it clear that the promisor also has available any defence or setoff, and any counterclaim not arising from the contract, which is specific to the third party. It can be illustrated as follows—

   (I) P1 contracts with P2 to pay £1000. P3 already owes P1 £600. P1 has a set-off to P3's claim so that P1 is only bound to pay P3 £400.

   (II) P3 induced P1 to enter into the contract with P2 by misrepresentation, but P2 has no actual or constructive notice of that misrepresentation. P1 may have a defence (or a counterclaim for damages) against P3 which would not have been available had the action been brought by P2.

19. *Subsection (5)* makes subsection (2) and (4) subject to any express term of the contract which narrows the defences or set-offs available under section 3(2) or narrows the defences, set-offs or counterclaims available under section 3(4). For example—

   (I) in relation to subsection (2), P2 agrees with P1 to purchase a painting, the painting to be delivered to P3, who is expressly given a right to enforce the delivery obligation. P2 owes P1 considerable sums for other art works purchased. P2 wishes to ensure that P3's right is not affected. P1 and P2 expressly agree that P1 may not raise against P3 defences and set-offs that would have been available to P1 in an action by P2.

   (II) in relation to subsection (4), P1 agrees with P2 to pay £5000 to P3 if P2 will transfer a number of cases of wine to P1. P3 is in dispute with P1 over a prior contract and P1 alleges that P3 owes P1 money. P2 is concerned the P1 may seek to withhold part of the £5000 payable to P3 by raising a set-off or counterclaim against P3 in relation to the prior contract. Consequently P1 and P2 include an express term that P1 may raise no defences, set-offs or counterclaims of any nature whatever against a claim by P3 to enforce P1's obligation to pay the £5000.

20. *Subsection (6)* ensures that an analogous approach to that set out in subsections (2) to (5) applies where the proceedings are brought against the third party and he seeks to avail himself of, for example, an exlusion section.

Financial Services and Markets Act 2000
(2000, c. 8)

[14th June 2000]

1 The Financial Services Authority

(1) The body corporate known as the Financial Services Authority ('the Authority') is to have the functions conferred on it by or under this Act.

2 The Authority's general duties

(1) In discharging its general functions the Authority must, so far as is reasonably possible, act in a way—

(a) which is compatible with the regulatory objectives; and

(b) which the Authority considers most appropriate for the purpose of meeting these objectives.

(2) The regulatory objectives are—

(a) market confidence;

(b) public awareness;

(c) the protection of consumers; and

(d) the reduction of financial crime.

(3) In discharging its general functions the Authority must have regard to—

(a) the need to use its resources in the most efficient and economic way;

(b) the responsibilities of those who manage the affairs of authorised persons;

(c) the principle that a burden or restriction which is imposed on a person, or on the carrying on of an activity, should be proportionate to the benefits, considered in general terms, which are expected to result from the imposition of that burden or restriction;

(d) the desirability of facilitating innovation in connection with regulated activities;

(e) the international character of financial services and markets and the desirability of maintaining the competitive position of the United Kingdom;

(f) the need to minimise the adverse effects on competition that may arise from anything done in the discharge of those functions;

(g) the desirability of facilitating competition between those who are subject to any form of regulation by the Authority.

(4) The Authority's general functions are—

(a) its function of making rules under this Act (considered as a whole);

(b) its function of preparing and issuing codes under this Act (considered as a whole);

(c) its functions in relation to the giving of general guidance (considered as a whole); and

(d) its function of determining the general policy and principles by reference to which it performs particular functions.

(5) 'General Guidance' has the meaning given in section 158(5).

3 Market confidence

(1) The market confidence objective is: maintaining confidence in the financial system.

(2) 'The financial system' means the financial system operating in the United Kingdom and includes—

(a) financial markets and exchanges;

(b) regulated activities; and

(c) other activities connected with financial markets and exchanges.

4 Public awareness

(1) The public awareness objective is: promoting public understanding of the financial system.

(2) It includes, in particular—

(a) promoting awareness of the benefits and risks associated with different kinds of investment or other financial dealing; and

(b) the provision of appropriate information and advice

(3) 'The financial system' has the same meaning as in section 3.

5 The protection of consumers

(1) The protection of consumers objective is: securing the appropriate degree of protection for consumers.

(2) In considering what degree of protection may be appropriate, the Authority must have regard to—

    (a) the differing degrees of risk involved in different kinds of investment or other transaction;

    (b) the differing degrees of experience and expertise that different consumers may have in relation to different kinds of regulated activity;

    (c) the needs that consumers may have for advice and accurate information; and

    (d) the general principle that consumers should take responsibility for their decisions.

(3) 'Consumers' means persons—

    (a) who are consumers for the purposes of section 138; or

    (b) who, in relation to regulated activities carried on otherwise than by authorised persons, would be consumers for those purposes if the activities were carried on by authorised persons.

6 The reduction of financial crime

(1) The reduction of financial crime objective is: reducing the extent to which it is possible for a business carried on—

    (a) by a regulated person, or

    (b) in contravention of the general prohibition, to be used for a purpose connected with financial crime.

(2) In considering that objective the Authority must, in particular, have regard to the desirability of—

    (a) regulated persons being aware of the risk of their businesses being used in connection with the commission of financial crime;

    (b) regulated persons taking appropriate measures (in relation to their administration and employment practices, the conduct of transactions by them and otherwise) to prevent financial crime, facilitate its detection and monitor its incidence;

    (c) regulated persons devoting adequate resources to the matters mentioned in paragraph (b).

(3) 'Financial crime' includes any offence involving—

    (a) fraud or dishonesty

    (b) misconduct in, or misuse of information relating to, a financial market; or

    (c) handling the proceeds of crime

(4) 'Offence' includes an act or omission which would be an offence if it had taken place in the United Kingdom.

(5) 'Regulated person' means an authorised person, a recognised investment exchange or a recognised clearing house.

7 Duty of Authority to follow principles of good governance

In managing its affairs, the Authority must have regard to such generally accepted principles of good corporate governance as it is reasonable to regard as applicable to it.

8 The Authority's general duty to consult

The Authority must make and maintain effective arrangements for consulting practitioners and consumers on the extent to which its general policies and practices are consistent with its general duties under section 2.

9 The Practitioner Panel

(1) Arrangements under section 8 must include the establishment and maintenance of a panel of persons (to be known as 'the Practitioner Panel') to represent the interests of practitioners.

10 The Consumer Panel

(1) Arrangements under section 8 must include the establishment and maintenance of a panel of persons (to be known as 'the Consumer Panel') to represent the interests of consumers.

(2) The Authority must appoint one of the members of the Consumer Panel to be its chairman.

(3) The Treasury's approval is required for the appointment or dismissal of the chairman.

(4) The Authority must have regard to any representations made to it by the Consumer Panel.

(5) The Authority must appoint to the Consumer Panel such consumers, or persons representing the interests of consumers, as it considers appropriate.

(6) The Authority must secure that the membership of the Consumer Panel is such as to give a fair degree of representation to those who are using, or are or may be contemplating using, services otherwise than in connection with businesses carried on by them.

(7) 'Consumers' means persons, other than authorised persons—

    (a) who are consumers for the purposes of section 138; or

    (b) who, in relation to regulated activities carried on otherwise than by authorised persons, would be consumers for those purposes if the activities were carried on by authorised persons.

11 Duty to consider representations by the Panels

(1) This section applies to a representation made, in accordance with arrangements under section 8, by the Practitioner Panel or by the Consumer Panel.

(2) The Authority must consider the representation.

(3) If the Authority disagrees with a view expressed, or proposal made, in the representation, it must give the Panel a statement in writing of its reasons for disagreeing.

19 The general prohibition

(1) No person may carry on a regulated activity in the United Kingdom, or purport to do so, unless he is—

    (a) an authorised person; or

    (b) an exempt person.

(2) The prohibition is referred to in this Act as the general prohibition.

21 Restrictions on financial promotion

(1) A person ('A') must not, in the course of business, communicate an invitation or inducement to engage in investment activity.

(2) But subsection (1) does not apply if—

    (a) A is an authorised person; or

    (b) the content of the communication is approved for the purposes of this section by an authorised person.

(3) In the case of a communication originating outside the United Kingdom, subsection (1) applies only if the communication is capable of having an effect in the United Kingdom.

(4) The Treasury may by order specify circumstances in which a person is to be regarded for the purposes of subsection (1) as—

    (a) acting in the course of business;

    (b) not acting in the course of business.

(5) The Treasury may by order specify circumstances (which may include compliance with financial promotion rules) in which subsection (1) does not apply.

(6) An order under subsection (5) may, in particular, provide that subsection (1) does not apply in relation to communications—

    (a) of a specified description;

    (b) originating in a specified country or territory outside the United Kingdom;

    (c) originating in a country or territory which falls within a specified description of country or territory outside the United Kingdom; or

    (d) originating outside the United Kingdom.

(7) The Treasury may by order repeal subsection (3).

(8) 'Engaging in investment activity' means—

    (a) entering or offering to enter into an agreement the making or performance of which by either party constitutes a controlled activity; or

    (b) exercising any rights conferred by a controlled investment to acquire, dispose of, underwrite or convert a controlled investment.

(9) An activity is a controlled activity if—

    (a) it is an activity of a specified kind or one which falls within a specified class of activity; and

    (b) it relates to an investment of a specified kind, or to one which falls within a specified class of investment.

(10) An investment is a controlled investment if it is an investment of a specified kind or one which falls within a specified class of investment.

22   The classes of activity and categories of investment

(1) An activity is a regulated activity for the purposes of this Act if it is an activity of a specified kind which is carried on by way of business and—

    (a) relates to an investment of a specified kind; or

    (b) in the case of an activity of a kind which is also specified for the purposes of this paragraph, is carried on in relation to property of any kind.

26   Agreements made by unauthorised persons

(1) An agreement made by a person in the course of carrying on a regulated activity in contravention of the general prohibition is unenforceable against the other party.

(2) The other party is entitled to recover—

    (a) any money or other property paid or transferred by him under the agreement; and

    (b) compensation for any loss sustained by him as a result of having parted with it.

(3) 'Agreement' means an agreement—

    (a) made after this section comes into force; and

    (b) the making or performance of which constitutes, or is part of, the regulated activity in question.

42   Giving permission

(1) 'The applicant' means an applicant for permission under section 40.

(2) The Authority may give permission for the applicant to carry on the regulated activity or activities to which his application relates or such of them as may be specified in the permission.

56   Prohibition orders

(1) Subsection (2) applies if it appears to the Authority that an individual is not a fit and proper person to perform functions in relation to a regulated activity carried on by an authorised person.

(2) The Authority may make an order ('a prohibition order') prohibiting the individual from performing a specified function, any function falling within a specified description or any function.

(4) An individual who performs or agrees to perform a function in breach of a prohibition order is guilty of an offence and liable on summary conviction to a fine not exceeding level 5 on the standard scale.

(5) In proceedings for an offence under subsection (4) it is a defence for the accused to show that he took all reasonable precautions and exercised all due diligence to avoid committing the offence.

(6) An authorised person must take reasonable care to ensure that no function of his, in relation to the carrying on of a regulated activity, is performed by a person who is prohibited from performing that function by a prohibition order.

64   Conduct: statements and codes

(1) The Authority may issue statements of principle with respect to the conduct expected of approved persons.

(2) If the Authority issues a statement of principle under subsection (1), it must also issue a code of practice for the purpose of helping to determine whether or not a person's conduct complies with the statement of principle.

(3) A code issued under subsection (2) may specify—

  (a) descriptions of conduct which, in the opinion of the Authority, comply with a statement of principle;

  (b) descriptions of conduct which, in the opinion of the Authority, do not comply with a statement of principle;

  (c) factors which, in the opinion of the Authority, are to be taken into account in determining whether or not a person's conduct complies with a statement of principle.

(4) The Authority may at any time alter or replace a statement or code issued under this section.

(5) If a statement or code is altered or replaced, the altered or replacement statement or code must be issued by the Authority.

(6) A statement or code issued under this section must be published by the Authority in the way appearing to the Authority to be best calculated to bring it to the attention of the public.

(7) A code published under this section and in force at the time when any particular conduct takes place may be relied on so far as it tends to establish whether or not that conduct complies with a statement of principle.

(8) Failure to comply with a statement of principle under this section does not of itself give rise to any right of action by persons affected or affect the validity of any transaction.

(9) A person is not to be taken to have failed to comply with a statement of principle if he shows that, at the time of the alleged failure, it or its associated code of practice had not been published.

(10) The Authority must, without delay, give the Treasury a copy of any statement or code which it publishes under this section.

90   [Compensation for false or misleading statements or omissions]

(1) Any person responsible for listing particulars is liable to pay compensation to a person who has—

  (a) acquired securities to which the particulars apply; and

  (b) suffered loss in respect of them as a result of—

    (i) any untrue or misleading statement in the particulars; or

    (ii) the omission from the particulars of any matter required to be included by section 80 or 81.

[118   Market abuse

(1) For the purposes of this Act, market abuse is behaviour (whether by one person alone or by two or more persons jointly or in concert) which—

  (a) occurs in relation to—

    (i) qualifying investments admitted to trading on a prescribed market,

    (ii) qualifying investments in respect of which a request for admission to trading on such a market has been made, or

        (iii) in the case of subsection (2) or (3) behaviour, investments which are related investments in relation to such qualifying investments, and

    (b) falls within any one or more of the types of behaviour set out in subsections (2) to (8).

(2) The first type of behaviour is where an insider deals, or attempts to deal, in a qualifying investment or related investment on the basis of inside information relating to the investment in question.

(3) The second is where an insider discloses inside information to another person otherwise than in the proper course of the exercise of his employment, profession or duties.

(4) The third is where the behaviour (not falling within subsection (2) or (3))—

    (a) is based on information which is not generally available to those using the market but which, if available to a regular user of the market, would be, or would be likely to be, regarded by him as relevant when deciding the terms on which transactions in qualifying investments should be effected, and

    (b) is likely to be regarded by a regular user of the market as a failure on the part of the person concerned to observe the standard of behaviour reasonably expected of a person in his position in relation to the market.

(5) The fourth is where the behaviour consists of effecting transactions or orders to trade (otherwise than for legitimate reasons and in conformity with accepted market practices on the relevant market) which—

    (a) give, or are likely to give, a false or misleading impression as to the supply of, or demand for, or as to the price of, one or more qualifying investments, or

    (b) secure the price of one or more such investments at an abnormal or artificial level.

(6) The fifth is where the behaviour consists of effecting transactions or orders to trade which employ fictitious devices or any other form of deception or contrivance.

(7) The sixth is where the behaviour consists of the dissemination of information by any means which gives, or is likely to give, a false or misleading impression as to a qualifying investment by a person who knew or could reasonably be expected to have known that the information was false or misleading.

(8) The seventh is where the behaviour (not falling within subsection (5), (6) or (7))—

    (a) is likely to give a regular user of the market a false or misleading impression as to the supply of, demand for or price or value of, qualifying investments, or

    (b) would be, or would be likely to be, regarded by a regular user of the market as behaviour that would distort, or would be likely to distort, the market in such an investment,

and the behaviour is likely to be regarded by a regular user of the market as a failure on the part of the person concerned to observe the standard of behaviour reasonably expected of a person in his position in relation to the market.

(9) Subsections (4) and (8) and the definition of "regular user" in section 130A(3) cease to have effect on 30 June 2008 and subsection (1)(b) is then to be read as no longer referring to those subsections.]

[*See also ss 118A (Supplementary provision about certain behaviour), 118B (Insiders) and 118C (Inside information).*]

119 The code

(1) The Authority must prepare and issue a code containing such provisions as the Authority considers will give appropriate guidance to those determining whether or not behaviour amounts to market abuse.

(2) The code may among other things specify—

    (a) descriptions of behaviour that, in the opinion of the Authority, amount to market abuse;

    (b) descriptions of behaviour that, in the opinion of the Authority, do not amount to market abuse;

(c) factors that, in the opinion of the Authority, are to be taken into account in determining whether or not behaviour amounts to market abuse

[(d) descriptions of behaviour that are accepted market practices in relation to one or more specified markets;

(e) descriptions of behaviour that are not accepted market practices in relation to one or more specified markets.].

[(2A) In determining, for the purposes of subsections (2)(d) and (2)(e) or otherwise, what are and what are not accepted market practices, the Authority must have regard to the factors and procedures laid down in Articles 2 and 3 respectively of Commission Directive 2004/72/EC of 29 April 2004 implementing Directive 2003/6/EC of the European Parliament and of the Council.]

122 Effect of the code

(1) If a person behaves in a way which is described (in the code in force under section 119 at the time of the behaviour) as behaviour that, in the Authority's opinion, does not amount to market abuse that behaviour of his is to be taken, for the purposes of this Act, as not amounting to market abuse.

(2) Otherwise, the code in force under section 119 at the time when particular behaviour occurs may be relied on so far as it indicates whether or not that behaviour should be taken to amount to market abuse.

138 General rule-making power

(1) The Authority may make such rules applying to authorised persons—
   (a) with respect to the carrying on by them of regulated activities, or
   (b) with respect to the carrying on by them of activities which are not regulated activities,
as appear to it to be necessary or expedient for the purpose of protecting the interests of consumers.

(7) 'Consumers' means persons—
   (a) who use, have used, or are or may be contemplating using, any of the services provided by—
      (i) authorised persons in carrying on regulated activities; or
      (ii) persons acting as appointed representatives;
   (b) who have rights or interests which are derived from, or are otherwise attributable to, the use of any such services by other persons; or
   (c) who have rights or interests which may be adversely affected by the use of any such services by persons acting on their behalf or in a fiduciary capacity in relation to them.

203 Power to prohibit the carrying on of Consumer Credit Act business

(1) If it appears to [the Office of Fair Trading ('the OFT')] that subsection (4) has been, or is likely to be, contravened as respects a consumer credit EEA firm, [it] may by written notice given to the firm impose on the firm a consumer credit prohibition.

(2) If it appears to the [OFT] that a restriction imposed under section 204 on an EEA consumer credit firm has not been complied with, [it] may by written notice given to the firm impose a consumer credit prohibition.

(3) 'Consumer credit prohibition' means a prohibition on carrying on, or purporting to carry on, in the United Kingdom any Consumer Credit Act business which consists of or includes carrying on one or more listed activities.

(4) This subsection is contravened as respects a firm if—
   (a) the firm or any of its employees, agents or associates (whether past or present), or
   (b) if the firm is a body corporate, any controller of the firm or an associate of any such controller,

does any of the things specified in paragraphs [(a) to (e) of section 25(2A)] of the Consumer Credit Act 1974.

(5) A consumer credit prohibition may be absolute or may be imposed—

(a) for such period,

(b) until the occurrence of such event, or

(c) until such conditions are complied with,

as may be specified in the notice given under subsection (1) or (2).

(6) Any period, event or condition so specified may be varied by the [OFT] on the application of the firm concerned.

(7) A consumer credit prohibition may be withdrawn by written notice served by the [OFT] on the firm concerned, and any such notice takes effect on such date as is specified in the notice.

(8) Schedule 16 has effect as respects consumer credit prohibitions and restrictions under section 204.

(9) A firm contravening a prohibition under this section is guilty of an offence and liable—

(a) on summary conviction, to a fine not exceeding the statutory maximum;

(b) on conviction on indictment, to a fine.

(10) In this section and section 204—

'a consumer credit EEA firm' means an EEA firm falling within any of paragraphs (a) to (c) of paragraph 5 of Schedule 3 whose EEA authorisation covers any Consumer Credit Act business;

'Consumer Credit Act business' means consumer credit business, consumer hire business or ancillary credit business;

'consumer credit business', 'consumer hire business' and 'ancillary credit business' have the same meaning as in the Consumer Credit Act 1974;

'listed activity' means an activity listed in [Annex 1 to the banking consolidation directive] or the Annex to the investment services directive;

'associate' has the same meaning as in section [25(2A)] of the Consumer Credit Act 1974;

'controller' has the meaning given by section 189(1) of that Act.

204 Power to restrict the carrying on of Consumer Credit Act business

(1) In this section 'restriction' means a direction that a consumer credit EEA firm may not carry on in the United Kingdom, otherwise than in accordance with such condition or conditions as may be specified in the direction, any Consumer Credit Act business which—

(a) consists of or includes carrying on any listed activity; and

(b) is specified in the direction.

(2) If it appears to the [OFT] that the situation as respects a consumer credit EEA firm is such that the powers conferred by section 203(1) are exercisable, the [OFT] may, instead of imposing a prohibition, impose such restriction as appears to [it] desirable.

(3) A restriction—

(a) may be withdrawn, or

(b) may be varied with the agreement of the firm concerned, by written notice served by the [OFT] on the firm, and any such notice takes effect on such date as is specified in the notice.

(4) A firm contravening a restriction is guilty of an offence and liable—

(a) on summary conviction, to a fine not exceeding the statutory maximum;

(b) on conviction on indictment, to a fine.

[226A Consumer credit jurisdiction

(1) A complaint which relates to an act or omission of a person ("the respondent") is to be dealt with under the ombudsman scheme if the conditions mentioned in subsection (2) are satisfied.

(2) The conditions are that—
  (a) the complainant is eligible and wishes to have the complaint dealt with under the scheme;
  (b) the complaint falls within a description specified in consumer credit rules;
  (c) at the time of the act or omission the respondent was the licensee under a standard licence or was authorised to carry on an activity by virtue of section 34A of the Consumer Credit Act 1974;
  (d) the act or omission occurred in the course of a business being carried on by the respondent which was of a type mentioned in subsection (3);
  (e) at the time of the act or omission that type of business was specified in an order made by the Secretary of State; and
  (f) the complaint cannot be dealt with under the compulsory jurisdiction.
(3) The types of business referred to in subsection (2)(d) are—
  (a) a consumer credit business;
  (b) a consumer hire business;
  (c) a business so far as it comprises or relates to credit brokerage;
  (d) a business so far as it comprises or relates to debt-adjusting;
  (e) a business so far as it comprises or relates to debt-counselling;
  (f) a business so far as it comprises or relates to debt-collecting;
  (g) a business so far as it comprises or relates to debt administration;
  (h) a business so far as it comprises or relates to the provision of credit (g) a business so far as it comprises or relates to debt administration;information services;
  (i) a business so far as it comprises or relates to the operation of a credit reference agency.
(4) A complainant is eligible if—
  (a) he is—
    (i) an individual; or
    (ii) a surety in relation to a security provided to the respondent in connection with the business mentioned in subsection (2)(d); and
  (b) he falls within a class of person specified in consumer credit rules.
(5) The approval of the Treasury is required for an order under subsection (2)(e).
(6) The jurisdiction of the scheme which results from this section is referred to in this Act as the "consumer credit jurisdiction".
(7) In this Act "consumer credit rules" means rules made by the scheme operator with the approval of the Authority for the purposes of the consumer credit jurisdiction.
(8) Consumer credit rules under this section may make different provision for different cases.
(9) Expressions used in the Consumer Credit Act 1974 have the same meaning in this section as they have in that Act.]

[234A   Funding by consumer credit licensees etc.
(1) For the purpose of funding-
  (a) the establishment of the ombudsman scheme so far as it relates to the consumer credit jurisdiction (whenever any relevant expense is incurred), and
  (b) its operation in relation to the consumer credit jurisdiction,
the scheme operator may from time to time with the approval of the Authority
the scheme operator may from time to time with the approval of the Authority determine a sum which is to be raised by way of contributions under this section.
(2) A sum determined under subsection (1) may include a component to cover the costs of the collection of contributions to that sum ("collection costs") under this section.
(3) The scheme operator must notify the OFT of every determination under subsection (1).
(4) The OFT must give general notice of every determination so notified
(5) The OFT may by general notice impose requirements on—

(a) licensees to whom this section applies, or

(b) persons who make applications to which this section applies,

to pay contributions to the OFT for the purpose of raising sums determined under sub-section (1).

(6) The amount of the contribution payable by a person under such a requirement—

(a) shall be the amount specified in or determined under the general notice; and

(b) shall be paid before the end of the period or at the time so specified or determined.

(7) A general notice under subsection (5) may—

(a) impose requirements only on descriptions of licensees or applicants specified in the notice;

(b) provide for exceptions from any requirement imposed on a description of licen-sees or applicants;

(c) impose different requirements on different descriptions of licensees or applicants;

(d) make provision for refunds in specified circumstances.

(8) Contributions received by the OFT must be paid to the scheme operator.

(9) As soon as practicable after the end of—

(a) each financial year of the scheme operator, or

(b) if the OFT and the scheme operator agree that this paragraph is to apply instead of paragraph (a) for the time being, each period agreed by them,

the scheme operator must pay to the OFT an amount representing the extent to which col-lection costs are covered in accordance with subsection (2) by the total amount of the con-tributions paid by the OFT to it during the year or (as the case may be) the agreed period.

(10) Amounts received by the OFT from the scheme operator are to be retained by it for the purpose of meeting its costs.

(11) The Secretary of State may by order provide that the functions of the OFT under this section are for the time being to be carried out by the scheme operator.

(12) An order under subsection (11) may provide that while the order is in force this section shall have effect subject to such modifications as may be set out in the order.

(13) The licensees to whom this section applies are licensees under standard licences which cover to any extent the carrying on of a type of business specified in an order under section 226A(2)(e).

(14) The applications to which this section applies are applications for—

(a) standard licences covering to any extent the carrying on of a business of such a type;

(b) the renewal of standard licences on terms covering to any extent the carrying on of a business of such a type.

(15) Expressions used in the Consumer Credit Act 1974 have the same meaning in this section as they have in that Act.]

380 Injunctions

(1) If, on the application of the Authority or the Secretary of State, the court is satisfied—

(a) that there is a reasonable likelihood that any person will contravene a relevant requirement, or

(b) that any person has contravened a relevant requirement and that there is a rea-sonable likelihood that the contravention will continue or be repeated,

the court may make an order restraining (or in Scotland an interdict prohibiting) the con-travention.

(2) If on the application of the Authority or the Secretary of State the court is satisfied—

(a) that any person has contravened a relevant requirement, and

(b) that there are steps which could be taken for remedying the contravention,

the court may make an order requiring that person, and any other person who appears to have been knowingly concerned in the contravention, to take such steps as the court may direct to remedy it.

381 Injunctions in cases of market abuse

(1) If, on the application of the Authority, the court is satisfied—

(a) that there is a reasonable likelihood that any person will engage in market abuse, or

(b) that any person is or has engaged in market abuse and that there is a reasonable likelihood that the market abuse will continue or be repeated,

the court may make an order restraining (or in Scotland an interdict prohibiting) the market abuse.

(2) If on the application of the Authority the court is satisfied—

(a) that any person is or has engaged in market abuse, and

(b) that there are steps which could be taken for remedying the market abuse,

the court may make an order requiring him to take such steps as the court may direct to remedy it.

382 Restitution orders

(1) The court may, on the application of the Authority or the Secretary of State, make an order under subsection (2) if it is satisfied that a person has contravened a relevant requirement, or been knowingly concerned in the contravention of such a requirement, and—

(a) that profits have accrued to him as a result of the contravention; or

(b) that one or more persons have suffered loss or been otherwise adversely affected as a result of the contravention.

(2) The court may order the person concerned to pay to the Authority such sum as appears to the court to be just having regard—

(a) in a case within paragraph (a) of subsection (1), to the profits appearing to the court to have accrued;

(b) in a case within paragraph (b) of that subsection, to the extent of the loss or other adverse effect;

(c) in a case within both of those paragraphs, to the profits appearing to the court to have accrued and to the extent of the loss or other adverse effect.

(3) Any amount paid to the Authority in pursuance of an order under subsection (2) must be paid by it to such qualifying person or distributed by it among such qualifying persons as the court may direct.

(8) 'Qualifying person' means a person appearing to the court to be someone—

(a) to whom the profits mentioned in subsection (1)(a) are attributable; or

(b) who has suffered the loss or adverse effect mentioned in subsection (1)(b).

Section 203(8)   SCHEDULE 16

PROHIBITIONS AND RESTRICTIONS IMPOSED BY
[OFFICE OF FAIR TRADING]

Preliminary

1. In this Schedule—

'appeal period' has the same meaning as in the Consumer Credit Act 1974;

'prohibition' means a consumer credit prohibition under section 203;

'restriction' means a restriction under section 204.

Notice of prohibition or restriction

2.—(1) This paragraph applies if the [OFT] proposes, in relation to a firm—

(a) to impose a prohibition;

(b) to impose a restriction; or

(c) to vary a restriction otherwise than with the agreement of the firm.

(2) The [OFT] must by notice—
  (a) inform the firm of [its] proposal, stating [its] reasons; and
  (b) invite the firm to submit representations in accordance with paragraph 4.

(3) If [the OFT] imposes the prohibition or restriction or varies the restriction, the [OFT] may give directions authorising the firm to carry into effect agreements made before the coming into force of the prohibition, restriction or variation.

(4) A prohibition, restriction or variation is not to come into force before the end of the appeal period.

(5) If the [OFT] imposes a prohibition or restriction or varies a restriction, [it] must serve a copy of the prohibition, restriction or variation—
  (a) on the Authority; and
  (b) on the firm's home state regulator.

Application to revoke prohibition or restriction

3.—(1) This paragraph applies if the [OFT] proposes to refuse an application made by a firm for the revocation of a prohibition or restriction.

(2) The [OFT] must by notice—
  (a) inform the firm of the proposed refusal, stating [its] reasons; and
  (b) invite the firm to submit representations in accordance with paragraph 4.

Representations to [OFT]

4.—(1) If this paragraph applies to an invitation to submit representations, the [OFT] must invite the firm, within 21 days after the notice containing the invitation is given to it or such longer period as [the OFT] may allow—
  (a) to submit its representations in writing to [it] and
  (b) to give notice to [it], if the firm thinks fit, that it wishes to make representations orally.

(2) If notice is given under sub-paragraph (1)(b), the [OFT] must arrange for the oral representations to be heard.

(3) The [OFT] must give the firm notice of [its] determination.

Appeals

5. Section 41 of the Consumer Credit Act 1974 (appeals to the Secretary of State) has effect as if—
  (a) the following determinations were mentioned in column 1 of the table set out at the end of that section—
    (i) imposition of a prohibition or restriction or the variation of a restriction; and
    (ii) refusal of an application for the revocation of a prohibition or restriction;
  (b) the firm concerned were mentioned in column 2 of that table in relation to those determinations.

Section 225(4)   SCHEDULE 17

THE OMBUDSMAN SCHEME

[PART 3A

THE CONSUMER CREDIT JURISDICTION

16A   Introduction
This Part of this Schedule applies only in relation to the consumer credit jurisdiction.

16B Procedure for complaints etc.

(1) Consumer credit rules—

(a) must provide that a complaint is not to be entertained unless the complainant has referred it under the ombudsman scheme before the applicable time limit (determined in accordance with the rules) has expired;

(b) may provide that an ombudsman may extend that time limit in specified circumstances;

(c) may provide that a complaint is not to be entertained (except in specified circumstances) if the complainant has not previously communicated its substance to the respondent and given him a reasonable opportunity to deal with it;

(d) may make provision about the procedure for the reference of complaints and for their investigation, consideration and determination by an ombudsman.

(2) Sub-paragraphs (2) and (3) of paragraph 14 apply in relation to consumer credit rules under sub-paragraph (1) of this paragraph as they apply in relation to scheme rules under that paragraph.

(3) Consumer credit rules may require persons falling within sub-paragraph (6) to establish such procedures as the scheme operator considers appropriate for the resolution of complaints which may be referred to the scheme.

(4) Consumer credit rules under sub-paragraph (3) may make different provision in relation to persons of different descriptions or to complaints of different descriptions.

(5) Consumer credit rules under sub-paragraph (3) may authorise the scheme operator to dispense with or modify the application of such rules in particular cases where the scheme operator—

(a) considers it appropriate to do so; and

(b) is satisfied that the specified conditions (if any) are met.

(6) A person falls within this sub-paragraph if he is licensed by a standard licence (within the meaning of the Consumer Credit Act 1974) to carry on to any extent a business of a type specified in an order under section 226A(2)(e) of this Act.

16C Fees

(1) Consumer credit rules may require a respondent to pay to the scheme operator such fees as may be specified in the rules.

(2) Sub-paragraph (2) of paragraph 15 applies in relation to consumer credit rules under this paragraph as it applies in relation to scheme rules under that paragraph.

16D Enforcement of money awards

A money award, including interest, which has been registered in accordance with consumer credit rules may—

(a) if a county court so orders in England and Wales, be recovered by execution issued from the county court (or otherwise) as if it were payable under an order of that court;

(b) be enforced in Northern Ireland as a money judgment under the Judgments Enforcement (Northern Ireland) Order 1981;

(c) be enforced in Scotland as if it were a decree of the sheriff and whether or not the sheriff could himself have granted such a decree.

16E Procedure for consumer credit rules

(1) If the scheme operator makes any consumer credit rules, it must give a copy of them to the Authority without delay.

(2) If the scheme operator revokes any such rules, it must give written notice to the Authority without delay.

(3) The power to make such rules is exercisable in writing.

(4) Immediately after the making of such rules, the scheme operator must arrange for them to be printed and made available to the public.

(5) The scheme operator may charge a reasonable fee for providing a person with a copy of any such rules.

16F   Verification of consumer credit rules

(1) The production of a printed copy of consumer credit rules purporting to be made by the scheme operator—

  (a) on which there is endorsed a certificate signed by a member of the scheme operator's staff authorised by the scheme operator for that purpose, and

  (b) which contains the required statements,

is evidence (or in Scotland sufficient evidence) of the facts stated in the certificate.

(2) The required statements are—

  (a) that the rules were made by the scheme operator;

  (b) that the copy is a true copy of the rules; and

  (c) that on a specified date the rules were made available to the public in accordance with paragraph 16E(4).

(3) A certificate purporting to be signed as mentioned in sub-paragraph (1) is to be taken to have been duly signed unless the contrary is shown.

16G   Consultation

(1) If the scheme operator proposes to make consumer credit rules, it must publish a draft of the proposed rules in the way appearing to it to be best calculated to bring the draft to the attention of the public.

(2) The draft must be accompanied by—

  (a) an explanation of the proposed rules; and

  (b) a statement that representations about the proposals may be made to the scheme operator within a specified time.

(3) Before making any consumer credit rules, the scheme operator must have regard to any representations made to it in accordance with sub-paragraph (2)(b).

(4) If consumer credit rules made by the scheme operator differ from the draft published under sub-paragraph (1) in a way which the scheme operator considers significant, the scheme operator must publish a statement of the difference.]

Limited Liability Partnerships Act 2000
(2000, c. 12)

An Act to make provision for limited liability partnerships.   [20th July 2000]

6   Members as agents

(1) Every member of a limited liability partnership is the agent of the limited liability partnership.

(2) But a limited liability partnership is not bound by anything done by a member in dealing with a person if—

  (a) the member in fact has no authority to act for the limited liability partnership by doing that thing, and

  (b) the person knows that he has no authority or does not know or believe him to be a member of the limited liability partnership.

(3) Where a person has ceased to be a member of a limited liability partnership, the former member is to be regarded (in relation to any person dealing with the limited liability partnership) as still being a member of the limited liability partnership unless—

  (a) the person has notice that the former member has ceased to be a member of the limited liability partnership, or

  (b) notice that the former member has ceased to be a member of the limited liability partnership has been delivered to the registrar.

(4) Where a member of a limited liability partnership is liable to any person (other than another member of the limited liability partnership) as a result of a wrongful act or omission of his in the course of the business of the limited liability partnership or with its authority, the limited liability partnership is liable to the same extent as the member.

Enterprise Act 2002
(2002, c. 40)

An Act to establish and provide for the functions of the Of?ce of Fair Trading, the Competition Appeal Tribunal and the Competition Service; to make provision about mergers and market structures and conduct; to amend the constitution and functions of the Competition Commission; to create an offence for those entering into certain anti-competitive agreements; to provide for the disquali?cation of directors of companies engaging in certain anti-competitive practices; to make other provision about competition law; to amend the law relating to the protection of the collective interests of consumers; to make further provision about the disclosure of information obtained under competition and consumer legislation; to amend the Insolvency Act 1986 and make other provision about insolvency; and for connected purposes. [7th November 2002]

PART 1

THE OFFICE OF FAIR TRADING

Establishment of OFT

1   The Office of Fair Trading

(1) There shall be a body corporate to be known as the Office of Fair Trading (in this Act referred to as 'the OFT').

(2) The functions of the OFT are carried out on behalf of the Crown.

(3) Schedule 1 (which makes further provision about the OFT) has effect.

(4) In managing its affairs the OFT shall have regard, in addition to any relevant general guidance as to the governance of public bodies, to such generally accepted principles of good corporate governance as it is reasonable to regard as applicable to the OFT.

2   The Director General of Fair Trading

(1) The functions of the Director General of Fair Trading (in this Act referred to as 'the Director'), and his property, rights and liabilities, are transferred to the OFT.

(2) The office of the Director is abolished.

(3) Any enactment, instrument or other document passed or made before the commencement of subsection (1) which refers to the Director shall have effect, so far as necessary for the purposes of or in consequence of anything being transferred, as if any reference to the Director were a reference to the OFT.

3   Annual plan

(1) The OFT shall, before each financial year, publish a document (the 'annual plan') containing a statement of its main objectives and priorities for the year.

(2) The OFT shall for the purposes of public consultation publish a document containing proposals for its annual plan at least two months before publishing the annual plan for any year.

(3) The OFT shall lay before Parliament a copy of each document published under subsection (2) and each annual plan.

4   Annual and other reports

(1) The OFT shall, as soon as practicable after the end of each financial year, make to the Secretary of State a report (the 'annual report') on its activities and performance during that year.

(2) The annual report for each year shall include—

    (a) a general survey of developments in respect of matters relating to the OFT's functions;

    (b) an assessment of the extent to which the OFT's main objectives and priorities for the year (as set out in the annual plan) have been met;

    (c) a summary of the significant decisions, investigations or other activities made or carried out by the OFT during the year;

    (d) a summary of the allocation of the OFT's financial resources to its various activities during the year; and

    (e) an assessment of the OFT's performance and practices in relation to its enforcement functions.

(3) The OFT shall lay a copy of each annual report before Parliament and arrange for the report to be published.

(4) The OFT may—

    (a) prepare other reports in respect of matters relating to any of its functions; and

    (b) arrange for any such report to be published.

General functions of OFT

5 Acquisition of information etc

(1) The OFT has the function of obtaining, compiling and keeping under review information about matters relating to the carrying out of its functions.

(2) That function is to be carried out with a view to (among other things) ensuring that the OFT has sufficient information to take informed decisions and to carry out its other functions effectively.

(3) In carrying out that function the OFT may carry out, commission or support (financially or otherwise) research.

6 Provision of information etc. to the public

(1) The OFT has the function of—

    (a) making the public aware of the ways in which competition may benefit consumers in, and the economy of, the United Kingdom; and

    (b) giving information or advice in respect of matters relating to any of its functions to the public.

(2) In carrying out those functions the OFT may—

    (a) publish educational materials or carry out other educational activities; or

    (b) support (financially or otherwise) the carrying out by others of such activities or the provision by others of information or advice.

7 Provision of information and advice to Ministers etc.

(1) The OFT has the function of—

    (a) making proposals, or

    (b) giving other information or advice,

on matters relating to any of its functions to any Minister of the Crown or other public authority (including proposals, information or advice as to any aspect of the law or a proposed change in the law).

(2) A Minister of the Crown may request the OFT to make proposals or give other information or advice on any matter relating to any of its functions; and the OFT shall, so far as is reasonably practicable and consistent with its other functions, comply with the request.

8 Promoting good consumer practice

(1) The OFT has the function of promoting good practice in the carrying out of activities which may affect the economic interests of consumers in the United Kingdom.

(2) In carrying out that function the OFT may (without prejudice to the generality of subsection (1)) make arrangements for approving consumer codes and may, in accordance

with the arrangements, give its approval to or withdraw its approval from any consumer code.

(3) Any such arrangements must specify the criteria to be applied by the OFT in determining whether to give approval to or withdraw approval from a consumer code.

(4) Any such arrangements may in particular—

(a) specify descriptions of consumer code which may be the subject of an application to the OFT for approval (and any such description may be framed by reference to any feature of a consumer code, including the persons who are, or are to be, subject to the code, the manner in which it is, or is to be, operated and the persons responsible for its operation); and

(b) provide for the use in accordance with the arrangements of an official symbol intended to signify that a consumer code is approved by the OFT.

(5) The OFT shall publish any arrangements under subsection (2) in such manner it considers appropriate.

(6) In this section 'consumer code' means a code of practice or other document (however described) intended, with a view to safeguarding or promoting the interests of consumers, to regulate by any means the conduct of persons engaged in the supply of goods or services to consumers (or the conduct of their employees or representatives).

Miscellaneous

11 Super-complaints to OFT

(1) This section applies where a designated consumer body makes a complaint to the OFT that any feature, or combination of features, of a market in the United Kingdom for goods or services is or appears to be significantly harming the interests of consumers.

(2) The OFT must, within 90 days after the day on which it receives the complaint, publish a response stating how it proposes to deal with the complaint, and in particular—

(a) whether it has decided to take any action, or to take no action, in response to the complaint, and

(b) if it has decided to take action, what action it proposes to take.

(3) The response must state the OFT's reasons for its proposals.

(4) The Secretary of State may by order amend subsection (2) by substituting any period for the period for the time being specified there.

(5) 'Designated consumer body' means a body designated by the Secretary of State by order.

(6) The Secretary of State—

(a) may designate a body only if it appears to him to represent the interests of consumers of any description, and

(b) must publish (and may from time to time vary) other criteria to be applied by him in determining whether to make or revoke a designation.

(7) The OFT—

(a) must issue guidance as to the presentation by the complainant of a reasoned case for the complaint, and

(b) may issue such other guidance as appears to it to be appropriate for the purposes of this section.

(8) An order under this section—

(a) shall be made by statutory instrument, and

(b) shall be subject to annulment in pursuance of a resolution of either House of Parliament.

(9) In this section—

(a) references to a feature of a market in the United Kingdom for goods or services have the same meaning as if contained in Part 4, and

(b) 'consumer' means an individual who is a consumer within the meaning of that Part.

PART 8

ENFORCEMENT OF CERTAIN CONSUMER LEGISLATION

Introduction

210 Consumers

(1) In this Part references to consumers must be construed in accordance with this section.

(2) In relation to a domestic infringement a consumer is an individual in respect of whom the first and second conditions are satisfied.

(3) The first condition is that—

(a) goods are or are sought to be supplied to the individual (whether by way of sale or otherwise) in the course of a business carried on by the person supplying or seeking to supply them, or

(b) services are or are sought to be supplied to the individual in the course of a business carried on by the person supplying or seeking to supply them.

(4) The second condition is that—

(a) the individual receives or seeks to receive the goods or services otherwise than in the course of a business carried on by him, or

(b) the individual receives or seeks to receive the goods or services with a view to carrying on a business but not in the course of a business carried on by him.

(5) For the purposes of a domestic infringement it is immaterial whether a person supplying goods or services has a place of business in the United Kingdom.

(6) In relation to a Community infringement a consumer is a person who is a consumer for the purposes of—

(a) the Injunctions Directive, and

(b) the listed Directive concerned.

(7) A Directive is a listed Directive—

(a) if it is a Directive of the Council of the European Communities or of the European Parliament and of the Council, and

(b) if it is specified in Schedule 13 or to the extent that any of its provisions is so specified.

(8) A business includes—

(a) a professional practice;

(b) any other undertaking carried on for gain or reward;

(c) any undertaking in the course of which goods or services are supplied otherwise than free of charge.

(9) The Secretary of State may by order modify Schedule 13.

(10) An order under this section must be made by statutory instrument subject to annulment in pursuance of a resolution of either House of Parliament.

211 Domestic infringements

(1) In this Part a domestic infringement is an act or omission which—

(a) is done or made by a person in the course of a business,

(b) falls within subsection (2), and

(c) harms the collective interests of consumers in the United Kingdom.

(2) An act or omission falls within this subsection if it is of a description specified by the Secretary of State by order and consists of any of the following—

(a) a contravention of an enactment which imposes a duty, prohibition or restriction enforceable by criminal proceedings;

(b) an act done or omission made in breach of contract;

(c) an act done or omission made in breach of a non-contractual duty owed to a person by virtue of an enactment or rule of law and enforceable by civil proceedings;

(d) an act or omission in respect of which an enactment provides for a remedy or sanction enforceable by civil proceedings;

(e) an act done or omission made by a person supplying or seeking to supply goods or services as a result of which an agreement or security relating to the supply is void or unenforceable to any extent;

(f) an act or omission by which a person supplying or seeking to supply goods or services purports or attempts to exercise a right or remedy relating to the supply in circumstances where the exercise of the right or remedy is restricted or excluded under or by virtue of an enactment;

(g) an act or omission by which a person supplying or seeking to supply goods or services purports or attempts to avoid (to any extent) liability relating to the supply in circumstances where such avoidance is restricted or prevented under an enactment.

(3) But an order under this section may provide that any description of act or omission falling within subsection (2) is not a domestic infringement.

(4) For the purposes of subsection (2) it is immaterial—

(a) whether or not any duty, prohibition or restriction exists in relation to consumers as such;

(b) whether or not any remedy or sanction is provided for the benefit of consumers as such;

(c) whether or not any proceedings have been brought in relation to the act or omission;

(d) whether or not any person has been convicted of an offence in respect of the contravention mentioned in subsection (2)(a);

(e) whether or not there is a waiver in respect of the breach of contract mentioned in subsection (2)(b).

(5) References to an enactment include references to subordinate legislation (within the meaning of the Interpretation Act 1978 (c. 30)).

(6) The power to make an order under this section must be exercised by statutory instrument.

(7) But no such order may be made unless a draft of it has been laid before Parliament and approved by a resolution of each House.

212 Community infringements

(1) In this Part a Community infringement is an act or omission which harms the collective interests of consumers and which—

(a) contravenes a listed Directive as given effect by the laws, regulations or administrative provisions of an EEA State, or

(b) contravenes such laws, regulations or administrative provisions which provide additional permitted protections.

(2) The laws, regulations or administrative provisions of an EEA State which give effect to a listed Directive provide additional permitted protections if—

(a) they provide protection for consumers which is in addition to the minimum protection required by the Directive concerned, and

(b) such additional protection is permitted by that Directive.

(3) The Secretary of State may by order specify for the purposes of this section the law in the United Kingdom which—

(a) gives effect to the listed Directives;

(b) provides additional permitted protections.

(4) References to a listed Directive must be construed in accordance with section 210.

(5) An EEA State is a State which is a contracting party to the Agreement on the European Economic Area signed at Oporto on 2nd May 1992 as adjusted by the Protocol signed at Brussels on 17th March 1993.

(6) An order under this section must be made by statutory instrument subject to annulment in pursuance of a resolution of either House of Parliament.

213 Enforcers

(1) Each of the following is a general enforcer—

(a) the OFT;

(b) every local weights and measures authority in Great Britain;

(c) the Department of Enterprise, Trade and Investment in Northern Ireland.

(2) A designated enforcer is any person or body (whether or not incorporated) which the Secretary of State—

(a) thinks has as one of its purposes the protection of the collective interests of consumers, and

(b) designates by order.

(3) The Secretary of State may designate a public body only if he is satisfied that it is independent.

(4) The Secretary of State may designate a person or body which is not a public body only if the person or body (as the case may be) satisfies such criteria as the Secretary of State specifies by order.

(5) A Community enforcer is a qualified entity for the purposes of the Injunctions Directive—

(a) which is for the time being specified in the list published in the Official Journal of the European Communities in pursuance of Article 4.3 of that Directive, but

(b) which is not a general enforcer or a designated enforcer.

(6) An order under this section may designate an enforcer in respect of—

(a) all infringements;

(b) infringements of such descriptions as are specified in the order.

(7) An order under this section may make different provision for different purposes.

(8) The designation of a body by virtue of subsection (3) is conclusive evidence for the purposes of any question arising under this Part that the body is a public body.

(9) An order under this section must be made by statutory instrument subject to annulment in pursuance of a resolution of either House of Parliament.

(10) If requested to do so by a designated enforcer which is designated in respect of one or more Community infringements the Secretary of State must notify the Commission of the European Communities—

(a) of its name and purpose;

(b) of the Community infringements in respect of which it is designated.

(11) The Secretary of State must also notify the Commission—

(a) of the fact that a person or body in respect of which he has given notice under subsection (10) ceases to be a designated enforcer;

(b) of any change in the name or purpose of a designated enforcer in respect of which he has given such notice;

(c) of any change to the Community infringements in respect of which a designated enforcer is designated.

Enforcement procedure

214 Consultation

(1) An enforcer must not make an application for an enforcement order unless he has engaged in appropriate consultation with—

(a) the person against whom the enforcement order would be made, and

(b) the OFT (if it is not the enforcer).

(2) Appropriate consultation is consultation for the purpose of—
  (a) achieving the cessation of the infringement in a case where an infringement is occurring;
  (b) ensuring that there will be no repetition of the infringement in a case where the infringement has occurred;
  (c) ensuring that there will be no repetition of the infringement in a case where the cessation of the infringement is achieved under paragraph (a);
  (d) ensuring that the infringement does not take place in the case of a Community infringement which the enforcer believes is likely to take place.

(3) Subsection (1) does not apply if the OFT thinks that an application for an enforcement order should be made without delay.

(4) Subsection (1) ceases to apply—
  (a) for the purposes of an application for an enforcement order at the end of the period of 14 days beginning with the day after the person against whom the enforcement order would be made receives a request for consultation from the enforcer;
  (b) for the purposes of an application for an interim enforcement order at the end of the period of seven days beginning with the day after the person against whom the interim enforcement order would be made receives a request for consultation from the enforcer.

(5) The Secretary of State may by order make rules in relation to consultation under this section.

(6) Such an order must be made by statutory instrument subject to annulment in pursuance of a resolution of either House of Parliament.

(7) In this section (except subsection (4)) and in sections 215 and 216 references to an enforcement order include references to an interim enforcement order.

215 Applications

(1) An application for an enforcement order must name the person the enforcer thinks—
  (a) has engaged or is engaging in conduct which constitutes a domestic or a Community infringement, or
  (b) is likely to engage in conduct which constitutes a Community infringement.

(2) A general enforcer may make an application for an enforcement order in respect of any infringement.

(3) A designated enforcer may make an application for an enforcement order in respect of any infringement to which his designation relates.

(4) A Community enforcer may make an application for an enforcement order in respect of a Community infringement.

(5) The following courts have jurisdiction to make an enforcement order—
  (a) the High Court or a county court if the person against whom the order is sought carries on business or has a place of business in England and Wales or Northern Ireland;
  (b) the Court of Session or the sheriff if the person against whom the order is sought carries on business or has a place of business in Scotland.

(6) If an application for an enforcement order is made by a Community enforcer the court may examine whether the purpose of the enforcer justifies its making the application.

(7) If the court thinks that the purpose of the Community enforcer does not justify its making the application the court may refuse the application on that ground alone.

(8) The purpose of a Community enforcer must be construed by reference to the Injunctions Directive.

(9) An enforcer which is not the OFT must notify the OFT of the result of an application under this section.

216 Applications: directions by OFT

(1) This section applies if the OFT believes that an enforcer other than the OFT intends to apply for an enforcement order.

(2) In such a case the OFT may direct that if an application in respect of a particular infringement is to be made it must be made—

(a) only by the OFT, or

(b) only by such other enforcer as the OFT directs.

(3) If the OFT directs that only it may make an application that does not prevent—

(a) the OFT or any enforcer from accepting an undertaking under section 219, or

(b) the OFT from taking such other steps it thinks appropriate (apart from making an application) for the purpose of securing that the infringement is not committed, continued or repeated.

(4) The OFT may vary or withdraw a direction given under this section.

(5) The OFT must take such steps as it thinks appropriate to bring a direction (or a variation or withdrawal of a direction) to the attention of enforcers it thinks may be affected by it.

(6) But this section does not prevent an application for an enforcement order being made by a Community enforcer.

217 Enforcement orders

(1) This section applies if an application for an enforcement order is made under section 215 and the court finds that the person named in the application has engaged in conduct which constitutes the infringement.

(2) This section also applies if such an application is made in relation to a Community infringement and the court finds that the person named in the application is likely to engage in conduct which constitutes the infringement.

(3) If this section applies the court may make an enforcement order against the person.

(4) In considering whether to make an enforcement order the court must have regard to whether the person named in the application—

(a) has given an undertaking under section 219 in respect of conduct such as is mentioned in subsection (3) of that section;

(b) has failed to comply with the undertaking.

(5) An enforcement order must—

(a) indicate the nature of the conduct to which the finding under subsection (1) or (2) relates, and

(b) direct the person to comply with subsection (6).

(6) A person complies with this subsection if he—

(a) does not continue or repeat the conduct;

(b) does not engage in such conduct in the course of his business or another business;

(c) does not consent to or connive in the carrying out of such conduct by a body corporate with which he has a special relationship (within the meaning of section 222(3)).

(7) But subsection (6)(a) does not apply in the case of a finding under subsection (2).

(8) An enforcement order may require a person against whom the order is made to publish in such form and manner and to such extent as the court thinks appropriate for the purpose of eliminating any continuing effects of the infringement—

(a) the order;

(b) a corrective statement.

(9) If the court makes a finding under subsection (1) or (2) it may accept an undertaking by the person—

(a) to comply with subsection (6), or

(b) to take steps which the court believes will secure that he complies with subsection (6).

(10) An undertaking under subsection (9) may include a further undertaking by the person to publish in such form and manner and to such extent as the court thinks appropriate for the purpose of eliminating any continuing effects of the infringement—

(a) the terms of the undertaking;

(b) a corrective statement.

(11) If the court—

    (a) makes a finding under subsection (1) or (2), and

    (b) accepts an undertaking under subsection (9),

it must not make an enforcement order in respect of the infringement to which the undertaking relates.

(12) An enforcement order made by a court in one part of the United Kingdom has effect in any other part of the United Kingdom as if made by a court in that part.

218   Interim enforcement order

(1) The court may make an interim enforcement order against a person named in the application for the order if it appears to the court—

    (a) that it is alleged that the person is engaged in conduct which constitutes a domestic or Community infringement or is likely to engage in conduct which constitutes a Community infringement,

    (b) that if the application had been an application for an enforcement order it would be likely to be granted,

    (c) that it is expedient that the conduct is prohibited or prevented (as the case may be) immediately, and

    (d) if no notice of the application has been given to the person named in the application that it is appropriate to make an interim enforcement order without notice.

(2) An interim enforcement order must—

    (a) indicate the nature of the alleged conduct, and

    (b) direct the person to comply with subsection (3).

(3) A person complies with this subsection if he—

    (a) does not continue or repeat the conduct;

    (b) does not engage in such conduct in the course of his business or another business;

    (c) does not consent to or connive in the carrying out of such conduct by a body corporate with which he has a special relationship (within the meaning of section 222(3)).

(4) But subsection (3)(a) does not apply in so far as the application is made in respect of an allegation that the person is likely to engage in conduct which constitutes a Community infringement.

(5) An application for an interim enforcement order against a person may be made at any time before an application for an enforcement order against the person in respect of the same conduct is determined.

(6) An application for an interim enforcement order must refer to all matters—

    (a) which are known to the applicant, and

    (b) which are material to the question whether or not the application is granted.

(7) If an application for an interim enforcement order is made without notice the application must state why no notice has been given.

(8) The court may vary or discharge an interim enforcement order on the application of—

    (a) the enforcer who applied for the order;

    (b) the person against whom it is made.

(9) An interim enforcement order against a person is discharged on the determination of an application for an enforcement order made against the person in respect of the same conduct.

(10) If it appears to the court as mentioned in subsection (1)(a) to (c) the court may instead of making an interim enforcement order accept an undertaking from the person named in the application—

    (a) to comply with subsection (3), or

(b) to take steps which the court believes will secure that he complies with subsection (3).

(11) An interim enforcement order made by a court in one part of the United Kingdom has effect in any other part of the United Kingdom as if made by a court in that part.

219   Undertakings

(1) This section applies if an enforcer has power to make an application under section 215.

(2) In such a case the enforcer may accept from a person to whom subsection (3) applies an undertaking that the person will comply with subsection (4).

(3) This subsection applies to a person who the enforcer believes—

(a) has engaged in conduct which constitutes an infringement;

(b) is engaging in such conduct;

(c) is likely to engage in conduct which constitutes a Community infringement.

(4) A person complies with this subsection if he—

(a) does not continue or repeat the conduct;

(b) does not engage in such conduct in the course of his business or another business;

(c) does not consent to or connive in the carrying out of such conduct by a body corporate with which he has a special relationship (within the meaning of section 222(3)).

(5) But subsection (4)(a) does not apply in the case of an undertaking given by a person in so far as subsection (3) applies to him by virtue of paragraph (c).

(6) If an enforcer accepts an undertaking under this section it must notify the OFT—

(a) of the terms of the undertaking;

(b) of the identity of the person who gave it.

220   Further proceedings

(1) This section applies if the court—

(a) makes an enforcement order under section 217,

(b) makes an interim enforcement order under section 218, or

(c) accepts an undertaking under either of those sections.

(2) In such a case the OFT has the same right to apply to the court in respect of a failure to comply with the order or undertaking as the enforcer who made the application for the order.

(3) An application to the court in respect of a failure to comply with an undertaking may include an application for an enforcement order or for an interim enforcement order.

(4) If the court finds that an undertaking is not being complied with it may make an enforcement order or an interim enforcement order (instead of making any other order it has power to make).

(5) In the case of an application for an enforcement order or for an interim enforcement order as mentioned in subsection (3) sections 214 and 216 must be ignored and sections 215 and 217 or 218 (as the case may be) apply subject to the following modifications—

(a) section 215(1)(b) must be ignored;

(b) section 215(5) must be ignored and the application must be made to the court which accepted the undertaking;

(c) section 217(9) to (11) must be ignored;

(d) section 218(10) must be ignored.

(6) If an enforcer which is not the OFT makes an application in respect of the failure of a person to comply with an enforcement order, an interim enforcement order or an undertaking given under section 217 or 218 the enforcer must notify the OFT—

(a) of the application;

(b) of any order made by the court on the application.

221   Community infringements: proceedings

(1) Subsection (2) applies to—

(a) every general enforcer;

(b) every designated enforcer which is a public body.

(2) An enforcer to which this subsection applies has power to take proceedings in EEA States other than the United Kingdom for the cessation or prohibition of a Community infringement.

(3) Subsection (4) applies to—

(a) every general enforcer;

(b) every designated enforcer.

(4) An enforcer to which this subsection applies may co-operate with a Community enforcer—

(a) for the purpose of bringing proceedings mentioned in subsection (2);

(b) in connection with the exercise by the Community enforcer of its functions under this Part.

(5) An EEA State is a State which is a contracting party to the Agreement on the European Economic Area signed at Oporto on 2nd May 1992 as adjusted by the Protocol signed at Brussels on 17th March 1993.

222 Bodies corporate: accessories

(1) This section applies if the person whose conduct constitutes a domestic infringement or a Community infringement is a body corporate.

(2) If the conduct takes place with the consent or connivance of a person (an accessory) who has a special relationship with the body corporate, the consent or connivance is also conduct which constitutes the infringement.

(3) A person has a special relationship with a body corporate if he is—

(a) a controller of the body corporate, or

(b) a director, manager, secretary or other similar officer of the body corporate or a person purporting to act in such a capacity.

(4) A person is a controller of a body corporate if—

(a) the directors of the body corporate or of another body corporate which is its controller are accustomed to act in accordance with the person's directions or instructions, or

(b) either alone or with an associate or associates he is entitled to exercise or control the exercise of one third or more of the voting power at any general meeting of the body corporate or of another body corporate which is its controller.

(5) An enforcement order or an interim enforcement order may be made against an accessory in respect of an infringement whether or not such an order is made against the body corporate.

(6) The court may accept an undertaking under section 217(9) or 218(10) from an accessory in respect of an infringement whether or not it accepts such an undertaking from the body corporate.

(7) An enforcer may accept an undertaking under section 219 from an accessory in respect of an infringement whether or not it accepts such an undertaking from the body corporate.

(8) Subsection (9) applies if—

(a) an order is made as mentioned in subsection (5), or

(b) an undertaking is accepted as mentioned in subsection (6) or (7).

(9) In such a case for subsection (6) of section 217, subsection (3) of section 218 or subsection (4) of section 219 (as the case may be) there is substituted the following subsection—

'( ) A person complies with this subsection if he—

(a) does not continue or repeat the conduct;

(b) does not in the course of any business carried on by him engage in conduct such as that which constitutes the infringement committed by the body corporate mentioned in section 222(1);

(c) does not consent to or connive in the carrying out of such conduct by another body corporate with which he has a special relationship (within the meaning of section 222(3)).'

(10) A person is an associate of an individual if—

(a) he is the spouse [or civil partner] of the individual;

(b) he is a relative of the individual;

(c) he is a relative of the individual's spouse [or civil partner];

(d) he is the spouse [or civil partner] of a relative of the individual;

(e) he is the spouse [or civil partner] of a relative of the individual's spouse;

(f) he lives in the same household as the individual otherwise than merely because he or the individual is the other's employer, tenant, lodger or boarder;

(g) he is a relative of a person who is an associate of the individual by virtue of paragraph (f);

(h) he has at some time in the past fallen within any of paragraphs (a) to (g).

(11) A person is also an associate of—

(a) an individual with whom he is in partnership;

(b) an individual who is an associate of the individual mentioned in paragraph (a);

(c) a body corporate if he is a controller of it or he is an associate of a person who is a controller of the body corporate.

(12) A body corporate is an associate of another body corporate if—

(a) the same person is a controller of both;

(b) a person is a controller of one and persons who are his associates are controllers of the other;

(c) a person is a controller of one and he and persons who are his associates are controllers of the other;

(d) a group of two or more persons is a controller of each company and the groups consist of the same persons;

(e) a group of two or more persons is a controller of each company and the groups may be regarded as consisting of the same persons by treating (in one or more cases) a member of either group as replaced by a person of whom he is an associate.

(13) A relative is a brother, sister, uncle, aunt, nephew, niece, lineal ancestor or lineal descendant.

223 Bodies corporate: orders

(1) This section applies if a court makes an enforcement order or an interim enforcement order against a body corporate and—

(a) at the time the order is made the body corporate is a member of a group of interconnected bodies corporate,

(b) at any time when the order is in force the body corporate becomes a member of a group of interconnected bodies corporate, or

(c) at any time when the order is in force a group of interconnected bodies corporate of which the body corporate is a member is increased by the addition of one or more further members.

(2) The court may direct that the order is binding upon all of the members of the group as if each of them were the body corporate against which the order is made.

(3) A group of interconnected bodies corporate is a group consisting of two or more bodies corporate all of whom are interconnected with each other.

(4) Any two bodies corporate are interconnected—

(a) if one of them is a subsidiary of the other, or

(b) if both of them are subsidiaries of the same body corporate.

(5) 'Subsidiary' must be construed in accordance with section 736 of the Companies Act 1985 (c. 6).

Information

224 OFT

(1) The OFT may for any of the purposes mentioned in subsection (2) give notice to any person requiring the person to provide it with the information specified in the notice.

(2) The purposes are—

(a) to enable the OFT to exercise or to consider whether to exercise any function it has under this Part;

(b) to enable a designated enforcer to which section 225 does not apply to consider whether to exercise any function it has under this Part;

(c) to enable a Community enforcer to consider whether to exercise any function it has under this Part;

(d) to ascertain whether a person has complied with or is complying with an enforcement order, an interim enforcement order or an undertaking given under section 217(9), 218(10) or 219.

225 Other enforcers

(1) This section applies to—

(a) every general enforcer (other than the OFT);

(b) every designated enforcer which is a public body.

(2) An enforcer to which this section applies may for any of the purposes mentioned in subsection (3) give notice to any person requiring the person to provide the enforcer with the information specified in the notice.

(3) The purposes are—

(a) to enable the enforcer to exercise or to consider whether to exercise any function it has under this Part;

(b) to ascertain whether a person has complied with or is complying with an enforcement order or an interim enforcement order made on the application of the enforcer or an undertaking given under section 217(9) or 218(10) (as the case may be) following such an application or an undertaking given to the enforcer under section 219.

226 Notices: procedure

(1) This section applies to a notice given under section 224 or 225.

(2) The notice must—

(a) be in writing;

(b) specify the purpose for which the information is required.

(3) If the purpose is as mentioned in section 224(2)(a), (b) or (c) or 225(3)(a) the notice must specify the function concerned.

(4) A notice may specify the time within which and manner in which it is to be complied with.

(5) A notice may require the production of documents or any description of documents.

(6) An enforcer may take copies of any documents produced in compliance with such a requirement.

(7) A notice may be varied or revoked by a subsequent notice.

(8) But a notice must not require a person to provide any information or produce any document which he would be entitled to refuse to provide or produce—

(a) in proceedings in the High Court on the grounds of legal professional privilege;

(b) in proceedings in the Court of Session on the grounds of confidentiality of communications.

227 Notices: enforcement

(1) If a person fails to comply with a notice given under section 224 or 225 the enforcer who gave the notice may make an application under this section.

(2) If it appears to the court that the person to whom the notice was given has failed to comply with the notice the court may make an order under this section.

(3) An order under this section may require the person to whom the notice was given to do anything the court thinks it is reasonable for him to do for any of the purposes mentioned in section 224 or 225 (as the case may be) to ensure that the notice is complied with.

(4) An order under this section may require the person to meet all the costs or expenses of the application.

(5) If the person is a company or association the court in proceeding under subsection (4) may require any officer of the company or association who is responsible for the failure to meet the costs or expenses.

(6) The court is a court which may make an enforcement order.

(7) In subsection (5) an officer of a company is a person who is a director, manager, secretary or other similar officer of the company.

Miscellaneous

228   Evidence

(1) Proceedings under this Part are civil proceedings for the purposes of—

(a) section 11 of the Civil Evidence Act 1968 (c. 64) (convictions admissible as evidence in civil proceedings);

(b) section 10 of the Law Reform (Miscellaneous Provisions) (Scotland) Act 1968 (c. 70) (corresponding provision in Scotland);

(c) section 7 of the Civil Evidence Act (Northern Ireland) 1971 (c. 36 (N.I.)) (corresponding provision in Northern Ireland).

(2) In proceedings under this Part any finding by a court in civil proceedings that an act or omission mentioned in section 211(2)(b), (c) or (d) or 212(1) has occurred—

(a) is admissible as evidence that the act or omission occurred;

(b) unless the contrary is proved, is sufficient evidence that the act or omission occurred.

(3) But subsection (2) does not apply to any finding—

(a) which has been reversed on appeal;

(b) which has been varied on appeal so as to negative it.

229   Advice and information

(1) As soon as is reasonably practicable after the passing of this Act the OFT must prepare and publish advice and information with a view to—

(a) explaining the provisions of this Part to persons who are likely to be affected by them, and

(b) indicating how the OFT expects such provisions to operate.

(2) The OFT may at any time publish revised or new advice or information.

(3) Advice or information published in pursuance of subsection (1)(b) may include advice or information about the factors which the OFT may take into account in considering how to exercise the functions conferred on it by this Part.

(4) Advice or information published by the OFT under this section is to be published in such form and in such manner as it considers appropriate.

(5) In preparing advice or information under this section the OFT must consult such persons as it thinks are representative of persons affected by this Part.

(6) If any proposed advice or information relates to a matter in respect of which another general enforcer or a designated enforcer may act the persons to be consulted must include that enforcer.

230   Notice to OFT of intended prosecution

(1) This section applies if a local weights and measures authority in England and Wales intends to start proceedings for an offence under an enactment or subordinate legislation specified by the Secretary of State by order for the purposes of this section.

(2) The authority must give the OFT—

    (a) notice of its intention to start the proceedings;

    (b) a summary of the evidence it intends to lead in respect of the charges.

(3) The authority must not start the proceedings until whichever is the earlier of the following—

    (a) the end of the period of 14 days starting with the day on which the authority gives the notice;

    (b) the day on which it is notified by the OFT that the OFT has received the notice and summary given under subsection (2).

(4) The authority must also notify the OFT of the outcome of the proceedings after they are finally determined.

(5) But such proceedings are not invalid by reason only of the failure of the authority to comply with this section.

(6) Subordinate legislation has the same meaning as in section 21(1) of the Interpretation Act 1978 (c. 30).

(7) An order under this section must be made by statutory instrument subject to annulment in pursuance of a resolution of either House of Parliament.

231 Notice of convictions and judgments to OFT

(1) This section applies if—

    (a) a person is convicted of an offence by or before a court in the United Kingdom, or

    (b) a judgment is given against a person by a court in civil proceedings in the United Kingdom.

(2) The court may make arrangements to bring the conviction or judgment to the attention of the OFT if it appears to the court—

    (a) having regard to the functions of the OFT under this Part or under the Estate Agents Act 1979 (c. 38) that it is expedient for the conviction or judgment to be brought to the attention of the OFT, and

    (b) without such arrangements the conviction or judgment may not be brought to the attention of the OFT.

(3) For the purposes of subsection (2) it is immaterial that the proceedings have been finally disposed of by the court.

(4) Judgment includes an order or decree and references to the giving of the judgment must be construed accordingly.

Interpretation

232 Goods and services

(1) References in this Part to goods and services must be construed in accordance with this section.

(2) Goods include—

    (a) buildings and other structures;

    (b) ships, aircraft and hovercraft.

(3) The supply of goods includes—

    (a) supply by way of sale, lease, hire or hire purchase;

    (b) in relation to buildings and other structures, construction of them by one person for another.

(4) Goods or services which are supplied wholly or partly outside the United Kingdom must be taken to be supplied to or for a person in the United Kingdom if they are supplied in accordance with arrangements falling within subsection (5).

(5) Arrangements fall within this subsection if they are made by any means and—

    (a) at the time the arrangements are made the person seeking the supply is in the United Kingdom, or

    (b) at the time the goods or services are supplied (or ought to be supplied in accordance with the arrangements) the person responsible under the arrangements for effecting the supply is in or has a place of business in the United Kingdom.

233 Person supplying goods
(1) This section has effect for the purpose of references in this Part to a person supplying or seeking to supply goods under—

    (a) a hire-purchase agreement;

    (b) a credit-sale agreement;

    (c) a conditional sale agreement.

(2) The references include references to a person who conducts any antecedent negotiations relating to the agreement.

(3) The following expressions must be construed in accordance with section 189 of the Consumer Credit Act 1974 (c. 39)—

    (a) hire-purchase agreement;

    (b) credit-sale agreement;

    (c) conditional sale agreement;

    (d) antecedent negotiations.

234 Supply of services
(1) References in this Part to the supply of services must be construed in accordance with this section.

(2) The supply of services does not include the provision of services under a contract of service or of apprenticeship whether it is express or implied and (if it is express) whether it is oral or in writing.

(3) The supply of services includes—

    (a) performing for gain or reward any activity other than the supply of goods;

    (b) rendering services to order;

    (c) the provision of services by making them available to potential users.

(4) The supply of services includes making arrangements for the use of computer software or for granting access to data stored in any form which is not readily accessible.

(5) The supply of services includes making arrangements by means of a relevant agreement (within the meaning of [paragraph 29 of Schedule 2 to the Telecommunications Act 1984]) for sharing the use of telecommunications apparatus.

(6) The supply of services includes permitting or making arrangements to permit the use of land in such circumstances as the Secretary of State specifies by order.

(7) The power to make an order under subsection (6) must be exercised by statutory instrument.

(8) But no such order may be made unless a draft of it has been laid before Parliament and approved by a resolution of each House.

235 Injunctions Directive
In this Part the Injunctions Directive is Directive 98/27/EC of the European Parliament and of the Council on injunctions for the protection of consumers' interests.

Crown

236 Crown
This Part binds the Crown.

Local Government Act 2003
(2003, c. 26)

[18th September 2003]

6 Protection of lenders
A person lending money to a local authority shall not be bound to enquire whether the authority has power to borrow the money and shall not be prejudiced by the absence of any such power.

12 Power to invest

A local authority may invest—

> (a) for any purpose relevant to its functions under any enactment, or
>
> (b) for the purposes of the prudent management of its financial affairs.

13 Security for money borrowed etc.

(1) Except as provided by subsection (3), a local authority may not mortgage or charge any of its property as security for money which it has borrowed or which it otherwise owes.

(2) Security given in breach of subsection (1) shall be unenforceable.

(3) All money borrowed by a local authority (whether before or after the coming into force of this section), together with any interest on the money borrowed, shall be charged indifferently on all the revenues of the authority.

(4) All securities created by a local authority shall rank equally without any priority.

Housing Act 2004
(2004, c. 34)

[18th November 2004]

PART 5   HOME INFORMATION PACKS

Preliminary

148 Meaning of 'residential property' and 'home information pack'

(1) In this Part—

'residential property' means premises in England and Wales consisting of a single dwelling-house, including any ancillary land; and

'dwelling-house' means a building or part of a building occupied or intended to be occupied as a separate dwelling (and includes one that is being or is to be constructed).

(2) References in this Part to a home information pack, in relation to a residential property, are to a collection of documents relating to the property or the terms on which it is or may become available for sale.

149 Meaning of 'on the market' and related expressions

(1) In this Part references to 'the market' are to the residential property market in England and Wales.

(2) A residential property is put on the market when the fact that it is or may become available for sale is, with the intention of marketing the property, first made public in England and Wales by or on behalf of the seller.

(3) A residential property which has been put on the market is to be regarded as remaining on the market until it is taken off the market or sold.

(4) A fact is made public when it is advertised or otherwise communicated (in whatever form and by whatever means) to the public or to a section of the public.

150 Acting as estate agent

(1) A person acts as estate agent for the seller of a residential property if he does anything, in the course of a business in England and Wales, in pursuance of marketing instructions from the seller.

(2) For this purpose—

'business in England and Wales' means a business carried on (in whole or in part) from a place in England and Wales; and

'marketing instructions' means instructions to carry out any activities with a view to—

> (a) effecting the introduction to the seller of a person wishing to buy the property; or
>
> (b) selling the property by auction or tender.

(3) It is immaterial for the purposes of this section whether or not a person describes himself as an estate agent.

Responsibility for marketing residential properties

151   Responsibility for marketing: general

(1) References in this Part to a responsible person, in relation to a residential property, are to any person who is for the time being responsible for marketing the property.

(2) Sections 152 and 153 identify for the purposes of this Part—

(a) the person or persons who are responsible for marketing a residential property which is on the market ('the property'); and

(b) when the responsibility of any such person arises and ceases.

(3) Only the seller or a person acting as estate agent for the seller may be responsible for marketing the property.

(4) A person may be responsible for marketing the property on more than one occasion.

152   Responsibility of person acting as estate agent

(1) A person acting as estate agent becomes responsible for marketing the property when action taken by him or on his behalf—

(a) puts the property on the market; or

(b) makes public the fact that the property is on the market.

(2) That responsibility ceases when the following conditions are satisfied, namely—

(a) his contract with the seller is terminated (whether by the withdrawal of his instructions or otherwise);

(b) he has ceased to take any action which makes public the fact that the property is on the market; and

(c) any such action being taken on his behalf has ceased.

(3) Any responsibility arising under this section also ceases when the property is taken off the market or sold.

153   Responsibility of the seller

(1) The seller becomes responsible for marketing the property when action taken by him or on his behalf—

(a) puts the property on the market; or

(b) makes public the fact that the property is on the market.

(2) That responsibility ceases when the following conditions are satisfied, namely—

(a) there is at least one person acting as his estate agent who is responsible for marketing the property;

(b) the seller has ceased to take any action which makes public the fact that the property is on the market; and

(c) any such action being taken on the seller's behalf has ceased.

(3) In this section the references to action taken on behalf of the seller exclude action taken by or on behalf of a person acting as his estate agent.

(4) Any responsibility arising under this section also ceases when the property is taken off the market or sold.

Duties of a responsible person where a property is on the market

154   Application of sections 155 to 158

(1) Where a residential property is on the market, a person responsible for marketing the property is subject to the duties relating to home information packs that are imposed by sections 155 to 158 until his responsibility ceases.

(2) Each of those duties is subject to any exception relating to that duty which is provided for in those sections.

(3) The duty under section 156(1) is also subject to any condition imposed under section 157.

155 Duty to have a home information pack

(1) It is the duty of a responsible person to have in his possession or under his control a home information pack for the property which complies with the requirements of any regulations under section 163.

(2) That duty does not apply where the responsible person is the seller at any time when—

  (a) there is another person who is responsible for marketing the property under section 152; and

  (b) the seller believes on reasonable grounds that the other responsible person has a home information pack for the property in his possession or under his control which complies with the requirements of any regulations under section 163.

156 Duty to provide copy of home information pack on request

(1) Where a potential buyer makes a request to a responsible person for a copy of the home information pack, or of a document (or part of a document) which is or ought to be included in that pack, it is the duty of the responsible person to comply with that request within the permitted period.

(2) The responsible person does not comply with that duty unless—

  (a) he provides the potential buyer with a document which is—

    (i) a copy of the home information pack for the property as it stands at the time when the document is provided, or

    (ii) a copy of a document (or part of a document) which is included in that pack, as the case may be; and

  (b) that pack or document complies with the requirements of any regulations under section 163 at that time.

(3) In subsection (2) 'the home information pack' means the home information pack intended by the responsible person to be the one required by section 155.

(4) That duty does not apply if, before the end of the permitted period, the responsible person believes on reasonable grounds that the person making the request—

  (a) is unlikely to have sufficient means to buy the property in question;

  (b) is not genuinely interested in buying a property of a general description which applies to the property; or

  (c) is not a person to whom the seller is likely to be prepared to sell the property.

Nothing in this subsection authorises the doing of anything which constitutes an unlawful act of discrimination.

(5) Subsection (4) does not apply if the responsible person knows or suspects that the person making the request is an officer of an enforcement authority.

(6) That duty does not apply where the responsible person is the seller if, when the request is made, the duty under section 155 does not (by virtue of subsection (2) of that section) apply to him.

(7) But where the duty under this section is excluded by subsection (6), it is the duty of the seller to take reasonable steps to inform the potential buyer that the request should be made to the other person.

(8) The responsible person may charge a sum not exceeding the reasonable cost of making and, if requested, sending a paper copy of the pack or document.

(9) The permitted period for the purposes of this section is (subject to section 157(5)) the period of 14 days beginning with the day on which the request is made.

(10) If the responsible person ceases to be responsible for marketing the property before the end of the permitted period (whether because the property has been taken off the market or sold or for any other reason), he ceases to be under any duty to comply with the request.

(11) A person does not comply with the duty under this section by providing a copy in electronic form unless the potential buyer consents to receiving it in that form.

157   Section 156(1) duty: imposition of conditions

(1) A potential buyer who has made a request to which section 156(1) applies may be required to comply with either or both of the following conditions before any copy is provided.

(2) The potential buyer may be required to pay a charge authorised by section 156(8).

(3) The potential buyer may be required to accept any terms specified in writing which—

(a) are proposed by the seller or in pursuance of his instructions; and

(b) relate to the use or disclosure of the copy (or any information contained in or derived from it).

(4) A condition is only effective if it is notified to the potential buyer before the end of the period of 14 days beginning with the day on which the request is made.

(5) Where the potential buyer has been so notified of either or both of the conditions authorised by this section, the permitted period for the purposes of section 156 is the period of 14 days beginning with—

(a) where one condition is involved, the day on which the potential buyer complies with it by—

(i)   making the payment demanded, or

(ii) accepting the terms proposed (or such other terms as may be agreed between the seller and the potential buyer in substitution for those proposed),

as the case may be; or

(b) where both conditions are involved, the day (or the later of the days) on which the potential buyer complies with them by taking the action mentioned in paragraph (a)(i) and (ii).

158   Duty to ensure authenticity of documents in other situations

(1) Where a responsible person provides a potential buyer with, or allows a potential buyer to inspect, any document purporting to be—

(a) a copy of the home information pack for the property, or

(b) a copy of a document (or part of a document) included in that pack,

the responsible person is under a duty to ensure that the document is authentic.

(2) A document is not authentic for the purposes of subsection (1) unless, at the time when it is provided or inspected—

(a) it is a copy of the home information pack for the property or a document (or part of a document) included in that pack, as the case may be; and

(b) that pack or document complies with the requirements of any regulations under section 163.

(3) In subsection (2) 'the home information pack' means the pack intended by the responsible person to be the one required by section 155.

(4) The duty under this section does not apply to anything provided in pursuance of the duty under section 156.

Other duties of person acting as estate agent

159   Other duties of person acting as estate agent

(1) This section applies to a person acting as estate agent for the seller of a residential property where—

(a) the property is not on the market; or

(b) the property is on the market but the person so acting is not a person responsible for marketing the property.

(2) It is the duty of a person to whom this section applies to have in his possession or under his control, when any qualifying action is taken by him or on his behalf, a home

information pack for the property which complies with the requirements of any regulations under section 163.

(3) In subsection (2) 'qualifying action' means action taken with the intention of marketing the property which—

(a) communicates to any person in England and Wales the fact that the property is or may become available for sale; but

(b) does not put the property on the market or make public the fact that the property is on the market.

(4) Where a person to whom this section applies provides a potential buyer with, or allows a potential buyer to inspect, any document purporting to be—

(a) a copy of the home information pack for the property; or

(b) a copy of a document (or part of a document) included in that pack;

it is his duty to ensure that it is an authentic copy.

(5) A document is not authentic for the purposes of subsection (4) unless, at the time when it is provided or inspected—

(a) it is a copy of the home information pack for the property or a document (or part of a document) included in that pack, as the case may be; and

(b) that pack or document complies with the requirements of any regulations under section 163.

(6) In subsection (5) 'the home information pack' means the home information pack intended by the person to whom this section applies to be the one required by subsection (2).

Exceptions from the duties

160 Residential properties not available with vacant possession

(1) The duties under sections 155 to 159 do not apply in relation to a residential property at any time when it is not available for sale with vacant possession.

(2) But for the purposes of this Part a residential property shall be presumed to be available with vacant possession, at any time when any of those duties would apply in relation to the property if it is so available, unless the contrary appears from the manner in which the property is being marketed at that time.

161 Power to provide for further exceptions

The Secretary of State may by regulations provide for other exceptions from any duty under sections 155 to 159 in such cases and circumstances, and to such extent, as may be specified in the regulations.

162 Suspension of duties under sections 155 to 159

(1) The Secretary of State may make an order suspending (or later reviving) the operation of any duty imposed by sections 155 to 159.

Contents of home information packs

163 Contents of home information packs

(1) The Secretary of State may make regulations prescribing—

(a) the documents which are required or authorised to be included in the home information pack for a residential property; and

(b) particular information which is required or authorised to be included in, or which is to be excluded from, any such document.

(2) A document prescribed under subsection (1) must be one that the Secretary of State considers would disclose relevant information.

(3) Any particular information required or authorised to be included in a prescribed document must be information that the Secretary of State considers to be relevant information.

(4) In this section 'relevant information' means information about any matter connected with the property (or the sale of the property) that would be of interest to potential buyers.

(5) Without prejudice to the generality of subsection (4), the information which the Secretary of State may consider to be relevant information includes any information about—

    (a) the interest which is for sale and the terms on which it is proposed to sell it;

    (b) the title to the property;

    (c) anything relating to or affecting the property that is contained in—

        (i) a register required to be kept by or under any enactment (whenever passed); or

        (ii) records kept by a person who can reasonably be expected to give information derived from those records to the seller at his request (on payment, if required, of a reasonable charge);

    (d) the physical condition of the property (including any particular characteristics or features of the property);

    (e) the energy efficiency of the property;

    (f) any warranties or guarantees subsisting in relation to the property;

    (g) any taxes, service charges or other charges payable in relation to the property.

(6) The regulations may require or authorise the home information pack to include—

    (a) replies the seller proposes to give to prescribed pre-contract enquiries; and

    (b) documents or particular information indexing or otherwise explaining the contents of the pack.

(7) The regulations may require a prescribed document—

    (a) to be in such form as may be prescribed; and

    (b) to be prepared by a person of a prescribed description on such terms (if any) as may be prescribed.

(8) The terms mentioned in subsection (7)(b) may include terms which enable provisions of the contract under which the document is to be prepared to be enforced by—

    (a) a potential or actual buyer;

    (b) a mortgage lender; or

    (c) any other person involved in the sale of the property who is not a party to that contract.

(9) The regulations may—

    (a) provide for the time at which any document is to be included in or removed from the home information pack; and

    (b) make different provision for different areas, for different descriptions of properties or for other different circumstances (including the manner in which a residential property is marketed).

(10) In this section 'prescribed' means prescribed by regulations under this section.

164 Home condition reports

(1) Regulations under section 163 may make the provision mentioned in this section in relation to any description of document dealing with matters mentioned in section 163(5)(d) or (e) (reports on physical condition or energy efficiency) which is to be included in the home information pack.

(2) In this section 'home condition report' means a document of that description.

(3) The regulations may require a home condition report to be made by an individual who is a member of an approved certification scheme following an inspection carried out by him in accordance with the provisions of the scheme.

(4) The regulations shall, if the provision mentioned in subsection (3) is made, make provision for the approval by the Secretary of State of one or more suitable certification schemes (and for the withdrawal by him of any such approval).

(5) The regulations shall require the Secretary of State to be satisfied, before approving a certification scheme, that the scheme contains appropriate provision—

(a) for ensuring that members of the scheme are fit and proper persons who are qualified (by their education, training and experience) to produce home condition reports;

(b) for ensuring that members of the scheme have in force suitable indemnity insurance;

(c) for facilitating the resolution of complaints against members of the scheme;

(d) for requiring home condition reports made by members of the scheme to be entered on the register mentioned in section 165;

(e) for the keeping of a public register of the members of the scheme; and

(f) for such other purposes as may be specified in the regulations.

(6) Subsection (5)(d) only applies where provision for a register of home condition reports is made under section 165.

(7) The regulations may require or authorise an approved certification scheme to contain provision about any matter relating to the home condition reports with which the scheme is concerned (including the terms on which members of the scheme may undertake to produce a home condition report).

(8) Nothing in this section limits the power under section 163 to make provision about home condition reports in the regulations.

Register of home condition reports

165 Register of home condition reports

(1) Where the provision mentioned in section 164(3) is made in relation to an approved certification scheme, regulations under section 163 may make provision for and in connection with a register of the home condition reports made by members of the scheme.

(2) The regulations may provide for the register to be kept—

(a) by (or on behalf of) the Secretary of State; or

(b) by such other person as the regulations may specify.

(3) The regulations may require a person wishing to enter a home condition report onto the register to pay such fee as may be prescribed.

(4) No person may disclose—

(a) the register or any document (or part of a document) contained in it; or

(b) any information contained in, or derived from, the register,

except in accordance with any provision of the regulations which authorises or requires such a disclosure to be made.

(5) The provision which may be made under subsection (1) includes (without prejudice to the generality of that subsection) provision as to circumstances in which or purposes for which a person or a person of a prescribed description—

(a) may (on payment of such fee, if any, as may be prescribed)—

(i) inspect the register or any document (or part of a document) contained in it;

(ii) take or be given copies of the register or any document (or part of a document) contained in it; or

(iii) be given information contained in, or derived from, the register; or

(b) may disclose anything obtained by virtue of provision made under paragraph (a).

(6) The purposes which may be so prescribed may be public purposes or purposes of private undertakings or other persons.

(7) A person who contravenes subsection (4) is guilty of an offence and liable on summary conviction to a fine not exceeding level 5 on the standard scale.

(8) Nothing in this section limits the power to make regulations under section 163.

Enforcement

166 Enforcement authorities

(1) Every local weights and measures authority is an enforcement authority for the purposes of this Part.

(2) It is the duty of each enforcement authority to enforce—

    (a) the duties under sections 155 to 159 and 167(4), and

    (b) any duty imposed under section 172(1),

in their area.

167 Power to require production of home information packs

(1) An authorised officer of an enforcement authority may require a person who appears to him to be or to have been subject to the duty under section 155 or 159(2), in relation to a residential property, to produce for inspection a copy of, or of any document included in, the home information pack for that property.

170 Right of private action

(1) This section applies where a person ('the responsible person') has committed a breach of duty under section 156 by failing to comply with a request from a potential buyer of a residential property for a copy of a prescribed document.

(2) If the potential buyer commissions his own version of the prescribed document at a time when both of the conditions mentioned below are satisfied, he is entitled to recover from the responsible person any reasonable fee paid by him in order to obtain the document.

172 Power to require estate agents to belong to a redress scheme

(1) The Secretary of State may by order require every estate agent to be a member of an approved redress scheme.

(2) Acting as estate agent for the seller of a residential property in contravention of such an order is a breach of duty under this Part.

Gambling Act 2005
(2005, c. 19)

[7th April 2005]

19 Non-commercial society

(1) For the purposes of this Act a society is non-commercial if it is established and conducted—

    (a) for charitable purposes,

    (b) for the purpose of enabling participation in, or of supporting, sport, athletics or a cultural activity, or

    (c) for any other non-commercial purpose other than that of private gain.

Mental Capacity Act 2005
(2005, c. 9)

[7th April 2005]

PART 1   PERSONS WHO LACK CAPACITY

The principles

1 The principles

(1) The following principles apply for the purposes of this Act.

(2) A person must be assumed to have capacity unless it is established that he lacks capacity.

(3) A person is not to be treated as unable to make a decision unless all practicable steps to help him to do so have been taken without success.

(4) A person is not to be treated as unable to make a decision merely because he makes an unwise decision.

(5) An act done, or decision made, under this Act for or on behalf of a person who lacks capacity must be done, or made, in his best interests.

(6) Before the act is done, or the decision is made, regard must be had to whether the purpose for which it is needed can be as effectively achieved in a way that is less restrictive of the person's rights and freedom of action.

Preliminary

2 People who lack capacity

(1) For the purposes of this Act, a person lacks capacity in relation to a matter if at the material time he is unable to make a decision for himself in relation to the matter because of an impairment of, or a disturbance in the functioning of, the mind or brain.

(2) It does not matter whether the impairment or disturbance is permanent or temporary.

(3) A lack of capacity cannot be established merely by reference to—

(a) a person's age or appearance, or

(b) a condition of his, or an aspect of his behaviour, which might lead others to make unjustified assumptions about his capacity.

(4) In proceedings under this Act or any other enactment, any question whether a person lacks capacity within the meaning of this Act must be decided on the balance of probabilities.

(5) No power which a person ('D') may exercise under this Act—

(a) in relation to a person who lacks capacity, or

(b) where D reasonably thinks that a person lacks capacity,

is exercisable in relation to a person under 16.

3 Inability to make decisions

(1) For the purposes of section 2, a person is unable to make a decision for himself if he is unable—

(a) to understand the information relevant to the decision,

(b) to retain that information,

(c) to use or weigh that information as part of the process of making the decision, or

(d) to communicate his decision (whether by talking, using sign language or any other means).

(2) A person is not to be regarded as unable to understand the information relevant to a decision if he is able to understand an explanation of it given to him in a way that is appropriate to his circumstances (using simple language, visual aids or any other means).

(3) The fact that a person is able to retain the information relevant to a decision for a short period only does not prevent him from being regarded as able to make the decision.

(4) The information relevant to a decision includes information about the reasonably foreseeable consequences of—

(a) deciding one way or another, or

(b) failing to make the decision.

4 Best interests

(1) In determining for the purposes of this Act what is in a person's best interests, the person making the determination must not make it merely on the basis of—

(a) the person's age or appearance, or

(b) a condition of his, or an aspect of his behaviour, which might lead others to make unjustified assumptions about what might be in his best interests.

(2) The person making the determination must consider all the relevant circumstances and, in particular, take the following steps.

(3) He must consider—

    (a) whether it is likely that the person will at some time have capacity in relation to the matter in question, and

    (b) if it appears likely that he will, when that is likely to be.

(4) He must, so far as reasonably practicable, permit and encourage the person to participate, or to improve his ability to participate, as fully as possible in any act done for him and any decision affecting him.

(5) Where the determination relates to life-sustaining treatment he must not, in considering whether the treatment is in the best interests of the person concerned, be motivated by a desire to bring about his death.

(6) He must consider, so far as is reasonably ascertainable—

    (a) the person's past and present wishes and feelings (and, in particular, any relevant written statement made by him when he had capacity),

    (b) the beliefs and values that would be likely to influence his decision if he had capacity, and

    (c) the other factors that he would be likely to consider if he were able to do so.

(7) He must take into account, if it is practicable and appropriate to consult them, the views of—

    (a) anyone named by the person as someone to be consulted on the matter in question or on matters of that kind,

    (b) anyone engaged in caring for the person or interested in his welfare,

    (c) any donee of a lasting power of attorney granted by the person, and

    (d) any deputy appointed for the person by the court,

as to what would be in the person's best interests and, in particular, as to the matters mentioned in subsection (6).

(8) The duties imposed by subsections (1) to (7) also apply in relation to the exercise of any powers which—

    (a) are exercisable under a lasting power of attorney, or

    (b) are exercisable by a person under this Act where he reasonably believes that another person lacks capacity.

(9) In the case of an act done, or a decision made, by a person other than the court, there is sufficient compliance with this section if (having complied with the requirements of subsections (1) to (7)) he reasonably believes that what he does or decides is in the best interests of the person concerned.

(10) 'Life-sustaining treatment' means treatment which in the view of a person providing health care for the person concerned is necessary to sustain life.

(11) 'Relevant circumstances' are those—

    (a) of which the person making the determination is aware, and

    (b) which it would be reasonable to regard as relevant.

Lasting powers of attorney

9   Lasting powers of attorney

(1) A lasting power of attorney is a power of attorney under which the donor ('P') confers on the donee (or donees) authority to make decisions about all or any of the following—

    (a) P's personal welfare or specified matters concerning P's personal welfare, and

    (b) P's property and affairs or specified matters concerning P's property and affairs,

and which includes authority to make such decisions in circumstances where P no longer has capacity.

(2) A lasting power of attorney is not created unless—

    (a) section 10 is complied with,

    (b) an instrument conferring authority of the kind mentioned in subsection (1) is made and registered in accordance with Schedule 1, and

(c) at the time when P executes the instrument, P has reached 18 and has capacity to execute it.

(3) An instrument which—

(a) purports to create a lasting power of attorney, but

(b) does not comply with this section, section 10 or Schedule 1,

confers no authority.

(4) The authority conferred by a lasting power of attorney is subject to—

(a) the provisions of this Act and, in particular, sections 1 (the principles) and 4 (best interests), and

(b) any conditions or restrictions specified in the instrument.

10 Appointment of donees

(1) A donee of a lasting power of attorney must be—

(a) an individual who has reached 18, or

(b) if the power relates only to P's property and affairs, either such an individual or a trust corporation.

(2) An individual who is bankrupt may not be appointed as donee of a lasting power of attorney in relation to P's property and affairs.

(3) Subsections (4) to (7) apply in relation to an instrument under which two or more persons are to act as donees of a lasting power of attorney.

(4) The instrument may appoint them to act—

(a) jointly,

(b) jointly and severally, or

(c) jointly in respect of some matters and jointly and severally in respect of others.

(5) To the extent to which it does not specify whether they are to act jointly or jointly and severally, the instrument is to be assumed to appoint them to act jointly.

(6) If they are to act jointly, a failure, as respects one of them, to comply with the requirements of subsection (1) or (2) or Part 1 or 2 of Schedule 1 prevents a lasting power of attorney from being created.

(7) If they are to act jointly and severally, a failure, as respects one of them, to comply with the requirements of subsection (1) or (2) or Part 1 or 2 of Schedule 1—

(a) prevents the appointment taking effect in his case, but

(b) does not prevent a lasting power of attorney from being created in the case of the other or others.

(8) An instrument used to create a lasting power of attorney—

(a) cannot give the donee (or, if more than one, any of them) power to appoint a substitute or successor, but

(b) may itself appoint a person to replace the donee (or, if more than one, any of them) on the occurrence of an event mentioned in section 13(6)(a) to (d) which has the effect of terminating the donee's appointment.

11 Lasting powers of attorney: restrictions

(1) A lasting power of attorney does not authorise the donee (or, if more than one, any of them) to do an act that is intended to restrain P, unless three conditions are satisfied.

(2) The first condition is that P lacks, or the donee reasonably believes that P lacks, capacity in relation to the matter in question.

(3) The second is that the donee reasonably believes that it is necessary to do the act in order to prevent harm to P.

(4) The third is that the act is a proportionate response to—

(a) the likelihood of P's suffering harm, and

(b) the seriousness of that harm.

(5) For the purposes of this section, the donee restrains P if he—

(a) uses, or threatens to use, force to secure the doing of an act which P resists, or

(b) restricts P's liberty of movement, whether or not P resists,

or if he authorises another person to do any of those things.

(6) But the donee does more than merely restrain P if he deprives P of his liberty within the meaning of Article 5(1) of the Human Rights Convention.

(7) Where a lasting power of attorney authorises the donee (or, if more than one, any of them) to make decisions about P's personal welfare, the authority—

    (a) does not extend to making such decisions in circumstances other than those where P lacks, or the donee reasonably believes that P lacks, capacity,

    (b) is subject to sections 24 to 26 (advance decisions to refuse treatment), and

    (c) extends to giving or refusing consent to the carrying out or continuation of a treatment by a person providing health care for P.

(8) But subsection (7)(c)—

    (a) does not authorise the giving or refusing of consent to the carrying out or continuation of life-sustaining treatment, unless the instrument contains express provision to that effect, and

    (b) is subject to any conditions or restrictions in the instrument.

12 Scope of lasting powers of attorney: gifts

(1) Where a lasting power of attorney confers authority to make decisions about P's property and affairs, it does not authorise a donee (or, if more than one, any of them) to dispose of the donor's property by making gifts except to the extent permitted by subsection (2).

(2) The donee may make gifts—

    (a) on customary occasions to persons (including himself) who are related to or connected with the donor, or

    (b) to any charity to whom the donor made or might have been expected to make gifts,

if the value of each such gift is not unreasonable having regard to all the circumstances and, in particular, the size of the donor's estate.

(3) 'Customary occasion' means—

    (a) the occasion or anniversary of a birth, a marriage or the formation of a civil partnership, or

    (b) any other occasion on which presents are customarily given within families or among friends or associates.

(4) Subsection (2) is subject to any conditions or restrictions in the instrument.

13 Revocation of lasting powers of attorney etc.

(1) This section applies if—

    (a) P has executed an instrument with a view to creating a lasting power of attorney, or

    (b) a lasting power of attorney is registered as having been conferred by P,

and in this section references to revoking the power include revoking the instrument.

(2) P may, at any time when he has capacity to do so, revoke the power.

(3) P's bankruptcy revokes the power so far as it relates to P's property and affairs.

(4) But where P is bankrupt merely because an interim bankruptcy restrictions order has effect in respect of him, the power is suspended, so far as it relates to P's property and affairs, for so long as the order has effect.

(5) The occurrence in relation to a donee of an event mentioned in subsection (6)—

    (a) terminates his appointment, and

    (b) except in the cases given in subsection (7), revokes the power.

(6) The events are—

    (a) the disclaimer of the appointment by the donee in accordance with such requirements as may be prescribed for the purposes of this section in regulations made by the Lord Chancellor,

    (b) subject to subsections (8) and (9), the death or bankruptcy of the donee or, if the donee is a trust corporation, its winding-up or dissolution,

    (c) subject to subsection (11), the dissolution or annulment of a marriage or civil partnership between the donor and the donee,

    (d) the lack of capacity of the donee.

(7) The cases are—

    (a) the donee is replaced under the terms of the instrument,

    (b) he is one of two or more persons appointed to act as donees jointly and severally in respect of any matter and, after the event, there is at least one remaining donee.

(8) The bankruptcy of a donee does not terminate his appointment, or revoke the power, in so far as his authority relates to P's personal welfare.

(9) Where the donee is bankrupt merely because an interim bankruptcy restrictions order has effect in respect of him, his appointment and the power are suspended, so far as they relate to P's property and affairs, for so long as the order has effect.

(10) Where the donee is one of two or more appointed to act jointly and severally under the power in respect of any matter, the reference in subsection (9) to the suspension of the power is to its suspension in so far as it relates to that donee.

(11) The dissolution or annulment of a marriage or civil partnership does not terminate the appointment of a donee, or revoke the power, if the instrument provided that it was not to do so.

14 Protection of donee and others if no power created or power revoked

(1) Subsections (2) and (3) apply if—

    (a) an instrument has been registered under Schedule 1 as a lasting power of attorney, but

    (b) a lasting power of attorney was not created,

whether or not the registration has been cancelled at the time of the act or transaction in question.

(2) A donee who acts in purported exercise of the power does not incur any liability (to P or any other person) because of the non-existence of the power unless at the time of acting he—

    (a) knows that a lasting power of attorney was not created, or

    (b) is aware of circumstances which, if a lasting power of attorney had been created, would have terminated his authority to act as a donee.

(3) Any transaction between the donee and another person is, in favour of that person, as valid as if the power had been in existence, unless at the time of the transaction that person has knowledge of a matter referred to in subsection (2).

(4) If the interest of a purchaser depends on whether a transaction between the donee and the other person was valid by virtue of subsection (3), it is conclusively presumed in favour of the purchaser that the transaction was valid if—

    (a) the transaction was completed within 12 months of the date on which the instrument was registered, or

    (b) the other person makes a statutory declaration, before or within 3 months after the completion of the purchase, that he had no reason at the time of the transaction to doubt that the donee had authority to dispose of the property which was the subject of the transaction.

(5) In its application to a lasting power of attorney which relates to matters in addition to P's property and affairs, section 5 of the Powers of Attorney Act 1971 (c. 27) (protection where power is revoked) has effect as if references to revocation included the cessation of the power in relation to P's property and affairs.

(6) Where two or more donees are appointed under a lasting power of attorney, this section applies as if references to the donee were to all or any of them.

Powers of the court in relation to lasting powers of attorney

22 Powers of court in relation to validity of lasting powers of attorney

   (1) This section and section 23 apply if—

      (a) a person ('P') has executed or purported to execute an instrument with a view to creating a lasting power of attorney, or

      (b) an instrument has been registered as a lasting power of attorney conferred by P.

   (2) The court may determine any question relating to—

      (a) whether one or more of the requirements for the creation of a lasting power of attorney have been met;

      (b) whether the power has been revoked or has otherwise come to an end.

   (3) Subsection (4) applies if the court is satisfied—

      (a) that fraud or undue pressure was used to induce P—

         (i) to execute an instrument for the purpose of creating a lasting power of attorney, or

         (ii) to create a lasting power of attorney, or

      (b) that the donee (or, if more than one, any of them) of a lasting power of attorney—

         (i) has behaved, or is behaving, in a way that contravenes his authority or is not in P's best interests, or

         (ii) proposes to behave in a way that would contravene his authority or would not be in P's best interests.

   (4) The court may—

      (a) direct that an instrument purporting to create the lasting power of attorney is not to be registered, or

      (b) if P lacks capacity to do so, revoke the instrument or the lasting power of attorney.

   (5) If there is more than one donee, the court may under subsection (4)(b) revoke the instrument or the lasting power of attorney so far as it relates to any of them.

   (6) 'Donee' includes an intended donee.

23 Powers of court in relation to operation of lasting powers of attorney

   (1) The court may determine any question as to the meaning or effect of a lasting power of attorney or an instrument purporting to create one.

   (2) The court may—

      (a) give directions with respect to decisions—

         (i) which the donee of a lasting power of attorney has authority to make, and

         (ii) which P lacks capacity to make;

      (b) give any consent or authorisation to act which the donee would have to obtain from P if P had capacity to give it.

   (3) The court may, if P lacks capacity to do so—

      (a) give directions to the donee with respect to the rendering by him of reports or accounts and the production of records kept by him for that purpose;

      (b) require the donee to supply information or produce documents or things in his possession as donee;

      (c) give directions with respect to the remuneration or expenses of the donee;

      (d) relieve the donee wholly or partly from any liability which he has or may have incurred on account of a breach of his duties as donee.

   (4) The court may authorise the making of gifts which are not within section 12(2) (permitted gifts).

   (5) Where two or more donees are appointed under a lasting power of attorney, this section applies as if references to the donee were to all or any of them.

PART II

Proposed Statutes

(Draft) Third Parties (Rights Against Insurers) Bill
(Law Com. No. 272)

A Bill to make provision about the rights of third parties against insurers of liabilities to third parties in the case where the insured is insolvent, and in certain other cases. [2001]

Transfer of rights to third parties

1 Rights against insurer of insolvent person etc.

(1) If—

    (a) a person to whom this section applies incurs a liability against which he is insured under a contract of insurance, or

    (b) a person who is subject to a liability against which he is so insured becomes a person to whom this section applies,

the person's rights under the contract against the insurer in respect of the liability are transferred to and vest in the person to whom the liability is or was incurred.

(2) An individual is a person to whom this section applies if—

    (a) a deed of arrangement registered in accordance with the Deeds of Arrangement Act 1914 (c. 47) is in force in respect of him;

    (b) a voluntary arrangement approved in accordance with Part VIII of the Insolvency Act 1986 (c. 45) is in force in respect of him;

    (c) a bankruptcy order made against him under Part IX of that Act is in force, and the individual has not been discharged under that Part;

    (d) an award of sequestration has been made under section 5 of the Bankruptcy (Scotland) Act 1985 (c. 66) in respect of his estate, and the individual has not been discharged under that Act;

    (e) a protected trust deed within the meaning of that Act is in force in respect of his estate; or

    (f) a composition approved in accordance with Schedule 4 to that Act is in force in respect of him.

(3) A body corporate or unincorporated body is a person to whom this section applies if—

    (a) a voluntary arrangement approved in accordance with Part I of the Insolvency Act 1986 is in force in respect of it;

    (b) an administration order made under Part II of that Act is in force in respect of it;

    (c) there is a person appointed in accordance with Part III of that Act who is acting as receiver or manager of the body's property (or there would be such a person so acting but for a temporary vacancy in the office of receiver or manager);

    (d) the body is, or is being, wound up voluntarily in accordance with Chapter II of Part IV of that Act;

    (e) there is a person appointed under section 135 of that Act who is acting as provisional liquidator in respect of the body (or there would be such a person so acting but for a temporary vacancy in the office of provisional liquidator);

(f) the body is, or is being, wound up by the court following the making of a winding-up order under Chapter VI of Part IV of that Act or Part V of that Act;

(g) a compromise or arrangement between the body and its creditors (or a class of them) is in force, having been sanctioned in accordance with section 425 of the Companies Act 1985 (c. 6);

(h) the body has been dissolved under section 652 or 652A of that Act, and a court has not declared the dissolution void under section 651 of that Act or ordered the body's name to be restored to the register under section 653 of that Act;

(i) an award of sequestration has been made under section 6 of the Bankruptcy (Scotland) Act 1985 (c. 66) in respect of the body's estate, and the body has not been discharged under that Act;

(j) the body has been dissolved and an award of sequestration has been made under that section in respect of its estate;

(k) a protected trust deed within the meaning of the Bankruptcy (Scotland) Act 1985 is in force in respect of the body's estate; or

(l) a composition approved in accordance with Schedule 4 to that Act is in force in respect of the body.

(4) A trustee of a Scottish trust is, in respect of a liability of his that falls to be met out of the trust estate, a person to whom this section applies if—

(a) an award of sequestration has been made under section 6 of the Bankruptcy (Scotland) Act 1985 in respect of the trust estate, and the trust has not been discharged under that Act;

(b) a protected trust deed within the meaning of that Act is in force in respect of the trust estate; or

(c) a composition approved in accordance with Schedule 4 to that Act is in force in respect of the trust.

(5) Subsection (1) does not apply by virtue of subsection (3)(g) in relation to a liability that is transferred to another body by the order sanctioning the compromise or arrangement.

(6) Where subsection (1) applies by virtue of subsection (3)(g), it has effect to transfer rights only to a person on whom the compromise or arrangement is binding.

(7) Where—

(a) an award of sequestration made under section 5 or 6 of the Bankruptcy (Scotland) Act 1985 is recalled or reduced, or

(b) an order discharging an individual, body or trust is recalled under paragraph 17 of Schedule 4 to that Act, or reduced under paragraph 18 of that Schedule,

the award or order is to be treated for the purposes of this section as never having been made.

(8) In this section—

(a) a reference to a person appointed in accordance with Part III of the Insolvency Act 1986 (c. 45) includes a reference to a person appointed under section 101 of the Law of Property Act 1925 (c. 20);

(b) a reference to a receiver or manager of a body's property includes a reference to a receiver or manager of part only of the property and to a receiver only of the income arising from the property or from part of it;

(c) for the purposes of subsection (3)(i) to (l) 'body corporate or unincorporated body' includes any entity, other than a trust, the estate of which may be sequestrated under section 6 of the Bankruptcy (Scotland) Act 1985 (c. 66);

(d) 'Scottish trust' means a trust the estate of which may be so sequestrated.

2 Rights against insurer of individual who dies insolvent

(1) Where an individual dies insolvent while subject to a liability against which he is insured under a contract of insurance, his rights under the contract against the insurer in respect of the liability are transferred to and vest in the person to whom the liability was incurred.

(2) For the purposes of this section an individual is to be regarded as having died insolvent if, following his death—

(a) his estate falls to be administered in accordance with an order under section 421 of the Insolvency Act 1986;

(b) an award of sequestration is made under section 5 of the Bankruptcy (Scotland) Act 1985 in respect of his estate and the award is not recalled or reduced; or

(c) a judicial factor is appointed under section 11A of the Judicial Factors (Scotland) Act 1889 (c. 39) in respect of his estate and the judicial factor certifies that the estate is absolutely insolvent within the meaning of the Bankruptcy (Scotland) Act 1985.

(3) In relation to a transfer under this section of an insured person's rights, references in this Act to an insured are, where the context so requires, to be read as references to his estate.

3 Transferred rights not to exceed insured's liability

Where the liability of an insured to a third party in respect of which there is a transfer of rights under section 1 or 2 is less than the liability (apart from that section) of the insurer to the insured, no rights are transferred under that section in respect of the difference.

4 Conditions affecting transferred rights

(1) Where—

(a) rights of an insured under a contract of insurance have been transferred to a third party under section 1 or 2, and

(b) under the contract, the rights are subject to a condition that the insured has to fulfil,

anything done by the third party which, if done by the insured, would have amounted to or contributed to fulfilment of the condition is to be treated as if done by the insured.

(2) Where—

(a) rights of an insured under a contract of insurance have been transferred to a third party under section 1,

(b) the insured is a body corporate that has been dissolved,

(c) under the contract, the rights are subject to a condition requiring the insured to provide information or assistance to the insurer, and

(d) the condition is not fulfilled, but only because of the body's inability to act after being dissolved,

the transferred rights are not subject to the condition.

(3) Where—

(a) rights of an insured under a contract of insurance have been transferred to a third party under section 1 or 2, and

(b) under the contract, the rights are subject to a condition requiring the prior discharge by the insured of his liability to the third party,

the transferred rights are not subject to the condition.

(4) In the case of a contract of marine insurance, subsection (3) applies only to the extent that the liability of the insured is a liability in respect of death or personal injury.

(5) In this section—

'contract of marine insurance' has the meaning given by section 1 of the Marine Insurance Act 1906 (c. 41);

'dissolved' means dissolved under Chapter IX of Part IV of the Insolvency Act 1986 (c. 45) or under section 652 or 652A of the Companies Act 1985 (c. 6);

'personal injury' includes any disease and any impairment of a person's physical or mental condition.

5 Insurer's right of set-off

Where—

(a) rights of an insured under a contract of insurance have been transferred to a third party under section 1 or 2,

(b) the insured is under any liability to the insurer under the contract ('the insured's liability'), and

(c) if there had been no transfer, the insurer would have been entitled to set off the amount of the insured's liability against the amount of his own liability to the insured,

the insurer is entitled to set off the amount of the insured's liability against the amount of his own liability to the third party.

6 Avoidance

(1) A provision of an insurance contract to which this section applies is of no effect in so far as it purports, whether directly or indirectly, to avoid the contract or to alter the rights of the parties under it in the event of the insured—

(a) becoming a person to whom section 1 applies; or

(b) dying insolvent (within the meaning given by section 2(2)).

(2) An insurance contract is one to which this section applies if the insured's rights under it are capable of being transferred under section 1 or 2.

Provision of information etc

7 Information and disclosure for third parties

Schedule 1 (which provides for entitlement to information and disclosure on the part of persons to whom rights have or may have been transferred under this Act) has effect.

Enforcement of transferred rights

8 Proceedings in England and Wales

(1) A person who claims that rights have vested in him under section 1 or 2, but who has not established the insured's liability, may take proceedings against the insurer for either or both of the following—

(a) a declaration as to the insured's liability to him;

(b) a declaration as to the insurer's potential liability to him.

(2) The claimant in such proceedings is entitled, subject to any defence on which the insurer may rely, to a declaration under subsection (1)(a) or (b) on proof of the insured's liability or (as the case may be) the insurer's potential liability.

(3) Where proceedings are taken under subsection (1)(a) the insurer may rely on any defence on which the insured could rely if those proceedings were proceedings taken against the insured in respect of his liability.

(4) Subsection (3) is subject to sections 11(1) and 12.

(5) Where—

(a) the court makes a declaration under each of paragraphs (a) and (b) of subsection (1), and

(b) the effect of the declarations is that the insurer is liable to the claimant,

the court may give the appropriate judgment against the insurer.

(6) Where a person applying for a declaration under subsection (1)(b) is entitled or required, by virtue of provision in the contract of insurance, to do so in arbitral proceedings, he may also apply in the same proceedings for a declaration under subsection (1)(a).

(7) In its application to arbitral proceedings, subsection (5) is to be read as if 'tribunal' were substituted for 'court' and 'make the appropriate award' for 'give the appropriate judgment'.

(8) The insured may be made a defendant to an application for a declaration under subsection (1)(a); and if he is (but not otherwise), a declaration under that subsection binds him as well as the insurer.

9 Proceedings in Scotland

(1) A person who claims that rights have vested in him under section 1 or 2, but who has not established the insured's liability, may take proceedings against the insurer for either or both of the following—

  (a) a declarator as to the insured's liability to him;

  (b) a declarator as to the insurer's potential liability to him.

(2) Where proceedings are taken under subsection (1)(a) the insurer may rely on any defence on which the insured could rely if those proceedings were proceedings taken against the insured in respect of his liability.

(3) Subsection (2) is subject to sections 11(1) and 12.

(4) Where—

  (a) the court grants a declarator under each of paragraphs (a) and (b) of subsection (1), and

  (b) the effect of the declarators is that the insurer is liable to the claimant, the court may grant the appropriate decree against the insurer.

(5) Where a person applying for a declarator under subsection (1)(b) is entitled or required, by virtue of provision in the contract of insurance, to do so in arbitral proceedings, he may also apply in the same proceedings for a declarator under subsection (1)(a).

(6) In its application to arbitral proceedings, subsection (4) is to be read as if 'arbiter' were substituted for 'court' and 'make the appropriate award' for 'grant the appropriate decree'.

(7) The insured may be made a defender to an application for a declarator under subsection (1)(a); and if he is (but not otherwise) a declarator under that subsection binds him as well as the insurer.

10 Interpretation of sections 8 and 9

(1) References in sections 8 and 9 to the insurer's potential liability are references to his liability in respect of the insured's liability, if established.

(2) For the purposes of those sections and this section, a liability is established only when both the existence and the amount of it is established.

(3) In those sections and this section 'establish' means establish by a judgment or decree, by an award in arbitral proceedings or by an enforceable agreement.

11 Limitation and prescription

(1) Where a person takes proceedings for a declaration under section 8(1)(a), or for a declarator under section 9(1)(a), and the proceedings are started—

  (a) after the expiry of a period of limitation applicable to an action against the insured to enforce his liability, or of a period of prescription applicable to that liability, but

  (b) while such an action is in progress,

the insurer may not rely as a defence on the expiry of that period unless the insured is able to rely on it in the action against him.

(2) For the purposes of subsection (1), where an action has been concluded by a judgment or decree, or by an award, it is no longer in progress even if there is an appeal or a right of appeal.

(3) In a case where a person who has already established an insured's liability to him takes proceedings under this Act against the insurer, nothing in this Act is to be read as meaning—

  (a) that, for the purposes of the law of limitation (in England and Wales), his cause of action accrued otherwise than at the time when he established that liability; or

  (b) that, for the purposes of the law of prescription (in Scotland), the obligation in respect of which the proceedings are taken became enforceable otherwise than at that time.

(4) Subsections (2) and (3) of section 10 apply also for the purposes of this section.

12   Discharge of insured

Where—
  (a) a person takes proceedings in respect of rights that he claims have vested in him under section 1 or 2, and
  (b) after the start of those proceedings, the insured is discharged—
      (i) under Part IX of the Insolvency Act 1986 (c. 45), or
      (ii) under the Bankruptcy (Scotland) Act 1985 (c. 66) or under a protected trust deed within the meaning of that Act,

the discharge is to be disregarded in determining the liability of the insured to the claimant for the purposes of this Act.

13   Jurisdiction within the UK

(1) Where a person domiciled in England and Wales or in Scotland is entitled to take court proceedings under this Act against an insurer domiciled in another part of the United Kingdom, he may do so in the part where he himself is domiciled or in the part where the insurer is domiciled (whatever the contract of insurance may stipulate as to where proceedings are to be taken).

(2) The following provisions of the Civil Jurisdiction and Judgments Act 1982 (c. 27) (which determine whether a person is domiciled in the United Kingdom and, if so, in which part) apply for the purposes of subsection (1)—
  (a) section 41(2), (3), (5) and (6) (individuals);
  (b) section 42(1), (3), (4) and (8) (corporations and associations);
  (c) section 46(1), (3) and (7) (the Crown).

(3) In Schedule 5 to that Act (proceedings excluded from general provisions as to allocation of jurisdiction within the United Kingdom) insert at the end—
  'Proceedings by third parties against insurers
  11. Proceedings under the Third Parties (Rights against Insurers) Act 2001.'

(4) If an Act of the Northern Ireland Assembly corresponding to this Act contains—
  (a) provision to the effect that a person domiciled in Northern Ireland who is entitled to take court proceedings under that Act against an insurer domiciled in another part of the United Kingdom may do so either in Northern Ireland or in the part where the insurer is domiciled (whatever the contract of insurance may stipulate as to where proceedings are to be taken), or
  (b) provision inserting a reference to proceedings under that Act into Schedule 5 to the Civil Jurisdiction and Judgments Act 1982 (c. 27),

the provision also has effect as part of the law of England and Wales and of Scotland.

Enforcement of insured's liability

14   Effect of transfer on insured's liability

(1) Where rights in respect of an insured's liability to a third party are transferred under section 1 or 2, the third party may enforce that liability only to the extent (if any) that it exceeds the amount recoverable from the insurer by virtue of the transfer.

(2) Where—
  (a) rights in respect of an insured's liability are transferred under section 1,
  (b) the transfer occurs by virtue of subsection (2)(a), (b) or (e), subsection (3)(a), (g) or (k) or subsection (4)(b) of that section, and
  (c) the liability is one that is subject to the arrangement, trust deed or compromise in question,

the liability is to be treated as subject to the arrangement, trust deed or compromise only to the extent (if any) that the liability exceeds the amount recoverable from the insurer by virtue of the transfer.

(3) Where—
  (a) rights in respect of an insured's liability are transferred under section 1, and

(b) the liability subsequently becomes one that is subject to a composition approved in accordance with Schedule 4 to the Bankruptcy (Scotland) Act 1985 (c. 66),

the liability is to be treated as subject to the composition only to the extent (if any) that the liability exceeds the amount recoverable from the insurer by virtue of the transfer.

(4) For the purposes of this section the amount recoverable from the insurer does not include any amount that the third party is unable to recover as a result of—

(a) a shortage of assets on the insurer's part, in a case where the insurer is himself a person to whom section 1 applies or an individual who has died insolvent (within the meaning given by section 2(2)); or

(b) a limit set by the insurance contract on the fund available to meet claims in respect of a particular description of liability of the insured.

(5) In ascertaining the amount given by subsection (4)(a), the third party is to be treated as able to recover any sum that is due to him, in respect of the insurer's liability, under or by virtue of rules made under Part XV of the Financial Services and Markets Act 2000 (c. 8) (the Financial Services Compensation Scheme).

Application of Act

15 Reinsurance

This Act does not apply to a case where the liability referred to in section 1(1) or 2(1) is itself a liability incurred by an insurer under a contract of insurance.

16 Voluntarily-incurred liabilities

It is irrelevant for the purposes of section 1 or 2 whether or not the liability of the insured is or was incurred voluntarily.

17 Cases with a foreign element

Except as expressly provided, the application of any provision of this Act does not depend on whether there is a connection with England and Wales or Scotland; and in particular it does not depend on—

(a) whether or not the liability (or the alleged liability) of the insured to the third party was incurred in, or under the law of, England and Wales or Scotland;

(b) the place of residence or domicile of any of the parties;

(c) whether or not the contract of insurance (or a part of it) is governed by the law of England and Wales or Scotland;

(d) the place where any sum due under the contract of insurance is payable.

Supplemental

18 Power to amend Act

(1) The Secretary of State may by order made by statutory instrument amend this Act for the purposes of redefining—

(a) the circumstances in which a person is one to whom section 1 applies;

(b) the circumstances in which an individual is to be regarded for the purposes of section 2 as having died insolvent.

(2) An order under this section may—

(a) make such transitional provision as the Secretary of State thinks fit;

(b) make consequential amendments to other enactments.

(3) No order under this section shall be made unless a draft of it has been laid before, and approved by a resolution of, each House of Parliament.

19 Consequential amendments and repeals

(1) In subsections (1) and (3) of section 153 of the Road Traffic Act 1988 (c. 52) (bankruptcy etc of insured or secured persons not to affect claims by third parties), for 'Third Parties (Rights against Insurers) Act 1930' substitute 'Third Parties (Rights against Insurers) Act 2001'.

(2) In section 165(5) of the Merchant Shipping Act 1995 (c. 21) (which excludes the application of the Third Parties (Rights against Insurers) Act 1930 (c. 25) in relation to certain contracts of compulsory insurance against liability for pollution), for 'Third Parties (Rights against Insurers) Act 1930' substitute 'Third Parties (Rights against Insurers) Act 2001'.

(3) The enactments mentioned in Schedule 2 are repealed or revoked to the extent specified.

20 Transitional provisions and savings

(1) Subsection (1)(a) of section 1 applies where the insured became a person to whom that section applies before, as well as when he becomes such a person on or after, commencement day.

(2) Section 1(1)(b) and section 2 apply where the liability was incurred before, as well as where it is incurred on or after, commencement day.

(3) Despite its repeal by this Act, the Third Parties (Rights against Insurers) Act 1930 continues to apply in relation to—

(a) cases where the event referred to in subsection (1) of section 1 of that Act and the incurring of the liability referred to in that subsection both happened before commencement day;

(b) cases where the death of the deceased person referred to in subsection (2) of that section happened before that day.

(4) In this section 'commencement day' means the day on which this Act comes into force.

21 Short title, commencement and extent

(1) This Act may be cited as the Third Parties (Rights against Insurers) Act 2001.

(2) This Act comes into force at the end of the period of three months beginning with the day on which it is passed.

(3) Section 8 and paragraphs 3 and 4 of Schedule 1 do not extend to Scotland.

(4) Section 9 extends only to Scotland.

(5) Only section 13(1) to (3) extends to Northern Ireland.

SCHEDULES

Section 7   SCHEDULE 1

INFORMATION AND DISCLOSURE FOR THIRD PARTIES

1 Notices requesting information

(1) If a person believes on reasonable grounds—

(a) that a liability has been incurred to him,

(b) that the party who incurred the liability is insured against it under a contract of insurance,

(c) that rights of that party under the contract have been transferred to him under section 1 or 2, and

(d) that there is a person who is able to provide any information falling within sub-paragraph (2),

he may by notice in writing request from that person such information falling within that sub-paragraph as the notice may specify.

(2) The following is the information that falls within this sub-paragraph—

(a) whether there is a contract of insurance that covers the supposed liability or might reasonably be regarded as covering it;

(b) if there is such a contract—

(i) who the insurer is;

    (ii) what the terms of the contract are;

    (iii) whether the insurer has informed the insured that he does not consider himself to be liable under the contract in respect of the supposed liability;

    (iv) whether there are or have been any proceedings between the insurer and the insured in respect of the supposed liability and, if so, relevant details of those proceedings;

    (v) in a case where the contract sets a limit on the fund available to meet claims in respect of the supposed liability and other liabilities, how much of it (if any) has been paid out in respect of other liabilities;

    (vi) whether there is a fixed charge to which any sums paid out under the contract in respect of the supposed liability would be subject.

    (3) For the purpose of sub-paragraph (2)(b)(iv), relevant details of proceedings are—

    (a) in the case of court proceedings—

      (i) the name of the court;

      (ii) the case number;

      (iii) the contents of all documents served in the proceedings in accordance with rules of court or with any orders made in the proceedings, and the contents of any such orders;

    (b) in the case of arbitral proceedings—

      (i) the name of the arbitrator or, in Scotland, the arbiter;

      (ii) information corresponding with that mentioned in paragraph (a)(iii).

    (4) In sub-paragraph (2)(b)(vi), in its application to Scotland, "fixed charge" means a fixed security within the meaning given by section 486(1) of the Companies Act 1985 (c. 6).

    (5) A notice given by a person under this paragraph must include particulars of the facts on which he relies for his entitlement to give the notice.

2 Provision of information where notice given under paragraph 1

    (1) A person who receives a notice under paragraph 1 shall, within the period of 28 days beginning with the day of receipt of the notice—

    (a) provide to the person who gave the notice any information specified in it that he is able to provide;

    (b) in relation to any such information that he is not able to provide, notify that person why he is not able to provide it.

    (2) Where—

    (a) a person receives a notice under paragraph 1,

    (b) there is information specified in the notice that he is not able to provide because it is contained in a document that is not in his control,

    (c) the document was at one time in his control, and

    (d) he knows or believes that it is now in another person's control,

he shall, within the period of 28 days beginning with the day of receipt of the notice, provide the person who gave the notice with whatever particulars he can as to the nature of the information and the identity of that other person.

    (3) No duty arises by virtue of this paragraph in respect of information as to which a claim to legal professional privilege or, in Scotland, to confidentiality as between client and professional legal adviser could be maintained in legal proceedings.

3 Notices requiring disclosure: defunct bodies

    (1) If—

    (a) a person has started proceedings under this Act against an insurer in respect of a liability that he claims has been incurred to him by a body corporate, and

    (b) the body is defunct,

he may by notice in writing require a person to whom sub-paragraph (2) applies to disclose to him any documents that are relevant to that liability.

(2) This sub-paragraph applies to a person if—

    (a) immediately before the time of the alleged transfer under section 1 or 2, he was an officer or employee of the body corporate; or

    (b) immediately before the body became defunct, he was—

        (i) acting as an insolvency practitioner in relation to the body (within the meaning given by section 388(1) of the Insolvency Act 1986 (c. 45)), or

        (ii) acting as the official receiver in relation to the winding up of the body.

(3) A notice under this paragraph must be accompanied by a copy of the particulars of claim required to be served in connection with the proceedings mentioned in sub-paragraph(1) or, where those proceedings are arbitral proceedings, the particulars of claim that would be required to be so served if they were court proceedings.

(4) For the purposes of this paragraph a body corporate is defunct if it has been dissolved under Chapter IX of Part IV of the Insolvency Act 1986, or under section 652 or 652A of the Companies Act 1985 (c. 6), and a court has not—

    (a) declared the dissolution void under section 651 of the Companies Act 1985; or

    (b) ordered the body's name to be restored to the register under section 653 of that Act.

4 Disclosure and inspection where notice given under paragraph 3

(1) Subject to the provisions of this paragraph and to any necessary modifications—

    (a) the duties of disclosure of a person who receives a notice under paragraph 3, and

    (b) the rights of inspection of the person giving the notice,

are the same as the corresponding duties and rights under Civil Procedure Rules of parties to court proceedings in which an order for standard disclosure has been made.

(2) A person who by virtue of sub-paragraph (1) has to serve a list of documents shall do so within the period of 28 days beginning with the day of receipt of the notice.

(3) A person who has received a notice under paragraph 3 and has served a list of documents in response to it is not under a duty of disclosure by reason of that notice in relation to any documents that he did not have to disclose at the time when he served the list.

5 Avoidance

A provision of an insurance contract is of no effect in so far as it purports, whether directly or indirectly—

    (a) to avoid the contract or to alter the rights of the parties under it in the event of a person providing any information, or giving any disclosure, that he is required to provide or give by virtue of a notice under paragraph 1 or 3; or

    (b) otherwise to prohibit or prevent a person from providing such information or giving such disclosure.

6 Other rights to information etc.

Rights to information, or to inspection of documents, that a person has by virtue of paragraph 1 or 3 are in addition to any such rights that he has apart from that paragraph.

7 Interpretation

For the purposes of this Schedule—

    (a) a person is able to provide information only if—

        (i) he can obtain it without undue difficulty from a document that is in his control, or

        (ii) where the person is an individual, the information is within his knowledge;

    (b) a thing is in a person's control if it is in his possession or if he has a right to possession of it or to inspect or take copies of it.

(Draft) Interest on Debts and Damages Bill
(Law Com. No. 287)

Draft of a Bill to amend the powers of courts to award interest on debts and damages; and for connected purposes. [2004]

1   Award of interest by High Court

For section 35A of the Supreme Court Act 1981 (c. 54) (power of High Court to award interest on debts and damages) substitute—

'35A   Power of high court to award interest on debts and damages

(1) Subsection (2) applies where, during proceedings in the High Court for the recovery of a debt, the defendant pays the whole debt to the claimant.

(2) The court may award simple or compound interest on some or all of the debt for some or all of the period—

    (a) beginning on the date when the cause of action arose, and

    (b) ending on the date of the payment.

(3) Subsections (4) and (5) apply where, in proceedings for the recovery of a debt or damages, the High Court gives judgment to any extent in favour of the claimant.

(4) In relation to an action for damages for personal injuries or death in which the court gives judgment for damages exceeding £200, it must, unless it thinks there are special reasons why it should not, award simple or compound interest on—

    (a) some or all of the damages for which it gives judgment, and

    (b) if any sum is paid in respect of damages during the proceedings, some or all of that sum, for some or all of the relevant period.

(5) Otherwise, the court may award simple or compound interest on—

    (a) some or all of the sum for which it gives judgment in respect of the debt or damages, and

    (b) if any sum is paid in that respect during the proceedings, some or all of that sum, for some or all of the relevant period.

(6) "Relevant period" means the period beginning on the date when the cause of action arose and ending—

    (a) in relation to any sum for which the court gives judgment, on the date of the judgment, and

    (b) in relation to any sum paid during the proceedings, on the date of the payment.

(7) This section is subject to rules of court.

35B   Section 35A: rate of interest, &c.

(1) In relation to an action for damages for personal injuries, interest awarded under section 35A on damages for non-pecuniary loss runs for the period for which it is awarded at such rate (or rates) as the court specifies.

(2) Otherwise, subject to rules of court, interest awarded under section 35A runs for the period for which it is awarded—

    (a) at such rate (or rates) as the Secretary of State may by order specify, or

    (b) if the court decides there are good reasons for awarding interest at some other rate (or rates), at such rate (or rates) as the court specifies.

(3) An order under subsection (2)(a) must be made by statutory instrument, which is subject to annulment in pursuance of a resolution of either House of Parliament.

(4) Where interest is awarded under section 35A, rules of court may make provision as to—

    (a) matters to which the court must have regard when deciding whether to award simple or compound interest;

    (b) circumstances in which, or heads of damage on which, compound interest may not be awarded;

    (c) the method of calculating any compound interest awarded (and, in particular, the rests to be used in the calculation);

    (d) matters to which the court must have regard when making a decision under subsection (2)(b) above.

(5) The court may not award interest under section 35A on a debt for a period during which, for whatever reason, interest already runs on it.

(6) But where interest on a debt is statutory interest under the Late Payment of Commercial Debts (Interest) Act 1998—

    (a) the court may, on the application of the claimant, award interest under section 35A for the period during which the statutory interest runs, and

    (b) if it does so, the claimant is not entitled to statutory interest under that Act for that period.

(7) Interest awarded under section 35A in respect of damages may be simple in respect of one head of damage and compound in respect of another.

(8) Interest under section 35A—

    (a) may be calculated at different rates in respect of different parts of the period for which it runs, but

    (b) may not be simple in respect of one part of that period and compound in respect of another.

(9) In section 35A and this section—

"claimant" means the person seeking the debt or damages,

"defendant" means the person from whom the claimant seeks the debt or damages, and

"personal injuries" includes any disease and any impairment of a person's physical or mental condition.

(10) Nothing in section 35A or this section affects the damages recoverable for the dishonour of a bill of exchange.'

4 Consequential amendments and repeals

(3) In section 1 of the Late Payment of Commercial Debts (Interest) Act 1998 (c. 20) (statutory interest), after subsection (2), insert—

'(2A) But that is subject to—

    (a) section 35B(6) of the Supreme Court Act 1981 (power of High Court to award interest under section 35A instead of statutory interest), and

    (b) section 69A(6) of the Country Courts Act 1984 (power of county courts to award interest under section 69 instead of statutory interest).'

PART III

....

Statutory Instruments

Consumer Transactions (Restrictions on Statements) Order 1976

(SI 1976, No. 1813)

2.—(1) In this Order—

'advertisement' includes a catalogue and a circular; 'consumer' means a person acquiring goods otherwise than in the course of a business but does not include a person who holds himself out as acquiring them in the course of a business;

'consumer transaction' means—

[(a) consumer sale, that is a sale of goods (other than an excepted sale) by a seller where the goods—

(i) are of a type ordinarily bought for private use or consumption, and

(ii) are sold to a person who does not buy or hold himself out as buying them in the course of a business.

For the purposes of this paragraph an excepted sale is a sale by auction, a sale by competitive tender and a sale arising by virtue of a contract for the international sale of goods as originally defined in section 62(1) of the Sale of Goods Act 1893 as amended by the Supply of Goods (Implied Terms) Act 1973;

(b) a hire-purchase agreement (within the meaning of section 189(1) of the Consumer Credit Act 1974) where the owner makes the agreement in the course of a business and the goods to which the agreement relates—

(i) are of a type ordinarily supplied for private use or consumption, and

(ii) are hired to a person who does not hire or hold himself out as hiring them in the course of a business;]

(c) an agreement for the redemption of trading stamps under a trading stamp scheme within section 10(1) of the Trading Stamps Act 1964 or, as the case may be, within section 9 of the Trading Stamps Act (Northern Ireland) 1965;

'container' includes any form of packaging of goods whether by way of wholly or partly enclosing the goods or by way of attaching the goods to, or winding the goods round, some other article, and in particular includes a wrapper or confining band;

'statutory rights' means the rights arising by virtue of sections 13 to 15 of the Sale of Goods Act 1893 as amended by the Act of 1973, sections 9 to 11 of the Act of 1973, or [sections 4, 9, 11D or 11J of the Supply of Goods and Services Act 1982].

(2) The Interpretation Act 1889 shall apply for the interpretation of this Order as it applies for the interpretation of an Act of Parliament.

3. A person shall not, in the course of a business—

(a) display, at any place where consumer transactions are effected (whether wholly or partly), a notice containing a statement which purports to apply, in relation to consumer transactions effected there, a term which would—

(i) [be void by virtue of section 6 or 20 of the Unfair Contract Terms Act 1977,]

(ii) be inconsistent with [a term implied by sections 4, 9, 11D or 11J of the Supply of Goods and Services Act 1982], if applied to some or all such consumer transactions;

(b) publish or cause to be published any advertisement which is intended to induce persons to enter into consumer transactions and which contains a statement purporting to apply in relation to such consumer transactions such a term as is mentioned in paragraph (a)(i) or (ii), being a term which would be void by virtue of, or as the case may be, inconsistent with, the provisions so mentioned if applied to some or all of those transactions;

(c) supply to a consumer pursuant to a consumer transaction goods bearing, or goods in a container bearing, a statement which is a term of that consumer transaction and which is void by virtue of, or inconsistent with, the said provisions, or if it were a term of that transaction, would be so void or inconsistent;

(d) furnish to a consumer in connection with the carrying out of a consumer transaction or to a person likely, as a consumer, to enter into such a transaction, a document which includes a statement which is a term of that transaction and is void or inconsistent as aforesaid, or, if it were a term of that transaction or were to become a term of a prospective transaction, would be so void or inconsistent.

4. A person shall not in the course of a business—

(i) supply to a consumer pursuant to a consumer transaction goods bearing, or goods in a container bearing, a statement about the rights that the consumer has against that person or about the obligations to the consumer accepted by that person in relation to the goods (whether legally enforceable or not), being rights or obligations that arise if the goods are defective or are not fit for a purpose or do not correspond with a description;

(ii) furnish to a consumer in connection with the carrying out of a consumer transaction or to a person likely, as a consumer, to enter into such a transaction with him or through his agency a document containing a statement about such rights and obligations,

unless there is in close proximity to any such statement another statement which is clear and conspicuous and to the effect that the first mentioned statement does not or will not affect the statutory rights of a consumer.

5.—(1) This Article applies to goods which are supplied in the course of a business by one person ('the supplier') to another where, at the time of the supply, the goods were intended by the supplier to be, or might reasonably be expected by him to be, the subject of a subsequent consumer transaction.

(2) A supplier shall not—

(a) supply goods to which this Article applies if the goods bear, or are in a container bearing, a statement which sets out or describes or limits obligations (whether legally enforceable or not) accepted or to be accepted by him in relation to the goods; or

(b) furnish a document in relation to the goods which contains such a statement, unless there is in close proximity to any such statement another statement which is clear and conspicuous and to the effect that the first mentioned statement does not or will not affect the statutory rights of a consumer.

(3) A person does not contravene paragraph (2) above—

(i) in a case to which sub-paragraph (a) of that paragraph applies, unless the goods have become the subject of a consumer transaction;

(ii) in a case to which sub-paragraph (b) applies, unless the document has been furnished to a consumer in relation to goods which were the subject of a consumer transaction, or to a person likely to become a consumer pursuant to such a transaction; or

(iii) by virtue of any statement if before the date on which this Article comes into operation the document containing, or the goods or container bearing, the statement has ceased to be in his possession.

Business Advertisements (Disclosure) Order 1977
(SI 1977, No. 1918)

2.—(1) Subject to paragraphs (2) and (3) below, a person who is seeking to sell goods that are being sold in the course of a business shall not publish or cause to be published an advertisement—
   (a) which indicates that the goods are for sale, and
   (b) which is likely to induce consumers to buy the goods, unless it is reasonably clear whether from the contents of the advertisement, its format or size, the place or manner of its publication or otherwise that the goods are to be sold in the course of a business.

(2) Paragraph (1) applies whether the person who is seeking to sell the goods is acting on his own behalf or that of another, and where he is acting as agent, whether he is acting in the course of a business carried on by him or not; but the reference in that paragraph to a business does not include any business carried on by the agent.

(3) Paragraph (1) above shall not apply in relation to advertisements—
   (a) which are concerned only with sales by auction or competitive tender; or
   (b) which are concerned only with the sale of flowers, fruit or vegetables, eggs or dead animals, fish or birds, gathered, produced or taken by the person seeking to sell the goods.

Consumer Protection (Cancellation of Contracts Concluded away from Business Premises) Regulations 1987
(SI 1987, No. 2117)

2 Interpretation
(1) In these Regulations—

'business' includes a trade or profession;

'consumer' means a person, other than a body corporate, who, in making a contract to which these Regulations apply, is acting for purposes which can be regarded as outside his business;

['enforcement authority' means, in Great Britain, a weights and measures authority and, in Northern Ireland, the Department of Economic Development;]

'goods' has the meaning given by section 61(1) of the Sale of Goods Act 1979;

'land mortgage' includes any security charged on land and in relation to Scotland includes any heritable security;

'notice of cancellation' has the meaning given by regulation 4(5) below;

'security' in relation to a contract means a mortgage, charge, pledge, bond, debenture, indemnity, guarantee, bill, note or other right provided by the consumer, or at his request (express or implied), to secure the carrying out of his obligations under the contract;

'signed' has the same meaning as in the Consumer Credit Act 1974; and

'trader' means a person who, in making a contract to which these Regulations apply, is acting for the purposes of his business, and anyone acting in the name or on behalf of such a person.

3 Contracts to which the Regulations apply
(1) These Regulations apply to a contract, other than an excepted contract, for the supply by a trader of goods or services to a consumer which is made—
   (a) during an unsolicited visit by a trader—
      (i) to the consumer's home or to the home of another person; or
      (ii) to the consumer's place of work;

(b) during a visit by a trader as mentioned in paragraph (a)(i) or (ii) above at the express request of the consumer where the goods or services to which the contract relates are other than those concerning which the consumer requested the visit of the trader, provided that when the visit was requested the consumer did not know, or could not reasonably have known, that the supply of those other goods or services formed part of the trader's business activities;

(c) after an offer was made by the consumer in respect of the supply by a trader of the goods or services in the circumstances mentioned in paragraph (a) or (b) above or (d) below; or

(d) during an excursion organised by the trader away from premises on which he is carrying on any business (whether on a permanent or temporary basis).

(2) For the purposes of this regulation an excepted contract means;

(a) any contract—
  (i) for the sale or other disposition of land, or for a lease or land mortgage;
  (ii) to finance the purchase of land;
  (iii) for a bridging loan in connection with the purchase of land; or
  (iv) for the construction or extension of a building or other erection on land: Provided that these Regulations shall apply to a contract for the supply of goods and their incorporation in any land or a contract for the repair or improvement of a building or other erection on land, where the contract is not financed by a loan secured by a land mortgage;

(b) any contract for the supply of food, drink or other goods intended for current consumption by use in the household and supplied by regular roundsmen;

(c) any contract for the supply of goods or services which satisfies all the following conditions, namely—
  (i) terms of the contract are contained in a trader's catalogue which is readily available to the consumer to read in the absence of the trader or his representative before the conclusion of the contract;
  (ii) the parties to the contract intend that there shall be maintained continuity of contact between the trader or his representative and the consumer in relation to the transaction in question or any subsequent transaction; and
  (iii) both the catalogue and the contract contain or are accompanied by a prominent notice indicating that the consumer has a right to return to the trader or his representative goods supplied to him within the period of not less than 7 days from the day on which the goods are received by the consumer and otherwise to cancel the contract within that period without the consumer incurring any liability, other than any liability which may arise from the failure of the consumer to take reasonable care of the goods while they are in his possession;

[(d) contracts of insurance;]

[(e) any agreement the making or performance by which of either party constitutes a relevant regulated activity;]

(f) any contract not falling within sub-paragraph (g) below under which the total payments to be made by the consumer do not exceed £35; and

(g) any contract under which credit within the meaning of the Consumer Credit Act 1974 is provided not exceeding £35 other than a hire-purchase or conditional sale agreement.

[(3) In this regulation 'unsolicited visit' means a visit by a trader, whether or not he is the trader who supplies the goods or services, which does not take place at the express request of the consumer and includes—

(a) a visit by a trader which takes place after he, or a person acting in his name or on his behalf, telephones the consumer (otherwise than at the consumer's express request) and indicates during the course of the telephone call (either expressly or by implication) that he, or the trader in whose name or on whose behalf he is acting, is willing to visit the consumer; and

(b) a visit by a trader which takes place after he, or a person acting in his name or on his behalf, visits the consumer (otherwise than at the consumer's express request) and indicates during the course of that visit (either expressly or by implication) that he, or the trader in whose name or on whose behalf he is acting, is willing to make a subsequent visit to the consumer.]

[(4) For the purposes of paragraph (2)(e)—

(a) 'a relevant regulated activity' means an activity of the following kind, namely—

    (i)   dealing in investments, as principal or as agent,

    (ii) arranging deals in investments,

    (iii) managing investments,

    (iv) safeguarding and administering investments,

    (v) establishing etc. a collective investment scheme; and

(b) 'investment' means—

    (i)   shares,

    (ii)   instruments creating or acknowledging indebtedness,

    (iii) government and public securities,

    (iv) instruments giving entitlement to investments,

    (v)   certificates representing securities,

    (vi) units in a collective investment scheme,

    (vii) options,

    (viii) futures,

    (ix) contracts for differences, and

    (x)   rights to or interests in investments.

(5) Paragraphs (2)(d) and (4) must be read with—

(a) section 22 of the Financial Services and Markets Act 2000;

(b) any relevant order under that section; and

(c) Schedule 2 to that Act,

but any restriction on or exclusion from the meaning of a regulated activity (which is a relevant regulated activity for the purposes of paragraph (2)(e)) which arises from the identity of the person carrying it on is to be disregarded.]

4 Cancellation of contract

(1) No contract to which these Regulations apply shall be enforceable against the consumer unless the trader has delivered to the consumer notice in writing in accordance with paragraphs (3) and (4) below indicating the right of the consumer to cancel the contract within the period of 7 days mentioned in paragraph (5) below containing both the information set out in Part I of the Schedule to these Regulations and a Cancellation Form in the form set out in Part II of the Schedule and completed in accordance with the footnotes.

(2) Paragraph (1) above does not apply to a cancellable agreement within the meaning of the Consumer Credit Act 1974 or to an agreement which may be cancelled by the consumer in accordance with terms of the agreement conferring upon him similar rights as if the agreement were such a cancellable agreement.

(3) The information to be contained in the notice under paragraph (1) above shall be easily legible and if incorporated in the contract or other document shall be afforded no less prominence than that given to any other information in the document apart from the heading to the document and the names of the parties to the contract and any information inserted in handwriting.

(4) The notice shall be dated and delivered to the consumer—

(a) in the cases mentioned in regulation 3(1)(a), (b) and (d) above, at the time of the making of the contract; and

(b) in the case mentioned in regulation 3(1)(c) above, at the time of the making of the offer by the consumer.

(5) If within the period of 7 days following the making of the contract the consumer serves a notice in writing (a 'notice of cancellation') on the trader or any other person specified in a notice referred to in paragraph (1) above as a person to whom notice of cancellation may be given which, however expressed and whether or not conforming to the cancellation form set out in Part II of the Schedule to these Regulations, indicates the intention of the consumer to cancel the contract, the notice of cancellation shall operate to cancel the contract.

(6) Except as otherwise provided under these Regulations, a contract cancelled under paragraph (5) above shall be treated as if it had never been entered into by the consumer.

(7) Notwithstanding anything in section 7 of the Interpretation Act 1978, a notice of cancellation sent by post by a consumer shall be deemed to have been served at the time of posting, whether or not it is actually received.

[4A   Offence relating to the failure to provide notice of cancellation rights

(1) A trader is guilty of an offence if he enters into a contract to which these Regulations apply (other than an agreement referred to in regulation 4(2) above) with a consumer but fails (or, in the case mentioned in regulation 3(1)(c) above, has failed) to deliver to the consumer the notice in writing referred to in regulation 4(1) above in accordance with paragraph (2) below.

(2) A notice is delivered in accordance with this paragraph if it—
  (a) contains what is required by regulation 4(1) above;
  (b) complies with the requirements of regulation 4(3) above; and
  (c) is dated and delivered to the consumer at the time specified in regulation 4(4) above.

(3) A person who is guilty of an offence under paragraph (1) above shall be liable on summary conviction to a fine not exceeding level 4 on the standard scale.]

[4B   Defence of due diligence

(1) In proceedings against any person for an offence under regulation 4A above it shall be a defence for that person to show that he took all reasonable steps and exercised all due diligence to avoid committing the offence.

(2) Where in proceedings against a person for such an offence the defence provided for by paragraph (1) above involves an allegation that the commission of the offence was due—
  (a) to the act or default of another, or
  (b) to reliance on information given by another,
that person shall not, without the leave of the court, be entitled to rely on the defence unless he has served a notice under paragraph (3) below on the person bringing the proceedings not less than seven clear days before the hearing of the proceedings or, in Scotland, the diet of the trial.

(3) A notice under this paragraph shall give such information identifying or assisting in the identification of the person who committed the act or default or gave the information as is in the possession of the person serving the notice at the time when he serves it.]

[4C   Liability of persons other than the principal offender

(1) Where the commission by a person of an offence under regulation 4A above is due to the act or default of some other person, that other person is guilty of the offence and may be proceeded against and punished by virtue of this regulation whether or not proceedings are taken against the first-mentioned person.

(2) Where a body corporate is guilty of an offence under regulation 4A above in respect of any act or default which is shown to have been committed with the consent or connivance of, or to be attributable to any neglect on the part of, any director, manager, secretary or other similar officer of the body corporate or any person who was purporting to act in any such capacity he, as well as the body corporate, shall be guilty of that offence and shall be liable to be proceeded against and punished accordingly.

(3) Where the affairs of a body corporate are managed by its members, paragraph (2) above shall apply in relation to the acts and defaults of a member in connection with his functions of management as if he were a director of the body corporate.

(4) Where an offence under regulation 4A above committed in Scotland by a Scottish partnership is proved to have been committed with the consent or connivance of, or to be attributable to neglect on the part of, a partner, he (as well as the partnership) is guilty of the offence and liable to be proceeded against and punished. accordingly.]

[4D   Duty to enforce regulation 4A

(1) Subject to paragraph (2) below—
  (a) it shall be the duty of every weights and measures authority in Great Britain to enforce regulation 4A above within its area; and
  (b) it shall be the duty of the Department of Economic Development to enforce regulation 4A above in Northern Ireland.

(2) Nothing in paragraph (1) above shall authorise any weights and measures authority to bring proceedings in Scotland for an offence.]

[4E   Enforcement powers, obstruction of authorised officers and restrictions on disclosure of information

(1) If a duly authorised officer of an enforcement authority has reasonable grounds for suspecting that an offence has been committed under regulation 4A above, he may—
  (a) require a person carrying on or employed in a business to produce any book, document or record in non-documentary form relating to the business, and take copies of it or any entry in it, or
  (b) require such a person to produce in a visible and legible documentary form any information so relating which is contained in a computer, and take copies of it, for the purposes of ascertaining whether such an offence has been committed.

(2) If such an officer has reasonable grounds for believing that any books, documents or records may be required as evidence in proceedings for such an offence, he may seize and detain them and shall, if he does so, inform the person from whom they are seized.

(3) The powers of an officer under this regulation may be exercised by him only at a reasonable hour and on production (if required) of his credentials.

(4) Nothing in this regulation requires a person to produce, or authorises the taking from a person of, a book, document or record which he could not be compelled to produce in civil proceedings before the High Court or (in Scotland) the Court of Session.]

[4F

(1) A person who—
  (a) intentionally obstructs an officer of an enforcement authority acting in pursuance of his functions under these Regulations,
  (b) without reasonable cause fails to comply with the requirement made of him by regulation 4E(1) above, or
  (c) without reasonable excuse fails to give an officer of an enforcement authority acting in pursuance of his functions under these Regulations any other assistance or information which the officer has reasonably required of him for the purpose of the performance of the officer's functions under these Regulations,
is guilty of an offence.

(2) If a person, in giving information to an officer of an enforcement authority who is acting in pursuance of his functions under these Regulations—
  (a) makes a statement which he knows is false in a material particular, or
  (b) recklessly makes a statement which is false in a material particular,
he is guilty of an offence.

(3) A person guilty of an offence under paragraph (1) or (2) above shall be liable on summary conviction to a fine not exceeding level 3 on the standard scale.]

[4H
Nothing in regulations 4E or 4F above requires a person to answer any question or give any information if to do so might incriminate him.]

5   Recovery of money paid by consumer

(1) Subject to regulation 7(2) below, on the cancellation of a contract under regulation 4 above, any sum paid by or on behalf of the consumer under or in contemplation of the contract shall become repayable.

(2) If under the terms of the cancelled contract the consumer or any person on his behalf is in possession of any goods, he shall have a lien on them for any sum repayable to him under paragraph (1) above.

(3) Where any security has been provided in relation to the cancelled contract, the security, so far as it is so provided, shall be treated as never having had effect and any property lodged with the trader solely for the purposes of the security as so provided shall be returned by him forthwith.

6   Repayment of credit

(1) Notwithstanding the cancellation of a contract under regulation 4 above under which credit is provided, the contract shall continue in force so far as it relates to repayment of credit and payment of interest.

(2) If, following the cancellation of the contract, the consumer repays the whole or a portion of the credit—

(a) before the expiry of one month following service of the notice of cancellation, or

(b) in the case of a credit repayable by instalments, before the date on which the first instalment is due,

no interest shall be payable on the amount repaid.

(3) If the whole of a credit repayable by instalments is not repaid on or before the date specified in paragraph (2)(b) above, the consumer shall not be liable to repay any of the credit except on receipt of a request in writing signed by the trader stating the amounts of the remaining instalments (recalculated by the trader as nearly as may be in accordance with the contract and without extending the repayment period), but excluding any sum other than principal and interest.

(4) Repayment of a credit, or payment of interest, under a cancelled contract shall be treated as duly made if it is made to any person on whom, under regulation 4(5) above, a notice of cancellation could have been served.

(5) Where any security has been provided in relation to the contract, the duty imposed on the consumer by this regulation shall not be enforceable before the trader has discharged any duty imposed on him by regulation 5(3) above.

[(6) In this regulation, the following expressions have the meanings hereby assigned to them:—

'cash' includes money in any form;

'credit' means a cash loan and any facility enabling the consumer to overdraw on a current account;

'current account' means an account under which the customer may, by means of cheques or similar orders payable to himself or to any other person, obtain or have the use of money held or made available by the person with whom the account is kept and which records alterations in the financial relationship betwen the said person and the customer; and

'repayment', in relation to credit, means the repayment of money—

(a) paid to a consumer before the cancellation of the contract; or

(b) to the extent that he was overdrawn on his current account before the cancellation.]

7   Return of goods by consumer after cancellation

(1) Subject to paragraph (2) below, a consumer who has before cancelling a contract under regulation 4 above acquired possession of any goods by virtue of the contract shall be

under a duty, subject to any lien, on the cancellation to restore the goods to the trader in accordance with this regulation, and meanwhile to retain possession of the goods and take reasonable care of them.

(2) The consumer shall not be under a duty to restore—

(i)   perishable goods;

(ii) goods which by their nature are consumed by use and which, before the cancellation, were so consumed;

(iii) goods supplied to meet an emergency; or

(iv) goods which, before the cancellation, had become incorporated in any land or thing not comprised in the cancelled contract,

but he shall be under a duty to pay in accordance with the cancelled contract for the supply of the goods and for the provision of any services in connection with the supply of the goods before the cancellation.

(3) The consumer shall not be under any duty to deliver the goods except at his own premises and in pursuance of a request in writing signed by the trader and served on the consumer either before, or at the time when, the goods are collected from those premises.

(4) If the consumer—

(i)   delivers the goods (whether at his own premises or elsewhere) to any person on whom, under regulation 4(5) above, a notice of cancellation could have been served; or

(ii) sends the goods at his own expense to such a person, he shall be discharged from any duty to retain possession of the goods or restore them to the trader.

(5) Where the consumer delivers the goods as mentioned in paragraph (4)(i) above, his obligation to take care of the goods shall cease; and if he sends the goods as mentioned in paragraph (4)(ii) above, he shall be under a duty to take reasonable care to see that they are received by the trader and not damaged in transit, but in other respects his duty to take care of the goods shall cease.

(6) Where, at any time during the period of 21 days following the cancellation, the consumer receives such a request as is mentioned in paragraph (3) above and unreasonably refuses or unreasonably fails to comply with it, his duty to retain possession and take reasonable care of the goods shall continue until he delivers or sends the goods as mentioned in paragraph (4) above, but if within that period he does not receive such a request his duty to take reasonable care of the goods shall cease at the end of that period.

(7) Where any security has been provided in relation to the cancelled contract, the duty imposed on the consumer to restore goods by this regulation shall not be enforceable before the trader has discharged any duty imposed on him by regulation 5(3) above.

(8) Breach of a duty imposed by this regulation on a consumer is actionable as a breach of statutory duty.

8   Goods given in part-exchange

(1) This regulation applies on the cancellation of a contract under regulation 4 above where the trader agreed to take goods in part-exchange (the 'part-exchange goods') and those goods have been delivered to him.

(2) Unless, before the end of the period of ten days beginning with the date of cancellation, the part-exchange goods are returned to the consumer in a condition substantially as good as when they were delivered to the trader, the consumer shall be entitled to recover from the trader a sum equal to the part-exchange allowance.

(3) During the period of ten days beginning with the date of cancellation, the consumer, if he is in possession of goods to which the cancelled contract relates, shall have a lien on them for—

(a) delivery of the part-exchange goods in a condition substantially as good as when they were deliverd to the trader; or

(b) a sum equal to the part-exchange allowance;

and if the lien continues to the end of that period it shall thereafter subsist only as a lien for a sum equal to the part-exchange allowance.

(4) In this regulation the part-exchange allowance means the sum agreed as such in the cancelled contract, or if no such sum was agreed, such sum as it would have been reasonable to allow in respect of the part-exchange goods if no notice of cancellation had been served.

10 No contracting-out

(1) A term contained in a contract to which these Regulations apply is void if, and to the extent that, it is inconsistent with a provision for the protection of the consumer contained in these Regulations.

(2) Where a provision of these Regulations specifies the duty or liability of the consumer in certain circumstances a term contained in a contract to which these Regulations apply is inconsistent with that provision if it purports to impose, directly or indirectly, an additional duty or liability on him in those circumstances.

11 Service of documents

(1) A document to be served under these Regulations on a person may be so served—

    (a) by delivering it to him, or by sending it by post to him, or by leaving it with him, at his proper address addressed to him by name;

    (b) if the person is a body corporate, by serving it in accordance with paragraph

    (a) above on the secretary or clerk of that body; or

    (c) if the person is a partnership, by serving it in accordance with paragraph (a) above on a partner or on a person having the control or management of the partnership business.

(2) For the purposes of these Regulations, a document sent by post to, or left at, the address last known to the server of the document as the address of a person shall be treated as sent by post to, or left at, his proper address.

Regulation 4(i)   SCHEDULE

PART I   INFORMATION TO BE CONTAINED IN NOTICE OF CANCELLATION RIGHTS

1. The name of the trader.

2. The trader's reference number, code or other details to enable the contract or offer to be identified.

3. A statement that the consumer has a right to cancel the contract if he wishes and that this right can be exercised by sending or taking a written notice of cancellation to the person mentioned in paragraph 4 within the period of 7 days following the making of the contract.

4. The name and address of a person to whom notice of cancellation may be given.

5. A statement that the consumer can use the cancellation form provided if he wishes.

PART II   CANCELLATION FORM TO BE INCLUDED IN NOTICE OF CANCELLATION RIGHTS

(Complete, detach and return this form ONLY IF YOU WISH TO CANCEL THE CONTRACT.)

To: 1

I/We* hereby give notice that I/We* wish to cancel my/our* contract   2

Signed

Date

*Delete as appropriate

Notes:
  1. Trader to insert name and address of person to whom notice may be given.
  2. Trader to insert reference number, code or other details to enable the contract or offer to be identified. He may also insert the name and address of the consumer.

Control of Misleading Advertisements Regulations 1988
(SI 1988, No. 915)

2 Interpretation
  (1) In these Regulations—
  'advertisement' means any form of representation which is made in connection with a trade, business, craft or profession in order to promote the supply or transfer of goods or services, immovable property, rights or obligations;
  [...]
  'court', in relation to England and Wales and Northern Ireland, means the High Court, and, in relation to Scotland, the Court of Session;
  'Director' means the Director General of Fair Trading;
  ['licensed service' means a service in respect of which a licence has been granted under Part I or III of the Broadcasting Act 1990 or under Part I or II of the Broadcasting Act 1996;].
  ['OFCOM' means the Office of Communications established by section 1(1) of the Office of Communications Act 2002;]
  ['products with designation of origin' are those products to which Council Regulation (EEC) No. 2081/92 of 14 July 1992 applies;]
  'publication' in relation to an advertisement means the dissemination of that advertisement whether to an individual person or a number of persons and whether orally or in writing or in any other way whatsoever, and "publish" shall be construed accordingly.
  ['S4C' and 'S4C Digital' have the same meaning as in Part 3 of the Communications Act 2003; . . .].
  (2) For the purposes of these Regulations an advertisement is misleading if in any way, including its presentation, it deceives or is likely to deceive the persons to whom it is addressed or whom it reaches and if, by reason of its deceptive nature, it is likely to affect their economic behaviour or, for those reasons, injures or is likely to injure a competitor of the person whose interests the advertisement seeks to promote.
  [(2A) For the purposes of these Regulations an advertisement is comparative if in any way, either explicitly or by implication, it identifies a competitor or goods or services offered by a competitor.]

4 Complaints to the Director
  (1) Subject to paragraphs (2) and (3) below, it shall be the duty of the Director to consider any complaint made to him that an advertisement is misleading [, or is a comparative advertisement and is not permitted under regulation 4A below], unless the complaint appears to the Director to be frivolous or vexatious.
  (2) The Director shall not consider any complaint which these Regulations require or would require, leaving aside any question as to the frivolous or vexatious nature of the complaint, [OFCOM] to consider.
  (3) Before considering any complaint under paragraph (1) above the Director may require the person making the complaint to satisfy him that—
    (a) there have been invoked in relation to the same or substantially the same complaint about the advertisement in question such established means of dealing with such complaints as the Director may consider appropriate, having regard to all the circumstances of the particular case;

(b) a reasonable opportunity has been allowed for those means to deal with the complaint in question; and

(c) those means have not dealt with the complaint adequately.

(4) In exercising the powers conferred on him by these Regulations the Director shall have regard to—

(a) all the interests involved and in particular the public interest; and

(b) the desirability of encouraging the control, by self-regulatory bodies, of advertisements.

[4A   Comparative Advertisements

(1) A comparative advertisement shall, as far as the comparison is concerned, be permitted only when the following conditions are met:—

(a) it is not misleading;

(b) it compares goods or services meeting the same needs or intended for the same purpose;

(c) it objectively compares one or more material, relevant, verifiable and representative features of those goods and services, which may include price;

(d) it does not create confusion in the market place between the advertiser and a competitor or between the advertiser's trade marks, trade names, other distinguishing marks, goods or services and those of a competitor;

(e) it does not discredit or denigrate the trade marks, trade names, other distinguishing marks, goods, services, activities, or circumstances of a competitor;

(f) for products with designation of origin, it relates in each case to products with the same designation;

(g) it does not take unfair advantage of the reputation of a trade mark, trade name or other distinguishing marks of a competitor or of the designation of origin of competing products;

(h) it does not present goods or services as imitations or replicas of goods or services bearing a protected trade mark or trade name.

(2) In the case of a comparative advertisement referring to a special offer, such an advertisement is not permitted unless it indicates in a clear and unequivocal way the date on which the offer ends or, where appropriate, that the special offer is subject to the availability of the goods and services, and, where the special offer has not yet begun, the date of the start of the period during which the special price or other specific conditions shall apply.

(3) The provisions of this regulation shall not be construed as—

(a) conferring a right of action in any civil proceedings in respect of any contravention of this regulation (save as provided for in these Regulations); or

(b) derogating from any right of action or other remedy (whether civil or criminal) in proceedings instituted otherwise than by virtue of these Regulations.]

5   Applications to the Court by the Director

(1) If, having considered a complaint about an advertisement pursuant to regulation 4(1) above, he considers that the advertisement is misleading [or is a comparative advertisement and is not permitted under regulation 4A], the Director may, if he thinks it appropriate to do so, bring proceedings for an injunction (in which proceedings he may also apply for an [interim injunction]) against any person appearing to him to be concerned or likely to be concerned with the publication of the advertisement.

(2) The Director shall give reasons for his decision to apply or not to apply, as the case may be, for an injunction in relation to any complaint which these Regulations require him to consider.

6   Functions of the Court

(1) The court on an application by the Director may grant an injunction on such terms as it may think fit but (except where it grants an [interim injunction]) only if the court is satisfied

that the advertisement to which the application relates is misleading [or is a comparative advertisement and is not permitted under regulation 4A]. Before granting an injunction the court shall have regard to all the interests involved and in particular the public interest.

(2) An injunction may relate not only to a particular advertisement but to any advertisement in similar terms or likely to convey a similar impression.

(3) In considering an application for an injunction the court may, whether or not on the application of any party to the proceedings, require any person appearing to the court to be responsible for the publication of the advertisement to which the application relates to furnish the court with evidence of the accuracy of any factual claim made in the advertisement. The court shall not make such a requirement unless it appears to the court to be appropriate in the circumstances of the particular case, having regard to the legitimate interests of the person who would be the subject of or affected by the requirement and of any other person concerned with the advertisement.

(4) If such evidence is not furnished to it following a requirement made by it under paragraph (3) above or if it considers such evidence inadequate, the court may decline to consider the factual claim mentioned in that paragraph accurate.

(5) The court shall not refuse to grant an injunction for lack of evidence that—

  (a) the publication of the advertisement in question has given rise to loss or damage to any person; or

  (b) the person responsible for the advertisement intended it to be misleading or failed to exercise proper care to prevent its being misleading [; or]

  [(c) the person responsible for the comparative advertisement intended to breach the conditions in regulation 4A(1) and (2) or failed to exercise proper care to meet the conditions in regulation 4A(1) and (2).]

(6) An injunction may prohibit the publication or the continued or further publication of an advertisement.

7 Powers of the Director to obtain and disclose information and disclosure of information generally

(1) For the purpose of facilitating the exercise by him of any functions conferred on him by these Regulations, the Director may, by notice in writing signed by him or on his behalf, require any person to furnish to him such information as may be specified or described in the notice or to produce to him any documents so specified or described.

(2) A notice under paragraph (1) above may—

  (a) specify the way in which and the time within which it is to be complied with; and

  (b) be varied or revoked by a subsequent notice.

(3) Nothing in this regulation compels the production or furnishing by any person of a document or of information which he would in an action in a court be entitled to refuse to produce or furnish on grounds of legal professional privilege or, in Scotland, on the grounds of confidentiality as between client and professional legal adviser.

(4) If a person makes default in complying with a notice under paragraph (1) above the court may, on the application of the Director, make such order as the court thinks fit for requiring the default to be made good, and any such order may provide that all the costs or expenses of and incidental to the application shall be borne by the person in default or by any officers of a company or other association who are responsible for its default.

(5) Subject to any provision to the contrary made by or under any enactment, where the Director considers it appropriate to do so for the purpose of controlling misleading advertisements [or comparative advertisements which do not comply with regulation 4A], he may refer to any person any complaint (including any related documentation) about an advertisement or disclose to any person any information (whether or not obtained by means of the exercise of the power conferred by paragraph (1) above).

(7) Subject to paragraph (5) above, any person, who knowingly discloses, otherwise than for the purposes of any legal proceedings or of a report of such proceedings or the

investigation of any criminal offence, any information obtained by means of the exercise of the power conferred by paragraph (1) above without the consent either of the person to whom the information relates, or, if the information relates to a business, the consent of the person for the time being carrying on that business, shall be guilty of an offence and liable on summary conviction to imprisonment for a term not exceeding 3 months or to a fine not exceeding [level 5 on the standard scale] or to both.

(8) The Director may arrange for the dissemination in such form and manner as he considers appropriate of such information and advice concerning the operation of these Regulations as may appear to him to be expedient to give to the public and to all persons likely to be affected by these Regulations.

[8   Complaints to OFCOM

(1) It shall be the duty of OFCOM to consider any complaint made to them that any advertisement included or proposed to be included in a licensed service is misleading or is a comparative advertisement and is not permitted under regulation 4A, unless the complaint appears to OFCOM to be frivolous or vexatious.

(3) OFCOM shall give reasons for their decisions.

(4) In exercising the powers conferred on them by these Regulations OFCOM shall have regard to all the interests involved and in particular the public interest.]

[9   Control by OFCOM of misleading advertisements and comparative advertising

(1) If, having considered a complaint about an advertisement pursuant to regulation 8(1) above, they consider that the advertisement is misleading, or is a comparative advertisement and is not permitted under regulation 4A, OFCOM may, if they think it appropriate to do so, exercise in relation to the advertisement any power conferred on them by virtue of a condition included in a licence in accordance with section 325(4) of the Communications Act 2003.

(2) OFCOM may require any person appearing to them to be responsible for an advertisement which OFCOM believe may be misleading or may be a comparative advertisement which is not permitted under regulation 4A to furnish them with evidence as to the accuracy of any factual claim made in the advertisement. In deciding whether or not to make such a requirement OFCOM shall have regard to the legitimate interests of any person who would be the subject of or affected by the requirement.

(3) If such evidence is not furnished to them following a requirement made by them under paragraph (2) above within a time specified by OFCOM or if they consider such evidence inadequate, OFCOM may consider the factual claim inaccurate.]

[10   Complaints about advertisement on S4C and S4C Digital

(1) It shall be the duty of OFCOM to consider any complaint made to them that any advertisement broadcast or proposed to be broadcast on S4C or S4C Digital is misleading, or is a comparative advertisement and is not permitted under regulation 4A, unless the complaint appears to OFCOM to be frivolous or vexatious.

(3) OFCOM shall give reasons for their decisions.

(4) In exercising the powers conferred on them by these Regulations OFCOM shall have regard to all the interests involved and in particular the public interest.]

[11   Control on S4C and S4C Digital of misleading advertisements and comparative advertisements

(1) If, having considered a complaint about an advertisement pursuant to regulation 10(1) above, they consider that the advertisement is misleading, or is a comparative advertisement and is not permitted under regulation 4A, OFCOM may, if they think it appropriate to do so, exercise in relation to the advertisement, the power conferred by paragraph 14 of Schedule 12 to the Communications Act 2003.

(2) OFCOM may require any person appearing to them to be responsible for an advertisement which OFCOM believe may be misleading or may be a comparative advertisement

which is not permitted under regulation 4A to furnish them with evidence as to the accuracy of any factual claim made in the advertisement. In deciding whether or not to make such a requirement OFCOM shall have regard to the legitimate interests of any person who would be the subject of or affected by the requirement.

(3) If such evidence is not furnished to them following a requirement made by them under paragraph (2) above within a time specified by the Welsh Authority or if they consider such evidence inadequate, the Welsh Authority may consider the factual claim inaccurate.]

Consumer Credit (Exempt Agreements) Order 1989
(SI 1989, No. 869)

1 Citation, commencement, interpretation and revocation
(2) In this Order—
'the Act' means the Consumer Credit Act 1974;
'business premises' means premises for occupation for the purposes of a business (including any activity carried on by a body of persons, whether corporate or unincorporate) or for those and other purposes;
and references to the total charge for credit and the rate thereof are respectively references to the total charge for credit and the rate thereof calculated in accordance with the Consumer Credit (Total Charge for Credit) Regulations 1980.

2 Exemption of certain consumer credit agreements secured on land
(1) The Act shall not regulate a consumer credit agreement which falls within section 16(2) of the Act, being an agreement to which this paragraph applies.
(2) Where the creditor is a body specified in Part 1 of Schedule 1 to this Order, [or a deposit taker (within the meaning given by section 16(10) of the Act),] paragraph (1) above applies only to—
(a) a debtor-creditor-supplier agreement falling within section 16(2)(a) or (c) of the Act;
(b) a debtor-creditor agreement secured by any land mortgage to finance—
  (i)   the purchase of land; or
  (ii) the provision of dwellings or business premises on any land; or
  (iii) subject to paragraph (3) below, the alteration, enlarging, repair or improvement of a dwelling or business premises on any land;
(c) a debtor-creditor agreement secured by any land mortgage to refinance any existing indebtedness of the debtor, whether to the creditor or another person, under any agreement by which the debtor was provided with credit for any of the purposes specified in heads (i) to (iii) of sub-paragraph (b) above.
(3) Head (iii) of sub-paragraph (b) of paragraph (2) above applies only—
  (i)   where the creditor is the creditor under—
    (a) an agreement (whenever made) by which the debtor is provided with credit for any of the purposes specified in head (i) and head (ii) of that sub-paragraph; or
    (b) an agreement (whenever made) refinancing an agreement under which the debtor is provided with credit for any of the said purposes,
being, in either case, an agreement relating to the land referred to in the said head (iii) and secured by a land mortgage on that land; or
  (ii) where a debtor-creditor agreement to finance the alteration, enlarging, repair or improvement of a dwelling, secured by a land mortgage on that dwelling, is made as a result of any such services as are described in [section 4(3)(e) of the Housing Associations Act 1985] which are certified as having been provided by—
    (a) a local authority;
    (b) a housing association within the meaning of section 1 of the Housing Associations Act 1985 or [Article 3 of the Housing (Northern Ireland) Order 1992];

(c) a body established by such a housing association for the purpose of providing such services as are described in the said [section 4(3)(e)];

(d) a charity;

(e) the National Home Improvement Council; [. . .]

(f) the Northern Ireland Housing Executive [; or

(g) a body, or a body of any description, that has been approved by the Secretary of State under section 169(4)(c) of the Local Government and Housing Act 1989 or the Department of the Environment for Northern Ireland under article 103(4)(c) of the Housing (Northern Ireland) Order 1992].

(4) Where the creditor is a body specified in Part II of Schedule 1 to this Order, paragraph (1) above applies only to an agreement of a description specified in that Part in relation to that body and made pursuant to an enactment or for a purpose so specified.

(5) Where the creditor is a body specified in Part III of Schedule 1 to this Order, paragraph (1) above applies only to an agreement of a description falling within Article 2(2)(a) to (c) above, being an agreement advancing money on the security of a dwelling-house.

3   Exemption of certain consumer credit agreements by reference to the number of payments to be made by the debtor

(1) The Act shall not regulate a consumer credit agreement which is an agreement of one of the following descriptions, that is to say—

(a) a debtor-creditor-supplier agreement being either—

(i)   an agreement for fixed-sum credit under which the total number of payments to be made by the debtor does not exceed four, and those payments are required to be made within a period not exceeding 12 months beginning with the date of the agreement; or

(ii) an agreement for running-account credit which provides for the making of payments by the debtor in relation to specified periods and requires that the number of payments to be made by the debtor in repayment of the whole amount of the credit provided in each such period shall not exceed one;

not being, in either case, an agreement of a description specified in paragraph (2) below; and in this sub-paragraph, 'payment' means a payment comprising an amount in respect of credit with or without any other amount;

(b) a debtor-creditor-supplier agreement financing the purchase of land being an agreement under which the number of payments to be made by the debtor does not exceed four; and in this sub-paragraph, 'payment' means a payment comprising or including an amount in respect of credit or the total charge for credit (if any);

(c) a debtor-creditor-supplier agreement for fixed-sum credit to finance a premium under a contract of insurance relating to any land or to anything thereon where—

(i)   the creditor is the creditor under an agreement secured by a land mortgage on that land which either is an exempt agreement by virtue of section 16(1) of the Act or of article 2 above, or is a personal credit agreement which would be an exempt agreement by virtue of either of those provisions if the credit provided were not to exceed £15,000;

(ii) the amount of the credit is to be repaid within the period to which the premium relates, not being a period exceeding 12 months; and

(iii) there is no charge forming part of the total charge for credit under the agreement other than interest at a rate not exceeding the rate of interest from time to time payable under the agreement mentioned in head (i) above,

and the number of payments to be made by the debtor does not exceed twelve; and in this sub-paragraph 'payment' has the same meaning as it has in paragraph (1)(b) above; and

(d) a debtor-creditor-supplier agreement for fixed-sum credit where—

(i)   the creditor is the creditor under an agreement secured by a land mortgage on any land which either is an exempt agreement by virtue of section 16(1) of the Act or of article 2 above, or is a personal credit agreement which would be an exempt agreement by virtue of either of those provisions if the credit provided were not to exceed £15,000;

(ii) the agreement is to finance a premium under a contract of life insurance which provides, in the event of the death before the credit under the agreement referred to in head (i) above has been repaid of the person on whose life the contract is effected, for payment of a sum not exceeding the amount sufficient to defray the sums which, immediately after that credit has been advanced, would be payable to the creditor in respect of that credit and of the total charge for that credit; and

(iii) there is no charge forming part of the total charge for credit under the agreement other than interest at a rate not exceeding the rate of interest from time to time payable under the agreement referred to in head (i) above,

and the number of payments to be made by the debtor does not exceed twelve; and in this sub-paragraph, 'payment' has the same meaning as it has in sub-paragraph (1)(b) above.

(2) The descriptions of agreement referred to in sub-paragraph (a) of paragraph (1) above and to which accordingly that sub-paragraph does not apply are—

(a) agreements financing the purchase of land;

(b) agreements which are conditional sale agreements or hire-purchase agreements; and

(c) agreements secured by a pledge (other than a pledge of documents of title or of bearer bonds).

[4   Exemption of certain consumer credit agreements by reference to the rate of the total charge for credit

(1) The Act shall not regulate—

(a) a debtor-creditor agreement where the creditor is a credit union and the rate of the total charge for credit does not exceed 12.7 per cent;

(b) (subject to paragraph (2) below) a debtor-creditor agreement—

(i)   which is an agreement of a type offered to a particular class, or particular classes, of individuals and not offered to the public generally; and

(ii) under the terms of which the only charge included in the total charge for credit is interest which cannot at any time exceed the sum of one per cent and the highest of the base rates published by the banks named in paragraph (3) below, being the latest rates in operation on the date 28 days before any such time; or

(c) (subject to paragraph (2) below) a debtor-creditor agreement—

(i)   which is an agreement of a type offered to a particular class, or particular classes, of individuals and not offered to the public generally;

(ii) under which there can be no increase after the relevant date in the rate or amount of any item which is included in the total charge for credit or which would be included but for regulation 14 of the Total Charge for Credit Regulations; and

(iii) in respect of which the rate of the total charge for credit does not exceed the sum of one per cent and the highest of the base rates published by the banks named in paragraph (3) below, being the latest rates in operation on the date 28 days before the date on which the agreement is made.

(2) Paragraph (1)(b) and (c) above does not apply to an agreement under which the total amount to be repaid by the debtor to discharge his indebtedness in respect of the amount of credit provided may vary according to a formula which is specified in the agreement and which has effect by reference to movements in the level of any index or to any other factor.

(3) The banks referred to in paragraph (1)(b) and (c) above are—

Bank of England

Bank of Scotland

Barclays Bank PLC
Clydesdale Bank PLC
Co-operative Bank Public Limited Company
Coutts & Co
Lloyds TSB Bank plc
Midland Bank Public Limited Company
National Westminster Bank Public Limited Company
The Royal Bank of Scotland p.l.c.
(4) In this article—
'credit union' means—

   (a) a society registered under the Industrial and Provident Societies Act 1965 by virtue of section 1 of the Credit Unions Act 1979; or

   (b) a society registered under the Credit Unions (Northern Ireland) Order 1985 or a society registered under the Industrial and Provident Societies Act (Northern Ireland) 1969 as a credit union;

'interest' means interest at a rate determined in accordance with the formula set out in regulation 7(1) of the Total Charge for Credit Regulations, and in that formula as applied by paragraph (1)(b) above;

'period rate of charge' has the meaning given in regulation 7(2) of those Regulations;

'the relevant date' has the meaning given in regulation 1(2) of the Total Charge for Credit Regulations; and

'the Total Charge for Credit Regulations' means the Consumer Credit (Total Charge for Credit) Regulations 1980.]

5   Exemption of certain consumer credit agreements having a connection with a country outside the United Kingdom
The Act shall not regulate a consumer credit agreement made—

   (a) in connection with trade in goods or services between the United Kingdom and a country outside the United Kingdom or within a country or between countries outside the United Kingdom, being an agreement under which credit is provided to the debtor in the course of a business carried on by him; or

   (b) between a creditor listed in Part IV of Schedule 1 to this Order and a debtor who is—

       (i)   a member of any of the armed forces of the United States of America;

       (ii) an employee not habitually resident in the United Kingdom of any of those forces; or

       (iii) any such member's or employee's wife or husband or any other person (whether or not a child of his) whom he wholly or partly maintains and treats as a child of the family.

6   Exemption of certain consumer hire agreements
The Act shall not regulate a consumer hire agreement where the owner is a body corporate authorised by or under any enactment to supply [gas] electricity or water and the subject of the agreement is a meter or metering equipment used or to be used in connection with the supply of [gas] electricity or water, as the case may be.

Package Travel, Package Holidays and Package Tours Regulations 1992
(SI 1992, No. 3288)

2   Interpretation
(1) In these Regulations—
'brochure' means any brochure in which packages are offered for sale;

'contract' means the agreement linking the consumer to the organiser or to the retailer, or to both, as the case may be;

'the Directive' means Council Directive 90/314/EEC on package travel, package holidays and package tours;

'offer' includes an invitation to treat whether by means of advertising or otherwise, and cognate expressions shall be construed accordingly;

'organiser' means the person who, otherwise than occasionally, organises packages and sells or offers them for sale, whether directly or through a retailer;

'the other party to the contract' means the party, other than the consumer, to the contract, that is, the organiser or the retailer, or both, as the case may be;

'package' means the pre-arranged combination of at least two of the following components when sold or offered for sale at an inclusive price and when the service covers a period of more than twenty-four hours or includes overnight accommodation—

    (a) transport;

    (b) accommodation;

    (c) other tourist services not ancillary to transport or accommodation and accounting for a significant proportion of the package,

    and

       (i) the submission of separate accounts for different components shall not cause the arrangements to be other than a package;

      (ii) the fact that a combination is arranged at the request of the consumer and in accordance with his specific instructions (whether modified or not) shall not of itself cause it to be treated as other than pre-arranged;

and

'retailer' means the person who sells or offers for sale the package put together by the organiser.

(2) In the definition of 'contract' in paragraph (1) above, 'consumer' means the person who takes or agrees to take the package ('the principal contractor') and elsewhere in these Regulations 'consumer' means, as the context requires, the principal contractor, any person on whose behalf the principal contractor agrees to purchase the package ('the other beneficiaries') or any person to whom the principal contractor or any of the other beneficiaries transfers the package ('the transferee').

3 Application of Regulations

(1) These Regulations apply to packages sold or offered for sale in the territory of the United Kingdom.

4 Descriptive matter relating to packages must not be misleading

(1) No organiser or retailer shall supply to a consumer any descriptive matter concerning a package, the price of a package or any other conditions applying to the contract which contains any misleading information.

(2) If an organiser or retailer is in breach of paragraph (1) he shall be liable to compensate the consumer for any loss which the consumer suffers in consequence.

5 Requirements as to brochures

(1) Subject to paragraph (4) below, no organiser shall make available a brochure to a possible consumer unless it indicates in a legible, comprehensive and accurate manner the price and adequate information about the matters specified in Schedule 1 to these Regulations in respect of the packages offered for sale in the brochure to the extent that those matters are relevant to the packages so offered.

(2) Subject to paragraph (4) below, no retailer shall make available to a possible consumer a brochure which he knows or has reasonable cause to believe does not comply with the requirements of paragraph (1).

(3) An organiser who contravenes paragraph (1) of this regulation and a retailer who contravenes paragraph (2) thereof shall be guilty of an offence and liable—

(a) on summary conviction, to a fine not exceeding level 5 on the standard scale; and

(b) on conviction on indictment, to a fine.

(4) Where a brochure was first made available to consumers generally before 31st December 1992 no liability shall arise under this regulation in respect of an identical brochure being made available to a consumer at any time.

6   Circumstances in which particulars in brochure are to be binding

(1) Subject to paragraphs (2) and (3) of this regulation, the particulars in the brochure (whether or not they are required by regulation 5(1) above to be included in the brochure) shall constitute implied warranties (or, as regards Scotland, implied terms) for the purposes of any contract to which the particulars relate.

(2) Paragraph (1) of this regulation does not apply—

(a) in relation to information required to be included by virtue of paragraph 9 of Schedule 1 to these Regulations; or

(b) where the brochure contains an express statement that changes may be made in the particulars contained in it before a contract is concluded and changes in the particulars so contained are clearly communicated to the consumer before a contract is concluded.

(3) Paragraph (1) of this regulation does not apply when the consumer and the other party to the contract agree after the contract has been made that the particulars in the brochure, or some of those particulars, should not form part of the contract.

7   Information to be provided before contract is concluded

(1) Before a contract is concluded, the other party to the contract shall provide the intending consumer with the information specified in paragraph (2) below in writing or in some other appropriate form.

(2) The information referred to in paragraph (1) is—

(a) general information about passport and visa requirements which apply to [nationals of the member State or States concerned] who purchase the package in question, including information about the length of time it is likely to take to obtain the appropriate passports and visas;

(b) information about health formalities required for the journey and the stay; and

(c) the arrangements for security for the money paid over and (where applicable) for the repatriation of the consumer in the event of insolvency.

(3) If the intending consumer is not provided with the information required by paragraph (1) in accordance with that paragraph the other party to the contract shall be guilty of an offence and liable—

(a) on summary conviction, to a fine not exceeding level 5 on the standard scale; and

(b) on conviction on indictment, to a fine.

8   Information to be provided in good time

(1) The other party to the contract shall in good time before the start of the journey provide the consumer with the information specified in paragraph (2) below in writing or in some other appropriate form.

(2) The information referred to in paragraph (1) is the following—

(a) the times and places of intermediate stops and transport connections and particulars of the place to be occupied by the traveller (for example, cabin or berth on ship, sleeper compartment on train);

(b) the name, address and telephone number—

(i)   of the representative of the other party to the contract in the locality where the consumer is to stay,

or, if there is no such representative,

(ii) of an agency in that locality on whose assistance a consumer in difficulty would be able to call,

or, if there is no such representative or agency, a telephone number or o
information which will enable the consumer to contact the other party to the
contract during the stay; and

(c) in the case of a journey or stay abroad by a child under the age of 16 on the day
when the journey or stay is due to start, information enabling direct contact to be
made with the child or the person responsible at the place where he is to stay; and

(d) except where the consumer is required as a term of the contract to take out an
insurance policy in order to cover the cost of cancellation by the consumer or the
cost of assistance, including repatriation, in the event of accident or illness,
information about an insurance policy which the consumer may, if he wishes,
take out in respect of the risk of those costs being incurred.

(3) If the consumer is not provided with the information required by paragraph (1) in
accordance with that paragraph the other party to the contract shall be guilty of an offence
and liable—

(a) on summary conviction, to a fine not exceeding level 5 on the standard scale; and

(b) on conviction on indictment, to a fine.

9 Contents and form of contract

(1) The other party to the contract shall ensure that—

(a) depending on the nature of the package being purchased, the contract contains at
least the elements specified in Schedule 2 to these Regulations;

(b) subject to paragraph (2) below, all the terms of the contract are set out in writing
or such other form as is comprehensible and accessible to the consumer and are
communicated to the consumer before the contract is made; and

(c) a written copy of these terms is supplied to the consumer.

(2) Paragraph (1)(b) above does not apply when the interval between the time when the
consumer approaches the other party to the contract with a view to entering into a contract
and the time of departure under the proposed contract is so short that it is impracticable to
comply with the sub-paragraph.

(3) It is an implied condition (or, as regards Scotland, an implied term) of the contract
that the other party to the contract complies with the provisions of paragraph (1).

10 Transfer of bookings

(1) In every contract there is an implied term that where the consumer is prevented from
proceeding with the package the consumer may transfer his booking to a person who satisfies
all the conditions applicable to the package, provided that the consumer gives reasonable
notice to the other party to the contract of his intention to transfer before the date when
departure is due to take place.

(2) Where a transfer is made in accordance with the implied term set out in paragraph (1)
above, the transferor and the transferee shall be jointly and severally liable to the other party
to the contract for payment of the price of the package (or, if part of the price has been paid,
for payment of the balance) and for any additional costs arising from such transfer.

11 Price revision

(1) Any term in a contract to the effect that the prices laid down in the contract may be
revised shall be void and of no effect unless the contract provides for the possibility of upward
or downward revision and satisfies the conditions laid down in paragraph (2) below.

(2) The conditions mentioned in paragraph (1) are that—

(a) the contract states precisely how the revised price is to be calculated;

(b) the contract provides that price revisions are to be made solely to allow for variations in—

(i) transportation costs, including the cost of fuel,

(ii) dues, taxes or fees chargeable for services such as landing taxes or embarkation or disembarkation fees at ports and airports, or

(iii) the exchange rates applied to the particular package; and

(3) Notwithstanding any terms of a contract,
   (i) no price increase may be made in a specified period which may not be less than 30 days before the departure date stipulated; and
   (ii) as against an individual consumer liable under the contract, no price increase may be made in respect of variations which would produce an increase of less than 2 per cent, or such greater percentage as the contract may specify, ('non-eligible variations') and that the non-eligible variations shall be left out of account in the calculation.

12 Significant alterations to essential terms

In every contract there are implied terms to the effect that—
   (a) where the organiser is constrained before the departure to alter significantly an essential term of the contract, such as the price (so far as regulation 11 permits him to do so), he will notify the consumer as quickly as possible in order to enable him to take appropriate decisions and in particular to withdraw from the contract without penalty or to accept a rider to the contract specifying the alterations made and their impact on the price; and
   (b) the consumer will inform the organiser or the retailer of his decision as soon as possible.

13 Withdrawal by consumer pursuant to regulation 12 and cancellation by organiser

(1) The terms set out in paragraphs (2) and (3) below are implied in every contract and apply where the consumer withdraws from the contract pursuant to the term in it implied by virtue of regulation 12(a), or where the organiser, for any reason other than the fault of the consumer, cancels the package before the agreed date of departure.

(2) The consumer is entitled—
   (a) to take a substitute package of equivalent or superior quality if the other party to the contract is able to offer him such a substitute; or
   (b) to take a substitute package of lower quality if the other party to the contract is able to offer him one and to recover from the organiser the difference in price between the price of the package purchased and that of the substitute package; or
   (c) to have repaid to him as soon as possible all the monies paid by him under the contract.

(3) The consumer is entitled, if appropriate, to be compensated by the organiser for non-performance of the contract except where—
   (a) the package is cancelled because the number of persons who agree to take it is less than the minimum number required and the consumer is informed of the cancellation, in writing, within the period indicated in the description of the package; or
   (b) the package is cancelled by reason of unusual and unforeseeable circumstances beyond the control of the party by whom this exception is pleaded, the consequences of which could not have been avoided even if all due care had been exercised.

(4) Overbooking shall not be regarded as a circumstance falling within the provisions of sub-paragraph (b) of paragraph (3) above.

14 Significant proportion of services not provided

(1) The terms set out in paragraphs (2) and (3) below are implied in every contract and apply where, after departure, a significant proportion of the services contracted for is not provided or the organiser becomes aware that he will be unable to procure a significant proportion of the services to be provided.

(2) The organiser will make suitable alternative arrangements, at no extra cost to the consumer, for the continuation of the package and will, where appropriate, compensate the consumer for the difference between the services to be supplied under the contract and those supplied.

(3) If it is impossible to make arrangements as described in paragraph (2), or these are not accepted by the consumer for good reasons, the organiser will, where appropriate, provide the consumer with equivalent transport back to the place of departure or to another place to which the consumer has agreed and will, where appropriate, compensate the consumer.

15 Liability of other party to the contract for proper performance of obligations under contract

(1) The other party to the contract is liable to the consumer for the proper performance of the obligations under the contract, irrespective of whether such obligations are to be performed by that other party or by other suppliers of services but this shall not affect any remedy or right of action which that other party may have against those other suppliers of services.

(2) The other party to the contract is liable to the consumer for any damage caused to him by the failure to perform the contract or the improper performance of the contract unless the failure or the improper performance is due neither to any fault of that other party nor to that of another supplier of services, because—

(a) the failures which occur in the performance of the contract are attributable to the consumer;

(b) such failures are attributable to a third party unconnected with the provision of the services contracted for, and are unforeseeable or unavoidable; or

(c) such failures are due to—

(i) unusual and unforeseeable circumstances beyond the control of the party by whom this exception is pleaded, the consequences of which could not have been avoided even if all due care had been exercised; or

(ii) an event which the other party to the contract or the supplier of services, even with all due care, could not foresee or forestall.

(3) In the case of damage arising from the non-performance or improper performance of the services involved in the package, the contract may provide for compensation to be limited in accordance with the international conventions which govern such services.

(4) In the case of damage other than personal injury resulting from the non-performance or improper performance of the services involved in the package, the contract may include a term limiting the amount of compensation which will be paid to the consumer, provided that the limitation is not unreasonable.

(5) Without prejudice to paragraph (3) and paragraph (4) above, liability under paragraphs (1) and (2) above cannot be excluded by any contractual term.

(6) The terms set out in paragraphs (7) and (8) below are implied in every contract.

(7) In the circumstances described in paragraph (2)(b) and (c) of this regulation, the other party to the contract will give prompt assistance to a consumer in difficulty.

(8) If the consumer complains about a defect in the performance of the contract, the other party to the contract, or his local representative, if there is one, will make prompt efforts to find appropriate solutions.

(9) The contract must clearly and explicitly oblige the consumer to communicate at the earliest opportunity, in writing or any other appropriate form, to the supplier of the services concerned and to the other party to the contract any failure which he perceives at the place where the services concerned are supplied.

23 Enforcement

Schedule 3 to these Regulations (which makes provision about the enforcement of regulations 5, 7, 8, 16 and 22 of these Regulations) shall have effect.

24 Due diligence defence

(1) Subject to the following provisions of this regulation, in proceedings against any person for an offence under regulation 5, 7, 8, 16 or 22 of these Regulations, it shall be a defence for that person to show that he took all reasonable steps and exercised all due diligence to avoid committing the offence.

(2) Where in any proceedings against any person for such an offence the defence provided by paragraph (1) above involves an allegation that the commission of the offence was due—

(a) to the act or default of another; or

(b) to reliance on information given by another,

that person shall not, without the leave of the court, be entitled to rely on the defence unless, not less than seven clear days before the hearing of the proceedings, or, in Scotland, the trial diet, he has served a notice under paragraph (3) below on the person bringing the proceedings.

(3) A notice under this paragraph shall give such information identifying or assisting in the identification of the person who committed the act or default or gave the information as is in the possession of the person serving the notice at the time he serves it.

(4) It is hereby declared that a person shall not be entitled to rely on the defence provided by paragraph (1) above by reason of his reliance on information supplied by another, unless he shows that it was reasonable in all the circumstances for him to have relied on the information, having regard in particular—

(a) to the steps which he took, and those which might reasonably have been taken, for the purpose of verifying the information; and

(b) to whether he had any reason to disbelieve the information.

25 Liability of persons other than principal offender

(1) Where the commission by any person of an offence under regulations 5, 7, 8, 16 or 22 of these Regulations is due to an act or default committed by some other person in the course of any business of his, the other person shall be guilty of the offence and may be proceeded against and punished by virtue of this paragraph whether or not proceedings are taken against the first-mentioned person.

(2) Where a body corporate is guilty of an offence under any of the provisions mentioned in paragraph (1) above (including where it is so guilty by virtue of the said paragraph (1)) in respect of any act or default which is shown to have been committed with the consent or connivance of, or to be attributable to any neglect on the part of, any director, manager, secretary or other similar officer of the body corporate or any person who was purporting to act in any such capacity he, as well as the body corporate, shall be guilty of that offence and shall be liable to be proceeded against and punished accordingly.

(3) Where the affairs of a body corporate are managed by its members, paragraph (2) above shall apply in relation to the acts and defaults of a member in connection with his functions of management as if he were a director of the body corporate.

(5) On proceedings for an offence under regulation 5 by virtue of paragraph (1) above committed by the making available of a brochure it shall be a defence for the person charged to prove that he is a person whose business it is to publish or arrange for the publication of brochures and that he received the brochure for publication in the ordinary course of business and did not know and had no reason to suspect that its publication would amount to an offence under these Regulations.

26 Prosecution time limit

(1) No proceedings for an offence under regulation 5, 7, 8, 16 or 22 of these Regulations or under paragraphs 5(3), 6 or 7 of Schedule 3 thereto shall be commenced after—

(a) the end of the period of three years beginning within the date of the commission of the offence; or

(b) the end of the period of one year beginning with the date of the discovery of the offence by the prosecutor,

whichever is the earlier.

(2) For the purposes of this regulation a certificate signed by or on behalf of the prosecutor and stating the date on which the offence was discovered by him shall be conclusive

evidence of that fact; and a certificate stating that matter and purporting to be so signed shall be treated as so signed unless the contrary is proved.

27 Saving for civil consequences
No contract shall be void or unenforceable, and no right of action in civil proceedings in respect of any loss shall arise, by reason only of the commission of an offence under regulations 5, 7, 8, 16 or 22 of these Regulations.

28 Terms implied in contract
Where it is provided in these Regulations that a term (whether so described or whether described as a condition or warranty) is implied in the contract it is so implied irrespective of the law which governs the contract.

Regulation 5   SCHEDULE 1

INFORMATION TO BE INCLUDED (IN ADDITION TO THE PRICE)
IN BROCHURES WHERE RELEVANT TO PACKAGES OFFERED

1. The destination and the means, characteristics and categories of transport used.
2. The type of accommodation, its location, category or degree of comfort and its main features and, where the accommodation is to be provided in a member State, its approval or tourist classification under the rules of that member State.
3. The meals which are included in the package.
4. The itinerary.
5. General information about passport and visa requirements which apply for [nationals of the member State or States in which the brochure is made available] and health formalities required for the journey and the stay.
6. Either the monetary amount or the percentage of the price which is to be paid on account and the timetable for payment of the balance.
7. Whether a minimum number of persons is required for the package to take place and, if so, the deadline for informing the consumer in the event of cancellation.
8. The arrangements (if any) which apply if consumers are delayed at the outward or homeward points of departure.
9. The arrangements for security for money paid over and for the repatriation of the consumer in the event of insolvency.

Regulation 9   SCHEDULE 2

ELEMENTS TO BE INCLUDED IN THE CONTRACT IF RELEVANT
TO THE PARTICULAR PACKAGE

1. The travel destination(s) and, where periods of stay are involved, the relevant periods, with dates.
2. The means, characteristics and categories of transport to be used and the dates, times and points of departure and return.
3. Where the package includes accommodation, its location, its tourist category or degree of comfort, its main features and, where the accommodation is to be provided in a member State, its compliance with the rules of that member State.
4. The meals which are included in the package.

5. Whether a minimum number of persons is required for the package to take place and, if so, the deadline for informing the consumer in the event of cancellation.

6. The itinerary.

7. Visits, excursions or other services which are included in the total price agreed for the package.

8. The name and address of the organiser, the retailer and, where appropriate, the insurer.

9. The price of the package, if the price may be revised in accordance with the term which may be included in the contract under regulation 11, an indication of the possibility of such price revisions, and an indication of any dues, taxes or fees chargeable for certain services (landing, embarkation or disembarkation fees at ports and airports and tourist taxes) where such costs are not included in the package.

10. The payment schedule and method of payment.

11. Special requirements which the consumer has communicated to the organiser or retailer when making the booking and which both have accepted.

12. The periods within which the consumer must make any complaint about the failure to perform or the inadequate performance of the contract.

Regulation 23   SCHEDULE 3

ENFORCEMENT

1   Enforcement authority

(1) Every local weights and measures authority in Great Britain shall be an enforcement authority for the purposes of regulations 5, 7, 8, 16 and 22 of these Regulations ('the relevant regulations'), and it shall be the duty of each such authority to enforce those provisions within their area.

Property Misdescriptions (Specified Matters) Order 1992
(SI 1992, No. 2834)

2. The matters contained in the Schedule to this Order are hereby specified to the extent described in that Schedule for the purposes of section 1(1) of the Property Misdescriptions Act 1991.

SCHEDULE   SPECIFIED MATTERS

1. Location or address.
2. Aspect, view, outlook or environment.
3. Availability and nature of services, facilities or amenities.
4. Proximity to any services, places, facilities or amenities.
5. Accommodation, measurements or sizes.
6. Fixtures and fittings.
7. Physical or structural characteristics, form of construction or condition.
8. Fitness for any purpose or strength of any buildings or other structures on land or of land itself.
9. Treatments, processes, repairs or improvements or the effects thereof.

10. Conformity of compliance with any scheme, standard, test or regulations or the existence of any guarantee.

11. Survey, inspection, investigation, valuation or appraisal by any person or the results thereof.

12. The grant or giving of any award or prize for design or construction.

13. History, including the age, ownership or use of land or any building or fixture and the date of any alterations thereto.

14. Person by whom any building, (or part of any building), fixture or component was designed, constructed, built, produced, treated, processed, repaired, reconditioned or tested.

15. The length of time during which land has been available for sale either generally or by or through a particular person.

16. Price (other than the price at which accommodation or facilities are available and are to be provided by means of the creation or disposal of an interest in land in the circumstances specified in section 23(1)(a) and (b) of the Consumer Protection Act 1987 or Article 16(1)(a) and (b) of the Consumer Protection (NI) Order 1987 (which relate to the creation or disposal of certain interests in new dwellings) and previous price.

17. Tenure or estate.

18. Length of any lease or of the unexpired term of any lease and the terms and conditions of a lease (and, in relation to land in Northern Ireland, any fee farm grant creating the relation of landlord and tenant shall be treated as a lease).

19. Amount of any ground-rent, rent or premium and frequency of any review.

20. Amount of any rent-charge.

21. Where all or any part of any land is let to a tenant or is subject to a licence, particulars of the tenancy or licence, including any rent, premium or other payment due and frequency of any review.

22. Amount of any service or maintenance charge or liability for common repairs.

23. Council tax payable in respect of a dwelling within the meaning of section 3, or in Scotland section 72, of the Local Government Finance Act 1992 or the basis or any part of the basis on which that tax is calculated.

24. Rates payable in respect of a non-domestic hereditament within the meaning of section 64 of the Local Government Finance Act 1988 or, in Scotland, in respect of lands and heritages shown on a valuation roll or the basis or any part of the basis on which those rates are calculated.

25. Rates payable in respect of a hereditament within the meaning of the Rates (Northern Ireland) Order 1977 or the basis or any part of the basis on which those rates are calculated.

26. Existence or nature of any planning permission or proposals for development, construction or change of use.

27. In relation to land in England and Wales, the passing or rejection of any plans of proposed building work in accordance with section 16 of the Building Act 1984 and the giving of any completion certificate in accordance with regulation 15 of the Building Regulations 1991.

28. In relation to land in Scotland, the granting of a warrant under section 6 of the Building (Scotland) Act 1959 or the granting of a certificate of completion under section 9 of that Act.

29. In relation to land in Northern Ireland, the passing or rejection of any plans of proposed building work in accordance with Article 13 of the Building Regulations (Northern Ireland) Order 1979 and the giving of any completion certificate in accordance with building regulations made under that Order.

30. Application of any statutory provision which restricts the use of land or which requires it to be preserved or maintained in a specified manner.

31. Existence or nature of any restrictive covenants, or of any restrictions on resale, restrictions on use, or pre-emption rights and, in relation to land in Scotland, (in addition to the matters mentioned previously in this paragraph) the existence or nature of any reservations or real conditions.

32. Easements, servitudes or wayleaves.

33. Existence and extent of any public or private right of way.

Commercial Agents (Council Directive) Regulations 1993
(SI 1993, No. 3053)

[As amended by the Commercial Agents (Council Directive) (Amendment) Regulation 1993 (S.I. 1993 No. 3173) and the Commercial Agents (Council Directive) (Amendment) Regulations 1998 (S.I. 1998 No. 2868).]

PART I   GENERAL

1   Citation, commencement and applicable law

(1) These Regulations may be cited as the Commercial Agents (Council Directive) Regulations 1993 and shall come into force on 1st January 1994.

(2) These Regulations govern the relations between commercial agents and their principals and, subject to paragraph (3), apply in relation to the activities of commercial agents in Great Britain.

[(3) A court or tribunal shall:
  (a) apply the law of the other member State concerned in place of regulations 3 to 22 where the parties have agreed that the agency contract is to be governed by the law of that member State;
  (b) (whether or not it would otherwise be required to do so) apply these Regulations where the law of another member State corresponding to these Regulations enables the parties to agree that the agency contract is to be governed by the law of a different member State and the parties have agreed that it is to be governed by the law of England and Wales or Scotland.]

2   Interpretation, application and extent

(1) In these Regulations—

'commercial agent' means a self-employed intermediary who has continuing authority to negotiate the sale or purchase of goods on behalf of another person (the 'principal'), or to negotiate and conclude the sale or purchase of goods on behalf of and in the name of that principal; but shall be understood as not including in particular:
  (i) a person who, in his capacity as an officer of a company or association, is empowered to enter into commitments binding on that company or association;
  (ii) a partner who is lawfully authorised to enter into commitments binding on his partners;
  (iii) a person who acts as an insolvency practitioner (as that expression is defined in section 388 of the Insolvency Act 1986) or the equivalent in any other jurisdiction;

'commission' means any part of the remuneration of a commercial agent which varies with the number or value of business transactions;

['EEA Agreement' means the Agreement on the European Economic Area signed at Oporto on 2nd May 1992 as adjusted by the Protocol signed at Brussels on 17th March 1993;

'member State' includes a State which is a contracting party to the EEA Agreement;]

'restraint of trade clause' means an agreement restricting the business activities of a commercial agent following termination of the agency contract.

(2) These Regulations do not apply to—

(a) commercial agents whose activities are unpaid;

(b) commercial agents when they operate on commodity exchanges or in the commodity market;

(c) the Crown Agents for Overseas Governments and Administrations, as set up under the Crown Agents Act 1979, or its subsidiaries.

(3) The provisions of the Schedule to these Regulations have effect for the purpose of determining the persons whose activities as commercial agents are to be considered secondary.

(4) These Regulations shall not apply to the persons referred to in paragraph (3) above.

(5) These Regulations do not extend to Northern Ireland.

PART II   RIGHTS AND OBLIGATIONS

3 Duties of a commercial agent to his principal

(1) In performing his activities a commercial agent must look after the interests of his principal and act dutifully and in good faith.

(2) In particular, a commercial agent must—

(a) make proper efforts to negotiate and, where appropriate, conclude the transactions he is instructed to take care of;

(b) communicate to his principal all the necessary information available to him;

(c) comply with reasonable instructions given by his principal.

4 Duties of a principal to his commercial agent

(1) In his relations with his commercial agent a principal must act dutifully and in good faith.

(2) In particular, a principal must—

(a) provide his commercial agent with the necessary documentation relating to the goods concerned;

(b) obtain for his commercial agent the information necessary for the performance of the agency contract, and in particular notify his commercial agent within a reasonable period once he anticipates that the volume of commercial transactions will be significantly lower than that which the commercial agent could normally have expected.

(3) A principal shall, in addition, inform his commercial agent within a reasonable period of his acceptance or refusal of, and of any non-execution by him of, a commercial transaction which the commercial agent has procured for him.

5 Prohibition on derogation from regulations 3 and 4 and consequence of breach

(1) The parties may not derogate from regulations 3 and 4 above.

(2) The law applicable to the contract shall govern the consequence of breach of the rights and obligations under regulations 3 and 4 above.

PART III   REMUNERATION

6 Form and amount of remuneration in absence of agreement

(1) In the absence of any agreement as to remuneration between the parties, a commercial agent shall be entitled to the remuneration that commercial agents appointed for the goods forming the subject of his agency contract are customarily allowed in the place where he carries on his activities and, if there is no such customary practice, a commercial agent shall be entitled to reasonable remuneration taking into account all the aspects of the transaction.

(2) This regulation is without prejudice to the application of any enactment or rule of law concerning the level of remuneration.

(3) Where a commercial agent is not remunerated (wholly or in part) by commission, regulations 7 to 12 below shall not apply.

7   Entitlement to commission on transactions concluded during agency contract

(1) A commercial agent shall be entitled to commission on commercial transactions concluded during the period covered by the agency contract—
  (a) where the transaction has been concluded as a result of his action; or
  (b) where the transaction is concluded with a third party whom he has previously acquired as a customer for transactions of the same kind.

(2) A commercial agent shall also be entitled to commission on transactions concluded during the period covered by the agency contract where he has an exclusive right to a specific geographical area or to a specific group of customers and where the transaction has been entered into with a customer belonging to that area or group.

8   Entitlement to commission on transactions concluded after agency contract has terminated

Subject to regulation 9 below, a commercial agent shall be entitled to commission on commercial transactions concluded after the agency contract has terminated if—
  (a) the transaction is mainly attributable to his efforts during the period covered by the agency contract and if the transaction was entered into within a reasonable period after that contract terminated; or
  (b) in accordance with the conditions mentioned in regulation 7 above, the order of the third party reached the principal or the commercial agent before the agency contract terminated.

9   Apportionment of commission between new and previous commercial agents

(1) A commercial agent shall not be entitled to the commission referred to in regulation 7 above if that commission is payable, by virtue of regulation 8 above, to the previous commercial agent, unless it is equitable because of the circumstances for the commission to be shared between the commercial agents.

(2) The principal shall be liable for any sum due under paragraph (1) above to the person entitled to it in accordance with that paragraph, and any sum which the other commercial agent receives to which he is not entitled shall be refunded to the principal.

10   When commission due and date for payment

(1) Commission shall become due as soon as, and to the extent that, one of the following circumstances occurs:
  (a) the principal has executed the transaction; or
  (b) the principal should, according to his agreement with the third party, have executed the transaction; or
  (c) the third party has executed the transaction.

(2) Commission shall become due at the latest when the third party has executed his part of the transaction or should have done so if the principal had executed his part of the transaction, as he should have.

(3) The commission shall be paid not later than on the last day of the month following the quarter in which it became due, and, for the purposes of these Regulations, unless otherwise agreed between the parties, the first quarter period shall run from the date the agency contract takes effect, and subsequent periods shall run from that date in the third month thereafter or the beginning of the fourth month, whichever is the sooner.

(4) Any agreement to derogate from paragraphs (2) and (3) above to the detriment of the commercial agent shall be void.

11   Extinction of right to commission

(1) The right to commission can be extinguished only if and to the extent that—

(a) it is established that the contract between the third party and the principal will not be executed; and

(b) that fact is due to a reason for which the principal is not to blame.

(2) Any commission which the commercial agent has already received shall be refunded if the right to it is extinguished.

(3) any agreement to derogate from paragraph (1) above to the detriment of the commercial agent shall be void.

12   Periodic supply of information as to commission due and right of inspection of principal's books

(1) The principal shall supply his commercial agent with a statement of the commission due, not later than the last day of the month following the quarter in which the commission has become due, and such statement shall set out the main components used in calculating the amount of the commission.

(2) A commercial agent shall be entitled to demand that he be provided with all the information (and in particular an extract from the books) which is available to his principal and which he needs in order to check the amount of the commission due to him.

(3) Any agreement to derogate from paragraphs (1) and (2) above shall be void.

(4) Nothing in this regulation shall remove or restrict the effect of, or prevent reliance upon, any enactment or rule of law which recognises the right of an agent to inspect the books of a principal.

PART IV   CONCLUSION AND TERMINATION OF THE AGENCY CONTRACT

13   Right to signed written statement of terms of agency contract

(1) The commercial agent and principal shall each be entitled to receive from the other, on request, a signed written document setting out the terms of the agency contract including any terms subsequently agreed.

(2) Any purported waiver of the right referred to in paragraph (1) above shall be void.

14   Conversion of agency contract after expiry of fixed period

An agency contract for a fixed period which continues to be performed by both parties after that period has expired shall be deemed to be converted into an agency contract for an indefinite period.

15   Minimum periods of notice for termination of agency contract

(1) Where an agency contract is concluded for an indefinite period either party may terminate it by notice.

(2) The period of notice shall be—

(a) 1 month for the first year of the contract;

(b) 2 months for the second year commenced;

(c) 3 months for the third year commenced and for the subsequent years; and the parties may not agree on any shorter periods of notice.

(3) If the parties agree on longer periods than those laid down in paragraph (2) above, the period of notice to be observed by the principal must not be shorter than that to be observed by the commercial agent.

(4) Unless otherwise agreed by the parties, the end of the period of notice must coincide with the end of a calendar month.

(5) The provisions of this regulation shall also apply to an agency contract for a fixed period where it is converted under regulation 14 above into an agency contract for an indefinite period subject to the proviso that the earlier fixed period must be taken into account in the calculation of the period of notice.

16   Savings with regard to immediate termination

These Regulations shall not affect the application of any enactment or rule of law which provides for the immediate termination of the agency contract—

> (a) because of the failure of one party to carry out all or part of his obligations under that contract; or
>
> (b) where exceptional circumstances arise.

17   Entitlement of commercial agent to indemnity or compensation on termination of agency contract

(1) This regulation has effect for the purpose of ensuring that the commercial agent is, after termination of the agency contract, indemnified in accordance with paragraphs (3) to (5) below or compensated for damage in accordance with paragraphs (6) and (7) below.

(2) Except where the agency [contract] otherwise provides, the commercial agent shall be entitled to be compensated rather than indemnified.

(3) Subject to paragraph (9) and to regulation 18 below, the commercial agent shall be entitled to an indemnity if and to the extent that—

> (a) he has brought the principal new customers or has significantly increased the volume of business with existing customers and the principal continues to derive substantial benefits from the business with such customers; and
>
> (b) the payment of this indemnity is equitable having regard to all the circumstances and, in particular, the commission lost by the commercial agent on the business transacted with such customers.

(4) The amount of the indemnity shall not exceed a figure equivalent to an indemnity for one year calculated from the commercial agent's average annual remuneration over the preceding five years and if the contract goes back less than five years the indemnity shall be calculated on the average for the period in question.

(5) The grant of an indemnity as mentioned above shall not prevent the commercial agent from seeking damages.

(6) Subject to paragraph (9) and to regulation 18 below, the commercial agent shall be entitled to compensation for the damage he suffers as a result of the termination of his relations with his principal.

(7) For the purpose of these Regulations such damage shall be deemed to occur particularly when the termination takes place in either or both of the following circumstances, namely circumstances which—

> (a) deprive the commercial agent of the commission which proper performance of the agency contract would have procured for him whilst providing his principal with substantial benefits linked to the activities of the commercial agent; or
>
> (b) have not enabled the commercial agent to amortize the costs and expenses that he had incurred in the performance of the agency contract on the advice of his principal.

(8) Entitlement to the indemnity or compensation for damage as provided for under paragraphs (2) to (7) above shall also arise where the agency contract is terminated as a result of the death of the commercial agent.

(9) The commercial agent shall lose his entitlement to the indemnity or compensation for damage in the instances provided for in paragraphs (2) to (8) above if within one year following termination of his agency contract he has not notified his principal that he intends pursuing his entitlement.

18   Grounds for excluding payment of indemnity or compensation under regulation 17

The [indemnity or] compensation referred to in regulation 17 above shall not be payable to the commercial agent where—

(a) the principal has terminated the agency contract because of default attributable to the commercial agent which would justify immediate termination of the agency contract pursuant to regulation 16 above; or

(b) the commercial agent has himself terminated the agency contract, unless such termination is justified—

    (i) by circumstances attributable to the principal, or

    (ii) on grounds of the age, infirmity or illness of the commercial agent in consequence of which he cannot reasonably be required to continue his activities; or

(c) the commercial agent, with the agreement of his principal, assigns his rights and duties under the agency contract to another person.

19 Prohibition on derogation from regulations 17 and 18

The parties may not derogate from regulations 17 and 18 to the detriment of the commercial agent before the agency contract expires.

20 Restraint of trade clauses

(1) A restraint of trade clause shall be valid only if and to the extent that—

    (a) it is concluded in writing; and

    (b) it relates to the geographical area or the group of customers and the geographical area entrusted to the commercial agent and to the kind of goods covered by his agency under the contract.

(2) A restraint of trade clause shall be valid for not more than two years after termination of the agency contract.

(3) Nothing in this regulation shall affect any enactment or rule of law which imposes other restrictions on the validity or enforceability of restraint of trade clauses or which enables a court to reduce the obligations on the parties resulting from such clauses.

PART V MISCELLANEOUS AND SUPPLEMENTAL

21 Disclosure of information

Nothing in these Regulations shall require information to be given where such disclosure would be contrary to public policy.

22 Service of notice etc

(1) Any notice, statement or other document to be given or supplied to a commercial agent or to be given or supplied to the principal under these Regulations may be so given or supplied:

    (a) by delivering it to him;

    (b) by leaving it at his proper address addressed to him by name;

    (c) by sending it by post to him addressed either to his registered address or to the address of his registered or principal office;

or by any other means provided for in the agency contract.

(2) Any such notice, statement or document may—

    (a) in the case of a body corporate, be given or served on the secretary or clerk of that body;

    (b) in the case of a partnership, be given to or served on any partner or on any person having the control or management of the partnership business.

23 Transitional provisions

(1) Notwithstanding any provision in an agency contract made before 1st January 1994, these Regulations shall apply to that contract after that date and, accordingly any provision which is inconsistent with these Regulations shall have effect subject to them.

(2) Nothing in these Regulations shall affect the rights and liabilities of a commercial agent or a principal which have accrued before 1st January 1994.

Regulation 2(3)   THE SCHEDULE

1. The activities of a person as a commercial agent are to be considered secondary where it may reasonably be taken that the primary purpose of the arrangement with his principal is other than as set out in paragraph 2 below.

2. An arrangement falls within this paragraph if—

    (a) the business of the principal is the sale, or as the case may be purchase, of goods of a particular kind; and

    (b) the goods concerned are such that—

        (i) transactions are normally individually negotiated and concluded on a commercial basis, and

        (ii) procuring a transaction on one occasion is likely to lead to further transactions in those goods with that customer on future occasions, or to transactions in those goods with other customers in the same geographical area or among the same group of customers, and

that accordingly it is in the commercial interests of the principal in developing the market in those goods to appoint a representative to such customers with a view to the representative devoting effort, skill and expenditure from his own resources to that end.

3. The following are indications that an arrangement falls within paragraph 2 above, and the absence of any of them is an indication to the contrary—

    (a) the principal is the manufacturer, importer or distributor of the goods;

    (b) the goods are specifically identified with the principal in the market in question rather than, or to a greater extent than, with any other person;

    (c) the agent devotes substantially the whole of his time to representative activities (whether for one principal or for a number of principals whose interests are not conflicting);

    (d) the goods are not normally available in the market in question other than by means of the agent;

    (e) the arrangement is described as one of commercial agency.

4. The following are indications that an arrangement does not fall within paragraph 2 above—

    (a) promotional material is supplied direct to potential customers;

    (b) persons are granted agencies without reference to existing agents in a particular area or in relation to a particular group;

    (c) customers normally select the goods for themselves and merely place their orders through the agent.

5. The activities of the following categories of persons are presumed, unless the contrary is established, not to fall within paragraph 2 above—

Mail order catalogue agents for consumer goods.

Consumer credit agents.

Unfair Terms in Consumer Contracts Regulations 1999
(SI 1999, No. 2083)

3 Interpretation

(1) In these Regulations—

'the Community' means the European Community;

'consumer' means any natural person who, in contracts covered by these Regulations, is acting for purposes which are outside his trade, business or profession;

'court' in relation to England and Wales and Northern Ireland means a county court or the High Court, and in relation to Scotland, the Sheriff or the Court of Session;

'Director' means the Director General of Fair Trading;

'EEA Agreement' means the Agreement on the European Economic Area signed at Oporto on 2nd May 1992 as adjusted by the protocol signed at Brussels on 17th March 1993;

'Member State' means a State which is a contracting party to the EEA Agreement;

'notified' means notified in writing;

'qualifying body' means a person specified in Schedule 1;

'seller or supplier' means any natural or legal person who, in contracts covered by these Regulations, is acting for purposes relating to his trade, business or profession, whether publicly owned or privately owned;

'unfair terms' means the contractual terms referred to in regulation 5.

[(1A) The references—

    (a) in regulation 4(1) to a seller or a supplier, and

    (b) in regulation 8(1) to a seller or supplier,

include references to a distance supplier and to an intermediary.

(1B) In paragraph (1A) and regulation 5(6)—

'distance supplier' means—

    (a) a supplier under a distance contract within the meaning of the Financial Services (Distance Marketing) Regulations 2004, or

    (b) a supplier of unsolicited financial services within regulation 15 of those Regulations; and

'intermediary' has the same meaning as in those Regulations.]

(2) In the application of these Regulations to Scotland for references to an 'injunction' or an 'interim injunction' there shall be substituted references to an 'interdict' or 'interim interdict' respectively.

4 Terms to which these Regulations apply

(1) These Regulations apply in relation to unfair terms in contracts concluded between a seller or a supplier and a consumer.

(2) These Regulations do not apply to contractual terms which reflect—

    (a) mandatory statutory or regulatory provisions (including such provisions under the law of any Member State or in Community legislation having effect in the United Kingdom without further enactment);

    (b) the provisions or principles of international conventions to which the Member States or the Community are party.

5 Unfair terms

(1) A contractual term which has not been individually negotiated shall be regarded as unfair if, contrary to the requirement of good faith, it causes a significant imbalance in the parties' rights and obligations arising under the contract, to the detriment of the consumer.

(2) A term shall always be regarded as not having been individually negotiated where it has been drafted in advance and the consumer has therefore not been able to influence the substance of the term.

(3) Notwithstanding that a specific term or certain aspects of it in a contract has been individually negotiated, these Regulations shall apply to the rest of a contract if an overall assessment of it indicates that it is a pre-formulated standard contract.

(4) It shall be for any seller or supplier who claims that a term was individually negotiated to show that it was.

(5) Schedule 2 to these Regulations contains an indicative and non-exhaustive list of the terms which may be regarded as unfair.

[(6) Any contractual term providing that a consumer bears the burden of proof in respect of showing whether a distance supplier or an intermediary complied with any or all of the obligations placed upon him resulting from the Directive and any rule or enactment implementing it shall always be regarded as unfair.

(7) In paragraph (6)—

'the Directive' means Directive 2002/65/EC of the European Parliament and of the Council of 23 September 2002 concerning the distance marketing of consumer financial services and amending Council Directive 90/619/EEC and Directives 97/7/EC and 98/27/EC; and

'rule' means a rule made by the Financial Services Authority under the Financial Services and Markets Act 2000 or by a designated professional body within the meaning of section 326(2) of that Act.]

6   Assessment of unfair terms

(1) Without prejudice to regulation 12, the unfairness of a contractual term shall be assessed, taking into account the nature of the goods or services for which the contract was concluded and by referring, at the time of conclusion of the contract, to all the circumstances attending the conclusion of the contract and to all the other terms of the contract or of another contract on which it is dependent.

(2) In so far as it is in plain intelligible language, the assessment of fairness of a term shall not relate—

(a) to the definition of the main subject matter of the contract, or

(b) to the adequacy of the price or remuneration, as against the goods or services supplied in exchange.

7   Written contracts

(1) A seller or supplier shall ensure that any written term of a contract is expressed in plain, intelligible language.

(2) If there is doubt about the meaning of a written term, the interpretation which is most favourable to the consumer shall prevail but this rule shall not apply in proceedings brought under regulation 12.

8   Effect of unfair term

(1) An unfair term in a contract concluded with a consumer by a seller or supplier shall not be binding on the consumer.

(2) The contract shall continue to bind the parties if it is capable of continuing in existence without the unfair term.

9   Choice of law clauses

These Regulations shall apply notwithstanding any contract term which applies or purports to apply the law of a non-Member State, if the contract has a close connection with the territory of the Member States.

10   Complaints—consideration by Director

(1) It shall be the duty of the Director to consider any complaint made to him that any contract term drawn up for general use is unfair, unless—

(a) the complaint appears to the Director to be frivolous or vexatious; or

(b) a qualifying body has notified the Director that it agrees to consider the complaint.

(2) The Director shall give reasons for his decision to apply or not to apply, as the case may be, for an injunction under regulation 12 in relation to any complaint which these Regulations require him to consider.

(3) In deciding whether or not to apply for an injunction in respect of a term which the Director considers to be unfair, he may, if he considers it appropriate to do so, have regard to any undertakings given to him by or on behalf of any person as to the continued use of such a term in contracts concluded with consumers.

11 Complaints—consideration by qualifying bodies

(1) If a qualifying body specified in Part One of Schedule 1 notifies the Director that it agrees to consider a complaint that any contract term drawn up for general use is unfair, it shall be under a duty to consider that complaint.

(2) Regulation 10(2) and (3) shall apply to a qualifying body which is under a duty to consider a complaint as they apply to the Director.

12 Injunctions to prevent continued use of unfair terms

(1) The Director or, subject to paragraph (2), any qualifying body may apply for an injunction (including an interim injunction) against any person appearing to the Director or that body to be using, or recommending use of, an unfair term drawn up for general use in contracts concluded with consumers.

(2) A qualifying body may apply for an injunction only where—

 (a) it has notified the Director of its intention to apply at least fourteen days before the date on which the application is made, beginning with the date on which the notification was given; or

 (b) the Director consents to the application being made within a shorter period.

(3) The court on an application under this regulation may grant an injunction on such terms as it thinks fit.

(4) An injunction may relate not only to use of a particular contract term drawn up for general use but to any similar term, or a term having like effect, used or recommended for use by any person.

13 Powers of the Director and qualifying bodies to obtain documents and information

(1) The Director may exercise the power conferred by this regulation for the purpose of—

 (a) facilitating his consideration of a complaint that a contract term drawn up for general use is unfair; or

 (b) ascertaining whether a person has complied with an undertaking or court order as to the continued use, or recommendation for use, of a term in contracts concluded with consumers.

(2) A qualifying body specified in Part One of Schedule 1 may exercise the power conferred by this regulation for the purpose of—

 (a) facilitating its consideration of a complaint that a contract term drawn up for general use is unfair; or

 (b) ascertaining whether a person has complied with—

  (i) an undertaking given to it or to the court following an application by that body, or

  (ii) a court order made on an application by that body,

   as to the continued use, or recommendation for use, of a term in contracts concluded with consumers.

(3) The Director may require any person to supply to him, and a qualifying body specified in Part One of Schedule 1 may require any person to supply to it—

 (a) a copy of any document which that person has used or recommended for use, at the time the notice referred to in paragraph (4) below is given, as a pre-formulated standard contract in dealings with consumers;

 (b) information about the use, or recommendation for use, by that person of that document or any other such document in dealings with consumers.

(4) The power conferred by this regulation is to be exercised by a notice in writing which may—

 (a) specify the way in which and the time within which it is to be complied with; and

 (b) be varied or revoked by a subsequent notice.

(5) Nothing in this regulation compels a person to supply any document or information which he would be entitled to refuse to produce or give in civil proceedings before the court.

(6) If a person makes default in complying with a notice under this regulation, the court may, on the application of the Director or of the qualifying body, make such order as the court thinks fit for requiring the default to be made good, and any such order may provide that all the costs or expenses of and incidental to the application shall be borne by the person in default or by any officers of a company or other association who are responsible for its default.

14   Notification of undertakings and orders to Director
A qualifying body shall notify the Director—
> (a) of any undertaking given to it by or on behalf of any person as to the continued use of a term which that body considers to be unfair in contracts concluded with consumers;
> (b) of the outcome of any application made by it under regulation 12, and of the terms of any undertaking given to, or order made by, the court;
> (c) of the outcome of any application made by it to enforce a previous order of the court.

15   Publication, information and advice
(1) The Director shall arrange for the publication in such form and manner as he considers appropriate, of—
> (a) details of any undertaking or order notified to him under regulation 14;
> (b) details of any undertaking given to him by or on behalf of any person as to the continued use of a term which the Director considers to be unfair in contracts concluded with consumers;
> (c) details of any application made by him under regulation 12, and of the terms of any undertaking given to, or order made by, the court;
> (d) details of any application made by the Director to enforce a previous order of the court.

(2) The Director shall inform any person on request whether a particular term to which these Regulations apply has been—
> (a) the subject of an undertaking given to the Director or notified to him by a qualifying body; or
> (b) the subject of an order of the court made upon application by him or notified to him by a qualifying body;

and shall give that person details of the undertaking or a copy of the order, as the case may be, together with a copy of any amendments which the person giving the undertaking has agreed to make to the term in question.

(3) The Director may arrange for the dissemination in such form and manner as he considers appropriate of such information and advice concerning the operation of these Regulations as may appear to him to be expedient to give to the public and to all persons likely to be affected by these Regulations.

[16   The functions of the Financial Services Authority
The functions of the Financial Services Authority under these Regulations shall be treated as functions of the Financial Services Authority under the Financial Services and Markets Act 2000.]

Regulation 3   SCHEDULE 1

QUALIFYING BODIES

PART ONE

[1.   The Information Commissioner.
2.   The Gas and Electricity Markets Authority.

3. The Director General of Electricity Supply for Northern Ireland.
4. The Director General of Gas for Northern Ireland.
5. [The Office of Communications].
6. [The Water Services Regulation Authority].
7. The Rail Regulator.
8. Every weights and measures authority in Great Britain.
9. The Department of Enterprise, Trade and Investment in Northern Ireland.
10. The Financial Services Authority.]

PART TWO
11. Consumers' Association.

Regulation 5(5)   SCHEDULE 2

INDICATIVE AND NON-EXHAUSTIVE LIST OF TERMS
WHICH MAY BE REGARDED AS UNFAIR

1. Terms which have the object or effect of—
    (a) excluding or limiting the legal liability of a seller or supplier in the event of the death of a consumer or personal injury to the latter resulting from an act or omission of that seller or supplier;
    (b) inappropriately excluding or limiting the legal rights of the consumer vis-à-vis the seller or supplier or another party in the event of total or partial non-performance or inadequate performance by the seller or supplier of any of the contractual obligations, including the option of offsetting a debt owed to the seller or supplier against any claim which the consumer may have against him;
    (c) making an agreement binding on the consumer whereas provision of services by the seller or supplier is subject to a condition whose realisation depends on his own will alone;
    (d) permitting the seller or supplier to retain sums paid by the consumer where the latter decides not to conclude or perform the contract, without providing for the consumer to receive compensation of an equivalent amount from the seller or supplier where the latter is the party cancelling the contract;
    (e) requiring any consumer who fails to fulfil his obligation to pay a disproportionately high sum in compensation;
    (f) authorising the seller or supplier to dissolve the contract on a discretionary basis where the same facility is not granted to the consumer, or permitting the seller or supplier to retain the sums paid for services not yet supplied by him where it is the seller or supplier himself who dissolves the contract;
    (g) enabling the seller or supplier to terminate a contract of indeterminate duration without reasonable notice except where there are serious grounds for doing so;
    (h) automatically extending a contract of fixed duration where the consumer does not indicate otherwise, when the deadline fixed for the consumer to express his desire not to extend the contract is unreasonably early;
    (i) irrevocably binding the consumer to terms with which he had no real opportunity of becoming acquainted before the conclusion of the contract;
    (j) enabling the seller or supplier to alter the terms of the contract unilaterally without a valid reason which is specified in the contract;
    (k) enabling the seller or supplier to alter unilaterally without a valid reason any characteristics of the product or service to be provided;

(l) providing for the price of goods to be determined at the time of delivery or allowing a seller of goods or supplier of services to increase their price without in both cases giving the consumer the corresponding right to cancel the contract if the final price is too high in relation to the price agreed when the contract was concluded;

(m) giving the seller or supplier the right to determine whether the goods or services supplied are in conformity with the contract, or giving him the exclusive right to interpret any term of the contract;

(n) limiting the seller's or supplier's obligation to respect commitments undertaken by his agents or making his commitments subject to compliance with a particular formality;

(o) obliging the consumer to fulfil all his obligations where the seller or supplier does not perform his;

(p) giving the seller or supplier the possibility of transferring his rights and obligations under the contract, where this may serve to reduce the guarantees for the consumer, without the latter's agreement;

(q) excluding or hindering the consumer's right to take legal action or exercise any other legal remedy, particularly by requiring the consumer to take disputes exclusively to arbitration not covered by legal provisions, unduly restricting the evidence available to him or imposing on him a burden of proof which, according to the applicable law, should lie with another party to the contract.

2. Scope of paragraphs 1(g), (j) and (l)—

(a) Paragraph 1(g) is without hindrance to terms by which a supplier of financial services reserves the right to terminate unilaterally a contract of indeterminate duration without notice where there is a valid reason provided that the supplier is required to inform the other contracting party or parties thereof immediately.

(b) Paragraph 1(j) is without hindrance to terms under which a supplier of financial services reserves the right to alter the rate of interest payable by the consumer or due to the latter, or the amount of other charges for financial services without notice where there is a valid reason, provided that the supplier is required to inform the other contracting party or parties thereof at the earliest opportunity and that the latter are free to dissolve the contract immediately.

Paragraph 1(j) is also without hindrance to terms under which a seller or supplier reserves the right to alter unilaterally the conditions of a contract of indeterminate duration, provided that he is required to inform the consumer with reasonable notice and that the consumer is free to dissolve the contract.

(c) Paragraphs 1(g), (j) and (l) do not apply to:
— transactions in transferable securities, financial instruments and other products or services where the price is linked to fluctuations in a stock exchange quotation or index or a financial market rate that the seller or supplier does not control;
— contracts for the purchase or sale of foreign currency, traveller's cheques or international money orders denominated in foreign currency;

(d) Paragraph 1(1) is without hindrance to price indexation clauses, where lawful, provided that the method by which prices vary is explicitly described.

Consumer Protection (Distance Selling) Regulations 2000
(SI 2000, No. 2334)

3 Interpretation
(1) In these Regulations—
['the 2000 Act' means the Financial Services and Markets Act 2000;

'appointed representative' has the same meaning as in section 39(2) of the 2000 Act;

'authorised person' has the same meaning as in section 31(2) of the 2000 Act;]

'breach' means contravention by a supplier of a prohibition in, or failure to comply with a requirement of, these Regulations;

'business' includes a trade or profession;

'consumer' means any natural person who, in contracts to which these Regulations apply, is acting for purposes which are outside his business;

'court' in relation to England and Wales and Northern Ireland means a county court or the High Court, and in relation to Scotland means the Sheriff Court or the Court of Session;

'credit' includes a cash loan and any other form of financial accommodation, and for this purpose 'cash' includes money in any form;

'Director' means the Director General of Fair Trading;

'distance contract' means any contract concerning goods or services concluded between a supplier and a consumer under an organised distance sales or service provision scheme run by the supplier who, for the purpose of the contract, makes exclusive use of one or more means of distance communication up to and including the moment at which the contract is concluded;

'EEA Agreement' means the Agreement on the European Economic Area signed at Oporto on 2 May 1992 as adjusted by the Protocol signed at Brussels on 17 March 1993;

'enactment' includes an enactment comprised in, or in an instrument made under, an Act of the Scottish Parliament;

'enforcement authority' means the Director, every weights and measures authority in Great Britain, and the Department of Enterprise, Trade and Investment in Northern Ireland;

'excepted contract' means a contract such as is mentioned in regulation 5(1);

['financial service' means any service of a banking, credit, insurance, personal pension, investment or payment nature;]

'means of distance communication' means any means which, without the simultaneous physical presence of the supplier and the consumer, may be used for the conclusion of a contract between those parties; and an indicative list of such means is contained in Schedule 1;

'Member State' means a State which is a contracting party to the EEA Agreement;

'operator of a means of communication' means any public or private person whose business involves making one or more means of distance communication available to suppliers;

'period for performance' has the meaning given by regulation 19(2);

'personal credit agreement' has the meaning given by regulation 14(8);

['regulated activity' has the same meaning as in section 22 of the 2000 Act;]

'related credit agreement' has the meaning given by regulation 15(5);

'supplier' means any person who, in contracts to which these Regulations apply, is acting in his commercial or professional capacity; and

'working days' means all days other than Saturdays, Sundays and public holidays.

(2) In the application of these Regulations to Scotland, for references to an 'injunction' or an 'interim injunction' there shall be substituted references to an 'interdict' or an 'interim interdict' respectively.

4   Contracts to which these Regulations apply

These Regulations apply, subject to regulation 6, to distance contracts other than excepted contracts.

5   Excepted contracts

(1) The following are excepted contracts, namely any contract—
  (a) for the sale or other disposition of an interest in land except for a rental agreement;
  (b) for the construction of a building where the contract also provides for a sale or other disposition of an interest in land on which the building is constructed, except for a rental agreement;
  (c) relating to financial services [. . .];

   (d) concluded by means of an automated vending machine or automated commercial premises;

   (e) concluded with a telecommunications operator through the use of a public payphone;

   (f) concluded at an auction.

  (2) References in paragraph (1) to a rental agreement—

   (a) if the land is situated in England and Wales, are references to any agreement which does not have to be made in writing (whether or not in fact made in writing) because of section 2(5)(a) of the Law of Property (Miscellaneous Provisions) Act 1989;

   (b) if the land is situated in Scotland, are references to any agreement for the creation, transfer, variation or extinction of an interest in land, which does not have to be made in writing (whether or not in fact made in writing) as provided for in section 1(2) and (7) of the Requirements of Writing (Scotland) Act 1995; and

   (c) if the land is situated in Northern Ireland, are references to any agreement which is not one to which section II of the Statute of Frauds, (Ireland) 1695 applies.

  (3) Paragraph (2) shall not be taken to mean that a rental agreement in respect of land situated outside the United Kingdom is not capable of being a distance contract to which these Regulations apply.

6   Contracts to which only part of these Regulations apply

  (1) Regulations 7 to 20 shall not apply to a contract which is a 'timeshare agreement' within the meaning of the Timeshare Act 1992 and to which that Act applies.

  (2) Regulations 7 to 19(1) shall not apply to—

   (a) contracts for the supply of food, beverages or other goods intended for everyday consumption supplied to the consumer's residence or to his workplace by regular roundsmen; or

   (b) contracts for the provision of accommodation, transport, catering or leisure services, where the supplier undertakes, when the contract is concluded, to provide these services on a specific date or within a specific period.

  (3) Regulations 19(2) to (8) and 20 do not apply to a contract for a 'package' within the meaning of the Package Travel, Package Holidays and Package Tours Regulations 1992 which is sold or offered for sale in the territory of the Member States.

  [(4) Regulations 7 to 14, 17 to 20 and 25 do not apply to any contract which is made, and regulation 24 does not apply to any unsolicited services which are supplied, by an authorised person where the making or performance of that contract or the supply of those services, as the case may be, constitutes or is part of a regulated activity carried on by him.

  (5) Regulations 7 to 9, 17 to 20 and 25 do not apply to any contract which is made, and regulation 24 does not apply to any unsolicited services which are supplied, by an appointed representative where the making or performance of that contract or the supply of those services, as the case may be, constitutes or is part of a regulated activity carried on by him.]

7   Information required prior to the conclusion of the contract

  (1) Subject to paragraph (4), in good time prior to the conclusion of the contract the supplier shall—

   (a) provide to the consumer the following information—

     (i) the identity of the supplier and, where the contract requires payment in advance, the supplier's address;

     (ii) a description of the main characteristics of the goods or services;

     (iii) the price of the goods or services including all taxes;

     (iv) delivery costs where appropriate;

     (v) the arrangements for payment, delivery or performance;

    (vi)   the existence of a right of cancellation except in the cases referred to in regulation 13;

    (vii) the cost of using the means of distance communication where it is calculated other than at the basic rate;

    (viii) the period for which the offer or the price remains valid; and

    (ix)   where appropriate, the minimum duration of the contract, in the case of contracts for the supply of goods or services to be performed permanently or recurrently;

(b) inform the consumer if he proposes, in the event of the goods or services ordered by the consumer being unavailable, to provide substitute goods or services (as the case may be) of equivalent quality and price; and

(c) inform the consumer that the cost of returning any such substitute goods to the supplier in the event of cancellation by the consumer would be met by the supplier.

(2) The supplier shall ensure that the information required by paragraph (1) is provided in a clear and comprehensible manner appropriate to the means of distance communication used, with due regard in particular to the principles of good faith in commercial transactions and the principles governing the protection of those who are unable to give their consent such as minors.

(3) Subject to paragraph (4), the supplier shall ensure that his commercial purpose is made clear when providing the information required by paragraph (1).

(4) In the case of a telephone communication, the identity of the supplier and the commercial purpose of the call shall be made clear at the beginning of the conversation with the consumer.

8 Written and additional information

(1) Subject to regulation 9, the supplier shall provide to the consumer in writing, or in another durable medium which is available and accessible to the consumer, the information referred to in paragraph (2), either—

(a) prior to the conclusion of the contract, or

(b) thereafter, in good time and in any event—

    (i)   during the performance of the contract, in the case of services; and

    (ii) at the latest at the time of delivery where goods not for delivery to third parties are concerned.

(2) The information required to be provided by paragraph (1) is—

(a) the information set out in paragraphs (i) to (vi) of Regulation 7(1)(a);

(b) information about the conditions and procedures for exercising the right to cancel under regulation 10, including—

    (i)   where a term of the contract requires (or the supplier intends that it will require) that the consumer shall return the goods to the supplier in the event of cancellation, notification of that requirement; [...]

    (ii) information as to whether the consumer or the supplier would be responsible under these Regulations for the cost of returning any goods to the supplier, or the cost of his recovering them, if the consumer cancels the contract under regulation 10;

    [(iii) in the case of a contract for the supply of services, information as to how the right to cancel may be affected by the consumer agreeing to performance of the services beginning before the end of the seven working day period referred to in regulation 12;]

(c) the geographical address of the place of business of the supplier to which the consumer may address any complaints;

(d) information about any after-sales services and guarantees; and

(e) the conditions for exercising any contractual right to cancel the contract, where the contract is of an unspecified duration or a duration exceeding one year.

9   Services performed through the use of a means of distance communication

(1) Regulation 8 shall not apply to a contract for the supply of services which are performed through the use of a means of distance communication, where those services are supplied on only one occasion and are invoiced by the operator of the means of distance communication.

(2) But the supplier shall take all necessary steps to ensure that a consumer who is a party to a contract to which paragraph (1) applies is able to obtain the supplier's geographical address and the place of business to which the consumer may address any complaints.

10   Right to cancel

(1) Subject to regulation 13, if within the cancellation period set out in regulations 11 and 12, the consumer gives a notice of cancellation to the supplier, or any other person previously notified by the supplier to the consumer as a person to whom notice of cancellation may be given, the notice of cancellation shall operate to cancel the contract.

(2) Except as otherwise provided by these Regulations, the effect of a notice of cancellation is that the contract shall be treated as if it had not been made.

(3) For the purposes of these Regulations, a notice of cancellation is a notice in writing or in another durable medium available and accessible to the supplier (or to the other person to whom it is given) which, however expressed, indicates the intention of the consumer to cancel the contract.

(4) A notice of cancellation given under this regulation by a consumer to a supplier or other person is to be treated as having been properly given if the consumer—

  (a) leaves it at the address last known to the consumer and addressed to the supplier or other person by name (in which case it is to be taken to have been given on the day on which it was left);

  (b) sends it by post to the address last known to the consumer and addressed to the supplier or other person by name (in which case, it is to be taken to have been given on the day on which it was posted);

  (c) sends it by facsimile to the business facsimile number last known to the consumer (in which case it is to be taken to have been given on the day on which it is sent); or

  (d) sends it by electronic mail, to the business electronic mail address last known to the consumer (in which case it is to be taken to have been given on the day on which it is sent).

(5) Where a consumer gives a notice in accordance with paragraph (4)(a) or (b) to a supplier who is a body corporate or a partnership, the notice is to be treated as having been properly given if—

  (a) in the case of a body corporate, it is left at the address of, or sent to, the secretary or clerk of that body; or

  (b) in the case of a partnership, it is left with or sent to a partner or a person having control or management of the partnership business.

11   Cancellation period in the case of contracts for the supply of goods

(1) For the purposes of regulation 10, the cancellation period in the case of contracts for the supply of goods begins with the day on which the contract is concluded and ends as provided in paragraphs (2) to (5).

(2) Where the supplier complies with regulation 8, the cancellation period ends on the expiry of the period of seven working days beginning with the day after the day on which the consumer receives the goods.

(3) Where a supplier who has not complied with regulation 8 provides to the consumer the information referred to in regulation 8(2), and does so in writing or in another durable medium available and accessible to the consumer, within the period of three months beginning with the day after the day on which the consumer receives the goods, the cancellation period ends on the expiry of the period of seven working days beginning with the day after the day on which the consumer receives the information.

(4) Where neither paragraph (2) nor (3) applies, the cancellation period ends on the expiry of the period of three months and seven working days beginning with the day after the day on which the consumer receives the goods.

(5) In the case of contracts for goods for delivery to third parties, paragraphs (2) to (4) shall apply as if the consumer had received the goods on the day on which they were received by the third party.

12   Cancellation period in the case of contracts for the supply of services

(1) For the purposes of regulation 10, the cancellation period in the case of contracts for the supply of services begins with the day on which the contract is concluded and ends as provided in paragraphs (2) to (4).

(2) Where the supplier complies with regulation 8 on or before the day on which the contract is concluded, the cancellation period ends on the expiry of the period of seven working days beginning with the day after the day on which the contract is concluded.

(3) [Subject to paragraph (3A)] Where a supplier who has not complied with regulation 8 on or before the day on which the contract is concluded provides to the consumer the information referred to in regulation 8(2) [. . .], and does so in writing or in another durable medium available and accessible to the consumer, within the period of three months beginning with the day after the day on which the contract is concluded, the cancellation period ends on the expiry of the period of seven working days beginning with the day after the day on which the consumer receives the information.

[(3A) Where the performance of the contract has begun with the consumer's agreement before the expiry of the period of seven working days beginning with the day after the day on which the contract was concluded and the supplier has not complied with regulation 8 on or before the day on which performance began, but provides to the consumer the information referred to in regulation 8(2) in good time during the performance of the contract, the cancellation period ends—

   (a) on the expiry of the period of seven working days beginning with the day after the day on which the consumer receives the information; or
   (b) if the performance of the contract is completed before the expiry of the period referred to in sub-paragraph (a), on the day when the performance of the contract is completed.]

(4) Where [none of paragraphs (2) to (3A) applies], the cancellation period ends on the expiry of the period of three months and seven working days beginning with the day after the day on which the contract is concluded.

13   Exceptions to the right to cancel

(1) Unless the parties have agreed otherwise, the consumer will not have the right to cancel the contract by giving notice of cancellation pursuant to regulation 10 in respect of contracts—

   [(a) for the supply of services if the performance of the contract has begun with the consumer's agreement—
      (i)   before the end of the cancellation period applicable under regulation 12(2); and
      (ii) after the supplier has provided the information referred to in regulation 8(2)];
   (b) for the supply of goods or services the price of which is dependent on fluctuations in the financial market which cannot be controlled by the supplier;
   (c) for the supply of goods made to the consumer's specifications or clearly personalised or which by reason of their nature cannot be returned or are liable to deteriorate or expire rapidly;
   (d) for the supply of audio or video recordings or computer software if they are unsealed by the consumer;
   (e) for the supply of newspapers, periodicals or magazines; or
   (f) for gaming, betting or lottery services.

14 Recovery of sums paid by or on behalf of the consumer on cancellation, and return of security

(1) On the cancellation of a contract under regulation 10, the supplier shall reimburse any sum paid by or on behalf of the consumer under or in relation to the contract to the person by whom it was made free of any charge, less any charge made in accordance with paragraph (5).

(2) The reference in paragraph (1) to any sum paid on behalf of the consumer includes any sum paid by a creditor who is not the same person as the supplier under a personal credit agreement with the consumer.

(3) The supplier shall make the reimbursement referred to in paragraph (1) as soon as possible and in any case within a period not exceeding 30 days beginning with the day on which the notice of cancellation was given.

(4) Where any security has been provided in relation to the contract, the security (so far as it is so provided) shall, on cancellation under regulation 10, be treated as never having had effect and any property lodged with the supplier solely for the purposes of the security as so provided shall be returned by him forthwith.

(5) Subject to paragraphs (6) and (7), the supplier may make a charge, not exceeding the direct costs of recovering any goods supplied under the contract, where a term of the contract provides that the consumer must return any goods supplied if he cancels the contract under regulation 10 but the consumer does not comply with this provision or returns the goods at the expense of the supplier.

(6) Paragraph (5) shall not apply where—

  (a) the consumer cancels in circumstances where he has the right to reject the goods under a term of the contract, including a term implied by virtue of any enactment, or

  (b) the term requiring the consumer to return any goods supplied if he cancels the contract is an 'unfair term' within the meaning of the Unfair Terms in Consumer Contracts Regulations 1999.

(7) Paragraph (5) shall not apply to the cost of recovering any goods which were supplied as substitutes for the goods ordered by the consumer.

(8) For the purposes of these Regulations, a personal credit agreement is an agreement between the consumer and any other person ('the creditor') by which the creditor provides the consumer with credit of any amount.

15 Automatic cancellation of a related credit agreement

(1) Where a notice of cancellation is given under regulation 10 which has the effect of cancelling the contract, the giving of the notice shall also have the effect of cancelling any related credit agreement.

(2) Where a related credit agreement is cancelled by virtue of paragraph (1), the supplier shall, if he is not the same person as the creditor under that agreement, forthwith on receipt of the notice of cancellation inform the creditor that the notice has been given.

(3) Where a related credit agreement is cancelled by virtue of paragraph (1)—

  (a) any sum paid by or on behalf of the consumer under, or in relation to, the credit agreement which the supplier is not obliged to reimburse under regulation 14(1) shall be reimbursed, except for any sum which, if it had not already been paid, would have to be paid under subparagraph (b);

  (b) the agreement shall continue in force so far as it relates to repayment of the credit and payment of interest, subject to regulation 16; and

  (c) subject to subparagraph (b), the agreement shall cease to be enforceable.

(4) Where any security has been provided under a related credit agreement, the security, so far as it is so provided, shall be treated as never having had effect and any property lodged with the creditor solely for the purposes of the security as so provided shall be returned by him forthwith.

(5) For the purposes of this regulation and regulation 16, a 'related credit agreement' means an agreement under which fixed sum credit which fully or partly covers the price

under a contract cancelled under regulation 10 is granted—

    (a) by the supplier, or

    (b) by another person, under an arrangement between that person and the supplier.

  (6) For the purposes of this regulation and regulation 16—

    (a) 'creditor' is a person who grants credit under a related credit agreement;

    (b) 'fixed sum credit' has the same meaning as in section 10 of the Consumer Credit Act 1974;

    (c) 'repayment' in relation to credit means repayment of money received by the consumer, and cognate expressions shall be construed accordingly; and

    (d) 'interest' means interest on money so received.

16 Repayment of credit and interest after cancellation of a related credit agreement

  (1) This regulation applies following the cancellation of a related credit agreement by virtue of regulation 15(1).

  (2) If the consumer repays the whole or a portion of the credit—

    (a) before the expiry of one month following the cancellation of the credit agreement, or

    (b) in the case of a credit repayable by instalments, before the date on which the first instalment is due,

no interest shall be payable on the amount repaid.

  (3) If the whole of a credit repayable by instalments is not repaid on or before the date referred to in paragraph (2)(b), the consumer shall not be liable to repay any of the credit except on receipt of a request in writing, signed by the creditor, stating the amounts of the remaining instalments (recalculated by the creditor as nearly as may be in accordance with the agreement and without extending the repayment period), but excluding any sum other than principal and interest.

  (4) Where any security has been provided under a related credit agreement the duty imposed on the consumer to repay credit and to pay interest shall not be enforceable before the creditor has discharged any duty imposed on him by regulation 15(4) to return any property lodged with him as security on cancellation.

17 Restoration of goods by consumer after cancellation

  (1) This regulation applies where a contract is cancelled under regulation 10 after the consumer has acquired possession of any goods under the contract other than any goods mentioned in regulation 13(1)(b) to (e).

  (2) The consumer shall be treated as having been under a duty throughout the period prior to cancellation—

    (a) to retain possession of the goods, and

    (b) to take reasonable care of them.

  (3) On cancellation, the consumer shall be under a duty to restore the goods to the supplier in accordance with this regulation, and in the meanwhile to retain possession of the goods and take reasonable care of them.

  (4) The consumer shall not be under any duty to deliver the goods except at his own premises and in pursuance of a request in writing, or in another durable medium available and accessible to the consumer, from the supplier and given to the consumer either before, or at the time when, the goods are collected from those premises.

  (5) If the consumer—

    (a) delivers the goods (whether at his own premises or elsewhere) to any person to whom, under regulation 10(1), a notice of cancellation could have been given; or

    (b) sends the goods at his own expense to such a person, he shall be discharged from any duty to retain possession of the goods or restore them to the supplier.

  (6) Where the consumer delivers the goods in accordance with paragraph (5)(a), his obligation to take care of the goods shall cease; and if he sends the goods in accordance with

paragraph (5)(b), he shall be under a duty to take reasonable care to see that they are received by the supplier and not damaged in transit, but in other respects his duty to take care of the goods shall cease when he sends them.

(7) Where, at any time during the period of 21 days beginning with the day notice of cancellation was given, the consumer receives such a request as is mentioned in paragraph (4), and unreasonably refuses or unreasonably fails to comply with it, his duty to retain possession and take reasonable care of the goods shall continue until he delivers or sends the goods as mentioned in paragraph (5), but if within that period he does not receive such a request his duty to take reasonable care of the goods shall cease at the end of that period.

(8) Where—

    (a) a term of the contract provides that if the consumer cancels the contract, he must return the goods to the supplier, and

    (b) the consumer is not otherwise entitled to reject the goods under the terms of the contract or by virtue of any enactment,

paragraph (7) shall apply as if for the period of 21 days there were substituted the period of 6 months.

(9) Where any security has been provided in relation to the cancelled contract, the duty to restore goods imposed on the consumer by this regulation shall not be enforceable before the supplier has discharged any duty imposed on him by regulation 14(4) to return any property lodged with him as security on cancellation.

(10) Breach of a duty imposed by this regulation on a consumer is actionable as a breach of statutory duty.

18 Goods given in part-exchange

(1) This regulation applies on the cancellation of a contract under regulation 10 where the supplier agreed to take goods in part-exchange (the 'part-exchange goods') and those goods have been delivered to him.

(2) Unless, before the end of the period of 10 days beginning with the date of cancellation, the part-exchange goods are returned to the consumer in a condition substantially as good as when they were delivered to the supplier, the consumer shall be entitled to recover from the supplier a sum equal to the part-exchange allowance.

(3) In this regulation the part-exchange allowance means the sum agreed as such in the cancelled contract, or if no such sum was agreed, such sum as it would have been reasonable to allow in respect of the part-exchange goods if no notice of cancellation had been served.

(4) Where the consumer recovers from the supplier a sum equal to the part-exchange allowance, the title of the consumer to the part-exchange goods shall vest in the supplier (if it has not already done so) on recovery of that sum.

19 Performance

(1) Unless the parties agree otherwise, the supplier shall perform the contract within a maximum of 30 days beginning with the day after the day the consumer sent his order to the supplier.

(2) Subject to paragraphs (7) and (8), where the supplier is unable to perform the contract because the goods or services ordered are not available, within the period for performance referred to in paragraph (1) or such other period as the parties agree ('the period for performance'), he shall—

    (a) inform the consumer; and

    (b) reimburse any sum paid by or on behalf of the consumer under or in relation to the contract to the person by whom it was made.

(3) The reference in paragraph (2)(b) to any sum paid on behalf of the consumer includes any sum paid by a creditor who is not the same person as the supplier under a personal credit agreement with the consumer.

(4) The supplier shall make the reimbursement referred to in paragraph (2)(b) as soon as possible and in any event within a period of 30 days beginning with the day after the day on which the period for performance expired.

(5) A contract which has not been performed within the period for performance shall be treated as if it had not been made, save for any rights or remedies which the consumer has under it as a result of the non-performance.

(6) Where any security has been provided in relation to the contract, the security (so far as it is so provided) shall, where the supplier is unable to perform the contract within the period for performance, be treated as never having had any effect and any property lodged with the supplier solely for the purposes of the security as so provided shall be returned by him forthwith.

(7) Where the supplier is unable to supply the goods or services ordered by the consumer, the supplier may perform the contract for the purposes of these Regulations by providing substitute goods or services (as the case may be) of equivalent quality and price provided that—

(a) this possibility was provided for in the contract;

(b) prior to the conclusion of the contract the supplier gave the consumer the information required by regulation 7(1)(b) and (c) in the manner required by regulation 7(2).

(8) In the case of outdoor leisure events which by their nature cannot be rescheduled, paragraph 2(b) shall not apply where the consumer and the supplier so agree.

20   Effect of non-performance on related credit agreement

Where a supplier is unable to perform the contract within the period for performance—

(a) regulations 15 and 16 shall apply to any related credit agreement as if the consumer had given a valid notice of cancellation under regulation 10 on the expiry of the period for performance; and

(b) the reference in regulation 15(3)(a) to regulation 14(1) shall be read, for the purposes of this regulation, as a reference to regulation 19(2).

21   Payment by card

(1) Subject to paragraph (4), the consumer shall be entitled to cancel a payment where fraudulent use has been made of his payment card in connection with a contract to which this regulation applies by another person not acting, or to be treated as acting, as his agent.

(2) Subject to paragraph (4), the consumer shall be entitled to be recredited, or to have all sums returned by the card issuer, in the event of fraudulent use of his payment card in connection with a contract to which this regulation applies by another person not acting, or to be treated as acting, as the consumer's agent.

(3) Where paragraphs (1) and (2) apply, in any proceedings if the consumer alleges that any use made of the payment card was not authorised by him it is for the card issuer to prove that the use was so authorised.

(4) Paragraphs (1) and (2) shall not apply to an agreement to which section 83(1) of the Consumer Credit Act 1974 applies.

(6) For the purposes of this regulation—

'card issuer' means the owner of the card; and

'payment card' includes credit cards, charge cards, debit cards and store cards.

24   Inertia Selling

(1) Paragraphs (2) and (3) apply if—

(a) unsolicited goods are sent to a person ('the recipient') with a view to his acquiring them;

(b) the recipient has no reasonable cause to believe that they were sent with a view to their being acquired for the purposes of a business; and

(c) the recipient has neither agreed to acquire nor agreed to return them.

(2) The recipient may, as between himself and the sender, use, deal with or dispose of the goods as if they were an unconditional gift to him.

(3) The rights of the sender to the goods are extinguished.

(4) A person who, not having reasonable cause to believe there is a right to payment, in the course of any business makes a demand for payment, or asserts a present or prospective right to payment, for what he knows are—

    (a) unsolicited goods sent to another person with a view to his acquiring them for purposes other than those of his business, or

    (b) unsolicited services supplied to another person for purposes other than those of his business,

is guilty of an offence and liable, on summary conviction, to a fine not exceeding level 4 on the standard scale.

    (5) A person who, not having reasonable cause to believe there is a right to payment, in the course of any business and with a view to obtaining payment for what he knows are unsolicited goods sent or services supplied as mentioned in paragraph (4)—

    (a) threatens to bring any legal proceedings, or

    (b) places or causes to be placed the name of any person on a list of defaulters or debtors or threatens to do so, or

    (c) invokes or causes to be invoked any other collection procedure or threatens to do so,

is guilty of an offence and liable, on summary conviction, to a fine not exceeding level 5 on the standard scale.

    (6) In this regulation—

'acquire' includes hire;

'send' includes deliver; '

sender', in relation to any goods, includes—

    (a) any person on whose behalf or with whose consent the goods are sent;

    (b) any other person claiming through or under the sender or any person mentioned in paragraph (a); and

    (c) any person who delivers the goods; and

'unsolicited' means, in relation to goods sent or services supplied to any person, that they are sent or supplied without any prior request made by or on behalf of the recipient.

    (7) For the purposes of this regulation, an invoice or similar document which—

    (a) states the amount of a payment, and

    (b) fails to comply with [the conditions set out in Part 2 of the Schedule to the Regulatory Reform (Unsolicited Goods and Services Act 1971) (Directory Entries and Demands for Payment) Order 2005] or, as the case may be, [the requirements of regulations made under] Article 6 of the Unsolicited Goods and Services (Northern Ireland) Order 1976 applicable to it, is to be regarded as asserting a right to the payment.

    (8) Section 3A of the Unsolicited Goods and Services Act 1971 applies for the purposes of this regulation in its application to England, Wales and Scotland as it applies for the purposes of that Act.

    (9) Article 6 of the Unsolicited Goods and Services (Northern Ireland) Order 1976 applies for the purposes of this regulation in its application to Northern Ireland as it applies for the purposes of that Order.

    (10) This regulation applies only to goods sent and services supplied after the date on which it comes into force.

25   No contracting-out

    (1) A term contained in any contract to which these Regulations apply is void if, and to the extent that, it is inconsistent with a provision for the protection of the consumer contained in these Regulations.

    (2) Where a provision of these Regulations specifies a duty or liability of the consumer in certain circumstances, a term contained in a contract to which these Regulations apply, other than a term to which paragraph (3) applies, is inconsistent with that provision if it purports to impose, directly or indirectly, an additional duty or liability on him in those circumstances.

    (3) This paragraph applies to a term which requires the consumer to return any goods supplied to him under the contract if he cancels it under regulation 10.

(4) A term to which paragraph (3) applies shall, in the event of cancellation by the consumer under regulation 10, have effect only for the purposes of regulation 14(5) and 17(8).

(5) These Regulations shall apply notwithstanding any contract term which applies or purports to apply the law of a non-Member State if the contract has a close connection with the territory of a Member State.

26 Consideration of complaints

(1) It shall be the duty of an enforcement authority to consider any complaint made to it about a breach unless—

    (a) the complaint appears to the authority to be frivolous or vexatious; or

    (b) another enforcement authority has notified the Director that it agrees to consider the complaint.

(2) If an enforcement authority notifies the Director that it agrees to consider a complaint made to another enforcement authority, the first mentioned authority shall be under a duty to consider the complaint.

(3) An enforcement authority which is under a duty to consider a complaint shall give reasons for its decision to apply or not to apply, as the case may be, for an injunction under regulation 27.

(4) In deciding whether or not to apply for an injunction in respect of a breach an enforcement authority may, if it considers it appropriate to do so, have regard to any undertaking given to it or another enforcement authority by or on behalf of any person as to compliance with these Regulations.

27 Injunctions to secure compliance with these Regulations

(1) The Director or, subject to paragraph (2), any other enforcement authority may apply for an injunction (including an interim injunction) against any person who appears to the Director or that authority to be responsible for a breach.

(2) An enforcement authority other than the Director may apply for an injunction only where—

    (a) it has notified the Director of its intention to apply at least fourteen days before the date on which the application is to be made, beginning with the date on which the notification was given; or

    (b) the Director consents to the application being made within a shorter period.

(3) The court on an application under this regulation may grant an injunction on such terms as it thinks fit to secure compliance with these Regulations.

28 Notification of undertakings and orders to the Director

An enforcement authority other than the Director shall notify the Director—

    (a) of any undertaking given to it by or on behalf of any person who appears to it to be responsible for a breach;

    (b) of the outcome of any application made by it under regulation 27 and of the terms of any undertaking given to or order made by the court;

    (c) of the outcome of any application made by it to enforce a previous order of the court.

29 Publication, information and advice

(1) The Director shall arrange for the publication in such form and manner as he considers appropriate of—

    (a) details of any undertaking or order notified to him under regulation 28;

    (b) details of any undertaking given to him by or on behalf of any person as to compliance with these Regulations;

    (c) details of any application made by him under regulation 27, and of the terms of any undertaking given to, or order made by, the court;

    (d) details of any application made by the Director to enforce a previous order of the court.

(2) The Director may arrange for the dissemination in such form and manner as he considers appropriate of such information and advice concerning the operation of these Regulations as it may appear to him to be expedient to give to the public and to all persons likely to be affected by these Regulations.

Regulation 3   SCHEDULE 1

INDICATIVE LIST OF MEANS OF DISTANCE COMMUNICATION

1. Unaddressed printed matter.
2. Addressed printed matter.
3. Letter.
4. Press advertising with order form.
5. Catalogue.
6. Telephone with human intervention.
7. Telephone without human intervention (automatic calling machine, audiotext).
8. Radio.
9. Videophone (telephone with screen).
10. Videotext (microcomputer and television screen) with keyboard or touch screen.
11. Electronic mail.
12. Facsimile machine (fax).
13. Television (teleshopping).

Electronic Commerce Directive (Financial Services and Markets) Regulations 2002
(SI 2002, No. 1775)

PART 1   GENERAL

2 Interpretation
(1) In these Regulations—
'the 2000 Act' means the Financial Services and Markets Act 2000;
'authorised incoming provider' means an incoming provider who is an authorised person within the meaning of the 2000 Act;
'the Authority' means the Financial Services Authority;
'commercial communication' means a communication, in any form, designed to promote, directly or indirectly, the goods, services or image of any person pursuing a commercial activity or exercising a regulated profession, other than a communication—
    (a) consisting only of information allowing direct access to the activity of that person, including a geographic address, domain name or electronic mail address; or
    (b) relating to the goods, services or image of that person provided that the communication has been prepared independently of the person making it (and for this purpose, a communication prepared without financial consideration is to be taken to have been prepared independently unless the contrary is shown);
'the Commission' means the Commission of the European Communities;
'consumer' means any individual who is acting for purposes other than those of his trade, business or profession;
'country of origin' in relation to an incoming electronic commerce activity means the EEA State in which is situated the establishment from which the information society service in question is provided;

'criminal conduct' means conduct which constitutes an offence in any part of the United Kingdom, or would constitute an offence in any part of the United Kingdom if it occurred there;

'direction' means a direction made, or proposed to be made, by the Authority under regulation 6;

'EEA regulator' means an authority in an EEA State other than the United Kingdom which exercises any function of a kind mentioned in section 195(4) of the 2000 Act;

'EEA State' means a State which is a contracting party to the agreement on the European Economic Area signed at Oporto on 2 May 1992, as adjusted by the Protocol signed at Brussels on 17 March 1993;

'electronic commerce directive' means Directive 2000/31/EC of the European Parliament and of the Council of 8 June 2000 on certain legal aspects of information society services, in particular electronic commerce, in the Internal Market (Directive on electronic commerce);

'financial instrument' includes an investment of a kind specified by any of articles 76 to 85 of the Regulated Activities Order;

'incoming electronic commerce activity' means an activity—

(a) which consists of the provision of an information society service from an establishment in an EEA State other than the United Kingdom to a person or persons in the United Kingdom, and

(b) which would, but for article 72A of the Regulated Activities Order (and irrespective of the effect of article 72 of that Order), be a regulated activity within the meaning of the 2000 Act;

'incoming provider' means a person carrying on an incoming electronic commerce activity;

'information society service' means an information society service within the meaning of Article 2(a) of the electronic commerce directive;

'investment' means an investment of a kind specified by any provision of Part III of the Regulated Activities Order;

'Regulated Activities Order' means the Financial Services and Markets Act 2000 (Regulated Activities) Order 2001;

'regulated profession' means any profession within the meaning of—

(a) Article 1(d) of Directive 89/48/EEC of the Council of the European Communities of 21 December 1988 on a general system for the recognition of higher-education diplomas awarded on completion of professional education and training of at least three years' duration, or

(b) Article 1(f) of Directive 92/51/EEC of the Council of the European Communities of 18 June 1992 on a second general system for the recognition of professional education and training to supplement Directive 89/48/EEC;

'relevant EEA regulator', in relation to a direction, means the EEA regulator in the country of origin of the incoming electronic commerce activity to which the direction does, or would if made, relate, and which is responsible in that country for the regulation of that activity;

'rule' means a rule made by the Authority under the 2000 Act;

'Tribunal' means the Financial Services and Markets Tribunal referred to in section 132 of the 2000 Act;

'UCITS Directive' means Directive 85/611/EEC of the Council of the European Communities of 20 December 1985 on the co-ordination of laws, regulations and administrative provisions relating to undertakings for collective investment in transferable securities;

'UCITS Directive scheme' means an undertaking for collective investment in transferable securities which is subject to the UCITS Directive, and has been authorised in accordance with Article 4 of that Directive;

'unauthorised incoming provider' means an incoming provider who is not an authorised person within the meaning of the 2000 Act.

(2) A reference in these Regulations to a requirement imposed by the Authority under these Regulations is a reference to—

(a) a requirement (including a requirement that a person no longer carry on an incoming electronic commerce activity) imposed by a direction; or

(b) a requirement imposed by a rule applicable to incoming providers in accordance with regulation 3(4).

(3) For the purposes of these Regulations—

(a) an establishment, in connection with an information society service, is the place at which the provider of the service (being a national of an EEA State or a company or firm as mentioned in Article 48 of the treaty establishing the European Community) effectively pursues an economic activity for an indefinite period;

(b) the presence or use in a particular place of equipment or other technical means of providing an information society service does not, of itself, constitute that place as an establishment of the kind mentioned in sub-paragraph (a);

(c) where it cannot be determined from which of a number of establishments a given information society service is provided, that service is to be regarded as provided from the establishment where the provider has the centre of his activities relating to the service;

(d) a communication by electronic mail is to be regarded as unsolicited, unless it is made in response to an express request from the recipient of the communication.

PART 2   MODIFICATION OF FUNCTIONS OF THE FINANCIAL SERVICES AUTHORITY

3   Consumer contract requirements: modification of rule-making power

(1) The power to make rules conferred by section 138 of the 2000 Act is to be taken to include a power to make rules applying to unauthorised incoming providers.

(2) In consequence of paragraph (1)—

(a) any reference in sections 138(4), (5) and (7) to (9), 148, 150 and 156 of the 2000 Act to an authorised person includes a reference to an unauthorised incoming provider;

(b) any reference in those sections to a regulated activity includes a reference to an incoming electronic commerce activity.

(3) For the purpose of the exercise by the Authority of the power conferred by section 138 of the 2000 Act to make rules applying to incoming providers with respect to the carrying on by them of incoming electronic commerce activities, subsections (7) and (9) of that section have effect as if the reference to 'person' where first occurring were a reference to an individual acting for purposes other than those of his trade, business or profession.

(4) Rules made by the Authority under section 138 of the 2000 Act do not apply to incoming providers with respect to the carrying on by them of incoming electronic commerce activities unless they—

(a) impose consumer contract requirements;

(b) apply with respect to communications that constitute an advertisement by the operator of a UCITS Directive scheme of units in that scheme; or

(c) relate to the permissibility of unsolicited commercial communications by electronic mail.

(5) A consumer contract rule may provide that conduct engaged in by a person to whom the rule applies, and which is in conformity with a provision corresponding to the rule made by a body or authority in an EEA State other than the United Kingdom, is to be treated as conduct in conformity with the rule.

(6) 'Consumer contract requirement' means a requirement—

(a) that information of a kind referred to in regulation 4 be provided to a consumer before he enters into a contract for the provision of one or more information society services, or

(b) as to the manner in which such information is to be provided.

(7) 'Consumer contract rule' means a rule made by the Authority under section 138 of the 2000 Act which imposes a consumer contract requirement on incoming providers.

4   Consumer contract requirements: information
The information which may be the subject of a consumer contract requirement is—

(a) the identity and description of the main business of the other party to the proposed contract ('the supplier'), the geographic address at which the supplier is established, and any other geographic address relevant to the consumer's relations with the supplier;

(b) if the supplier has a representative established in the consumer's country of residence with whom the consumer is to have dealings, the identity and geographic address of the representative, and any other geographic address relevant to the consumer's relations with the representative;

(c) if the consumer is to have dealings with any professional person in connection with the contract, the identity of that person, a statement of the capacity in which he is to act, and the geographic address relevant to the consumer's relations with him;

(d) if the supplier is registered on any public register in connection with the carrying on of his business (or such of his business as is relevant to the contract), the name of that register, and any registration number or other means of identifying the relevant entry on the register;

(e) if the carrying on of the supplier's business (or such of it as is relevant to the contract) is subject to a requirement that he be authorised by a person or body in order to carry it on, the name and geographic address of that person or body;

(f) a description of the main features of the service or services to which the contract relates;

(g) either—

    (aa) the total price to be paid by the consumer under the contract, including all related fees, charges and expenses, and all taxes paid by or through the supplier (in so far as these are reflected in the total price); or

    (bb) if the total price cannot be given, the basis for the calculation of the total price, in a form enabling the consumer to verify the total price when calculated by the supplier;

(h) where the service to be provided under the contract relates to one or more financial instruments—

    (aa) if the instruments are subject to special risks relating to their specific features or operations to be executed in relation to them, notice of the existence of those risks,

    (bb) if the price of the instruments is subject to fluctuation depending on market conditions outside the supplier's control, notice of that fact, and

    (cc) notice that movements in the price of the instruments in the past are not necessarily an indicator of future performance;

(i) notice of the possibility that taxes or other costs may exist which are not imposed or paid by or through the supplier;

(j) the arrangements for payment under, and the performance of, the contract;

(k) any specific additional cost imposed by the supplier on the consumer in relation to the consumer's use of the means for concluding the contract or communicating with the supplier;

(l) the existence or absence of any legal right of the consumer to withdraw from the contract after it has been entered into, the conditions attached to the exercise of any such right, and the consequences for the consumer of not exercising it;

(m) where the contract relates to services to be performed on an indefinite or recurrent basis, the minimum duration of the contract;

(n) any rights of the consumer or the supplier to terminate the contract in accordance with one of its express terms, any contractual penalties which may apply in that event, and the procedure to be followed by the consumer in that event (including the address to which any notification of withdrawal from the contract should be sent);

(o) the state or states whose laws are taken by the supplier as a basis for the establishment of relations with the consumer before the contract is concluded;

(p) any express term in the contract relating to the law governing it, or to the jurisdiction of courts;

(q) the language or languages in which the supplier—

(aa) proposes to offer the terms of, and information concerning, the contract, and

(bb) undertakes (with the agreement of the consumer) to communicate with the consumer during the existence of the contract;

(r) whether any mechanism other than redress through a court (including guarantee funds and compensation schemes and arrangements) is available to the consumer in relation to matters arising in connection with the contract, and if so, the procedure to be followed by the consumer in order to gain access to it;

(s) any limitations, of which the supplier could reasonably be taken to be aware, of the period for which any information referred to in paragraphs (a) to (r) will be valid.

5 Application of certain rules

Rules made by the Authority under section 140 or 141 of the 2000 Act do not apply to incoming providers to the extent that they specify an activity which is an incoming electronic commerce activity.

Electronic Commerce (EC Directive) Regulations 2002
(SI 2002, No. 2013)

2 Interpretation

(1) In these Regulations and in the Schedule—

'commercial communication' means a communication, in any form, designed to promote, directly or indirectly, the goods, services or image of any person pursuing a commercial, industrial or craft activity or exercising a regulated profession, other than a communication—

(a) consisting only of information allowing direct access to the activity of that person including a geographic address, a domain name or an electronic mail address; or

(b) relating to the goods, services or image of that person provided that the communication has been prepared independently of the person making it (and for this purpose, a communication prepared without financial consideration is to be taken to have been prepared independently unless the contrary is shown);

'the Commission' means the Commission of the European Communities;

'consumer' means any natural person who is acting for purposes other than those of his trade, business or profession;

'coordinated field' means requirements applicable to information society service providers or information society services, regardless of whether they are of a general nature or specifically designed for them, and covers requirements with which the service provider has to comply in respect of—

(a) the taking up of the activity of an information society service, such as requirements concerning qualifications, authorisation or notification, and

(b) the pursuit of the activity of an information society service, such as requirements concerning the behaviour of the service provider, requirements regarding the quality or content of the service including those applicable to advertising and contracts, or requirements concerning the liability of the service provider, but does not cover requirements such as those applicable to goods as such, to the delivery of goods or to services not provided by electronic means;

'the Directive' means Directive 2000/31/EC of the European Parliament and of the Council of 8 June 2000 on certain legal aspects of information society services, in particular electronic commerce, in the Internal Market (Directive on electronic commerce);

'EEA Agreement' means the Agreement on the European Economic Area signed at Oporto on 2 May 1992 as adjusted by the Protocol signed at Brussels on 17 March 1993;

'enactment' includes an enactment comprised in Northern Ireland legislation and comprised in, or an instrument made under, an Act of the Scottish Parliament;

'enforcement action' means any form of enforcement action including, in particular—

    (a) in relation to any legal requirement imposed by or under any enactment, any action taken with a view to or in connection with imposing any sanction (whether criminal or otherwise) for failure to observe or comply with it; and

    (b) in relation to a permission or authorisation, anything done with a view to removing or restricting that permission or authorisation;

'enforcement authority' does not include courts but, subject to that, means any person who is authorised, whether by or under an enactment or otherwise, to take enforcement action;

'established service provider' means a service provider who is a national of a member State or a company or firm as mentioned in Article 48 of the Treaty and who effectively pursues an economic activity by virtue of which he is a service provider using a fixed establishment in a member State for an indefinite period, but the presence and use of the technical means and technologies required to provide the information society service do not, in themselves, constitute an establishment of the provider; in cases where it cannot be determined from which of a number of places of establishment a given service is provided, that service is to be regarded as provided from the place of establishment where the provider has the centre of his activities relating to that service; references to a service provider being established or to the establishment of a service provider shall be construed accordingly;

'information society services' (which is summarised in recital 17 of the Directive as covering 'any service normally provided for remuneration, at a distance, by means of electronic equipment for the processing (including digital compression) and storage of data, and at the individual request of a recipient of a service') has the meaning set out in Article 2(a) of the Directive, (which refers to Article 1(2) of Directive 98/34/EC of the European Parliament and of the Council of 22 June 1998 laying down a procedure for the provision of information in the field of technical standards and regulations, as amended by Directive 98/48/EC of 20 July 1998);

'member State' includes a State which is a contracting party to the EEA Agreement;

'recipient of the service' means any person who, for professional ends or otherwise, uses an information society service, in particular for the purposes of seeking information or making it accessible;

'regulated profession' means any profession within the meaning of either Article 1(d) of Council Directive 89/48/EEC of 21 December 1988 on a general system for the recognition of higher-education diplomas awarded on completion of professional education and training of at least three years' duration or of Article 1(f) of Council Directive 92/51/EEC of 18 June 1992 on a second general system for the recognition of professional education and training to supplement Directive 89/48/EEC;

'service provider' means any person providing an information society service;

'the Treaty' means the treaty establishing the European Community.

(2) In regulation 4 and 5, 'requirement' means any legal requirement under the law of the United Kingdom, or any part of it, imposed by or under any enactment or otherwise.

(3) Terms used in the Directive other than those in paragraph (1) above shall have the same meaning as in the Directive.

3 Exclusions

(1) Nothing in these Regulations shall apply in respect of—

(a) the field of taxation;

(b) questions relating to information society services covered by the Data Protection Directive and the Telecommunications Data Protection Directive and Directive 2002/58/EC of the European Parliament and of the Council of 12th July 2002 concerning the processing of personal data and the protection of privacy in the electronic communications sector (Directive on privacy and electronic communications);

(c) questions relating to agreements or practices governed by cartel law; and

(d) the following activities of information society services—

   (i) the activities of a public notary or equivalent professions to the extent that they involve a direct and specific connection with the exercise of public authority,

   (ii) the representation of a client and defence of his interests before the courts, and

   (iii) betting, gaming or lotteries which involve wagering a stake with monetary value.

[(2) These Regulations shall not apply in relation to any Act passed on or after the date these Regulations are made or in relation to the exercise of a power to legislate after that date.]

(3) In this regulation—

'cartel law' means so much of the law relating to agreements between undertakings, decisions by associations of undertakings or concerted practices as relates to agreements to divide the market or fix prices;

'Data Protection Directive' means Directive 95/46/EC of the European Parliament and of the Council of 24 October 1995 on the protection of individuals with regard to the processing of personal data and on the free movement of such data; and

'Telecommunications Data Protection Directive' means Directive 97/66/EC of the European Parliament and of the Council of 15 December 1997 concerning the processing of personal data and the protection of privacy in the telecommunications sector.

4   Internal market

(1) Subject to paragraph (4) below, any requirement which falls within the coordinated field shall apply to the provision of an information society service by a service provider established in the United Kingdom irrespective of whether that information society service is provided in the United Kingdom or another member State.

(2) Subject to paragraph (4) below, an enforcement authority with responsibility in relation to any requirement in paragraph (1) shall ensure that the provision of an information society service by a service provider established in the United Kingdom complies with that requirement irrespective of whether that service is provided in the United Kingdom or another member State and any power, remedy or procedure for taking enforcement action shall be available to secure compliance.

(3) Subject to paragraphs (4), (5) and (6) below, any requirement shall not be applied to the provision of an information society service by a service provider established in a member State other than the United Kingdom for reasons which fall within the coordinated field where its application would restrict the freedom to provide information society services to a person in the United Kingdom from that member State.

(4) Paragraphs (1), (2) and (3) shall not apply to those fields in the annex to the Directive set out in the Schedule.

(5) The reference to any requirements the application of which would restrict the freedom to provide information society services from another member State in paragraph (3) above does not include any requirement maintaining the level of protection for public health and consumer interests established by Community acts.

(6) To the extent that anything in these Regulations creates any new criminal offence, it shall not be punishable with imprisonment for more than two years or punishable on

summary conviction with imprisonment for more than three months or with a fine of more than level 5 on the standard scale (if not calculated on a daily basis) or with a fine of more than £100 a day.

5   Derogations from Regulation 4

(1) Notwithstanding regulation 4(3), an enforcement authority may take measures, including applying any requirement which would otherwise not apply by virtue of regulation 4(3) in respect of a given information society service, where those measures are necessary for reasons of—

(a) public policy, in particular the prevention, investigation, detection and prosecution of criminal offences, including the protection of minors and the fight against any incitement to hatred on grounds of race, sex, religion or nationality, and violations of human dignity concerning individual persons;

(b) the protection of public health;

(c) public security, including the safeguarding of national security and defence, or

(d) the protection of consumers, including investors,

and proportionate to those objectives.

(2) Notwithstanding regulation 4(3), in any case where an enforcement authority with responsibility in relation to the requirement in question is not party to the proceedings, a court may, on the application of any person or of its own motion, apply any requirement which would otherwise not apply by virtue of regulation 4(3) in respect of a given information society service, if the application of that enactment or requirement is necessary for and proportionate to any of the objectives set out in paragraph (1) above.

(3) Paragraphs (1) and (2) shall only apply where the information society service prejudices or presents a serious and grave risk of prejudice to an objective in paragraph (1)(a) to (d).

(4) Subject to paragraphs (5) and (6), an enforcement authority shall not take the measures in paragraph (1) above, unless it—

(a) asks the member State in which the service provider is established to take measures and the member State does not take such measures or they are inadequate; and

(b) notifies the Commission and the member State in which the service provider is established of its intention to take such measures.

(5) Paragraph (4) shall not apply to court proceedings, including preliminary proceedings and acts carried out in the course of a criminal investigation.

(6) If it appears to the enforcement authority that the matter is one of urgency, it may take the measures under paragraph (1) without first asking the member State in which the service provider is established to take measures and notifying the Commission and the member State in derogation from paragraph (4).

(7) In a case where a measure is taken pursuant to paragraph (6) above, the enforcement authority shall notify the measures taken to the Commission and to the member State concerned in the shortest possible time thereafter and indicate the reasons for urgency.

(8) In paragraph (2), 'court' means any court or tribunal.

6   General information to be provided by a person providing an information society service

(1) A person providing an information society service shall make available to the recipient of the service and any relevant enforcement authority, in a form and manner which is easily, directly and permanently accessible, the following information—

(a) the name of the service provider;

(b) the geographic address at which the service provider is established;

(c) the details of the service provider, including his electronic mail address, which make it possible to contact him rapidly and communicate with him in a direct and effective manner;

(d) where the service provider is registered in a trade or similar register available to the public, details of the register in which the service provider is entered and his registration number, or equivalent means of identification in that register;

(e) where the provision of the service is subject to an authorisation scheme, the particulars of the relevant supervisory authority;

(f) where the service provider exercises a regulated profession—
  (i) the details of any professional body or similar institution with which the service provider is registered;
  (ii) his professional title and the member State where that title has been granted;
  (iii) a reference to the professional rules applicable to the service provider in the member State of establishment and the means to access them; and

(g) where the service provider undertakes an activity that is subject to value added tax, the identification number referred to in Article 22(1) of the sixth Council Directive 77/388/EEC of 17 May 1977 on the harmonisation of the laws of the member States relating to turnover taxes—Common system of value added tax: uniform basis of assessment.

(2) Where a person providing an information society service refers to prices, these shall be indicated clearly and unambiguously and, in particular, shall indicate whether they are inclusive of tax and delivery costs.

7   Commercial communications

A service provider shall ensure that any commercial communication provided by him and which constitutes or forms part of an information society service shall—

(a) be clearly identifiable as a commercial communication;

(b) clearly identify the person on whose behalf the commercial communication is made;

(c) clearly identify as such any promotional offer (including any discount, premium or gift) and ensure that any conditions which must be met to qualify for it are easily accessible, and presented clearly and unambiguously; and

(d) clearly identify as such any promotional competition or game and ensure that any conditions for participation are easily accessible and presented clearly and unambiguously.

8   Unsolicited commercial communications

A service provider shall ensure that any unsolicited commercial communication sent by him by electronic mail is clearly and unambiguously identifiable as such as soon as it is received.

9   Information to be provided where contracts are concluded by electronic means

(1) Unless parties who are not consumers have agreed otherwise, where a contract is to be concluded by electronic means a service provider shall, prior to an order being placed by the recipient of a service, provide to that recipient in a clear, comprehensible and unambiguous manner the information set out in (a) to (d) below—

(a) the different technical steps to follow to conclude the contract;

(b) whether or not the concluded contract will be filed by the service provider and whether it will be accessible;

(c) the technical means for identifying and correcting input errors prior to the placing of the order; and

(d) the languages offered for the conclusion of the contract.

(2) Unless parties who are not consumers have agreed otherwise, a service provider shall indicate which relevant codes of conduct he subscribes to and give information on how those codes can be consulted electronically.

(3) Where the service provider provides terms and conditions applicable to the contract to the recipient, the service provider shall make them available to him in a way that allows him to store and reproduce them.

(4) The requirements of paragraphs (1) and (2) above shall not apply to contracts concluded exclusively by exchange of electronic mail or by equivalent individual communications.

10   Other information requirements

Regulations 6, 7, 8 and 9(1) have effect in addition to any other information requirements in legislation giving effect to Community law.

11   Placing of the order

(1) Unless parties who are not consumers have agreed otherwise, where the recipient of the service places his order through technological means, a service provider shall—

    (a) acknowledge receipt of the order to the recipient of the service without undue delay and by electronic means; and

    (b) make available to the recipient of the service appropriate, effective and accessible technical means allowing him to identify and correct input errors prior to the placing of the order.

(2) For the purposes of paragraph (1)(a) above—

    (a) the order and the acknowledgement of receipt will be deemed to be received when the parties to whom they are addressed are able to access them; and

    (b) the acknowledgement of receipt may take the form of the provision of the service paid for where that service is an information society service.

(3) The requirements of paragraph (1) above shall not apply to contracts concluded exclusively by exchange of electronic mail or by equivalent individual communications.

12   Meaning of the term 'order'

Except in relation to regulation 9(1)(c) and regulation 11(1)(b) where 'order' shall be the contractual offer, 'order' may be but need not be the contractual offer for the purposes of regulations 9 and 11.

13   Liability of the service provider

The duties imposed by regulations 6, 7, 8, 9(1) and 11(1)(a) shall be enforceable, at the suit of any recipient of a service, by an action against the service provider for damages for breach of statutory duty.

14   Compliance with Regulation 9(3)

Where on request a service provider has failed to comply with the requirement in regulation 9(3), the recipient may seek an order from any court having jurisdiction in relation to the contract requiring that service provider to comply with that requirement.

15   Right to rescind contract

Where a person—

    (a) has entered into a contract to which these Regulations apply, and

    (b) the service provider has not made available means of allowing him to identify and correct input errors in compliance with regulation 11(1)(b),

he shall be entitled to rescind the contract unless any court having jurisdiction in relation to the contract in question orders otherwise on the application of the service provider.

17   Mere conduit

(1) Where an information society service is provided which consists of the transmission in a communication network of information provided by a recipient of the service or the provision of access to a communication network, the service provider (if he otherwise would) shall not be liable for damages or for any other pecuniary remedy or for any criminal sanction as a result of that transmission where the service provider—

    (a) did not initiate the transmission;

    (b) did not select the receiver of the transmission; and

    (c) did not select or modify the information contained in the transmission.

(2) The acts of transmission and of provision of access referred to in paragraph (1) include the automatic, intermediate and transient storage of the information transmitted where:

(a) this takes place for the sole purpose of carrying out the transmission in the communication network, and

(b) the information is not stored for any period longer than is reasonably necessary for the transmission.

18 Caching

Where an information society service is provided which consists of the transmission in a communication network of information provided by a recipient of the service, the service provider (if he otherwise would) shall not be liable for damages or for any other pecuniary remedy or for any criminal sanction as a result of that transmission where—

(a) the information is the subject of automatic, intermediate and temporary storage where that storage is for the sole purpose of making more efficient onward transmission of the information to other recipients of the service upon their request, and

(b) the service provider—

(i)   does not modify the information;

(ii) complies with conditions on access to the information;

(iii) complies with any rules regarding the updating of the information, specified in a manner widely recognised and used by industry;

(iv) does not interfere with the lawful use of technology, widely recognised and used by industry, to obtain data on the use of the information; and

(v) acts expeditiously to remove or to disable access to the information he has stored upon obtaining actual knowledge of the fact that the information at the initial source of the transmission has been removed from the network, or access to it has been disabled, or that a court or an administrative authority has ordered such removal or disablement.

19 Hosting

Where an information society service is provided which consists of the storage of information provided by a recipient of the service, the service provider (if he otherwise would) shall not be liable for damages or for any other pecuniary remedy or for any criminal sanction as a result of that storage where—

(a) the service provider—

(i)   does not have actual knowledge of unlawful activity or information and, where a claim for damages is made, is not aware of facts or circumstances from which it would have been apparent to the service provider that the activity or information was unlawful; or

(ii) upon obtaining such knowledge or awareness, acts expeditiously to remove or to disable access to the information, and

(b) the recipient of the service was not acting under the authority or the control of the service provider.

20 Protection of rights

(1) Nothing in regulations 17, 18 and 19 shall—

(a) prevent a person agreeing different contractual terms; or

(b) affect the rights of any party to apply to a court for relief to prevent or stop infringement of any rights.

(2) Any power of an administrative authority to prevent or stop infringement of any rights shall continue to apply notwithstanding regulations 17, 18 and 19.

21 Defence in criminal proceedings: burden of proof

(1) This regulation applies where a service provider charged with an offence in criminal proceedings arising out of any transmission, provision of access or storage falling within regulation 17, 18 or 19 relies on a defence under any of regulations 17, 18 and 19.

(2) Where evidence is adduced which is sufficient to raise an issue with respect to that defence, the court or jury shall assume that the defence is satisfied unless the prosecution proves beyond reasonable doubt that it is not.

22 Notice for the purposes of actual knowledge

In determining whether a service provider has actual knowledge for the purposes of regulations 18(b)(v) and 19(a)(i), a court shall take into account all matters which appear to it in the particular circumstances to be relevant and, among other things, shall have regard to—

    (a) whether a service provider has received a notice through a means of contact made available in accordance with regulation 6(1)(c), and

    (b) the extent to which any notice includes—

        (i)   the full name and address of the sender of the notice;

        (ii) details of the location of the information in question; and

        (iii) details of the unlawful nature of the activity or information in question.

Regulation 4   SCHEDULE

1. Copyright, neighbouring rights, rights referred to in Directive 87/54/EEC and Directive 96/9/EC and industrial property rights.

2. The freedom of the parties to a contract to choose the applicable law.

3. Contractual obligations concerning consumer contracts.

4. Formal validity of contracts creating or transferring rights in real estate where such contracts are subject to mandatory formal requirements of the law of the member State where the real estate is situated.

5. The permissibility of unsolicited commercial communications by electronic mail.

Late Payment of Commercial Debts Regulations 2002
(SI 2002, No. 1674)

3 Proceedings restraining use of grossly unfair terms

(1) In this regulation:

    (a) 'small and medium-sized enterprises' means those enterprises defined in Annex 1 to Commission Regulation (EC) No 70/2001 of 12th January 2001 on the application of Articles 87 and 88 of the EC Treaty to State aid to small and medium-sized enterprises;

    (b) 'representative body' means an organisation established to represent the collective interests of small and medium-sized enterprises in general or in a particular sector or area.

(2) This regulation applies where a person acting in the course of a business has written standard terms on which he enters (or intends to enter) as purchaser into contracts to which the Late Payment of Commercial Debts (Interest) Act 1998 applies which include a term purporting to oust or vary the right to statutory interest in relation to qualifying debts created by those contracts.

(3) If it appears to the High Court that in all or any circumstances the purported use of such a term in a relevant contract would be void under the Late Payment of Commercial Debts (Interest) Act 1998, the court on the application of a representative body may grant an injunction against that person restraining him in those circumstances from using the offending term, on such terms as the court may think fit.

(4) Only a representative body may apply to the High Court under this regulation.

Sale and Supply of Goods to Consumers Regulations 2002
(SI 2002, No. 3045)

1   Title, commencement and extent

(1) These Regulations may be cited as the Sale and Supply of Goods to Consumers Regulations 2002 and shall come into force on 31st March 2003.

(2) These Regulations extend to Northern Ireland.

2   Interpretation

In these Regulations—

'consumer' means any natural person who, in the contracts covered by these Regulations, is acting for purposes which are outside his trade, business or profession;

'consumer guarantee' means any undertaking to a consumer by a person acting in the course of his business, given without extra charge, to reimburse the price paid or to replace, repair or handle consumer goods in any way if they do not meet the specifications set out in the guarantee statement or in the relevant advertising;

'court' in relation to England and Wales and Northern Ireland means a county court or the High Court, and in relation to Scotland, the sheriff or the Court of Session;

'enforcement authority' means the Director General of Fair Trading, every local weights and measures authority in Great Britain and the Department of Enterprise, Trade and Investment for Northern Ireland;

'goods' has the same meaning as in section 61 of the Sale of Goods Act 1979;

'guarantor' means a person who offers a consumer guarantee to a consumer; and

'supply' includes supply by way of sale, lease, hire or hire-purchase.

15   Consumer guarantees

(1) Where goods are sold or otherwise supplied to a consumer which are offered with a consumer guarantee, the consumer guarantee takes effect at the time the goods are delivered as a contractual obligation owed by the guarantor under the conditions set out in the guarantee statement and the associated advertising.

(2) The guarantor shall ensure that the guarantee sets out in plain intelligible language the contents of the guarantee and the essential particulars necessary for making claims under the guarantee, notably the duration and territorial scope of the guarantee as well as the name and address of the guarantor.

(3) On request by the consumer to a person to whom paragraph (4) applies, the guarantee shall within a reasonable time be made available in writing or in another durable medium available and accessible to him.

(4) This paragraph applies to the guarantor and any other person who offers to consumers the goods which are the subject of the guarantee for sale or supply.

(5) Where consumer goods are offered with a consumer guarantee, and where those goods are offered within the territory of the United Kingdom, then the guarantor shall ensure that the consumer guarantee is written in English.

(6) If the guarantor fails to comply with the provisions of paragraphs (2) or (5) above, or a person to whom paragraph (4) applies fails to comply with paragraph (3) then the enforcement authority may apply for an injunction or (in Scotland) an order of specific implement against that person requiring him to comply.

(7) The court on application under this Regulation may grant an injunction or (in Scotland) an order of specific implement on such terms as it thinks fit.

Insolvency Act 1986 (Prescribed Part) Order 2003
(SI 2003, No. 2097)

1   Citation, Commencement and Interpretation

(2) In this order 'the 1986 Act' means the Insolvency Act 1986.

2 Minimum value of the company's net property

For the purposes of section 176A(3)(a) of the 1986 Act the minimum value of the company's net property is £10,000.

3 Calculation of prescribed part

(1) The prescribed part of the company's net property to be made available for the satisfaction of unsecured debts of the company pursuant to section 176A of the 1986 Act shall be calculated as follows—

(a) where the company's net property does not exceed £10,000 in value, 50% of that property;

(b) subject to paragraph (2), where the company's net property exceeds £10,000 in value the sum of—

(i) 50% of the first £10,000 in value; and

(ii) 20% of that part of the company's net property which exceeds £10,000 in value.

(2) The value of the prescribed part of the company's net property to be made available for the satisfaction of unsecured debts of the company pursuant to section 176A shall not exceed £600,000.

Timeshare (Cancellation Information) Order 2003
(SI 2003, No. 2579)

2 Interpretation

In this Order—

'the Act' means the Timeshare Act 1992;

'blank cancellation notice', in the case of a timeshare agreement, means a blank notice of cancellation which the agreement is required to contain by section 2(2F) of the Act, and, in the case of a timeshare credit agreement, means a blank notice of cancellation which a timeshare credit agreement is required to contain by section 3(6) of the Act;

'required information', in the case of a timeshare agreement, means information which the agreement is required to contain by section 2 of the Act and, in the case of a timeshare credit agreement, means information which the agreement is required to contain by section 3 of the Act.

3 Form of timeshare agreements

(1) A timeshare agreement shall include the required information in the form set out—

(a) in Part I of Schedule 1 to this Order, unless the agreement fulfils the conditions set out in either subsection (2B) or subsection (2D) of section 2 of the Act;

(b) in Part II of that Schedule, if the agreement fulfils the conditions set out in subsection (2D), but does not fulfil the conditions set out in subsection (2B), of that section; or

(c) in Part III of that Schedule, if the agreement fulfils the conditions set out in subsection (2B) of that section.

(2) If a timeshare agreement includes provision for providing credit for or in respect of the offeree, it shall also include the information which it is required to contain by section 2(2A) of the Act in the form set out in Schedule 2 to this Order.

(3) A timeshare agreement shall include a blank cancellation notice in the form set out in Part I of Schedule 4 to this Order.

(4) The required information and the blank cancellation notice shall be set out at the end of the timeshare agreement.

(5) A timeshare agreement shall include, immediately adjacent to the place where the offeree signs the agreement, the statement, 'YOU HAVE THE RIGHT TO CANCEL THIS

AGREEMENT. YOU HAVE UNTIL   IN WHICH TO DO SO. (THIS DATE MUST BE AT LEAST FOURTEEN DAYS AFTER THE DAY YOU SIGNED THE AGREEMENT). PLEASE REFER TO THE END OF THE AGREEMENT FOR FURTHER DETAILS OF YOUR CANCELLATION RIGHTS.'

4   Form of timeshare credit agreements

(1) A timeshare agreement shall include the required information in the form set out—

(a) in Part I of Schedule 3 to this Order, or

(b) in Part II of that Schedule, if the agreement fulfils the conditions set out in sub-section (4) of section 3 of the Act.

(2) A timeshare credit agreement shall include a blank cancellation notice in the form set out in Part II of Schedule 4 to this Order.

(3) The required information and the blank cancellation notice shall be set out at the end of the timeshare credit agreement.

(4) A timeshare credit agreement shall include, immediately adjacent to the place where the offeree signs the agreement, the statement, 'YOU HAVE THE RIGHT TO CANCEL THIS AGREEMENT. YOU HAVE UNTIL   IN WHICH TO DO SO (THIS DATE MUST BE AT LEAST FOURTEEN DAYS AFTER THE DAY YOU SIGNED THE AGREEMENT). PLEASE REFER TO THE END OF THE AGREEMENT FOR FURTHER DETAILS OF YOUR CANCELLATION RIGHTS.'

5   Lettering requirements

(1) The lettering of the required information, of the blank cancellation notices and of the statements referred to in articles 3(5) and 4(4) shall be of a size and type that is easily legible and of a colour which is easily distinguishable from the background on which they are set out.

(2) For the required information and the blank cancellation notices, capital letters shall be used in all the places in which they are shown in each Schedule and words shall be in bold lettering in accordance with the Schedules.

(3) Capital letters shall be used for all the words in the statements referred to in articles 3(5) and 4(4).

(4) The lettering of the words 'IMPORTANT—YOU SHOULD READ THIS CAREFULLY' and 'YOUR RIGHT TO CANCEL THIS AGREEMENT' in the required information shall be larger than any other lettering in the required information.

6   Information to be inserted

(1) In the required information and the blank cancellation notices, there shall be inserted in the blank spaces in the form set out in the appropriate Schedule the information referred to in the square brackets besides the blank spaces.

(2) In the statement referred to in article 3(5), there shall be inserted in the blank space after the word 'until' the date which must be specified in the agreement by virtue of section 2(2)(a) of the Act.

(3) In the statement referred to in article 4(4), there shall be inserted in the blank space after the word 'until' the date which must be specified in the agreement by virtue of section 3(2)(a) of the Act.

Article 3(1)   SCHEDULE 1

PART I   IMPORTANT—YOU SHOULD READ THIS CAREFULLY YOUR
RIGHT TO CANCEL THIS AGREEMENT

You can cancel this timeshare agreement by sending or taking a written notice of cancellation to . . . [name and address of person to whom notice of cancellation may be given] on or before. . . [date specified under section 2 (2)(a) of the Timeshare Act 1992]. You therefore have at least fourteen days in which to cancel this agreement. If you post the notice in a properly addressed and fully pre-paid letter, the notice will be treated as given at the time of posting.

You may use the cancellation notice provided in this agreement, but this is not obligatory.

If you cancel this agreement in the way described above, you will have no further rights or obligations under it, but you will have the right to recover any sums paid under or in contemplation of this agreement.

PART II   IMPORTANT—YOU SHOULD READ THIS CAREFULLY YOUR RIGHT TO CANCEL THIS AGREEMENT

You can cancel this timeshare agreement by sending or taking a written notice of cancellation to . . . [name and address of person to whom notice of cancellation may be given] on or before . . . [date specified under section 2 (2)(a) of the Timeshare Act 1992]. You therefore have at least fourteen days in which to cancel this agreement. If you post the notice in a properly addressed and fully pre-paid letter, the notice will be treated as given at the time of posting.

You may use the cancellation notice provided in this agreement, but this is not obligatory.

If you cancel this agreement in the way described above, you will have no further rights or obligations under it, but you will have the right to recover any sums paid under or in contemplation of this agreement.

You may have further rights to cancel, if this agreement does not include certain required information.

PART III   IMPORTANT—YOU SHOULD READ THIS CAREFULLY YOUR RIGHT TO CANCEL THIS AGREEMENT

You can cancel this timeshare agreement by sending or taking a written notice of cancellation to . . . [name and address of person to whom notice of cancellation may be given] on or before . . . [date specified under section 2 (2)(a) of the Timeshare Act 1992]. You therefore have at least fourteen days in which to cancel this agreement. If you post the notice in a properly addressed and fully pre-paid letter, the notice will be treated as given at the time of posting.

You may use the cancellation notice provided in this agreement, but this is not obligatory.

If you cancel this agreement in the way described above, you will have no further rights or obligations under it, but you will have the right to recover any sums paid under or in contemplation of this agreement.

You may have further rights to cancel, if this agreement does not include certain required information.

Purchase of Timeshare using credit under a related agreement

If you have purchased a timeshare using credit under a related credit agreement, then the related credit agreement will be automatically cancelled, if you cancel the timeshare agreement in the way described above.

If you have received any monies under a related credit agreement, you will need to repay these. If you are repaying by instalments and you repay any monies by the date your first repayment is due, then you will not be liable to pay interest on the amount repaid. If you do not repay the whole of the amount you have borrowed in that time then you will be sent a statement showing the amount outstanding and the repayments due, including interest, and you do not have to make any repayment until you receive this. If you are not repaying by instalments and you repay any monies within one month of the date you gave notice to cancel then you will not be liable to pay interest on the amount repaid. Subject to the above, you will have no further rights and obligations under the credit agreement.

Article 3(2)   SCHEDULE 2

If your timeshare agreement includes provision for credit with which to pay for the time-share, then you will need to repay the credit. If you are repaying by instalments and you repay any monies by the date your first repayment is due, then you will not be liable to pay interest on the amount repaid. If you do not repay the whole of the amount you have borrowed in that time then you will be sent a statement showing the amount outstanding and the repayments due, including interest, and you do not have to make any repayment until you receive this. If you are not repaying by instalments and you repay any monies within one month of the date you gave notice to cancel then you will not be liable to pay interest on the amount repaid. Subject to the above, you will have no further rights and obligations under the credit agreement.

Article 4(1)   SCHEDULE 3

PART I   IMPORTANT—YOU SHOULD READ THIS CAREFULLY
YOUR RIGHT TO CANCEL THIS AGREEMENT

This is a timeshare credit agreement for the purposes of the Timeshare Act 1992. You can cancel this credit agreement by sending or taking a written notice of cancellation to . . . [name and address of person to whom notice of cancellation may be given] on or before . . . [date specified under section 3(2)(a) of the Timeshare Act 1992]. You therefore have at least fourteen days in which to cancel this agreement. If you post the notice in a properly addressed and fully pre-paid letter, the notice will be treated as given at the time of posting.

    You may use the cancellation notice provided in this agreement, but this is not obligatory.

    Cancelling your timeshare credit agreement does not cancel your timeshare agreement. If you wish to cancel your timeshare agreement, you must do that separately.

    If you have received any monies under this credit agreement, you will need to repay these. If you are repaying by instalments and you repay any monies by the date your first repayment is due, then you will not be liable to pay interest on the amount repaid. If you do not repay the whole of the amount you have borrowed in that time then you will be sent a statement showing the amount outstanding and the repayments due, including interest, and you do not have to make any repayment until you receive this. If you are not repaying by instalments and you repay any monies within one month of the date you gave notice to cancel then you will not be liable to pay interest on the amount repaid. Subject to the above, you will have no further rights and obligations under the credit agreement.

PART II   IMPORTANT—YOU SHOULD READ THIS CAREFULLY
YOUR RIGHT TO CANCEL THIS AGREEMENT

This is a timeshare credit agreement for the purposes of the Timeshare Act 1992. You can cancel this credit agreement by sending or taking a written notice of cancellation to . . . [name and address of person to whom notice of cancellation may be given] on or before . . . [date specified under section 3(2)(a) of the Timeshare Act 1992]. You therefore have at least fourteen days in which to cancel this agreement. If you post the notice in a properly addressed and fully pre-paid letter, the notice will be treated as given at the time of posting.

    You may use the cancellation notice provided in this agreement, but this is not obligatory.

    Cancelling your timeshare credit agreement does not cancel your timeshare agreement. If you wish to cancel your timeshare agreement, you must do that separately.

If you cancel the timeshare agreement in the way described in that agreement, then this credit agreement will be automatically cancelled.

If you have received any monies under this credit agreement, you will need to repay these. If you are repaying by instalments and you repay any monies by the date your first repayment is due, then you will not be liable to pay interest on the amount repaid. If you do not repay the whole of the amount you have borrowed in that time then you will be sent a statement showing the amount outstanding and the repayments due, including interest, and you do not have to make any repayment until you receive this. If you are not repaying by instalments and you repay any monies within one month of the date you gave notice to cancel then you will not be liable to pay interest on the amount repaid. Subject to the above, you will have no further rights and obligations under the credit agreement.

Articles 3(3) and 4(2)   SCHEDULE 4

PART I   NOTICE OF CANCELLATION OF TIMESHARE AGREEMENT GIVEN UNDER SECTION 5 OR SECTION 5A OF THE TIMESHARE ACT 1992

Complete and return this notice ONLY if you wish to cancel the timeshare agreement.

To . . . [name and address of person to whom notice of cancellation may be given]

I/we (delete as appropriate) hereby give notice that I/we (delete as appropriate) wish to cancel my/our (delete as appropriate) timeshare agreement.

Reference . . . [offeror's reference number, code or other details to enable the timeshare agreement to be identified]

Signed . . .

Dated . . .

If this notice is sent by post in a properly addressed and pre-paid letter, the notice is treated as given at the time of posting.

PART II   NOTICE OF CANCELLATION OF TIMESHARE CREDIT AGREEMENT GIVEN UNDER SECTION 6 OF THE TIMESHARE ACT 1992

Complete and return this notice ONLY if you wish to cancel the timeshare credit agreement.

To . . . [name and address of person to whom notice of cancellation may be given]

I/we (delete as appropriate) hereby give notice that I/we (delete as appropriate) wish to cancel my/our (delete as appropriate) timeshare credit agreement.

Reference . . . [creditor's reference number, code or other details to enable the timeshare credit agreement to be identified]

Signed . . .

Dated . . .

If this notice is sent by post in a properly addressed and pre-paid letter, the notice is treated as given at the time of posting.

Consumer Credit (Disclosure of Information) Regulations 2004

(SI 2004, No. 1481)

1   Citation, commencement and interpretation

(2) In these Regulations—

'the Agreements Regulations' mean the Consumer Credit (Agreements) Regulations 1983;

'distance contract' means any regulated agreement made under an organised distance sales or service-provision scheme run by the creditor or owner or by an intermediary of the creditor or owner who, in any such case, for the purpose of that agreement makes exclusive use of one or more means of distance communication up to and including the time at which the agreement is made and for this purpose any means of communication is a means of distance communication if, without the simultaneous physical presence of the creditor or owner or any intermediary of the creditor or owner and of the debtor or hirer, it may be used for the distance marketing of a regulated agreement between the parties to that agreement;

'durable medium' means any instrument which enables the debtor or hirer to store information addressed personally to him in a way accessible for future reference for a period of time adequate for the purposes of the information and which allows the unchanged reproduction of the information stored.

2   Agreements to which these Regulations apply

These Regulations apply in respect of all regulated agreements except—

    (a) agreements to which section 58 of the Consumer Credit Act 1974 (opportunity for withdrawal from prospective land mortgage) applies; and

    (b) distance contracts.

3   Information to be disclosed to a debtor or hirer before a regulated agreement is made

(1) Before a regulated agreement ('the relevant agreement') is made, the creditor or owner must disclose to the debtor or hirer in the manner set out in regulation 4 the information and statements of protection and remedies that are required to be given—

    (a) in the case of a regulated consumer credit agreement, under regulation 2 of the Agreements Regulations;

    (b) in the case of a regulated consumer hire agreement, under regulation 3 of the Agreements Regulations;

    (c) in the case of a modifying agreement which is, or is treated as, a regulated consumer credit agreement, under regulations 2(3) and 7(2) of the Agreements Regulations;

    (d) in the case of a modifying agreement which is or is treated as a regulated consumer hirer agreement, under regulations 3(3) and 7(9) of the Agreements Regulations.

(2) The information and statements of protection required to be disclosed under paragraph (1) shall be the information and statements that will be included in the document embodying the relevant agreement save that, where any of the information is not known at the time of disclosure, the creditor or owner shall disclose estimated information based on such assumptions as he may reasonably make in all the circumstances of the case.

4   Manner of disclosure

The information and statements of protection and remedies required to be disclosed under regulation 3 must be—

    (a) easily legible and, where applicable, of a colour which is readily distinguishable from the background medium upon which they are displayed;

    (b) not interspersed with any other information or wording apart from subtotals of total amounts and cross references to the terms of the agreement;

    (c) of equal prominence except that headings may be afforded more prominence whether by capital letters, underlining, larger or bold print or otherwise; and

    (d) contained in a document which:

        (i) is separate from the document embodying the relevant agreement (within the meaning of regulation 3) and any other document referred to in the document embodying that agreement;

        (ii) is headed with the words 'Pre-contract Information';

        (iii) does not contain any other information or wording apart from the heading referred to in sub-paragraph (ii);

(iv) is on paper or on another durable medium which is available and accessible to the debtor or hirer; and

(v) is of a nature that enables the debtor or hirer to remove it from the place where it is disclosed to him.

Financial Services (Distance Marketing) Regulations 2004
(SI 2004, No. 2095)

2 Interpretation

(1) In these Regulations—

'the 1974 Act' means the Consumer Credit Act 1974;

'the 2000 Act' means the Financial Services and Markets Act 2000;

'the Authority' means the Financial Services Authority;

'appointed representative' has the same meaning as in section 39(2) of the 2000 Act (exemption of appointed representatives);

'authorised person' has the same meaning as in section 31(2) of the 2000 Act (authorised persons);

'breach' means a contravention by a supplier of a prohibition in, or a failure by a supplier to comply with a requirement of, these Regulations;

'business' includes a trade or profession;

'consumer' means any individual who, in contracts to which these Regulations apply, is acting for purposes which are outside any business he may carry on;

'court' in relation to England and Wales and Northern Ireland means a county court or the High Court, and in relation to Scotland means the Sheriff Court or the Court of Session;

'credit' includes a cash loan and any other form of financial accommodation, and for this purpose 'cash' includes money in any form;

'designated professional body' has the same meaning as in section 326(2) of the 2000 Act (designation of professional bodies);

'the Directive' means Directive 2002/65/EC of the European Parliament and of the Council of 23 September 2002 concerning the distance marketing of consumer financial services and amending Council Directive 90/619/EEC and Directives 97/7/EC and 98/27/EC;

'distance contract' means any contract concerning one or more financial services concluded between a supplier and a consumer under an organised distance sales or service-provision scheme run by the supplier or by an intermediary, who, for the purpose of that contract, makes exclusive use of one or more means of distance communication up to and including the time at which the contract is concluded;

'durable medium' means any instrument which enables a consumer to store information addressed personally to him in a way accessible for future reference for a period of time adequate for the purposes of the information and which allows the unchanged reproduction of the information stored;

'EEA supplier' means a supplier who is a national of an EEA State, or a company or firm (within the meaning of Article 48 of the Treaty establishing the European Community) formed in accordance with the law of an EEA State;

'EEA State' means a State which is a contracting party to the Agreement on the European Economic Area signed at Oporto on 2nd May 1992, as adjusted by the Protocol signed at Brussels on 17th March 1993;

'exempt regulated activity' has the same meaning as in section 325(2) of the 2000 Act;

'financial service' means any service of a banking, credit, insurance, personal pension, investment or payment nature;

'means of distance communication' means any means which, without the simultaneous physical presence of the supplier and the consumer, may be used for the marketing of a service between those parties;

'the OFT' means the Office of Fair Trading;

'regulated activity' has the same meaning as in section 22 of the 2000 Act (the classes of activity and categories of investment);

'Regulated Activities Order' means the Financial Services and Markets Act 2000 (Regulated Activities) Order 2001;

'rule' means a rule—

(a) made by the Authority under the 2000 Act, or

(b) made by a designated professional body, and approved by the Authority, under section 332 of the 2000 Act,

as the context requires;

'supplier' means any person who, acting in his commercial or professional capacity, is the contractual provider of services.

(2) In these Regulations, subject to paragraph (1), any expression used in these Regulations which is also used in the Directive has the same meaning as in the Directive.

Scope of these Regulations

3—(1) Regulations 7 to 14 apply, subject to regulations 4 and 5, in relation to distance contracts made on or after 31st October 2004.

(2) Regulation 15 applies in relation to financial services supplied on or after 31st October 2004 under an organised distance sales or service-provision scheme run by the supplier or by an intermediary, who, for the purpose of that supply, makes exclusive use of one or more means of distance communication up to and including the time at which the financial services are supplied.

4—(1) Where an EEA State, other than the United Kingdom, has transposed the Directive or has obligations in its domestic law corresponding to those provided for in the Directive—

(a) regulations 7 to 14 do not apply in relation to any contract made between an EEA supplier contracting from an establishment in that EEA State and a consumer in the United Kingdom, and

(b) regulation 15 does not apply to any supply of financial services by an EEA supplier from an establishment in that EEA State to a consumer in the United Kingdom,

if the provisions by which that State has transposed the Directive, or the obligations in the domestic law of that State corresponding to those provided for in the Directive, as the case may be, apply to that contract or that supply.

(2) Subject to paragraph (5) and regulation 6(3) and (4)—

(a) regulations 7 to 11 do not apply in relation to any contract made by a supplier who is an authorised person, the making or performance of which constitutes or is part of a regulated activity carried on by him;

(b) regulation 15 does not apply to any supply of financial services by a supplier who is an authorised person, where that supply constitutes or is part of a regulated activity carried on by him.

(3) Subject to regulation 6(3) and (4)—

(a) regulations 7 and 8 do not apply in relation to any contract made by a supplier who is an appointed representative, the making or performance of which constitutes or is part of a regulated activity (other than an exempt regulated activity) carried on by him;

(b) regulation 15 does not apply to any supply of financial services by a supplier who is an appointed representative, where that supply constitutes or is part of a regulated activity (other than an exempt regulated activity) carried on by him.

(4) Subject to regulation 6(3) and (4)—

(a) regulations 7 and 8 do not apply in relation to any contract where—

(i) the supplier is bound, or is controlled or managed by one or more persons who are bound, by rules of a designated professional body which are equivalent to those regulations, and

        (ii) the making or performance of that contract constitutes or is part of an exempt regulated activity carried on by the supplier;

    (b) regulation 15 does not apply to any supply of financial services where—

        (i) the supplier is bound, or is controlled or managed by one or more persons who are bound, by rules of a designated professional body which are equivalent to that regulation, and

        (ii) that supply constitutes or is part of an exempt regulated activity carried on by the supplier.

(5) Paragraph (2) does not apply in relation to any contract or supply of financial services made by a supplier who is the operator, trustee or depositary of a scheme which is a recognised scheme by virtue of section 264 of the 2000 Act (schemes constituted in other EEA States), where the making or performance of the contract or the supply of the financial services constitutes or is part of a regulated activity for which he has permission in that capacity.

(6) In paragraph (5)—

'the operator', 'trustee' and 'depositary' each has the same meaning as in section 237(2) of the 2000 Act (other definitions); and

'permission' has the same meaning as in section 266 of that Act (disapplication of rules).

5—(1) Where a consumer and a supplier enter an initial service agreement and—

    (a) successive operations of the same nature, or

    (b) a series of separate operations of the same nature,

are subsequently performed between them over time and within the framework of that agreement, then, if any of regulations 7 to 14 apply, they apply only to the initial service agreement.

(2) Where a consumer and a supplier do not enter an initial service agreement and—

    (a) successive operations of the same nature, or

    (b) a series of separate operations of the same nature,

are performed between them over time, then, if regulations 7 and 8 apply, they apply only—

        (i) when the first operation is performed, and

        (ii) to any operation which is performed more than one year after the previous operation.

(3) For the purposes of this regulation, 'initial service agreement' includes, for example, an agreement for the provision of—

    (a) a bank account;

    (b) a credit card; or

    (c) portfolio management services.

(4) For the purposes of this regulation, 'operations' includes, for example—

    (a) deposits to or withdrawals from a bank account;

    (b) payments by a credit card;

    (c) transactions carried out within the framework of an initial service agreement for portfolio management services; and

    (d) subscriptions to new units of the same collective investment fund,

but does not include adding new elements to an existing initial service agreement, for example adding the possibility of using an electronic payment instrument together with an existing bank account.

6 Financial services marketed by an intermediary

(1) This regulation applies where a financial service is marketed by an intermediary.

(2) These Regulations have effect as if—

    (a) each reference to a supplier in the definition of 'breach' in regulation 2(1) were a reference to a supplier or an intermediary;

    (b) the reference to the supplier in the definition of 'means of distance communication' in regulation 2(1), each reference to the supplier in regulations 7, 8(1) and (2), 10 and 11(3)(b), and the first reference to the supplier in regulation 8(4), were a reference to the intermediary;

(c) the reference to the supplier in regulation 8(3) were a reference to the supplier or the intermediary;

(d) for regulation 11(2) there were substituted—

'(2) Paragraph (1) does not apply to a distance contract if the intermediary has not complied with regulation 8(1) (and the supplier has not done what the intermediary was required to do by regulation 8(1)), unless—

(a) the circumstances fall within regulation 8(1)(b); and

(b) either—

(i) the intermediary has complied with regulation 7(1) and (2) or, if applicable, regulation 7(4)(b), and with regulation 7(5), or

(ii) the supplier has done what the intermediary was required to do by regulation 7(1) and (2) or, if applicable, regulation 7(4)(b), and by regulation 7(5).';

(e) the reference to a supplier in regulation 22(1) were a reference to an intermediary; and

(f) each reference to the supplier in paragraphs 2, 4, 5 and 19 of Schedule 1 were a reference to the supplier and the intermediary.

(3) Notwithstanding paragraphs (2) to (4) of regulation 4, regulations 7 and 8 apply in relation to the intermediary unless—

(a) the intermediary is an authorised person and the marketing of the financial service constitutes or is part of a regulated activity carried on by him;

(b) the intermediary is an appointed representative and the marketing of the financial service constitutes or is part of a regulated activity (other than an exempt regulated activity) carried on by him; or

(c) the intermediary is not an authorised person, but—

(i) he is bound, or is controlled or managed by one or more persons who are bound, by rules of a designated professional body which are equivalent to regulations 7 and 8, and

(ii) the marketing of the financial service constitutes or is part of an exempt regulated activity carried on by him.

(4) Notwithstanding paragraphs (2) to (4) of regulation 4, regulation 15 applies to the intermediary unless—

(a) the intermediary is an authorised person and is acting in the course of a regulated activity carried on by him;

(b) the intermediary is an appointed representative and is acting in the course of a regulated activity (other than an exempt regulated activity) carried on by him; or

(c) the intermediary is not an authorised person, but—

(i) he is bound, or is controlled or managed by one or more persons who are bound, by rules of a designated professional body which are equivalent to regulation 15, and

(ii) he is acting in the course an exempt regulated activity carried on by him.

7   Information required prior to the conclusion of the contract

(1) Subject to paragraph (4), in good time prior to the consumer being bound by any distance contract, the supplier shall provide to the consumer the information specified in Schedule 1.

(2) The supplier shall provide the information specified in Schedule 1 in a clear and comprehensible manner appropriate to the means of distance communication used, with due regard in particular to the principles of good faith in commercial transactions and the principles governing the protection of those who are unable to give their consent such as minors.

(3) Subject to paragraph (4), the supplier shall make clear his commercial purpose when providing the information specified in Schedule 1.

(4) In the case of a voice telephone communication—

(a) the supplier shall make clear his identity and the commercial purpose of any call initiated by him at the beginning of any conversation with the consumer; and

(b) if the consumer explicitly consents, only the information specified in Schedule 2 need be given.

(5) The supplier shall ensure that the information he provides to the consumer pursuant to this regulation, regarding the contractual obligations which would arise if the distance contract were concluded, accurately reflects the contractual obligations which would arise under the law presumed to be applicable to that contract.

8   Written and additional information

(1) The supplier under a distance contract shall communicate to the consumer on paper, or in another durable medium which is available and accessible to the consumer, all the contractual terms and conditions and the information specified in Schedule 1, either—

> (a) in good time prior to the consumer being bound by that distance contract; or
>
> (b) immediately after the conclusion of the contract, where the contract has been concluded at the consumer's request using a means of distance communication which does not enable provision in accordance with sub-paragraph (a) of the contractual terms and conditions and the information specified in Schedule 1.

(2) The supplier shall communicate the contractual terms and conditions to the consumer on paper, if the consumer so requests at any time during their contractual relationship.

(3) Paragraph (2) does not apply if the supplier has already communicated the contractual terms and conditions to the consumer on paper during that contractual relationship, and those terms and conditions have not changed since they were so communicated.

(4) The supplier shall change the means of distance communication with the consumer if the consumer so requests at any time during his contractual relationship with the supplier, unless that is incompatible with the distance contract or the nature of the financial service provided to the consumer.

9   Right to cancel

(1) Subject to regulation 11, if within the cancellation period set out in regulation 10 notice of cancellation is properly given by the consumer to the supplier, the notice of cancellation shall operate to cancel the distance contract.

(2) Cancelling the contract has the effect of terminating the contract at the time at which the notice of cancellation is given.

(3) For the purposes of these Regulations, a notice of cancellation is a notification given—

> (a) orally (where the supplier has informed the consumer that notice of cancellation may be given orally),
>
> (b) in writing, or
>
> (c) in another durable medium available and accessible to the supplier,

which, however expressed, indicates the intention of the consumer to cancel the contract by that notification.

(4) Notice of cancellation given under this regulation by a consumer to a supplier is to be treated as having been properly given if the consumer—

> (a) gives it orally to the supplier (where the supplier has informed the consumer that notice of cancellation may be given orally);
>
> (b) leaves it at the address of the supplier last known to the consumer and addressed to the supplier by name (in which case it is to be taken to have been given on the day on which it was left);
>
> (c) sends it by post to the address of the supplier last known to the consumer and addressed to the supplier by name (in which case it is to be taken to have been given on the day on which it was posted);
>
> (d) sends it by facsimile to the business facsimile number of the supplier last known to the consumer (in which case it is to be taken to have been given on the day on which it was sent);

(e) sends it by electronic mail to the business electronic mail address of the supplier last known to the consumer (in which case it is to be taken to have been given on the day on which it is sent); or

(f) by other electronic means—

(i) sends it to an internet address or web-site which the supplier has notified the consumer may be used for the purpose, or

(ii) indicates it on such a web-site in accordance with instructions which are on the web-site or which the supplier has provided to the consumer, (in which case it is to be taken to have been given on the day on which it is sent to that address or web-site or indicated on that web-site).

(5) The references in paragraph (4)(b) and (c) to the address of the supplier shall, in the case of a supplier which is a body corporate, be treated as including a reference to the address of the secretary or clerk of that body.

(6) The references in paragraph (4)(b) and (c) to the address of the supplier shall, in the case of a supplier which is a partnership, be treated as including a reference to the address of a partner or a person having control or management of the partnership business.

(7) In this regulation—

(a) every reference to the supplier includes a reference to any other person previously notified by or on behalf of the supplier to the consumer as a person to whom notice of cancellation may be given;

(b) the references to giving notice of cancellation orally include giving such notice by voice telephone communication, where the supplier has informed the consumer that notice of cancellation may be given in that way; and

(c) 'electronic mail' has the same meaning as in regulation 2(1) of the Privacy and Electronic Communications (EC Directive) Regulations 2003 (interpretation).

10 Cancellation period

(1) For the purposes of regulation 9, the cancellation period begins on the day on which the distance contract is concluded ('conclusion day') and ends as provided for in paragraphs (2) to (5).

(2) Where the supplier complies with regulation 8(1) on or before conclusion day, the cancellation period ends on the expiry of fourteen calendar days beginning with the day after conclusion day.

(3) Where the supplier does not comply with regulation 8(1) on or before conclusion day, but subsequently communicates to the consumer on paper, or in another durable medium which is available and accessible to the consumer, all the contractual terms and conditions and the information required under regulation 8(1), the cancellation period ends on the expiry of fourteen calendar days beginning with the day after the day on which the consumer receives the last of those terms and conditions and that information.

(4) In the case of a distance contract relating to life insurance, for the references to conclusion day in paragraphs (2) and (3) there are substituted references to the day on which the consumer is informed that the distance contract has been concluded.

(5) In the case of a distance contract relating to life insurance or a personal pension, for the references to fourteen calendar days in paragraphs (2) and (3) there are substituted references to thirty calendar days.

11 Exceptions to the right to cancel

(1) Subject to paragraphs (2) and (3), regulation 9 does not confer on a consumer a right to cancel a distance contract which is—

(a) a contract for a financial service where the price of that service depends on fluctuations in the financial market outside the supplier's control, which may occur during the cancellation period, such as services related to—

  (i)   foreign exchange,
  (ii) money market instruments,
  (iii) transferable securities,
  (iv) units in collective investment undertakings,
  (v)   financial-futures contracts, including equivalent cash-settled instruments,
  (vi) forward interest-rate agreements,
  (vii) interest-rate, currency and equity swaps,
  (viii)options to acquire or dispose of any instruments referred to in sub- para-
        graphs (i) to (vii), including cash-settled instruments and options on cur-
        rency and on interest rates;
  (b) a contract whose performance has been fully completed by both parties at the
      consumer's express request before the consumer gives notice of cancellation;
  (c) a contract which—
      (i)   is a connected contract of insurance within the meaning of article 72B(1) of
            the Regulated Activities Order (activities carried on by a provider of relevant
            goods or services),
      (ii) covers travel risks within the meaning of article 72B(1)(d)(ii) of that Order, and
      (iii) has a total duration of less than one month;
  (d) a contract under which a supplier provides credit to a consumer and the con-
      sumer's obligation to repay is secured by a legal mortgage on land;
  (e) a credit agreement cancelled under regulation 15(1) of the Consumer Protection
      (Distance Selling) Regulations 2000 (automatic cancellation of a related credit
      agreement);
  (f) a credit agreement cancelled under section 6A of the Timeshare Act 1992 (auto-
      matic cancellation of timeshare credit agreement); or
  (g) a restricted-use credit agreement (within the meaning of the 1974 Act) to finance
      the purchase of land or an existing building, or an agreement for a bridging loan
      in connection with the purchase of land or an existing building.
  (2) Paragraph (1) does not apply to a distance contract if the supplier has not complied
with regulation 8(1), unless—
  (a) the circumstances fall within regulation 8(1)(b); and
  (b) the supplier has complied with regulation 7(1) and (2) or, if applicable, regulation
      7(4)(b), and with regulation 7(5).
  (3) Where—
  (a) the conditions in sub-paragraphs (a) and (b) of paragraph (2) are satisfied in
      relation to a distance contract falling within paragraph (1),
  (b) the supplier has not complied with regulation 8(1), and
  (c) the consumer has not, by the end of the sixth day after the day on which the
      distance contract is concluded, received all the contractual terms and conditions
      and the information required under regulation 8(1),
the consumer may cancel the contract under regulation 9 during the period beginning on the
seventh day after the day on which the distance contract is concluded and ending when he
receives the last of the contractual terms and conditions and the information required under
regulation 8(1).

12 Automatic cancellation of an attached distance contract
  (1) For the purposes of this regulation, where there is a distance contract for the provision of a financial service by a supplier to a consumer ('the main contract') and there is a
further distance contract ('the secondary contract') for the provision to that consumer of a
further financial service by—
  (a) the same supplier, or
  (b) a third party, the further financial service being provided pursuant to an agree-
      ment between the third party and the supplier under the main contract,

then the secondary contract (referred to in these Regulations as an 'attached contract') is attached to the main contract if any of the conditions in paragraph (2) are satisfied.

(2) The conditions referred to in paragraph (1) are—

(a) the secondary contract is entered into in compliance with a term of the main contract;

(b) the main contract is, or is to be, financed by the secondary contract;

(c) the main contract is a debtor-creditor-supplier agreement within the meaning of the 1974 Act, and the secondary contract is, or is to be, financed by the main contract;

(d) the secondary contract is entered into by the consumer to induce the supplier to enter into the main contract;

(e) performance of the secondary contract requires performance of the main contract.

(3) Where a main contract is cancelled by a notice of cancellation given under regulation 9—

(a) the cancellation of the main contract also operates to cancel, at the time at which the main contract is cancelled, any attached contract which is not a contract or agreement of a type listed in regulation 11(1); and

(b) the supplier under the main contract shall, if he is not the supplier under the attached contract, forthwith on receipt of the notice of cancellation inform the supplier under the attached contract.

(4) Paragraph (3)(a) does not apply to an attached contract if, at or before the time at which the notice of cancellation in respect of the main contract is given, the consumer has given and not withdrawn a notice to the supplier under the main contract that cancellation of the main contract is not to operate to cancel that attached contract.

(5) Where a main contract made by an authorised person, the making or performance of which constitutes or is part of a regulated activity carried on by him, is cancelled under rules made by the Authority corresponding to regulation 9—

(a) the cancellation of the main contract also operates to cancel, at the time at which the main contract is cancelled, any attached contract which is not a contract or agreement of a type listed in regulation 11(1); and

(b) the supplier under the main contract shall, if he is not the supplier under the attached contract, inform the supplier under the attached contract forthwith on receiving notification of the consumer's intention to cancel the main contract by that notification.

(6) Paragraph (5)(a) does not apply to an attached contract if, at or before the time at which the consumer gives notification of his intention to cancel the main contract by that notification, the consumer has given and not withdrawn a notice to the supplier under the main contract that cancellation of the main contract is not to operate to cancel that attached contract.

13   Payment for services provided before cancellation

(1) This regulation applies where a cancellation event occurs in relation to a distance contract.

(2) In this regulation, 'cancellation event' means the cancellation of a distance contract under regulation 9 or 12.

(3) The supplier shall refund any sum paid by or on behalf of the consumer under or in relation to the contract to the person by whom it was paid, less any charge made in accordance with paragraph (6), as soon as possible and in any event within a period not exceeding 30 calendar days beginning with—

(a) the day on which the cancellation event occurred; or

(b) if the supplier proves that this is later—

    (i) in the case of a contract cancelled under regulation 9, the day on which the supplier in fact received the notice of cancellation, or

    (ii) in the case of an attached contract under which the supplier is not the supplier under the main contract, the day on which, pursuant to regulation 12(3)(b) or (5)(b), he was in fact informed by the supplier under the main contract of the cancellation of the main contract.

(4) The reference in paragraph (3) to any sum paid on behalf of the consumer includes any sum paid by any other person ('the creditor'), who is not the supplier, under an agreement between the consumer and the creditor by which the creditor provides the consumer with credit of any amount.

(5) Where any security has been provided in relation to the contract, the security (so far as it has been provided) shall, on cancellation under regulation 9 or 12, be treated as never having had effect; and any property lodged solely for the purposes of the security as so provided shall be returned forthwith by the person with whom it is lodged.

(6) Subject to paragraphs (7), (8) and (9), the supplier may make a charge for any service actually provided by the supplier in accordance with the contract.

(7) The charge shall not exceed an amount which is in proportion to the extent of the service provided to the consumer prior to the time at which the cancellation event occurred (including the service of arranging to provide the financial service) in comparison with the full coverage of the contract, and in any event shall not be such that it could be construed as a penalty.

(8) The supplier may not make any charge unless he can prove on the balance of probabilities that the consumer was informed about the amount payable in accordance with—

    (a) regulation 7(1) and paragraph 13 of Schedule 1,

    (b) regulation 7(4) and paragraph 5 of Schedule 2, or

    (c) rules corresponding to those provisions,

as the case may be.

(9) The supplier may not make any charge if, without the consumer's prior request, he commenced performance of the contract prior to the expiry of the relevant cancellation period.

(10) In paragraph (9), the relevant cancellation period is the cancellation period which—

    (a) in the case of a main contract, is applicable to that contract, or

    (b) in the case of an attached contract, would be applicable to that contract if that contract were a main contract,

under regulation 10, or under rules corresponding to that regulation, as the case may be.

(11) The consumer shall, as soon as possible and in any event within a period not exceeding 30 calendar days beginning with the day on which the cancellation event occurred—

    (a) refund any sum paid by or on behalf of the supplier under or in relation to that contract to the person by whom it was paid; and

    (b) either restore to the supplier any property of which he has acquired possession under that contract, or deliver or send that property to any person to whom, under regulation 9, a notice of cancellation could have been given in respect of that contract.

(12) Breach of a duty imposed by paragraph (11) on a consumer is actionable as a breach of statutory duty.

14 Payment by card

(1) Subject to paragraph (2), where—

    (a) a payment card has been issued to an individual who, when entering the contract for the provision of that card, was acting for purposes which were outside any business he may carry on ('the card-holder'), and

    (b) fraudulent use is made of that card to make a payment under or in connection with a distance contract to which these Regulations apply, by another person who is neither acting, nor to be treated as acting, as the card-holder's agent, the card-holder may request cancellation of that payment, and is entitled to be recredited with the sum paid, or to have it returned, by the card issuer.

(2) Where paragraph (1) applies and, in any proceedings, the card-holder alleges that any use made of the payment card was not authorised by him, it is for the card issuer to prove that the use was so authorised.

(3) Paragraph (1) does not apply if the contract for the provision of the payment card is an agreement to which section 83(1) of the 1974 Act (liability for misuse of credit facilities) applies.

(5) For the purposes of this regulation—

'card issuer' means the owner of the card;

'payment card' includes a credit card, a charge card, a debit card and a store card.

15   Unsolicited services

(1) A person ('the recipient') who receives unsolicited financial services for purposes other than those of his business from another person who supplies those services in the course of his business, shall not thereby become subject to any obligation (to make payment, or otherwise).

(2) Where, in the course of any business—

   (a) unsolicited financial services are supplied for purposes other than those of the recipient's business, and

   (b) a person includes with the supply of those services a demand for payment, or an assertion of a present or prospective right to payment in respect of those services,

that person is guilty of an offence and liable, on summary conviction, to a fine not exceeding level 4 on the standard scale.

(3) A person who, not having reasonable cause to believe that there is a right to payment, in the course of any business and with a view to obtaining payment for what he knows are unsolicited financial services supplied as mentioned in paragraph (2)—

   (a) threatens to bring any legal proceedings,

   (b) places or causes to be placed the name of any person on a list of defaulters or debtors or threatens to do so, or

   (c) invokes or causes to be invoked any other collection procedure or threatens to do so,

is guilty of an offence and liable, on summary conviction, to a fine not exceeding level 5 on the standard scale.

(4) In this regulation, 'unsolicited' means, in relation to financial services supplied to any person, that they are supplied without any prior request made by or on behalf of that person.

(5) For the purposes of this regulation, a person who sends to a recipient an invoice or similar document which—

   (a) states the amount of a payment, and

   (b) does not comply with the requirements, applicable to invoices and similar documents, of regulations made under section 3A of the Unsolicited Goods and Services Act 1971 (contents and form of notes of agreement, invoices and similar documents) or, as the case may be, article 6 of the Unsolicited Goods and Services (Northern Ireland) Order 1976 (contents and form of notes of agreement, invoices and similar documents),

is to be regarded as asserting a right to the payment.

(6) Section 3A of the Unsolicited Goods and Services Act 1971 applies for the purposes of this regulation in its application to England, Wales and Scotland as it applies for the purposes of that Act.

(7) Article 6 of the Unsolicited Goods and Services (Northern Ireland) Order 1976 applies for the purposes of this regulation in its application to Northern Ireland as it applies for the purposes of that Order.

(8) This regulation is without prejudice to any right a supplier may have at any time, by contract or otherwise, to renew a distance contract with a consumer without any request made by or on behalf of that consumer prior to the renewal of that contract.

16 Prevention of contracting-out

(1) A term contained in any contract is void if, and to the extent that, it is inconsistent with the application of a provision of these Regulations to a distance contract or the application of regulation 15 to a supply of unsolicited financial services.

(2) Where a provision of these Regulations specifies a duty or liability of the consumer in certain circumstances, a term contained in a contract is inconsistent with that provision if it purports to impose, directly or indirectly, an additional or greater duty or liability on him in those circumstances.

(3) These Regulations apply notwithstanding any contract term which applies or purports to apply the law of a State which is not an EEA State if the contract or supply has a close connection with the territory of an EEA State.

17 Enforcement authorities

(1) For the purposes of regulations 18 to 21—

(a) in relation to any alleged breach concerning a specified contract, the Authority is the enforcement authority;

(b) in relation to any alleged breach concerning a contract under which the supplier is a local authority, but which is not a specified contract, the OFT is the enforcement authority;

(c) in relation to any other alleged breach—

(i) the OFT, and

(ii) in Great Britain every local weights and measures authority, and in Northern Ireland the Department of Enterprise, Trade and Investment,

is an enforcement authority.

(2) For the purposes of paragraph (1) and regulation 22(6), each of the following is a specified contract—

(a) a contract the making or performance of which constitutes or is part of a regulated activity carried on by the supplier;

(b) a contract for the provision of a debit card;

(c) a contract relating to the issuing of electronic money by a supplier to whom the Authority has given a certificate under article 9C of the Regulated Activities Order (persons certified as small issuers etc.);

(d) a contract the effecting or carrying out of which is excluded from article 10(1) or (2) of the Regulated Activities Order (effecting and carrying out contracts of insurance) by article 12 of that order (breakdown insurance), where the supplier is a person who does not otherwise carry on an activity of the kind specified by article 10 of that order;

(e) a contract under which a supplier provides credit to a consumer and the obligation of the consumer to repay is secured by a first legal mortgage on land;

(f) a contract, made before 14th January 2005, for insurance mediation activity other than in respect of a contract of long-term care insurance.

(3) For the purposes of the application of this regulation and regulations 18 to 22 in relation to breaches of, and offences under, regulation 15, 'contract'—

(a) wherever it appears in this regulation other than in the expression 'contract of long-term care insurance', and

(b) in regulation 22(6),

is to be taken to mean 'supply of financial services'.

(4) For the purposes of this regulation—

'contract of long-term care insurance' has the same meaning as in the Financial Services and Markets Act 2000 (Regulated Activities) (Amendment) (No. 2) Order 2003;

'insurance mediation activity' means any activity which is not a regulated activity at the time the contract is made but will be a regulated activity of the kind specified by article 21, 25(1) or (2), 39A or 53 of the Regulated Activities Order when the amendments to that order made by the Financial Services and Markets Act 2000 (Regulated Activities) (Amendment) (No. 2) Order 2003 come into force;

'local authority' means—

(a) in England and Wales, a local authority within the meaning of the Local Government Act 1972, the Greater London Authority, the Common Council of the City of London or the Council of the Isles of Scilly,

(b) in Scotland, a council constituted under section 2 of the Local Government etc. (Scotland) Act 1994, and

(c) in Northern Ireland, a district council within the meaning of the Local Government Act (Northern Ireland) 1972.

18   Consideration of complaints

(1) An enforcement authority shall consider any complaint made to it about a breach unless—

(a) the complaint appears to that authority to be frivolous or vexatious; or

(b) that authority is aware that another enforcement authority has notified the OFT that it agrees to consider the complaint.

(2) If an enforcement authority notifies the OFT that it agrees to consider a complaint made to another enforcement authority, the first mentioned authority shall be under a duty to consider the complaint.

19   Injunctions to secure compliance with these Regulations

(1) Subject to paragraph (2), an enforcement authority may apply for an injunction (including an interim injunction) against any person who appears to that authority to be responsible for a breach.

(2) An enforcement authority, other than the OFT or the Authority, may apply for an injunction only where—

(a) that authority has notified the OFT, at least fourteen days before the date on which the application is to be made, of its intention to apply; or

(b) the OFT consents to the application being made within a shorter period.

(3) On an application made under this regulation, the court may grant an injunction on such terms as it thinks fit to secure compliance with these Regulations.

(4) An enforcement authority which has a duty under regulation 18 to consider a complaint shall give reasons for its decision to apply or not to apply, as the case may be, for an injunction.

(5) In deciding whether or not to apply for an injunction in respect of a breach, an enforcement authority may, if it considers it appropriate to do so, have regard to any undertaking as to compliance with these Regulations given to it or to another enforcement authority by or on behalf of any person.

(6) In the application of this regulation to Scotland, for references to an 'injunction' or an 'interim injunction' there are substituted references to an 'interdict' or an 'interim interdict' respectively.

20   Notification of undertakings and orders to the OFT

An enforcement authority, other than the OFT and the Authority, shall notify the OFT of—

(a) any undertaking given to it by or on behalf of any person who appears to it to be responsible for a breach;

(b) the outcome of any application made by it under regulation 19 and the terms of any undertaking given to, or order made by, the court; and

(c) the outcome of any application made by it to enforce a previous order of the court.

21 Publication, information and advice

(1) The OFT shall arrange for the publication, in such form and manner as it considers appropriate, of details of any undertaking or order notified to it under regulation 20.

(2) Each of the OFT and the Authority shall arrange for the publication in such form and manner as it considers appropriate of—

(a) details of any undertaking as to compliance with these Regulations given to it by or on behalf of any person;

(b) details of any application made by it under regulation 19, and of the terms of any undertaking given to, or order made by, the court; and

(c) details of any application made by it to enforce a previous order of the court.

(3) Each of the OFT and the Authority may arrange for the dissemination, in such form and manner as it considers appropriate, of such information and advice concerning the operation of these Regulations as may appear to it to be expedient to give to the public and to all persons likely to be affected by these Regulations.

22 Offences

(1) A supplier under a distance contract who fails to comply with regulation 7(3) or (4)(a) or regulation 8(2) or (4) is guilty of an offence and liable, on summary conviction, to a fine not exceeding level 3 on the standard scale.

(2) If an offence under paragraph (1), or under regulation 15(2) or (3), committed by a body corporate is shown—

(a) to have been committed with the consent or connivance of any director, manager, secretary or other similar officer of the body corporate, or any person who was purporting to act in any such capacity, or

(b) to be attributable to any neglect on his part,

he as well as the body corporate is guilty of the offence and liable to be proceeded against and punished accordingly.

(3) If the affairs of a body corporate are managed by its members, paragraph (2) applies in relation to the acts and defaults of a member in connection with his functions of management as if he were a director of the body.

(4) If an offence under paragraph (1), or under regulation 15(2) or (3), committed by a partnership is shown—

(a) to have been committed with the consent or connivance of any partner, or any person who was purporting to act as a partner, or

(b) to be attributable to any neglect on his part,

he as well as the partnership is guilty of an offence and liable to be proceeded against and punished accordingly.

(5) If an offence under paragraph (1), or under regulation 15(2) or (3), committed by an unincorporated association (other than a partnership) is shown—

(a) to have been committed with the consent or connivance of an officer of the association or a member of its governing body, or any person who was purporting to act in any such capacity, or

(b) to be attributable to any neglect on his part,

he as well as the association is guilty of an offence and liable to be proceeded against and punished accordingly.

(6) Except in Scotland—

(a) the Authority may institute proceedings for an offence under these Regulations which relates to a specified contract;

(b) the OFT, and—

(i) in Great Britain, every local weights and measures authority,

(ii) in Northern Ireland, the Department of Enterprise, Trade and Investment,

may institute proceedings for any other offence under these Regulations.

23   Functions of the Authority

The functions conferred on the Authority by these Regulations shall be treated as if they were conferred by the 2000 Act.

29   Transitional provisions

(1) In relation to any contract made before 31st May 2005 which is a consumer credit agreement within the meaning of the 1974 Act and a regulated agreement within the meaning of that Act—

>   (a) regulations 7, 8, 10 and 11 apply subject to the modifications in paragraphs (2) to (5); and

>   (b) references in these Regulations to regulations 7, 8, 10 and 11 or to provisions contained in them shall be construed accordingly.

(2) In regulation 7—

>   (a) in paragraphs (1) to (3), before 'Schedule 1' at each place where it occurs insert 'paragraph 13 of'; and

>   (b) in paragraph (4)(b), before 'Schedule 2' insert 'paragraph 5 of'.

(3) In regulation 8(1), for 'contractual terms and conditions and the information specified in' at each place where it occurs substitute 'information specified in paragraph 13 of'.

(4) In regulation 10(3), omit—

>   (a) 'the contractual terms and conditions and'; and

>   (b) 'those terms and conditions and'.

(5) In regulation 11(3), omit 'the contractual terms and conditions and' at each place where it occurs.

Regulations 7(1) and 8(1)   SCHEDULE 1

Information required prior to the conclusion of the contract

1. The identity and the main business of the supplier, the geographical address at which the supplier is established and any other geographical address relevant to the consumer's relations with the supplier.

2. Where the supplier has a representative established in the consumer's State of residence, the identity of that representative and the geographical address relevant to the consumer's relations with him.

3. Where the consumer's dealings are with any professional other than the supplier, the identity of that professional, the capacity in which he is acting with respect to the consumer, and the geographical address relevant to the consumer's relations with that professional.

4. Where the supplier is registered in a trade or similar public register, the particulars of the register in which the supplier is entered and his registration number or an equivalent means of identification in that register.

5. Where the supplier's activity is subject to an authorisation scheme, the particulars of the relevant supervisory authority.

6. A description of the main characteristics of the financial service.

7. The total price to be paid by the consumer to the supplier for the financial service, including all related fees, charges and expenses, and all taxes paid via the supplier or, where an exact price cannot be indicated, the basis for the calculation of the price enabling the consumer to verify it.

8. Where relevant, notice indicating that: (i) the financial service is related to instruments involving special risks related to their specific features or the operations to be executed or whose price depends on fluctuations in the financial markets outside the supplier's control; and (ii) historical performances are no indicators for future performances.

9. Notice of the possibility that other taxes or costs may exist that are not paid via the supplier or imposed by him.

10. Any limitations of the period for which the information provided is valid.

11. The arrangements for payment and for performance.

12. Any specific additional cost for the consumer of using the means of distance communication, if such additional cost is charged.

13. Whether or not there is a right of cancellation and, where there is a right of cancellation, its duration and the conditions for exercising it, including information on the amount which the consumer may be required to pay in accordance with regulation 13, as well as the consequences of not exercising that right.

14. The minimum duration of the distance contract in the case of financial services to be performed indefinitely or recurrently.

15. Information on any rights the parties may have to terminate the distance contract early or unilaterally by virtue of the terms of the contract, including any penalties imposed by the contract in such cases.

16. Practical instructions for exercising the right to cancel in accordance with regulation 9 indicating, among other things, the address at which the notice of cancellation should be left or to which it should be sent by post, and any facsimile number or electronic mail address to which it should be sent.

17. The EEA State or States whose laws are taken by the supplier as a basis for the establishment of relations with the consumer prior to the conclusion of the distance contract.

18. Any contractual clause on the law applicable to the distance contract or on the competent court.

19. In which language, or languages: (i) the contractual terms and conditions, and the prior information specified in this Schedule, are supplied; and (ii) the supplier, with the agreement of the consumer, undertakes to communicate during the duration of the distance contract.

20. Whether or not there is an out-of-court complaint and redress mechanism for the consumer and, if so, the methods for having access to it.

21. The existence of guarantee funds or other compensation arrangements, except to the extent that they are required by Directive 94/19/EC of the European Parliament and of the Council of 30 May 1994 on deposit guarantee schemes or Directive 97/9/EC of the European Parliament and of the Council of 3 March 1997 on investor compensation schemes.

Regulation 7(4)(b)   SCHEDULE 2

Information required in the case of voice telephone communications

1. The identity of the person in contact with the consumer and his link with the supplier.

2. A description of the main characteristics of the financial service.

3. The total price to be paid by the consumer to the supplier for the financial service including all taxes paid via the supplier or, if an exact price cannot be indicated, the basis for the calculation of the price enabling the consumer to verify it.

4. Notice of the possibility that other taxes or costs may exist that are not paid via the supplier or imposed by him.

5. Whether or not there is a right to cancel and, where there is such a right, its duration and the conditions for exercising it, including information on the amount which the consumer may be required to pay in accordance with regulation 13, as well as the consequences of not exercising that right.

6. That other information is available on request and the nature of that information.

General Product Safety Regulations 2005

(SI 2005, No. 1803)

PART 1

GENERAL

1. Citation, commencement and revocation

(1) These Regulations may be cited as the General Product Safety Regulations 2005 and shall come into force on 1st October 2005 with the exception of the reference to a civil partner in regulation 43(2) which shall come into force on 5th December 2005.

(2) The General Product Safety Regulations 1994 are hereby revoked.

2. Interpretation

In these Regulations:—

"the 1987 Act" means the Consumer Protection Act 1987;

"Community law" includes a law in any part of the United Kingdom which implements a Community obligation;

"contravention" includes a failure to comply and cognate expressions shall be construed accordingly;

"dangerous product" means a product other than a safe product;

"distributor" means a professional in the supply chain whose activity does not affect the safety properties of a product;

"enforcement authority" means the Secretary of State, any other Minister of the Crown in charge of a government department, any such department and any authority or council mentioned in regulation 10;

"general safety requirement" means the requirement that only safe products should be placed on the market;

"the GPS Directive" means Directive 2001/95/EC of the European Parliament and of the Council of 3 December 2001 on general product safety;

"magistrates' court" in relation to Northern Ireland, means a court of summary jurisdiction;

"Member State" means a member State, Norway, Iceland or Liechtenstein;

"notice" means a notice in writing;

"officer", in relation to an enforcement authority, means a person authorised in writing to assist the authority in carrying out its functions under or for the purposes of the enforcement of these Regulations and safety notices, except in relation to an enforcement authority which is a government department where it means an officer of that department;

"producer" means—

    (a) the manufacturer of a product, when he is established in a Member State and any other person presenting himself as the manufacturer by affixing to the product his name, trade mark or other distinctive mark, or the person who reconditions the product;

    (b) when the manufacturer is not established in a Member State—

        (i) if he has a representative established in a Member State, the representative,

        (ii) in any other case, the importer of the product from a state that is not a Member State into a Member State;

    (c) other professionals in the supply chain, insofar as their activities may affect the safety properties of a product;

"product" means a product which is intended for consumers or likely, under reasonably foreseeable conditions, to be used by consumers even if not intended for them and which is supplied or made available, whether for consideration or not, in the course of a commercial activity and whether it is new, used or reconditioned and includes a product that is supplied or made available to consumers for their own use in the context of providing a service. "product" does not include equipment used by service providers themselves to supply a service to consumers, in particular equipment on which consumers ride or travel which is operated by a service provider;

"recall" means any measure aimed at achieving the return of a dangerous product that has already been supplied or made available to consumers;

"recall notice" means a notice under regulation 15;

"record" includes any book or document and any record in any form;

"requirement to mark" means a notice under regulation 12;

"requirement to warn" means a notice under regulation 13;

"safe product" means a product which, under normal or reasonably foreseeable conditions of use including duration and, where applicable, putting into service, installation and maintenance requirements, does not present any risk or only the minimum risks compatible with the product's use, considered to be acceptable and consistent with a high level of protection for the safety and health of persons. In determining the foregoing, the following shall be taken into account in particular—

(a) the characteristics of the product, including its composition, packaging, instructions for assembly and, where applicable, instructions for installation and maintenance,

(b) the effect of the product on other products, where it is reasonably foreseeable that it will be used with other products,

(c) the presentation of the product, the labelling, any warnings and instructions for its use and disposal and any other indication or information regarding the product, and

(d) the categories of consumers at risk when using the product, in particular children and the elderly.

The feasibility of obtaining higher levels of safety or the availability of other products presenting a lesser degree of risk shall not constitute grounds for considering a product to be a dangerous product;

"safety notice" means a suspension notice, a requirement to mark, a requirement to warn, a withdrawal notice or a recall notice;

"serious risk" means a serious risk, including one the effects of which are not immediate, requiring rapid intervention;

"supply" in relation to a product includes making it available, in the context of providing a service, for use by consumers;

"suspension notice" means a notice under regulation 11;

"withdrawal" means any measure aimed at preventing the distribution, display or offer of a dangerous product to a consumer;

"withdrawal notice" means a notice under regulation 14.

3. Application

(1) Each provision of these Regulations applies to a product in so far as there are no specific provisions with the same objective in rules of Community law governing the safety of the product other than the GPS Directive.

(2) Where a product is subject to specific safety requirements imposed by rules of Community law other than the GPS Directive, these Regulations shall apply only to the aspects and risks or category of risks not covered by those requirements. This means that:

(a) the definition of "safe product" and "dangerous product" in regulation 2 and regulations 5 and 6 shall not apply to such a product in so far as concerns the risks or category of risks covered by the specific rules, and

(b) the remainder of these Regulations shall apply except where there are specific provisions governing the aspects covered by those regulations with the same objective.

4. These Regulations do not apply to a second-hand product supplied as a product to be repaired or reconditioned prior to being used, provided the supplier clearly informs the person to whom he supplies the product to that effect.

PART 2

OBLIGATIONS OF PRODUCERS AND DISTRIBUTORS

5.   General safety requirement

(1) No producer shall place a product on the market unless the product is a safe product.

(2) No producer shall offer or agree to place a product on the market or expose or possess a product for placing on the market unless the product is a safe product.

(3) No producer shall offer or agree to supply a product or expose or possess a product for supply unless the product is a safe product.

(4) No producer shall supply a product unless the product is a safe product.

6.   Presumption of conformity

(1) Where, in the absence of specific provisions in rules of Community law governing the safety of a product, the product conforms to the specific rules of the law of part of the United Kingdom laying down the health and safety requirements which the product must satisfy in order to be marketed in the United Kingdom, the product shall be deemed safe so far as concerns the aspects covered by such rules.

(2) Where a product conforms to a voluntary national standard of the United Kingdom giving effect to a European standard the reference of which has been published in the Official Journal of the European Union in accordance with Article 4 of the GPS Directive, the product shall be presumed to be a safe product so far as concerns the risks and categories of risk covered by that national standard. The Secretary of State shall publish the reference number of such national standards in such manner as he considers appropriate.

(3) In circumstances other than those referred to in paragraphs (1) and (2), the conformity of a product to the general safety requirement shall be assessed taking into account—

(a) any voluntary national standard of the United Kingdom giving effect to a European standard, other than one referred to in paragraph (2),

(b) other national standards drawn up in the United Kingdom,

(c) recommendations of the European Commission setting guidelines on product safety assessment,

(d) product safety codes of good practice in the sector concerned,

(e) the state of the art and technology, and

(f) reasonable consumer expectations concerning safety.

(4) Conformity of a product with the criteria designed to ensure the general safety requirement is complied with, in particular the provisions mentioned in paragraphs (1) to (3), shall not bar an enforcement authority from exercising its powers under these Regulations in relation to that product where there is evidence that, despite such conformity, it is dangerous.

7.   Other obligations of producers

(1) Within the limits of his activities, a producer shall provide consumers with the relevant information to enable them—

(a) to assess the risks inherent in a product throughout the normal or reasonably foreseeable period of its use, where such risks are not immediately obvious without adequate warnings, and

(b) to take precautions against those risks.

(2) The presence of warnings does not exempt any person from compliance with the other requirements of these Regulations.

(3) Within the limits of his activities, a producer shall adopt measures commensurate with the characteristics of the products which he supplies to enable him to—

(a) be informed of the risks which the products might pose, and

(b) take appropriate action including, where necessary to avoid such risks, withdrawal, adequately and effectively warning consumers as to the risks or, as a last resort, recall.

(4) The measures referred to in paragraph (3) include—

(a) except where it is not reasonable to do so, an indication by means of the product or its packaging of—

(i) the name and address of the producer, and

(ii) the product reference or where applicable the batch of products to which it belongs; and

(b) where and to the extent that it is reasonable to do so—

(i) sample testing of marketed products,

(ii) investigating and if necessary keeping a register of complaints concerning the safety of the product, and

(iii) keeping distributors informed of the results of such monitoring where a product presents a risk or may present a risk.

8. Obligations of distributors

(1) A distributor shall act with due care in order to help ensure compliance with the applicable safety requirements and in particular he—

(a) shall not expose or possess for supply or offer or agree to supply, or supply, a product to any person which he knows or should have presumed, on the basis of the information in his possession and as a professional, is a dangerous product; and

(b) shall, within the limits of his activities, participate in monitoring the safety of a product placed on the market, in particular by—

(i) passing on information on the risks posed by the product,

(ii) keeping the documentation necessary for tracing the origin of the product,

(iii) producing the documentation necessary for tracing the origin of the product, and cooperating in action taken by a producer or an enforcement authority to avoid the risks.

(2) Within the limits of his activities, a distributor shall take measures enabling him to cooperate efficiently in the action referred to in paragraph (1)(b)(iii).

9. Obligations of producers and distributors

(1) Subject to paragraph (2), where a producer or a distributor knows that a product he has placed on the market or supplied poses risks to the consumer that are incompatible with the general safety requirement, he shall forthwith notify an enforcement authority in writing of that information and—

(a) the action taken to prevent risk to the consumer; and

(b) where the product is being or has been marketed or otherwise supplied to consumers outside the United Kingdom, of the identity of each Member State in which, to the best of his knowledge, it is being or has been so marketed or supplied.

(2) Paragraph (1) shall not apply—

(a) in the case of a second-hand product supplied as an antique or as a product to be repaired or reconditioned prior to being used, provided the supplier clearly informed the person to whom he supplied the product to that effect,

(b) in conditions concerning isolated circumstances or products.

(3) In the event of a serious risk the notification under paragraph (1) shall include the following—

(a) information enabling a precise identification of the product or batch of products in question,

(b) a full description of the risks that the product presents,

(c) all available information relevant for tracing the product, and

(d) a description of the action undertaken to prevent risks to the consumer.

(4) Within the limits of his activities, a person who is a producer or a distributor shall co-operate with an enforcement authority (at the enforcement authority's request) in action taken to avoid the risks posed by a product which he supplies or has supplied. Every enforcement authority shall maintain procedures for such co-operation, including procedures for dialogue with the producers and distributors concerned on issues related to product safety.

PART 3

ENFORCEMENT

10. Enforcement

(1) It shall be the duty of every authority to which paragraph (4) applies to enforce within its area these Regulations and safety notices.

(2) An authority in England or Wales to which paragraph (4) applies shall have the power to investigate and prosecute for an alleged contravention of any provision imposed by or under these Regulations which was committed outside its area in any part of England and Wales.

(3) A district council in Northern Ireland shall have the power to investigate and prosecute for an alleged contravention of any provision imposed by or under these Regulations which was committed outside its area in any part of Northern Ireland.

(4) The authorities to which this paragraph applies are:

(a) in England, a county council, district council, London Borough Council, the Common Council of the City of London in its capacity as a local authority and the Council of the Isles of Scilly,

(b) in Wales, a county council or a county borough council,

(c) in Scotland, a council constituted under section 2 of the Local Government etc. (Scotland) Act 1994,

(d) in Northern Ireland any district council.

(5) An enforcement authority shall in enforcing these Regulations act in a manner proportionate to the seriousness of the risk and shall take due account of the precautionary principle. In this context, it shall encourage and promote voluntary action by producers and distributors. Notwithstanding the foregoing, an enforcement authority may take any action under these Regulations urgently and without first encouraging and promoting voluntary action if a product poses a serious risk.

11. Suspension notices

(1) Where an enforcement authority has reasonable grounds for suspecting that a requirement of these Regulations has been contravened in relation to a product, the authority may, for the period needed to organise appropriate safety evaluations, checks and controls, serve a notice ("a suspension notice") prohibiting the person on whom it is served from doing any of the following things without the consent of the authority, that is to say—

(a) placing the product on the market, offering to place it on the market, agreeing to place it on the market or exposing it for placing on the market, or

(b) supplying the product, offering to supply it, agreeing to supply it or exposing it for supply.

(2) A suspension notice served by an enforcement authority in relation to a product may require the person on whom it is served to keep the authority informed of the whereabouts of any such product in which he has an interest.

(3) A consent given by the enforcement authority for the purposes of paragraph (1) may impose such conditions on the doing of anything for which the consent is required as the authority considers appropriate.

12.   Requirements to mark

(1) Where an enforcement authority has reasonable grounds for believing that a product is a dangerous product in that it could pose risks in certain conditions, the authority may serve a notice ("a requirement to mark") requiring the person on whom the notice is served at his own expense to undertake either or both of the following, as specified in the notice—

> (a) to ensure that the product is marked in accordance with requirements specified in the notice with warnings as to the risks it may present,
>
> (b) to make the marketing of the product subject to prior conditions as specified in the notice so as to ensure the product is a safe product.

(2) The requirements referred to in paragraph (1)(a) shall be such as to ensure that the product is marked with a warning which is suitable, clearly worded and easily comprehensible.

13.   Requirements to warn

Where an enforcement authority has reasonable grounds for believing that a product is a dangerous product in that it could pose risks for certain persons, the authority may serve a notice ("a requirement to warn") requiring the person on whom the notice is served at his own expense to undertake one or more of the following, as specified in the notice—

> (a) where and to the extent it is practicable to do so, to ensure that any person who could be subject to such risks and who has been supplied with the product be given warning of the risks in good time and in a form specified in the notice,
>
> (b) to publish a warning of the risks in such form and manner as is likely to bring those risks to the attention of any such person,
>
> (c) to ensure that the product carries a warning of the risks in a form specified in the notice.

14.   Withdrawal notices

(1) Where an enforcement authority has reasonable grounds for believing that a product is a dangerous product, the authority may serve a notice ("a withdrawal notice") prohibiting the person on whom it is served from doing any of the following things without the consent of the authority, that is to say—

> (a) placing the product on the market, offering to place it on the market, agreeing to place it on the market or exposing it for placing on the market, or
>
> (b) supplying the product, offering to supply it, agreeing to supply it or exposing it for supply.

(2) A withdrawal notice may require the person on whom it is served to take action to alert consumers to the risks that the product presents.

(3) In relation to a product that is already on the market, a withdrawal notice may only be served by an enforcement authority where the action being undertaken by the producer or the distributor concerned in fulfilment of his obligations under these Regulations is unsatisfactory or insufficient to prevent the risks concerned to the health and safety of persons.

(4) Paragraph (3) shall not apply in the case of a product posing a serious risk requiring, in the view of the enforcement authority, urgent action.

(5) A withdrawal notice served by an enforcement authority in relation to a product may require the person on whom it is served to keep the authority informed of the whereabouts of any such product in which he has an interest.

(6) A consent given by the enforcement authority for the purposes of paragraph (1) may impose such conditions on the doing of anything for which the consent is required as the authority considers appropriate.

15.   Recall notices

(1) Subject to paragraph (4), where an enforcement authority has reasonable grounds for believing that a product is a dangerous product and that it has already been supplied or made available to consumers, the authority may serve a notice ("a recall notice") requiring the person on whom it is served to use his reasonable endeavours to organise the return of the

product from consumers to that person or to such other person as is specified in the notice.

(2) A recall notice may require—

    (a) the recall to be effected in accordance with a code of practice applicable to the product concerned, or

    (b) the recipient of the recall notice to—

        (i) contact consumers who have purchased the product in order to inform them of the recall, where and to the extent it is practicable to do so,

        (ii) publish a notice in such form and such manner as is likely to bring to the attention of purchasers of the product the risk the product poses and the fact of the recall, or

        (iii) make arrangements for the collection or return of the product from consumers who have purchased it or for its disposal,

and may impose such additional requirements on the recipient of the notice as are reasonable and practicable with a view to achieving the return of the product from consumers to the person specified in the notice or its disposal.

(3) In determining what requirements to include in a recall notice, the enforcement authority shall take into consideration the need to encourage distributors, users and consumers to contribute to its implementation.

(4) A recall notice may only be issued by an enforcement authority where—

    (a) other action which it may require under these Regulations would not suffice to prevent the risks concerned to the health and safety of persons,

    (b) the action being undertaken by the producer or the distributor concerned in fulfilment of his obligations under these Regulations is unsatisfactory or insufficient to prevent the risks concerned to the health and safety of persons, and

    (c) the authority has given not less than seven days notice to the person on whom the recall notice is to be served of its intention to serve such a notice and where that person has before the expiry of that period by notice required the authority to seek the advice of such person as the Institute determines on the questions of—

        (i) whether the product is a dangerous product,

        (ii) whether the issue of a recall notice is proportionate to the seriousness of the risk, and

the authority has taken account of such advice.

(5) Paragraphs (4)(b) and (c) shall not apply in the case of a product posing a serious risk requiring, in the view of the enforcement authority, urgent action.

(6) Where a person requires an enforcement authority to seek advice as referred to in paragraph (4)(c), that person shall be responsible for the fees, costs and expenses of the Institute and of the person appointed by the Institute to advise the authority.

(7) In paragraphs 4(c) and (6) "the Institute" means the charitable organisation with registered number 803725 and known as the Chartered Institute of Arbitrators.

(8) A recall notice served by an enforcement authority in relation to a product may require the person on whom it is served to keep the authority informed of the whereabouts of any such product to which the recall notice relates, so far as he is able to do so.

(9) Where the conditions in paragraph (1) for serving a recall notice are satisfied and either the enforcement authority has been unable to identify any person on whom to serve a recall notice, or the person on whom such a notice has been served has failed to comply with it, then the authority may itself take such action as could have been required by a recall notice.

(10) Where—

    (a) an authority has complied with the requirements of paragraph (4); and

    (b) the authority has exercised its powers under paragraph (9) to take action following the failure of the person on whom the recall notice has been served to comply with that notice, then the authority may recover from the person on whom the notice was served summarily as a civil debt, any costs or expenses reasonably incurred by it in undertaking the action referred to in sub-paragraph (b).

    (11) A civil debt recoverable under the preceding paragraph may be recovered—

        (a) in England and Wales by way of complaint (as mentioned in section 58 of the Magistrates' Courts Act 1980,

        (b) in Northern Ireland in proceedings under Article 62 of the Magistrate's Court (Northern Ireland) Order 1981.

16. Supplementary provisions relating to safety notices

    (1) Whenever feasible, prior to serving a safety notice the authority shall give an opportunity to the person on whom the notice is to be served to submit his views to the authority. Where, due to the urgency of the situation, this is not feasible the person shall be given an opportunity to submit his views to the authority after service of the notice.

    (2) A safety notice served by an enforcement authority in respect of a product shall—

        (a) describe the product in a manner sufficient to identify it;

        (b) state the reasons on which the notice is based;

        (c) indicate the rights available to the recipient of the notice under these Regulations and (where applicable) the time limits applying to their exercise; and

        (d) in the case of a suspension notice, state the period of time for which it applies.

    (3) A safety notice shall have effect throughout the United Kingdom.

    (4) Where an enforcement authority serves a suspension notice in respect of a product, the authority shall be liable to pay compensation to a person having an interest in the product in respect of any loss or damage suffered by reason of the notice if—

        (a) there has been no contravention of any requirement of these Regulations in relation to the product; and

        (b) the exercise by the authority of the power to serve the suspension notice was not attributable to any neglect or default by that person.

    (5) Where an enforcement authority serves a withdrawal notice in respect of a product, the authority shall be liable to pay compensation to a person having an interest in the product in respect of any loss or damage suffered by reason of the notice if—

        (a) the product was not a dangerous product; and

        (b) the exercise by the authority of the power to serve the withdrawal notice was not attributable to any neglect or default by that person.

    (6) Where an enforcement authority serves a recall notice in respect of a product, the authority shall be liable to pay compensation to the person on whom the notice was served in respect of any loss or damage suffered by reason of the notice if—

        (a) the product was not a dangerous product; and

        (b) the exercise by the authority of the power to serve the recall notice was not attributable to any neglect or default by that person.

    (7) An enforcement authority may vary or revoke a safety notice which it has served provided that the notice is not made more restrictive for the person on whom it is served or more onerous for that person to comply with.

    (8) Wherever feasible prior to varying a safety notice the authority shall give an opportunity to the person on whom the original notice was served to submit his views to the authority.

17. Appeals against safety notices

    (1) A person on whom a safety notice has been served and a person having an interest in a product in respect of which a safety notice (other than a recall notice) has been served may, before the end of the period of 21 days beginning with the day on which the notice was served, apply for an order to vary or set aside the terms of the notice.

    (2) On an application under paragraph (1) the court or the sheriff, as the case may be, shall make an order setting aside the notice only if satisfied that—

    (a) in the case of a suspension notice, there has been no contravention in relation to the product of any requirement of these Regulations,

    (b) in the case of a requirement to mark or a requirement to warn, the product is not a dangerous product,

    (c) in the case of a withdrawal notice—

       (i) the product is not a dangerous product, or

       (ii) where applicable, regulation 14(3) has not been complied with by the enforcement authority concerned,

    (d) in the case of a recall notice—

       (i) the product is not a dangerous product, or

       (ii) regulation 15(4) has not been complied with,

    (e) in any case, the serving of the safety notice concerned was not proportionate to the seriousness of the risk.

(3) On an application concerning the period of time specified in a suspension notice as the period for which it applies, the court or the sheriff, as the case may be, may reduce the period to such period as it considers sufficient for organising appropriate safety evaluations, checks and controls.

(4) On an application to vary the terms of a notice, the court or the sheriff, as the case may be, may vary the requirements specified in the notice as it considers appropriate.

(5) A person on whom a recall notice has been served and who proposes to make an application under paragraph (1) in relation to the notice may, before the end of the period of seven days beginning with the day on which the notice was served, apply to the court or the sheriff for an order suspending the effect of the notice and the court or the sheriff may, in any case where it considers it appropriate to do so, make an order suspending the effect of the notice.

(6) If the court or the sheriff makes an order suspending the effect of a recall notice under paragraph (5) in the absence of the enforcement authority, the enforcement authority may apply for the revocation of such order.

(7) An order under paragraph (5) shall take effect from the time it is made until—

    (a) it is revoked under paragraph (6),

    (b) where no application is made under paragraph (1) in respect of the recall notice within the time specified in that paragraph, the expiration of that time,

    (c) where such an application is made but is withdrawn or dismissed for want of prosecution, the date of dismissal or withdrawal of the application, or

    (d) where such an application is made and is not withdrawn or dismissed for want of prosecution, the determination of the application.

(8) Subject to paragraph (6), in Scotland the sheriff's decision under paragraph (5) shall be final.

(9) An application under this regulation may be made—

    (a) by way of complaint to any magistrates' court in which proceedings have been brought in England and Wales or Northern Ireland—

       (i) in respect of a contravention in relation to the product of a requirement imposed by or under these Regulations; or

       (ii) for the forfeiture of the product under regulation 18;

    (b) where no such proceedings have been brought, by way of complaint to any magistrates' court; or

    (c) in Scotland, by summary application to the sheriff.

(10) A person aggrieved by an order made pursuant to an application under paragraph (1) by a magistrates' court in England, Wales or Northern Ireland, or by a decision of such a court not to make such an order, may appeal against that order or decision—

    (a) in England and Wales, to the Crown Court;

    (b) in Northern Ireland, to the county court.

18.   Forfeiture: England and Wales and Northern Ireland

(1) An enforcement authority in England and Wales or Northern Ireland may apply for an order for the forfeiture of a product on the grounds that the product is a dangerous product.

(2) An application under paragraph (1) may be made—

(a) where proceedings have been brought in a magistrates' court for an offence in respect of a contravention in relation to the product of a requirement imposed by or under these Regulations, to that court,

(b) where an application with respect to the product has been made to a magistrates' court under regulation 17 (appeals against safety notices) or 25 (appeals against detention of products and records) to that court, and

(c) otherwise, by way of complaint to a magistrates' court.

(3) An enforcement authority making an application under paragraph (1) shall serve a copy of the application on any person appearing to it to be the owner of, or otherwise to have an interest in, the product to which the application relates, together with a notice giving him the opportunity to appear at the hearing of the application to show cause why the product should not be forfeited.

(4) A person on whom notice is served under paragraph (3) and any other person claiming to be the owner of, or otherwise to have an interest in, the product to which the application relates shall be entitled to appear at the hearing of the application and show cause why the product should not be forfeited.

(5) The court shall not make an order for the forfeiture of a product—

(a) if any person on whom notice is served under paragraph (3) does not appear, unless service of the notice on that person is proved, or

(b) if no notice under paragraph (3) has been served, unless the court is satisfied that in the circumstances it was reasonable not to serve notice on any person.

(6) The court may make an order for the forfeiture of a product only if it is satisfied that the product is a dangerous product.

(7) Any person aggrieved by an order made by a magistrates' court for the forfeiture of a product, or by a decision of such a court not to make such an order, may appeal against that order or decision—

(a) in England and Wales, to the Crown Court;

(b) in Northern Ireland, to the county court.

(8) An order for the forfeiture of a product shall not take effect until the later of—

(i) the end of the period within which an appeal under paragraph (7) may be brought or within which an application under section 111 of the Magistrates' Courts Act 1980 or article 146 of the Magistrates' Courts (Northern Ireland) Order 1981 (statement of case) may be made, or

(ii) if an appeal or an application is so made, when the appeal or application is determined or abandoned.

(9) Subject to the following paragraph, where a product is forfeited it shall be destroyed in accordance with such directions as the court may give.

(10) On making an order for forfeiture of a product a magistrates' court may, if it considers it appropriate to do so, direct that the product shall (instead of being destroyed) be delivered up to such person as the court may specify, on condition that the person—

(a) does not supply the product to any person otherwise than as mentioned in paragraph (11), and

(b) on condition, if the court considers it appropriate, that he complies with any order to pay costs or expenses (including any order under regulation 28) which has been made against him in the proceedings for the order for forfeiture.

(11) The supplies which may be permitted under the preceding paragraph are—

(a) a supply to a person who carries on a business of buying products of the same description as the product concerned and repairing or reconditioning them,

(b) a supply to a person as scrap (that is to say, for the value of materials included in the product rather than for the value of the product itself),

(c) a supply to any person, provided that being so supplied the product is repaired by or on behalf of the person to whom the product was delivered up by direction of the court and that following such repair it is not a dangerous product.

19. Forfeiture: Scotland

(1) In Scotland a sheriff may make an order for forfeiture of a product on the grounds that the product is a dangerous product—

(a) on an application by a procurator-fiscal made in the manner specified in section 134 of the Criminal Procedure (Scotland) Act 1995, or

(b) where a person is convicted of any offence in respect of a contravention in relation to the product of a requirement imposed by or under these Regulations, in addition to any other penalty which the sheriff may impose.

(2) The procurator-fiscal making an application under paragraph (1)(a) shall serve on any person appearing to him to be the owner of, or otherwise to have an interest in, the product to which the application relates a copy of the application, together with a notice giving him the opportunity to appear at the hearing of the application to show cause why the product should not be forfeited.

(3) Service under paragraph (2) shall be carried out, and such service may be proved, in the manner specified for citation of an accused in summary proceedings under the Criminal Procedure (Scotland) Act 1995.

(4) A person upon whom notice is served under paragraph (2) and any other person claiming to be the owner of, or otherwise to have an interest in, the product to which the application relates shall be entitled to appear at the hearing of the application to show cause why the product should not be forfeited.

(5) The sheriff shall not make an order following an application under paragraph (1)(a)—

(a) if any person on whom notice is served under paragraph (2) does not appear, unless service of the notice on that person is proved; or

(b) if no notice under paragraph (2) has been served, unless the sheriff is satisfied that in the circumstances it was reasonable not to serve notice on any person.

(6) The sheriff may make an order under this regulation only if he is satisfied that the product is a dangerous product.

(7) Where an order for the forfeiture of a product is made following an application by the procurator-fiscal under paragraph (1)(a), any person who appeared, or was entitled to appear to show cause why the product should not be forfeited may, within twenty-one days of the making of the order, appeal to the High Court by Bill of Suspension on the ground of an alleged miscarriage of justice; and section 182(5)(a) to (e) of the Criminal Procedure (Scotland) Act 1995 shall apply to an appeal under this paragraph as it applies to a stated case under Part X of that Act.

(8) An order following an application under paragraph (1)(a) shall not take effect—

(a) until the end of the period of twenty-one days beginning with the day after the day on which the order is made; or

(b) if an appeal is made under paragraph (7) within that period, until the appeal is determined or abandoned.

(9) An order under paragraph (1)(b) shall not take effect—

(a) until the end of the period within which an appeal against the order could be brought under the Criminal Procedure (Scotland) Act 1995; or

(b) if an appeal is made within that period, until the appeal is determined or abandoned.

(10) Subject to paragraph (11), a product forfeited under this regulation shall be destroyed in accordance with such directions as the sheriff may give.

(11) If he thinks fit, the sheriff may direct that the product be released to such person as he may specify, on condition that that person does not supply the product to any other person otherwise than as mentioned in paragraph (11) of regulation 18.

20.   Offences

(1) A person who contravenes regulations 5 or 8(1)(a) shall be guilty of an offence and liable on conviction on indictment to imprisonment for a term not exceeding 12 months or to a fine not exceeding £20,000 or to both, or on summary conviction to imprisonment for a term not exceeding three months or to a fine not exceeding the statutory maximum or to both.

(2) A person who contravenes regulation 7(1), 7(3) (by failing to take any of the measures specified in regulation 7(4)), 8(1)(b)(i), (ii) or (iii) or 9(1) shall be guilty of an offence and liable on summary conviction to imprisonment for a term not exceeding three months or to a fine not exceeding level 5 on the standard scale or to both.

(3) A producer or distributor who does not give notice to an enforcement authority under regulation 9(1) in respect of a product he has placed on the market or supplied commits an offence where it is proved that he ought to have known that the product poses risks to consumers that are incompatible with the general safety requirement and he shall be liable on summary conviction to imprisonment for a term not exceeding three months or to a fine not exceeding level 5 on the standard scale or to both.

(4) A person who contravenes a safety notice shall be guilty of an offence and liable on conviction on indictment to imprisonment for a term not exceeding 12 months or to a fine not exceeding £20,000 or to both, or on summary conviction to imprisonment for a term not exceeding three months or to a fine not exceeding the statutory maximum or to both.

21.   Test purchases

(1) An enforcement authority shall have power to organise appropriate checks on the safety properties of a product, on an adequate scale, up to the final stage of use or consumption and for that purpose may make a purchase of a product or authorise an officer of the authority to make a purchase of a product.

(2) Where a product purchased under paragraph (1) is submitted to a test and the test leads to—

- (a) the bringing of proceedings for an offence in respect of a contravention in relation to the product of any requirement imposed by or under these Regulations or for the forfeiture of the product under regulation 18 or 19, or
- (b) the serving of a safety notice in respect of the product, and
- (c) the authority is requested to do so and it is practicable for the authority to comply with the request,

then the authority shall allow the person from whom the product was purchased, a person who is a party to the proceedings, on whom the notice was served or who has an interest in the product to which the notice relates, to have the product tested.

22.   Powers of entry and search etc.

(1) An officer of an enforcement authority may at any reasonable hour and on production, if required, of his credentials exercise any of the powers conferred by the following provisions of this regulation.

(2) The officer may, for the purposes of ascertaining whether there has been a contravention of a requirement imposed by or under these Regulations, enter any premises other than premises occupied only as a person's residence and inspect any record or product.

(3) The officer may, for the purpose of ascertaining whether there has been a contravention of a requirement imposed by or under these Regulations, examine any procedure (including any arrangements for carrying out a test) connected with the production of a product.

(4) If the officer has reasonable grounds for suspecting that the product has not been placed on the market or supplied in the United Kingdom since it was manufactured or

imported he may for the purpose of ascertaining whether there has been a contravention in relation to the product of a requirement imposed by or under these Regulations—

    (a) require a person carrying on a commercial activity, or employed in connection with a commercial activity, to supply all necessary information relating to the activity, including by the production of records,

    (b) require any record which is stored in an electronic form and is accessible from the premises to be produced in a form —

        (i) in which it can be taken away, and

        (ii) in which it is visible and legible.

    (c) for the purpose of ascertaining (by testing or otherwise) whether there has been any such contravention, seize and detain samples of the product,

    (d) take copies of, or of an entry in, any records produced by virtue of sub-paragraph (a).

(5) If the officer has reasonable grounds for suspecting that there has been a contravention in relation to a product of a requirement imposed by or under these Regulations, he may—

    (a) for the purpose of ascertaining whether there has been any such contravention, require a person carrying on a commercial activity, or employed in connection with a commercial activity, to supply all necessary information relating to the activity, including by the production of records,

    (b) for the purpose of ascertaining whether there has been any such contravention, require any record which is stored in an electronic form and is accessible from the premises to be produced in a form—

        (i) in which it can be taken away, and

        (ii) in which it is visible and legible,

    (c) for the purpose of ascertaining (by testing or otherwise) whether there has been any such contravention, seize and detain samples of the product,

    (d) take copies of, or of an entry in, any records produced by virtue of sub-paragraph (a).

(6) The officer may seize and detain any products or records which he has reasonable grounds for believing may be required as evidence in proceedings for an offence in respect of a contravention of any requirement imposed by or under these Regulations.

(7) If and to the extent that it is reasonably necessary to do so to prevent a contravention of any requirement imposed by or under these Regulations, the officer may, for the purpose of exercising his power under paragraphs (4) to (6) to seize products or records—

    (a) require any person having authority to do so to open any container or to open any vending machine; and

    (b) himself open or break open any such container or machine where a requirement made under sub-paragraph (a) in relation to the container or machine has not been complied with.

23.   Provisions supplemental to regulation 22 and search warrants etc.

(1) An officer seizing any products or records shall, before he leaves the premises, provide to the person from whom they were seized a written notice—

    (a) specifying the products (including the quantity thereof) and records seized,

    (b) stating the reasons for their seizure, and

    (c) explaining the right of appeal under regulation 25.

(2) References in paragraph (1) and regulation 25 to the person from whom something has been seized, in relation to a case in which the power of seizure was exercisable by reason of the product having been found on any premises, are references to the occupier of the premises at the time of the seizure.

(3) If a justice of the peace—

(a) is satisfied by written information on oath that there are reasonable grounds for believing either—

(i) that any products or records which an officer has power to inspect under regulation 22 are on any premises and that their inspection is likely to disclose evidence that there has been a contravention of any requirement imposed by or under these Regulations, or

(ii) that such a contravention has taken place, is taking place or is about to take place on any premises, and

(b) is also satisfied by such information either—

(i) that admission to the premises has been or is likely to be refused and that notice of the intention to apply for a warrant under this paragraph has been given to the occupier, or

(ii) that an application for admission, or the giving of such a notice, would defeat the object of the entry or that the premises are unoccupied or that the occupier is temporarily absent and it might defeat the object of the entry to await his return.

the justice may by warrant under his hand, which shall continue in force for a period of one month, authorise any officer of an enforcement authority to enter the premises, if need be by force.

(4) An officer entering premises by virtue of regulation 22 or a warrant under paragraph (3) may take him such other persons and equipment as may appear to him necessary.

(5) On leaving any premises which a person is authorised to enter by a warrant under paragraph (3), that person shall, if the premises are unoccupied or the occupier is temporarily absent—

(a) leave the premises as effectively secured against trespassers as he found them,

(b) attach a notice such as is mentioned in paragraph (1) in a prominent place at the premises.

(6) Where a product seized by an officer of an enforcement authority under regulation 22 or 23 is submitted to a test, the authority shall inform the person mentioned in paragraph (1) of the result of the test and, if—

(a) proceedings are brought for an offence in respect of a contravention in relation to the product of any requirement imposed by or under these Regulations or for the forfeiture of the product under regulation 18 or 19; or

(b) a safety notice is served in respect of the product; and

(c) the authority is requested to do so and it is practicable for him to comply with the request,

then the authority shall allow a person who is a party to the proceedings or, on whom the notice was served or who has an interest in the product to which the notice relates to have the product tested.

(7) If a person who is not an officer of an enforcement authority purports to act as such under regulation 22 or under this regulation he shall be guilty of an offence and liable on summary conviction to a fine not exceeding level 5 on the standard scale.

(8) In the application of this section to Scotland, the reference in paragraph (3) to a justice of the peace shall include a reference to a sheriff and the reference to written information on oath shall be construed as a reference to evidence on oath.

(9) In the application of this section to Northern Ireland, the reference in paragraph (3) to a justice of the peace shall include a reference to a lay magistrate and the references to an information on oath shall be construed as a reference to a complaint on oath.

24. Obstruction of officers

(1) A person who—

(a) intentionally obstructs an officer of an enforcement authority who is acting in pursuance of any provision of regulations 22 or 23; or

    (b) intentionally fails to comply with a requirement made of him by an officer of an enforcement authority under any provision of those regulations; or

    (c) without reasonable cause fails to give an officer of an enforcement authority who is so acting any other assistance or information which the officer may reasonably require of him for the purposes of the exercise of the officer's functions under any provision of those regulations,

shall be guilty of an offence and liable on summary conviction to a fine not exceeding level 5 on the standard scale.

    (2) A person shall be guilty of an offence if, in giving any information which is required by him by virtue of paragraph (1)(c)—

    (a) he makes a statement which he knows is false in a material particular; or

    (b) he recklessly makes a statement which is false in a material particular.

    (3) A person guilty of an offence under paragraph (2) shall be liable—

    (a) on conviction on indictment, to a fine;

    (b) on summary conviction, to a fine not exceeding the statutory maximum.

25. Appeals against detention of products and records

    (1) A person referred to in regulation 23(1) may apply for an order requiring any product or record which is for the time being detained under regulation 22 or 23 by an enforcement authority or by an officer of such an authority to be released to him or to another person.

    (2) An application under the preceding paragraph may be made—

    (a) to any magistrates' court in which proceedings have been brought in England and Wales or Northern Ireland—

        (i) for an offence in respect of a contravention in relation to the product of a requirement imposed by or under these Regulation, or

        (ii) for the forfeiture of the product under regulation 18,

    (b) where no such proceedings have been brought, by way of complaint to a magistrates' court;

    (c) in Scotland, by summary application to the sheriff.

    (3) On an application under paragraph (1) to a magistrates' court or to the sheriff, the court or the sheriff may make an order requiring a product or record to be released only if the court or sheriff is satisfied—

    (a) that proceedings

        (i) for an offence in respect of any contravention in relation to the product or, in the case of a record, the product to which the record relates, of any requirement imposed by or under these Regulations; or

        (ii) for the forfeiture of the product or, in the case of a record, the product to which the record relate, under regulation 18 or 19,

    have not been brought or, having been brought, have been concluded without the product being forfeited; and

    (b) where no such proceedings have been brought, that more than six months have elapsed since the product or records was seized.

    (4) In determining whether to make an order under this regulation requiring the release of a product or record the court or sheriff shall take all the circumstances into account including the results of any tests on the product which have been carried out by or on behalf of the enforcement authority and any statement made by the enforcement authority to the court or sheriff as to its intention to bring proceedings for an offence in respect of a contravention in relation to the product of any requirement imposed by or under these Regulations.

    (5) Where—

    (a) more than 12 months have elapsed since a product or records were seized and the enforcement authority has not commenced proceedings for an offence in respect of a contravention in relation to the product (or, in the case of records, the product to which the records relate) of any requirement imposed by or under these Regulations or for the forfeiture of the product under regulation 18 or 19, or

(b) an enforcement authority has brought proceedings for an offence as mentioned in sub-paragraph (a) and the proceedings were dismissed and all rights of appeal have been exercised or the time for appealing has expired,

the authority shall be under a duty to return the product or records detained under regulation 22 or 23 to the person from whom they were seized.

(6) Where the authority is satisfied that some other person has a better right to a product or record than the person from whom they were seized, the authority shall, instead of the duty in paragraph (5), be under a duty to return it to that other person or, as the case may be, to the person appearing to the authority to have the best right to the product or record in question.

(7) Where different persons claim to be entitled to the return of a product or record that is required to be returned under paragraph (5), then it may be retained for as long as it reasonably necessary for the determination in accordance with paragraph (6) of the person to whom it must be returned.

(8) A person aggrieved by an order made under this regulation by a magistrates' court in England and Wales or Northern Ireland, or by a decision of such a court not to make such an order, may appeal against that order or decision—

(a) in England and Wales, to the Crown Court;

(b) in Northern Ireland, to the county court;

and an order so made may contain such provision as appears to the court to be appropriate for delaying the coming into force of the order pending the making and determination of any appeal (including any application under section 111 of the Magistrates' Courts Act 1980 or article 146 of the Magistrates' Courts (Northern Ireland) Order 1981 (statement of case)).

26. Compensation for seizure and detention

Where an officer of an enforcement authority exercises any power under regulation 22 or 23 to seize and detain a product, the enforcement authority shall be liable to pay compensation to any person having an interest in the product in respect of any loss or damage caused by reason of the exercise of the power if—

(a) there has been no contravention in relation to the product of any requirement imposed by or under these Regulations, and

(b) the exercise of the power is not attributable to any neglect or default by that person.

27. Recovery of expenses of enforcement

(1) This regulation shall apply where a court—

(a) convicts a person of an offence in respect of a contravention in relation to a product of any requirement imposed by or under these Regulations, or

(b) makes an order under regulation 18 or 19 for the forfeiture of a product.

(2) The court may (in addition to any other order it may make as to costs or expenses) order the person convicted or, as the case may be, any person having an interest in the product to reimburse an enforcement authority for any expenditure which has been or may be incurred by that authority—

(a) in connection with any seizure or detention of the product by or on behalf of the authority, or

(b) in connection with any compliance by the authority with directions given by the court for the purposes of any order for the forfeiture of the product.

28. Power of Secretary of State to obtain information

(1) If the Secretary of State considers that, for the purposes of deciding whether to serve a safety notice, or to vary or revoke a safety notice which he has already served, he requires information or a sample of a product he may serve on a person a notice requiring him:

(a) to furnish to the Secretary of State, within a period specified in the notice, such information as is specified;

(b) to produce such records as are specified in the notice at a time and place so specified (and to produce any such records which are stored in any electronic form in a form in which they are visible and legible) and to permit a person appointed by the Secretary of State for that purpose to take copies of the records at that time and place;

(c) to produce such samples of a product as are specified in the notice at a time and place so specified.

(2) A person shall be guilty of an offence if he—

(a) fails, without reasonable cause, to comply with a notice served on him under paragraph (1); or

(b) in purporting to comply with a requirement which by virtue of paragraph (1)(a) or (b) is contained in such a notice—

(i) furnishes information or records which he knows are false in a material particular, or

(ii) recklessly furnishes information or records which are false in a material particular.

(3) A person guilty of an offence under paragraph (2) shall—

(a) in the case of an offence under sub-paragraph (a) of that paragraph, be liable on summary conviction to a fine not exceeding level 5 on the standard scale; and

(b) in the case of an offence under sub-paragraph (b) of that paragraph, be liable—

(i) on conviction on indictment, to a fine;

(ii) on summary conviction, to a fine not exceeding the statutory maximum.

29. Defence of due diligence

(1) Subject to the following provisions of this regulation, in proceedings against a person for an offence under these Regulations it shall be a defence for that person to show that he took all reasonable steps and exercised all due diligence to avoid committing the offence.

(2) Where in any proceedings against any person for such an offence the defence provided by paragraph (1) involves an allegation that the commission of the offence was due—

(a) to the act or default of another, or

(b) to reliance on information given by another,

that person shall not, without the leave of the court, be entitled to rely on the defence unless, not less than seven clear days before, in England, Wales and Northern Ireland, the hearing of the proceedings or, in Scotland, the trial diet, he has served a notice under paragraph (3) on the person bringing the proceedings.

(3) A notice under this paragraph shall give such information identifying or assisting in the identification of the person who—

(a) committed the act or default, or

(b) gave the information,

as is in the possession of the person serving the notice at the time he serves it.

(4) A person may not rely on the defence provided by paragraph (1) by reason of his reliance on information supplied by another, unless he shows that it was reasonable in all the circumstances to have relied on the information, having regard in particular—

(a) to the steps which he took, and those which might reasonably have been taken, for the purpose of verifying the information; and

(b) to whether he had any reason to disbelieve the information.

30. Defence in relation to antiques

(1) This regulation shall apply in proceedings against any person for an offence under regulation 20(1) in respect of the supply, offer or agreement to supply or exposure or possession for supply of second hand products supplied as antiques.

(2) It shall be a defence for that person to show that the terms on which he supplied the product or agreed or offered to supply the product or, in the case of a product which he exposed or possessed for supply, the terms on which he intended to supply the product, contemplated the acquisition of an interest in the product by the person supplied or to be supplied.

(3) Paragraph (2) applies only if the producer or distributor clearly informed the person to whom he supplied the product, or offered or agreed to supply the product or, in the case of a product which he exposed or possessed for supply, he intended to so inform that person, that the product is an antique.

31. Liability of person other than principal offender

(1) Where the commission by a person of an offence under these Regulations is due to an act or default committed by some other person in the course of a commercial activity of his, the other person shall be guilty of the offence and may be proceeded against and punished by virtue of this paragraph whether or not proceedings are taken against the first-mentioned person.

(2) Where a body corporate is guilty of an offence under these Regulations (including where it is so guilty by virtue of paragraph (1)) in respect of any act or default which is shown to have been committed with the consent or connivance of, or to be attributable to any neglect on the part of, any director, manager, secretary or other similar officer of the body corporate or any person who was purporting to act in any such capacity he, as well as the body corporate, shall be guilty of that offence and shall be liable to be proceeded against and punished accordingly.

(3) Where the affairs of a body corporate are managed by its members, paragraph (2) shall apply in relation to the acts and defaults of a member in connection with his functions of management as if he were a director of the body corporate.

(4) Where a Scottish partnership is guilty of an offence under these Regulations (including where it is so guilty by virtue of paragraph (1)) in respect of any act or default which is shown to have been committed with the consent or connivance of, or to be attributable to any neglect on the part of, a partner in the partnership, he, as well as the partnership, shall be guilty of that offence and shall be liable to be proceeded against and punished accordingly.

PART 4

MISCELLANEOUS

32. Reports

(1) It shall be the duty of the Secretary of State to lay before each House of Parliament a report on the exercise during the period to which the report relates of the functions which are exercisable by enforcement authorities under these Regulations.

(2) The first such report shall relate to the period beginning on the day on which these Regulations come into force and ending on 31 March 2008 and subsequent reports shall relate to a period of not more than five years beginning on the day after the day on which the period to which the previous report relates ends.

(3) The Secretary of State may from time to time prepare and lay before each House of Parliament such other reports on the exercise of those functions as he considers appropriate.

(4) The Secretary of State may direct an enforcement authority to report at such intervals as he may specify in the direction on the discharge by that authority of the functions exercisable by it under these Regulations.

(5) A report under paragraph (4) shall be in such form and shall contain such particulars as are specified in the direction of the Secretary of State.

33. Duty to notify Secretary of State and Commission

(1) An enforcement authority which has received a notification under regulation 9(1) shall immediately pass the same on to the Secretary of State, who shall immediately pass it on

to the competent authorities appointed for the purpose in the Member States where the product in question is or has been marketed or otherwise supplied to consumers.

(2) Where an enforcement authority takes a measure which restricts the placing on the market of a product, or requires its withdrawal or recall, it shall immediately notify the Secretary of State, specifying its reasons for taking the action. It shall also immediately notify the Secretary of State of any modification or lifting of such a measure.

(3) On receiving a notification under paragraph (2), or if he takes a measure which restricts the placing on the market of a product, or requires its withdrawal or recall, the Secretary of State shall (to the extent that such notification is not required under article 12 of the GPS Directive or any other Community legislation) immediately notify the European Commission of the measure taken, specifying the reasons for taking it. The Secretary of State shall also immediately notify the European Commission of any modification or lifting of such a measure. If the Secretary of State considers that the effects of the risk do not or cannot go beyond the territory of the United Kingdom, he shall notify the European Commission of the measure concerned insofar as it involves information likely to be of interest to Member States from the product safety standpoint, and in particular if it is in response to a new risk which has not yet been reported in other notifications.

(4) Where an enforcement authority adopts or decides to adopt, recommend or agree with producers and distributors, whether on a compulsory or voluntary basis, a measure or action to prevent, restrict or impose specific conditions on the possible marketing or use of a product (other than a pharmaceutical product) by reason of a serious risk, it shall immediately notify the Secretary of State. It shall also immediately notify the Secretary of State of any modification or withdrawal of any such measure or action.

(5) On receiving a notification under paragraph (4), or if he adopts or decides to adopt, recommend or agree with producers and distributors, whether on a compulsory or voluntary basis, a measure or action to prevent, restrict or impose specific conditions on the possible marketing or use of a product (other than a pharmaceutical product) by reason of a serious risk, the Secretary of State shall immediately notify the European Commission of it through the Community Rapid Information System, known as RAPEX. The Secretary of State shall also inform the European Commission without delay of any modification or withdrawal of any such measure or action.

(6) If the Secretary of State considers that the effects of the risk do not or cannot go beyond the territory of the United Kingdom, he shall notify the European Commission of the measures or action concerned insofar as they involve information likely to be of interest to Member States of the European Union from the product safety standpoint, and in particular if they are in response to a new risk which has not been reported in other notifications.

(7) Before deciding to adopt such a measure or take such an action as is referred to in paragraph (5), the Secretary of State may pass on to the European Commission any information in his possession regarding the existence of a serious risk. Where he does so, he must inform the European Commission, within 45 days of the day of passing the information to it, whether he confirms or modifies that information.

(8) Upon receipt of a notification from the European Commission under article 12(2) of the GPS Directive, the Secretary of State shall notify the Commission of the following—

    (a) whether the product the subject of the notification has been marketed in the United Kingdom;

    (b) what measure concerning the product the enforcement authorities in the United Kingdom may be adopting, stating the reasons, including any differing assessment of risk or any other special circumstance justifying the decision as to the measure, in particular lack of action or follow-up; and

    (c) any relevant supplementary information he has obtained on the risk involved, including the results of any test or analysis carried out.

(9) The Secretary of State shall notify the European Commission without delay of any modification or withdrawal of any measures notified to it under paragraph (8)(b).

(10) In this regulation—
  (a) references to a product excludes a second hand product supplied as an antique or as a product to be repaired or reconditioned prior to being used, provided the supplier clearly informs the person to whom he supplies the product to that effect;
  (b) "pharmaceutical product" means a product falling within Council Directive 2001/83/EC of the European Parliament and of the Council on the Community code relating to medicinal products for human use.

34. Provisions supplemental to regulation 33

(1) A notification under regulation 33(2) to (6), (8) or (9) to the Secretary of State or the Commission shall be in writing and shall provide all available details and at least the following information—
  (a) information enabling the product to be identified,
  (b) a description of the risk involved, including a summary of the results of any test or analysis and of their conclusions which are relevant to assessing the level of risk,
  (c) the nature and the duration of the measures or action taken or decided on, if applicable,
  (d) information on supply chains and distribution of the product, in particular on destination countries.

(2) Where a measure notified to the Commission under regulation 33 seeks to limit the marketing or use of a chemical substance or preparation, the Secretary of State shall provide to the Commission as soon as possible either a summary or the references of the relevant data relating to the substance or preparation considered and to known and available substitutes, where such information is available. The Secretary of State shall also notify the Commission of the anticipated effects of the measure on consumer health and safety together with the assessment of the risk carried out in accordance with the general principles for the risk evaluation of chemical substances as referred to in article 10(4) of Council Regulation (EEC) No. 793/93 of 23 March 1993 on the evaluation and control of the risks of existing substances, in the case of an existing substance, or in article 3(2) of Council Directive 67/548/EEC on the approximation of laws, regulations and administrative provisions relating to the classification, packaging and labelling of dangerous substances in the case of a new substance.

(3) Where the Commission carries out an investigation under paragraph 5 of Annex II to the GPS Directive, the Secretary of State shall supply the Commission with such information as it requests, to the best of his ability.

35. Implementation of Commission decisions

(1) This regulation applies where the Commission adopts a decision pursuant to article 13 of the GPS Directive.

(2) The Secretary of State shall—
  (a) take such action under these Regulations, or
  (b) direct another enforcement authority to take such action under these Regulations as is necessary to comply with the decision.

(3) Where an enforcement authority serves a safety notice pursuant to paragraph (2), the following provisions of these Regulations shall not apply in relation to that notice, namely regulations 14(3), 15(4) to (6) and 16(1), 16(2)(c) and (d), 16(5) to (7) and 17.

(4) Unless the Commission's decision provides otherwise, export from the Community of a dangerous product which is the subject of such a decision is prohibited with effect from the date the decision comes into force.

(5) The enforcement of the prohibition in paragraph (4) shall be treated as an assigned matter within the meaning of section 1(1) of the Customs and Excise Management Act 1979.

(6) The measures necessary to implement the decision shall be taken within 20 days, unless the decision specifies a different period.

(7) The Secretary of State or, where the Secretary of State has directed another enforcement authority to take action under paragraph (2)(b), that enforcement authority shall,

within one month, give the parties concerned an opportunity to submit their views and shall inform the Commission accordingly.

36. Market surveillance

In order to ensure a high level of consumer health and safety protection, enforcement authorities shall within the limits of their responsibility and to the extent of their ability undertake market surveillance of products employing appropriate means and procedures and co-operating with other enforcement authorities and competent authorities of other Member States which may include:

(a) establishment, periodical updating and implementation of sectoral surveillance programmes by categories of products or risks and the monitoring of surveillance activities, findings and results,

(b) follow-up and updating of scientific and technical knowledge concerning the safety of products,

(c) the periodical review and assessment of the functioning of the control activities and their effectiveness and, if necessary revision of the surveillance approach and organisation put in place.

37. Complaints procedures

An enforcement authority shall maintain and publish a procedure by which complaints may be submitted by any person on product safety and on surveillance and control activities, which complaints shall be followed up as appropriate.

38. Co-operation between enforcement authorities

(1) It shall be the duty of an enforcement authority to co-operate with other enforcement authorities in carrying out the functions conferred on them by these Regulations. In particular—

(a) enforcement authorities shall share their expertise and best practices with each other;

(b) enforcement authorities shall undertake collaborative working where they have a shared interest.

(2) The Secretary of State shall inform the European Commission as to the arrangements for the enforcement of these Regulations, including which bodies are enforcement authorities.

39. Information

(1) An enforcement authority shall in general make available to the public such information as is available to it on the following matters relating to the risks to consumer health and safety posed by a product—

(a) the nature of the risk,

(b) the product identification,

and the measures taken in respect of the risk, without prejudice to the need not to disclose information for effective monitoring and investigation activities.

(2) Paragraph (1) shall not apply to any information obtained by an enforcement authority for the purposes of these Regulations which, by its nature, is covered by professional secrecy, unless the circumstances require such information to be made public in order to protect the health and safety of consumers.

40. Service of documents

(1) A document required or authorised by virtue of these Regulations to be served on a person may be so served—

(a) on an individual by delivering it to him or by leaving it at his proper address or by sending it by post to him at that address;

(b) on a body corporate other than a limited liability partnership, by serving it in accordance with sub-paragraph (a) on the secretary of the body;

(c) on a limited liability partnership, by serving it in accordance with sub-paragraph (a) on a member of the partnership; or

(d) on a partnership, by serving it in accordance with sub-paragraph (a) on a partner or a person having the control or management of the partnership business;

(e) on any other person by leaving it at his proper address or by sending it by post to him at that address.

(2) For the purposes of paragraph (1), and for the purposes of section 7 of the Interpretation Act 1978 (which relates to the service of documents by post) in its application to that paragraph, the proper address of a person on whom a document is to be served by virtue of these Regulations shall be his last known address except that—

(a) in the case of a body corporate (other than a limited liability partnership) or its secretary, it shall be the address of the registered or principal office of the body;

(b) in the case of a limited liability partnership or a member of the partnership, it shall be the address of the registered or principal office of the partnership;

(c) in the case of a partnership or a partner or a person having the control or management of a partnership business, it shall be the address of the principal office of the partnership,

and for the purposes of this paragraph the principal officer of a company constituted under the law of a country or territory outside the United Kingdom or of a partnership carrying on business outside the United Kingdom is its principal office within the United Kingdom.

(3) A document required or authorised by virtue of these Regulations to be served on a person may also be served by transmitting the request by any means of electronic communication to an electronic address (which includes a fax number and an e-mail address) being an address which the person has held out as an address at which he or it can be contacted for the purposes of receiving such documents.

(4) A document transmitted by any means of electronic communication in accordance with the preceding paragraph is, unless the contrary is proved, deemed to be received on the business day after the notice was transmitted over a public electronic communications network.

41. Extension of time for bringing summary proceedings

(1) Notwithstanding section 127 of the Magistrates' Courts Act 1980 or article 19 of the Magistrates' Courts (Northern Ireland) Order 1981, in England, Wales and Northern Ireland a magistrates' court may try an information (in the case of England and Wales) or a complaint (in the case of Northern Ireland) in respect of an offence under these Regulations if (in the case of England and Wales) the information is laid or (in the case of Northern Ireland) the complaint is made within three years from the date of the offence or within one year from the discovery of the offence by the prosecutor whichever is the earlier.

(2) Notwithstanding section 136 of the Criminal Procedure (Scotland) Act 1995, in Scotland summary proceedings for an offence under these Regulations may be commenced within three years from the date of the offence or within one year from the discovery of the offence by the prosecutor whichever is the earlier.

(3) For the purposes of paragraph (2), section 136(3) of the Criminal Procedure (Scotland) Act 1995 shall apply as it applies for the purposes of that section.

42. Civil proceedings

These Regulations shall not be construed as conferring any right of action in civil proceedings in respect of any loss or damage suffered in consequence of a contravention of these Regulations.

43. Privileged information

(1) Nothing in these Regulations shall be taken as requiring a person to produce any records if he would be entitled to refuse to produce those records in any proceedings in any court on the grounds that they are the subject of legal professional privilege or, in Scotland,

that they contain a confidential communication made by or to an advocate or solicitor in that capacity, or as authorising a person to take possession of any records which are in the possession of a person who would be so entitled.

(2) Nothing in these Regulations shall be construed as requiring a person to answer any question or give any information if to do so would incriminate that person or that person's spouse or civil partner.

44. Evidence in proceedings for offence relating to regulation 9(1)

(1) This regulation applies where a person has given a notification to an enforcement authority pursuant to regulation 9(1).

(2) No evidence relating to that statement may be adduced and no question relating to it may be asked by the prosecution in any criminal proceedings (other than proceedings in which that person is charged with an offence under regulation 20 for a contravention of regulation 9(1)), unless evidence relating to it is adduced, or a question relating to it is asked, in the proceedings by or on behalf of that person.

45. Transitional provisions

Where, in relation to a product, a suspension notice (within the meaning of the 1987 Act) has (by virtue of regulation 11(b) of the General Product Safety Regulations 1994) been served under section 14 of the 1987 Act and is in force immediately prior to the coming into force of these Regulations, it shall continue in force notwithstanding the revocation of the General Product Safety Regulations 1994 by these Regulations, and those Regulations shall continue to apply accordingly.

Regulatory Reform (Unsolicited Goods and Services Act 1971) (Directory Entries and Demands for Payment) Order 2005

(SI 2005, No. 55)

1 Citation, commencement, extent and interpretation

(2) This Order does not extend to Northern Ireland.

(3) Expressions used in this Order which are also used in the Unsolicited Goods and Services Act 1971 have the same meaning as in that Act.

3 Subordinate Provisions

(1) The provisions of the Schedule are subordinate provisions for the purposes of section 4 of the Regulatory Reform Act 2001.

5 The Electronic Commerce (EC Directive) Regulations 2002

The Electronic Commerce (EC Directive) Regulations 2002 apply to—

(a) this Order; and

(b) any subordinate provisions order (within the meaning of section 4(4) of the Regulatory Reform Act 2001) made in respect of the Schedule to this Order.

Article 3   SCHEDULE

PART 1   PARTICULARS OF DIRECTORY OR PROPOSED DIRECTORY WHICH MUST BE GIVEN IN A NOTE

The particulars referred to in section 3(3) of the Unsolicited Goods and Services Act 1971 are:

(a) the amount of the charge;

(b) the name of the directory or proposed directory;

(c) the name of the person producing the directory;

(d) the geographic address at which that person is established;

(e) if the directory is to be available in printed form, the proposed date of publication of the directory or of the issue in which the entry is to be included;

(f) if the directory or the issue in which the entry is to be included is to be put on sale, the price at which it is to be offered for sale and the minimum number of copies which are to be available for sale;

(g) if the directory or the issue of the directory in which the entry is to be included is to be distributed free of charge (whether or not it is also to be put on sale), the minimum numbers of copies which are to be so distributed; and

(h) if the directory is or is to be made available in a form other than printed form, adequate details of how it may be accessed.

PART 2   CONDITIONS APPLYING TO INVOICE OR SIMILAR DOCUMENT WHICH DOES NOT ASSERT RIGHT TO PAYMENT

The conditions referred to in section 6(2) of the Unsolicited Goods and Services Act 1971 are that the invoice or similar document must:

(a) be clear, legible and comprehensible; and

(b) contain the following statement, displayed in uppercase lettering and in a manner that makes that statement readily apparent to a reasonable person reading that invoice or similar document—

'THIS IS NOT A DEMAND FOR PAYMENT
THERE IS NO OBLIGATION TO PAY
THIS IS NOT A BILL'

PART 3   INFORMATION REQUIRED IN WRITTEN NOTICE

The notice referred to in section 3B(1)(h)(i) of the Unsolicited Goods and Services Act 1971 must specify the following information:

(a) the fact that the earlier contract is to be renewed or extended;

(b) the commencement date of the new contract;

(c) the cost to the purchaser of the new contract; and

(d) the fact that the purchaser may, within 21 days, write to the person by whom the notice is given withdrawing his consent to the renewal or extension of the contract.

PART 4   INFORMATION TO BE GIVEN TO A PURCHASER

The following information must be given to the purchaser pursuant to section 3B(1)(i)(ii) of the Unsolicited Goods and Services Act 1971:

(a) the name of the relevant publisher; and

(b) the fact that, if the purchaser enters into the new contract:

(i)   the other party to the new contract will be the relevant publisher; and

(ii) the parties to the earlier contract and the new contract will be different.

PART IV

....

EU Materials*

Treaty Establishing the European Community
(Treaty of Rome, 25 March 1957, revised)

CONSUMER PROTECTION

Art. 153   (ex Art. 129a)

1. In order to promote the interests of consumers and to ensure a high level of consumer protection, the Community shall contribute to protecting the health, safety and economic interests of consumers, as well as to promoting their right to information, education and to organise themselves in order to safeguard their interests.

2. Consumer protection requirements shall be taken into account in defining and implementing other Community policies and activities.

3. The Community shall contribute to the attainment of the objectives referred to in paragraph 1 through:

   (a) measures adopted pursuant to Article 95 in the context of the completion of the internal market;

   (b) measures which support, supplement and monitor the policy pursued by the Member States.

4. The Council, acting in accordance with the procedure referred to in Article 251 and after consulting the Economic and Social Committee, shall adopt the measures referred to in paragraph 3(b).

5. Measures adopted pursuant to paragraph 4 shall not prevent any Member State from maintaining or introducing more stringent protective measures. Such measures must be compatible with this Treaty. The Commission shall be notified of them.

Council Directive
of 25 July 1985

on the approximation of the laws, regulations and administrative provisions of the Member States concerning liability for defective products (85/374/EEC: L 210/29)

THE COUNCIL OF THE EUROPEAN COMMUNITIES,

Having regard to the Treaty establishing the European Economic Community, and in particular Article 100 thereof,

   Having regard to the proposal from the Commission,

   Having regard to the opinion of the European Parliament,

Materials to be found at and taken from http://europa.eu/index_en.htm and whose permission to reproduce them is gratefully acknowledged. Please note that 'only European Community official Documents printed in the Official Journal of the European Union are deemed authentic'.

Having regard to the opinion of the Economic and Social Committee,

Whereas approximation of the laws of the Member States concerning the liability of the producer for damage caused by the defectiveness of his products is necessary because the existing divergences may distort competition and affect the movement of goods within the common market and entail a differing degree of protection of the consumer against damage caused by a defective product to his health or property;

Whereas liability without fault on the part of the producer is the sole means of adequately solving the problem, peculiar to our age of increasing technicality, of a fair apportionment of the risks inherent in modern technological production;

Whereas liability without fault should apply only to movables which have been industrially produced; whereas, as a result, it is appropriate to exclude liability for agricultural products and game, except where they have undergone a processing of an industrial nature which could cause a defect in these products; whereas the liability provided for in this Directive should also apply to movables which are used in the construction of immovables or are installed in immovables;

Whereas protection of the consumer requires that all producers involved in the production process should be made liable, in so far as their finished product, component part or any raw material supplied by them was defective; whereas, for the same reason, liability should extend to importers of products into the Community and to persons who present themselves as producers by affixing their name, trade mark or other distinguishing feature or who supply a product the producer of which cannot be identified;

Whereas, in situations where several persons are liable for the same damage, the protection of the consumer requires that the injured person should be able to claim full compensation for the damage from any one of them;

Whereas, to protect the physical well-being and property of the consumer, the defectiveness of the product should be determined by reference not to its fitness for use but to the lack of the safety which the public at large is entitled to expect; whereas the safety is assessed by excluding any misuse of the product not reasonable under the circumstances;

Whereas a fair apportionment of risk between the injured person and the producer implies that the producer should be able to free himself from liability if he furnishes proof as to the existence of certain exonerating circumstances;

Whereas the protection of the consumer requires that the liability of the producer remains unaffected by acts or omissions of other persons having contributed to cause the damage; whereas, however, the contributory negligence of the injured person may be taken into account to reduce or disallow such liability;

Whereas the protection of the consumer requires compensation for death and personal injury as well as compensation for damage to property; whereas the latter should nevertheless be limited to goods for private use or consumption and be subject to a deduction of a lower threshold of a fixed amount in order to avoid litigation in an excessive number of cases; whereas this Directive should not prejudice compensation for pain and suffering and other non-material damages payable, where appropriate, under the law applicable to the case;

Whereas a uniform period of limitation for the bringing of action for compensation is in the interests both of the injured person and of the producer;

Whereas products age in the course of time, higher safety standards are developed and the state of science and technology progresses; whereas, therefore, it would not be reasonable to make the producer liable for an unlimited period for the defectiveness of his product; whereas therefore, liability should expire after a reasonable length of time, without prejudice to claims pending at law;

Whereas, to achieve effective protection of consumers, no contractual derogation should be permitted as regards the liability of the producer in relation to the injured person;

Whereas under the legal systems of the Member States an injured party may have a claim for damages based on grounds of contractual liability or on grounds of non-contractual liability other than that provided for in this Directive; in so far as these provisions also serve to attain the objective of effective protection of consumers, they should remain unaffected by this Directive; whereas, in so far as effective protection of consumers in the sector of pharmaceutical products is already also attained in a Member State under a special liability system, claims based on this system should similarly remain possible;

Whereas, to the extent that liability for nuclear injury or damage is already covered in all Member States by adequate special rules, it has been possible to exclude damage of this type from the scope of this Directive;

Whereas, since the exclusion of primary agricultural products and game from the scope of this Directive may be felt, in certain Member States, in view of what is expected for the protection of consumers, to restrict unduly such protection, it should be possible for a Member State to extend liability to such products;

Whereas, for similar reasons, the possibility offered to a producer to free himself from liability if he proves that the state of scientific and technical knowledge at the time when he put the product into circulation was not such as to enable the existence of a defect to be discovered may be felt in certain Member States to restrict unduly the protection of the consumer; whereas it should therefore be possible for a Member State to maintain in its legislation or to provide by new legislation that this exonerating circumstance is not admitted; whereas, in the case of new legislation, making use of this derogation should, however, be subject to a Community stand-still procedure, in order to raise, if possible, the level of protection in a uniform manner throughout the Community;

Whereas, taking into account the legal traditions in most of the Member States, it is inappropriate to set any financial ceiling on the producer's liability without fault; whereas, in so far as there are, however, differing traditions, it seems possible to admit that a Member State may derogate from the principle of unlimited liability by providing a limit for the total liability of the producer for damage resulting from a death or personal injury and caused by identical items with the same defect, provided that this limit is established at a level sufficiently high to guarantee adequate protection of the consumer and the correct functioning of the common market;

Whereas the harmonization resulting from this cannot be total at the present stage, but opens the way towards greater harmonization; whereas it is therefore necessary that the Council receive at regular intervals, reports from the Commission on the application of this Directive, accompanied, as the case may be, by appropriate proposals;

Whereas it is particularly important in this respect that a re-examination be carried out of those parts of the Directive relating to the derogations open to the Member States, at the expiry of a period of sufficient length to gather practical experience on the effects of these derogations on the protection of consumers and on the functioning of the common market, HAS ADOPTED THIS DIRECTIVE:

Art.1. The producer shall be liable for damage caused by a defect in his product.

Art.2. For the purpose of this Directive 'product' means all movables, with the exception of primary agricultural products and game, even though incorporated into another movable or into an immovable. 'Primary agricultural products' means the products of the soil, of stock-farming and of fisheries, excluding products which have undergone initial processing. 'Product' includes electricity.

Art.3. 1. 'Producer' means the manufacturer of a finished product, the producer of any raw material or the manufacturer of a component part and any person who, by putting his name, trade mark or other distinguishing feature on the product presents himself as its producer.

Without prejudice to the liability of the producer, any person who imports into the Community a product for sale, hire, leasing or any form of distribution in the course of his business shall be deemed to be a producer within the meaning of this Directive and shall be responsible as a producer.

3. Where the producer of the product cannot be identified, each supplier of the product shall be treated as its producer unless he informs the injured person, within a reasonable

time, of the identity of the producer or of the person who supplied him with the product. The same shall apply, in the case of an imported product, if this product does not indicate the identity of the importer referred to in paragraph 2, even if the name of the producer is indicated.

Art.4. The injured person shall be required to prove the damage, the defect and the causal relationship between defect and damage.

Art.5. Where, as a result of the provisions of this Directive, two or more persons are liable for the same damage, they shall be liable jointly and severally, without prejudice to the provisions of national law concerning the rights of contribution or recourse.

Art.6. 1. A product is defective when it does not provide the safety which a person is entitled to expect, taking all circumstances into account, including:

(a) the presentation of the product;

(b) the use to which it could reasonably be expected that the product would be put;

(c) the time when the product was put into circulation.

2. A product shall not be considered defective for the sole reason that a better product is subsequently put into circulation.

Art.7. The producer shall not be liable as a result of this Directive if he proves:

(a) that he did not put the product into circulation; or

(b) that, having regard to the circumstances, it is probable that the defect which caused the damage did not exist at the time when the product was put into circulation by him or that this defect came into being afterwards; or

(c) that the product was neither manufactured by him for sale or any form of distribution for economic purpose nor manufactured or distributed by him in the course of his business; or

(d) that the defect is due to compliance of the product with mandatory regulations issued by the public authorities; or

(e) that the state of scientific and technical knowledge at the time when he put the product into circulation was not such as to enable the existence of the defect to be discovered; or

(f) in the case of a manufacturer of a component, that the defect is attributable to the design of the product in which the component has been fitted or to the instructions given by the manufacturer of the product.

Art.8. 1. Without prejudice to the provisions of national law concerning the right of contribution or recourse, the liability of the producer shall not be reduced when the damage is caused both by a defect in product and by the act or omission of a third party.

2. The liability of the producer may be reduced or disallowed when, having regard to all the circumstances, the damage is caused both by a defect in the product and by the fault of the injured person or any person for whom the injured person is responsible.

Art.9. For the purpose of Article 1, 'damage' means:

(a) damage caused by death or by personal injuries;

(b) damage to, or destruction of, any item of property other than the defective product itself, with a lower threshold of 500 ECU, provided that the item of property:

(i) is of a type ordinarily intended for private use or consumption, and

(ii) was used by the injured person mainly for his own private use or consumption.

This Article shall be without prejudice to national provisions relating to non-material damage.

Art.10. 1. Member States shall provide in their legislation that a limitation period of three years shall apply to proceedings for the recovery of damages as provided for in this Directive. The limitation period shall begin to run from the day on which the plaintiff became aware, or should reasonably have become aware, of the damage, the defect and the identity of the producer.

2. The laws of Member States regulating suspension or interruption of the limitation period shall not be affected by this Directive.

Art.11. Member States shall provide in their legislation that the rights conferred upon the injured person pursuant to this Directive shall be extinguished upon the expiry of a period of 10 years from the date on which the producer put into circulation the actual product which caused the damage, unless the injured person has in the meantime instituted proceedings against the producer.

Art.12. The liability of the producer arising from this Directive may not, in relation to the injured person, be limited or excluded by a provision limiting his liability or exempting him from liability.

Art.13. This Directive shall not affect any rights which an injured person may have according to the rules of the law of contractual or non-contractual liability or a special liability system existing at the moment when this Directive is notified.

Art.14. This Directive shall not apply to injury or damage arising from nuclear accidents and covered by international conventions ratified by the Member States.

Art.15. 1. Each Member State may:

    (a) by way of derogation from Article 2, provide in its legislation that within the meaning of Article 1 of this Directive 'product' also means primary agricultural products and game;

    (b) by way of derogation from Article 7(e), maintain or, subject to the procedure set out in paragraph 2 of this Article, provide in this legislation that the producer shall be liable even if he proves that the state of scientific and technical knowledge at the time when he put the product into circulation was not such as to enable the existence of a defect to be discovered.

2. A Member State wishing to introduce the measure specified in paragraph 1(b) shall communicate the text of the proposed measure to the Commission. The Commission shall inform the other Member States thereof.

The Member State concerned shall hold the proposed measure in abeyance for nine months after the Commission is informed and provided that in the meantime the Commission has not submitted to the Council a proposal amending this Directive on the relevant matter. However, if within three months of receiving the said information, the Commission does not advise the Member State concerned that it intends submitting such a proposal to the Council, the Member State may take the proposed measure immediately.

If the Commission does submit to the Council such a proposal amending this Directive within the aforementioned nine months, the Member State concerned shall hold the proposed measure in abeyance for a further period of 18 months from the date on which the proposal is submitted.

3. Ten years after the date of notification of this Directive, the Commission shall submit to the Council a report on the effect that rulings by the courts as to the application of Article 7(e) and of paragraph 1(b) of this Article have on consumer protection and the functioning of the common market. In the light of this report the Council, acting on a proposal from the Commission and pursuant to the terms of Article 100 of the Treaty, shall decide whether to repeal Article 7(e).

Art.16. 1. Any Member State may provide that a producer's total liability for damage resulting from a death or personal injury and caused by identical items with the same defect shall be limited to an amount which may not be less than 70 million ECU.

2. Ten years after the date of notification of this Directive, the Commission shall submit to the Council a report on the effect on consumer protection and the functioning of the common market of the implementation of the financial limit on liability by those Member States which have used the option provided for in paragraph 1. In the light of this report the Council, acting on a proposal from the Commission and pursuant to the terms of Article 100 of the Treaty, shall decide whether to repeal paragraph 1.

Art.17. This Directive shall not apply to products put into circulation before the date on which the provisions referred to in Article 19 enter into force.

Art.18. 1. For the purposes of this Directive, the ECU shall be that defined by Regulation (EEC) No. 3180/78, as amended by Regulation (EEC) No. 2626/84. The equivalent in national currency shall initially be calculated at the rate obtaining on the date of adoption of this Directive.

2. Every five years the Council, acting on a proposal from the Commission, shall examine and, if need be, revise the amounts in this Directive, in the light of economic and monetary trends in the Community.

Art.19. 1. Member States shall bring into force, not later than three years from the date of notification of this Directive, the laws, regulations and administrative provisions necessary to comply with this Directive. They shall forthwith inform the Commission thereof.

2. The procedure set out in Article 15(2) shall apply from the date of notification of this Directive.

Art.20. Member States shall communicate to the Commission the texts of the main provisions of national law which they subsequently adopt in the field governed by this Directive.

Art.21. Every five years the Commission shall present a report to the Council on the application of this Directive and, if necessary, shall submit appropriate proposals to it.

Art.22. This Directive is addressed to the Member States.

Done at Brussels, 25 July 1985.

Decision No. 283/1999/EC of the European Parliament and of the Council

of 25 January 1999

establishing a general framework for Community activities in favour of consumers

THE EUROPEAN PARLIAMENT AND THE COUNCIL OF THE EUROPEAN UNION,

Having regard to the Treaty establishing the European Community, and in particular Article 129a thereof,

Having regard to the proposal from the Commission,

Having regard to the opinion of the Economic and Social Committee,

Acting in accordance with the procedure laid down in Article 189b of the Treaty,

(1) Whereas Community action contributes to achieving a high level of consumer protection and thus also contributes to promoting economic and social cohesion in the Community and to strengthening consumer confidence, which is essential for the smooth functioning of the internal market;

(2) Whereas these objectives cannot be achieved effectively without the cooperation and participation of all the institutions and parties concerned;

(3) Whereas the Community is committed in particular to giving new impetus to its action in favour of consumers and their health in order to enable them to become a driving and innovatory force;

(4) Whereas the statement of the European Council meeting in Luxembourg on 12 and 13 December 1997 on food safety recognises that everything must be done to restore public confidence, severely shaken by the BSE crisis; whereas activities to be undertaken within a general framework are essential for achieving this aim;

(5) Whereas the Community needs to plan the actions required by grouping them together in a general framework that identifies the activities and areas of activity which must

be tackled as a matter of priority in order to achieve maximum effectiveness throughout the period covered;

(6) Whereas this general framework aims in particular to bring together the initiatives carried out for the benefit of consumers in order to optimise their effects for consumers;

(7) Whereas this general framework must provide both for initiatives taken by the Community, in compliance with the principle of subsidiarity, and for actions to support organisations and bodies which work to defend consumer interests at Community or national level;

(8) Whereas the initiatives undertaken by the Community and the actions to support other private or public initiatives complement one another and should form part of an integrated approach; whereas it is necessary to strengthen the bodies and organisations that are active in the area of consumer protection so that they can be a more effective driving force for making consumers aware of the priorities set by the Community;

(9) Whereas the other policies of the Community are also responsible and accountable for the integration of consumer interests and should also contribute in financial terms to the implementation of policy in the field of consumer protection;

(10) Whereas the implementation of this general framework should make it possible to take better account of the interests of consumers in the other relevant policies of the Community, and should ensure the development of consumer participation in the standardisation process;

(11) Whereas a harmonised approach to matters related to the protection of consumers and their health is indispensable and whereas this general framework is to provide the necessary financial support to ensure the provision of high-quality independent scientific advice, globally recognised risk-assessment methods and effective control and inspection methods; whereas the Community also has at its disposal the expertise of the joint Research Centre;

(12) Whereas this general framework is open to the participation of the associated countries of central and eastern Europe in accordance with the relevant European Agreements or their Additional Protocols, and also to Cyprus in accordance with procedures to be agreed, as well as to the EFTA/EEA countries on the basis of additional appropriations in accordance with the rules set out in the Agreement on the European Economic Area;

(13) Whereas action under this general framework should also contribute to promoting the interests of consumers at international level;

(14) Whereas it is necessary to evaluate past achievements and draw up a policy priority programme to implement this general framework in order to help achieve maximum effectiveness throughout the period covered; whereas an action plan should be included;

(15) Whereas it is necessary to ensure that the interests of consumers are represented at Community level and to provide significant support to European organisations and bodies which represent the interests of consumers effectively and actively;

(16) Whereas it is necessary, at the same time, to support organisations and bodies which are active at national or regional level by encouraging them to take part in concerted action in the areas recognised as priorities;

(17) Whereas it is therefore necessary to set out the arrangements for the financial support provided by the Community to the organisations and bodies that are representative of consumer interests, out of a constant concern for maximum transparency and for effectiveness in the use of the funds allocated by the Community;

(18) Whereas a modus vivendi was concluded on 20 December 1994 between the European Parliament, the Council and the Commission concerning the implementing measures for acts adopted in accordance with the procedure laid down in Article 189b of the Treaty;

(19) Whereas it is necessary to lay down selection criteria for the provision of financial support;

(20) Whereas it is necessary to establish effective methods for evaluation and monitoring and to make provision for informing the target groups concerned in an appropriate way;

(21) Whereas the implementation of the activities provided for under this general framework must be evaluated in the light of the experience gained in the first three years;

(22) Whereas this Decision lays down, for the whole of the planned duration, a financial framework constituting the principal point of reference, within the meaning of point 1 of the Declaration by the European Parliament, the Council and the Commission of 6 March 1995, for the budgetary authority in the annual budgetary procedure,

HAVE DECIDED AS FOLLOWS:

CHAPTER I

General objectives and approach

Art. 1

1. This Decision establishes, at Community level, a general framework for activities for promoting the interests of consumers and providing them with a high level of protection.

2. This general framework of activities consists of actions designed to help protect the health, safety and economic interests of consumers and to promote their right to information and education and their right to join forces in order to protect their interests.

3. This general framework of activities is hereby adopted for the period from 1 January 1999 to 31 December 2003.

4. The financial framework for the implementation of this general framework for the period 1999–2003 is hereby set at EUR 112,5 million.

5. The annual appropriations shall be authorised by the budgetary authority within the limits of the financial perspective.

Art. 2

The activities to support and supplement the policy conducted by the Member States shall consist of:

(a) actions taken by the Commission;

(b) actions providing financial support for the activities of European consumer organ-isations, under the conditions set out in Article 5;

(c) actions providing financial support for specific projects to promote the interests of consumers in the Member States presented under the conditions set out in Article 6, in particular by consumer organisations and appropriate independent public bodies.

Art. 3

The Commission shall ensure that there is consistency and complementarity between the Community activities and projects under this general framework and the other Community programmes and initiatives, such as the triennial action programmes, and shall in accordance with its action plan 1999–2001 lay down the priorities to be applied in the activities listed in the Annex.

Art. 4

The actions referred to in Article 2 shall concern the following specific areas in particular:

(a) the health and safety of consumers as regards products and services;

(b) protecting the economic and legal interests of consumers, including access to dispute resolution, as regards products and services, taking into account horizontal aspects;

(c) educating and informing consumers about their protection and rights;

(d) promotion and representation of the interests of consumers.

The Annex sets out a list of the activities by area.

CHAPTER II

Implementing arrangements

Art. 5

1. The financial support referred to in Article 2(b) may be granted to European consumer organisations which:

— are non-governmental, non-profit-making organisations whose main objectives are to promote and protect the interests and health of consumers, and
— have been mandated to represent the interests of consumers at European level by national organisations of at least half the Member States of the Community that are representative, in accordance with national rules or practice, of consumers and are active at national or regional level.

2. The financial support referred to in Article 2(b) may be granted to support the activities of European consumer organisations that are planned in the annual programme of their activities, where these activities relate to one or more of the areas mentioned in Article 4.

3. The conditions for granting financial support are set out in Articles 7, 8 and 10. In addition, the financial support may not, in principle, exceed 50% of the expenditure involved in carrying out eligible activities. Administrative costs related to eligible activities shall be taken into account in so far as they are in conformity with Article 6(3).

Art. 6

1. The financial support referred to in Article 2(c) may be granted to any natural or legal person or association of natural persons that acts independently of industry and commerce and is actually responsible for the implementation of the projects, where the main objectives of these projects are to promote and protect the interests and health of consumers.

2. The financial support referred to in Article 2(c) shall be granted on the basis of the description of the project, where it relates to one or more of the areas mentioned in Article 4.

Unpaid work or donations in kind, if properly documented, may be taken into account, up to a level of 20 % of total eligible costs, when assessing the organisations' revenue and costs.

3. The conditions for granting financial support are set out in Articles 7, 8 and 10. In addition, the financial support may not, in principle, exceed 50% of the expenditure involved in implementing the project(s), excluding all operating expenses, except where these are directly related to the proposed project.

Art. 7

The financial support referred to in Article 2(b) and (c) shall be granted to actions selected in particular on the basis of the following criteria, where appropriate, taking into account the variety of consumer organisations in Member States in order to ensure an adequate balance of consumer interests in the Community:

— a satisfactory level of cost-effectiveness,
— an added value ensuring a high and uniform level of the representation of the interests of consumers,
— a lasting multiplier effect at national or European level,
— effective and balanced cooperation between the various parties for planning and carrying out activities and for financial participation,
— the development of lasting transnational cooperation, especially through the exchange of experience to raise the awareness of consumers and economic operators and by joint utilisation of their results,
— the widest possible dissemination of the results of the activities and projects supported,
— the ability to analyse the situations to be covered, the means earmarked for evaluating the activities and projects and their suitability for best practice.

CHAPTER III

Procedures, evaluation and monitoring

Art. 8

1. Each year the Commission shall, for the actions referred to in Article 2(b) and (c), at a date, if possible before 30 September, of which it will inform all interested parties and Member States in an appropriate way, publish a notice in the *Official Journal of the European Communities* describing the areas for funding and setting out the selection and award criteria and the procedures for application and approval.

2. Having assessed the proposals, the Commission shall, within five months of the publication referred to in paragraph 1, select such activities and projects referred to in Chapter II as are to receive financial support. The Commission decision shall lead to the conclusion of a contract with the recipients responsible for implementation concerning the rights and obligations of the parties.

3. Community support shall relate to actions to be carried out in the year of the financial contribution or in the following year.

4. A list of the recipients and of the actions funded under this framework shall be published each year in the *Official Journal of the European Communities* with an indication of the amount of the support.

Art. 9

1. In defining the criteria for the selection of activities and projects referred to in Article 2(b) and (c) and in selecting these activities and projects, the Commission shall be assisted by a committee of an advisory nature composed of the representatives of the Member States and chaired by the representative of the Commission.

2. The representative of the Commission shall submit to the committee a draft of the measures to be taken. The committee shall deliver its opinion on the draft, within a time limit which the chairman may lay down according to the urgency of the matter, if necessary by taking a vote.

The opinion shall be recorded in the minutes; in addition, each Member State shall have the right to ask to have its position recorded in the minutes.

The Commission shall take the utmost account of the opinion delivered by the committee. It shall inform the committee of the manner in which its opinion has been taken into account.

3. In addition, at the beginning of each year, the Commission shall provide the Committee with information about the activities financed under Article 2(a).

Art. 10

1. The Commission shall ensure the monitoring and supervision of effective implementation of the activities financed by the Community. This shall be done on the basis of reports using procedures agreed between the Commission and the recipient; it shall include checks *in situ* by means of sampling.

2. Recipients shall submit a report to the Commission for each action within three months of its completion. The Commission shall determine the form and content of this report.

3. Recipients of financial support shall keep at the Commission's disposal all the documentary evidence of expenditure for a period of five years from the last payment concerning an action.

Art. 11

The Commission shall ensure that the actions funded by the Community are evaluated regularly. These evaluations may be carried out by the Commission and/or by independent experts engaged for this purpose.

Art. 12

1. The Commission may reduce, suspend or recover financial support granted for an activity if it detects irregularities or learns that the activity has, without its approval, been significantly modified so that it is incompatible with the objectives of the agreed implementing arrangements.

2. If the deadlines are not met or if the state of progress of an activity warrants only partial use of the appropriations granted, the Commission shall ask the recipient concerned to provide an explanation within a given period of time. If the recipient's reply is not satisfactory, the Commission may cancel the balance of the financial support and demand that the sums already paid be refunded immediately.

3. All undue payments shall be refunded to the Commission. Any sums not refunded in good time may be increased by default interest. The Commission shall determine the arrangements for the application of this paragraph.

Art. 13

1. Each year, the Commission shall submit a report to the European Parliament and to the Council on the implementation of this general framework.

This report shall include the results of the evaluation of the actions, activities and projects carried out under this framework as well as, where appropriate, under other budgetary frameworks.

2. By 30 June 2002 at the latest, the Commission shall submit an evaluation report to the European Parliament and to the Council on the first three years of implementation of activities under this general framework.

Art. 14

This Decision shall enter into force on the day of its publication in the *Official Journal of the European Communities*.

ANNEX   LIST OF ACTIVITIES BY AREA

1   Consumer health and safety
   — Actions undertaken for the preparation and drawing up of opinions of the scientific committees,
   — expertise and inspections relating to controls in the food, veterinary and phytosanitary sectors,
   — technical expertise to assess, adopting a preventive approach, risks relating to products, in particular for foodstuffs,
   — making best use of scientific and technical elements relating to consumer protection actions, in particular through the use of expertise of the Joint Research Centre,
   — actions relating to consumer products and services causing danger to consumers,
   — dissemination of information about dangerous products and services as well as about potential risks.

2   Protecting the economic and legal interests of consumers, including access to dispute resolution, as regards products and services, taking into account horizontal aspects
   — Actions to improve cooperation between the bodies participating in market surveillance,
   — actions to ensure the respect of consumer rights in the supply of products and services, including mechanisms for improving the settlement of consumer disputes, in particular through pilot projects and setting up databases,

— actions to ensure a level playing field in consumer transactions, taking into account the impact of new technologies, the development of financial services and the impact of the euro on the consumer,

— actions to monitor environmental claims on product labels, on packaging and, in general, in advertising and through other types of marketing,

— improving common extra-judicial procedures,

— development of, and support for, actions aimed at facilitating access to justice,

— actions to assess the specific risks and potential benefits for consumers in the information society including pilot projects to establish cross-border dispute resolution systems applicable to electronic commerce and on-line contracts,

— actions to promote data protection and the protection of privacy including the protection of minors.

3 Educating and informing consumers

— Improving information to consumers about their rights and how to enforce them and raising awareness of manufacturers and consumers about safety aspects of products and services,

— raising awareness of consumers for the need for sustainable production and consumption patterns,

— improving information to consumers about features of specific products and services in particular through comparative testing,

— developing the education and training of consumers, particularly in schools,

— development of, and support for, European centres providing information and advice to cross-border consumers in the Community.

4 Promotion and representation of the interests of consumers

— Strengthening the representation of the interests of consumers at the Community and international level,

— supporting consumer organisations in the Member States, in particular where their means are limited,

— promotion and coordination of consumer participation at the European level in standardisation,

— pilot projects promoting sustainable consumption models, in particular those that are environmentally friendly.

Directive 1999/44/EC of the European Parliament and of the Council
of 25 May 1999

on certain aspects of the sale of consumer goods and associated guarantees

THE EUROPEAN PARLIAMENT AND THE COUNCIL OF THE EUROPEAN UNION,

Having regard to the Treaty establishing the European Community, and in particular Article 95 thereof,

Having regard to the proposal from the Commission,

Having regard to the opinion of the Economic and Social Committee,

Acting in accordance with the procedure laid down in Article 251 of the Treaty in the light of the joint text approved by the Conciliation Committee on 18 May 1999,

(1) Whereas Article 153(1) and (3) of the Treaty provides that the Community should contribute to the achievement of a high level of consumer protection by the measures it adopts pursuant to Article 95 thereof;

(2) Whereas the internal market comprises an area without internal frontiers in which the free movement of goods, persons, services and capital is guaranteed; whereas free movement of goods concerns not only transactions by persons acting in the course of a business but also transactions by private individuals; whereas it implies that consumers resident in one Member State should be free to purchase goods in the territory of another Member State on the basis of a uniform minimum set of fair rules governing the sale of consumer goods;

(3) Whereas the laws of the Member States concerning the sale of consumer goods are somewhat disparate, with the result that national consumer goods markets differ from one another and that competition between sellers may be distorted;

(4) Whereas consumers who are keen to benefit from the large market by purchasing goods in Member States other than their State of residence play a fundamental role in the completion of the internal market; whereas the artificial reconstruction of frontiers and the compartmentalisation of markets should be prevented; whereas the opportunities available to consumers have been greatly broadened by new communication technologies which allow ready access to distribution systems in other Member States or in third countries; whereas, in the absence of minimum harmonisation of the rules governing the sale of consumer goods, the development of the sale of goods through the medium of new distance communication technologies risks being impeded;

(5) Whereas the creation of a common set of minimum rules of consumer law, valid no matter where goods are purchased within the Community, will strengthen consumer confidence and enable consumers to make the most of the internal market;

(6) Whereas the main difficulties encountered by consumers and the main source of disputes with sellers concern the non-conformity of goods with the contract; whereas it is therefore appropriate to approximate national legislation governing the sale of consumer goods in this respect, without however impinging on provisions and principles of national law relating to contractual and non-contractual liability;

(7) Whereas the goods must, above all, conform with the contractual specifications; whereas the principle of conformity with the contract may be considered as common to the different national legal traditions whereas in certain national legal traditions it may not be possible to rely solely on this principle to ensure a minimum level of protection for the consumer; whereas under such legal traditions, in particular, additional national provisions may be useful to ensure that the consumer is protected in cases where the parties have agreed no specific contractual terms or where the parties have concluded contractual terms or agreements which directly or indirectly waive or restrict the rights of the consumer and which, to the extent that these rights result from this Directive, are not binding on the consumer;

(8) Whereas, in order to facilitate the application of the principle of conformity with the contract, it is useful to introduce a rebuttable presumption of conformity with the contract covering the most common situations, whereas that presumption does not restrict the principle of freedom of contract; whereas, furthermore, in the absence of specific contractual terms, as well as where the minimum protection clause is applied, the elements mentioned in this presumption may be used to determine the lack of conformity of the goods with the contract; whereas the quality and performance which consumers can reasonably expect will depend *inter alia* on whether the goods are new or second-hand; whereas the elements mentioned in the presumption are cumulative; whereas, if the circumstances of the case render any particular element manifestly inappropriate, the remaining elements of the presumption nevertheless still apply;

(9) Whereas the seller should be directly liable to the consumer for the conformity of the goods with the contract; whereas this is the traditional solution enshrined in the legal orders of the Member States whereas nevertheless the seller should be free, as provided for by national law, to pursue remedies against the producer, a previous seller in the same chain of contracts or any other intermediary, unless he has renounced that entitlement; whereas this Directive does not affect the principle of freedom of contract between the seller, the producer, a previous seller or any other intermediary; whereas the rules

governing against whom and how the seller may pursue such remedies are to be determined by national law;

(10) Whereas, in the case of non-conformity of the goods with the contract, consumers should be entitled to have the goods restored to conformity with the contract free of charge, choosing either repair or replacement, or, failing this, to have the price reduced or the contract rescinded;

(11) Whereas the consumer in the first place may require the seller to repair the goods or to replace them unless those remedies are impossible or disproportionate; whereas whether a remedy is disproportionate should be determined objectively; whereas a remedy would be disproportionate if it imposed, in comparison with the other remedy, unreasonable costs; whereas, in order to determine whether the costs are unreasonable, the costs of one remedy should be significantly higher than the costs of the other remedy;

(12) Whereas in cases of a lack of conformity, the seller may always offer the consumer, by way of settlement, any available remedy; whereas it is for the consumer to decide whether to accept or reject this proposal;

(13) Whereas, in order to enable consumers to take advantage of the internal market and to buy consumer goods in another Member State, it should be recommended that, in the interests of consumers, the producers of consumer goods that are marketed in several Member States attach to the product a list with at least one contact address in every Member State where the product is marketed;

(14) Whereas the references to the time of delivery do not imply that Member States have to change their rules on the passing of the risk;

(15) Whereas Member States may provide that any reimbursement to the consumer may be reduced to take account of the use the consumer has had of the goods since they were delivered to him: whereas the detailed arrangements whereby rescission of the contract is effected may be laid down in national law:

(16) Whereas the specific nature of second-hand goods makes it generally impossible to replace them; whereas therefore the consumer's right of replacement is generally not available for these goods; whereas for such goods, Member States may enable the parties to agree a shortened period of liability;

(17) Whereas it is appropriate to limit in time the period during which the seller is liable for any lack of conformity which exists at the time of delivery of the goods; whereas Member States may also provide for a limitation on the period during which consumers can exercise their rights, provided such a period does not expire within two years from the time of delivery; whereas where, under national legislation, the time when a limitation period starts is not the time of delivery of the goods, the total duration of the limitation period provided for by national law may not be shorter than two years from the time of delivery;

(18) Whereas Member States may provide for suspension or interruption of the period during which any lack of conformity must become apparent and of the limitation period, where applicable and in accordance with their national law, in the event of repair, replacement or negotiations between seller and consumer with a view to an amicable settlement;

(19) Whereas Member States should be allowed to set a period within which the consumer must inform the seller of any lack of conformity; whereas Member States may ensure a higher level of protection for the consumer by not introducing such an obligation; whereas in any case consumers throughout the Community should have at least two months in which to inform the seller that a lack of conformity exists;

(20) Whereas Member States should guard against such a period placing at a disadvantage consumers shopping across borders; whereas all Member States should inform the Commission of their use of this provision; whereas the Commission should monitor the effect of the varied application of this provision on consumers and on the internal market; whereas information on the use made of this provision by a Member State should be available to the other Member States and to consumers and consumer organisations throughout the

Community; whereas a summary of the situation in all Member States should therefore be published in the *Official Journal of the European Communities;*

(21) Whereas, for certain categories of goods, it is current practice for sellers and producers to offer guarantees on goods against any defect which becomes apparent within a certain period; whereas this practice can stimulate competition; whereas, while such guarantees are legitimate marketing tools, they should not mislead the consumer whereas, to ensure that consumers are not misled, guarantees should contain certain information, including a statement that the guarantee does not affect the consumer's legal rights;

(22) Whereas the parties may not, by common consent, restrict or waive the rights granted to consumers, since otherwise the legal protection afforded would be thwarted; whereas this principle should apply also to clauses which imply that the consumer was aware of any lack of conformity of the consumer goods existing at the time the contract was concluded; whereas the protection granted to consumers under this Directive should not be reduced on the grounds that the law of a non-member State has been chosen as being applicable to the contract:

(23) Whereas legislation and case-law in this area in the various Member States show that there is growing concern to ensure a high level of consumer protection; whereas, in the light of this trend and the experience acquired in implementing this Directive, it may be necessary to envisage more far-reaching harmonisation, notably by providing for the producer's direct liability for defects for which he is responsible;

(24) Whereas Member States should be allowed to adopt or maintain in force more stringent provisions in the field covered by this Directive to ensure an even higher level of consumer protection;

(25) Whereas, according to the Commission recommendation of 30 March 1998 on the principles applicable to the bodies responsible for out-of-court settlement of consumer disputes, Member States can create bodies that ensure impartial and efficient handling of complaints in a national and cross-border context and which consumers can use as mediators;

(26) Whereas it is appropriate, in order to protect the collective interests of consumers, to add this Directive to the list of Directives contained in the Annex to Directive 98/27/EC of the European Parliament and of the Council of 19 May 1998 on injunctions for the protection of consumers interests,
HAVE ADOPTED THIS DIRECTIVE:

Art. 1   Scope and definitions
1. The purpose of this Directive is the approximation of the laws, regulations and administrative provisions of the Member States on certain aspects of the sale of consumer goods and associated guarantees in order to ensure a uniform minimum level of consumer protection in the context of the internal market.
2. For the purposes of this Directive:
   (a) *consumer:* shall mean any natural person who, in the contracts covered by this Directive, is acting for purposes which are not related to his trade, business or profession:
   (b) *consumer goods:* shall mean any tangible movable item, with the exception of:
       — goods sold by way of execution or otherwise by authority of law,
       — water and gas where they are not put up for sale in a limited volume or set quantity,
       — electricity;
   (c) *seller:* shall mean any natural or legal person who, under a contract, sells consumer goods in the course of his trade, business or profession;
   (d) *producer:* shall mean the manufacturer of consumer goods the importer of consumer goods into the territory of the Community or any person purporting to be a

producer by placing his name, trade mark or other distinctive sign to the consumer goods;

(e) *guarantee:* shall mean any undertaking by a seller or producer to the consumer, given without extra charge to reimburse the price paid or to replace, repair or handle consumer goods in any way if they do not meet the specifications set out in the guarantee statement or in the relevant advertising;

(f) *repair:* shall mean, in the event of lack of conformity bringing consumer goods into conformity with the contract of sale.

3. Member States may provide that the expression 'consumer goods' does not cover second-hand goods sold at public auction where consumers have the opportunity of attending the sale in person.

4. Contracts for the supply of consumer goods to be manufactured or produced shall also be deemed contracts of sale for the purpose of this Directive.

Art. 2   Conformity with the contract

1. The seller must deliver goods to the consumer which are in conformity with the contract of sale.

2. Consumer goods are presumed to be in conformity with the contract if they:

(a) comply with the description given by the seller and possess the qualities of the goods which the seller has held out in the consumer as a sample or model;

(b) are fit for any particular purpose for which the consumer requires them and which he made known to the seller as the time of conclusion of the contract and which the seller has accepted;

(c) are fit for the purposes for which goods of the same type are normally used;

(d) show the quality and performance which are normal in goods of the same type and which the consumer can reasonably expect, given the nature of the goods and taking into account any public statements on the specific characteristics of the goods made about them by the seller, the producer or his representative, particularly in advertising or on labelling.

3. There shall be deemed not to be a lack of conformity for the purposes of this Article if, at the time the contract was concluded, the consumer was aware, or could not reasonably be unaware of, the lack of conformity, or if the lack of conformity has its origin in materials supplied by the consumer.

4. The seller shall not be bound by public statements, as referred to in paragraph 2(d) if he:

— shows that he was not, and could not reasonably have been aware of the statement in question,

— shows that by the time of conclusion of the contract the statement had been corrected, or

— shows that the decision to buy the consumer goods could not have been influenced by the statement.

5. Any lack of conformity resulting from incorrect installation of the consumer goods shall be deemed to be equivalent to lack of conformity of the goods if installation forms part of the contract of sale of the goods and the goods were installed by the seller or under his responsibility. This shall apply equally if the product, intended to be installed by the consumer, is installed by the consumer and the incorrect installation is due to a shortcoming in the installation instructions.

Art. 3   Rights of the consumer

1. The seller shall be liable to the consumer for any lack of conformity which exists at the time the goods were delivered.

2. In the case of a lack of conformity, the consumer shall be entitled to have the goods brought into conformity free of charge by repair or replacement, in accordance with paragraph 3, or to have an appropriate reduction made in the price or the contract rescinded with regard to those goods, in accordance with paragraphs 5 and 6.

3. In the first place, the consumer may require the seller to repair the goods or he may require the seller to replace them, in either case free of charge, unless this is impossible or disproportionate.

A remedy shall be deemed to be disproportionate if it improves costs on the seller which, in comparison with the alternative remedy, are unreasonable, taking into account:
— the value the goods would have if there were no lack of conformity,
— the significance of the lack of conformity, and
— whether the alternative remedy could be completed without significant inconvenience to the consumer.

Any repair or replacement shall be completed within a reasonable time and without any significant inconvenience to the consumer, taking account of the nature of the goods and the purpose for which the consumer required the goods.

4. The terms 'free of charge' in paragraphs 2 and 3 refer to the necessary costs incurred to bring the goods into conformity, particularly the cost of postage, labour and materials.

5. The consumer may require an appropriate reduction of the price or have the contract rescinded:
— if the consumer is entitled to neither repair nor replacement, or
— if the seller has not completed the remedy within a reasonable time, or
— if the seller has not completed the remedy without significant inconvenience to the consumer.

6. The consumer is not entitled to have the contract rescinded if the lack of conformity is minor.

Art. 4   Right of redress
Where the final seller is liable to the consumer because of a lack of conformity resulting from an act or omission by the producer, a previous seller in the same chain of contracts or any other intermediary, the final seller shall be entitled to pursue remedies against the person or persons liable in the contractual chain, the person or persons liable against whom the final seller may pursue remedies, together with the relevant actions and conditions of exercise, shall be determined by national law.

Art. 5   Time limits
1. The seller shall be held liable under Article 3 where the lack of conformity becomes apparent within two years as from delivery of the goods. If, under national legislation, the rights laid down in Article 3(2) are subject to a limitation period, that period shall not expire within a period of two years from the time of delivery.

2. Member States may provide that, in order to benefit from his rights, the consumer must inform the seller of the lack of conformity within a period of two months from the date on which he detected such lack of conformity.

Member States shall inform the Commission of their use of this paragraph. The Commission shall monitor the effect of the existence of this option for the Member States on consumers and on the internal market.

Not later than 7 January 2003, the Commission shall prepare a report on the use made by Member States of this paragraph. This report shall be published in the *Official Journal of the European Communities*.

3. Unless proved otherwise, any lack of conformity which becomes apparent within six months of delivery of the goods shall be presumed to have existed at the time of delivery unless this presumption is incompatible with the nature of the goods or the nature of the lack of conformity.

Art.   6 Guarantees
1. A guarantee shall be legally binding on the offerer under the conditions laid down in the guarantee statement and the associated advertising.

2. The guarantee shall:
— state that the consumer has legal rights under applicable national legislation governing the sale of consumer goods and make clear that those rights are not affected by the guarantee,
— set out in plain intelligible language the contents of the guarantee and the essential particulars necessary for making claims under the guarantee, notably the duration and territorial scope of the guarantee as well as the name and address of the guarantor.

3. On request by the consumer, the guarantee shall be made available in writing or feature in another durable medium available and accessible to him.

4. Within its own territory, the Member State in which the consumer goods are marketed may, in accordance with the rules of the Treaty, provide that the guarantee be drafted in one or more languages which it shall determine from among the official languages of the Community.

5. Should a guarantee infringe the requirements of paragraphs 2, 3 or 4, the validity of this guarantee shall in no way be affected, and the consumer can still rely on the guarantee and require that it be honoured.

Art. 7 Binding nature

1. Any contractual terms or agreements concluded with the seller before the lack of conformity is brought to the seller's attention which directly or indirectly waive or restrict the rights resulting from this Directive shall, as provided for by national law, not be binding on the consumer.

Member States may provide that, in the case of second-hand goods, the seller and consumer may agree contractual terms or agreements which have a shorter time period for the liability of the seller than that set down in Article 5(1). Such period may not be less than one year.

2. Member States shall take the necessary measures to ensure that consumers are not deprived of the protection afforded by this Directive as a result of opting for the law of a non-member State as the law applicable to the contract where the contract has a close connection with the territory of the Member States.

Art. 8 National law and minimum protection

1. The rights resulting from this Directive shall be exercised without prejudice to other rights which the consumer may invoke under the national rules governing contractual or non-contractual liability.

2. Member States may adopt or maintain in force more stringent provisions, compatible with the Treaty in the field covered by this Directive, to ensure a higher level of consumer protection.

Art. 9

Member States shall take appropriate measures to inform the consumer of the national law transposing this Directive and shall encourage, where appropriate, professional organisations to inform consumers of their rights.

Art. 11 Transposition

1. Member States shall bring into force the laws, regulations and administrative provisions necessary to comply with this Directive not later than 1 January 2002. They shall forthwith inform the Commission thereof.

When Member States adopt these measures, they shall contain a reference to this Directive, or shall be accompanied by such reference at the time of their official publication. The procedure for such reference shall be adopted by Member States.

2. Member States shall communicate to the Commission the provisions of national law which they adopt in the field covered by this Directive.

Art. 12   Review

The Commission shall, not later than 7 July 2006, review the application of this Directive and submit to the European Parliament and the Council a report. The report shall examine, *inter alia*, the case for introducing the producer's direct liability and if appropriate, shall be accompanied by proposals.

Directive 2000/31/EC of the European Parliament and of the Council
of 8 June 2000
on certain legal aspects of information society services, in particular electronic commerce, in the Internal Market
(Directive on electronic commerce)

THE EUROPEAN PARLIAMENT AND THE COUNCIL OF THE EUROPEAN UNION,

Having regard to the Treaty establishing the European Community, and in particular Articles 47(2), 55 and 95 thereof,

Having regard to the proposal from the Commission,

Having regard to the opinion of the Economic and Social Committee,

Acting in accordance with the procedure laid down in Article 251 of the Treaty, Whereas:

(1) The European Union is seeking to forge ever closer links between the States and peoples of Europe, to ensure economic and social progress; in accordance with Article 14(2) of the Treaty, the internal market comprises an area without internal frontiers in which the free movements of goods, services and the freedom of establishment are ensured; the development of information society services within the area without internal frontiers is vital to eliminating the barriers which divide the European peoples.

(2) The development of electronic commerce within the information society offers significant employment opportunities in the Community, particularly in small and mediumsized enterprises, and will stimulate economic growth and investment in innovation by European companies, and can also enhance the competitiveness of European industry, provided that everyone has access to the Internet.

(3) Community law and the characteristics of the Community legal order are a vital asset to enable European citizens and operators to take full advantage, without consideration of borders, of the opportunities afforded by electronic commerce; this Directive therefore has the purpose of ensuring a high level of Community legal integration in order to establish a real area without internal borders for information society services.

(4) It is important to ensure that electronic commerce could fully benefit from the internal market and therefore that, as with Council Directive 89/552/EEC of 3 October 1989 on the coordination of certain provisions laid down by law, regulation or administrative action in Member States concerning the pursuit of television broadcasting activities, a high level of Community integration is achieved.

(5) The development of information society services within the Community is hampered by a number of legal obstacles to the proper functioning of the internal market which make less attractive the exercise of the freedom of establishment and the freedom to provide services; these obstacles arise from divergences in legislation and from the legal uncertainty as to which national rules apply to such services; in the absence of coordination and adjustment of legislation in the relevant areas, obstacles might be justified in the light of the case-law of the Court of Justice of the European Communities; legal uncertainty exists with regard to the extent to which Member States may control services originating from another Member State.

(6) In the light of Community objectives, of Articles 43 and 49 of the Treaty and of secondary Community law, these obstacles should be eliminated by coordinating certain

national laws and by clarifying certain legal concepts at Community level to the extent necessary for the proper functioning of the internal market; by dealing only with certain specific matters which give rise to problems for the internal market, this Directive is fully consistent with the need to respect the principle of subsidiarity as set out in Article 5 of the Treaty.

(7) In order to ensure legal certainty and consumer confidence, this Directive must lay down a clear and general framework to cover certain legal aspects of electronic commerce in the internal market.

(8) The objective of this Directive is to create a legal framework to ensure the free movement of information society services between Member States and not to harmonise the field of criminal law as such.

(9) The free movement of information society services can in many cases be a specific reflection in Community law of a more general principle, namely freedom of expression as enshrined in Article 10(1) of the Convention for the Protection of Human Rights and Fundamental Freedoms, which has been ratified by all the Member States; for this reason, directives covering the supply of information society services must ensure that this activity may be engaged in freely in the light of that Article, subject only to the restrictions laid down in paragraph 2 of that Article and in Article 46(1) of the Treaty; this Directive is not intended to affect national fundamental rules and principles relating to freedom of expression.

(10) In accordance with the principle of proportionality, the measures provided for in this Directive are strictly limited to the minimum needed to achieve the objective of the proper functioning of the internal market; where action at Community level is necessary, and in order to guarantee an area which is truly without internal frontiers as far as electronic commerce is concerned, the Directive must ensure a high level of protection of objectives of general interest, in particular the protection of minors and human dignity, consumer protection and the protection of public health; according to Article 152 of the Treaty, the protection of public health is an essential component of other Community policies.

(11) This Directive is without prejudice to the level of protection for, in particular, public health and consumer interests, as established by Community acts; amongst others, Council Directive 93/13/EEC of 5 April 1993 on unfair terms in consumer contracts and Directive 97/ 7/EC of the European Parliament and of the Council of 20 May 1997 on the protection of consumers in respect of distance contracts form a vital element for protecting consumers in contractual matters; those Directives also apply in their entirety to information society services; that same Community acquis, which is fully applicable to information society services, also embraces in particular Council Directive 84/450/EEC of 10 September 1984 concerning misleading and comparative advertising, Council Directive 87/102/EEC of 22 December 1986 for the approximation of the laws, regulations and administrative provisions of the Member States concerning consumer credit, Council Directive 93/22/EEC of 10 May 1993 on investment services in the securities field, Council Directive 90/314/EEC of 13 June 1990 on package travel, package holidays and package tours, Directive 98/6/EC of the European Parliament and of the Council of 16 February 1998 on consumer production in the indication of prices of products offered to consumers, Council Directive 92/59/EEC of 29 June 1992 on general product safety, Directive 94/47/EC of the European Parliament and of the Council of 26 October 1994 on the protection of purchasers in respect of certain aspects on contracts relating to the purchase of the right to use immovable properties on a timeshare basis, Directive 98/27/EC of the European Parliament and of the Council of 19 May 1998 on injunctions for the protection of consumers' interests, Council Directive 85/374/EEC of 25 July 1985 on the approximation of the laws, regulations and administrative provisions concerning liability for defective products, Directive 1999/44/EC of the European Parliament and of the Council of 25 May 1999 on certain aspects of the sale of consumer goods and associated guarantees, the future Directive of the European Parliament and of the Council concerning the distance marketing of consumer financial services and Council Directive 92/28/EEC of 31 March 1992 on the advertising of medicinal products; this Directive should

be without prejudice to Directive 98/ 43/EC of the European Parliament and of the Council of 6 July 1998 on the approximation of the laws, regulations and administrative provisions of the Member States relating to the advertising and sponsorship of tobacco products adopted within the framework of the internal market, or to directives on the protection of public health; this Directive complements information requirements established by the above-mentioned Directives and in particular Directive 97/7/EC.

(12) It is necessary to exclude certain activities from the scope of this Directive, on the grounds that the freedom to provide services in these fields cannot, at this stage, be guaranteed under the Treaty or existing secondary legislation; excluding these activities does not preclude any instruments which might prove necessary for the proper functioning of the internal market; taxation, particularly value added tax imposed on a large number of the services covered by this Directive, must be excluded from the scope of this Directive.

(13) This Directive does not aim to establish rules on fiscal obligations nor does it pre-empt the drawing up of Community instruments concerning fiscal aspects of electronic commerce.

(14) The protection of individuals with regard to the processing of personal data is solely governed by Directive 95/46/EC of the European Parliament and of the Council of 24 October 1995 on the protection of individuals with regard to the processing of personal data and on the free movement of such data, and Directive 97/66/EC of the European Parliament and of the Council of 15 December 1997 concerning the processing of personal data and the protection of privacy in the telecommunications sector which are fully applicable to information society services; these Directives already establish a Community legal framework in the field of personal data and therefore it is not necessary to cover this issue in this Directive in order to ensure the smooth functioning of the internal market, in particular the free movement of personal data between Member States; the implementation and application of this Directive should be made in full compliance with the principles relating to the protection of personal data, in particular as regards unsolicited commercial communication and the liability of intermediaries; this Directive cannot prevent the anonymous use of open networks such as the Internet.

(15) The confidentiality of communications is guaranteed by Article 5 Directive 97/66/ EC; in accordance with that Directive, Member States must prohibit any kind of interception or surveillance of such communications by others than the senders and receivers, except when legally authorised.

(16) The exclusion of gambling activities from the scope of application of this Directive covers only games of chance, lotteries and betting transactions, which involve wagering a stake with monetary value; this does not cover promotional competitions or games where the purpose is to encourage the sale of goods or services and where payments, if they arise, serve only to acquire the promoted goods or services.

(17) The definition of information society services already exists in Community law in Directive 98/34/EC of the European Parliament and of the Council of 22 June 1998 laying down a procedure for the provision of information in the field of technical standards and regulations and of rules on information society services and in Directive 98/84/EC of the European Parliament and of the Council of 20 November 1998 on the legal protection of services based on, or consisting of, conditional access; this definition covers any service normally provided for remuneration, at a distance, by means of electronic equipment for the processing (including digital compression) and storage of data, and at the individual request of a recipient of a service; those services referred to in the indicative list in Annex V to Directive 98/34/EC which do not imply data processing and storage are not covered by this definition.

(18) Information society services span a wide range of economic activities which take place on-line; these activities can, in particular, consist of selling goods on-line; activities such as the delivery of goods as such or the provision of services off-line are not covered; information society services are not solely restricted to services giving rise to on-line

contracting but also, in so far as they represent an economic activity, extend to services which are not remunerated by those who receive them, such as those offering on-line information or commercial communications, or those providing tools allowing for search, access and retrieval of data; information society services also include services consisting of the transmission of information via a communication network, in providing access to a communication network or in hosting information provided by a recipient of the service; television broadcasting within the meaning of Directive EEC/89/552 and radio broadcasting are not information society services because they are not provided at individual request; by contrast, services which are transmitted point to point, such as video-on-demand or the provision of commercial communications by electronic mail are information society services; the use of electronic mail or equivalent individual communications for instance by natural persons acting outside their trade, business or profession including their use for the conclusion of contracts between such persons is not an information society service; the contractual relationship between an employee and his employer is not an information society service; activities which by their very nature cannot be carried out at a distance and by electronic means, such as the statutory auditing of company accounts or medical advice requiring the physical examination of a patient are not information society services.

(19) The place at which a service provider is established should be determined in conformity with the case-law of the Court of Justice according to which the concept of establishment involves the actual pursuit of an economic activity through a fixed establishment for an indefinite period; this requirement is also fulfilled where a company is constituted for a given period; the place of establishment of a company providing services via an Internet website is not the place at which the technology supporting its website is located or the place at which its website is accessible but the place where it pursues its economic activity; in cases where a provider has several places of establishment it is important to determine from which place of establishment the service concerned is provided; in cases where it is difficult to determine from which of several places of establishment a given service is provided, this is the place where the provider has the centre of his activities relating to this particular service.

(20) The definition of 'recipient of a service' covers all types of usage of information society services, both by persons who provide information on open networks such as the Internet and by persons who seek information on the Internet for private or professional reasons.

(21) The scope of the coordinated field is without prejudice to future Community harmonisation relating to information society services and to future legislation adopted at national level in accordance with Community law; the coordinated field covers only requirements relating to on-line activities such as on-line information, on-line advertising, on-line shopping, on-line contracting and does not concern Member States' legal requirements relating to goods such as safety standards, labelling obligations, or liability for goods, or Member States' requirements relating to the delivery or the transport of goods, including the distribution of medicinal products; the coordinated field does not cover the exercise of rights of preemption by public authorities concerning certain goods such as works of art.

(22) Information society services should be supervised at the source of the activity, in order to ensure an effective protection of public interest objectives; to that end, it is necessary to ensure that the competent authority provides such protection not only for the citizens of its own country but for all Community citizens; in order to improve mutual trust between Member States, it is essential to state clearly this responsibility on the part of the Member State where the services originate; moreover, in order to effectively guarantee freedom to provide services and legal certainty for suppliers and recipients of services, such information society services should in principle be subject to the law of the Member State in which the service provider is established.

(23) This Directive neither aims to establish additional rules on private international law relating to conflicts of law nor does it deal with the jurisdiction of Courts; provisions of the applicable law designated by rules of private international law must not restrict the freedom

to provide information society services as established in this Directive.

(24) In the context of this Directive, notwithstanding the rule on the control at source of information society services, it is legitimate under the conditions established in this Directive for Member States to take measures to restrict the free movement of information society services.

(25) National courts, including civil courts, dealing with private law disputes can take measures to derogate from the freedom to provide information society services in conformity with conditions established in this Directive.

(26) Member States, in conformity with conditions established in this Directive, may apply their national rules on criminal law and criminal proceedings with a view to taking all investigative and other measures necessary for the detection and prosecution of criminal offences, without there being a need to notify such measures to the Commission.

(27) This Directive, together with the future Directive of the European Parliament and of the Council concerning the distance marketing of consumer financial services, contributes to the creating of a legal framework for the online provision of financial services; this Directive does not pre-empt future initiatives in the area of financial services in particular with regard to the harmonisation of rules of conduct in this field; the possibility for Member States, established in this Directive, under certain circumstances of restricting the freedom to provide information society services in order to protect consumers also covers measures in the area of financial services in particular measures aiming at protecting investors.

(28) The Member States' obligation not to subject access to the activity of an information society service provider to prior authorisation does not concern postal services covered by Directive 97167/EC of the European Parliament and of the Council of 15 December 1997 on common rules for the development of the internal market of Community postal services and the improvement of quality of service consisting of the physical delivery of a printed electronic mail message and does not affect voluntary accreditation systems, in particular for providers of electronic signature certification service.

(29) Commercial communications are essential for the financing of information society services and for developing a wide variety of new, charge-free services; in the interests of consumer protection and fair trading, commercial communications, including discounts, promotional offers and promotional competitions or games, must meet a number of transparency requirements; these requirements are without prejudice to Directive 97/7/EC; this Directive should not affect existing Directives on commercial communications, in particular Directive 98/43/EC.

(30) The sending of unsolicited commercial communications by electronic mail may be undesirable for consumers and information society service providers and may disrupt the smooth functioning of interactive networks; the question of consent by recipient of certain forms of unsolicited commercial communications is not addressed by this Directive, but has already been addressed, in particular, by Directive 97/7/EC and by Directive 97/66/EC; in Member States which authorise unsolicited commercial communications by electronic mail, the setting up of appropriate industry filtering initiatives should be encouraged and facilitated; in addition it is necessary that in any event unsolicited commercial communities are clearly identifiable as such in order to improve transparency and to facilitate the functioning of such industry initiatives; unsolicited commercial communications by electronic mail should not result in additional communication costs for the recipient.

(31) Member States which allow the sending of unsolicited commercial communications by electronic mail without prior consent of the recipient by service providers established in their territory have to ensure that the service providers consult regularly and respect the optout registers in which natural persons not wishing to receive such commercial communications can register themselves.

(32) In order to remove barriers to the development of cross-border services within the Community which members of the regulated professions might offer on the Internet, it is necessary that compliance be guaranteed at Community level with professional rules aiming,

in particular, to protect consumers or public health; codes of conduct at Community level would be the best means of determining the rules on professional ethics applicable to commercial communication; the drawing-up or, where appropriate, the adaptation of such rules should be encouraged without prejudice to the autonomy of professional bodies and associations.

(33) This Directive complements Community law and national law relating to regulated professions maintaining a coherent set of applicable rules in this field.

(34) Each Member State is to amend its legislation containing requirements, and in particular requirements as to form, which are likely to curb the use of contracts by electronic means; the examination of the legislation requiring such adjustment should be systematic and should cover all the necessary stages and acts of the contractual process, including the filing of the contract; the result of this amendment should be to make contracts concluded electronically workable; the legal effect of electronic signatures is dealt with by Directive 1999/93/EC of the European Parliament and of the Council of 13 December 1999 on a Community framework for electronic signatures; the acknowledgement of receipt by a service provider may take the form of the on-line provision of the service paid for.

(35) This Directive does not affect Member States' possibility of maintaining or establishing general or specific legal requirements for contracts which can be fulfilled by electronic means, in particular requirements concerning secure electronic signatures.

(36) Member States may maintain restrictions for the use of electronic contracts with regard to contracts requiring by law the involvement of courts, public authorities, or professions exercising public authority; this possibility also covers contracts which require the involvement of courts, public authorities, or professions exercising public authority in order to have an effect with regard to third parties as well as contracts requiring by law certification or attestation by a notary.

(37) Member States' obligation to remove obstacles to the use of electronic contracts concerns only obstacles resulting from legal requirements and not practical obstacles resulting from the impossibility of using electronic means in certain cases.

(38) Member States' obligation to remove obstacles to the use of electronic contracts is to be implemented in conformity with legal requirements for contracts enshrined in Community law.

(39) The exceptions to the provisions concerning the contracts concluded exclusively by electronic mail or by equivalent individual communications provided for by this Directive, in relation to information to be provided and the placing of orders, should not enable, as a result, the by-passing of those provisions by providers of information society services.

(40) Both existing and emerging disparities in Member States' legislation and case-law concerning liability of service providers acting as intermediaries prevent the smooth functioning of the internal market, in particular by impairing the development of cross-border services and producing distortions of competition; service providers have a duty to act, under certain circumstances, with a view to preventing or stopping illegal activities; this Directive should constitute the appropriate basis for the development of rapid and reliable procedures for removing and disabling access to illegal information; such mechanisms could be developed on the basis of voluntary agreements between all parties concerned and should be encouraged by Member States; it is in the interest of all parties involved in the provision of information society services to adopt and implement such procedures; the provisions of this Directive relating to liability should not preclude the development and effective operation, by the different interested parties, of technical systems of protection and identification and of technical surveillance instruments made possible by digital technology within the limits laid down by Directives 95/46/EC and 97/66/EC.

(41) This Directive strikes a balance between the different interests at stake and establishes principles upon which industry agreements and standards can be based.

(42) The exemptions from liability established in this Directive cover only cases where the activity of the information society service provider is limited to the technical process of

operating and giving access to a communication network over which information made available by third parties is transmitted or temporarily stored, for the sole purpose of making the transmission more efficient; this activity is of a mere technical, automatic and passive nature, which implies that the information society service provider has neither knowledge of nor control over the information which is transmitted or stored.

(43) A service provider can benefit from the exemptions for 'mere conduit' and for 'caching' when he is in no way involved with the information transmitted; this requires among other things that he does not modify the information that he transmits; this requirement does not cover manipulations of a technical nature which take place in the course of the transmission as they do not alter the integrity of the information contained in the transmission.

(44) A service provider who deliberately collaborates with one of the recipients of his service in order to undertake illegal acts goes beyond the activities of 'mere conduit' or 'caching' and as a result cannot benefit from the liability exemptions established for these activities.

(45) The limitations of the liability of intermediary service providers established in this Directive do not affect the possibility of injunctions of different kinds; such injunctions can in particular consist of orders by courts or administrative authorities requiring the termination or prevention of any infringement, including the removal of illegal information or the disabling of access to it.

(46) In order to benefit from a limitation of liability, the provider of an information society service, consisting of the storage of information, upon obtaining actual knowledge or awareness of illegal activities has to act expeditiously to remove or to disable access to the information concerned; the removal or disabling of access has to be undertaken in the observance of the principle of freedom of expression and of procedures established for this purpose at national level; this Directive does not affect Member States' possibility of establishing specific requirements which must be fulfilled expeditiously prior to the removal or disabling of information.

(47) Member States are prevented from imposing a monitoring obligation on service providers only with respect to obligations of a general nature; this does not concern monitoring obligations in a specific case and, in particular, does not affect orders by national authorities in accordance with national legislation.

(48) This Directive does not affect the possibility for Member States of requiring service providers, who host information provided by recipients of their service, to apply duties of care, which can reasonably be expected from them and which are specified by national law, in order to detect and prevent certain types of illegal activities.

(49) Member States and the Commission are to encourage the drawing-up of codes of conduct; this is not to impair the voluntary nature of such codes and the possibility for interested parties of deciding freely whether to adhere to such codes.

(50) It is important that the proposed directive on the harmonisation of certain aspects of copyright and related rights in the information society and this Directive come into force within a similar time scale with a view to establishing a clear framework of rules relevant to the issue of liability of intermediaries for copyright and relating rights infringements at Community level.

(51) Each Member State should be required, where necessary, to amend any legislation which is liable to hamper the use of schemes for the out-of-court settlement of disputes through electronic channels; the result of this amendment must be to make the functioning of such schemes genuinely and effectively possible in law and in practice, even across borders.

(52) The effective exercise of the freedoms of the internal market makes it necessary to guarantee victims effective access to means of settling disputes; damage which may arise in connection with information society services is characterised both by its rapidity and by its geographical extent; in view of this specific character and the need to ensure that national

authorities do not endanger the mutual confidence which they should have in one another, this Directive requests Member States to ensure that appropriate court actions are available; Member States should examine the need to provide access to judicial procedures by appropriate electronic means.

(53) Directive 98/27/EC, which is applicable to information society services, provides a mechanism relating to actions for an injunction aimed at the protection of the collective interests of consumers; this mechanism will contribute to the free movement of information society services by ensuring a high level of consumer protection.

(54) The sanctions provided for under this Directive are without prejudice to any other sanction or remedy provided under national law; Member States are not obliged to provide criminal sanctions for infringement of national provisions adopted pursuant to this Directive.

(55) This Directive does not affect the law applicable to contractual obligations relating to consumer contracts; accordingly, this Directive cannot have the result of depriving the consumer of the protection afforded to him by the mandatory rules relating to contractual obligations of the law of the Member State in which he has his habitual residence.

(56) As regards the derogation contained in this Directive regarding contractual obligations concerning contracts concluded by consumers, those obligations should be interpreted as including information on the essential elements of the content of the contract, including consumer rights, which have a determining influence on the decision to contract.

(57) The Court of Justice has consistently held that a Member State retains the right to take measures against a service provider that is established in another Member State but directs all or most of his activity to the territory of the first Member State if the choice of establishment was made with a view to evading the legislation that would have applied to the provider had he been established on the territory of the first Member State.

(58) This Directive should not apply to services supplied by service providers established in a third country; in view of the global dimension of electronic commerce, it is, however, appropriate to ensure that the Community rules are consistent with international rules; this Directive is without prejudice to the results of discussions within international organisations (amongst others WTO, OECD, Uncitral) on legal issues.

(59) Despite the global nature of electronic communications, coordination of national regulatory measures at European Union level is necessary in order to avoid fragmentation of the internal market, and for the establishment of an appropriate European regulatory framework; such coordination should also contribute to the establishment of a common and strong negotiating position in international forums.

(60) In order to allow the unhampered development of electronic commerce, the legal framework must be clear and simple, predictable and consistent with the rules applicable at international level so that it does not adversely affect the competitiveness of European industry or impede innovation in that sector.

(61) If the market is actually to operate by electronic means in the context of globalisation, the European Union and the major non-European areas need to consult each other with a view to making laws and procedures compatible.

(62) Cooperation with third countries should be strengthened in the area of electronic commerce, in particular with applicant countries, the developing countries and the European Union's other trading partners.

(63) The adoption of this Directive will not prevent the Member States from taking into account the various social, societal and cultural implications which are inherent in the advent of the information society; in particular it should not hinder measures which Member States might adopt in conformity with Community law to achieve social, cultural and democratic goals taking into account their linguistic diversity, national and regional specificities as well as their cultural heritage, and to ensure and maintain public access to the widest possible range of information society services; in any case, the development of the

information society is to ensure that Community citizens can have access to the cultural European heritage provided in the digital environment.

(64) Electronic communication offers the Member States an excellent means of providing public services in the cultural, educational and linguistic fields.

(65) The Council, in its resolution of 19 January 1999 on the consumer dimension of the information society stressed that the protection of consumers deserved special attention in this field; the Commission will examine the degree to which existing consumer protection rules provide insufficient protection in the context of the information society and will identify, where necessary, the deficiencies of this legislation and those issues which could require additional measures; if need be, the Commission should make specific additional proposals to resolve such deficiencies that will thereby have been identified,
HAVE ADOPTED THIS DIRECTIVE:

CHAPTER I   GENERAL PROVISIONS

Art. 1   **Objective and scope**

1. This Directive seeks to contribute to the proper functioning of the internal market by ensuring the free movement of information society services between the Member States.

2. This Directive approximates, to the extent necessary for the achievement of the objective set out in paragraph 1, certain national provisions on information society services relating to the internal market, the establishment of service providers, commercial communications, electronic contracts, the liability of intermediaries, codes of conduct, out-of-court dispute settlements, court actions and cooperation between Member States.

3. This Directive complements Community law applicable to information society services without prejudice to the level of protection for, in particular, public health and consumer interests, as established by Community acts and national legislation implementing them in so far as this does not restrict the freedom to provide information society services.

4. This Directive does not establish additional rules on private international law nor does it deal with the jurisdiction of Courts.

5. This Directive shall not apply to:
   (a) the field of taxation;
   (b) questions relating to information society services covered by Directives 95/46/EC and 97/66/EC;
   (c) questions relating to agreements or practices governed by cartel law;
   (d) the following activities of information society services:
      — the activities of notaries or equivalent professions to the extent that they involve a direct and specific connection with the exercise of public authority,
      — the representation of a client and defence of his interests before the courts,
      — gambling activities which involve wagering a stake with monetary value in games of chance, including lotteries and betting transactions.

6. This Directive does not affect measures taken at Community or national level, in the respect of Community law, in order to promote cultural and linguistic diversity and to ensure the defence of pluralism.

Art. 2   **Definitions**

For the purpose of this Directive, the following terms shall bear the following meanings:
   (a) 'information society services': services within the meaning of Article 1(2) of Directive 98/34/EC as amended by Directive 98/48/EC;
   (b) 'service provider': any natural or legal person providing an information society service;
   (c) 'established service provider': a service provider who effectively pursues an economic activity using a fixed establishment for an indefinite period. The presence

and use of the technical means and technologies required to provide the service do not, in themselves, constitute an establishment of the provider;

(d) 'recipient of the service': any natural or legal person who, for professional ends or otherwise, uses an information society service, in particular for the purposes of seeking information or making it accessible;

(e) 'consumer': any natural person who is acting for purposes which are outside his or her trade, business or profession;

(f) 'commercial communication': any form of communication designed to promote, directly or indirectly, the goods, services or image of a company, organisation or person pursuing a commercial, industrial or craft activity or exercising a regulated profession. The following do not in themselves constitute commercial communications:
— information allowing direct access to the activity of the company, organisation or person, in particular a domain name or an electronic-mail address,
— communications relating to the goods, services or image of the company, organisation or person compiled in an independent manner, particularly when this is without financial consideration;

(g) 'regulated profession': any profession within the meaning of either Article 1(d) of Council Directive 89/48/EEC of 21 December 1988 on a general system for the recognition of higher-education diplomas awarded on completion of professional education and training of at least three-years' duration or of Article 1(f) of Council Directive 92/51/EEC of 18 June 1992 on a second general system for the recognition of professional education and training to supplement Directive 89/48/EEC;

(h) 'coordinated field': requirements laid down in Member States' legal systems applicable to information society service providers or information society services, regardless of whether they are of a general nature or specifically designed for them.

(i) The coordinated field concerns requirements with which the service provider has to comply in respect of:
— the taking up of the activity of an information society service, such as requirements concerning qualifications, authorisation or notification,
— the pursuit of the activity of an information society service, such as requirements concerning the behaviour of the service provider, requirements regarding the quality or content of the service including those applicable to advertising and contracts, or requirements concerning the liability of the service provider;

(j) The coordinated field does not cover requirements such as:
— requirements applicable to goods as such,
— requirements applicable to the delivery of goods,
— requirements applicable to services not provided by electronic means.

Art. 3 Internal market

1. Each Member State shall ensure that the information society services provided by a service provider established on its territory comply with the national provisions applicable in the Member State in question which fall within the coordinated field.

2. Member States may not, for reasons falling within the coordinated field, restrict the freedom to provide information society services from another Member State.

3. Paragraphs 1 and 2 shall not apply to the fields referred to in the Annex.

4. Member States may take measures to derogate from paragraph 2 in respect of a given information society service if the following conditions are fulfilled:
(a) the measures shall be:
(i) necessary for one of the following reasons:
— public policy, in particular the prevention, investigation, detection and prosecution of criminal offences, including the protection of minors and the fight

against any incitement to hatred on grounds of race, sex, religion or nationality, and violations of human dignity concerning individual persons,
— the protection of public health,
— public security, including the safeguarding of national security and defence,
— the protection of consumers, including investors;
(ii) taken against a given information society service which prejudices the objectives referred to in point (i) or which presents a serious and grave risk of prejudice to those objectives;
(iii) proportionate to those objectives;
(b) before taking the measures in question and without prejudice to court proceedings, including preliminary proceedings and acts carried out in the framework of a criminal investigation, the Member State has:
— asked the Member State referred to in paragraph 1 to take measures and the latter did not take such measures, or they were inadequate,
— notified the Commission and the Member State referred to in paragraph 1 of its intention to take such measures.

5. Member States may, in the case of urgency, derogate from the conditions stipulated in paragraph 4(b). Where this is the case, the measures shall be notified in the shortest possible time to the Commission and to the Member State referred to in paragraph 1, indicating the reasons for which the Member State considers that there is urgency.

6. Without prejudice to the Member State's possibility of proceeding with the measures in question, the Commission shall examine the compatibility of the notified measures with Community law in the shortest possible time; where it comes to the conclusion that the measure is incompatible with Community law, the Commission shall ask the Member State in question to refrain from taking any proposed measures or urgently to put an end to the measures in question.

CHAPTER II   PRINCIPLES

Section 1   Establishment and information requirements

Art. 4   Principle excluding prior authorisation
1. Member States shall ensure that the taking up and pursuit of the activity of an information society service provider may not be made subject to prior authorisation or any other requirement having equivalent effect.

2. Paragraph 1 shall be without prejudice to authorisation schemes which are not specifically and exclusively targeted at information society services, or which are covered by Directive 97/13/EC of the European Parliament and of the Council of 10 April 1997 on a common framework for general authorisations and individual licences in the field of telecommunications services.

Art. 5   General information to be provided
1. In addition to other information requirements established by Community law, Member States shall ensure that the service provider shall render easily, directly and permanently accessible to the recipients of the service and competent authorities, at least the following information:
(a) the name of the service provider;
(b) the geographic address at which the service provider is established;
(c) the details of the service provider, including his electronic mail address, which allow him to be contacted rapidly and communicated with in a direct and effective manner;

(d) where the service provider is registered in a trade or similar public register, the trade register in which the service provider is entered and his registration number, or equivalent means of identification in that register;

(e) where the activity is subject to an authorisation scheme, the particulars of the relevant supervisory authority;

(f) as concerns the regulated professions:
   — any professional body or similar institution with which the service provider is registered,
   — the professional title and the Member State where it has been granted,
   — a reference to the applicable professional rules in the Member State of establishment and the means to access them;

(g) where the service provider undertakes an activity that is subject to VAT, the identification number referred to in Article 22(1) of the sixth Council Directive 77/388/ EEC of 17 May 1977 on the harmonisation of the laws of the Member States relating to turnover taxes—Common system of value added tax: uniform basis of assessment.

2. In addition to other information requirements established by Community law, Member States shall at least ensure that, where information society services refer to prices, these are to be indicated clearly and unambiguously and, in particular, must indicate whether they are inclusive of tax and delivery costs.

Section 2   Commercial communications

Art. 6   Information to be provided
In addition to other information requirements established by Community law, Member States shall ensure that commercial communications which are part of, or constitute, an information society service comply at least with the following conditions:
   (a) the commercial communication shall be clearly identifiable as such;
   (b) the natural or legal person on whose behalf the commercial communication is made shall be clearly identifiable;
   (c) promotional offers, such as discounts, premiums and gifts, where permitted in the Member State where the service provider is established, shall be clearly identifiable as such, and the conditions which are to be met to qualify for them shall be easily accessible and be presented clearly and unambiguously;
   (d) promotional competitions or games, where permitted in the Member State where the service provider is established, shall be clearly identifiable as such, and the conditions for participation shall be easily accessible and be presented clearly and unambiguously.

Art. 7   Unsolicited commercial communication
1. In addition to other requirements established by Community law, Member States which permit unsolicited commercial communication by electronic mail shall ensure that such commercial communication by a service provider established in their territory shall be identifiable clearly and unambiguously as such as soon as it is received by the recipient.

2. Without prejudice to Directive 97/7/EC and Directive 97/66/EC, Member States shall take measures to ensure that service providers undertaking unsolicited commercial communications by electronic mail consult regularly and respect the opt-out registers in which natural persons not wishing to receive such commercial communications can register themselves.

Art. 8   Regulated professions
1. Member States shall ensure that the use of commercial communications which are part of, or constitute, an information society service provided by a member of a regulated profession is permitted subject to compliance with the professional rules regarding, in

particular, the independence, dignity and honour of the profession, professional secrecy and fairness towards clients and other members of the profession.

2. Without prejudice to the autonomy of professional bodies and associations, Member States and the Commission shall encourage professional associations and June 2000 bodies to establish codes of conduct at Community level in order to determine the types of information that can be given for the purposes of commercial communication in conformity with the rules referred to in paragraph 1.

3. When drawing up proposals for Community initiatives which may become necessary to ensure the proper functioning of the Internal Market with regard to the information referred to in paragraph 2, the Commission shall take due account of codes of conduct applicable at Community level and shall act in close cooperation with the relevant professional associations and bodies.

4. This Directive shall apply in addition to Community Directives concerning access to, and the exercise of, activities of the regulated professions.

Section 3   Contracts concluded by electronic means

Art. 9   Treatment of contracts

1. Member States shall ensure that their legal system allows contracts to be concluded by electronic means. Member States shall in particular ensure that the legal requirements applicable to the contractual process neither create obstacles for the use of electronic contracts nor result in such contracts being deprived of legal effectiveness and validity on account of their having been made by electronic means.

2. Member States may lay down that paragraph 1 shall not apply to all or certain contracts falling into one of the following categories:

(a) contracts that create or transfer rights in real estate, except for rental rights;

(b) contracts requiring by law the involvement of courts, public authorities or professions exercising public authority;

(c) contracts of suretyship granted and on collateral securities furnished by persons acting for purposes outside their trade, business or profession;

(d) contracts governed by family law or by the law of succession.

3. Member States shall indicate to the Commission the categories referred to in paragraph 2 to which they do not apply paragraph 1. Member States shall submit to the Commission every five years a report on the application of paragraph 2 explaining the reasons why they consider it necessary to maintain the category referred to in paragraph 2(b) to which they do not apply paragraph 1.

Art. 10   Information to be provided

1. In addition to other information requirements established by Community law, Member States shall ensure, except when otherwise agreed by parties who are not consumers, that at least the following information is given by the service provider clearly, comprehensibly and unambiguously and prior to the order being placed by the recipient of the service:

(a) the different technical steps to follow to conclude the contract;

(b) whether or not the concluded contract will be filed by the service provider and whether it will be accessible;

(c) the technical means for identifying and correcting input errors prior to the placing of the order;

(d) the languages offered for the conclusion of the contract.

2. Member States shall ensure that, except when otherwise agreed by parties who are not consumers, the service provider indicates any relevant codes of conduct to which he subscribes and information on how those codes can be consulted electronically.

3. Contract terms and general conditions provided to the recipient must be made available in a way that allows him to store and reproduce them.

4. Paragraphs 1 and 2 shall not apply to contracts concluded exclusively by exchange of electronic mail or by equivalent individual communications.

Art. 11   Placing of the order

1. Member States shall ensure, except when otherwise agreed by parties who are not consumers, that in cases where the recipient of the service places his order through technological means, the following principles apply:

— the service provider has to acknowledge the receipt of the recipient's order without undue delay and by electronic means,

— the order and the acknowledgement of receipt are deemed to be received when the parties to whom they are addressed are able to access them.

2. Member States shall ensure that, except when otherwise agreed by parties who are not consumers, the service provider makes available to the recipient of the service appropriate, effective and accessible technical means allowing him to identify and correct input errors, prior to the placing of the order.

3. Paragraph 1, first indent, and paragraph 2 shall not apply to contracts concluded exclusively by exchange of electronic mail or by equivalent individual communications.

Section 4   Liability of intermediary service providers

Art. 12   'Mere conduit'

1. Where an information society service is provided that consists of the transmission in a communication network of information provided by a recipient of the service, or the provision of access to a communication network, Member States shall ensure that the service provider is not liable for the information transmitted, on condition that the provider:

(a) does not initiate the transmission;

(b) does not select the receiver of the transmission; and

(c) does not select or modify the information contained in the transmission.

2. The acts of transmission and of provision of access referred to in paragraph 1 include the automatic, intermediate and transient storage of the information transmitted in so far as this takes place for the sole purpose of carrying out the transmission in the communication network, and provided that the information is not stored for any period longer than is reasonably necessary for the transmission.

3. This Article shall not affect the possibility for a court or administrative authority, in accordance with Member States' legal systems, of requiring the service provider to terminate or prevent an infringement.

Art. 13   'Caching'

1. Where an information society service is provided that consists of the transmission in a communication network of information provided by a recipient of the service, Member States shall ensure that the service provider is not liable for the automatic, intermediate and temporary storage of that information, performed for the sole purpose of making more efficient the information's onward transmission to other recipients of the service upon their request, on condition that:

(a) the provider does not modify the information;

(b) the provider complies with conditions on access to the information;

(c) the provider complies with rules regarding the updating of the information, specified in a manner widely recognised and used by industry;

(d) the provider does not interfere with the lawful use of technology, widely recognised and used by industry, to obtain data on the use of the information; and

(e) the provider acts expeditiously to remove or to disable access to the information it has stored upon obtaining actual knowledge of the fact that the information at the initial source of the transmission has been removed from the network, or access to it has been disabled, or that a court or an administrative authority has ordered such removal or disablement.

2. This Article shall not affect the possibility for a court or administrative authority, in accordance with Member States' legal systems, of requiring the service provider to terminate or prevent an infringement.

Art. 14   Hosting

1. Where an information society service is provided that consists of the storage of information provided by a recipient of the service, Member States shall ensure that the service provider is not liable for the information stored at the request of a recipient of the service, on condition that:

    (a) the provider does not have actual knowledge of illegal activity or information and, as regards claims for damages, is not aware of facts or circumstances from which the illegal activity or information is apparent; or

    (b) the provider, upon obtaining such knowledge or awareness, acts expeditiously to remove or to disable access to the information.

2. Paragraph 1 shall not apply when the recipient of the service is acting under the authority or the control of the provider.

3. This Article shall not affect the possibility for a court or administrative authority, in accordance with Member States' legal systems, of requiring the service provider to terminate or prevent an infringement, nor does it affect the possibility for Member States of establishing procedures governing the removal or disabling of access to information.

Art. 15   No general obligation to monitor

1. Member States shall not impose a general obligation on providers, when providing the services covered by Articles 12, 13 and 14, to monitor the information which they transmit or store, nor a general obligation actively to seek facts or circumstances indicating illegal activity.

2. Member States may establish obligations for information society service providers promptly to inform the competent public authorities of alleged illegal activities undertaken or information provided by recipients of their service or obligations to communicate to the competent authorities, at their request, information enabling the identification of recipients of their service with whom they have storage agreements.

CHAPTER III   IMPLEMENTATION

Art. 16   Codes of conduct

1. Member States and the Commission shall encourage:

    (a) the drawing up of codes of conduct at Community level, by trade, professional and consumer associations or organisations, designed to contribute to the proper implementation of Articles 5 to 15;

    (b) the voluntary transmission of draft codes of conduct at national or Community level to the Commission;

    (c) the accessibility of these codes of conduct in the Community languages by electronic means;

    (d) the communication to the Member States and the Commission, by trade, professional and consumer associations or organisations, of their assessment of the application of their codes of conduct and their impact upon practices, habits or customs relating to electronic commerce;

    (e) the drawing up of codes of conduct regarding the protection of minors and human dignity.

2. Member States and the Commission shall encourage the involvement of associations or organisations representing consumers in the drafting and implementation of codes of

conduct affecting their interests and drawn up in accordance with paragraph 1(a). Where appropriate, to take account of their specific needs, associations representing the visually impaired and disabled should be consulted.

Art. 17   Out-of-court dispute settlement

1. Member States shall ensure that, in the event of disagreement between an information society service provider and the recipient of the service, their legislation does not hamper the use of out-of-court schemes, available under national law, for dispute settlement, including appropriate electronic means.

2. Member States shall encourage bodies responsible for the out-of-court settlement of, in particular, consumer disputes to operate in a way which provides adequate procedural guarantees for the parties concerned.

3. Member States shall encourage bodies responsible for out-of-court dispute settlement to inform the Commission of the significant decisions they take regarding information society services and to transmit any other information on the practices, usages or customs relating to electronic commerce.

Art. 18   Court actions

1. Member States shall ensure that court actions available under national law concerning information society services' activities allow for the rapid adoption of measures, including interim measures, designed to terminate any alleged infringement and to prevent any further impairment of the interests involved.

2. The Annex to Directive 98127/EC shall be supplemented as follows:

'11. Directive 2000/3 1/EC of the European Parliament and of the Council of 8 June 2000 on certain legal aspects on information society services, in particular electronic commerce, in the internal market (Directive on electronic commerce) (OJL 178, 17.7.2000, p. 1).'

Art. 19   Cooperation

1. Member States shall have adequate means of supervision and investigation necessary to implement this Directive effectively and shall ensure that service providers supply them with the requisite information.

2. Member States shall cooperate with other Member States; they shall, to that end, appoint one or several contact points, whose details they shall communicate to the other Member States and to the Commission.

3. Member States shall, as quickly as possible, and in conformity with national law, provide the assistance and information requested by other Member States or by the Commission, including by appropriate electronic means.

4. Member States shall establish contact points which shall be accessible at least by electronic means and from which recipients and service providers may:

  (a) obtain general information on contractual rights and obligations as well as on the complaint and redress mechanisms available in the event of disputes, including practical aspects involved in the use of such mechanisms;

  (b) obtain the details of authorities, associations or organisations from which they may obtain further information or practical assistance.

5. Member States shall encourage the communication to the Commission of any significant administrative or judicial decisions taken in their territory regarding disputes relating to information society services and practices, usages and customs relating to electronic commerce. The Commission shall communicate these decisions to the other Member States.

Art. 20   Sanctions

Member States shall determine the sanctions applicable to infringements of national provisions adopted pursuant to this Directive and shall take all measures necessary to ensure that they are enforced. The sanctions they provide for shall be effective, proportionate and dissuasive.

CHAPTER IV   FINAL PROVISIONS

Art. 21   Re-examination

1. Before 17 July 2003, and thereafter every two years, the Commission shall submit to the European Parliament, the Council and the Economic and Social Committee a report on the application of this Directive, accompanied, where necessary, by proposals for adapting it to legal, technical and economic developments in the field of information society services, in particular with respect to crime prevention, the protection of minors, consumer protection and to the proper functioning of the internal market.

2. In examining the need for an adaptation of this Directive, the report shall in particular analyse the need for proposals concerning the liability of providers of hyperlinks and location tool services, 'notice and take down' procedures and the attribution of liability following the taking down of content. The report shall also analyse the need for additional conditions for the exemption from liability, provided for in Articles 12 and 13, in the light of technical developments, and the possibility of applying the internal market principles to unsolicited commercial communications by electronic mail.

Art. 22   Transposition

1. Member States shall bring into force the laws, regulations and administrative provisions necessary to comply with this Directive before 17 January 2002. They shall forthwith inform the Commission thereof.

2. When Member States adopt the measures referred to in paragraph 1, these shall contain a reference to this Directive or shall be accompanied by such reference at the time of their official publication. The methods of making such reference shall be laid down by Member States.

ANNEX   DEROGATIONS FROM ARTICLE 3

As provided for in Article 3(3), Article 3(1) and (2) do not apply to:
- copyright, neighbouring rights, rights referred to in Directive 87/54/EEC and Directive 96/9/EC as well as industrial property rights,
- the emission of electronic money by institutions in respect of which Member States have applied one of the derogations provided for in Article 8(1) of Directive 2000/46/EC,
- Article 44(2) of Directive 85/611/EEC,
- Article 30 and Title IV of Directive 92/49/EEC, Title IV of Directive 92/96/EEC, Articles 7 and 8 of Directive 88/357/EEC and Article 4 of Directive 90/619/EEC,
- the freedom of the parties to choose the law applicable to their contract,
- contractual obligations concerning consumer contacts,
- formal validity of contracts creating or transferring rights in real estate where such contracts are subject to mandatory formal requirements of the law of the Member State where the real estate is situated,
- the permissibility of unsolicited commercial communications by electronic mail.

Directive 2000/35/EC of the European Parliament and of the Council
of 29 June 2000

on combating late payment in commercial transactions

THE EUROPEAN PARLIAMENT AND THE COUNCIL OF THE EUROPEAN UNION,

Having regard to the Treaty establishing the European Community, and in particular Article 95 thereof,

Having regard to the proposal from the Commission,

Having regard to the opinion of the Economic and Social Committee,

Acting in accordance with the procedure laid down in Article 251 of the Treaty, in the light of the joint text approved by the Conciliation Committee on 4 May 2000,

Whereas:

(1) In its resolution on the integrated programme in favour of SMEs and the craft sector, the European Parliament urged the Commission to submit proposals to deal with the problem of late payment.

(2) On 12 May 1995 the Commission adopted a recommendation on payment periods in commercial transactions.

(3) In its resolution on the Commission recommendation on payment periods in commercial transactions, the European Parliament called on the Commission to consider transforming its recommendation into a proposal for a Council directive to be submitted as soon as possible.

(4) On 29 May 1997 the Economic and Social Committee adopted an opinion on the Commission's Green Paper on Public procurement in the European Union: Exploring the way forward.

(5) On 4 June 1997 the Commission published an action plan for the single market, which underlined that late payment represents an increasingly serious obstacle for the success of the single market.

(6) On 17 July 1997 the Commission published a report on late payments in commercial transactions, summarising the results of an evaluation of the effects of the Commission's recommendation of 12 May 1995.

(7) Heavy administrative and financial burdens are placed on businesses, particularly small and medium-sized ones, as a result of excessive payment periods and late payment. Moreover, these problems are a major cause of insolvencies threatening the survival of businesses and result in numerous job losses.

(8) In some Member States contractual payment periods differ significantly from the Community average.

(9) The differences between payment rules and practices in the Member States constitute an obstacle to the proper functioning of the internal market.

(10) This has the effect of considerably limiting commercial transactions between Member States. This is in contradiction with Article 14 of the Treaty as entrepreneurs should be able to trade throughout the internal market under conditions which ensure that transborder operations do not entail greater risks than domestic sales. Distortions of competition would ensue if substantially different rules applied to domestic and transborder operations.

(11) The most recent statistics indicate that there has been, at best, no improvement in late payments in many Member States since the adoption of the recommendation of 12 May 1995.

(12) The objective of combating late payments in the internal market cannot be sufficiently achieved by the Member States acting individually and can, therefore, be better achieved by the Community. This Directive does not go beyond what is necessary to achieve that objective. This Directive complies therefore, in its entirety, with the requirements of the principles of subsidiarity and proportionality as laid down in Article 5 of the Treaty.

(13) This Directive should be limited to payments made as remuneration for commercial transactions and does not regulate transactions with consumers, interest in connection with other payments, e.g. payments under the laws on cheques and bills of exchange, payments made as compensation for damages including payments from insurance companies.

(14) The fact that the liberal professions are covered by this Directive does not mean that Member States have to treat them as undertakings or merchants for purposes not covered by this Directive.

(15) This Directive only defines the term 'enforceable title' but does not regulate the various procedures of forced execution of such a title and the conditions under which forced execution of such a title can be stopped or suspended.

(16) Late payment constitutes a breach of contract which has been made financially attractive to debtors in most Member States by low interest rates on late payments and/or slow procedures for redress. A decisive shift, including compensation of creditors for the costs incurred, is necessary to reverse this trend and to ensure that the consequences of late payments are such as to discourage late payment.

(17) The reasonable compensation for the recovery costs has to be considered without prejudice to national provisions according to which a national judge can award to the creditor any additional damage caused by the debtor's late payment, taking also into account that such incurred costs may be already compensated for by the interest for late payment.

(18) This Directive takes into account the issue of long contractual payment periods and, in particular, the existence of certain categories of contracts where a longer payment period in combination with a restriction of freedom of contract or a higher interest rate can be justified.

(19) This Directive should prohibit abuse of freedom of contract to the disadvantage of the creditor. Where an agreement mainly serves the purpose of procuring the debtor additional liquidity at the expense of the creditor, or where the main contractor imposes on his suppliers and subcontractors terms of payment which are not justified on the grounds of the terms granted to himself, these may be considered to be factors constituting such an abuse. This Directive does not affect national provisions relating to the way contracts are concluded or regulating the validity of contractual terms which are unfair to the debtor.

(20) The consequences of late payment can be dissuasive only if they are accompanied by procedures for redress which are rapid and effective for the creditor. In conformity with the principle of non-discrimination contained in Article 12 of the Treaty, those procedures should be available to all creditors who are established in the Community.

(21) It is desirable to ensure that creditors are in a position to exercise a retention of title on a non-discriminatory basis throughout the Community, if the retention of title clause is valid under the applicable national provisions designated by private international law.

(22) This Directive should regulate all commercial transactions irrespective of whether they are carried out between private or public undertakings or between undertakings and public authorities, having regard to the fact that the latter handle a considerable volume of payments to business. It should therefore also regulate all commercial transactions between main contractors and their suppliers and subcontractors.

(23) Article 5 of this Directive requires that the recovery procedure for unchallenged claims be completed within a short period of time in conformity with national legislation, but does not require Member States to adopt a specific procedure or to amend their existing legal procedures in a specific way,
HAVE ADOPTED THIS DIRECTIVE:

Art. 1   Scope
This Directive shall apply to all payments made as remuneration for commercial transactions.

Art. 2   Definitions
For the purposes of this Directive:

1. 'commercial transactions' means transactions between undertakings or between undertakings and public authorities which lead to the delivery of goods or the provision of services for remuneration,

'public authority' means any contracting authority or entity, as defined by the Public Procurement Directives (92/50/EEC, 93/36/EEC, 93/37/EEC and 93/38/EEC),

'undertaking' means any organisation acting in the course of its independent economic or professional activity, even where it is carried on by a single person;

2. 'late payment' means exceeding the contractual or statutory period of payment;

3. 'retention of title' means the contractual agreement according to which the seller retains title to the goods in question until the price has been paid in full;

4. 'interest rate applied by the European Central Bank to its main refinancing operations' means the interest rate applied to such operations in the case of fixed-rate tenders. In the event that a main refinancing operation was conducted according to a variable-rate tender procedure, this interest rate refers to the marginal interest rate which resulted from that tender. This applies both in the case of single-rate and variable-rate auctions;

5. 'enforceable title' means any decision, judgment or order for payment issued by a court or other competent authority, whether for immediate payment or payment by instalments, which permits the creditor to have his claim against the debtor collected by means of forced execution; it shall include a decision, judgment or order for payment that is provisionally enforceable and remains so even if the debtor appeals against it.

Art. 3   Interest in case of late payment

1. Member States shall ensure that:
   (a) interest in accordance with point (d) shall become payable from the day following the date or the end of the period for payment fixed in the contract;
   (b) if the date or period for payment is not fixed in the contract, interest shall become payable automatically without the necessity of a reminder:
      (i)   30 days following the date of receipt by the debtor of the invoice or an equivalent request for payment; or
      (ii) if the date of the receipt of the invoice or the equivalent request for payment is uncertain, 30 days after the date of receipt of the goods or services; or
      (iii) if the debtor receives the invoice or the equivalent request for payment earlier than the goods or the services, 30 days after the receipt of the goods or services; or
      (iv) if a procedure of acceptance or verification, by which the conformity of the goods or services with the contract is to be ascertained, is provided for by statute or in the contract and if the debtor receives the invoice or the equivalent request for payment earlier or on the date on which such acceptance or verification takes place, 30 days after this latter date;
   (c) the creditor shall be entitled to interest for late payment to the extent that:
      (i) he has fulfilled his contractual and legal obligations; and
      (ii) he has not received the amount due on time, unless the debtor is not responsible for the delay;
   (d) the level of interest for late payment ('the statutory rate'), which the debtor is obliged to pay, shall be the sum of the interest rate applied by the European Central Bank to its most recent main refinancing operation carried out before the first calendar day of the half-year in question ('the reference rate'), plus at least seven percentage points ('the margin'), unless otherwise specified in the contract. For a Member State which is not participating in the third stage of economic and monetary union, the reference rate referred to above shall be the equivalent rate set by its national central bank. In both cases, the reference rate in force on the first calendar day of the half-year in question shall apply for the following six months;
   (e) unless the debtor is not responsible for the delay, the creditor shall be entitled to claim reasonable compensation from the debtor for all relevant recovery costs incurred through the latter's late payment. Such recovery costs shall respect the principles of transparency and proportionality as regards the debt in question. Member States may, while respecting the principles referred to above, fix maximum amounts as regards the recovery costs for different levels of debt.

2. For certain categories of contracts to be defined by national law, Member States may fix the period after which interest becomes payable to a maximum of 60 days provided that they either restrain the parties to the contract from exceeding this period or fix a mandatory interest rate that substantially exceeds the statutory rate.

3. Member States shall provide that an agreement on the date for payment or on the consequences of late payment which is not in line with the provisions of paragraphs

1(b) to (d) and 2 either shall not be enforceable or shall give rise to a claim for damages if, when all circumstances of the case, including good commercial practice and the nature of the product, are considered, it is grossly unfair to the creditor. In determining whether an agreement is grossly unfair to the creditor, it will be taken, inter alia, into account whether the debtor has any objective reason to deviate from the provisions of paragraphs 1(b) to (d) and 2. If such an agreement is determined to be grossly unfair, the statutory terms will apply, unless the national courts determine different conditions which are fair.

4. Member States shall ensure that, in the interests of creditors and of competitors, adequate and effective means exist to prevent the continued use of terms which are grossly unfair within the meaning of paragraph 3.

5. The means referred to in paragraph 4 shall include provisions whereby organisations officially recognised as, or having a legitimate interest in, representing small and mediumsized enterprises may take action according to the national law concerned before the courts or before competent administrative bodies on the grounds that contractual terms drawn up for general use are grossly unfair within the meaning of paragraph 3, so that they can apply appropriate and effective means to prevent the continued use of such terms.

Art. 4   Retention of title

1. Member States shall provide in conformity with the applicable national provisions designated by private international law that the seller retains title to goods until they are fully paid for if a retention of title clause has been expressly agreed between the buyer and the seller before the delivery of the goods.

2. Member States may adopt or retain provisions dealing with down payments already made by the debtor.

Art. 5   Recovery procedures for unchallenged claims

1. Member States shall ensure that an enforceable title can be obtained, irrespective of the amount of the debt, normally within 90 calendar days of the lodging of the creditor's action or application at the court or other competent authority, provided that the debt or aspects of the procedure are not disputed. This duty shall be carried out by Member States in conformity with their respective national legislation, regulations and administrative provisions.

2. The respective national legislation, regulations and administrative provisions shall apply the same conditions for all creditors who are established in the European Community.

3. The 90 calendar day period referred to in paragraph 1 shall not include the following:
    (a) periods for service of documents;
    (b) any delays caused by the creditor, such as periods devoted to correcting applications.

4. This Article shall be without prejudice to the provisions of the Brussels Convention on jurisdiction and enforcement of judgments in civil and commercial matters.

Art. 6   Transposition

1. Member States shall bring into force the laws, regulations and administrative provisions necessary to comply with this Directive before 8 August 2002. They shall forthwith inform the Commission thereof.

When Member States adopt these measures, they shall contain a reference to this Directive or shall be accompanied by such reference on the occasion of their official publication. The methods of making such reference shall be laid down by Member States.

2. Member States may maintain or bring into force provisions which are more favourable to the creditor than the provisions necessary to comply with this Directive.

3. In transposing this Directive, Member States may exclude:
    (a) debts that are subject to insolvency proceedings instituted against the debtor;
    (b) contracts that have been concluded prior to 8 August 2002; and
    (c) claims for interest of less than EUR 5.

4. Member States shall communicate to the Commission the text of the main provisions of national law which they adopt in the field covered by this Directive.

5. The Commission shall undertake two years after 8 August 2002 a review of, inter alia, the statutory rate, contractual payment periods and late payments, to assess the impact on commercial transactions and the operation of the legislation in practice. The results of this review and of other reviews will be made known to the European Parliament and the Council, accompanied where appropriate by proposals for improvement of this Directive.

Directive 2001/95/EC of the European Parliament and of the Council
of 3 December 2001
on general product safety

THE EUROPEAN PARLIAMENT AND THE COUNCIL OF THE EUROPEAN UNION,

Having regard to the Treaty establishing the European Community, and in particular Article 95 thereof,

Having regard to the proposal from the Commission,

Having regard to the opinion of the Economic and Social Committee,

Acting in accordance with the procedure referred to in Article 251 of the Treaty, in the light of the joint text approved by the Conciliation Committee on 2 August 2001,

Whereas:

(1) Under Article 16 of Council Directive 92/59/EEC of 29 June 1992 on general product safety, the Council was to decide, four years after the date set for the implementation of the said Directive, on the basis of a report of the Commission on the experience acquired, together with appropriate proposals, whether to adjust Directive 92/59/EEC. It is necessary to amend Directive 92/59/EEC in several respects, in order to complete, reinforce or clarify some of its provisions in the light of experience as well as new and relevant developments on consumer product safety, together with the changes made to the Treaty, especially in Articles 152 concerning public health and 153 concerning consumer protection, and in the light of the precautionary principle. Directive 92/59/EEC should therefore be recast in the interest of clarity. This recasting leaves the safety of services outside the scope of this Directive, since the Commission intends to identify the needs, possibilities and priorities for Community action on the safety of services and liability of service providers, with a view to presenting appropriate proposals.

(2) It is important to adopt measures with the aim of improving the functioning of the internal market, comprising an area without internal frontiers in which the free movement of goods, persons, services and capital is assured.

(3) In the absence of Community provisions, horizontal legislation of the Member States on product safety, imposing in particular a general obligation on economic operators to market only safe products, might differ in the level of protection afforded to consumers. Such disparities, and the absence of horizontal legislation in some Member States, would be liable to create barriers to trade and distortion of competition within the internal market.

(4) In order to ensure a high level of consumer protection, the Community must contribute to protecting the health and safety of consumers. Horizontal Community legislation introducing a general product safety requirement, and containing provisions on the general obligations of producers and distributors, on the enforcement of Community product safety requirements and on rapid exchange of information and action at Community level in certain cases, should contribute to that aim.

(5) It is very difficult to adopt Community legislation for every product which exists or which may be developed; there is a need for a broad-based, legislative framework of a horizontal nature to deal with such products, and also to cover lacunae, in particular pending

revision of the existing specific legislation, and to complement provisions in existing or forthcoming specific legislation, in particular with a view to ensuring a high level of protection of safety and health of consumers, as required by Article 95 of the Treaty.

(6) It is therefore necessary to establish at Community level a general safety requirement for any product placed on the market, or otherwise supplied or made available to consumers, intended for consumers, or likely to be used by consumers under reasonably foreseeable conditions even if not intended for them. In all these cases the products under consideration can pose risks for the health and safety of consumers which must be prevented. Certain secondhand goods should nevertheless be excluded by their very nature.

(7) This Directive should apply to products irrespective of the selling techniques, including distance and electronic selling.

(8) The safety of products should be assessed taking into account all the relevant aspects, in particular the categories of consumers which can be particularly vulnerable to the risks posed by the products under consideration, in particular children and the elderly.

(9) This Directive does not cover services, but in order to secure the attainment of the protection objectives in question, its provisions should also apply to products that are supplied or made available to consumers in the context of service provision for use by them. The safety of the equipment used by service providers themselves to supply a service to consumers does not come within the scope of this Directive since it has to be dealt with in conjunction with the safety of the service provided. In particular, equipment on which consumers ride or travel which is operated by a service provider is excluded from the scope of this Directive.

(10) Products which are designed exclusively for professional use but have subsequently migrated to the consumer market should be subject to the requirements of this Directive because they can pose risks to consumer health and safety when used under reasonably foreseeable conditions.

(11) In the absence of more specific provisions, within the framework of Community legislation covering safety of the products concerned, all the provisions of this Directive should apply in order to ensure consumer health and safety.

(12) If specific Community legislation sets out safety requirements covering only certain risks or categories of risks, with regard to the products concerned the obligations of economic operators in respect of these risks are those determined by the provisions of the specific legislation, while the general safety requirement of this Directive should apply to the other risks.

(13) The provisions of this Directive relating to the other obligations of producers and distributors, the obligations and powers of the Member States, the exchanges of information and rapid intervention situations and dissemination of information and confidentiality apply in the case of products covered by specific rules of Community law, if those rules do not already contain such obligations.

(14) In order to facilitate the effective and consistent application of the general safety requirement of this Directive, it is important to establish European voluntary standards covering certain products and risks in such a way that a product which conforms to a national standard transposing a European standard is to be presumed to be in compliance with the said requirement.

(15) With regard to the aims of this Directive, European standards should be established by European standardisation bodies, under mandates set by the Commission assisted by appropriate Committees. In order to ensure that products in compliance with the standards fulfil the general safety requirement, the Commission assisted by a committee composed of representatives of the Member States, should fix the requirements that the standards must meet. These requirements should be included in the mandates to the standardisation bodies.

(16) In the absence of specific regulations and when the European standards established under mandates set by the Commission are not available or recourse is not made to such standards, the safety of products should be assessed taking into account in particular national standards transposing any other relevant European or international standards, Commission

recommendations or national standards, international standards, codes of good practice, the state of the art and the safety which consumers may reasonably expect. In this context, the Commission's recommendations may facilitate the consistent and effective application of this Directive pending the introduction of European standards or as regards the risks and/or products for which such standards are deemed not to be possible or appropriate.

(17) Appropriate independent certification recognised by the competent authorities may facilitate proof of compliance with the applicable product safety criteria.

(18) It is appropriate to supplement the duty to observe the general safety requirement by other obligations on economic operators because action by such operators is necessary to prevent risks to consumers under certain circumstances.

(19) The additional obligations on producers should include the duty to adopt measures commensurate with the characteristics of the products, enabling them to be informed of the risks that these products may present, to supply consumers with information enabling them to assess and prevent risks, to warn consumers of the risks posed by dangerous products already supplied to them, to withdraw those products from the market and, as a last resort, to recall them when necessary, which may involve, depending on the provisions applicable in the Member States, an appropriate form of compensation, for example exchange or reimbursement.

(20) Distributors should help in ensuring compliance with the applicable safety requirements. The obligations placed on distributors apply in proportion to their respective responsibilities. In particular, it may prove impossible, in the context of charitable activities, to provide the competent authorities with information and documentation on possible risks and origin of the product in the case of isolated used objects provided by private individuals.

(21) Both producers and distributors should cooperate with the competent authorities in action aimed at preventing risks and inform them when they conclude that certain products supplied are dangerous. The conditions regarding the provision of such information should be set in this Directive to facilitate its effective application, while avoiding an excessive burden for economic operators and the authorities.

(22) In order to ensure the effective enforcement of the obligations incumbent on producers and distributors, the Member States should establish or designate authorities which are responsible for monitoring product safety and have powers to take appropriate measures, including the power to impose effective, proportionate and dissuasive penalties, and ensure appropriate coordination between the various designated authorities.

(23) It is necessary in particular for the appropriate measures to include the power for Member States to order or organise, immediately and efficiently, the withdrawal of dangerous products already placed on the market and as a last resort to order, coordinate or organise the recall from consumers of dangerous products already supplied to them. Those powers should be applied when producers and distributors fail to prevent risks to consumers in accordance with their obligations. Where necessary, the appropriate powers and procedures should be available to the authorities to decide and apply any necessary measures rapidly.

(24) The safety of consumers depends to a great extent on the active enforcement of Community product safety requirements. The Member States should, therefore, establish systematic approaches to ensure the effectiveness of market surveillance and other enforcement activities and should ensure their openness to the public and interested parties.

(25) Collaboration between the enforcement authorities of the Member States is necessary in ensuring the attainment of the protection objectives of this Directive. It is, therefore, appropriate to promote the operation of a European network of the enforcement authorities of the Member States to facilitate, in a coordinated manner with other Community procedures, in particular the Community Rapid Information System (RAPEX), improved collaboration at operational level on market surveillance and other enforcement activities, in particular risk assessment, testing of products, exchange of expertise and scientific knowledge, execution of joint surveillance projects and tracing, withdrawing or recalling dangerous products.

(26) It is necessary, for the purpose of ensuring a consistent, high level of consumer health and safety protection and preserving the unity of the internal market, that the Commission be informed of any measure restricting the placing on the market of a product or requiring its withdrawal or recall from the market. Such measures should be taken in compliance with the provisions of the Treaty, and in particular Articles 28, 29 and 30 thereof.

(27) Effective supervision of product safety requires the setting-up at national and Community levels of a system of rapid exchange of information in situations of serious risk requiring rapid intervention in respect of the safety of a product. It is also appropriate in this Directive to set out detailed procedures for the operation of the system and to give the Commission, assisted by an advisory committee, power to adapt them.

(28) This Directive provides for the establishment of non-binding guidelines aimed at indicating simple and clear criteria and practical rules which may change, in particular for the purpose of allowing efficient notification of measures restricting the placing on the market of products in the cases referred to in this Directive, whilst taking into account the range of situations dealt with by Member States and economic operators. The guidelines should in particular include criteria for the application of the definition of serious risks in order to facilitate consistent implementation of the relevant provisions in case of such risks.

(29) It is primarily for Member States, in compliance with the Treaty and in particular with Articles 28, 29 and 30 thereof, to take appropriate measures with regard to dangerous products located within their territory.

(30) However, if the Member States differ as regards the approach to dealing with the risk posed by certain products, such differences could entail unacceptable disparities in consumer protection and constitute a barrier to intra-Community trade.

(31) It may be necessary to deal with serious product-safety problems requiring rapid intervention which affect or could affect, in the immediate future, all or a significant part of the Community and which, in view of the nature of the safety problem posed by the product, cannot be dealt with effectively in a manner commensurate with the degree of urgency, under the procedures laid down in the specific rules of Community law applicable to the products or category of products in question.

(32) It is therefore necessary to provide for an adequate mechanism allowing, as a last resort, for the adoption of measures applicable throughout the Community, in the form of a decision addressed to the Member States, to cope with situations created by products presenting a serious risk. Such a decision should entail a ban on the export of the product in question, unless in the case in point exceptional circumstances allow a partial ban or even no ban to be decided upon, particularly when a system of prior consent is established. In addition, the banning of exports should be examined with a view to preventing risks to the health and safety of consumers. Since such a decision is not directly applicable to economic operators, Member States should take all necessary measures for its implementation. Measures adopted under such a procedure are interim measures, save when they apply to individually identified products or batches of products. In order to ensure the appropriate assessment of the need for, and the best preparation of such measures, they should be taken by the Commission, assisted by a committee, in the light of consultations with the Member States, and, if scientific questions are involved falling within the competence of a Community scientific committee, with the scientific committee competent for the risk concerned.

(33) The measures necessary for the implementation of this Directive should be adopted in accordance with Council Decision 1999/468/EC of 28 June 1999 laying down the procedures for the exercise of implementing powers conferred on the Commission.

(34) In order to facilitate effective and consistent application of this Directive, the various aspects of its application may need to be discussed within a committee.

(35) Public access to the information available to the authorities on product safety should be ensured. However, professional secrecy, as referred to in Article 287 of the Treaty, must be protected in a way which is compatible with the need to ensure the effectiveness of market surveillance activities and of protection measures.

(36) This Directive should not affect victims' rights within the meaning of Council Directive 85/374/EEC of 25 July 1985 on the approximation of the laws, regulations and administrative provisions of the Member States concerning liability for defective products.

(37) It is necessary for Member States to provide for appropriate means of redress before the competent courts in respect of measures taken by the competent authorities which restrict the placing on the market of a product or require its withdrawal or recall.

(38) In addition, the adoption of measures concerning imported products, like those concerning the banning of exports, with a view to preventing risks to the safety and health of consumers must comply with the Community's international obligations.

(39) The Commission should periodically examine the manner in which this Directive is applied and the results obtained, in particular in relation to the functioning of market surveillance systems, the rapid exchange of information and measures adopted at Community level, together with other issues relevant for consumer product safety in the Community, and submit regular reports to the European Parliament and the Council on the subject.

(40) This Directive should not affect the obligations of Member States concerning the deadline for transposition and application of Directive 92/59/EEC,
HAVE ADOPTED THIS DIRECTIVE:

CHAPTER I

Objective—Scope—Definitions

Article 1
1. The purpose of this Directive is to ensure that products placed on the market are safe.
2. This Directive shall apply to all the products defined in Article 2(a). Each of its provisions shall apply in so far as there are no specific provisions with the same objective in rules of Community law governing the safety of the products concerned.

Where products are subject to specific safety requirements imposed by Community legislation, this Directive shall apply only to the aspects and risks or categories of risks not covered by those requirements. This means that:
    (a) Articles 2(b) and (c), 3 and 4 shall not apply to those products insofar as concerns the risks or categories of risks covered by the specific legislation;
    (b) Articles 5 to 18 shall apply except where there are specific provisions governing the aspects covered by the said Articles with the same objective.

Article 2
For the purposes of this Directive:
    (a) 'product' shall mean any product—including in the context of providing a service—which is intended for consumers or likely, under reasonably foreseeable conditions, to be used by consumers even if not intended for them, and is supplied or made available, whether for consideration or not, in the course of a commercial activity, and whether new, used or reconditioned.
    This definition shall not apply to second-hand products supplied as antiques or as products to be repaired or reconditioned prior to being used, provided that the supplier clearly informs the person to whom he supplies the product to that effect;
    (b) 'safe product' shall mean any product which, under normal or reasonably foreseeable conditions of use including duration and, where applicable, putting into service, installation and maintenance requirements, does not present any risk or only the minimum risks compatible with the product's use, considered to be acceptable and consistent with a high level of protection for the safety and health of persons, taking into account the following points in particular:
        (i) the characteristics of the product, including its composition, packaging, instructions for assembly and, where applicable, for installation and maintenance;

   (ii) the effect on other products, where it is reasonably foreseeable that it will be used with other products;
   (iii) the presentation of the product, the labelling, any warnings and instructions for its use and disposal and any other indication or information regarding the product;
   (iv) the categories of consumers at risk when using the product, in particular children and the elderly.

The feasibility of obtaining higher levels of safety or the availability of other products presenting a lesser degree of risk shall not constitute grounds for considering a product to be 'dangerous';

   (c) 'dangerous product' shall mean any product which does not meet the definition of 'safe product' in (b);
   (d) 'serious risk' shall mean any serious risk, including those the effects of which are not immediate, requiring rapid intervention by the public authorities;
   (e) 'producer' shall mean:
      (i) the manufacturer of the product, when he is established in the Community, and any other person presenting himself as the manufacturer by affixing to the product his name, trade mark or other distinctive mark, or the person who reconditions the product;
      (ii) the manufacturer's representative, when the manufacturer is not established in the Community or, if there is no representative established in the Community, the importer of the product;
      (iii) other professionals in the supply chain, insofar as their activities may affect the safety properties of a product;
   (f) 'distributor' shall mean any professional in the supply chain whose activity does not affect the safety properties of a product;
   (g) 'recall' shall mean any measure aimed at achieving the return of a dangerous product that has already been supplied or made available to consumers by the producer or distributor;
   (h) 'withdrawal' shall mean any measure aimed at preventing the distribution, display and offer of a product dangerous to the consumer.

CHAPTER II

General safety requirement, conformity assessment criteria and European standards

Article 3

1. Producers shall be obliged to place only safe products on the market.

2. A product shall be deemed safe, as far as the aspects covered by the relevant national legislation are concerned, when, in the absence of specific Community provisions governing the safety of the product in question, it conforms to the specific rules of national law of the Member State in whose territory the product is marketed, such rules being drawn up in conformity with the Treaty, and in particular Articles 28 and 30 thereof, and laying down the health and safety requirements which the product must satisfy in order to be marketed.

A product shall be presumed safe as far as the risks and risk categories covered by relevant national standards are concerned when it conforms to voluntary national standards transposing European standards, the references of which have been published by the Commission in the Official Journal of the European Communities in accordance with Article 4. The Member States shall publish the references of such national standards.

3. In circumstances other than those referred to in paragraph 2, the conformity of a product to the general safety requirement shall be assessed by taking into account the following elements in particular, where they exist:

(a) voluntary national standards transposing relevant European standards other than those referred to in paragraph 2;

(b) the standards drawn up in the Member State in which the product is marketed;

(c) Commission recommendations setting guidelines on product safety assessment;

(d) product safety codes of good practice in force in the sector concerned;

(e) the state of the art and technology;

(f) reasonable consumer expectations concerning safety.

4. Conformity of a product with the criteria designed to ensure the general safety requirement, in particular the provisions mentioned in paragraphs 2 or 3, shall not bar the competent authorities of the Member States from taking appropriate measures to impose restrictions on its being placed on the market or to require its withdrawal from the market or recall where there is evidence that, despite such conformity, it is dangerous.

Article 4

1. For the purposes of this Directive, the European standards referred to in the second subparagraph of Article 3(2) shall be drawn up as follows:

(a) the requirements intended to ensure that products which conform to these standards satisfy the general safety requirement shall be determined in accordance with the procedure laid down in Article 15(2);

(b) on the basis of those requirements, the Commission shall, in accordance with Directive 98/34/EC of the European Parliament and of the Council of 22 June 1998 laying down a procedure for the provision of information in the field of technical standards and regulations and of rules on information society services call on the European standardisation bodies to draw up standards which satisfy these requirements;

(c) on the basis of those mandates, the European standardisation bodies shall adopt the standards in accordance with the principles contained in the general guidelines for cooperation between the Commission and those bodies;

(d) the Commission shall report every three years to the European Parliament and the Council, within the framework of the report referred to in Article 19(2), on its programmes for setting the requirements and the mandates for standardisation provided for in subparagraphs (a) and (b) above. This report will, in particular, include an analysis of the decisions taken regarding requirements and mandates for standardisation referred to in subparagraphs (a) and (b) and regarding the standards referred to in subparagraph (c). It will also include information on the products for which the Commission intends to set the requirements and the mandates in question, the product risks to be considered and the results of any preparatory work launched in this area.

2. The Commission shall publish in the Official Journal of the European Communities the references of the European standards adopted in this way and drawn up in accordance with the requirements referred to in paragraph 1.

If a standard adopted by the European standardisation bodies before the entry into force of this Directive ensures compliance with the general safety requirement, the Commission shall decide to publish its references in the Official Journal of the European Communities.

If a standard does not ensure compliance with the general safety requirement, the Commission shall withdraw reference to the standard from publication in whole or in part.

In the cases referred to in the second and third subparagraphs, the Commission shall, on its own initiative or at the request of a Member State, decide in accordance with the procedure laid down in Article 15(2) whether the standard in question meets the general safety requirement. The Commission shall decide to publish or withdraw after consulting the

Committee established by Article 5 of Directive 98/34/EC. The Commission shall notify the Member States of its decision.

CHAPTER III

Other obligations of producers and obligations of distributors

Article 5

1. Within the limits of their respective activities, producers shall provide consumers with the relevant information to enable them to assess the risks inherent in a product throughout the normal or reasonably foreseeable period of its use, where such risks are not immediately obvious without adequate warnings, and to take precautions against those risks.

The presence of warnings does not exempt any person from compliance with the other requirements laid down in this Directive.

Within the limits of their respective activities, producers shall adopt measures commensurate with the characteristics of the products which they supply, enabling them to:

(a) be informed of risks which these products might pose;

(b) choose to take appropriate action including, if necessary to avoid these risks, withdrawal from the market, adequately and effectively warning consumers or recall from consumers.

The measures referred to in the third subparagraph shall include, for example:

(a) an indication, by means of the product or its packaging, of the identity and details of the producer and the product reference or, where applicable, the batch of products to which it belongs, except where not to give such indication is justified and

(b) in all cases where appropriate, the carrying out of sample testing of marketed products, investigating and, if necessary, keeping a register of complaints and keeping distributors informed of such monitoring.

Action such as that referred to in (b) of the third subparagraph shall be undertaken on a voluntary basis or at the request of the competent authorities in accordance with Article 8(1)(f). Recall shall take place as a last resort, where other measures would not suffice to prevent the risks involved, in instances where the producers consider it necessary or where they are obliged to do so further to a measure taken by the competent authority. It may be effected within the framework of codes of good practice on the matter in the Member State concerned, where such codes exist.

2. Distributors shall be required to act with due care to help to ensure compliance with the applicable safety requirements, in particular by not supplying products which they know or should have presumed, on the basis of the information in their possession and as professionals, do not comply with those requirements. Moreover, within the limits of their respective activities, they shall participate in monitoring the safety of products placed on the market, especially by passing on information on product risks, keeping and providing the documentation necessary for tracing the origin of products, and cooperating in the action taken by producers and competent authorities to avoid the risks. Within the limits of their respective activities they shall take measures enabling them to cooperate efficiently.

3. Where producers and distributors know or ought to know, on the basis of the information in their possession and as professionals, that a product that they have placed on the market poses risks to the consumer that are incompatible with the general safety requirement, they shall immediately inform the competent authorities of the Member States thereof under the conditions laid down in Annex I, giving details, in particular, of action taken to prevent risk to the consumer.

The Commission shall, in accordance with the procedure referred to in Article 15(3), adapt the specific requirements relating to the obligation to provide information laid down in Annex I.

4. Producers and distributors shall, within the limits of their respective activities, cooperate with the competent authorities, at the request of the latter, on action taken to avoid the risks posed by products which they supply or have supplied. The procedures for such cooperation, including procedures for dialogue with the producers and distributors concerned on issues related to product safety, shall be established by the competent authorities.

CHAPTER IV

Specific obligations and powers of the Member States

Article 6

1. Member States shall ensure that producers and distributors comply with their obligations under this Directive in such a way that products placed on the market are safe.

2. Member States shall establish or nominate authorities competent to monitor the compliance of products with the general safety requirements and arrange for such authorities to have and use the necessary powers to take the appropriate measures incumbent upon them under this Directive.

3. Member States shall define the tasks, powers, organisation and cooperation arrangements of the competent authorities. They shall keep the Commission informed, and the Commission shall pass on such information to the other Member States.

Article 7

Member States shall lay down the rules on penalties applicable to infringements of the national provisions adopted pursuant to this Directive and shall take all measures necessary to ensure that they are implemented. The penalties provided for shall be effective, proportionate and dissuasive. Member States shall notify those provisions to the Commission by 15 January 2004 and shall also notify it, without delay, of any amendment affecting them.

Article 8

1. For the purposes of this Directive, and in particular of Article 6 thereof, the competent authorities of the Member States shall be entitled to take, inter alia, the measures in (a) and in (b) to (f) below, where appropriate:

(a) for any product:
   (i)   to organise, even after its being placed on the market as being safe, appropriate checks on its safety properties, on an adequate scale, up to the final stage of use or consumption;
   (ii) to require all necessary information from the parties concerned;
   (iii) to take samples of products and subject them to safety checks;

(b) for any product that could pose risks in certain conditions:
   (i)   to require that it be marked with suitable, clearly worded and easily comprehensible warnings, in the official languages of the Member State in which the product is marketed, on the risks it may present;
   (ii) to make its marketing subject to prior conditions so as to make it safe;

(c) for any product that could pose risks for certain persons: to order that they be given warning of the risk in good time and in an appropriate form, including the publication of special warnings;

(d) for any product that could be dangerous: for the period needed for the various safety evaluations, checks and controls, temporarily to ban its supply, the offer to supply it or its display;

(e) for any dangerous product:
   to ban its marketing and introduce the accompanying measures required to ensure the ban is complied with;

(f) for any dangerous product already on the market:
   (i)   to order or organise its actual and immediate withdrawal, and alert con-
         sumers to the risks it presents;
   (ii) to order or coordinate or, if appropriate, to organise together with producers and
         distributors its recall from consumers and its destruction in suitable conditions.

2. When the competent authorities of the Member States take measures such as those
provided for in paragraph 1, in particular those referred to in (d) to (f), they shall act in
accordance with the Treaty, and in particular Articles 28 and 30 thereof, in such a way as to
implement the measures in a manner proportional to the seriousness of the risk, and taking
due account of the precautionary principle.

In this context, they shall encourage and promote voluntary action by producers and
distributors, in accordance with the obligations incumbent on them under this Directive,
and in particular Chapter III thereof, including where applicable by the development of
codes of good practice.

If necessary, they shall organise or order the measures provided for in paragraph 1(f) if the
action undertaken by the producers and distributors in fulfilment of their obligations is
unsatisfactory or insufficient. Recall shall take place as a last resort. It may be effected within
the framework of codes of good practice on the matter in the Member State concerned; where
such codes exist.

3. In particular, the competent authorities shall have the power to take the necessary
action to apply with due dispatch appropriate measures such as those mentioned in paragraph 1, (b) to (f), in the case of products posing a serious risk. These circumstances shall be
determined by the Member States, assessing each individual case on its merits, taking into
account the guidelines referred to in point 8 of Annex II.

4. The measures to be taken by the competent authorities under this Article shall be
addressed, as appropriate, to:
   (a) the producer;
   (b) within the limits of their respective activities, distributors and in particular the
       party responsible for the first stage of distribution on the national market;
   (c) any other person, where necessary, with a view to cooperation in action taken to
       avoid risks arising from a product.

Article 9

1. In order to ensure effective market surveillance, aimed at guaranteeing a high level of
consumer health and safety protection, which entails cooperation between their competent
authorities, Member States shall ensure that approaches employing appropriate means and
procedures are put in place, which may include in particular:
   (a) establishment, periodical updating and implementation of sectoral surveillance
       programmes by categories of products or risks and the monitoring of surveillance
       activities, findings and results;
   (b) follow-up and updating of scientific and technical knowledge concerning the
       safety of products;
   (c) periodical review and assessment of the functioning of the control activities and
       their effectiveness and, if necessary, revision of the surveillance approach and
       organisation put in place.

2. Member States shall ensure that consumers and other interested parties are given an
opportunity to submit complaints to the competent authorities on product safety and on
surveillance and control activities and that these complaints are followed up as appropriate.
Member States shall actively inform consumers and other interested parties of the procedures
established to that end.

Article 10

1. The Commission shall promote and take part in the operation in a European network
of the authorities of the Member States competent for product safety, in particular in the

form of administrative cooperation.

2. This network operation shall develop in a coordinated manner with the other existing Community procedures, particularly RAPEX. Its objective shall be, in particular, to facilitate:

    (a) the exchange of information on risk assessment, dangerous products, test methods and results, recent scientific developments as well as other aspects relevant for control activities;

    (b) the establishment and execution of joint surveillance and testing projects;

    (c) the exchange of expertise and best practices and cooperation in training activities;

    (d) improved cooperation at Community level with regard to the tracing, withdrawal and recall of dangerous products.

CHAPTER V

Exchanges of information and rapid intervention situations

Article 11

1. Where a Member State takes measures which restrict the placing on the market of products—or require their withdrawal or recall—such as those provided for in Article 8(1)(b) to (f), the Member State shall, to the extent that such notification is not required under Article 12 or any specific Community legislation, inform the Commission of the measures, specifying its reasons for adopting them. It shall also inform the Commission of any modification or lifting of such measures.

If the notifying Member State considers that the effects of the risk do not or cannot go beyond its territory, it shall notify the measures concerned insofar as they involve information likely to be of interest to Member States from the product safety standpoint, and in particular if they are in response to a new risk which has not yet been reported in other notifications.

In accordance with the procedure laid down in Article 15(3) of this Directive, the Commission shall, while ensuring the effectiveness and proper functioning of the system, adopt the guidelines referred to in point 8 of Annex II. These shall propose the content and standard form for the notifications provided for in this Article, and, in particular, shall provide precise criteria for determining the conditions for which notification is relevant for the purposes of the second subparagraph.

2. The Commission shall forward the notification to the other Member States, unless it concludes, after examination on the basis of the information contained in the notification, that the measure does not comply with Community law. In such a case, it shall immediately inform the Member State which initiated the action.

Article 12

1. Where a Member State adopts or decides to adopt, recommend or agree with producers and distributors, whether on a compulsory or voluntary basis, measures or actions to prevent, restrict or impose specific conditions on the possible marketing or use, within its own territory, of products by reason of a serious risk, it shall immediately notify the Commission thereof through RAPEX. It shall also inform the Commission without delay of modification or withdrawal of any such measure or action.

If the notifying Member State considers that the effects of the risk do not or cannot go beyond its territory, it shall follow the procedure laid down in Article 11, taking into account the relevant criteria proposed in the guidelines referred to in point 8 of Annex II.

Without prejudice to the first subparagraph, before deciding to adopt such measures or to take such action, Member States may pass on to the Commission any information in their possession regarding the existence of a serious risk.

In the case of a serious risk, they shall notify the Commission of the voluntary measures laid down in Article 5 of this Directive taken by producers and distributors.

2. On receiving such notifications, the Commission shall check whether they comply with this Article and with the requirements applicable to the functioning of RAPEX, and shall forward them to the other Member States, which, in turn, shall immediately inform the Commission of any measures adopted.

3. Detailed procedures for RAPEX are set out in Annex II. They shall be adapted by the Commission in accordance with the procedure referred to in Article 15(3).

4. Access to RAPEX shall be open to applicant countries, third countries or international organisations, within the framework of agreements between the Community and those countries or international organisations, according to arrangements defined in these agreements. Any such agreements shall be based on reciprocity and include provisions on confidentiality corresponding to those applicable in the Community.

Article 13

1. If the Commission becomes aware of a serious risk from certain products to the health and safety of consumers in various Member States, it may, after consulting the Member States, and, if scientific questions arise which fall within the competence of a Community Scientific Committee, the Scientific Committee competent to deal with the risk concerned, adopt a decision in the light of the result of those consultations, in accordance with the procedure laid down in Article 15(2), requiring Member States to take measures from among those listed in Article 8(1)(b) to (f) if, at one and the same time:

  (a) it emerges from prior consultations with the Member States that they differ significantly on the approach adopted or to be adopted to deal with the risk; and

  (b) the risk cannot be dealt with, in view of the nature of the safety issue posed by the product, in a manner compatible with the degree of urgency of the case, under other procedures laid down by the specific Community legislation applicable to the products concerned; and

  (c) the risk can be eliminated effectively only by adopting appropriate measures applicable at Community level, in order to ensure a consistent and high level of protection of the health and safety of consumers and the proper functioning of the internal market.

2. The decisions referred to in paragraph 1 shall be valid for a period not exceeding one year and may be confirmed, under the same procedure, for additional periods none of which shall exceed one year.

However, decisions concerning specific, individually identified products or batches of products shall be valid without a time limit.

3. Export from the Community of dangerous products which have been the subject of a decision referred to in paragraph 1 shall be prohibited unless the decision provides otherwise.

4. Member States shall take all necessary measures to implement the decisions referred to in paragraph 1 within less than 20 days, unless a different period is specified in those decisions.

5. The competent authorities responsible for carrying out the measures referred to in paragraph 1 shall, within one month, give the parties concerned an opportunity to submit their views and shall inform the Commission accordingly.

CHAPTER VI

Committee procedures

Article 14

1. The measures necessary for the implementation of this Directive relating to the matters referred to below shall be adopted in accordance with the regulatory procedure provided for in Article 15(2):

  (a) the measures referred to in Article 4 concerning standards adopted by the European standardisation bodies;

(b) the decisions referred to in Article 13 requiring Member States to take measures as listed in Article 8(1)(b) to (f).

2. The measures necessary for the implementation of this Directive in respect of all other matters shall be adopted in accordance with the advisory procedure provided for in Article 15(3).

Article 15

1. The Commission shall be assisted by a Committee.

2. Where reference is made to this paragraph, Articles 5 and 7 of Decision 1999/468/EC shall apply, having regard to the provisions of Article 8 thereof.

The period laid down in Article 5(6) of Decision 1999/468/EC shall be set at 15 days.

3. Where reference is made to this paragraph, Articles 3 and 7 of Decision 1999/468/EC shall apply, having regard to the provisions of Article 8 thereof.

4. The Committee shall adopt its rules of procedure.

CHAPTER VII

Final provisions

Article 16

1. Information available to the authorities of the Member States or the Commission relating to risks to consumer health and safety posed by products shall in general be available to the public, in accordance with the requirements of transparency and without prejudice to the restrictions required for monitoring and investigation activities. In particular the public shall have access to information on product identification, the nature of the risk and the measures taken.

However, Member States and the Commission shall take the steps necessary to ensure that their officials and agents are required not to disclose information obtained for the purposes of this Directive which, by its nature, is covered by professional secrecy in duly justified cases, except for information relating to the safety properties of products which must be made public if circumstances so require, in order to protect the health and safety of consumers.

2. Protection of professional secrecy shall not prevent the dissemination to the competent authorities of information relevant for ensuring the effectiveness of market monitoring and surveillance activities. The authorities receiving information covered by professional secrecy shall ensure its protection.

Article 17

This Directive shall be without prejudice to the application of Directive 85/374/EEC.

Article 18

1. Any measure adopted under this Directive and involving restrictions on the placing of a product on the market or requiring its withdrawal or recall must state the appropriate reasons on which it is based. It shall be notified as soon as possible to the party concerned and shall indicate the remedies available under the provisions in force in the Member State in question and the time limits applying to such remedies.

The parties concerned shall, whenever feasible, be given an opportunity to submit their views before the adoption of the measure. If this has not been done in advance because of the urgency of the measures to be taken, they shall be given such opportunity in due course after the measure has been implemented.

Measures requiring the withdrawal of a product or its recall shall take into consideration the need to encourage distributors, users and consumers to contribute to the implementation of such measures.

2. Member States shall ensure that any measure taken by the competent authorities involving restrictions on the placing of a product on the market or requiring its withdrawal or recall can be challenged before the competent courts.

3. Any decision taken by virtue of this Directive and involving restrictions on the placing of a product on the market or requiring its withdrawal or its recall shall be without prejudice to assessment of the liability of the party concerned, in the light of the national criminal law applying in the case in question.

Article 19

1. The Commission may bring before the Committee referred to in Article 15 any matter concerning the application of this Directive and particularly those relating to market monitoring and surveillance activities.

2. Every three years, following 15 January 2004, the Commission shall submit a report on the implementation of this Directive to the European Parliament and the Council.

The report shall in particular include information on the safety of consumer products, in particular on improved traceability of products, the functioning of market surveillance, standardisation work, the functioning of RAPEX and Community measures taken on the basis of Article 13. To this end the Commission shall conduct assessments of the relevant issues, in particular the approaches, systems and practices put in place in the Member States, in the light of the requirements of this Directive and the other Community legislation relating to product safety. The Member States shall provide the Commission with all the necessary assistance and information for carrying out the assessments and preparing the reports.

Article 20

The Commission shall identify the needs, possibilities and priorities for Community action on the safety of services and submit to the European Parliament and the Council, before 1 January 2003, a report, accompanied by proposals on the subject as appropriate.

Article 21

1. Member States shall bring into force the laws, regulations and administrative provisions necessary in order to comply with this Directive with effect from 15 January 2004. They shall forthwith inform the Commission thereof.

When Member States adopt those measures, they shall contain a reference to this Directive or be accompanied by such reference on the occasion of their official publication. The methods of making such reference shall be laid down by Member States.

2. Member States shall communicate to the Commission the provisions of national law which they adopt in the field covered by this Directive.

Article 22

Directive 92/59/EEC is hereby repealed from 15 January 2004, without prejudice to the obligations of Member States concerning the deadlines for transposition and application of the said Directive as indicated in Annex III.

References to Directive 92/59/EEC shall be construed as references to this Directive and shall be read in accordance with the correlation table in Annex IV.

Council Regulation (EC) No. 44/2001
of 22 December 2000

on jurisdiction and the recognition and enforcement of judgments in civil and commercial matters

THE COUNCIL OF THE EUROPEAN UNION.

Having regard to the Treaty establishing the European Community, and in particular Article 61(c) and Article 67(1) thereof,

Having regard to the proposal from the Commission (1),

Having regard to the opinion of the European Parliament (2),

Having regard to the opinion of the Economic and Social Committee (3), Whereas:

(1) The Community has set itself the objective of maintaining and developing an area of freedom, security and justice, in which the free movement of persons is ensured. In order to establish progressively such an area, the Community should adopt, amongst other things, the measures relating to judicial cooperation in civil matters which are necessary for the sound operation of the internal market.

(2) Certain differences between national rules governing jurisdiction and recognition of judgments hamper the sound operation of the internal market. Provisions to unify the rules of conflict of jurisdiction in civil and commercial matters and to simplify the formalities with a view to rapid and simple recognition and enforcement of judgments from Member States bound by this Regulation are essential.

(3) This area is within the field of judicial cooperation in civil matters within the meaning of Article 65 of the Treaty.

(4) In accordance with the principles of subsidiarity and proportionality as set out in Article 5 of the Treaty, the objectives of this Regulation cannot be sufficiently achieved by the Member States and can therefore be better achieved by the Community. This Regulation confines itself to the minimum required in order to achieve those objectives and does not go beyond what is necessary for that purpose.

(5) On 27 September 1968 the Member States, acting under Article 293, fourth indent, of the Treaty, concluded the Brussels Convention on Jurisdiction and the Enforcement of Judgments in Civil and Commercial Matters, as amended by Conventions on the Accession of the New Member States to that Convention (hereinafter referred to as the 'Brussels Convention') (4). On 16 September 1988 Member States and EFTA States concluded the Lugano Convention on Jurisdiction and the Enforcement of Judgments in Civil and Commercial Matters, which is a parallel Convention to the 1968 Brussels Convention. Work has been undertaken for the revision of those Conventions, and the Council has approved the content of the revised texts. Continuity in the results achieved in that revision should be ensured.

(6) In order to attain the objective of free movement of judgments in civil and commercial matters, it is necessary and appropriate that the rules governing jurisdiction and the recognition and enforcement of judgments be governed by a Community legal instrument which is binding and directly applicable.

(7) The scope of this Regulation must cover all the main civil and commercial matters apart from certain well-defined matters.

(8) There must be a link between proceedings to which this Regulation applies and the territory of the Member States bound by this Regulation. Accordingly common rules on jurisdiction should, in principle, apply when the defendant is domiciled in one of those Member States.

(9) A defendant not domiciled in a Member State is in general subject to national rules of jurisdiction applicable in the territory of the Member State of the court seised, and a defendant domiciled in a Member State not bound by this Regulation must remain subject to the Brussels Convention.

(10) For the purposes of the free movement of judgments, judgments given in a Member State bound by this Regulation should be recognised and enforced in another Member State bound by this Regulation, even if the judgment debtor is domiciled in a third State.

(11) The rules of jurisdiction must be highly predictable and founded on the principle that jurisdiction is generally based on the defendant's domicile and jurisdiction must always be available on this ground save in a few well-defined situations in which the subject-matter of the litigation or the autonomy of the parties warrants a different linking factor. The domicile of a legal person must be defined autonomously so as to make the common rules more transparent and avoid conflicts of jurisdiction.

(12) In addition to the defendant's domicile, there should be alternative grounds of jurisdiction based on a close link between the court and the action or in order to facilitate the sound administration of justice.

(13) In relation to insurance, consumer contracts and employment, the weaker party should be protected by rules of jurisdiction more favourable to his interests than the general rules provide for.

(14) The autonomy of the parties to a contract, other than an insurance, consumer or employment contract, where only limited autonomy to determine the courts having jurisdiction is allowed, must be respected subject to the exclusive grounds of jurisdiction laid down in this Regulation.

(15) In the interests of the harmonious administration of justice it is necessary to minimise the possibility of concurrent proceedings and to ensure that irreconcilable judgments will not be given in two Member States. There must be a clear and effective mechanism for resolving cases of lis pendens and related actions and for obviating problems flowing from national differences as to the determination of the time when a case is regarded as pending. For the purposes of this Regulation that time should be defined autonomously.

(16) Mutual trust in the administration of justice in the Community justifies judgments given in a Member State being recognised automatically without the need for any procedure except in cases of dispute.

(17) By virtue of the same principle of mutual trust, the procedure for making enforceable in one Member State a judgment given in another must be efficient and rapid. To that end, the declaration that a judgment is enforceable should be issued virtually automatically after purely formal checks of the documents supplied, without there being any possibility for the court to raise of its own motion any of the grounds for non-enforcement provided for by this Regulation.

(18) However, respect for the rights of the defence means that the defendant should be able to appeal in an adversarial procedure, against the declaration of enforceability, if he considers one of the grounds for non-enforcement to be present. Redress procedures should also be available to the claimant where his application for a declaration of enforceability has been rejected.

(19) Continuity between the Brussels Convention and this Regulation should be ensured, and transitional provisions should be laid down to that end. The same need for continuity applies as regards the interpretation of the Brussels Convention by the Court of Justice of the European Communities and the 1971 Protocol (5) should remain applicable also to cases already pending when this Regulation enters into force.

(20) The United Kingdom and Ireland, in accordance with Article 3 of the Protocol on the position of the United Kingdom and Ireland annexed to the Treaty on European Union and to the Treaty establishing the European Community, have given notice of their wish to take part in the adoption and application of this Regulation.

(21) Denmark, in accordance with Articles 1 and 2 of the Protocol on the position of Denmark annexed to the Treaty on European Union and to the Treaty establishing the European Community, is not participating in the adoption of this Regulation, and is therefore not bound by it nor subject to its application.

(22) Since the Brussels Convention remains in force in relations between Denmark and the Member States that are bound by this Regulation, both the Convention and the 1971 Protocol continue to apply between Denmark and the Member States bound by this Regulation.

(23) The Brussels Convention also continues to apply to the territories of the Member States which fall within the territorial scope of that Convention and which are excluded from this Regulation pursuant to Article 299 of the Treaty.

(24) Likewise for the sake of consistency, this Regulation should not affect rules governing jurisdiction and the recognition of judgments contained in specific Community instruments.

(25) Respect for international commitments entered into by the Member States means that this Regulation should not affect conventions relating to specific matters to which the Member States are parties.

(26) The necessary flexibility should be provided for in the basic rules of this Regulation in order to take account of the specific procedural rules of certain Member States. Certain provisions of the Protocol annexed to the Brussels Convention should accordingly be incorporated in this Regulation.

(27) In order to allow a harmonious transition in certain areas which were the subject of special provisions in the Protocol annexed to the Brussels Convention, this Regulation lays down, for a transitional period, provisions taking into consideration the specific situation in certain Member States.

(28) No later than five years after entry into force of this Regulation the Commission will present a report on its application and, if need be, submit proposals for adaptations.

(29) The Commission will have to adjust Annexes I to IV on the rules of national jurisdiction, the courts or competent authorities and redress procedures available on the basis of the amendments forwarded by the Member State concerned; amendments made to Annexes V and VI should be adopted in accordance with Council Decision 1999/468/EC of 28 June 1999 laying down the procedures for the exercise of implementing powers conferred on the Commission (6),

HAS ADOPTED THIS REGULATION:

CHAPTER I   SCOPE

Article 1

1. This Regulation shall apply in civil and commercial matters whatever the nature of the court or tribunal. It shall not extend, in particular, to revenue, customs or administrative matters.

2. The Regulation shall not apply to:
    (a) the status or legal capacity of natural persons, rights in property arising out of a matrimonial relationship, wills and succession;
    (b) bankruptcy, proceedings relating to the winding-up of insolvent companies or other legal persons, judicial arrangements, compositions and analogous proceedings;
    (c) social security;
    (d) arbitration.

3. In this Regulation, the term 'Member State' shall mean Member States with the exception of Denmark.

CHAPTER II   JURISDICTION

Section 1   General provisions

Article 2

1. Subject to this Regulation, persons domiciled in a Member State shall, whatever their nationality, be sued in the courts of that Member State.

2. Persons who are not nationals of the Member State in which they are domiciled shall be governed by the rules of jurisdiction applicable to nationals of that State.

Article 3

1. Persons domiciled in a Member State may be sued in the courts of another Member State only by virtue of the rules set out in Sections 2 to 7 of this Chapter.

2. In particular the rules of national jurisdiction set out in Annex I shall not be applicable as against them.

Article 4

1. If the defendant is not domiciled in a Member State, the jurisdiction of the courts of each Member State shall, subject to Articles 22 and 23, be determined by the law of that Member State.

2. As against such a defendant, any person domiciled in a Member State may, whatever his nationality, avail himself in that State of the rules of jurisdiction there in force, and in particular those specified in Annex I, in the same way as the nationals of that State.

Section 2   Special jurisdiction

Article 5

A person domiciled in a Member State may, in another Member State, be sued:

1. (a) in matters relating to a contract, in the courts for the place of performance of the obligation in question;

   (b) for the purpose of this provision and unless otherwise agreed, the place of performance of the obligation in question shall be:
  — in the case of the sale of goods, the place in a Member State where, under the contract, the goods were delivered or should have been delivered,
  — in the case of the provision of services, the place in a Member State where, under the contract, the services were provided or should have been provided.

   (c) if subparagraph (b) does not apply then subparagraph (a) applies;

2. In matters relating to maintenance, in the courts for the place where the maintenance creditor is domiciled or habitually resident or, if the matter is ancillary to proceedings concerning the status of a person, in the court which, according to its own law, has jurisdiction to entertain those proceedings, unless that jurisdiction is based solely on the nationality of one of the parties;

3. In matters relating to tort, delict or quasi-delict, in the courts for the place where the harmful event occurred or may occur;

4. As regards a civil claim for damages or restitution which is based on an act giving rise to criminal proceedings, in the court seised of those proceedings, to the extent that that court has jurisdiction under its own law to entertain civil proceedings;

5. As regards a dispute arising out of the operations of a branch, agency or other establishment, in the courts for the place in which the branch, agency or other establishment is situated;

6. As settlor, trustee or beneficiary of a trust created by the operation of a statute, or by a written instrument, or created orally and evidenced in writing, in the courts of the Member State in which the trust is domiciled;

7. As regards a dispute concerning the payment of remuneration claimed in respect of the salvage of a cargo or freight, in the court under the authority of which the cargo or freight in question:

   (a) has been arrested to secure such payment, or

   (b) could have been so arrested, but bail or other security has been given;

provided that this provision shall apply only if it is claimed that the defendant has an interest in the cargo or freight or had such an interest at the time of salvage.

Article 6

A person domiciled in a Member State may also be sued:

1. Where he is one of a number of defendants, in the courts for the place where any one of them is domiciled, provided the claims are so closely connected that it is expedient to hear and determine them together to avoid the risk of irreconcilable judgments resulting from separate proceedings;

2. As a third party in an action on a warranty or guarantee or in any other third party proceedings, in the court scised of the original proceedings, unless these were instituted

solely with the object of removing him from the jurisdiction of the court which would be competent in his case;

3. On a counter-claim arising from the same contract or facts on which the original claim was based, in the court in which the original claim is pending;

4. In matters relating to a contract, if the action may be combined with an action against the same defendant in matters relating to rights in rem in immovable property, in the court of the Member State in which the property is situated.

Article 7

Where by virtue of this Regulation a court of a Member State has jurisdiction in actions relating to liability from the use or operation of a ship, that court, or any other court substituted for this purpose by the internal law of that Member State, shall also have jurisdiction over claims for limitation of such liability.

Section 4   Jurisdiction over consumer contracts

Article 15

1. In matters relating to a contract concluded by a person, the consumer, for a purpose which can be regarded as being outside his trade or profession, jurisdiction shall be determined by this Section, without prejudice to Article 4 and point 5 of Article 5, if:
   (a) it is a contract for the sale of goods on instalment credit terms; or
   (b) it is a contract for a loan repayable by instalments, or for any other form of credit, made to finance the sale of goods; or
   (c) in all other cases, the contract has been concluded with a person who pursues commercial or professional activities in the Member State of the consumer's domicile or, by any means, directs such activities to that Member State or to several States including that Member State, and the contract falls within the scope of such activities.

2. Where a consumer enters into a contract with a party who is not domiciled in the Member State but has a branch, agency or other establishment in one of the Member States, that party shall, in disputes arising out of the operations of the branch, agency or establishment, be deemed to be domiciled in that State.

3. This Section shall not apply to a contract of transport other than a contract which, for an inclusive price, provides for a combination of travel and accommodation.

Article 16

1. A consumer may bring proceedings against the other party to a contract either in the courts of the Member State in which that party is domiciled or in the courts for the place where the consumer is domiciled.

2. Proceedings may be brought against a consumer by the other party to the contract only in the courts of the Member State in which the consumer is domiciled.

3. This Article shall not affect the right to bring a counter-claim in the court in which, in accordance with this Section, the original claim is pending.

Article 17

The provisions of this Section may be departed from only by an agreement:

1. Which is entered into after the dispute has arisen; or

2. Which allows the consumer to bring proceedings in courts other than those indicated in this Section; or

3. Which is entered into by the consumer and the other party to the contract, both of whom are at the time of conclusion of the contract domiciled or habitually resident in the same Member State, and which confers jurisdiction on the courts of that Member State, provided that such an agreement is not contrary to the law of that Member State.

Section 6   Exclusive jurisdiction

Article 22

The following courts shall have exclusive jurisdiction, regardless of domicile:

1. In proceedings which have as their object rights in rem in immovable property or tenancies of immovable property, the courts of the Member State in which the property is situated.

However, in proceedings which have as their object tenancies of immovable property concluded for temporary private use for a maximum period of six consecutive months, the courts of the Member State in which the defendant is domiciled shall also have jurisdiction, provided that the tenant is a natural person and that the landlord and the tenant are domiciled in the same Member State;

2. In proceedings which have as their object the validity of the constitution, the nullity or the dissolution of companies or other legal persons or associations of natural or legal persons, or of the validity of the decisions of their organs, the courts of the Member State in which the company, legal person or association has its seat. In order to determine that seat, the court shall apply its rules of private international law;

3. In proceedings which have as their object the validity of entries in public registers, the courts of the Member State in which the register is kept;

4. In proceedings concerned with the registration or validity of patents, trade marks, designs, or other similar rights required to be deposited or registered, the courts of the Member State in which the deposit or registration has been applied for, has taken place or is under the terms of a Community instrument or an international convention deemed to have taken place.

Without prejudice to the jurisdiction of the European Patent Office under the Convention on the Grant of European Patents, signed at Munich on 5 October 1973, the courts of each Member State shall have exclusive jurisdiction, regardless of domicile, in proceedings concerned with the registration or validity of any European patent granted for that State;

5. In proceedings concerned with the enforcement of judgments, the courts of the Member State in which the judgment has been or is to be enforced.

Section 7   Prorogation of jurisdiction

Article 23

1. If the parties, one or more of whom is domiciled in a Member State, have agreed that a court or the courts of a Member State are to have jurisdiction to settle any disputes which have arisen or which may arise in connection with a particular legal relationship, that court or those courts shall have jurisdiction. Such jurisdiction shall be exclusive unless the parties have agreed otherwise. Such an agreement conferring jurisdiction shall be either:

(a) in writing or evidenced in writing; or
(b) in a form which accords with practices which the parties have established between themselves; or
(c) in international trade or commerce, in a form which accords with a usage of which the parties are or ought to have been aware and which in such trade or commerce is widely known to, and regularly observed by, parties to contracts of the type involved in the particular trade or commerce concerned.

2. Any communication by electronic means which provides a durable record of the agreement shall be equivalent to 'writing'.

3. Where such an agreement is concluded by parties, none of whom is domiciled in a Member State, the courts of other Member States shall have no jurisdiction over their disputes unless the court or courts chosen have declined jurisdiction.

4. The court or courts of a Member State on which a trust instrument has conferred jurisdiction shall have exclusive jurisdiction in any proceedings brought against a settlor, trustee or beneficiary, if relations between these persons or their rights or obligations under the trust are involved.

5. Agreements or provisions of a trust instrument conferring jurisdiction shall have no legal force if they are contrary to Articles 13, 17 or 21, or if the courts whose jurisdiction they purport to exclude have exclusive jurisdiction by virtue of Article 22.

Article 24
Apart from jurisdiction derived from other provisions of this Regulation, a court of a Member State before which a defendant enters an appearance shall have jurisdiction. This rule shall not apply where appearance was entered to contest the jurisdiction, or where another court has exclusive jurisdiction by virtue of Article 22.

CHAPTER III   RECOGNITION AND ENFORCEMENT

Article 32
For the purposes of this Regulation, 'judgment' means any judgment given by a court or tribunal of a Member State, whatever the judgment may be called, including a decree, order, decision or writ of execution, as well as the determination of costs or expenses by an officer of the court.

Section 1 Recognition

Article 33
1. A judgment given in a Member State shall be recognised in the other Member States without any special procedure being required.
2. Any interested party who raises the recognition of a judgment as the principal issue in a dispute may, in accordance with the procedures provided for in Sections 2 and 3 of this Chapter, apply for a decision that the judgment be recognised.
3. If the outcome of proceedings in a court of a Member State depends on the determination of an incidental question of recognition that court shall have jurisdiction over that question.

Article 34
A judgment shall not be recognised:
1. If such recognition is manifestly contrary to public policy in the Member State in which recognition is sought;
2. Where it was given in default of appearance, if the defendant was not served with the document which instituted the proceedings or with an equivalent document in sufficient time and in such a way as to enable him to arrange for his defence, unless the defendant failed to commence proceedings to challenge the judgment when it was possible for him to do so;
3. If it is irreconcilable with a judgment given in a dispute between the same parties in the Member State in which recognition is sought;
4. If it is irreconcilable with an earlier judgment given in another Member State or in a third State involving the same cause of action and between the same parties, provided that the earlier judgment fulfils the conditions necessary for its recognition in the Member State addressed.

Article 36
Under no circumstances may a foreign judgment be reviewed as to its substance.

CHAPTER V   GENERAL PROVISIONS

Article 59
1. In order to determine whether a party is domiciled in the Member State whose courts are seised of a matter, the court shall apply its internal law.

2. If a party is not domiciled in the Member State whose courts are seised of the matter, then, in order to determine whether the party is domiciled in another Member State, the court shall apply the law of that Member State.

Article 60

1. For the purposes of this Regulation, a company or other legal person or association of natural or legal persons is domiciled at the place where it has its:
    (a) statutory seat, or
    (b) central administration, or
    (c) principal place of business.

2. For the purposes of the United Kingdom and Ireland 'statutory seat' means the registered office or, where there is no such office anywhere, the place of incorporation or, where there is no such place anywhere, the place under the law of which the formation took place.

3. In order to determine whether a trust is domiciled in the Member State whose courts are seised of the matter, the court shall apply its rules of private international law.

Article 61

Without prejudice to any more favourable provisions of national laws, persons domiciled in a Member State who are being prosecuted in the criminal courts of another Member State of which they are not nationals for an offence which was not intentionally committed may be defended by persons qualified to do so, even if they do not appear in person. However, the court seised of the matter may order appearance in person; in the case of failure to appear, a judgment given in the civil action without the person concerned having had the opportunity to arrange for his defence need not be recognised or enforced in the other Member States.

CHAPTER VII   RELATIONS WITH OTHER INSTRUMENTS

Article 67

This Regulation shall not prejudice the application of provisions governing jurisdiction and the recognition and enforcement of judgments in specific matters which are contained in Community instruments or in national legislation harmonised pursuant to such instruments.

Article 68

1. This Regulation shall, as between the Member States, supersede the Brussels Convention, except as regards the territories of the Member States which fall within the territorial scope of that Convention and which are excluded from this Regulation pursuant to Article 299 of the Treaty.

2. In so far as this Regulation replaces the provisions of the Brussels Convention between Member States, any reference to the Convention shall be understood as a reference to this Regulation.

Article 76

This Regulation shall enter into force on 1 March 2002.

This Regulation is binding in its entirety and directly applicable in the Member States in accordance with the Treaty establishing the European Community.

Done at Brussels, 22 December 2000.

ANNEX 1

The rules of jurisdiction referred to in Article 3(2) and Article 4(2) are the following:

    ...

    — in the United Kingdom: rules which enable jurisdiction to be founded on:
        (a) the document instituting the proceedings having been served on the defendant during his temporary presence in the United Kingdom; or

(b) the presence within the United Kingdom of property belonging to the defendant; or

(c) the seizure by the plaintiff of property situated in the United Kingdom.

Directive 2005/29/EC of the European Parliament and of the Council
of 11 May 2005

concerning unfair business-to-consumer commercial practices in the internal market and amending Council Directive 84/450/EEC, Directives 97/7/EC, 98/27/EC and 2002/65/EC of the European Parliament and of the Council and Regulation (EC) No 2006/2004 of the European Parliament and of the Council ('Unfair Commercial Practices Directive') (Text with EEA relevance)

THE EUROPEAN PARLIAMENT AND THE COUNCIL OF THE EUROPEAN UNION,

Having regard to the Treaty establishing the European Community, and in particular Article 95 thereof,

Having regard to the proposal from the Commission,

Having regard to the Opinion of the European Economic and Social Committee,

Acting in accordance with the procedure laid down in Article 251 of the Treaty, Whereas:

(1) Article 153(1) and (3)(a) of the Treaty provides that the Community is to contribute to the attainment of a high level of consumer protection by the measures it adopts pursuant to Article 95 thereof.

(2) In accordance with Article 14(2) of the Treaty, the internal market comprises an area without internal frontiers in which the free movement of goods and services and freedom of establishment are ensured. The development of fair commercial practices within the area without internal frontiers is vital for the promotion of the development of cross-border activities.

(3) The laws of the Member States relating to unfair commercial practices show marked differences which can generate appreciable distortions of competition and obstacles to the smooth functioning of the internal market. In the field of advertising, Council Directive 84/450/EEC of 10 September 1984 concerning misleading and comparative advertising establishes minimum criteria for harmonising legislation on misleading advertising, but does not prevent the Member States from retaining or adopting measures which provide more extensive protection for consumers. As a result, Member States' provisions on misleading advertising diverge significantly.

(4) These disparities cause uncertainty as to which national rules apply to unfair commercial practices harming consumers' economic interests and create many barriers affecting business and consumers. These barriers increase the cost to business of exercising internal market freedoms, in particular when businesses wish to engage in cross border marketing, advertising campaigns and sales promotions. Such barriers also make consumers uncertain of their rights and undermine their confidence in the internal market.

(5) In the absence of uniform rules at Community level, obstacles to the free movement of services and goods across borders or the freedom of establishment could be justified in the light of the case-law of the Court of Justice of the European Communities as long as they seek to protect recognised public interest objectives and are proportionate to those objectives. In view of the Community's objectives, as set out in the provisions of the Treaty and in secondary Community law relating to freedom of movement, and in accordance with the Commission's policy on commercial communications as indicated in the Communication

from the Commission entitled 'The follow-up to the Green Paper on Commercial Communications in the Internal Market', such obstacles should be eliminated. These obstacles can only be eliminated by establishing uniform rules at Community level which establish a high level of consumer protection and by clarifying certain legal concepts at Community level to the extent necessary for the proper functioning of the internal market and to meet the requirement of legal certainty.

(6) This Directive therefore approximates the laws of the Member States on unfair commercial practices, including unfair advertising, which directly harm consumers' economic interests and thereby indirectly harm the economic interests of legitimate competitors. In line with the principle of proportionality, this Directive protects consumers from the consequences of such unfair commercial practices where they are material but recognises that in some cases the impact on consumers may be negligible. It neither covers nor affects the national laws on unfair commercial practices which harm only competitors' economic interests or which relate to a transaction between traders; taking full account of the principle of subsidiarity, Member States will continue to be able to regulate such practices, in conformity with Community law, if they choose to do so. Nor does this Directive cover or affect the provisions of Directive 84/450/EEC on advertising which misleads business but which is not misleading for consumers and on comparative advertising. Further, this Directive does not affect accepted advertising and marketing practices, such as legitimate product placement, brand differentiation or the offering of incentives which may legitimately affect consumers' perceptions of products and influence their behaviour without impairing the consumer's ability to make an informed decision.

(7) This Directive addresses commercial practices directly related to influencing consumers' transactional decisions in relation to products. It does not address commercial practices carried out primarily for other purposes, including for example commercial communication aimed at investors, such as annual reports and corporate promotional literature. It does not address legal requirements related to taste and decency which vary widely among the Member States. Commercial practices such as, for example, commercial solicitation in the streets, may be undesirable in Member States for cultural reasons. Member States should accordingly be able to continue to ban commercial practices in their territory, in conformity with Community law, for reasons of taste and decency even where such practices do not limit consumers' freedom of choice. Full account should be taken of the context of the individual case concerned in applying this Directive, in particular the general clauses thereof.

(8) This Directive directly protects consumer economic interests from unfair business-to-consumer commercial practices. Thereby, it also indirectly protects legitimate businesses from their competitors who do not play by the rules in this Directive and thus guarantees fair competition in fields coordinated by it. It is understood that there are other commercial practices which, although not harming consumers, may hurt competitors and business customers. The Commission should carefully examine the need for Community action in the field of unfair competition beyond the remit of this Directive and, if necessary, make a legislative proposal to cover these other aspects of unfair competition.

(9) This Directive is without prejudice to individual actions brought by those who have been harmed by an unfair commercial practice. It is also without prejudice to Community and national rules on contract law, on intellectual property rights, on the health and safety aspects of products, on conditions of establishment and authorisation regimes, including those rules which, in conformity with Community law, relate to gambling activities, and to Community competition rules and the national provisions implementing them. The Member States will thus be able to retain or introduce restrictions and prohibitions of commercial practices on grounds of the protection of the health and safety of consumers in their territory wherever the trader is based, for example in relation to alcohol, tobacco or pharmaceuticals. Financial services and immovable property, by reason of their complexity and inherent serious risks, necessitate detailed requirements, including positive obligations on traders. For this reason, in the field of financial services and immovable property, this

Directive is without prejudice to the right of Member States to go beyond its provisions to protect the economic interests of consumers. It is not appropriate to regulate here the certification and indication of the standard of fineness of articles of precious metal.

(10) It is necessary to ensure that the relationship between this Directive and existing Community law is coherent, particularly where detailed provisions on unfair commercial practices apply to specific sectors. This Directive therefore amends Directive 84/450/EEC, Directive 97/7/EC of the European Parliament and of the Council of 20 May 1997 on the protection of consumers in respect of distance contracts, Directive 98/27/EC of the European Parliament and of the Council of 19 May 1998 on injunctions for the protection of consumers' interests and Directive 2002/65/EC of the European Parliament and of the Council of 23 September 2002 concerning the distance marketing of consumer financial services. This Directive accordingly applies only in so far as there are no specific Community law provisions regulating specific aspects of unfair commercial practices, such as information requirements and rules on the way the information is presented to the consumer. It provides protection for consumers where there is no specific sectoral legislation at Community level and prohibits traders from creating a false impression of the nature of products. This is particularly important for complex products with high levels of risk to consumers, such as certain financial services products. This Directive consequently complements the Community acquis, which is applicable to commercial practices harming consumers' economic interests.

(11) The high level of convergence achieved by the approximation of national provisions through this Directive creates a high common level of consumer protection. This Directive establishes a single general prohibition of those unfair commercial practices distorting consumers' economic behaviour. It also sets rules on aggressive commercial practices, which are currently not regulated at Community level.

(12) Harmonisation will considerably increase legal certainty for both consumers and business. Both consumers and business will be able to rely on a single regulatory framework based on clearly defined legal concepts regulating all aspects of unfair commercial practices across the EU. The effect will be to eliminate the barriers stemming from the fragmentation of the rules on unfair commercial practices harming consumer economic interests and to enable the internal market to be achieved in this area.

(13) In order to achieve the Community's objectives through the removal of internal market barriers, it is necessary to replace Member States' existing, divergent general clauses and legal principles. The single, common general prohibition established by this Directive therefore covers unfair commercial practices distorting consumers' economic behaviour. In order to support consumer confidence the general prohibition should apply equally to unfair commercial practices which occur outside any contractual relationship between a trader and a consumer or following the conclusion of a contract and during its execution. The general prohibition is elaborated by rules on the two types of commercial practices which are by far the most common, namely misleading commercial practices and aggressive commercial practices.

(14) It is desirable that misleading commercial practices cover those practices, including misleading advertising, which by deceiving the consumer prevent him from making an informed and thus efficient choice. In conformity with the laws and practices of Member States on misleading advertising, this Directive classifies misleading practices into misleading actions and misleading omissions. In respect of omissions, this Directive sets out a limited number of key items of information which the consumer needs to make an informed transactional decision. Such information will not have to be disclosed in all advertisements, but only where the trader makes an invitation to purchase, which is a concept clearly defined in this Directive. The full harmonisation approach adopted in this Directive does not preclude the Member States from specifying in national law the main characteristics of particular products such as, for example, collectors' items or electrical goods, the omission of which would be material when an invitation to purchase is made. It is not the intention of this Directive to reduce consumer choice by prohibiting the promotion of products which

look similar to other products unless this similarity confuses consumers as to the commercial origin of the product and is therefore misleading. This Directive should be without prejudice to existing Community law which expressly affords Member States the choice between several regulatory options for the protection of consumers in the field of commercial practices. In particular, this Directive should be without prejudice to Article 13(3) of Directive 2002/58/EC of the European Parliament and of the Council of 12 July 2002 concerning the processing of personal data and the protection of privacy in the electronic communications sector.

(15) Where Community law sets out information requirements in relation to commercial communication, advertising and marketing that information is considered as material under this Directive. Member States will be able to retain or add information requirements relating to contract law and having contract law consequences where this is allowed by the minimum clauses in the existing Community law instruments. A non-exhaustive list of such information requirements in the acquis is contained in Annex II. Given the full harmonisation introduced by this Directive only the information required in Community law is considered as material for the purpose of Article 7(5) thereof. Where Member States have introduced information requirements over and above what is specified in Community law, on the basis of minimum clauses, the omission of that extra information will not constitute a misleading omission under this Directive. By contrast Member States will be able, when allowed by the minimum clauses in Community law, to maintain or introduce more stringent provisions in conformity with Community law so as to ensure a higher level of protection of consumers' individual contractual rights.

(16) The provisions on aggressive commercial practices should cover those practices which significantly impair the consumer's freedom of choice. Those are practices using harassment, coercion, including the use of physical force, and undue influence.

(17) It is desirable that those commercial practices which are in all circumstances unfair be identified to provide greater legal certainty. Annex I therefore contains the full list of all such practices. These are the only commercial practices which can be deemed to be unfair without a case-by-case assessment against the provisions of Articles 5 to 9. The list may only be modified by revision of the Directive.

(18) It is appropriate to protect all consumers from unfair commercial practices; however the Court of Justice has found it necessary in adjudicating on advertising cases since the enactment of Directive 84/450/EEC to examine the effect on a notional, typical consumer. In line with the principle of proportionality, and to permit the effective application of the protections contained in it, this Directive takes as a benchmark the average consumer, who is reasonably well-informed and reasonably observant and circumspect, taking into account social, cultural and linguistic factors, as interpreted by the Court of Justice, but also contains provisions aimed at preventing the exploitation of consumers whose characteristics make them particularly vulnerable to unfair commercial practices. Where a commercial practice is specifically aimed at a particular group of consumers, such as children, it is desirable that the impact of the commercial practice be assessed from the perspective of the average member of that group. It is therefore appropriate to include in the list of practices which are in all circumstances unfair a provision which, without imposing an outright ban on advertising directed at children, protects them from direct exhortations to purchase. The average consumer test is not a statistical test. National courts and authorities will have to exercise their own faculty of judgement, having regard to the case-law of the Court of Justice, to determine the typical reaction of the average consumer in a given case.

(19) Where certain characteristics such as age, physical or mental infirmity or credulity make consumers particularly susceptible to a commercial practice or to the underlying product and the economic behaviour only of such consumers is likely to be distorted by the practice in a way that the trader can reasonably foresee, it is appropriate to ensure that they are adequately protected by assessing the practice from the perspective of the average member of that group.

(20) It is appropriate to provide a role for codes of conduct, which enable traders to apply the principles of this Directive effectively in specific economic fields. In sectors where there are specific mandatory requirements regulating the behaviour of traders, it is appropriate that these will also provide evidence as to the requirements of professional diligence in that sector. The control exercised by code owners at national or Community level to eliminate unfair commercial practices may avoid the need for recourse to administrative or judicial action and should therefore be encouraged. With the aim of pursuing a high level of consumer protection, consumers' organisations could be informed and involved in the drafting of codes of conduct.

(21) Persons or organisations regarded under national law as having a legitimate interest in the matter must have legal remedies for initiating proceedings against unfair commercial practices, either before a court or before an administrative authority which is competent to decide upon complaints or to initiate appropriate legal proceedings. While it is for national law to determine the burden of proof, it is appropriate to enable courts and administrative authorities to require traders to produce evidence as to the accuracy of factual claims they have made.

(22) It is necessary that Member States lay down penalties for infringements of the provisions of this Directive and they must ensure that these are enforced. The penalties must be effective, proportionate and dissuasive.

(23) Since the objectives of this Directive, namely to eliminate the barriers to the functioning of the internal market represented by national laws on unfair commercial practices and to provide a high common level of consumer protection, by approximating the laws, regulations and administrative provisions of the Member States on unfair commercial practices, cannot be sufficiently achieved by the Member States and can therefore be better achieved at Community level, the Community may adopt measures, in accordance with the principle of subsidiarity as set out in Article 5 of the Treaty. In accordance with the principle of proportionality, as set out in that Article, this Directive does not go beyond what is necessary in order to eliminate the internal market barriers and achieve a high common level of consumer protection.

(24) It is appropriate to review this Directive to ensure that barriers to the internal market have been addressed and a high level of consumer protection achieved. The review could lead to a Commission proposal to amend this Directive, which may include a limited extension to the derogation in Article 3(5), and/or amendments to other consumer protection legislation reflecting the Commission's Consumer Policy Strategy commitment to review the existing acquis in order to achieve a high, common level of consumer protection.

(25) This Directive respects the fundamental rights and observes the principles recognised in particular by the Charter of Fundamental Rights of the European Union,
HAVE ADOPTED THIS DIRECTIVE:

CHAPTER 1   GENERAL PROVISIONS

Art. 1   Purpose
The purpose of this Directive is to contribute to the proper functioning of the internal market and achieve a high level of consumer protection by approximating the laws, regulations and administrative provisions of the Member States on unfair commercial practices harming consumers' economic interests.

Art. 2   Definitions
For the purposes of this Directive:
> (a) 'consumer' means any natural person who, in commercial practices covered by this Directive, is acting for purposes which are outside his trade, business, craft or profession;

(b) 'trader' means any natural or legal person who, in commercial practices covered by this Directive, is acting for purposes relating to his trade, business, craft or profession and anyone acting in the name of or on behalf of a trader;

(c) 'product' means any goods or service including immovable property, rights and obligations;

(d) 'business-to-consumer commercial practices' (hereinafter also referred to as 'commercial practices') means any act, omission, course of conduct or representation, commercial communication including advertising and marketing, by a trader, directly connected with the promotion, sale or supply of a product to consumers;

(e) 'to materially distort the economic behaviour of consumers' means using a commercial practice to appreciably impair the consumer's ability to make an informed decision, thereby causing the consumer to take a transactional decision that he would not have taken otherwise;

(f) 'code of conduct' means an agreement or set of rules not imposed by law, regulation or administrative provision of a Member State which defines the behaviour of traders who undertake to be bound by the code in relation to one or more particular commercial practices or business sectors;

(g) 'code owner' means any entity, including a trader or group of traders, which is responsible for the formulation and revision of a code of conduct and/or for monitoring compliance with the code by those who have undertaken to be bound by it;

(h) 'professional diligence' means the standard of special skill and care which a trader may reasonably be expected to exercise towards consumers, commensurate with honest market practice and/or the general principle of good faith in the trader's field of activity;

(i) 'invitation to purchase' means a commercial communication which indicates characteristics of the product and the price in a way appropriate to the means of the commercial communication used and thereby enables the consumer to make a purchase;

(j) 'undue influence' means exploiting a position of power in relation to the consumer so as to apply pressure, even without using or threatening to use physical force, in a way which significantly limits the consumer's ability to make an informed decision;

(k) 'transactional decision' means any decision taken by a consumer concerning whether, how and on what terms to purchase, make payment in whole or in part for, retain or dispose of a product or to exercise a contractual right in relation to the product, whether the consumer decides to act or to refrain from acting;

(l) 'regulated profession' means a professional activity or a group of professional activities, access to which or the pursuit of which, or one of the modes of pursuing which, is conditional, directly or indirectly, upon possession of specific professional qualifications, pursuant to laws, regulations or administrative provisions.

Art. 3 Scope

1. This Directive shall apply to unfair business-to-consumer commercial practices, as laid down in Article 5, before, during and after a commercial transaction in relation to a product.

2. This Directive is without prejudice to contract law and, in particular, to the rules on the validity, formation or effect of a contract.

3. This Directive is without prejudice to Community or national rules relating to the health and safety aspects of products.

4. In the case of conflict between the provisions of this Directive and other Community rules regulating specific aspects of unfair commercial practices, the latter shall prevail and apply to those specific aspects.

5. For a period of six years from 12 June 2007, Member States shall be able to continue to apply national provisions within the field approximated by this Directive which are more

restrictive or prescriptive than this Directive and which implement directives containing minimum harmonisation clauses. These measures must be essential to ensure that consumers are adequately protected against unfair commercial practices and must be proportionate to the attainment of this objective. The review referred to in Article 18 may, if considered appropriate, include a proposal to prolong this derogation for a further limited period.

6. Member States shall notify the Commission without delay of any national provisions applied on the basis of paragraph 5.

7. This Directive is without prejudice to the rules determining the jurisdiction of the courts.

8. This Directive is without prejudice to any conditions of establishment or of authorisation regimes, or to the deontological codes of conduct or other specific rules governing regulated professions in order to uphold high standards of integrity on the part of the professional, which Member States may, in conformity with Community law, impose on professionals.

9. In relation to 'financial services', as defined in Directive 2002/65/EC, and immovable property, Member States may impose requirements which are more restrictive or prescriptive than this Directive in the field which it approximates.

10. This Directive shall not apply to the application of the laws, regulations and administrative provisions of Member States relating to the certification and indication of the standard of fineness of articles of precious metal.

Art. 4   Internal market

Member States shall neither restrict the freedom to provide services nor restrict the free movement of goods for reasons falling within the field approximated by this Directive.

CHAPTER 2   UNFAIR COMMERCIAL PRACTICES

Art. 5   Prohibition of unfair commercial practices

1. Unfair commercial practices shall be prohibited.

2. A commercial practice shall be unfair if:
   (a) it is contrary to the requirements of professional diligence, and
   (b) it materially distorts or is likely to materially distort the economic behaviour with regard to the product of the average consumer whom it reaches or to whom it is addressed, or of the average member of the group when a commercial practice is directed to a particular group of consumers.

3. Commercial practices which are likely to materially distort the economic behaviour only of a clearly identifiable group of consumers who are particularly vulnerable to the practice or the underlying product because of their mental or physical infirmity, age or credulity in a way which the trader could reasonably be expected to foresee, shall be assessed from the perspective of the average member of that group. This is without prejudice to the common and legitimate advertising practice of making exaggerated statements or statements which are not meant to be taken literally.

4. In particular, commercial practices shall be unfair which:
   (a) are misleading as set out in Articles 6 and 7, or
   (b) are aggressive as set out in Articles 8 and 9.

5. Annex I contains the list of those commercial practices which shall in all circumstances be regarded as unfair. The same single list shall apply in all Member States and may only be modified by revision of this Directive.

Section 1   Misleading commercial practices

Art. 6   Misleading actions

1. A commercial practice shall be regarded as misleading if it contains false information and is therefore untruthful or in any way, including overall presentation, deceives or is likely

to deceive the average consumer, even if the information is factually correct, in relation to one or more of the following elements, and in either case causes or is likely to cause him to take a transactional decision that he would not have taken otherwise:

(a) the existence or nature of the product;

(b) the main characteristics of the product, such as its availability, benefits, risks, execution, composition, accessories, after-sale customer assistance and complaint handling, method and date of manufacture or provision, delivery, fitness for purpose, usage, quantity, specification, geographical or commercial origin or the results to be expected from its use, or the results and material features of tests or checks carried out on the product;

(c) the extent of the trader's commitments, the motives for the commercial practice and the nature of the sales process, any statement or symbol in relation to direct or indirect sponsorship or approval of the trader or the product;

(d) the price or the manner in which the price is calculated, or the existence of a specific price advantage;

(e) the need for a service, part, replacement or repair;

(f) the nature, attributes and rights of the trader or his agent, such as his identity and assets, his qualifications, status, approval, affiliation or connection and ownership of industrial, commercial or intellectual property rights or his awards and distinctions;

(g) the consumer's rights, including the right to replacement or reimbursement under Directive 1999/44/EC of the European Parliament and of the Council of 25 May 1999 on certain aspects of the sale of consumer goods and associated guarantees, or the risks he may face.

2. A commercial practice shall also be regarded as misleading if, in its factual context, taking account of all its features and circumstances, it causes or is likely to cause the average consumer to take a transactional decision that he would not have taken otherwise, and it involves:

(a) any marketing of a product, including comparative advertising, which creates confusion with any products, trade marks, trade names or other distinguishing marks of a competitor;

(b) non-compliance by the trader with commitments contained in codes of conduct by which the trader has undertaken to be bound, where:

(i) the commitment is not aspirational but is firm and is capable of being verified, and

(ii) the trader indicates in a commercial practice that he is bound by the code.

Art. 7   Misleading omissions

1. A commercial practice shall be regarded as misleading if, in its factual context, taking account of all its features and circumstances and the limitations of the communication medium, it omits material information that the average consumer needs, according to the context, to take an informed transactional decision and thereby causes or is likely to cause the average consumer to take a transactional decision that he would not have taken otherwise.

2. It shall also be regarded as a misleading omission when, taking account of the matters described in paragraph 1, a trader hides or provides in an unclear, unintelligible, ambiguous or untimely manner such material information as referred to in that paragraph or fails to identify the commercial intent of the commercial practice if not already apparent from the context, and where, in either case, this causes or is likely to cause the average consumer to take a transactional decision that he would not have taken otherwise.

3. Where the medium used to communicate the commercial practice imposes limitations of space or time, these limitations and any measures taken by the trader to make the information available to consumers by other means shall be taken into account in deciding whether information has been omitted.

4. In the case of an invitation to purchase, the following information shall be regarded as material, if not already apparent from the context:

    (a) the main characteristics of the product, to an extent appropriate to the medium and the product;

    (b) the geographical address and the identity of the trader, such as his trading name and, where applicable, the geographical address and the identity of the trader on whose behalf he is acting;

    (c) the price inclusive of taxes, or where the nature of the product means that the price cannot reasonably be calculated in advance, the manner in which the price is calculated, as well as, where appropriate, all additional freight, delivery or postal charges or, where these charges cannot reasonably be calculated in advance, the fact that such additional charges may be payable;

    (d) the arrangements for payment, delivery, performance and the complaint handling policy, if they depart from the requirements of professional diligence;

    (e) for products and transactions involving a right of withdrawal or cancellation, the existence of such a right.

5. Information requirements established by Community law in relation to commercial communication including advertising or marketing, a non-exhaustive list of which is contained in Annex II, shall be regarded as material.

Section 2   Aggressive commercial practices

Art. 8   Aggressive commercial practices
A commercial practice shall be regarded as aggressive if, in its factual context, taking account of all its features and circumstances, by harassment, coercion, including the use of physical force, or undue influence, it significantly impairs or is likely to significantly impair the average consumer's freedom of choice or conduct with regard to the product and thereby causes him or is likely to cause him to take a transactional decision that he would not have taken otherwise.

Art. 9   Use of harassment, coercion and undue influence
In determining whether a commercial practice uses harassment, coercion, including the use of physical force, or undue influence, account shall be taken of:

    (a) its timing, location, nature or persistence;

    (b) the use of threatening or abusive language or behaviour;

    (c) the exploitation by the trader of any specific misfortune or circumstance of such gravity as to impair the consumer's judgement, of which the trader is aware, to influence the consumer's decision with regard to the product;

    (d) any onerous or disproportionate non-contractual barriers imposed by the trader where a consumer wishes to exercise rights under the contract, including rights to terminate a contract or to switch to another product or another trader;

    (e) any threat to take any action that cannot legally be taken.

CHAPTER 3   CODES OF CONDUCT

Art. 10   Codes of conduct
This Directive does not exclude the control, which Member States may encourage, of unfair commercial practices by code owners and recourse to such bodies by the persons or organisations referred to in Article 11 if proceedings before such bodies are in addition to the court or administrative proceedings referred to in that Article.

Recourse to such control bodies shall never be deemed the equivalent of foregoing a means of judicial or administrative recourse as provided for in Article 11.

CHAPTER 4   FINAL PROVISIONS

Art. 11   Enforcement

1. Member States shall ensure that adequate and effective means exist to combat unfair commercial practices in order to enforce compliance with the provisions of this Directive in the interest of consumers.

Such means shall include legal provisions under which persons or organisations regarded under national law as having a legitimate interest in combating unfair commercial practices, including competitors, may:

    (a) take legal action against such unfair commercial practices; and/or

    (b) bring such unfair commercial practices before an administrative authority competent either to decide on complaints or to initiate appropriate legal proceedings.

It shall be for each Member State to decide which of these facilities shall be available and whether to enable the courts or administrative authorities to require prior recourse to other established means of dealing with complaints, including those referred to in Article 10. These facilities shall be available regardless of whether the consumers affected are in the territory of the Member State where the trader is located or in another Member State.

It shall be for each Member State to decide:

    (a) whether these legal facilities may be directed separately or jointly against a number of traders from the same economic sector; and

    (b) whether these legal facilities may be directed against a code owner where the relevant code promotes non-compliance with legal requirements.

2. Under the legal provisions referred to in paragraph 1, Member States shall confer upon the courts or administrative authorities powers enabling them, in cases where they deem such measures to be necessary taking into account all the interests involved and in particular the public interest:

    (a) to order the cessation of, or to institute appropriate legal proceedings for an order for the cessation of, unfair commercial practices, or

    (b) if the unfair commercial practice has not yet been carried out but is imminent, to order the prohibition of the practice, or to institute appropriate legal proceedings for an order for the prohibition of the practice,

even without proof of actual loss or damage or of intention or negligence on the part of the trader.

Member States shall also make provision for the measures referred to in the first subparagraph to be taken under an accelerated procedure:

    — either with interim effect, or

    — with definitive effect,

on the understanding that it is for each Member State to decide which of the two options to select.

Furthermore, Member States may confer upon the courts or administrative authorities powers enabling them, with a view to eliminating the continuing effects of unfair commercial practices the cessation of which has been ordered by a final decision:

    (a) to require publication of that decision in full or in part and in such form as they deem adequate,

    (b) to require in addition the publication of a corrective statement.

3. The administrative authorities referred to in paragraph 1 must:

    (a) be composed so as not to cast doubt on their impartiality;

    (b) have adequate powers, where they decide on complaints, to monitor and enforce the observance of their decisions effectively;

    (c) normally give reasons for their decisions.

Where the powers referred to in paragraph 2 are exercised exclusively by an administrative authority, reasons for its decisions shall always be given. Furthermore, in this case, provision must be made for procedures whereby improper or unreasonable exercise of its powers by the administrative authority or improper or unreasonable failure to exercise the said powers can be the subject of judicial review.

Art. 12   Courts and administrative authorities: substantiation of claims
Member States shall confer upon the courts or administrative authorities powers enabling them in the civil or administrative proceedings provided for in Article 11:

    (a) to require the trader to furnish evidence as to the accuracy of factual claims in relation to a commercial practice if, taking into account the legitimate interest of the trader and any other party to the proceedings, such a requirement appears appropriate on the basis of the circumstances of the particular case; and

    (b) to consider factual claims as inaccurate if the evidence demanded in accordance with (a) is not furnished or is deemed insufficient by the court or administrative authority.

Art. 13   Penalties
Member States shall lay down penalties for infringements of national provisions adopted in application of this Directive and shall take all necessary measures to ensure that these are enforced. These penalties must be effective, proportionate and dissuasive.

Art. 17   Information
Member States shall take appropriate measures to inform consumers of the national law transposing this Directive and shall, where appropriate, encourage traders and code owners to inform consumers of their codes of conduct.

Art. 18   Review
    1. By 12 June 2011 the Commission shall submit to the European Parliament and the Council a comprehensive report on the application of this Directive, in particular of Articles 3(9) and 4 and Annex I, on the scope for further harmonisation and simplification of Community law relating to consumer protection, and, having regard to Article 3(5), on any measures that need to be taken at Community level to ensure that appropriate levels of consumer protection are maintained. The report shall be accompanied, if necessary, by a proposal to revise this Directive or other relevant parts of Community law.

    2. The European Parliament and the Council shall endeavour to act, in accordance with the Treaty, within two years of the presentation by the Commission of any proposal submitted under paragraph 1.

Art. 19   Transposition
Member States shall adopt and publish the laws, regulations and administrative provisions necessary to comply with this Directive by 12 June 2007. They shall forthwith inform the Commission thereof and inform the Commission of any subsequent amendments without delay.

    They shall apply those measures by 12 December 2007. When Member States adopt those measures, they shall contain a reference to this Directive or be accompanied by such a reference on the occasion of their official publication. Member States shall determine how such reference is to be made.

Art. 20   Entry into force
This Directive shall enter into force on the day following that of its publication in the Official Journal of the European Union.

ANNEX I

Commercial practices which are in all circumstances considered unfair

Misleading commercial practices

    (1) Claiming to be a signatory to a code of conduct when the trader is not.

(2) Displaying a trust mark, quality mark or equivalent without having obtained the necessary authorisation.

(3) Claiming that a code of conduct has an endorsement from a public or other body which it does not have.

(4) Claiming that a trader (including his commercial practices) or a product has been approved, endorsed or authorised by a public or private body when he/it has not or making such a claim without complying with the terms of the approval, endorsement or authorisation.

(5) Making an invitation to purchase products at a specified price without disclosing the existence of any reasonable grounds the trader may have for believing that he will not be able to offer for supply or to procure another trader to supply, those products or equivalent products at that price for a period that is, and in quantities that are, reasonable having regard to the product, the scale of advertising of the product and the price offered (bait advertising).

(6) Making an invitation to purchase products at a specified price and then:

    (a) refusing to show the advertised item to consumers, or

    (b) refusing to take orders for it or deliver it within a reasonable time, or

    (c) demonstrating a defective sample of it,

with the intention of promoting a different product (bait and switch).

(7) Falsely stating that a product will only be available for a very limited time, or that it will only be available on particular terms for a very limited time, in order to elicit an immediate decision and deprive consumers of sufficient opportunity or time to make an informed choice.

(8) Undertaking to provide after-sales service to consumers with whom the trader has communicated prior to a transaction in a language which is not an official language of the Member State where the trader is located and then making such service available only in another language without clearly disclosing this to the consumer before the consumer is committed to the transaction.

(9) Stating or otherwise creating the impression that a product can legally be sold when it cannot.

(10) Presenting rights given to consumers in law as a distinctive feature of the trader's offer.

(11) Using editorial content in the media to promote a product where a trader has paid for the promotion without making that clear in the content or by images or sounds clearly identifiable by the consumer (advertorial). This is without prejudice to Council Directive 89/552/EEC.

(12) Making a materially inaccurate claim concerning the nature and extent of the risk to the personal security of the consumer or his family if the consumer does not purchase the product.

(13) Promoting a product similar to a product made by a particular manufacturer in such a manner as deliberately to mislead the consumer into believing that the product is made by that same manufacturer when it is not.

(14) Establishing, operating or promoting a pyramid promotional scheme where a consumer gives consideration for the opportunity to receive compensation that is derived primarily from the introduction of other consumers into the scheme rather than from the sale or consumption of products.

(15) Claiming that the trader is about to cease trading or move premises when he is not.

(16) Claiming that products are able to facilitate winning in games of chance.

(17) Falsely claiming that a product is able to cure illnesses, dysfunction or malformations.

(18) Passing on materially inaccurate information on market conditions or on the possibility of finding the product with the intention of inducing the consumer to acquire the product at conditions less favourable than normal market conditions.

(19) Claiming in a commercial practice to offer a competition or prize promotion without awarding the prizes described or a reasonable equivalent.

(20) Describing a product as 'gratis', 'free', 'without charge' or similar if the consumer has to pay anything other than the unavoidable cost of responding to the commercial practice and collecting or paying for delivery of the item.

(21) Including in marketing material an invoice or similar document seeking payment which gives the consumer the impression that he has already ordered the marketed product when he has not.

(22) Falsely claiming or creating the impression that the trader is not acting for purposes relating to his trade, business, craft or profession, or falsely representing oneself as a consumer.

(23) Creating the false impression that after-sales service in relation to a product is available in a Member State other than the one in which the product is sold.

Aggressive commercial practices

(24) Creating the impression that the consumer cannot leave the premises until a contract is formed.

(25) Conducting personal visits to the consumer's home ignoring the consumer's request to leave or not to return except in circumstances and to the extent justified, under national law, to enforce a contractual obligation.

(26) Making persistent and unwanted solicitations by telephone, fax, e-mail or other remote media except in circumstances and to the extent justified under national law to enforce a contractual obligation. This is without prejudice to Article 10 of Directive 97/7/EC and Directives 95/46/EC and 2002/58/EC.

(27) Requiring a consumer who wishes to claim on an insurance policy to produce documents which could not reasonably be considered relevant as to whether the claim was valid, or failing systematically to respond to pertinent correspondence, in order to dissuade a consumer from exercising his contractual rights.

(28) Including in an advertisement a direct exhortation to children to buy advertised products or persuade their parents or other adults to buy advertised products for them. This provision is without prejudice to Article 16 of Directive 89/552/EEC on television broadcasting.

(29) Demanding immediate or deferred payment for or the return or safekeeping of products supplied by the trader, but not solicited by the consumer except where the product is a substitute supplied in conformity with Article 7(3) of Directive 97/7/EC (inertia selling).

(30) Explicitly informing a consumer that if he does not buy the product or service, the trader's job or livelihood will be in jeopardy.

(31) Creating the false impression that the consumer has already won, will win, or will on doing a particular act win, a prize or other equivalent benefit, when in fact either:
— there is no prize or other equivalent benefit, or
— taking any action in relation to claiming the prize or other equivalent benefit is subject to the consumer paying money or incurring a cost.

ANNEX II

Community law provisions setting out rules for advertising and commercial communication

Articles 4 and 5 of Directive 97/7/EC

Article 3 of Council Directive 90/314/EEC of 13 June 1990 on package travel, package holidays and package tours *[[1990] OJ L158/59]*

Article 3(3) of Directive 94/47/EC of the European Parliament and of the Council of 26 October 1994 on the protection of purchasers in respect of certain aspects of contracts relating to the purchase of a right to use immovable properties on a timeshare basis *[[1994] OJ L280/83]*

Article 3(4) of Directive 98/6/EC of the European Parliament and of the Council of 16 February 1998 on consumer protection in the indication of the prices of products offered to consumers *[[2001] OJ L311/67 as last amended by Directive 2004/27/EC [2004] OJ L136/34]*

Articles 86 to 100 of Directive 2001/83/EC of the European Parliament and of the Council of 6 November 2001 on the Community code relating to medicinal products for human use

Articles 5 and 6 of Directive 2000/31/EC of the European Parliament and of the Council of 8 June 2000 on certain legal aspects of information society services, in particular electronic commerce, in the Internal Market ('Directive on electronic commerce') *[[2000] OJ L178/1]*

Article 1(d) of Directive 98/7/EC of the European Parliament and of the Council of 16 February 1998 amending Council Directive 87/102/EEC for the approximation of the laws, regulations and administrative provisions of the Member States concerning consumer credit *[[1998] OJ L101/17]*

Articles 3 and 4 of Directive 2002/65/EC

Article 1(9) of Directive 2001/107/EC of the European Parliament and of the Council of 21 January 2002 amending Council Directive 85/611/EEC on the coordination of laws, regulations and administrative provisions relating to undertakings for collective investment in transferable securities (UCITS) with a view to regulating management companies and simplified prospectuses *[[2002] OJ L41/20]*

Articles 12 and 13 of Directive 2002/92/EC of the European Parliament and of the Council of 9 December 2002 on insurance mediation *[[2003] OJ L9/3]*

Article 36 of Directive 2002/83/EC of the European Parliament and of the Council of 5 November 2002 concerning life assurance *[[2002] OJ L345/1 as amended by Council Directive 2004/66/EC [2004] OJ L168/35]*

Article 19 of Directive 2004/39/EC of the European Parliament and of the Council of 21 April 2004 on markets in financial instruments *[[2004] OJ L145/1]*

Articles 31 and 43 of Council Directive 92/49/EEC of 18 June 1992 on the coordination of laws, regulations and administrative provisions relating to direct insurance other than life assurance (third non-life insurance Directive) *[[1992] OJ L228/1 as amended by Directive 2002/87/EC of the European Parliament and of the Council [2003] OJ L35/1]*

Articles 5, 7 and 8 of Directive 2003/71/EC of the European Parliament and of the Council of 4 November 2003 on the prospectus to be published when securities are offered to the public or admitted to trading *[[2003] OJ L345/64]*.

PART V

International Materials

United Nations Convention on the Carriage of Goods by Sea 1978

Preamble

THE states parties to this convention,
HAVING recognized the desirability of determining by agreement certain rules relating to the carriage of goods by sea,
HAVE decided to conclude a Convention for this purpose and have thereto agreed as follows:

PART I GENERAL PROVISIONS

Article 1 Definitions

In this Convention:

1. 'Carrier' means any person by whom or in whose name a contract of carriage of goods by sea has been concluded with a shipper.

2. 'Actual carrier' means any person to whom the performance of the carriage of the goods, or of part of the carriage, has been entrusted by the carrier, and includes any other person to whom such performance has been entrusted.

3. 'Shipper' means any person by whom or in whose name or on whose behalf a contract of carriage of goods by sea has been concluded with a carrier, or any person by whom or in whose name or on whose behalf the goods are actually delivered to the carrier in relation to the contract of carriage by sea.

4. 'Consignee' means the person entitled to take delivery of the goods.

5. 'Goods' includes live animals; where the goods are consolidated in a container, pallet or similar article of transport or where they are packed, 'goods' includes such article of transport or packaging if supplied by the shipper.

6. 'Contract of carriage by sea' means any contract whereby the carrier undertakes against payment of freight to carry goods by sea from one port to another; however, a contract which involves carriage by sea and also carriage by some other means is deemed to be a contract of carriage by sea for the purposes of this Convention only in so far as it relates to the carriage by sea.

7. 'Bill of lading' means a document which evidences a contract of carriage by sea and the taking over or loading of the goods by the carrier, and by which the carrier undertakes to deliver the goods against surrender of the document. A provision in the document that the goods are to be delivered to the order of a named person, or to order, or to bearer, constitutes such an undertaking.

8. 'Writing' includes, inter alia, telegram and telex.

Article 2 Scope of application

1. The provisions of this Convention are applicable to all contracts of carriage by sea between two different States, if:

   (a) the port of loading as provided for in the contract of carriage by sea is located in a Contracting State, or

(b) the port of discharge as provided for in the contract of carriage by sea is located in a Contracting State, or

(c) one of the optional ports of discharge provided for in the contract of carriage by sea is the actual port of discharge and such port is located in a Contracting State, or

(d) the bill of lading or other document evidencing the contract of carriage by sea is issued in a Contracting State, or

(e) the bill of lading or other document evidencing the contract of carriage by sea provides that the provisions of this Convention or the legislation of any State giving effect to them are to govern the contract.

2. The provisions of this Convention are applicable without regard to the nationality of the ship, the carrier, the actual carrier, the shipper, the consignee or any other interested person.

3. The provisions of this Convention are not applicable to charter-parties. However, where a bill of lading is issued pursuant to a charter-party, the provisions of the Convention apply to such a bill of lading if it governs the relation between the carrier and the holder of the bill of lading, not being the charterer.

4. If a contract provides for future carriage of goods in a series of shipments during an agreed period, the provisions of this Convention apply to each shipment. However, where a shipment is made under a charter-party, the provisions of para 3 of this Article apply.

Article 3   Interpretation of the Convention
In the interpretation and application of the provisions of this Convention regard shall be had to its international character and to the need to promote uniformity.

PART II   LIABILITY OF THE CARRIER

Article 4   Period of responsibility
1. The responsibility of the carrier for the goods under this Convention covers the period during which the carrier is in charge of the goods at the port of loading, during the carriage and at the port of discharge.

2. For the purpose of para 1 of this Article, the carrier is deemed to be in charge of the goods

(a) from the time he has taken over the goods from:
   (i)   the shipper, or a person acting on his behalf; or
   (ii) an authority or other third party to whom: pursuant to law or regulations applicable at the port of loading, the goods must be handed over for shipment;

(b) until the time he has delivered the goods:
   (i)   by handing over the goods to the consignee; or
   (ii) in cases where the consignee does not receive the goods from the carrier, by placing them at the disposal of the consignee in accordance with the contract or with the law or with the usage of the particular trade, applicable at the port of discharge; or
   (iii) by handing over the goods to an authority or other third party to whom, pursuant to law or regulations applicable at the port of discharge, the goods must be handed over.

3. In paras 1 and 2 of this Article, reference to the carrier or to the consignee means, in addition to the carrier or the consignee, the servants or agents, respectively of the carrier or the consignee.

Article 5   Basis of liability
1. The carrier is liable for loss resulting from loss of or damage to the goods, as well as from delay in delivery, if the occurrence which caused the loss, damage or delay took place while the goods were in his charge as defined in art 4, unless the carrier proves that he, his

servants or agents took all measures that could reasonably be required to avoid the occurrence and its consequences.

2. Delay in delivery occurs when the goods have not been delivered at the port of discharge provided for in the contract of carriage by sea within the time expressly agreed upon or, in the absence of such agreement, within the time which it would be reasonable to require of a diligent carrier, having regard to the circumstances of the case.

3. The person entitled to make a claim for the loss of goods may treat the goods as lost if they have not been delivered as required by art 4 within 60 consecutive days following the expiry of the time for delivery according to para 2 of this Article.

4. (a) The carrier is liable
    (i) for loss of or damage to the goods or delay in delivery caused by fire, if the claimant proves that the fire arose from fault or neglect on the part of the carrier, his servants or agents;
    (ii) for such loss, damage or delay in delivery which is proved by the claimant to have resulted from the fault or neglect of the carrier, his servants or agents, in taking all measures that could reasonably be required to put out the fire and avoid or mitigate its consequences.
(b) In case of fire on board the ship affecting the goods, if the claimant or the carrier so desires, a survey in accordance with shipping practices must be held into the cause and circumstances of the fire, and a copy of the surveyor's report shall be made available on demand to the carrier and the claimant.

5. With respect to live animals, the carrier is not liable for loss, damage or delay in delivery resulting from any special risks inherent in that kind of carriage. If the carrier proves that he has complied with any special instructions given to him by the shipper respecting the animals and that, in the circumstances of the case, the loss, damage or delay in delivery could be attributed to such risks, it is presumed that the loss, damage or delay in delivery was so caused, unless there is proof that all or a part of the loss, damage or delay in delivery resulted from fault or neglect on the part of the carrier, his servants or agents.

6. The carrier is not liable, except in general average, where loss, damage or delay in delivery resulted from measures to save life or from reasonable measures to save property at sea.

7. Where fault or neglect on the part of the carrier, his servants or agents combines with another cause to produce loss, damage or delay in delivery the carrier is liable only to the extent that the loss, damage or delay in delivery is attributable to such fault or neglect, provided that the carrier proves the amount of the loss, damage or delay in delivery not attributable thereto.

Article 6 **Limits of liability**

1. (a) The liability of the carrier for loss resulting from loss of or damage to goods according to the provisions of art 5 is limited to an amount equivalent to 835 units of account per package or other shipping unit or 2.5 units of account per kilogramme of gross weight of the goods lost or damaged, whichever is the higher.
(b) The liability of the carrier for delay in delivery according to the provisions of art 5 is limited to an amount equivalent to two and a half times the freight payable for the goods delayed, but not exceeding the total freight payable under the contract of carriage of goods by sea.
(c) In no case shall the aggregate liability of the carrier, under both sub-paras (a) and (b) of this paragraph, exceed the limitation which would be established under sub-para (a) of this paragraph for total loss of the goods with respect to which such liability was incurred.

2. For the purpose of calculating which amount is the higher in accordance with para 1(a) of this Article the following rules apply:
(a) Where a container, pallet or similar article of transport is used to consolidate goods, the package or other shipping units enumerated in the bill of lading, if

issued, or otherwise in any other document evidencing the contract of carriage by sea, as packed in such article of transport are deemed packages or shipping units. Except as aforesaid the goods in such article of transport are deemed one shipping unit.

(b) In cases where the article of transport itself has been lost or damaged, that article of transport, if not owned or otherwise supplied by the carrier, is considered one separate shipping unit.

3. Unit of account means the unit of account mentioned in art 26.

4. By agreement between the carrier and the shipper, limits of liability exceeding those provided for in para 1 may be fixed.

Article 7   **Application to non-contractual claims**

1. The defences and limits of liability provided for in this Convention apply in any action against the carrier in respect of loss or damage to the goods covered by the contract of carriage by sea, as well as of delay in delivery whether the action is founded in contract, in tort or otherwise.

2. If such an action is brought against a servant or agent of the carrier, such servant or agent, if he proves that he acted within the scope of his employment, is entitled to avail himself of the defences and limits of liability which the carrier is entitled to invoke under this Convention.

3. Except as provided in art 8, the aggregate of the amounts recoverable from the carrier and from any persons referred to in para 2 of this Article shall not exceed the limits of liability provided for in this Convention.

Article 8   **Loss of right to limit responsibility**

1. The carrier is not entitled to the benefit of the limitation of liability provided for in art 6 if it is proved that the loss, damage or delay in delivery resulted from an act or omission of the carrier done with the intent to cause such loss, damage or delay, or recklessly and with knowledge that such loss, damage or delay would probably result.

2. Notwithstanding the provisions of para 2 of art 7, a servant or agent of the carrier is not entitled to the benefit of the limitation of liability provided for in art 6 if it is proved that the loss, damage or delay in delivery resulted from an act or omission of such servant or agent, done with the intent to cause such loss, damage or delay, or recklessly and with knowledge that such loss, damage or delay would probably result.

Article 9   **Deck cargo**

1. The carrier is entitled to carry the goods on deck only if such carriage is in accordance with an agreement with the shipper or with the usage of the particular trade or is required by statutory rules or regulations.

2. If the carrier and the shipper have agreed that the goods shall or may be carried on deck, the carrier must insert in the bill of lading or other document evidencing the contract of carriage by sea a statement to that effect. In the absence of such a statement the carrier has the burden of proving that an agreement for carriage on deck has been entered into; however, the carrier is not entitled to invoke such an agreement against a third party, including a consignee, who has acquired the bill of lading in good faith.

3. Where the goods have been carried on deck contrary to the provisions of para 1 of this Article or where the carrier may not under para 2 of this Article invoke an agreement for carriage on deck, the carrier, notwithstanding the provisions of para 1 of art 5, is liable for loss of or damage to the goods, as well as for delay in delivery, resulting solely from the carriage on deck, and the extent of his liability is to be determined in accordance with the provisions of art 6 or art 8 of this Convention as the case may be.

4. Carriage of goods on deck contrary to express agreement for carriage under deck is deemed to be an act or omission of the carrier within the meaning of art 8.

Article 10   Liability of the carrier and actual carrier

1. Where the performance of the carriage or part thereof has been entrusted to an actual carrier, whether or not in pursuance of a liberty under the contract of carriage by sea to do so, the carrier nevertheless remains responsible for the entire carriage according to the provisions of this Convention. The carrier is responsible, in relation to the carriage performed by the actual carrier, for the acts and omissions of the actual carrier and of his servants and agents acting within the scope of their employment.

2. All the provisions of this Convention governing the responsibility of the carrier also apply to the responsibility of the actual carrier for the carriage performed by him. The provisions of paras 2 and 3 of art 7 and of para 2 of art 8 apply if an action is brought against a servant or agent of the actual carrier.

3. Any special agreement under which the carrier assumes obligations not imposed by this Convention or waives rights conferred by this Convention affects the actual carrier only if agreed to by him expressly and in writing. Whether or not the actual carrier has so agreed, the carrier nevertheless remains bound by the obligations or waivers resulting from such special agreement.

4. Where and to the extent that both the carrier and the actual carrier are liable, their liability is joint and several.

5. The aggregate of the amounts recoverable from the carrier, the actual carrier and their servants and agents shall not exceed the limits of liability provided for in this Convention.

6. Nothing in this Article shall prejudice any right of recourse as between the carrier and the actual carrier.

Article 11   Through carriage

1. Notwithstanding the provisions of para 1 of art 10, where a contract of carriage by sea provides explicitly that a specified part of the carriage covered by the said contract is to be performed by a named person other than the carrier, the contract may also provide that the carrier is not liable for loss, damage or delay in delivery caused by an occurrence which takes place while the goods are in the charge of the actual carrier during such part of the carriage. Nevertheless, any stipulation limiting or excluding such liability is without effect if no judicial proceedings can be instituted against the actual carrier in a court competent under paras 1 or 2 of art 21. The burden of proving that any loss, damage or delay in delivery has been caused by such an occurrence rests upon the carrier.

2. The actual carrier is responsible in accordance with the provisions of para 2 of art 10 for loss, damage or delay in delivery caused by an occurrence which takes place while the goods are in his charge.

PART III   LIABILITY OF THE SHIPPER

Article 12   General rule

The shipper is not liable for loss sustained by the carrier or the actual carrier, or for damage sustained by the ship, unless such loss or damage was caused by the fault or neglect of the shipper, his servants or agents. Nor is any servant or agent of the shipper liable for such loss or damage unless the loss or damage was caused by fault or neglect on his part.

Article 13   Special rules on dangerous goods

1. The shipper must mark or label in a suitable manner dangerous goods as dangerous.

2. Where the shipper hands over dangerous goods to the carrier or an actual carrier, as the case may be, the shipper must inform him of the dangerous character of the goods and, if necessary, of the precautions to be taken. If the shipper fails to do so and such carrier or actual carrier does not otherwise have knowledge of their dangerous character:

    (a) the shipper is liable to the carrier and any actual carrier for the loss resulting from the shipment of such goods, and

(b) the goods may at any time be unloaded, destroyed or rendered innocuous, as the circumstances may require, without payment of compensation.

3. The provisions of para 2 of this Article may not be invoked by any person if during the carriage he has taken the goods in his charge with knowledge of their dangerous character.

4. If, in cases where the provisions of para 2, sub-para (b), of this Article do not apply or may not be invoked, dangerous goods become an actual danger to life or property, they may be unloaded, destroyed or rendered innocuous, as the circumstances may require, without payment of compensation except where there is an obligation to contribute in general average or where the carrier is liable in accordance with the provisions of art 5.

PART IV   TRANSPORT DOCUMENTS

Article 14   Issue of bill of lading

1. When the carrier or the actual carrier takes the goods in his charge the carrier must, on demand of the shipper, issue to the shipper a bill of lading.

2. The bill of lading may be signed by a person having authority from the carrier. A bill of lading signed by the master of the ship carrying the goods is deemed to have been signed on behalf of the carrier.

3. The signature on the bill of lading may be in handwriting, printed in facsimile, perforated, stamped, in symbols, or made by any other mechanical or electronic means, if not inconsistent with the law of the country where the bill of lading is issued.

Article 15   Contents of bill of lading

1. The bill of lading must include, inter alia, the following particulars:
   - (a) the general nature of the goods, the leading marks necessary for identification of the goods, an express statement, if applicable, as to the dangerous character of the goods, the number of packages or pieces, and the weight of the goods or their quantity otherwise expressed, all such particulars as furnished by the shipper;
   - (b) the apparent condition of the goods;
   - (c) the name and principal place of business of the carrier;
   - (d) the name of the shipper;
   - (e) the consignee if named by the shipper;
   - (f) the port of loading under the contract of carriage by sea and the date on which the goods were taken over by the carrier at the port of loading;
   - (g) the port of discharge under the contract of carriage by sea;
   - (h) the number of originals of the bill of lading, if more than one;
   - (i) the place of issuance of the bill of lading;
   - (j) the signature of the carrier or a person acting on his behalf;
   - (k) the freight to the extent payable by the consignee or other indication that freight is payable by him;
   - (l) the statement referred to in para 3 of art 23;
   - (m) the statement, if applicable, that the goods shall or may be carried on deck;
   - (n) the date or the period of delivery of the goods at the port of discharge if expressly agreed upon between the parties; and
   - (o) any increased limit or limits of liability where agreed in accordance with para 4 of art 6.

2. After the goods have been loaded on board, if the shipper so demands, the carrier must issue to the shipper a 'shipped' bill of lading which, in addition to the particulars required under para 1 of this Article, must state that the goods are on board a named ship or ships, and the date or dates of loading. If the carrier has previously issued to the shipper a bill of lading or other document of title with respect to any of such goods, on request of the carrier, the shipper must surrender such document in exchange for a 'shipped' bill of lading. The carrier may amend any previously issued document in order to meet the shipper's demand for a

'shipped' bill of lading if, as amended, such document includes all the information required to be contained in a 'shipped' bill of lading.

3. The absence in the bill of lading of one or more particulars referred to in this Article does not affect the legal character of the document as a bill of lading provided that it nevertheless meets the requirements set out in para 7 of art 1.

Article 16   Bills of lading: reservations and evidentiary effect

1. If the bill of lading contains particulars concerning the general nature, leading marks, number of packages or pieces, weight or quantity of the goods which the carrier or other person issuing the bill of lading on his behalf knows or has reasonable grounds to suspect do not accurately represent the goods actually taken over or, where a 'shipped' bill of lading is issued, loaded, or if he had no reasonable means of checking such particulars, the carrier or such other person must insert in the bill of lading a reservation specifying these inaccuracies, grounds of suspicion or the absence of reasonable means of checking.

2. If the carrier or other person issuing the bill of lading on his behalf fails to note on the bill of lading the apparent condition of the goods, he is deemed to have noted on the bill of lading that the goods were in apparent good condition.

3. Except for particulars in respect of which and to the extent to which a reservation permitted under para 1 of this Article has been entered:
  (a) the bill of lading is prima facie evidence of the taking over or, where a 'shipped' bill of lading is issued, loading, by the carrier of the goods as described in the bill of lading; and
  (b) proof to the contrary by the carrier is not admissible if the bill of lading has been transferred to a third party, including a consignee, who in good faith has acted in reliance on the description of the goods therein.

4. A bill of lading which does not, as provided in para 1, sub-para (k) of art 15, set forth the freight or otherwise indicate that freight is payable by the consignee or does not set forth demurrage incurred at the port of loading payable by the consignee, is prima facie evidence that no freight or such demurrage is payable by him. However, proof to the contrary by the carrier is not admissible when the bill of lading has been transferred to a third party, including a consignee, who in good faith has acted in reliance on the absence in the bill of lading of any such indication.

Article 17   Guarantees by the shipper

1. The shipper is deemed to have guaranteed to the carrier the accuracy of particulars relating to the general nature of the goods, their marks, number, weight and quantity as furnished by him for insertion in the bill of lading. The shipper must indemnify the carrier against the loss resulting from inaccuracies in such particulars. The shipper remains liable even if the bill of lading has been transferred by him. The right of the carrier to such indemnity in no way limits his liability under the contract of carriage by sea to any person other than the shipper.

2. Any letter of guarantee or agreement by which the shipper undertakes to indemnify the carrier against loss resulting from the issuance of the bill of lading by the carrier, or by a person acting on his behalf, without entering a reservation relating to particulars furnished by the shipper for insertion in the bill of lading, or to the apparent condition of the goods, is void and of no effect as against any third party, including a consignee, to whom the bill of lading has been transferred.

3. Such letter of guarantee or agreement is valid as against the shipper unless the carrier or the person acting on his behalf, by omitting the reservation referred to in para 2 of this Article, intends to defraud a third party, including a consignee, who acts in reliance on the description of the goods in the bill of lading. In the latter case, if the reservation omitted relates to particulars furnished by the shipper for insertion in the bill of lading, the carrier has no right of indemnity from the shipper pursuant to para 1 of this Article.

4. In the case of intended fraud referred to in para 3 of this Article the carrier is liable, without the benefit of the limitation of liability provided for in this Convention, for the loss incurred by a third party, including a consignee, because he has acted in reliance on the description of the goods in the bill of lading.

Article 18   Documents other than bills of lading

Where a carrier issues a document other than a bill of lading to evidence the receipt of the goods to be carried, such a document is prima facie evidence of the conclusion of the contract of carriage by sea and the taking over by the carrier of the goods as therein described.

PART V   CLAIMS AND ACTIONS

Article 19   Notice of loss, damage or delay

1. Unless notice of loss or damage, specifying the general nature of such loss or damage, is given in writing by the consignee to the carrier not later than the working day after the day when the goods were handed over to the consignee, such handing over is prima facie evidence of the delivery by the carrier of the goods as described in the document of transport or, if no such document has been issued, in good condition.

2. Where the loss or damage is not apparent, the provisions of para 1 of this Article apply correspondingly if notice in writing is not given within 15 consecutive days after the day when the goods were handed over to the consignee.

3. If the state of the goods at the time they were handed over to the consignee has been the subject of a joint survey or inspection by the parties, notice in writing need not be given of loss or damage ascertained during such survey or inspection.

4. In the case of any actual or apprehended loss or damage the carrier and the consignee must give all reasonable facilities to each other for inspecting and tallying the goods.

5. No compensation shall be payable for loss resulting from delay in delivery unless a notice has been given in writing to the carrier within 60 consecutive days after the day when the goods were handed over to the consignee.

6. If the goods have been delivered by an actual carrier, any notice given under this Article to him shall have the same effect as if it had been given to the carrier, and any notice given to the carrier shall have effect as if given to such actual carrier.

7. Unless notice of loss or damage, specifying the general nature of the loss or damage, is given in writing by the carrier or actual carrier to the shipper not later than 90 consecutive days after the occurrence of such loss or damage or after the delivery of the goods in accordance with para 2 of art 4, whichever is later, the failure to give such notice is prima facie evidence that the carrier or the actual carrier has sustained no loss or damage due to the fault or neglect of the shipper, his servants or agents.

8. For the purpose of this Article, notice given to a person acting on the carrier's or the actual carrier's behalf, including the master or the officer in charge of the ship, or to a person acting on the shipper's behalf is deemed to have been given to the carrier, to the actual carrier or to the shipper, respectively.

Article 20   Limitation of actions

1. Any action relating to carriage of goods under this Convention is time-barred if judicial or arbitral proceedings have not been instituted within a period of two years.

2. The limitation period commences on the day on which the carrier has delivered the goods or part thereof or, in cases where no goods have been delivered, on the last day on which the goods should have been delivered.

3. The day on which the limitation period commences is not included in the period.

4. The person against whom a claim is made may at any time during the running of the limitation period extend that period by a declaration in writing to the claimant. This period may be further extended by another declaration or declarations.

5. An action for indemnity by a person held liable may be instituted even after the expiration of the limitation period provided for in the preceding paragraphs if instituted within the time allowed by the law of the State where proceedings are instituted. However, the time allowed shall not be less than 90 days commencing from the day when the person instituting such action for indemnity has settled the claim or has been served with process in the action against himself.

Article 21 Jurisdiction

1. In judicial proceedings relating to carriage of goods under this Convention the plaintiff, at his option, may institute an action in a court which, according to the law of the State where the court is situated, is competent and within the jurisdiction of which is situated one of the following places:

  (a) the principal place of business or, in the absence thereof, the habitual residence of the defendant; or

  (b) the place where the contract was made provided that the defendant has there a place of business, branch or agency through which the contract was made; or

  (c) the port of loading or the port of discharge; or

  (d) any additional place designated for that purpose in the contract of carriage by sea.

2. (a) Notwithstanding the preceding provisions of this Article, an action may be instituted in the courts of any port or place in a Contracting State at which the carrying vessel or any other vessel of the same ownership may have been arrested in accordance with applicable rules of the law of that State and of international law. However, in such a case, at the petition of the defendant, the claimant must remove the action, at his choice, to one of the jurisdictions referred to in para 1 of this Article for the determination of the claim, but before such removal the defendant must furnish security sufficient to ensure payment of any judgment that may subsequently be awarded to the claimant in the action.

  (b) All questions relating to the sufficiency or otherwise of the security shall be determined by the court of the port or place of the arrest.

3. No judicial proceedings relating to carriage of goods under this Convention may be instituted in a place not specified in paras 1 or 2 of this Article. The provision of this paragraph do not constitute an obstacle to the jurisdiction of the Contracting States for provisional or protective measures.

4. (a) Where an action has been instituted in a court competent under paras 1 or 2 of this Article or where judgment has been delivered by such a court, no new action may be started between the same parties on the same grounds unless the judgment of the court before which the first action was instituted is not enforceable in the country in which the new proceedings are instituted:

  (b) for the purpose of this Article the institution of measures with a view to obtaining enforcement of a judgment is not to be considered as the starting of a new action;

  (c) for the purpose of this Article, the removal of an action to a different court within the same country, or to a court in another country, in accordance with para 2(a) of this Article, is not to be considered as the starting of a new action.

5. Notwithstanding the provisions of the preceding paragraphs, an agreement made by the parties, after a claim under the contact of carriage by sea has arisen, which designates the place where the claimant may institute an action, is effective.

Article 22 Arbitration

1. Subject to the provisions of this Article, parties may provide by agreement evidenced in writing that any dispute that may arise relating to carriage of goods under this Convention shall be referred to arbitration.

2. Where a charter-party contains a provision that disputes arising thereunder shall be referred to arbitration and a bill of lading issued pursuant to the charter-party does not contain a special annotation providing that such provision shall be binding upon the holder

of the bill of lading, the carrier may not invoke such provision as against a holder having acquired the bill of lading in good faith.

3. The arbitration proceedings shall at the option of the claimant, be instituted at one of the following places:

    (a) a place in a State within whose territory is situated:

        (i) the principal place of business of the defendant or, in the absence thereof, the habitual residence of the defendant; or

        (ii) the place where the contract was made, provided that the defendant has there a place of business, branch or agency through which the contract was made; or

        (iii) the port of loading or the port of discharge; or

    (b) any place designated for that purpose in the arbitration clause or agreement.

4. The arbitrator or arbitration tribunal shall apply the rules of this Convention.

5. The provisions of paras 3 and 4 of this Article are deemed to be part of every arbitration clause or agreement, and any term of such clause or agreement which is inconsistent therewith is null and void.

6. Nothing in this Article affects the validity of an agreement relating to arbitration made by the parties after the claim under the contract of carriage by sea has arisen.

PART VI   SUPPLEMENTARY PROVISIONS

Article 23   Contractual stipulations

1. Any stipulation in a contract of carriage by sea, in a bill of lading, or in any other document evidencing the contract of carriage by sea is null and void to the extent that it derogates, directly or indirectly, from the provisions of this Convention. The nullity of such a stipulation does not affect the validity of the other provisions of the contract or document of which it forms a part. A clause assigning benefit of insurance of the goods in favour of the carrier, or any similar clause, is null and void.

2. Notwithstanding the provisions of para 1 of this Article, a carrier may increase his responsibilities and obligation under this Convention.

3. Where a bill of lading or any other document evidencing the contract of carriage by sea is issued, it must contain a statement that the carriage is subject to the provisions of this Convention which nullify any stipulation derogating therefrom to the detriment of the shipper or the consignee.

4. Where the claimant in respect of the goods has incurred loss as a result of a stipulation which is null and void by virtue of the present Article, or as a result of the omission of the statement referred to in para 3 of this Article, the carrier must pay compensation to the extent required in order to give the claimant compensation in accordance with the provisions of this Convention for any loss of or damage to the goods as well as for delay in delivery. The carrier must, in addition, pay compensation for costs incurred by the claimant for the purpose of exercising his right, provided that costs incurred in the action where the foregoing provision is invoked are to be determined in accordance with the law of the State where proceedings are instituted.

Article 24   General average

1. Nothing in this Convention shall prevent the application of provisions in the contract of carriage by sea or national law regarding the adjustment of general average.

2. With the exception of art 20, the provisions of this Convention relating to the liability of the carrier for loss of or damage to the goods also determine whether the consignee may refuse contribution in general average and the liability of the carrier to indemnify the consignee in respect of any such contribution made or any salvage paid.

Article 25   Other conventions

1. This Convention does not modify the rights or duties of the carrier, the actual carrier and their servants and agents, provided for in international conventions or national law relating to the limitation of liability of owners of seagoing ships.

2. The provisions of arts 21 and 22 of this Convention do not prevent the application of the mandatory provisions of any other multi-lateral convention already in force at the date of this Convention relating to matters dealt within the said Articles, provided that the dispute arises exclusively between parties having their principal place of business in States members of such other convention. However, this paragraph does not affect the application of para 4 of art 22 of this Convention.

3. No liability shall arise under the provisions of this Convention for damage caused by a nuclear incident if the operator of a nuclear installation is liable for such damage:

   (a) under either the Paris Convention of 29 July 1960, on Third Party Liability in the Field of Nuclear Energy as amended by the Additional Protocol of 28 January 1964, or the Vienna Convention of 21 May 1963, on Civil Liability for Nuclear Damage, or

   (b) by virtue of national law governing the liability for such damage, provided that such law is in all respects as favourable to persons who may suffer damage as either the Paris or Vienna Conventions.

4. No liability shall arise under the provisions of this Convention for any loss of or damage to or delay in delivery of luggage for which the carrier is responsible under any international convention or national law relating to the carriage of passengers and their luggage by sea.

5. Nothing contained in this Convention prevents a Contracting State from applying any other international convention which is already in force at the date of this Convention and which applies mandatorily to contracts of carriage of goods primarily by a mode of transport other than transport by sea. This provision also applies to any subsequent revision or amendment of such international convention.

Article 26   Unit of account

1. The unit of account referred to in art 6 of this Convention is the Special Drawing Right as defined by the International Monetary Fund. The amounts mentioned in art 6 are to be converted into the national currency of a State according to the value of such currency at the date of judgment or the date agreed upon by the parties. The value of a national currency, in terms of the Special Drawing Right, of a Contracting State which is a member of the International Monetary Fund is to be calculated in accordance with the method of valuation applied by the International Monetary Fund in effect at the date in question for its operations and transactions. The value of a national currency in terms of the Special Drawing Right of a Contracting State which is not a member of the International Monetary Fund is to be calculated in a manner determined by that State.

2. Nevertheless, those States which are not members of the International Monetary Fund and whose law does not permit the application of the provisions of para 1 of this Article may, at the time of signature, or at the time of ratification, acceptance, approval or accession or at any time thereafter, declare that the limits of liability provided for in this Convention to be applied in their territories shall be fixed as: 12,500 monetary units per package or other shipping unit or 37.5 monetary units per kilogramme of gross weight of the goods.

3. The monetary unit referred to in para 2 of this Article corresponds to sixty-five and a half milligrammes of gold of millesimal fineness nine hundred. The conversion of the amounts referred to in para 2 into the national currency is to be made according to the law of the State concerned.

4. The calculation mentioned in the last sentence of para 1 and the conversion mentioned in para 3 of this Article is to be made in such a manner as to express in the national currency of the Contracting State as far as possible the same real value for the amounts in art

6 as is expressed there in units of account. Contracting States must communicate to the depositary the manner of calculation pursuant to para 1 of this Article, or the result of the conversion mentioned in para 3 of this Article, as the case may be, at the time of signature or when depositing their instruments of ratification, acceptance, approval or accession, or when availing themselves of the option provided for in para 2 of this Article and whenever there is a change in the manner of such calculation or in the result of such conversion.

PART VII   FINAL CLAUSES

Article 27   Depositary

. . .

Article 28   Signature, ratification, acceptance, approval, accession

. . .

Article 29   Reservations

No reservations may be made to this Convention.

Article 30   Entry into force

1. This Convention enters into force on the first day of the month following the expiration of one year from the date of deposit of the 20th instrument of ratification, acceptance, approval or accession.

2. For each State which becomes a Contracting State to this Convention after the date of the deposit of the 20th instrument of ratification, acceptance, approval or accession, this Convention enters into force on the first day of the month following the expiration of one year after the deposit of the appropriate instrument on behalf of that State.

3. Each Contracting State shall apply the provisions of this Convention to contracts of carriage by sea concluded on or after the date of the entry into force of this Convention in respect of that State.

Article 31   Denunciation of other conventions

1. Upon becoming a Contracting State to this Convention, any State party to the International Convention for the Unification of Certain Rules relating to Bills of Lading signed at Brussels on 25 August 1924 (1924 Convention) must notify the Government of Belgium as the depositary of the 1924 Convention of its denunciation of the said Convention with a declaration that the denunciation is to take effect as from the date when this Convention enters into force in respect of that State.

2. Upon the entry into force of this Convention under para 1 of art 30, the depositary of this Convention must notify the Government of Belgium as the depositary of the 1924 Convention of the date of such entry into force, and of the names of the Contracting States in respect of which the Convention has entered into force.

3. The provisions of paras 1 and 2 of this Article apply correspondingly in respect of States parties to the Protocol signed on 23 February 1968, to amend the International Convention for the Unification of Certain Rules relating to Bills of Lading signed at Brussels on 25 August 1924.

4. Notwithstanding art 2 of this Convention, for the purposes of para 1 of this Article, a Contracting State may, if it deems it desirable, defer the denunciation of the 1924 Convention and of the 1924 Convention as modified by the 1968 Protocol for a maximum period of five years from the entry into force of this Convention. It will then notify the Government of Belgium of its intention. During this transitory period, it must apply to the Contracting States this Convention to the exclusion of any other one.

Article 32   Revision and amendment

. . .

Article 33   **Revision of the limitation amounts and unit of account of monetary unit**

1. Notwithstanding the provisions of art 32, a conference only for the purpose of altering the amount specified in art 6 and para 2 of art 26, or of substituting either or both of the units defined in paras 1 and 3 of art 26 by other units is to be convened by the depositary in accordance with para 2 of this Article. An alteration of the amounts shall be made only because of a significant change in their real value.

2. A revision conference is to be convened by the depositary when not less than one-fourth of the Contracting States so request.

3. Any decision by the conference must be taken by a two-thirds majority of the participating States. The amendment is communicated by the depositary to all the Contracting States for acceptance and to all the States signatories of the Convention for information.

4. Any amendment adopted enters into force on the first day of the month following one year after its acceptance by two-thirds of the Contracting States. Acceptance is to be effected by the deposit of a formal instrument to that effect, with the depositary.

5. After entry into force of an amendment a Contracting State which has accepted the amendment is entitled to apply the Convention as amended in its relations with Contracting States which have not within six months after the adoption of the amendment notified the depositary that they are not bound by the amendment.

6. Any instrument of ratification, acceptance, approval or accession deposited after the entry into force of an amendment to this Convention, is deemed to apply to the Convention as amended.

Article 34   Denunciation

. . .

Done at Hamburg, this thirty-first day of March one thousand nine hundred and seventy-eight, in a single original, of which the Arabic, Chinese, English, French, Russian and Spanish texts are equally authentic . . .

COMMON UNDERSTANDING ADOPTED BY THE UNITED NATIONS CONFERENCE ON THE CARRIAGE OF GOODS BY SEA

It is the common understanding that the liability of the carrier under this Convention is based on the principle of presumed fault or neglect. This means that as a rule, the burden of proof rests on the carrier but, with respect to certain cases, the provisions of the Convention modify this rule.

United Nations Convention on Contracts for the International Sale of Goods 1980

THE STATES PARTIES TO THIS CONVENTION,

BEARING IN MIND the broad objectives in the resolutions adopted by the sixth special session of the General Assembly of the United Nations on the establishment of a New International Economic Order,

CONSIDERING that the development of international trade on the basis of equality and mutual benefit is an important element in promoting friendly relations among States,

BEING OF THE OPINION that the adoption of uniform rules which govern contracts for the international sale of goods and take into account the different social, economic and legal systems would contribute to the removal of legal barriers in international trade and promote the development of international trade,

HAVE AGREED as follows:

PART I   SPHERE OF APPLICATION AND GENERAL PROVISIONS

CHAPTER I   SPHERE OF APPLICATION

Article 1

1. This Convention applies to contracts of sale of goods between parties whose places of business are in different States:
   (a) when the States are Contracting States; or
   (b) when the rules of private international law lead to the application of the law of a Contracting State.

2. The fact that the parties have their places of business in different States is to be disregarded whenever this fact does not appear either from the contract or from any dealings between, or from information disclosed by, the parties at any time before or at the conclusion of the contract.

3. Neither the nationality of the parties nor the civil or commercial character of the parties or of the contract is to be taken into consideration in determining the application of this Convention.

Article 2

This Convention does not apply to sales:
   (a) of goods bought for personal, family or household use unless the seller, at any time before or at the conclusion of the contract, neither knew nor ought to have known that the goods were bought for any such use;
   (b) by auction;
   (c) on execution or otherwise by authority of law;
   (d) of stocks, shares, investment securities, negotiable instruments or money;
   (e) of ships, vessels, hovercraft or aircraft;
   (f) of electricity.

Article 3

1. Contracts for the supply of goods to be manufactured or produced are to be considered sales unless the party who orders the goods undertakes to supply a substantial part of the materials necessary for such manufacture or production.

2. This Convention does not apply to contracts in which the preponderant part of the obligations of the party who furnishes the goods consists in the supply of labour or other services.

Article 4

This Convention governs only the formation of the contract of sale and the rights and obligations of the seller and the buyer arising from such a contract. In particular, except as otherwise expressly provided in this Convention, it is not concerned with:
   (a) the validity of the contract or of any of its provisions or of any usage;
   (b) the effect which the contract may have on the property in the goods sold.

Article 5

This Convention does not apply to the liability of the seller for death or personal injury caused by the goods to any person.

Article 6

The parties may exclude the application of this Convention or, subject to article 12, derogate from or vary the effect of any of its provisions.

CHAPTER II   GENERAL PROVISIONS

Article 7

1. In the interpretation of this Convention, regard is to be had to its international character and to the need to promote uniformity in its application and the observance of good faith in international trade.

2. Questions concerning matters governed by this Convention which are not expressly settled in it are to be settled in conformity with the general principles on which it is based or, in the absence of such principles, in conformity with the law applicable by virtue of the rules of private international law.

Article 8

1. For the purposes of this Convention statements made by and other conduct of a party are to be interpreted according to his intent where the other party knew or could not have been unaware what that intent was.

2. If the preceding paragraph is not applicable, statements made by and other conduct of a party are to be interpreted according to the understanding that a reasonable person of the same kind as the other party would have had in the same circumstances.

3. In determining the intent of a party or the understanding a reasonable person would have had, due consideration is to be given to all relevant circumstances of the case including the negotiations, any practices which the parties have established between themselves, usages and any subsequent conduct of the parties.

Article 9

1. The parties are bound by any usage to which they have agreed and by any practices which they have established between themselves.

2. The parties are considered, unless otherwise agreed, to have impliedly made applicable to their contract or its formation a usage of which the parties knew or ought to have known and which in international trade is widely known to, and regularly observed by, parties to contracts of the type involved in the particular trade concerned.

Article 10

For the purposes of this Convention:
  (a) if a party has more than one place of business, the place of business is that which has the closest relationship to the contract and its performance, having regard to the circumstances known to or contemplated by the parties at any time before or at the conclusion of the contract;
  (b) if a party does not have a place of business, reference is to be made to his habitual residence.

Article 11

A contract of sale need not be concluded in or evidenced by writing and is not subject to any other requirement as to form. It may be proved by any means, including witnesses.

Article 12

Any provision of article 11, article 29 or Part II of this Convention that allows a contract of sale or its modification or termination by agreement or any offer, acceptance or other indication of intention to be made in any form other than in writing does not apply where any party has his place of business in a Contracting State which has made a declaration under article 96 of this Convention. The parties may not derogate from or vary the effect of this article.

Article 13

For the purposes of this Convention 'writing' includes telegram and telex.

PART II   FORMATION OF THE CONTRACT

Article 14

1. A proposal for concluding a contract addressed to one or more specific persons constitutes an offer if it is sufficiently definite and indicates the intention of the offeror to be bound in case of acceptance. A proposal is sufficiently definite if it indicates the goods and expressly or implicitly fixes or makes provision for determining the quantity and the price.

2. A proposal other than one addressed to one or more specific persons is to be considered merely as an invitation to make offers, unless the contrary is clearly indicated by the person making the proposal.

Article 15

1. An offer becomes effective when it reaches the offeree.

2. An offer, even if it is irrevocable, may be withdrawn if the withdrawal reaches the offeree before or at the same time as the offer.

Article 16

1. Until a contract is concluded an offer may be revoked if the revocation reaches the offeree before he has dispatched an acceptance.

2. However, an offer cannot be revoked:
   (a) if it indicates, whether by stating a fixed time for acceptance or otherwise, that it is irrevocable; or
   (b) if it was reasonable for the offeree to rely on the offer as being irrevocable and the offeree has acted in reliance on the offer.

Article 17

An offer, even if it is irrevocable, is terminated when a rejection reaches the offeror.

Article 18

1. A statement made by or other conduct of the offeree indicating assent to an offer is an acceptance. Silence or inactivity does not itself amount to acceptance.

2. An acceptance of an offer becomes effective at the moment the indication of assent reaches the offeror. An acceptance is not effective if the indication of assent does not reach the offeror within the time he has fixed or, if no time is fixed, within a reasonable time, due account being taken of the circumstances of the transaction, including the rapidity of the means of communication employed by the offeror. An oral offer must be accepted immediately unless the circumstances indicate otherwise.

3. However, if, by virtue of the offer or as a result of practices which the parties have established between themselves or of usage, the offeree may indicate assent by performing an act, such as one relating to the dispatch of the goods or payment of the price, without notice to the offeror, the acceptance is effective at the moment the act is performed, provided that the act is performed within the period of time laid down in the preceding paragraph.

Article 19

1. A reply to an offer which purports to be an acceptance but contains additions, limitations or other modifications is a rejection of the offer and constitutes a counter-offer.

2. However, a reply to an offer which purports to be an acceptance but contains additional or different terms which do not materially alter the terms of the offer constitutes an acceptance, unless the offeror, without undue delay, objects orally to the discrepancy or dispatches a notice to the effect. If he does not so object, the terms of the contract are the terms of the offer with the modifications contained in the acceptance.

3. Additional or different terms relating, among other things, to the price, payment, quality and quantity of the goods, place and time of delivery, extent of one party's liability to the other or the settlement of disputes are considered to alter the terms of the offer materially.

Article 20

1. A period of time for acceptance fixed by the offeror in a telegram or a letter begins to run from the moment the telegram is handed in for dispatch or from the date shown on the letter or, if no such date is shown on the letter or, if no such date is shown, from the date shown on the envelope. A period of time for acceptance fixed by the offeror by telephone, telex or other means of instantaneous communication, begins to run from the moment that the offer reaches the offeree.

2. Official holidays or non-business days occurring during the period for acceptance are included in calculating the period. However, if a notice of acceptance cannot be delivered at the address of the offeror on the last day of the period because that day falls on an official holiday or a non-business day at the place of business of the offeror, the period is extended until the first business day which follows.

Article 21

1. A late acceptance is nevertheless effective as an acceptance if without delay the offeror orally so informs the offeree or dispatches a notice to that effect.

2. If a letter or other writing containing a late acceptance shows that it has been sent in such circumstances that if its transmission had been normal it would have reached the offeror in due time, the late acceptance is effective as an acceptance unless, without delay, the offeror orally informs the offeree that he considers his offer as having lapsed or dispatches a notice to that effect.

Article 22

An acceptance may be withdrawn if the withdrawal reaches the offeror before or at the same time as the acceptance would have become effective.

Article 23

A contract is concluded at the moment when an acceptance of an offer becomes effective in accordance with the provisions of this Convention.

Article 24

For the purposes of this Part of the Convention, an offer, declaration of acceptance or any other indication of intention 'reaches' the addressee when it is made orally to him or delivered by any other means to him personally, to his place of business or mailing address or, if he does not have a place of business or mailing address, to his habitual residence.

PART III   SALE OF GOODS

CHAPTER I   GENERAL PROVISIONS

Article 25

A breach of contract committed by one of the parties is fundamental if it results in such detriment to the other party as substantially to deprive him of what he is entitled to expect under the contract, unless the party in breach did not foresee and a reasonable person of the same kind in the same circumstances would not have foreseen such a result.

Article 26

A declaration of avoidance of the contract is effective only if made by notice to the other party.

Article 27

Unless otherwise expressly provided in this Part of the Convention, if any notice, request or other communication is given or made by a party in accordance with this Part and by means appropriate in the circumstances, a delay or error in the transmission of the communication or its failure to arrive does not deprive that party of the right to rely on the communication.

Article 28

If, in accordance with the provisions of this Convention, one party is entitled to require performance of any obligation by the other party, a court is not bound to enter a judgment for specific performance unless the court would do so under its own law in respect of similar contracts of sale not governed by this Convention.

Article 29

1. A contract may be modified or terminated by the mere agreement of the parties.

2. A contract in writing which contains a provision requiring any modification or termination by agreement to be in writing may not be otherwise modified or terminated by agreement. However, a party may be precluded by his conduct from asserting such a provision to the extent that the other party has relied on that conduct.

CHAPTER II   OBLIGATIONS OF THE SELLER

Article 30
The seller must deliver the goods, hand over any documents relating to them and transfer the property in the goods, as required by the contract and this Convention.

Section I   Delivery of the goods and handing over of documents

Article 31
If the seller is not bound to deliver the goods at any other particular place, his obligation to deliver consists:
    (a) if the contract of sale involves carriage of the goods—in handing the goods over to the first carrier for transmission to the buyer;
    (b) if, in cases not within the preceding sub-paragraph, the contract relates to specific goods, or unidentified goods to be drawn from a specific stock or to be manufactured or produced, and at the time of the conclusion of the contract the parties knew that the goods were at, or were to be manufactured or produced at, a particular place—in placing the goods at the buyer's disposal at that place;
    (c) in other cases—in placing the goods at the buyer's disposal at the place where the seller had his place of business at the time of the conclusion of the contract.

Article 32
1. If the seller, in accordance with the contract or this Convention, hands the goods over to a carrier and if the goods are not clearly identified to the contract by markings on the goods, by shipping documents or otherwise, the seller must give the buyer notice of the consignment specifying the goods.

2. If the seller is bound to arrange for carriage of the goods, he must make such contracts as are necessary for carriage to the place fixed by means of transportation appropriate in the circumstances and according to the usual terms for such transportation.

3. If the seller is not bound to effect insurance in respect of the carriage of the goods, he must, at the buyer's request, provide him with all available information necessary to enable him to effect such insurance.

Article 33
The seller must deliver the goods:
    (a) if a date is fixed by or determinable from the contract, on that date;
    (b) if a period of time is fixed by or determinable from the contract, at any time within that period unless circumstances indicate that the buyer is to choose a date; or
    (c) in any other case, within a reasonable time after the conclusion of the contract.

Article 34
If the seller is bound to hand over documents relating to the goods, he must hand them over at the time and place and in the form required by the contract. If the seller has handed over documents before that time, he may, up to that time, cure any lack of conformity in the documents, if the exercise of this right does not cause the buyer unreasonable inconvenience or unreasonable expense. However, the buyer retains any right to claim damages as provided for in this Convention.

Section II   Conformity of the goods and third party claims

Article 35

1. The seller must deliver goods which are of the quantity, quality and description required by the contract and which are contained or packaged in the manner required by the contract.

2. Except where the parties have agreed otherwise, the goods do not conform with the contract unless they:

    (a) are fit for the purposes for which goods of the same description would ordinarily be used

    (b) are fit for any particular purpose expressly or impliedly made known to the seller at the time of the conclusion of the contract, except where the circumstances show that the buyer did not rely, or that it was unreasonable for him to rely, on the seller's skill and judgment;

    (c) possess the qualities of goods which the seller has held out to the buyer as a sample or model;

    (d) are contained or packaged in the manner usual for such goods or, where there is no such manner, in a manner adequate to preserve and protect the goods.

3. The seller is not liable under subparagraphs (a) to (d) of the preceding paragraph for any lack of conformity of the goods if at the time of the conclusion of the contract the buyer knew or could not have been unaware of such lack of conformity.

Article 36

1. The seller is liable in accordance with the contract and this Convention for any lack of conformity which exists at the time when the risk passes to the buyer, even though the lack of conformity becomes apparent only after that time.

2. The seller is also liable for any lack of conformity which occurs after the time indicated in the preceding paragraph and which is due to a breach of any of his obligations, including a breach of any guarantee that for a period of time the goods will remain fit for their ordinary purpose or for some particular purpose or will retain specified qualities or characteristics.

Article 37

If the seller has delivered goods before the date for delivery, he may, up to that date, deliver any missing part or make up any deficiency in the quantity of the goods delivered, or deliver goods in replacement of any non-conforming goods delivered or remedy any lack of conformity in the goods delivered, provided that the exercise of this right does not cause the buyer unreasonable inconvenience or unreasonable expense. However, the buyer retains any right to claim damages as provided for in this Convention.

Article 38

1. The buyer must examine the goods, or cause them to be examined, within as short a period as is practicable in the circumstances.

2. If the contract involves carriage of the goods, examination may be deferred until after the goods have arrived at their destination.

3. If the goods are redirected in transit or redispatched by the buyer without a reasonable opportunity for examination by him and at the time of the conclusion of the contract the seller knew or ought to have known of the possibility of such redirection or redispatch, examination may be deferred until after the goods have arrived at the new destination.

Article 39

1. The buyer loses the right to rely on a lack of conformity of the goods if he does not give notice to the seller specifying the nature of the lack of conformity within a reasonable time after he has discovered it or ought to have discovered it.

2. In any event, the buyer loses the right to rely on a lack of conformity of the goods if he does not give the seller notice thereof at the latest within a period of two years from the

date on which the goods were actually handed over to the buyer, unless this time-limit is inconsistent with a contractual period of guarantee.

Article 40
The seller is not entitled to rely on the provisions of articles 38 and 39 if the lack of conformity relates to facts of which he knew or could not have been unaware and which he did not disclose to the buyer.

Article 41
The seller must deliver goods which are free from any right or claim of a third party, unless the buyer agreed to take the goods subject to that right or claim. However, if such right or claim is based on industrial property or other intellectual property, the seller's obligation is governed by article 42.

Article 42
1. The seller must deliver goods which are free from any right or claim of a third party based on industrial property or other intellectual property, of which at the time of the conclusion of the contract the seller knew or could not have been unaware, provided that the right or claim is based on industrial property or other intellectual property:
>   (a) under the law of the State where the goods will be resold or otherwise used, if it was contemplated by the parties at the time of the conclusion of the contract that the goods would be resold or otherwise used in that State; or
>   (b) in any other case, under the law of the State where the buyer has his place of business.

2. The obligation of the seller under the preceding paragraph does not extend to cases where:
>   (a) at the time of the conclusion of the contract the buyer knew or could not have been unaware of the right or claim; or
>   (b) the right or claim results from the seller's compliance with technical drawings, designs, formulae or other such specifications furnished by the buyer.

Article 43
1. The buyer loses the right to rely on the provisions of article 41 or article 42 if he does not give notice to the seller specifying the nature of the right or claim of the third party within a reasonable time after he has become aware or ought to have become aware of the right or claim.

2. The seller is not entitled to rely on the provisions of the preceding paragraph if he knew of the right or claim of the third party and the nature of it.

Article 44
Notwithstanding the provisions of paragraph 1 of article 39 and paragraph 1 of article 43, the buyer may reduce the price in accordance with article 50 or claim damages, except for loss of profit, if he has a reasonable excuse for his failure to give the required notice.

Section III   Remedies for breach of contract by the seller

Article 45
1. If the seller fails to perform any of his obligations under the contract or this Convention, the buyer may:
>   (a) exercise the rights provided in articles 46 to 52;
>   (b) claim damages as provided in articles 74 to 77.

2. The buyer is not deprived of any right he may have to claim damages by exercising his right to other remedies.

3. No period of grace may be granted to the seller by a court or arbitral tribunal when the buyer resorts to a remedy for breach of contract.

Article 46
1. The buyer may require performance by the seller of his obligations unless the buyer has resorted to a remedy which is inconsistent with this requirement.
2. If the goods do not conform with the contract, the buyer may require delivery of substitute goods only if the lack of conformity constitutes a fundamental breach of contract and a request for substitute goods is made either in conjunction with notice given under article 39 or within a reasonable time thereafter.
3. If the goods do not conform with the contract, the buyer may require the seller to remedy the lack of conformity by repair, unless this is unreasonable having regard to all the circumstances. A request for repair must be made either in conjunction with notice given under article 39 or within a reasonable time thereafter.

Article 47
1. The buyer may fix an additional period of time of reasonable length for performance by the seller of his obligations.
2. Unless the buyer has received notice from the seller that he will not perform within the period so fixed, the buyer may not, during that period, resort to any remedy for breach of contract. However, the buyer is not deprived thereby of any right he may have to claim damages for delay in performance.

Article 48
1. Subject to article 49, the seller may, even after the date for delivery, remedy at his own expense any failure to perform his obligations, if he can do so without unreasonable delay and without causing the buyer unreasonable inconvenience or uncertainty of reimbursement by the seller of expenses advanced by the buyer. However, the buyer retains any right to claim damages as provided for in this Convention.
2. If the seller requests the buyer to make known whether he will accept performance and the buyer does not comply with the request within a reasonable time, the seller may perform within the time indicated in his request. The buyer may not, during that period of time, resort to any remedy which is inconsistent with performance by the seller.
3. A notice by the seller that he will perform within a specified period of time is assumed to include a request, under the preceding paragraph, that the buyer make known his decision.
4. A request or notice by the seller under paragraph 2 or 3 of this article is not effective unless received by the buyer.

Article 49
1. The buyer may declare the contract avoided:
   (a) if the failure by the seller to perform any of his obligations under the contract or this Convention amounts to a fundamental breach of contract; or
   (b) in case of non-delivery, if the seller does not deliver the goods within the additional period of time fixed by the buyer in accordance with paragraph 1 of article 47 or declares that he will not deliver within the period so fixed.
2. However, in cases where the seller has delivered the goods, the buyer loses the right to declare the contract avoided unless he does so:
   (a) in respect of late delivery, within a reasonable time after he has become aware that delivery has been made;
   (b) in respect of any breach other than late delivery, within a reasonable time:
      (i) after he new or ought to have nown of the breach;
      (ii) after the expiration of any additional period of time fixed by the buyer in accordance with paragraph 1 of article 47, or after the seller has declared that he will not perform his obligations within such an additional period; or
      (iii) after the expiration of any additional period of time indicated by the seller in accordance with paragraph 2 of article 48, or after the buyer has declared that he will not accept performance.

Article 50

If the goods do not conform with the contract and whether or not the price has already been paid, the buyer may reduce the price in the same proportion as the value that the goods actually delivered had at the time of the delivery bears to the value that conforming goods would have had at that time. However, if the seller remedies any failure to perform his obligations in accordance with article 37 or article 48 or if the buyer refuses to accept performance by the seller in accordance with those articles, the buyer may not reduce the price.

Article 51

1. If the seller delivers only a part of the goods or if only a part of the goods delivered is in conformity with the contract, articles 46 to 50 apply in respect of the part which is missing or which does not conform.

2. The buyer may declare the contract avoided in its entirety only if the failure to make delivery completely or in conformity with the contract amounts to a fundamental breach of the contract.

Article 52

1. If the seller delivers the goods before the date fixed, the buyer may take delivery or refuse to take delivery.

2. If the seller delivers a quantity of goods greater than that provided for in the contract, the buyer may take delivery or refuse to take delivery of the excess quantity. If the buyer takes delivery of all or part of the excess quantity, he must pay for it at the contract rate.

CHAPTER III   OBLIGATIONS OF THE BUYER

Article 53

The buyer must pay the price for the goods and take delivery of them as required by the contract and this Convention.

Section I   Payment of the price

Article 54

The buyer's obligation to pay the price includes taking such steps and complying with such formalities as may be required under the contract or any laws and regulations to enable payment to be made.

Article 55

Where a contract has been validly concluded but does not expressly or implicitly fix or make provision for determining the price, the parties are considered, in the absence of any indication to the contrary, to have impliedly made reference to the price generally charged at the time of the conclusion of the contract for such goods sold under comparable circumstances in the trade concerned.

Article 56

If the price is fixed according to the weight of the goods, in case of doubt it is to be determined by the net weight.

Article 57

1. If the buyer is not bound to pay the price at any other particular place, he must pay it to the seller:
> (a) at the seller's place of business; or
> (b) if the payment is to be made against the handing over of the goods or of documents, at the place where the handing over takes place.

2. The seller must bear any increase in the expenses incidental to payment which is caused by a change in his place of business subsequent to the conclusion of the contract.

Article 58

1. If the buyer is not bound to pay the price at any other specific time, he must pay it when the seller places either the goods or documents controlling their disposition at the buyer's disposal in accordance with the contract and this Convention. The seller may make such payment a condition for handing over the goods or documents.

2. If the contract involves carriage of the goods, the seller may dispatch the goods on terms whereby the goods, or documents controlling their disposition, will not be handed over to the buyer except against payment of the price.

3. The buyer is not bound to pay the price until he has had an opportunity to examine the goods, unless the procedures for delivery or payment agreed upon by the parties are inconsistent with his having such an opportunity.

Article 59

The buyer must pay the price on the date fixed by or determinable from the contract and this Convention without the need for any request or compliance with any formality on the part of the seller.

Section II   Taking delivery

Article 60

The buyer's obligation to take delivery consists:

    (a) in doing all the acts which could reasonably be expected of him in order to enable the seller to make delivery, and

    (b) in taking over the goods.

Section III   Remedies for breach of contract by the buyer

Article 61

1. If the buyer fails to perform any of his obligations under the contract or this Convention, the seller may:

    (a) exercise the rights provided in articles 62 to 65;

    (b) claim damages as provided in articles 74 to 77.

2. The seller is not deprived of any right he may have to claim damages by exercising his right to other remedies.

3. No period of grace may be granted to the buyer by a court or arbitral tribunal when the seller resorts to a remedy for breach of contract.

Article 62

The seller may require the buyer to pay the price, take delivery or perform his other obligations, unless the seller has resorted to a remedy which is inconsistent with this requirement.

Article 63

1. The seller may fix an additional period of time of reasonable length for performance by the buyer of his obligations.

2. Unless the seller has received notice from the buyer that he will not perform within the period so fixed, the seller may not, during that period, resort to any remedy for breach of contract. However, the seller is not deprived thereby of any right he may have to claim damages for delay in performance.

Article 64

1. The seller may declare the contract avoided:

    (a) if the failure by the buyer to perform any of his obligations under the contract or this Convention amounts to a fundamental breach of contract, or

    (b) if the buyer does not, within the additional period of time fixed by the seller in accordance with paragraph 1 of article 63, perform his obligation to pay the price or take delivery of the goods, or if he declares that he will not do so within the period so fixed.

2. However, in cases where the buyer has paid the price, the seller loses the right to declare the contract avoided unless he does so:

(a) in respect of late performance by the buyer, before the seller has become aware that performance has been rendered; or

(b) in respect of any breach other than late performance by the buyer, within a reasonable time:

(i) after the seller knew or ought to have known the breach; or

(ii) after the expiration of any additional period of time fixed by the seller in accordance with paragraph 1 of article 63, or after the buyer has declared that he will not perform his obligations within such an additional period.

Article 65

1. If under the contract the buyer is to specify the form, measurement or other features of the goods and he fails to make such specification either on the date agreed upon or within a reasonable time after receipt of a request from the seller, the seller may, without prejudice to any other rights he may have, make the specification himself in accordance with the requirements of the buyer that may be known to him.

2. If the seller makes the specification himself, he must inform the buyer of the details thereof and must fix a reasonable time within which the buyer may make a different specification. If, after receipt of such a communication, the buyer fails to do so within the time so fixed, the specification made by the seller is binding.

CHAPTER IV   PASSING OF RISK

Article 66

Loss of or damage to the goods after the risk has passed to the buyer does not discharge him from his obligation to pay the price, unless the loss or damage is due to an act or omission of the seller.

Article 67

1. If the contract of sale involves carriage of the goods and the seller is not bound to hand them over at a particular place, the risk passes to the buyer when the goods are handed over to the first carrier for transmission to the buyer in accordance with the contract of sale. If the seller is bound to hand the goods over to a carrier at a particular place, the risk does not pass to the buyer until the goods are handed over to the carrier at that place. The fact that the seller is authorized to retain documents controlling the disposition of the goods does not affect the passage of the risk.

2. Nevertheless, the risk does not pass to the buyer until the goods are clearly identified to the contract, whether by markings on the goods, by shipping documents, by notice given to the buyer or otherwise.

Article 68

The risk in respect of goods sold in transit passes to the buyer from the time of the conclusion of the contract. However, if the circumstances so indicate, the risk is assumed by the buyer from the time the goods were handed over to the carrier who issued the documents embodying the contract of carriage. Nevertheless, if at the time of the conclusion of the contract of sale the seller knew or ought to have known that the goods had been lost or damaged and did not disclose this to the buyer, the loss or damage is at the risk of the seller.

Article 69

1. In cases not within articles 67 and 68, the risk passes to the buyer when he takes over the goods or, if he does not do so in due time, from the time when the goods are placed at his disposal and he commits a breach of contract by failing to take delivery.

2. However, if the buyer is bound to take over the goods at a place other than a place of business of the seller, the risk passes when delivery is due and the buyer is aware of the fact that the goods are placed at his disposal at that place.

3. If the contract relates to goods not then identified, the goods are considered not to be placed at the disposal of the buyer until they are clearly identified to the contract.

Article 70

If the seller has committed a fundamental breach of contract, articles 67, 68 and 69 do not impair the remedies available to the buyer on account of the breach.

CHAPTER V   PROVISIONS COMMON TO THE OBLIGATIONS OF THE SELLER AND OF THE BUYER

Section I   Anticipatory breach and instalment contracts

Article 71

1. A party may suspend the performance of his obligations if, after the conclusion of the contract, it becomes apparent that the other party will not perform a substantial part of his obligations as a result of:

(a) a serious deficiency in his ability to perform or in is creditworthiness; or

(b) his conduct in preparing to perform or in performing the contract.

2. If the seller has already dispatched the goods before the grounds described in the preceding paragraph become evident, he may prevent the handing over of the goods to the buyer even though the buyer holds a document which entitles him to obtain them. The present paragraph relates only to the rights in the goods as between the buyer and the seller.

3. A party suspending performance, whether before or after dispatch of the goods, must imediately give notice of the suspension to the other party and must continue with performance if the other party provides adequate assurance of his performance.

Article 72

1. If prior to the date for performance of the contract it is clear that one of the parties will commit a fundamental breach of contract, the other party may declare the contract avoided.

2. If time allows, the party intending to declare the contract avoided must give reasonable notice to the other party in order to permit him to provide adequate assurance of his performance.

3. The requirements of the preceding paragraph do not apply if the other party has declared that he will not perform his obligations.

Article 73

1. In the case of a contract for delivery of goods by instalments, if the failure of one party to perform any of his obligations in respect of any instalment, the other party constitutes a fundamental breach of contract with respect to that instalment, the other party may declare the contract avoided with respect to that instalment.

2. If one party's failure to perform any of his obligations in respect of any instalment gives the other party good grounds to conclude that a fundamental breach of contract will occur with respect to future instalments, he may declare the contract avoided for the future, provided that he does so within a reasonable time.

3. A buyer who declares the contract avoided in respect of any delivery may, at the same time, declare it avoided in respect of deliveries already made or of future deliveries if, by reason of their interdependence, those deliveries could not be used for the purpose contemplated by the parties at the time of the conclusion of the contract.

Section II   Damages

Article 74

Damages for breach of contract by one party consist of a sum equal to the loss, including loss of profit, suffered by the other party as a consequence of the breach. Such damages may not exceed the loss which the party in breach foresaw or ought to have foreseen at the time of the conclusion of the contract, in the light of the facts and matters of which he then knew or ought to have known, as a possible consequence of the breach of contract.

Article 75

If the contract is avoided and if, in a reasonable manner and with a reasonable time after avoidance, the buyer has bought goods in replacement or the seller has resold the goods, the party claiming damages may recover the difference between the contract price and the price in the substitute transaction as well as any further damages recoverable under article 74.

Article 76

1. If the contract is avoided and there is a current price for the goods, the party claiming damages may, if he has not made a purchase or resale under article 75, recover the difference between the price fixed by the contract and the current price at the time of avoidance as well as any further damages recoverable under article 74. If, however, the party claiming damages has avoided the contract after taking over the goods, the current price at the time of such taking over shall be applied instead of the current price at the time of avoidance.

2. For the purposes of the preceding paragraph, the current price is the price prevailing at the place where delivery of the goods should have been made or, if there is no current price at that place, the price at such other place as serves as a reasonable substitute, making due allowance for differences in the cost of transporting the goods.

Article 77

A party who relies on a breach of contract must take such measures as are reasonable in the circumstances to mitigate the loss, including loss of profit, resulting from the breach. If he fails to take such measures, the party in breach may claim a reduction in the damages in the amount by which the loss should have been mitigated.

Section III   Interest

Article 78

If a party fails to pay the price or any other sum that is in arrears, the other party is entitled to interest on it, without prejudice to any claim for damages recoverable under article 74.

Section IV   Exemptions

Article 79

1. A party is not liable for a failure to perform any of his obligations if he proves that the failure was due to an impediment beyond his control and he could not reasonably be expected to have taken the impediment into account at the time of the conclusion of the contract or to have avoided or overcome it or its consequences.

2. If the party's failure is due to the failure by a third person whom he has engaged to perform the whole or a part of the contract, that party is exempt from liability only if:
   (a) he is exempt under the preceding paragraph; and
   (b) the person whom he has so engaged would be so exempt if the provisions of that paragraph were applied to him.

3. The exemption provided by this article has effect for the period during which the impediment exists.

4. The party who fails to perform must give notice to the other party of the impediment and its effect on his ability to perform. If the notice is not received by the other party within a

reasonable time after the party who fails to perform knew or ought to have known of the impediment, he is liable for damages resulting from such non-receipt.

5. Nothing in this article prevents either party from exercising any right other than to claim damages under this Convention.

Article 80

A party may not rely on a failure of the other party to perform, to the extent the such failure was caused by the first party's act or omission.

Section V   Effects of avoidance

Article 81

1. Avoidance of the contract releases both parties from their obligations under it, subject to any damages which may be due. Avoidance does not affect any provision of the contract for the settlement of disputes or any other provision of the contract governing the rights and obligations of the parties consequent upon the avoidance of the contract.

2. A party who has performed the contract either wholly or in part may claim restitution from the other party of whatever the first party has supplied or paid under the contract. If both parties are bound to make restitution, they must do so concurrently.

Article 82

1. The buyer loses the right to declare the contract avoided or to require the seller to deliver substitute goods if it is impossible for him to make restitution of the goods substantially in the condition in which he received them.

2. The preceding paragraph does not apply:
   (a) if the impossibility of making restitution of the goods or of making restitution of the goods substantially in the condition in which the buyer received them is not due to his act or omission;
   (b) if the goods or part of the goods have perished or deteriorated as a result of the examination provided for in article 38; or
   (c) if the goods or part of the goods have been sold in the normal course of business or have been consumed or transformed by the buyer in the course of normal use before he discovered or ought to have discovered the lack of conformity.

Article 83

A buyer who has lost the right to declare the contract avoided or to require the seller to deliver substitute goods in accordance with article 82 retains all other remedies under the contract and this Convention.

Article 84

1. If the seller is bound to refund the price, he must also pay interest on it, from the date on which the price was paid.

2. The buyer must account to the seller for all benefits which he has derived from the goods or part of them:
   (a) if he must make restitution of the goods or part of them; or
   (b) if it is impossible for him to make restitution of all or part of the goods or to make restitution of all or part of the goods substantially in the condition in which he received them, but he has nevertheless declared the contract avoided or required the seller to deliver substitute goods.

Section VI   Preservation of the goods

Article 85

If the buyer is in delay in taking delivery of the goods or, where payment of the price and delivery of the goods are to be made concurrently, if he fails to pay the price, and the seller is either in possession of the goods or otherwise able to control their disposition, the seller must take such steps as are reasonable in the circumstances to preserve them. He is entitled to retain them until he has been reimbursed his reasonable expenses by the buyer.

Article 86

1. If the buyer has received the goods and intends to exercise any right under the contract or this Convention to reject them, he must take such steps to preserve them as are reasonable in the circumstances. He is entitled to retain them until he has been reimbursed his reasonable expenses by the seller.

2. If goods dispatched to the buyer have been placed at his disposal at their destination and he exercises the right to reject them, he must take possession of them on behalf of the seller, provided that this can be done without payment of the price and without unreasonable inconvenience or unreasonable expense. This provision does not apply if the seller or a person authorized to take charge of the goods on his behalf is present at the destination. If the buyer takes possession of the goods under this paragraph, his rights and obligations are governed by the preceding paragraph.

Article 87

A party who is bound to take steps to preserve the goods may deposit them in a warehouse of a third person at the expense of the other party provided that the expense incurred is not unreasonable.

Article 88

1. A party who is bound to preserve the goods in accordance with article 85 or 86 may sell them by an appropriate means if there has been an unreasonable delay by the other party in taking possession of the goods or in taking them back or in paying the price or the cost of preservation, provided that reasonable notice of the intention to sell has been given to the other party.

2. If the goods are subject to rapid deterioration or their preservation would involve unreasonable expense, a party who is bound to preserve the goods in accordance with article 85 or 86 must take reasonable measures to sell them. To the extent possible he must give notice to the other party of his intention to sell.

3. A party selling the goods has the right to retain out of the proceeds of sale an amount equal to the reasonable expenses of preserving the goods and of selling them. He must account to the other party for the balance.

PART IV   FINAL PROVISIONS

Article 89

...

Article 90

This Convention does not prevail over any international agreement which has already been or may be entered into and which contains provisions concerning the matters governed by this Convention, provided that the parties have their places of business in States parties to such agreement.

Article 91

...

Article 92

1. A Contracting State may declare at the time of signature, ratification, acceptance, approval or accession that it will not be bound by Part II of this Convention or that it will not be bound by Part III of this Convention.

2. A Contracting State which makes a declaration in accordance with the preceding paragraph in respect of Part 11 or Part III of this Convention is not to be considered a

Contracting State within paragraph 1 of article 1 of this Convention in respect of matters governed by the Part to which the declaration applies.

Article 93

1. If a Contracting State has two or more territorial units in which, according to its constitution, different systems of law are applicable in relation to the matters dealt within this Convention, it may, at the time of signature, ratification, acceptance, approval or accession, declare that this Convention is to extend to all its territorial units or only to one or more of them, and may amend its declaration by submitting another declaration at any time.

. . .

Article 94

1. Two or more Contracting States which have the same or closely related legal rules on matters governed by this Convention may at any time declare that the Convention is not to apply to contracts of sale or to their formation where the parties have their places of business in those States. Such declaration may be made jointly or by reciprocal unilateral declarations.

2. A Contracting State which has the same or closely related legal rules on matters governed by this Convention as one or more non-Contracting States may at any time declare that the Convention is not to apply to contracts of sale or to their formation where the parties have their places of business in those States.

3. If a State which is the object of a declaration under the preceding paragraph subsequently becomes a Contracting State, the declaration made will, as from the date on which the Convention enters into force in respect of the new Contracting State, have the effect of a declaration made under paragraph 1, provided that the new Contracting State joins in such declaration or makes a reciprocal unilateral declaration.

Article 95

Any State may declare at the time of the deposit of its instrument of ratification, acceptance, approval or accession that it will not be bound by sub-paragraph 1(b) of article 1 of this Convention.

Article 96

A Contracting State whose legislation requires contracts of sale to be concluded in or evidenced by writing may at any time make a declaration in accordance with article 12 that any provision of article 11, article 29, or Part II of this Convention, that allows a contract of sale or its modification or termination by agreement or any offer, acceptance, or other indication of intention to be made in any form other than in writing, does not apply where any party has his place of business in that State.

Article 97

. . .

Article 98

No reservations are permitted except those expressly authorized in this Convention.

Article 99

1. This Convention enters into force, subject to the provisions of paragraph 6 of this article, on the first day of the month following the expiration of twelve months after the date of deposit of the tenth instrument of ratification, acceptance, approval or accession, including an instrument which contains a declaration made under article 92.

. . .

Article 100

. . .

Article 101

. . .

Done at Vienna, this day of eleventh day of April, one thousand nine hundred and eighty, in a single original, of which the Arabic, Chinese, English, French, Russian and Spanish texts are equally authentic.

...

CMI Rules for Electronic Bills of Lading

1 Scope of Application

These rules shall apply whenever the parties so agree.

2 Definitions

(a) 'Contract of Carriage', means any agreement to carry goods wholly or partly by sea.

(b) 'EDI', means Electronic Data Interchange, i.e. the interchange of trade data effected by teletransmission.

(c) 'UN/EDIFACT' means the United Nations Rules for Electronic Data Interchange for Administration, Commerce and Transport.

(d) 'Transmission' means one or more messages electronically sent together as one unit of dispatch which includes heading and terminating data.

(e) 'Confirmation' means a Transmission which advises that the content of a Transmission appears to be complete and correct, without prejudice to any subsequent consideration or action that the content may warrant.

(f) 'Private Key' means any technically appropriate form, such as a combination of numbers and/or letters, which the parties may agree for securing the authenticity and integrity of a Transmission.

(g) 'Holder' means the party who is entitled to the rights described in Article 7(a) by virtue of its possession of a valid Private Key.

(h) 'Electronic Monitoring System' means the device by which a computer system can be examined for the transactions that it recorded, such as a Trade Data Log or an Audit Trail.

(i) 'Electronic Storage' means any temporary, intermediate or permanent storage of electronic data including the primary and the back-up storage of such data.

3 Rules of procedure

(a) When not in conflict with these Rules, the Uniform Rules of Conduct for Interchange of Trade Data by Teletransmission, 1987 (UNCID) shall govern the conduct between the parties.

(b) The EDI under these Rules should conform with the relevant UN/EDIFACT standards. However, the parties may use any other method of trade data interchange acceptable to all of the users.

(c) Unless otherwise agreed, the document format for the Contract of Carriage shall conform to the UN Layout Key or compatible national standard for bills of lading.

(d) Unless otherwise agreed, a recipient of a Transmission is not authorised to act on a Transmission unless he has sent a Confirmation.

(e) In the event of a dispute arising between the parties as to the data actually transmitted, an Electronic Monitoring System may be used to verify the data received. Data concerning other transactions not related to the data in dispute are to be considered as trade secrets and thus not available for examination. If such data are unavoidably revealed as part of the examination of the Electronic Monitoring System, they must be treated as confidential and not released to any outside party or used for any other purpose.

(f) Any transfer of rights to the goods shall be considered to be private information, and shall not be released to any outside party not connected to the transport or clearance of the goods.

4 Form and content of the receipt message

(a) The carrier, upon receiving the goods from the shipper, shall give notice of the receipt of the goods to the shipper by a message at the electronic address specified by the shipper.

(b) This receipt message shall include:

   (i)   the name of the shipper;

   (ii) the description of the goods, with any representations and reservations, in the same tenor as would be required if a paper bill of lading were issued;

   (iii) the date and place of the receipt of the goods;

   (iv) a reference to the carrier's terms and conditions of carriage; and

   (v) the Private Key to be used in subsequent Transmissions.

The shipper must confirm this receipt message to the carrier, upon which Confirmation the shipper shall be the Holder.

(c) Upon demand of the Holder, the receipt message shall be updated with the date and place of shipment as soon as the goods have been loaded on board.

(d) The information contained in (ii), (iii) and (iv) of paragraph (b) above including the date and place of shipment if updated in accordance with paragraph (c) of this Rule, shall have the same force and effect as if the receipt message were contained in a paper bill of lading.

5 Terms and conditions of the Contract of Carriage

(a) It is agreed and understood that whenever the carrier makes a reference to its terms and conditions of carriage, these terms and conditions shall form part of the Contract of Carriage.

(b) Such terms and conditions must be readily available to the parties to the Contract of Carriage.

(c) In the event of any conflict or inconsistency between such terms and conditions and these Rules, these Rules shall prevail.

6 Applicable law

The Contract of Carriage shall be subject to any international convention or national law which would have been compulsorily applicable if a paper bill of lading had been issued.

7 Right of Control and Transfer

(a) The Holder is the only party who may, as against the carrier:

   (1) claim delivery of the goods;

   (2) nominate the consignee or substitute a nominated consignee for any other party, including itself;

   (3) transfer the Right of Control and Transfer to another party;

   (4) instruct the carrier on any other subject concerning the goods, in accordance with the terms and conditions of the Contract of Carriage, as if he were the holder of a paper bill of lading.

(b) A transfer of the Right of Control and Transfer shall be effected: (i) by notification of the current Holder to the carrier of its intention to transfer its Right of Control and Transfer to a proposed new Holder, and (ii) confirmation by the carrier of such notification message, whereupon (iii) the carrier shall transmit the information as referred to in article 4 (except for the Private Key) to the proposed new Holder, whereafter (iv) the proposed new Holder shall advise the carrier of its acceptance of the Right of Control and Transfer, whereupon

(v) the carrier shall cancel the current Private Key and issue a new Private Key to the new Holder.

(c) If the proposed new Holder advises the carrier that it does not accept the Right of Control and Transfer or fails to advise the carrier of such acceptance within a reasonable time, the proposed transfer of the Right of Control and Transfer shall not take place. The carrier shall notify the current Holder accordingly and the current Private Key shall retain its validity.

(d) The transfer of the Right of Control and Transfer in the manner described above shall have the same effects as the transfer of such rights under a paper bill of lading.

8   The Private Key

(a) The Private Key is unique to each successive Holder. It is not transferable by the Holder. The carrier and the Holder shall each maintain the security of the Private Key.

(b) The carrier shall only be obliged to send a Confirmation of an electronic message to the last Holder to whom it issued a Private Key, when such Holder secures the Transmission containing such electronic message by the use of the Private Key.

(c) The Private Key must be separate and distinct from any means used to identify the Contract of Carriage, and any security password or identification used to access the computer network.

9   Delivery

(a) The carrier shall notify the Holder of the place and date of intended delivery of the goods. Upon such notification the Holder has a duty to nominate a consignee and to give adequate delivery instructions to the carrier with verification by the Private Key. In the absence of such nomination, the Holder will be deemed to be the consignee.

(b) The carrier shall deliver the goods to the consignee upon production of proper identification in accordance with the delivery instructions specified in para-graph (a) above; such delivery shall automatically cancel the Private Key.

(c) The carrier shall be under no liability for misdelivery if it can prove that it exer-cised reasonable care to ascertain that the party who claimed to be the consignee was in fact that party.

10   Option to receive a paper document

(a) The Holder has the option at any time prior to delivery of the goods to demand from the carrier a paper bill of lading. Such document shall be made available at a location to be determined by the Holder, provided that no carrier shall be obliged to make such document available at a place where it has no facilities and in such instance the carrier shall only be obliged to make the document available at the facility nearest to the location determined by the Holder. The carrier shall not be responsible for delays in delivering the goods resulting from the Holder exercising the above option.

(b) The carrier has the option at any time prior to delivery of the goods to issue to the Holder a paper bill of lading unless the exercise of such option could result in undue delay or disrupts the delivery of the goods.

(c) A bill of lading issued under Rules 10(a) or (b) shall include: the information set out in the receipt message referred to in Rule 4 (except for the Private Key); and (ii) a statement to the effect that the bill of lading has been issued upon termination of the procedures for EDI under the CMI Rules for Electronic Bills of Lading. The aforementioned bill of lading shall be issued at the option of the Holder either to the order of the Holder whose name for this purpose shall then be inserted in the bill of lading or 'to bearer'.

(d) The issuance of a paper bill of lading under Rule 10(a) or (b) shall cancel the Private Key and terminate the procedures for EDI under these Rules. Termination of these procedures by the Holder or the carrier will not relieve any of the parties to the Contract of Carriage of their rights, obligations or liabilities while performing under the present Rules nor of their rights, obligations or liabilities under the Contract of Carriage.

(e) The Holder may demand at any time the issuance of a print-out of the receipt message referred to in Rule 4 (except for the Private Key) marked as 'non- negotiable copy'. The issuance of such a print-out shall not cancel the Private Key nor terminate the procedures for EDI.

11   Electronic data is equivalent to writing

The carrier and the shipper and all subsequent parties utilizing these procedures agree that any national or local law, custom or practice requiring the Contract of Carriage to be evidenced in writing and signed, is satisfied by the transmitted and confirmed electronic data residing on computer data storage media displayable in human language on a video screen or as printed out by a computer. In agreeing to adopt these Rules, the parties shall be taken to have agreed not to raise the defence that this contract is not in writing.

CMI Uniform Rules for Sea Waybills

1   Scope of Application

(i)   These Rules shall be called the 'CMI Uniform Rules for Sea Waybills'.

(ii) They shall apply when adopted by a contract of carriage which is not covered by a bill of lading or similar document of title, whether the contract be in writing or not.

2   Definitions

In these Rules:

'Contract of carriage' shall mean any contract of carriage subject to these Rules which is to be performed wholly or partly by sea.

'Goods' shall mean any goods carried or received for carriage under a contract of carriage.

'Carrier' and 'Shipper' shall mean the parties named in or identifiable as such from the contract of carriage.

'Consignee' shall mean the party named in or identifiable as such from the contract of carriage, or any person substituted as consignee in accordance with rule 6(i).

'Right of Control' shall mean the rights and obligations referred to in rule 6.

3   Agency

(i)   The shipper on entering into the contract of carriage does so not only on his own behalf but also as agent for and on behalf of the consignee, and warrants to the carrier that he has authority so to do.

(ii) This rule shall apply if, and only if, it be necessary by the law applicable to the contract of carriage so as to enable the consignee to sue and be sued thereon. The consignee shall be under no greater liability than he would have been had the contract of carriage been covered by a bill of lading or similar document of title.

4   Rights and Responsibilities

(i)   The contract of carriage shall be subject to any International Convention or National Law which is, or if the contract of carriage had been covered by a bill of lading or similar document of title would have been, compulsorily applicable thereto. Such convention or law shall apply notwithstanding anything inconsistent therewith in the contract of carriage.

(ii) Subject always to subrule (i), the contract of carriage is governed by:

(a) these Rules;

(b) unless otherwise agreed by the parties, the carrier's standard terms and conditions for the trade, if any, including any terms and conditions relating to the non-sea part of the carriage;

(c) any other terms and conditions agreed by the parties.

(iii) In the event of any inconsistency between the terms and conditions mentioned under subrule (ii)(b) or (c) and these Rules, these Rules shall prevail.

5 Description of the Goods

(i) The shipper warrants the accuracy of the particulars furnished by him relating to the goods, and shall indemnify the carrier against any loss, damage or expense resulting from any inaccuracy.

(ii) In the absence of reservation by the carrier, any statement in a sea waybill or similar document as to the quantity or condition of the goods shall

(a) as between the carrier and the shipper be *prima facie* evidence of receipt of the goods as so stated;

(b) as between the carrier and the consignee be conclusive evidence of receipt of the goods as so stated, and proof to the contrary shall not be permitted, provided always that the consignee has acted in good faith.

6 Right of Control

(i) Unless the shipper has exercised his option under subrule (ii) below, he shall be the only party entitled to give the carrier instructions in relation to the contract of carriage. Unless prohibited by the applicable law, he shall be entitled to change the name of the consignee at any time up to the consignee claiming delivery of the goods after their arrival at destination, provided he gives the carrier reasonable notice in writing, or by some other means acceptable to the carrier, thereby undertaking to indemnify the carrier against any additional expense caused thereby.

(ii) The shipper shall have the option, to be exercised not later than the receipt of the goods by the carrier, to transfer the right of control to the consignee. The exercise of this option must be noted on the sea waybill or similar document, if any. Where the option has been exercised the consignee shall have such rights as are referred to in subrule (i) above and the shipper shall cease to have such rights.

7 Delivery

(i) The carrier shall deliver the goods to the consignee upon production of proper identification.

(ii) The carrier shall be under no liability for wrong delivery if he can prove that he has exercised reasonable care to ascertain that the party claiming to be the consignee is in fact that party.

8 Validity

In the event of anything contained in these Rules or any such provisions as are incorporated into the contract of carriage by virtue of rule 4, being inconsistent with the provisions of any International Convention or National Law compulsorily appli-cable to the contract of car-riage, such Rules and provisions shall to that extent but no further be null and void.

ICC Uniform Customs and Practice for Documentary Credits
(1993 Revision)

(ICC Publication No. 500E—ISBN 92.842.1155.7)

Notes:
Published in its official English version by the International Chamber of Commerce
Copyright © 1993—International Chamber of Commerce (ICC), Paris.

Available from: ICC Services SAS, 38 Cours Albert 1er, 75008 Paris, France; and iccbooks.com.

A. GENERAL PROVISIONS AND DEFINITIONS

Article 1 Application of UC
The Uniform Customs and Practice for Documentary Credits, 1993 Revision, ICC Publication No. 500, shall apply to all Documentary Credits (including to the extent to which they may be applicable, Standby Letter(s) of Credit) where they are incorporated into the text of the Credit. They are binding on all parties thereto, unless otherwise expressly stipulated in the Credit.

Article 2 Meaning of Credit
For the purposes of these Articles, the expressions 'Documentary Credits(s)' and 'Standby Letter(s) of Credit' (hereinafter referred to as 'Credit(s)'), mean any arrangement, however named or described, whereby a bank (the 'Issuing Bank') acting at the request and on the instructions of a customer (the 'Applicant') or on its own behalf,

 (i)   is to make a payment to or to the order of a third party (the 'Beneficiary'), or is to accept and pay bills of exchange (Draft(s)) drawn by the Beneficiary, or

 (ii) authorises another bank to effect such payment, or to accept and pay such bills of exchange (Draft(s)), or

 (iii) authorises another bank to negotiate, against stipulated document(s), provided that the terms and conditions of the Credit are complied with.

For the purposes of these Articles, branches of a bank in different countries are considered another bank.

Article 3 Credits v. Contracts

 (a) Credits, by their nature, are separate transactions from the sales or other contract(s) on which they may be based and banks are in no way concerned with or bound by such contract(s), even it any reference whatsoever to such contract(s) is included in the Credit. Consequently, the undertaking of a bank to pay, accept and pay Draft(s) or negotiate and/or to fulfil any other obligation under the Credit, is not subject to claims or defences by the Applicant resulting from his relationships with the Issuing Bank or the Beneficiary.

 (b) A Beneficiary can in no case avail himself of the contractual relationships existing between the banks or between the Applicant and the Issuing Bank.

Article 4 Documents v. Goods/Services/Performances
In Credit operations all parties concerned deal with documents, and not with goods, services and/or other performances to which the documents may relate.

Article 5 Instructions to Issue/Amend Credits

 (a) Instructions for the Issuance of a Credit, the Credit itself, instructions for an amendment thereto, and the amendment itself, must be complete and precise.
     In order to guard against confusion and misunderstanding, banks should discourage any attempt:

 (i)   to include excessive detail in the Credit or in any amendment thereto;

 (ii) to give instructions to issue, advise or confirm a Credit by reference to a Credit previously issued (similar Credit) where such previous Credit has been subject to accepted amendment(s), and/or unaccepted amendment(s).

 (b) All instructions for the issuance of a Credit and the Credit itself and, where applicable, all instructions for an amendment thereto and the amendment itself, must state precisely the document(s) against which payment, acceptance of negotiation is to be made.

B.   FORM AND NOTIFICATION OF CREDITS

Article 6   Revocable v. Irrevocable Credits
(a) A Credit may be either
(i)   revocable, or
(ii) irrevocable.
(b) The Credit, therefore, should clearly indicate whether it is revocable or irrevocable.
(c) In the absence of such indication the Credit shall be deemed to be irrevocable.

Article 7   Advising Bank's Liability
(a) A Credit may be advised to a Beneficiary through another bank (the 'Advising Bank') without engagement on the part of the Advising Bank, but that bank, if it elects to advise the Credit, shall take reasonable care to check the apparent authenticity of the Credit which it advises. If the bank elects not to advise the Credit, it must so inform the Issuing Bank without delay.
(b) If the Advising Bank cannot establish such apparent authenticity It must inform, without delay, the bank from which the Instructions appear to have been received that it has been unable to establish the authenticity of the Credit and if it elects nonetheless to advise the Credit it must Inform the Beneficiary that it has not been able to establish the authenticity of the Credit.

Article 8   Revocation of a Credit
(a) A revocable Credit may be amended or cancelled by the Issuing Bank at any moment and without prior notice to the Beneficiary.
(b) However, the Issuing Bank must:
(i)   reimburse another bank with which a revocable Credit has been made available for sight payment, acceptance or negotiation—for any payment, acceptance or negotiation made by such bank—prior to receipt by it of notice of amendment or cancellation, against documents which appear on their face to be in compliance with the terms and conditions of the Credit;
(ii) reimburse another bank with which a revocable Credit has been made available for deferred payment, if such a bank has, prior to receipt by it of notice of amendment or cancellation, taken up documents which appear on their lace to be In compliance with the terms and conditions of the Credit.

Article 9   Liability of Issuing and Confirming Banks
(a) An irrevocable Credit constitutes a definite undertaking of the Issuing Bank, provided that the stipulated documents are presented to the Nominated Bank or to the Issuing Bank and that the terms and conditions of the Credit are complied with:
(i)   if the Credit provides for sight payment—to pay at sight;
(ii) if the Credit provides for deferred payment—to pay on the maturity date(s) determinable in accordance with the stipulations of the Credit;
(iii) if the Credit provides for acceptance:
(a) by the Issuing Bank—to accept Draft(s) drawn by the Beneficiary on the Issuing Bank and pay them at maturity, or
(b) by another drawee bank—to accept and pay at maturity Draft(s) drawn by the Beneficiary on the Issuing Bank in the event the drawee bank stipulated in the Credit does not accept Draft(s) drawn on it, or to pay Draft(s) accepted but not paid by such drawee bank at maturity;
(iv) if the Credit provides for negotiation—to pay without recourse to drawers and/or bona fide holders, Draft(s) drawn by the Beneficiary and/or documents(s) presented under the Credit. A Credit should not be issued available by Draft(s) on the Applicant. If the Credit nevertheless calls for Draft(s) on the Applicant, banks will consider such Draft(s) as an additional document(s).

(b) A confirmation of an irrevocable Credit by another bank (the 'Confirming Bank') upon the authorisation or request of the Issuing Bank, constitutes a definite undertaking of the Confirming Bank, in addition to that of the Issuing Bank, provided that the stipulated documents are presented to the Confirming Bank or to any other Nominated Bank and that the terms and conditions of the Credit are complied with:

(i)   if the Credit provides for sight payment—to pay at sight

(ii) if the Credit provides for deferred payment—to pay on the maturity date(s) determinable in accordance with the stipulations of the Credit;

(iii) if the Credit provides for acceptance:

(a) by the Confirming Bank—to accept Draft(s) drawn by the Beneficiary on the Confirming Bank and pay them at maturity, or

(b) by another drawee bank—to accept and pay at maturity Draft(s) drawn on it, or to pay Draft(s) accepted but not paid by such drawee bank at maturity;

(iv) if the Credit provides for negotiation—to negotiate without recourse to drawers and/or bona fide holders, Draft(s) drawn by the Beneficiary and/or document(s) presented under the Credit. A Credit should not be issued available by Draft(s) on the Applicant. If the Credit nevertheless calls for Draft(s) on the Applicant, banks will consider such Draft(s) as an additional document(s).

(c) (i) If another bank is authorised or requested by the Issuing Bank to add its confirmation to a Credit but is not prepared to do so, it must so inform the Issuing Bank without delay.

(ii) Unless the Issuing Bank specifies otherwise in its authorisation or request to add confirmation, the Advising Bank may advise the Credit to the Beneficiary without adding its confirmation.

(d) (i) Except as otherwise provided by Article 48, an irrevocable Credit can neither be amended not cancelled without agreement of the Issuing Bank, the Confirming Bank, if any, and the Beneficiary.

(ii) The Issuing Bank shall be irrevocably bound by an amendment(s) issued by it from the time of the issuance of such amendment(s). A Confirming Bank may extend its confirmation to an amendment and shall be irrevocably bound as one of the time of its advice of the amendment. A confirming Bank may, however, choose to advise an amendment to the Beneficiary without extending its confirmation and if so, must inform the Issuing Bank and the Beneficiary without delay.

(iii) The terms of the original Credit (or a Credit incorporating previously accepted amendment(s)) will remain in force for the Beneficiary until the Beneficiary communicates his acceptance of the amendment to the bank that advised such amendment. The Beneficiary should give notification of acceptance or rejection of amendment(s). If the Beneficiary fails to give such notification, the lender of documents to the Nominated Bank or Issuing Bank, that conform to the Credit and to not yet accepted amendment(s), will be deemed to be notification of acceptance by the Beneficiary of such amendment(s) and as of that moment the Credit will be amended.

(iv) Partial acceptance of amendments contained in one and the same advice of amendment is not allowed and consequently will not be given any effect.

Article 10 Types of Credits

(a) All Credits must clearly indicate whether they are available by sight payment, by deferred payment, by acceptance or by negotiation.

(b) (i) Unless the Credit stipulates that it is available only with the Issuing Bank, all Credits must nominate the Bank (the 'Nominated Bank') which is authorised to pay, to incur a deferred payment undertaking, to accept Draft(s) or to negotiate. In a freely negotiable Credit, any bank is a Nominated Bank.

Presentation of documents must be made to the Issuing Bank or the Confirming Bank, if any, or any other Nominated Bank.

   (ii) Negotiation means the giving of value for Draft(s) and/or document(s) by the bank authorised to negotiate. Mere examinations of the documents without giving of value does not constitute a negotiation.

(c) Unless the Nominated Bank is the Confirming Bank, nominated by the Issuing Bank does not constitute any undertaking by the Nominated Bank to pay, to incur a deferred payment undertaking, to accept Draft(s), or to negotiate. Except where expressly agreed to by the Nominated Bank and so communicated to the Beneficiary, the Nominated Bank's receipt of and/or examination and/or forwarding of the documents does not make that bank liable to pay, to incur a deferred payment undertaking, to accept Draft(s), or to negotiate.

(d) By nominating another bank, or by allowing for negotiation by another bank, or by authorising or requesting another bank to add its confirmation, the Issuing Bank authorises such bank to pay, accept Draft(s) or negotiate as the case may be, against documents which appear on their face to be in compliance with the terms and conditions of the Credit and undertakes to reimburse such bank in accordance with the provisions of these Articles.

Article 11   Teletransmitted and Pre-advised Credits

(a) (i)   When an Issuing Bank instructs an advising Bank by an authenticated teletransmission to advise a Credit or an amendment to a Credit, the teletrans- mission will be deemed to be the operative Credit instrument or the operative amendment, and no mail confirmation nevertheless be sent, it will have no effect and the Advising Bank will have no obligation to check such mail confirmation against the operative Credit instrument or the operative amendment received by teletransmission.

   (ii) If the teletransmission states 'full details to follow' (or words of similar effect) or states that the mail confirmation is to be the operative Credit instrument or the operative amendment, then the teletransmission will not be deemed to be the operative Credit instrument or the operative Credit instrument or the operative amendment. The Issuing Bank must forward the operative Credit instrument or the operative amendment to such Advising Bank without delay.

(b) If a bank uses the services of an Advising Bank to have the Credit advised to the Beneficiary, it must also use the services of the same bank for advising an amendment(s).

(c) A preliminary advice of the issuance or amendment of an irrevocable Credit (pre-advice), shall only be given by an Issuing Bank if such bank is prepared to issue the operative Credit instrument or the operative amendment thereto. Unless otherwise stated in such preliminary advice by the Issuing Bank, an Issuing Bank having given such pre-advice shall be irrevocably committed to issue or amend the Credit, in terms not inconsistent with the pre-advice, without delay.

Article 12   Incomplete or Unclear Instructions

If incomplete or unclear instructions are received to advise, confirm or amend a Credit, the bank requested to act on such instructions may give preliminary notification to the Beneficiary for information only and without responsibility. This preliminary notification should state clearly that the notification is provided for information only and without the responsibility of the Advising Bank. In any event, the Advising Bank must inform the Issuing Bank of the action taken and request it to provide the necessary information.

The Issuing Bank must provide the necessary information without delay. The Credit will be advised, confirmed or amended, only when complete and clear instructions have been received and if the Advising Bank is then prepared to act on the instructions.

C.   LIABILITIES AND RESPONSIBILITIES

Article 13   **Standard for Examination of Documents**

(a) Banks must examine all documents stipulated in the Credit with reasonable care, to ascertain whether or not they appear, on their face, to be in compliance with the terms and conditions of the Credit. Compliance of the stipulated documents on their face with the terms and conditions of the Credit, shall be determined by international standard banking practice as reflected in these Articles. Documents which appear on their face to be inconsistent with one another will be considered as not appearing on their face to be in compliance with the terms and conditions of the Credit.

Documents not stipulated in the Credit will not be examined by banks. If they receive such documents, they shall return them to the presenter or pass them on without responsibility.

(b) The Issuing Bank, the Confirming Bank, if any, or a Nominated Bank acting on their behalf, shall each have a reasonable time, not to exceed seven banking days following the day of receipt of the documents, to examine the documents and examine the documents and determine whether to take up or refuse the documents and to inform the party from which it received the documents accordingly.

(c) If a Credit contains conditions without stating the document(s) to be presented in compliance therewith, banks will deem such conditions as not stated and will disregard them.

Article 14   **Discrepant Documents and Notice**

(a) When the Issuing Bank authorises another bank to pay, incur a deferred payment undertaking, accept Draft(s), or negotiate against documents which appear on their face to be in compliance with the terms and conditions of the Credit, the Issuing Bank and the Confirming Bank, if any, are bound:

(i)   to reimburse the Nominated Bank which has paid, incurred a deferred payment undertaking, accepted Draft(s), or negotiated,

(ii)   to take up the documents.

(b) Upon receipt of the documents the Issuing Bank and/or Confirming Bank, if any, or a Nominated Bank acting on their behalf, must determine on the basis of the documents alone whether or not they appear on their face to be in compliance with the terms and conditions of the Credit. If the documents appear on their face not to be in compliance with the terms and conditions of the Credit, such banks may refuse to take up the documents.

(c) If the Issuing Bank determines that the documents appear on their face not to be in compliance with the terms and conditions of the Credit, it may in its sole judgment approach the Applicant for a waiver of the discrepancy(ies). This does not, however, extend the period mentioned in sub-Article 13(b).

(d) (i) If the Issuing Bank and/or Confirming Bank, if any, or a Nominated Bank acting on their behalf, decides to refuse the documents, it must give notice to that effect by telecommunication or, if that is not possible, by other expeditious means, without delay but no later than the close of the seventh banking day following the day of receipt of the documents. Such notice shall be given to the bank from which it received the documents, or to the Beneficiary, if it received the documents directly from him.

> (ii) Such notice must state all discrepancies in respect of which the bank refuses the documents and must also state whether it is holding the documents at the disposal of, or is returning them to, the presenter.
>
> (iii) The Issuing Bank and/or Confirming Bank, if any, shall then be entitled to claim from the remitting bank refund, with interest, of any reimbursement which has been made to that bank.

(e) If the Issuing Bank and/or Confirming Bank, if any, fails to act in accordance with the provisions of this Article and/or fails to hold the documents at the disposal of, or return them to the presenter, the Issuing Bank and/or Confirming Bank, if any, shall be precluded from claiming that the documents are not in compliance with the terms and conditions of the Credit.

(f) If the remitting bank draws the attention of the Issuing Bank and/or Confirming Bank, if any, to any discrepancy(ies) in the document(s) or advises such banks that it has paid, incurred a deferred payment undertaking, accepted Draft(s) or negotiated under reserve or against an indemnity in respect of such discrepancy(ies), the Issuing Bank and/or Confirming Bank, if any, shall not be thereby relieved from any of their obligations under any provision of this Article. Such reserve or indemnity concerns only the relations between the remitting bank and the party towards whom the reserve was made, or from whom, or on whose behalf, the indemnity was obtained.

Article 15   Disclaimer on Effectiveness of Documents

Banks assume no liability or responsibility for the form, sufficiency, accuracy, genuineness, falsification or legal effect of any document(s), or for the general and/or particular conditions stipulated in the document(s) or superimposed thereon; nor do they assume any liability or responsibility for the description, quantity, weight, quality, condition, packing, delivery, value or existence of the goods represented by any document(s), or for the good faith or acts and/or omissions, solvency, performance or standing of the consignors, the carriers, the forwarders, the consignees or the insurers of the goods, or any other person whomsoever.

Article 16   Disclaimer on the Transmission of Messages

Banks assume no liability or responsibility for the consequences arising out of delay and/or loss in transit of any message(s), letter(s) or document(s), or for delay, mutilation or other error(s) arising in the transmission of any telecommunication. Banks assume no liability or responsibility for errors in translation and/or interpretation of technical terms, and reserve the right to transmit Credit terms without translating them.

Article 17   Force Majeure

Banks assume no liability or responsibility for the consequences arising out of the interruption of their business by Acts of God, riots, civil commotions, insurrections, wars or any other causes beyond their control, or by any strikes or lockouts. Unless specifically authorised, banks will not, upon resumption of their business, pay, incur a deferred payment undertaking, accept Draft(s) or negotiate under Credits which expired during such interruption of their business.

Article 18   Disclaimer for Acts of an Instructed Party

(a) Banks utilizing the services of another bank or other banks for the purpose of giving effect to the instructions of the Applicant do so for the account and at the risk of such Applicant.

(b) Banks assume no liability or responsibility should the instructions they transmit not be carried out, even if they have themselves taken the initiative in the choice of such other bank(s).

(c) (i) A party instructing another party to perform services is liable for any charges, including commissions, fees, costs or expenses incurred by the instructed party in connection with its instructions.

(i) Where a Credit stipulates that such charges are for the account of a party other than the instructing party, and charges cannot be collected, the instructing party remains ultimately liable for the payment thereof.

(d) The Applicant shall be bound by and liable to indemnify the banks against all obligations and responsibilities imposed by foreign laws and usages.

Article 19   Bank-to-Bank Reimbursement Arrangements

(a) If an Issuing Bank intends that the reimbursement to which a paying, accepting or negotiating bank is entitled, shall be obtained by such bank (the 'Claiming Bank'), claiming on another party (the 'Reimbursing Bank'). It shall provide such Reimbursing Bank in good time with the proper instructions or authorisation to honour such reimbursement claims.

(b) Issuing Banks shall not require a Claiming Bank to supply a certificate of compliance with the terms and conditions of the Credit to the Reimbursing Bank.

(c) An issuing Bank shall not be relieved from any of its obligations to provide reimbursement if and when reimbursement is not received by the Claiming Bank from the Reimbursing Bank.

(d) The Issuing Bank shall be responsible to the Claiming Bank for any loss of interest if reimbursement is not provided by the Reimbursing Bank on first demand, or as otherwise specified in the Credit, or mutually agreed, as the case may be.

(e) The Reimbursing Bank's charges should be for the account of the Issuing Bank. However, in cases where the charges are for the account of another party, it is the responsibility of the Issuing Bank to so indicate in the original Credit and in the reimbursement authorisation. In cases where the Reimbursing Bank's charges are for the account of another party they shall be collected from the Claiming Bank when the Credit is drawn under. In cases where the Credit is not drawn under, the Reimbursing Bank's charges remain the obligation of the Issuing Bank.

D.   DOCUMENTS

Article 20   Ambiguity as to the Issuers of Documents

(a) Terms such as 'first class', 'well known', 'qualified', 'independent', 'official', 'competent', 'local' and the like, shall not be used to describe the issuers of any document(s) as presented, provided that it appears on its face to be in compliance with the other terms and conditions of the Credit and not to have been issued by the Beneficiary.

(b) Unless otherwise stipulated in the Credit, banks will also accept as an original document(s), a document(s) produced or appearing to have been produced:

(i)   by reprographic, automated or computerised systems;

(ii)   as carbon copies;

provided that it is marked as original and, where necessary, appears to be signed.

A document may be signed by handwriting, by facsimile signature, by perforated signature, by stamp, by symbol, or by any other mechanical or electronic method of authentication.

(c) (i) Unless otherwise stipulated in the Credit, banks will accept as a copy(ies), a document(s) either labelled copy or not marked as an original—a copy(ies) need not be signed.

(ii) Credits that require multiple document(s) such as 'duplicate', 'two fold', 'two copies' and the like, will be satisfied by the presentation of one original and the remaining number in copies except where the document itself indicates otherwise.

(d) Unless otherwise stipulated in the Credit, a condition under a Credit calling for a document to be authenticated, validated, legalised, visaed, certified or indicating a similar requirement, will be satisfied by any signature, mark, stamp or label on such document that on its face appears to satisfy the above condition.

Article 21   Unspecified Issuers or Contents of Documents

When documents other than transport documents, insurance documents and commercial invoices are called for, the Credit should stipulate by whom such documents are to be issued and their wording or data content. If the Credit does not so stipulate, banks will accept such documents as presented, provided that their data content is not inconsistent with any other stipulated document presented.

Article 22   Issuance Date of Documents v. Credit Date

Unless otherwise stipulated in the Credit, banks will accept a document bearing a date of issuance prior to that of the Credit, subject to such document being presented within the time limits set out in the Credit and in these Articles.

Article 23   Marine/Ocean Bill of Lading

(a) If a Credit calls for a bill of lading covering a port-to-port shipment, banks will, unless otherwise stipulated in the Credit, accept a document, however named, which:

    (i) appears on its face to indicate the name of the carrier and to have been signed or otherwise authenticated by:

        — the carrier or a named agent for or on behalf of the carrier, or

        — the master or a named agent for or on behalf of the master.

Any signature or authentication of the carrier or master must be identified as carrier or master, as the case may be. An agent signing or authenticating for the carrier or master must also indicate the name and the capacity of the party, i.e. carrier or master, on whose behalf that agent is acting.

    and

    (ii) indicates that the goods have been loaded on board, or shipped on a named vessel.

Loading on board or shipment on a named vessel may be indicated by pre-printed wording on the bill of lading that the goods have been loaded on board a named vessel or shipped on a named vessel, in which case the date of issuance of the bill of lading will be deemed to be the date of loading on board and the date of shipment.

In all other cases loading on board a named vessel must be evidenced by a notation on the bill of lading which gives the date on which the goods have been loaded on board, in which case the date of the on board notation will be deemed to be the date of shipment.

If the bill of lading contains the indication 'intended vessel', or similar qualification in relation to the vessel, loading on board a named vessel must be evidenced by an on board notation on the bill of lading which, in addition to the date on which the goods have been loaded on board, also includes the name of the vessel on which the goods have been loaded, even if they have been loaded on the vessel named as the 'intended vessel'.

If the bill of lading indicates a place of receipt or taking in charge different from the port of loading, the on board notation must also include the port of loading stipulated in the Credit and the name of the vessel on which the goods have been loaded, even if they have been loaded on the vessel named in the bill of lading. This provision also applies whenever loading on board the vessel is indicated by pre-printed wording on the bill of lading.

and

    (iii) indicates the port of loading and the port of discharge stipulated in the Credit, notwithstanding that it:

        (a) indicates a place of taking in charge different from the port of loading, and/or a place of final destination different from the port of discharge,

        and/or

(b) contains the indication 'intended or similar qualification in relation to the port of loading and/or port of discharge, as long as the document also states the ports of loading and/or discharge stipulated in the Credit,

and

(iv) consists of a sole original bill of lading or, if issued in more than one original, the full set as so issued,

and

(v) appears to contain all of the terms and conditions of carriage, or some of such terms and conditions by reference to a source or document other than the bill of lading (short form/blank back bill of lading); banks will not examine the contents of such terms and conditions,

and

(vi) contains no indication that it is subject to a charter party and/or no indication that the carrying vessel is propelled by sail only,

and

(vii) in all other respects meets the stipulations of the Credit.

(b) For the purpose of this Article, transhipment means unloading and reloading from one vessel to another vessel during the course of ocean carriage from the port of loading to the port of discharge stipulated in the Credit.

(c) Unless transhipment is prohibited by the terms of the Credit, banks will accept a bill of lading which indicates that the goods will be transhipped, provided that the entire ocean carriage is covered by one and the same bill of lading.

(d) Even if the Credit prohibits transhipment, banks will accept a bill of lading which:

(i) indicates that transhipment will take place as long as the relevant cargo is shipped in Container(s), Trailer(s) and/or 'LASH' barge(s) as evidenced by the bill of lading, provided that the entire ocean carriage is covered by one and the same bill of lading.

and/or

(ii) incorporates clauses stating that the carrier resolves the right to tranship.

Article 24   Non-Negotiable Sea Waybill

(a) If a Credit calls for a non-negotiable sea waybill covering a port-to-port shipment, banks will, unless otherwise stipulated In the Credit, accept a document, however named, which:

(i) appears on its face to indicate the name of the carrier and to have been signed or otherwise authenticated by:
— the carrier or a named agent for or on behalf of the carrier, or
— the master or a named agent for or on behalf of the master,

any signature or authentication of the carrier or master must be identified as carrier or master, as the case may be. An agent signing or authenticating for the carrier or master must also indicate file name and the capacity of the party, i.e. carrier or master, on whose behalf that agent is acting,

and

(ii) indicates that the goods have been loaded on board, or shipped on a named vessel.

Loading on board or shipment on a named vessel maybe indicated by pre-printed wording on the non-negotiable sea waybill that the goods have been loaded on board a named vessel or shipped on a named vessel. In which case the date of issuance of the non-negotiable sea waybill will be deemed to be the date of loading on board and the date of shipment.

In all other cases loading on board a named vessel must be evidenced by a notation on the non-negotiable sea waybill which gives the date on which the goods have been loaded on board, in which case the date of the on board notation will be deemed to be the date of shipment.

If the non-negotiable sea waybill contains the indication 'intended vessel', or similar qualification in relation to the vessel, loading on board a named vessel must be evidenced by an on board notation on the non-negotiable sea waybill which, in addition to the date on which the goods have been loaded on board, includes the name of the vessel on which the goods have been loaded, even it they have been loaded on the vessel named as the 'intended vessel'.

If the non-negotiable sea waybill indicates a place of receipt or taking in charge different from the port of loading, the on board notation must also include the port of loading stipulated in the Credit and the name of the vessel on which the goods have been loaded, oven it they have been loaded on a vessel named in the non-negotiable sea waybill. This provision also applies whenever loading on board the vessel is indicated by pre-printed wording on the non-negotiable sea waybill,

and

> (iii) indicates the port of loading and the port of discharge stipulated in the Credit, notwithstanding that it:
>
> > (a) indicates a place of taking in charge different from the port of loading, and/or a place of final destination different from the port of discharge.
> >
> > and/or
> >
> > (b) contains the indication 'intended' or similar qualification in relation to the port of loading and/or port of discharge, as long as the document also states the ports of loading and/or discharge stipulated in the Credit.
>
> and
>
> (iv) consists of a sole original non-negotiable sea waybill, or it issued in more than one original, the full set as so issued,
>
> and
>
> (v) appears to contain all of the terms and conditions of carriage, or some of such terms and conditions by reference to a source or document other than the non-negotiable sea waybill (short form/blank back non-negotiable sea waybill); banks will not examine the contents of such terms and conditions,
>
> and
>
> (vi) contains no indication that it is subject to a charter party and/or no indication that the carrying vessel is propelled by sail only.
>
> and
>
> (vii) in all other respects meets the stipulations of the Credit.

(b) For the purpose of this Article, transhipment means unloading and reloading from one vessel to another vessel during the course of ocean carriage from the port of loading to the port of discharge stipulated in the Credit.

(c) Unless transhipment is prohibited by the terms of the Credit, banks will accept a non-negotiable sea waybill which indicates that the goods will be transhipped, provided that the entire ocean carriage is covered by one and the same non-negotiable sea waybill.

(d) Even if the Credit prohibits transhipment, banks will accept a non-negotiable sea waybill which:

> (i) indicates that transhipment will take place as long as the relevant cargo is shipped in Container(s). Trailer(s) and/or 'LASH' barge(s) as evidenced by the non-negotiable sea waybill, provided that the entire ocean carriage is covered by one and the same non-negotiable sea waybill,
>
> and/or
>
> (ii) incorporates clauses stating that the carrier reserves the right to tranship.

Article 25   Charter Party Bill of Lading

(a) If a Credit calls for or permits a charter party bill of lading, banks will, unless otherwise stipulated in the Credit, accept a document, however named, which:

  (i)   contains any indication that it is subject to a charter party, and

  (ii) appears on its face to have been signed or otherwise authenticated by:

  — the master or a named agent for or on behalf of the master, or

  — the owner or a named agent for or on behalf of the owner.

Any signature or authentication of the master or owner must be identified as master or owner as the case may be. An agent signing or authenticating for the master or owner must also indicate the name and the capacity of the party, i.e. master or owner, on whose behalf that agent is acting,

and

  (iii) does or does not indicate the name of the carrier. and

  (iv) indicates that the goods have been loaded on board or shipped an a named vessel.

Loading on board or shipment on a named vessel may be indicated by pre-printed wording on the bill of lading that the goods have been loaded on board a named vessel or shipped on a named vessel, in which case the date of issuance of the bill of lading will be deemed to be the date of loading on board and the date of shipment.

In all other cases loading on board a named vessel most be evidenced by a notation on the bill of lading which gives the date on which the goods have been loaded on board, in which case the date of the on board notation will be deemed to be the date of shipment.

and

  (v)   indicates the port of loading and the port of discharge stipulated in the Credit, and

  (vi) onsists of a sole original bill of lading or, if issued in more than one original, the full set as so issued, and

  (vii) contains no indication that the carrying vessel is propelled by sail only, and

  (viii) in all other respects meets the stipulations of the Credit.

(b) Even if the Credit requires the presentation of a charter party contract in connection with a charter party bill of lading, banks will not examine such charter party contract, but will pass it on without responsibility on their part.

Article 26   Multimodal Transport Document

(a) If a Credit calls for a transport document covering at least two different modes of transport (multimodal transport), banks will, unless otherwise stipulated in the Credit, accept a document, however named, which:

  (i)   appears on its face to indicate the name of the carrier or multimodal transport operator and to have been signed or otherwise authenticated by:

  — the carrier or multimodal transport operator or a named agent for or on behalf of the carrier or multimodal transport operator, or

  — the master or a named agent for or on behalf of the master.

Any signature or authentication of the carrier, multimodal transport operator or master must be identified as carrier, multimodal transport operator or master, as the case may be. An agent signing or authenticating for the carrier, multimodal transport operator or master must also indicate the name and the capacity of the party, i.e. carrier, multimodal transport operator or master, on whose behalf that agent is acting, and

  (ii) indicates that the goods have been dispatched, taken in charge or loaded on board.

Dispatch, taking in charge or loading on board may be indicated by wording to that effect on the multimodal transport document and the date of issuance will be deemed to be the

date of dispatch, taking in charge or loading on board and the date of shipment. However, if the document indicates, by stamp or otherwise, a date of dispatch, taking in charge or loading on board, such date will be deemed to be the date of shipment.
and

    (iii) (a) indicates the place of taking in charge stipulated in the Credit which may be different from the port, airport or place of loading, and the place of final destination stipulated in the Credit which may be different from the port, airport or place of discharge.
             and/or

        (b) contains the indication 'intended' or similar qualification in relation to the vessel and/or port of loading and/or port of discharge,
      and

    (iv) consists of a sole original multimodal transport document or, if issued in more than one original, the full set as so issued.
      and

    (v) appears to contain all of the terms and conditions of carriage, or some of such terms and conditions by reference to a source or document other than the multimodal transport document (short form/blank back multimodal transport document); banks will not examine the contents of such terms and conditions,
      and

    (vi) contains no indication that it is subject to a charter party and/or no indication that the carrying vessel is propelled by sail only,
      and

    (vii) in all other respects meets the stipulations of the Credit.

  (b) Even if the Credit prohibits transhipment, banks will accept a multimodal transport document which indicates that transhipment will or may take place, provided that the entire carriage is covered by one and the same multimodal transport document.

Article 27   Air Transport Document

  (a) If a Credit calls for an air transport document, banks will, unless otherwise stipulated in the Credit, accept a document, however named, which:

    (i) appears on its face to indicate the name of the carrier and to have been signed or otherwise authenticated by:
      — the carrier, or
      — a named agent for or on behalf of the carrier.

Any signature or authentication of the carrier must be identified as carrier. An agent signing or authenticating for the carrier must also indicate the name and the capacity of the party, i.e. carrier, on whose behalf that agent is acting,
and

    (ii) indicates that the goods have been accepted for carriage,
      and

    (iii) where the Credit calls for an actual date of dispatch, indicates a specific notation of such date, the date of dispatch so indicated on the air transport document will be deemed to be the date of shipment.

For the purpose of this Article, the information appearing in the box on the air transport document (marked 'For Carrier Use Only' or similar expression) relative to the flight number and date will not be considered as a specific notation of such date of dispatch.

In all other cases, the date of issuance of the air transport document will be deemed to be the date of shipment,
and

(iv) indicates the airport of departure and the airport of destination stipulated in the Credit,

(v) appears to be the original for consignor/shipper even if the Credit stipulates a full set of originals, or similar expressions, and

(vi) appears to contain all of the terms and conditions of carriage, or some of such terms and conditions, by reference to a source or document other than the air transport document; banks will not examine the contents of such terms and conditions, and

(vii) in all other respects meets the stipulations of the Credit.

(b) For the purpose of this Article, transhipment means unloading and reloading from one aircraft to another aircraft during the course of carriage from the airport of departure to the airport of destination stipulated in the Credit.

(c) Even if the Credit prohibits transhipment, banks will accept an air transport document which indicates that transhipment will or may take place, provided that the entire carriage is covered by one and the same air transport document.

Article 28   Road, Rail or Inland Waterway Transport Documents
If a Credit calls for a road, rail, or inland waterway transport document, banks will, unless otherwise stipulated in the Credit, accept a document of the type called for, however named, which:

(i) appears on its face to indicate the name of the carrier and to have been signed or otherwise authenticated by the carrier or a named agent for or on behalf of the carrier and/or to bear a reception stamp or other indication of receipt by the carrier or a named agent for or on behalf of the carrier.

Any signature, authentication, reception stamp or other indication of receipt of the carrier, must be identified on its face as that of the carrier. An agent signing or authenticating for the carrier, must also indicate the name and the capacity of the party, i.e. carrier, on whose behalf that agent is acting.
and

(ii) indicates that the goods have been received for shipment, dispatch or carriage or wording to this effect. The date of issuance will be deemed to be the date of shipment unless the transport document contains a reception stamp, in which case the date of the reception stamp will be deemed to be the date of shipment, and

(iii) indicates the place of shipment and the place of destination stipulated in the Credit, and

(iv) in all other respects meets the stipulations of the Credit.

(b) In the absence of any indication on the transport document as to the numbers issued, banks will accept the transport document(s) presented as constituting a full set. Banks will accept as original(s) the transport document(s) whether marked as original(s) or not.

(c) For the purpose of this Article, transhipment means unloading and reloading from one means of conveyance to another means of conveyance, in different modes of transport, during the course of carriage from the place of shipment to the place of destination stipulated in the Credit.

(d) Even if the Credit prohibits transhipment, banks will accept a road, rail, or inland waterway transport document which indicates that transhipment will or may take place, provided that the entire carriage is covered by one and the same transport document and within the same mode of transport.

Article 29   Courier and Post Receipts

(a) If a Credit calls for a post receipt or certificate of posting, banks will, unless otherwise stipulated in the Credit, accept a post receipt or certificate of posting which:

  (i) appears on its face to have been stamped or otherwise authenticated and dated in the place from which the Credit stipulates the goods are to be shipped or dispatched and such date will be deemed to be the date of shipment or dispatch.

  and

  (ii) in all other respects meets the stipulations of the Credit.

(b) If a Credit calls for a document issued by a courier or expedited delivery service evidencing receipt of the goods for delivery, banks will, unless otherwise stipulated in the Credit, accept a document, however named, which:

  (i) appears on its face to indicate the name of the courier service, and to have been stamped, signed or otherwise authenticated by such named courier service (unless the Credit specifically calls for a document issued by a named Courier/Service, banks will accept a document issued by any Courier/Service), and

  (ii) indicates a date of pick-up or of receipt or wording to this effect, such date being deemed to be the date of shipment or dispatch.

  and

  (iii) in all other respects meets the stipulations of the Credit.

Article 30   Transport Documents issued by Freight Forwarders

Unless otherwise authorised in the Credit, banks will only accept a transport document issued by a freight forwarder if it appears on its face to indicate:

  (i) the name of the freight forwarder as a carrier or multimodal transport operator and to have been signed or otherwise authenticated by the freight forwarder as carrier or multimodal transport operator,

  or

  (ii) the name of the carrier or multimodal transport operator and to have been signed or otherwise authenticated by the freight forwarder is a named agent for or on behalf of the carrier or multimodal transport operator.

Article 31   'On Deck', 'Shipper's Load and Count', Name of Consignor

Unless otherwise stipulated in the Credit, banks will accept a transport document which:

  (i) does not indicate, in the case of carriage by sea or by more than one means of conveyance including carriage by sea, that the goods are or will be loaded on deck. Nevertheless, banks will accept a transport document which contains a provision that the goods may be carried on deck, provided that it does not specifically state that they are or will be loaded on deck.

  and/or

  (ii) bears a clause on the face thereof such as 'shipper's load and count' or 'said by shipper to contain' or words of similar effect.

  and/or

  (iii) indicates as the consignor of the goods a party other than the Beneficiary of the Credit.

Article 32   Clean Transport Documents

(a) A clean transport document is one which bears no clause or notation which expressly declares a defective condition of the goods and/or the packaging.

(b) Banks will not accept transport documents bearing such clauses or notations unless the Credit expressly stipulates the clauses or notations which may be accepted.

(c) Banks will regard a requirement in a Credit for a transport document to bear the clause 'clean on board' as complied with if such transport document meets the requirements of this Article and of Articles 23, 24, 25, 26, 27, 28 or 30.

Article 33   Freight Payable/Prepaid Transport Documents

(a) Unless otherwise stipulated in the Credit, or inconsistent with any of the documents presented under the Credit, banks will accept transport documents stating that freight or transportation charges (hereafter referred to as 'freight') have still to be paid.

(b) If a Credit stipulates that the transport document has to indicate that freight has been paid or prepaid, banks will accept a transport document on which words clearly indicating payment or prepayment of freight appear by stamp or otherwise, or on which payment or prepayment of freight is indicated by other means. If the Credit requires courier charges to be paid or prepaid banks will also accept a transport document issued by a courier or expedited delivery service evidencing that courier charges are for the account of a party other than the consignee.

(c) The words 'freight prepayable' or 'freight to be prepaid' or words of similar effect, if appearing on transport documents, will not be accepted as constituting evidence of the payment of freight.

(d) Banks will accept transport documents bearing reference by stamp or otherwise to costs additional to the freight, such as costs of, or disbursements incurred in connection with, loading, unloading or similar operations, unless the conditions of the Credit specifically prohibit such reference.

Article 34   Insurance Documents

(a) Insurance documents must appear on their face to be issued and signed by insurance companies or underwriters or their agents.

(b) If the insurance document indicates that it has been issued in more than one original, all the originals must be presented unless otherwise authorised in the Credit.

(c) Cover notes issued by brokers will not be accepted, unless specifically authorised in the Credit.

(d) Unless otherwise stipulated in the Credit, banks will accept an insurance certificate or a declaration under an open cover pre-signed by insurance companies or underwriters or their agents, if a Credit specifically calls for an insurance certificate or a declaration under an open cover, banks will accept, in lieu thereof, an insurance policy.

(e) Unless otherwise stipulated in the Credit, or unless it appears from the insurance document that the cover is effective at the latest from the date of loading on board or dispatch or taking in charge of the goods, banks will not accept an insurance document which bears a date of issuance later than the date of loading on board or dispatch or taking in charge as indicated in such transport document.

(f) (i) Unless otherwise stipulated in the Credit, the insurance document must be expressed in the same currency as the Credit.

(ii) Unless otherwise stipulated in the Credit, the minimum amount for which the insurance document must indicate the insurance cover to have been effected is the CIF (cost, insurance and freight (. . . 'named port of destination')) or CIP (carriage and insurance paid to (. . . 'named place of destination')) value of the goods, as the case may be, plus 10%, but only when the CIF or CIP value can be determined from the documents on their face. Otherwise, banks will accept as such minimum amount 110% of the amount for which payment, acceptance or negotiation is requested under the Credit, or 110% of the gross amount of the invoice, whichever is the greater.

Article 35 Type of insurance Cover

(a) Credits should stipulate the type of insurance required and, if any, the additional risks which are to be covered. Imprecise terms such as 'usual risks' or 'customary risks' shall not be used; if they are used, banks will accept insurance documents as presented, without responsibility for any risks not being covered.

(b) Failing specific stipulations in the Credit, banks will accept insurance documents as presented, without responsibility for any risks not being covered.

(c) Unless otherwise stipulated in the Credit, banks will accept an insurance document which indicates that the cover is subject to a franchise or an excess (deductible).

Article 36 All Risks Insurance Cover

Where a Credit stipulates 'insurance against all risks', banks will accept an insurance document which contains any 'all risks' notation or clause, whether or not bearing the heading 'all risks', even if the insurance document indicates that certain risks are excluded, without responsibility for any risk(s) not being covered.

Article 37 Commercial Invoices

(a) Unless otherwise stipulated in the Credit, commercial invoices:

  (i) must appear on their face to be issued by the Beneficiary named in the Credit (except as provided in Article 46),
    and

  (ii) must be made out in the name of the Applicant (except as provided in sub-Article 48(h)),
    and

  (iii) need not be signed.

(b) Unless otherwise stipulated in the Credit, banks may refuse commercial invoices issued for amounts in excess of the amount permitted by the Credit. Nevertheless, if a bank authorised to pay, incur a deferred payment undertaking, accept Draft(s), or negotiate under a Credit accepts such invoices, its decision will be binding upon all parties, provided that such bank has not paid, incurred a deferred payment undertaking, accepted Draft(s) or negotiated for an amount in excess of that permitted by the Credit.

(c) The description of the goods in the commercial invoice must correspond with the description in the Credit. In all other documents, the goods may be described in general terms not inconsistent with the description of the goods in the Credit.

Article 38 Other Documents

If a Credit calls for an attestation or certification of weight in the case of transport other than by sea, banks will accept a weight stamp or declaration of weight which appears to have been superimposed on the transport document by the carrier or his agent unless the Credit specifically stipulates that the attestation or certification of weight must be by means of a separate document.

E. MISCELLANEOUS PROVISIONS

Article 39 Allowances in Credit Amount, Quantity and Unit Price

(a) The words 'about', 'approximately', 'circa' or similar expressions used in connection with the amount of the Credit or the quantity or the unit price stated in the Credit are to be construed as allowing a difference not to exceed 10% more or 10% less than the amount or the quantity or the unit price to which they refer.

(b) Unless a Credit stipulates that the quantify of the goods specified must not be exceeded or reduced, a tolerance of 5% more or 5% less will be permissible, always provided that the amount of the drawings does not exceed the amount of the Credit. This tolerance does not apply when the Credit stipulates the quantity in terms of a stated number of packing units or individual items.

(c) Unless a Credit which prohibits partial shipments stipulates otherwise, or unless sub-Article (b) above is applicable, a tolerance of 5% less in the amount of the drawing will be permissible, provided that if the Credit stipulates the quantity of the goods, such quantity of goods, is shipped in full, and if the Credit stipulates a unit price, such price is not reduced. This provision does not apply when expressions referred to in sub-Article (a) above are used in the Credit.

Article 40   Partial Shipments/Drawings

(a) Partial drawings and/or shipments are allowed, unless the Credit stipulates otherwise.

(b) Transport documents which appear on their face to indicate that shipment has been made on the same means of conveyance and for the same journey, provided they indicate the same destination, will not be regarded as covering partial shipments, even if the transport documents indicate different dates of shipment and/ or different ports of loading, places of taking in charge, or despatch.

(c) Shipments made by post or by courier will not be regarded as partial shipments if the post receipts or certificates of posting or courier's receipts or dispatch notes appear to have been stamped, signed or otherwise authenticated in the place from which the Credit stipulates the goods are to be dispatched, and on the same date.

Article 41   Instalment Shipments/Drawings

If drawings and/or shipments by instalments within given periods are stipulated in the Credit and any instalment is not drawn and/or shipped within the period allowed for that instalment, the Credit ceases to be available for that and any subsequent instalments, unless otherwise stipulated in the Credit.

Article 42   Expiry Date and Place for Presentation of Documents

(a) All Credits must stipulate an expiry date and a place for presentation of documents for payment, acceptance, or with the exception of freely negotiable Credits, a place for presentation of documents for negotiation. An expiry date stipulated for payment, acceptance or negotiation will be construed to express an expiry date for presentation of documents.

(b) Except as provided in sub-Article 44(a), documents must be presented on or before such expiry date.

(c) If an issuing Bank states that the Credit is to be available 'for one month', 'for six months', or the like, but does not specify the date from which the time is to run, the date of issuance of the Credit by the Issuing Bank will be deemed to be the first day from which such time is to run. Banks should discourage indication of the expiry date of the Credit in this manner.

Article 43   Limitation on the Expiry Date

(a) In addition to stipulating an expiry date for presentation of documents, every Credit which calls for a transport document(s) should also stipulate a specified period of time after the date of shipment during which presentation must be made in compliance with the terms and conditions of the Credit. If no such period of time is stipulated, banks will not accept documents presented to them later than 21 days after the date of shipment, in any event, documents must be presented not later than the expiry date of the Credit.

(b) In cases in which sub-Article 40(b) applies, the date of shipment will be considered to be the latest shipment date on any of the transport documents presented.

Article 44   Extension of Expiry Date

   (a) If the expiry date of the Credit and/or the last day of the period of time for presentation of documents stipulated by the Credit or applicable by virtue of Article 43 falls on a day on which the bank to which presentation has to be made is closed for reasons other than those referred to in Article 17, the stipulated expiry date and/or the last day of the period of time after the date of shipment for presentation of documents, as the case may be, shall be extended to the first following day on which such bank is open.

   (b) The latest date for shipment shall not be extended by reason of the extension of the expiry date and/or the period of time after the date of shipment for presentation of documents in accordance with sub-Article (a) above. If no such latest date for shipment is stipulated in the Credit or amendments thereto, banks will not accept transport documents indicating a date of shipment later than the expiry date stipulated in the Credit or amendments thereto.

   (c) The bank to which presentation is made on such first following business day must provide a statement that the documents were presented within the time limits extended in accordance with sub-Article 44(a) on the Uniform Customs and Practice for Documentary Credits, 1993 Revision, ICC Publication No. 500.

Article 45   Hours of Presentation

Banks are under no obligation to accept presentation of documents outside their banking hours.

Article 46   General Expressions as to Dates for Shipment

   (a) Unless otherwise stipulated in the Credit, the expression 'shipment' used in stipulating an earliest and/or a latest date for shipment will be understood to include expressions such as, 'loading on board', 'dispatch', 'accepted for carriage', 'date of post receipt', 'date of pick-up', and the like, and in the case of a Credit calling for a multimodal transport document the expression 'taking in charge'.

   (b) Expressions such as 'Prompt', 'immediately', 'as soon as possible', and the like should not be used. If they are used banks will disregard them.

   (c) If the expression 'on or about' or similar expressions are used, banks will interpret them as a stipulation that shipment is to be made during the period from five days before to five days after the specified date, both end days included.

Article 47   Date Terminology for Periods of Shipment

   (a) The words 'to', 'until', 'till', 'from' and words of similar import applying to any date or period in the Credit referring to shipment will be understood to include the date mentioned.

   (b) The word 'after' will be understood to exclude the date mentioned.

   (c) The terms 'first half', 'second half' of a month shall be construed respectively as the 1st to the 15th, and the 16th to the last day of such month, all dates inclusive.

   (d) The terms 'beginning', 'middle', or 'end' of a month shall be construed respectively as the 1st to the 10th, the 11th to the 20th, and the 21st to the last day of such month, all dates inclusive.

F.   TRANSFERABLE CREDIT

Article 48   Transferable Credit

   (a) A transferable Credit is a Credit under which the Beneficiary (First Beneficiary) may request the bank authorised to pay, incur a deferred payment undertaking, accept or negotiate (the 'Transferring Bank'), or in the case of a freely negotiable Credit, the bank specifically authorised in the Credit as a Transferring Bank, to make the Credit available in whole or in part to one or more other Beneficiary(ies) (Second Beneficiary(ies)).

(b) A Credit can be transferred only if it is expressly designated as 'transferable' by the Issuing Bank. Terms such as 'divisible', 'tractionable', 'assignable', and 'transmissible' do not render the Credit transferable. If such terms are used they shall be disregarded.

(c) The Transferring Bank shall be under no obligation to effect such transfer except to the extent and in the manner expressly consented to by such bank.

(d) At the time of making a request for transfer and prior to transfer of the Credit, the First Beneficiary must irrevocably instruct the Transferring Bank whether or not he retains the right to refuse to allow the Transferring Bank to advise amendments to the Second Beneficiary(ies). If the Transferring Bank consents to the transfer under these conditions. It must, at the time of transfer, advise the Second Beneficiary(ies) of the First Beneficiary's instructions regarding amendments.

(e) If a Credit is transferred to more than one Second Beneficiary(ies), refusal of an amendment by one or more Second Beneficiary(ies) does not invalidate the acceptance(s) by the other Second Beneficiary(ies) with respect to whom the Credit will be amended accordingly. With respect to the Second Beneficiary(ies) who rejected the amendment, the Credit will remain unamended.

(f) Transferring Bank charges in respect of transfers including commissions, fees, costs or expenses are payable by the First Beneficiary, unless otherwise agreed. If the Transferring Bank agrees to transfer the Credit it shall be under no obligation to effect the transfer until such charges are paid.

(g) Unless otherwise stated in the Credit, a transferable Credit can be transferred once only. Consequently, the Credit cannot be transferred at the request of the Second Beneficiary to any subsequent Third Beneficiary. For the purpose of this Article, a retransfer to the First Beneficiary does not constitute a prohibited transfer.

Fractions of a transferable Credit (not exceeding in the aggregate file amount of the Credit) can be transferred separately, provided partial shipments/drawings are not prohibited, and the aggregate of such transfers will be considered as constituting only one transfer of the Credit.

(h) The Credit can be transferred only on the terms and conditions specified in the original Credit, with the exception of:
— the amount of the Credit,
— any unit price stated therein,
— the expiry date,
— the last date for presentation of documents in accordance with Article 43,
— the period for shipment,
any or all of which may be reduced or curtailed.

The percentage for which insurance cover must be effected may be increased in such a way as to provide the amount of cover stipulated in the original Credit, or these Articles.

In addition, the name of the First Beneficiary can be substituted for that of file Applicant, but if the name of the Applicant is specifically required by the original Credit to appear in any document(s) other than the invoice, such requirement must be fulfilled.

(i) The First Beneficiary has the right to substitute his own invoice(s) (and Draft(s)) for those of the Second Beneficiary(ies), for amounts not in excess of the original amount stipulated in the Credit and for the original unit prices if stipulated in the Credit, and upon such substitution of invoice(s) (and Draft(s)) the First Beneficiary can draw under the Credit for the difference, if any, between his invoice(s) and the Second Beneficiary's(ies') invoice(s).

When a Credit has been transferred and the First Beneficiary is to supply his own invoice(s) (and Draft(s)) in exchange for the Second Beneficiary's(ies') invoice(s) (and Draft(s)) but fails to do so on first demand, the Transferring Bank has the right to deliver to the Issuing Bank the documents received under the transferred Credit, including the Second Beneficiary's(ies') invoice(s) (and Draft(s)) without further responsibility to the First Beneficiary.

(j) The First Beneficiary may request that payment or negotiation be effected to the Second Beneficiary(ies) at the place to which the Credit has been transferred up to and including the expiry date of the Credit, unless the original Credit expressly states that it may not be made available for payment or negotiation at a place other than that stipulated in the Credit. This is without prejudice to the First Beneficiary's right to substitute subsequently his own invoice(s) (and Draft(s)) for those of the Second Beneficiary(ies) and to claim any difference due to him.

G.   ASSIGNMENT OF PROCEEDS

Article 49   **Assignment of Proceeds**
The fact that a Credit is not stated to be transferable shall not affect the Beneficiary's right to assign any proceeds to which he may be, or may become, entitled under such Credit, in accordance with the provisions of the applicable law. This Article relates only to the assignment of proceeds and not to the assignment of the right to perform under the Credit itself.

ICC ARBITRATION

Contracting parties that wish to have the possibility of resorting to ICC Arbitration in the event of a dispute with their contracting partner should specifically and clearly agree upon ICC Arbitration in their contract or, in the event no single contractual document exists, in the exchange of correspondence which constitutes the agreement between them. The fact of issuing a letter of credit subject to the UCP 500 does NOT by itself constitute an agreement to have resort to ICC Arbitration. The following standard arbitration clause is recommended by the ICC:
'All disputes arising in connection with the present contract shall be finally settled under the Rules of Conciliation and Arbitration of the International Chamber of Commerce by one or more arbitrators appointed in accordance with the said Rules'.

Draft Convention on the Carriage of Goods [Wholly or Partly] [By Sea]
UNCITRAL A/CN.9/WG.III/WP.56

[8 September 2005]

CHAPTER 1.   GENERAL PROVISIONS

Article 1.   **Definitions**
For the purposes of this Convention:
(a) "Contract of carriage" means a contract in which a carrier, against the payment of freight, undertakes to carry goods from one place to another. The contract must provide for carriage by sea and may provide for carriage by other modes of transport in addition to the sea carriage.
(b) "Volume contract" means a contract that provides for the carriage of a specified quantity of cargo in a series of shipments during an agreed period of time. The specification of the quantity may include a minimum, a maximum or a certain range.
(c) "Non-liner transportation" means any transportation that is not liner transportation. For the purpose of this paragraph, "liner transportation" means a transportation service that (i) is offered to the public through publication or similar means and (ii) includes transportation by ships operating on a regular schedule between specified ports in accordance with publicly available timetables of sailing dates.

(d) "Carrier" means a person that enters into a contract of carriage with a shipper.

(e) "Performing party" means a person other than the carrier that physically performs or undertakes to perform any of the carrier's responsibilities under a contract of carriage with respect to the receipt, loading, handling, stowage, carriage, care, discharge or delivery of the goods, to the extent that such person acts, either directly or indirectly, at the carrier's request or under the carrier's supervision or control. The term "performing party" includes maritime performing parties and nonmaritime performing parties as defined in subparagraphs (f) and (g) of this paragraph but does not include any person that is retained by a shipper, a person referred to in article 34, consignor, controlling party or consignee, or is an employee, agent, contractor, or subcontractor of a person (other than the carrier) who is retained by a shipper, a person referred to in article 34, consignor, controlling party or consignee.

(f) "Maritime performing party" means a performing party that performs any of the carrier's responsibilities during the period between the arrival of the goods at the port of loading [or, in case of trans-shipment, at the first port of loading] of a ship and their departure from the port of discharge from a ship [or final port of discharge as the case may be]. In the event of a trans-shipment, the performing parties that perform any of the carrier's responsibilities inland during the period between the departure of the goods from a port and their arrival at another port of loading are not maritime performing parties.

(g) "Non-maritime performing party" means a performing party that performs any of the carrier's responsibilities prior to the arrival of the goods at the port of loading or after the departure of the goods from the port of discharge.

(h) "Shipper" means a person that enters into a contract of carriage with a carrier.

(i) "Consignor" means a person that delivers the goods to the carrier or a performing party for carriage.

(j) "Holder" means
  (i) a person that is for the time being in possession of a negotiable transport document and
      (a) if the document is an order document, is identified in it as the shipper or the consignee, or is the person to which the document is duly endorsed, or
      (b) if the document is a blank endorsed order document or bearer document, is the bearer thereof; or
  (ii) the person to which a negotiable electronic transport record has been issued or transferred and that has exclusive control of that negotiable electronic transport record.

(k) "Consignee" means a person entitled to take delivery of the goods under a contract of carriage or a transport document or electronic transport record.

(l) "Right of control" has the meaning given in article 54.

(m) "Controlling party" means the person that pursuant to article 56 is entitled to exercise the right of control.

(n) "Transport document" means a document issued pursuant to a contract of carriage by the carrier or a performing party that satisfies one or both of the following conditions:
  (i) it evidences the carrier's or a performing party's receipt of goods under a contract of carriage, or
  (ii) it evidences or contains a contract of carriage.

(o) "Negotiable transport document" means a transport document that indicates, by wording such as "to order" or "negotiable" or other appropriate wording recognized as having the same effect by the law governing the document, that the goods have been consigned to the order of the shipper, to the order of the consignee, or to bearer, and is not explicitly stated as being "non-negotiable" or "not negotiable".

(p) "Non-negotiable transport document" means a transport document that does not qualify as a negotiable transport document.

(q) "Electronic communication" means information generated, sent, received or stored by electronic, optical, digital or similar means with the result that the information communicated is accessible so as to be usable for subsequent reference.

(r) "Electronic transport record" means information in one or more messages issued by electronic communication pursuant to a contract of carriage by a carrier or a performing party, including information logically associated with the electronic transport record by attachments or otherwise linked to the electronic transport record contemporaneously with or subsequent to its issue by the carrier or a performing party, so as to become part of the electronic transport record, that satisfies one or both of the following conditions:

(i) it evidences the carrier's or a performing party's receipt of goods under a contract of carriage, or

(ii) it evidences or contains a contract of carriage.

(s) "Negotiable electronic transport record" means an electronic transport record

(i) that indicates, by statements such as "to order", or "negotiable", or other appropriate statements recognized as having the same effect by the law governing the record, that the goods have been consigned to the order of the shipper or to the order of the consignee, and is not explicitly stated as being "non-negotiable" or "not negotiable", and

(ii) the use of which meets the requirements of article 6(1).

(t) "Non-negotiable electronic transport record" means an electronic transport record that does not qualify as a negotiable electronic transport record.

(u) The "issuance" and the "transfer" of a negotiable electronic transport record means the issuance and the transfer of exclusive control over the record. [A person has exclusive control of an electronic transport record if the procedure employed under article 6 reliably establishes that person as the person that has the rights in the negotiable electronic transport record.]

(v) "Contract particulars" means any information relating to the contract of carriage or to the goods (including terms, notations, signatures and endorsements) that is in a transport document or an electronic transport record.

(w) "Goods" means the wares, merchandise, and articles of every kind [whatsoever that a carrier or a performing party [received for carriage] [undertakes to carry under a contract of carriage]] and includes the packing and any equipment and container not supplied by or on behalf of the carrier or a performing party.

(x) "Ship" means any vessel used to carry goods by sea.

(y) "Container" means any type of container, transportable tank or flat, swapbody, or any similar unit load used to consolidate goods, and any equipment ancillary to such unit load.

(z) "Freight" means the remuneration payable to the carrier for the carriage of goods under a contract of carriage.

(aa) "Domicile" means the place where (a) a company or other legal person [or association of natural or legal persons] has its (i) statutory seat or place of incorporation or registered office, as appropriate, (ii) central administration, or (iii) principal place of business, and (b) a natural person has her or his habitual residence.

[(bb) [Unless otherwise provided in this Convention] "the time of receipt" and "the place of the receipt" means the time and the place agreed to in the contract of carriage or, failing any specific provision relating to the receipt of the goods in such contract, the time and place that is in accordance with the customs, practices, or usages in the trade. In the absence of any such provisions in the contract of carriage or of such customs, practices, or usages, the time and place of receipt of the goods is when and where the carrier or a performing party actually takes custody of the goods.]

[(cc) [Unless otherwise provided in this Convention,] "the time of delivery" and "the place of delivery" means the time and the place agreed to in the contract of carriage, or, failing any specific provision relating to the delivery of the goods in such contract, the time and place that is in accordance with the customs, practices, or usages in the trade. In the absence of any such specific provision in the contract of carriage or of such customs, practices, or usages, the time and place of delivery is that of the discharge or unloading of the goods from the final means of transport in which they are carried under the contract of carriage.]

Article 2. Interpretation of this Convention

In the interpretation of this Convention, regard is to be had to its international character and to the need to promote uniformity in its application and the observance of good faith in international trade.

Article 3. Form requirements

The notices, confirmation, consent, agreement, declaration and other communications referred to in articles 20(2), 24(1), 24(2), 24(3), 38(1)(b) and (c), 41(c), 47, 52, 56(1), 63(2), 64(1), 71, 76, 95(1) and 95(6)(b) must be in writing. Electronic communications may be used for these purposes, provided the use of such means is with the express or implied consent of the party by which it is communicated and of the party to which it is communicated."

Article 4. Applicability of defences and limitations

1. The defences and limitations of liability provided for in this Convention and the responsibilities imposed by this Convention apply in any action against the carrier or a maritime performing party for loss of, or damage to, the goods covered by a contract of carriage and delay in delivery of such goods, or for the breach of any other obligation under this Convention, whether the action is founded in contract, in tort, or otherwise.

2. If an action is brought34 against an employee or agent of the carrier or a maritime performing party, that person is entitled to the benefit of the defences and limitations of liability available to the carrier under this Convention if [that person proves that] 35 it acted within the scope of its employment or agency.

CHAPTER 2.   ELECTRONIC COMMUNICATION

Article 5. Use and effect of electronic communications

Subject to the requirements set out in this Convention:

(a) Anything that is to be in or on a transport document in pursuance of this Convention may be recorded or communicated by using electronic communications instead of by means of the transport document, provided the issuance and subsequent use of an electronic transport record is with the express or implied consent of the carrier and the shipper; and

(b) The issuance, control, or transfer of an electronic transport record has the same effect as the issuance, possession, or transfer of a transport document.

Article 6. Procedures for use of negotiable electronic transport records

1. The use of a negotiable electronic transport record must be subject to procedures that provide for:

(a) The method for the issuance and the transfer of that record to an intended holder;

(b) An assurance that the negotiable electronic transport record retains its integrity;

(c) The manner in which the holder is able to demonstrate that it is the holder; and

(d) The way in which confirmation is given that delivery to the holder has been effected; or that, pursuant to articles 7(2) or 49(a)(ii), the negotiable electronic transport record has ceased to have any effect or validity.

2. The procedures in paragraph 1 must be referred to in the contract particulars and be readily ascertainable.

Article 7. **Replacement of negotiable transport document or negotiable electronic transport record**

1. If a negotiable transport document has been issued and the carrier and the holder agree to replace that document by a negotiable electronic transport record:

(a) The holder must surrender the negotiable transport document, or all of them if more than one has been issued, to the carrier;

(b) The carrier must issue to the holder a negotiable electronic transport record that includes a statement that it is issued in substitution for the negotiable transport document; and

(c) The negotiable transport document ceases thereafter to have any effect or validity.

2. If a negotiable electronic transport record has been issued and the carrier and the holder agree to replace that electronic transport record by a negotiable transport document:

(a) The carrier must issue to the holder, in substitution for that electronic transport record, a negotiable transport document that includes a statement that it is issued in substitution for the negotiable electronic transport record; and

(b) Upon such substitution, the electronic transport record ceases to have any effect or validity.

CHAPTER 3.   SCOPE OF APPLICATION

Article 8.   General scope of application

1. Subject to article 9(1), this Convention applies to contracts of carriage in which the place of receipt and the place of delivery are in different States, and the port of loading [of a sea carriage] and the port of discharge [of the same sea carriage] are in different States, if:

(a) The place of receipt [or port of loading] is located in a Contracting State; or

(b) The place of delivery [or port of discharge] is located in a Contracting State; or

[(c) The contract of carriage provides that this Convention, or the law of any State giving effect to it, is to govern the contract.]

References to [places and] ports mean the [places and] ports agreed in the contract of carriage.

2. This Convention applies without regard to the nationality of the vessel, the carrier, the performing parties, the shipper, the consignee, or any other interested parties.

Article 9.   Specific exclusions and inclusions

1. This Convention does not apply to:

(a) Charterparties;

(b) Contracts for the use of a ship or of any space thereon;

(c) Except as provided in paragraph 2, other contracts in non-liner transportation; and

(d) Except as provided in paragraph 3, volume contracts.

2. Without prejudice to subparagraphs 1(a) and (b), this Convention applies to contracts of carriage in non-liner transportation when evidenced by or contained in a transport document or an electronic transport record that also evidences the carrier's or a performing party's receipt of the goods, except as between the parties to a charterparty or to a contract for the use of a ship or of any space thereon.

3. (a) This Convention applies to the terms that regulate each shipment under a volume contract to the extent that the provisions of this chapter so specify.

(b) This Convention applies to the terms of a volume contract to the extent that they regulate a shipment under that volume contract that is governed by this Convention under subparagraph (a).

Article 10.   Application to certain parties

Notwithstanding article 9, if a transport document or an electronic transport record is issued pursuant to a charterparty or a contract under article 9 (1)(b) or (c), this Convention applies to the contract evidenced by or contained in the transport document or electronic transport record as between the carrier and the consignor, consignee, controlling party, holder, or person referred to in article 34 that is not the charterer or the party to the contract under article 9 (1)(b) or (c).

CHAPTER 4.   PERIOD OF RESPONSIBILITY

Article 11.   Period of responsibility of the carrier

1. Subject to article 12, the responsibility of the carrier for the goods under this Convention covers the period from the time when the carrier or a performing party has received the goods for carriage until the time when the goods are delivered to the consignee.

2. The time and location of receipt of the goods is the time and location agreed in the contract of carriage or, failing such agreement, the time and location that is in accordance with the customs, practices, or usages in the trade. In the absence of such agreement or of such customs, practices, or usages, the time and location of receipt of the goods is when and where the carrier or a performing party actually takes custody of the goods.

3. If the consignor is required to hand over the goods at the place of receipt to an authority or other third party to which, pursuant to applicable law or regulation, the goods must be handed over and from which the carrier may collect them, the time and location of the carrier's collection of the goods from the authority or other third party is the time and location of the receipt of the goods by the carrier under paragraph 2.

4. The time and location of delivery of the goods is the time and location agreed in the contract of carriage, or, failing such agreement, the time and location that is in accordance with the customs, practices, or usages in the trade. In the absence of such agreement or of such customs, practices, or usages, the time and location of delivery is that of the discharge or unloading of the goods from the final means of transport in which they are carried under the contract of carriage.

5. If the carrier is required to hand over the goods at the place of delivery to an authority or other third party to which, pursuant to applicable law or regulation, the goods must be handed over and from which the consignee may collect them, such handing over is a delivery of the goods by the carrier to the consignee under paragraph 4.

6. For the purposes of determining the carrier's period of responsibility and subject to paragraph 14(2), the contract of carriage may not provide that:

(a) The time of receipt of the goods is subsequent to the commencement of their initial loading under the contract of carriage, or

(b) The time of delivery of the goods is prior to the completion of their final discharge under the contract of carriage.

Article 12.   Transport beyond the contract of carriage

Variant A of article 12

1. The parties may expressly agree in the contract of carriage that in respect of a specified part or parts of the transport of the goods the carrier, acting as agent, will arrange carriage by another carrier or carriers.

2. In such event the carrier must exercise due diligence in selecting the other carrier, conclude a contract with such other carrier on usual and normal terms, and do everything that is reasonably required to enable such other carrier to perform duly under its contract.

Variant B of article 12

On the request of the shipper, the carrier may agree to issue a single transport document or an electronic transport record that includes specified transport that is not covered by the contract of carriage.In such an event, the responsibility of the carrier covers the period of the contract of carriage and, unless otherwise agreed, the carrier, on behalf of the shipper, must arrange the additional transport as provided in such transport document or electronic transport record.

CHAPTER 5.   OBLIGATIONS OF THE CARRIER

Article 13.   Carriage and delivery of the goods

The carrier must, subject to this Convention and in accordance with the terms of the contract of carriage, carry the goods to the place of destination and deliver them to the consignee.

Article 14.   Specific obligations

1. The carrier must during the period of its responsibility as defined in article 11, and subject to article 27, properly and carefully receive, load, handle, stow, carry, keep, care for, discharge and deliver the goods.

[2. The parties may agree that the loading, stowing and discharging of the goods is to be performed by the shipper or any person referred to in article 35, the controlling party or the consignee. Such an agreement must be referred to in the contract particulars.]

Article 15.   Goods that may become a danger

Variant A

Notwithstanding articles 13, 14, and 16(1), the carrier may decline to load, or may unload, destroy, or render goods harmless or take such other measures as are reasonable if goods are, or reasonably appear likely during its period of responsibility to become, an actual danger to persons or property or an illegal or unacceptable danger to the environment.

Variant B

Notwithstanding articles 13, 14, and 16(1), the carrier may unload, destroy or render goods harmless if they become an actual danger to persons or property.

Article 16.   Specific obligations applicable to the voyage by sea

1. The carrier is bound, before, at the beginning of, and during61 the voyage by sea, to exercise due diligence to:

(a) Make and keep the ship seaworthy;

(b) Properly man, equip and supply the ship and keep the ship so manned, equipped and supplied throughout the voyage;

(c) Make and keep the holds and all other parts of the ship in which the goods are carried, including containers when supplied by the carrier, in or upon which the goods are carried fit and safe for their reception, carriage and preservation.

[2. Notwithstanding articles 13, 14, and 16(1), the carrier may sacrifice goods when the sacrifice is reasonably made for the common safety or for the purpose of preserving from peril human life or other property involved in the common adventure.]

CHAPTER 6.   LIABILITY OF THE CARRIER FOR LOSS, DAMAGE OR DELAY

Article 17.   Basis of liability

1. The carrier is liable for loss of or damage to the goods, as well as for delay in delivery, if the claimant proves that

(a) the loss, damage, or delay; or

(b) the occurrence that caused or contributed to the loss, damage, or delay

took place during the period of the carrier's responsibility as defined in chapter 4. The carrier is relieved of all or part of its liability if it proves that the cause or one of the causes of the loss, damage, or delay is not attributable to its fault or to the fault of any person referred to in article 19.

2. If the carrier, alternatively to proving the absence of fault as provided in paragraph 1, proves that an event listed in paragraph 3 caused or contributed to the loss, damage, or delay, then the carrier is relieved of all or part of its liability subject to the following provisions:

(a) If the claimant proves that the fault of the carrier or of a person referred to in article 19 caused or contributed to the event on which the carrier relies, then the carrier is liable for all or part of the loss, damage, or delay.

(b) If the claimant proves that an event not listed in paragraph 3 contributed to the loss, damage, or delay, and the carrier cannot prove that this event is not attributable to its fault or to the fault of any person referred to in article 19, then the carrier is liable for part of the loss, damage, or delay.

(c) If the claimant proves that the loss, damage, or delay was or was probably caused by or contributed to by

(i)   the unseaworthiness of the ship;

(ii) the improper manning, equipping, and supplying of the ship; or

(iii) the fact that the holds or other parts of the ship in which the goods are carried (including containers, when supplied by the carrier, in or upon which the goods are carried) were not fit and safe for reception, carriage, and preservation of the goods, and the carrier cannot prove that;

(A) it complied with its obligation to exercise due diligence as required under article 16(1); or

(B) the loss, damage, or delay was not caused by any of the circumstances referred to in (i), (ii), and (iii) above,

then the carrier is liable for part or all of the loss, damage, or delay.

3. The events mentioned in paragraph 2 are:

(a) Act of God;

(b) Perils, dangers, and accidents of the sea or other navigable waters;

(c) War, hostilities, armed conflict, piracy, terrorism, riots, and civil commotions;

(d) Quarantine restrictions; interference by or impediments created by governments, public authorities, rulers, or people including detention, arrest, or seizure not attributable to the carrier or any person referred to in article 19;

(e) Strikes, lockouts, stoppages, or restraints of labour;

(f) Fire on the ship;

(g) Latent defects in the [ship][vessel][means of transport] not discoverable by due diligence;

(h) Act or omission of the shipper or any person referred to in article 35, the controlling party, or the consignee;

(i) Handling, loading, [stowage,] or discharging of the goods [actually performed] by the shipper or any person referred to in article 35, the controlling party, or the consignee;

(j) Wastage in bulk or weight or any other loss or damage arising from inherent quality, defect, or vice of the goods;

(k) Insufficiency or defective condition of packing or marking not performed by [or on behalf of] the carrier;

(l) Saving or attempting to save life at sea;

(m) Reasonable measures to save or attempt to save property at sea;

(n) Reasonable measures to avoid or attempt to avoid damage to the environment;

[(o) Acts of the carrier or a performing party in pursuance of the powers conferred by articles 15 and 16(2) when the goods have become a danger to persons, property, or the environment or have been sacrificed.]

4. When the carrier is relieved of part of its liability pursuant to the previous paragraphs of this article, then the carrier is liable only for that part of the loss, damage, or delay that is attributable to the event or occurrence for which it is liable under the previous paragraphs, and liability must be apportioned on the basis established in the previous paragraphs.

Article 18.   Carrier's liability for failure to provide information and instructions

The carrier is liable for loss, damage [, delay] or injury caused by a breach of its obligations under article 29, unless [and to the extent] the carrier proves that neither its fault nor the fault of any person referred to in article 19 caused [or contributed to] the loss, damage [, delay] or injury.

Article 19.   Vicarious liability of the carrier

1. Subject to paragraph 20(4), the carrier is liable for the acts and omissions of:

(a) Any performing party, and

(b) Any other person, including a performing party's subcontractors, employees and agents, that performs or undertakes to perform any of the carrier's responsibilities under the contract of carriage, to the extent that the person acts, either directly or indirectly, at the carrier's request or under the carrier's supervision or control, as if such acts or omissions were its own.

2. The carrier is liable under paragraph 1 only when the performing party's or other person's act or omission is within the scope of its contract, employment, or agency.

Article 20.   Liability of maritime performing parties

1. A maritime performing party is subject to the responsibilities and liabilities imposed on the carrier under this Convention, and entitled to the carrier's rights and immunities provided by this Convention if the occurrence that caused the loss, damage or delay took place (a) during the period in which it has custody of the goods; or (b) at any other time to the extent that it is participating in the performance of any of the activities contemplated by the contract of carriage.

2. If the carrier agrees to assume responsibilities other than those imposed on the carrier under this Convention, or agrees that its liability for the delay in delivery of, loss of, or damage to or in connection with the goods is higher than the limits imposed under articles 65, 64 and 26(4), a maritime performing party is not bound by this agreement unless the maritime performing party expressly agrees to accept such responsibilities or such limits.

3. Subject to paragraph 4, a maritime performing party is liable for the acts and omissions of any person to which it has delegated the performance of any of the carrier's responsibilities under the contract of carriage, including its subcontractors, employees, and agents, as if such acts or omissions were its own. A maritime performing party is liable under this paragraph only when the act or omission of the person concerned is within the scope of its contract, employment, or agency.

Variant A of paragraph 4

4. If an action under this Convention is brought against a maritime performing party, that party is entitled to the benefit of the defences and limitations of liability available to the carrier under this Convention if [it proves that]86 it acted within the scope of its contract, employment or agency.

4. If an action under this Convention is brought against any person, other than the carrier, referred to in article 19 or paragraph 3, [, including employees or agents of the contracting carrier or of a maritime performing party,] that person is entitled to the benefit of the defences and limitations of liability available to the carrier under this Convention if [it proves that] it acted within the scope of its contract, employment, or agency.

Article 21.   Joint and several liability and set-off
1. If the carrier and one or more maritime performing parties are liable for the loss of, damage to, or delay in delivery of the goods, their liability is joint and several [, such that each such party is liable for compensating the entire amount of such loss, damage or delay, without prejudice to any right of recourse it may have against other liable parties,] but only up to the limits provided for in articles 22, 64 and 26.

2. Without prejudice to article 66, the aggregate liability of all such persons must not exceed the overall limits of liability under this Convention.

[3. When a claimant has made a successful claim against a non-maritime performing party for the loss of, damage to, or delay in delivery of the goods, the amount received by the claimant is set off against any subsequent claim for that loss, damage or delay that the claimant makes against a carrier or a maritime performing party.]

Article 22.   Delay
Delay in delivery occurs when the goods are not delivered at the place of destination provided for in the contract of carriage within the time expressly agreed upon or, in the absence of such agreement, within the time it would be reasonable to expect of a diligent carrier, having regard to the terms of the contract, the characteristics of the transport, and the circumstances of the voyage or journey.

Article 23.   Calculation of compensation
1. Subject to article 64, the compensation payable by the carrier for loss of or damage to the goods is calculated by reference to the value of such goods at the place and time of delivery established in accordance with article 11.

2. The value of the goods is fixed according to the commodity exchange price or, if there is no such price, according to their market price or, if there is no commodity exchange price or market price, by reference to the normal value of the goods of the same kind and quality at the place of delivery.

3. In case of loss of or damage to the goods, the carrier is not liable for payment of any compensation beyond what is provided for in paragraphs 1 and 2 except when the carrier and the shipper have agreed to calculate compensation in a different manner within the limits of chapter 20.

Article 24.   Notice of loss, damage, or delay

[Variant A of paragraph 1
1. The carrier is presumed, in absence of proof to the contrary, to have delivered the goods according to their description in the contract particulars unless notice of loss of or damage to the goods, indicating the general nature of such loss or damage, was given [by or on behalf of the consignee] to the carrier or the performing party that delivered the goods before or at the time of the delivery, or, if the loss or damage is not apparent, within [three working days][seven days][seven working days at the place of delivery][seven consecutive days] after the delivery of the goods. Such a notice is not required in respect of loss or damage that is ascertained in a joint inspection of the goods by the consignee and the carrier or the performing party against which liability is being asserted.]

[Variant B of paragraph 1

   1. Notice of loss of or damage to the goods, indicating the general nature of such loss or damage, must be given [by or on behalf of the consignee] to the carrier or the performing party that delivered the goods before or at the time of the delivery, or, if the loss or damage is not apparent, within [three working days][__working days at the place of delivery] [__consecutive days] after the delivery of the goods. [A court [may] [must] consider the failure to give such notice in deciding whether the claimant has carried its burden of proof under article 17(1).] Such a notice is not required in respect of loss or damage that is ascertained in a joint inspection of the goods by the consignee and the carrier or the performing party against which liability is being asserted.]

   2. No compensation is payable under article 22 unless notice of loss due to delay was given to the carrier within 21 consecutive days following delivery of the goods.

   3. When the notice referred to in this article is given to the performing party that delivered the goods, it has the same effect as if that notice was given to the carrier, and notice given to the carrier has the same effect as a notice given to a maritime performing party.

   4. In the case of any actual or apprehended loss or damage, the parties to the claim or dispute must give all reasonable facilities to each other for inspecting and tallying the goods and must provide access to records and documents relevant to the carriage of the goods.

CHAPTER 7. ADDITIONAL PROVISIONS RELATING TO PARTICULAR STAGES OF CARRIAGE

Article 25. Deviation during sea carriage

[Variant A

   1. The carrier is not liable for loss, damage, or delay in delivery caused by a deviation to save or attempt to save life [or property] at sea[, or by any other [reasonable] deviation].

   2. When under national law a deviation of itself constitutes a breach of the carrier's obligations, such breach only has effect consistently with this Convention.]

[Variant B

   1. The carrier is not liable for loss, damage, or delay in delivery caused by any deviation to save or attempt to save life or property at sea, or by any other reasonable deviation.

   2. To the extent that a deviation constitutes a breach of the carrier's obligations under a legal doctrine recognized by national law or in this Convention, that doctrine applies only when there has been an unreasonable deviation with respect to the routing of a ship.

   3. To the extent that a deviation constitutes a breach of the carrier's obligations, the breach has effect only under the terms of this Convention. In particular, a deviation does not deprive the carrier of its rights under this Convention except to the extent provided in article 66.]

Article 26. Deck cargo on ships
   1. Goods may be carried on or above the deck of a ship only if:
      (a) Such carriage is required by applicable laws or administrative rules or regulations, or
      (b) They are carried in or on containers [fitted to carry cargo on deck] on decks that are specially fitted to carry such containers, or
      (c) [In cases not covered by subparagraphs (a) or (b) of this paragraph,] the carriage on deck [is in accordance with the contract of carriage, or] complies with the customs, usages, and practices of the trade, or follows from other usages or practices in the trade in question.

2. If the goods have been shipped in accordance with subparagraphs 1(a) or (c), the carrier is not liable for loss of or damage to these goods or delay in delivery caused by the special risks involved in their carriage on deck. If the goods are carried on or above deck pursuant to subparagraph 1(b), the carrier is liable for loss of or damage to such goods, or for delay in delivery, under the terms of this Convention without regard to whether they are carried on or above deck. If the goods are carried on deck in cases other than those permitted under paragraph 1, the carrier is liable, irrespective of article 17, for loss of or damage to the goods or delay in delivery that are exclusively the consequence of their carriage on deck.

3. If the goods have been shipped in accordance with subparagraph 1(c), the fact that particular goods are carried on deck must be included in the contract particulars. Failing this, the carrier has the burden of proving that carriage on deck complies with subparagraph 1(c) and, if a negotiable transport document or a negotiable electronic transport record is issued, is not entitled to invoke that subparagraph against a third party that has acquired such negotiable transport document or electronic transport record in good faith.

[4. If the carrier is liable under this article for loss or damage to goods carried on deck or for delay in their delivery, its liability is limited to the extent provided in articles 22, 64 and 66(1); but, if the carrier and shipper [expressly] agreed that the goods would be carried under deck, the carrier is not entitled to limit its liability for any loss of or damage to the goods [[that exclusively][to the extent that such damage] resulted from their carriage on deck].]

[**Article 27.   Carriage preceding or subsequent to sea carriage**

1. When a claim or dispute arises out of loss of or damage to goods or delay occurring solely during the carrier's period of responsibility but:

(a) Before the time of their loading on to the ship;

(b) After their discharge from the ship to the time of their delivery to the consignee;
and, at the time of such loss, damage or delay, provisions of an international convention [or national law]:

(i)   according to their terms apply to all or any of the carrier's activities under the contract of carriage during that period, [irrespective whether the issuance of any particular document is needed in order to make such international convention applicable], and

(ii) specifically provide for carrier's liability, limitation of liability, or time for suit, and

(iii) cannot be departed from by private contract either at all or to the detriment of the shipper,

such provisions, to the extent that they are mandatory as indicated in (iii) above, prevail over the provisions of this Convention.]

[2. Paragraph 1 does not affect the application of article 64(2).]

[3. Article 27 applies regardless of the national law otherwise applicable to the contract of carriage.]

CHAPTER 8.   OBLIGATIONS OF THE SHIPPER

Article 28.   Delivery for carriage

The shipper must deliver the goods ready for carriage, unless otherwise agreed in the contract of carriage, and in such condition that they will withstand the intended carriage, including their loading, handling, stowage, lashing and securing, and discharge, and that they will not cause injury or damage. In the event the goods are delivered in or on a container or trailer packed by the shipper, the shipper must stow, lash and secure the goods in or on the container or trailer in such a way that the goods will withstand the intended carriage, including loading, handling and discharge of the container or trailer, and that they will not cause injury or damage.

Article 29.   Carrier's obligation to provide information and instructions

The carrier must provide to the shipper, on its request [and in a timely manner], such information as is within the carrier's knowledge and instructions that are reasonably necessary or of importance to the shipper in order to comply with its obligations under article 28. [The information and instructions so provided must be accurate and complete.]

Article 30.   Shipper's obligation to provide information, instructions and documents

The shipper must provide to the carrier [in a timely manner, such accurate and complete] information, instructions, and documents as are reasonably necessary for:

(a) The handling and carriage of the goods, including precautions to be taken by the carrier or a performing party, except to the extent that the shipper may reasonably assume that such information is already known to the carrier;

(b) Compliance with rules, regulations, and other requirements of authorities in connection with the intended carriage, including filings, applications, and licences relating to the goods;

(c) The compilation of the contract particulars and the issuance of the transport documents or electronic transport records, including the particulars referred to in article 38(1)(b) and (c); the name of the party to be identified as the shipper in the contract particulars; the name of the consignee, if any; and the name of the person to whose order the transport document or electronic transport record is to be issued, if any, unless the shipper may reasonably assume that such information is already known to the carrier.

Article 31.   Basis of shipper's liability

1. The shipper is liable for loss, damage [, delay] or injury caused by the goods, and for breach of its obligations under article 28 and paragraph 30(a), [unless][unless and to the extent that][except to the extent that] the shipper proves that neither its fault nor the fault of any person referred to in article 35 caused or contributed to the loss, damage [, delay] or injury.

[Variant A of paragraph 2

2. The shipper is liable for loss or damage caused by a breach of its obligations under paragraphs 30(b) and (c).]

[Variant B of paragraph 2

2. The shipper is deemed to have guaranteed to the carrier the timeliness, accuracy and completeness at the time of receipt by the carrier of the information, instructions and documents that the shipper is required to provide under paragraphs 30(b) and (c). The shipper must indemnify the carrier against all loss, damages and expenses arising or resulting from any breach of obligations under paragraphs 30(b) and (c). The right of the carrier to such indemnity in no way limits its responsibility under the contract of carriage to any person other than the shipper.]

3. When loss or damage [or injury] is caused jointly by the failure of the shipper and of the carrier to comply with their respective obligations, the shipper and the carrier are jointly liable to the consignee or the controlling party for any such loss or damage [or injury].

[Article 32.   Material misstatement by shipper

A carrier is not liable for delay in the delivery of, the loss of, or damage to or in connection with the goods if the nature or value of the goods was knowingly and materially misstated by the shipper in the contract of carriage or a transport document or electronic transport record.]

Article 33.   Special rules on dangerous goods

1. "Dangerous goods" means goods which by their nature or character are, or reasonably appear likely to become, a danger to persons or property or an illegal or unacceptable danger to the environment.

2. The shipper must mark or label dangerous goods in accordance with any rules, regulations or other requirements of authorities that apply during any stage of the intended carriage of the goods. If the shipper fails to do so, it is liable to the carrier and any performing party for all loss, damages, delay and expenses directly or indirectly arising out of or resulting from such failure.

3. The shipper must inform the carrier of the dangerous nature or character of the goods in a timely manner before the consignor delivers them to the carrier or a performing party. If the shipper fails to do so and the carrier or performing party does not otherwise have knowledge of their dangerous nature or character, the shipper is liable to the carrier and any performing party for all loss, damages, delay and expenses directly or indirectly arising out of or resulting from such shipment.

Article 34.   Assumption of shipper's rights and obligations

If a person identified as "shipper" in the contract particulars, although not the shipper as defined in paragraph 1(h), [accepts][receives][becomes a holder of] the transport document or electronic transport record, then such person is (a) [subject to the responsibilities and liabilities] imposed on the shipper under this chapter and under article 59, and (b) entitled to the shipper's rights and immunities provided by this chapter and by chapter 14.

Article 35.   Vicarious liability of the shipper

The shipper is liable for the acts and omissions of any person to which it has delegated the performance of any of its responsibilities under this chapter, including its sub-contractors, employees, agents, and any other persons [except the carrier or performing parties] that act, either directly or indirectly, at its request, or under its supervision or control, as if such acts or omissions were its own. Liability is imposed on the shipper under this article only when the act or omission of the person concerned is within the scope of that person's contract, employment, or agency.

[Article 36.   Cessation of shipper's liability

If the contract of carriage provides that the liability of the shipper or any other person identified in the contract particulars as the shipper will cease, wholly or partly, upon a certain event or after a certain time, such cessation is not valid:

(a) With respect to any liability under this chapter of the shipper or a person referred to in article 34; or

(b) With respect to any amounts payable to the carrier under the contract of carriage, except to the extent that the carrier has adequate security for the payment of such amounts.

(c) To the extent that it conflicts with article 63.]

CHAPTER 9.   TRANSPORT DOCUMENTS AND ELECTRONIC TRANSPORT RECORDS

Article 37.   Issuance of the transport document or the electronic transport record

Upon delivery of the goods to the carrier or performing party:

(a) The consignor is entitled to obtain a transport document or, subject to article 5(a), an electronic transport record evidencing the carrier's or performing party's receipt of the goods; and

(b) The shipper or, if the shipper instructs the carrier, the person referred to in article 34, is entitled to obtain from the carrier an appropriate negotiable transport document or, subject to paragraph 5(a), electronic transport record, unless the shipper and the carrier, expressly or impliedly, have agreed not to use a negotiable transport document or electronic transport record, or it is the custom, usage, or practice in the trade not to use one.

Article 38.   Contract Particulars

1. The contract particulars in the transport document or electronic transport record referred to in article 37 must include:

(a) A description of the goods;

(b) The leading marks necessary for identification of the goods as furnished by the shipper before the carrier or a performing party receives the goods;

(c) (i) The number of packages, the number of pieces, or the quantity, as furnished by the shipper before the carrier or a performing party receives the goods and

(ii) The weight as furnished by the shipper before the carrier or a performing party receives the goods;

(d) A statement of the apparent order and condition of the goods at the time the carrier or a performing party receives them for shipment;

(e) The name and address of the carrier; and

(f) The date

(i) on which the carrier or a performing party received the goods, or

(ii) on which the goods were loaded on board the ship, or

(iii) on which the transport document or electronic transport record was issued.

2. The phrase "apparent order and condition of the goods" in paragraph 1 refers to the order and condition of the goods based on:

(a) A reasonable external inspection of the goods as packaged at the time the shipper delivers them to the carrier or a performing party and

(b) Any additional inspection that the carrier or a performing party actually performs before issuing the transport document or the electronic transport record.

Article 39. Signature

1. A transport document must be signed by the carrier or a person having authority from the carrier.

2. An electronic transport record must include the electronic signature of the carrier or a person having authority from the carrier. Such electronic signature must identify the signatory in relation to the electronic transport record and indicate the carrier's authorization of the electronic transport record.

Article 40. Deficiencies in the contract particulars

1. The absence of one or more of the contract particulars referred to in article 38(1), or the inaccuracy of one or more of those particulars, does not of itself affect the legal character or validity of the transport document or of the electronic transport record.

2. If the contract particulars include the date but fail to indicate its significance, then the date is considered to be:

(a) If the contract particulars indicate that the goods have been loaded on board a ship, the date on which all of the goods indicated in the transport document or electronic transport record were loaded on board the ship; or

(b) If the contract particulars do not indicate that the goods have been loaded on board a ship, the date on which the carrier or a performing party received the goods.

[3. If the contract particulars fail to identify the carrier but indicate that the goods have been loaded on board a named ship, then the registered owner of the ship is presumed to be the carrier. The registered owner can defeat this presumption if it proves that the ship was under a bareboat charter at the time of the carriage that transfers contractual responsibility for the carriage of the goods to an identified bareboat charterer. [If the registered owner defeats the presumption that it is the carrier under this article, then the bareboat charterer at the time of the carriage is presumed to be the carrier in the same manner as that in which the registered owner was presumed to be the carrier.]]

4. If the contract particulars fail to state the apparent order and condition of the goods at the time the carrier or a performing party receives them from the consignor, the transport document or electronic transport record is either prima facie or conclusive evidence under article 43, as the case may be, that the goods were in apparent good order and condition at the time the consignor delivered them to the carrier or a performing party.

Article 41.   Qualifying the description of the goods in the contract particulars

The carrier, if acting in good faith when issuing a transport document or an electronic transport record, may qualify the information referred to in article 38(1)(a), 38(1)(b) or 38(1)(c) in the circumstances and in the manner set out below in order to indicate that the carrier does not assume responsibility for the accuracy of the information furnished by the shipper:

(a) For non-containerized goods

(i)   if the carrier can show that it had no reasonable means of checking the information furnished by the shipper, it may so state in the contract particulars, indicating the information to which it refers, or

(ii) if the carrier reasonably considers the information furnished by the shipper to be inaccurate, it may include a clause providing what it reasonably considers accurate information.

(b) For goods delivered to the carrier or a performing party in a closed container, unless the carrier or a performing party in fact inspects the goods inside the container or otherwise has actual knowledge of the contents of the container before issuing the transport document or the electronic transport record, provided, however, that in such case the carrier may include such clause if it reasonably considers the information furnished by the shipper regarding the contents of the container to be inaccurate, the carrier may include a qualifying clause in the contract particulars with respect to

(i)   the leading marks on the goods inside the container, or

(ii) the number of packages, the number of pieces, or the quantity of the goods inside the container.

(c) For goods delivered to the carrier or a performing party in a closed container, the carrier may qualify any statement of the weight of goods or the weight of a container and its contents with an explicit statement that the carrier has not weighed the container if

(i)   the carrier can show that neither the carrier nor a performing party weighed the container, and the shipper and the carrier did not agree prior to the shipment that the container would be weighed and the weight would be included in the contract particulars, or

(ii) the carrier can show that there was no reasonable means of checking the weight of the container.

Article 42.   Reasonable means of checking and good faith

For purposes of article 41:

(a) A "reasonable means of checking" must be not only physically practicable but also commercially reasonable.

(b) The carrier acts in "good faith" when issuing a transport document or an electronic transport record if

(i)   the carrier has no actual knowledge that any material statement in the transport document or electronic transport record is materially false or misleading, and

(ii) the carrier has not intentionally failed to determine whether a material statement in the transport document or electronic transport record is materially false or misleading because it believes that the statement is likely to be false or misleading.

(c) The burden of proving whether the carrier acted in good faith when issuing a transport document or an electronic transport record is on the party claiming that the carrier did not act in good faith.

Article 43.   Prima facie and conclusive evidence

Except as otherwise provided in article 44, a transport document or an electronic transport record that evidences receipt of the goods is:

(a) Prima facie evidence of the carrier's receipt of the goods as described in the contract particulars; and

(b) Conclusive evidence of the carrier's receipt of the goods as described in the contract particulars

[(i)] if a negotiable transport document or a negotiable electronic transport record has been transferred to a third party acting in good faith [or

(ii) Variant A of paragraph (b)(ii)

if a person acting in good faith has paid value or otherwise altered its position in reliance on the description of the goods in the contract particulars.]

(iii) Variant B of paragraph (b)(ii)

if no negotiable transport document or no negotiable electronic transport record has been issued and the consignee has purchased and paid for the goods in reliance on the description of the goods in the contract particulars.]

Article 44.   Evidentiary effect of qualifying clauses

If the contract particulars include a qualifying clause that complies with the requirements of article 41, then the transport document or electronic transport document does not constitute prima facie or conclusive evidence under article 43 to the extent that the description of the goods is qualified by the clause.

[Article 45.   "Freight prepaid"

If the contract particulars in a negotiable transport document or a negotiable electronic transport record contain the statement "freight prepaid" or a statement of a similar nature, then neither the holder nor the consignee, is liable for the payment of the freight. This article does not apply if the holder or the consignee is also the shipper.]

CHAPTER 10.   DELIVERY TO THE CONSIGNEE

Article 46.   Obligation to accept delivery

When the goods have arrived at their destination, the consignee [that exercises any of its rights under the contract of carriage] must accept delivery of the goods at the time and location referred to in article 11(4). [If the consignee, in breach of this obligation, leaves the goods in the custody of the carrier or the performing party, the carrier or performing party acts in respect of the goods as an agent of the consignee, but without any liability for loss or damage to these goods, unless the loss or damage results from a personal act or omission of the carrier [or of the performing party] done with the intent to cause such loss or damage, or recklessly, with the knowledge that such loss or damage probably would result.]

Article 47.   Obligation to acknowledge receipt

On request of the carrier or the performing party that delivers the goods, the consignee must acknowledge receipt of the goods from the carrier or the performing party in the manner that is customary at the place of destination.

Article 48.   Delivery when no negotiable transport document or negotiable electronic transport record is issued

When no negotiable transport document or no negotiable electronic transport record has been issued, the following paragraphs apply:

(a) If the name and address of the consignee is not referred to in the contract particulars the controlling party must advise the carrier thereof, prior to or upon the arrival of the goods at the place of destination;

(b) Variant A of paragraph (b)
The carrier must deliver the goods at the time and location mentioned in article 11(4) to the consignee upon the consignee's production of proper identification;
Variant B of paragraph (b)
The carrier must deliver the goods at the time and location mentioned in article 11(4) to the consignee. As a prerequisite for delivery, the consignee must produce proper identification.
Variant C of paragraph (b)
The carrier must deliver the goods at the time and location mentioned in article 11(4) to the consignee. The carrier may refuse delivery if the consignee does not produce proper identification.

(c) If the consignee does not claim delivery of the goods from the carrierafter their arrival at the place of destination, the carrier must so advise the controlling party or, if it, after reasonable effort, is unable to identify the controlling party, the shipper. In such event, the controlling party or shipper must give instructions in respect of the delivery of the goods. If the carrier is unable, after reasonable effort, to identify and find the controlling party or the shipper, then the person referred to in article 34 is deemed to be the shipper for purposes of this paragraph. The carrier that delivers the goods upon instruction of the controlling party or the shipper under this paragraph is discharged from its obligations to deliver the goods under the contract of carriage.

Article 49.   Delivery when negotiable transport document or negotiable electronic transport record is issued
When a negotiable transport document or a negotiable electronic transport record has been issued, the following paragraphs apply:

(a)   (i)   Without prejudice to article 46 the holder of a negotiable transport document is entitled to claim delivery of the goods from the carrier after they have arrived at the place of destination, in which event the carrier must deliver the goods at the time and location referred to in article 11(4) to such holder upon surrender of the negotiable transport document. In the event that more than one original of the negotiable transport document has been issued, the surrender of one original will suffice and the other originals cease to have any effect or validity.

(ii)   Without prejudice to article 46 the holder of a negotiable electronic transport record is entitled to claim delivery of the goods from the carrier after they have arrived at the place of destination, in which event the carrier must deliver the goods at the time and location referred to in article 11(4) to such holder if it demonstrates in accordance with the procedures referred to in article 6 that it is the holder of the electronic transport record. Upon such delivery, the electronic transport record ceases to have any effect or validity.

(b) If the holder does not claim delivery of the goods from the carrier after their arrival at the place of destination, the carrier must so advise the controlling party or, if, after reasonable effort, it is unable to identify or find the controlling party, the shipper. In such event the controlling party or shipper must give the carrier instructions in respect of the delivery of the goods. If the carrier is unable, after reasonable effort, to identify and find the controlling party or the shipper, then the person referred to in article 34 shall be deemed to be the shipper for purposes of this paragraph.

(c) [Notwithstanding paragraph (d),] the carrier that delivers the goods upon instruction of the controlling party or the shipper in accordance with paragraph (b) is discharged from its obligation to deliver the goods under the contract of carriage to the holder, irrespective of whether the negotiable transport document has been surrendered to it, or the person claiming delivery under a negotiable electronic transport record has demonstrated, in accordance with the procedures referred to in article 6, that it is the holder.

Variant A of paragraph (d)

(d) [Except as provided in paragraph (c)] if the delivery of the goods by the carrier at the place of destination occurs without the surrender of the negotiable transport document to the carrier or without the demonstration referred to in paragraph (a)(ii), a person that becomes a holder after the carrier has delivered the goods to the consignee or to a person entitled to them pursuant to any contractual or other arrangement other than the contract of carriage acquires rights [against the carrier] under the contract of carriage only if: (i) the passing of the negotiable transport document or negotiable electronic transport record was effected in pursuance of contractual or other arrangements made before such delivery of the goods; or (ii) unless such person at the time it became a holder did not have and could not reasonably have had knowledge of such delivery. [This paragraph does not apply when the goods are delivered by the carrier pursuant to paragraph (c).]

Variant B of paragraph (d), which comprises (d) and (e)

(d) If the goods are delivered pursuant to paragraph (c), a person that becomes a holder after the carrier has delivered the goods to the consignee or to a person entitled to them pursuant to any contractual or other arrangement other than the contract of carriage acquires rights against the carrier under the contract of carriage, other than the right to claim delivery of the goods, when only the transfer of the negotiable transport document or negotiable electronic transport record was effected in pursuance of contractual or other arrangements made before such delivery of the goods.

(e) Notwithstanding paragraphs (c) and (d), the holder that did not have or could not reasonably have had knowledge of such delivery at the time it became a holder acquires the rights incorporated in the negotiable transport document or negotiable electronic transport record.

Article 50. Failure to give adequate instruction

If the controlling party or the shipper does not give the carrier adequate instructions under articles 48 and 49 or if the controlling party or the shipper cannot be found, the carrier is entitled, without prejudice to any other remedies that the carrier may have against such controlling party or shipper, to exercise its rights under articles 51, 52 and 53.

Article 51. When goods are undeliverable

1. The carrier is entitled to exercise the rights and remedies referred to in paragraph 2 at the risk and expense of the person entitled to the goods, if the goods have arrived at the place of destination and:

(a) The consignee did not actually accept delivery of the goods under this chapter at the time and location referred to in article 11(4) [and no express or implied contract has been concluded between the carrier or the performing party and the consignee with respect to the custody of the goods]; or

(b) The carrier is not allowed under applicable law or regulations to deliver the goods to the consignee.

2. The rights and remedies referred to in paragraph 1 are:

(a) To store the goods at any suitable place;

(b) To unpack the goods if they are packed in containers, or to act otherwise in respect of the goods as, in the opinion of the carrier, circumstances reasonably may require; or

(c) To cause the goods to be sold in accordance with the practices, or the requirements under the law or regulations, of the place where the goods are located at the time.

3. If the goods are sold under paragraph 2(c), the carrier must hold the proceeds of the sale for the benefit of the person entitled to the goods, subject to the deduction of any costs incurred in respect of the goods and any other amounts that are due to the carrier.

Article 52.   Notice of arrival at destination

The carrier is allowed to exercise the rights referred to in article 51 only after it has given reasonable advance notice that the goods have arrived at the place of destination to the person stated in the contract particulars as the person to be notified of the arrival of the goods at the place of destination, if any, or to the consignee, or otherwise to the controlling party or the shipper.

Article 53.   Carrier's liability for undeliverable goods

When exercising its rights referred to in article 51(2), the carrier or a performing party is liable for loss of or damage to the goods, only if the loss or damage results from [an act or omission of the carrier or of the performing party done with the intent to cause such loss or damage, or recklessly, with the knowledge that such loss or damage probably would result].

CHAPTER 11.   RIGHT OF CONTROL

Article 54.   Definition of right of control

The right of control of the goods [means][is] the right under the contract of carriage to give the carrier instructions in respect of the goods during the period of its responsibility as stated in article 11(1).] Such right includes and is limited to:

(a) The right to give or modify instructions in respect of the goods that do not constitute a variation of the contract of carriage;

(b) The right to demand delivery of the goods [before their arrival at the place of destination][at an intermediate port or place en route]; and

(c) The right to replace the consignee by any other person including the controlling party.

[Article 55.   Variations to the contract of carriage

1. The controlling party is the exclusive person that may exercise the right of control and may agree with the carrier to a variation of the contract of carriage other than the variations referred to in article 54 (b) and (c).

2. Any variation to the contract of carriage, including those referred to in article 54 (b) and (c), upon becoming effective, must be stated in the [negotiable] transport document or incorporated in the [negotiable] electronic transport record and be initialed or signed in accordance with article 39.]

Article 56.   Applicable rules based on transport document or electronic transport record issued

1. When no negotiable transport document or no negotiable electronic transport record is issued, the following rules apply:

(a) The shipper is the controlling party unless the shipper [and consignee agree that another person is to be the controlling party and the shipper so notifies the carrier. The shipper and consignee may agree that the consignee is the controlling party] [designates the consignee or another person as the controlling party].

(b) The controlling party is entitled to transfer the right of control to another person, upon which transfer the transferor loses its right of control. The transferor [or the transferee][or, if applicable law permits, the transferee] must notify the carrier of such transfer.

(c) When the controlling party exercises the right of control in accordance with article 54, it must produce proper identification.

(d) [The right of control [terminates] [is transferred to the consignee] when the goods have arrived at destination and the consignee has requested delivery of the goods.]

2. When a negotiable transport document is issued, the following rules apply:

(a) The holder or, in the event that more than one original of the negotiable transport document is issued, the holder of all originals is the sole controlling party.

(b) The holder is entitled to transfer the right of control by passing the negotiable transport document to another person in accordance with article 61, upon which transfer the transferor loses its right of control. If more than one original of that document was issued, all originals must be passed in order to effect a transfer of the right of control.

(c) In order to exercise the right of control, the holder must, if the carrier so requires, produce the negotiable transport document to the carrier. If more than one original of the document was issued, all originals [except those that the carrier already holds on behalf of the person seeking to exercise a right of control] must be produced, failing which the right of control cannot be exercised.

3. When a negotiable electronic transport record is issued:

(a) The holder is the sole controlling party and is entitled to transfer the right of control to another person by transferring the negotiable electronic transport record in accordance with the procedures referred to in article 6, upon which transfer the transferor loses its right of control.

(b) In order to exercise the right of control, the holder must, if the carrier so requires, demonstrate, in accordance with the procedures referred to in article 6, that it is the holder.

4. Notwithstanding article 63, a person, not being the shipper or the person referred to in article 34, that transferred the right of control without having exercised that right, is upon such transfer discharged from the liabilities imposed on the controlling party by the contract of carriage or by this Convention.

Article 57.   Carrier's execution of instruction

1.
Variant A of paragraph 1, including para. 1 *bis*

Subject to paragraphs 1 *bis*, 2 and 3, the carrier must execute any instruction referred to in article 54 if it:

(a) Can reasonably be executed according to its terms at the moment that the instruction reaches the person to perform it;

(b) Will not interfere with the normal operations of the carrier or a performing party; and

(c) Would not cause any additional expense, loss, or damage to the carrier, the performing party, or any person interested in other goods carried on the same voyage.

1 bis. If it is reasonably expected that one or more of the conditions referred to in sub-paragraphs (a), (b) and (c) is not satisfied, then the carrier is under no obligation to execute the instruction.

Variant B of paragraph 1

Subject to paragraphs 2 and 3, the carrier is bound to execute the instructions referred to in article 54 if:

(a) The person giving such instructions is entitled to exercise the right of control;

(b) The instructions can reasonably be executed according to their terms at the moment that they reach the carrier; and

(c) The instructions will not interfere with the normal operations of the carrier or a performing party.

2. In any event, the controlling party must reimburse the carrier, performing parties, and any persons interested in other goods carried on the same voyage or journey for any additional expense that they may incur and must indemnify them against any loss or damage that they may suffer as a result of executing any instruction under this article.

3. At the request of the carrier, the controlling party must provide security for the amount of the reasonably expected additional expense, loss or damage. [The carrier is entitled to obtain security from the controlling party if it:

(a) Reasonably expects that the execution of an instruction under this article will cause additional expense, loss, or damage; and

(b) Is nevertheless willing to execute the instruction.]

4. The carrier is liable for loss of or damage to the goods resulting from its failure to comply with the instructions of the controlling party in breach of its obligation under paragraph 1.

Article 58.   Deemed delivery

Goods that are delivered pursuant to an instruction in accordance with article 54(b) are deemed to be delivered at the place of destination and the provisions of chapter 10 relating to such delivery are applicable to such goods.

Article 59.   Obligation to provide information, instructions or documents to carrier

If the carrier or a performing party during the period that it has custody of the goods reasonably requires information, instructions, or documents in addition to those referred to in article 30(a), the controlling party, on request of the carrier or such performing party, must provide such information. If the carrier, after reasonable effort, is unable to identify and find the controlling party or the controlling party is unable to provide adequate information, instructions, or documents to the carrier, the shipper or the person referred to in article 34 must do so.

Article 60.   Variation by agreement

Articles 54(b) and (c), and 57 may be varied by agreement between the parties. The parties may also restrict or exclude the transferability of the right of control referred to in article 56(1)(b). If a negotiable transport document or a negotiable electronic transport record is issued, any agreement referred to in this article must be stated or incorporated in the contract particulars.

CHAPTER 12.   TRANSFER OF RIGHTS

Article 61.   When a negotiable transport document or negotiable electronic transport record is issued

1. If a negotiable transport document is issued, the holder is entitled to transfer the rights incorporated in such document by transferring such document to another person:
    (a) If an order document, duly endorsed either to such other person or in blank, or,
    (b) If a bearer document or a blank endorsed document, without endorsement, or,
    (c) If a document made out to the order of a named person and the transfer is between the first holder and such named person, without endorsement.

2. If a negotiable electronic transport record is issued, its holder is entitled to transfer the rights incorporated in such electronic transport record, whether it be made out to order or to the order of a named person, by transferring the electronic transport record in accordance with the procedures referred to in article 6.

Article 62.   Liability of holder

1. Without prejudice to article 59, any holder that is not the shipper and that does not exercise any right under the contract of carriage, does not assume any liability under the contract of carriage solely by reason of being a holder.

2. Any holder that is not the shipper and that exercises any right under the contract of carriage, assumes [any liabilities imposed on it under the contract of carriage to the extent that such liabilities are incorporated in or ascertainable from the negotiable transport document or the negotiable electronic transport record] [the liabilities imposed on the controlling party under chapter 11 and the liabilities imposed on the shipper for the payment of freight, dead freight, demurrage and damages for detention to the extent that such liabilities are incorporated in the negotiable transport document or the negotiable electronic transport record].

3. For the purpose of paragraphs 1 and 2 [and article 46], any holder that is not the shipper does not exercise any right under the contract of carriage solely by reason of the fact that it:

(a) Under article 7 agrees with the carrier to replace a negotiable transport document by a negotiable electronic transport record or to replace a negotiable electronic transport record by a negotiable transport document, or

(b) Under article 61 transfers its rights.

Article 63   **When no negotiable transport document or negotiable electronic transport record is issued**

If no negotiable transport document or no negotiable electronic transport record is issued, the following paragraphs apply to the transfer of rights under a contract of carriage:

(a) The transfer is subject to the law governing the contract for the transfer of such rights or, if the rights are transferred otherwise than by contract, to the law governing such transfer;

(b) The transferability of the rights purported to be transferred is governed by the law applicable to the contract of carriage; and

(c) Regardless of the law applicable pursuant to paragraphs (a) and (b),

   (i) A transfer that is otherwise permissible under the applicable law may be made by electronic means,

   (ii) A transfer must be notified to the carrier by the transferor or, if applicable law permits, by the transferee, and

   (iii) If a transfer includes liabilities that are connected to or flow from the right that is transferred, the transferor and the transferee are jointly and severally liable in respect of such liabilities.

CHAPTER 13:   LIMITATION OF LIABILITY

Article 64.   **Basis of limitation of liability**

1.   Subject to articles 65 and 66(1), the carrier's liability for breaches of its obligations under this Convention is limited to [...] units of account per package or other shipping unit, or [...] units of account per kilogram of the gross weight of the goods lost or damaged, whichever is the higher, except when the nature and value of the goods have been declared by the shipper before shipment and included in the contract particulars, or when a higher amount than the amount of limitation of liability set out in this article has been agreed upon between the carrier and the shipper.

Variant A of paragraph 2

[2. Notwithstanding paragraph 1, if (a) the carrier cannot establish whether the goods were lost or damaged [or whether the delay in delivery was caused] during the sea carriage or during the carriage preceding or subsequent to the sea carriage and (b) provisions of an international convention [or national law] would be applicable under article 27 if the loss, damage, [or delay] occurred during the carriage preceding or subsequent to the sea carriage, then the carrier's liability for such loss, damage, [or delay] is limited according to the limitation terms of any international convention [or national law] that would have been applicable if the place where the damage occurred had been established, or the limitation terms of this Convention, whichever would result in the highest limitation amount.]

Variant B of paragraph 2

[2. Notwithstanding paragraph 1, if the carrier cannot establish whether the goods were lost or damaged [or whether the delay in delivery was caused] during the sea carriage or during the carriage preceding or subsequent to the sea carriage, the highest limit of liability in the international [and national] mandatory provisions that govern the different parts of the transport applies.]

3.   When goods are carried in or on a container, pallet, or similar article of transport used to consolidate goods, the packages or shipping units enumerated in the contract particulars as packed in or on such article of transport are deemed packages or shipping units. If not so enumerated, the goods in or on such article of transport are deemed one shipping unit.

4.   The unit of account referred to in this article is the Special Drawing Right as defined by the International Monetary Fund. The amounts referred to in this article are to be converted into the national currency of a State according to the value of such currency at the date of judgement or the date agreed upon by the parties. The value of a national currency, in terms of the Special Drawing Right, of a Contracting State that is a member of the International Monetary Fund is to be calculated in accordance with the method of valuation applied by the International Monetary Fund in effect at the date in question for its operations and transactions. The value of a national currency, in terms of the Special Drawing Right, of a Contracting State that is not a member of the International Monetary Fund is to be calculated in a manner to be determined by that State.

Article 65.   Liability for loss caused by delay

Variant A

Subject to paragraph 66(2), compensation for physical loss of or damage to the goods caused by delay must be calculated in accordance with article 23 and [, unless otherwise agreed,] liability for economic loss caused by delay is limited to an amount equivalent to [one times] the freight payable on the goods delayed. The total amount payable under this article and paragraph 64(1) may not exceed the limit that would be established under paragraph 64(1) in respect of the total loss of the goods concerned.

Variant B

Subject to paragraph 66(2), unless otherwise agreed, if delay in delivery causes [consequential] loss not resulting from loss of or damage to the goods carried and hence not covered by article 23, the liability for such loss is limited to an amount equivalent to [one times] the freight payable on the goods delayed. The total amount payable under this article and article 64(1) may not exceed the limit that would be established under article 64(1) in respect of the total loss of the goods concerned.

Article 66.   Loss of the right to limit liability

1.   Neither the carrier nor any of the persons referred to in article 19 may limit their liability as provided in articles 64 and 26(4), [or as provided in the contract of carriage,] if the claimant proves that the loss of, or the damage to the goods or the breach of the carrier's obligation under this Convention resulted from a personal act or omission of the person claiming a right to limit done with the intent to cause such loss or damage, or recklessly and with knowledge that such loss or damage would probably result.

2.   Neither the carrier nor any of the persons mentioned in article 19 may limit their liability as provided in article 65 if the claimant proves that the delay in delivery resulted from a personal act or omission of the person claiming a right to limit done with the intent to cause the loss due to delay or recklessly and with knowledge that such loss would probably result.

CHAPTER 14. RIGHTS OF SUIT

Article 67. Parties

<u>Variant A</u>

1. Without prejudice to articles 68 and 68(b), rights under the contract of carriage may be asserted against the carrier or a performing party only by:

(a) The shipper, to the extent that it has suffered loss or damage in consequence of a breach of the contract of carriage;

(b) The consignee, to the extent that it has suffered loss or damage in consequence of a breach of the contract of carriage; or

(c) Any person to which the shipper or the consignee has transferred its rights, or that has acquired rights under the contract of carriage by subrogation under the applicable national law, such as an insurer, to the extent that the person whose rights it has acquired by transfer or subrogation suffered loss or damage in consequence of a breach of the contract of carriage.

2. In case of any passing of rights of suit through transfer or subrogation under sub-paragraph 1(c), the carrier and the performing party are entitled to all defences and limitations of liability that are available to it against such third party under the contract of carriage and under this Convention.

<u>Variant B</u>

Any right under or in connection with a contract of carriage may be asserted by any person having a legitimate interest in the performance of any obligation arising under or in connection with such contract, when that person suffered loss or damage.

Article 68. When negotiable transport document or negotiable electronic transport record is issued

In the event that a negotiable transport document or negotiable electronic transport record is issued:

(a) The holder is entitled to assert rights under the contract of carriage against the carrier or a performing party, irrespective of whether it suffered loss or damage itself; and

(b) When the claimant is not the holder, it must, in addition to proving that it suffered loss or damage in consequence of a breach of the contract of carriage, prove that the holder did not suffer the loss or damage in respect of which the claim is made.

CHAPTER 15. TIME FOR SUIT

Article 69. Limitation of actions

<u>Variant A</u>

The carrier is discharged from all liability under this Convention if judicial or arbitral proceedings have not been instituted within a period of [one] year. The shipper is discharged from all liability under chapter 8 of this Convention if judicial or arbitral proceedings have not been instituted within a period of [one] year.

<u>Variant B</u>

All [rights] [actions] under this Convention are extinguished [timebarred] if judicial or arbitral proceedings have not been commenced within the period of [one] year.

Article 70. Commencement of limitation period

The period referred to in article 69 commences on the day on which the carrier has completed delivery of the goods concerned pursuant to article 11(4) or 11(5) or, in cases in which no goods have been delivered, on the [last] day on which the goods should have been delivered. The day on which the period commences is not included in the period.

Article 71. Extension of limitation period

The person against which a claim is made may at any time during the running of the period extend that period by a declaration to the claimant. This period may be further extended by another declaration or declarations.

Article 72. Action for indemnity

An action for indemnity by a person held liable under this Convention may be instituted even after the expiration of the period referred to in article 69 if the indemnity action is instituted within the later of:

   (a) The time allowed by applicable law in the jurisdiction where proceedings are instituted; or

   (b) Variant A of paragraph (b)

      90 days commencing from the day when the person instituting the action for indemnity has either

      (i)   settled the claim; or

      (ii) been served with process in the action against itself.

   Variant B of paragraph (b)

      90 days commencing from the day when either

      (i)   the person instituting the action for indemnity has settled the claim; or

      (ii) a final judgment not subject to further appeal has been issued against the person instituting the action for indemnity.

Article 73. Counterclaims

A counterclaim by a person held liable under this Convention may be instituted even after the expiration of the period referred to in article 69 if it is instituted within 90 days commencing from the day when the person making the counterclaim has been served with process in the action against itself.

Article 74. Actions against the bareboat charterer

[If the registered owner of a ship defeats the presumption that it is the carrier under article 40(3), an action against the bareboat charterer may be instituted even after the expiration of the period referred to in article 69 if the action is instituted within the later of:

   (a) The time allowed by the applicable law in the jurisdiction where proceedings are instituted; or

   (a) 90 days commencing from the day when the registered owner [both

      (i)   proves that the ship was under a bareboat charter at the time of the carriage; and]

      [(ii)] adequately identifies the bareboat charterer.]

CHAPTER 16.   JURISDICTION

Article 75. Actions against the carrier

In judicial proceedings against the carrier relating to carriage of goods under this Convention the plaintiff, at its option, may institute an action in a court in a Contracting State that, according to the law of the State where the court is situated, is competent and within the jurisdiction of which is situated one of the following places:

   (a) The domicile of the defendant; or

   (b) The contractual place of receipt or the contractual place of delivery; or

   [(c) the port where the goods are initially loaded on a ship; or the port where the goods are finally discharged from a ship; or]

   (d) Any additional place [designated][agreed upon] for that purpose in the transport document or electronic transport record.

[**Article 76.**   Exclusive jurisdiction agreements

1. If the shipper and the carrier agree that the courts of one Contracting State or one or more specific courts in one Contracting State have jurisdiction to decide disputes that have arisen or may arise under this Convention, that court or those courts have jurisdiction. Such jurisdiction is exclusive, provided that the agreement conferring it:

(a) Is evidenced in writing or by electronic communication;

(b) Clearly states the name and location of the chosen court or courts as well as the names and addresses of the parties; and

(c) Expressly provides that the jurisdiction of the chosen court is to be exclusive.

2. When an exclusive forum is agreed under paragraph 1, the shipper and the carrier may also expressly agree that the exclusive choice of forum is binding on any other person bringing an action under this Convention, and it is so binding, provided that:

Variant A of subparagraph 2(a)

(a) Such agreement is included in the contract particulars [or incorporated by reference in the transport document or electronic transport record]; and

Variant B of subparagraph 2(a)

(a) Such person is given adequate notice of the place where the action can be brought; and

Variant C of subparagraph 2(a)

(a) Such person expressly consents to the agreement, and such consent complies with the requirements of article 95(6)(b); and

(b) The forum is in one of the places designated under paragraphs 75(a), (b) or (c).]

Article 77.   Actions against the maritime performing party

In judicial proceedings against the maritime performing party relating to carriage of goods under this Convention, the plaintiff, at its option, may institute an action in a court in a Contracting State that, according to the law of the State where the court is situated, is competent and within the jurisdiction of which is situated one of the following places:

(a) The domicile of the maritime performing party; or

(b) The place where the goods are [initially] received by the maritime performing party; and the place where the goods are [ultimately] delivered by the maritime performing party.

Article 78.   No additional bases of jurisdiction

Subject to article 80, no judicial proceedings relating to carriage of goods under this Convention may be instituted in a place not designated under article 75 or 77.

Article 79.   Arrest and provisional or protective measures

1. Nothing in this Convention affects jurisdiction with regard to:

(a) Arrest [pursuant to applicable rules of international law [or the law of the forum state]]; or

(b) Provisional or protective measures.

[2. For the purpose of this article "provisional or protective measures" means:

(a) Orders for the preservation, interim custody, or sale of any goods which are the subject-matter of the dispute; or

(b) An order securing the amount in dispute; or

(c) An order appointing a receiver; or

(d) Any other orders to ensure that any judgment or arbitral is not rendered ineffectual by the dissipation of assets by the other party; or

(e) An interim injunction or other interim order.]

Article 80. Consolidation and removal of actions
Variant A of paragraph 1
[1. Any action against both the carrier and the maritime performing party arising out of the same occurrence must be instituted in one of the places specified in article 77, whether or not that place is specified in article 75.]
Variant B of paragraph 1
[1. Any action against both the carrier and the maritime performing party arising out of the same occurrence must be instituted in a place designated under both article 75 and article 77. If no place is specified in both articles, then such action must be instituted in one of the places designated under article 77.]
Variant C of paragraph 1
[1. If the cargo claimant institutes actions *in solidum* against the contracting carrier and the maritime performing party, this must be done in one of the places mentioned in article 77, where actions can be instituted against the maritime performing party.]

2. If the carrier or maritime performing party institutes an action under this Convention, then the claimant, at the request of the defendant, must withdraw the action and recommence it in one of the places designated under articles 75 or 77, whichever is applicable, at the choice of the defendant.

Article 81. Agreement after dispute has arisen
Notwithstanding the preceding articles of this chapter, an agreement made by the parties to the dispute under the contract of carriage after the dispute has arisen, that designates the place where the claimant may institute an action, is effective.

CHAPTER 17. ARBITRATION

Variant A

Article 82.
Subject to this chapter, the parties may provide by agreement evidenced in writing that any dispute that may arise relating to the contract of carriage to which this Convention applies must be referred to arbitration.

Article 83.
If a negotiable transport document or a negotiable electronic transport record has been issued the arbitration clause or agreement must be contained in the documents or record or expressly incorporated therein by reference. When a charterparty contains a provision that disputes arising thereunder must be referred to arbitration and a negotiable transport document or a negotiable electronic transport record issued pursuant to the charterparty does not contain a special annotation providing that such provision is binding upon the holder, the carrier may not invoke such provision as against a holder having acquired the negotiable transport document or the negotiable electronic transport record in good faith.

Article 84.
The arbitration proceedings must, at the option of the claimant, be instituted at one of the following places:
(a) A place in a State within whose territory is situated:
    (i) The principal place of business of the defendant or, in the absence thereof, the habitual residence of the defendant; or
    (ii) [(ii) The place where the contract of carriage was made, provided that the defendant has there a place of business, branch or agency through which the contract was made; or]

         (iii) The place where the carrier or a performing party has received the goods for carriage or the place of delivery; or

    (b) Any other place designated for that purpose in the arbitration clause or agreement.

Article 85.

The arbitrator or arbitration tribunal must apply the rules of this Convention.

Article 85 bis.

Article 83 and 84 are deemed to be part of every arbitration clause or agreement, and any term of such clause or agreement that is inconsistent therewith is void.

Article 86.

Nothing in this chapter affects the validity of an agreement on arbitration made by the parties after the claim relating to the contract of carriage has arisen.

Variant B

Article 82.

Subject to this chapter, the parties may provide by agreement evidenced in writing that any dispute that may arise relating to the contract of carriage to which this Convention applies must be referred to arbitration.

Article 83.

If a negotiable transport document or a negotiable electronic transport record has been issued the arbitration clause or agreement must be contained in the documents or record or expressly incorporated therein by reference. When a charterparty contains a provision that disputes arising thereunder must be referred to arbitration and a negotiable transport document or a negotiable electronic transport record issued pursuant to the charterparty does not contain a special annotation providing that such provision is binding upon the holder, the carrier may not invoke such provision as against a holder having acquired the negotiable transport document or the negotiable electronic transport record in good faith.

Article 84.

Article 85.

The arbitrator or arbitration tribunal must apply the rules of this Convention.

Article 86.

Nothing in this chapter shall affect the validity of an agreement on arbitration made by the parties after the claim relating to the contract of carriage has arisen.

CHAPTER 18.   GENERAL AVERAGE

Article 87.   Provisions on general average

Nothing in this Convention prevents the application of provisions in the contract of carriage or national law regarding the adjustment of general average.

Article 88.   Contribution in general average

1. [With the exception of the chapter on time for suit,] the provisions of this Convention relating to the liability of the carrier for loss of or damage to the goods also determine whether the consignee may refuse to contribute in general average and the liability of the carrier to indemnify the consignee in respect of any such contribution made or any salvage paid.

2. All [actions for] [rights to] contribution in general average are [time-barred] [extinguished] if judicial or arbitral proceedings are not instituted within a period of [one year] from the date of the issuance of the general average statement.

CHAPTER 19.   OTHER CONVENTIONS

Article 89.   International instruments governing other modes of transport

Subject to article 92, nothing contained in this Convention prevents a Contracting State from applying any other international instrument which is already in force at the date of this Convention and that applies mandatorily to contracts of carriage of goods primarily by a mode of transport other than carriage by sea.

Article 90.   Prevalence over earlier conventions

[As between parties to this Convention, it prevails over those][Subject to article 102, this Convention prevails between its parties over those] of an earlier convention to which they may be parties [that are incompatible with those of this Convention].

Article 91.   Global limitation of liability

This Convention does not modify the rights or obligations of the carrier, or the performing party provided for in international conventions or national law governing the limitation of liability relating to the operation of vessels.

Article 92.   Other provisions on carriage of passengers and luggage

No liability arises under this Convention for any loss of or damage to or delay in delivery of luggage for which the carrier is liable under any convention or national law relating to the carriage of passengers and their luggage.

Article 93.   Other provisions on damage caused by nuclear incident

No liability arises under this Convention for damage caused by a nuclear incident if the operator of a nuclear installation is liable for such damage:

(a) under the Paris Convention on Third Party Liability in the Field of Nuclear Energy of 29 July 1960 as amended by the additional Protocol of 28 January 1964, the Vienna Convention on Civil Liability for Nuclear Damage of 21 May 1963, as amended by the Joint Protocol Relating to the Application of the Vienna Convention and the Paris Convention of 21 September 1988, and as amended by the Protocol to Amend the 1963 Vienna Convention on Civil Liability for Nuclear Damage of 12 September 1997, or the Convention on Supplementary Compensation for Nuclear Damage of 12 September 1997, or

(b) by virtue of national law governing the liability for such damage, provided that such law is in all respects as favourable to persons that may suffer damage as either the Paris or Vienna Conventions or the Convention on Supplementary Compensation for Nuclear Damage.

CHAPTER 20.   VALIDITY OF CONTRACTUAL STIPULATIONS

Article 20.   General provisions

1. Unless otherwise specified in this Convention, any provision is void if:

(a) It directly or indirectly excludes or limits the obligations of the carrier or a maritime performing party under this Convention;

(c) It directly or indirectly excludes or limits the liability of the carrier or a maritime performing party for breach of an obligation under this Convention; or

(d) It assigns a benefit of insurance of the goods in favour of the carrier or a person referred to in article 19.

[2. Unless otherwise specified in this Convention, any provision is void if:

(a) It directly or indirectly excludes, limits, [or increases] the obligations under chapter 8 of the shipper, consignor, consignee, controlling party, holder, or person referred to in article 34; or

(b) It directly or indirectly excludes, limits, [or increases] the liability of the shipper, consignor, consignee, controlling party, holder, or person referred to in article 34 for breach of any of their obligations under chapter 8.]

Article 95.   Special rules for volume contracts

1. Notwithstanding article 94, if terms of a volume contract are subject to this Convention under article 9(3)(b), the volume contract may provide for greater or lesser duties, rights, obligations, and liabilities than those set forth in the Convention provided that the volume contract [is agreed to in writing or electronically], contains a prominent statement that it derogates from this Convention, and:

(a) Is individually negotiated; or

(b) Prominently specifies the sections of the volume contract containing the derogations.

2. A derogation under paragraph 1 must be set forth in the contract and may not be incorporated by reference from another document.

3. A [carrier's public schedule of prices and services,] transport document, electronic transport record, or similar document is not a volume contract under paragraph 1, but a volume contract may incorporate such documents by reference as terms of the contract.

4. The right of derogation under this article applies to the terms that regulate shipments under the volume contract to the extent these terms are subject to this Convention under article 9(3)(a).

5. Paragraph 1 is not applicable to:

(a) Obligations stipulated in article 16(1)(a) and (b) [and liability arising from the breach thereof or limitation of that liability];

(b) [Rights and obligations stipulated in articles, [28], [29], [30], [33] and [66] [and the liability arising from the breach thereof]].

6. Paragraph 1 applies:

(a) Between the carrier and the shipper;

(b) Between the carrier and any other party that has expressly consented [in writing or electronically] to be bound by the terms of the volume contract that derogate from this Convention. [The express consent must demonstrate that the consenting party received a notice that prominently states that the volume contract derogates from this Convention and the consent shall not be set forth in a [carrier's public schedule of prices and services,] transport document, or electronic transport record. The burden is on the carrier to prove that the conditions for derogation have been fulfilled.]

Article 96.   Special rules for live animals and certain other goods

Notwithstanding chapters 5 and 6 of this Convention and the obligations of the carrier, the terms of the contract of carriage may exclude or limit the liability of both the carrier and a maritime performing party if:

(a) The goods are live animals except when it is proved that the loss, damage, or delay resulted from an action or omission of the carrier [or of a person referred to in article 19] or of a maritime performing party done recklessly and with knowledge that such loss, damage, or delay would probably occur; or

(b) The character or condition of the goods or the circumstances and terms and conditions under which the carriage is to be performed are such as reasonably to justify a special agreement, provided that ordinary commercial shipments made in the ordinary course of trade are not concerned and no negotiable transport document or negotiable electronic transport record is issued for the carriage of the goods.

CHAPTER 21.   FINAL CLAUSES

Article 97.   Depositary

The Secretary-General of the United Nations is hereby designated as the depositary of this Convention.

Article 98.   Signature, ratification, acceptance, approval or accession

1. This Convention is open for signature by all States [at [...] from [...] to [...] and thereafter] at the United Nations Headquarters in New York from [...] to [...].

2. This Convention is subject to ratification, acceptance or approval by the signatory States.

3. This Convention is open for accession by all States that are not signatory States as from the date it is open for signature.

4. Instruments of ratification, acceptance, approval and accession are to be deposited with the Secretary-General of the United Nations.

Article 99.   Reservations

No reservations may be made to this Convention.

Article 100.   Effect in domestic territorial units

1. If a Contracting State has two or more territorial units in which different systems of law are applicable in relation to the matters dealt with in this Convention, it may, at the time of signature, ratification, acceptance, approval or accession, declare that this Convention is to extend to all its territorial units or only to one or more of them, and may amend its declaration by submitting another declaration at any time.

2. These declarations are to be notified to the depositary and are to state expressly the territorial units to which the Convention extends.

3. If, by virtue of a declaration under this article, this Convention extends to one or more but not all of the territorial units of a Contracting State, and if the place of business of a party is located in that State, this place of business, for the purposes of this Convention, is considered not to be in a Contracting State, unless it is in a territorial unit to which the Convention extends.

4. If a Contracting State makes no declaration under paragraph (1) of this article, the Convention is to extend to all territorial units of that State.

Article 101.   Entry into force

1. This Convention enters into force on the first day of the month following the expiration of [one year from] [six months after] the date of deposit of the [twentieth] [third] instrument of ratification, acceptance, approval or accession.

2. For each State that becomes a Contracting State to this Convention after the date of the deposit of the [twentieth] [third] instrument of ratification, acceptance, approval or accession, this Convention enters into force on the first day of the month following the expiration of [one year] [six months] after the deposit of the appropriate instrument on behalf of that State.

3. Each Contracting State must apply this Convention to contracts of carriage concluded on or after the date of the entry into force of this Convention in respect of that State.

Article 102.   Denunciation of other conventions

1. A State that ratifies, accepts, approves or accedes to this Convention and is a party to any or all of the following instruments: the International Convention for the Unification of certain Rules relating to Bills of Lading signed at Brussels on 25 August 1924; the Protocol signed on 23 February 1968 to amend the International Convention for the Unification of certain Rules relating to Bills of Lading signed at Brussels on 25 August 1924; and the Protocol to amend the International Convention for the Unification of certain Rules relating to Bills of Lading as Modified by the Amending Protocol of 23 February 1968, signed at Brussels on 21 December 1979; or, alternatively, to the United Nations Convention on the Carriage of Goods by Sea concluded at Hamburg on 31 March 1978, must at the same time denounce, as the case may be, the relevant international agreements to that effect.

2.   For the purpose of this article, ratifications, acceptances, approvals and accessions in respect of this Convention by States parties to the instruments listed in paragraph 1 are not effective until such denunciations as may be required on the part of those States in respect of these instruments have themselves become effective. The depositary of this Convention must consult with the Government of Belgium, as the depositary of other relevant conventions, so as to ensure necessary co-ordination in this respect.

Article 103.   Revision and amendment

1.   At the request of not less than one third of the Contracting States to this Convention, the depositary must convene a conference of the Contracting States for revising or amending it.

2.   Any instrument of ratification, acceptance, approval or accession deposited after the entry into force of an amendment to this Convention is deemed to apply to the Convention as amended.

Article 104.   Amendment of limitation amounts

1.   Without prejudice to article 103, the special procedure in this article applies solely for the purposes of amending the limitation amount set out in paragraph 64(1) of this Convention.

2.   Upon the request of at least [one quarter] of the Contracting States to this Convention, the depositary must circulate any proposal to amend the limitation amount specified in paragraph 64(1) of this Convention to all of the Contracting States and must convene a meeting of a Committee composed of a representative from each of the Contracting States to consider the proposed amendment.

3.   The meeting of the Committee must take place on the occasion and at the location of the next session of the United Nations Commission on International Trade Law.

4.   Amendments must be adopted by the Committee by a two-thirds majority of its members present and voting.

5.   When acting on a proposal to amend the limits, the Committee will take into account the experience of incidents and, in particular, the amount of damage resulting therefrom, changes in the monetary values and the effect of the proposed amendment on the cost of insurance.

6.   (a) No amendment of the limit under this article may be considered less than [five] years from the date on which this Convention was opened for signature nor less than [five] years from the date of entry into force of a previous amendment under this article.

      (b) No limit may be increased so as to exceed an amount that corresponds to the limit laid down in this Convention increased by [six] per cent per year calculated on a compound basis from the date on which this Convention was opened for signature.

      (c) No limit may be increased so as to exceed an amount that corresponds to the limit laid down in this Convention multiplied by [three].

7.   Any amendment adopted in accordance with paragraph 4 must be notified by the depositary to all Contracting States. The amendment is deemed to have been accepted at the end of a period of [eighteen] months after the date of notification, unless within that period not less than [one fourth] of the States that were Contracting States at the time of the adoption of the amendment have communicated to the depositary that they do not accept the amendment, in which case the amendment is rejected and has no effect.

8.   An amendment deemed to have been accepted in accordance with paragraph 7 enters into force [eighteen] months after its acceptance.

9.   All Contracting States are bound by the amendment unless they denounce this Convention in accordance with article 105 at least six months before the amendment enters into force. Such denunciation takes effect when the amendment enters into force.

10.   When an amendment has been adopted but the [eighteen]-month period for its acceptance has not yet expired, a State that becomes a Contracting State during that period is bound by the amendment if it enters into force. A State that becomes a Contracting State

after that period is bound by an amendment that has been accepted in accordance with paragraph 7. In the cases referred to in this paragraph, a State becomes bound by an amendment when that amendment enters into force, or when this Convention enters into force for that State, if later.

Article 105. Denunciation of this Convention

1.   A Contracting State may denounce this Convention at any time by means of a notification in writing addressed to the depositary.

2.   The denunciation takes effect on the first day of the month following the expiration of one year after the notification is received by the depositary. If a longer period is specified in the notification, the denunciation takes effect upon the expiration of such longer period after the notification is received by the depositary.

PART VI

....

Codes

The Banking Code

[Issued by and reproduced with the permission of:
British Bankers' Association, *Pinners Hall, 105–108 Old Broad Street, London EC2N 1EX (phone: 020 7216 8800; fax: 020 7216 8811; website: www.bba.org.uk).*
The Building Societies Association, *3 Savile Row, London W1X 1AF (phone: 020 7437 0655; fax: 020 7734 6416; website: www.bsa.org.uk).*
Association for Payment Clearing Services (APACS), *Mercury House, Triton Court, 14 Finsbury Square, London EC2A 1BR (phone: 020 7711 6200; fax: 020 7256 5527; website: www.pacs. org.uk).]*

[1 March 2005]

Throughout this Code, words in the text which are shown in **bold** print are defined in the glossary at the end of the Code.

1 Introduction

What the Code covers

1.1 This is a voluntary code which sets standards of good banking practice for financial institutions to follow when they are dealing with **personal customers** in the United Kingdom. It provides valuable protection for you and explains how financial institutions are expected to deal with you day-to-day and in times of financial difficulty.

The Code applies to:

- current accounts, including **basic bank accounts** (section 3);
- savings and deposit accounts (sections 3 and 4), including mini cash and Tessa ISAs, and cash deposit Child Trust Funds;
- payment services, including foreign-exchange services (section 9);
- **cards and PINs** (section 10); and
- loans and overdrafts (section 13).

It does not cover mortgages, investments, insurance, Premium Bonds or currency accounts.

About this Code

1.2 As a voluntary code, it allows competition and market forces to work to encourage higher standards for the benefit of customers.

Within the Code, 'you' means the customer and 'we', 'us' and 'our' means the financial institution the customer deals with.

You can check which financial institutions follow the Code by contacting the Banking Code Standards Board, the independent organisation which monitors how well financial institutions are meeting the Code. (You can find their contact details later in the Code— section 16.2.) The types of financial institution currently include:

- banks;
- building societies;

- **credit card** companies; and
- National Savings & Investments.

The standards of the Code are covered by the six key commitments found in section 2.

Not all the financial institutions covered by this Code offer all the products and services listed in section 1.1 above.

Unless it says otherwise, all parts of this Code apply to all the products and services listed above, whether they are provided by branches, over the phone, by post, through interactive TV, on the internet or by any other method.

This revised edition is effective from 1 March 2005 unless otherwise shown.

2 Our key commitments to you

We promise that we will act fairly and reasonably in all our dealings with you by meeting all the commitments and standards in this Code. The key commitments are shown below.

- We will make sure that our advertising and promotional literature is clear and not misleading and that you are given clear information about our products and services.
- When you have chosen an account or service, we will give you clear information about how it works, the terms and conditions and the interest rates which apply to it.
- We will help you use your account or service by sending you regular statements (where appropriate) and we will keep you informed about changes to the interest rates, charges or terms and conditions.
- We will deal quickly and sympathetically with things that go wrong and consider all cases of financial difficulty sympathetically and positively.
- We will treat all your personal information as private and confidential, and operate secure and reliable banking and payment systems.
- We will publicise this Code, have copies available and make sure that our staff are trained to put it into practice.

3 Helping you to choose products and services which meet your needs

3.1 Before you become a customer, we will:

- give you clear information explaining the key features of the services and products you tell us you are interested in;
- assess whether your needs are suited to a **basic bank account** (if we offer one) and if they are we will offer you this product;
- offer you a **basic bank account** if you specifically ask, and meet the qualifying conditions for one;
- give you information on a single product or service, if you have already made up your mind; and
- tell you what information we need from you to prove your identity (by law, we have to check your identity).

3.2 We will tell you if we offer products and services in more than one way (for example, on the internet, over the phone, in branches and so on) and tell you how to find out more about them. Where we offer **basic bank accounts**, we will tell you if they can be used at post offices.

3.3 Once you have chosen an account or service, we will tell you how it works.

3.4 When you open a joint account, we will give you extra information on your rights and responsibilities.

3.5 **Personal customers** are protected by the European Distance Marketing Directive (DMD) in relation to deposit taking. This gives you rights when opening current, savings and deposit accounts, and doing financial services business in relation to these types of account at a distance (typically by post, telephone or electronically). In summary, the major types of protection are:

- detailed information before you commit to a contract;
- a 14-day right of cancellation; and
- restrictions on how a financial service is supplied if you have not asked for it.

4   Interest rates

4.1 You can find out about our interest rates by:
- phoning our helpline;
- looking on our website;
- looking at the notices in our branches; or
- asking our staff.

4.2 When you become a customer, we will give you information on the interest rates which apply to your accounts, and when we will take interest or pay it to you. We will also tell you our website address, our helpline numbers and the other ways in which you can find out about changes in interest rates on your accounts.

4.3 If you ask us, we will also give you a full explanation of how we work out interest.

Changes in interest rates

4.4 We will keep you informed about changes to the interest rates on your accounts and we will tell you about the ways we will do this.

4.5 When we change the interest rates on your accounts, we will update the information on our phone helpline and our website within three **working days**. To help you compare rates, the old rate will also be available on our website and our helpline.

Interest on savings accounts

4.6 To help you compare interest rates on all our savings accounts more easily, at least once a year we will send you a summary of these products and their current interest rates unless your account has less than £500 in it. This summary will also include:
- accounts that are no longer available; and
- details of how you can find out about the current interest rates that apply to your accounts.

4.7 We will also tell you the different interest rates which have applied to your account during the year and any changes in the **Bank of England base rate** (unless we have already told you personally about these or if your account has less than £500 in it).

4.8 If you have a variable-rate savings account with £250 or more in it and the interest rate has fallen significantly compared with the **Bank of England base rate**, we will contact you within a reasonable period of time to:
- tell you that this has happened;
- tell you about our other savings accounts and offer to help you to switch to one of these accounts if you want to;
- tell you that you can withdraw all the money in your account; and
- give you a reasonable period of time to switch to another account or withdraw the money without any notice period or any charges.

5   Charges

5.1 When you become a customer, we will give you details of any charges for the day-to-day running of the account you have chosen.

5.2 You can also find out about these charges by:
- phoning our helpline;
- looking on our website; or
- asking our staff.

5.3 If we increase any of these charges or introduce a new charge, we will tell you personally at least 30 days before the change takes effect.

5.4 We will tell you the charge for any other service or product before we provide that service or product, and at any time you ask.

5.5 Before we take interest or charges for **standard account services** from your current or savings account, we will give you at least 14 days' notice of how much we will take.

Cash machine charges

5.6 We will give you details of any charges we make for using **cash machines** when we issue the **card**.

5.7 You will not be charged more than once for any transaction at one of our **cash machines**.

5.8 When you use a **cash card** at one of our **cash machines**, a message on the screen will tell you, before you commit to making a withdrawal, the amount (if any) you will be charged for the transaction and who is making the charge.

5.9 When you use a **card** other than a **cash card** at one of our **cash machines**, a message on the screen will tell you, before you commit to making a withdrawal, the amount (if any) we will charge you for the transaction. The message will also tell you that your **card** issuer may charge you for the transaction.

5.10 We will show **cash machine** charges on your statement of account.

6 Terms and conditions

6.1 We will give you any relevant terms and conditions for the product you have asked us to provide when you apply to become a customer or accept a product for the first time.

6.2 All written terms and conditions will be fair and will set out your rights and responsibilities clearly, legibly and in plain language. We will only use legal or technical language where necessary.

Changes to terms and conditions

6.3 When you become a customer, we will tell you how we will let you know about changes to terms and conditions.

6.4 If the change is to your disadvantage, we will tell you about it personally at least 30 days before we make the change. At any time up to 60 days from the date of the notice you may, without notice, switch your account or close it without having to pay any extra charges or any interest for doing this.

6.5 We may make any other change immediately and tell you about it within 30 days.

6.6 If we have made a major change or a lot of minor changes in any one year, we will give you a copy of the new terms and conditions or a summary of the changes.

7 Changing your account

Cooling off

7.1 If you are not happy about your choice of current or savings account, you may cancel it within 14 days of:
- the day the contract is entered into; or
- the day on which you receive the contract terms and conditions and other information on paper or electronically;

whichever is later.

We will help you switch to another of our accounts or we will give all your money back with any interest it has earned. We will ignore any notice period and any extra charges.

This does not apply to:
- a **fixed-rate** account; or
- an account or contract for financial services where the price depends on rises and falls in financial markets outside our control that may happen during the cancellation period; or
- a branch-based Child Trust Fund cash deposit account (in other words, not sold at a distance).

Moving your account

7.2 If you decide to move your current account to another financial institution, we will give them information on your standing orders and direct debits within three **working days**

of receiving their request to do this. Also, we will close or move your current account, without charge, when you ask us to do so.

7.3 If you want to transfer your current account to us, we will tell you:

- how the process for transferring your account will work and who is responsible for each step in the process;
- what information your old financial institution will pass to us;
- what features you will be offered with the new account so that you can compare your new account with features on your old account; and
- how long the transfer is likely to take.

We will give you what you need to operate the account within 10 **working days** of approving your application.

7.4 We will cancel any bank charges you will have to pay as a result of any mistake or unnecessary delay by us when you transfer your current account to or from us.

Closing your account

7.5 Under normal circumstances, we will not close your account without giving you at least 30 days' notice. Examples of circumstances which are not 'normal' include threatening or abusive behaviour towards staff.

7.6 If we plan to close or move your branch, we will tell you at least eight weeks beforehand, and 12 weeks beforehand if yours is the last bank or building society branch within a one-mile radius (four miles in rural areas). We will tell you how we will continue to provide banking services to you.

8   Advertising and marketing

8.1 We will make sure that all advertising and promotional material is clear, fair, reasonable and not misleading.

8.2 We will take care when sending marketing material to you, particularly if it relates to loans or overdrafts, or if you are under 18.

8.3 Unless you specifically give your permission or ask us to, we will not pass your name and address to any company, including other companies in our group, for marketing purposes. We will not ask you to give your permission in return for **standard account services**.

8.4 We may tell you about another company's services or products. If you agree, that company may contact you directly.

8.5 When you become a customer, we will give you the opportunity to say that you do not want us to contact you for marketing purposes. At least once every three years, we will remind you that you can do this.

8.6 We will not insist that you buy an insurance product from us when we agree to provide you with a lending product.

9   Running your account

Statements

9.1 To help you manage your account and check entries on it, we will give you regular account statements unless this is not appropriate for the type of account you have (such as an account where you have a passbook).

9.2 We will normally give you a statement every month, every three months or, in any case, at least once a year. You can ask us to give you account statements more often than is normally available on your type of account, but there may be a charge for this service.

9.3 If you have a **card** which allows you to withdraw money from your account, we will provide you with account statements at least every three months if the **card** has been used.

Clearing cycle

9.4 We will tell you about the **central clearing cycle**—normally three **working days**—for cheques and automated payments, including those over the phone or internet, and whether we add extra days to this **central clearing cycle**. We will tell you when you can withdraw money after paying into your account, and when you will start to earn interest. We will do this when you open your account and whenever you ask us.

Direct debits, standing orders and recurring transactions

9.5 We will tell you how direct debits, standing orders and **recurring transactions** work and how you may cancel one of these when you no longer need it.

9.6 We will tell you about the Direct Debit Guarantee, which protects you if a direct debit you have not authorised is taken from your account. If any money is wrongly taken from your account under a direct debit, we will refund your account as soon as you tell us about it.

Cheques

9.7 We will keep original cheques paid from your account, or copies, for at least six years unless we have already returned these to you.

9.8 If, within a reasonable period after the entry has been made on your statement, there is a dispute with us about a cheque paid from your account, we will give you the cheque or a copy as evidence. If there is an unreasonable delay after you have told us about it, we will add the amount of the cheque to your account until we have sorted the matter out.

9.9 We will tell you how we will deal with **unpaid cheques** and **out-of-date cheques**.

9.10 If we need to tell you that a cheque you have written (or another item) has been returned unpaid, we will do this either by letter or in another private and confidential way.

Foreign-exchange services

9.11 When you buy or sell foreign currency, we will give you an explanation of the service, details of the exchange rate and an explanation of the charges which apply to foreign- exchange transactions.

9.12 If you want to transfer money abroad, we will tell you how to do this and will give you:

- a description of the services and how to use them;
- details of when the money you have sent abroad should get there and the reasons for possible delays;
- the exchange rate applied when converting to the foreign currency (if this is not possible at the time of the transaction, we will let you know later what the rate is); and
- details of any commission or charges which you will have to pay and a warning that the person receiving the money may also have to pay the foreign bank's charges.

9.13 If money is transferred to your bank account from abroad, we will tell you the original amount received and any charges. If the sender has agreed to pay all charges, we will not take off charges when we pay the money into your account.

Protecting your account

9.14 We will tell you what you can do to help protect your accounts. You can find out more about what you can do to help in section 12 of this Code.

9.15 If you tell us that your cheque book, passbook, **card** or **electronic purse** has been lost or stolen, or that someone else knows your **PIN** or **other security information**, we will take immediate steps to try to prevent these from being used.

Dormant and lost accounts, and unclaimed assets

9.16 If you have money in a **dormant account**, it will always be your property (or if you die, it will become part of your estate). This is the case no matter how many years pass.

9.17 If you ask us, we will tell you how to access these accounts either directly, or via the British Bankers' Association, The Building Societies Association or National Savings & Investment **dormant account** schemes (see section 17.6).

10   Cards and PINs

This section applies to **cards** as defined in the glossary.

General features of cards

10.1 We will only send you a **card** if you ask for one or to replace a **card** you already have.

10.2 If you do not recognise a **card** transaction which appears on your statement, we will give you more details if you ask us. In some cases, we will need you to give us confirmation or evidence that you have not authorised a transaction.

10.3 If we confirm a transaction is unauthorised, any interest charged will be refunded, unless you have acted fraudulently or without reasonable care (see under sections 12.5 and 12.11).

10.4 Your statement will show the rate of commission or charge (if any) we apply to foreign-currency **card** transactions.

PINs

10.5 We will give you your **PIN** (personal identification number) separately from your **card**. We will not reveal your **PIN** to anyone else.

10.6 We will tell you about our systems, which allow you to choose and change your **PIN**. This should make it easier for you to remember.

Credit cards

10.7 Before you become a customer, we will give you the main features of the **credit card** in a **Summary Box**.

10.8 When you apply for a **credit card**, we will tell you how it works and give you the terms and conditions.

10.9 Before we give you a credit limit, we will assess whether we feel you will be able to repay it.

10.10 We may increase your credit limit on your **credit card**.
- You can contact us at any time if you want to reduce your credit limit or opt out of receiving credit limit increases.
- You can ask us to increase your credit limit and we will consider this when we have made the appropriate checks.
- Sometimes, we may decide to reduce your limit.

10.11 You will receive a monthly statement for your **credit card**, unless your account has a nil balance and has not been used. The monthly statement will include information about transactions since the last statement date, any interest which applies, the minimum repayment and other useful information including the 'allocation of payments' (how we use your payment to reduce your balance).

10.12 We will make sure that your minimum repayment covers more than that month's interest.

10.13 We will warn you when an introductory promotional interest rate on your **credit card** is about to come to an end.

10.14 If you make a cash withdrawal with a **credit card**, it will be treated as a cash advance and we may charge you a handling fee and interest at the cash advance rate from the date of the withdrawal.

10.15 You have the opportunity to say you do not want to receive **credit card cheques** and we will let you know about any fees if you use these cheques. You may not have the same level of protection when you use a **credit card cheque** as you do with a **credit card**.

11   Your personal information

Confidentiality

11.1 We will treat all your personal information as private and confidential (even when you are no longer a customer). We will not reveal your name and address or details about your accounts to anyone, including other companies in our group, other than in the following four exceptional cases when we are allowed to do this by law.
- If we have to give the information by law.
- If there is a duty to the public to reveal the information.
- If our interests mean we must give the information (for example, to prevent fraud). However, we will not use this as a reason for giving information about you or your accounts (including your name and address) to anyone else, including other companies in our group for marketing purposes.
- If you ask us to reveal the information, or if we have your permission.

Bankers' references

11.2 If we are asked to give a **banker's reference** about you, we will need your written permission before we give it.

Data protection

11.3 We will explain to you that, under the Data Protection Act, you have the right to see the personal records we hold about you.
11.4 We will tell you if we record your telephone conversations with us.

12   Protecting your accounts

Secure and reliable banking and payment systems

12.1 We will co-operate as an industry so that you enjoy secure and reliable **banking and payment systems** you can trust.
The rest of this section is all about what you can do to help prevent your accounts being misused.

Keeping us up to date

12.2 Please make sure you let us know as soon as possible when you change your:
- name;
- address;
- phone number; or
- e-mail address (if this is how we communicate with you).

If we do not hold correct information we may make your account **dormant** to protect us both (see section 9.16 and section 17.6).

Checking your account

12.3 We recommend that you check your statement or passbook regularly. If there is an entry which seems to be wrong, you should tell us as soon as possible so that we can sort it out. Regular checks on direct debits and standing orders will help you be sure the money is going where you want it to.

12.4 If we need to investigate a transaction on your account, you should co-operate with us and the police, if we need to involve them.

Taking care

12.5 The care of your cheques, passbook, **cards**, **electronic purse**, **PINs** and **other security information** is essential to help prevent fraud and protect your accounts. Please make sure that you follow the advice given below.

- Do not keep your cheque book and **cards** together.
- Do not allow anyone else to use your **card**, and do not tell anyone else your **PIN**, **password** or **other security information**.
- If you change your **PIN**, you should choose your new **PIN** carefully.
- Try to remember your **PIN**, **password** and **other security information**, and destroy the notice as soon as you receive it.
- Never write down or record your **PIN**, **password** or **other security information**.
- Always take reasonable steps to keep your **card** safe and your **PIN**, **password** and **other security information** secret at all times.
- Never give your account details or **other security information** to anyone unless you know who they are and why they need them.
- Keep your **card** receipts and other information about your account containing personal details (for example, statements) safe and get rid of them carefully.
- Take care when storing or getting rid of information about your accounts. People who commit fraud use many methods, such as 'bin raiding', to get this type of information. You should take simple steps such as shredding printed material.
- You will find the APACS website (www.cardwatch.org.uk) a helpful guide on what to do if you suspect **card** fraud.

12.6 When you write a cheque, it will help to prevent fraud if you clearly write the name of the person you are paying the cheque to and put extra information about them on the cheque especially if you are not personally paying a cheque in (for example, because you are sending a cheque by post).

- If you are paying a cheque to a large organisation such as the Inland Revenue, do not make the cheque payable simply to that organisation. Add further details into the payee line (for example, Inland Revenue re: J Jones, your reference xxxyyz). You should draw a line through unused space on the cheque so unauthorised people cannot add extra numbers or names.
- If you are making a cheque payable to a bank or a building society, do not make the cheque payable simply to that organisation. Add further details in the payee line (for example, XYZ Bank, re: J Jones, account number xxxxxx). You should draw a line through unused space on the cheque so unauthorised people cannot add extra numbers or names.

What to do if you lose your cheque book, passbook, electronic purse or card, or if someone else knows your PIN

12.7 It is essential that you tell us as soon as you can if you suspect or discover that:

- your cheque book, passbook, **card** or **electronic purse** has been lost or stolen; or
- someone else knows your **PIN**, **password** or **other security information**.

12.8 The best way of telling us about the loss will usually be by phone, using the numbers we have given you, or by e-mail if we have given you an address for this purpose.

Online banking

12.9 Online banking is safe and convenient as long as you take a number of simple precautions. Please make sure you follow the advice given below.

- Keep your PC secure. Use up-to-date anti-virus and spyware software and a personal firewall.
- Keep your **passwords** and **PINs** secret.
- Treat e-mails you receive with caution and be wary of e-mails or calls asking you to reveal any personal security details. Neither the police nor we will ever contact you to ask you to reveal your online banking or payment **card PINs**, or your **password** information.
- Follow our advice—our websites are usually a good place to get help and guidance on how to stay safe online.
- Visit www.banksafeonline.org.uk for useful information.

Cancelling payments

12.10 If you want to cancel a payment or series of payments you have authorised, you should do the following.

- To cancel a cheque or standing order, you must tell us (we cannot cancel cheques covered by a cheque guarantee **card**).
- To cancel a direct debit, you can either tell the **originator** of the direct debit or tell us. We recommend you do both.
- To cancel a **recurring transaction**, you must tell the **originator**. We recommend you keep proof of cancellation.
- It may not be possible to cancel payments if you do not give enough notice of your decision to cancel.

Liability for losses

12.11 If you act fraudulently, you will be responsible for all losses on your account. If you act without reasonable care, and this causes losses, you may be responsible for them. (This may apply if you do not follow section 12.5 or you do not keep to your account's terms and conditions.)

12.12 Unless we can show that you have acted fraudulently or without reasonable care, your liability for the misuse of your **card** will be limited as follows.

- If someone else uses your **card**, before you tell us it has been lost or stolen or that someone else knows your **PIN**, the most you will have to pay is £50.
- If someone else uses your **card** details without your permission, and your **card** has not been lost or stolen, you will not have to pay anything.
- If someone else uses your **card** details without your permission for a transaction where the cardholder does not need to be present, you will not have to pay anything.
- If your **card** is used before you have received it, you will not have to pay anything.

Account aggregation services

12.13 If you use an **account aggregation** service, you may be liable for any fraud or mistakes that happen on your accounts as a result.

Electronic purse

12.14 You should treat your **electronic purse** like cash in a wallet. If you lose your **electronic purse** or it is stolen, you will lose any money in it, in just the same way as if you lost your wallet.

12.15 However, unless we can show that you have acted fraudulently or without reasonable care, your liability for the misuse of your **electronic purse** will be as follows. If money is transferred to your **electronic purse** by unauthorised withdrawals from your account before you tell us it has been lost, stolen or misused, the most you will lose is £50.

12.16 You will not lose anything if money is transferred from your account to your **electronic purse** after you have told us it has been lost or stolen or that someone else knows your **PIN**.

13   Lending

Borrowing money

13.1 Before we lend you any money or increase your overdraft, or other borrowing, we will assess whether we feel you will be able to repay it.

(For **credit cards** see also section 10.9.)

13.2 If we offer you an overdraft, or an increase in your existing overdraft limit, we will tell you if your overdraft is repayable on demand.

13.3 If we cannot help you, we will explain the main reason why if you ask us to. We will give you this, in writing or electronically, if you ask.

13.4 If you want us to accept a **guarantee** or other **security** from someone for any amounts you owe, we may ask you for your permission to give confidential information about your finances to the person giving the **guarantee** or other **security**, or to their legal adviser. We will also:

- encourage them to take independent legal advice to make sure that they understand their commitment and the possible consequences of their decision (where appropriate, the documents we ask them to sign will contain this recommendation as a clear and obvious notice);
- tell them that, by giving the **guarantee** or other **security**, they may become liable instead of, or as well as, you; and
- tell them what their liability will be.

We will not take an unlimited **guarantee**.

Credit reference agencies

13.5 When you open your account or apply for a **card**, we will tell you when we may pass your details to **credit reference agencies** and the checks we may make with them.

13.6 We may give information to **credit reference agencies** about the personal debts you owe us if:

- you have fallen behind with your payments;
- the amount owed is not in dispute; and
- you have not made proposals we are satisfied with for repaying your debt, following our formal demand.

13.7 In these cases, we will give you at least 28 days' notice that we plan to give information about the debts you owe us to **credit reference agencies**. At the same time, we will explain to you the role of **credit reference agencies** and the effect the information they provide can have on your ability to get credit.

13.8 We may give **credit reference agencies** other information about the day-to-day running of your account if you have given us your permission to do so.

13.9 If you ask, we will tell you how to get a copy of the information that **credit reference agencies** have about you, or their leaflets that explain how credit referencing works. You should contact the customer service teams at:

Experian Ltd	Equifax	Plc Call credit Plc
PO Box 8000	PO Box 1140	PO Box 491
Nottingham	Bradford	Leeds
NG807WF	BD1 5US	LS1 1WX
www.experian.co.uk	www.equifax.co.uk	www.callcredit.co.uk

We may also ask you to give your permission to use the information held by **credit reference agencies** to check identity for anti-money-laundering and fraud purposes—this does not affect your credit history.

14   Financial difficulties—how we can help

14.1 We will consider cases of financial difficulty sympathetically and positively. Our first step will be to try to contact you to discuss the matter.

14.2 If you find yourself in financial difficulties, you should let us know as soon as possible. We will do all we can to help you to overcome your difficulties. With your coop-eration, we will develop a plan with you for dealing with your financial difficulties and we will tell you in writing what we have agreed.

14.3 The sooner we discuss your problems, the easier it will be for both of us to find a solution. The more you tell us about your full financial circumstances, the more we may be able to help.

14.4 If you are in difficulties, you can also get help and advice from debt-counselling organisations. We will tell you where you can get free money advice. If you ask us to, we will work with debt-counselling organisations, such as Citizens Advice Bureaux, money advice centres or the Consumer Credit Counselling Service. Their contact details are as follows.

- Advice UK—020 7407 4070 (www.adviceuk.org.uk)
- Citizens Advice Bureaux—You can get the phone number of your local bureau from the phone book, the local library or www.citizensadvice.org.uk
- Citizens Advice Scotland—0131 550 1000 (www.cas.org.uk)
- Consumer Credit Counselling Service—0800 138 1111 (www.cccs.co.uk)
- Money Advice Scotland—0141 572 0237 (www.moneyadvicescotland.org.uk)
- National Debtline—0808 808 4000 (www.nationaldebtline.co.uk)
- Payplan—0800 085 4298 (www.payplan.com)

You should also be aware that there are other companies that charge a fee for managing your debts. It is your responsibility to check the fees that may be charged before asking these companies to act on your behalf.

14.5 If you have debts with many creditors, a debt-counselling organisation may complete a **Common Financial Statement** (or equivalent acceptable to us) on your behalf, which we will accept as the basis for negotiations with you in drawing up a **debt-management plan**.

14.6 In certain circumstances we may pass your debt to another organisation or debt-collection agency. We will always choose reputable firms which also agree to follow the Code when arranging repayment.

14.7 In other circumstances, we may sell your debt. We will always choose reputable firms if we do this.

15   Complaints

Internal procedures

15.1 If you want to make a complaint, we will tell you how to do this and what to do if you are not happy about the outcome. Our staff will help you with any questions you have.

15.2 When you become a customer, we will tell you where to find details of our proce-dures for handling complaints fairly and quickly. These procedures meet the requirements of the Financial Services Authority.

15.3 Within five **working days** of receiving your complaint, we will send you a written acknowledgement.

15.4 Within four weeks, we will write to you again with our final response, or to explain why we need more time to respond.

15.5 If we have not already sent it, we will send you our final or other response within eight weeks and will tell you how to take your complaint further if you are still not satisfied.

Financial Ombudsman Service

15.6 We will display on our website and in all our branches a notice explaining that we are covered by the Financial Ombudsman Service (FOS). The FOS is available to settle certain complaints you make if they cannot be settled through our own complaints procedures. The contact details of the FOS are as follows.

- The Financial Ombudsman Service
  South Quay Plaza
  183 Marsh Wall
  London E14 9SR
  Phone: 0845 080 1800
  Website: www.financial-ombudsman.org.uk

15.7 National Savings & Investments (NS& I) has an independent arbitration scheme to settle disputes between NS&I and its customers. Their contact details are as follows.

- The Independent Adjudicator for National Savings & Investments
  1st Floor, South Quay Plaza
  183 Marsh Wall
  London E14 9SR

16   Monitoring

16.1 We have a 'Code Compliance Officer' and our own auditing procedures make sure we meet the Code.

Banking Code Standards Board

16.2 The Code is monitored by the Banking Code Standards Board whose directors include a majority of independent members as well as representatives of financial institutions. Their contact details are as follows.

- Banking Code Standards Board
  6 Frederick's Place
  London EC2R 8BT
  Phone: 0845 230 9694
  Website: www.bankingcode.org.uk

17   Getting help

17.1 If you have any enquiries about the Code, you should contact the British Bankers' Association, The Building Societies Association or APACS. Their addresses and phone numbers are shown at the front of this booklet. Or, contact the Banking Code Standards Board at the address above.

Copies of the Code

17.2 All financial institutions that follow this Code will make copies of it available to all their **personal customers** and have notices in all their branches and on their websites explaining that copies of the Code are available and how you can get one.

17.3 You can get a copy of this Code and guidance notes on how this Code should be followed from the Banking Code Standards Board, whose contact details are given in section 16.2, or from the British Bankers' Association or The Building Societies Association at the addresses shown at the front of this Code.

Further information

17.4 You can get more information on a range of banking matters from the British Bankers' Association's (BBA) 'BankFacts' leaflets, and factsheets and information leaflets from the Building Societies Association (BSA) and APACS. Also, the BBA, BSA and APACS have customer helplines. (The phone numbers are given at the front of this Code.)

17.5 Financial Services Compensation Scheme

We are part of the Financial Services Compensation Scheme (FSCS) set up under the Financial Services and Markets Act 2000. The FSCS is a fund of last resort for customers of financial services firms. The FSCS pays compensation if an authorised firm cannot pay claims against it. The scheme is governed by FSA rules. For more details on the scheme, go to the FSCS website— www.fscs.org.uk or phone 020 7892 7300.

17.6 Dormant account schemes

You can get copies of the **dormant account**, lost account, unclaimed assets tracing forms from us or from the following.

FOR BANKS

British Bankers' Association, phone 020 7216 8909 or download a copy from www.bba.org.uk or write to BBA Dormant Accounts, Pinners Hall, 105–108 Old Broad Street, London, EC2N 1EX.

FOR BUILDING SOCIETIES

The Building Societies Association, phone 020 7437 0655 or download a copy from www.bsa.org.uk or write to BSA Dormant Accounts, 3 Savile Row, London, W1S 3PB.

FOR NATIONAL SAVINGS & INVESTMENTS

National Savings & Investments, phone 0845 964 5000 or download a copy from www.nsandi.com or write to National Savings & Investments, FREEPOST BJ 2092, Blackpool, FY3 9XR.

Glossary

These definitions explain the meaning of words and terms used in the Code. They are not precise legal or technical definitions.

Account aggregation

Account aggregation services allow you to have details of some or all of the online accounts you hold with financial institutions, and other information, presented on one web page. These services may be operated by a financial institution (with whom you may already hold an account) or they may be provided by a website not owned by a financial institution.

Banker's reference

An opinion about a particular customer's ability to enter into, or repay, a financial commitment.

Banking and payment systems

This refers to the underlying clearing, money transmission and computer systems which the financial institutions that follow the Code control.

Base rate or Bank of England base rate

This refers to the Bank of England Repo Rate. This is the rate the Bank of England considers every month and publicly announces any changes to.

Basic bank account

A basic bank account will normally have the following features.
- Employers can pay income directly into the account.
- The Government can pay pensions, tax credits and benefits directly into the account.
- Cheques and cash can be paid into the account.
- Bills can be paid by direct debit, by transferring money to another account or by a payment to a linked account.
- Cash can be withdrawn at cash machines.
- There is no overdraft facility.
- The last penny in the account can be withdrawn.

Card

A general term for any plastic card which a customer may use to pay for goods and services or to withdraw cash. In this Code, it includes debit, credit, cheque guarantee, charge cards and cash cards. It does not include electronic purses or store cards.

Cash card

A card, other than a charge card or credit card, which allows the cardholder to withdraw cash from a cash machine.

Cash machine

An automated teller machine (ATM) or freestanding machine in which a customer can use their card to get cash, information and other services.

Central clearing cycle

CHEQUES
- The central cheque clearing cycle normally takes three working days.
- If the cheque you pay in was written by a customer of your own bank, this process may be faster. This varies from bank to bank.
- The cycle may also be longer when paying in via some financial institutions or agents (such as post offices).

AUTOMATED PAYMENTS (for example, internet, telephone and standing orders)
When you give an instruction to your bank to make an automated payment (including payments over the phone or internet), the money will normally be taken from your account on the same day.
- The central clearing cycle is normally three working days.
- If the person you are paying banks at the same bank as you, the amount will usually be credited on the same day.
- Payments may take longer than three working days through some financial institutions.

Charge card

A card which allows you to make purchases and to draw cash up to an arranged credit limit. The terms include paying the balance in full at the end of a set period. You will normally be charged a fee each year.

Common Financial Statement

A full review of the financial position of a customer in financial difficulties. This is filled in with the help of a money adviser. It allows you to offer repayments from your available income to a group of creditors. Although it exists in a standard format agreed by the industry, we may also agree to accept an equivalent form.

Credit card

A card which allows you to make purchases and to draw cash up to an arranged credit limit. You can pay off the credit granted in full or in part by a set date. Interest is usually charged on the amount of any balance left owing. In the case of cash withdrawals, interest is normally charged from the transaction date. You may also have to pay an annual fee.

Credit card cheque

A cheque drawn against a credit card account that gives the cardholder another way of accessing funds—up to their credit limit—usually to make transactions where credit cards are not accepted. Interest is normally charged from the transaction date.

Credit reference agencies

Organisations, licensed under the Consumer Credit Act 1974, which hold information about people that is useful to lenders. Financial institutions may contact these agencies for information to help them make various decisions, for example, whether or not to open an account or provide loans or grant credit. Financial institutions may also give the agencies information.

Dormant accounts

Accounts which are lost or which contain assets that have not been claimed.

Electronic purse

Any card, or function of a card, which contains real value in the form of electronic money which someone has paid for beforehand. Some cards can be reloaded with more money and can be used for a range of purposes.

Fixed rate

An interest rate which is guaranteed not to change over a set period of time.

Fixed term

This applies to products and services which have a set lifetime. The customer may be charged if the financial institution agrees to alter the product or service before the end of its life.

Guarantee

A promise given by a person called 'the guarantor' to pay another person's debts if that person does not pay them.

Originator

A company (either a retail or service organisation) which collects payments from a customer's account in line with the customers instructions. This only applies to direct debits or recurring transactions.

Other security information

A selection of facts and information (which only you know) which is used for identification when using accounts.

Out-of-date cheque

A cheque which has not been paid because the date written on the cheque is too old (normally older than six months).

Password

A word or an access code which you have chosen, to allow you to use a phone or internet banking service.

Personal customer

Any person who is acting for purposes which are not linked to their trade, business or profession. (This definition is based on the one used in European legislation and by the Financial Services Authority with the title of either 'consumer' or 'retail customer'.)

In practice, personal customers may act in a number of capacities. The above definition does not include an individual acting, for example:

- as trustee of a trust such as a housing or NHS trust; or
- as a member of the governing body of a club or other unincorporated association such as a trade body or a student union; or
- as a pension trustee.

Examples of personal customers acting in capacities that are included in the above definition are:

- personal representatives, including executors, unless they are acting in a professional capacity, for example, a solicitor acting as executor; and
- private individuals acting in personal or other family circumstances, for example, as trustee of a family trust.

PIN (personal identification number)

A confidential number which allows customers to buy things, withdraw cash and use other services at a cash machine. You will often have to enter your **PIN** into a point of sale terminal, instead of signing a receipt, to authorise a transaction.

Recurring transaction

A regular payment (other than a **direct debit** or standing order) collected from a customer's card account by an originator, in line with the customer's instruction. Recurring transactions are not covered by the Direct Debit Guarantee.

Security

A word used to describe valuable items such as title deeds to houses, share certificates, life policies and so on, which represent assets used as support for a loan or other liability. Under a secured loan, the lender has the right to sell the security if the loan is not repaid.

Standard account services

Opening, maintaining and running accounts for transmitting money (for example, by cheque or debit card). These services would normally be provided in basic or current accounts.

Summary Box

This gives you a brief summary in a standard format of the key features of the credit card you are considering so you can compare different products more easily.

Unpaid cheque

This is a cheque which, after being paid into the account of the person it is written out to, is returned 'unpaid' (bounced) by the financial institution whose customer issued the cheque. This leaves the person the cheque was written out to without the money in their account.

Working days

Monday to Friday, not including bank holidays.

INDEX